YOU HAVE THE BOOK. NOW IT'S TIME TO *TAKE ACTION!*

FUNDAMENTALS OF INTERMEDIATE ACCOUNTING offers you a comprehensive understanding of Intermediate Accounting:

- The text gives you a strong conceptual foundation to build on in your career
- *TAKE ACTION*, the Interactive CD, helps you develop practical skills to use on the job!

WHEN YOU POP THE TAKE ACTION CD IN YOUR COMPUTER YOU WILL LEARN:

HOW TO STUDY

Everybody learns in different ways. Understanding how you learn best will help you get the best possible grade from this course. *TAKE ACTION* offers an Interactive Learning Style Quiz that shows you how you learn best, and how to pinpoint the study aids in the text that are most effective based on your learning style. You also get special help on Surviving the Group Project.

WHAT TO STUDY

TAKE ACTION includes a special tutorial to help you master the Accounting Cycle, one of the most important keys to success. In fact, *TAKE ACTION* features a total of eight interactive tutorials to help you ace the most difficult topics:
- Accounting Cycle
- Accounting for Bad Debt
- Transfer of Receivables
- Inventory Methods
- LIFO Inventory Issues
- Interest Capitalization
- Depreciation of Long-Lived Assets
- Impairment of Long-Lived Assets

- So you can check your progress through the course, *TAKE ACTION* offers a special Self-Test feature for each chapter.
- *TAKE ACTION* helps you expand your skills and apply your growing knowledge with a Writing Handbook, Database of more than 20 Real Companies, Ethics in Accounting feature, Financial Analysis Primer, Additional Disclosures, Expanded Discussions, Spreadsheet Tools and more!

WHY YOU STUDY!

When you ace this course, you're on the road to a successful career. *TAKE ACTION* helps you figure out where to go from here by:
- Offering insight into Why Accounting Is Important
- Exploring the opportunities available in Careers in Accounting
- Meeting business professionals in the Professional Profiles section

All of this is designed to help you get the best grade you can in the course and to give you the tools you need to take you wherever you want to go in your career!

2006 FASB UPDATE

FUNDAMENTALS OF INTERMEDIATE ACCOUNTING

Donald E. Kieso Ph.D., C.P.A.
KPMG Emeritus Professor of Accounting
Northern Illinois University
DeKalb, Illinois

Jerry J. Weygandt Ph.D., C.P.A.
Arthur Anderson Alumni Professor of Accounting
University of Wisconsin
Madison, Wisconsin

Terry D. Warfield Ph.D.
Associate Professor of Accounting
University of Wisconsin
Madison, Wisconsin

WILEY

John Wiley & Sons, Inc.

PUBLISHER	Susan Elbe
ACQUISITIONS EDITOR	Mark Bonadeo
SENIOR MARKETING MANAGER	Steven Herdegen
OUTSIDE DEVELOPMENT EDITOR	Ann Torbert
PRODUCTION SERVICES MANAGER	Jeanine Furino
SUPPLEMENTS EDITOR	Ed Brislin
PROJECT EDITOR	Brian Kamins
MEDIA EDITOR	Allison Morris
SENIOR DESIGNER	Karin Kincheloe
ILLUSTRATION EDITOR	Anna Melhorn
COVER PHOTOS	© www.danheller.com

This book was set in Palatino by Techbooks and printed and bound by Von Hoffmann Press. The cover was printed by Lehigh Press.

This book is printed on acid-free paper. ∞

To order books or for customer service please, call 1-800-CALL WILEY (225-5945).

ISBN: 0-471-75272-X
ISBN-13: 978-0471-75272-1

Printed in the United States of America

10 9 8 7 6 5 4 3 2 1

Contents

....

This update booklet contains discussions of key accounting standards that have been issued since the publication of *Fundamentals of Intermediate Accounting*, by Kieso, Weygandt, and Warfield. These standards are discussed, by topic, in seven sections, as outlined below. See the following page for a visual display of how these sections relate to the textbook chapters.

Section 1   **Asset Exchanges** (revision of *APB Opinion No. 29, SFAS No. 153*)

Section 2   **Consolidation of Variable Interest Entities** (*FASB Interpretation No. 46R*)

Section 3   **Other-than-Temporary Impairments** (*EITF 03-01*)

Section 4   **Stock-Based Compensation** (amendment of *SFAS No. 123, SFAS No. 123R*)

Section 5   **Pension Disclosures** (*SFAS No. 132R*)

Section 6   **Accounting Changes** (replacement of *APB Opinion No. 20, SFAS No. 154*)

Section 7   **Miscellaneous Update Topics:**

      Income Statement Reporting of Changes in Accounting Principle (replacement of *APB Opinion No. 20, SFAS No. 154*)

      Inventory Costs (amendment of *ARB No. 43, SFAS No. 151*)

      Preferred Stock (*SFAS No. 150*)

OTHER WAYS TO STAY UP-TO-DATE

A **quarterly eNewsletter** is distributed to users of *Fundamentals of Intermediate Accounting*, to provide information that updates and complements material in the textbook. Each newsletter contains four parts: (1) *Updates* provide the latest information about new accounting standards. (2) *Financial Reporting Challenges* address a contemporary issue being debated by accounting professionals and standard setters. (3) *"By the Way"* provides a "heads-up" to instructors on topics that have implications for the intermediate accounting course. (4) *CPA Exam Update*, prepared by Debra R. Hopkins, CPA, CIA, Director of the Northern Illinois University CPA Review, shares information useful for preparing student for the new CPA exam.

FARS Online (Educational Version) gives students six complete infobases: Original Pronouncements, Current Text, EITF Abstracts, Staff Implementation Guides (Q&A), Derivative Instruments and Hedging Activities, and a Comprehensive Topical Index. To learn more or to access FARS Online, visit www.wiley.com/college/farsonline.

Key to Using this Update

The following chapters in *Fundamentals of Intermediate Accounting* are affected by the update information described in the callout boxes below.

5 Income Statement and Related Information

> SECTION 7 contains MISCELLANEOUS UPDATE TOPICS. The first part of Section 7, about **INCOME STATEMENT REPORTING OF CHANGE IN ACCOUNTING PRINCIPLE,** should be used IN PLACE OF the discussion on pages 187–193 of Chapter 5.

8 Accounting for Inventories

> The second part of SECTION 7, about **INVENTORY COSTS,** should be used AS A COMPLEMENT TO the discussion on pages 351–352 of Chapter 8.

9 Accounting for Property, Plant, and Equipment

> SECTION 1 of the Update, about **ASSET EXCHANGES,** should be used IN PLACE OF the discussion on pages 428–432 of Chapter 9.

12 Stockholders' Equity

> The third part of SECTION 7, about **PREFERRED STOCK,** should be used IN PLACE OF footnote 10, page 590, of Chapter 12.

13 Investments

> SECTION 2 of the Update, about **CONSOLIDATION OF VARIABLE INTEREST ENTITIES,** should be used AS A SUPPLEMENT TO the discussion on page 650 of Chapter 13.

> SECTION 3 of the Update, about **OTHER-THAN-TEMPORARY IMPAIRMENTS,** should be used AS AN APPENDIX TO Chapter 13.

15 Accounting for Compensation

> SECTION 4 of the Update, about **STOCK-BASED COMPENSATION,** should be used IN PLACE OF the discussion on pages 743–750 of Chapter 15.

> SECTION 5 of the Update, about **PENSION DISCLOSURES,** should be used IN PLACE OF the discussion on pages 760–762 of Chapter 15.

17 Additional Reporting Issues

> SECTION 6 of the Update, about **ACCOUNTING CHANGES,** should be used IN PLACE OF the discussion on pages 824–834 of Chapter 17. In addition, throughout Chapter 17, references to *APB Opinion No. 20* should be replaced with *SFAS No. 154.*

In 2004, the FASB issued a new standard addressing the accounting for exchanges of productive assets. This new standard, "Exchanges of Nonmonetary Assets, an Amendment of *APB Opinion No. 29*," *Statement of Financial Accounting Standards No. 153* (Norwalk, Conn.: FASB, 2004), is part of the FASB's short-term international convergence project and amends *APB Opinion No. 29*.

The following material should be used **in place of** the discussion in Chapter 9, pages 428–432, of *Fundamentals of Intermediate Accounting*.

Exchanges of Nonmonetary Assets

The proper accounting for exchanges of nonmonetary assets (such as inventories and property, plant, and equipment) is controversial.[1] Some argue that the accounting for these types of exchanges should be based on the fair value of the asset given up or the fair value of the asset received, with a gain or loss recognized. Others believe that the accounting should be based on the recorded amount (book value) of the asset given up, with no gain or loss recognized. Still others favor an approach that would recognize losses in all cases, but defer gains in special situations.

Ordinarily accounting for the exchange of nonmonetary assets should be based on **the fair value of the asset given up or the fair value of the asset received, whichever is clearly more evident**.[2] Thus, any gains or losses on the exchange **should be recognized immediately**. The rationale for this approach is that most transactions have **commercial substance** and therefore should be recognized.

Meaning of Commercial Substance

As indicated above, fair value is the basis for measuring an asset acquired in a nonmonetary exchange, **if the transaction has commercial substance**. An exchange has commercial substance if the future cash flows change as a result of the transaction. That is, if the two parties' economic positions change, the transaction has commercial substance. For example, Andrew Co. exchanges some of its equipment for land held by Roddick Inc. It is likely that the timing and amount of the cash flows arising from the land received in the exchange will be significantly different from the cash flows from the equipment. As a result, both Andrew Co. and Roddick Inc. are in **different economic positions**. Therefore the exchange has commercial substance, and the companies should recognize a gain or loss on the exchange.

Even if similar assets are exchanged (e.g., an exchange of a truck for another truck), a change in the economic position of the company can result. For example, let's say the useful life of the truck received is significantly longer than the truck given up. In this case the cash flows for the trucks can be significantly different. As a result, the transaction has commercial substance and fair value should be used as a basis for measuring the asset received in the exchange. However, if the difference in cash flows is not

---

[1]Nonmonetary assets are items whose price in terms of the monetary unit may change over time. Monetary assets—cash and short- or long-term accounts and notes receivable—are fixed in terms of units of currency by contract or otherwise.

[2]"Accounting for Nonmonetary Transactions," *Opinions of the Accounting Principles Board No. 29* (New York: AICPA, 1973), par 18, and "Exchanges of Nonmonetary Assets, an Amendment of *APB Opinion No. 29*," *Statement of Financial Accounting Standards No. 153* (Norwalk, Conn.: FASB, 2004).

significant, then the company is in the same economic position as before the exchange.[3] In this case, losses are recognized but gains are generally deferred.

As we will see in the examples below, use of fair value generally results in recognition of a gain or loss at the time of the exchange. Consequently companies must carefully evaluate the cash flow characteristics of the assets exchanged to determine if the transaction has commercial substance.[4] Asset exchange situations and the related accounting are summarized in Illustration U9-1.

ILLUSTRATION U9-1
Accounting for Exchanges

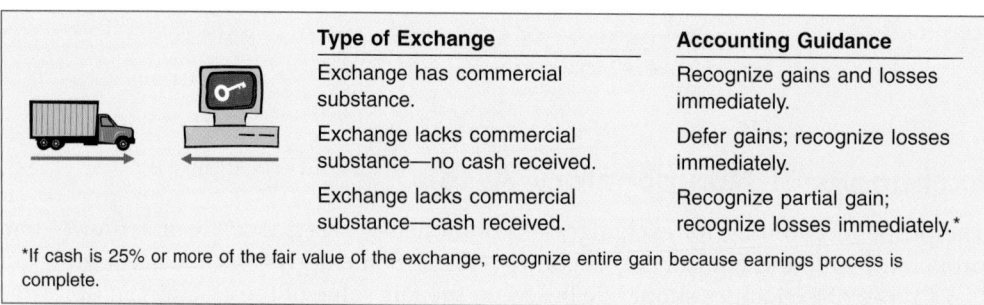

Type of Exchange	Accounting Guidance
Exchange has commercial substance.	Recognize gains and losses immediately.
Exchange lacks commercial substance—no cash received.	Defer gains; recognize losses immediately.
Exchange lacks commercial substance—cash received.	Recognize partial gain; recognize losses immediately.*

*If cash is 25% or more of the fair value of the exchange, recognize entire gain because earnings process is complete.

As Illustration U9-1 indicates, losses are reported on all exchanges. However, the accounting for gains depends on whether the exchange has commercial substance. The profession modifies the general rule for immediate recognition of a gain when exchanges lack commercial substance. If no cash is received, a gain is not recognized but is deferred. If cash is received, then a portion of the gain is recognized immediately. To illustrate the accounting for these different types of transactions, we will examine various loss and gain exchange situations.

Exchanges—Loss Situation

When nonmonetary assets are exchanged and a loss results, the loss is recognized immediately. The rationale: Assets should not be valued at more than their cash equivalent price. If the loss is deferred, assets are overstated. A loss is therefore recognized immediately whether the exchange has commercial substance or lacks commercial substance.

For example, Information Processing, Inc. trades its used machine for a new model; the exchange has commercial substance. The machine given up has a book value of $8,000 (original cost $12,000 less $4,000 accumulated depreciation) and a fair value of $6,000. It is traded for a new model that has a list price of $16,000. In negotiations with the seller, a trade-in allowance of $9,000 is finally agreed on for the used machine. The cash payment that must be made for the new asset and the cost of the new machine are computed as shown in Illustration U9-2.

---

[3]According to previous accounting standards, the primary factor in determining whether to recognize gains on exchanges was based on whether the assets exchanged were "similar" in nature. This approach was criticized due to the subjectivity of determining similarity in the assets being exchanged. Adopting the commercial-substance condition addresses this concern and contributes to international accounting convergence. The FASB and the IASB are collaborating on a project in which they have agreed to converge around high-quality solutions to resolve differences between U.S. GAAP and International Financial Reporting Standards (IFRS). By adopting the commercial-substance approach, U.S. GAAP and IFRS are now in agreement.

[4]The determination of the commercial substance of a transaction requires significant judgment. In determining whether future cash flows change, it is necessary to either (1) determine whether the risk, timing, and amount of cash flows arising for the asset received is different from the cash flows associated with the outbound asset, or (2) evaluate whether cash flows are affected with the exchange versus without the exchange. Also note that if fair values of the assets exchanged are not determinable, then the recorded book values are used to record the exchange.

List price of new machine	$16,000
Less: Trade-in allowance for used machine	9,000
Cash payment due	7,000
Fair value of used machine	6,000
Cost of new machine	$13,000

ILLUSTRATION U9-2
Computation of Cost of
New Machine

The journal entry to record this transaction is:

Equipment	13,000	
Accumulated Depreciation—Equipment	4,000	
Loss on Disposal of Equipment	2,000	
Equipment		12,000
Cash		7,000

The loss on the disposal of the used machine can be verified as follows.

Fair value of used machine	$6,000
Book value of used machine	8,000
Loss on disposal of used machine	$2,000

ILLUSTRATION U9-3
Computation of Loss on
Disposal of Used
Machine

Why was the trade-in allowance or the book value of the old asset not used as a basis for the new equipment? The trade-in allowance is not used because it included a price concession (similar to a price discount) to the purchaser. For example, few individuals pay list price for a new car. Trade-in allowances on the used car are often inflated so that actual selling prices are below list prices. To record the car at list price would state it at an amount in excess of its cash equivalent price because the new car's list price is usually inflated. Similarly, use of book value in this situation would overstate the value of the new machine by $2,000.

Exchanges—Gain Situation

Has Commercial Substance. If an exchange has commercial substance, the cost of a nonmonetary asset acquired in exchange for another nonmonetary asset is usually recorded at the **fair value of the asset given up**, and a gain or loss is recognized. The **fair value of the asset received** should be used only if it is more clearly evident than the fair value of the asset given up.

To illustrate, Interstate Transportation Company exchanged a number of used trucks plus cash for vacant land that might be used for a future plant site. The trucks have a combined book value of $42,000 (cost $64,000 less $22,000 accumulated depreciation). Interstate's purchasing agent, who has had previous dealings in the second-hand market, indicates that the trucks have a fair market value of $49,000. In addition to the trucks, Interstate must pay $17,000 cash for the land. The cost of the land to Interstate is $66,000 computed as follows.

Fair value of trucks exchanged	$49,000
Cash paid	17,000
Cost of land	$66,000

ILLUSTRATION U9-4
Computation of Land
Cost

The journal entry to record the exchange transaction is:

Land	66,000	
Accumulated Depreciation—Trucks	22,000	
Trucks		64,000
Gain on Disposal of Trucks		7,000
Cash		17,000

The gain is the difference between the fair value of the trucks and their book value. It is verified as shown in Illustration U9-5.

ILLUSTRATION U9-5
Computation of Gain on
Disposal of Used Trucks

Fair value of trucks		$49,000
Cost of trucks	$64,000	
Less: Accumulated depreciation	22,000	
Book value of trucks		42,000
Gain on disposal of used trucks		$ 7,000

In this case, the company is in a different economic position, and therefore the transaction has commercial substance. Thus, **a gain is recognized**.

Lacks Commercial Substance—No Cash Received. We now assume that the Interstate Transportation Company exchange lacks commercial substance. That is, the economic position of Interstate did not change significantly as a result of this exchange. In this case, the gain of $7,000 is deferred, and the basis of the vacant land is reduced. Two different but acceptable computations are shown below to illustrate this reduction.

ILLUSTRATION U9-6
Basis of Land—Fair Value
vs. Book Value

Fair value of land	$66,000		Book value of trucks		$42,000
Less: Gain deferred	7,000	**or**	Plus: Cash paid		17,000
Basis of land	$59,000		Basis of land		$59,000

The entry by Interstate to record this transaction is as follows:

Land	59,000	
Accumulated Depreciation—Trucks	22,000	
Trucks		64,000
Cash		17,000

The gain that reduced the basis of the land is recognized when the land is sold, not at the time of the exchange if the exchange lacks commercial substance.

Lacks Commercial Substance—Some Cash Received. An exception to the rule that gains are deferred when the exchange lacks commercial substance occurs when cash (sometimes referred to as "boot") is received. In this situation, a portion of the gain should be recognized.[5] Illustration U9-7 shows the general formula for gain recognition when some cash is received.

ILLUSTRATION U9-7
Formula for Gain
Recognition, Some Cash
Received

$$\frac{\text{Cash Received (Boot)}}{\text{Cash Received (Boot)} + \text{Fair Value of Other Assets Received}} \times \text{Total Gain} = \text{Recognized Gain}$$

To illustrate, assume that Queenan Corporation traded in used machinery with a book value of $60,000 (cost $110,000 less accumulated depreciation $50,000) and a fair value of $100,000. It receives in exchange a machine with a fair value of $90,000 and cash of $10,000. The total gain on the exchange is computed as follows.

ILLUSTRATION U9-8
Computation of Total
Gain

Fair value of machine exchanged	$100,000
Book value of machine exchanged	60,000
Total gain	$ 40,000

---

[5]When the monetary consideration is significant, i.e., **25 percent or more** of the fair value of the exchange, the transaction is considered a **monetary exchange** by both parties. In such monetary exchanges the fair values are used to measure the gains or losses that are recognized in their entirety. *EITF Issue No. 86–29,* "Nonmonetary Transactions: Magnitude of Boot and the Exception to the Use of Fair Value," *Emerging Issues Task Force Abstracts* (October 1, 1987).

Generally, when a transaction lacks commercial substance, any gain is deferred. But because Queenan received $10,000 in cash, a partial gain is recognized, computed as follows.

$$\frac{\$10,000}{\$10,000 + \$90,000} \times \$40,000 = \$4,000$$

ILLUSTRATION U9-9
Computation of Gain Based on Ratio of Cash Received

The ratio of monetary assets ($10,000) to the total consideration received ($10,000/$100,000) is the portion of the total gain ($40,000) to be recognized—that is, $4,000. Because only a gain of $4,000 is recognized on this transaction, the remaining $36,000 ($40,000 – $4,000) is deferred and reduces the basis (recorded cost) of the new machine. The computation of the basis is as follows.

Fair value of new machine	$90,000	Book value of old machine	$60,000
Less: Gain deferred	36,000	Portion of book value presumed sold	6,000*
Basis of new machine	$54,000	Basis of new machine	$54,000

$$\frac{*\$10,000}{\$100,000} \times \$60,000 = \$6,000$$

ILLUSTRATION U9-10
Computation of Gain Based on Ratio of Cost Received

The entry by Queenan to record this transaction is as follows.

Cash	10,000	
Machine (New)	54,000	
Accumulated Depreciation—Machine	50,000	
Machine (Old)		110,000
Gain on Disposal of Machine		4,000

The rationale for this treatment is as follows: Before the exchange, Queenan had an unrecognized gain of $40,000, as evidenced by the difference between the book value ($60,000) and the fair value ($100,000) of its old machine. When the exchange occurred, a portion of the fair value ($10,000/$100,000) or 1/10 was converted to a more liquid asset. The ratio of this liquid asset ($10,000) to the total consideration received ($10,000 + $90,000) is the portion of the total gain realized. Thus the gain of $4,000 (1/10 × $40,000) is recognized and recorded.

Presented below in summary form are the accounting requirements for recognizing gains and losses on exchanges of nonmonetary assets.[6]

1. Compute the total gain or loss on the transaction. This amount is equal to the difference between the fair value of the asset given up and the book value of the asset given up.

2. If a loss is computed in step 1, always recognize the entire loss.

3. If a gain is computed in step 1,
  (a) and the exchange has commercial substance, the entire gain is recognized.
  (b) and the exchange lacks commercial substance,
    (1) and no cash is involved, no gain is recognized.
    (2) and some cash is given, no gain is recognized.
    (3) and some cash is received, the following portion of the gain is recognized:

$$\frac{\text{Cash Received (Boot)}}{\text{Cash Received (Boot)} + \text{Fair Value of Other Assets Received}} \times \text{Total Gain*}$$

*If the amount of cash exchanged is 25% or more, recognize entire gain.

ILLUSTRATION U9-11
Summary of Gain and Loss Recognition on Exchanges of Nonmonetary Assets

---

[6]Adapted from an article by Robert Capettini and Thomas E. King, "Exchanges of Nonmonetary Assets: Some Changes," *The Accounting Review* (January 1976).

An enterprise that engages in nonmonetary exchanges in a period should disclose in financial statements for the period the nature of the transactions, the method of accounting for the assets transferred, and gains or losses recognized on transfers.[7]

WHAT DO THE NUMBERS MEAN?

ABOUT THOSE SWAPS

Roy Olofson, former vice president of finance for Global Crossing, accused company executives of improperly describing the company's revenue to the public. Olofson said Global Crossing had improperly recorded long-term sales immediately rather than over the term of the contract, that it improperly booked swaps of capacity with other carriers as cash transactions, and that it fired him when he blew the whistle.

The accounting for the swaps is of particular interest. The accounting for swaps involves exchanges of similar network capacity. Companies said they engaged in such deals because it was less costly and quicker than building segments that their own networks lacked, or because such pacts provided redundancies to make their own networks more reliable. In one expert's view, an exchange of similar network capacity is the equivalent of trading a blue truck for a red truck—it shouldn't boost a company's revenue.

But Global Crossing and Qwest, among others, used the transactions to do just that, counting as revenue the money received from the company on the other end of the deal. (In general, in transactions involving leased capacity, the companies booked the revenue over the life of the contract.) Some of these companies then treated their own purchases as capital expenditures, which weren't run through the income statement. Instead, the spending led to the addition of assets on the balance sheet.

Both congressional and SEC investigators are seeking to determine whether some of these capacity exchanges may have been a device to pad revenue. Revenue growth was a key factor in the valuation of some of these companies, such as Global Crossing and Qwest, throughout the tech stock craze in the late 1990s and 2000.

Source: Adapted from Henny Sender, "Telecoms Draw Focus for Moves in Accounting," *Wall Street Journal* (March 26, 2002), p. C7.

EXERCISES

UE9-1 (Nonmonetary Exchange) Cannondale Company purchased an electric wax melter on April 30, 2005, by trading in its old gas model and paying the balance in cash. The following data relate to the purchase.

List price of new melter	$15,800
Cash paid	10,000
Cost of old melter (5-year life, $700 residual value)	11,200
Accumulated depreciation—old melter (straight-line)	6,300
Second-hand market value of old melter	5,200

Instructions

Prepare the journal entry(ies) necessary to record this exchange, assuming that the exchange **(a)** has commercial substance, and **(b)** lacks commercial substance. Cannondale's fiscal year ends on December 31, and depreciation has been recorded through December 31, 2004.

UE9-2 (Nonmonetary Exchange) Carlos Arruza Company exchanged equipment used in its manufacturing operations plus $3,000 in cash for similar equipment used in the operations of Tony LoBianco Company. The following information pertains to the exchange.

---

[7]"Accounting for Nonmonetary Transactions," op. cit., par. 28.

	Carlos Arruza Co.	Tony LoBianco Co.
Equipment (cost)	$28,000	$28,000
Accumulated depreciation	19,000	10,000
Fair value of equipment	12,500	15,500
Cash given up	3,000	

Instructions

(a) Prepare the journal entries to record the exchange on the books of both companies. Assume that the exchange lacks commercial substance.

(b) Prepare the journal entries to record the exchange on the books of both companies. Assume that the exchange has commercial substance.

UE9-3 (Nonmonetary Exchange) Busytown Corporation, which manufactures shoes, hired a recent college graduate to work in its accounting department. On the first day of work, the accountant was assigned to total a batch of invoices with the use of an adding machine. Before long, the accountant, who had never before seen such a machine, managed to break the machine. Busytown Corporation gave the machine plus $340 to Dick Tracy Business Machine Company (dealer) in exchange for a new machine. Assume the following information about the machines. (The difference in expected cash flows between the exchanged machines is significant.)

	Busytown Corp. (Old Machine)	Dick Tracy Co. (New Machine)
Machine cost	$290	$270
Accumulated depreciation	140	–0–
Fair value	85	425

Instructions

For each company, prepare the necessary journal entry to record the exchange.

UE9-4 (Nonmonetary Exchange) Dana Ashbrook Inc. has negotiated the purchase of a new piece of equipment at a price of $8,000 plus trade-in, f.o.b. factory. Dana Ashbrook Inc. paid $8,000 cash and traded in used equipment. The used equipment had originally cost $62,000; it had a book value of $42,000 and a secondhand market value of $47,800, as indicated by recent transactions involving similar equipment. Freight and installation charges for the new equipment required a cash payment of $1,100.

Instructions

(a) Prepare the general journal entry to record this transaction, assuming that the exchange has commercial substance.

(b) Assume the same facts as in (a) except that fair value information for the assets exchanged is not determinable. Prepare the general journal entry to record this transaction.

PROBLEMS

UP9-1 (Nonmonetary Exchanges) Susquehanna Corporation wishes to exchange a machine used in its operations. Susquehanna has received the following offers from other companies in the industry.

1. Choctaw Company offered to exchange a similar machine plus $23,000 (exchange has commercial substance).
2. Powhatan Company offered to exchange a similar machine (exchange lacks commercial substance).
3. Shawnee Company offered to exchange a similar machine, but wanted $8,000 in addition to Susquehanna's machine (exchange has commercial substance).

	Susquehanna	Choctaw	Powhatan	Shawnee
Machine cost	$160,000	$120,000	$147,000	$160,000
Accumulated depreciation	50,000	45,000	71,000	75,000
Fair value	92,000	69,000	92,000	100,000

Instructions

For each of the three independent situations, prepare the journal entries to record the exchange on the books of each company.

UP9-2 (Nonmonetary Exchanges) On August 1, Arna, Inc. exchanged productive assets with Bontemps, Inc. Arna's asset is referred to below as "Asset A," and Bontemps' is referred to as "Asset B." The following facts pertain to these assets.

	Asset A	Asset B
Original cost	$96,000	$110,000
Accumulated depreciation (to date of exchange)	45,000	52,000
Fair market value at date of exchange	60,000	75,000
Cash paid by Arna, Inc.	15,000	
Cash received by Bontemps, Inc.		15,000

Instructions

(a) Assuming that the exchange of Assets A and B has commercial substance, record the exchange for both Arna, Inc. and Bontemps, Inc. in accordance with generally accepted accounting principles.

(b) Assuming that the exchange of Assets A and B lacks commercial substance, record the exchange for both Arna, Inc. and Bontemps, Inc. in accordance with generally accepted accounting principles.

UP9-3 (Nonmonetary Exchanges) During the current year, Garrison Construction trades an old crane that has a book value of $80,000 (original cost $140,000 less accumulated depreciation $60,000) for a new crane from Keillor Manufacturing Co. The new crane cost Keillor $165,000 to manufacture and is classified as inventory. The following information is also available.

	Garrison Const.	Keillor Mfg. Co.
Fair market value of old crane	$ 72,000	
Fair market value of new crane		$190,000
Cash paid	118,000	
Cash received		118,000

Instructions

(a) Assuming that this exchange is considered to have commercial substance, prepare the journal entries on the books of (1) Garrison Construction and (2) Keillor Manufacturing.

(b) Assuming that this exchange lacks commercial substance for Garrison, prepare the journal entries on the books of Garrison Construction.

(c) Assuming the same facts as those in (a), except that the fair market value of the old crane is $98,000 and the cash paid is $92,000, prepare the journal entries on the books of (1) Garrison Construction and (2) Keillor Manufacturing.

(d) Assuming the same facts as those in (b), except that the fair market value of the old crane is $87,000 and the cash paid $103,000. Prepare the journal entries on the books of Garrison Construction.

SECTION 2 CONSOLIDATION OF VARIABLE INTEREST ENTITIES

Late in 2003, the FASB issued an interpretation of *ARB No. 51*. That document, *FASB Interpretation No. 46 (Revised)*, "Consolidation of Variable Interest Entities," addresses the concern that some companies were not reporting the risks and rewards of certain investments and other financial arrangements in their consolidated financial statements. While preparation of consolidated financial statements is generally beyond the scope of most intermediate accounting courses, many of the investments and arrangements addressed in the interpretation are topics in intermediate accounting.

The following discussion can be used **as a supplement** to the section "Holdings of More than 50%" in Chapter 13, on page 650, of *Fundamentals of Intermediate Accounting*.

CONSOLIDATED FINANCIAL STATEMENTS: ADDITIONAL REPORTING ISSUES

As one analyst noted, **Enron** showed the world the power of the idea that "if investors can't see it, they can't ask you about it—the 'it' being assets and liabilities." What exactly did Enron do? For starters, it created a number of entities whose purpose was to hide debt, avoid taxes, and enrich certain management personnel to the detriment of the company and its stockholders. In effect, these entities, often dubbed **special purpose entities (SPEs)**, appeared to be separate entities for which Enron had a limited economic interest. Unfortunately, for many of these arrangements, Enron actually had a substantial economic interest because the risks and rewards of ownership were not shifted to the entities but remained with Enron. In short, Enron was obligated to repay investors in these SPEs when they were unsuccessful. Once Enron's problems were discovered, it soon became apparent that many other companies had similar problems.

What About GAAP?

A reasonable question to ask with regard to SPEs is, "Why didn't GAAP prevent companies from hiding SPE debt and other risks, by forcing companies to include these obligations in their consolidated financial statements?" To understand why, we have to look at the basic rules of consolidation. The GAAP rules indicate that consolidated financial statements are "usually necessary for a fair presentation when one of the companies in the group directly or indirectly has a controlling financial interest in other companies." It further notes that "the usual condition for a controlling financial interest is ownership of a majority voting interest." In other words, if a company like Intel owns more than 50 percent of the voting stock of another company, Intel consolidates that company. GAAP also indicates that controlling financial interest may be achieved through arrangements that do not involve voting interests. However, applying these guidelines in practice is difficult.

Whenever a clear line, like "greater than 50 percent" is used, the criterion is sometimes exploited. For example, some companies set up joint ventures in which each party owns exactly 50 percent. In that case, neither party consolidates. Or the company owns less than 50 percent of the voting stock, but maintains effective control through board of director relationships or supply relationships, or through some other type of financial arrangement.

So the FASB realized that changes had to be made to GAAP for consolidations, and it issued *SFAS Interpretation No. 46 (Revised)*, "Consolidation of Variable Interest Entities." This interpretation (*FIN No. 46R*) defines when a company should use factors other than voting interest to determine controlling financial interest. In this interpretation, the FASB created a new risk-and-reward model to be used in situations where voting interests were unclear. The risk-and-reward model answers the basic question of who stands to gain or lose the most from ownership in an SPE when ownership is uncertain.

In other words, we now have two models for consolidation:

1. **Voting-interest model**—If a company owns more than 50 percent of another company, then consolidate in most cases.
2. **Risk-and-reward model**—If a company is involved substantially in the economics of another company, then consolidate.

Operationally, the voting-interest model is easily applied: It sets a "bright line" ownership standard of more than 50 percent of the voting stock. However, if control can not be determined based on voting interest, the risk-and-reward model may be used.

A Closer Look at the New GAAP

To answer the question of who gains or loses when voting rights do not determine consolidation, the FASB developed a risk-and-reward model. In this model, the FASB introduced the notion of a variable interest entity. A **variable interest entity (VIE)** is an entity that has **one** of the following characteristics:

1. **Insufficient equity investment at risk**. Stockholders are assumed to have sufficient capital investment to support the entity's operations. If thinly capitalized, the entity is considered a VIE and is subject to the risk-and-reward model.
2. **Stockholders lack decision-making rights**. In some cases, stockholders do not have the influence to control the company's destiny.

❸ **Stockholders do not absorb the losses or receive the benefits of a normal stock-holder**. In some entities, stockholders are shielded from losses related to their primary risks, or their returns are capped or must be shared by other parties.

Once it is determined that an entity is a variable interest entity, the voting-interest model is no longer appropriate. The question that must then be asked is, "What party is exposed to the majority of the risks and rewards associated with the VIE?" This party is called the **primary beneficiary** and must consolidate the VIE. The decision model for the VIE consolidation model is shown in Illustration U13-1.

ILLUSTRATION U13-1
VIE Consolidation Model

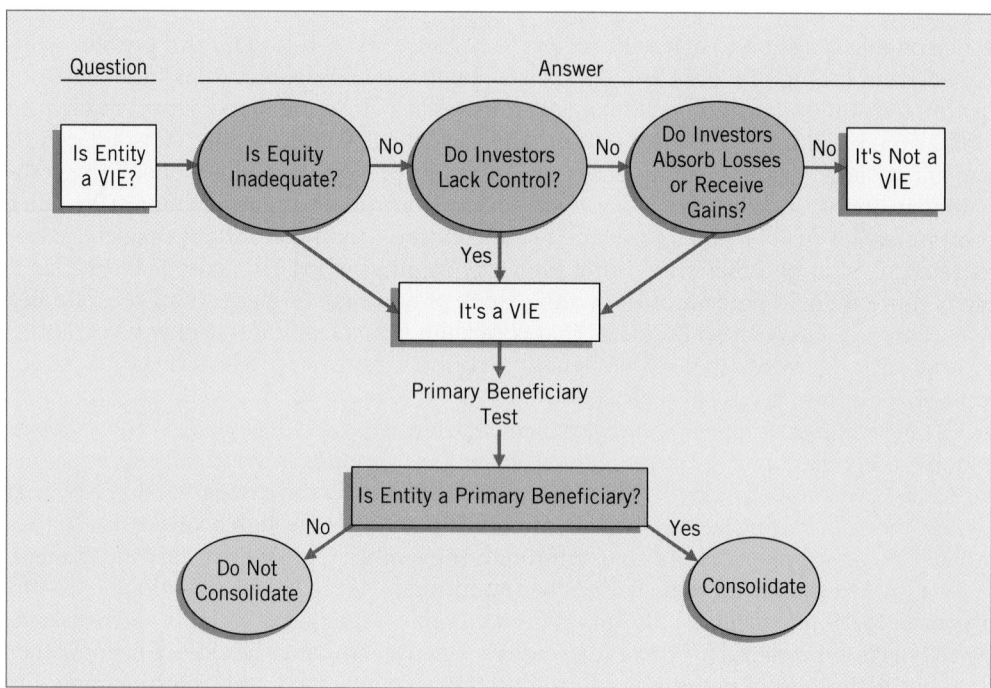

Note that the primary beneficiary may have the risks and rewards of ownership through use of a variety of instruments and financial arrangements, such as equity investments, loans to the VIE, leases, derivatives, and guarantees. Potential VIEs include the following: corporations, partnerships, limited liability companies, and majority-owned subsidiaries.

ILLUSTRATION U13-2
Impact of *FIN No. 46 R*

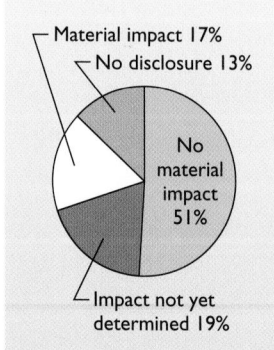

SOURCE: Company Reports, *Glass, Lewis, & Co. Research Report* (November 6, 2003).

WHAT IS HAPPENING IN PRACTICE?

As shown in Illustration U13-2, one study of 509 companies with total market values over $500 million found that 17 percent of the companies reviewed have a material impact from *FIN No. 46R*.

Of the material VIEs disclosed, the most common types (42%) were related to joint-venture equity investments, followed by off-balance-sheet lease arrangements (22%). In some cases, companies are restructuring transactions to avoid consolidation. For example, **Pep Boys, Choice Point, Inc.**, and **Anadarko** all appear to have restructured their lease transactions to avoid consolidation. On the other hand, companies like **eBay, Kimberly-Clark**, and **Williams-Sonoma Inc.** intend to or have consolidated their VIEs.

In summary, *FIN No. 46R* introduces a new model for determining if certain investments or other financial arrangements should be included in consolidated financial statements. As a result, financial statements should be more complete in reporting the risks and rewards of these transactions.

Since publication of *Fundamentals of Intermediate Accounting*, the Emerging Issues Task Force (EITF) reached a consensus on "Other-Than-Temporary Impairment" of debt and equity investments (*EITF Issue No. 03-1*, "The Meaning of Other-Than-Temporary Impairment and Its Application to Certain Investments"). This new standard is described below.

This discussion should be considered **an appendix to Chapter 13**. It provides additional analysis as to the recognition of impairments.

APPENDIX 13B: OTHER-THAN-TEMPORARY IMPAIRMENTS OF CERTAIN INVESTMENTS

As discussed in the chapter, determination of whether an equity or debt investment is impaired is predicated on the notion of "other than temporary." However, conflicting guidance in the accounting literature about the meaning of "other than temporary" has resulted in inconsistent application in practice. Consequently, the EITF addressed this issue to develop a common approach for evaluating other-than-temporary impairments. In brief, the EITF provides guidance based on application of the following three-step model:

- **Step 1:** Determine whether an investment is impaired.
- **Step 2:** Evaluate whether an impairment is other than temporary.
- **Step 3:** If the impairment is other than temporary, recognize an impairment loss equal to the difference between the investment's cost and its fair value.

Also addressed in the consensus is the accounting subsequent to the recognition of the impairment and required disclosures about unrealized losses not recognized as other-than-temporary impairments.

Three-Step Model

Recall that **debt investments** are classified into three categories: (1) held-to-maturity, (2) trading securities, and (3) available-for-sale securities. **Investments in equity securities** are classified into four categories: (1) available-for-sale, (2) trading, (3) equity method, and (4) full consolidation. The general guidelines in accounting for investments in securities are that available-for-sale or trading securities are adjusted to fair value, and the related income or loss amount is reported as part of income or as part of comprehensive income.

Every investment should be evaluated at each reporting date to determine if it has suffered an **impairment**—a loss in value that is other-than-temporary. If the decline is judged to be other-than-temporary, the cost basis of the individual security is written down to a new cost basis. The amount of the write-down is accounted for as a realized loss and, therefore, is included in net income.

In practice, the notion of "other-than-temporary" has been interpreted in different ways, and inconsistencies in accounting for impairments have developed. The accounting now is based on the application of a three-step model.

Step 1: Determine Whether an Investment Is Impaired

Consistent with other authoritative literature, an investment is **impaired if the fair value of the investment is less than its cost.** This assessment should be performed each reporting period. Because the fair value of most cost method investments is not readily determinable, impairment evaluation may be triggered by **impairment indicators**. Examples of such indicators are a significant deterioration in the earnings performance, credit rating, asset quality, business prospects of the investee, or a significant adverse change in the regulatory, economic, or technological environment of the investee. If an impairment indicator is present, the investor should estimate the fair value of the investment.

Step 2: Evaluate Whether an Impairment Is Other-Than-Temporary

In general, an **impairment should be recorded** unless:

a. The investor has the ability and intent to hold an investment for a reasonable period of time sufficient for a forecasted recovery of fair value up to (or beyond) the cost of the investment,

   and

b. Evidence indicating that the cost of the investment is recoverable within a reasonable period of time outweighs evidence to the contrary.

The "ability and intent" to hold an investment is assessed based on a couple of guidelines. The first is whether the investor's cash or working capital requirements and contractual or regulatory obligations indicate that the investment may need to be sold before the forecasted recovery of fair value occurs. The second guideline is whether the issuer has the ability to settle the security during the forecasted recovery period.

To evaluate the amount of the impairment, the investor should assess (a) the extent to which fair value is below cost, and (b) the nature of the event (or events) that gave rise to the impairment. Thus, an other-than-temporary impairment may occur if, based on all available evidence, the cost of the investment is not recoverable within a reasonable period of time.

Step 3: Recognize an Impairment Loss

If it is determined in Step 2 that the impairment is other-than-temporary, then an impairment loss should be recognized in earnings equal to the difference between the investment's cost and its fair value at the balance sheet date for which the assessment is made. The **fair value of the investment would then become the new cost basis** of the investment. That amount **should not be adjusted for subsequent recoveries in fair value**.

Here is an example that illustrates the above points.

Example

Amclone Company is developing a product that is highly anticipated by the market. On January 1, 2004, Costello Inc. purchased 200,000 shares of Amclone stock at a cost of $20 per share. On May 1, 2004, a regulatory body informed Amclone that the product did not meet certain regulatory requirements and therefore would not receive the regulatory approval required to sell the product.

On May 2, 2004, Amclone issued a press release announcing the regulator's decision. The company also reiterated its belief that it will ultimately obtain regulatory approval. However, no evidence exists to support its assertion at this time. Amclone's share price immediately declined from $34 per share to $10 per share, and it traded in the $10 to $12 range through June 30, 2004. At June 30, 2004, the price was $11. No information is available to support a recovery of fair value up to (or beyond) the cost of the investment. Costello has the ability and intent to hold the investment for an indefinite period.

Solution

If we use the three-step model for assessing impairments, we have the following:

Step 1: Determine whether Costello's investment in Amclone is impaired. The investment is impaired because the cost of the investment, $4,000,000 (200,000 × $20) is higher than its fair value of $2,200,000 (200,000 × $11) on June 30, 2004.

Step 2: Determine whether Costello's investment is other-than-temporary. Even though Costello has the ability and intent to hold the investment for an indefinite period, Costello should deem the investment as other-than-temporarily impaired, given:

❶ The severity of the decline.

❷ The cause of the decline (that is, failure to obtain regulatory approval of a product).

❸ The absence of evidence to support a recovery of fair value up to (or beyond) the cost of the investment within a reasonable period of time.

Consequently, at June 30, 2004, Costello would record an impairment of $1,800,000 ($4,000,000 − $2,200,000) for the Amclone stock held.

Step 3: If the impairment is other-than-temporary, recognize an impairment loss equal to the difference between the investment's cost and its fair value. As noted above, Costello would report a loss on the impairment of $1,800,000. Once the investment is recognized as impaired, the investment now has a new cost basis. The entry to record this loss will depend on classification of the investment (e.g., as trading or available for sale). **This cost basis cannot be adjusted upward** even if the fair value of Amclone stock increases in the next reporting period.

DISCLOSURES RELATED TO INVESTMENTS

Also addressed by the EITF is the topic of additional disclosures related to investments. These additional disclosures were mandated due to concerns expressed regarding the lack of transparency involving unrealized losses on investment accounts. There are three major requirements related to the disclosures of unrealized losses, discussed below.

Tabular Information

Investments with an unrealized loss should be reported in a table, which provides fair value information and the amount of the unrealized loss. In addition, investments should be segregated between investments that have had continuous losses for fewer than 12 months, and those for 12 months or more.

By providing this disclosure, users of the financial statements can better understand how many securities have unrealized losses and how long the fair value of these securities have been below cost. The longer the time the company has this loss, the greater the likelihood the investment is impaired. That is, the greater the likelihood that the loss is other-than-temporary.

Narrative

In addition to the tabular summary, the company is required to explain why the unrealized losses are considered temporary. The disclosure might include a discussion of the nature of the investment, the causes for the unrealized losses, the severity and duration of the unrealized losses, the number of investments in this position, and other substantial evidence used by management in making its impairment judgment.

Cost-Method Investments

Also required is a disclosure of the aggregate carrying amount of cost-method investments and an explanation as to why any cost-based investment was not evaluated for impairment. In other words, the disclosure indicates whether impairment was not considered because estimating fair values was not practical, or because there were no significant adverse effects on the investment.

SECTION 4 STOCK-BASED COMPENSATION

In December 2004 the FASB issued a standard on stock compensation plans. The new standard, "Share-Based Payment," *Statement of Financial Accounting Standards No. 123R* (Norwalk, Conn.: FASB, 2004), is a revision of *SFAS No. 123* and supercedes *APB Opinion No. 25*. In April 2005, the SEC approved an additional six-month delay in adoption of these rules for SEC registrants with December 31 year-ends. Thus, mandatory expensing of stock-based compensation would not begin for most companies until the first quarter of 2006. Many attribute the delay to questions related to the valuation models used to value stock options.

The following material provides information necessary to understand the new standard and can be used **in place of** the discussion in Chapter 15, pages 743–750, of *Fundamentals of Intermediate Accounting*.

STOCK COMPENSATION PLANS

Another form of warrant arises in stock compensation plans used to pay and motivate employees. This warrant is a **stock option**, which gives selected employees the option to purchase common stock at a given price over an extended period of time. As indicated in the opening story, stock options are very popular. For example, the following chart shows stock options as a percentage of total compensation for 1999–2000 given to the top 200 CEOs and to 100 dot-com company CEOs.

ILLUSTRATION U15-1
Stock Options as a Portion of Total Compensation

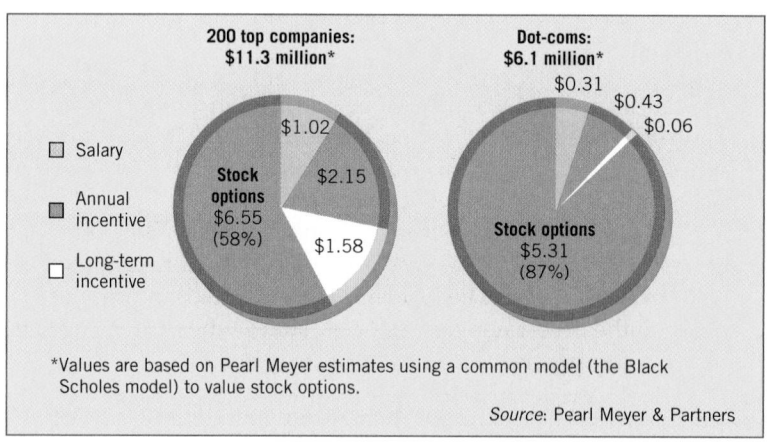

These figures show the dramatic change in the way many top executives (and for that matter, regular employees) are compensated.

Effective compensation has been a subject of considerable interest lately. A consensus of opinion is that effective compensation programs are ones that (1) motivate employees to high levels of performance, (2) help retain executives and allow for recruitment of new talent, (3) base compensation on employee and company performance, (4) maximize the employee's after-tax benefit and minimize the employee's after-tax cost, and (5) use performance criteria over which the employee has control. Although straight cash compensation plans (salary and, perhaps, bonus) are an important part of any compensation program, they are oriented to the short run. Many companies recognize that a more long-run compensation plan is often needed in addition to a cash component.

Long-term compensation plans attempt to develop in key employees a strong loyalty toward the company. An effective way to accomplish this goal is to give the employees "a piece of the action"—that is, an equity interest based on changes in long-term measures such as increases in earnings per share, revenues, stock price, or market share. These plans, generally referred to as **stock option plans**, come in many different forms. Essentially, they provide the employee with the opportunity to receive stock or cash in the future if the performance of the company (by whatever measure) is satisfactory.

The Major Reporting Issue

Suppose that you are an employee for Hurdle Inc. and you are granted options to purchase 10,000 shares of the firm's common stock as part of your compensation. The date you receive the options is referred to as the **grant date**. The options are good for 10 years. The market price and the exercise price for the stock are both $20 at the grant date. **What is the value of the compensation you just received?**

Some believe you have not received anything: That is, the difference between the market price and the exercise price is zero, and therefore no compensation results. Others argue these options have value: If the stock price goes above $20 any time over the next 10 years and you exercise these options, substantial compensation results. For example, if at the end of the fourth year, the market price of the stock is $30 and you exercise your options, you will have earned $100,000 [10,000 options × ($30 − $20)], ignoring income taxes.

How should the granting of these options be reported by Hurdle Inc.? In the past, GAAP required that compensation cost be measured by the excess of the market price of the stock over its exercise price at the grant date. This approach is referred to as the **intrinsic value method** because the computation is not dependent on external circumstances: **The compensation cost is the difference between the market price of the stock and the exercise price of the options at the grant date.** Hurdle would therefore not recognize any compensation expense related to your options because at the grant date the market price and exercise price were the same.

Under previous accounting standards, companies could use **either** the intrinsic or fair value methods for recognizing stock-based compensation. Fair value represents the market value of the option at the date of grant. Most companies adopted the intrinsic value approach because it generally results in lower compensation expense. However, during 2002 a number of companies began voluntarily to switch to the fair value method for recording compensation expense related to stock options. By March 2004 over 500 public companies were using the fair value method. A major reason for this change was that these companies wanted to show the investing community that they believe in fair and transparent financial reporting, particularly in the aftermath of the many financial reporting scandals. Because some companies included stock-based compensation expense in income based on fair value and others only disclosed the pro-forma effects, comparability concerns were raised, and the FASB developed a new standard for stock-based compensation.

The FASB now **requires recognition of compensation cost for the fair value of stock-based compensation paid to employees for their services.**[1] The FASB position is that the accounting for the cost of employee services should be based on the value of compensation paid, which is presumed to be a measure of the value of the services received. Accordingly, the compensation cost arising from employee stock options should be measured based on the fair value of the stock options granted.[2] To determine this value, acceptable option pricing models are used to value options at the date

---

[1]"Accounting for Stock-Based Compensation," *Statement of Financial Accounting Standards No. 123* (Norwalk, Conn.: FASB, 1995). "Share-Based Payment, an Amendment of FASB Statements No. 123 and 95," *Statement of Financial Accounting Standards No. 123R* (Norwalk, Conn.: FASB, 2004).

Note that in 2004 the International Accounting Standards Board (IASB) also issued a statement, titled "Share-Based Payment," which requires the expensing of stock-based compensation based on fair values. Thus the FASB's new standard contributes to international accounting convergence.

[2]Stock options issued to non-employees in exchange for other goods or services must be recognized according to the fair value method in *SFAS 123R*.

of grant. This approach is referred to as the fair value method because the option value is estimated based on the many factors that determine its underlying value.[3]

Accounting for Stock Compensation

Stock option plans involve two main accounting issues:

1. How should compensation expense be determined?
2. Over what periods should compensation expense be allocated?

Determining Expense

Under the fair value method, total compensation expense is computed based on the fair value of the options expected to vest[4] on the date the options are granted to the employee(s) (i.e., the **grant date**). Fair value for public companies is to be estimated using an option pricing model, with some adjustments for the unique factors of employee stock options. No adjustments are made after the grant date, in response to subsequent changes in the stock price—either up or down.

WHAT DO THE NUMBERS MEAN?

A LITTLE HONESTY GOES A LONG WAY

You might think investors would punish companies that have decided to expense stock options. After all, most of corporate America has been battling for years to avoid such a fate, worried that accounting for those perks would destroy earnings. And indeed, Merrill Lynch estimates that if all S&P 500 companies were to expense options [in 2002], reported profits would fall 10 percent.

And yet, as a small but growing band of big-name companies makes the switch, investors have for the most part showered them with love. With a few exceptions, the stock prices of the expensers, from **Cinergy** to **Fannie Mae**, have outpaced the market since they announced the change.

The few, the brave

	Estimated 2002 EPS		% change since announcement**
	Without options	With options expensed*	Company stock price
Cinergy	$ 2.80	$ 2.77	22.4%
Washington Post	20.48	20.10	16.4
Computer Associates	−0.46	−0.62	11.1
Fannie Mae	6.15	6.02	6.7
Bank One	2.77	2.61	2.6
General Motors	5.84	5.45	2.6
Procter & Gamble	3.57	3.35	−2.3
Coca-Cola	1.79	1.70	−6.2
General Electric	1.65	1.61	−6.2
Amazon	0.04	−0.99	−11.4

*Assumes options expenses for 2002 are the same as 2001 and that all outstanding grants are counted.

**As of 8/6/02.

Data sources: Merrill Lynch; company reports.

Source: David Stires, "A Little Honesty Goes a Long Way," *Fortune* (September 2, 2002), p. 186. Reprinted by permission.

---

[3]These factors include the volatility of the underlying stock, the expected life of the options, the risk-free rate during the option life, and expected dividends during the option life.

[4]"To vest" means "to earn the rights to." An employee's award becomes vested at the date that the employee's right to receive or retain shares of stock or cash under the award is no longer contingent on remaining in the service of the employer.

Allocating Compensation Expense

In general, compensation expense is recognized in the periods in which the employee performs the service—the **service period**. Unless otherwise specified, the service period is the vesting period—the time between the grant date and the vesting date. Thus, total compensation cost is determined at the grant date and allocated to the periods benefited by the employees' services.

Illustration

To illustrate the accounting for a stock option plan, assume that on November 1, 2002, the stockholders of Chen Company approve a plan that grants the company's five executives options to purchase 2,000 shares each of the company's $1 par value common stock. The options are granted on January 1, 2003, and may be exercised at any time within the next 10 years. The option price per share is $60, and the market price of the stock at the date of grant is $70 per share.

   Under the fair value method, total compensation expense is computed by applying an acceptable fair value option pricing model (such as the Black-Scholes option pricing model). To keep this illustration simple, we will assume that the fair value option pricing model determines total compensation expense to be $220,000.

Basic Entries. The value of the options is recognized as an expense in the periods in which the employee performs services. In the case of Chen Company, assume that the expected period of benefit is 2 years, starting with the grant date. The journal entries to record the transactions related to this option contract are shown below.

At date of grant (January 1, 2003)

No entry

To record compensation expense for 2003 (December 31, 2003)

Compensation Expense	110,000	
Paid-in Capital—Stock Options		
($220,000 ÷ 2)		110,000

To record compensation expense for 2004 (December 31, 2004)

Compensation Expense	110,000	
Paid-in Capital—Stock Options		110,000

As indicated, compensation expense is allocated evenly over the 2-year service period.

Exercise. If 20 percent, or 2,000, of the 10,000 options were exercised on June 1, 2006 (3 years and 5 months after date of grant), the following journal entry would be recorded.

June 1, 2006

Cash (2,000 × $60)	120,000	
Paid-in Capital—Stock Options (20% × $220,000)	44,000	
Common Stock (2,000 × $1)		2,000
Paid-in Capital in Excess of Par		162,000

Expiration. If the remaining stock options are not exercised before their expiration date, the balance in the Paid-in Capital—Stock Options account should be transferred to a more properly titled paid-in capital account, such as Paid-in Capital from Expired Stock Options. The entry to record this transaction at the date of expiration would be as follows.

January 1, 2013 (expiration date)

Paid-in Capital—Stock Options	176,000	
Paid-in Capital from Expired Stock		
Options (80% × $220,000)		176,000

Adjustment. The fact that a stock option is not exercised does not nullify the propriety of recording the costs of services received from executives and attributable to the stock option plan. Under GAAP, compensation expense is, therefore, not adjusted upon expiration of the options.

However, if a stock option is forfeited because **an employee fails to satisfy a service requirement** (e.g., leaves employment), the estimate of compensation expense recorded in the current period should be adjusted (as a change in estimate). This change in estimate would be recorded by debiting Paid-in Capital—Stock Options and crediting Compensation Expense, thereby decreasing compensation expense in the period of forfeiture.

Types of Plans

Many different types of plans are used to compensate key employees. In all these plans the amount of the reward depends upon future events. Consequently, continued employment is a necessary element in almost all types of plans. The popularity of a given plan usually depends on the firm's prospects in the stock market and on tax considerations. For example, if it appears that appreciation will occur in a company's stock, a plan that offers the option to purchase stock is attractive. Conversely, if it appears that price appreciation is unlikely, then compensation might be tied to some performance measure such as an increase in book value or earnings per share.

Three common compensation plans that illustrate different objectives are:

1. Stock option plans (incentive or nonqualified).
2. Stock appreciation rights plans.
3. Performance-type plans.

Most plans follow the general guidelines for reporting established in the previous sections.

Noncompensatory Plans

In some companies, employee share purchase plans permit all employees to purchase stock at a discounted price for a short period of time. These plans are usually classified as noncompensatory. Noncompensatory means that the primary purpose of the plan is not to compensate the employees but, rather, to enable the employer to secure equity capital or to induce widespread ownership of an enterprise's common stock among employees. Thus, compensation expense is not reported for these plans. Noncompensatory plans have three characteristics:

1. Substantially all full-time employees may participate on an equitable basis.
2. The discount from market price is small. That is, it does not exceed the greater of a per share discount reasonably offered to stockholders or the per share amount of costs avoided by not having to raise cash in a public offering.
3. The plan offers no substantive option feature.

For example, Masthead Company had a stock purchase plan under which employees who meet minimal employment qualifications are entitled to purchase Masthead stock at a 5 percent reduction from market price for a short period of time. The reduction from market price is not considered compensatory because the per share amount of the costs avoided by not having to raise the cash in a public offering is equal to 5 percent. **Plans that do not possess all of the above mentioned three characteristics are classified as compensatory.**

Disclosure of Compensation Plans

Full disclosure should be made about the status of these plans at the end of the periods presented, including the number of shares under option, options exercised and forfeited, the weighted average option prices for these categories, the weighted average fair value of options granted during the year, and the average remaining contractual life of the options outstanding.[5] In addition to information about the status of the stock

---

[5]These data should be reported separately for each different type of plan offered to employees.

option plans, companies must also disclose the method and significant assumptions used to estimate the fair values of the stock options.

Page UP-XX shows the types of information to be disclosed related to stock-based compensation.

Page UP-XX shows the types of information to be disclosed related to stock-based compensation.

ILLUSTRATION U15-2
Stock Option Plan
Disclosure

The Company has a share-based compensation plan. The compensation cost that has been charged against income for the plan was $29.4 million, and $28.7 million for 2004 and 2003, respectively.

The Company's 2004 Employee Share Option Plan (the Plan), which is shareholder-approved, permits the grant of share options and shares to its employees for up to 8 million shares of common stock. The Company believes that such awards better align the interests of its employees with those of its shareholders. Option awards are generally granted with an exercise price equal to the market price of the Company's stock at the date of grant; those option awards generally vest based on 5 years of continuous service and have 10-year contractual terms. Share awards generally vest over five years. Certain option and share awards provide for accelerated vesting if there is a change in control (as defined by the Plan).

The fair value of each option award is estimated on the date of grant using an option valuation model based on the assumptions noted in the following table.

	2004	2003
Expected volatility	25%–40%	24%–38%
Weighted-average volatility	33%	30%
Expected dividends	1.5%	1.5%
Expected term (in years)	5.3–7.8	5.5–8.0
Risk-free rate	6.3%–11.2%	6.0%–10.0%

A summary of option activity under the Plan as of December 31, 2004, and changes during the year then ended are presented below.

Options	Shares (000)	Weighted-Average Exercise Price	Weighted-Average Remaining Contractual Term	Aggregate Intrinsic Value ($000)
Outstanding at January 1, 2004	4,660	42		
Granted	950	60		
Exercised	(800)	36		
Forfeited or expired	(80)	59		
Outstanding at December 31, 2004	4,730	47	6.5	85,140
Exercisable at December 31, 2004	3,159	41	4.0	75,816

The weighted-average grant-date fair value of options granted during the years 2004 and 2003 was $19.57 and $17.46, respectively. The total intrinsic value of options exercised during the years ended December 31, 2004 and 2003, was $25.2 million, and $20.9 million, respectively.

As of December 31, 2004, there was $25.9 million of total unrecognized compensation cost related to nonvested share-based compensation arrangements granted under the Plan. That cost is expected to be recognized over a weighted-average period of 4.9 years. The total fair value of shares vested during the years ended December 31, 2004 and 2003, was $22.8 million and $21 million, respectively.

Debate over Stock Option Accounting

The FASB faced considerable opposition when it proposed the fair value method for accounting for stock options. This is not surprising, given that use of the fair value approach results in greater compensation costs relative to the intrinsic value model. As indicated in the story on page UP-16, a study of the companies in the Standard & Poor's 500 stock index documented that, on average, earnings in 2002 could be overstated by 10 percent through the use of the intrinsic value method. However, a number of companies, such as **Coca-Cola**, **General Electric**, **Wachovia**, **Bank One**, and **The Washington Post**, decided to use the fair value method. As the CFO of Coke stated, "There is no doubt that stock options are compensation. If they weren't, none of us would want them."

OBJECTIVE U2
Explain the controversy involving stock compensation plans.

Even given the exemplary behavior of certain companies, many in corporate America resist the fair value method. Many small high-technology companies are particularly vocal in their opposition, arguing that only through offering stock options can they attract top professional management. They contend that if they are forced to recognize large amounts of compensation expense under these plans, they will be at a competitive disadvantage with larger companies that can withstand higher compensation charges. As one high-tech executive stated, "If your goal is to attack fat-cat executive compensation in multi-billion dollar firms, then please do so! But not at the expense of the people who are 'running lean and mean,' trying to build businesses and creating jobs in the process."

The stock option saga is a classic example of the difficulty the FASB faces in issuing an accounting standard. Many powerful interests aligned against the Board; even some who initially appeared to support the Board's actions later reversed themselves. These efforts are unfortunate because they undermine the authority of the FASB at a time when it is essential that we restore faith in our financial reporting system. It must be emphasized that transparent financial reporting—including recognizing stock-based compensation expense—should not be criticized because companies will report lower income. We may not like what the financial statements say, but we are always better off when the statements are representationally faithful to the underlying economic substance of transactions.

By leaving stock-based compensation expense out of income, reported income is biased. It may be in the interests of managers of some companies to report biased income numbers, but doing so does not serve financial reporting or our capital markets well. Biased reporting not only raises concerns about the credibility of companies' reports, but also of financial reporting in general. Consider companies that do not use stock options. Why should they be made to look worse because they use a different form of compensation? As we have learned from **Enron**, **WorldCom**, **Xerox**, **MicroStrategy**, **Lucent**, and other recent failures, credibility of financial reporting is fundamental to the efficient operation of our capital markets. Even good companies get tainted by biased reporting of a few "bad apples."[6] If we continue to write standards so that some social, economic, or public policy goal is achieved, financial reporting will lose its credibility.

SECTION 5 PENSION DISCLOSURES

In 2003, the FASB issued a new standard addressing pension disclosures, *Statement of Financial Accounting Standard No. 132* (Stamford, Conn.: FASB, revised 2003) entitled "Employers' Disclosures about Pensions and other Postretirement Benefits." This new standard provides for enhanced financial disclosures related to defined benefit plans.

The following material should be used **in place of** the discussion in Chapter 15, pages 760–762, of *Fundamentals of Intermediate Accounting*.

REPORTING PENSION PLANS IN FINANCIAL STATEMENTS

OBJECTIVE U1

Describe the reporting requirements for pension plans in financial statements.

One might suspect that a phenomenon as significant and complex as pensions would involve extensive reporting and disclosure requirements. We will cover these requirements in two categories: (1) those within the financial statements, and (2) those within the notes to the financial statements.

---

[6]Congress reacted to these events with passage of the **Sarbanes-Oxley Act of 2002**. The Act affirmed the role of the FASB as an independent private sector accounting standard-setter. However, recent actions by Congress in the stock option controversy have undermined the Act's support for independent accounting standard-setting by the FASB.

Within the Financial Statements

If the amount funded (credit to Cash) by the employer to the pension trust is **less than the annual expense** (debit to Pension Expense), a credit balance accrual of the difference arises in the long-term liabilities section. It might be described as Accrued Pension Cost, Liability for Pension Expense Not Funded, or Pension Liability. A liability is classified as current when it requires the disbursement of cash within the next year.

If the amount funded to the pension trust during the period is **greater than the amount charged to expense**, an asset equal to the difference arises. This asset is reported as Prepaid Pension Cost, Deferred Pension Expense, or Prepaid Pension Expense in the current assets section if it is current in nature, and in the other assets section if it is long-term in nature.

If the **accumulated benefit obligation exceeds the fair value of pension plan assets**, an additional liability is recorded. The debit is either to an Intangible Asset—Deferred Pension Cost or to a contra account to stockholders' equity entitled Excess of Additional Pension Liability Over Unrecognized Prior Service Cost. If the debit is less than unrecognized prior service cost, it is reported as an intangible asset. If the debit is greater than unrecognized prior service cost, the excess debit is reported as part of other comprehensive income and the accumulated balance as a component of accumulated other comprehensive income.

Within the Notes to the Financial Statements

Pension plans are frequently important to an understanding of financial position, results of operations, and cash flows of a company. Therefore, the following information, if not disclosed in the body of the financial statements, should be disclosed in the notes.[1]

❶ A schedule showing all the major components of pension expense should be reported. *Rationale:* Information provided about the components of pension expense helps users better understand how pension expense is determined and is useful in forecasting a company's net income.

❷ A **reconciliation** showing how the projected benefit obligation and the fair value of the plan assets changed from the beginning to the end of the period is required. *Rationale:* Disclosing the projected benefit obligation, the fair value of the plan assets, and changes in them helps users understand the economics underlying the obligations and resources of these plans. The Board believes that explaining the changes in the projected benefit obligation and fair value of plan assets in the form of a reconciliation provides a more complete disclosure and makes the financial statements more understandable.

❸ The **funded status** of the plan (difference between the projected benefit obligation and fair value of the plan assets) and the amounts recognized and not recognized in the financial statements must be disclosed. *Rationale:* Providing a reconciliation of the plan's funded status to the amount reported in the balance sheet highlights the difference between the funded status and the balance sheet presentation.[2]

---

[1]"Employers' Disclosures about Pensions and Other Postretirement Benefits," *Financial Accounting Standard No. 132* (Stamford, Conn.: FASB, 1998; revised 2003). This statement and its revision modify the disclosure requirements of *SFAS No. 87.* The revised statement was issued because concerns were raised recently about the lack of transparency in pension information. This new standard amends the existing disclosure requirements related to pensions by (1) continuing the existing disclosure requirements, while (2) requiring companies to provide more details about their plan assets, benefit obligations, cash flows, benefit costs, and other relevant information.

[2]The vested benefit obligation does not need to be disclosed, since it is not used in the accounting for the fund. The accumulated benefit obligation (ABO) under *FAS 87* for all plans combined should be disclosed. Information on the ABO is useful because it is relevant to assessing the minimum liability (whether the company has recognized the minimum liability or not). In addition, it provides another measure for assessing the overall funded status of the plan.

4 A disclosure of the rates used in measuring the benefit amounts (discount rate, expected return on plan assets, rate of compensation increases) should be disclosed. *Rationale:* Disclosure of these rates permits the reader to determine the reasonableness of the assumptions applied in measuring the pension liability and pension expense.

5 A table is required indicating the allocation of pension plan assets by category (equity securities, debt securities, real estate, and other assets), and showing the percentage of the fair value to total plan assets. In addition, a narrative description of investment policies and strategies, including the target allocation percentages (if used by the company), must be disclosed. *Rationale:* Such information is useful to users of the financial statements in evaluating the pension plan's exposure to market risk and possible cash flow demands on the company. In addition, it will help users to better understand and assess the reasonableness of the company's expected rate of return assumption.

6 The company must disclose the **expected benefit payments** to be paid to current plan participants for each of the next five fiscal years and in the aggregate for the five fiscal years thereafter, based on the same assumptions used to measure the company's benefit obligation at the end of the year. Also required is disclosure of a company's best **estimate of expected contributions** to be paid to the plan during the next year. *Rationale:* These disclosures provide information related to the cash outflows of the company. With this information, financial statement users can better understand the potential cash outflows related to the pension plan. As a result, users can better assess the liquidity and solvency of the company, which helps in assessing the company's overall financial flexibility.

In summary, the disclosure requirements are extensive, and purposely so. One factor that has been a challenge for useful pension reporting in the past has been the lack of consistency in terminology. Furthermore, a substantial amount of offsetting is inherent in the measurement of pension expense and the pension liability. These disclosures are designed to address these concerns and take some of the mystery out of pension reporting.

Illustration of Pension Note Disclosure

In the following sections we provide illustrations and explain the key pension disclosure elements.

Components of Pension Expense

The FASB requires disclosure of the individual pension expense components—(1) service cost, (2) interest cost, (3) expected return on assets, (4) other deferrals and amortization—so that more sophisticated readers can understand how pension expense is determined. Providing information on the components should also be useful in predicting future pension expense. Using the information from the Zarle Company illustration—specifically, the expense component information taken from the left-hand column of the work sheet in Illustration U15-3—an example of this part of the disclosure in presented in the following schedule.

ILLUSTRATION U15-3
Summary of Expense Components—2003, 2004, 2005

ZARLE COMPANY			
	2003	2004	2005
Components of Net Periodic Pension Expense			
Service cost	$ 9,000	$ 9,500	$13,000
Interest cost	10,000	19,200	$21,270
Expected return on plan assets	(10,000)	(11,100)	(13,410)*
Amortization of prior service cost	–0–	27,200	20,800
Net periodic pension expense	$ 9,000	$44,800	$41,660

*Note that the expected return must be disclosed, not the actual. In 2005, the expected return is $13,410, which is the actual gain ($12,000) adjusted by the unrecognized loss ($1,410).

Reconciliation and Funded Status of Plan

A reconciliation of the changes in the assets and liabilities from the beginning of the year to the end of the year is provided to enable statement readers to better understand the underlying economics of the plan. In essence, this disclosure (reconciliation) contains the information in the pension work sheet for the projected benefit obligation and plan asset columns.

In addition, the FASB also requires a disclosure of the funded status of the plan. That is, the off-balance-sheet assets, liabilities, and unrecognized gains and losses must be reconciled with the on-balance-sheet liability or asset. Many believe this is the key to understanding the accounting for pensions. Why is such a disclosure important? The FASB acknowledged that the delayed recognition of some pension elements may exclude the most current and the most relevant information about the pension plan from the financial statements. This important information, however, is provided within this disclosure.

Using the information for Zarle Company, the following schedule provides an example of the reconciliation.

UNDERLYING CONCEPTS

This represents another compromise between relevance and reliability. The disclosure of the unrecognized items attempts to balance these objectives.

ILLUSTRATION U15-4
Pension Disclosure for Zarle Company—2003, 2004, 2005

ZARLE COMPANY
PENSION DISCLOSURE

	2003	2004	2005
Change in benefit obligation			
Benefit obligation at beginning of year	$100,000	$112,000	$212,700
Service cost	9,000	9,500	13,000
Interest cost	10,000	19,200	21,270
Amendments (Prior service cost)	–0–	80,000	–0–
Actuarial loss	–0–	–0–	28,530
Benefits paid	(7,000)	(8,000)	(10,500)
Benefit obligation at end of year	112,000	212,700	265,000
Change in plan assets			
Fair value of plan assets at beginning of year	100,000	111,000	134,100
Actual return on plan assets	10,000	11,100	12,000
Contributions	8,000	20,000	24,000
Benefits paid	(7,000)	(8,000)	(10,500)
Fair value of plan assets at end of year	111,000	134,100	159,600
Funded status	(1,000)	(78,600)	(105,400)
Unrecognized net actuarial loss	–0–	–0–	29,940
Unrecognized prior service cost	–0–	52,800	32,000
Prepaid (accrued) benefit cost	**(1,000)**	**(25,800)**	**(43,460)**
Minimum liability adjustment included in:			
Intangible assets	–0–	(4,100)	(32,000)
Stockholders' equity	–0–	–0–	(5,540)
Accrued pension cost liability in the balance sheet	$ (1,000)	$ (29,900)	$ (81,000)

The 2003 column reveals that the projected benefit obligation is underfunded by $1,000. The 2004 column reveals that the underfunded liability of $78,600 is reported in the balance sheet at $29,900, due to the unrecognized prior service cost of $52,800 and the $4,100 additional liability. Finally, the 2005 column indicates that underfunded liability of $105,400 is recognized in the balance sheet at only $81,000 because of $32,000 in unrecognized prior service costs, $29,940 of unrecognized net loss, and $37,540 additional liability (with $5,540 of the minimum liability recorded in stockholders' equity).

Illustration U15-5 (next page) provides a representative postretirement benefit disclosure for **Gillette Company**.[3] This disclosure shows how companies are providing information on the rates used in measuring the benefit amounts.

UNDERLYING CONCEPTS

Does it make a difference to users of financial statements whether pension information is recognized in the financial statements or disclosed only in the notes? The FASB was not sure, so in accord with the full disclosure principle, it decided to provide extensive pension plan disclosures.

---

[3]Note that the Gillette disclosure combines the disclosures for pensions and other postretirement benefits in one disclosure. This is one way the new standard streamlined the reporting on benefit plans.

Gillette Company

Pensions and Other Retiree Benefits. The Company has various retirement programs, including defined benefit, defined contribution, and other plans, that cover most employees worldwide. Other retiree benefits are health care and life insurance benefits provided to eligible retired employees, principally in the United States. The components of defined benefit expense for continuing operations follow.

Years ended December 31, (millions)	Pensions			Other Retiree Benefits		
	2001	2000	1999	2001	2000	1999
Components of net benefit expense:						
Service cost-benefits earned	$ 61	$ 64	$ 67	$ 6	$ 6	$ 6
Interest cost on benefit obligation	130	122	112	18	19	16
Estimated return on assets	(166)	(171)	(159)	(4)	(4)	(4)
Net amortization	9	5	13	(5)	(7)	(7)
Plan curtailments and other	—	(3)	(7)	—	—	—
	34	17	26	15	14	11
Other	12	9	9	–	–	–
Net defined benefit expense	$ 46	$ 26	$ 35	$15	$14	$11

The funded status of the Company's principal defined benefit and other retiree benefit plans and the amounts recognized in the balance sheet follow.

Years ended December 31, (millions)	Pension Benefits		Other Retiree Benefits	
	2001	2000	2001	2000
Change in benefit obligation:				
Balance at beginning of year	$1,961	$1,956	$ 259	$ 261
Benefit payments	(113)	(111)	(21)	(17)
Service and interest costs	191	185	24	24
Amendments	12	26	(14)	—
Actuarial (gains) losses	(57)	78	135	(7)
Plan curtailments	(3)	(33)	—	—
Divestitures	—	(71)	—	—
Currency translation adjustment	(41)	(69)	(3)	(2)
Balance at end of year	$1,950	$1,961	$ 380	$ 259
Change in fair value of plan assets:				
Balance at beginning of year	$1,878	$2,052	$ 40	$ 41
Actual return on plan assets	(168)	42	(2)	(1)
Employer contribution	35	31	—	—
Benefit payments	(92)	(91)	—	—
Divestitures	—	(87)	—	—
Currency translation adjustment	(35)	(69)	—	—
Balance at end of year	$1,618	$1,878	$ 38	$ 40
Benefit obligations in excess of plan assets	$ (332)	$ (83)	$(342)	$(219)
Unrecognized prior service cost and transition obligation	41	44	2	18
Unrecognized net loss (gain)	399	128	57	(90)
Minimum liability adjustment included in:				
Intangible assets	(12)	(6)	—	—
Stockholders' equity	(87)	(34)	—	—
Net prepaid (accrued) benefit cost	$ 9	$ 49	$(283)	$(291)

Additional Postretirement
Benefit Disclosures

The values for pension plans with accumulated benefit obligations in excess of plan assets follow.

At December 31, (millions)	2001	2000
Projected benefit obligation	$550	$513
Accumulated benefit obligation	490	445
Fair value of plan assets	276	277

The weighted average assumptions used in determining related obligations of pension benefit plans are shown below.

At December 31, (percent)	2001	2000	1999
Discount rate	6.8	7.0	6.8
Long-term rate of return on assets	8.6	9.1	9.1
Rate of compensation increases	4.2	4.7	4.7

The weighted average assumptions used in determining related obligations of other retiree benefit plans are shown below.

At December 31, (percent)	2001	2000	1999
Discount rate	7.2	7.2	7.5
Long-term rate of return on assets	9.0	10.0	10.0

The assumed health care cost trend rate for 2002 is 12%, decreasing to 5% by 2007. A one percentage point increase in the trend rate would have increased the accumulated postretirement benefit obligation by 14%, and interest and service cost by 21%. A one percentage point decrease in the trend rate would have decreased the accumulated postretirement benefit obligation by 12%, and interest and service cost by 17%. . . . In addition to the defined benefit and other retiree benefit plans, the Company also sponsors defined contribution plans, primarily covering U.S. employees. The Company's expense for defined contribution plans in 2001, 2000 and 1999 totaled $34 million, $35 million and $36 million, respectively.

Illustration U15-6 provides an example of the disclosures on pension plan asset allocations and expected cash flows for the pension plan, as reported by **Procter & Gamble**. These disclosures, mandated by the revision of *SFAS No. 132*, should help users compare the riskiness of companies' pension plan investments and the future cash requirements for the pension plan.

PROCTER & GAMBLE COMPANY

Plan Assets. The Company's target asset allocation for the year ending June 30, 2005, and actual asset allocation by asset category as of June 30, 2004, and 2003, are as follows:

	Target Allocation	
	Pension Benefits	Other Retiree Benefits
Asset Category	2005	2005
Equity securities[1]	64%	99%
Debt securities	32%	1%
Real estate	4%	0%
Total	100%	100%

	Plan Asset Allocation at June 30			
	Pension Benefits		Other Retiree Benefits	
Asset Category	**2004**	2003	**2004**	2003
Equity securities[1]	**64%**	62%	**99%**	99%
Debt securities	**32%**	35%	**1%**	1%
Real estate	**4%**	3%	**0%**	0%
Total	**100%**	100%	**100%**	100%

The Company's investment objective for defined benefit plan assets is to meet the plans' benefit obligations, while minimizing the potential for future required Company plan contributions. The investment strategies focus on asset class diversification, liquidity to meet benefit payments, and an appropriate balance of long-term investment return and risk. Target ranges for asset allocations are determined by matching the actuarial projections of the plans' future liabilities and benefit payments with expected long-term rates of return on the assets, taking into account investment return volatility and correlations across asset classes.

Cash Flows ($ millions). Management's best estimate of its cash requirements for the defined benefit plans and other retiree benefit plans for the year ending June 30, 2005 is $237 and $20, respectively.

Total benefit payments expected to be paid to participants, which include payments funded from the Company's assets, as discussed above, as well as payments paid from the plans are as follows:

	Years ended June 30	
	Pension Benefits	Other Retiree Benefits
Expected benefit payments		
2005	$ 191	$ 144
2006	177	152
2007	193	166
2008	207	176
2009	207	185
2010–2014	1,180	1,058

ILLUSTRATION U15-6
Procter & Gamble Co. Pension Disclosure of Asset Allocation and Expected Cash Flows

SECTION 6 ACCOUNTING CHANGES ···

In 2005, the FASB issued a new standard addressing accounting changes and error corrections. This new standard, "Accounting Changes and Error Corrections," *Statement of Financial Accounting Standards No. 154* (Norwalk, Conn.: FASB, 2005), is part of the FASB's short-term international convergence project and replaces *APB Opinion No. 20 and FASB Statement No. 3.*

The following material should be used **in place of** the discussion in Chapter 17, pages 824–834, of *Fundamentals of Intermediate Accounting.* Throughout Chapter 17, references to *APB Opinion No. 20* should be replaced with this new standard.

OBJECTIVE U1

Identify the types of accounting changes.

UNDERLYING CONCEPTS

While the qualitative characteristic of *usefulness* may be enhanced by changes in accounting, the characteristics of *comparability* and *consistency* may be adversely affected.

When accounting alternatives exist, comparability of the statements between periods and between companies is diminished and useful historical trend data are obscured. For example, if **Ford** revises its estimates for equipment useful lives, depreciation expense for the current year will not be comparable to depreciation expense reported by Ford in prior years. Similarly, if **Best Buy** changes to FIFO inventory pricing while **Circuit City** uses LIFO, it will be difficult to compare these companies' reported results. Thus a reporting framework is needed to preserve the usefulness of accounting when there is an accounting change. The first step in this area, then, is to establish categories for the different types of changes and corrections that occur in practice.[1] The three types of accounting changes are:

❶ *Change in Accounting Principle.* A change from one generally accepted accounting principle to another generally accepted accounting principle. Example: A change in the basis of inventory pricing from average cost to FIFO.

❷ *Change in Accounting Estimate.* A change that occurs as the result of new information or as additional experience is acquired. Example: A change in the estimate of the useful lives of depreciable assets.

❸ *Change in Reporting Entity.* A change from reporting as one type of entity to another type of entity. Example: changing specific subsidiaries that constitute the group of companies for which consolidated financial statements are prepared.[2]

A fourth category necessitates changes in the accounting, though it is not classified as an accounting change.

❹ **Errors in Financial Statements.** Errors occur as a result of mathematical mistakes, mistakes in the application of accounting principles, or oversight or misuse of facts that existed at the time financial statements were prepared. Example: the incorrect application of the retail inventory method for determining the final inventory value.

Changes are classified in these four categories because the individual characteristics of each category necessitate different methods of recognizing these changes in the

---

[1]"Accounting Changes and Error Corrections," *Statement of Financial Accounting Standards No. 154* (Norwalk, Conn.: FASB, 2005).

[2]*Accounting Trends and Techniques—2004* in its survey of 600 annual reports identified the following specific types of accounting changes reported.

Cost of exit or disposal activities, impairments	249	Asset-retirement obligations	125
Consolidation of variable-interest entities	200	Stock compensation	122
Debt/equity financial instruments	188	Revenue recognition	76
Guarantees	172	Goodwill and intangibles	57
Derivatives	158	Other	116

financial statements. Each of these items is discussed separately, to investigate its unusual characteristics and to determine how each item should be reported in the accounts and how the information should be disclosed in comparative statements.

CHANGES IN ACCOUNTING PRINCIPLE

A change in accounting principle involves a change from one generally accepted accounting principle to another. For example, a company might change the basis of inventory pricing from average cost to LIFO. Or it might change from the completed-contract to percentage-of-completion method of accounting for construction contracts.

A careful examination must be made in each circumstance to ensure that a change in principle has actually occurred. **A change in accounting principle is not considered to result from the adoption of a new principle in recognition of events that have occurred for the first time or that were previously immaterial.** For example, when an inventory pricing method that is adopted for a new line of products is different from the method or methods used for **previously recorded** inventories, a change in accounting principle has **not occurred**. As another example, certain marketing expenditures that were previously immaterial and expensed in the period incurred may become material and acceptably deferred and amortized without a change in accounting principle occurring.

Finally, **if the accounting principle previously followed was not acceptable, or if the principle was applied incorrectly, a change to a generally accepted accounting principle is considered a correction of an error.** A switch from the cash or income tax basis of accounting to the accrual basis is considered a correction of an error. If the company deducted salvage value when computing double-declining depreciation on plant assets and later recomputed depreciation without deduction of estimated salvage value, an error is corrected.

Three approaches have been suggested for reporting changes in accounting principles in the accounts:

Currently.   The **cumulative effect** of the change, which measures the cumulative difference in prior years' income between the newly adopted and prior accounting method, is reported in the current year's income statement as a special item. Under this approach, the effect of change on prior years' income is reported on the current-year income statement; **prior-year financial statements are not restated.**

Advocates of this position argue that restating financial statements for prior years results in a loss of confidence by investors in financial reports. Restatement, if permitted, also might upset many contractual and other arrangements that were based on the old figures. For example, profit-sharing arrangements computed on the old basis might have to be recomputed and completely new distributions made, which might create numerous legal problems. Many practical difficulties also exist; the cost of restatement may be excessive, or restatement may be impossible on the basis of data available.

Retrospectively.   Under this approach, a **retroactive adjustment** of the financial statements is made such that the **prior years' statements are recast** on a basis consistent with the newly adopted principle. Any cumulative effect of the change for periods prior to those presented is recorded as an adjustment to beginning retained earnings of the earliest year presented.

Advocates of this position argue that only by restatement of prior periods can changes in accounting principles lead to comparable financial statements. If this approach is not used, the year previous to the change will be on the old method; the year of the change will report the entire cumulative adjustment in income; and the following year will present financial statements on the new basis without the cumulative effect of the change. Consistency is considered essential in providing meaningful earnings-trend data and other financial relationships necessary to evaluate the business.

Prospectively (in the future). Previously reported results remain; no change is made. Opening balances are not adjusted, and no attempt is made to allocate charges or credits for prior events.

Advocates of this position argue that once management presents financial statements based on acceptable accounting principles, they are final; management cannot change prior periods by adopting a new principle. According to this line of reasoning, the cumulative adjustment in the current year is not appropriate, because such an approach includes amounts that have little or no relationship to the current year's income or economic events.

INTERNATIONAL
INSIGHT

IAS 8 generally requires restatement of prior years for accounting changes. However, *IAS 8* permits the cumulative-effect method or prospective method if the amounts to restate prior periods are not reasonably determinable.

The FASB now believes that the retrospective approach provides financial statement users with more useful information than the current or prospective approaches.[3] The rationale? First, through restatement, the retrospective approach results in greater consistency across accounting periods. As a result, users can better compare results from one period to the next. Furthermore, reporting the cumulative adjustment in the period of the change might have such a large effect on net income that the income figure would be misleading. A perfect illustration is the experience of **Chrysler Corporation** (now **DaimlerChrysler**) when it changed its inventory accounting from LIFO to FIFO. If the change had been handled on a current basis, Chrysler would have had to report a $53,500,000 adjustment to net income, which would have resulted in net income of $45,900,000 instead of a net loss of $7,600,000.

As another illustration, in the early 1980s the railroad industry switched from the retirement-replacement method of depreciating railroad equipment to a more generally used method such as straight-line depreciation. Cumulative-effect treatment meant that a substantial adjustment would be made to income in the period of change. Many in the railroad industry argued that the adjustment was so large that to include the cumulative effect in the current year instead of restating prior years would distort the information and make it less useful. Such situations lend support to restatement so that comparability is not seriously affected.[4]

In the following sections we illustrate application of the retrospective approach for accounting changes and how the prospective approach is applied to changes in accounting estimates.

Retrospective Accounting Change Approach

OBJECTIVE U3
Understand how to apply the retrospective accounting approach.

Under the retrospective approach, the cumulative effect of the new method on the financial statements at the beginning of the period is computed. A retroactive adjustment of the financial statements presented is made by **recasting prior years on a basis consistent with the newly adopted accounting principle**. We first illustrate application of the retrospective approach followed by a situation when it is impracticable to apply the retrospective approach—the change to the LIFO method.

Illustration

To illustrate the retrospective approach, assume that Denson Construction Co. has accounted for its income from long-term construction contracts using the completed-contract method. In 2005 the company changed to the percentage-of-completion method

---

[3]The new standard carries forward many of the provisions in the previous accounting change standard (*APB Opinion No. 20*), including the accounting for errors, changes in estimates, and the disclosures related to accounting changes.

[4]Adoption of the retrospective approach contributes to international accounting convergence. The FASB and the IASB are collaborating on a project in which they have agreed to converge around high-quality solutions to resolve differences between U.S. GAAP and International Financial Reporting Standards (IFRS). By adopting the retrospective approach, which is the method used in IFRS, the FASB agreed that this approach is superior to the current approach.

because management believes that this approach provides a more appropriate measure of the income earned. For tax purposes (assume a 40 percent enacted tax rate), the company has employed the completed-contract method and plans to continue using this method in the future.

Illustration U17-1 provides the information for analysis.

Year	Pretax Income from		Difference in Income		
	Percentage-of-Completion	Completed-Contract	Difference	Tax Effect 40%	Income Effect (net of tax)
Prior to 2004	$600,000	$400,000	$200,000	$80,000	$120,000
In 2004	180,000	160,000	20,000	8,000	12,000
Total at beginning of 2005	$780,000	$560,000	$220,000	$88,000	$132,000
Total in 2005	$200,000	$190,000	$ 10,000	$ 4,000	$ 6,000

ILLUSTRATION U17-1
Data for Change in Accounting for Long-Term Construction Contracts

The entry to record the change in 2005 would be:

Construction in Process	220,000	
Deferred Tax Liability		88,000
Retained Earnings		132,000

The Construction in Process account is increased by $220,000 (as indicated in the first column under "Difference in Income" in Illustration U17-1). The credit to Retained Earnings of $132,000 reflects the cumulative income effects prior to 2005 (third column under "Difference in Income" in Illustration U17-1). Retained Earnings is credited because prior years' income is closed to this account each year. The credit to Deferred Tax Liability represents the adjustment to prior years' tax expense, which is now recognized as a tax liability for future taxable amounts. That is, in future periods taxable income will be higher than book income as a result of current temporary differences, and therefore a deferred tax liability must be reported in the current year.

Income Statement Presentation

The bottom portion of the income statement for Denson Construction Co., **before giving effect to the change in accounting principle**, would be as follows.

Income Statement	2005	2004
Net income	$114,000[a]	$96,000[a]
Per Share Amounts		
Earnings per share (100,000 shares)	$1.14	$0.96

[a]The net income for the two periods is computed as follows:
2005 $190,000 − .40($190,000) = $114,000
2004 $160,000 − .40($160,000) = $96,000

ILLUSTRATION U17-2
Income Statement before Retroactive Change

The bottom portion of the income statement for Denson Construction Co., **after giving effect to the change in accounting principle,** would be as follows.

Income Statement	2005	2004
Net income	$120,000[a]	$108,000[a]
Per Share Amounts		
Earnings per share (100,000 shares)	$1.20	$1.08

[a]The net income for the two periods is computed as follows:
2005 $200,000 − .40($200,000) = $120,000
2004 $180,000 − .40($180,000) = $108,000

ILLUSTRATION U17-3
Income Statement after Retroactive Change

Retained Earnings Statement

Assuming a retained earnings balance of $1,600,000 at the beginning of 2004, the retained earnings statement **before giving effect to the change in accounting principle**, would appear as follows.

ILLUSTRATION U17-4
Retained Earnings
Statement before
Retroactive Change

RETAINED EARNINGS STATEMENT		
	2005	2004
Balance at beginning of year	$1,696,000	$1,600,000
Net income	114,000	96,000
Balance at end of year	$1,810,000	$1,696,000

To develop a comparative retained earnings statement, after giving effect to the change in accounting principle, the beginning retained earnings for earliest period presented must be adjusted for the cumulative prior years' effects, as indicated in Illustration U17-5.

ILLUSTRATION U17-5
Retained Earnings
Statement after
Retroactive Change

RETAINED EARNINGS STATEMENT		
	2005	2004
Balance at beginning of year, as previously reported		$1,600,000
Add: Adjustment for the cumulative effect on prior years of applying retrospectively the new method of accounting for long-term contracts (Note A)		120,000
Balance at beginning of year, as adjusted	$1,828,000	1,720,000
Net income	120,000	108,000
Balance at end of year	$1,948,000	$1,828,000

Note A: Change in Method of Accounting for Long-Term Contracts. The company has accounted for revenue and costs for long-term construction contracts by the percentage-of-completion method in 2005, whereas in all prior years revenue and costs were determined by the completed-contract method. The new method of accounting for long-term contracts was adopted to recognize . . . [state justification for change in accounting principle] . . . and financial statements of prior years have been restated to apply the new method retroactively. For income tax purposes, the completed-contract method has been continued. The effect of the accounting change on income of 2005 was an increase of $6,000 net of related taxes and on income of 2004 as previously reported was an increase of $12,000 net of related taxes. The balances of retained earnings for 2004 and 2005 have been adjusted for the effect of applying retrospectively the new method of accounting.

In 2004, the beginning balance was adjusted for the excess of the percentage-of-completion income over the completed-contract income prior to 2004 ($120,000). Under the newly adopted method, income for 2004 ($108,000) is added to the adjusted beginning balance, resulting in the ending retained earnings for 2004 ($1,828,000). This amount is also the beginning Retained Earnings for 2005. Adding 2005 income of $120,000 (as measured under the newly adopted method) results in the 2005 ending Retained Earnings balance. Thus, after adjusting beginning 2004 for the cumulative effect from prior periods, and recording income based on the newly adopted method, comparable Retained Earnings amounts are reported for 2004 and 2005.

OBJECTIVE U4
Understand how to account for changes to LIFO.

Change to LIFO Method

As indicated above, **unless it is impracticable to do so, changes in accounting principles should be reported by retrospective application.** Three conditions are considered in assessing impracticality:

① The effects of the retrospective application are not determinable.

② Retrospective application requires assumptions about management's intent in a prior period.

③ Retrospective application requires significant estimates for a prior period, and the availability of the necessary information to develop these estimates cannot be objectively verified.

If any of the above conditions exists, it is deemed impracticable to apply the retrospective approach. In this case, the new accounting principle is **applied prospectively** as of the earliest date it is practicable to do so.

CHANGE MANAGEMENT

WHAT DO THE NUMBERS MEAN?

The recent experience at Halliburton offers a case study in the importance of good reporting of an accounting change. Recall from Chapter 18 that Halliburton uses percentage-of-completion accounting for its long-term construction services contracts. Recently, the SEC questioned the company about its change in accounting for disputed claims.

Prior to 1998 Halliburton took a very conservative approach to its accounting for disputed claims. That is, the company waited until all disputes were resolved before recognizing associated revenues. In contrast, in 1998 the company recognized revenue for disputed claims before their resolution, using estimates of amounts expected to be recovered. Such revenue and its related profit are more tentative and subject to possible later adjustment. The accounting method in 1998 is more aggressive than the company's former policy but is still within the boundaries of GAAP.

It appears that the problem with Halliburton's accounting stems more from the way it handled its accounting change than from the new accounting method itself. That is, an overt reference to the company's change in accounting method was not provided in its 1998 annual report. In fact, rather than stating its new policy, the company simply deleted the sentence that described how it accounted for disputed claims. Then later, in its 1999 annual report, the new accounting policy was stated.

When such changes in accounting are made, investors need to be apprised of them and their effects on the company's financial results and position. With such information, current results can be compared with those of prior periods and a more informed assessment can be made about the company's future prospects.

Source: Adapted from "Accounting Ace Charles Mulford Answers Accounting Questions," *Wall Street Journal Online* (June 7, 2002).

An example of the impracticable condition is the change to the LIFO method. In such a situation, **the base-year inventory for all subsequent LIFO calculations is the opening inventory in the year the method is adopted. There is no restatement of prior years' income because it is just too impractical.** A restatement to LIFO would be subject to assumptions as to the different years that the layers were established, and these assumptions would ordinarily result in the computation of a number of different earnings figures. The only adjustment necessary may be to restate the beginning inventory to a cost basis from a lower of cost or market approach.

Disclosure then is limited to showing the effect of the change on the results of operations in the period of change. Also, the reasons for omitting the computations of the cumulative effect and the pro forma amounts for prior years should be explained. Finally, the company should disclose the justification for the change to LIFO. As shown in Illustration U17-6 on the next page, the Annual Report of **Quaker Oats Company** indicates the type of disclosure necessary.

In practice, many companies defer the formal adoption of LIFO until year-end. Management thus has an opportunity to assess the impact that a change to LIFO will have on the financial statements and to evaluate the desirability of a change for tax purposes. As indicated in Chapter 8, many companies use LIFO because of the advantages of this inventory valuation method in a period of inflation.

ILLUSTRATION U17-6
Disclosure of Change
to LIFO

The Quaker Oats Company

Note 1 (In Part): Summary of Significant Accounting Policies

Inventories. Inventories are valued at the lower of cost or market, using various cost methods, and include the cost of raw materials, labor and overhead. The percentage of year-end inventories valued using each of the methods is as follows:

June 30	1989	1988	1987
Average quarterly cost	21%	54%	52%
Last-in, first-out (LIFO)	65%	29%	31%
First-in, first-out (FIFO)	14%	17%	17%

Effective July 1, 1988, the Company adopted the LIFO cost flow assumption for valuing the majority of remaining U.S. Grocery Products inventories. The Company believes that the use of the LIFO method better matches current costs with current revenues. The cumulative effect of this change on retained earnings at the beginning of the year is not determinable, nor are the pro-forma effects of retroactive application of LIFO to prior years. The effect of this change on fiscal 1989 was to decrease net income by $16.0 million, or $.20 per share.

If the LIFO method of valuing certain inventories were not used, total inventories would have been $60.1 million, $24.0 million and $14.6 million higher than reported at June 30, 1989, 1988, and 1987, respectively.

CHANGES IN ACCOUNTING ESTIMATE

OBJECTIVE U5
Describe the accounting for changes in estimates.

The preparation of financial statements requires estimating the effects of future conditions and events. The following are examples of items that require estimates:

1 Uncollectible receivables.
2 Inventory obsolescence.
3 Useful lives and salvage values of assets.
4 Periods benefited by deferred costs.
5 Liabilities for warranty costs and income taxes.
6 Recoverable mineral reserves.

Future conditions and events and their effects cannot be perceived with certainty; therefore, estimating requires the exercise of judgment. Accounting estimates will change as new events occur, as more experience is acquired, or as additional information is obtained.

Changes in estimates must be handled prospectively. That is, no changes should be made in previously reported results. Opening balances are not adjusted, and no attempt is made to "catch-up" for prior periods. Financial statements of prior periods are not restated. Instead, the effects of all changes in estimate are accounted for in (1) the period of change if the change affects that period only, or (2) the period of change and future periods if the change affects both. As a result, changes in estimates are viewed as **normal recurring corrections and adjustments**, the natural result of the accounting process. Retrospective treatment is prohibited.

The circumstances related to a change in estimate are different from those surrounding a change in accounting principle. If changes in estimates were handled on a retrospective basis, continual adjustments of prior years' income would occur. It seems proper to accept the view that because new conditions or circumstances exist, the revision fits the new situation and should be handled in the current and future periods.

To illustrate, Underwriters Labs Inc. purchased a building for $300,000 which was originally estimated to have a useful life of 15 years and no salvage value. Depreciation has been recorded for 5 years on a straight-line basis. On January 1, 2005, the estimate of the useful life is revised so that the asset is considered to have a total life

INTERNATIONAL INSIGHT

In most nations, changes in accounting estimates are treated prospectively. International differences occur in the degree of disclosure required.

of 25 years. Assume that the useful life for financial reporting and tax purposes is the same. The accounts at the beginning of the sixth year are as follows.

Building	$300,000
Less: Accumulated depreciation—building (5 × $20,000)	100,000
Book value of building	$200,000

ILLUSTRATION U17-7
Book Value after Five Years' Depreciation

The entry to record depreciation for the year 2005 is:

Depreciation Expense	10,000	
Accumulated Depreciation—Building		10,000

The $10,000 depreciation charge is computed as follows.

$$\text{Depreciation charge} = \frac{\text{Book value of asset}}{\text{Remaining service live}} = \frac{\$200,000}{25 \text{ years} - 5 \text{ years}} = \$10,000$$

ILLUSTRATION U17-8
Depreciation after Change in Estimate

The disclosure of a change in estimated useful lives appeared in the Annual Report of **Ampco–Pittsburgh Corporation.**

Ampco–Pittsburgh Corporation

Note 11: Change in Accounting Estimate. The Corporation revised its estimate of the useful lives of certain machinery and equipment. Previously, all machinery and equipment, whether new when placed in use or not, were in one class and depreciated over 15 years. The change principally applies to assets purchased new when placed in use. Those lives are now extended to 20 years. These changes were made to better reflect the estimated periods during which such assets will remain in service. The change had the effect of reducing depreciation expense and increasing net income by approximately $991,000 ($.10 per share).

ILLUSTRATION U17-9
Disclosure of Change in Estimated Useful Lives

Differentiating between a change in an estimate and a change in an accounting principle is sometimes difficult. Is it a change in principle or a change in estimate when a company changes from deferring and amortizing certain marketing costs to recording them as an expense as incurred because future benefits of these costs have become doubtful? In such a case, **whenever it is impossible to determine whether a change in principle or a change in estimate has occurred, the change should be considered a change in estimate**.

The FASB relied on this rationale for "...a change in estimate that is effected by a change in accounting principle." An example of this type of change is a change in depreciation (as well as amortization or depletion) methods. Because changes in depreciation methods are made based on changes in estimates about future benefits arising from long-lived assets, it is not possible to separate the effect of the accounting principle change from that of the estimates. **As a result, the FASB decided to account for a change in depreciation methods as a change in estimate.**[5]

A similar problem occurs in differentiating between a change in estimate and a correction of an error, although the answer is more clear cut. How do we determine whether the information was overlooked in earlier periods (an error) or whether the information is now available for the first time (change in estimate)? Proper classification is important because corrections of errors have a different accounting treatment from that given changes in estimates. The general rule is that **careful estimates that**

---

[5]"Accounting Changes and Error Corrections," *Statement of Financial Accounting Standards No. 154* (Norwalk, Conn.: FASB. 2005).

later prove to be incorrect should be considered changes in estimate. Only when the estimate was obviously computed incorrectly because of lack of expertise or in bad faith should the adjustment be considered an error. There is no clear demarcation line here, and good judgment must be used in light of all the circumstances.[6]

EXERCISES

UE17-1 (Change in Principle—Long-term Contracts) Pam Erickson Construction Company changed from the completed-contract to the percentage-of-completion method of accounting for long-term construction contracts during 2005. For tax purposes, the company employs the completed-contract method and will continue this approach in the future. (*Hint:* Adjust all tax consequences through the Deferred Tax Liability account.) The appropriate information related to this change is as follows.

	Pretax Income from:		
	Percentage-of-Completion	Completed-Contract	Difference
2004	$780,000	$590,000	$190,000
2005	700,000	480,000	220,000

Instructions

(a) Assuming that the tax rate is 35%, what is the amount of net income that would be reported in 2005?

(b) What entry(ies) are necessary to adjust the accounting records for the change in accounting principle?

UE17-2 (Change in Principle—Inventory Methods) Holder-Webb Company began operations on January 1, 2002, and uses the average cost method of pricing inventory. Management is contemplating a change in inventory methods for 2005. The following information is available for the years 2002–2004.

	Net Income Computed Using		
	Average Cost Method	FIFO Method	LIFO Method
2002	$15,000	$19,000	$12,000
2003	18,000	23,000	14,000
2004	20,000	25,000	17,000

Instructions

(a) Prepare the journal entry necessary to record a change from the average cost method to the FIFO method in 2005.

(b) Determine net income to be reported for 2002, 2003, and 2004, after giving effect to the change in accounting principle.

(c) Assume Holder-Webb Company used the LIFO method instead of the average cost method during the years 2002–2004. In 2005, Holder-Webb changed to the FIFO method. Prepare the journal entry necessary to record the change in principle.

UE17-3 (Accounting Changes—Depreciation) Kathleen Cole Inc. acquired the following assets in January of 2002.

Equipment, estimated service life, 5 years; salvage value, $15,000	$525,000
Building, estimated service life, 30 years; no salvage value	$693,000

The equipment has been depreciated using the sum-of-the-years'-digits method for the first 3 years for financial reporting purposes. In 2005, the company decided to change the method of computing depreciation to the straight-line method for the equipment, but no change was made in the estimated service life or salvage value. It was also decided to change the total estimated service life of the building from 30

---

[6]In evaluating reasonableness, the auditor should use one or a combination of the following approaches:

(a) Review and test the process used by management to develop the estimate.

(b) Develop an independent expectation of the estimate to corroborate the reasonableness of management's estimate.

(c) Review subsequent events or transactions occurring prior to completion of fieldwork. "Auditing Accounting Estimates," *Statement on Auditing Standards No. 57* (New York: AICPA, 1988).

years to 40 years, with no change in the estimated salvage value. The building is depreciated on the straight-line method.

Instructions
  (a) Prepare the general journal entry to record depreciation expense for the equipment in 2005.
  (b) Prepare the journal entry to record depreciation expense for the building in 2005. (Round all computations to two decimal places.)

UE17-4 (Change in Principle and Error; Financial Statements) Presented below are the comparative statements for Denise Habbe Inc.

	2005	2004
Sales	$340,000	$270,000
Cost of sales	200,000	142,000
Gross profit	140,000	128,000
Expenses	88,000	50,000
Net income	$ 52,000	$ 78,000
Retained earnings (Jan. 1)	$125,000	$ 72,000
Net income	52,000	78,000
Dividends	(30,000)	(25,000)
Retained earnings (Dec. 31)	$147,000	$125,000

The following additional information is provided:

  1. In 2005, Denise Habbe Inc. decided to switch its depreciation method from sum-of-the-years'-digits to the straight-line method. The assets were purchased at the beginning of 2004 for $100,000 with an estimated useful life of 4 years and no salvage value. (The 2005 income statement contains depreciation expense of $30,000.)
  2. In 2005, the company discovered that the ending inventory for 2004 was overstated by $24,000; ending inventory for 2005 is correctly stated.

Instructions
Prepare the revised income and retained earnings statement for 2004 and 2005, assuming comparative statements.

UE17-5 (Accounting for Accounting Changes and Errors) Listed below are various types of accounting changes and errors.

  _____ 1. Change in a plant asset's salvage value.
  _____ 2. Change due to overstatement of inventory.
  _____ 3. Change from sum-of-the-years'-digits to straight-line method of depreciation.
  _____ 4. Change from presenting unconsolidated to consolidated financial statements.
  _____ 5. Change from LIFO to FIFO inventory method.
  _____ 6. Change in the rate used to compute warranty costs.
  _____ 7. Change from an unacceptable accounting principle to an acceptable accounting principle.
  _____ 8. Change in a patent's amortization period.
  _____ 9. Change from completed-contract to percentage-of-completion method on construction contracts.
  _____ 10. Change from FIFO to average-cost inventory method.

Instructions
For each change or error, indicate how it would be accounted for using the following code letters:

  a. Accounted for prospectively.
  b. Accounted for retrospectively.
  c. Neither of the above.

PROBLEMS

UP17-1 (Change in Estimate, Principle, and Error Correction) Brueggen Company is in the process of preparing its financial statements for 2004. Assume that no entries for depreciation have been recorded in 2004. The following information related to depreciation of fixed assets is provided to you:

  1. Brueggen purchased equipment on January 2, 2001, for $65,000. At that time, the equipment had an estimated useful life of 10 years with a $5,000 salvage value. The equipment is depreciated

on a straight-line basis. On January 2, 2004, as a result of additional information, the company determined that the equipment has a remaining useful life of 4 years with a $3,000 salvage value.

2. During 2004 Brueggen changed from the double-declining balance method for its building to the straight-line method. The building originally cost $300,000. It had a useful life of 10 years and a salvage value of $30,000. The following computations present depreciation on both bases for 2002 and 2003.

	2003	2002
Straight-line	$27,000	$27,000
Declining-balance	48,000	60,000

3. Brueggen purchased a machine on July 1, 2002, at a cost of $80,000. The machine has a salvage value of $8,000 and a useful life of 8 years. Brueggen's bookkeeper recorded straight-line depreciation in 2002 and 2003 but failed to consider the salvage value.

Instructions

(a) Prepare the journal entries to record depreciation expense for 2004 and correct any errors made to date related to the information provided. (Round all computations to two decimal places.)

(b) Show comparative net income for 2003 and 2004. Income before depreciation expense was $300,000 in 2004, and was $310,000 in 2003. Ignore taxes.

UP17-2 **(Comprehensive Accounting Change and Error Analysis Problem)** Larry Kingston Inc. was organized in late 2002 to manufacture and sell hosiery. At the end of its fourth year of operation, the company has been fairly successful, as indicated by the following reported net incomes.

2002	$140,000[a]	2004	$205,000
2003	160,000[b]	2005	276,000

[a]Includes a $12,000 increase because of change in bad debt experience rate.
[b]Includes extraordinary gain of $40,000.

The company has decided to expand operations and has applied for a sizable bank loan. The bank officer has indicated that the records should be audited and presented in comparative statements to facilitate analysis by the bank. Larry Kingston Inc. therefore hired the auditing firm of Check & Doublecheck Co. and has provided the following additional information.

1. In early 2003, Larry Kingston Inc. changed its estimate from 2% to 1% on the amount of bad debt expense to be charged to operations. Bad debt expense for 2002, if a 1% rate had been used, would have been $12,000. The company therefore restated its net income for 2002.

2. In 2005, the auditor discovered that the company had changed its method of inventory pricing from LIFO to FIFO. The effect on the income statements for the previous years is as follows.

	2002	2003	2004	2005
Net income unadjusted—LIFO basis	$140,000	$160,000	$205,000	$276,000
Net income unadjusted—FIFO basis	155,000	165,000	215,000	260,000
	$ 15,000	$ 5,000	$ 10,000	($ 16,000)

3. In 2005, the auditor discovered that:
   a. The company incorrectly overstated the ending inventory by $11,000 in 2004.
   b. A dispute developed in 2003 with the Internal Revenue Service over the deductibility of entertainment expenses. In 2002, the company was not permitted these deductions, but a tax settlement was reached in 2005 that allowed these expenses. As a result of the court's finding, tax expenses in 2005 were reduced by $60,000.

Instructions

(a) Indicate how each of these changes or corrections should be handled in the accounting records. Ignore income tax considerations.

(b) Present comparative income statements for the years 2002 to 2005, starting with income before extraordinary items. Ignore income tax considerations.

UP17-3 **(Error Corrections and Accounting Changes)** Patricia Voga Company is in the process of adjusting and correcting its books at the end of 2005. In reviewing its records, the following information is compiled.

1. Voga has failed to accrue sales commissions payable at the end of each of the last 2 years, as follows.

December 31, 2004	$4,000
December 31, 2005	$2,500

2. In reviewing the December 31, 2005, inventory, Voga discovered errors in its inventory-taking procedures that have caused inventories for the last 3 years to be incorrect, as follows.

December 31, 2003	Understated	$16,000
December 31, 2004	Understated	$21,000
December 31, 2005	Overstated	$ 6,700

Voga has already made an entry that established the incorrect December 31, 2005, inventory amount.

3. At December 31, 2005, Voga decided to change the depreciation method on its office equipment from double-declining balance to straight-line. The equipment has an original cost of $100,000 when purchased on January 1, 2003. It has a 10-year useful life and no salvage value. Depreciation expense recorded prior to 2005 under the double-declining balance method was $36,000. Voga has already recorded 2005 depreciation expense of $12,800 using the double-declining balance method.

4. Before 2005, Voga accounted for its income from long-term construction contracts on the completed-contract basis. Early in 2005, Voga changed to the percentage-of-completion basis for both accounting and tax purposes. Income for 2005 has been recorded using the percentage-of-completion method. The income tax rate is 40%. The following information is available.

	Pretax Income	
	Percentage-of-Completion	Completed-Contract
Prior to 2005	$150,000	$95,000
2005	60,000	20,000

Instructions

Prepare the journal entries necessary at December 31, 2005, to record the above corrections and changes. The books are still open for 2005. Voga has not yet recorded its 2005 income tax expense and payable amounts so current year-tax effects may be ignored. Prior-year tax effects must be considered in item 4.

UP17-4   (Change in Principle)   Plato Corporation performs year-end planning in November of each year before their calendar year ends in December. The preliminary estimated net income is $3 million. The CFO, Mary Sheets, meets with the company president, S. A. Plato, to review the projected numbers. She presents the following projected information.

PLATO CORPORATION PROJECTED INCOME STATEMENT FOR THE YEAR ENDED DECEMBER 31, 2004		
Sales		$29,000,000
Cost of goods sold	$14,000,000	
Depreciation	2,600,000	
Operating expenses	6,400,000	23,000,000
Income before income taxes		$ 6,000,000
Provision for income taxes		3,000,000
Net income		$ 3,000,000

PLATO CORPORATION SELECTED BALANCE SHEET INFORMATION AT DECEMBER 31, 2004	
Estimated cash balance	$ 5,000,000
Available-for-sale securities (at cost)	10,000,000
Security fair value adjustment account (1/1/04)	200,000

Estimated market value at December 31, 2004:

Security	Cost	Estimated Market
A	$ 2,000,000	$ 2,200,000
B	4,000,000	3,900,000
C	3,000,000	3,000,000
D	1,000,000	2,800,000
Total	$10,000,000	$11,900,000

Other information at December 31, 2004:

Equipment	$3,000,000
Accumulated depreciation (5-year SL)	1,200,000
New robotic equipment (purchased 1/1/04)	5,000,000
Accumulated depreciation (5-year DDB)	2,000,000

The corporation has never used robotic equipment before, and Sheets assumed an accelerated method because of the rapidly changing technology in robotic equipment. The company normally uses straight-line depreciation for production equipment.

Plato explains to Sheets that it is important for the corporation to show an $8,000,000 net income before taxes because Plato receives a $1,000,000 bonus if the income before taxes and bonus reaches $8,000,000. He also cautions that he will not pay more than $3,000,000 in income taxes to the government.

Instructions
(a) What can Sheets do within GAAP to accommodate the president's wishes to achieve $8,000,000 income before taxes and bonus? Present the revised income statement based on your decision.
(b) Are the actions ethical? Who are the stakeholders in this decision, and what effect does Sheets' actions have on their interests?

SECTION 7 MISCELLANEOUS UPDATE TOPICS

Income Statement Reporting of Change in Accounting Principle

In 2005, the FASB issued a new standard addressing accounting changes and error corrections. This new standard, "Accounting Changes and Error Corrections," *Statement of Financial Accounting Standards No. 154* (Norwalk, Conn.: FASB, 2005), is part of the FASB's short-term international convergence project and replaces *APB Opinion No. 20* and *FASB Statement No. 3*.

The following material should be used **in place of** the discussion in Chapter 5, pages 187–193, of *Fundamentals of Intermediate Accounting*.

UNDERLYING CONCEPTS

Companies can change principles, but it must be demonstrated that the newly adopted principle is preferable to the old one. Such changes mean that consistency from period to period is lost.

Changes in Accounting Principle

Changes in accounting occur frequently in practice, because important events or conditions may be in dispute or uncertain at the statement date. One type of accounting change, therefore, comprises the normal recurring corrections and adjustments that are made by every business enterprise. Another accounting change results when an accounting principle is adopted that is different from the one previously used. Changes in accounting principle would include a change in the method of inventory pricing from FIFO to average cost or a change in accounting for construction contracts from percentage of completion to completed contract.[1]

Changes in accounting principle are recognized by making a **retroactive adjustment** of the financial statements such that the **prior years' statements are recast** on a basis consistent with the newly adopted principle. Any cumulative effect of the change

[1]"Accounting Changes and Error Corrections," *Statement of Financial Accounting Standards No. 154* (Norwalk, Conn.: FASB, 2005). In Chapter 17, we examine in greater detail the problems related to accounting changes.

for periods prior to those presented is recorded as an adjustment to beginning retained earnings of the earliest year presented.

To illustrate, Gaubert Inc. decided in March 2004 to change from FIFO to weighted-average inventory pricing. Gaubert's income before taxes, using the new weighted-average method in 2004, is $30,000. The pretax income data for 2002 and 2003 for this example are shown in Illustration U5-1.

Year	FIFO	Weighted-Average Method	Excess of FIFO over Weighted-Average Method
2002	$40,000	$35,000	$5,000
2003	30,000	27,000	3,000
Total			$8,000

ILLUSTRATION U5-1
Calculation of a Change in Accounting Principle

The information presented in the 2004 financial statements is shown in Illustration U5-2. (The tax rate was 30 percent.)

	2004	2003	2002
Income before taxes	$30,000	$27,000	$35,000
Income tax	9,000	8,100	10,500
Net income	$21,000	$18,900	$24,500

ILLUSTRATION U5-2
Income Statement Presentation of a Change in Accounting Principle

Thus, under the retrospective approach, the prior year's income numbers are restated under the newly adopted method in the current year; comparability across years is preserved.

Changes in Estimates

Estimates are inherent in the accounting process. Estimates are made, for example, of useful lives and salvage values of depreciable assets, of uncollectible receivables, of inventory obsolescence, and of the number of periods expected to benefit from a particular expenditure. Not infrequently, as time passes, as circumstances change, or as additional information is obtained, even estimates originally made in good faith must be changed. Such **changes in estimates** are accounted for in the period of change if they affect only that period, or in the period of change and future periods if the change affects both.

To illustrate a change in estimate that affects only the period of change, assume that DuPage Materials Corp. has consistently estimated its bad debt expense at 1 percent of credit sales. In 2003, however, DuPage's controller determines that the estimate of bad debts for the current year's credit sales must be revised upward to 2 percent, or double the prior years' percentage. Using 2 percent results in a bad debt charge of $240,000, or double the amount using the 1 percent estimate for prior years. The 2 percent rate is necessary to reduce accounts receivable to net realizable value. The provision is recorded at December 31, 2003, as follows.

Bad Debt Expense	240,000	
Allowance for Doubtful Accounts		240,000

The entire change in estimate is included in 2003 income because no future periods are affected by the change. **Changes in estimate are not handled retrospectively.** That is, they are not carried back to adjust prior years. (Changes in estimate that affect both the current and future periods are examined in greater detail in Chapter 17.) **Changes in estimate are not considered errors (prior period adjustments) or extraordinary items.**

Summary of Irregular Items

The modified all-inclusive income concept is accepted in practice. Except for a couple of items (discussed later in this chapter) that are charged or credited directly to retained earnings, all other irregular gains or losses or nonrecurring items are closed to Income Summary and are included in the income statement. Of these, **discontinued operations of a component** of a business is classified as a separate item in the income statement after continuing operations. The **unusual, material, nonrecurring items** that are significantly different from the typical or customary business activities are shown in a separate section for "Extraordinary items" below discontinued operations. Other items of a material amount that are of an **unusual or nonrecurring** nature and are **not considered extraordinary** are separately disclosed.

Because of the numerous intermediate income figures that are created by the reporting of these irregular items, careful evaluation of earnings information reported by the financial press is needed. Illustration U5-3 summarizes the basic concepts previously discussed. Although the chart is simplified, it provides a useful framework for determining the treatment of special items affecting the income statement.

ILLUSTRATION U5-3
Summary of Irregular Items in the Income Statement

Type of Situation[a]	Criteria	Examples	Placement on Financial Statements
Discontinued operations	Disposal of a component of a business for which the operations and cash flows can be clearly distinguished from the rest of the company's operations.	Sale by diversified company of major division that represents only activities in electronics industry. Food distributor that sells wholesale to supermarket chains and through fast-food restaurants decides to discontinue the division that sells to one of two classes of customers.	Shown in separate section of the income statement after continuing operations but before extraordinary items. (Shown net of tax.)
Extraordinary items	Material, and both unusual and infrequent (nonrecurring).	Gains or losses resulting from casualties, an expropriation, or a prohibition under a new law.	Separate section in the income statement entitled "Extraordinary items." (Shown net of tax.)
Unusual gains or losses, not considered extraordinary	Material; character typical of the customary business activities; unusual or infrequent but not both.	Write-downs of receivables, inventories; adjustments of accrued contract prices; gains or losses from fluctuations of foreign exchange; gains or losses from sales of assets used in business.	Separate section in income statement above income before extraordinary items. Often reported in "Other revenues and gains" or "Other expenses and losses" section. (Not shown net of tax.)
Changes in principle	Change from one generally accepted principle to another.	Change in the basis of inventory pricing from FIFO to average cost.	Prior years' income statements are restated on the same basis as the newly adopted principle.
Changes in estimates	Normal, recurring corrections and adjustments.	Changes in the realizability of receivables and inventories; changes in estimated lives of equipment, intangible assets; changes in estimated liability for warranty costs, income taxes, and salary payments.	Change in income statement only in the account affected. (Not shown net of tax.)

[a]This summary provides only the general rules to be followed in accounting for the various situations described above. Exceptions do exist in some of these situations.

SPECIAL REPORTING ISSUES

Intraperiod Tax Allocation

We noted that certain irregular items are shown on the income statement net of tax. Many believe that the resulting income tax effect should be directly associated with that event or item. In other words, the tax expense for the year should be related, where possible, to **specific items** on the income statement to provide a more informative disclosure to statement users. This procedure is called **intraperiod tax allocation**, that is, allocation within a period. Its main purpose is to relate the income tax expense of the period to the items that affect the amount of the tax expense. Intraperiod tax allocation is used for the following items: (1) income from continuing operations, (2) discontinued operations, (3) extraordinary items, and (4) changes in accounting principle. The general concept is, "**Let the tax follow the income.**"

The income tax expense attributable to "income from continuing operations" is computed by finding the income tax expense related to revenue and to expense transactions used in determining this income. In this tax computation, no effect is given to the tax consequences of the items excluded from the determination of "income from continuing operations." A separate tax effect is then associated with each irregular item.

> **OBJECTIVE U1**
> Explain intraperiod tax allocation.

Extraordinary Gains

In applying the concept of intraperiod tax allocation, assume that Schindler Co. has income before income tax and extraordinary item of $250,000 and an extraordinary gain from the sale of a single stock investment of $100,000. If the income tax rate is assumed to be 30 percent, the following information is presented on the income statement.

Income before income tax and extraordinary item		$250,000
Income tax		75,000
Income before extraordinary item		175,000
Extraordinary gain—sale of investment	$100,000	
Less: Applicable income tax	30,000	70,000
Net income		$245,000

ILLUSTRATION U5-4
Intraperiod Tax Allocation, Extraordinary Gain

The income tax of $75,000 ($250,000 × 30%) attributable to "Income before income tax and extraordinary item" is determined from revenue and expense transactions related to this income. In this income tax computation, the tax consequences of items excluded from the determination of "Income before income tax and extraordinary item" are not considered. The "Extraordinary gain—sale of investment" then shows a separate tax effect of $30,000.

Extraordinary Losses

To illustrate the reporting of an extraordinary loss, assume that Schindler Co. has income before income tax and extraordinary item of $250,000 and an extraordinary loss from a major casualty of $100,000. Assuming a 30 percent tax rate, the presentation of income tax on the income statement would be as shown in Illustration U5-5. In this case, the loss provides a positive tax benefit of $30,000 and, therefore, is subtracted from the $100,000 loss.

Income before income tax and extraordinary item		$250,000
Income tax		75,000
Income before extraordinary item		175,000
Extraordinary item—loss from casualty	$100,000	
Less: Applicable income tax reduction	30,000	70,000
Net income		$105,000

ILLUSTRATION U5-5
Intraperiod Tax Allocation, Extraordinary Loss

An extraordinary item may be reported "net of tax" with note disclosure, as shown in Illustration U5-6.

ILLUSTRATION U5-6
Note Disclosure of
Intraperiod Tax Allocation

Income before income tax and extraordinary item	$250,000
Income tax	75,000
Income before extraordinary item	175,000
Extraordinary item, less applicable income tax reduction (Note 1)	70,000
Net income	$105,000

Note 1: During the year the Company suffered a major casualty loss of $70,000, net of applicable income tax reduction of $30,000.

OBJECTIVE U2

Explain where earnings per share information is reported.

Earnings per Share

The results of a company's operations are customarily summed up in one important figure: net income. As if this condensation were not enough of a simplification, the financial world has widely accepted an even more distilled and compact figure as its most significant business indicator—**earnings per share (EPS)**.

The computation of earnings per share is usually straightforward. **Net income minus preferred dividends (income available to common stockholders) is divided by the weighted average of common shares outstanding to arrive at earnings per share.**[2] To illustrate, assume that Lancer, Inc. reports net income of $350,000 and declares and pays preferred dividends of $50,000 for the year. The weighted average number of common shares outstanding during the year is 100,000 shares. Earnings per share is $3, as computed in Illustration U5-7.

ILLUSTRATION U5-7
Equation Illustrating
Computation of Earnings
per Share

$$\frac{\text{Net Income} - \text{Preferred Dividends}}{\text{Weighted Average of Common Shares Outstanding}} = \text{Earnings per Share}$$

$$\frac{\$350,000 - \$50,000}{100,000} = \$3$$

Note that the EPS figure measures the number of dollars earned by each share of common stock—not the dollar amount paid to stockholders in the form of dividends.

"Net income per share" or "earnings per share" is a ratio commonly used in prospectuses, proxy material, and annual reports to stockholders. It is also highlighted in the financial press, by statistical services like Standard & Poor's, and by Wall Street securities analysts. Because of its importance, **earnings per share is required to be disclosed on the face of the income statement**. A company that reports a discontinued operation or an extraordinary item must report per share amounts for these line items either on the face of the income statement or in the notes to the financial statements.[3]

To illustrate the income statement order of presentation and the earnings per share data, we present an income statement for Poquito Industries Inc. in Illustration U5-8 (next page). Notice the order in which data are shown. In addition, per share information is shown at the bottom. Assume that the company had 100,000 shares outstanding for the entire year. The Poquito Industries Inc. income statement, in Illustration U5-8, is highly condensed. Items such as "Unusual charge," "Discontinued operations," and "Extraordinary item" would have to be described fully and appropriately in the statement or related notes.

[2]In the calculation of earnings per share, preferred dividends are deducted from net income if declared or if cumulative though not declared.

[3]"Earnings Per Share," *Statement of Financial Accounting Standards No. 128* (Norwalk, Conn.: FASB, 1996).

POQUITO INDUSTRIES INC.
INCOME STATEMENT
FOR THE YEAR ENDED DECEMBER 31, 2004

Sales revenue		$1,420,000
Cost of goods sold		600,000
Gross profit		820,000
Selling and administrative expenses		320,000
Income from operations		500,000
Other revenues and gains		
Interest revenue		10,000
Other expenses and losses		
Loss on disposal of part of Textile Division	$ (5,000)	
Unusual charge—loss on sale of investments	(45,000)	(50,000)
Income from continuing operations before income tax		460,000
Income tax		208,000
Income from continuing operations		252,000
Discontinued operations		
Income from operations of Pizza Division, less		
applicable income tax of $24,800	54,000	
Loss on disposal of Pizza Division, less		
applicable income tax of $41,000	(90,000)	(36,000)
Income before extraordinary item		216,000
Extraordinary item—loss from earthquake, less		
applicable income tax of $23,000		(45,000)
Net income		$ 171,000
Per share of common stock		
Income from continuing operations		$3.12
Income from operations of discontinued division, net of tax		0.54
Loss on disposal of discontinued operation, net of tax		(0.90)
Income before extraordinary item		2.76
Extraordinary loss, net of tax		(0.45)
Net income		$1.71

Many corporations have simple capital structures that include only common stock. For these companies, a presentation such as "earnings per common share" is appropriate on the income statement. In many instances, however, companies' earnings per share are subject to dilution (reduction) in the future because existing contingencies permit the issuance of additional common shares.[4]

In summary, the simplicity and availability of figures for per share earnings lead inevitably to their widespread use. Because of the undue importance that the public, even the well-informed public, attaches to earnings per share, the EPS figure must be made as meaningful as possible.

Inventory Costs

In 2004, the FASB issued a new standard addressing the accounting for inventory costs. This new standard is titled "Inventory Costs: An Amendment of *ARB No. 43*, Chapter 4," *Statement of Financial Accounting Standards No. 151* (Norwalk, Conn.: FASB, 2004). It is part of the FASB's short-term international convergence project.

The following material **complements** the discussion on product and period costs in Chapter 8, pages 351–352, of *Fundamentals of Intermediate Accounting*.

---

[4]Ibid. The computational problems involved in accounting for these dilutive securities in earnings per share computations are discussed in Chapter 17.

COSTS INCLUDED IN INVENTORY

U.S. GAAP has not required that certain abnormal inventory costs, such as those related to idle capacity and spoilage, double freight, and re-handling, be excluded from the cost of inventory. As a result, companies following U.S. GAAP may include such costs in inventory, whereas companies following International Financial Reporting Standards would treat these items as period costs.

The FASB has now decided to be consistent with the IASB position, to require that these costs, when abnormal, should be **excluded from the cost of inventory**. This change should improve the comparability of financial statements prepared under U.S. and international GAAP.

Preferred Stock

Late in 2003, the FASB issued a new standard that affects the accounting for certain "hybrid" financial instruments, which have characteristics of both liabilities and equity. This standard, "Accounting for Certain Financial Instruments with Characteristics of Both Liabilities and Equity," *Statement of Financial Accounting Standards No. 150,* is one part of the FASB Debt-Equity Project.

The following discussion **replaces** the discussion in Chapter 12, page 590, footnote 10, in *Fundamentals of Intermediate Accounting*.

REDEEMABLE PREFERRED STOCK

Recently, more and more issuances of preferred stock have features that make the security more like debt (a legal obligation to pay) than an equity instrument. For example, **redeemable preferred stock** is a preferred stock that has a mandatory redemption period or redemption feature that is outside the control of the issuer. Previously, public companies were not permitted to report these debt-like preferreds in equity, but they were not required to report them as a liability either. There were concerns about classification of these debt-like securities, which may have been reported as equity or in the "mezzanine" section of balance sheets between debt and equity. There also was diversity in practice as to how dividends on these securities were reported. The new standard addresses these concerns by requiring that such instruments be **classified as liabilities** and be measured and accounted for similar to liabilities.

Note that *SFAS No. 150* represents completion of the first phase in a broader project on liabilities and equity. In phase two of the project, the FASB will deal with the accounting for compound financial instruments (e.g., convertible debt covered in Chapter 16) that have characteristics of liabilities and equity, the definition of an ownership relationship, and the definition of liabilities (an amendment to FASB Concepts Statement No. 6, *Elements of Financial Statements.*)

0-555-02305-2

FUNDAMENTALS OF
INTERMEDIATE
ACCOUNTING

FUNDAMENTALS OF INTERMEDIATE ACCOUNTING

Donald E. Kieso, Ph.D., C.P.A.
KPMG Peat Marwick
Emeritus Professor of Accounting
Northern Illinois University
DeKalb, Illinois

Jerry J. Weygandt, Ph.D., C.P.A.
Arthur Andersen Alumni Professor of Accounting
University of Wisconsin
Madison, Wisconsin

Terry D. Warfield, Ph.D.
PricewaterhouseCoopers Research Scholar
University of Wisconsin
Madison, Wisconsin

John Wiley & Sons, Inc.

PUBLISHER Susan Elbe
ACQUISITIONS EDITOR Mark Bonadeo
MARKETING MANAGER Keari Bedford
OUTSIDE DEVELOPMENT EDITOR Ann Torbert
PRODUCTION SERVICES MANAGER Jeanine Furino
SENIOR DESIGNER Harry Nolan
ILLUSTRATION EDITOR Anna Melhorn
PRODUCTION MANAGEMENT SERVICES Ingrao Associates
MEDIA EDITOR David Kear
COVER DESIGNER Howard Grossman
INTERIOR DESIGN Fearn De Vicq De Cumptich
COVER PHOTO ©Sally Beyer/Stone/Getty Images

This book was set in Palatino by Techbooks. The cover and the interior were printed and bound by Von Hoffmann.

This book is printed on acid-free paper. ∞

To order books or for customer service please, call 1(800)-CALL-WILEY (225-5945).

Library of Congress Cataloging-in-Publication Data

Kieso, Donald E.
    Fundamentals of intermediate accounting/Donald E. Kieso, Jerry J. Weygandt,
Terry D. Warfield.
        p.   cm.
    Includes index.
    ISBN 0-471-07203-6 (cloth: alk. paper)
    1. Accounting. I. Weygandt, Jerry J. II. Warfield, Terry D. III. Title.
HF5635.K498   2002
657'.044—dc21
                                                                    2002032390
                                                                    CIP

ISBN 0-471-07203-6

WIE ISBN 0-471-42899-x

Printed in the United States of America

10 9 8 7 6 5 4 3 2

Dedicated to our wives,

Donna, Enid, and Mary,

and to our children,

Douglas and Debra,

Matt, Erin, and Lia,

Andrew, Lauren, and Katie,

for their

love, support, and encouragement

ABOUT THE AUTHORS

Donald E. Kieso, Ph.D., C.P.A., received his bachelor's degree from Aurora University and his doctorate in accounting from the University of Illinois. He has served as chairman of the Department of Accountancy and is currently the KPMG Peat Marwick Emeritus Professor of Accounting at Northern Illinois University. He has public accounting experience with Price Waterhouse & Co. (San Francisco and Chicago) and Arthur Andersen & Co. (Chicago) and research experience with the Research Division of the American Institute of Certified Public Accountants (New York). He has done postdoctorate work as a Visiting Scholar at the University of California at Berkeley and is a recipient of NIU's Teaching Excellence Award and four Golden Apple Teaching Awards. Professor Kieso is the author of other accounting and business books and is a member of the American Accounting Association, the American Institute of Certified Public Accountants, and the Illinois CPA Society. He has served as a member of the Board of Directors of the Illinois CPA Society, the AACSB's Accounting Accreditation Committees, the State of Illinois Comptroller's Commission, as Secretary-Treasurer of the Federation of Schools of Accountancy, and as Secretary-Treasurer of the American Accounting Association. Professor Kieso served as a charter member of the national Accounting Education Change Commission. He is the recipient of the Outstanding Accounting Educator Award from the Illinois CPA Society, the FSA's Joseph A. Silvoso Award of Merit, and the NIU Foundation's Humanitarian Award for Service to Higher Education.

Jerry J. Weygandt, Ph.D., C.P.A., is Arthur Andersen Alumni Professor of Accounting at the University of Wisconsin-Madison. He holds a Ph.D. in accounting from the University of Illinois. Articles by Professor Weygandt have appeared in the *Accounting Review, Journal of Accounting Research, Accounting Horizons, Journal of Accountancy,* and other academic and professional journals. These articles have examined such financial reporting issues as accounting for price-level adjustments, pensions, convertible securities, stock option contracts, and interim reports. Professor Weygandt is author of other accounting and financial reporting books and is a member of the American Accounting Association, the American Institute of Certified Public Accountants, and the Wisconsin Society of Certified Public Accountants. He has served on numerous committees of the American Accounting Association and as a member of the editorial board of the *Accounting Review;* he also has served as President and Secretary-Treasurer of the American Accounting Association. In addition, he has been actively involved with the American Institute of Certified Public Accountants and has been a member of the Accounting Standards Executive Committee (AcSEC) of that organization. He has served on the FASB task force that examined the reporting issues related to accounting for income taxes and is presently a trustee of the Financial Accounting Foundation. Professor Weygandt has received the Chancellor's Award for Excellence in Teaching and the Beta Gamma Sigma Dean's Teaching Award. He is on the board of directors of M & I Bank of Southern Wisconsin and the Dean Foundation. He is the recipient of the Wisconsin Institute of CPA's Outstanding Educator's Award and the Lifetime Achievement Award. In 2001 he received the American Accounting Association's Outstanding Accounting Educator Award.

Terry D. Warfield, Ph.D., is PricewaterhouseCoopers Research Scholar at the University of Wisconsin—Madison. He received a B.S. and M.B.A. from Indiana University and a Ph.D. in accounting from the University of Iowa. Professor Warfield's area of expertise is financial reporting, and prior to his academic career, he worked for five years in the banking industry. He served as the Academic Accounting Fellow in the Office of the Chief Accountant at the U.S. Securities and Exchange Commission in Washington, D.C. from 1995–1996. While on the staff, he worked on projects related to financial instruments and financial institutions, and he helped coordinate a symposium on intangible asset financial reporting. Professor Warfield's primary research interests concern financial accounting standards and disclosure policies. He has published scholarly articles in *The Accounting Review, Journal of Accounting and Economics, Research in Accounting Regulation,* and *Accounting Horizons,* and he has served on the editorial boards of *The Accounting Review, Accounting Horizons,* and *Issues in Accounting Education.* He has served on the Financial Accounting Standards Committee of the American Accounting Association (Chair 1995–1996) and the Nominations

Committee, and on the AAA-FASB Research Conference Committee. Professor Warfield has taught accounting courses at the introductory, intermediate, and graduate levels. He has received teaching awards at both the University of Iowa and the University of Wisconsin, and he was named to the Teaching Academy at the University of Wisconsin in 1995. Professor Warfield has developed and published several case studies based on his research for use in accounting classes. These cases have been selected for the AICPA Professor-Practitioner Case Development Program, and a case on hybrid securities has been published in *Issues in Accounting Education*. Professor Warfield also has developed materials on cooperative learning in accounting that have been presented at teaching workshops and included in instructor materials for accounting textbooks.

PREFACE

Intermediate Accounting was first published approximately 30 years ago. Our intent at that time was to write a book in which students would understand the *how* as well as the *why* of intermediate accounting. Ten editions have now gone by, and *Intermediate* continues to be the market leader. Several features of *Intermediate* have contributed to its long-lasting success. We believe that students best learn to account for and analyze financial events and phenomena if they fully understand the nature of business transactions and comprehend the behavioral and economic consequences of the events for which companies account and report. As a result, we have always strived to show how important accounting is to the functions of an efficient capital market. In addition, we have attempted to provide the most up-to-date, complete, and authoritative book in the marketplace.

Although *Intermediate* continues to have outstanding success, some have suggested that they would prefer a shorter text in order to have more time to develop various professional competencies, such as analysis and oral and written communication skills. Others have indicated that a shorter text will help them to develop a course in which more emphasis can be placed on accounting concepts. With less content to get through, these instructors are seeking to apply the fundamental concepts in various settings, such as in oral and written presentations, and with introduction of more technology and other enhancements.

On the other hand, many of our users have indicated that they prefer no changes in *Intermediate* because it is complete, up-to-date, and authoritative. In addition, *Intermediate* gives flexibility in selecting topics, provides a useful long-term reference for students, and offers materials that students can pursue on their own.

We believe both viewpoints have merit, and as a result there is a need to find a balance among these various demands in the intermediate accounting course. Therefore we decided to develop *Fundamentals of Intermediate Accounting*. We hope this shorter, more concise text will be helpful to instructors and students alike. Our overriding goal has been to craft a book that helps students understand the *significance* of the numbers they are working with.

◆ FINDING THE BALANCE

In developing *Fundamentals*, one of the first issues we considered was whether to eliminate topics or to eliminate the rigor and depth found in *Intermediate*. We decided that it was important to find the right balance between the number of topics to cover and the depth and rigor necessary to ensure that essential concepts were understood. As a consequence, we spent significant time considering topics that could be deleted or reduced significantly in scope. Because these omitted topics may be important for some, many of the omitted topics can be found on our *Take Action!* CD-ROM, which accompanies the book.

The key difference, therefore, between *Intermediate* and *Fundamentals* is that *Fundamentals* is shorter. Although the chapters in *Fundamentals* are similar to those found in *Intermediate,* a number of chapters have been combined and material omitted, so that the text is more streamlined. At the same time, *Fundamentals* examines and explains the core concepts for understanding (1) the conceptual framework, (2) financial statements, (3) the institutional framework, and (4) major accounting and reporting issues related to assets, liabilities, stockholders' equity, revenues, and expenses. It is our hope that with a better understanding of the framework and core concepts comes the opportunity for students to better understand the significance of the material presented in the course.

Like *Intermediate, Fundamentals* is intended for the second course in financial accounting and reporting, which in many cases covers three quarters or two semesters. However, *Fundamentals* is a much shorter book. For example, *Intermediate* has 25 chapters, whereas *Fundamentals* has 17. As a result, *Fundamentals* can be covered in a single semester, provided some omission of subject material. For those instructors who intend to use *Fundamentals* over two semesters, it should be possible to enhance the fundamental material with additional readings, cases, exercises, or other professional competency activities. A shorter book also provides additional flexibility to instructors who are interested in teaching a corporate reporting course. Because we provide the core concepts covered in intermediate accounting, many instructors can use this textbook in graduate, masters, and MBA courses.

◆ CONTENT AND ORGANIZATION OF *FUNDAMENTALS*

Content

Fundamentals of Intermediate Accounting has 17 chapters and 7 end-of-book appendixes:

Chapter 1	Financial Accounting and Accounting Standards
Chapter 2	Conceptual Framework Underlying Financial Accounting
Chapter 3	The Accounting Information System
Chapter 4	Balance Sheet
Chapter 5	Income Statement and Related Information
Chapter 6	Revenues and Cash Flows
Chapter 7	Cash and Receivables
Chapter 8	Accounting for Inventories
Chapter 9	Accounting for Property, Plant, and Equipment
Chapter 10	Intangible Assets
Chapter 11	Accounting for Liabilities
Chapter 12	Stockholders' Equity
Chapter 13	Investments
Chapter 14	Accounting for Income Taxes
Chapter 15	Accounting for Compensation
Chapter 16	Accounting for Leases
Chapter 17	Additional Reporting Issues
Appendix A	Accounting and the Time Value of Money
Appendix B	Using Financial Calculators
Appendix C	Retail Inventory Method
Appendix D	Accounting for Natural Resources
Appendix E	Accounting for Computer Software Costs
Appendix F	Accounting for Troubled Debt
Appendix G	Accounting for Derivative Instruments

These chapters are very similar to the ones in *Intermediate*. We continue to strive for a balanced discussion of concepts and applications so that these elements are mutually reinforcing. In addition, discussion focuses on explaining the rationale behind business transactions before addressing the accounting and reporting for those activities.

The importance of accounting to the capital market has never been more important. A recent *Wall Street Journal* ran the following headlines:

- "The SEC Checks Whether Microsoft Was Too Conservative in Booking Revenues"
- "Qwest Communications Acknowledges Some Off-Balance-Sheet Transactions"
- "SEC Reviews Allegations That EMC Improperly Accounted for Some Sales"
- "Krispy Kreme Makes Changes After an Accounting Technique Is Questioned"
- "Marriott Is Set to Disclose Details of Write-Offs Related to Developer Financing"

An important feature of *Fundamentals* is an enhanced effort to provide more perspective on the financial information provided. As a result, special boxed insights entitled "What Do the Numbers Mean?" illustrate how reporting methods affect the decisions of financial statement users. By means of these boxes we hope to convey the excitement and ever-changing nature of accounting, illuminating its significance and highlighting its importance. Over the years of teaching, we have found that many students, when introduced to the issues involved in financial reporting, genuinely enjoy the subject area.

We have made every effort to provide an integrated framework in which to study *Fundamentals*. Similar to *Intermediate*, the first two chapters discuss the standards-setting process, starting with the institutional structure and following with the conceptual framework. Following this foundational material is a review of the accounting cycle for those who wish a refresher on basic understanding of the recording process. The next three chapters address the three major financial statements—the balance sheet, income statement, and statement of cash flows. In addition, since a significant number of our users have requested that revenue recognition be developed early in the textbook, *Fundamentals* covers revenue recognition in Chapter 6, along with cash flows.

What then follows is a group of chapters addressing the basic issues at the intermediate level: cash and receivables, inventories, plant assets, intangible assets, liabilities, stockholders' equity, and investments.

The next three chapters focus on accounting issues related to the important topics of deferred taxes, compensation, and leases. The new chapter on compensation addresses not only pensions but also the basic issues related to payroll and to stock options.

We complete the text with a discussion related to disclosure issues of various kinds, dealing with accounting changes, earnings per share, and additional issues related to the statement of cash flows.

At the end of the book are seven appendixes on topics that some instructors may want to cover. The first two appendixes discuss time value of money concepts and the use of financial calculators in making time value of money calculations. The remaining five appendixes present a variety of industry reporting issues: the retail inventory method, accounting for natural resources, accounting for computer software costs, accounting for troubled debt, and accounting for derivative instruments.

Organizational Highlights

A New Chapter on Revenues and Cash Flows   A significant number of users of *Intermediate* have requested that revenue recognition be discussed earlier in the textbook. *Fundamentals* provides us with the opportunity to provide a streamlined discussion of revenue recognition in Chapter 6. Here, we interface revenue recognition with its accrual concepts and the statement of cash flows, to provide a perspective on the *use* of various performance measurements. Given that many companies have chosen to report pro-forma earnings numbers that range from cash flow per share to earnings before interest and taxes, the logic of discussing revenue recognition and cash flow in one chapter seemed appropriate.

Updated Chapter on Intangibles   *Intermediate Accounting, 10e, Updated Edition* provides a new chapter on intangible assets. This new chapter, with modifications, is now also found in *Fundamentals*. The major changes from the *Updated Edition* are that the impairment discussion is enhanced, as it now addresses not only intangibles, but also property, plant, and equipment. In addition, the "Other Costs" section has been streamlined. Coverage of the accounting issues related to computer software costs now appears in Appendix E at the back of the book.

Chapter on Compensation   New Chapter 15 gathers together in one place the various topics related to compensation: payroll, stock options, and pensions. The content in the area is very similar to the treatment in *Intermediate*. The biggest change is in the pension discussion, which has been streamlined and rewritten to clearly present the fundamental concepts but still ensure adequate coverage.

Combined Chapters

Chapter on Inventories   *Intermediate* covers inventories in two chapters because of the many complexities associated with the topic. *Fundamentals* omits certain topics related to managerial accounting and therefore is able to cover inventories in one chapter. In addition, the specialized topic of the retail inventory method is discussed in Appendix C at the back of the book.

Chapter on Property, Plant, and Equipment   *Fundamentals* also combines two chapters related to plant assets—"Property, Plant, and Equipment," and "Depreciation." Discussions related to interest capitalization, exchanges of plant assets, contributions, costs subsequent to acquisition, and special depreciation methods have been streamlined. The important topic of impairments has been moved to the intangibles chapter, so that this subject can be discussed fully in one place. The subject matter related to depletion has been moved to Appendix D at the back of the book.

Chapters on Liabilities and on Equity   The two liabilities chapters and the two chapters related to stockholders' equity have been streamlined and rewritten and are now presented in one chapter on each of these topics.

◆ OTHER FEATURES

We have continued, and enhanced, many of the features that have been used so successfully in *Intermediate*, including the following.

Chapter-Opening Vignettes

We have updated chapter-opening vignettes and introduced many new ones, to provide a real-world context that helps motivate student interest in the chapter topic.

Review Exercises

A Review Exercise, with solution, is presented at the end of the text portion of each chapter (following the Summary of Learning Objectives). The exercise and solution give students a chance to check their understanding of chapter concepts before they begin homework assignments.

Using Your Judgment

The Using Your Judgment section appears at the end of each chapter and contains problem features that link the chapter content to real-world situations. These features are: a Financial Reporting Problem (questions about the financial statements of 3M Company); a Financial Statement Analysis Case (dealing with various companies), a Comparative Analysis (comparison of the statements of The Coca-Cola Company and PepsiCo, Inc.), and an International Reporting Case (see the following elaboration). In *Fundamentals*, writing and group assignments (which have been part of the Using Your Judgment section in *Intermediate*) are integrated into the exercises, problems, and cases, where they are identified by icons. Ethics cases are also identified with an icon (a balance).

International Reporting Cases

We have extended the international coverage in the text by introducing a number of International Reporting Cases that are based on various real companies and that are designed to illustrate international accounting differences. A particular emphasis is on the implications of these differences for analysis, which reinforces the user orientation of the Using Your Judgment elements.

Take Action! CD

The *Take Action!* CD is an electronic gateway for students to a comprehensive set of materials that supplement the already-comprehensive coverage of accounting topics in the textbook. Major elements of the *Take Action!* CD (similar to the features contained in the *Gateway to the Profession* Digital Tool for *Intermediate Accounting*) are as follows.

Analyst Toolkit

Database of Real Companies Numerous annual reports of well-known companies, including three international companies, are provided on the *Take Action!* CD. These annual reports can be used in a variety of ways. For example, they can be used as illustrations of different presentations of financial information or for comparing note disclosures across companies. In addition, these reports can be used to analyze a company's financial condition and compare its prospects with other companies in the same industry. Assignment material is included to provide some examples of different types of analysis that can be performed.

Company Web Links Each of the companies in the database of real companies is identified by a Web address to facilitate the gathering of additional information, if desired.

Additional Enrichment Material A chapter on Financial Statement Analysis is provided, along with related assignment material. This chapter can also be used in conjunction with the database of annual reports of real companies.

Spreadsheet Tools Present value templates are provided which can be used to solve time value of money problems.

Additional Internet Links A number of useful links related to financial analysis are provided to expand expertise in this area.

Professional Toolkit

Consistent with expanding beyond technical accounting knowledge, the *Take Action!* CD emphasizes certain skills necessary to become a successful accountant and financial manager.

Writing Materials A primer on professional communications is provided that will give students a framework for writing professional materials. This primer discusses issues such as the top ten writing problems, strategies for rewriting, how to do revisions, and tips on clarity. This primer has been class-tested and is effective in helping students enhance their writing skills.

Group Work Materials Recent evaluation of accounting education has identified the need to develop more skills in group problem solving. The *Take Action!* CD contains a second primer dealing with the role that groups play in organizations. Information on what makes a successful group, how can you participate effectively in the group, and the do's and don'ts of group formation, is included.

Ethics The Professional Toolkit contains expanded materials on the role of ethics in the profession, including references to:

- Speeches and articles on ethics in accounting.
- Codes of ethics for major professional bodies.
- Examples and additional case studies on ethics.

Career Professional Spotlights   Every student should have a good understanding of the profession he or she is entering. These vignettes indicate the types of work accountants do. Other aspects of the spotlights on careers are included on the *Take Action!* CD to help students make successful career choices. These include professional Web links—important links to Web sites that can provide useful career information to facilitate the student's efforts in this area.

Student Toolkit

Also included on the *Take Action!* CD are features that help students process and understand the course materials. These are:

Interactive Tutorials   To help students better understand some of the more difficult topics in intermediate accounting, we have developed several interactive tutorials that provide expanded discussion and explanation in a visual and narrative context. Topics addressed include the accounting cycle; inventory methods, including dollar-value LIFO; depreciation and impairment of long-lived assets; and interest capitalization. Note that these tutorials are for the benefit of the student and should require no use of class time on the part of instructors.

Expanded Discussions and Illustrations   This section provides additional topics not covered in depth in the textbook. The *Take Action!* CD gives the flexibility to discuss topics not covered in detail in the textbook.

International Accounting   An expanded discussion of international accounting institutions, the evolution of international accounting standards, and a framework for understanding differences in accounting practice is provided. This discussion is designed to complement the international reporting problems in the text.

Take Action! CD Topics   Topics included on the *Take Action!* CD are as follows (with appropriate chapter linkage identified).

Chapter 1—Financial Accounting and Accounting Standards
- Expanded discussion of international accounting
- Expanded discussion of ethical issues in financial reporting

Chapter 2—Conceptual Framework Underlying Financial Accounting
- Expanded discussion of inflation accounting approaches

Chapter 3—The Accounting Information System
- Expanded discussion of special journals
- Expanded discussion of cash basis versus accrual basis accounting
- *Tutorial* on the accounting cycle
- Presentation of worksheet using the periodic inventory method

Chapter 4—Balance Sheet
- Presentation of balance sheet formats for various real companies

Chapter 5—Income Statement and Related Information
- Income statements for real companies
- Examples of comprehensive income reporting

Chapter 6—Revenues and Cash Flows
- Additional disclosures of revenue recognition policies
- Expanded discussion of the accounting for franchises
- Additional disclosures of cash flow reporting
- Expanded discussion of financial statement analysis (Appendix 6A)

Chapter 7—Cash and Receivables
- Additional disclosures of restricted cash
- *Tutorial* on recording uncollectible accounts
- Comprehensive illustration of sale without recourse
- *Tutorial* on disposition of receivables
- Additional disclosure of receivables
- Expanded discussion of a four-column bank reconciliation (Appendix 7A)

Chapter 8—Accounting for Inventories
- *Tutorial* on inventory methods
- *Tutorial* on LIFO inventory issues
- Additional inventory disclosures
- Additional LIFO reserve disclosures
- Discussion of inventory errors
- Discussion of LIFO retail methods (in end-of-book Appendix C)

Chapter 9—Accounting for Property, Plant, and Equipment
- *Tutorial* on interest capitalization
- *Tutorial* on depreciation methods
- Expanded discussion of special depreciation methods
- Expanded discussion of gains on exchanges of similar assets
- Additional property, plant, and equipment disclosures

Chapter 10—Intangible Assets
- *Tutorial* on impairments
- Additional disclosures of intangibles and R&D costs
- Discussion on valuing goodwill

Chapter 11—Accounting for Liabilities
- Additional disclosures of current liabilities and contingencies

Chapter 12—Stockholders' Equity
- Expanded discussion of quasi-reorganization
- Financial analysis primer

Chapter 13—Investments
- Disclosures related to investments and comprehensive income
- Disclosures related to equity investments
- Examples of entries for transfers between categories
- Discussion of special issues related to investments

Chapter 14—Accounting for Income Taxes
- Expanded discussion of intraperiod tax allocation
- Additional examples of deferred tax disclosures
- Comprehensive illustration of interperiod tax allocation
- Discussion of the conceptual aspects of interperiod tax allocation, including the deferred and net-of-tax methods

Chapter 15—Accounting for Compensation
- Additional discussion on bonus computations
- Expanded discussion of stock compensation plans
- Disclosures for defined compensation plans
- Expanded discussion of other postretirement benefits
- Examples of pension and other postretirement benefit disclosures

Chapter 16—Accounting for Leases
- Expanded discussion of real estate and leveraged leases
- Additional lease disclosures

Chapter 17—Additional Reporting Issues
- Examples of cash flow statements, including disclosure of significant non-cash transactions
- Example of antidilution with multiple securities
- Discussion of the T-account method for preparing a statement of cash flows, including a detailed example

Appendix C—Retail Inventory Method
- Discussion of LIFO retail method

In addition to these materials, illustrative disclosures of financial reporting practices are provided throughout.

Self-Tests Each chapter includes two sets of self-tests to allow students to check their understanding of key concepts from the chapter.

Glossary   A complete glossary of all the key terms used in the text in alphabetical order is provided on the *Take Action!* CD. Page numbers where these key terms and concepts appear in the text are also shown.

Learning Style Survey   Research on left brain/right brain differences and on learning and personality differences suggests that each person has preferred ways to receive and communicate information. After taking this quiz, students will be able to pinpoint the study aids in the text that will help them learn the material based on their own learning style.

In summary, the *Take Action!* CD is a comprehensive complement to the first edition of *Fundamentals of Intermediate Accounting*, providing new materials as well as a new way to communicate that material.

◆ SUPPLEMENTARY MATERIALS

Accompanying this textbook is an extensive package of active-teaching supplements for instructors and active-learning supplements for students. The *Fundamentals of Intermediate Accounting* package includes the following additional tools.

Active-Teaching Supplements

Take Action! CD

The *Take Action!* CD, previously described, provides numerous tools for students and instructors. It contains the professional, analyst, and student toolkits, as well as other features such as interactive self-study and self-test questions, and the Accounting Cycle Tutorial. The new CD also contains new voice-guided tutorials covering securitization, LIFO, bad debts, basic inventory issues, depreciation, interest capitalization, and impairments.

Instructor's Resource CD (IR CD)

The Instructor's Resource CD-ROM (IR CD) contains the instructor's manual, solutions manual, teaching transparencies, text art, computerized test bank, solutions to Excel workbook problems, PowerPoint presentations, and Checklist of Key Figures.

Solutions Manual

The Solutions Manual (Volumes 1 and 2) provides answers to all questions, brief exercises, exercises, problems, and case materials in the end-of-chapter problems. Each chapter contains an *assignment classification table*, an *assignment characteristics table,* and a *Bloom's taxonomy table.* Print is large and bold for easy readability in lecture settings. (Also available online at *www.wiley.com/college/kieso* and on the IR CD.)

Solutions Transparencies

Acetates of the brief exercises, exercises, and problems are provided in an organizer box with chapter file folders. PDF files of the cases and materials in the Using Your Judgment section are on the Web site and available for download.

Instructor's Manual

The Instructor's Manual is designed to assist professors in preparing lectures and assignment. The manual contains chapter reviews, study objectives for each chapter, sample syllabi, lecture outlines, and print teaching transparency masters. Each chapter also provides quizzing exercises, a Bloom's taxonomy table, and much more. (Also available online at *www.wiley.com/college/kieso* and on the IR CD.)

Teaching Transparencies

These four-color acetates provide illustrations of text concepts discussed in the Instructor's Manual.

Examination Book and Test Bank

True-false, multiple-choice, and essay questions help instructors test students' knowledge and communication skills. The Test Bank is designed to allow instructors to tailor examinations according to study objectives, learning skills, and content. In addition to chapter tests, achievement tests, and comprehensive tests, a final exam is provided. (Also available online at *www.wiley.com/college/kieso* and on the IR CD.)

Computerized Test Bank

This easy-to-use program allows instructors to create multiple versions of the same test. This computerized test bank also has authoring capabilities and randomizing functions. (Also available online and on the IR CD.)

PowerPoint Presentation Material

The electronic PowerPoint slides emphasize the key concepts in each chapter. (Available at HYPERLINK *"http://www.wiley.com/college/kieso"*, *www.wiley.com/college/kieso,* and on the IR CD.)

Nightly Business Report Video

This video contains segments from the "Nightly Business Report" that have been selected for the applicability to intermediate accounting. An Instructor's Manual with suggestions for integrating the material into the classroom accompanies the video.

Checklist of Key Figures

Available for download on the Web site only, the check figures are partial or complete answers (not solutions) to select end-of-chapter materials.

Web CT/Blackboard Course Management Resources

Web CT and Blackboard course management systems are tools that facilitate the organization and delivery of course materials on the Web. Easy to use, they provide powerful communication, loaded content, easy and flexible course administration, and sophisticated online testing and diagnostic systems.

Solutions to Excel Templates

Available for download from the Web site only, these are solutions to the Excel problem templates discussed in the Kieso *Fundamentals Excel Workbook.* (Also available at *www.wiley.com/college/kieso* and on the IR CD.)

Solutions to Rockford Practice Set

Available for print or download from the Kieso *Fundamentals* Web site (*www.wiley.com/college/kieso*), this supplement provides solutions to the Rockford Practice Set.

Student Active-Learning Supplements

Excel Working Papers

This CD contains all solution forms and partially completed solution forms for all end-of-chapter problems and exercises. Solution forms are available as Excel templates. Solutions can be typed directly into the templates which are saved onto a hard drive or written manually after forms are printed. By entering data electronically, students can now paste homework to a new file and e-mail the worksheet to their instructor.

Working Papers

These are solution forms and partially completed solution forms for all end-of-chapter problems and exercises. This resource demonstrates how to correctly set up solution formats.

Study Guide

The Study Guide is a useful tool for students to use in the classroom and an excellent resource when preparing for exams. It contains chapter outlines, chapter reviews of key concepts, and a glossary of key terms. Demonstration problems, multiple-choice, true-false, matching, and other self-testing opportunities are included.

Problem-Solving Survival Guide

This guide is a very useful tool for students, as it provides additional questions and problems to develop students' problem-solving skills. Explanations assist in the approach, set-up, and completion of problems. Tips alert students to common pitfalls and misconceptions.

Solving Intermediate Accounting Problems Using Excel Workbook

This workbook contains Excel templates that allow students to complete select end-of-chapter exercises and problems identified by a spreadsheet icon in the margin of the main text. A useful introduction to Excel, this package details how students can work with preprogrammed spreadsheets, and it instructs students on how to design their own spreadsheets.

Rockford Practice Set

This revised practice set has been designed as a student review and update of the accounting cycle and the preparation of financial statements.

Computerized Rockford Practice Set

This computerized practice set allows students to apply concepts of the accounting cycle and prepare financial statements using general ledger software (GLS).

Interactive Web Quizzing Powered by eGrade

Available at the book's Web site, these interactive questions are derived from end-of-chapter exercises. These practice questions are powered by eGrade.

Business Extra Web Site

The Business Extra Web site gives professors and students instant access to a wealth of current articles dealing with all aspects of accounting. The articles are organized by topic, and discussion questions follow each article.

◆ ACKNOWLEDGMENTS

We thank the many users of the ten editions of *Intermediate Accounting* who contributed to the book's success through their comments and instructive criticism. Special thanks are extended to the following people for their various contributions.

Focus Group Participants

Larry Bergin
Winona State University

Robert Bloom
John Carroll University

Phillip Buchanan
George Mason University

Tom Buchman
University of Colorado, Boulder

Tom Carment
Northeastern State University

Joanne Duke
San Francisco State University

Julia Higgs
Florida Atlantic University

Kathy Hsu
University of Louisiana, Lafayette

James Johnston
Louisiana Tech University

Gary Luoma
University of South Carolina

Richard Parker
Olivet College

Debbie Rankin
Lincoln University

John Rossi
Moravian College

Jerry Siebel
University of South Florida

Ron Stunda
Birmingham Southern College

Gary Taylor
University of Alabama

Elizabeth Venuti
Hofstra University

Jeannie Welsh
La Salle University

Content Providers

Clyde Galbraith
West Chester University

Patricia Parker
Columbus State Community College

Marlene Plumlee
University of Utah

Paul Robertson
New Mexico State University

Larry Roman
Cuyahoga Community College

Other colleagues who have provided helpful criticisms and made valuable suggestions as members of focus groups and telesession participants, as adopters, or as reviewers of previous editions include:

Charlene Abendroth
Californina State University, Hayward

Roberta Allen
Texas Tech University

Jon Booker
Tennessee Technological University

Robert Cluskey
Tennessee State University

Edwin Cohen
DePaul University

W. Terry Dancer
Arkansas State University

Lee Dexter
Moorhead State University

Judith Doing
University of Arizona

Susan Gill
Washington State University

John Gribble
PriceWaterhouseCoopers

Zafar Iqbal
California Poly State University, San Luis Obispo

Jeff Jones
Auburn University

Celina Jozsi
University of South Florida

Paul Kimmel
University of Wisconsin, Milwaukee

Mark Kohlbeck
University of Wisconsin, Madison

Lisa Koonce
University of Texas at Austin

Brian Leventhal
University of Illinois, Chicago

Timothy Lindquist
University of Northern Iowa

Tom Linsmeier
Michigan State University

Daphne Main
University of New Orleans

Mostafa Maksy
Northeastern Illinois University

Siva Nathan
Georgia State University

Ray Pfeiffer
University of Massachusetts, Amherst

Tom Porter
Georgia State University

Vernon Richardson
University of Kansas

Richard Riley
West Virginia University

Paul Robertson
New Mexico State University

Steven Rock
University of Colorado

Victoria Rymer
University of Maryland

Jon Sander
University of Southern Maine

Carlton Stolle
Texas A & M

William Stout
University of Louisville

Iris Stuart
California State University, Fullerton

Eric Sussman
University of California, Los Angeles

Diane Tanner
University of North Florida

Paula Thomas
Middle Tennessee State University

James Waddington
Hawaii Pacific University

Michael Willenborg
University of Connecticut

Joni Young
University of New Mexico

Paul Zarowin
New York University

Ancillary Authors, Contributors, and Accuracy Checkers

Maryann Benson

John C. Borke
University of Wisconsin, Platteville

Michelle Ephraim
Worcester Polytechnic Institute

Larry Falcetto
Emporia State University

Sarah Frank
University of West Florida

Clyde Galbraith
West Chester University

Marc Giullian
Montana State University

Bonnie Harrison
College of Southern Maryland

Wayne Higley
Buena Vista College

Marilyn F. Hunt
University of Central Florida

Heather Johnson
Elm Street Publishing Services

Douglas W. Kieso
University of California, Irvine

Edwin Hackleman

Jennifer Laudermilch

Gary Lubin

Don Newell
Delta Software

Andrew Prewitt
KPMG LLP—Chicago

Rex A. Schildhouse
University of Phoenix, San Diego

Jeff Seymour
KPMG—Minneapolis

Alice Sineath
Forsyth Technical Community College

Iris Stuart
California State University

Erin Viel
PriceWaterhouseCoopers—Milwaukee

Dick D. Wasson
Southwestern College

Stuart Weiss
Stuart Weiss Business Writing, Inc.

Edward Wertheim
Northeastern University

We appreciate the outstanding support and professional commitment given us by the development, marketing, production, and editorial staffs of John Wiley & Sons, including Susan Elbe, Jay O'Callaghan, Mark Bonadeo, Jeanine Furino, Johnna Barto, David Kear, Ed Brislin, Brian Kamins, and Cynthia Taylor. Thanks, too, to development editor Ann Torbert, project editor Suzanne Ingrao, and the management and staff at TechBooks. Finally, thanks to Maris Technologies for developing the *Take Action!* CD.

We appreciate the cooperation of the American Institute of Certified Public Accountants and the Financial Accounting Standards Board in permitting us to quote from their pronouncements. We thank 3M Company for permitting us to use its 2001 Annual Report for our specimen financial statements. We also acknowledge permission from the American Institute of Certified Public Accountants, the Institute of Management Accountants, and the Institute of Internal Auditors to adapt and use material from the Uniform CPA Examinations, the CMA Examinations, and the CIA Examinations, respectively.

If this book helps teachers instill in their students an appreciation for the challenges, worth, and limitations of accounting, if it encourages students to evaluate critically and understand financial accounting theory and practice, and if it prepares students for advanced study, professional examinations, and the successful and ethical pursuit of their careers in accounting or business, then we will have achieved our objective.

We appreciate and welcome suggestions and comments from users of this book.

Donald E. Kieso, *Somonauk, Illinois*
Jerry J. Weygandt, *Madison, Wisconsin*
Terry D. Warfield, *Madison, Wisconsin*

Brief Contents

Chapter 1
FINANCIAL ACCOUNTING AND ACCOUNTING STANDARDS 1

Chapter 2
CONCEPTUAL FRAMEWORK UNDERLYING FINANCIAL ACCOUNTING 25

Chapter 3
THE ACCOUNTING INFORMATION SYSTEM 61

Chapter 4
BALANCE SHEET 123

Chapter 5
INCOME STATEMENT AND RELATED INFORMATION 171

Chapter 6
REVENUES AND CASH FLOWS 221

Chapter 7
CASH AND RECEIVABLES 285

Chapter 8
ACCOUNTING FOR INVENTORIES 345

Chapter 9
ACCOUNTING FOR PROPERTY, PLANT, AND EQUIPMENT 407

Chapter 10
INTANGIBLE ASSETS 471

Chapter 11
ACCOUNTING FOR LIABILITIES 515

Chapter 12
STOCKHOLDERS' EQUITY 575

Chapter 13
INVESTMENTS 633

Chapter 14
ACCOUNTING FOR INCOME TAXES 683

Chapter 15
ACCOUNTING FOR COMPENSATION 737

Chapter 16
ACCOUNTING FOR LEASES 779

Chapter 17
ADDITIONAL REPORTING ISSUES 823

Appendix A
ACCOUNTING AND THE TIME VALUE OF MONEY A1

Appendix B
FINANCIAL CALCULATORS B1

Appendix C
RETAIL INVENTORY METHOD C2

Appendix D
ACCOUNTING FOR NATURAL RESOURCES D1

Appendix E
ACCOUNTING FOR COMPUTER SOFTWARE COSTS E1

Appendix F
ACCOUNTING FOR TROUBLED DEBT F1

Appendix G
ACCOUNTING FOR DERIVATIVE INSTRUMENTS G1

CONTENTS

CHAPTER 1
FINANCIAL ACCOUNTING AND ACCOUNTING STANDARDS, 1
THE SIZE OF THE NEW YORK PHONE BOOK, IF NECESSARY, 1

◆ **Financial Statements and Financial Reporting, 2**

Accounting and Capital Allocation, 3
The Challenges Facing Financial Accounting, 3
Objectives of Financial Reporting, 4
The Need to Develop Standards, 5

◆ **Parties Involved in Standards Setting, 6**

Securities and Exchange Commission (SEC), 6
American Institute of Certified Public Accountants (AICPA), 7
Financial Accounting Standards Board (FASB), 8
Changing Role of the AICPA, 11

◆ **Generally Accepted Accounting Principles, 12**

◆ **Issues in Financial Reporting, 13**

Standards Setting in a Political Environment, 13
The Expectations Gap, 14
International Accounting Standards, 15
Ethics in the Environment of Financial Accounting, 15

CHAPTER 2
CONCEPTUAL FRAMEWORK UNDERLYING FINANCIAL ACCOUNTING, 25
SHOW ME THE EARNINGS!, 25

◆ **Conceptual Framework, 26**

Need for Conceptual Framework, 26
Development of Conceptual Framework, 27

◆ **First Level: Basic Objectives, 28**

◆ **Second Level: Fundamental Concepts, 29**

Qualitative Characteristics of Accounting Information, 29
Basic Elements, 32

◆ **Third Level: Recognition and Measurement Concepts, 33**

Basic Assumptions, 34
Basic Principles of Accounting, 35
Constraints, 41
Summary of the Structure, 44

CHAPTER 3
THE ACCOUNTING INFORMATION SYSTEM, 61
NEEDED: A RELIABLE INFORMATION SYSTEM, 61

◆ **Accounting Information System, 62**

Basic Terminology, 63
Debits and Credits, 64
Basic Equation, 64
Financial Statements and Ownership Structure, 66

◆ **The Accounting Cycle, 68**

Identifying and Recording Transactions and Other Events, 68
Journalizing, 69
Posting, 70
Trial Balance, 71
Adjusting Entries, 72
Adjusted Trial Balance, 82
Closing, 83
Post-Closing Trial Balance, 85
Reversing Entries, 85
The Accounting Cycle Summarized, 86

◆ **Using a Work Sheet, 86**

Adjustments Entered on the Work Sheet, 86
Work Sheet Columns, 88
Preparing Financial Statements from a Work Sheet, 89
Closing Entries, 92
Monthly Statements, Yearly Closing, 92

Behind the Numbers: Appendix 3A
Using Reversing Entries, 96

◆ **Illustration of Reversing Entries— Accruals, 96**

◆ **Illustration of Reversing Entries— Prepayments, 97**

◆ **Summary of Reversing Entries, 98**

CHAPTER 4
BALANCE SHEET, 123
"THERE OUGHT TO BE A LAW", 123

◆ **Uses and Limitations, 124**

Usefulness of the Balance Sheet, 124
Limitations of the Balance Sheet, 125

◆ **Classification in the Balance Sheet, 126**

Current Assets, 127
Non-Current Assets, 131
Liabilities, 133

Owners' Equity, 136
Balance Sheet Format, 136

◆ **Additional Information Reported, 138**

Contingencies, 139
Accounting Policies, 139
Contractual Situations, 140
Post-Balance Sheet Events (Subsequent Events), 140
Fair Values, 143

◆ **Techniques of Disclosure, 143**

Parenthetical Explanations, 143
Notes, 143
Cross Reference and Contra Items, 145
Supporting Schedules, 145
Terminology, 145

CHAPTER 5
INCOME STATEMENT AND RELATED INFORMATION, 171
WHICH INCOME NUMBER?, 171

◆ **Income Statement, 172**

Usefulness of the Income Statement, 172
Limitations of the Income Statement, 173
Quality of Earnings, 173

◆ **Format of the Income Statement, 175**

Elements of the Income Statement, 175
Single-Step Income Statements, 176
Multiple-Step Income Statements, 177
Condensed Income Statements, 178

◆ **Reporting Irregular Items, 180**

Discontinued Operations, 182
Extraordinary Items, 183
Unusual Gains and Losses, 185
Changes in Accounting Principle, 187
Changes in Estimates, 188
Summary of Irregular Items, 188

◆ **Special Reporting Issues, 190**

Intraperiod Tax Allocation, 190
Earnings per Share, 191
Retained Earnings Statement, 193
Comprehensive Income, 194

CHAPTER 6
REVENUES AND CASH FLOWS, 221
BOEING BOUNCING BACK, 221

◆ **Revenue Recognition, 222**

Revenue Recognition at Point of Sale (Delivery), 223
Revenue Recognition Before Delivery, 226
Revenue Recognition After Delivery, 230
Summary, 235
Observations, 236

◆ **Cash Flows, 236**

Purpose of the Statement of Cash Flows, 237
Content and Format of the Statement of Cash Flows, 238
Preparation of the Statement of Cash Flows, 239
Usefulness of the Statement of Cash Flows, 240

Behind the Numbers: Appendix 6A
Ratio Analysis—A Reference, 247

◆ **Using Ratios to Analyze Financial Performance, 247**

Behind the Numbers: Appendix 6B
Revenue Recognition Procedures, 249

◆ **Long-Term Contracts, 249**

Percentage of Completion Method, 251
Completed-Contract Method, 252

◆ **Installment Sales, 253**

Additional Problems of Installment Sales Accounting, 257
Financial Statement Presentation of Installment-Sales Transactions, 259

CHAPTER 7
CASH AND RECEIVABLES, 285
UGLY DUCKLING OR SWAN? 285

SECTION 1: CASH, 286

◆ **What Is Cash? 286**

◆ **Management and Control of Cash, 287**

◆ **Reporting Cash, 288**

Restricted Cash, 288
Bank Overdrafts, 289
Cash Equivalents, 289

◆ **Summary of Cash-Related Items, 290**

SECTION 2: RECEIVABLES, 290

◆ **Recognition of Accounts Receivable, 292**

Trade Discounts, 292
Cash Discounts (Sales Discounts), 292
Nonrecognition of Interest Element, 293

◆ **Valuation of Accounts Receivable, 294**

Uncollectible Accounts Receivable, 294

◆ **Recognition of Notes Receivable, 298**

Note Issued at Face Value, 299
Note Not Issued at Face Value, 300
Choice of Interest Rate, 303

◆ **Valuation of Notes Receivable, 303**

◆ **Disposition of Accounts and Notes Receivable, 304**

Secured Borrowing, 305
Sales of Receivables, 306
Secured Borrowing versus Sale, 308

◆ **Presentation and Analysis, 309**

Presentation of Receivables, 309
Analysis of Receivables, 310

Behind the Numbers: Appendix 7A
Cash Controls, 314

◆ **Using Bank Accounts, 314**

◆ **The Imprest Petty Cash System, 314**

◆ **Physical Protection of Cash Balances, 316**

◆ **Reconciliation of Bank Balances, 316**

CHAPTER 8
ACCOUNTING FOR INVENTORIES, 345
INVENTORIES IN THE CRYSTAL BALL, 345

◆ **Inventory Classification and Systems, 346**

Classification, 346
Inventory Systems, 347

◆ **Basic Issues in Inventory Valuation, 350**

Physical Goods Included in Inventory, 350
Costs Included in Inventory, 351
What Cost Flow Assumption Should Be
Adopted? 353

◆ **Special Issues Related to LIFO, 357**

LIFO Reserve, 357
LIFO Liquidation, 358
Dollar-Value LIFO, 360
Comparison of LIFO Approaches, 362
Basis for Selection of Inventory Method, 363

◆ **Lower of Cost or Market, 367**

Lower of Cost or Market—Ceiling and Floor,
368
How Lower of Cost or Market Works, 369
Methods of Applying Lower of Cost or
Market, 370
Evaluation of the Lower of Cost or Market
Rule, 371

◆ **Presentation and Analysis, 372**

Presentation of Inventories, 372
Analysis of Inventories, 373

Behind the Numbers: Appendix 8A
Gross Profit Method, 378

◆ **Computation of Gross Profit Percentage, 379**

◆ **Evaluation of Gross Profit Method, 381**

CHAPTER 9
ACCOUNTING FOR PROPERTY, PLANT, AND EQUIPMENT, 407
WHERE HAVE ALL THE ASSETS GONE? 407

◆ **Acquisition and Valuation of Property, Plant, and Equipment, 408**

Cost of Land, 409

Cost of Buildings, 409
Cost of Equipment, 410
Self-Constructed Assets, 410
Interest Costs Duting Construction, 410
Other Valuation Issues, 412
Summary, 415

◆ **Costs Subsequent to Acquisition, 415**

Additions, 416
Improvements and Replacements, 416
Rearrangement and Reinstallation, 417
Repairs, 417
Summary of Costs Subsequent to
Acquisition, 418

◆ **Use of Property, Plant, and Equipment, 418**

Factors Involved in the Depreciation Process,
419
Methods of Depreciation, 420
Special Depreciation Issues, 424

◆ **Dispositions of Plant Assets, 427**

Sale of Plant Assets, 427
Involuntary Conversion, 428
Exchanges, 428

◆ **Presentation and Analysis, 432**

Presentation of Property, Plant, and
Equipment, 432
Analysis of Property, Plant, and Equipment,
433

Behind the Numbers: Appendix 9A
Interest Capitalization Procedures, 439

◆ **Interest Capitalization, 439**

Qualifying Assets, 439
Capitalization Period, 439
Amount to Capitalize, 440
Comprehensive Illustration of Interest
Capitalization, 441

CHAPTER 10
INTANGIBLE ASSETS, 471
TRYING TO GRASP THE INTANGIBLE, 471

◆ **Intangible Asset Issues, 472**

Characteristics, 472
Valuation, 473
Amortization of Intangibles, 473

◆ **Categories of Intangible Assets, 475**

Marketing-Related Intangible Assets, 475
Customer-Related Intangible Assets, 476
Artistic-Related Intangible Assets, 476
Contract-Related Intangible Assets, 477
Technology-Related Intangible Assets, 478
Goodwill, 479

◆ **Impairments, 483**

Impairment of Property, Plant, and Equipment, 484

Impairment of Limited-Life Intangibles, 485

Indefinite-Life Intangibles Other Than Goodwill, 486

Impairment of Goodwill, 486

Restoration of Impairment Loss, 487

Assets to Be Disposed Of, 488

◆ **Research and Development Costs, 488**

Identifying R&D Activities, 489

Accounting for R&D Activities, 489

Start-Up Costs, 491

Conceptual Questions, 491

◆ **Presentation of Intangibles and Related Items, 492**

Intangible Assets, 492

Research and Development Costs, 492

CHAPTER 11
ACCOUNTING FOR LIABILITIES, 515
YOUR DEBT IS KILLING MY STOCK, 515

SECTION I: CURRENT LIABILITIES, 516

◆ **What Is a Liability? 516**

◆ **What Is a Current Liability? 517**

Accounts Payable, 518

Notes Payable, 518

Current Maturities of Long-Term Debt, 520

Dividends Payable, 520

Unearned Revenues, 521

SECTION 2: LONG-TERM LIABILITIES, 522

◆ **Issuing Bonds, 523**

◆ **Types of Bonds, 523**

◆ **Valuation of Bonds Payable—Discount and Premium, 524**

Bonds Issued at Par on Interest Date, 526

Bonds Issued at Discount or Premium on Interest Date, 527

Classification of Discount and Premium, 527

Costs of Issuing Bonds, 528

Extinguishment of Debt, 530

SECTION 3: SPECIAL ISSUES, 530

◆ **Contingencies, 530**

Gain Contingencies, 530

Loss Contingencies, 531

◆ **Off-Balance-Sheet Financing, 539**

Different Forms, 539

Rationale, 540

◆ **Presentation and Analysis, 541**

Presentation of Current Liabilities, 541

Presentation of Long-Term Debt, 541

Presentation of Contingencies, 541

Analysis of Current Liabilities, 543

Analysis of Long-Term Debt, 544

Behind the Numbers: Appendix 11A
Effective Interest Amortization, 549

◆ **Bonds Issued at a Discount, 549**

◆ **Bonds Issued at a Premium, 551**

◆ **Accruing Interest, 552**

CHAPTER 12
STOCKHOLDERS' EQUITY, 575
STOCKING UP, 575

◆ **The Corporate Form, 576**

State Corporate Law, 576

Capital Stock or Share System, 577

Variety of Ownership Interests, 578

◆ **Corporate Capital, 579**

Issuance of Stock, 579

Reacquisition of Shares, 584

◆ **Preferred Stock, 588**

Features of Preferred Stock, 589

Accounting for and Reporting of Preferred Stock, 590

◆ **Dividend Policy, 590**

Financial Condition and Dividend Distributions, 591

Types of Dividends, 592

Stock Split, 597

Disclosure of Restrictions on Retained Earnings, 600

◆ **Presentation and Analysis of Stockholders' Equity, 600**

Presentation, 600

Analysis, 602

Behind the Numbers: Appendix 12A
Accounting for Financial Instruments with Both Debt and Equity Characteristics, 608

◆ **Convertible Debt, 608**

At Time of Issuance, 609

At Time of Conversion, 609

◆ **Stock Warrants Issued with Other Securities, 609**

Proportional Method, 610

Incremental Method, 611

◆ **Conceptual Questions, 611**

CHAPTER 13
INVESTMENTS, 633
IS COKE IN CONTROL HERE? 633

SECTION 1: INVESTMENTS IN DEBT
SECURITIES, 635

◆ **Held-to-Maturity Securities, 636**

◆ **Available-for-Sale Securities, 637**

Illustration: Single Security, 637
Illustration: Portfolio of Securities, 638
Sale of Available-for-Sale Securities, 639
Financial Statement Presentation, 640

◆ **Trading Securities, 641**

SECTION 2: INVESTMENTS IN EQUITY
SECURITIES, 642

◆ **Holdings of Less Than 20%, 643**

Available-for-Sale Securities, 644
Trading Securities, 646

◆ **Holdings Between 20% and 50%, 646**

Equity Method, 647

◆ **Holdings of More Than 50%, 649**

SECTION 3: OTHER REPORTING ISSUES, 650

◆ **Financial Statement Presentation of
Investments, 650**

Disclosures Required Under the Equity
Method, 651
Reclassification Adjustments, 651
Comprehensive Illustration, 653

◆ **Impairment of Value, 655**

◆ **Transfers Between Categories, 656**

◆ **Summary, 658**

CHAPTER 14
ACCOUNTING FOR INCOME TAXES, 683
USE IT, BUT DON'T ABUSE IT, 683

◆ **Fundamentals of Accounting for Income
Taxes, 684**

Future Taxable Amounts and Deferred Taxes,
686
Future Deductible Amounts and Deferred
Taxes, 690
Income Statement Presentation, 694
Specific Differences, 695
Tax Rate Considerations, 698

◆ **Accounting for Net Operating Losses, 699**

Loss Carryback, 700
Loss Carryforward, 700
Loss Carryback Illustrated, 701
Loss Carryforward Illustrated, 701

◆ **Financial Statement Presentation, 706**

Balance Sheet, 706
Income Statement, 708

◆ **Review of the Asset-Liability Method, 710**

CHAPTER 15
ACCOUNTING FOR COMPENSATION, 737
MORE DEPENDS ON THE MARKET, 737

◆ **Salary and Bonuses, 738**

Payroll Deductions, 738
Compensated Absences, 741

◆ **Stock Compensation Plans, 743**

The Major Reporting Issue, 743
Accounting for Stock Compensation, 744
Types of Plans, 747
Noncompensatory Plans, 748
Disclosure of Compensation Plans, 748
Debate Over Stock Option Accounting, 749

◆ **Postretirement Benefits, 750**

Defined Contribution Plan, 750
Defined Benefit Plan, 751
Components of Pension Expense, 752
Using a Pension Work Sheet, 754
Reporting Pension Amounts, 760
Other Postretirement Expenses, 763

◆ **Concluding Remarks, 764**

CHAPTER 16
ACCOUNTING FOR LEASES, 779
MORE COMPANIES ASK, "WHY BUY?", 779

◆ **Advantages of Leasing, 780**

Conceptual Nature of a Lease, 782

◆ **Accounting by Lessee, 783**

Capitalization Criteria, 784
Asset and Liability Accounted for Differently,
786
Capital Lease Method (Lessee), 787
Operating Method (Lessee), 791
Comparison of Capital Lease with Operating
Lease, 791

◆ **Accounting by Lessor, 793**

Economics of Leasing, 794
Classification of Leases by the Lessor, 794
Direct Financing Method (Lessor), 796
Operating Method (Lessor), 799
Sales-Type Leases (Lessor), 799

◆ **Special Issues, 800**

Disclosing Lease Data, 800
Unsolved Problems, 803

CHAPTER 17
ADDITIONAL REPORTING ISSUES, 823
WHEN DO I GET MY MONEY BACK? 823

◆ **Reporting Accounting Changes, 824**

Changes in Accounting Principle, 825

Changes in Accounting Estimate, 832
Reporting a Correction of an Error, 834
Summary of Accounting Changes and
Corrections of Errors, 836

◆ **Reporting Earnings Per Share, 837**

Earnings Per Share—Simple Capital
Structure, 838
Earnings Per Share—Complex Capital
Structure, 842
Summary of EPS Computation, 849

Behind the Numbers: Appendix 17A
Reporting Cash Flows, 852

◆ **Classification of Cash Flows, 852**

◆ **Format of the Statement of Cash Flows, 853**

◆ **Steps in Preparation, 854**

◆ **Illustration, 855**

◆ **More Complex Illustration, 857**

◆ **Special Problems in Statement Preparation, 861**

Adjustments Similar to Depreciation, 861
Accounts Receivable (Net), 862
Other Working Capital Changes, 863
Net Losses, 864
Gains, 864
Significant Noncash Transactions, 865

APPENDIX A
ACCOUNTING AND THE TIME VALUE OF MONEY, A1

◆ **Applications of Time Value Concepts, A1**

◆ **The Nature of Interest, A2**

◆ **Simple Interest, A2**

◆ **Compound Interest, A3**

Compound Interest Tables, A4

◆ **Fundamental Variables, A7**

◆ **Single-Sum Problems, A7**

Future Value of a Single Sum, A8
Present Value of a Single Sum, A9
Solving for Other Unknowns in Single-Sum
Problems, A11

◆ **Annuities, A13**

Future Value of an Ordinary Annuity, A13
Future Value of an Annuity Due, A15
Illustrations of Future Value of Annuity
Problems, A17
Present Value of an Ordinary Annuity, A19
Present Value of an Annuity Due, A20
Illustrations of Present Value of Annuity
Problems, A21

◆ **More Complex Situations, A23**

Deferred Annuities, A23
Valuation of Long-Term Bonds, A26

◆ **Present Value Measurement, A26**

Expected Cash Flow Illustration, A27

◆ **Table 1 Future Value of 1, A40**

◆ **Table 2 Present Value of 1, A42**

◆ **Table 3 Future Value of an Ordinary Annuity of 1, A44**

◆ **Table 4 Present Value of an Ordinary Annuity of 1, A46**

◆ **Table 5 Present Value of an Annuity Due of 1, A48**

APPENDIX B
USING FINANCIAL CALCULATORS, B1

◆ **Future Value of a Single Sum, B1**

Plus and Minus, B2
Compounding Periods, B2
Rounding, B2

◆ **Present Value of a Single Sum, B2**

◆ **Future Value of an Ordinary Annuity, B2**

◆ **Future Value of an Annuity Due, B3**

◆ **Present Value of an Ordinary Annuity, B3**

◆ **Useful Features of the Financial Calculator, B4**

Auto Loan, B4
Mortgage Loan Amount, B4
Individual Retirement Account (IRA), B5

APPENDIX C
RETAIL INVENTORY METHOD, C2

◆ **Retail Method Terminology, C3**

◆ **Retail Inventory Method with Markups and Markdowns—Conventional Method, C3**

◆ **Special Items Relating to Retail Method, C6**

◆ **Evaluation of Retail Inventory Method, C7**

APPENDIX D
ACCOUNTING FOR NATURAL RESOURCES, D1

◆ **Establishing a Depletion Base, D1**

Acquisition Costs, D1
Exploration Costs, D1
Development Costs, D1
Restoration Costs, D2

◆ **Write-Off of Resource Cost, D2**

◆ **Continuing Controversy, D3**

◆ **Special Problems in Depletion Accounting, D4**

Estimating Recoverable Reserves, D5
Discovery Value, D5
Tax Aspects of Natural Resources, D5
Liquidating Dividends, D5

◆ **Presentation of Natural Resources, D6**

APPENDIX E
ACCOUNTING FOR COMPUTER SOFTWARE COSTS, E1

◆ **Diversity in Practice, E1**

◆ **The Profession's Position, E1**

◆ **Accounting for Capitalized Software Costs, E2**

◆ **Reporting Software Costs, E2**

◆ **Setting Standards for Software Accounting, E3**

APPENDIX F
ACCOUNTING FOR TROUBLED DEBT, F1

◆ **Accounting Issues, F1**

◆ **Impairments, F2**

Illustration of Loss on Impairment, F3

◆ **Troubled Debt Restructurings, F5**

Settlement of Debt, F5
Modification of Terms, F7

APPENDIX G
ACCOUNTING FOR DERIVATIVE INSTRUMENTS, G1

◆ **Understanding Derivatives, G1**

Who Uses Derivatives, and Why?, G2

◆ **Basic Principles in Accounting for Derivatives, G3**

Illustration of Derivative Financial Instrument—Speculation, G4
Differences between Traditional and Derivative Financial Instruments, G6

◆ **Derivatives Used for Hedging, G7**

Fair Value Hedge, G7
Interest Rate Swap—A Fair Value Hedge, G8
Cash Flow Hedge, G11

◆ **Other Reporting Issues, G13**

Embedded Derivatives, G13
Qualifying Hedge Criteria, G14
Disclosure Provisions, G15

◆ **Comprehensive Hedge Accounting Example, G17**

◆ **Controversy and Concluding Remarks, G19**

LOGO CREDITS, LC-1

COMPANY INDEX, CI-1

SUBJECT INDEX, SI-1

FINANCIAL ACCOUNTING AND ACCOUNTING STANDARDS

CHAPTER

1

THE SIZE OF THE NEW YORK PHONE BOOK, IF NECESSARY

Enron, Global Crossing, Kmart, WorldCom, Williams Cos., and Xerox are examples of companies that have come under the scrutiny of the Securities and Exchange Commission recently because of accounting issues. Share prices of all these companies have declined substantially, as investors punish any company whose quality of earning is in doubt.

The unfortunate part of accounting scandals is that we all pay. Enron, for example, at one time had a market capitalization of $80 billion before disclosure of its accounting irregularities. Today it is bankrupt. Employees have lost their pension money, investors have lost their savings, and the entire stock market has been caught up in "Enronitis," which has led to substantial declines in the overall stock market. At one point, there were at least 10 congressional committees involved in inquiries regarding corporate governance issues. Over 30 Enron-related bills have addressed matters such as regulation of derivative securities, auditor–client conflicts, and development of an oversight body to regulate the accounting profession.

As a result of the many concerns expressed by investors about the completeness and reliability of the accounting numbers, many companies have expanded the financial disclosures in their annual reports. For example, General Electric's CEO Jeffrey Immelt stated, "I want people to think about GE as we think of GE—as a transparent company." He noted that GE's annual report will be "the size of New York City's phone book, if necessary" to provide the information needed to help investors and creditors make the proper investing decisions.

It is our hope that meaningful reform will come out of these recent investigations into sloppy or fraudulent accounting. Although the United States is still considered to have the finest financial reporting system in the world, we must do better. As former chair of the FASB Ed Jenkins remarked recently, "If anything positive results . . . it may be that [these accounting issues] serve as an indelible reminder to all that transparent financial reporting does matter and that lack of transparency imposes significant costs on all who participate [in our markets]."

LEARNING OBJECTIVES

After studying this chapter, you should be able to:

1. Identify the major financial statements and other means of financial reporting.

2. Explain how accounting assists in the efficient use of scarce resources.

3. Identify some of the challenges facing accounting.

4. Identify the objectives of financial reporting.

5. Explain the need for accounting standards.

6. Identify the major policy-setting bodies and their role in the standards-setting process.

7. Explain the meaning of generally accepted accounting principles.

8. Describe the impact of user groups on the standards-setting process.

9. Understand issues related to ethics and financial accounting.

As the opening story indicates, the U.S. financial reporting system is one of the best in the world. But it will continue to be challenged as the business world experiences unprecedented change caused by globalization, deregulation, and computerization. In the middle of this changing business world, relevant and reliable information must be provided so that our capital markets work efficiently.

The purpose of this chapter is to explain the environment of financial reporting and the many factors affecting it. The content and organization of the chapter are as follows.

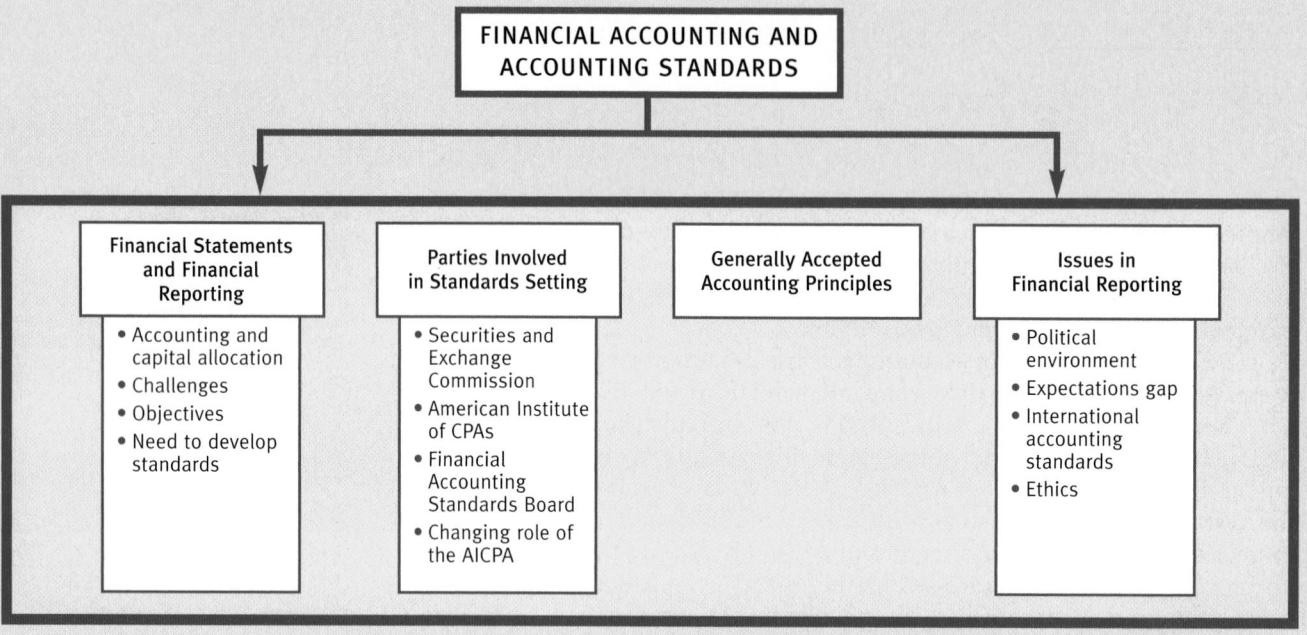

FINANCIAL STATEMENTS AND FINANCIAL REPORTING

The essential characteristics of accounting are: (1) identification, measurement, and communication of financial information about (2) economic entities to (3) interested parties. **Financial accounting** is the process that culminates in the preparation of financial reports on the enterprise as a whole for use by both internal and external parties. Users of these financial reports include investors, creditors, managers, unions, and government agencies. In contrast, **managerial accounting** is the process of identifying, measuring, analyzing, and communicating financial information needed by management to plan, evaluate, and control an organization's operations.

OBJECTIVE 1
Identify the major financial statements and other means of financial reporting.

Financial statements are the principal means through which financial information is communicated to those outside an enterprise. These statements provide the firm's history quantified in money terms. The **financial statements** most frequently provided are (1) the balance sheet, (2) the income statement, (3) the statement of cash flows, and (4) the statement of owners' or stockholders' equity. In addition, note disclosures are an integral part of each financial statement.

Some financial information is better provided, or can be provided only, by means of **financial reporting** other than formal financial statements. Examples include the president's letter or supplementary schedules in the corporate annual report, prospectuses, reports filed with government agencies, news releases, management's forecasts, and descriptions of an enterprise's social or environmental impact. Such information may be required by authoritative pronouncement, regulatory rule, or custom. Or it may be supplied because management wishes to disclose it voluntarily.

The primary focus of this textbook concerns the development of two types of financial information: (1) the basic financial statements and (2) related disclosures.

Accounting and Capital Allocation

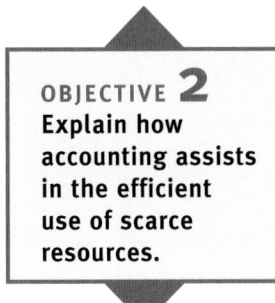

OBJECTIVE **2**
Explain how accounting assists in the efficient use of scarce resources.

Because resources are limited, people try to conserve them, to use them effectively, and to identify and encourage those who can make efficient use of them. Through an efficient use of resources, our standard of living increases.

Markets, free enterprise, and competition determine whether a business is to be successful and thrive. This fact places a substantial burden on the accounting profession to measure performance accurately and fairly on a timely basis, so that the right managers and companies are able to attract investment capital. For example, relevant and reliable financial information enables investors and creditors to compare the income and assets employed by such companies as **IBM**, **McDonald's**, **Microsoft**, and **Ford**. As a result, they can assess the relative return and risks associated with investment opportunities and so channel resources more effectively. This process of capital allocation works as follows.

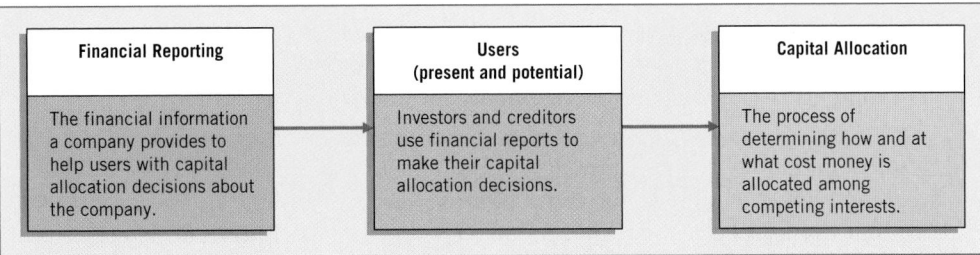

Illustration 1-1
Capital Allocation Process

An effective process of capital allocation is critical to a healthy economy. It promotes productivity, encourages innovation, and provides an efficient and liquid market for buying and selling securities and obtaining and granting credit.[1] As indicated in our opening story, unreliable and irrelevant information leads to poor capital allocation, which adversely affects the securities markets.

The Challenges Facing Financial Accounting

OBJECTIVE **3**
Identify some of the challenges facing accounting.

Much is right about financial reporting in the United States. We presently have the most liquid, deep, secure, and efficient public capital markets of any country at any time in history. One reason for this success is that our financial statements and related disclosures have captured and organized financial information in a useful and reliable fashion. However, much still needs to be done. For example, suppose you could move to the year 2020 and look back at financial reporting today. Here is what you might read.

- **Non-financial Measurements.** Financial reports failed to provide some key performance measures widely used by management. For example, nonfinancial measures such as customer satisfaction indexes, backlog information, and reject rates on goods purchased, all now used to evaluate the long-term stability of the company, were provided on an ad hoc basis, if at all.

- **Forward-looking Information.** Financial reports failed to provide forward-looking information needed by present and potential investors and creditors. One individual noted that financial statements in 2000 should have started with the phrase, "Once upon a time," to signify their use of historical cost and their accumulation of past events.

[1]AICPA Special Committee on Financial Reporting, "Improving Business Reporting—A Customer Focus," *Journal of Accountancy,* Supplement (October 1994).

- **Soft Assets.** Financial reports focused on hard assets (inventory, plant assets) but failed to provide much information on a company's soft assets (intangibles). For example, often the best assets are intangible, such as **Microsoft**'s know-how and market dominance, **Dell**'s unique marketing setup and well-trained employees, and **J.Crew**'s brand image.
- **Timeliness.** Financial statements were prepared only quarterly, and audited financials were provided annually. Little to no real-time financial statement information was available.

We believe each of these challenges must be met for the accounting profession to continue to provide the type of information needed for an efficient capital allocation process. We are confident that changes will occur. Here are some positive signs.

INTERNATIONAL INSIGHT

The objectives of financial reporting differ across nations. Traditionally, the primary objective of accounting in many continental European nations and in Japan was conformity with the law. In contrast, Canada, the U.K., the Netherlands, and many other nations have shared the U.S. view that the primary objective is to provide information for investors. Insights into international standards and practices will be presented throughout the text.

- Already some companies are making voluntary disclosures on information deemed relevant to investors. Often such information is of a non-financial nature. Regional banking companies, like **BankOne Corp.**, **Fifth Third Bancorp**, **Sun Trust Banks**, and others, for example, now include, in addition to traditional financial information, data on loan growth, credit quality, fee income, operating efficiency, capital management, and management strategy.
- The World Wide Web was first used to provide limited financial data. Now most companies offer their annual reports in several formats on the Web. The most innovative companies are now offering sections of their annual reports in a format that can be readily manipulated by the user, such as in an Excel spreadsheet format.
- More accounting standards are now requiring the recording or disclosing of fair value information. For example, either investments in stocks and bonds, debt obligations, and derivatives are recorded at fair value, or information related to fair values is shown in the notes to the financial statements.

Changes in these directions will enhance the relevance of financial reporting and provide useful information to users of the financial statements.

Objectives of Financial Reporting

OBJECTIVE **4**
Identify the objectives of financial reporting.

In an attempt to establish a foundation for financial accounting and reporting, the accounting profession identified a set of **objectives of financial reporting** by business enterprises. Financial reporting should provide information that:

1. Is useful to present and potential investors and creditors and other users **in making rational investment, credit, and similar decisions**. The information should be comprehensible to those who have a **reasonable understanding** of business and economic activities and are willing to study the information with reasonable diligence.

2. Helps present and potential investors, creditors, and other users **assess the amounts, timing, and uncertainty of prospective cash receipts** from dividends or interest and the proceeds from the sale, redemption, or maturity of securities or loans. Since investors' and creditors' cash flows are related to enterprise cash flows, financial reporting should provide information to help investors, creditors, and others assess the amounts, timing, and uncertainty of prospective net cash inflows to the related enterprise.

⟨3⟩ **Clearly portrays the economic resources of an enterprise, the claims to those resources** (obligations of the enterprise to transfer resources to other entities and owners' equity), and the effects of transactions, events, and circumstances that change its resources and claims to those resources.[2]

In brief, the objectives of financial reporting are to provide (1) information that is useful in investment and credit decisions, (2) information that is useful in assessing cash flow prospects, and (3) information about enterprise resources, claims to those resources, and changes in them.

The emphasis on "assessing cash flow prospects" might lead one to suppose that the cash basis is preferred over the accrual basis of accounting. That is not the case. Information based on **accrual accounting generally provides a better indication of an enterprise's present and continuing ability to generate favorable cash flows** than does information limited to the financial effects of cash receipts and payments.[3]

Recall from your first accounting course that the objective of **accrual basis accounting** is to ensure that events that change an entity's financial statements are recorded in the periods in which the events occur, rather than only in the periods in which the entity receives or pays cash. Using the accrual basis to determine net income means recognizing revenues when earned rather than when cash is received, and recognizing expenses when incurred rather than when paid. Under accrual accounting, revenues, for the most part, are recognized when sales are made so they can be related to the economic environment of the period in which they occurred. Over the long run, trends in revenues are generally more meaningful than trends in cash receipts.

The Need to Develop Standards

The main controversy in setting accounting standards is, "Whose rules should we play by, and what should they be?" The answer is not immediately clear because the users of financial accounting statements have both coinciding and conflicting needs for information of various types. To meet these needs, and to satisfy the fiduciary[4] reporting responsibility of management, a single set of **general-purpose financial statements** is prepared. These statements are expected to present fairly, clearly, and completely the financial operations of the enterprise.

As a result, the accounting profession has attempted to develop a set of standards that are generally accepted and universally practiced. Without these standards, each enterprise would have to develop its own standards, and readers of financial statements would have to familiarize themselves with every company's peculiar accounting and reporting practices. It would be almost impossible to prepare statements that could be compared.

This common set of standards and procedures is called **generally accepted accounting principles (GAAP)**. The term "generally accepted" means either that an authoritative accounting rule-making body has established a principle of reporting in a given area or that over time a given practice has been accepted as appropriate because

OBJECTIVE 5
Explain the need for accounting standards.

[2]"Objectives of Financial Reporting by Business Enterprises," *Statement of Financial Accounting Concepts No. 1* (Stamford, Conn.: FASB, November 1978), pars. 5–8.

[3]*SFAC No. 1*, p. iv. As used here, cash flow means "cash generated and used in operations." The term **cash flows** is frequently used also to include cash obtained by borrowing and used to repay borrowing, cash used for investments in resources and obtained from the disposal of investments, and cash contributed by or distributed to owners.

[4]Management's responsibility to manage assets with care and trust is its **fiduciary** responsibility.

of its universal application.[5] Although principles and practices have provoked both debate and criticism, most members of the financial community recognize them as the standards that over time have proven to be most useful. A more extensive discussion of what constitutes GAAP is presented later in this chapter.

PARTIES INVOLVED IN STANDARDS SETTING

OBJECTIVE 6
Identify the major policy-setting bodies and their role in the standards-setting process.

A number of organizations are instrumental in the development of financial accounting standards (GAAP) in the United States. Three major organizations are as follows.

1. Securities and Exchange Commission (SEC)
2. American Institute of Certified Public Accountants (AICPA)
3. Financial Accounting Standards Board (FASB)

Securities and Exchange Commission (SEC)

Prior to 1900, single ownership was the predominant form of business organization in our economy. Financial reports emphasized solvency and liquidity and were limited to internal use and scrutiny by banks and other lending institutions. From 1900 to 1929, the growth of large corporations, with their absentee ownership, led to increasing investment and speculation in corporate stock. Unfortunately, after a couple of days on which stock prices dropped rapidly, both individual and institutional investors panicked, and sold over 16 million shares of stock at huge losses. This 1929 stock market crash contributed to the Great Depression.

As a result of these events, the federal government established the **Securities and Exchange Commission (SEC)** to help develop and standardize financial information presented to stockholders. The SEC is a federal agency. It administers the Securities Exchange Act of 1934 and several other acts. Most companies that issue securities to the public or are listed on a stock exchange are required to file audited financial statements with the SEC. In addition, the SEC has broad powers to prescribe, in whatever detail it desires, the accounting practices and standards to be employed by companies that fall within its jurisdiction. As a result, the SEC exercises oversight over 12,000 companies that are listed on the major exchanges (such as the New York Stock Exchange and the American Stock Exchange).

INTERNATIONAL INSIGHT

The International Organization of Securities Commissions (IOSCO) is a group of more than 100 securities regulatory agencies or securities exchanges from all over the world. IOSCO was established in 1987. Collectively, its members represent a substantial proportion of the world's capital markets. The SEC is a member of IOSCO.

Public/Private Partnership

At the time the SEC was created, no group—public or private—was issuing accounting standards. The SEC encouraged the creation of a private standards-setting body because it believed that the private sector had the resources and talent to develop appropriate accounting standards. As a result, accounting standards have generally developed in the private sector either through the American Institute of Certified Public Accountants (AICPA) or the Financial Accounting Standards Board (FASB).

The SEC has affirmed its support for the FASB by indicating that financial statements conforming to standards set by the FASB will be presumed to have substantial authoritative support. In short, the **SEC requires registrants to adhere to GAAP**. In addition, it has indicated in its reports to Congress that "it continues to believe that the initiative for establishing and improving accounting standards should remain in the private sector, subject to Commission oversight."

---

[5]The terms **principles** and **standards** are used interchangeably in practice and throughout this textbook.

SEC Oversight

The SEC's partnership with the private sector has worked well. The SEC has acted with remarkable restraint in the area of developing accounting standards. Generally, **the SEC has relied on the AICPA and FASB to regulate the accounting profession and develop and enforce accounting standards**.

Over its history, however, the SEC's involvement in the development of accounting standards has varied. In some cases the private sector has attempted to establish a standard, but the SEC has refused to accept it. In other cases the SEC has prodded the private sector into taking quicker action on certain reporting problems, such as accounting for investments in debt and equity securities and the reporting of derivative instruments. In still other situations the SEC communicates problems to the FASB, responds to FASB exposure drafts, and provides the FASB with counsel and advice upon request.

The SEC has the mandate to establish accounting principles. The private sector, therefore, must listen carefully to the views of the SEC. In some sense the private sector is the formulator and the implementor of the standards.[6] While the partnership between the SEC and the private sector has worked well, it can be strained when accounting problems are not addressed as quickly as the SEC would like. This was apparent in the recent deliberations on the accounting for business combinations and intangible assets and concerns over the accounting for special-purpose entities, highlighted in the failure of Enron.

Enforcement

As indicated earlier, companies listed on a stock exchange are required to submit their financial statements to the SEC. If the SEC believes that an accounting or disclosure irregularity exists regarding the form or content of the financial statements, it sends a deficiency letter to the company. Usually these deficiency letters are resolved quickly. However, if disagreement continues, the SEC has the power to issue a "stop order," which prevents the registrant from issuing securities or trading securities on the exchanges. Criminal charges may also be brought by the Department of Justice for violations of certain laws. The SEC program, private sector initiatives, and civil and criminal litigation help to ensure the integrity of financial reporting for public companies.

INTERNATIONAL INSIGHT

Nations also differ in the degree to which they have developed national standards and consistent accounting practices. One indicator of the level of a nation's accounting is the nature of the accounting profession within the country. Professional accounting bodies were established in the Netherlands, the U.K., Canada, and the U.S. in the nineteenth century. In contrast, public accountancy bodies were established in Hong Kong, Singapore, and Korea only in the last half century.

American Institute of Certified Public Accountants (AICPA)

As indicated earlier, the **American Institute of Certified Public Accountants (AICPA)**, which is the national professional organization of practicing Certified Public Accountants (CPAs), has been vital to the development of GAAP. Various committees and boards established since the founding of the AICPA have contributed to this effort.

Committee on Accounting Procedure

At the urging of the SEC, the AICPA appointed the Committee on Accounting Procedure in 1939. The **Committee on Accounting Procedure (CAP)**, composed of practicing CPAs, issued 51 **Accounting Research Bulletins** during the years 1939 to 1959. These bulletins deal with a variety of accounting problems. But this problem-by-

---

[6]One writer has described the relationship of the FASB and SEC and the development of financial reporting standards using the analogy of a pearl. The pearl (financial reporting standard) "is formed by the reaction of certain oysters (FASB) to an irritant (the SEC)—usually a grain of sand—that becomes embedded inside the shell. The oyster coats this grain with layers of nacre, and ultimately a pearl is formed. The pearl is a joint result of the irritant (SEC) and oyster (FASB); without both, it cannot be created." John C. Burton, "Government Regulation of Accounting and Information," *Journal of Accountancy* (June 1982).

problem approach failed to provide the structured body of accounting principles that was both needed and desired. In response, in 1959 the AICPA created the Accounting Principles Board.

Accounting Principles Board

The major purposes of the **Accounting Principles Board (APB)** were (1) to advance the written expression of accounting principles, (2) to determine appropriate practices, and (3) to narrow the areas of difference and inconsistency in practice. To achieve these objectives, the APB's mission was to develop an overall conceptual framework to assist in the resolution of problems as they become evident and to do substantive research on individual issues before pronouncements were issued.

The Board's 18 to 21 members, selected primarily from public accounting, also included representatives from industry and the academic community. The Board's official pronouncements, called **APB Opinions**, were intended to be based mainly on research studies and be supported by reasons and analysis. Between its inception in 1959 and its dissolution in 1973, the APB issued 31 opinions.

Unfortunately, the APB came under fire early, charged with lack of productivity and failing to act promptly to correct alleged accounting abuses. Later the APB tackled numerous thorny accounting issues, only to meet a buzz saw of opposition from industry and CPA firms and occasional governmental interference. In 1971 the accounting profession's leaders, anxious to avoid governmental rule-making, appointed a Study Group on Establishment of Accounting Principles. Commonly known as the **Wheat Committee** for its chair Francis Wheat, this group was to examine the organization and operation of the APB and determine what changes would be necessary to attain better results. The Study Group's recommendations were submitted to the AICPA Council in the spring of 1972, adopted in total, and implemented by early 1973.

Financial Accounting Standards Board (FASB)

The Wheat Committee's recommendations resulted in the demise of the APB and the creation of a new standards-setting structure composed of three organizations—the Financial Accounting Foundation (FAF), the Financial Accounting Standards Board (FASB), and the Financial Accounting Standards Advisory Council (FASAC). The **Financial Accounting Foundation** selects the members of the FASB and the Advisory Council, funds their activities, and generally oversees the FASB's activities.

The major operating organization in this three-part structure is the **Financial Accounting Standards Board (FASB)**. Its mission is to establish and improve standards of financial accounting and reporting for the guidance and education of the public, which includes issuers, auditors, and users of financial information. The expectations of success and support for the new FASB were based upon several significant differences between it and its predecessor, the APB:

1 **Smaller Membership.** The FASB is composed of seven members, replacing the relatively large 18-member APB.

2 **Full-time, Remunerated Membership.** FASB members are well-paid, full-time members appointed for renewable 5-year terms. The APB members were unpaid and part-time.

3 **Greater Autonomy.** The APB was a senior committee of the AICPA, whereas the FASB is not an organ of any single professional organization. It is appointed by and answerable only to the Financial Accounting Foundation.

4 **Increased Independence.** APB members retained their private positions with firms, companies, or institutions. FASB members must sever all such ties.

⑤ **Broader Representation.** All APB members were required to be CPAs and members of the AICPA. Currently, it is not necessary to be a CPA to be a member of the FASB.

In addition to research help from its own staff, the FASB relies on the expertise of various task force groups formed for various projects and on the **Financial Accounting Standards Advisory Council (FASAC)**. FASAC consults with the FASB on major policy and technical issues and also helps select task force members.

Due Process

In establishing financial accounting standards, two basic premises of the FASB are: (1) The FASB should be responsive to the needs and viewpoints of the entire economic community, not just the public accounting profession. (2) It should operate in full view of the public through a "due process" system that gives interested persons ample opportunity to make their views known. To ensure the achievement of these goals, the steps shown in Illustration 1-2 are taken in the evolution of a typical FASB Statement of Financial Accounting Standards.

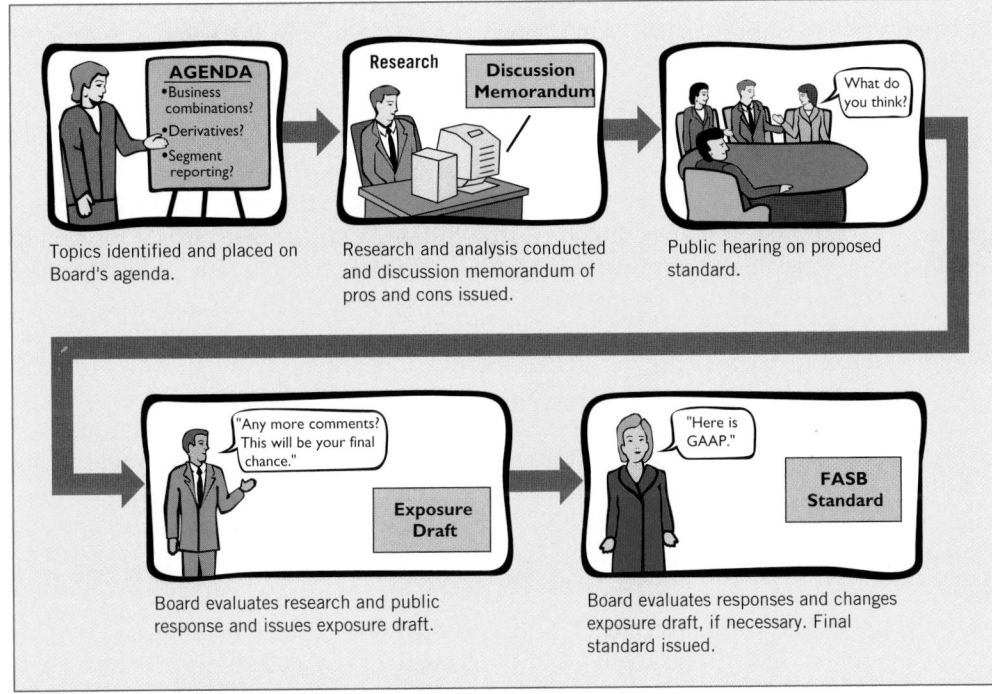

Illustration 1-2
Due Process

Topics identified and placed on Board's agenda.

Research and analysis conducted and discussion memorandum of pros and cons issued.

Public hearing on proposed standard.

Board evaluates research and public response and issues exposure draft.

Board evaluates responses and changes exposure draft, if necessary. Final standard issued.

The passage of a new FASB **Standards Statement** requires the support of four of the seven Board members. FASB Statements are considered GAAP and thereby binding in practice. All ARBs and APB Opinions that were in effect in 1973 when the FASB became effective continue to be effective until amended or superseded by FASB pronouncements. In recognition of possible misconceptions of the term "principles," the FASB uses the term **financial accounting standards** in its pronouncements.

Types of Pronouncements

The major types of pronouncements that the FASB issues are:

① Standards and Interpretations.
② Financial Accounting Concepts.
③ Technical Bulletins.
④ Emerging Issues Task Force Statements.

Standards and Interpretations.   Financial accounting **standards** issued by the FASB are considered generally accepted accounting principles. In addition, the FASB also issues **interpretations** that represent modifications or extensions of existing standards. The interpretations have the same authority as standards and require the same votes for passage as standards. However, interpretations do not require the FASB to operate in full view of the public through the due process system that is required for FASB Standards. The APB also issued interpretations of APB Opinions. Both types of interpretations are now considered authoritative support for purposes of determining GAAP. Since replacing the APB, the FASB has issued 145 standards and 44 interpretations.

Financial Accounting Concepts.   As part of a long-range effort to move away from the problem-by-problem approach, the FASB in November 1978 issued the first in a series of **Statements of Financial Accounting Concepts** as part of its conceptual framework project. (See list at the back of the book.) The purpose of the series is to set forth fundamental objectives and concepts that the Board will use in developing future standards of financial accounting and reporting. They are intended to form a cohesive set of interrelated concepts, a conceptual framework, that will serve as tools for solving existing and emerging problems in a consistent manner. Unlike a Statement of Financial Accounting Standards, **a Statement of Financial Accounting Concepts does not establish GAAP**. Concepts statements, however, pass through the same due process system (discussion memo, public hearing, exposure draft, etc.) as do standards statements.

FASB Technical Bulletins.   The FASB receives many requests from various sources for guidelines on implementing or applying FASB Standards or Interpretations, APB Opinions, and Accounting Research Bulletins. In addition, a strong need exists for timely guidance on financial accounting and reporting problems. For example, in one tax law change, certain income taxes that companies had accrued as liabilities were forgiven. The immediate question was: How should the forgiven taxes be reported—as a reduction of income tax expense, as a prior period adjustment, or as an extraordinary item? A technical bulletin was quickly issued that required the tax reduction be reported as a reduction of the current period's income tax expense. Note that a **technical bulletin** is issued only when (1) **it is not expected to cause a major change in accounting practice for a number of enterprises**, (2) **its cost of implementation is low**, and (3) **the guidance provided by the bulletin does not conflict with any broad fundamental accounting principle.**[7]

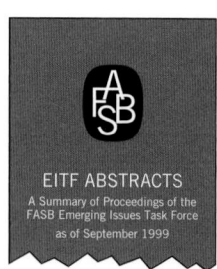

Emerging Issues Task Force Statements.   In 1984 the FASB created the **Emerging Issues Task Force (EITF)**. The EITF is composed of 13 members, representing CPA firms and preparers of financial statements. Also attending EITF meetings are observers from the SEC and AICPA. The purpose of the task force is to reach a consensus on how to account for new and unusual financial transactions that have the potential for creating differing financial reporting practices. Examples include how to account for pension plan terminations; how to account for revenue from barter transactions by Internet companies; and how to account for excessive amounts paid to takeover specialists. The EITF also provided timely guidance for the reporting of the losses arising from the terrorist attacks on the World Trade Center on 9/11/01.

We cannot overestimate the importance of the EITF. In one year, for example, the task force examined 61 emerging financial reporting issues and arrived at a consensus on approximately 75 percent of them. The SEC has indicated that it will view consensus solutions as preferred accounting and will require persuasive justification for departing from them.

---

[7]"Purpose and Scope of FASB Technical Bulletins and Procedures for Issuance," *FASB Technical Bulletin No. 79-1* (Revised) (Stamford, Conn.: FASB, June 1984).

The EITF helps the FASB in many ways. For example, emerging issues often attract public attention. If they are not resolved quickly, they can lead to financial crises and scandal and can undercut public confidence in current reporting practices. The next step, possible governmental intervention, would threaten the continuance of standards setting in the private sector. In addition, the EITF identifies controversial accounting problems as they arise and determines whether they can be quickly resolved, or whether the FASB should become involved in solving them. In essence, it becomes a "problem filter" for the FASB. Thus, it is hoped that the FASB will be able to work on more pervasive long-term problems, while the EITF deals with short-term emerging issues.

The formal organizational structure as it currently exists for the development of financial reporting standards is presented in Illustration 1-3.

Illustration 1-3

Organizational Structure for Setting Accounting Standards

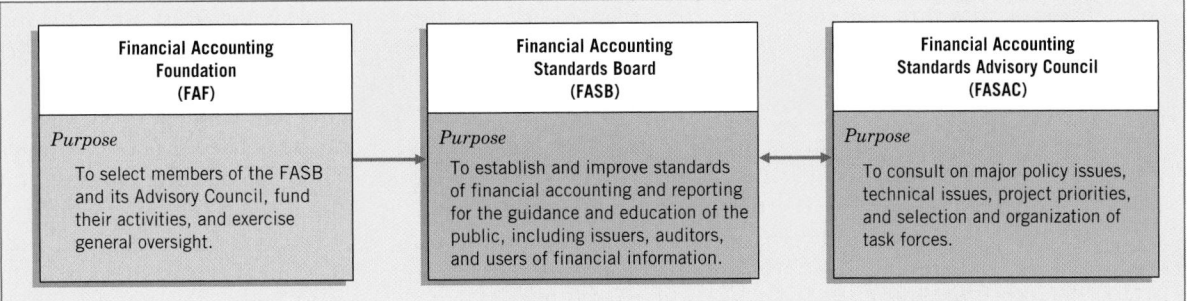

Changing Role of the AICPA

For several decades the AICPA provided the leadership in the development of accounting principles and rules. It regulated the accounting profession and developed and enforced accounting practice more than did any other professional organization. When the Accounting Principles Board was dissolved and replaced with the FASB, the AICPA established the Accounting Standards Division to act as its official voice on accounting and reporting issues.

The **Accounting Standards Executive Committee (AcSEC)** was established within the Division and was designated as the senior technical committee authorized to speak for the AICPA in the area of financial accounting and reporting. It does so through various written communications:

Audit and Accounting Guidelines summarize the accounting practices of specific industries and provide specific guidance on matters not addressed by the FASB. Examples are accounting for casinos, airlines, colleges and universities, banks, insurance companies, and many others.

Statements of Position (SOP) provide guidance on financial reporting topics until the FASB sets standards on the issue in question. SOPs may update, revise, and clarify audit and accounting guides or provide free-standing guidance.

Practice Bulletins indicate AcSEC's views on narrow financial reporting issues not considered by the FASB.

The AICPA is still the leader in developing auditing standards through its **Auditing Standards Board** and in regulating auditing practice. It also takes a lead in developing and enforcing professional ethics and in providing continuing professional education programs. In addition, the AICPA develops and grades the CPA examination, which is administered in all 50 states.

GENERALLY ACCEPTED ACCOUNTING PRINCIPLES

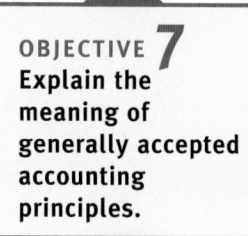

OBJECTIVE 7
Explain the meaning of generally accepted accounting principles.

Generally accepted accounting principles are those principles that have "substantial authoritative support." The AICPA's Code of Professional Conduct requires that members prepare financial statements in accordance with generally accepted accounting principles. Specifically, Rule 203 of this Code prohibits a member from expressing an opinion that financial statements conform with GAAP if those statements contain a material departure from a generally accepted accounting principle, unless the member can demonstrate that because of unusual circumstances the financial statements would otherwise have been misleading. Failure to follow Rule 203 can lead to loss of a CPA's license to practice.

The meaning of generally accepted accounting principles is defined by *Statement on Auditing Standards (SAS) No. 69*, "The Meaning of 'Present Fairly in Conformity With Generally Accepted Accounting Principles' in the Independent Auditor's Report." **Under this standard, generally accepted accounting principles covered by Rule 203 are construed to be FASB Standards and Interpretations, APB Opinions, and AICPA Accounting Research Bulletins.**

Often, however, a specific accounting transaction occurs that is not covered by any of these documents. In this case, other authoritative literature is used. Major examples are: FASB Technical Bulletins; AICPA Industry Auditing and Accounting Guides; and Statements of Position that have been "cleared" by the FASB.[8] These documents are considered to have substantial authoritative support because the recognized professional bodies, after giving interested and affected parties the opportunity to react to exposure drafts and respond at public hearings, have voted their issuance. If these pronouncements are lacking in guidance, then other sources might be considered. The hierarchy of these sources is presented in Illustration 1-4.[9] If the accounting treatment of an event is not specified by a Category (a) pronouncement, then Categories (b) through (d) should be investigated. If there is a conflict between pronouncements in (b) through (d), the higher category is to be followed. For example, (b) is higher than (c).

Illustration 1-4
The House of GAAP

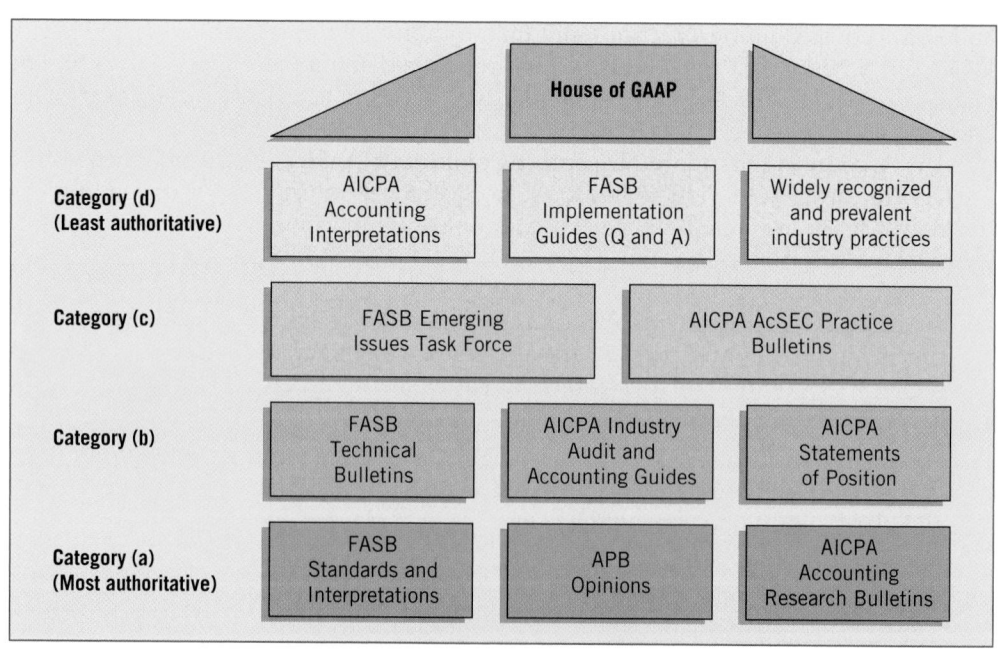

[8]*SAS No. 69* states that Audit Guides and Statements of Position are assumed to be cleared (approved) by the FASB unless the pronouncement states otherwise.

[9]See for example, "Remodeling the House of GAAP," by Douglas Sauter, *Journal of Accountancy* (July 1991), pp. 30–37.

If none of these pronouncements addresses the event, the support is sought from other accounting literature. Examples of other accounting literature include FASB Concepts Statements, International Accounting Standards, and accounting articles.

ISSUES IN FINANCIAL REPORTING

Since many interests may be affected by the implementation of an accounting standard, it is not surprising that there is much discussion about who should develop these standards and to whom they should apply. Some of the major issues are discussed below.

Standards Setting in a Political Environment

Possibly the most powerful force influencing the development of accounting standards is user groups. User groups consist of the parties who are most interested in or affected by accounting standards, rules, and procedures. Like lobbyists in our state and national capitals, user groups play a significant role. **Accounting standards are as much a product of political action as they are of careful logic or empirical findings.**

OBJECTIVE **8**
Describe the impact of user groups on the standards-setting process.

User groups may want particular economic events accounted for or reported in a particular way, and they fight hard to get what they want. They know that the most effective way to influence the standards that dictate accounting practice is to participate in the formulation of these standards or to try to influence or persuade the formulator of them. Therefore, the FASB has become the target of many pressures and efforts to influence changes in the existing standards and the development of new ones.[10] To top it off, these pressures have been multiplying. Some influential groups demand that the accounting profession act more quickly and decisively to solve its problems and remedy its deficiencies. Other groups resist such action, preferring to implement change more slowly, if at all. Illustration 1-5 shows the various user groups that apply pressure.

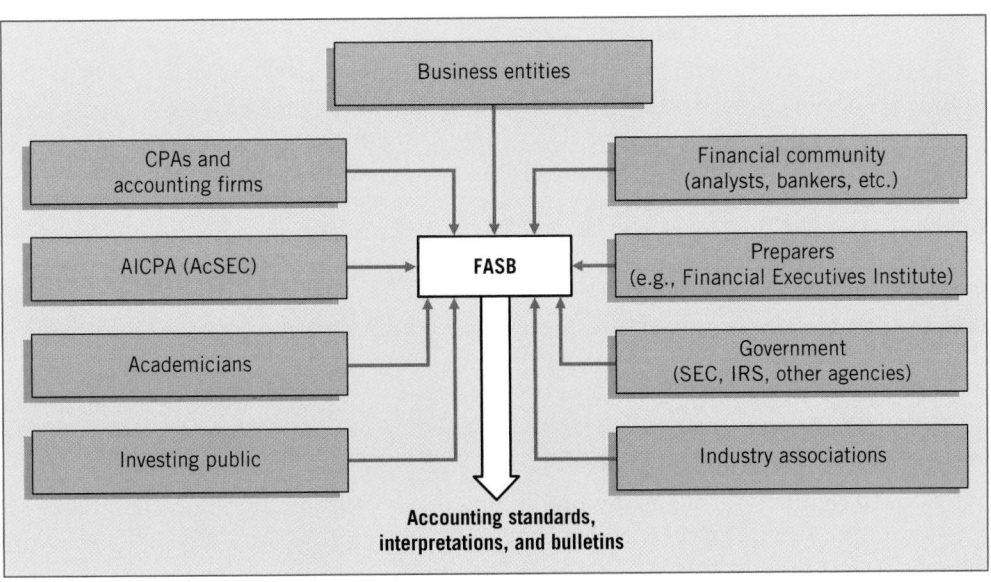

Illustration 1-5
User Groups that Influence the Formulation of Accounting Standards

Should there be politics in setting standards for financial accounting and reporting? We have politics at home; at school; at the fraternity, sorority, and dormitory; at the office; at church, temple, and mosque—politics is everywhere. The FASB does not

---

[10]FASB board members have acknowledged that many of the Board's projects, such as "Accounting for Contingencies," "Accounting for Pensions," "Statement of Cash Flows," and "Accounting for Derivatives," were targets of political pressure.

exist in a vacuum. Standards setting is part of the real world, and it cannot escape politics and political pressures.

That is not to say that politics in standards setting is evil. Considering the **economic consequences**[11] of many accounting standards, it is not surprising that special interest groups become vocal when standards are being formulated. The Board must be attentive to the economic consequences of its actions. What the Board should *not* do is issue pronouncements that are primarily politically motivated. While paying attention to its constituencies, the Board should base its standards on sound research and a conceptual framework that has its foundation in economic reality.

WHAT DO THE NUMBERS MEAN?

THE ECONOMIC CONSEQUENCES OF GOODWILL

Investors generally ignore an accounting change. But when it substantially affects net income, stockholders pay attention. One change that will affect many companies is the new goodwill rules. Under current GAAP, companies that had goodwill must charge it against revenues over time. Under new rules, companies no longer have to write off this cost. The effect on the bottom line for some companies is substantial. For example, assuming no goodwill amortization, **International Paper** estimates an income increase of 21 percent, **Johnson Controls** 16 percent, and **Pepsi Bottling Group** 30 percent.

Some believe this change in the rules will make their stock more attractive. Others argue that it should have no effect because the write-off is a mere bookkeeping charge. Others argue that the change in the rules has no effect on cash flows, but that investors will perceive the company to be more profitable, and therefore a good buy in the marketplace. In short, the numbers have consequences. What do you think?

The Expectations Gap

All professions have come under increasing scrutiny by the government, whether it be the investment banking profession because of insider trading, the medical profession because of high costs and Medicare or Medicaid frauds, or engineers because of their failure to consider environmental consequences in their work.

Recently, it has been the accounting profession's turn. As indicated earlier, recent accounting scandals have attracted the attention of Congress. Congress has already substantially increased the resources for the SEC to combat fraud and curb poor reporting practices. The SEC has increased its policing efforts, approving new auditor independence rules and materiality guidelines for financial reporting. In addition, both the SEC and Congress are considering sweeping changes to the institutional structure of the accounting profession. In July 2002 Congress passed legislation with provisions that:

- Establish an oversight board for accounting practices, with investigative and disciplinary powers.
- Increase penalties for securities fraud.
- Reduce conflicts of interest by prohibiting auditors from offering certain types of consulting services to corporate clients.
- Require CEOs and CFOs to personally certify financial results.
- Prohibit investment banks from retaliating against analysts who criticize companies that are clients of the investment bank.

---

[11]"Economic consequences" means the impact of accounting reports on the wealth positions of issuers and users of financial information and the decision-making behavior resulting from that impact. The resulting behavior of these individuals and groups could have detrimental financial effects on the providers of the financial information. See Stephen A. Zeff, "The Rise of 'Economic Consequences'," *Journal of Accountancy* (December 1978), pp. 56–63. Appreciation is extended to Professor Zeff for his insights on this chapter.

But is it enough? The **expectations gap**—what the public thinks accountants should be doing and what accountants think they can do—is a difficult one to close. The instances of fraudulent reporting have caused some to question whether the profession is doing enough. Although the profession can argue rightfully that they cannot be responsible for every financial catastrophe, it must continue to strive to meet the needs of society. Efforts to meet these needs will become more costly to society because the development of a highly transparent, clear, and reliable system will require considerable resources.

International Accounting Standards

In the comment quoted in the opening story, Lawrence Summers, former Secretary of the Treasury, indicated that the single most important innovation shaping the capital market was the idea of generally accepted accounting principles. Summers went on to say that we need something similar internationally.

Most countries have recognized the need for more global standards. As a result, the **International Accounting Standards Committee (IASC)** was formed in 1973—the same year the FASB was born—to attempt to narrow the areas of divergence between standards of different countries.

The objective of the IASC in terms of standards setting was "to work generally for the improvement and harmonization of regulations, accounting standards and procedures relating to the presentation of financial statements." Eliminating differences is not easy. The objectives of financial reporting in the United States often differ from those in foreign countries, the institutional structures are often not comparable, and strong national tendencies are pervasive. Nevertheless, much headway has been made since IASC's inception.

Recently, the IASC has been restructured and renamed the **International Accounting Standards Board (IASB)**. This new body will work toward the development of a **single set of high-quality global standards**. The IASB has a structure similar to that of the FASB. It is hoped that the establishment of a fully independent international accounting standards setter will provide the essential convergence needed as we move to a global capital market system.

It should be emphasized that the United States has a major voice in how international standards are being developed. As a result, there are many similarities between IASB- and U.S.-based standards. Throughout this textbook, international considerations are presented to help you understand the international reporting environment.

Expanded Discussion of International Accounting

Ethics in the Environment of Financial Accounting

Robert Sack, a commentator on the subject of accounting ethics, noted that, "Based on my experience, new graduates tend to be idealistic . . . thank goodness for that! Still it is very dangerous to think that your armor is all in place and say to yourself 'I would have never given in to that.' The pressures don't explode on us; they build, and we often don't recognize them until they have us."

OBJECTIVE **9**
Understand issues related to ethics and financial accounting.

These observations are particularly appropriate for anyone entering the business world. In accounting, as in other areas of business, ethical dilemmas are encountered frequently. Some of these dilemmas are simple and easy to resolve. However, many are complex, requiring choices among allowable alternatives, and solutions are not obvious. Businesses' concentration on "maximizing the bottom line," "facing the challenges of competition," and "stressing short-term results" places accountants in an environment of conflict and pressure. Basic questions such as, "Is this way of communicating financial information good or bad?" "Is it right or wrong?" "What should I do in the circumstance?" cannot always be answered by simply adhering to GAAP or following the rules of the profession. Technical competence is not enough when ethical decisions are encountered.

Doing the right thing, making the right decision, is not always easy. Right is not always obvious. And the pressures "to bend the rules," "to play the game," "to just ignore it" can be considerable. For example, "Will my decision affect my job performance negatively?" "Will my superiors be upset?" "Will my colleagues be unhappy with me?" are often questions faced in making a tough ethical decision. The decision is more difficult because a public consensus has not emerged to formulate a comprehensive ethical system to provide guidelines.

This whole process of ethical sensitivity and selection among alternatives can be complicated by pressures that may take the form of time pressures, job pressures, client pressures, personal pressures, and peer pressures. Throughout this textbook, **ethical considerations are presented for the purpose of sensitizing you** to the type of situations you may encounter in the performance of your professional responsibility.

Expanded Discussion of Ethical Issues in Financial Reporting

Conclusion

The FASB is in its twenty-ninth year as this textbook is written. Will the FASB survive in its present state, or will it be restructured or changed as its predecessors were? As indicated, some people in government, some in the financial community, and some in the profession itself are continually challenging the accounting profession to assume more responsibility and to be more responsive to the needs of its constituencies.

At present, we believe that the accounting profession is reacting responsibly to remedy identified shortcomings. Because of its substantive resources and expertise, the private sector should be able to develop and maintain high standards. But it is a difficult process requiring time, logic, and diplomacy. By a judicious mix of these three ingredients, the profession may be able to continue to develop its own standards and regulate itself with minimal intervention.

SUMMARY OF LEARNING OBJECTIVES

❶ Identify the major financial statements and other means of financial reporting. The financial statements most frequently provided are (1) the balance sheet, (2) the income statement, (3) the statement of cash flows, and (4) the statement of owners' or stockholders' equity. Financial reporting other than financial statements may take various forms. Examples include the president's letter and supplementary schedules in the corporate annual report, prospectuses, reports filed with government agencies, news releases, management's forecasts, and descriptions of an enterprise's social or environmental impact.

❷ Explain how accounting assists in the efficient use of scarce resources. Accounting provides reliable, relevant, and timely information to managers, investors, and creditors so that resources are allocated to the most efficient enterprises. Accounting also provides measurements of efficiency (profitability) and financial soundness.

❸ Identify some of the challenges facing accounting. Financial reports fail to provide (1) some key performance measures widely used by management, (2) forward-looking information needed by investors and creditors, (3) sufficient information on a company's soft assets (intangibles), and (4) real-time financial information.

❹ Identify the objectives of financial reporting. The objectives of financial reporting are to provide (1) information that is useful in investment and credit decisions, (2) information that is useful in assessing cash flow prospects, and (3) information about enterprise resources, claims to those resources, and changes in them.

❺ Explain the need for accounting standards. The accounting profession has attempted to develop a set of standards that is generally accepted and universally practiced. Without this set of standards, each enterprise would have to develop its own standards, and readers of financial statements would have to familiarize themselves with every company's peculiar accounting and reporting practices. As a result, it would be almost impossible to prepare statements that could be compared.

❻ Identify the major policy-setting bodies and their role in the standards-setting process. The *Securities and Exchange Commission (SEC)* is an agency of the federal gov-

KEY TERMS

Accounting Principles Board (APB), 8

Accounting Research Bulletins, 7

accrual basis accounting, 5

American Institute of Certified Public Accountants (AICPA), 7

APB Opinions, 8

Auditing Standards Board, 11

Committee on Accounting Procedure (CAP), 7

Emerging Issues Task Force (EITF), 10

expectations gap, 14

financial accounting, 2

Financial Accounting Standards Board (FASB), 8

financial reporting, 2

financial statements, 2

generally accepted accounting principles (GAAP), 5

International Accounting Standards Board (IASB), 15

interpretations, 10

objectives of financial reporting, 4

Securities and Exchange Commission (SEC), 6

Standards Statement, 9

Statement of Financial Accounting Concepts, 10

technical bulletin, 10

Wheat Committee, 8

ernment that has the broad powers to prescribe, in whatever detail it desires, the accounting standards to be employed by companies that fall within its jurisdiction. The *American Institute of Certified Public Accountants (AICPA)* issued standards through its Committee on Accounting Procedure and Accounting Principles Board. The *Financial Accounting Standards Board (FASB)* establishes and improves standards of financial accounting and reporting for the guidance and education of the public.

7 Explain the meaning of generally accepted accounting principles. Generally accepted accounting principles are those principles that have substantial authoritative support, such as FASB Standards and Interpretations, APB Opinions and Interpretations, AICPA Accounting Research Bulletins, and other authoritative pronouncements.

8 Describe the impact of user groups on the standards-setting process. User groups may want particular economic events accounted for or reported in a particular way, and they fight hard to get what they want. The FASB has become the target of many pressures and efforts to influence changes in the existing standards and the development of new ones. Because of the accelerated rate of change and the increased complexity of our economy, these pressures have been multiplying. Accounting standards are as much a product of political action as they are of careful logic or empirical findings.

9 Understand issues related to ethics and financial accounting. Financial accountants are called on for moral discernment and ethical decision making. The decision is more difficult because a public consensus has not emerged to formulate a comprehensive ethical system that provides guidelines in making ethical judgments.

QUESTIONS

1 Differentiate broadly between financial accounting and managerial accounting.

2 Differentiate between "financial statements" and "financial reporting."

3 How does accounting help the capital allocation process?

4 What are some of the major challenges facing the accounting profession?

5 What are the major objectives of financial reporting?

6 Of what value is a common set of standards in financial accounting and reporting?

7 What is the likely limitation of "general-purpose financial statements"?

8 What are some of the developments or events that occurred between 1900 and 1930 that helped bring about changes in accounting theory or practice?

9 In what way is the Securities and Exchange Commission concerned about and supportive of accounting principles and standards?

10 What was the Committee on Accounting Procedure, and what were its accomplishments and failings?

11 For what purposes did the AICPA in 1959 create the Accounting Principles Board?

12 Distinguish among Accounting Research Bulletins, Opinions of the Accounting Principles Board, and Statements of the Financial Accounting Standards Board.

13 If you had to explain or define "generally accepted accounting principles or standards," what essential characteristics would you include in your explanation?

14 In what ways was it felt that the statements issued by the Financial Accounting Standards Board would carry greater weight than the opinions issued by the Accounting Principles Board?

15 How are FASB discussion memoranda and FASB exposure drafts related to FASB "statements"?

16 Distinguish between FASB "statements of financial accounting standards" and FASB "statements of financial accounting concepts."

17 What is Rule 203 of the Code of Professional Conduct?

18 Rank from the most authoritative to the least authoritative, the following three items: FASB Technical Bulletins, AICPA Practice Bulletins, and FASB Standards.

19 The chairman of the FASB at one time noted that "the flow of standards can only be slowed if (1) producers focus less on quarterly earnings per share and tax benefits and more on quality products, and (2) accountants and lawyers rely less on rules and law and more on professional judgment and conduct." Explain his comment.

20 What is the purpose of FASB Technical Bulletins? How do FASB Technical Bulletins differ from FASB Interpretations?

21 Explain the role of the Emerging Issues Task Force in establishing generally accepted accounting principles.

22 What is AcSEC and what is its relationship to the FASB?

23 What are the sources of pressure that change and influence the development of accounting principles and standards?

24 Some individuals have indicated that the FASB must be cognizant of the economic consequences of its pronouncements. What is meant by "economic consequences"? What dangers exist if politics play too much of a role in the development of financial reporting standards?

25 If you were given complete authority in the matter, how would you propose that accounting principles or standards should be developed and enforced?

26 One writer recently noted that 99.4 percent of all companies prepare statements that are in accordance with GAAP. Why then is there such concern about fraudulent financial reporting?

27 What is the "expectations gap"? What is the profession doing to try to close this gap?

28 A number of foreign countries have reporting standards that differ from those in the United States. What are some of the main reasons why reporting standards are often different among countries?

29 How are financial accountants challenged in their work to make ethical decisions? Is technical mastery of GAAP not sufficient to the practice of financial accounting?

CONCEPTUAL CASES

C1-1 **(Financial Accounting)** Alan Rodriquez has recently completed his first year of studying accounting. His instructor for next semester has indicated that the primary focus will be the area of financial accounting.

Instructions
(a) Differentiate between financial accounting and managerial accounting.
(b) One part of financial accounting involves the preparation of financial statements. What are the financial statements most frequently provided?
(c) What is the difference between financial statements and financial reporting?

C1-2 **(Objectives of Financial Reporting)** Celia Cruz, a recent graduate of the local state university, is presently employed by a large manufacturing company. She has been asked by Angeles Ochoa, controller, to prepare the company's response to a current Discussion Memorandum published by the Financial Accounting Standards Board (FASB). Cruz knows that the FASB has issued seven *Statements of Financial Accounting Concepts*, and she believes that these concept statements could be used to support the company's response to the Discussion Memorandum. She has prepared a rough draft of the response citing *Statement of Financial Accounting Concepts No. 1*, "Objectives of Financial Reporting by Business Enterprises."

Instructions
(a) Identify the three objectives of financial reporting as presented in *Statement of Financial Accounting Concepts No. 1 (SFAC No. 1)*.
(b) Describe the level of sophistication expected of the users of financial information by *SFAC No. 1*.

(CMA adapted)

C1-3 **(Accounting Numbers and the Environment)** Hardly a day goes by without an article appearing on the crises affecting many of our financial institutions in the United States. It is estimated that the savings and loan (S&L) debacle of the 1980s, for example, ended up costing $500 billion ($2,000 for every man, woman, and child in the United States). Some argue that if the S&Ls had been required to report their investments at market value instead of cost, large losses would have been reported earlier, which would have signaled regulators to close those S&Ls and, therefore, minimize the losses to U.S. taxpayers.

Instructions
Explain how reported accounting numbers might affect an individual's perceptions and actions. Cite two examples.

C1-4 **(Need for Accounting Standards)** Some argue that having various organizations establish accounting principles is wasteful and inefficient. Rather than mandating accounting standards, each company could voluntarily disclose the type of information it considered important. In addition, if an investor wants additional information, the investor could contact the company and pay to receive the additional information desired.

Instructions
Comment on the appropriateness of this viewpoint.

C1-5 (AICPA's Role in Standards Setting) One of the major groups involved in the standards-setting process is the American Institute of Certified Public Accountants. Initially it was the primary organization that established accounting principles in the United States. Subsequently it relinquished most of its power to the FASB.

Instructions
(a) Identify the two committees of the AICPA that established accounting principles prior to the establishment of the FASB.
(b) Speculate as to why these two organizations failed. In your answer, identify steps the FASB has taken to avoid failure.
(c) What is the present role of the AICPA in the standards-setting environment?

C1-6 (FASB Role in Standards Setting) A press release announcing the appointment of the trustees of the new Financial Accounting Foundation stated that the Financial Accounting Standards Board (to be appointed by the trustees) ". . . will become the established authority for setting accounting principles under which corporations report to the shareholders and others" (AICPA news release July 20, 1972).

Instructions
(a) Identify the sponsoring organization of the FASB and the process by which the FASB arrives at a decision and issues an accounting standard.
(b) Indicate the major types of pronouncements issued by the FASB and the purposes of each of these pronouncements.

C1-7 (Government Role in Standards Setting) Recently an article stated "the setting of accounting standards in the United States is now about 60 years old. It is a unique process in our society, one that has undergone numerous changes over the years. The standards are established by a private sector entity that has no dominant sponsor and is not part of any professional organization or trade association. The governmental entity that provides oversight, on the other hand, is far more a friend than a competitor or an antagonist."

Instructions
Identify the governmental entity that provides oversight and indicate its role in the standards-setting process.

C1-8 (Meaning of Generally Accepted Accounting Principles) At the completion of Bloom Company's audit, the president, Judy Bloom, asks about the meaning of the phrase "in conformity with generally accepted accounting principles" that appears in your audit report on the management's financial statements. Judy observes that the meaning of the phrase must include something more and different than what she thinks of as "principles."

Instructions
(a) Explain the meaning of the term "accounting principles" as used in the audit report. (Do not discuss in this part the significance of "generally accepted.")
(b) President Bloom wants to know how you determine whether or not an accounting principle is generally accepted. Discuss the sources of evidence for determining whether an accounting principle has substantial authoritative support. Do not merely list the titles of publications.

C1-9 (Politicization of Standards Setting) Some accountants have said that politicization in the development and acceptance of generally accepted accounting principles (i.e., standards setting) is taking place. Some use the term "politicization" in a narrow sense to mean the influence by governmental agencies, particularly the Securities and Exchange Commission, on the development of generally accepted accounting principles. Others use it more broadly to mean the compromise that results when the bodies responsible for developing generally accepted accounting principles are pressured by interest groups (SEC, American Accounting Association, businesses through their various organizations, Institute of Management Accountants, financial analysts, bankers, lawyers, and so on).

Instructions

(a) The Committee on Accounting Procedures of the AICPA was established in the mid to late 1930s and functioned until 1959, at which time the Accounting Principles Board came into existence. In 1973, the Financial Accounting Standards Board was formed and the APB went out of existence. Do the reasons these groups were formed, their methods of operation while in existence, and the reasons for the demise of the first two indicate an increasing politicization (as the term is used in the broad sense) of accounting standards setting? Explain your answer by indicating how the CAP, the APB, and the FASB operated or operate. Cite specific developments that tend to support your answer.

(b) What arguments can be raised to support the "politicization" of accounting standards setting?

(c) What arguments can be raised against the "politicization" of accounting standards setting?

(CMA adapted)

C1-10 (Models for Setting Accounting Standards) Presented below are three models for setting accounting standards.

1. The purely political approach, where national legislative action decrees accounting standards.

2. The private, professional approach, where financial accounting standards are set and enforced by private professional actions only.

3. The public/private mixed approach, where standards are basically set by private-sector bodies that behave as though they were public agencies and whose standards to a great extent are enforced through governmental agencies.

Instructions

(a) Which of these three models best describes standards setting in the United States? Comment on your answer.

(b) Why do companies, financial analysts, labor unions, industry trade associations, and others take such an active interest in standards setting?

(c) Cite an example of a group other than the FASB that attempts to establish accounting standards. Speculate as to why another group might wish to set its own standards.

 **C1-11 (Standards-Setting Terminology)** Andrew Wyeth, an administrator at a major university, recently said, "I've got some CDs in my IRA, which I set up to beat the IRS." As elsewhere, in the world of accounting and finance, it often helps to be fluent in abbreviations and acronyms.

Instructions

Presented below is a list of common accounting acronyms. Identify the term for which each acronym stands, and provide a brief definition of each term.

C1-12 (Accounting Organizations and Documents Issued) Presented below are a number of accounting organizations and type of documents they have issued.

(a) AICPA	**(e)** FAF	**(i)** CPA
(b) CAP	**(f)** FASAC	**(j)** FASB
(c) ARB	**(g)** SOP	**(k)** SEC
(d) APB	**(h)** GAAP	**(l)** IASB

Instructions

Match the appropriate document to the organization involved. Note that more than one document may be issued by the same organization. If no document is provided for an organization, write in "0."

Organization	*Document*
1. _____ Securities and Exchange Commission	**(a)** Opinions
2. _____ Accounting Standards Executive Committee	**(b)** Practice Bulletins
3. _____ Accounting Principles Board	**(c)** Accounting Research Bulletins
4. _____ Committee on Accounting Procedure	**(d)** Financial Reporting Releases
5. _____ Financial Accounting Standards Board	**(e)** Financial Accounting Standards
	(f) Statements of Position
	(g) Technical Bulletins

C1-13 **(Accounting Pronouncements)** A number of authoritative pronouncements have been issued by standards-setting bodies in the last 50 years. A list is provided on the left, below, with a description of these pronouncements on the right.

Instructions

Match the description to the pronouncements.

1. _____ Technical Bulletin
2. _____ Interpretations (of the Financial Accounting Standards Board)
3. _____ Statement of Financial Accounting Standards
4. _____ EITF Statements
5. _____ Opinions
6. _____ Statement of Financial Accounting Concepts

(a) Official pronouncements of the APB.

(b) Sets forth fundamental objectives and concepts that will be used in developing future standards.

(c) Primary document of the FASB that establishes GAAP.

(d) Provides additional guidance on implementing or applying FASB Standards or Interpretations.

(e) Provides guidance on how to account for new and unusual financial transactions that have the potential for creating diversity in financial reporting practices.

(f) Represent extensions or modifications of existing standards.

C1-14 **(Issues Involving Standards Setting)** When the FASB issues new standards, the implementation date is usually 12 months from date of issuance, with early implementation encouraged. Paula Popovich, controller, discusses with her financial vice president the need for early implementation of a standard that would result in a fairer presentation of the company's financial condition and earnings. When the financial vice president determines that early implementation of the standard will adversely affect the reported net income for the year, he discourages Popovich from implementing the standard until it is required.

Instructions

Answer the following questions.

(a) What, if any, is the ethical issue involved in this case?
(b) Is the financial vice president acting improperly or immorally?
(c) What does Popovich have to gain by advocacy of early implementation?
(d) Which stakeholders might be affected by the decision against early implementation?

(CMA adapted)

C1-15 **(Securities and Exchange Commission)** The U.S. Securities and Exchange Commission (SEC) was created in 1934 and consists of five commissioners and a large professional staff. The SEC professional staff is organized into five divisions and several principal offices. The primary objective of the SEC is to support fair securities markets. The SEC also strives to foster enlightened shareholder participation in corporate decisions of publicly traded companies. The SEC has a significant presence in financial markets, the development of accounting practices, and corporation-shareholder relations, and has the power to exert influence on entities whose actions lie within the scope of its authority.

Instructions

(a) Explain from where the Securities and Exchange Commission receives its authority.
(b) Describe the official role of the Securities and Exchange Commission in the development of financial accounting theory and practices.
(c) Discuss the interrelationship between the Securities and Exchange Commission and the Financial Accounting Standards Board with respect to the development and establishment of financial accounting theory and practices.

(CMA adapted)

C1-16 **(Standards-Setting Process)** In 1973, the responsibility for developing and issuing rules on accounting practices was given to the Financial Accounting Foundation and, in particular, to an arm of the foundation called the Financial Accounting Standards Board (FASB). The generally accepted accounting principles established by the FASB are enunciated through a publication series entitled *Statements of Financial Ac-*

counting Standards. These statements are issued periodically, and over 140 are currently in force. The statements have a significant influence on the way in which financial statements are prepared by U.S. corporations.

Instructions

(a) Describe the process by which a topic is selected or identified as appropriate for study by the Financial Accounting Standards Board (FASB).

(b) Once a topic is considered appropriate for consideration by the FASB, a series of steps is followed before a *Statement of Financial Accounting Standards* is issued. Describe the major steps in the process leading to the issuance of a standard.

(c) Identify at least three other organizations that influence the setting of generally accepted accounting principles (GAAP).

(CMA adapted)

C1-17 (History of Standards-Setting Organizations) Beta Alpha Psi, your university's accounting society, has decided to publish a brief pamphlet for seniors in high school, detailing the various facets of the accountancy profession. As a junior accounting major, you have been asked to contribute an article for this publication. Your topic is the evolution of accounting standards-setting organizations in the United States.

Instructions

Write a 1–2 page article on the historical development of the organizations responsible for giving us GAAP. (The most appropriate introduction would explain the increasing need for a more standardized approach to accounting for a company's assets.)

C1-18 (Economic Consequences) Presented below are comments made in the financial press.

Instructions

Prepare responses to the requirements in each item.

(a) Rep. John Dingell, the ranking Democrat on the House Commerce Committee, threw his support behind the FASB's controversial derivatives accounting standard and encouraged the FASB to adopt the rule promptly. Indicate why a member of Congress might feel obligated to comment on this proposed FASB standard.

(b) In a strongly worded letter to Senator Lauch Faircloth (R-NC) and House Banking Committee Chairman Jim Leach (R-IA), the American Institute of Certified Public Accountants (AICPA) cautioned against government intervention in the accounting standards-setting process, warning that it had the potential of jeopardizing U.S. capital markets. Explain how government intervention could possibly affect capital markets adversely.

C1-19 (Standards-Setting Process, Economic Consequences) The following letter was sent to the SEC and the FASB by leaders of the business community.

Dear Sirs:

The FASB has been struggling with accounting for derivatives and hedging for many years. The FASB has now developed, over the last few weeks, a new approach that it proposes to adopt as a final standard. We understand that the Board intends to adopt this new approach as a final standard without exposing it for public comment and debate, despite the evident complexity of the new approach, the speed with which it has been developed and the significant changes to the exposure draft since it was released more than one year ago. Instead, the Board plans to allow only a brief review by selected parties, limited to issues of operationality and clarity, and would exclude questions as to the merits of the proposed approach.

As the FASB itself has said throughout this process, its mission does not permit it to consider matters that go beyond accounting and reporting considerations. Accordingly, the FASB may not have adequately considered the wide range of concerns that have been expressed about the derivatives and hedging proposal, including concerns related to the potential impact on the capital markets, the weakening of companies' ability to manage risk, and the adverse control implications of implementing costly and complex new rules imposed at the same time as other major initiatives, including the Year 2000 issues and a single European currency. We believe that these crucial issues must be considered, if not by the FASB, then by the Securities and Exchange Commission, other regulatory agencies, or Congress.

We believe it is essential that the FASB solicit all comments in order to identify and address all material issues that may exist before issuing a final standard. We understand the desire to bring this process to a prompt conclusion, but the underlying issues are so important to this nation's businesses, the customers they serve and the economy as a whole that expediency cannot be the dominant consideration. As a result, we urge the FASB to expose its new proposal for public comment, following the established due process procedures that are essential to acceptance of its standards, and providing sufficient time to affected parties to understand and assess the new approach.

We also urge the SEC to study the comments received in order to assess the impact that these proposed rules may have on the capital markets, on companies' risk management practices, and on management and financial controls. These vital public policy matters deserve consideration as part of the Commission's oversight responsibilities.

We believe that these steps are essential if the FASB is to produce the best possible accounting standard while minimizing adverse economic effects and maintaining the competitiveness of U.S. businesses in the international marketplace.

Very truly yours,

(This letter was signed by the chairs of 22 of the largest U.S. companies.)

Instructions

Answer the following questions.

(a) Explain the "due process" procedures followed by the FASB in developing a financial reporting standard.
(b) What is meant by the term "economic consequences" in accounting standards setting?
(c) What economic consequences arguments are used in this letter?
(d) What do you believe is the main point of the letter?
(e) Why do you believe a copy of this letter was sent by the business community to influential members of the United States Congress?

USING YOUR JUDGMENT

FINANCIAL REPORTING PROBLEM

Kate Jackson, a new staff accountant, is confused because of the complexities involving accounting standards setting. Specifically, she is confused by the number of bodies issuing financial reporting standards of one kind or another and the level of authoritative support that can be attached to these reporting standards. Kate decides that she must review the environment in which accounting standards are set, if she is to increase her understanding of the accounting profession.

Kate recalls that during her accounting education there was a chapter or two regarding the environment of financial accounting and the development of accounting standards. However, she remembers that little emphasis was placed on these chapters by her instructor.

Instructions

(a) Help Kate by identifying key organizations involved in accounting standards setting.
(b) Kate asks for guidance regarding authoritative support. Please assist her by explaining what is meant by authoritative support.
(c) Give Kate a historical overview of how standards setting has evolved so that she will not feel that she is the only one to be confused.
(d) What authority for compliance with GAAP has existed throughout the period of standards setting?

INTERNATIONAL REPORTING CASE

Michael Sharpe, former Deputy Chairman of the International Accounting Standards Committee (IASC), made the following comments before the 63rd Annual Conference of the Financial Executives Institute (FEI).

There is an irreversible movement towards the harmonization of financial reporting throughout the world. The international capital markets require an end to:

1 The confusion caused by international companies announcing different results depending on the set of accounting standards applied. Recent announcements by Daimler-Benz [now **DaimlerChrysler**] highlight the confusion that this causes.

2 Companies in some countries obtaining unfair commercial advantages from the use of particular national accounting standards.

3 The complications in negotiating commercial arrangements for international joint ventures caused by different accounting requirements.

4 The inefficiency of international companies having to understand and use a myriad of different accounting standards depending on the countries in which they operate and the countries in which they raise capital and debt. Executive talent is wasted on keeping up to date with numerous sets of accounting standards and the never-ending changes to them.

5 The inefficiency of investment managers, bankers, and financial analysts as they seek to compare financial reporting drawn up in accordance with different sets of accounting standards.

6 Failure of many stock exchanges and regulators to require companies subject to their jurisdiction to provide comparable, comprehensive, and transparent financial reporting frameworks giving international comparability.

7 Difficulty for developing countries and countries entering the free market economy such as China and Russia in accessing foreign capital markets because of the complexity of and differences between national standards.

8 The restriction on the mobility of financial service providers across the world as a result of different accounting standards.

Clearly the elimination of these inefficiencies by having comparable high-quality financial reporting used across the world would benefit international businesses.

Instructions

(a) What is the International Accounting Standards Board, and what is its relation to the International Accounting Standards Committee?

(b) What stakeholders might benefit from the use of International Accounting Standards?

(c) What do you believe are some of the major obstacles to harmonization?

*Remember to check the **Take Action! CD**
and the book's **companion Web site**
to find additional resources for this chapter.*

SHOW ME THE EARNINGS!

The growth of new-economy business on the Internet has led to the development of new measures of performance. When Priceline.com splashed on the dot-com scene, it touted steady growth in a measure called "unique offers by users" to explain its heady stock price. And Drugstore.com focused on "unique customers" at its Web site to draw investors to its stock. After all, new businesses call for new performance measures, right?

Not necessarily. The problem with such indicators is that they do not exhibit any consistent relationship with the ability of these companies to earn profits from the customers visiting their Web sites. Eventually, as the graphs below show, the profits never materialized, and stock prices fell.

After studying this chapter, you should be able to:

① Describe the usefulness of a conceptual framework.

② Describe the FASB's efforts to construct a conceptual framework.

③ Understand the objectives of financial reporting.

④ Identify the qualitative characteristics of accounting information.

⑤ Define the basic elements of financial statements.

⑥ Describe the basic assumptions of accounting.

⑦ Explain the application of the basic principles of accounting.

⑧ Describe the impact that constraints have on reporting accounting information.

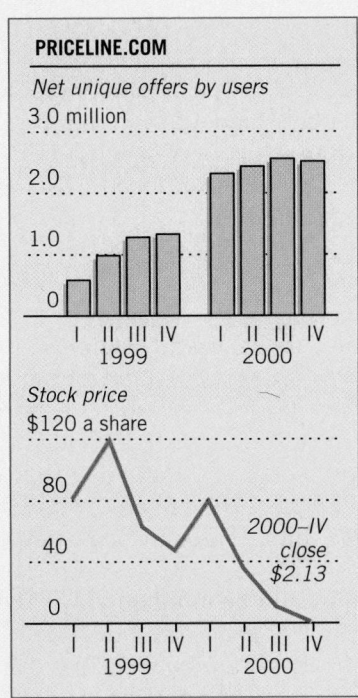

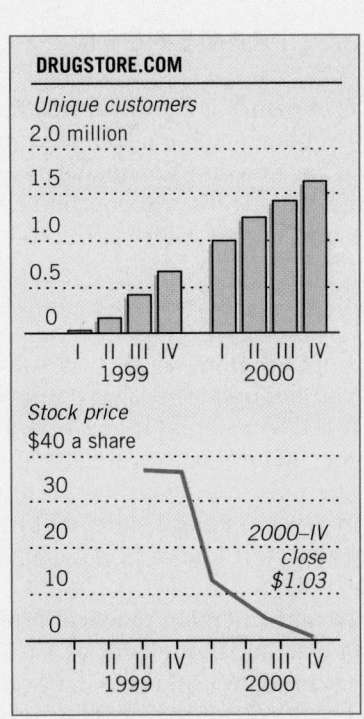

According to one accounting expert, investors' use of nonfinancial measures is not detrimental when combined with financial analysis, which is based on measures such as earnings and cash flows. The problem is that during the recent Internet craze, investors placed too much emphasis on nonfinancial data. Thus, the new economy may require some new measures, but investors need to be careful not to forget the relevant and reliable traditional ones.[1]

---

[1]Story and graphs adapted from Gretchen Morgenson, "How Did They Value Stocks? Count the Absurd Ways," *New York Times* (March 18, 2001), section 3, p. 1.

As indicated in the opening story about dot-com reporting, users of financial statements need relevant and reliable information. To help develop this type of financial information, a conceptual framework that guides financial accounting and reporting is used. This chapter discusses the basic concepts underlying this conceptual framework. The content and organization of this chapter are as follows.

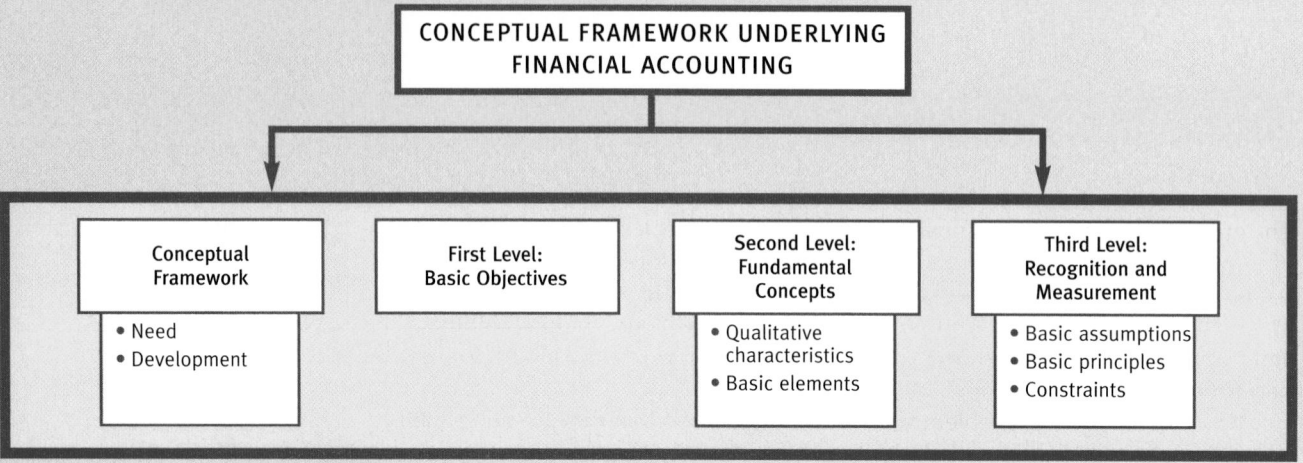

CONCEPTUAL FRAMEWORK

A **conceptual framework** is like a **constitution**: It is "a coherent system of interrelated objectives and fundamentals that can lead to consistent standards and that prescribes the nature, function, and limits of financial accounting and financial statements."[2] Many have considered the FASB's real contribution—and even its continued existence—to depend on the quality and utility of the conceptual framework.

Need for Conceptual Framework

OBJECTIVE **1**
Describe the usefulness of a conceptual framework.

Why is a conceptual framework necessary? First, to be useful, standard setting should build on and relate to an established body of concepts and objectives. A soundly developed conceptual framework should enable the FASB to issue more useful and consistent standards over time. **A coherent set of standards and rules should be the result**, because they would be built upon the same foundation. The framework should increase financial statement users' understanding of and confidence in financial reporting, and it should enhance comparability among companies' financial statements.

Second, new and emerging **practical problems should be more quickly solved by reference to an existing framework of basic theory**. For example, **Sunshine Mining** (a silver mining company) sold two issues of bonds that it would redeem either with $1,000 in cash or with 50 ounces of silver, whichever was worth more at maturity. Both bond issues had a stated interest rate of 8.5%. At what amounts should the bonds have been recorded by Sunshine or the buyers of the bonds? What is the amount of the pre-

---

[2]"Conceptual Framework for Financial Accounting and Reporting: Elements of Financial Statements and Their Measurement," *FASB Discussion Memorandum* (Stamford, Conn.: FASB, 1976), page 1 of the "Scope and Implications of the Conceptual Framework Project" section. For an excellent discussion of the functions of the conceptual framework, see Reed K. Storey and Sylvia Storey, Special Report, "The Framework of Financial Accounting and Concepts" (Norwalk, Conn.: FASB, 1998), pp. 85–88.

mium or discount on the bonds and how should it be amortized, if the bond redemption payments are to be made in silver (the future value of which was unknown at the date of issuance)?

It is difficult, if not impossible, for the FASB to prescribe the proper accounting treatment quickly for situations like this. Practicing accountants, however, must resolve such problems on a day-to-day basis. Through the exercise of good judgment and with the help of a universally accepted conceptual framework, practitioners can dismiss certain alternatives quickly and then focus on an acceptable treatment.

Development of Conceptual Framework

Over the years numerous organizations, committees, and interested individuals developed and published their own conceptual frameworks. But no single framework was universally accepted and relied on in practice. Recognizing the need for a generally accepted framework, the FASB in 1976 began work to develop a conceptual framework that would be a basis for setting accounting standards and for resolving financial reporting controversies. Since the publication of that document, the FASB has issued six Statements of Financial Accounting Concepts that relate to financial reporting for business enterprises.[3] They are:

OBJECTIVE **2**
Describe the FASB's efforts to construct a conceptual framework.

1. *SFAC No. 1*, "Objectives of Financial Reporting by Business Enterprises," presents the goals and purposes of accounting.
2. *SFAC No. 2*, "Qualitative Characteristics of Accounting Information," examines the characteristics that make accounting information useful.
3. *SFAC No. 3*, "Elements of Financial Statements of Business Enterprises," provides definitions of items in financial statements, such as assets, liabilities, revenues, and expenses.
4. *SFAC No. 5*, "Recognition and Measurement in Financial Statements of Business Enterprises," sets forth fundamental recognition and measurement criteria and guidance on what information should be formally incorporated into financial statements and when.
5. *SFAC No. 6*, "Elements of Financial Statements," replaces *SFAC No. 3* and expands its scope to include not-for-profit organizations.
6. *SFAC No. 7*, "Using Cash Flow Information and Present Value in Accounting Measurements," provides a framework for using expected future cash flows and present values as a basis for measurement.

INTERNATIONAL INSIGHT

The IASC has issued a conceptual framework that is broadly consistent with that of the United States.

Illustration 2-1 (on page 28) provides an overview of the conceptual framework.[4] At the first level, the **objectives** identify the goals and purposes of accounting. Ideally, accounting standards developed according to a conceptual framework will result in accounting reports that are more useful. At the second level are the **qualitative characteristics** that make accounting information useful and the **elements** of financial statements (assets, liabilities, and so on). At the third level are the **measurement and recognition concepts** used in establishing and applying accounting standards. These concepts include assumptions, principles, and constraints that describe the present reporting environment. The remainder of the chapter examines these three levels of the conceptual framework.

---

[3]The FASB has also issued a Statement of Financial Accounting Concepts that relates to nonbusiness organizations: *Statement of Financial Accounting Concepts No. 4*, "Objectives of Financial Reporting by Nonbusiness Organizations" (December 1980).

[4]Adapted from William C. Norby, *The Financial Analysts Journal* (March–April 1982), p. 22.

Illustration 2-1
Conceptual Framework
for Financial Reporting

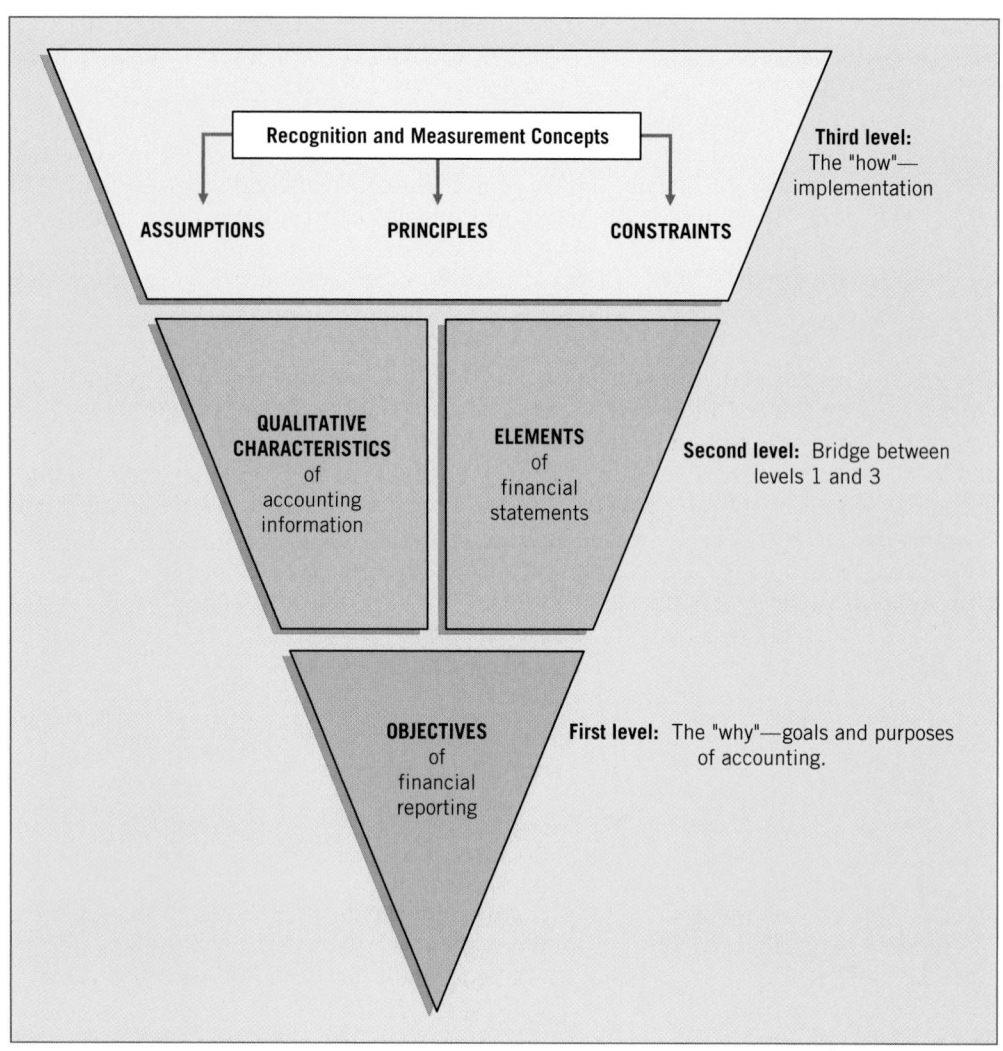

FIRST LEVEL: BASIC OBJECTIVES

OBJECTIVE 3
Understand the objectives of financial reporting.

As we discussed in Chapter 1, the **objectives of financial reporting** are to provide information that is: (1) useful to those making investment and credit decisions who have a reasonable understanding of business and economic activities; (2) helpful to present and potential investors, creditors, and other users in assessing the amounts, timing, and uncertainty of future cash flows; and (3) about economic resources, the claims to those resources, and the changes in them.

The objectives, therefore, begin with a broad concern about information that is useful to investor and creditor decisions. That concern narrows to the investors' and creditors' interest in the prospect of receiving cash from their investments in, or loans to, business enterprises. Finally, the objectives focus on the financial statements that provide information useful in the assessment of prospective cash flows to the business enterprise. This approach is referred to as **decision usefulness**. It has been said that the golden rule is the message of the Bible and the rest is elaboration. Similarly, decision usefulness is the message of the conceptual framework and the rest is elaboration.

In providing information to users of financial statements, general-purpose financial statements are prepared. These statements provide the most useful information possible at minimal cost to various user groups. Underlying these objectives is the notion that users need reasonable knowledge of business and financial accounting matters to understand the information contained in financial statements. This point is important. It means that in the preparation of financial statements a level of reasonable competence on the part of users can be assumed. This has an impact on the way and the extent to which information is reported.

Second Level: Fundamental Concepts

The objectives (first level) are concerned with the goals and purposes of accounting. Later, we will discuss the ways these goals and purposes are implemented (third level). Between these two levels it is necessary to provide certain conceptual building blocks that explain the qualitative characteristics of accounting information and define the elements of financial statements. These conceptual building blocks form a bridge between the **why** of accounting (the objectives) and the **how** of accounting (recognition and measurement).

Qualitative Characteristics of Accounting Information

How does one decide whether financial reports should provide information on how much a firm's assets cost to acquire (historical cost basis) or how much they are currently worth (current value basis)? Or how does one decide whether the three main segments that constitute **PepsiCo**—PepsiCola, Frito Lay, and Tropicana—should be combined and shown as one company, or disaggregated and reported as three separate segments for financial reporting purposes?

   Choosing an acceptable accounting method, the amount and types of information to be disclosed, and the format in which information should be presented involves determining **which alternative provides the most useful information for decision making purposes (decision usefulness)**. The FASB has identified the **qualitative characteristics** of accounting information that distinguish better (more useful) information from inferior (less useful) information for decision making purposes.[5] In addition, the FASB has identified certain constraints (cost-benefit and materiality) as part of the conceptual framework; these are discussed later in the chapter. The characteristics may be viewed as a hierarchy, as shown in Illustration 2-2 on the next page.

Decision Makers (Users) and Understandability
Decision makers vary widely in the types of decisions they make, how they make decisions, the information they already possess or can obtain from other sources, and their ability to process the information. For information to be useful, there must be a connection (linkage) between these users and the decisions they make. This link, **understandability**, is the quality of information that permits reasonably informed users to perceive its significance. To illustrate the importance of this linkage, assume that **IBM Corp.** issues a three-months' earnings report (interim report) that shows interim earnings way down. This report provides relevant and reliable information for decision making purposes. Some users, upon reading the report, decide to sell their stock. Other users do not understand the report's content and significance. They are surprised when IBM declares a smaller year-end dividend and the value of the stock declines. Thus, although the information presented was highly relevant and reliable, it was useless to those who did not understand it.

Primary Qualities: Relevance and Reliability
Relevance and **reliability** are the two primary qualities that make accounting information useful for decision making.** As stated in FASB *Concepts Statement No. 2*, "the qualities that distinguish 'better' (more useful) information from 'inferior' (less useful)

OBJECTIVE **4**
Identify the qualitative characteristics of accounting information.

---

[5]"Qualitative Characteristics of Accounting Information," *Statement of Financial Accounting Concepts No. 2* (Stamford, Conn.: FASB, May 1980).

Illustration 2-2

Hierarchy of Accounting
Qualities

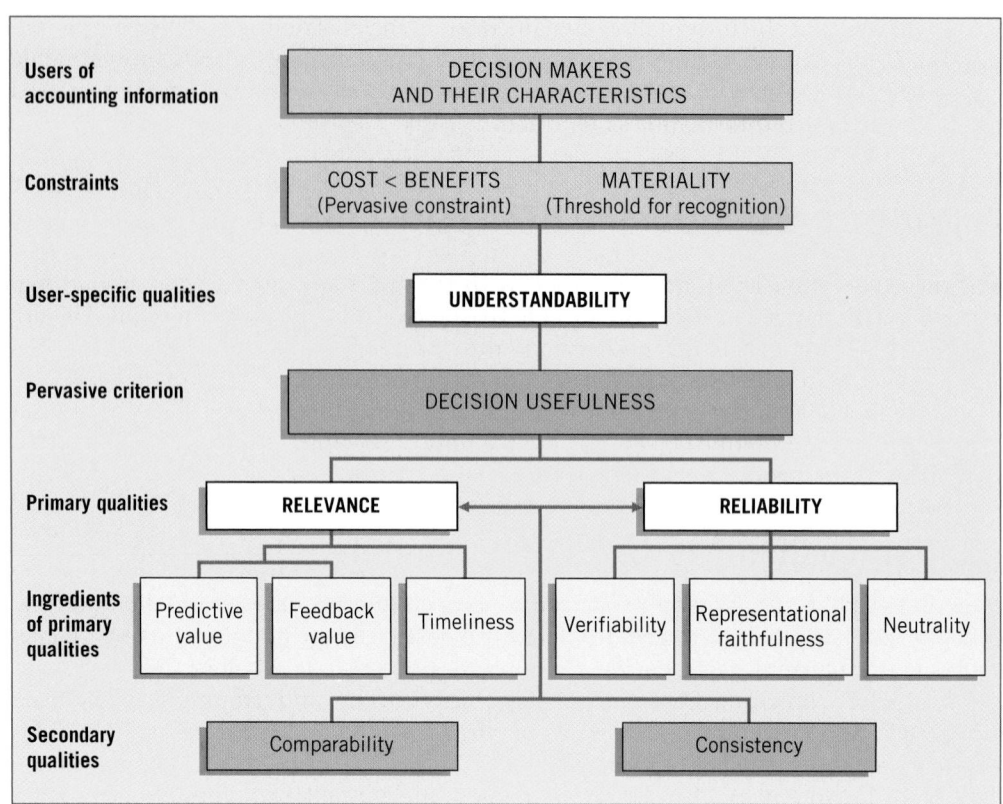

information are primarily the qualities of relevance and reliability, with some other characteristics that those qualities imply."[6]

Relevance. To be relevant, accounting information must be capable of making a difference in a decision.[7] If certain information has no bearing on a decision, it is irrelevant to that decision. Relevant information helps users make predictions about the ultimate outcome of past, present, and future events; that is, it has **predictive value**. Relevant information also helps users confirm or correct prior expectations; it has **feedback value**. For example, when **UPS (United Parcel Service)** issues an interim report, this information is considered relevant because it provides a basis for forecasting annual earnings and provides feedback on past performance. For information to be relevant, it must also be available to decision makers before it loses its capacity to influence their decisions. Thus **timeliness** is a primary ingredient. If UPS did not report its interim results until six months after the end of the period, the information would be much less useful for decision making purposes. **For information to be relevant, it should have predictive or feedback value, and it must be presented on a timely basis.**

Reliability. Accounting information is reliable to the extent that **it is verifiable, is a faithful representation, and is reasonably free of error and bias**. Reliability is a necessity for individuals who have neither the time nor the expertise to evaluate the factual content of the information.

    Verifiability is demonstrated when independent measurers, using the same measurement methods, obtain similar results. For example, would several independent auditors come to the same conclusion about a set of financial statements? If outside parties using the same measurement methods arrive at different conclusions, then the statements are not verifiable. Auditors could not render an opinion on such statements.

---

[6]Ibid., par. 15.

[7]Ibid., par. 47.

Representational faithfulness means that the numbers and descriptions represent what really existed or happened. The accounting numbers and descriptions agree with the resources or events that these numbers and descriptions purport to represent. If **General Motors'** income statement reports sales of $150 billion when it had sales of $138.2 billion, then the statement is not a faithful representation.

Neutrality means that information cannot be selected to favor one set of interested parties over another. Factual, truthful, unbiased information must be the overriding consideration. For example, **R. J. Reynolds** should not be permitted to suppress information in the notes to its financial statements about the numerous lawsuits that have been filed against it because of tobacco-related health concerns—even though such disclosure is damaging to the company.

Neutrality in standard setting has come under increasing attack. Some argue that standards should not be issued if they cause undesirable economic effects on an industry or company. We disagree. Standards must be free from bias or we will no longer have credible financial statements. Without credible financial statements, individuals will no longer use this information. An analogy demonstrates the point: In the United States, we have both boxing and wrestling matches. Many individuals bet on boxing matches because such contests are assumed not to be fixed. But nobody bets on wrestling matches. Why? Because the public assumes that wrestling matches are rigged. If financial information is biased (rigged), the public will lose confidence and no longer use this information.

Secondary Qualities: Comparability and Consistency

Information about an enterprise is more useful if it can be compared with similar information about another enterprise **(comparability)** and with similar information about the same enterprise at other points in time **(consistency)**.

Comparability.   Information that has been measured and reported in a similar manner for different enterprises is considered comparable. Comparability enables users to identify the real similarities and differences in economic phenomena because these differences and similarities have not been obscured by the use of noncomparable accounting methods. For example, the accounting for pensions is different in the United States and Japan. In the U.S., pension cost is recorded as it is incurred, whereas in Japan there is little or no charge to income for these costs. As a result, it is difficult to compare and evaluate the financial results of **General Motors** or **Ford** to **Nissan** or **Honda**. Also, resource allocation decisions involve evaluations of alternatives; a valid evaluation can be made only if comparable information is available.

Consistency.   When an entity applies the same accounting treatment to similar events, from period to period, the entity is considered to be consistent in its use of accounting standards. It does not mean that companies cannot switch from one method of accounting to another. Companies can change methods, but the changes are restricted to situations in which it can be demonstrated that the newly adopted method is preferable to the old. Then the nature and effect of the accounting change, as well as the justification for it, must be disclosed in the financial statements for the period in which the change is made.[8]

When there has been a change in accounting principles, the auditor refers to it in an explanatory paragraph of the audit report. This paragraph identifies the nature of the change and refers the reader to the note in the financial statements that discusses the change in detail.[9]

---

[8]Surveys of users indicate that users highly value consistency. They note that a change tends to destroy the comparability of data before and after the change. Some companies take the time to assist users to understand the pre- and post-change data. Generally, however, users say they lose the ability to analyze over time.

[9]"Reports on Audited Financial Statements," *Statement on Auditing Standards No. 58* (New York: AICPA, April 1988), par. 34.

In summary, accounting reports for any given year are more useful if they can be compared with reports from other companies and with prior reports of the same entity.

WHAT DO THE NUMBERS MEAN?

CAN YOU COMPARE PRO FORMAS?

Beyond touting nonfinancial measures to investors (see opening story), many companies are increasingly promoting the performance of their companies through the reporting of various "pro-forma" earnings measures. A recent survey of newswire reports found 36 instances of the reporting of pro-forma measures in just a three-day period.

Pro-forma measures are standard measures, such as earnings, that are adjusted, usually for one-time or nonrecurring items. For example, it is standard practice to adjust earnings for the effects of an extraordinary item. Such adjustments make the numbers more comparable to numbers reported in periods without the unusual item.

However, rather than increasing comparability, it appears that recent pro-forma reporting is designed to accentuate the positive in company results. Examples of such reporting include **Yahoo!** and **Cisco**, which define pro-forma income after adding back payroll tax expense. And **Level 8 Systems** transformed an operating loss into a pro-forma profit by adding back expenses for depreciation and amortization of intangible assets.

Lynn Turner, former Chief Accountant at the SEC, calls such earnings measures EBS— "everything but bad stuff." He admonishes investors to view such reporting with caution and appropriate skepticism.

Source: Adapted from Gretchen Morgenson, "How Did They Value Stocks? Count the Absurd Ways," *New York Times* (March 18, 2001), section 3, p. 1; and Gretchen Morgenson, "Expert Advice: Focus on Profit," *New York Times* (March 18, 2001), section 3, p. 14.

Basic Elements

OBJECTIVE 5
Define the basic elements of financial statements.

An important aspect of developing any theoretical structure is the body of **basic elements** or definitions to be included in the structure. At present, accounting uses many terms that have distinctive and specific meanings. These terms constitute the language of business or the jargon of accounting.

One such term is **asset**. Is it something we own? If the answer is yes, can we assume that any leased asset would not be shown on the balance sheet? Is an asset something we have the right to use, or is it anything of value used by the enterprise to generate revenues? If the answer is yes, then why should the managers of the enterprise not be considered an asset? It seems necessary, therefore, to develop basic definitions for the elements of financial statements. *Concepts Statement No. 6* defines the ten interrelated elements that are most directly related to measuring the performance and financial status of an enterprise. We list them here for review and information purposes; you need not memorize these definitions at this point. Each of these elements will be explained and examined in more detail in subsequent chapters.

ELEMENTS OF FINANCIAL STATEMENTS

ASSETS. Probable future economic benefits obtained or controlled by a particular entity as a result of past transactions or events.

LIABILITIES. Probable future sacrifices of economic benefits arising from present obligations of a particular entity to transfer assets or provide services to other entities in the future as a result of past transactions or events.

EQUITY. Residual interest in the assets of an entity that remains after deducting its liabilities. In a business enterprise, the equity is the ownership interest.

INVESTMENTS BY OWNERS. Increases in net assets of a particular enterprise resulting from transfers to it from other entities of something of value to obtain or increase ownership interests (or equity) in it. Assets are most commonly received as investments by owners, but that which is received may also include services or satisfaction or conversion of liabilities of the enterprise.

DISTRIBUTIONS TO OWNERS. Decreases in net assets of a particular enterprise resulting from transferring assets, rendering services, or incurring liabilities by the enterprise to owners. Distributions to owners decrease ownership interests (or equity) in an enterprise.

COMPREHENSIVE INCOME. Change in equity (net assets) of an entity during a period from transactions and other events and circumstances from nonowner sources. It includes all changes in equity during a period except those resulting from investments by owners and distributions to owners.

REVENUES. Inflows or other enhancements of assets of an entity or settlement of its liabilities (or a combination of both) during a period from delivering or producing goods, rendering services, or other activities that constitute the entity's ongoing major or central operations.

EXPENSES. Outflows or other using up of assets or incurrences of liabilities (or a combination of both) during a period from delivering or producing goods, rendering services, or carrying out other activities that constitute the entity's ongoing major or central operations.

GAINS. Increases in equity (net assets) from peripheral or incidental transactions of an entity and from all other transactions and other events and circumstances affecting the entity during a period except those that result from revenues or investments by owners.

LOSSES. Decreases in equity (net assets) from peripheral or incidental transactions of an entity and from all other transactions and other events and circumstances affecting the entity during a period except those that result from expenses or distributions to owners.[10]

The FASB classifies the elements into two distinct groups. The first group of three elements (assets, liabilities, and equity) describes amounts of resources and claims to resources at a **moment in time**. The other seven elements (comprehensive income and its components—revenues, expenses, gains, and losses—as well as investments by owners and distributions to owners) describe transactions, events, and circumstances that affect an enterprise during a **period of time**. The first class is changed by elements of the second class, and at any time is the cumulative result of all changes. This interaction is referred to as "articulation." That is, key figures in one statement correspond to balances in another.

THIRD LEVEL: RECOGNITION AND MEASUREMENT CONCEPTS

The third level of the framework consists of concepts that implement the basic objectives of level one. These concepts explain which, when, and how financial elements and events should be recognized, measured, and reported by the accounting system. Most of them are set forth in FASB *Statement of Financial Accounting Concepts No. 5,*

[10]"Elements of Financial Statements," *Statement of Financial Accounting Concepts No. 6* (Stamford, Conn.: FASB, December 1985), pp. ix and x.

"Recognition and Measurement in Financial Statements of Business Enterprises." According to *SFAC No. 5*, to be recognized, an item (event or transaction) must meet the definition of an "element of financial statements" as defined in *SFAC No. 6* and must be measurable. Most aspects of current practice are consistent with this recognition and measurement concept.

The accounting profession continues to use the concepts in *SFAC No. 5* as operational guidelines. For discussion purposes, we have chosen to identify the concepts as basic assumptions, principles, and constraints. Not everyone uses this classification system, so it is best to focus your attention more on **understanding the concepts** than on how they are classified and organized. These concepts serve as guidelines in developing rational responses to controversial financial reporting issues.

Basic Assumptions

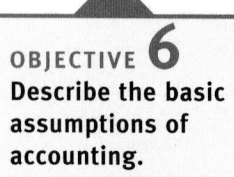

OBJECTIVE **6**
Describe the basic assumptions of accounting.

Four basic **assumptions** underlie the financial accounting structure: (1) **economic entity**, (2) **going concern**, (3) **monetary unit**, and (4) **periodicity**.

Economic Entity Assumption

The **economic entity assumption** **means that economic activity can be identified with a particular unit of accountability.** In other words, the activity of a business enterprise can be kept separate and distinct from its owners and any other business unit. For example, if the activities and elements of **General Motors** could not be distinguished from those of **Ford** or **DaimlerChrysler**, then it would be impossible to know which company financially outperformed the other two in recent years. If there were no meaningful way to separate all of the economic events that occur, no basis for accounting would exist.

The entity concept does not apply solely to the segregation of activities among given business enterprises. An individual, a department or division, or an entire industry could be considered a separate entity if we chose to define the unit in such a manner. Thus, **the entity concept does not necessarily refer to a legal entity**. A parent and its subsidiaries are separate **legal** entities, but merging their activities for accounting and reporting purposes does not violate the **economic entity** assumption.[11]

Going Concern Assumption

Most accounting methods are based on the **going concern assumption—that the business enterprise will have a long life**. Experience indicates that, in spite of numerous business failures, companies have a fairly high continuance rate. Although accountants do not believe that business firms will last indefinitely, they do expect them to last long enough to fulfill their objectives and commitments.

The implications of this assumption are profound. The historical cost principle would be of limited usefulness if eventual liquidation were assumed. Under a liquidation approach, for example, asset values are better stated at net realizable value (sales price less costs of disposal) than at acquisition cost. **Depreciation and amortization policies are justifiable and appropriate only if we assume some permanence to the enterprise.** If a liquidation approach were adopted, the current-noncurrent classification of assets and liabilities would lose much of its significance. Labeling anything a

---

[11]The concept of the entity is changing. For example, it is now harder to define the outer edges of companies. There are public companies, such as **Enron**, with multiple public subsidiaries, each with joint ventures, licensing arrangements, and other affiliations. Increasingly, loose affiliations of enterprises in joint ventures or customer-supplier relationships are formed and dissolved in a matter of months or weeks. These "virtual companies" raise accounting issues about how to account for the entity. See Steven H. Wallman, "The Future of Accounting and Disclosure in an Evolving World: The Need for Dramatic Change," *Accounting Horizons* (September 1995).

fixed or long-term asset would be difficult to justify. Indeed, listing liabilities on the basis of priority in liquidation would be more reasonable.

The going concern assumption applies in most business situations. **Only where liquidation appears imminent is the assumption inapplicable.** In these cases a total revaluation of assets and liabilities can provide information that closely approximates the entity's net realizable value. Accounting problems related to an enterprise in liquidation are presented in advanced accounting courses.

Monetary Unit Assumption

The **monetary unit assumption** means that money is the common denominator of economic activity and provides an appropriate basis for accounting measurement and analysis. This assumption implies that the monetary unit is the most effective means of expressing to interested parties changes in capital and exchanges of goods and services. **The monetary unit is relevant, simple, universally available, understandable, and useful.** Application of this assumption depends on the even more basic assumption that quantitative data are useful in communicating economic information and in making rational economic decisions.

In the United States, price-level changes (inflation and deflation) are ignored in accounting, and the unit of measure—the dollar—is assumed to remain reasonably stable. This assumption about the monetary unit has been used to justify adding 1970 dollars to 2004 dollars without any adjustment. The FASB in *SFAC No. 5* indicated that it expects the dollar, unadjusted for inflation or deflation, to continue to be used to measure items recognized in financial statements. Only if circumstances change dramatically (such as if the United States were to experience high inflation similar to that in many South American countries) will the FASB again consider "inflation accounting."

Accounting for Changing Prices

Periodicity Assumption

The most accurate way to measure the results of enterprise activity would be to measure them at the time of the enterprise's eventual liquidation. Business, government, investors, and various other user groups, however, cannot wait that long for such information. Users need to be apprised of performance and economic status on a timely basis so that they can evaluate and compare firms, and take appropriate actions. Therefore, information must be reported periodically.

The **periodicity** (or **time period**) **assumption** implies that **the economic activities of an enterprise can be divided into artificial time periods**. These time periods vary, but the most common are monthly, quarterly, and yearly.

The shorter the time period, the more difficult it becomes to determine the proper net income for the period. A month's results are usually less reliable than a quarter's results, and a quarter's results are likely to be less reliable than a year's results. Investors desire and demand that information be quickly processed and disseminated; yet the quicker the information is released, the more it is subject to error. **This phenomenon provides an interesting example of the trade-off between relevance and reliability in preparing financial data.**

The problem of defining the time period is becoming more serious because product cycles are shorter and products become obsolete more quickly. Many believe that, given technology advances, more online, real-time financial information needs to be provided to ensure that relevant information is available.

Basic Principles of Accounting

Four basic **principles of accounting** are used to record transactions: (1) **historical cost**, (2) **revenue recognition**, (3) **matching**, and (4) **full disclosure**.

Historical Cost Principle

GAAP requires that most assets and liabilities be accounted for and reported on the basis of acquisition price. This is often referred to as the **historical cost principle**.

OBJECTIVE **7**
Explain the application of the basic principles of accounting.

Cost has an important advantage over other valuations: **it is reliable**. To illustrate the importance of this advantage, consider the problems that would arise if we adopted some other basis for keeping records. If we were to select current selling price, for instance, we might have a difficult time in attempting to establish a sales value for a given item until it was sold. Every member of the accounting department might have a different opinion regarding an asset's value, and management might desire still another figure. And how often would it be necessary to establish sales value? All companies close their accounts at least annually, and some compute their net income every month. These companies would find it necessary to place a sales value on every asset each time they wished to determine income—a laborious task and one that would result in a figure of net income materially affected by opinion. Similar objections have been leveled against current cost (replacement cost, present value of future cash flows) and any other basis of valuation **except cost**.

What about liabilities? Are they accounted for on a cost basis? Yes, they are. **If we convert the term "cost" to "exchange price," we find that it applies to liabilities as well.** Liabilities, such as bonds, notes, and accounts payable, are issued by a business enterprise in exchange for assets, or perhaps services, upon which an agreed price has usually been placed. This price, established by the exchange transaction, is the "cost" of the liability and provides the figure at which it should be recorded in the accounts and reported in financial statements.

In general, users have indicated a preference for historical cost because it provides them a stable and consistent benchmark that can be relied upon to measure historical trends. However, fair value information is thought to be more useful for certain types of assets and liabilities and in certain industries. For example, many financial instruments, including derivatives, are reported at fair value, and inventories are reported at lower of cost or market. Certain industries, such as brokerage houses and mutual funds, prepare their basic financial statements on a fair value basis.

At initial acquisition, historical cost and fair value are the same. In subsequent periods, as market and economic conditions change, historical cost and fair value often diverge. Some believe that fair value measures or estimates are needed to provide relevant information about the expected future cash flows related to the asset or liability. For example, when long-lived assets decline in value, a fair value measure is needed to determine any impairment loss.

Statement of Financial Accounting Concepts No. 7 (SFAC No. 7), "Using Cash Flow Information and Present Value in Accounting Measurements," provides a framework for using expected cash flows and present value techniques to develop fair value estimates. These concepts are applied when reliable fair value information is not available for certain assets and liabilities. In the case of an impairment, reliable market values of long-lived assets often are not readily available. In this situation, the principles in *SFAC No. 7* can be applied to derive a fair value estimate for the asset.

As indicated, we presently have a "mixed attribute" system that permits the use of historical cost, fair value, and other valuation bases. Although the historical cost principle continues to be the primary basis for valuation, recording and reporting of fair value information is increasing.[12]

Revenue Recognition Principle

A crucial question for many enterprises is **when** revenue should be recognized. Revenue is generally recognized (1) when **realized** or **realizable** and (2) when **earned**. This approach has often been referred to as the **revenue recognition principle**. Revenues are **realized** when products (goods or services), merchandise, or other assets are exchanged for cash or claims to cash. Revenues are **realizable** when assets received or held are readily convertible into cash or claims to cash. Assets are readily convertible

---

[12]The FASB and IASB currently are working on a project that will result in reporting all financial instruments, both assets and liabilities, at fair value. See for example, FASB, *Financial Accounting Series*, "Preliminary Views on Major Issues Related to Reporting Financial Instruments and Related Assets and Liabilities at Fair Value," No. 204B (December 14, 1999).

when they are salable or interchangeable in an active market at readily determinable prices without significant additional cost.

In addition to the first test (realized or realizable), revenues are not recognized until earned. Revenues are considered **earned** when the entity has substantially accomplished what it must do to be entitled to the benefits represented by the revenues.[13]

Generally, an objective test—confirmation by a sale to independent interests—is used to indicate the point at which revenue is recognized. Usually, only at the date of sale is there an objective and verifiable measure of revenue—the sales price. Any basis for revenue recognition short of actual sale opens the door to wide variations in practice. To give accounting reports uniform meaning, a rule of revenue recognition comparable to the cost rule for asset valuation is essential. **Recognition at the time of sale provides a uniform and reasonable test.**

There are, however, exceptions to the rule, as shown in Illustration 2-3.

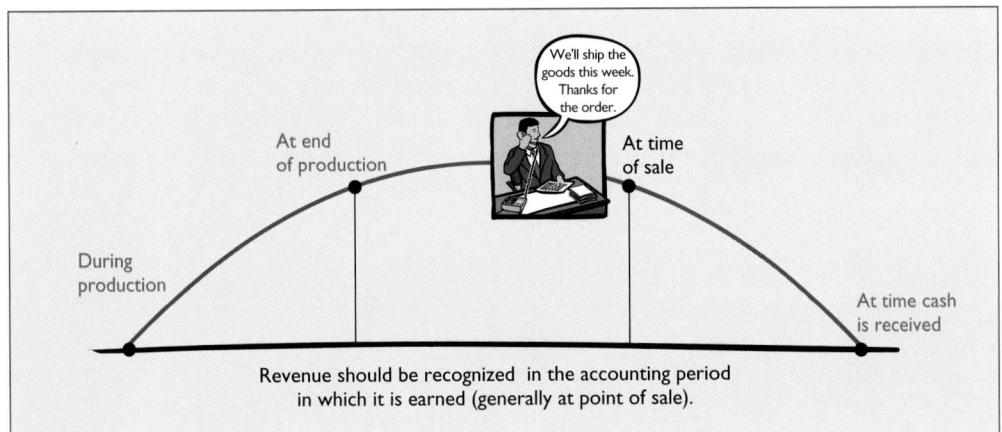

Illustration 2-3
Timing of Revenue Recognition

During Production. **Recognition of revenue is allowed before the contract is completed in certain long-term construction contracts.** In this method revenue is recognized periodically based on the percentage of the job that has been completed, instead of waiting until the entire job has been finished. Although technically a transfer of ownership has not occurred, the earning process is considered substantially completed at various stages as construction progresses. If it is not possible to obtain dependable estimates of cost and progress, then revenue recognition is delayed until the job is completed.

At End of Production. At times, **revenue might be recognized after the production cycle has ended but before the sale takes place.** This is the case when the selling price and the amount are certain. For instance, if products or other assets are salable in an active market at readily determinable prices without significant additional cost, then revenue can be recognized at the completion of production. An example would be the mining of certain minerals for which, once the mineral is mined, a ready market at a standard price exists. The same holds true for some artificial price supports set by the government in establishing agricultural prices.

Upon Receipt of Cash. **Receipt of cash is another basis for revenue recognition.** The cash basis approach is used only when it is impossible to establish the revenue figure at the time of sale because of the uncertainty of collection. One form of the cash basis is the installment sales method, in which payment is required in periodic installments over a long period of time. Its most common use is in the retail field. Farm and home

[13]"Recognition and Measurement in Financial Statements of Business Enterprises," *Statement of Financial Accounting Concepts No. 5* (Stamford, Conn.: FASB, December 1984), par. 83(a) and (b).

equipment and furnishings are typically sold on an installment basis. The installment method is frequently justified on the basis that the risk of not collecting an account receivable is so great that the sale is not sufficient evidence for recognition to take place. In some instances, this reasoning may be valid. Generally, though, if a sale has been completed, it should be recognized; if bad debts are expected, they should be recorded as separate estimates.

Revenue, then, is recorded in the period when realized or realizable and earned. Normally, this is the date of sale. But circumstances may dictate application of the percentage-of-completion approach, the end-of-production approach, or the receipt-of-cash approach.

WHAT DO THE NUMBERS MEAN?

NO TAKE BACKS!

Investors in **Lucent Technologies** got an unpleasant surprise when the company was forced to restate its financial results in a recent quarter. What happened? Lucent violated one of the fundamental criteria for revenue recognition—the "no take-back" rule. This rule holds that revenue should not be booked on inventory that is shipped if the customer can return it at some point in the future. In this particular case, Lucent agreed to take back shipped inventory from its distributors, if the distributors are unable to sell the items to their customers.

Lucent booked the sales on the shipped goods, which helped it report continued sales growth. However, Lucent investors got a nasty surprise when those goods were returned by the distributors. The restatement erased $679 million in revenues, turning an operating profit into a loss. In response to this bad news, Lucent's stock price declined $1.31 per share or 8.5 percent.

Lucent has since changed its policy so that it will now record inventory as sold only if the final customer has bought the equipment, not when the inventory is shipped to the distributor. The lesson for investors is to review a company's revenue recognition policy for indications that revenues are being overstated due to generous return provisions for inventory. And remember, no take-backs!

Source: Adapted from S. Young, "Lucent Slashes First Quarter Outlook, Erases Revenue from Latest Quarter," *Wall Street Journal, Interactive Edition* (December 22, 2000).

Matching Principle

In recognizing expenses, the approach followed is, "Let the expense follow the revenues." Expenses are recognized not when wages are paid, or when the work is performed, or when a product is produced, but when the work (service) or the product actually makes its contribution to revenue. Thus, expense recognition is tied to revenue recognition. This practice is referred to as the **matching principle** because it dictates that **efforts (expenses) be matched with accomplishment (revenues) whenever it is reasonable and practicable to do so**.

For those costs for which it is difficult to adopt some type of rational association with revenue, some other approach must be developed. Often, a "rational and systematic" allocation policy is used that will approximate the matching principle. This type of expense recognition pattern involves assumptions about the benefits that are being received as well as the cost associated with those benefits. The cost of a long-lived asset, for example, must be allocated over all of the accounting periods during which the asset is used because the asset contributes to the generation of revenue throughout its useful life.

Some costs are charged to the current period as expenses (or losses) simply because no connection with revenue can be determined. Examples of these types of costs are officers' salaries and other administrative expenses.

Costs are generally classified into two groups: **product costs** and **period costs**. **Product costs** such as material, labor, and overhead attach to the product. They are carried into future periods if the revenue from the product is recognized in subsequent periods. **Period costs** such as officers' salaries and other administrative expenses are charged off immediately, even though benefits associated with these costs occur in the future, because no direct relationship between cost and revenue can be determined. These expense recognition procedures are summarized in Illustration 2-4.

Type of Cost	Relationship	Recognition
Product costs: • Material • Labor • Overhead	Direct relationship between cost and revenue.	Recognize in period of revenue (matching).
Period costs: • Salaries • Administrative costs	No direct relationship between cost and revenue.	Expense as incurred.

Illustration 2-4
Expense Recognition

The conceptual validity of the matching principle has been a subject of debate. **A major concern is that matching permits certain costs to be deferred and treated as assets on the balance sheet when in fact these costs may not have future benefits.** If abused, this principle permits the balance sheet to become a "dumping ground" for unmatched costs. In addition, there appears to be no objective definition of "systematic and rational."

HOLLYWOOD ACCOUNTING

WHAT DO THE NUMBERS MEAN?

The problem of expense recognition is as complex as that of revenue recognition, as illustrated by Hollywood accounting. Major motion picture studios have been allowed to capitalize advertising and marketing costs and to amortize these costs against revenues over the life of the film. As a result, many investors have suggested that the studios' profit numbers were overstated. Under a new GAAP standard, these costs now must be amortized over no more than three months; in many cases, they have to be expensed immediately. Similarly, the costs related to abandoned projects often were allocated to overhead and spread out over the lives of the successful projects. Not anymore. These costs now must be expensed as they are incurred.

Here is a rough estimate of the amounts of capitalized advertising costs some major studios will have to write off.

Studio (Parent Company)	Capitalized Advertising (in millions)
Columbia Tri-Star (Sony)	$200
Paramount (Viacom)	200
20th Century Fox (News Corp)	150

Why the more conservative approach? A lot has to do with a stricter application of the definitions of assets and expenses. While many argue that advertising and marketing costs have future service potential, difficulty in reliably measuring these benefits suggests they are not assets. Therefore, a very short amortization period or immediate write-off is justified.

Under these new guidelines, investors will have more reliable measures for assessing the performance of companies in this industry.

Full Disclosure Principle

In deciding what information to report, the general practice of providing information that is of sufficient importance to influence the judgment and decisions of an informed user is followed. Often referred to as the **full disclosure principle**, it recognizes that the nature and amount of information included in financial reports reflects a series of judgmental trade-offs. These trade-offs strive for (1) sufficient detail to disclose matters that **make a difference** to users, yet (2) sufficient condensation to make the **information understandable**, keeping in mind costs of preparing and using it.

Information about financial position, income, cash flows, and investments can be found in one of three places: (1) within the main body of financial statements, (2) in the notes to those statements, or (3) as supplementary information.

The **financial statements** are a formalized, structured means of communicating financial information. To be recognized in the main body of financial statements, **an item should meet the definition of a basic element, be measurable with sufficient certainty, and be relevant and reliable.**[14]

Disclosure is not a substitute for proper accounting. As a former chief accountant of the SEC recently noted: Good disclosure does not cure bad accounting any more than an adjective or adverb can be used without, or in place of, a noun or verb. Thus, for example, cash basis accounting for cost of goods sold is misleading, even if accrual basis amounts were disclosed in the notes to the financial statements.

The **notes to financial statements** generally amplify or explain the items presented in the main body of the statements. If the information in the main body of the financial statements gives an incomplete picture of the performance and position of the enterprise, additional information that is needed to complete the picture should be included in the notes. Information in the notes does not have to be quantifiable, nor does it need to qualify as an element. Notes can be partially or totally narrative. Examples of notes are: descriptions of the accounting policies and methods used in measuring the elements reported in the statements; explanations of uncertainties and contingencies; and statistics and details too voluminous for inclusion in the statements. The notes are not only helpful but also essential to understanding the enterprise's performance and position.

WHAT DO THE NUMBERS MEAN?

HOW'S YOUR LEVERAGE?

A classic illustration of the problem of determining adequate disclosure guidelines is the question on what banks should disclose about loans made for highly leveraged transactions such as leveraged buyouts. Investors want to know what percentage of a bank's loans are of this risky type. The problem is what do we mean by "leveraged"? As one regulator noted, "If it looks leveraged, it probably is leveraged, but most of us would be hard-pressed to come up with a definition." Is a loan to a company with a debt to equity ratio of 4 to 1 highly leveraged? Or is high leverage 8 to 1 or 10 to 1? The problem is complicated because some highly leveraged companies have cash flows that cover interest payments. Therefore, they are not as risky as they might appear. In short, providing the appropriate disclosure to help investors and regulators differentiate risky from safe is difficult.

Supplementary information may include details or amounts that present a different perspective from that adopted in the financial statements. It may be quantifiable information that is high in relevance but low in reliability. Or it may be information that is helpful but not essential. One example of supplementary information is the data

[14]*SFAC No. 5,* par. 63.

and schedules provided by oil and gas companies: Typically they provide information on proven reserves as well as the related discounted cash flows.

Supplementary information may also include management's explanation of the financial information and its discussion of the significance of that information. For example, many business combinations have produced innumerable conglomerate-type business organizations and financing arrangements that demand new and peculiar accounting and reporting practices and principles. In each of these situations, the same problem must be faced: making sure that enough information is presented to ensure that the **reasonably prudent investor** will not be misled.

The content, arrangement, and display of financial statements, along with other facets of full disclosure, are discussed in Chapters 4, 5, 6, and 17.

Constraints

In providing information with the qualitative characteristics that make it useful, two overriding **constraints** must be considered: (1) the **cost-benefit relationship** and (2) **materiality**. Two other less dominant yet important constraints that are part of the reporting environment are **industry practices** and **conservatism**.

OBJECTIVE 8
Describe the impact that constraints have on reporting accounting information.

Cost-Benefit Relationship

Too often, users assume that information is a cost-free commodity. But preparers and providers of accounting information know that it is not. Therefore, the **cost-benefit relationship** must be considered: The costs of providing the information must be weighed against the benefits that can be derived from using the information. Standards-setting bodies and governmental agencies use cost-benefit analysis before making their informational requirements final. In order to justify requiring a particular measurement or disclosure, the benefits perceived to be derived from it must exceed the costs perceived to be associated with it.

The following remark, made by a corporate executive about a proposed standard, was addressed to the FASB: "In all my years in the financial arena, I have never seen such an absolutely ridiculous proposal. . . . To dignify these 'actuarial' estimates by recording them as assets and liabilities would be virtually unthinkable except for the fact that the FASB has done equally stupid things in the past. . . . For God's sake, use common sense just this once."[15] Although this remark is extreme, it does indicate the frustration expressed by members of the business community about standards setting and whether the benefits of a given standard exceed the costs.

The difficulty in cost-benefit analysis is that the costs and especially the benefits are not always evident or measurable. The costs are of several kinds, including costs of collecting and processing, costs of disseminating, costs of auditing, costs of potential litigation, costs of disclosure to competitors, and costs of analysis and interpretation. Benefits accrue to preparers (in terms of greater management control and access to capital) and to users (in terms of better information for allocation of resources, tax assessment, and rate regulation). But benefits are generally more difficult to quantify than are costs.

Most recently, the AICPA Special Committee on Financial Reporting submitted the following **constraints to limit the costs of reporting**.

1. Business reporting should exclude information outside of management's expertise or for which management is not the best source, such as information about competitors.

2. Management should not be required to report information that would significantly harm the company's competitive position.

---

[15]"Decision-Usefulness: The Overriding Objective," *FASB Viewpoints*, October 19, 1983, p. 4.

③ Management should not be required to provide forecasted financial statements. Rather, management should provide information that helps users forecast for themselves the company's financial future.

④ Other than for financial statements, management need only report the information it knows. That is, management should be under no obligation to gather information it does not have, or need, to manage the business.

⑤ Certain elements of business reporting should be presented only if users and management agree they should be reported—a concept of flexible reporting.

⑥ Companies should not have to report forward-looking information unless there are effective deterrents to unwarranted litigation that discourages companies from doing so.

Materiality

The constraint of **materiality** relates to an item's impact on a firm's overall financial operations. An item is material if its inclusion or omission would influence or change the judgment of a reasonable person.[16] It is immaterial and, therefore, irrelevant if it would have no impact on a decision maker. In short, **it must make a difference** or it need not be disclosed. The point involved here is one of **relative size and importance**. If the amount involved is significant when compared with the other revenues and expenses, assets and liabilities, or net income of the entity, sound and acceptable standards should be followed. If the amount is so small that it is unimportant when compared with other items, application of a particular standard may be considered of less importance.

It is difficult to provide firm guides in judging when a given item is or is not material because materiality varies both with relative amount and with relative importance. For example, the two sets of numbers presented below illustrate relative size.

Illustration 2-5

Materiality Comparison

	Company A	Company B
Sales	$10,000,000	$100,000
Costs and expenses	9,000,000	90,000
Income from operations	$ 1,000,000	$ 10,000
Unusual gain	$ 20,000	$ 5,000

During the period in question, the revenues and expenses, and therefore the net incomes of Company A and Company B, have been proportional. Each has had an unusual gain. In looking at the abbreviated income figures for Company A, it does not appear significant whether the amount of the unusual gain is set out separately or merged with the regular operating income. It is only 2 percent of the net income and, if merged, would not seriously distort the net income figure. Company B has had an unusual gain of only $5,000, but it is relatively much more significant than the larger gain realized by A. For Company B, an item of $5,000 amounts to 50 percent of its net income. Obviously, the inclusion of such an item in ordinary operating income would

---

[16]*SFAC No. 2* (par. 132) sets forth the essence of materiality: "The omission or misstatement of an item in a financial report is material if, in the light of surrounding circumstances, the magnitude of the item is such that it is probable that the judgment of a reasonable person relying upon the report would have been changed or influenced by the inclusion or correction of the item." This same concept of materiality has been adopted by the auditing profession. See "Audit Risk and Materiality in Conducting an Audit," *Statement on Auditing Standards No. 47* (New York: AICPA, 1983), par. 6.

affect the amount of that income materially. Thus we see the importance of the **relative size** of an item in determining its materiality.

Companies and their auditors for the most part have adopted the general rule of thumb that anything under 5 percent of net income is considered not material. Recently the SEC has indicated that it is acceptable to use this percentage for an initial assessment of materiality, but that other factors must also be considered.[17] For example, companies can no longer fail to record items in order to meet consensus analysts' earnings numbers, preserve a positive earnings trend, convert a loss to a profit or vice versa, increase management compensation, or hide an illegal transaction like a bribe. In other words, **both quantitative and qualitative factors must be considered in determining whether an item is material**.

The SEC has also indicated that in determining materiality companies must consider each misstatement separately and the aggregate effect of all misstatements. For example, at one time, **General Dynamics** disclosed that its Resources Group had improved its earnings by $5.8 million at the same time that one of its other subsidiaries had taken write-offs of $6.7 million. Although both numbers were far larger than the $2.5 million that General Dynamics as a whole earned for the year, neither was disclosed as unusual because the net effect on earnings was considered immaterial. This practice is now prohibited because each item must be considered separately. In addition, even though an individual item may be immaterial, it may be considered material when added to other immaterial items. Such items must be disclosed.

Materiality is a factor in a great many internal accounting decisions, too. The amount of classification required in a subsidiary expense ledger, the degree of accuracy required in prorating expenses among the departments of a business, and the extent to which adjustments should be made for accrued and deferred items, are examples of judgments that should finally be determined on a basis of reasonableness and practicability, which is the materiality constraint sensibly applied. Only by **the exercise of good judgment and professional expertise** can reasonable and appropriate answers be found.

Industry Practices

Another practical consideration is **industry practices**. **The peculiar nature of some industries and business concerns** sometimes requires departure from basic theory. In the public utility industry, noncurrent assets are reported first on the balance sheet to highlight the industry's capital-intensive nature. Agricultural crops are often reported at market value because it is costly to develop accurate cost figures on individual crops. Such variations from basic theory are not many, yet they do exist. Whenever we find what appears to be a violation of basic accounting theory, we should determine whether it is explained by some peculiar feature of the type of business involved before we criticize the procedures followed.

Conservatism

Few conventions in accounting are as misunderstood as the constraint of conservatism. **Conservatism** means **when in doubt choose the solution that will be least likely to overstate assets and income**. Note that there is nothing in the conservatism convention urging that net assets or net income be *understated*. Unfortunately it has been interpreted by some to mean just that. All that conservatism does, properly applied, is provide a very reasonable guide in difficult situations: refrain from overstatement of net income and net assets. Examples of conservatism in accounting are the use of the lower of cost or market approach in valuing inventories and the rule that accrued net losses should be recognized on firm purchase commitments for goods for inventory. If the issue is in doubt, it is better to understate than overstate net income and net assets. Of course, if there is no doubt, there is no need to apply this constraint.

INTERNATIONAL INSIGHT

In Japan, assets are often undervalued and liabilities overvalued by companies. These practices reduce the demand for dividends and protect creditors in event of a default.

---

[17]"Materiality," *SEC Staff Accounting Bulletin No. 99* (Washington, D.C.: SEC, 1999).

Summary of the Structure

Illustration 2-6 presents the conceptual framework discussed in this chapter. It is similar to Illustration 2-1, except that it provides additional information for each level. We cannot overemphasize the usefulness of this conceptual framework in helping to understand many of the problem areas that are examined in subsequent chapters.

Illustration 2-6

Conceptual Framework
for Financial Reporting

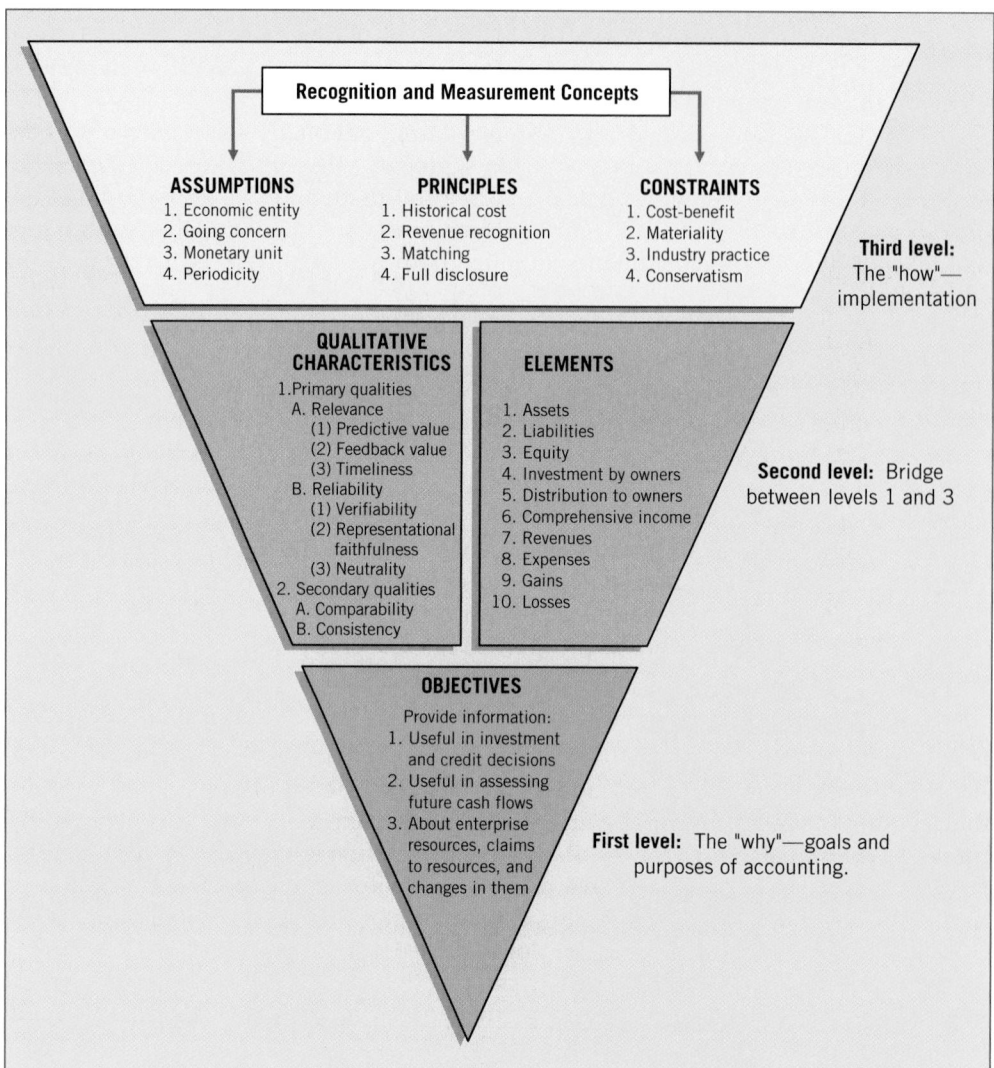

SUMMARY OF LEARNING OBJECTIVES

❶ **Describe the usefulness of a conceptual framework.** A conceptual framework is needed to (1) build on and relate to an established body of concepts and objectives, (2) provide a framework for solving new and emerging practical problems, (3) increase financial statement users' understanding of and confidence in financial reporting, and (4) enhance comparability among companies' financial statements.

❷ **Describe the FASB's efforts to construct a conceptual framework.** The FASB has issued six Statements of Financial Accounting Concepts that relate to financial reporting for business enterprises. These concept statements provide the framework for the conceptual framework. They include objectives, qualitative characteristics, and elements. In addition, measurement and recognition concepts are developed.

❸ Understand the objectives of financial reporting. The objectives of financial reporting are to provide information that is (1) useful to those making investment and credit decisions who have a reasonable understanding of business activities; (2) helpful to present and potential investors, creditors, and others in assessing future cash flows; and (3) about economic resources and the claims to and changes in them.

❹ Identify the qualitative characteristics of accounting information. The overriding criterion by which accounting choices can be judged is decision usefulness—that is, providing information that is most useful for decision making. Relevance and reliability are the two primary qualities, and comparability and consistency are the secondary qualities, that make accounting information useful for decision making.

❺ Define the basic elements of financial statements. The basic elements of financial statements are: (1) assets, (2) liabilities, (3) equity, (4) investments by owners, (5) distributions to owners, (6) comprehensive income, (7) revenues, (8) expenses, (9) gains, and (10) losses. These ten elements are defined on pages 32 and 33.

❻ Describe the basic assumptions of accounting. Four basic assumptions underlying the financial accounting structure are: (1) *Economic entity:* the assumption that the activity of a business enterprise can be kept separate and distinct from its owners and any other business unit. (2) *Going concern:* the assumption that the business enterprise will have a long life. (3) *Monetary unit:* the assumption that money is the common denominator by which economic activity is conducted, and that the monetary unit provides an appropriate basis for measurement and analysis. (4) *Periodicity:* the assumption that the economic activities of an enterprise can be divided into artificial time periods.

❼ Explain the application of the basic principles of accounting. (1) *Historical cost principle:* Existing GAAP requires that most assets and liabilities be accounted for and reported on the basis of acquisition price. (2) *Revenue recognition:* Revenue is generally recognized when (a) realized or realizable and (b) earned. (3) *Matching principle:* Expenses are recognized when the work (service) or the product actually makes its contribution to revenue. (4) *Full disclosure principle:* Accountants follow the general practice of providing information that is of sufficient importance to influence the judgment and decisions of an informed user.

❽ Describe the impact that constraints have on reporting accounting information. The constraints and their impact are: (1) *Cost-benefit relationship:* The costs of providing the information must be weighed against the benefits that can be derived from using the information. (2) *Materiality:* Sound and acceptable standards should be followed if the amount involved is significant when compared with the other revenues and expenses, assets and liabilities, or net income of the entity. (3) *Industry practices:* Follow the general practices in the firm's industry, which sometimes requires departure from basic theory. (4) *Conservatism:* When in doubt, choose the solution that will be least likely to overstate net assets and net income.

KEY TERMS

assumption, *34*
comparability, *31*
conceptual framework, *26*
conservatism, *43*
consistency, *31*
constraints, *41*
cost-benefit relationship, *41*
decision usefulness, *28*
earned (revenue), *37*
economic entity
   assumption, *34*
elements, basic, *32*
feedback value, *30*
financial statements, *40*
full disclosure principle, *40*
going concern
   assumption, *34*
historical cost principle, *35*
industry practices, *43*
matching principle, *38*
materiality, *42*
monetary unit
   assumption, *35*
neutrality, *31*
notes to financial
   statements, *40*
objectives of financial
   reporting, *28*
period costs, *39*
periodicity assumption, *35*
predictive value, *30*
principles of accounting, *35*
product costs, *39*
qualitative
   characteristics, *29*
realizable (revenue), *36*
realized (revenue), *36*
relevance, *29*
reliability, *29*
representational
   faithfulness, *31*
revenue recognition
   principle, *36*
supplementary
   information, *40*
timeliness, *30*
understandability, *29*
verifiability, *30*

REVIEW EXERCISE

You are engaged to review the accounting records of Jeremy Roenick Corporation prior to the closing of the revenue and expense accounts as of December 31, the end of the current fiscal year. The following information comes to your attention.

1. During the current year, Jeremy Roenick Corporation changed its policy in regard to expensing purchases of small tools. In the past, these purchases had been expensed because they amounted to less than 2% of net income. Now, the president has decided that capitalization and subsequent depreciation should be followed. It is expected that purchases of small tools will not fluctuate greatly from year to year.

2. Jeremy Roenick Corporation constructed a warehouse at a cost of $1,000,000. The company had been depreciating the asset on a straight-line basis over 10 years. In the current year, the controller doubled depreciation expense because the replacement cost of the warehouse had increased significantly.

3. When the balance sheet was prepared, detailed information as to the amount of cash on deposit in each of several banks was omitted. Only the total amount of cash under a caption "Cash in banks" was presented.

4. On July 15 of the current year, Jeremy Roenick Corporation purchased an undeveloped tract of land at a cost of $320,000. The company spent $80,000 in subdividing the land and getting it ready for sale. An appraisal of the property at the end of the year indicated that the land was now worth $500,000. Although none of the lots were sold, the company recognized revenue of $180,000, less related expenses of $80,000, for a net income on the project of $100,000.

5. For a number of years the company used the FIFO method for inventory valuation purposes. During the current year, the president noted that all the other companies in their industry had switched to the LIFO method. The company decided not to switch to LIFO because net income would decrease $830,000.

Instructions

State whether or not you agree with the decisions made by Jeremy Roenick Corporation. Support your answers with reference, whenever possible, to the generally accepted principles, assumptions, and constraints applicable in the circumstances.

SOLUTION TO REVIEW EXERCISE

1. From the facts it is difficult to determine whether to agree or disagree. Consistency, of course, is violated in this situation, although its violation may not be material. Furthermore, that the corporation changed accounting policies regarding the treatment of small tools cannot be judged good or bad, but would depend on the circumstances. In this case, it seems that the result will be approximately the same whether the corporation capitalizes and expenses, or simply expenses each period, since the purchases are fairly uniform. Perhaps from a cost standpoint (expediency), it might be best to continue the present policy rather than become involved in detailed depreciation schedules, assuming that purchases remain fairly uniform. On the other hand, the president may believe there is a significant unrecorded asset that should be shown on the balance sheet. If such is the case, capitalization and subsequent depreciation would be more appropriate.

2. Disagree. At the present time, accountants do not recognize price level or current value adjustments in the accounts. Hence it is misleading to deviate from the cost principle, because conjecture or opinion can take place. Also, depreciation is not so much a matter of valuation as it is a means of cost allocation. Assets are not depreciated on the basis of a decline in their fair market value, but are depreciated on the basis of a systematic charge of expired cost against revenues.

3. Agree. The full disclosure principle recognizes that reasonable condensation and summarization of the details of a corporation's operations and financial position are essential to readability and comprehension. Thus, in determining what is full disclosure, the accountant must decide whether omission will cause a misleading inference by the reader of the financial statements. Only the total amount of cash is generally presented on a balance sheet, unless some special circumstance is involved (such as a possible restriction on the use of the cash). In most cases, however, the company's presentation would be considered appropriate and in accordance with the full disclosure principle.

4. Disagree. The historical cost principle indicates that assets and liabilities are accounted for on the basis of cost. If sales value were selected, for example, it would be extremely

difficult to establish an appraisal value for the given item without selling it. Note, too, that the revenue recognition principle provides guidance on when revenue should be recognized. Revenue should be recognized when (1) realized or realizable and (2) earned. In this case, the revenue was not earned because the critical event "sale of the land" had not occurred.

5. From the facts it is difficult to determine whether to agree or disagree with the president. The president's approach is not a violation of any principle. Consistency requires that accounting entities give accountable events the same accounting treatment from period to period for a given business enterprise. It says nothing concerning consistency of accounting principles among business enterprises. From a comparability viewpoint, it might be useful to report the information on a LIFO basis, but as indicated above, there is no requirement to do so.

QUESTIONS

1 What is a conceptual framework? Why is a conceptual framework necessary in financial accounting?

2 What are the primary objectives of financial reporting as indicated in *Statement of Financial Accounting Concepts No. 1?*

3 What is meant by the term "qualitative characteristics of accounting information"?

4 Briefly describe the two primary qualities of useful accounting information.

5 According to the FASB conceptual framework, the objectives of financial reporting for business enterprises are based on the needs of the users of financial statements. Explain the level of sophistication that the Board assumes about the users of financial statements.

6 What is the distinction between comparability and consistency?

7 Why is it necessary to develop a definitional framework for the basic elements of accounting?

8 Expenses, losses, and distributions to owners are all decreases in net assets. What are the distinctions among them?

9 Revenues, gains, and investments by owners are all increases in net assets. What are the distinctions among them?

10 What are the four basic assumptions that underlie the financial accounting structure?

11 The life of a business is divided into specific time periods, usually a year, to measure results of operations for each such time period and to portray financial conditions at the end of each period.

(a) This practice is based on the accounting assumption that the life of the business consists of a series of time periods and that it is possible to measure accurately the results of operations for each period. Comment on the validity and necessity of this assumption.

(b) What has been the effect of this practice on accounting? What is its relation to the accrual system? What influence has it had on accounting entries and methodology?

12 What is the basic accounting problem created by the monetary unit assumption when there is significant inflation? What appears to be the FASB position on a stable monetary unit?

13 The chairman of the board of directors of the company for which you are chief accountant has told you that he has little use for accounting figures based on cost. He believes that replacement values are of far more significance to the board of directors than "out-of-date costs." Present some arguments to convince him that accounting data should still be based on cost.

14 When is revenue generally recognized? Why has that date been chosen as the point at which to recognize the revenue resulting from the entire producing and selling process?

15 Magnus Eatery operates a catering service specializing in business luncheons for large corporations. Magnus requires customers to place their orders 2 weeks in advance of the scheduled events. Magnus bills its customers on the tenth day of the month following the date of service and requires that payment be made within 30 days of the billing date. Conceptually, when should Magnus recognize revenue related to its catering service?

16 What is the difference between realized and realizable? Give an example of where the concept of realizable is used to recognize revenue.

17 What is the justification for the following deviations from recognizing revenue at the time of sale?

(a) Installment sales method of recognizing revenue.

(b) Recognition of revenue at completion of production for certain agricultural products.

(c) The percentage-of-completion basis in long-term construction contracts.

18 Jane Hull Company paid $135,000 for a machine in 2003. The Accumulated Depreciation account has a balance of $46,500 at the present time. The company could sell the machine today for $150,000. The company president believes that the company has a "right to this gain." What does the president mean by this statement? Do you agree?

19 Three expense recognition methods (associating cause and effect, systematic and rational allocation, and immediate recognition) were discussed in the text under the matching principle. Indicate the basic nature of each of these types of expenses and give two examples of each.

20 *Statement of Financial Accounting Concepts No. 5* identifies four characteristics that an item must have before it is recognized in the financial statements. What are these four characteristics?

21 Briefly describe the types of information concerning financial position, income, and cash flows that might be provided: (a) within the main body of the financial statements, (b) in the notes to the financial statements, or (c) as supplementary information.

22 In January 2003, Alan Jackson Inc. doubled the amount of its outstanding stock by selling on the market an additional 10,000 shares to finance an expansion of the business. You propose that this information be shown by a footnote on the balance sheet as of December 31, 2002. The president objects, claiming that this sale took place after December 31, 2002, and, therefore, should not be shown. Explain your position.

23 Describe the two major constraints inherent in the presentation of accounting information.

24 What are some of the costs of providing accounting information? What are some of the benefits of accounting information? Describe the cost-benefit factors that should be considered when new accounting standards are being proposed.

25 How are materiality (and immateriality) related to the proper presentation of financial statements? What factors and measures should be considered in assessing the materiality of a misstatement in the presentation of a financial statement?

26 The treasurer of Joan Osborne Co. has heard that conservatism is a doctrine that is followed in accounting and, therefore, proposes that several policies be followed that are conservative in nature. State your opinion with respect to each of the policies listed below.

(a) The company gives a 2-year warranty to its customers on all products sold. The estimated warranty costs incurred from this year's sales should be entered as an expense this year instead of an expense in the period in the future when the warranty is made good.

(b) When sales are made on account, there is always uncertainty about whether the accounts are collectible. Therefore, the treasurer recommends recording the sale when the cash is received from the customers.

(c) A personal liability lawsuit is pending against the company. The treasurer believes there is an even chance that the company will lose the suit and have to pay damages of $200,000 to $300,000. The treasurer recommends that a loss be recorded and a liability created in the amount of $300,000.

(d) The inventory should be valued at "cost or market, whichever is lower" because the losses from price declines should be recognized in the accounts in the period in which the price decline takes place.

BRIEF EXERCISES

BE2-1 Discuss whether the changes described in each of the cases below require recognition in the CPA's report as to consistency. (Assume that the amounts are material.)

(a) After 3 years of computing depreciation under an accelerated method for income tax purposes and under the straight-line method for reporting purposes, the company adopted an accelerated method for reporting purposes.

(b) The company disposed of one of the two subsidiaries that had been included in its consolidated statements for prior years.

(c) The estimated remaining useful life of plant property was reduced because of obsolescence.

(d) The company is using an inventory valuation method that is different from those used by all other companies in its industry.

BE2-2 Identify which qualitative characteristic of accounting information is best described in each item below. (Do not use relevance and reliability.)

(a) The annual reports of Garbo Corp. are audited by certified public accountants.

(b) Klamoth Corp. and Kutenai, Inc. both use the FIFO cost flow assumption.
(c) Claudio Abbado Corp. has used straight-line depreciation since it began operations.
(d) Augusta Corp. issues its quarterly reports immediately after each quarter ends.

BE2-3 For each item below, indicate to which category of elements of financial statements it belongs.

(a) Retained earnings	**(e)** Depreciation	**(h)** Dividends
(b) Sales	**(f)** Loss on sale of equipment	**(i)** Gain on sale of investment
(c) Additional paid-in capital	**(g)** Interest payable	**(j)** Issuance of common stock
(d) Inventory		

BE2-4 Identify which basic assumption of accounting is best described in each item below.

(a) The economic activities of Kristi Thomas Corp. are divided into 12-month periods for the purpose of issuing annual reports.
(b) Watson Brewer, Inc. does not adjust amounts in its financial statements for the effects of inflation.
(c) Jessi Ramsey Company reports current and noncurrent classifications in its balance sheet.
(d) The economic activities of Mallory Pike Corporation and its subsidiaries are merged for accounting and reporting purposes.

BE2-5 Identify which basic principle of accounting is best described in each item below.

(a) New Hampshire Corporation reports revenue in its income statement when it is earned instead of when the cash is collected.
(b) Vermont Enterprise recognizes depreciation expense for a machine over the 5-year period during which that machine helps the company earn revenue.
(c) Massachusetts, Inc. reports information about pending lawsuits in the notes to its financial statements.
(d) Rhode Island Farms reports land on its balance sheet at the amount paid to acquire it, even though the estimated fair market value is greater.

BE2-6 Which constraints on accounting information are illustrated by the items below?

(a) Zip's Farms, Inc. reports agricultural crops on its balance sheet at market value.
(b) Crimson Tide Corporation does not accrue a contingent lawsuit gain of $650,000.
(c) Wildcat Company does not disclose any information in the notes to the financial statements unless the value of the information to financial statement users exceeds the expense of gathering it.
(d) Sun Devil Corporation expenses the cost of wastebaskets in the year they are acquired.

BE2-7 Presented below are three different transactions related to materiality. Explain whether you would classify these transactions as material.

(a) Marcus Co. has reported a positive trend in earnings over the last 3 years. In the current year, it reduces its bad debt allowance to ensure another positive earnings year. The impact of this adjustment is equal to 3% of net income.
(b) Sosa Co. has an extraordinary gain of $3.1 million on the sale of plant assets and a $3.3 million loss on the sale of investments. It decides to net the gain and loss because the net effect is considered immaterial. Sosa Co.'s income for the current year was $10 million.
(c) Seliz Co. expenses all capital equipment under $25,000 on the basis that it is immaterial. The company has followed this practice for a number of years.

BE2-8 If the going concern assumption is not made in accounting, what difference does it make in the amounts shown in the financial statements for the following items?

(a) Land.
(b) Unamortized bond premium.
(c) Depreciation expense on equipment.
(d) Merchandise inventory.
(e) Prepaid insurance.

BE2-9 What accounting assumption, principle, or modifying convention does Accra Co. use in each of the situations below?

(a) Accra Co. uses the lower of cost or market basis to value inventories.
(b) Accra was involved in litigation with Kinshasa Co. over a product malfunction. This litigation is disclosed in the financial statements.
(c) Accra allocates the cost of its depreciable assets over the life it expects to receive revenue from these assets.
(d) Accra records the purchase of a new IBM PC at its cash equivalent price.

BE2-10 Explain how you would decide whether to record each of the following expenditures as an asset or an expense. Assume all items are material.

(a) Legal fees paid in connection with the purchase of land are $1,500.
(b) Benjamin Bratt, Inc. paves the driveway leading to the office building at a cost of $21,000.
(c) A meat market purchases a meat-grinding machine at a cost of $3,500.
(d) On June 30, Alan and Alda, medical doctors, pay 6 months' office rent to cover the month of July and the next 5 months.
(e) Tim Taylor's Hardware Company pays $9,000 in wages to laborers for construction on a building to be used in the business.
(f) Nancy Kwan's Florists pays wages of $2,100 for November to an employee who serves as driver of their delivery truck.

EXERCISES

E2-1 **(Qualitative Characteristics)** *SFAC No. 2* identifies the qualitative characteristics that make accounting information useful. Presented below are a number of questions related to these qualitative characteristics and underlying constraints.

(a) What is the quality of information that enables users to confirm or correct prior expectations?
(b) Identify the two overall or pervasive constraints developed in *SFAC No. 2*.
(c) The chairman of the SEC at one time noted, "If it becomes accepted or expected that accounting principles are determined or modified in order to secure purposes other than economic measurement, we assume a grave risk that confidence in the credibility of our financial information system will be undermined." Which qualitative characteristic of accounting information should ensure that such a situation will not occur? (Do not use reliability.)
(d) Billy Owens Corp. switches from FIFO to average cost to FIFO over a 2-year period. Which qualitative characteristic of accounting information is not followed?
(e) Assume that the profession permits the savings and loan industry to defer losses on investments it sells, because immediate recognition of the loss may have adverse economic consequences on the industry. Which qualitative characteristic of accounting information is not followed? (Do not use relevance or reliability.)
(f) What are the two primary qualities that make accounting information useful for decision making?
(g) Rex Chapman, Inc. does not issue its first-quarter report until after the second quarter's results are reported. Which qualitative characteristic of accounting is not followed? (Do not use relevance.)
(h) Predictive value is an ingredient of which of the two primary qualities that make accounting information useful for decision making purposes?
(i) Ronald Coles, Inc. is the only company in its industry to depreciate its plant assets on a straight-line basis. Which qualitative characteristic of accounting information may not be followed? (Do not use industry practices.)
(j) Jeff Malone Company has attempted to determine the replacement cost of its inventory. Three different appraisers arrive at substantially different amounts for this value. The president, nevertheless, decides to report the middle value for external reporting purposes. Which qualitative characteristic of information is lacking in these data? (Do not use reliability or representational faithfulness.)

 **E2-2 (Qualitative Characteristics)** The qualitative characteristics that make accounting information useful for decision-making purposes are as follows.

Relevance	Timeliness	Representational faithfulness
Reliability	Verifiability	Comparability
Predictive value	Neutrality	Consistency
Feedback value		

Instructions
Identify the appropriate qualitative characteristic(s) to be used given the information provided below.

(a) Qualitative characteristic being employed when companies in the same industry are using the same accounting principles.
(b) Quality of information that confirms users' earlier expectations.
(c) Imperative for providing comparisons of a firm from period to period.
(d) Ignores the economic consequences of a standard or rule.
(e) Requires a high degree of consensus among individuals on a given measurement.
(f) Predictive value is an ingredient of this primary quality of information.
(g) Two qualitative characteristics that are related to both relevance and reliability.
(h) Neutrality is an ingredient of this primary quality of accounting information.
(i) Two primary qualities that make accounting information useful for decision-making purposes.
(j) Issuance of interim reports is an example of what primary ingredient of relevance?

E2-3 (Elements of Financial Statements) Ten interrelated elements that are most directly related to measuring the performance and financial status of an enterprise are provided below.

Assets	Distributions to owners	Expenses
Liabilities	Comprehensive income	Gains
Equity	Revenues	Losses
Investments by owners		

Instructions
Identify the element or elements associated with the 12 items below.

(a) Arises from peripheral or incidental transactions.
(b) Obligation to transfer resources arising from a past transaction.
(c) Increases ownership interest.
(d) Declares and pays cash dividends to owners.
(e) Increases in net assets in a period from nonowner sources.
(f) Items characterized by service potential or future economic benefit.
(g) Equals increase in assets less liabilities during the year, after adding distributions to owners and subtracting investments by owners.
(h) Arises from income statement activities that constitute the entity's ongoing major or central operations.
(i) Residual interest in the assets of the enterprise after deducting its liabilities.
(j) Increases assets during a period through sale of product.
(k) Decreases assets during the period by transferring enterprise assets to owners.
(l) Includes all changes in equity during the period, except those resulting from investments by owners and distributions to owners.

 **E2-4 (Assumptions, Principles, and Constraints)** Presented below are the assumptions, principles, and constraints used in this chapter.

1. Economic entity assumption	5. Historical cost principle	9. Materiality
2. Going concern assumption	6. Matching principle	10. Industry practices
3. Monetary unit assumption	7. Full disclosure principle	11. Conservatism
4. Periodicity assumption	8. Cost-benefit relationship	

Instructions

Identify by number the accounting assumption, principle, or constraint that describes each situation below. Do not use a number more than once.

(a) Allocates expenses to revenues in the proper period.
(b) Indicates that market value changes subsequent to purchase are not recorded in the accounts. (Do not use revenue recognition principle.)
(c) Ensures that all relevant financial information is reported.
(d) Rationale why plant assets are not reported at liquidation value. (Do not use historical cost principle.)
(e) Anticipates all losses, but reports no gains.
(f) Indicates that personal and business record keeping should be separately maintained.
(g) Separates financial information into time periods for reporting purposes.
(h) Permits the use of market value valuation in certain specific situations.
(i) Requires that information significant enough to affect the decision of reasonably informed users should be disclosed. (Do not use full disclosure principle.)
(j) Assumes that the dollar is the "measuring stick" used to report on financial performance.

E2-5 **(Assumptions, Principles, and Constraints)** Presented below are a number of operational guidelines and practices that have developed over time.

Instructions

Select the assumption, principle, or constraint that most appropriately justifies these procedures and practices. (Do not use qualitative characteristics.)

(a) Price-level changes are not recognized in the accounting records.
(b) Lower of cost or market is used to value inventories.
(c) Financial information is presented so that reasonably prudent investors will not be misled.
(d) Intangibles are capitalized and amortized over periods benefited.
(e) Repair tools are expensed when purchased.
(f) Brokerage firms use market value for purposes of valuation of all marketable securities.
(g) Each enterprise is kept as a unit distinct from its owner or owners.
(h) All significant postbalance sheet events are reported.
(i) Revenue is recorded at point of sale.
(j) All important aspects of bond indentures are presented in financial statements.
(k) Rationale for accrual accounting is stated.
(l) The use of consolidated statements is justified.
(m) Reporting must be done at defined time intervals.
(n) An allowance for doubtful accounts is established.
(o) All payments out of petty cash are charged to Miscellaneous Expense. (Do not use conservatism.)
(p) Goodwill is recorded only at time of purchase.
(q) No profits are anticipated and all possible losses are recognized.
(r) A company charges its sales commission costs to expense.

E2-6 **(Full Disclosure Principle)** Presented below are a number of facts related to R. Kelly, Inc. Assume that no mention of these facts was made in the financial statements and the related notes.

Instructions

Assume that you are the auditor of R. Kelly, Inc. and that you have been asked to explain the appropriate accounting and related disclosure necessary for each of these items.

(a) The company decided that, for the sake of conciseness, only net income should be reported on the income statement. Details as to revenues, cost of goods sold, and expenses were omitted.
(b) Equipment purchases of $170,000 were partly financed during the year through the issuance of a $110,000 notes payable. The company offset the equipment against the notes payable and reported plant assets at $60,000.

(c) During the year, an assistant controller for the company embezzled $15,000. R. Kelly's net income for the year was $2,300,000. Neither the assistant controller nor the money have been found.

(d) R. Kelly has reported its ending inventory at $2,100,000 in the financial statements. No other information related to inventories is presented in the financial statements and related notes.

(e) The company changed its method of depreciating equipment from the double-declining balance to the straight-line method. No mention of this change was made in the financial statements.

E2-7 (Accounting Principles—Comprehensive) Presented below are a number of business transactions that occurred during the current year for Fresh Horses, Inc.

Instructions
In each of the situations, discuss the appropriateness of the journal entries in terms of generally accepted accounting principles.

(a) The president of Fresh Horses, Inc. used his expense account to purchase a new Suburban solely for personal use. The following journal entry was made.

Miscellaneous Expense	29,000	
Cash		29,000

(b) Merchandise inventory that cost $620,000 is reported on the balance sheet at $690,000, the expected selling price less estimated selling costs. The following entry was made to record this increase in value.

Merchandise Inventory	70,000	
Revenue		70,000

(c) The company is being sued for $500,000 by a customer who claims damages for personal injury apparently caused by a defective product. Company attorneys feel extremely confident that the company will have no liability for damages resulting from the situation. Nevertheless, the company decides to make the following entry.

Loss from Lawsuit	500,000	
Liability for Lawsuit		500,000

(d) Because the general level of prices increased during the current year, Fresh Horses, Inc. determined that there was a $16,000 understatement of depreciation expense on its equipment and decided to record it in its accounts. The following entry was made.

Depreciation Expense	16,000	
Accumulated Depreciation		16,000

(e) Fresh Horses, Inc. has been concerned about whether intangible assets could generate cash in case of liquidation. As a consequence, goodwill arising from a purchase transaction during the current year and recorded at $800,000 was written off as follows.

Retained Earnings	800,000	
Goodwill		800,000

(f) Because of a "fire sale," equipment obviously worth $200,000 was acquired at a cost of $155,000. The following entry was made.

Equipment	200,000	
Cash		155,000
Revenue		45,000

E2-8 (Accounting Principles—Comprehensive) Presented on the next page is information related to Garth Brooks, Inc.

Instructions

Comment on the appropriateness of the accounting procedures followed by Garth Brooks, Inc.

(a) Depreciation expense on the building for the year was $60,000. Because the building was increasing in value during the year, the controller decided to charge the depreciation expense to retained earnings instead of to net income. The following entry is recorded.

Retained Earnings	60,000	
Accumulated Depreciation — Buildings		60,000

(b) Materials were purchased on January 1, 2003, for $120,000 and this amount was entered in the Inventory account. On December 31, 2003, the materials would have cost $141,000, so the following entry is made.

Inventory	21,000	
Gain on Inventories		21,000

(c) During the year, the company purchased equipment through the issuance of common stock. The stock had a par value of $135,000 and a fair market value of $450,000. The fair market value of the equipment was not easily determinable. The company recorded this transaction as follows.

Equipment	135,000	
Common Stock		135,000

(d) During the year, the company sold certain equipment for $285,000, recognizing a gain of $69,000. Because the controller believed that new equipment would be needed in the near future, she decided to defer the gain and amortize it over the life of any new equipment purchased.

(e) An order for $61,500 has been received from a customer for products on hand. This order was shipped on January 9, 2004. The company made the following entry in 2003.

Accounts Receivable	61,500	
Sales		61,500

CONCEPTUAL CASES

C2-1 (Conceptual Framework—General) Roger Morgan has some questions regarding the theoretical framework in which standards are set. He knows that the FASB and other predecessor organizations have attempted to develop a conceptual framework for accounting theory formulation. Yet, Roger's supervisors have indicated that these theoretical frameworks have little value in the practical sense (i.e., in the real world). Roger did notice that accounting standards seem to be established after the fact rather than before. He thought this indicated a lack of theory structure but never really questioned the process at school because he was too busy doing the homework.

Roger feels that some of his anxiety about accounting theory and accounting semantics could be alleviated by identifying the basic concepts and definitions accepted by the profession and considering them in light of his current work. By doing this, he hopes to develop an appropriate connection between theory and practice.

Instructions

(a) Help Roger recognize the purpose of and benefit of a conceptual framework.

(b) Identify any *Statements of Financial Accounting Concepts* issued by FASB that may be helpful to Roger in developing his theoretical background.

C2-2 (Conceptual Framework—General) The Financial Accounting Standards Board (FASB) has developed a conceptual framework for financial accounting and reporting. The FASB has issued seven *Statements of Financial Accounting Concepts*. These statements are intended to set forth objectives and fundamentals that will be the basis for developing financial accounting and reporting standards. The objectives identify the goals and purposes of financial reporting. The fundamentals are the underlying concepts of financial accounting—concepts that guide the selection of transactions, events, and circumstances to be accounted for; their recognition and measurement; and the means of summarizing and communicating them to interested parties.

The purpose of *Statement of Financial Accounting Concepts No. 2*, "Qualitative Characteristics of Accounting Information," is to examine the characteristics that make accounting information useful. The characteristics or qualities of information discussed in *SFAC No. 2* are the ingredients that make information useful and the qualities to be sought when accounting choices are made.

Instructions

(a) Identify and discuss the benefits that can be expected to be derived from the FASB's conceptual framework study.

(b) What is the most important quality for accounting information as identified in *Statement of Financial Accounting Concepts No. 2*? Explain why it is the most important.

(c) *Statement of Financial Accounting Concepts No. 2* describes a number of key characteristics or qualities for accounting information. Briefly discuss the importance of any three of these qualities for financial reporting purposes.

(CMA adapted)

C2-3 (Objectives of Financial Reporting) Regis Gordon and Kathy Medford are discussing various aspects of the FASB's pronouncement, *Statement of Financial Accounting Concepts No. 1*, "Objectives of Financial Reporting by Business Enterprises." Regis indicates that this pronouncement provides little, if any, guidance to the practicing professional in resolving accounting controversies. He believes that the statement provides such broad guidelines that it would be impossible to apply the objectives to present-day reporting problems. Kathy concedes this point but indicates that objectives are still needed to provide a starting point for the FASB in helping to improve financial reporting.

Instructions

(a) Indicate the basic objectives established in *Statement of Financial Accounting Concepts No. 1*.

(b) What do you think is the meaning of Kathy's statement that the FASB needs a starting point to resolve accounting controversies?

C2-4 (Qualitative Characteristics) Accounting information provides useful information about business transactions and events. Those who provide and use financial reports must often select and evaluate accounting alternatives. *FASB Statement of Financial Accounting Concepts No. 2*, "Qualitative Characteristics of Accounting Information," examines the characteristics of accounting information that make it useful for decision making. It also points out that various limitations inherent in the measurement and reporting process may necessitate trade-offs or sacrifices among the characteristics of useful information.

Instructions

(a) Describe briefly the following characteristics of useful accounting information.

    (1) Relevance   **(4)** Comparability.

    (2) Reliability   **(5)** Consistency.

    (3) Understandability

(b) For each of the following pairs of information characteristics, give an example of a situation in which one of the characteristics may be sacrificed in return for a gain in the other.

    (1) Relevance and reliability.   **(3)** Comparability and consistency.

    (2) Relevance and consistency.   **(4)** Relevance and understandability.

(c) What criterion should be used to evaluate trade-offs between information characteristics?

C2-5 (Revenue Recognition and Matching Principle) After the presentation of your report on the examination of the financial statements to the board of directors of Bones Publishing Company, one of the new directors expresses surprise that the income statement assumes that an equal proportion of the revenue is earned with the publication of every issue of the company's magazine. She feels that the "crucial event" in the process of earning revenue in the magazine business is the cash sale of the subscription. She says that she does not understand why most of the revenue cannot be "recognized" in the period of the sale.

Instructions

(a) List the various accepted times for recognizing revenue in the accounts and explain when the methods are appropriate.

(b) Discuss the propriety of timing the recognition of revenue in Bones Publishing Company's accounts with:

(1) The cash sale of the magazine subscription.

(2) The publication of the magazine every month.

(3) Both events, by recognizing a portion of the revenue with cash sale of the magazine subscription and a portion of the revenue with the publication of the magazine every month.

C2-6 (Revenue Recognition and Matching Principle) On June 5, 2003, McCoy Corporation signed a contract with Sulu Associates under which Sulu agreed (1) to construct an office building on land owned by McCoy, (2) to accept responsibility for procuring financing for the project and finding tenants, and (3) to manage the property for 35 years. The annual net income from the project, after debt service, was to be divided equally between McCoy Corporation and Sulu Associates. Sulu was to accept its share of future net income as full payment for its services in construction, obtaining finances and tenants, and management of the project.

By May 31, 2004, the project was nearly completed and tenants had signed leases to occupy 90% of the available space at annual rentals totaling $4,000,000. It is estimated that, after operating expenses and debt service, the annual net income will amount to $1,500,000.

The management of Sulu Associates believed that (a) the economic benefit derived from the contract with McCoy should be reflected on its financial statements for the fiscal year ended May 31, 2004, and directed that revenue be accrued in an amount equal to the commercial value of the services Sulu had rendered during the year, (b) this amount be carried in contracts receivable, and (c) all related expenditures be charged against the revenue.

Instructions

(a) Explain the main difference between the economic concept of business income as reflected by Sulu's management and the measurement of income under generally accepted accounting principles.

(b) Discuss the factors to be considered in determining when revenue should be recognized for the purpose of accounting measurement of periodic income.

(c) Is the belief of Sulu's management in accordance with generally accepted accounting principles for the measurement of revenue and expense for the year ended May 31, 2004? Support your opinion by discussing the application to this case of the factors to be considered for asset measurement and revenue and expense recognition.

(AICPA adapted)

C2-7 (Matching Principle) An accountant must be familiar with the concepts involved in determining earnings of a business entity. The amount of earnings reported for a business entity is dependent on the proper recognition, in general, of revenue and expense for a given time period. In some situations, costs are recognized as expenses at the time of product sale. In other situations, guidelines have been developed for recognizing costs as expenses or losses by other criteria.

Instructions

(a) Explain the rationale for recognizing costs as expenses at the time of product sale.

(b) What is the rationale underlying the appropriateness of treating costs as expenses of a period instead of assigning the costs to an asset? Explain.

(c) In what general circumstances would it be appropriate to treat a cost as an asset instead of as an expense? Explain.

(d) Some expenses are assigned to specific accounting periods on the basis of systematic and rational allocation of asset cost. Explain the underlying rationale for recognizing expenses on the basis of systematic and rational allocation of asset cost.

(e) Identify the conditions in which it would be appropriate to treat a cost as a loss.

(AICPA adapted)

C2-8 (Matching Principle) Accountants try to prepare income statements that are as accurate as possible. A basic requirement in preparing accurate income statements is to match costs against revenues properly.

Proper matching of costs against revenues requires that costs resulting from typical business operations be recognized in the period in which they expired.

Instructions

(a) List three criteria that can be used to determine whether such costs should appear as charges in the income statement for the current period.

(b) As generally presented in financial statements, the following items or procedures have been criticized as improperly matching costs with revenues. Briefly discuss each item from the viewpoint of matching costs with revenues and suggest corrective or alternative means of presenting the financial information.

    (1) Receiving and handling costs.

    (2) Valuation of inventories at the lower of cost or market.

    (3) Cash discounts on purchases.

C2-9 (Matching Principle) Carlos Rodriguez sells and erects shell houses, that is, frame structures that are completely finished on the outside but are unfinished on the inside except for flooring, partition studding, and ceiling joists. Shell houses are sold chiefly to customers who are handy with tools and who have time to do the interior wiring, plumbing, wall completion and finishing, and other work necessary to make the shell houses livable dwellings.

Rodriguez buys shell houses from a manufacturer in unassembled packages consisting of all lumber, roofing, doors, windows, and similar materials necessary to complete a shell house. Upon commencing operations in a new area, Rodriguez buys or leases land as a site for its local warehouse, field office, and display houses. Sample display houses are erected at a total cost of $20,000 to $29,000 including the cost of the unassembled packages. The chief element of cost of the display houses is the unassembled packages, inasmuch as erection is a short, low-cost operation. Old sample models are torn down or altered into new models every 3 to 7 years. Sample display houses have little salvage value because dismantling and moving costs amount to nearly as much as the cost of an unassembled package.

Instructions

(a) A choice must be made between (1) expensing the costs of sample display houses in the periods in which the expenditure is made and (2) spreading the costs over more than one period. Discuss the advantages of each method.

(b) Would it be preferable to amortize the cost of display houses on the basis of (1) the passage of time or (2) the number of shell houses sold? Explain.

(AICPA adapted)

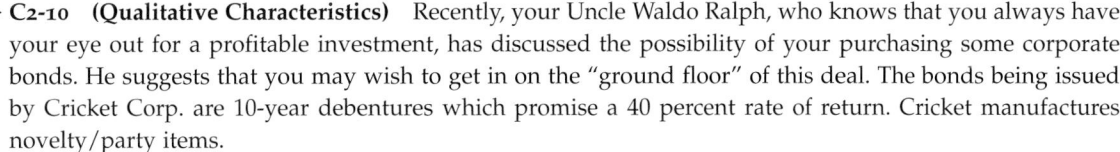

C2-10 (Qualitative Characteristics) Recently, your Uncle Waldo Ralph, who knows that you always have your eye out for a profitable investment, has discussed the possibility of your purchasing some corporate bonds. He suggests that you may wish to get in on the "ground floor" of this deal. The bonds being issued by Cricket Corp. are 10-year debentures which promise a 40 percent rate of return. Cricket manufactures novelty/party items.

You have told Waldo that, unless you can take a look at Cricket's financial statements, you would not feel comfortable about such an investment. Believing that this is the chance of a lifetime, Uncle Waldo has procured a copy of Cricket's most recent, unaudited financial statements which are a year old. These statements were prepared by Mrs. John Cricket. You peruse these statements, and they are quite impressive. The balance sheet showed a debt-to-equity ratio of 0.10 and, for the year shown, the company reported net income of $2,424,240.

The financial statements are not shown in comparison with amounts from other years. In addition, no significant note disclosures about inventory valuation, depreciation methods, loan agreements, etc. are available.

Instructions

Write a letter to Uncle Waldo explaining why it would be unwise to base an investment decision on the financial statements that he has provided to you. Be sure to explain why these financial statements are neither relevant nor reliable.

C2-11 (Matching) Hinckley Nuclear Power Plant will be "mothballed" at the end of its useful life (approximately 20 years) at great expense. The matching principle requires that expenses be matched to revenue. Accountants Jana Kingston and Pete Henning argue whether it is better to allocate the expense of mothballing over the next 20 years or ignore it until mothballing occurs.

Instructions

Answer the following questions.

(a) What stakeholders should be considered?

(b) What ethical issue, if any, underlies the dispute?

(c) What alternatives should be considered?

(d) Assess the consequences of the alternatives.

(e) What decision would you recommend?

USING YOUR JUDGMENT

FINANCIAL REPORTING PROBLEM

3M COMPANY

The financial statements of **3M** were provided with your book or can be accessed on the Take Action! CD.

Instructions

Refer to 3M's financial statements and the accompanying notes to answer the following questions.

(a) Using the notes to the consolidated financial statements, determine 3M's revenue recognition policies. Comment on the impact of SEC *SAB No. 101* on 3M's financial statements.

(b) Give two examples of where historical cost information is reported in 3M's financial statements and related notes. Give two examples of the use of fair value information reported in either the financial statements or related notes.

(c) How can we determine that the accounting principles used by 3M are prepared on a basis consistent with those of last year?

(d) What is 3M's accounting policy related to advertising? What accounting principle does 3M follow regarding accounting for advertising?

FINANCIAL STATEMENT ANALYSIS CASE

WEYERHAEUSER COMPANY

Presented below is a statement that appeared about **Weyerhaeuser Company** in a financial magazine.

> The land and timber holdings are now carried on the company's books at a mere $422 million. The value of the timber alone is variously estimated at $3 billion to $7 billion and is rising all the time. "The understatement of the company is pretty severe," conceded Charles W. Bingham, a senior vice-president. Adds Robert L. Schuyler, another senior vice-president: "We have a whole stream of profit nobody sees and there is no way to show it on our books."

Instructions

(a) What does Schuyler mean when he says, "We have a whole stream of profit nobody sees and there is no way to show it on our books"?

(b) If the understatement of the company's assets is severe, why does accounting not report this information?

COMPARATIVE ANALYSIS CASE

THE COCA-COLA COMPANY AND PEPSICO, INC.

Instructions

Go to the Take Action! CD, and use information found there to answer the following questions related to The Coca-Cola Company and PepsiCo, Inc.

(a) What are the primary lines of business of these two companies as shown in their notes to the financial statements?

(b) Which company has the dominant position in beverage sales?

(c) How are inventories for these two companies valued? What cost allocation method is used to report inventory? How does their accounting for inventories affect comparability between the two companies?

(d) Which company changed its accounting policies during 2001 which affected the consistency of the financial results from the previous year? What were these changes?

INTERNATIONAL REPORTING CASE

As discussed in Chapter 1, the **International Accounting Standards Board** (IASB) develops accounting standards for many international companies. The IASB also has developed a conceptual framework to help guide the setting of accounting standards. Following is an Overview of the IASB Framework.

Objective of Financial Statements
    To provide information about the financial position, performance, and changes in financial position of an enterprise that is useful to a wide range of users in making economic decisions.

Underlying Assumptions
    Accrual basis
    Going concern

Qualitative Characteristics of Financial Statements
    Understandability
    Relevance
        Materiality
    Reliability
        Faithful representation
        Substance over form
        Neutrality
        Prudence
        Completeness
    Comparability

Constraints on Relevant and Reliable Information
    Timeliness
    Balance between benefit and cost
    Balance between qualitative characteristics

True and Fair Presentation

<u>Elements of Financial Statements</u>

Asset: A resource controlled by the enterprise as a result of past events and from which future economic benefits are expected to flow to the enterprise.

Liability: A present obligation of the enterprise arising from past events, the settlement of which is expected to result in an outflow from the enterprise of resources embodying economic benefits.

Equity: The residual interest in the assets of the enterprise after deducting all its liabilities.

Income: Increases in economic benefits during the accounting period in the form of inflows or enhancements of assets or decreases of liabilities that result in increases in equity, other than those relating to contributions from equity participants.

Expenses: Decreases in economic benefits during the accounting period in the form of outflows or depletions of assets or incurrences of liabilities that result in decreases in equity, other than those relating to distributions to equity participants.

Instructions

Identify at least three similarities and at least three differences between the FASB and ISAB conceptual frameworks as revealed in the preceding Overview.

*Remember to check the **Take Action! CD**
and the book's **companion Web site**
to find additional resources for this chapter.*

THE ACCOUNTING INFORMATION SYSTEM

NEEDED: A RELIABLE INFORMATION SYSTEM

Maintaining a set of accounting records is not optional. The Internal Revenue Service requires that businesses prepare and retain a set of records and documents that can be audited. The Foreign Corrupt Practices Act (federal legislation) requires public companies to ". . . make and keep books, records, and accounts, which, in reasonable detail, accurately and fairly reflect the transactions and dispositions of the assets. . . ." But beyond these two reasons, a company that does not keep an accurate record of its business transactions may lose revenue and is more likely to operate inefficiently.

Some companies are inefficient partly because of poor accounting systems. Consider, for example, the **Long Island Railroad**, once one of the nation's busiest commuter lines. The LIRR lost money because its cash position was unknown: Large amounts of money owed the railroad had not been billed; some payables were erroneously paid twice; and redemptions of bonds were not recorded. Also, consider **Gould Inc.**, an electronics conglomerate, where accounting and record keeping became so chaotic that results from operations had to be restated for five of seven years.

Similarly, when the **International Gold Bullion Exchange** (IGBE), one of the largest gold and silver retailers, was forced to declare bankruptcy, its records were in such shambles that it was difficult to determine how much money it lost. The company had failed to keep track of its revenues and had written checks on uncollected funds. IGBE had even allowed its employee health insurance to lapse while continuing to collect premiums from workers. Although these situations are not common in large enterprises, they illustrate our point: accounts and detailed records must be kept by every business enterprise.

Even the use of computers is no assurance of accuracy and efficiency. "The conversion to a new system called MasterNet fouled up data processing records to the extent that **Bank of America** was frequently unable to produce or deliver customer statements on a timely basis," said an executive at one of the country's largest banks.

LEARNING OBJECTIVES

After studying this chapter, you should be able to:

1. Understand basic accounting terminology.
2. Explain double-entry rules.
3. Identify steps in the accounting cycle.
4. Record transactions in journals, post to ledger accounts, and prepare a trial balance.
5. Explain the reasons for preparing adjusting entries.
6. Prepare closing entries.
7. Explain how inventory accounts are adjusted at year-end.
8. Prepare a 10-column work sheet.

As the opening story indicates, a reliable information system is a necessity for all companies. The purpose of this chapter is to explain and illustrate the features of an accounting information system. The content and organization of this chapter are as follows.

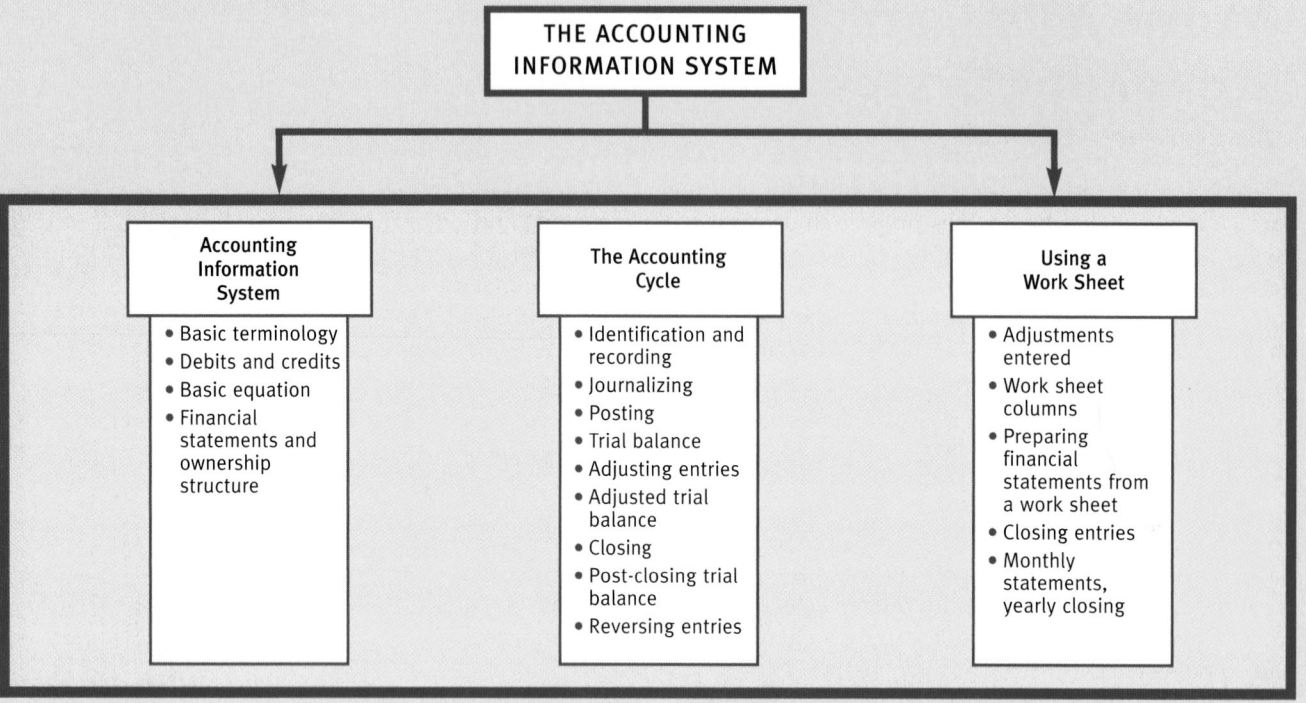

ACCOUNTING INFORMATION SYSTEM

The system of collecting and processing transaction data and disseminating financial information to interested parties is known as the **accounting information system**. Accounting information systems vary widely from one business to another. Factors that shape these systems are the **nature of the business** and the transactions in which it engages, the **size of the firm**, the **volume of data** to be handled, and the **informational demands** that management and others place on the system.

A good accounting information system helps management answer such questions as:

How much and what kind of debt is outstanding?

Were our sales higher this period than last?

What assets do we have?

What were our cash inflows and outflows?

Did we make a profit last period?

Are any of our product lines or divisions operating at a loss?

Can we safely increase our dividends to stockholders?

Is our rate of return on net assets increasing?

Many other questions can be answered when there is an efficient accounting system to provide the data. A well-devised accounting information system is beneficial for every business enterprise.

Basic Terminology

Financial accounting rests on a set of concepts (discussed in Chapters 1 and 2) for iden-tifying, recording, classifying, and interpreting transactions and other events relating to enterprises. It is important to understand the **basic terminology employed in col-lecting accounting data**.

BASIC TERMINOLOGY

EVENT. A happening of consequence. An event generally is the source or cause of changes in assets, liabilities, and equity. Events may be external or internal.

TRANSACTION. An **external event** involving a transfer or exchange between two or more entities.

ACCOUNT. A systematic arrangement that shows the effect of transactions and other events on a specific asset or equity. A separate account is kept for each asset, liability, revenue, expense, and for capital (owners' equity).

REAL AND NOMINAL ACCOUNTS. Real (permanent) **accounts** are asset, lia-bility, and equity accounts; they appear on the balance sheet. **Nominal** (tem-porary) **accounts** are revenue, expense, and dividend accounts; except for dividends, they appear on the income statement. Nominal accounts are peri-odically closed; real accounts are not.

LEDGER. The book (or computer printouts) containing the accounts. Each ac-count usually has a separate page. A **general ledger** is a collection of all the asset, liability, owners' equity, revenue, and expense accounts. A **subsidiary ledger** contains the details related to a given general ledger account.

JOURNAL. The book of original entry where transactions and selected other events are initially recorded. Various amounts are transferred to the ledger from the book of original entry, the journal.

POSTING. The process of transferring the essential facts and figures from the book of original entry to the ledger accounts.

TRIAL BALANCE. A list of all open accounts in the ledger and their balances. A trial balance taken immediately after all adjustments have been posted is called an **adjusted trial balance**. A trial balance taken immediately after clos-ing entries have been posted is designated as a **post-closing** or **after-closing trial balance**. A trial balance may be prepared at any time.

ADJUSTING ENTRIES. Entries made at the end of an accounting period to bring all accounts up to date on an accrual accounting basis so that correct financial statements can be prepared.

FINANCIAL STATEMENTS. Statements that reflect the collection, tabulation, and final summarization of the accounting data. Four statements are involved: (1) The **balance sheet** shows the financial condition of the enterprise at the end of a period. (2) The **income statement** measures the results of operations dur-ing the period. (3) The **statement of cash flows** reports the cash provided and used by operating, investing, and financing activities during the period. (4) The **statement of retained earnings** reconciles the balance of the retained earn-ings account from the beginning to the end of the period.

CLOSING ENTRIES. The formal process by which all nominal accounts are re-duced to zero and the net income or net loss is determined and transferred to an owners' equity account; also known as "closing the ledger," "closing the books," or merely "closing."

OBJECTIVE **1**
Understand basic accounting terminology.

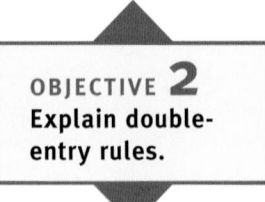

Debits and Credits

The terms **debit** and **credit** mean left and right, respectively. They are commonly abbreviated as Dr. for debit and Cr. for credit. These terms do not mean increase or decrease. The terms debit and credit are used repeatedly in the recording process to describe where entries are made. For example, the act of entering an amount on the left side of an account is called **debiting** the account, and making an entry on the right side is **crediting** the account. When the totals of the two sides are compared, an account will have a **debit balance** if the total of the debit amounts exceeds the credits. An account will have a **credit balance** if the credit amounts exceed the debits.

The procedure of having debits on the left and credits on the right is an accounting custom or rule. We could function just as well if debits and credits were reversed. However, the custom of having debits on the left side of an account and credits on the right side (like the custom of driving on the right-hand side of the road) has been adopted in the United States. **This rule applies to all accounts.**

The equality of debits and credits provides the basis for the double-entry system of recording transactions (sometimes referred to as double-entry bookkeeping). Under the universally used **double-entry accounting system**, the dual (two-sided) effect of each transaction is recorded in appropriate accounts. This system provides a logical method for recording transactions. It also offers a means of proving the accuracy of the recorded amounts. If every transaction is recorded with equal debits and credits, then the sum of all the debits to the accounts must equal the sum of all the credits.

All asset and expense accounts are increased on the left (or debit side) and decreased on the right (or credit side). Conversely, all liability and revenue accounts are increased on the right (or credit side) and decreased on the left (or debit side). Stockholders' equity accounts, such as Common Stock and Retained Earnings, are increased on the credit side, whereas Dividends is increased on the debit side. The basic guidelines for an accounting system are presented in Illustration 3-1.

Illustration 3-1

Double-entry (Debit and Credit) Accounting System

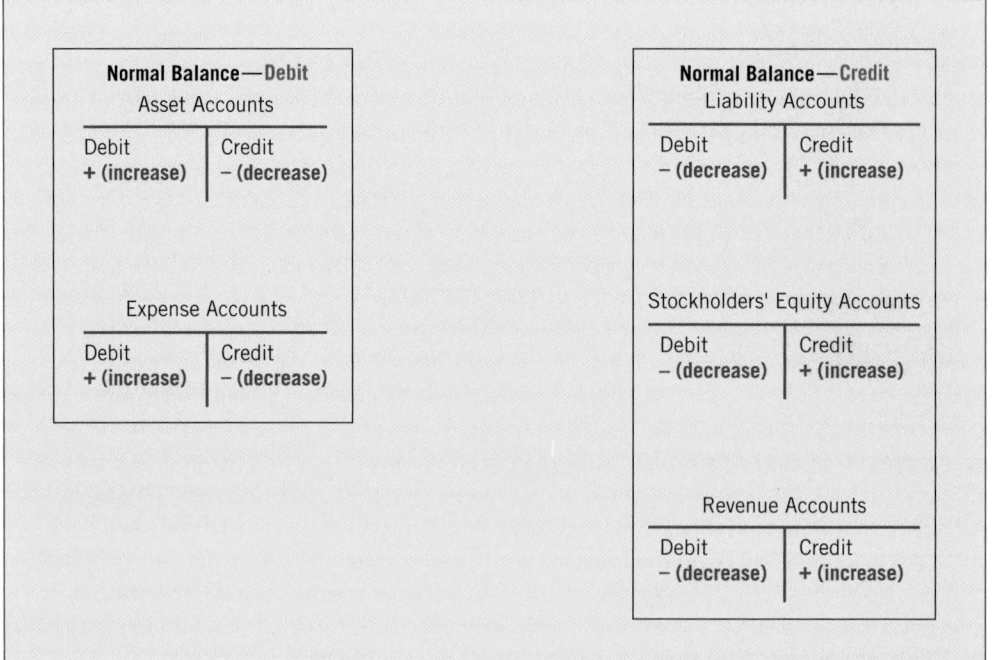

Basic Equation

In a double-entry system, for every debit there must be a credit, and vice versa. This leads us, then, to the basic equation in accounting (Illustration 3-2).

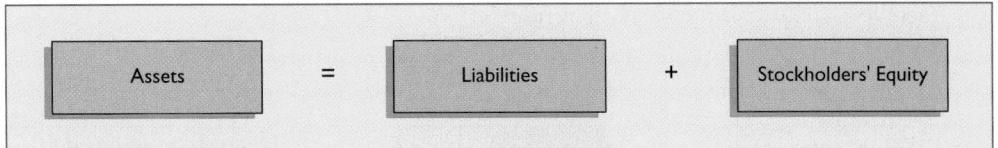

Illustration 3-2
The Basic Accounting Equation

Illustration 3-3 expands this equation to show the accounts that comprise stockholders' equity. In addition, the debit/credit rules and effects on each type of account are illustrated. Study this diagram carefully. It will help you understand the fundamentals of the double-entry system. Like the basic equation, the expanded basic equation must be in balance (total debits equal total credits).

Illustration 3-3
Expanded Basic Equation and Debit/Credit Rules and Effects

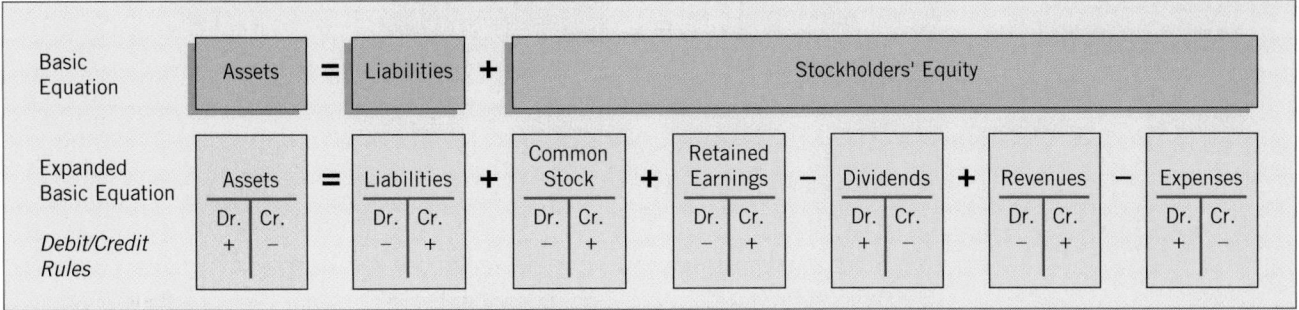

Every time a transaction occurs, the elements of the equation change, but the basic equality remains. To illustrate, here are eight different transactions for Perez Inc.

① Owners invest $40,000 in exchange for common stock.

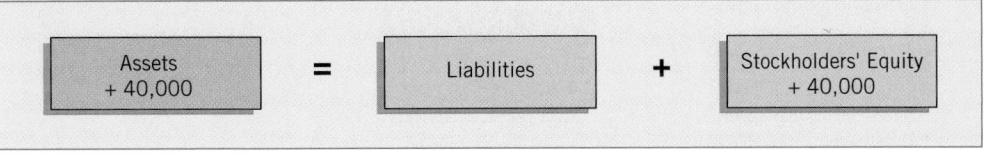

② Disburse $600 cash for secretarial wages.

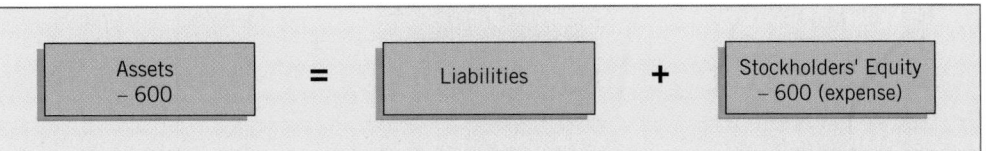

③ Purchase office equipment priced at $5,200, giving a 10 percent promissory note in exchange.

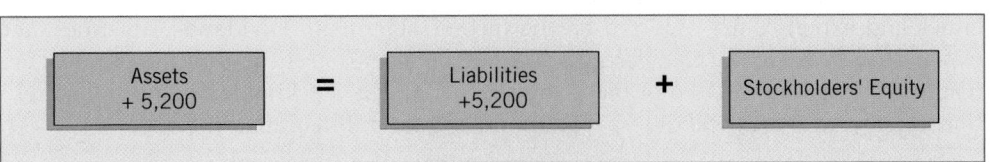

④ Receive $4,000 cash for services rendered.

Assets + 4,000	=	Liabilities	+	Stockholders' Equity + 4,000 (revenue)

⑤ Pay off a short-term liability of $7,000.

Assets − 7,000	=	Liabilities − 7,000	+	Stockholders' Equity

⑥ Declare a cash dividend of $5,000.

Assets	=	Liabilities + 5,000	+	Stockholders' Equity − 5,000

⑦ Convert a long-term liability of $80,000 into common stock.

Assets	=	Liabilities − 80,000	+	Stockholders' Equity + 80,000

⑧ Pay cash of $16,000 for a delivery van.

Assets −16,000 +16,000	=	Liabilities	+	Stockholders' Equity

Financial Statements and Ownership Structure

Common stock and retained earnings are reported in the stockholders' equity section of the balance sheet. Dividends are reported on the statement of retained earnings. Revenues and expenses are reported on the income statement. Dividends, revenues, and expenses are eventually transferred to retained earnings at the end of the period. As a result, a change in any one of these three items affects stockholders' equity. The relationships related to stockholders' equity are shown in Illustration 3-4.

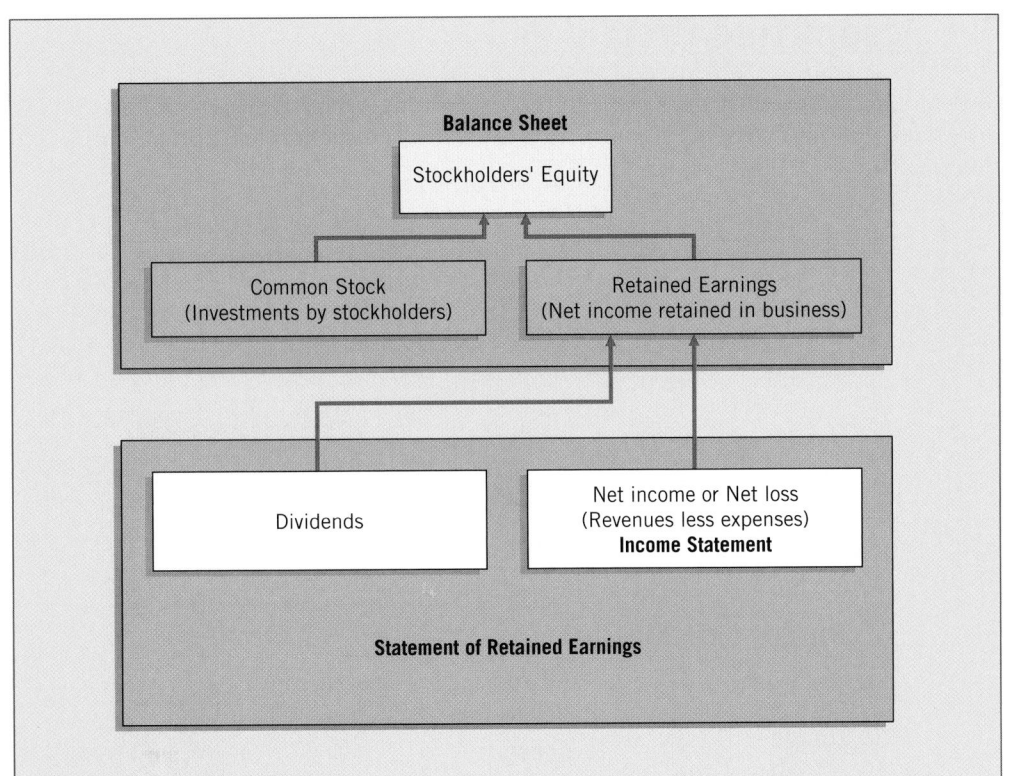

Illustration 3-4
Financial Statements and
Ownership Structure

The type of ownership structure employed by a business enterprise dictates the types of accounts that are part of or affect the equity section. In a corporation, **Common Stock**, **Additional Paid-in Capital**, **Dividends**, and **Retained Earnings** are accounts commonly used. In a proprietorship or partnership, a Capital account is used to indicate the owner's or owners' investment in the company. A Drawing account is used to indicate withdrawals by the owner(s).

Illustration 3-5 summarizes and relates the transactions affecting owners' equity to the nominal (temporary) and real (permanent) classifications and to the types of business ownership.

Illustration 3-5
Effects of Transactions on
Owners' Equity Accounts

		Ownership Structure			
		Proprietorships and Partnerships		Corporations	
Transactions Affecting Owners' Equity	Impact on Owners' Equity	Nominal (Temporary) Accounts	Real (Permanent) Accounts	Nominal (Temporary) Accounts	Real (Permanent) Accounts
Investment by owner(s)	Increase		Capital		Common Stock and related accounts
Revenues earned	Increase	Revenue		Revenue	
Expenses incurred	Decrease	Expense	Capital	Expense	Retained Earnings
Withdrawal by owner(s)	Decrease	Drawing		Dividends	

THE ACCOUNTING CYCLE

Illustration 3-6 flowcharts the steps in the **accounting cycle**. These are the accounting procedures normally used by enterprises to record transactions and prepare financial statements.

Illustration 3-6
The Accounting Cycle

Identification and Measurement of Transactions and Other Events
Journalization
General journal
Cash receipts journal
Cash disbursements journal
Purchases journal
Sales journal
Other special journals
Posting
General ledger (usually monthly)
Subsidiary ledgers (usually daily)
Trial balance preparation
Adjustments
Accruals
Prepayments
Estimated items
Work Sheet (optional)
Adjusted trial balance
Statement preparation
Income statement
Retained earnings
Balance sheet
Cash flows
Closing
(nominal accounts)
Post-closing trial balance (optional)
Reversing entries (optional)
THE ACCOUNTING CYCLE
When the steps have been completed, the sequence starts over again in the next accounting period.

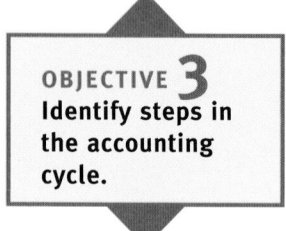

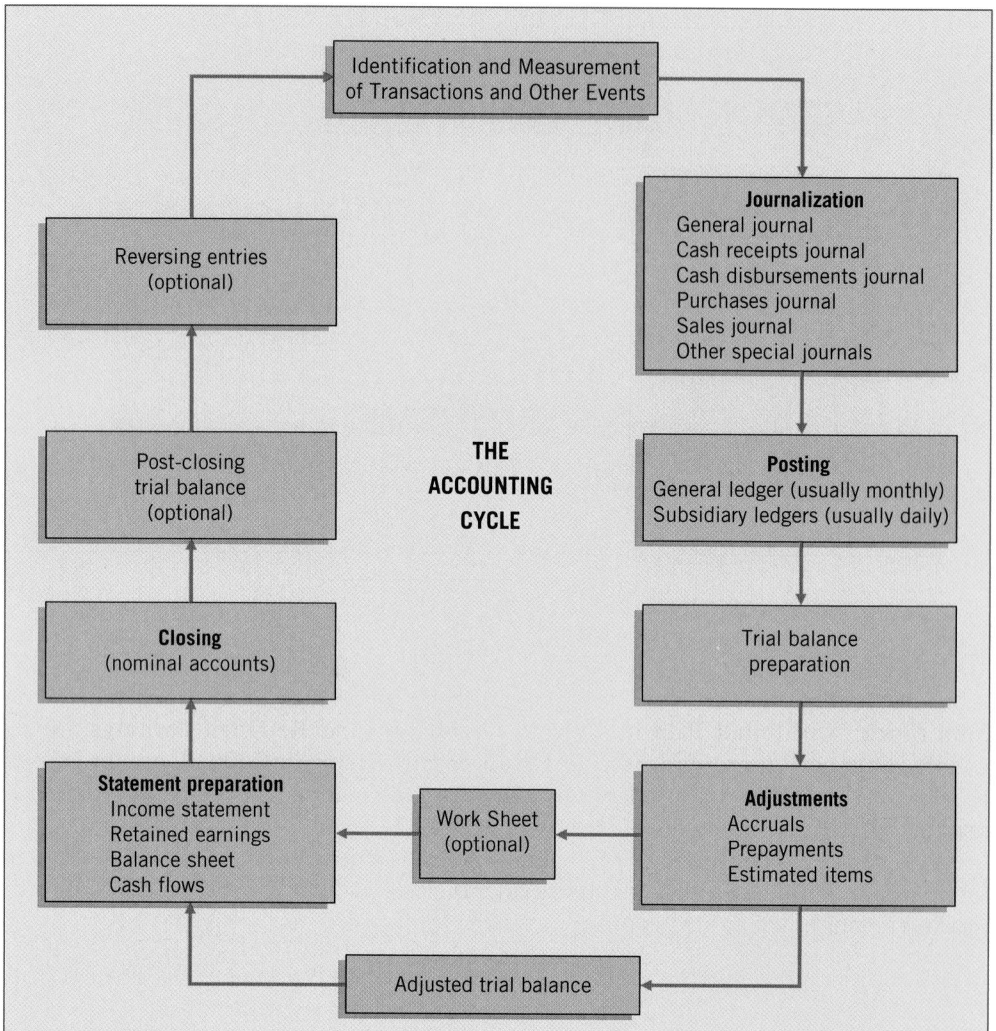

OBJECTIVE 3
Identify steps in the accounting cycle.

Identifying and Recording Transactions and Other Events

The first step in the accounting cycle is analysis of transactions and selected other events. The problem is to determine **what to record**. No simple rules exist that state whether an event should be recorded. Most agree that changes in personnel, changes in managerial policies, and the value of human resources, though important, should not be recorded in the accounts. On the other hand, when the company makes a cash sale or purchase—no matter how small—it should be recorded.

UNDERLYING CONCEPTS

Assets are probable economic benefits controlled by a particular entity as a result of a past transaction or event. Do human resources of a company meet this definition?

The treatment relates to the accounting concepts presented in Chapter 2. **An item should be recognized in the financial statements if it is an element, is measurable, and is relevant and reliable.** Consider human resources. **R.G. Barry & Co.** at one time reported as supplemental data total assets of $14,055,926, including $986,094 for "Net investments in human resources." **AT&T** and **Exxon Mobil Company** have also experimented with human resource accounting. Should we value employees for balance sheet and income statement purposes? Certainly skilled employees are an important asset (highly relevant), but the problems of **determining their value and measuring it reliably have not yet been solved**. Consequently, human resources are not recorded. Perhaps when measurement techniques become more sophisticated and accepted, such information will be presented, if only in supplemental form.

The phrase "transactions and other events and circumstances that affect a business enterprise" is used to describe the sources or causes of changes in an entity's assets, liabilities, and equity.[1] **Events** are of two types: (1) **External events** involve interaction between an entity and its environment, such as a transaction with another entity, a change in the price of a good or service that an entity buys or sells, a flood or earthquake, or an improvement in technology by a competitor. (2) **Internal events** occur within an entity, such as using buildings and machinery in operations or transferring or consuming raw materials in production processes.

Many events have both external and internal elements. For example, acquiring the services of employees or others involves exchange transactions, which are external events. Using those services (labor), often simultaneously with their acquisition, is part of production, which is internal. Events may be initiated and controlled by an entity, such as the purchase of merchandise or the use of a machine. Or they may be beyond its control, such as an interest rate change, a theft or vandalism, or the imposition of taxes.

Transactions, as particular kinds of external events, may be an exchange in which each entity both receives and sacrifices value, such as purchases and sales of goods or services. Or transactions may be transfers in one direction in which an entity incurs a liability or transfers an asset to another entity without directly receiving (or giving) value in exchange. Examples include investments by owners, distributions to owners, payment of taxes, gifts, charitable contributions, casualty losses, and thefts.

In short, as many events as possible that affect the financial position of the enterprise are recorded. Some events are omitted because of tradition and others because the problems of measuring them are too complex. The accounting profession in recent years has shown signs of breaking with age-old traditions and is more receptive than ever to accepting the challenge of measuring and reporting events and phenomena previously viewed as too complex and immeasurable.

Journalizing

Differing effects on the basic business elements (assets, liabilities, and equities) are categorized and collected in **accounts**. The **general ledger** is a collection of all the asset, liability, stockholders' equity, revenue, and expense accounts. A **T-account** (as shown in Illustration 3-8, on page 71) is a convenient method of illustrating the effect of transactions on particular asset, liability, equity, revenue, and expense items.

In practice, transactions and selected other events are not recorded originally in the ledger because a transaction affects two or more accounts, each of which is on a different page in the ledger. To circumvent this deficiency and to have a complete record of each transaction or other event in one place, a **journal** (also called "the book of original entry") is employed. The simplest journal form is a chronological listing of transactions and other events expressed in terms of debits and credits to particular accounts. This is called a **general journal**. It is illustrated on the next page for the following transactions.

OBJECTIVE **4**
Record transactions in journals, post to ledger accounts, and prepare a trial balance.

Nov. 1   Buys a new delivery truck on account from Auto Sales Co., $22,400.
    3   Receives an invoice from the *Evening Graphic* for advertising, $280.
    4   Returns merchandise to Yankee Supply for credit, $175.
  16   Receives a $95 debit memo from Confederate Co., indicating that freight on a purchase from Confederate Co. was prepaid but is our obligation.

[1]"Elements of Financial Statements of Business Enterprises," *Statement of Financial Accounting Concepts No. 6* (Stamford, Conn.: FASB, 1985), pp. 259–60.

*Expanded Discussion of
Special Journals*

Each **general journal entry** consists of four parts: (1) the accounts and amounts to be debited (Dr.), (2) the accounts and amounts to be credited (Cr.), (3) a date, and (4) an explanation. Debits are entered first, followed by the credits, which are slightly indented. The explanation is begun below the name of the last account to be credited and may take one or more lines. The "Ref." column is completed at the time the accounts are posted.

In some cases, businesses use **special journals** in addition to the general journal. Special journals summarize transactions possessing a common characteristic (e.g., cash receipts, sales, purchases, cash payments), thereby reducing the time necessary to accomplish the various bookkeeping tasks.

Posting

The items entered in a general journal must be transferred to the general ledger. This procedure, **posting**, is part of the summarizing and classifying process.

For example, the November 1 entry in the general journal in Illustration 3-7 shows a debit to Delivery Equipment of $22,400 and a credit to Accounts Payable of $22,400. The amount in the debit column is posted from the journal to the debit side of the ledger account (Delivery Equipment). The amount in the credit column is posted from the journal to the credit side of the ledger account (Accounts Payable).

Illustration 3-7
General Journal with
Sample Entries

	GENERAL JOURNAL				PAGE 12
Date 2004	Account Title and Explanation	Ref.	Debit	Credit
Nov. 1	Delivery Equipment	8	22,400	
	Accounts Payable	34		22,400
	(Purchased delivery truck on account from Auto Sales Co.)			
3	Advertising Expense	65	280	
	Accounts Payable	34		280
	(Received invoice for advertising from *Evening Graphic*)			
4	Accounts Payable	34	175	
	Purchase Returns	53		175
	(Returned merchandise for credit to Yankee Supply)			
16	Transportation-In	55	95	
	Accounts Payable	34		95
	(Received debit memo for freight on merchandise purchased from Confederate Co.)			

The numbers in the "Ref." column of the general journal refer to the accounts in the ledger to which the respective items are posted. For example, the "34" placed in the column to the right of "Accounts Payable" indicates that this $22,400 item was posted to Account No. 34 in the ledger.

The posting of the general journal is completed when all of the posting reference numbers have been recorded opposite the account titles in the journal. Thus the number in the posting reference column serves two purposes: (1) It indicates the ledger account number of the account involved. And (2) it indicates that the posting has been completed for the particular item. Each business enterprise selects its own numbering system for its ledger accounts. One practice is to begin numbering with asset accounts and to follow with liabilities, owners' equity, revenue, and expense accounts, in that order.

The various ledger accounts in Illustration 3-8 show the accounts after the posting process is completed. The source of the data transferred to the ledger account is indicated by the reference GJ 12 (General Journal, page 12).

	Delivery Equipment		No. 8				
Nov. 1	GJ 12	22,400					

	Accounts Payable		No. 34				
Nov. 4	GJ 12	175	Nov. 1	GJ 12	22,400		
			3	GJ 12	280		
			16	GJ 12	95		

	Purchase Returns		No. 53				
			Nov. 4	GJ 12	175		

	Transportation-In		No. 55				
Nov. 16	GJ 12	95					

	Advertising Expense		No. 65				
Nov. 3	GJ 12	280					

Illustration 3-8

Ledger Accounts, in T-Account Format

Trial Balance

A **trial balance** is a list of accounts and their balances at a given time. Customarily, a trial balance is prepared at the end of an accounting period. The accounts are listed in the order in which they appear in the ledger, with debit balances listed in the left column and credit balances in the right column. The totals of the two columns must be in agreement.

The primary purpose of a trial balance is to prove the mathematical equality of debits and credits after posting. Under the double-entry system this equality will occur when the sum of the debit account balances equals the sum of the credit account balances. **A trial balance also uncovers errors in journalizing and posting. In addition, it is useful in the preparation of financial statements.** The procedures for preparing a trial balance consist of:

1. Listing the account titles and their balances.
2. Totaling the debit and credit columns.
3. Proving the equality of the two columns.

The trial balance prepared from the ledger of Pioneer Advertising Agency Inc. is presented in Illustration 3-9 (page 72). Note that the total debits $287,000 equal the total credits $287,000. Account numbers to the left of the account titles in the trial balance are also often shown.

A trial balance does not prove that all transactions have been recorded or that the ledger is correct. Numerous errors may exist even though the trial balance columns agree. For example, the trial balance may balance even when (1) a transaction is not

Illustration 3-9
Trial Balance
(Unadjusted)

PIONEER ADVERTISING AGENCY INC. TRIAL BALANCE OCTOBER 31, 2004		
	Debit	Credit
Cash	$ 80,000	
Accounts Receivable	72,000	
Advertising Supplies	25,000	
Prepaid Insurance	6,000	
Office Equipment	50,000	
Notes Payable		$ 50,000
Accounts Payable		25,000
Unearned Service Revenue		12,000
Common Stock		100,000
Dividends	5,000	
Service Revenue		100,000
Salaries Expense	40,000	
Rent Expense	9,000	
	$287,000	$287,000

journalized, (2) a correct journal entry is not posted, (3) a journal entry is posted twice, (4) incorrect accounts are used in journalizing or posting, or (5) offsetting errors are made in recording the amount of a transaction. In other words, as long as equal debits and credits are posted, even to the wrong account or in the wrong amount, the total debits will equal the total credits.

Adjusting Entries

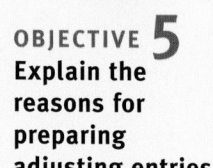

OBJECTIVE 5
Explain the reasons for preparing adjusting entries.

In order for revenues to be recorded in the period in which they are earned, and for expenses to be recognized in the period in which they are incurred, **adjusting entries** are made at the end of the accounting period. In short, **adjustments are needed to ensure that the revenue recognition and matching principles are followed**.

The use of adjusting entries makes it possible to report on the balance sheet the appropriate assets, liabilities, and owners' equity at the statement date and to report on the income statement the proper net income (or loss) for the period. However, the trial balance—the first pulling together of the transaction data—may not contain up-to-date and complete data. This is true for the following reasons.

1. Some events are not journalized daily because it is not expedient. Examples are the consumption of supplies and the earning of wages by employees.

2. Some costs are not journalized during the accounting period because these costs expire with the passage of time rather than as a result of recurring daily transactions. Examples of such costs are building and equipment deterioration and rent and insurance.

3. Some items may be unrecorded. An example is a utility service bill that will not be received until the next accounting period.

Adjusting entries are required every time financial statements are prepared. An essential starting point is an analysis of each account in the trial balance to determine whether it is complete and up-to-date for financial statement purposes. The analysis requires a thorough understanding of the company's operations and the interrelationship of accounts. The preparation of adjusting entries is often an involved process that requires the services of a skilled professional. In accumulating the adjustment data, the company may need to make inventory counts of supplies and repair parts. Also it may be desirable to prepare supporting schedules of insurance policies, rental agreements, and other contractual commitments. Adjustments are often prepared after the balance sheet date. However, the entries are dated as of the balance sheet date.

Types of Adjusting Entries

Adjusting entries can be classified as either prepayments or accruals. Each of these classes has two subcategories as shown below.

Prepayments	Accruals
1. **Prepaid Expenses.** Expenses paid in cash and recorded as assets before they are used or consumed.	3. **Accrued Revenues.** Revenues earned but not yet received in cash or recorded.
2. **Unearned Revenues.** Revenues received in cash and recorded as liabilities before they are earned.	4. **Accrued Expenses.** Expenses incurred but not yet paid in cash or recorded.

Specific examples and explanations of each type of adjustment are given in subsequent sections. Each example is based on the October 31 trial balance of Pioneer Advertising Agency Inc. (Illustration 3-9). We assume that Pioneer Advertising uses an accounting period of one month. Thus, monthly adjusting entries will be made. The entries will be dated October 31.

Adjusting Entries for Prepayments

As indicated earlier, prepayments are either prepaid expenses or unearned revenues. Adjusting entries for prepayments are required at the statement date to record the portion of the prepayment that represents the **expense incurred or the revenue earned** in the current accounting period. Assuming an adjustment is needed for both types of prepayments, the asset and liability are overstated and the related expense and revenue are understated. For example, in the trial balance, the balance in the asset Supplies shows only supplies purchased. This balance is overstated; the related expense account, Supplies Expense, is understated because the cost of supplies used has not been recognized. Thus the adjusting entry for prepayments will decrease a balance sheet account and increase an income statement account. The effects of adjusting entries for prepayments are graphically depicted in Illustration 3-10 (page 74).

Prepaid Expenses. Expenses paid in cash and recorded as assets before they are used or consumed are identified as **prepaid expenses**. When a cost is incurred, an asset account is debited to show the service or benefit that will be received in the future. Prepayments often occur in regard to insurance, supplies, advertising, and rent. In addition, prepayments are made when buildings and equipment are purchased.

Prepaid expenses expire either with the passage of time (e.g., rent and insurance) or through use and consumption (e.g., supplies). The expiration of these costs does not require daily recurring entries, which would be unnecessary and impractical. Accordingly, it is customary to postpone the recognition of such cost expirations until financial statements are prepared. At each statement date, adjusting entries are made to record the expenses that apply to the current accounting period and to show the unexpired costs in the asset accounts.

Prior to adjustment, assets are overstated and expenses are understated. **Thus, the prepaid expense adjusting entry results in a debit to an expense account and a credit to an asset account.**

Illustration 3-10
Adjusting Entries for
Prepayments

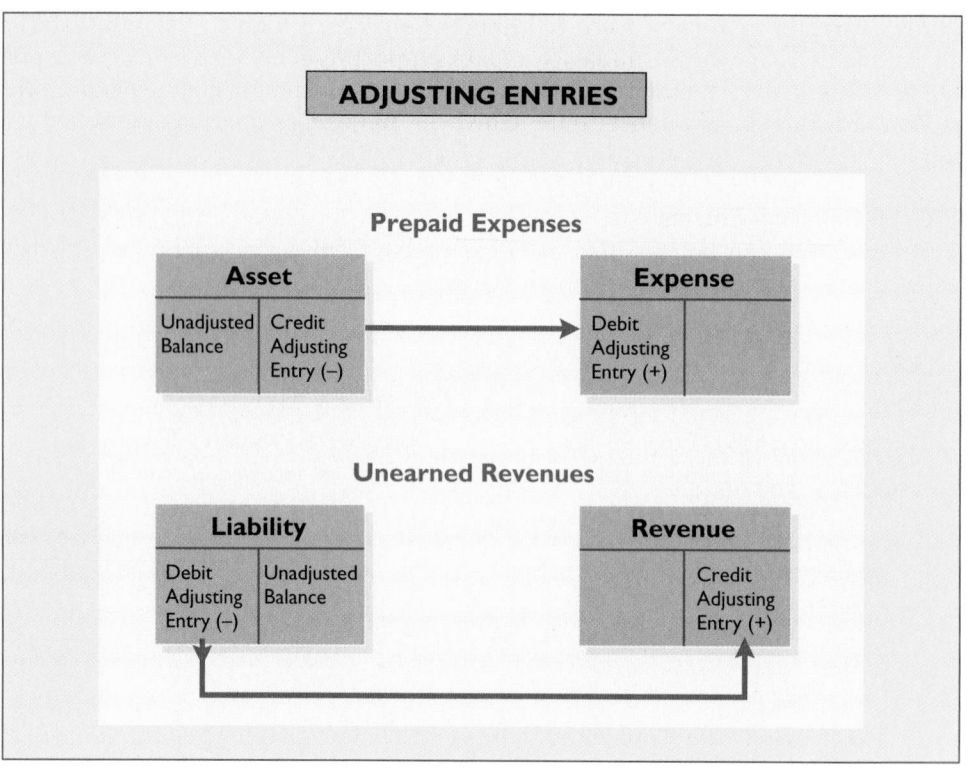

ADJUSTING ENTRIES

Prepaid Expenses

Asset		
Unadjusted Balance	Credit Adjusting Entry (−)	

Expense	
Debit Adjusting Entry (+)	

Unearned Revenues

Liability	
Debit Adjusting Entry (−)	Unadjusted Balance

Revenue	
	Credit Adjusting Entry (+)

Supplies

Oct. 5

Supplies purchased;
record asset

Oct. 31

Supplies used;
record supplies expense

Supplies. Several different types of supplies are used in a business enterprise. For example, a CPA firm will have **office supplies** such as stationery, envelopes, and accounting paper. An advertising firm will have **advertising supplies** such as graph paper, video film, and poster paper. Supplies are generally debited to an asset account when they are acquired. During the course of operations, supplies are depleted or entirely consumed. However, recognition of supplies used is deferred until the adjustment process, when a physical inventory (count) of supplies is taken. The difference between the balance in the Supplies (asset) account and the cost of supplies on hand represents the supplies used (expense) for the period.

Pioneer Advertising Agency (see Illustration 3-9) purchased advertising supplies costing $25,000 on October 5. The debit was made to the asset Advertising Supplies. This account shows a balance of $25,000 in the October 31 trial balance. An inventory count at the close of business on October 31 reveals that $10,000 of supplies are still on hand. Thus, the cost of supplies used is $15,000 ($25,000 − $10,000), and the following adjusting entry is made.

A	=	L	+	SE
−15,000				−15,000

Oct. 31
Advertising Supplies Expense 15,000
　Advertising Supplies 15,000
　　(To record supplies used)

After the adjusting entry is posted, the two supplies accounts in T-account form show the following.

Illustration 3-11
Supplies Accounts after
Adjustment

Advertising Supplies		Advertising Supplies Expense	
10/ 5　　25,000	10/31　Adj. 15,000	10/31　Adj. 15,000	
10/31　Bal. 10,000			

The asset account Advertising Supplies now shows a balance of $10,000, which is equal to the cost of supplies on hand at the statement date. In addition, Advertising Supplies Expense shows a balance of $15,000, which equals the cost of supplies used in October. **If the adjusting entry is not made, October expenses will be understated and net income overstated by $15,000. Moreover, both assets and owners' equity will be overstated by $15,000 on the October 31 balance sheet.**

Insurance. Most companies have fire and theft insurance on merchandise and equipment, personal liability insurance for accidents suffered by customers, and automobile insurance on company cars and trucks. The cost of insurance protection is determined by the payment of insurance premiums. The term and coverage are specified in the insurance policy. The minimum term is usually one year, but three- to five-year terms are available and offer lower annual premiums. Insurance premiums normally are charged to the asset account Prepaid Insurance when paid. At the financial statement date it is necessary to debit Insurance Expense and credit Prepaid Insurance for the cost that has expired during the period.

On October 4, Pioneer Advertising Agency Inc. paid $6,000 for a one-year fire insurance policy. The effective date of coverage was October 1. The premium was charged to Prepaid Insurance when it was paid, and this account shows a balance of $6,000 in the October 31 trial balance. An analysis of the policy reveals that $500 ($6,000 ÷ 12) of insurance expires each month. Thus, the following adjusting entry is made.

Insurance

Oct. 4

Insurance purchased;
record asset

Insurance Policy			
Oct	Nov	Dec	Jan
$500	$500	$500	$500
Feb	March	April	May
$500	$500	$500	$500
June	July	Aug	Sept
$500	$500	$500	$500
I YEAR $6,000			

Oct. 31
    Insurance expired;
record insurance expense

A	=	L	+	SE
−500				−500

	Oct. 31		
Insurance Expense		500	
Prepaid Insurance			500
(To record insurance expired)			

After the adjusting entry is posted, the accounts show:

Prepaid Insurance			Insurance Expense	
10/4 6,000	10/31 Adj. 500	10/31 Adj. 500	
10/31 Bal. 5,500			

Illustration 3-12
Insurance Accounts after Adjustment

The asset Prepaid Insurance shows a balance of $5,500, which represents the unexpired cost applicable to the remaining 11 months of coverage. At the same time, the balance in Insurance Expense is equal to the insurance cost that has expired in October. **If this adjustment is not made, October expenses will be understated by $500 and net income overstated by $500. Moreover, both assets and owners' equity also will be overstated by $500 on the October 31 balance sheet.**

Depreciation. A business enterprise typically owns a variety of productive facilities such as buildings, equipment, and motor vehicles. These assets provide a service for a number of years. The term of service is commonly referred to as the **useful life** of the asset. Because an asset such as a building is expected to provide service for many years, it is recorded as an asset, rather than an expense, in the year it is acquired. Such assets are recorded at cost, as required by the cost principle.

According to the matching principle, a portion of the cost of a long-lived asset should be reported as an expense during each period of the asset's useful life. **Depreciation** is the process of allocating the cost of an asset to expense over its useful life in a rational and systematic manner.

Depreciation

Oct.1

Office equipment purchased; record asset ($50,000)

Office Equipment			
Oct	Nov	Dec	Jan
$400	$400	$400	$400
Feb	March	April	May
$400	$400	$400	$400
June	July	Aug	Sept
$400	$400	$400	$400
Depreciation = $4,800/year			

Oct. 31
Depreciation recognized; record depreciation expense

A	=	L	+	SE
−400				−400

Need for depreciation adjustment. From an accounting standpoint, the acquisition of productive facilities is viewed essentially as a long-term prepayment for services. The need for making periodic adjusting entries for depreciation is, therefore, the same as described before for other prepaid expenses—that is, to recognize the cost that has expired (expense) during the period and to report the unexpired cost (asset) at the end of the period.

In determining the useful life of a productive facility, the primary causes of depreciation are actual use, deterioration due to the elements, and obsolescence. At the time an asset is acquired, the effects of these factors cannot be known with certainty, so they must be estimated. Thus, you should recognize that depreciation is an **estimate** rather than a factual measurement of the cost that has expired. A common procedure in computing depreciation expense is to divide the cost of the asset by its useful life. For example, if cost is $10,000 and useful life is expected to be 10 years, annual depreciation is $1,000.

For Pioneer Advertising, depreciation on the office equipment is estimated to be $4,800 a year (cost $50,000 less salvage value $2,000 divided by useful life of 10 years), or $400 per month. Accordingly, depreciation for October is recognized by the following adjusting entry.

Oct. 31

Depreciation Expense	400	
Accumulated Depreciation—Office Equipment		400
(To record monthly depreciation)		

After the adjusting entry is posted, the accounts show the following.

Illustration 3-13
Accounts after Adjustment for Depreciation

Office Equipment

10/1 50,000	

Accumulated Depreciation—Office Equipment

	10/31 Adj. 400

Depreciation Expense

10/31 Adj. 400	

The balance in the accumulated depreciation account will increase $400 each month. Therefore, after journalizing and posting the adjusting entry at November 30, the balance will be $800.

Statement presentation. Accumulated Depreciation—Office Equipment is a contra asset account. A **contra asset account** is an account that is offset against an asset account on the balance sheet. This means that the accumulated depreciation account is offset against Office Equipment on the balance sheet and that its normal balance is a credit. This account is used instead of crediting Office Equipment in order to permit disclosure of **both the original cost** of the equipment **and the total cost that has expired to date**. In the balance sheet, Accumulated Depreciation—Office Equipment is deducted from the related asset account as follows.

Illustration 3-14
Balance Sheet Presentation of Accumulated Depreciation

Office equipment	$50,000	
Less: Accumulated depreciation—office equipment	400	$49,600

The difference between the cost of any depreciable asset and its related accumulated depreciation is referred to as the **book value** of that asset. In Illustration 3-14, the book value of the equipment at the balance sheet date is $49,600. It is important to realize that the book value and the market value of the asset are generally two different amounts. The reason the two are different is that depreciation is not a matter of valuation but rather a means of cost allocation.

Note also that depreciation expense identifies that portion of the asset's cost that has expired in October. As in the case of other prepaid adjustments, the omission of this adjusting entry would cause total assets, total owners' equity, and net income to be overstated and depreciation expense to be understated.

If additional equipment is involved, such as delivery or store equipment, or if the company has buildings, depreciation expense is recorded on each of these items. Related accumulated depreciation accounts also are established. These accumulated depreciation accounts would be described in the ledger as follows: Accumulated Depreciation—Delivery Equipment; Accumulated Depreciation—Store Equipment; and Accumulated Depreciation—Buildings.

Unearned Revenues. Revenues received in cash and recorded as liabilities before they are earned are called **unearned revenues**. Such items as rent, magazine subscriptions, and customer deposits for further service may result in unearned revenues. Airlines such as **United**, **American**, and **Delta** treat receipts from the sale of tickets as unearned revenue until the flight service is provided. Similarly, tuition received prior to the start of a semester is considered to be unearned revenue. Unearned revenues are the opposite of prepaid expenses. Indeed, unearned revenue on the books of one company is likely to be a prepayment on the books of the company that has made the advance payment. For example, if identical accounting periods are assumed, a landlord will have unearned rent revenue when a tenant has prepaid rent.

Unearned Revenues

Oct. 2

Cash is received in advance; liability is recorded

Oct. 31
Service is provided; revenue is recorded

When the payment is received for services to be provided in a future accounting period, an unearned revenue (a liability) account should be credited to recognize the obligation that exists. Unearned revenues are subsequently earned through rendering service to a customer. During the accounting period it may not be practical to make daily recurring entries as the revenue is earned. In such cases, the recognition of earned revenue is delayed until the adjustment process. Then an adjusting entry is made to record the revenue that has been earned and to show the liability that remains. In the typical case, liabilities are overstated and revenues are understated prior to adjustment. Thus, **the adjusting entry for unearned revenues results in a debit (decrease) to a liability account and a credit (increase) to a revenue account**.

Pioneer Advertising Agency received $12,000 on October 2 from R. Knox for advertising services expected to be completed by December 31. The payment was credited to Unearned Service Revenue, and this account shows a balance of $12,000 in the October 31 trial balance. When analysis reveals that $4,000 of these services have been earned in October, the following adjusting entry is made.

	Oct. 31		
Unearned Service Revenue		4,000	
Service Revenue			4,000
(To record revenue for services provided)			

After the adjusting entry is posted, the accounts show the following.

Unearned Service Revenue		Service Revenue	
10/31 Adj. 4,000	10/2 12,000		10/31 Bal. 100,000
	10/31 Bal. 8,000		31 Adj. 4,000

Illustration 3-15
Service Revenue Accounts after Prepayments Adjustment

Expanded Discussion of Cash Basis versus Accrual Basis Accounting

The liability Unearned Service Revenue now shows a balance of $8,000, which represents the remaining advertising services expected to be performed in the future. At the same time, Service Revenue shows total revenue earned in October of $104,000. **If this adjustment is not made, revenues and net income will be understated by $4,000 in the income statement. Moreover, liabilities will be overstated and owners' equity will be understated by $4,000 on the October 31 balance sheet.**

Adjusting Entries for Accruals

The second category of adjusting entries is **accruals**. Adjusting entries for accruals are required to record revenues earned and expenses incurred in the current accounting period that have not been recognized through daily entries. If an accrual adjustment is needed, the revenue account (and the related asset account) and/or the expense account (and the related liability account) is understated. Thus, the adjusting entry for accruals will **increase both a balance sheet and an income statement account**. Adjusting entries for accruals are graphically depicted in Illustration 3-16.

Illustration 3-16
Adjusting Entries for Accruals

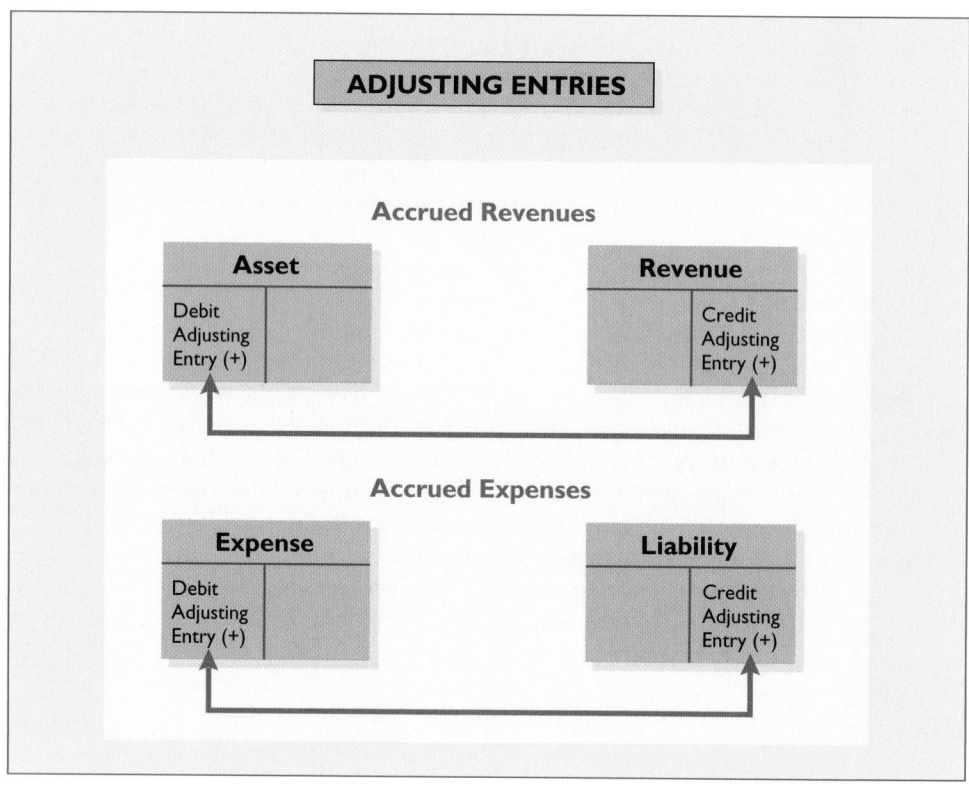

Accrued Revenues

Oct. 31

My fee is $2,000

Service is provided; revenue and receivable are recorded

Nov.
Cash is received; receivable is reduced

Accrued Revenues. Revenues earned but not yet received in cash or recorded at the statement date are **accrued revenues**. Accrued revenues may accumulate (accrue) with the passing of time, as in the case of interest revenue and rent revenue. Or they may result from services that have been performed but neither billed nor collected, as in the case of commissions and fees. The former are unrecorded because the earning of interest and rent does not involve daily transactions. The latter may be unrecorded because only a portion of the total service has been provided.

An adjusting entry is required to show the receivable that exists at the balance sheet date and to record the revenue that has been earned during the period. Prior to adjustment both assets and revenues are understated. Accordingly, **an adjusting entry for accrued revenues results in a debit (increase) to an asset account and a credit (increase) to a revenue account.**

In October Pioneer Advertising Agency earned $2,000 for advertising services that were not billed to clients before October 31. Because these services have not been billed, they have not been recorded. Thus, the following adjusting entry is made.

	Oct. 31		
Accounts Receivable		2,000	
Service Revenue			2,000
(To record revenue for services provided)			

After the adjusting entry is posted, the accounts show the following.

<table>
<tr><td colspan="2" align="center">Accounts Receivable</td><td colspan="2" align="center">Service Revenue</td></tr>
<tr><td>10/31</td><td>72,000</td><td>10/31</td><td>100,000</td></tr>
<tr><td>31 Adj.</td><td>2,000</td><td>31</td><td>4,000</td></tr>
<tr><td></td><td></td><td>31 Adj.</td><td>2,000</td></tr>
<tr><td></td><td></td><td>10/31 Bal.</td><td>106,000</td></tr>
</table>

Illustration 3-17
Receivable and Revenue Accounts after Accrual Adjustment

The asset Accounts Receivable shows that $74,000 is owed by clients at the balance sheet date. The balance of $106,000 in Service Revenue represents the total revenue earned during the month ($100,000 + $4,000 + $2,000). **If the adjusting entry is not made, assets and owners' equity on the balance sheet, and revenues and net income on the income statement, will all be understated.**

Accrued Expenses. Expenses incurred but not yet paid or recorded at the statement date are called **accrued expenses**. Interest, rent, taxes, and salaries can be accrued expenses. Accrued expenses result from the same causes as accrued revenues. In fact, an accrued expense on the books of one company is an accrued revenue to another company. For example, the $2,000 accrual of service revenue by Pioneer is an accrued expense to the client that received the service.

Adjustments for accrued expenses are necessary to record the obligations that exist at the balance sheet date and to recognize the expenses that apply to the current accounting period. Prior to adjustment, both liabilities and expenses are understated. Therefore, **the adjusting entry for accrued expenses results in a debit (increase) to an expense account and a credit (increase) to a liability account.**

Accrued Interest. Pioneer Advertising Agency signed a three-month note payable in the amount of $50,000 on October 1. The note requires interest at an annual rate of 12 percent. The amount of the interest accumulation is determined by three factors: (1) the face value of the note, (2) the interest rate, which is always expressed as an annual rate, and (3) the length of time the note is outstanding. The total interest due on Pioneer's $50,000 note at its due date three months hence is $1,500 ($50,000 × 12% × 3/12), or $500 for one month. The formula for computing interest and its application to Pioneer Advertising Agency for October are shown in Illustration 3-18.

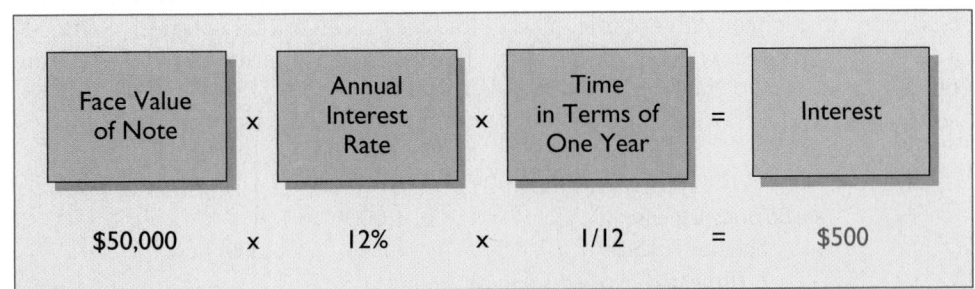

Illustration 3-18
Formula for Computing Interest

Face Value of Note	×	Annual Interest Rate	×	Time in Terms of One Year	=	Interest
$50,000	×	12%	×	1/12	=	$500

Note that the time period is expressed as a fraction of a year. The accrued expense adjusting entry at October 31 is as follows.

A	=	L	+	SE
		+500		−500

Oct. 31

Interest Expense	500	
Interest Payable		500
(To record interest on notes payable)		

After this adjusting entry is posted, the accounts show the following.

Illustration 3-19
Interest Accounts after
Adjustment

Interest Expense		Interest Payable	
10/31	500	10/31	500

Interest Expense shows the interest charges applicable to the month of October. The amount of interest owed at the statement date is shown in Interest Payable. It will not be paid until the note comes due at the end of three months. The Interest Payable account is used instead of crediting Notes Payable to disclose the two types of obligations (interest and principal) in the accounts and statements. **If this adjusting entry is not made, liabilities and interest expense will be understated, and net income and owners' equity will be overstated.**

Accrued Salaries.   Some types of expenses, such as employee salaries and commissions, are paid for after the services have been performed. At Pioneer Advertising, salaries were last paid on October 26; the next payment of salaries will not occur until November 9. As shown in the calendar below, three working days remain in October (October 29–31).

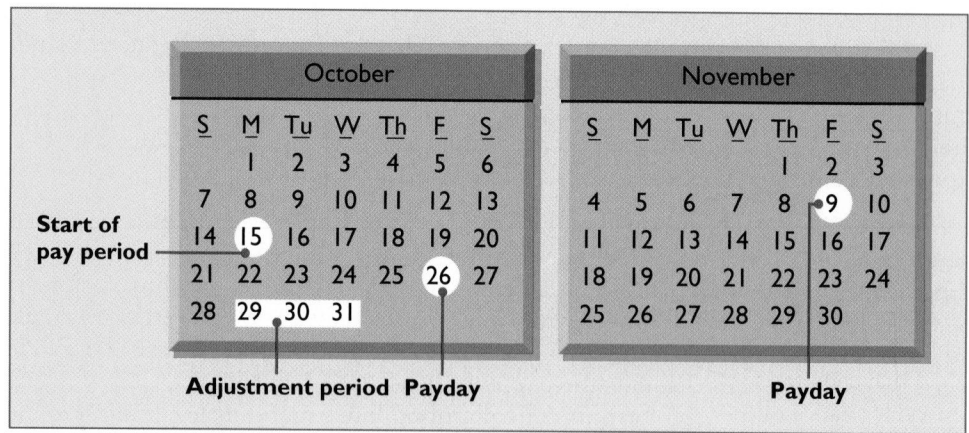

At October 31, the salaries for these days represent an accrued expense and a related liability to Pioneer Advertising. The employees receive total salaries of $10,000 for a five-day work week, or $2,000 per day. Thus, accrued salaries at October 31 are $6,000 ($2,000 × 3), and the adjusting entry is as follows.

A	=	L	+	SE
		+6,000		−6,000

Oct. 31

Salaries Expense	6,000	
Salaries Payable		6,000
(To record accrued salaries)		

After this adjusting entry is posted, the accounts show the following.

Salaries Expense		Salaries Payable	
10/26 40,000			10/31 Adj. 6,000
31 Adj. 6,000			
10/31 Bal. 46,000			

Illustration 3-20
Salary Accounts after Adjustment

After this adjustment, the balance in Salaries Expense of $46,000 (23 days × $2,000) is the actual salary expense for October. The balance in Salaries Payable of $6,000 is the amount of the liability for salaries owed as of October 31. **If the $6,000 adjustment for salaries is not recorded, Pioneer's expenses will be understated $6,000, and its liabilities will be understated $6,000.**

At Pioneer Advertising, salaries are payable every two weeks. Consequently, the next payday is November 9, when total salaries of $20,000 will again be paid. The payment consists of $6,000 of salaries payable at October 31 plus $14,000 of salaries expense for November (7 working days as shown in the November calendar × $2,000). Therefore, the following entry is made on November 9.

	Nov. 9		
Salaries Payable		6,000	
Salaries Expense		14,000	
Cash			20,000
(To record November 9 payroll)			

A	=	L	+	SE
−20,000		−6,000		−14,000

This entry eliminates the liability for Salaries Payable that was recorded in the October 31 adjusting entry and records the proper amount of Salaries Expense for the period between November 1 and November 9.

Bad Debts. Proper matching of revenues and expenses dictates recording bad debts as an expense of the period in which revenue is earned instead of the period in which the accounts or notes are written off. The proper valuation of the receivable balance also requires recognition of uncollectible, worthless receivables. Proper matching and valuation require an adjusting entry.

At the end of each period an estimate is made of the amount of current period revenue on account that will later prove to be uncollectible. The estimate is based on the amount of bad debts experienced in past years, general economic conditions, how long the receivables are past due, and other factors that indicate the element of uncollectibility. Usually it is expressed as a percentage of the revenue on account for the period. Or it may be computed by adjusting the Allowance for Doubtful Accounts to a certain percentage of the trade accounts receivable and trade notes receivable at the end of the period.

To illustrate, assume that experience indicates a reasonable estimate for bad debt expense for the month is $1,600. The adjusting entry for bad debts is:

Bad Debts

Oct. 31
Uncollectible accounts; record bad debt expense

	Oct. 31		
Bad Debt Expense		1,600	
Allowance for Doubtful Accounts			1,600
(To record monthly bad debt expense)			

After the adjusting entry is posted, the accounts show the following.

Illustration 3-21
Accounts after
Adjustment for Bad
Debt Expense

Accounts Receivable	
10/ 1 72,000	
31 Adj. 2,000	

Allowance for Doubtful Accounts		Bad Debt Expense	
	10/31 Adj. 1,600	10/31 Adj. 1,600	

Adjusted Trial Balance

After all adjusting entries have been journalized and posted, another trial balance is prepared from the ledger accounts. This trial balance is called an **adjusted trial balance**. It shows the balance of all accounts, including those that have been adjusted, at the end of the accounting period. The purpose of an adjusted trial balance is to show the effects of all financial events that have occurred during the accounting period.

Illustration 3-22
Adjusted Trial Balance

PIONEER ADVERTISING AGENCY, INC.
ADJUSTED TRIAL BALANCE
OCTOBER 31, 2004

	Debit	Credit
Cash	$ 80,000	
Accounts Receivable	74,000	
Allowance for Doubtful Accounts		$ 1,600
Advertising Supplies	10,000	
Prepaid Insurance	5,500	
Office Equipment	50,000	
Accumulated Depreciation—		
Office Equipment		400
Notes Payable		50,000
Accounts Payable		25,000
Interest Payable		500
Unearned Service Revenue		8,000
Salaries Payable		6,000
Common Stock		100,000
Dividends	5,000	
Service Revenue		106,000
Salaries Expense	46,000	
Advertising Supplies Expense	15,000	
Rent Expense	9,000	
Insurance Expense	500	
Interest Expense	500	
Depreciation Expense	400	
Bad Debt Expense	1,600	
	$297,500	$297,500

Closing

Basic Process

The procedure generally followed to reduce the balance of nominal (temporary) accounts to zero in order to prepare the accounts for the next period's transactions is known as the **closing process**. In the closing process all of the revenue and expense account balances (income statement items) are transferred to a clearing or suspense account called Income Summary, which is used only at the end of each accounting period (yearly). Revenues and expenses are matched in the Income Summary account. The net result of this matching, which represents the net income or net loss for the period, is then transferred to an owners' equity account (retained earnings for a corporation, and capital accounts normally for proprietorships and partnerships). All such **closing entries** are posted to the appropriate general ledger accounts.

> **OBJECTIVE 6**
> **Prepare closing entries.**

For example, assume that revenue accounts of Collegiate Apparel Shop have the following balances, after adjustments, at the end of the year.

Sales Revenue	$280,000
Rental Revenue	27,000
Interest Revenue	5,000

These **revenue accounts** would be closed and the balances transferred by the following closing journal entry.

Sales Revenue	280,000	
Rental Revenue	27,000	
Interest Revenue	5,000	
Income Summary		312,000
(To close revenue accounts to Income Summary)		

Assume that the expense accounts, including Cost of Goods Sold, have the following balances, after adjustments, at the end of the year.

Cost of Goods Sold	$206,000
Selling Expenses	25,000
General and Adm. Expenses	40,600
Interest Expense	4,400
Income Tax Expense	13,000

These **expense accounts** would be closed and the balances transferred through the following closing journal entry.

Income Summary	289,000	
Cost of Goods Sold		206,000
Selling Expenses		25,000
General and Adm. Expenses		40,600
Interest Expense		4,400
Income Tax Expense		13,000
(To close expense accounts to Income Summary)		

The Income Summary account now has a credit balance of $23,000, which is net income. The **net income is transferred to owners' equity** by closing the Income Summary account to Retained Earnings as follows.

A	=	L	+	SE
				−23,000
				+23,000

Income Summary	23,000	
Retained Earnings		23,000
(To close Income Summary to Retained Earnings)		

Assuming that dividends of $7,000 were declared and distributed during the year, the Dividends account is closed directly to Retained Earnings as follows.

A	=	L	+	SE
				−7,000
				+7,000

Retained Earnings	7,000	
Dividends		7,000
(To close Dividends to Retained Earnings)		

After the closing process is completed, each income statement (i.e., nominal) account is balanced out to zero and is ready for use in the next accounting period. Illustration 3-23 shows the closing process in T-account form.

Illustration 3-23
The Closing Process

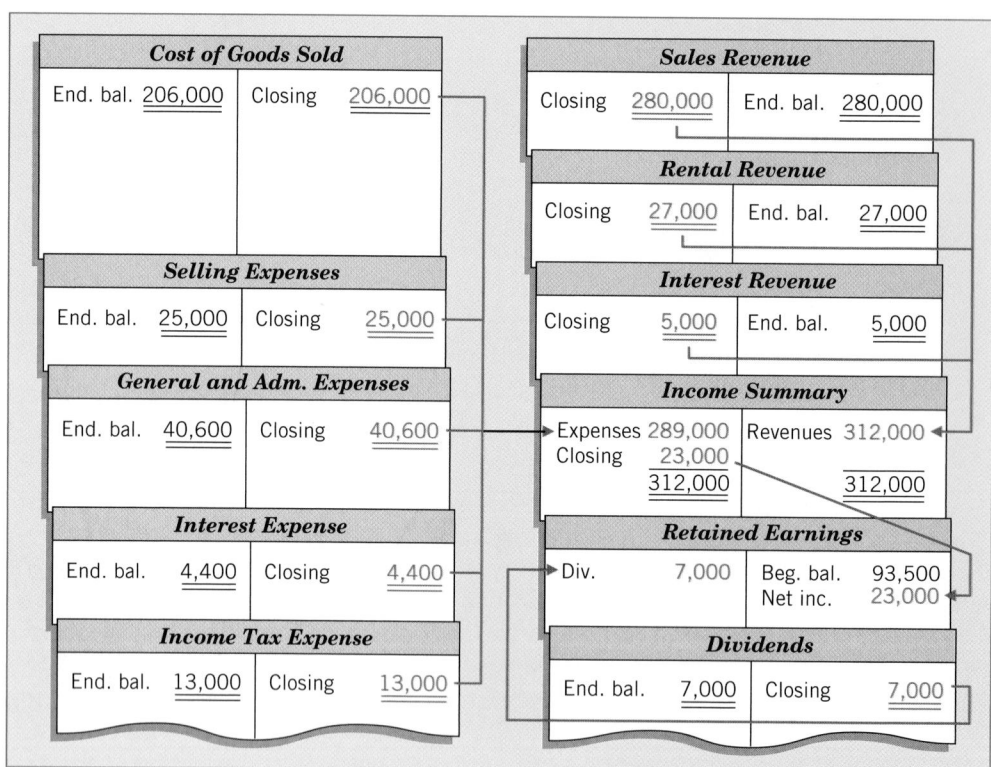

Inventory and Cost of Goods Sold

The closing procedures illustrated above assumed the use of the perpetual inventory system. With a **perpetual inventory system**, purchases and sales are recorded **directly in the Inventory account** as the purchases and sales occur. Therefore, the balance in the Inventory account should represent the ending inventory amount, and no adjusting entries are needed. To ensure this accuracy, a physical count of the items in the inventory is generally made annually. No Purchases account is used because the purchases are debited directly to the Inventory account. However, a Cost of Goods Sold account is used to accumulate the issuances from inventory. That is, when inventory items are sold, the cost of the sold goods is credited to Inventory and debited to Cost of Goods Sold.

With a **periodic inventory system**, a Purchases account is used, and the Inventory account is unchanged during the period. The Inventory account represents the beginning inventory amount throughout the period. At the end of the accounting period the Inventory account must be adjusted by **closing out the beginning inventory** amount and **recording the ending inventory** amount. The ending inventory is determined by physically counting the items on hand and valuing them at cost or at the lower of cost or market. Under the periodic inventory system, cost of goods sold is, therefore, determined by adding the beginning inventory together with net purchases and deducting the ending inventory.

To illustrate how cost of goods sold is computed with a periodic inventory system, assume that Collegiate Apparel Shop has a beginning inventory of $30,000; Purchases $200,000; Transportation-In $6,000; Purchase Returns and Allowances $1,000; Purchase Discounts $3,000; and the ending inventory is $26,000. The computation of cost of goods sold is as follows.

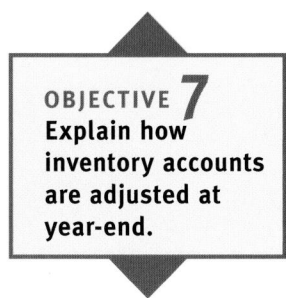

OBJECTIVE **7**
Explain how inventory accounts are adjusted at year-end.

Beginning inventory			$ 30,000
Purchases		$200,000	
Less: Purchase returns and allowances	$1,000		
Purchase discounts	3,000	4,000	
Net purchases		196,000	
Plus: Transportation-in		6,000	
Cost of goods purchased			202,000
Cost of goods available for sale			232,000
Less: Ending inventory			26,000
Cost of goods sold			$206,000

Illustration 3-24
Computation of Cost of Goods Sold Under Periodic Inventory System

Cost of goods sold will be the same whether the perpetual or periodic method is used.

Post-Closing Trial Balance

We already mentioned that a trial balance is taken after the regular transactions of the period have been entered and that a second trial balance (the adjusted trial balance) is taken after the adjusting entries have been posted. A third trial balance may be taken after posting the closing entries. The trial balance after closing, called the **post-closing trial balance**, shows that equal debits and credits have been posted to the Income Summary account. The post-closing trial balance consists only of asset, liability, and owners' equity (the real) accounts.

Reversing Entries

After the financial statements have been prepared and the books have been closed, it is often helpful to reverse some of the adjusting entries before recording the regular transactions of the next period. Such entries are called **reversing entries**. **A reversing entry is made at the beginning of the next accounting period and is the exact opposite of the related adjusting entry made in the previous period.** The recording of reversing entries is an **optional** step in the accounting cycle that may be performed at the beginning of the next accounting period. Appendix 3A discusses reversing entries in more detail.

The Accounting Cycle Summarized

A summary of the steps in the accounting cycle shows a logical sequence of the accounting procedures used during a fiscal period:

① Enter the transactions of the period in appropriate journals.

② Post from the journals to the ledger (or ledgers).

③ Take an unadjusted trial balance (trial balance).

④ Prepare adjusting journal entries and post to the ledger(s).

⑤ Take a trial balance after adjusting (adjusted trial balance).

⑥ Prepare the financial statements from the second trial balance.

⑦ Prepare closing journal entries and post to the ledger(s).

⑧ Take a trial balance after closing (post-closing trial balance).

⑨ Prepare reversing entries (optional) and post to the ledger(s).

This list of procedures constitutes a complete accounting cycle that is normally performed in every fiscal period.

USING A WORK SHEET

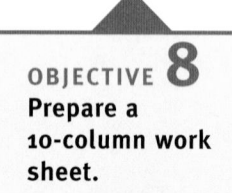

OBJECTIVE **8**
Prepare a
10-column work
sheet.

To facilitate the end-of-period (monthly, quarterly, or annually) accounting and reporting process, a work sheet is often used. A **work sheet** is a columnar sheet of paper used to adjust the account balances and prepare the financial statements. Use of a work sheet helps the accountant prepare the financial statements on a more timely basis. It is not necessary to delay preparation of the financial statements until the adjusting and closing entries are journalized and posted. The **10-column work sheet** illustrated in this chapter (Illustration 3-25 on page 87) provides columns for the first trial balance, adjustments, adjusted trial balance, income statement, and balance sheet.

The work sheet does not replace the financial statements. Instead, it is an informal device for accumulating and sorting information needed for the financial statements. Completing the work sheet provides considerable assurance that all of the details related to the end-of-period accounting and statement preparation have been properly brought together.

Adjustments Entered on the Work Sheet

Items (a) through (f) below serve as the basis for the adjusting entries made in the work sheet shown in Illustration 3-25.

(a) Furniture and equipment is depreciated at the rate of 10% per year based on original cost of $67,000.

(b) Estimated bad debts, one-quarter of 1% of sales ($400,000).

(c) Insurance expired during the year, $360.

(d) Interest accrued on notes receivable as of December 31, $800.

(e) The Rent Expense account contains $500 rent paid in advance, which is applicable to next year.

(f) Property taxes accrued December 31, $2,000.

Illustration 3-25
Use of a Work Sheet

UPTOWN CABINET CORP.
TEN-COLUMN WORK SHEET
FOR THE YEAR ENDED DECEMBER 31, 2004

Accounts	Trial Balance Dr.	Trial Balance Cr.	Adjustments Dr.	Adjustments Cr.	Adjusted Trial Balance Dr.	Adjusted Trial Balance Cr.	Income Statement Dr.	Income Statement Cr.	Balance Sheet Dr.	Balance Sheet Cr.
Cash	1,200				1,200				1,200	
Notes receivable	16,000				16,000				16,000	
Accounts receivable	41,000				41,000				41,000	
Allowance for doubtful accounts		2,000		(b) 1,000		3,000				3,000
Merchandise inventory	40,000				40,000				40,000	
Prepaid insurance	900			(c) 360	540				540	
Furniture and equipment	67,000				67,000				67,000	
Accumulated depreciation— furniture and equipment		12,000		(a) 6,700		18,700				18,700
Notes payable		20,000				20,000				20,000
Accounts payable		13,500				13,500				13,500
Bonds payable		30,000				30,000				30,000
Common stock		50,000				50,000				50,000
Retained earnings, Jan. 1, 2004		14,200				14,200				14,200
Sales		400,000				400,000		400,000		
Cost of goods sold	316,000				316,000		316,000			
Sales salaries expense	20,000				20,000		20,000			
Advertising expense	2,200				2,200		2,200			
Traveling expense	8,000				8,000		8,000			
Salaries, office and general	19,000				19,000		19,000			
Telephone and Internet expense	600				600		600			
Rent expense	4,800			(e) 500	4,300		4,300			
Property tax expense	3,300		(f) 2,000		5,300		5,300			
Interest expense	1,700				1,700		1,700			
Totals	541,700	541,700								
Depreciation expense— furniture and equipment			(a) 6,700		6,700		6,700			
Bad debt expense			(b) 1,000		1,000		1,000			
Insurance expense			(c) 360		360		360			
Interest receivable			(d) 800		800				800	
Interest revenue				(d) 800		800		800		
Prepaid rent expense			(e) 500		500				500	
Property tax payable				(f) 2,000		2,000				2,000
Totals			11,360	11,360	552,200	552,200	385,160	400,800		
Income before income taxes							15,640			
Totals							400,800	400,800		
Income before income taxes								15,640		
Income tax expense			(g) 3,440				3,440			
Income tax payable				(g) 3,440						3,440
Net income							12,200			12,200
Totals							15,640	15,640	167,040	167,040

The adjusting entries shown on the December 31, 2004, work sheet are as follows.

(a)		
Depreciation Expense—Furniture and Equipment	6,700	
Accumulated Depreciation—Furniture and Equipment		6,700
(b)		
Bad Debt Expense	1,000	
Allowance for Doubtful Accounts		1,000
(c)		
Insurance Expense	360	
Prepaid Insurance		360
(d)		
Interest Receivable	800	
Interest Revenue		800
(e)		
Prepaid Rent Expense	500	
Rent Expense		500
(f)		
Property Tax Expense	2,000	
Property Tax Payable		2,000

These adjusting entries are transferred to the Adjustments columns of the work sheet, and each may be designated by letter. The accounts that are set up as a result of the adjusting entries and that are not already in the trial balance are listed below the totals of the trial balance, as illustrated on the work sheet. The Adjustments columns are then totaled and balanced.

Work Sheet Columns

Trial Balance Columns

Data for the trial balance are obtained from the ledger balances of Uptown Cabinet Corp. at December 31. The amount for Merchandise Inventory, $40,000, is the year-end inventory amount, which results from the application of a perpetual inventory system.

Adjustments Columns

After all adjustment data are entered on the work sheet, the equality of the adjustment columns is established. The balances in all accounts are then extended to the adjusted trial balance columns.

Adjusted Trial Balance

The adjusted trial balance shows the balance of all accounts after adjustment at the end of the accounting period. For example, the $2,000 shown opposite the Allowance for Doubtful Accounts in the Trial Balance Cr. column is added to the $1,000 in the Adjustments Cr. column. The $3,000 total is then extended to the Adjusted Trial Balance Cr. column. Similarly, the $900 debit opposite Prepaid Insurance is reduced by the $360 credit in the Adjustments column. The result, $540, is shown in the Adjusted Trial Balance Dr. column.

Income Statement and Balance Sheet Columns

All the debit items in the Adjusted Trial Balance columns are extended into the Income Statement or Balance Sheet columns to the right. All the credit items are similarly extended.

The next step is to total the Income Statement columns; the figure necessary to balance the debit and credit columns is the pretax income or loss for the period. The income before income taxes of $15,640 is shown in the Income Statement Dr. column because revenues exceeded expenses by that amount.

Income Taxes and Net Income

The federal and state income tax expense and related tax liability are computed next. The company applies an effective rate of 22 percent to arrive at $3,440. Because the Adjustments columns have been balanced, this adjustment is entered in the Income Statement Dr. column as Income Tax Expense and in the Balance Sheet Cr. column as Income Tax Payable. The following adjusting journal entry is recorded on December 31, 2004, and posted to the general ledger as well as entered on the work sheet.

	(g)	
Income Tax Expense	3,440	
Income Tax Payable		3,440

A	=	L	+	SE
		+3,440		−3,440

Next, the Income Statement columns are balanced with the income taxes included. The $12,200 difference between the debit and credit columns in this illustration represents net income. The net income of $12,200 is entered in the Income Statement Dr. column to achieve equality and in the Balance Sheet Cr. column as the increase in retained earnings.

Preparing Financial Statements from a Work Sheet

The work sheet provides the information needed for preparation of the financial statements without reference to the ledger or other records. In addition, the data have been sorted into appropriate columns, which facilitates the preparation of the statements.

The financial statements prepared from the 10-column work sheet illustrated are as follows:

Using a Worksheet— Periodic Inventory

1 Income Statement for the Year Ended December 31, 2004 (Illustration 3-26).

2 Statement of Retained Earnings for the Year Ended December 31, 2004 (Illustration 3-27).

3 Balance Sheet as of December 31, 2004 (Illustration 3-28).

These illustrations are shown on the following pages.

Income Statement

The income statement presented is that of a trading or merchandising concern. If a manufacturing concern were illustrated, three inventory accounts would be involved: Raw Materials, Work in Process, and Finished Goods. When these accounts are used, a supplementary statement entitled Cost of Goods Manufactured must be prepared.

Statement of Retained Earnings

The net income earned by a corporation may be retained in the business, or it may be distributed to stockholders by payment of dividends. In the illustration, the net income earned during the year was added to the balance of retained earnings on January 1,

Illustration 3-26
An Income Statement

UPTOWN CABINET CORP. INCOME STATEMENT FOR THE YEAR ENDED DECEMBER 31, 2004			
Net sales			$400,000
Cost of goods sold			316,000
Gross profit on sales			84,000
Selling expenses			
Sales salaries expense		$20,000	
Advertising expense		2,200	
Traveling expense		8,000	
Total selling expenses		30,200	
Administrative expenses			
Salaries, office and general	$19,000		
Telephone and Internet expense	600		
Rent expense	4,300		
Property tax expense	5,300		
Depreciation expense—furniture and equipment	6,700		
Bad debt expense	1,000		
Insurance expense	360		
Total administrative expenses		37,260	
Total selling and administrative expenses			67,460
Income from operations			16,540
Other revenues and gains			
Interest revenue			800
			17,340
Other expenses and losses			
Interest expense			1,700
Income before income taxes			15,640
Income taxes			3,440
Net income			$ 12,200
Earnings per share			$1.22

thereby increasing the balance of retained earnings to $26,400 on December 31. No dividends were declared during the year.

Illustration 3-27
A Statement of Retained Earnings

UPTOWN CABINET CORP. STATEMENT OF RETAINED EARNINGS FOR THE YEAR ENDED DECEMBER 31, 2004	
Retained earnings, Jan. 1, 2004	$14,200
Add: Net income for 2004	12,200
Retained earnings, Dec. 31, 2004	$26,400

Balance Sheet

The balance sheet prepared from the 10-column work sheet contains new items resulting from year-end adjusting entries. Interest receivable, unexpired insurance, and prepaid rent expense are included as current assets. These assets are considered current because they will be converted into cash or consumed in the ordinary routine of the

Illustration 3-28
A Balance Sheet

UPTOWN CABINET CORP.
BALANCE SHEET
AS OF DECEMBER 31, 2004

Assets

Current assets			
Cash			$ 1,200
Notes receivable	$16,000		
Accounts receivable	41,000		
Interest receivable	800	$57,800	
Less: Allowance for doubtful accounts		3,000	54,800
Merchandise inventory			40,000
Prepaid insurance			540
Prepaid rent			500
Total current assets			97,040
Property, plant, and equipment			
Furniture and equipment		67,000	
Less: Accumulated depreciation		18,700	
Total property, plant, and equipment			48,300
Total assets			$145,340

Liabilities and Stockholders' Equity

Current liabilities			
Notes payable			$ 20,000
Accounts payable			13,500
Property tax payable			2,000
Income tax payable			3,440
Total current liabilities			38,940
Long-term liabilities			
Bonds payable, due June 30, 2009			30,000
Total liabilities			68,940
Stockholders' equity			
Common stock, $5.00 par value, issued and outstanding, 10,000 shares		$50,000	
Retained earnings		26,400	
Total stockholders' equity			76,400
Total liabilities and stockholders' equity			$145,340

business within a relatively short period of time. The amount of Allowance for Doubtful Accounts is deducted from the total of accounts, notes, and interest receivable because it is estimated that only $54,800 of $57,800 will be collected in cash.

In the property, plant, and equipment section the accumulated depreciation is deducted from the cost of the furniture and equipment. The difference represents the book or carrying value of the furniture and equipment.

Property tax payable is shown as a current liability because it is an obligation that is payable within a year. Other short-term accrued liabilities would also be shown as current liabilities.

The bonds payable, due in 2009, are long-term liabilities and are shown in a separate section. (Interest on the bonds was paid on December 31.)

Because Uptown Cabinet Corp. is a corporation, the capital section of the balance sheet, called the stockholders' equity section in the illustration, is somewhat different from the capital section for a proprietorship. Total stockholders' equity consists of the common stock, which is the original investment by stockholders, and the earnings retained in the business.

Closing Entries

The entries for the closing process are as follows.

General Journal
December 31, 2004

Interest Revenue	800	
Sales	400,000	
Cost of Goods Sold		316,000
Sales Salaries Expense		20,000
Advertising Expense		2,200
Traveling Expense		8,000
Salaries, Office and General		19,000
Telephone and Internet Expense		600
Rent Expense		4,300
Property Tax Expense		5,300
Depreciation Expense—Furniture and Equipment		6,700
Bad Debt Expense		1,000
Insurance Expense		360
Interest Expense		1,700
Income Tax Expense		3,440
Income Summary		12,200
(To close revenues and expenses to Income Summary)		
Income Summary	12,200	
Retained Earnings		12,200
(To close Income Summary to Retained Earnings)		

Monthly Statements, Yearly Closing

The use of a work sheet at the end of each month or quarter permits the preparation of interim financial statements even though the books are closed only at the end of each year. For example, assume that a business closes its books on December 31 but that monthly financial statements are desired. At the end of January, a work sheet similar to the one illustrated in this chapter can be prepared to supply the information needed for statements for January. At the end of February, a work sheet can be used again. Note that because the accounts were not closed at the end of January, the income statement taken from the work sheet on February 28 will present the net income for two months. If an income statement for only the month of February is wanted, it can be obtained by subtracting the items in the January income statement from the corresponding items in the income statement for the two months of January and February.

A statement of retained earnings for February only also may be obtained by subtracting the January items. The balance sheet prepared from the February work sheet, however, shows assets, liabilities, and stockholders' equity as of February 28, the specific date for which a balance sheet is desired.

The March work sheet would show the revenues and expenses for three months. The subtraction of the revenues and expenses for the first two months could be made to supply the amounts needed for an income statement for the month of March only, and so on throughout the year.

SUMMARY OF LEARNING OBJECTIVES

❶ Understand basic accounting terminology. It is important to understand the following eleven terms: (1) Event. (2) Transaction. (3) Account. (4) Real and nominal accounts. (5) Ledger. (6) Journal. (7) Posting. (8) Trial balance. (9) Adjusting entries. (10) Financial statements. (11) Closing entries.

❷ Explain double-entry rules. The left side of any account is the debit side; the right side is the credit side. All asset and expense accounts are increased on the left or debit side and decreased on the right or credit side. Conversely, all liability and revenue accounts are increased on the right or credit side and decreased on the left or debit side. Stockholders' equity accounts, Common Stock and Retained Earnings, are increased on the credit side. Dividends is increased on the debit side.

❸ Identify steps in the accounting cycle. The basic steps in the accounting cycle are (1) identification and measurement of transactions and other events; (2) journalization; (3) posting; (4) unadjusted trial balance; (5) adjustments; (6) adjusted trial balance; (7) statement preparation; and (8) closing.

❹ Record transactions in journals, post to ledger accounts, and prepare a trial balance. The simplest journal form is a chronological listing of transactions and events expressed in terms of debits and credits to particular accounts. The items entered in a general journal must be transferred (posted) to the general ledger. An unadjusted trial balance should be prepared at the end of a given period after the entries have been recorded in the journal and posted to the ledger.

❺ Explain the reasons for preparing adjusting entries. Adjustments are necessary to achieve a proper matching of revenues and expenses, so as to determine net income for the current period and to achieve an accurate statement of end-of-the-period balances in assets, liabilities, and owners' equity accounts.

❻ Prepare closing entries. In the closing process all of the revenue and expense account balances (income statement items) are transferred to a clearing account called Income Summary, which is used only at the end of the fiscal year. Revenues and expenses are matched in the Income Summary account. The net result of this matching represents the net income or net loss for the period. It is then transferred to an owners' equity account (retained earnings for a corporation and capital accounts for proprietorships and partnerships).

❼ Explain how inventory accounts are adjusted at year-end. Under a perpetual inventory system the balance in the Inventory account should represent the ending inventory amount. When the inventory records are maintained in a periodic inventory system, a Purchases account is used; the Inventory account is unchanged during the period. The Inventory account represents the beginning inventory amount throughout the period. At the end of the accounting period the inventory account must be adjusted by closing out the beginning inventory amount and recording the ending inventory amount.

❽ Prepare a 10-column work sheet. The 10-column work sheet provides columns for the first trial balance, adjustments, adjusted trial balance, income statement, and balance sheet. The work sheet does not replace the financial statements. Instead, it is the accountant's informal device for accumulating and sorting information needed for the financial statements.

KEY TERMS

account, *63*
accounting cycle, *68*
accounting information
  system, *62*
accrued expenses, *79*
accrued revenues, *78*
adjusted trial balance, *63*,
  82
adjusting entry, *63*, *72*
balance sheet, *63*
book value, *76*
closing entries, *63*, *83*
closing process, *83*
contra asset account, *76*
credit, *64*
debit, *64*
depreciation, *75*
double-entry accounting, *64*
event, *63*
financial statements, *63*
general journal, *69*
general ledger, *69*
income statement, *63*
journal, *63*
ledger, *63*
nominal accounts, *63*
periodic inventory
  system, *85*
perpetual inventory
  system, *84*
post-closing trial balance,
  63, *85*
posting, *63*, *70*
prepaid expense, *73*
real accounts, *63*
reversing entries, *85*
special journals, *70*
statement of cash flows, *63*
statement of retained
  earnings, *63*
T-account, *69*
transaction, *63*
trial balance, *63*, *71*
unearned revenues, *77*
useful life, *75*
work sheet, *86*

REVIEW EXERCISE

Nalezny Advertising Agency was founded by Casey Hayward in January 2000. Presented below are both the adjusted and unadjusted trial balances as of December 31, 2003.

NALEZNY ADVERTISING AGENCY
TRIAL BALANCE
DECEMBER 31, 2003

	Unadjusted Dr.	Unadjusted Cr.	Adjusted Dr.	Adjusted Cr.
Cash	$ 11,000		$ 11,000	
Accounts Receivable	20,000		21,500	
Art Supplies	8,400		5,000	
Printing Equipment	60,000		60,000	
Accumulated Depreciation		$ 28,000		$ 35,000
Accounts Payable		5,000		5,000
Unearned Advertising Revenue		7,000		5,600
Salaries Payable		—0—		1,300
Common Stock		10,000		10,000
Retained Earnings		4,800		4,800
Advertising Revenue		58,600		61,500
Salaries Expense	10,000		11,300	
Depreciation Expense			7,000	
Art Supplies Expense			3,400	
Rent Expense	4,000		4,000	
	$113,400	$113,400	$123,200	$123,200

Instructions

(a) Journalize the annual adjusting entries that were made.
(b) Prepare an income statement for the year ending December 31, 2003, and a balance sheet at December 31.
(c) Describe the remaining steps in the accounting cycle to be completed by Nalezny for 2003.

SOLUTION TO REVIEW EXERCISE

(a)

Dec. 31	Accounts Receivable	1,500	
	Advertising Revenue		1,500
31	Unearned Advertising Revenue	1,400	
	Advertising Revenue		1,400
31	Art Supplies Expense	3,400	
	Art Supplies		3,400
31	Depreciation Expense	7,000	
	Accumulated Depreciation		7,000
31	Salaries Expense	1,300	
	Salaries Payable		1,300

(b)

NALEZNY ADVERTISING AGENCY
INCOME STATEMENT
FOR THE YEAR ENDED DECEMBER 31, 2003

Revenues		
Advertising revenue		$61,500
Expenses		
Salaries expense	$11,300	
Depreciation expense	7,000	
Rent expense	4,000	
Art supplies expense	3,400	
Total expenses		25,700
Net income		$35,800

NALEZNY ADVERTISING AGENCY
BALANCE SHEET
DECEMBER 31, 2003

Assets

Cash		$11,000
Accounts receivable		21,500
Art supplies		5,000
Printing equipment	$60,000	
Less: Accumulated depreciation—printing equipment	35,000	25,000
Total assets		$62,500

Liabilities and Owners' Equity

Liabilities		
Accounts payable		$5,000
Unearned advertising revenue		5,600
Salaries payable		1,300
Total liabilities		11,900
Owners' equity		
Common stock	$10,000	
Retained earnings	40,600*	50,600
Total liabilities and owners' equity		$62,500

*Retained earnings, Jan. 1, 2003	$ 4,800	
Add: Net income	35,800	
Retained earnings, Dec. 31, 2003	$40,600	

(c) Following preparation of financial statements (see Illustration 3-6), Nalezny would prepare closing entries to reduce the temporary accounts to zero. Some companies prepare a post-closing trial balance and reversing entries.

USING REVERSING ENTRIES

The purpose of reversing entries is to simplify the recording of transactions in the next accounting period. The use of reversing entries does not change the amounts reported in the financial statements for the previous period.

Illustration of Reversing Entries—Accruals

Reversing entries are most often used to reverse two types of adjusting entries: accrued revenues and accrued expenses. To illustrate the optional use of reversing entries for accrued expenses, we will use the following transaction and adjustment data.

① October 24 (initial salary entry): $4,000 of salaries incurred between October 1 and October 24 are paid.

② October 31 (adjusting entry): Salaries incurred between October 25 and October 31 are $1,200. These will be paid in the November 8 payroll.

③ November 8 (subsequent salary entry): Salaries paid are $2,500. Of this amount, $1,200 applied to accrued wages payable at October 31 and $1,300 was incurred between November 1 and November 8.

The comparative entries are shown in Illustration 3A-1.

Illustration 3A-1

Comparison of Entries for Accruals, with and without Reversing Entries

REVERSING ENTRIES NOT USED				REVERSING ENTRIES USED			
Initial Salary Entry							
Oct. 24	Salaries Expense	4,000		Oct. 24	Salaries Expense	4,000	
	Cash		4,000		Cash		4,000
Adjusting Entry							
Oct. 31	Salaries Expense	1,200		Oct. 31	Salaries Expense	1,200	
	Salaries Payable		1,200		Salaries Payable		1,200
Closing Entry							
Oct. 31	Income Summary	5,200		Oct. 31	Income Summary	5,200	
	Salaries Expense		5,200		Salaries Expense		5,200
Reversing Entry							
Nov. 1	No entry is made.			Nov. 1	Salaries Payable	1,200	
					Salaries Expense		1,200
Subsequent Salary Entry							
Nov. 8	Salaries Payable	1,200		Nov. 8	Salaries Expense	2,500	
	Salaries Expense	1,300			Cash		2,500
	Cash		2,500				

The comparative entries show that the first three entries are the same whether or not reversing entries are used. The last two entries are different. The November 1 reversing entry eliminates the $1,200 balance in Salaries Payable that was created by the

October 31 adjusting entry. The reversing entry also creates a $1,200 credit balance in the Salaries Expense account. As you know, it is unusual for an expense account to have a credit balance; however, the balance is correct in this instance. It is correct because the entire amount of the first salary payment in the new accounting period will be debited to Salaries Expense. This debit will eliminate the credit balance, and the resulting debit balance in the expense account will equal the salaries expense incurred in the new accounting period ($1,300 in this example).

When reversing entries are made, all cash payments of expenses can be debited to the expense account. This means that on November 8 (and every payday) Salaries Expense can be debited for the amount paid without regard to the existence of any accrued salaries payable. Being able to make the same entry each time simplifies the recording process in an accounting system.

Illustration of Reversing Entries — Prepayments

Up to this point, we have assumed that all prepayments are recorded as prepaid expense or unearned revenue. In some cases, prepayments are recorded directly in expense or revenue accounts. When this occurs, prepayments may also be reversed.

To illustrate the use of reversing entries for prepaid expenses, we will use the following transaction and adjustment data:

① December 10 (initial entry): $20,000 of office supplies are purchased with cash.
② December 31 (adjusting entry): $5,000 of office supplies on hand.

The comparative entries are shown in Illustration 3A-2.

Illustration 3A-2

Comparison of Entries for Prepayments, with and without Reversing Entries

REVERSING ENTRIES NOT USED				REVERSING ENTRIES USED			
Initial Purchase of Supplies Entry							
Dec. 10	Office Supplies	20,000		Dec. 10	Office Supplies Expense	20,000	
	Cash		20,000		Cash		20,000
Adjusting Entry							
Dec. 31	Office Supplies Expense	15,000		Dec. 31	Office Supplies	5,000	
	Office Supplies		15,000		Office Supplies Expense		5,000
Closing Entry							
Dec. 31	Income Summary	15,000		Dec. 31	Income Summary	15,000	
	Office Supplies Expense		15,000		Office Supplies Expense		15,000
Reversing Entry							
Jan. 1	No entry			Jan. 1	Office Supplies Expense	5,000	
					Office Supplies		5,000

After the adjusting entry on December 31 (regardless of whether reversing entries are used) the asset account Office Supplies shows a balance of $5,000 and Office Supplies Expense a balance of $15,000. If Office Supplies Expense initially was debited when the supplies were purchased, a reversing entry is made to return to the expense account the cost of unconsumed supplies. The company then continues to debit Office Supplies Expense for additional purchases of office supplies during the next period.

With respect to prepaid items, why are all such items not entered originally into real accounts (assets and liabilities), thus making reversing entries unnecessary? Sometimes this practice is followed. It is particularly advantageous for items that need to be apportioned over several periods (e.g., supplies and parts inventories). However, items that do not follow this regular pattern and that may or may not involve two or more periods are ordinarily entered initially in revenue or expense accounts. The revenue and expense accounts may not require adjusting and are systematically closed to Income Summary. Using the nominal accounts adds consistency to the accounting system. It also makes the recording more efficient, particularly when a large number of such transactions occur during the year. For example, the bookkeeper knows that when an invoice is received for other than a capital asset acquisition, the amount is expensed. The bookkeeper need not worry at the time the invoice is received whether or not the item will result in a prepaid expense at the end of the period, because adjustments will be made at the end of the period.

Summary of Reversing Entries

A summary of guidelines for reversing entries is as follows.

1 All accrued items should be reversed.
2 All prepaid items for which the original cash transaction was debited or credited to an expense or revenue account should be reversed.
3 Adjusting entries for depreciation and bad debts are not reversed.

Recognize that reversing entries do not have to be used. Therefore, some accountants avoid them entirely.

SUMMARY OF LEARNING OBJECTIVE FOR APPENDIX 3A

9 Identify adjusting entries that may be reversed. Reversing entries are most often used to reverse two types of adjusting entries: accrued revenues and accrued expenses. Prepayments may also be reversed if the initial entry to record the transaction is made to an expense or revenue account.

Note: All **asterisked** Questions, Exercises, Problems, and Cases relate to material contained in the appendix to the chapter.

QUESTIONS

1 Give an example of a transaction that results in:

(a) A decrease in an asset and a decrease in a liability.

(b) A decrease in one asset and an increase in another asset.

(c) A decrease in one liability and an increase in another liability.

2 Do the following events represent business transactions? Explain your answer in each case.

(a) A computer is purchased on account.

(b) A customer returns merchandise and is given credit on account.

(c) A prospective employee is interviewed.

(d) The owner of the business withdraws cash from the business for personal use.

(e) Merchandise is ordered for delivery next month.

3 Name the accounts debited and credited for each of the following transactions.

(a) Billing a customer for work done.

(b) Receipt of cash from customer on account.

(c) Purchase of office supplies on account.

(d) Purchase of 15 gallons of gasoline for the delivery truck.

4 Why are revenue and expense accounts called temporary or nominal accounts?

5 Omar Morena, a fellow student, contends that the double-entry system means that each transaction must be recorded twice. Is Omar correct? Explain.

6 Is it necessary that a trial balance be taken periodically? What purpose does it serve?

7 Indicate whether each of the items below is a real or nominal account and whether it appears in the balance sheet or the income statement.

(a) Prepaid Rent.

(b) Salaries and Wages Payable.

(c) Merchandise Inventory.

(d) Accumulated Depreciation.

(e) Office Equipment.

(f) Income from Services.

(g) Office Salaries Expense.

(h) Supplies on Hand.

8 Employees are paid every Saturday for the preceding work week. If a balance sheet is prepared on Wednesday, December 31, what does the amount of wages earned during the first three days of the week (12/29, 12/30, 12/31) represent? Explain.

9 (a) How do the components of revenues and expenses differ between a merchandising company and a service enterprise? (b) Explain the income measurement process of a merchandising company.

10 What is the purpose of the Cost of Goods Sold account? (Assume a periodic inventory system.)

11 Under a perpetual system, what is the purpose of the Cost of Goods Sold account?

12 If the $3,900 cost of a new microcomputer and printer purchased for office use were recorded as a debit to Purchases, what would be the effect of the error on the balance sheet and income statement in the period in which the error was made?

13 What differences are there between the trial balance before closing and the trial balance after closing with respect to the following accounts?

(a) Accounts Payable.

(b) Expense accounts.

(c) Revenue accounts.

(d) Retained Earnings account.

(e) Cash.

14 What are adjusting entries and why are they necessary?

15 What are closing entries and why are they necessary?

16 Paul Molitor, maintenance supervisor for Blue Jay Insurance Co., has purchased a riding lawnmower and accessories to be used in maintaining the grounds around corporate headquarters. He has sent the following information to the accounting department.

Cost of mower and		Date purchased	7/1/03
accessories	$3,000	Monthly salary of	
Estimated useful life	5 yrs	groundskeeper	$1,100
		Estimated annual	
		fuel cost	$150

Compute the amount of depreciation expense (related to the mower and accessories) that should be reported on Blue Jay's December 31, 2003, income statement. Assume straight-line depreciation.

17 Selanne Enterprises made the following entry on December 31, 2003.

Dec. 31, 2003	Interest Expense	10,000	
	Interest Payable		10,000
	(To record interest expense due		
	on loan from Anaheim National Bank.)		

What entry would Anaheim National Bank make regarding its outstanding loan to Selanne Enterprises? Explain why this must be the case.

18 "A worksheet is a permanent accounting record, and its use is required in the accounting cycle." Do you agree? Explain.

*19 What are reversing entries, and why are they used?

BRIEF EXERCISES

BE3-1 Transactions for Argot Company for the month of May are presented below. Prepare journal entries for each of these transactions. (You may omit explanations.)

May	1	B.D. Argot invests $3,000 cash in exchange for common stock in a small welding corporation.
	3	Buys equipment on account for $1,100.
	13	Pays $400 to landlord for May rent.
	21	Bills Noble Corp. $500 for welding work done.

BE3-2 Brett Favre Repair Shop had the following transactions during the first month of business. Journalize the transactions.

August	2	Invested $12,000 cash and $2,500 of equipment in the business.
	7	Purchased supplies on account for $400. (Debit asset account.)
	12	Performed services for clients, for which $1,300 was collected in cash and $670 was billed to the clients.
	15	Paid August rent, $600.
	19	Counted supplies and determined that only $270 of the supplies purchased on August 7 are still on hand.

BE3-3 On July 1, 2004, Blair Co. pays $18,000 to Hindi Insurance Co. for a 3-year insurance contract. Both companies have fiscal years ending December 31. For Blair Co. journalize the entry on July 1 and the adjusting entry on December 31.

BE3-4 Using the data in BE3-3, journalize the entry on July 1 and the adjusting entry on December 31 for Hindi Insurance Co. Hindi uses the accounts Unearned Insurance Revenue and Insurance Revenue.

BE3-5 On August 1, George Bell Company paid $8,400 in advance for 2 years' insurance coverage. Prepare Bell's August 1 journal entry and the annual adjusting entry on December 31.

BE3-6 Mogilny Corporation owns a warehouse. On November 1, it rented storage space to a lessee (tenant) for 3 months for a total cash payment of $2,700 received in advance. Prepare Mogilny's November 1 journal entry and the December 31 annual adjusting entry.

BE3-7 Catherine Janeway Company's weekly payroll, paid on Fridays, totals $6,000. Employees work a 5-day week. Prepare Janeway's adjusting entry on Wednesday, December 31, and the journal entry to record the $6,000 cash payment on Friday, January 2.

BE3-8 Included in Martinez Company's December 31 trial balance is a note receivable of $10,000. The note is a 4-month, 12% note dated October 1. Prepare Martinez's December 31 adjusting entry to record $300 of accrued interest, and the February 1 journal entry to record receipt of $10,400 from the borrower.

BE3-9 Prepare the following adjusting entries at December 31 for DeGads Co.

(a) Interest on notes payable of $400 is accrued.
(b) Fees earned but unbilled total $1,400.
(c) Salaries earned by employees of $700 have not been recorded.
(d) Bad debt expense for year is $900.

Use the following account titles: Service Revenue, Accounts Receivable, Interest Expense, Interest Payable, Salaries Expense, Salaries Payable, Allowance for Doubtful Accounts, and Bad Debt Expense.

BE3-10 At the end of its first year of operations, the trial balance of Rafael Company shows Equipment $30,000 and zero balances in Accumulated Depreciation—Equipment and Depreciation Expense. Depreciation for the year is estimated to be $3,000. Prepare the adjusting entry for depreciation at December 31, and indicate the balance sheet presentation for the equipment at December 31.

BE3-11 Willis Corporation has beginning inventory $81,000; Purchases $540,000; Freight-in $16,200; Purchase Returns $5,800; Purchase Discounts $5,000; and ending inventory $70,200. Compute cost of goods sold.

BE3-12 Karen Sepaniak has year-end account balances of Sales $828,900; Interest Revenue $13,500; Cost of Goods Sold $556,200; Operating Expenses $189,000; Income Tax Expense $35,100; and Dividends $18,900. Prepare the year-end closing entries.

***BE3-13** Pelican Company made a December 31 adjusting entry to debit Salaries Expense and credit Salaries Payable for $3,600. On January 2, Pelican paid the weekly payroll of $6,000. Prepare Pelican's (a) January 1 reversing entry; (b) January 2 entry (assuming the reversing entry was prepared); and (c) January 2 entry (assuming the reversing entry was not prepared).

EXERCISES

E3-1 (Transaction Analysis—Service Company) Beverly Crusher is a licensed CPA. During the first month of operations of her business (a sole proprietorship), the following events and transactions occurred.

April	2	Invested $32,000 cash and equipment valued at $14,000 in the business.
	2	Hired a secretary-receptionist at a salary of $290 per week payable monthly.
	3	Purchased supplies on account $700 (debit an asset account).
	7	Paid office rent of $600 for the month.
	11	Completed a tax assignment and billed client $1,100 for services rendered. (Use Service Revenue account.)
	12	Received $3,200 advance on a management consulting engagement.
	17	Received cash of $2,300 for services completed for Ferengi Co.
	21	Paid insurance expense $110.
	30	Paid secretary-receptionist $1,160 for the month.
	30	A count of supplies indicated that $120 of supplies had been used.
	30	Purchased a new computer for $6,100 with personal funds. (The computer will be used exclusively for business purposes.)

Instructions

Journalize the transactions in the general journal. (Omit explanations.)

E3-2 (Corrected Trial Balance) The trial balance of Wanda Landowska Company shown below does not balance. Your review of the ledger reveals the following: (a) each account had a normal balance; (b) the debit footings in Prepaid Insurance, Accounts Payable, and Property Tax Expense were each understated $100; (c) a transposition error was made in Accounts Receivable; the correct balances are $2,750 and $6,690, respectively; (d) a debit posting to Advertising Expense of $300 was omitted; and (e) a $1,500 cash drawing by the owner was debited to Wanda Landowska, Capital, and credited to Cash.

WANDA LANDOWSKA COMPANY
TRIAL BALANCE
APRIL 30, 2003

	Debit	Credit
Cash	$ 4,800	
Accounts Receivable	2,570	
Prepaid Insurance	700	
Equipment		$ 8,000
Accounts Payable		4,500
Property Tax Payable	560	
Wanda Landowska, Capital		11,200
Service Revenue	6,960	
Salaries Expense	4,200	
Advertising Expense	1,100	
Property Tax Expense		800
	$20,890	$24,500

Instructions

Prepare a correct trial balance.

E3-3 (Corrected Trial Balance) The trial balance of Blues Traveler Corporation (see next page) does not balance.

BLUES TRAVELER CORPORATION
TRIAL BALANCE
APRIL 30

	Debit	Credit
Cash	$ 5,912	
Accounts Receivable	5,240	
Supplies on Hand	2,967	
Furniture and Equipment	6,100	
Accounts Payable		$ 7,044
Common Stock		8,000
Retained Earnings		2,000
Service Revenue		5,200
Office Expense	4,320	
	$24,539	$22,244

An examination of the ledger shows these errors.

1. Cash received from a customer on account was recorded (both debit and credit) as $1,380 instead of $1,830.
2. The purchase on account of a computer costing $3,200 was recorded as a debit to Office Expense and a credit to Accounts Payable.
3. Services were performed on account for a client, $2,250, for which Accounts Receivable was debited $2,250 and Service Revenue was credited $225.
4. A payment of $95 for telephone charges was entered as a debit to Office Expenses and a debit to Cash.
5. The Service Revenue account was totaled at $5,200 instead of $5,280.

Instructions
From this information prepare a corrected trial balance.

 **E3-4 (Corrected Trial Balance)** The trial balance of Antoine Watteau Co. shown below does not balance.

ANTOINE WATTEAU CO.
TRIAL BALANCE
JUNE 30, 2004

	Debit	Credit
Cash		$ 2,870
Accounts Receivable	$ 3,231	
Supplies	800	
Equipment	3,800	
Accounts Payable		2,666
Unearned Service Revenue	1,200	
Common Stock		6,000
Retained Earnings		3,000
Service Revenue		2,380
Wages Expense	3,400	
Office Expense	940	
	$13,371	$16,916

Each of the listed accounts has a normal balance per the general ledger. An examination of the ledger and journal reveals the following errors.

1. Cash received from a customer on account was debited for $570, and Accounts Receivable was credited for the same amount. The actual collection was for $750.
2. The purchase of a computer printer on account for $500 was recorded as a debit to Supplies for $500 and a credit to Accounts Payable for $500.
3. Services were performed on account for a client for $890. Accounts Receivable was debited for $890 and Service Revenue was credited for $89.
4. A payment of $65 for telephone charges was recorded as a debit to Office Expense for $65 and a debit to Cash for $65.
5. When the Unearned Service Revenue account was reviewed, it was found that $325 of the balance was earned prior to June 30.
6. A debit posting to Wages Expense of $670 was omitted.
7. A payment on account for $206 was credited to Cash for $206 and credited to Accounts Payable for $260.
8. A dividend of $575 was debited to Wages Expense for $575 and credited to Cash for $575.

Instructions
Prepare a correct trial balance. (Note: It may be necessary to add one or more accounts to the trial balance.)

 E3-5 (Adjusting Entries) The ledger of Duggan Rental Agency on March 31 of the current year includes the following selected accounts before adjusting entries have been prepared.

	Debit	Credit
Prepaid Insurance	$ 3,600	
Supplies	2,800	
Equipment	25,000	
Accumulated Depreciation—Equipment		$ 8,400
Notes Payable		20,000
Unearned Rent Revenue		9,300
Rent Revenue		60,000
Interest Expense	–0–	
Wage Expense	14,000	

An analysis of the accounts shows the following.

1. The equipment depreciates $250 per month.
2. One-third of the unearned rent was earned during the quarter.
3. Interest of $500 is accrued on the notes payable.
4. Supplies on hand total $850.
5. Insurance expires at the rate of $300 per month.

Instructions
Prepare the adjusting entries at March 31, assuming that adjusting entries are made quarterly. Additional accounts are: Depreciation Expense; Insurance Expense; Interest Payable; and Supplies Expense.

E3-6 (Adjusting Entries) Karen Weller, D.D.S., opened a dental practice on January 1, 2004. During the first month of operations the following transactions occurred.

1. Performed services for patients who had dental plan insurance. At January 31, $750 of such services was earned but not yet billed to the insurance companies.
2. Utility expenses incurred but not paid prior to January 31 totaled $520.

3. Purchased dental equipment on January 1 for $80,000, paying $20,000 in cash and signing a $60,000, 3-year note payable. The equipment depreciates $400 per month. Interest is $500 per month.
4. Purchased a one-year malpractice insurance policy on January 1 for $12,000.
5. Purchased $1,600 of dental supplies. On January 31, determined that $500 of supplies were on hand.

Instructions

Prepare the adjusting entries on January 31. Account titles are: Accumulated Depreciation—Dental Equipment; Depreciation Expense; Service Revenue; Accounts Receivable; Insurance Expense; Interest Expense; Interest Payable; Prepaid Insurance; Supplies; Supplies Expense; Utilities Expense; and Utilities Payable.

E3-7 (Analyze Adjusted Data) A partial adjusted trial balance of Piper Company at January 31, 2004, shows the following.

PIPER COMPANY
ADJUSTED TRIAL BALANCE
JANUARY 31, 2004

	Debit	Credit
Supplies	$ 700	
Prepaid Insurance	2,400	
Salaries Payable		$ 800
Unearned Revenue		750
Supplies Expense	950	
Insurance Expense	400	
Salaries Expense	1,800	
Service Revenue		2,000

Instructions

Answer the following questions, assuming the year begins January 1.

(a) If the amount in Supplies Expense is the January 31 adjusting entry, and $850 of supplies was purchased in January, what was the balance in Supplies on January 1?
(b) If the amount in Insurance Expense is the January 31 adjusting entry, and the original insurance premium was for one year, what was the total premium and when was the policy purchased?
(c) If $2,500 of salaries was paid in January, what was the balance in Salaries Payable at December 31, 2003?
(d) If $1,600 was received in January for services performed in January, what was the balance in Unearned Revenue at December 31, 2003?

E3-8 (Adjusting Entries) Bjorn Borg is the new owner of Ace Computer Services. At the end of August 2003, his first month of ownership, Bjorn is trying to prepare monthly financial statements. Below is some information related to unrecorded expenses that the business incurred during August.

1. At August 31, Mr. Borg owed his employees $1,900 in wages that will be paid on September 1.
2. At the end of the month he had not yet received the month's utility bill. Based on past experience, he estimated the bill would be approximately $600.
3. On August 1, Mr. Borg borrowed $30,000 from a local bank on a 15-year mortgage. The annual interest rate is 8%.
4. A telephone bill in the amount of $117 covering August charges is unpaid at August 31.

Instructions
Prepare the adjusting journal entries as of August 31, 2003, suggested by the information above.

E3-9 (Adjusting Entries) Selected accounts of Urdu Company are shown below.

Supplies			
Beg. Bal.	800	10/31	470

Accounts Receivable		
10/17	2,400	
10/31	1,650	

Salaries Expense		
10/15	800	
10/31	600	

Salaries Payable		
	10/31	600

Unearned Service Revenue			
10/31	400	10/20	650

Supplies Expense		
10/31	470	

Service Revenue		
	10/17	2,400
	10/31	1,650
	10/31	400

Instructions
From an analysis of the T-accounts, reconstruct (a) the October transaction entries, and (b) the adjusting journal entries that were made on October 31, 2003.

E3-10 (Adjusting Entries) Greco Resort opened for business on June 1 with eight air-conditioned units. Its trial balance on August 31 is as follows.

GRECO RESORT
TRIAL BALANCE
AUGUST 31, 2003

	Debit	Credit
Cash	$ 19,600	
Prepaid Insurance	4,500	
Supplies	2,600	
Land	20,000	
Cottages	120,000	
Furniture	16,000	
Accounts Payable		$ 4,500
Unearned Rent Revenue		4,600
Mortgage Payable		60,000
Common Stock		91,000
Retained Earnings		9,000
Dividends	5,000	
Rent Revenue		76,200
Salaries Expense	44,800	
Utilities Expense	9,200	
Repair Expense	3,600	
	$245,300	$245,300

Other data:

1. The balance in prepaid insurance is a one-year premium paid on June 1, 2003.
2. An inventory count on August 31 shows $450 of supplies on hand.
3. Annual depreciation rates are cottages (4%) and furniture (10%). Salvage value is estimated to be 10% of cost.
4. Unearned Rent Revenue of $3,800 was earned prior to August 31.
5. Salaries of $375 were unpaid at August 31.
6. Rentals of $800 were due from tenants at August 31.
7. The mortgage interest rate is 8% per year.

Instructions
(a) Journalize the adjusting entries on August 31 for the 3-month period June 1–August 31.
(b) Prepare an adjusted trial balance on August 31.

E3-11 **(Closing Entries)** The adjusted trial balance of Lopez Company shows the following data pertaining to sales at the end of its fiscal year, October 31, 2004: Sales $800,000, Freight-out $12,000, Sales Returns and Allowances $24,000, and Sales Discounts $15,000.

Instructions
(a) Prepare the sales revenue section of the income statement.
(b) Prepare separate closing entries for (1) sales, and (2) the contra accounts to sales.

E3-12 **(Closing Entries)** Presented is information related to Gonzales Corporation for the month of January 2003.

Cost of goods sold	$208,000	Salary expense	$ 61,000
Freight-out	7,000	Sales discounts	8,000
Insurance expense	12,000	Sales returns and allowances	13,000
Rent expense	20,000	Sales	350,000

Instructions
Prepare the necessary closing entries.

E3-13 **(Work Sheet)** Presented below are selected accounts for Alvarez Company as reported in the work sheet at the end of May 2003.

Accounts	Adjusted Trial Balance		Income Statement		Balance Sheet	
	Dr.	Cr.	Dr.	Cr.	Dr.	Cr.
Cash	9,000					
Merchandise Inventory	80,000					
Sales		450,000				
Sales Returns and Allowances	10,000					
Sales Discounts	5,000					
Cost of Goods Sold	250,000					

Instructions
Complete the work sheet by extending amounts reported in the adjusted trial balance to the appropriate columns in the work sheet. Do not total individual columns.

E3-14 (Missing Amounts) Presented below is financial information for two different companies.

	Alatorre Company	Eduardo Company
Sales	$90,000	(d)
Sales returns	(a)	$ 5,000
Net sales	81,000	95,000
Cost of goods sold	56,000	(e)
Gross profit	(b)	38,000
Operating expenses	15,000	23,000
Net income	(c)	15,000

Instructions

Compute the missing amounts.

E3-15 (Find Missing Amounts—Periodic Inventory) Financial information is presented below for four different companies.

	Pamela's Cosmetics	Dean's Grocery	Anderson Wholesalers	Baywatch Supply Co.
Sales	$78,000	(c)	$144,000	$100,000
Sales returns	(a)	$ 5,000	12,000	9,000
Net sales	74,000	94,000	132,000	(g)
Beginning inventory	16,000	(d)	44,000	24,000
Purchases	88,000	100,000	(e)	85,000
Purchase returns	6,000	10,000	8,000	(h)
Ending inventory	(b)	48,000	30,000	28,000
Cost of goods sold	64,000	72,000	(f)	72,000
Gross profit	10,000	22,000	18,000	(i)

Instructions

Determine the missing amounts (a–i). Show all computations.

E3-16 (Cost of Goods Sold Section—Periodic Inventory) The trial balance of the Neville Mariner Company at the end of its fiscal year, August 31, 2004, includes the following accounts: Merchandise Inventory $17,500; Purchases $149,400; Sales $200,000; Freight-in $4,000; Sales Returns and Allowances $4,000; Freight-out $1,000; and Purchase Returns and Allowances $2,000. The ending merchandise inventory is $25,000.

Instructions

Prepare a cost of goods sold section for the year ending August 31.

E3-17 (Closing Entries for a Corporation) Presented below are selected account balances for Homer Winslow Co. as of December 31, 2004.

Merchandise Inventory 12/31/04	$ 60,000	Cost of Goods Sold	$225,700
Common Stock	75,000	Selling Expenses	16,000
Retained Earnings	45,000	Administrative Expenses	38,000
Dividends	18,000	Income Tax Expense	30,000
Sales Returns and Allowances	12,000		
Sales Discounts	15,000		
Sales	410,000		

Instructions

Prepare closing entries for Homer Winslow Co. on December 31, 2004.

E3-18 (Work Sheet Preparation) The trial balance of R. L. Stein Roofing at March 31, 2004, is as follows.

R. L. STEIN ROOFING
TRIAL BALANCE
MARCH 31, 2004

	Debit	Credit
Cash	$ 2,300	
Accounts Receivable	2,600	
Roofing Supplies	1,100	
Equipment	6,000	
Accumulated Depreciation—Equipment		$ 1,200
Accounts Payable		1,100
Unearned Service Revenue		300
Common Stock		6,400
Retained Earnings		600
Service Revenue		3,000
Salaries Expense	500	
Miscellaneous Expense	100	
	$12,600	$12,600

Other data:

1. A physical count reveals only $520 of roofing supplies on hand.
2. Equipment is depreciated at a rate of $120 per month.
3. Unearned service revenue amounted to $100 on March 31.
4. Accrued salaries are $850.

Instructions

Enter the trial balance on a work sheet and complete the work sheet, assuming that the adjustments relate only to the month of March. (Ignore income taxes.)

E3-19 (Work Sheet and Balance Sheet Presentation) The adjusted trial balance of Ed Bradley Co. work sheet for the month ended April 30, 2003, contains the following.

ED BRADLEY CO.
WORK SHEET (PARTIAL)
FOR THE MONTH ENDED APRIL 30, 2003

Account Titles	Adjusted Trial Balance Dr.	Cr.	Income Statement Dr.	Cr.	Balance Sheet Dr.	Cr.
Cash	$19,472					
Accounts Receivable	6,920					
Prepaid Rent	2,280					
Equipment	18,050					
Accumulated Depreciation		$ 4,895				
Notes Payable		5,700				
Accounts Payable		5,472				
Bradley, Capital		34,960				
Bradley, Drawing	6,650					
Service Revenue		11,590				
Salaries Expense	6,840					
Rent Expense	2,260					
Depreciation Expense	145					
Interest Expense	83					
Interest Payable		83				

Instructions

Complete the work sheet, and prepare a balance sheet as illustrated in this chapter.

E3-20 (Partial Work Sheet Preparation) Jurassic Park Co. prepares monthly financial statements from a work sheet. Selected portions of the January work sheet showed the following data.

JURASSIC PARK CO.						
WORK SHEET (PARTIAL)						
FOR MONTH ENDED JANUARY 31, 2004						

Account Title	Trial Balance		Adjustments		Adjusted Trial Balance	
	Dr.	Cr.	Dr.	Cr.	Dr.	Cr.
Supplies	3,256			(a) 1,500	1,756	
Accumulated Depreciation		6,682		(b) 257		6,939
Interest Payable		100		(c) 50		150
Supplies Expense			(a) 1,500		1,500	
Depreciation Expense			(b) 257		257	
Interest Expense			(c) 50		50	

During February no events occurred that affected these accounts, but at the end of February the following information was available.

(a) Supplies on hand	$715
(b) Monthly depreciation	$257
(c) Accrued interest	$ 50

Instructions

Reproduce the data that would appear in the February work sheet, and indicate the amounts that would be shown in the February income statement.

E3-21 (Transactions of a Corporation, Including Investment and Dividend) Scratch Miniature Golf and Driving Range Inc. was opened on March 1 by Scott Verplank. The following selected events and transactions occurred during March.

Mar.	1	Invested $50,000 cash in the business in exchange for common stock.
	3	Purchased Lee Janzen's Golf Land for $38,000 cash. The price consists of land $10,000; building $22,000; and equipment $6,000. (Make one compound entry.)
	5	Advertised the opening of the driving range and miniature golf course, paying advertising expenses of $1,600.
	6	Paid cash $1,480 for a one-year insurance policy.
	10	Purchased golf equipment for $2,500 from Sluman Company payable in 30 days.
	18	Received golf fees of $1,200 in cash.
	25	Declared and paid a $500 cash dividend.
	30	Paid wages of $900.
	30	Paid Sluman Company in full.
	31	Received $750 of fees in cash.

Scratch uses the following accounts: Cash; Prepaid Insurance; Land; Buildings; Equipment; Accounts Payable; Common Stock; Dividends; Service Revenue; Advertising Expense; and Wages Expense.

Instructions

Journalize the March transactions.

*E3-22 **(Closing and Reversing Entries)** On December 31, the adjusted trial balance of Cree Co. Inc. shows the following selected data.

Accounts Receivable	$4,300	Service Revenue	$96,000
Interest Expense	7,800	Interest Payable	2,400

Analysis shows that adjusting entries were made for (1) $4,300 of services performed but not billed, and (2) $2,400 of accrued but unpaid interest.

Instructions

(a) Prepare the closing entries for the temporary accounts at December 31.

(b) Prepare the reversing entries on January 1.

(c) Enter the adjusted trial balance data in the four accounts. Post the entries in (a) and (b) and rule and balance the accounts. (Use T-accounts.)

(d) Prepare the entries to record (1) the collection of the accrued commissions on January 10, and (2) the payment of all interest due ($3,000) on January 15.

(e) Post the entries in (d) to the temporary accounts.

*E3-23 **(Adjusting and Reversing Entries)** When the accounts of Daniel Barenboim Inc. are examined, the adjusting data listed below are uncovered on December 31, the end of an annual fiscal period.

1. The prepaid insurance account shows a debit of $5,280, representing the cost of a 2-year fire insurance policy dated August 1 of the current year.

2. On November 1, Rental Revenue was credited for $1,800, representing revenue from a subrental for a 3-month period beginning on that date.

3. Purchase of advertising materials for $800 during the year was recorded in the Advertising Expense account. On December 31, advertising materials of $290 are on hand.

4. Interest of $770 has accrued on notes payable.

Instructions

Prepare in general journal form: (a) the adjusting entry for each item; (b) the reversing entry for each item where appropriate.

PROBLEMS

 P3-1 (Transactions, Financial Statements—Service Company) Listed below are the transactions of Isao Aoki, D.D.S., for the month of September.

Sept.	1	Isao Aoki begins practice as a dentist and invests $20,000 cash.
	2	Purchases furniture and dental equipment on account from Green Jacket Co. for $17,280.
	4	Pays rent for office space, $680 for the month.
	4	Employs a receptionist, Michael Bradley.
	5	Purchases dental supplies for cash, $942.
	8	Receives cash of $1,690 from patients for services performed.
	10	Pays miscellaneous office expenses, $430.
	14	Bills patients $5,120 for services performed.
	18	Pays Green Jacket Co. on account, $3,600.
	19	Withdraws $3,000 cash from the business for personal use.
	20	Receives $980 from patients on account.
	25	Bills patients $2,110 for services performed.
	30	Pays the following expenses in cash: office salaries, $1,400; miscellaneous office expenses, $85.
	30	Dental supplies used during September, $330.

Instructions

(a) Enter the transactions shown above in appropriate general ledger accounts. Use the following ledger accounts: Cash; Accounts Receivable; Supplies on Hand; Furniture and Equipment; Accumulated Depreciation; Accounts Payable; Isao Aoki, Capital; Service Revenue; Rent Expense; Miscellaneous Office

Expense; Office Salaries Expense; Supplies Expense; Depreciation Expense; and Income Summary. Allow 10 lines for the Cash and Income Summary accounts, and 5 lines for each of the other accounts needed. Record depreciation using a 5-year life on the furniture and equipment, the straight-line method, and no salvage value. Do not use a drawing account.

(b) Prepare a trial balance.
(c) Prepare an income statement, a balance sheet, and a statement of owner's equity.
(d) Close the ledger.
(e) Prepare a post-closing trial balance.

P3-2 (Adjusting Entries and Financial Statements) Yount Advertising Agency was founded by Thomas Grant in January 1999. Presented below are both the adjusted and unadjusted trial balances as of December 31, 2003.

	Unadjusted Dr.	Unadjusted Cr.	Adjusted Dr.	Adjusted Cr.
YOUNT ADVERTISING AGENCY TRIAL BALANCE DECEMBER 31, 2003				
Cash	$ 11,000		$ 11,000	
Accounts Receivable	20,000		21,500	
Art Supplies	8,400		5,000	
Prepaid Insurance	3,350		2,500	
Printing Equipment	60,000		60,000	
Accumulated Depreciation		$ 28,000		$ 35,000
Accounts Payable		5,000		5,000
Interest Payable		–0–		150
Notes Payable		5,000		5,000
Unearned Advertising Revenue		7,000		5,600
Salaries Payable		–0–		1,300
Common Stock		10,000		10,000
Retained Earnings		3,500		3,500
Advertising Revenue		58,600		61,500
Salaries Expense	10,000		11,300	
Insurance Expense			850	
Interest Expense	350		500	
Depreciation Expense			7,000	
Art Supplies Expense			3,400	
Rent Expense	4,000		4,000	
	$117,100	$117,100	$127,050	$127,050

Instructions

(a) Journalize the annual adjusting entries that were made.
(b) Prepare an income statement and a statement of retained earnings for the year ending December 31, 2003, and a balance sheet at December 31.
(c) Answer the following questions.
  (1) If the note has been outstanding 3 months, what is the annual interest rate on that note?
  (2) If the company paid $13,500 in salaries in 2003, what was the balance in Salaries Payable on December 31, 2002?

P3-3 (Adjusting Entries) A review of the ledger of Oklahoma Company at December 31, 2003, produces the following data pertaining to the preparation of annual adjusting entries.

1. Salaries Payable $0. There are eight salaried employees. Salaries are paid every Friday for the current week. Five employees receive a salary of $700 each per week, and three employees earn $500 each per

week. December 31 is a Tuesday. Employees do not work weekends. All employees worked the last 2 days of December.

2. Unearned Rent Revenue $369,000. The company began subleasing office space in its new building on November 1. Each tenant is required to make a $5,000 security deposit that is not refundable until occupancy is terminated. At December 31, the company had the following rental contracts that are paid in full for the entire term of the lease.

Date	Term (in months)	Monthly Rent	Number of Leases
Nov. 1	6	$4,000	5
Dec. 1	6	$8,500	4

3. Prepaid Advertising $13,200. This balance consists of payments on two advertising contracts. The contracts provide for monthly advertising in two trade magazines. The terms of the contracts are as follows.

Contract	Date	Amount	Number of Magazine Issues
A650	May 1	$6,000	12
B974	Oct. 1	7,200	24

The first advertisement runs in the month in which the contract is signed.

4. Notes Payable $80,000. This balance consists of a note for one year at an annual interest rate of 12%, dated June 1.

Instructions

Prepare the adjusting entries at December 31, 2003. (Show all computations).

P3-4 (Financial Statements and Closing Entries) The completed financial statement columns of the work sheet for Parsons Company are shown below.

PARSONS COMPANY
WORK SHEET
FOR THE YEAR ENDED DECEMBER 31, 2004

Account No.	Account Titles	Income Statement Dr.	Income Statement Cr.	Balance Sheet Dr.	Balance Sheet Cr.
101	Cash			8,200	
112	Accounts Receivable			7,500	
130	Prepaid Insurance			1,800	
157	Equipment			28,000	
167	Accumulated Depreciation				8,600
201	Accounts Payable				12,000
212	Salaries Payable				3,000
301	Common Stock				20,000
306	Retained Earnings				6,800
400	Service Revenue		42,000		
622	Repair Expense	3,200			
711	Depreciation Expense	2,800			
722	Insurance Expense	1,200			
726	Salaries Expense	36,000			
732	Utilities Expense	3,700			
	Totals	46,900	42,000	45,500	50,400
	Net Loss		4,900	4,900	
		46,900	46,900	50,400	50,400

Instructions

(a) Prepare an income statement, retained earnings statement, and a classified balance sheet.
(b) Prepare the closing entries.
(c) Post the closing entries and rule and balance the accounts. Use T-accounts. Income Summary is No. 350.
(d) Prepare a post-closing trial balance.

P3-5 (Work Sheet, Balance Sheet, Adjusting and Closing Entries) Noah's Ark has a fiscal year ending on September 30. Selected data from the September 30 work sheet are presented below.

NOAH'S ARK
WORK SHEET
FOR THE YEAR ENDED SEPTEMBER 30, 2004

	Trial Balance Dr.	Trial Balance Cr.	Adjusted Trial Balance Dr.	Adjusted Trial Balance Cr.
Cash	37,400		37,400	
Supplies	18,600		1,200	
Prepaid Insurance	31,900		3,900	
Land	80,000		80,000	
Equipment	120,000		120,000	
Accumulated Depreciation		36,200		43,000
Accounts Payable		14,600		14,600
Unearned Admissions Revenue		2,700		1,700
Mortgage Payable		50,000		50,000
N. Y. Berge, Capital		109,700		109,700
N. Y. Berge, Drawing	14,000		14,000	
Admissions Revenue		278,500		279,500
Salaries Expense	109,000		109,000	
Repair Expense	30,500		30,500	
Advertising Expense	9,400		9,400	
Utilities Expense	16,900		16,900	
Property Taxes Expense	18,000		21,000	
Interest Expense	6,000		12,000	
Totals	491,700	491,700		
Insurance Expense			28,000	
Supplies Expense			17,400	
Interest Payable				6,000
Depreciation Expense			6,800	
Property Taxes Payable				3,000
Totals			507,500	507,500

Instructions

(a) Prepare a complete work sheet.
(b) Prepare a classified balance sheet. (Note: $10,000 of the mortgage payable is due for payment in the next fiscal year.)
(c) Journalize the adjusting entries using the work sheet as a basis.
(d) Journalize the closing entries using the work sheet as a basis.
(e) Prepare a post-closing trial balance.

P3-6 (Financial Statements, Adjusting and Closing Entries) The trial balance of Becky Bishop Fashion Center contained the following accounts at November 30, the end of the company's fiscal year.

BECKY BISHOP FASHION CENTER TRIAL BALANCE NOVEMBER 30, 2004		
	Debit	Credit
Cash	$ 26,700	
Accounts Receivable	33,700	
Merchandise Inventory	45,000	
Store Supplies	5,500	
Store Equipment	85,000	
Accumulated Depreciation—Store Equipment		$ 18,000
Delivery Equipment	48,000	
Accumulated Depreciation—Delivery Equipment		6,000
Notes Payable		51,000
Accounts Payable		48,500
Common Stock		90,000
Retained Earnings		8,000
Sales		757,200
Sales Returns and Allowances	4,200	
Cost of Goods Sold	497,400	
Salaries Expense	140,000	
Advertising Expense	26,400	
Utilities Expense	14,000	
Repair Expense	12,100	
Delivery Expense	16,700	
Rent Expense	24,000	
	$978,700	$978,700

Adjustment data:

1. Store supplies on hand totaled $3,500.
2. Depreciation is $9,000 on the store equipment and $7,000 on the delivery equipment.
3. Interest of $11,000 is accrued on notes payable at November 30.

Other data:

1. Salaries expense is 70% selling and 30% administrative.
2. Rent expense and utilities expense are 80% selling and 20% administrative.
3. $30,000 of notes payable are due for payment next year.
4. Repair expense is 100% administrative.

Instructions
(a) Enter the trial balance on a work sheet and complete the work sheet.
(b) Prepare a multiple-step income statement and retained earnings statement for the year and a classified balance sheet as of November 30, 2004.
(c) Journalize the adjusting entries.
(d) Journalize the closing entries.
(e) Prepare a post-closing trial balance.

P3-7 (Financial Statements, Adjusting and Closing Entries) Rusch Department Store is located near the Village shopping mall. At the end of the company's fiscal year on December 31, 2004, the following accounts appeared in two of its trial balances.

	Unadjusted	Adjusted
Accounts Payable	$ 79,300	$ 79,300
Accounts Receivable	50,300	50,300
Accumulated Depreciation—Building	42,100	52,500
Accumulated Depreciation—Equipment	29,600	42,900
Building	190,000	190,000
Cash	23,000	23,000
Common Stock	160,000	160,000
Retained Earnings	16,600	16,600
Cost of Goods Sold	412,700	412,700
Depreciation Expense—Building		10,400
Depreciation Expense—Equipment		13,300
Dividends	28,000	28,000
Equipment	110,000	110,000
Insurance Expense		7,200
Interest Expense	3,000	11,000
Interest Payable		8,000
Interest Revenue	4,000	4,000
Merchandise Inventory	75,000	75,000
Mortgage Payable	80,000	80,000
Office Salaries Expense	32,000	32,000
Prepaid Insurance	9,600	2,400
Property Taxes Expense		4,800
Property Taxes Payable		4,800
Sales Salaries Expense	76,000	76,000
Sales	628,000	628,000
Sales Commissions Expense	11,000	14,500
Sales Commissions Payable		3,500
Sales Returns and Allowances	8,000	8,000
Utilities Expense	11,000	11,000

Analysis reveals the following additional data.

1. Insurance expense and utilities expense are 60% selling and 40% administrative.
2. $20,000 of the mortgage payable is due for payment next year.
3. Depreciation on the building and property tax expense are administrative expenses; depreciation on the equipment is a selling expense.

Instructions

(a) Prepare a multiple-step income statement, a retained earnings statement, and a classified balance sheet.
(b) Journalize the adjusting entries that were made.
(c) Journalize the closing entries that are necessary.

P3-8 (Adjusting Entries) The accounts listed below appeared in the December 31 trial balance of the Jane Alexander Theater.

	Debit	Credit
Equipment	$192,000	
Accumulated Depreciation—Equipment		$ 60,000
Notes Payable		90,000
Admissions Revenue		380,000
Advertising Expense	13,680	
Salaries Expense	57,600	
Interest Expense	1,400	

Instructions

(a) From the account balances listed above and the information given below, prepare the annual adjusting entries necessary on December 31.

  (1) The equipment has an estimated life of 16 years and a salvage value of $40,000 at the end of that time. (Use straight-line method.)

  (2) The note payable is a 90-day note given to the bank October 20 and bearing interest at 10%. (Use 360 days for denominator.)

  (3) In December 2,000 coupon admission books were sold at $25 each. They could be used for admission any time after January 1.

  (4) Advertising expense paid in advance and included in Advertising Expense, $1,100.

  (5) Salaries accrued but unpaid, $4,700.

(b) What amounts should be shown for each of the following on the income statement for the year?

  (1) Interest expense.

  (2) Admissions revenue.

  (3) Advertising expense.

  (4) Salaries expense.

P3-9 (Adjusting Entries and Financial Statements) Presented below are the trial balance and the other information related to Muhammad Ali, a consulting engineer.

MUHAMMAD ALI, CONSULTING ENGINEER
TRIAL BALANCE
DECEMBER 31, 2003

	Debit	Credit
Cash	$ 31,500	
Accounts Receivable	49,600	
Allowance for Doubtful Accounts		$ 750
Engineering Supplies Inventory	1,960	
Unexpired Insurance	1,100	
Furniture and Equipment	25,000	
Accumulated Depreciation—Furniture and Equipment		6,250
Notes Payable		7,200
Muhammad Ali, Capital		35,010
Service Revenue		100,000
Rent Expense	9,750	
Office Salaries Expense	28,500	
Heat, Light, and Water Expense	1,080	
Miscellaneous Office Expense	720	
	$149,210	$149,210

---

1. Fees received in advance from clients, $6,900.
2. Services performed for clients that were not recorded by December 31, $4,900.
3. Bad debt expense for the year is $1,430.
4. Insurance expired during the year, $480.
5. Furniture and equipment is being depreciated at $12\frac{1}{2}$% per year.
6. Muhammad Ali gave the bank a 90-day, 10% note for $7,200 on December 1, 2003.
7. Rent of the building is $750 per month. The rent for 2003 has been paid, as has that for January 2004.
8. Office salaries earned but unpaid December 31, 2003, $2,510.

Instructions

(a) From the trial balance and other information given, prepare annual adjusting entries as of December 31, 2003.

(b) Prepare an income statement for 2003, a balance sheet, and a statement of owner's equity. Muhammad Ali withdrew $17,000 cash for personal use during the year.

P3-10 (Adjusting Entries and Financial Statements) Ana Alicia Advertising Corporation was founded by Ana Alicia in January 2000. Presented below are both the adjusted and unadjusted trial balances as of December 31, 2004.

ANA ALICIA ADVERTISING CORPORATION
TRIAL BALANCE
DECEMBER 31, 2004

	Unadjusted Dr.	Unadjusted Cr.	Adjusted Dr.	Adjusted Cr.
Cash	$ 7,000		$ 7,000	
Accounts Receivable	19,000		22,000	
Art Supplies	8,500		5,500	
Prepaid Insurance	3,250		2,500	
Printing Equipment	60,000		60,000	
Accumulated Depreciation		$ 27,000		$ 33,750
Accounts Payable		5,000		5,000
Interest Payable				150
Notes Payable		5,000		5,000
Unearned Service Revenue		7,000		5,600
Salaries Payable				1,500
Common Stock		10,000		10,000
Retained Earnings		4,500		4,500
Service Revenue		58,600		63,000
Salaries Expense	10,000		11,500	
Insurance Expense			750	
Interest Expense	350		500	
Depreciation Expense			6,750	
Art Supplies Expense	5,000		8,000	
Rent Expense	4,000		4,000	
	$117,100	$117,100	$128,500	$128,500

Instructions

(a) Journalize the annual adjusting entries that were made.
(b) Prepare an income statement and a statement of retained earnings for the year ending December 31, 2004, and a balance sheet at December 31.
(c) Answer the following questions.
   (1) If the useful life of equipment is 8 years, what is the expected salvage value?
   (2) If the note has been outstanding 3 months, what is the annual interest rate on that note?
   (3) If the company paid $12,500 in salaries in 2004, what was the balance in Salaries Payable on December 31, 2003?

P3-11 (Adjusting Entries) Presented below is information related to Jillian Anderson, Realtor, at the close of the fiscal year ending December 31.

1. Jillian had paid the local newspaper $335 for an advertisement to be run in January of the next year, charging it to Advertising Expense.
2. On November 1 Jillian borrowed $9,000 from Yorkville Bank issuing a 90-day, 10% note.
3. Salaries and wages due and unpaid December 31: sales, $1,420; office clerks, $1,060.
4. Interest accrued to date on Grant Muldaur's note, which Jillian holds, $500.

5. Estimated loss on bad debts, $1,210 for the period.
6. Stamps and stationery on hand, $110, charged to Stationery and Postage Expense account when purchased.
7. Jillian has not yet paid the December rent on the building her business occupies, $1,000.
8. Insurance paid November 1 for one year, $930, charged to Prepaid Insurance when paid.
9. Property taxes accrued, $1,670.
10. On December 1 Jillian gave Laura Palmer her (Jillian's) 60-day, 12% note for $6,000 on account.
11. On October 31 Jillian received $2,580 from Douglas Raines in payment of 6 months' rent for office space occupied by him in the building and credited Unearned Rent Revenue.
12. On September 1 she paid 6 months' rent in advance on a warehouse, $6,600, and debited the asset account Prepaid Rent Expense.
13. The bill from the Twin Peaks Light & Power Company for December has been received but not yet entered or paid, $510.
14. Estimated depreciation on furniture and equipment, $1,400.

Instructions

Prepare annual adjusting entries as of December 31.

 P3-12 (Adjusting and Closing) Following is the trial balance of the Platteville Golf Club, Inc. as of December 31. The books are closed annually on December 31.

PLATTEVILLE GOLF CLUB, INC. TRIAL BALANCE DECEMBER 31		
	Debit	Credit
Cash	$ 15,000	
Accounts Receivable	13,000	
Allowance for Doubtful Accounts		$ 1,100
Land	350,000	
Buildings	120,000	
Accumulated Depreciation of Buildings		38,400
Equipment	150,000	
Accumulated Depreciation of Equipment		70,000
Unexpired Insurance	9,000	
Common Stock		400,000
Retained Earnings		82,000
Dues Revenue		200,000
Greens Fee Revenue		8,100
Rental Revenue		15,400
Utilities Expense	54,000	
Salaries Expense	80,000	
Maintenance Expense	24,000	
	$815,000	$815,000

Instructions

(a) Enter the balances in ledger accounts. Allow five lines for each account.
(b) From the trial balance and the information given, prepare annual adjusting entries and post to the ledger accounts.
   (1) The buildings have an estimated life of 25 years with no salvage value (straight-line method).
   (2) The equipment is depreciated at 10% per year.
   (3) Insurance expired during the year, $3,500.
   (4) The rental revenue represents the amount received for 11 months for dining facilities. The December rent has not yet been received.

(5) It is estimated that 15% of the accounts receivable will be uncollectible.

(6) Salaries earned but not paid by December 31, $3,600.

(7) Dues paid in advance by members, $8,900.

(c) Prepare an adjusted trial balance.

(d) Prepare closing entries and post.

P3-13 **(Adjusting and Closing)** Presented below is the December 31 trial balance of Nancy Drew Boutique.

NANCY DREW BOUTIQUE TRIAL BALANCE DECEMBER 31		
	Debit	Credit
Cash	$ 18,500	
Accounts Receivable	42,000	
Allowance for Doubtful Accounts		$ 700
Inventory, December 31	80,000	
Furniture and Equipment	84,000	
Accumulated Depreciation of Furniture and Equipment		35,000
Prepaid Insurance	5,100	
Notes Payable		28,000
Common Stock		80,600
Retained Earnings		10,000
Sales		600,000
Cost of Goods Sold	398,000	
Sales Salaries Expense	50,000	
Advertising Expense	6,700	
Administrative Salaries Expense	65,000	
Office Expense	5,000	
	$754,300	$754,300

Instructions

(a) Construct T-accounts and enter the balances shown.

(b) Prepare adjusting journal entries for the following and post to the T-accounts. Open additional T-accounts as necessary. (The books are closed yearly on December 31.)

(1) Bad debts are estimated to be $1,400.

(2) Furniture and equipment is depreciated based on a 6-year life (no salvage).

(3) Insurance expired during the year, $2,550.

(4) Interest accrued on notes payable, $3,360.

(5) Sales salaries earned but not paid, $2,400.

(6) Advertising paid in advance, $700.

(7) Office supplies on hand, $1,500, charged to Office Expense when purchased.

(c) Prepare closing entries and post to the accounts.

USING YOUR JUDGMENT

FINANCIAL REPORTING PROBLEM

3M COMPANY

The financial statements of 3M were provided with your book or can be accessed on the Take Action! CD.

Instructions

Refer to these financial statements and the accompanying notes to answer the following questions.

(a) What were 3M's total assets at December 30, 2001? At December 31, 2000?

(b) How much cash (and cash equivalents) did 3M have on December 30, 2001?

(c) What were 3M's research and development costs in 1999? In 2001?

(d) What were 3M's revenues in 1999? In 2001?

(e) Using 3M's financial statements and related notes, identify items that may result in adjusting entries for prepayments and accruals.

(f) What were the amounts of 3M's depreciation expense in 1999, 2000, and 2001?

FINANCIAL STATEMENT ANALYSIS CASE

KELLOGG COMPANY

Kellogg Company has its headquarters in Battle Creek, Michigan. The company manufactures and sells ready-to-eat breakfast cereals and convenience foods including toaster pastries and cereal bars.

Selected data from Kellogg Company's 1998 annual report follows (dollar amounts and share data in millions).

	1998	1997	1996
Net sales	$6,762.1	$6,830.1	$6,676.6
Cost of goods sold	3,282.6	3,270.1	3,122.9
Selling and administrative expense	2,513.9	2,366.8	2,458.7
Net income	502.6	546.0	531.0

In its 1998 annual report, Kellogg Company outlined its plans for the future, which it described as its five point "strategy for growth." A brief description of these plans follows.

1. **Leading the food industry in innovation**—Kellogg Company is rolling out a broader grain-based product portfolio, including great-tasting new cereals, innovative convenience foods, and new grain-based products outside our traditional lines.

2. **Investing in our largest cereal markets**—During 1999, Kellogg will invest in growth in our seven largest cereal markets.

3. **Accelerating the global growth of our convenience foods business**—Kellogg is focusing both on an expanded geographic distribution and new distribution channels, particularly single-serve channels.

4. **Continuing to reduce cost**—From ongoing cost-reduction programs, we anticipate more than $50 million in incremental savings in 1999.

5. **Creating a more focused and accountable organization**—Kellogg's objective is to develop a talented, diverse global workforce with every person focused on the largest, most important activities.

Instructions

(a) For each of the strategies, describe how gross profit and net income are likely to be affected.

(b) Compute the percentage change in sales, gross profit, operating costs (cost of goods sold plus selling and administrative expenses), and net income from year to year for each of the three years shown. Evaluate Kellogg Company's performance. Which trend seems to be least favorable? Do you think the global strategies described will improve that trend? Explain.

COMPARATIVE ANALYSIS CASE

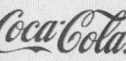

THE COCA-COLA COMPANY AND PEPSICO, INC.

Instructions

Go to the Take Action! CD and use information found there to answer the following questions related to The Coca-Cola Company and PepsiCo, Inc.

(a) Which company had the greater percentage increase in total assets from 2000 to 2001?

(b) Using the Selected Financial Data section of these two companies, determine their 5-year compound growth rates related to net sales and income from continuing operations.

(c) What company had more depreciation and amortization expense for 2001? Provide a rationale as to why there is a difference in these amounts between the two companies.

*Remember to check the **Take Action! CD**
and the book's **companion Web site**
to find additional resources for this chapter.*

"THERE OUGHT TO BE A LAW"

LEARNING OBJECTIVES

After studying this chapter, you should be able to:

1. Identify the uses and limitations of a balance sheet.

2. Identify the major classifications of the balance sheet.

3. Prepare a classified balance sheet using the report and account formats.

4. Identify balance sheet information requiring supplemental disclosure.

5. Identify major disclosure techniques for the balance sheet.

When the Internet stock bubble burst during 2000, many investors learned the importance of analysis based on information in the balance sheet. As one money-manager noted, "There ought to be a law in this country that before you are allowed to buy a stock, you have to be able to read its balance sheet." Analysis based on balance sheet information was clearly missing during much of the bull market of late 1990s. Many investors in companies such as **Gateway 2000**, **Cisco Systems**, and **Alcatel** missed the information in the balance sheet indicating that inventories and receivables were growing. Increases in these assets indicate that sales are slowing and customers are facing more difficult economic times, both of which generally foretell declining future sales and profitability.[1]

Information on liabilities also is important for financial analysis, especially when the economy begins to slow. As shown in the graph below, in 2001 nonfinancial companies reported debt levels (as a percent of net worth) of nearly 60 percent. By comparsion, debt levels during the previous recession in 1990–91 were only 51 percent.

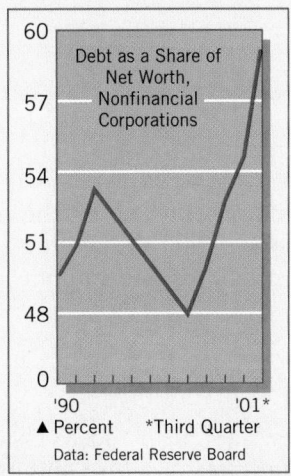

Debt as a Share of Net Worth, Nonfinancial Corporations

▲ Percent   *Third Quarter

Data: Federal Reserve Board

These high debt levels are troublesome because they indicate less of a financial cushion, making a company more vulnerable to unexpected shocks. For example, if inflation slows more than expected and companies cannot increase prices, the debt will be harder to pay. This situation further reduces a company's financial flexibility and reduces income as higher interest is paid on its risky debt.

Thus, these earnings declines (and falling stock prices) for many companies during the recent economic slowdown could have been predicted, based on the information in the balance sheet. And just as deteriorating balance sheets warned of trouble, improving balance sheet information is a leading indicator for improved future earnings.

[1]Adapted from Gretchen Morgenson, "How Did They Value Stocks? Count the Absurd Ways," *New York Times on the Web* (March 18, 2001).

Readers of the financial statements sometimes ignore important information in the balance sheet. As shown in the opening story involving **Cisco Systems**, **Gateway 2000**, and **Alcatel**, surprises in earnings could have been anticipated if the balance sheet had not been overlooked. The purpose of this chapter is to examine the many different types of assets, liabilities, and stockholders' equity items that affect the balance sheet. The content and organization of this chapter are as follows.

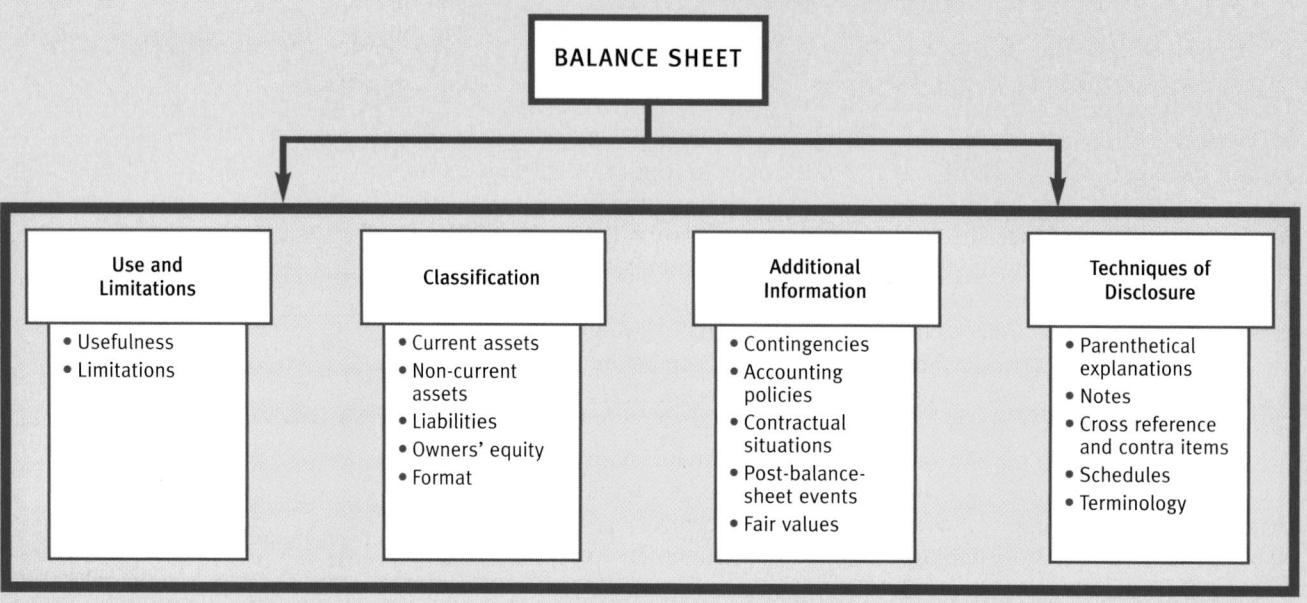

BALANCE SHEET			
Use and Limitations	**Classification**	**Additional Information**	**Techniques of Disclosure**
• Usefulness • Limitations	• Current assets • Non-current assets • Liabilities • Owners' equity • Format	• Contingencies • Accounting policies • Contractual situations • Post-balance-sheet events • Fair values	• Parenthetical explanations • Notes • Cross reference and contra items • Schedules • Terminology

USE AND LIMITATIONS

OBJECTIVE 1
Identify the uses and limitations of a balance sheet.

The **balance sheet**, sometimes referred to as the statement of financial position, reports the assets, liabilities, and stockholders' equity of a business enterprise at a specific date. This financial statement provides information about the nature and amounts of investments in enterprise resources, obligations to creditors, and the owners' equity in net resources.[2] It therefore helps in predicting the amounts, timing, and uncertainty of future cash flows.

Usefulness of the Balance Sheet

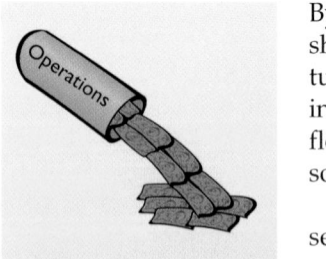

How quickly will my assets convert to cash?

By providing information on assets, liabilities, and stockholders' equity, the balance sheet provides a basis for computing rates of return and evaluating the capital structure of the enterprise. As illustrated in the opening story about new-economy stocks, information in the balance sheet is also used to assess enterprise risk[3] and future cash flows. In this regard, the balance sheet is useful for analyzing a company's liquidity, solvency, and financial flexibility.

    Liquidity describes "the amount of time that is expected to elapse until an asset is realized or otherwise converted into cash or until a liability has to be paid."[4]

---

[2]*Accounting Trends and Techniques—2001* indicates that approximately 95 percent of the companies surveyed used the term "balance sheet." The term "statement of financial position" is used infrequently, although it is conceptually appealing.

[3]Risk is an expression of the unpredictability of future events, transactions, circumstances, and results of the enterprise.

[4]"Reporting Income, Cash Flows, and Financial Position of Business Enterprises," *Proposed Statement of Financial Accounting Concepts* (Stamford, Conn.: FASB, 1981), par. 29.

Creditors are interested in short-term liquidity ratios, such as the ratio of cash (or near cash) to short-term liabilities, because they indicate whether the enterprise will have the resources to pay its current and maturing obligations. Similarly, stockholders assess liquidity to evaluate the possibility of future cash dividends or the buyback of shares. In general, the greater the liquidity, the lower the risk of enterprise failure.

Solvency refers to the ability of an enterprise to pay its debts as they mature. For example, when a company carries a high level of long-term debt relative to assets, it has lower solvency than a similar company with a low level of long-term debt. Companies with higher debt are relatively more risky because more of their assets will be required to meet these fixed obligations (such as interest and principal payments).

Liquidity and solvency affect an entity's **financial flexibility**, which measures the "ability of an enterprise to take effective actions to alter the amounts and timing of cash flows so it can respond to unexpected needs and opportunities."[5] For example, a company may become so loaded with debt—so financially inflexible—that its sources of cash to finance expansion or to pay off maturing debt are limited or nonexistent. An enterprise with a high degree of financial flexibility is better able to survive bad times, to recover from unexpected setbacks, and to take advantage of profitable and unexpected investment opportunities. Generally, the greater the financial flexibility, the lower the risk of enterprise failure.

Obligation Ocean

We are drowning in a sea of debt!

GROUNDED

WHAT DO THE NUMBERS MEAN?

Lack of liquidity and solvency, and inadequate financial flexibility seriously affected the U.S. airline industry over the last 25 years. For example, in the 1980s and again in the early 1990s, American, Eastern, United, and TWA all reported quarterly operating losses that stemmed primarily from high interest costs, increased fuel costs, and price cutting resulting from deregulation. In response to operating losses and lowered liquidity, some airlines asked their employees to sign labor contracts that provided no wage increases. Other airlines, already heavily in debt and lacking financial flexibility and liquidity, had to cancel orders for new, more efficient aircraft. TWA had to sell routes and planes to raise cash. Some of the major airlines (such as Braniff, Continental, Eastern, Midway, and America West) even declared bankruptcy. And the terrorist attacks of September 11, 2001, have shown how vulnerable the major airlines are to reduced demand for their services. This financial distress was not an insiders' secret. The airlines' balance sheets clearly revealed their financial inflexibility and low liquidity.

Limitations of the Balance Sheet

Some of the major limitations of the balance sheet are:

①   Most assets and liabilities are stated at **historical cost**. As a result, the information reported in the balance sheet has higher reliability but is subject to the criticism that a more relevant current fair value is not reported. For example, Georgia Pacific owns timber and other assets that may appreciate in value after they are purchased; this increase is not reported unless the assets are sold.

②   **Judgments and estimates** are used in determining many of the items reported in the balance sheet. For example, Gateway 2000 makes estimates of the amount of

Hmm... I wonder if they will pay me back?

[5]"Reporting Income, Cash Flows, and Financial Position of Business Enterprises," *Proposed Statement of Financial Accounting Concepts* (Stamford, Conn.: FASB, 1981), par. 25.

receivables that it will collect, the useful life of its warehouses, and the number of computers that will be returned under warranty in arriving at the amounts reported in its balance sheet.

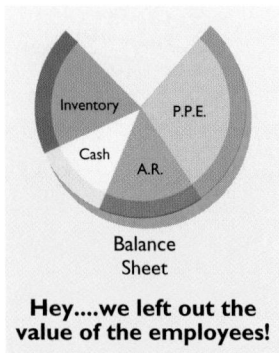

Balance Sheet

Hey....we left out the value of the employees!

③ The balance sheet necessarily **omits many items that are of financial value** to the business but cannot be recorded objectively. For example, the knowledge and skill of **Intel** employees in developing new computer chips are arguably the company's most significant asset. However, because it is difficult to reliably measure the value of employees and other intangible assets (such as customer base, research superiority, and reputation), these items are not recognized in the balance sheet. Similarly, many liabilities are also reported in an "off-balance-sheet" manner, if reported at all.[6]

The recent bankruptcy of the seventh largest U.S. company, **Enron**, highlights the fact that not all items of importance are reported in the balance sheet. In Enron's case, it had certain off-balance-sheet financing obligations which were not disclosed in the main financial statements.

CLASSIFICATION IN THE BALANCE SHEET

OBJECTIVE 2
Identify the major classifications of the balance sheet.

Balance sheet accounts are **classified** so that similar items are grouped together to arrive at significant subtotals. Furthermore, the material is arranged so that important relationships are shown.

The FASB has often noted that the parts and subsections of financial statements can be more informative than the whole. Therefore, as one would expect, the reporting of summary accounts alone (total assets, net assets, total liabilities, etc.) is discouraged. Individual items should be separately reported and classified in sufficient detail to permit users to assess the amounts, timing, and uncertainty of future cash flows, as well as the evaluation of liquidity and financial flexibility, profitability, and risk.

Classification in financial statements helps analysts by grouping items with similar characteristics and separating items with different characteristics:[7]

① Assets that differ in their **type or expected function** in the central operations or other activities of the enterprise should be reported as separate items. For example, merchandise inventories should be reported separately from property, plant, and equipment.

② Assets and liabilities with **different implications for the financial flexibility** of the enterprise should be reported as separate items. For example, assets used in operations should be reported separately from assets held for investment and assets subject to restrictions such as leased equipment.

③ Assets and liabilities with **different general liquidity characteristics** should be reported as separate items. For example, cash should be reported separately from inventories.

[6]Several of these omitted items (such as leases and other off-balance-sheet arrangements) are discussed in later chapters. See AICPA Special Committee on Financial Reporting, "Improving Business Reporting—A Customer Focus," *Journal of Accountancy*, Supplement (October 1994), for a discussion of issues surrounding off-balance-sheet items; and Wayne Upton, Jr., Special Report: *Business and Financial Reporting, Challenges from the New Economy* (Norwalk, Conn.: FASB, 2001).

[7]"Reporting Income, Cash Flows, and Financial Positions of Business Enterprises," *Proposed Statement of Financial Accounting Concepts* (Stamford, Conn.: FASB, 1981), par. 51.

The three general classes of items included in the balance sheet are assets, liabilities, and equity. We defined them in Chapter 2 as follows.

ELEMENTS OF THE BALANCE SHEET

◇1 *Assets.* Probable future economic benefits obtained or controlled by a particular entity as a result of past transactions or events.

◇2 *Liabilities.* Probable future sacrifices of economic benefits arising from present obligations of a particular entity to transfer assets or provide services to other entities in the future as a result of past transactions or events.

◇3 *Equity.* Residual interest in the assets of an entity that remains after deducting its liabilities. In a business enterprise, the equity is the ownership interest.[8]

These items are then divided into several subclassifications. Illustration 4-1 indicates the general format of balance sheet presentation.

Assets	Liabilities and Owners' Equity
Current assets	Current liabilities
Long-term investments	Long-term debt
Property, plant, and equipment	Owners' equity
Intangible assets	Capital stock
Other assets	Additional paid-in capital
	Retained earnings

Illustration 4-1
Balance Sheet
Classifications

The balance sheet may be classified in some other manner, but there is very little departure from these major subdivisions in practice. If a proprietorship or partnership is involved, the classifications within the owners' equity section are presented a little differently, as will be shown later in the chapter.

Current Assets

Current assets are cash and other assets expected to be converted into cash, sold, or consumed either in one year or in the operating cycle, whichever is longer. The operating cycle is the average time between the acquisition of materials and supplies and the realization of cash through sales of the product for which the materials and supplies were acquired. The cycle operates from cash through inventory, production, receivables, and back to cash. When there are several operating cycles within one year, the one-year period is used. If the operating cycle is more than one year, the longer period is used.

---

[8]"Elements of Financial Statements of Business Enterprises," *Statement of Financial Accounting Concepts No. 6* (Stamford, Conn.: FASB, 1985), paras. 25, 35 and 49.

Current assets are presented in the balance sheet in order of liquidity. The five major items found in the current assets section are cash, short-term investments, receivables, inventories, and prepayments. Valuation of these items is as follows: **Cash** is included at its stated value. **Short-term investments** are generally valued at fair value. **Accounts receivable** are stated at the estimated amount collectible. **Inventories** generally are included at cost or the lower of cost or market. **Prepaid items** are valued at cost.

These five items are not considered current assets if they are not expected to be realized in one year or in the operating cycle, whichever is longer. For example, cash restricted for purposes other than payment of current obligations or for use in current operations is excluded from the current assets section. **Generally, the rule is that if an asset is to be turned into cash or is to be used to pay a current liability within a year or the operating cycle, whichever is longer, it is classified as current.** This requirement is subject to exceptions. An investment in common stock is classified as either a current asset or a noncurrent asset depending on management's intent. When a company has small holdings of common stocks or bonds that are going to be held long-term, they should not be classified as current.

Although a current asset is well defined, certain theoretical problems develop. One problem is justifying the inclusion of prepaid expense in the current assets section. The normal justification is that if these items had not been paid in advance, they would require the use of current assets during the operating cycle. If we follow this logic to its ultimate conclusion, however, any asset purchased previously saves the use of current assets during the operating cycle and would be considered current.

Another problem occurs in the current asset definition when fixed assets are consumed during the operating cycle. A literal interpretation of the accounting profession's position on this matter would indicate that an amount equal to the current depreciation and amortization charges on the noncurrent assets should be placed in the current assets section at the beginning of the year, because they will be consumed in the next operating cycle. This conceptual problem is ignored, which illustrates that the formal distinction made between current and noncurrent assets is somewhat arbitrary.

Cash

Any restrictions on the general availability of cash or any commitments on its probable disposition must be disclosed. An example of such a presentation is excerpted from the Annual Report of **Alterra Healthcare Corp.** below.

Illustration 4-2
Balance Sheet
Presentation of
Restricted Cash

Alterra
AGING WITH CHOICE

ALTERRA HEALTHCARE CORP.

Current assets	
Cash	$18,728,000
Restricted cash and investments (Note 7)	7,191,000

Note 7: Restricted Cash and Investments. Restricted cash and investments consist of certificates of deposit restricted as collateral for lease arrangements and debt service with interest rates ranging from 4.0% to 5.5%.

For Alterra Healthcare, cash was restricted to meet an obligation due currently and, therefore, was included under current assets. If cash is restricted for purposes other than current obligations, it is excluded from current assets. An example of current and noncurrent presentation is excerpted from the Annual Report of **Owens Corning, Inc.** in Illustration 4-3.

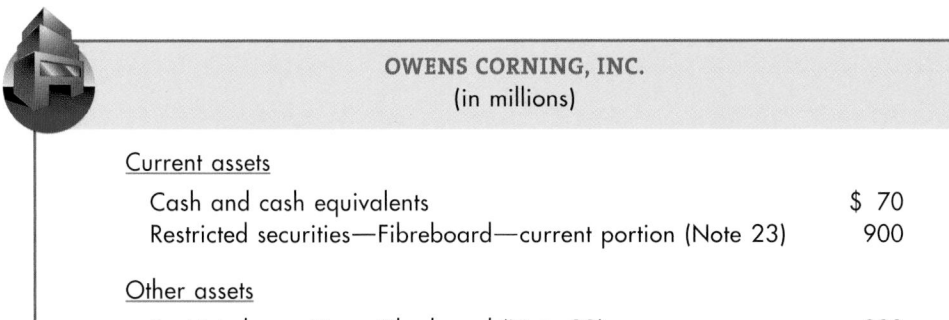

Illustration 4-3
Balance Sheet
Presentation of Current
and Noncurrent
Restricted Cash

OWENS CORNING, INC. (in millions)	
Current assets	
Cash and cash equivalents	$ 70
Restricted securities—Fibreboard—current portion (Note 23)	900
Other assets	
Restricted securities—Fibreboard (Note 23)	938

Note 23 (in part). The Insurance Settlement funds are held in and invested by the Fibreboard Settlement Trust (the "Trust") and are available to satisfy Fibreboard's pending and future asbestos related liabilities. . . . The assets of the Trust are comprised of cash and marketable securities (collectively, the "Trust Assets") and are reflected on Owens Corning's consolidated balance sheet as restricted assets. These assets are reflected as current assets or other assets, with each category denoted "Restricted securities—Fibreboard."

Short-Term Investments

Investments in debt and equity securities are grouped into three separate portfolios for valuation and reporting purposes. These portfolios are categorized as follows.

Held-to-maturity: Debt securities that the enterprise has the positive intent and ability to hold to maturity.

Trading: Debt and equity securities bought and held primarily for sale in the near term to generate income on short-term price differences.

Available-for-sale: Debt and equity securities not classified as held-to-maturity or trading securities.

Trading securities (whether debt or equity) should be reported as current assets. Individual held-to-maturity and available-for-sale securities are classified as current or noncurrent depending upon the circumstances. All trading and available-for-sale securities are to be reported at fair value.[9]

The example below is excerpted from the Annual Report of **Anchor BanCorp Wisconsin Inc.**

Illustration 4-4
Balance Sheet
Presentation of
Investments in Securities

ANCHOR BANCORP WISCONSIN INC. (in thousands)	
Assets	
Cash and cash equivalents	$ 105,042
Investment securities available for sale	22,216
Investment securities held to maturity (fair value of $34,096)	33,913
Mortgage-related securities available for sale	173,968
Mortgage-related securities held to maturity (fair value of $207,669)	205,191
Loans receivable, net	
Held for sale	17,622
Held for investment	2,414,976
Foreclosed properties and repossessed assets, net	313

[9]"Accounting for Certain Investments in Debt and Equity Securities," *Statement of Financial Accounting Standards No. 115* (Norwalk, Conn.: FASB, 1993).

Receivables

Any anticipated loss due to uncollectibles, the amount and nature of any nontrade receivables, and any receivables designated or pledged as collateral should be clearly identified. **Mack Trucks, Inc.** reported its receivables as follows.

Illustration 4-5
Balance Sheet
Presentation of
Receivables

MACK TRUCKS, INC.	
Current assets	
Trade receivables	
Accounts receivable	$102,212,000
Affiliated companies	1,157,000
Installment notes and contracts	625,000
Total	103,994,000
Less: Allowance for uncollectible accounts	8,194,000
Trade receivables—net	95,800,000
Receivables from unconsolidated financial subsidiaries	22,106,000

UNDERLYING CONCEPTS

The lower of cost or market valuation is an example of the use of conservatism in accounting.

Inventories

For a proper presentation of inventories, the basis of valuation (i.e., lower of cost or market) and the method of pricing (FIFO or LIFO) are disclosed. For a manufacturing concern (like **Abbott Laboratories**, shown below), the stage of completion of the inventories is also indicated.

Illustration 4-6
Balance Sheet
Presentation of
Inventories, Showing
Stage of Completion

ABBOTT LABORATORIES (in thousands)		
Current assets		
Inventories		
Finished products	$ 772,478	
Work in process	338,818	
Materials	384,148	
Total inventories	1,495,444	

Note 1 (in part): Inventories. Inventories are stated at the lower of cost (first-in, first-out basis) or market.

Weyerhaeuser Company, a forestry company and lumber manufacturer with several finished-goods product lines, reported its inventory as follows.

Illustration 4-7
Balance Sheet
Presentation of
Inventories, Showing
Product Lines

WEYERHAEUSER COMPANY	
Current assets	
Inventories—at FIFO lower of cost or market	
Logs and chips	$ 68,471,000
Lumber, plywood and panels	86,741,000
Pulp, newsprint and paper	47,377,000
Containerboard, paperboard, containers and cartons	59,682,000
Other products	161,717,000
Total product inventories	423,988,000
Materials and supplies	175,540,000

Prepaid Expenses

Prepaid expenses included in current assets are expenditures already made for benefits (usually services) to be received within one year or the operating cycle, whichever is longer.[10] These items are current assets because if they had not already been paid, they would require the use of cash during the next year or the operating cycle. A common example is the payment in advance for an insurance policy. It is classified as a prepaid expense at the time of the expenditure because the payment precedes the receipt of the benefit of coverage. Other common prepaid expenses include prepaid rent, advertising, taxes, and office or operating supplies. Prepaid expenses are reported at the amount of the unexpired or unconsumed cost. **Knight Ridder, Inc.**, for example, listed its prepaid expenses in current assets as follows.

KNIGHT RIDDER, INC. (in thousands)	
Current assets	
Cash, including short-term cash investments of $7,001	$ 41,661
Accounts receivable, net of allowances of $20,238	416,498
Inventories	52,786
Prepaids	30,767
Other current assets	34,382

Illustration 4-8

Balance Sheet Presentation of Prepaid Expenses

Companies often include insurance and other prepayments for two or three years in current assets even though part of the advance payment applies to periods beyond one year or the current operating cycle.

Non-Current Assets

Non-current assets are those not meeting the definition of current assets. They include a variety of items, as discussed in the following sections.

Long-Term Investments

Long-term investments, often referred to simply as investments, normally consist of one of four types:

1. Investments in securities, such as bonds, common stock, or long-term notes.
2. Investments in tangible fixed assets not currently used in operations, such as land held for speculation.
3. Investments set aside in special funds such as a sinking fund, pension fund, or plant expansion fund. The cash surrender value of life insurance is included here.
4. Investments in nonconsolidated subsidiaries or affiliated companies.

Long-term investments are to be held for many years. They are not acquired with the intention of disposing of them in the near future. They are usually presented on the balance sheet just below "Current assets," in a separate section called Investments. Many securities that are properly shown among long-term investments are, in fact, readily marketable. But they are not included as current assets unless the intent is to convert them to cash in the short-term—within a year or in the operating

---

[10]*Accounting Trends and Techniques—2001* in its survey of 600 annual reports identified 343 companies that reported prepaid expenses.

cycle, whichever is longer. Securities classified as available-for-sale should be reported at fair value. Securities classified as held-to-maturity are reported at amortized cost.

Motorola, Inc. reported its investments section between "Property, plant, and equipment" and "Other assets" in the following manner.

Illustration 4-9
Balance Sheet
Presentation of Long-
Term Investments

MOTOROLA, INC. (in millions)	
Investments	
Equity investments	$ 872
Other investments	2,567
Fair value adjustment to available-for-sale securities	2,487
Total	$5,926

Property, Plant, and Equipment

Property, plant, and equipment are properties of a durable nature used in the regular operations of the business. These assets consist of physical property such as land, buildings, machinery, furniture, tools, and wasting resources (timberland, minerals). With the exception of land, most assets are either depreciable (such as buildings) or depletable (such as timberlands or oil reserves).

Mattel, Inc., a manufacturer of toys and games, presented its property, plant, and equipment in its balance sheet as follows.

Illustration 4-10
Balance Sheet
Presentation of Property,
Plant, and Equipment

MATTEL, INC.	
Property, plant, and equipment	
Land	$ 32,793,000
Buildings	257,430,000
Machinery and equipment	564,244,000
Capitalized leases	23,271,000
Leasehold improvements	74,988,000
	952,726,000
Less: Accumulated depreciation	472,986,000
	479,740,000
Tools, dies and molds, net	168,092,000
Property, plant, and equipment, net	647,832,000

The basis of valuing the property, plant, and equipment, any liens against the properties, and accumulated depreciation should be disclosed—usually in notes to the statements.

Intangible Assets

Intangible assets lack physical substance and are not financial instruments (see definition on page 142). They include patents, copyrights, franchises, goodwill, trademarks, trade names, and secret processes. Limited-life intangible assets are written off (amortized) over their useful lives. Indefinite-life intangibles (such as goodwill) are not amortized but, instead, are assessed periodically for impairment. Intangibles can represent significant economic resources, yet financial analysts often ignore them, and accountants write them down or off arbitrarily because valuation is difficult.

PepsiCo, Inc. reported intangible assets in its balance sheet as follows.

PEPSICO	PEPSICO, INC. (in millions)	
Intangible assets		
Goodwill		$3,374
Trademarks		1,320
Other identifiable intangibles		147
Total intangibles		$4,841

Illustration 4-11
Balance Sheet
Presentation of
Intangible Assets

Other Assets

The items included in the section "Other assets" vary widely in practice. Some of the items commonly included are deferred charges (long-term prepaid expenses), noncurrent receivables, intangible assets, assets in special funds, deferred income taxes, property held for sale, and advances to subsidiaries. Such a section unfortunately is too general a classification. Instead, it should be restricted to unusual items sufficiently different from assets included in specific categories.

Liabilities

Similar to assets, liabilities are classified as current or long-term.

Current Liabilities

Current liabilities are the obligations that are reasonably expected to be liquidated either through the use of current assets or the creation of other current liabilities. This concept includes:

1. Payables resulting from the acquisition of goods and services: accounts payable, wages payable, taxes payable, and so on.

2. Collections received in advance for the delivery of goods or performance of services such as unearned rent revenue or unearned subscriptions revenue.

3. Other liabilities whose liquidation will take place within the operating cycle such as the portion of long-term bonds to be paid in the current period, or short-term obligations arising from purchase of equipment.

At times, a liability payable next year is not included in the current liabilities section. This occurs either when the debt is expected to be refinanced through another long-term issue,[11] or when the debt is retired out of noncurrent assets. This approach is used because liquidation does not result from the use of current assets or the creation of other current liabilities.

Current liabilities are not reported in any consistent order. The items most commonly listed first are notes payable, accounts payable, or short-term debt. Income taxes payable, current maturities of long-term debt, or other current liabilities are commonly

---

[11]"Classification of Short-term Obligations Expected to Be Refinanced," *Statement of Financial Accounting Standards No. 6* (Stamford, Conn.: FASB, 1975).

listed last. An example of **Halliburton Company**'s current liabilities section is shown below.

Illustration 4-12
Balance Sheet
Presentation of Current
Liabilities

HALLIBURTON COMPANY (in millions)	
Current liabilities	
Short-term notes payable	$1,570
Accounts payable	782
Accrued employee compensation and benefits	267
Unearned revenues	386
Income taxes payable	113
Accrued special charges	6
Current maturities of long-term debt	8
Other current liabilities	694
Total current liabilities	3,826

Current liabilities include such items as trade and nontrade notes and accounts payable, advances received from customers, and current maturities of long-term debt. Income taxes and other accrued items are classified separately, if material. Any secured liability—for example, stock held as collateral on notes payable—is fully described in the notes so that the assets providing the security can be identified.

The excess of total current assets over total current liabilities is referred to as **working capital** (sometimes called **net working capital**). Working capital represents the net amount of a company's relatively liquid resources. That is, it is the liquid buffer available to meet the financial demands of the operating cycle. Working capital as an amount is seldom disclosed on the balance sheet, but it is computed by bankers and other creditors as an indicator of the short-run liquidity of a company. In order to determine the actual liquidity and availability of working capital to meet current obligations, however, one must analyze the composition of the current assets and their nearness to cash.

WHAT DO THE NUMBERS MEAN?

"SHOW ME THE ASSETS!"

Recently, concerns about liquidity and solvency of many dot-com companies have led creditors to demand more assurance that these companies can pay their bills when due. A key indicator for creditors is the amount of working capital. For example, when a report published early in 2001 predicted that **Amazon.com**'s working capital would turn negative, vendors who sell goods to Amazon on credit began to explore steps that could be taken to ensure that they will be paid.

Some vendors demanded that their Internet customers sign notes stating that the goods shipped to them serve as collateral for the transaction. Other vendors began shipping goods on consignment—an arrangement whereby the vendor retains ownership of the goods until they are bought and paid for by a third party. Such creditor protection measures for dot-coms arise from creditors' concerns about Internet companies' lack of tangible assets that can be converted to cash to meet short-term obligations. For example, the primary asset for many Internet companies is its customer list. However, these lists have little resale value because privacy agreements stipulate that the customer information is provided for the Internet company's use only.

Thus, with fewer hard assets that can be converted to cash, Internet companies can experience a more severe credit squeeze as vendors curtail shipments or take other measures to limit their financial risk to Internet customers. Such actions can further erode a company's liquidity and financial flexibility.

Long-Term Liabilities

Long-term liabilities are obligations that are not reasonably expected to be liquidated within the normal operating cycle but, instead, are payable at some date beyond that time. Bonds payable, notes payable, some deferred income tax amounts, lease obligations, and pension obligations are the most common examples. Generally, a great deal of supplementary disclosure is needed for this section, because most long-term debt is subject to various covenants and restrictions for the protection of lenders.[12] Long-term liabilities that mature within the current operating cycle are classified as current liabilities if their liquidation requires the use of current assets.

Generally, long-term liabilities are of three types:

1 Obligations arising from specific financing situations, such as the issuance of bonds, long-term lease obligations, and long-term notes payable.

2 Obligations arising from the ordinary operations of the enterprise, such as pension obligations and deferred income tax liabilities.

3 Obligations that are dependent upon the occurrence or nonoccurrence of one or more future events to confirm the amount payable, or the payee, or the date payable, such as service or product warranties and other contingencies.

It is desirable to report any premium or discount separately as an addition to or subtraction from the bonds payable. The terms of all long-term liability agreements (including maturity date or dates, rates of interest, nature of obligation, and any security pledged to support the debt) are frequently described in notes to the financial statements. An example of the financial statement and accompanying note presentation is shown in Illustration 4-13 in the excerpt from **The Great Atlantic & Pacific Tea Company**'s financials.

Illustration 4-13
Balance Sheet Presentation of Long-Term Debt

THE GREAT ATLANTIC & PACIFIC TEA COMPANY, INC.

Total current liabilities	$978,109,000
Long-term debt (See note)	254,312,000
Obligations under capital leases	252,618,000
Deferred income taxes	57,167,000
Other non-current liabilities	127,321,000

Note: Indebtedness. Debt consists of:

9.5% Senior notes, due in annual installments of $10,000,000	$ 40,000,000
Mortgages and other notes due through 2011 (average interest rate of 9.9%)	107,604,000
Bank borrowings at 9.7%	67,225,000
Commercial paper at 9.4%	100,102,000
	314,931,000
Less: Current portion	(60,619,000)
Total long-term debt	$254,312,000

---

[12]The pertinent rights and privileges of the various securities (both debt and equity) outstanding are usually explained in the notes to the financial statements. Examples of information that should be disclosed are dividend and liquidation preferences, participation rights, call prices and dates, conversion or exercise prices or rates and pertinent dates, sinking fund requirements, unusual voting rights, and significant terms of contracts to issue additional shares. "Disclosure of Information about Capital Structure," *Statement of Financial Accounting Standards No. 129* (Norwalk: FASB, 1997), par. 4.

Owners' Equity

The **owners' equity** (stockholders' equity) section is one of the most difficult sections to prepare and understand. This is due to the complexity of capital stock agreements and the various restrictions on residual equity imposed by state corporation laws, liability agreements, and boards of directors. The section is usually divided into three parts:

STOCKHOLDERS' EQUITY SECTION

1. *Capital Stock.* The par or stated value of the shares issued.
2. *Additional Paid-In Capital.* The excess of amounts paid in over the par or stated value.
3. *Retained Earnings.* The corporation's undistributed earnings.

The major disclosure requirements for capital stock are the authorized, issued, and outstanding par value amounts. The additional paid-in capital is usually presented in one amount, although subtotals are informative if the sources of additional capital are varied and material. The retained earnings section may be divided between the unappropriated (the amount that is usually available for dividend distribution) and restricted (e.g., by bond indentures or other loan agreements) amounts. In addition, any capital stock reacquired (treasury stock) is shown as a reduction of stockholders' equity.

The ownership or stockholders' equity accounts in a corporation are considerably different from those in a partnership or proprietorship. Partners' permanent capital accounts and the balance in their temporary accounts (drawing accounts) are shown separately. Proprietorships ordinarily use a single capital account that handles all of the owner's equity transactions.

Presented below is an example of the stockholders' equity section from **Quanex Corporation**.

Illustration 4-14
Balance Sheet
Presentation of
Stockholders' Equity

QUANEX CORPORATION (in thousands)	
Stockholders' equity	
Preferred stock, no par value, 1,000,000 shares authorized; 345,000 issued and outstanding	$ 86,250
Common stock, $0.50 par value, 25,000,000 shares authorized; 13,638,005 shares issued and outstanding	6,819
Additional paid-in capital	87,260
Retained earnings	57,263
	$237,592

Balance Sheet Format

OBJECTIVE 3
Prepare a classified balance sheet using the report and account formats.

One common arrangement followed in the presentation of a classified balance sheet is called the **account form**. It lists assets by sections on the left side and liabilities and stockholders' equity by sections on the right side. The main disadvantage is the need for two facing pages.

To avoid the use of facing pages, the **report form**, shown in Illustration 4-15 (page 137), lists liabilities and stockholders' equity directly below assets on the same page.[13]

[13]*Accounting Trends and Techniques—2001* indicates that all of the 600 companies surveyed use either the "report form" (502) or the "account form" (98), sometimes collectively referred to as the "customary form."

SCIENTIFIC PRODUCTS, INC.
BALANCE SHEET
DECEMBER 31, 2003

Assets

Current assets

Cash		$ 42,485
Available-for-sale securities—at fair value		28,250
Accounts receivable	$165,824	
Less: Allowance for doubtful accounts	1,850	163,974
Notes receivable		23,000
Inventories—at average cost		489,713
Supplies on hand		9,780
Prepaid expenses		16,252
Total current assets		$ 773,454

Long-term investments

Investments in Warren Co.		87,500

Property, plant, and equipment

Land—at cost		125,000
Buildings—at cost	975,800	
Less: Accumulated depreciation	341,200	634,600
Total property, plant, and equipment		759,600

Intangible assets

Goodwill		100,000
Total assets		$1,720,554

Liabilities and Stockholders' Equity

Current liabilities

Notes payable to banks		$ 50,000
Accounts payable		197,532
Accrued interest on notes payable		500
Income taxes payable		62,520
Accrued salaries, wages, and other liabilities		9,500
Deposits received from customers		420
Total current liabilities		$ 320,472

Long-term debt

Twenty-year 12% debentures, due January 1, 2013		500,000
Total liabilities		820,472

Stockholders' equity

Paid in on capital stock		
Preferred, 7%, cumulative		
Authorized, issued, and outstanding, 30,000 shares of $10 par value	$300,000	
Common		
Authorized, 500,000 shares of $1.00 par value; issued and outstanding, 400,000 shares	400,000	
Additional paid-in capital	37,500	737,500
Earnings retained in the business		162,582
Total stockholders' equity		900,082
Total liabilities and stockholders' equity		$1,720,554

Illustration 4-15
Classified Report Form
Balance Sheet

UNDERLYING CONCEPTS

The presentation of balance sheet information meets one of the objectives of financial reporting—to provide information about enterprise resources, claims to resources, and changes in them.

Presentation of Balance Sheet Formats for Various Real Companies

Other balance sheet formats are used infrequently. For example, current liabilities are sometimes deducted from current assets to arrive at working capital, or all liabilities are deducted from all assets.

WHAT DO THE NUMBERS MEAN?

WARNING SIGNALS

One of the uses of balance sheet information is in models used to predict financial distress. A bankruptcy-prediction model pioneered by Altman combines balance sheet and income measures in the following equation to derive a "Z-score."

$$Z = \frac{\text{Working capital}}{\text{Total assets}} \times 1.2 + \frac{\text{Retained earnings}}{\text{Total assets}} \times 1.4 + \frac{\text{EBIT}}{\text{Total assets}} \times 3.3$$

$$+ \frac{\text{Sales}}{\text{Total assets}} \times 0.99 + \frac{\text{MV equity}}{\text{Total liabilities}} \times 0.6$$

Following extensive testing, Altman found that companies with Z-scores above 3.0 are unlikely to fail. Those with Z-scores below 1.81 are very likely to fail. While the original model was developed for publicly held manufacturing companies, the model has been modified to apply to companies in various industries, emerging companies, and companies not traded in public markets.

Until recently, the use of Z-scores was virtually unheard of among practicing accountants. Today this measure is used by auditors, management consultants, and courts of law, and as part of many database systems used for loan evaluation. While a low score does not guarantee bankruptcy, the model has been proven accurate in many situations in the past, and can be used to help evaluate the overall financial position and trends of a firm.

Source: Adapted from E. I. Altman, *Corporate Financial Distress and Bankruptcy,* 2nd edition (New York: John Wiley and Sons, 1993).

UNDERLYING CONCEPTS

The basis for inclusion of additional information should meet the full disclosure principle; that is, the information should be of sufficient importance to influence the judgment of an informed user.

ADDITIONAL INFORMATION REPORTED

The balance sheet is not complete simply because the assets, liabilities, and owners' equity accounts have been listed. Great importance is given to supplemental information. It may be information not presented elsewhere in the statement, or it may be an elaboration or qualification of items in the balance sheet. There are normally five types of information that are supplemental to account titles and amounts presented in the balance sheet.

OBJECTIVE 4
Identify balance sheet information requiring supplemental disclosure.

SUPPLEMENTAL BALANCE SHEET INFORMATION

1. *Contingencies.* Material events that have an uncertain outcome.
2. *Accounting Policies.* Explanations of the valuation methods used or the basic assumptions made concerning inventory valuations, depreciation methods, investments in subsidiaries, etc.
3. *Contractual Situations.* Explanations of certain restrictions or covenants attached to specific assets or, more likely, to liabilities.
4. *Post-Balance Sheet Disclosures.* Disclosures of certain events that have occurred after the balance sheet date but before the financial statements have been issued.
5. *Fair Values.* Disclosures of fair values, particularly for financial instruments.

Contingencies

A **contingency** is defined as an existing situation involving uncertainty as to possible gain (gain contingency) or loss (loss contingency) that will ultimately be resolved when one or more future events occur or fail to occur. In short, they are material events that have an uncertain future. Examples of gain contingencies are tax operating loss carryforwards or company litigation against another party. Typical loss contingencies relate to litigation, environmental issues, possible tax assessments, or government investigation. The accounting and reporting requirements involving contingencies are examined fully in Chapter 11 and, therefore, additional discussion is not provided here.

Accounting Policies

APB Opinion No. 22 recommends disclosure for all significant accounting principles and methods that involve selection from among alternatives or those that are peculiar to a given industry.[14] For instance, inventories can be computed under several cost flow assumptions (such as LIFO and FIFO); plant and equipment can be depreciated under several accepted methods of cost allocation (such as double-declining balance and straight-line); and investments can be carried at different valuations (such as cost, equity, and fair value). Sophisticated users of financial statements know of these possibilities and examine the statements closely to determine the methods used.

Companies also are required to disclose information about the nature of their operations, the use of estimates in preparing financial statements, certain significant estimates, and vulnerabilities due to certain concentrations.[15] An example of such a disclosure is shown in Illustration 4-16.

CHESAPEAKE CORPORATION

Risks and Uncertainties. Chesapeake operates in three business segments which offer a diversity of products over a broad geographic base. The Company is not dependent on any single customer, group of customers, market, geographic area or supplier of materials, labor or services. Financial statements include, where necessary, amounts based on the judgments and estimates of management. These estimates include allowances for bad debts, accruals for landfill closing costs, environmental remediation costs, loss contingencies for litigation, self-insured medical and workers' compensation insurance and income taxes and determinations of discount and other rate assumptions for pensions and postretirement benefit expenses.

Illustration 4-16
Balance Sheet Disclosure of Significant Risks and Uncertainties

Disclosure of significant accounting principles and methods and of risks and uncertainties is particularly useful if given in a separate **Summary of Significant Accounting Policies** preceding the notes to the financial statements or as the initial note.

---

[14]"Disclosure of Accounting Policies," *Opinions of the Accounting Principles Board No. 22* (New York: AICPA, 1972).

[15]"Disclosure of Certain Significant Risks and Uncertainties," *Statement of Position 94-6* (New York: AICPA, 1994).

Contractual Situations

In addition to contingencies and different methods of valuation, contractual situations of significance should be disclosed in the notes to the financial statements. It is mandatory, for example, that the essential provisions of lease contracts, pension obligations, and stock option plans be clearly stated in the notes. The analyst who examines a set of financial statements wants to know not only the amount of the liabilities, but also how the different contractual provisions affect the company at present and in the future.

Commitments related to obligations to maintain working capital, to limit the payment of dividends, to restrict the use of assets, and to require the maintenance of certain financial ratios must all be disclosed if material. Considerable judgment is necessary to determine whether omission of such information is misleading. The axiom in this situation is, "When in doubt, disclose." It is better to disclose a little too much information than not enough.

Post–Balance-Sheet Events (Subsequent Events)

Notes to the financial statements should explain any significant financial events that took place after the formal balance sheet date, but before it is finally issued. These events are referred to as **post–balance-sheet events**, events subsequent to the balance sheet date, or just plain **subsequent events**. The subsequent events period is time-diagrammed as shown in Illustration 4-17.

Illustration 4-17

Time Periods for
Subsequent Events

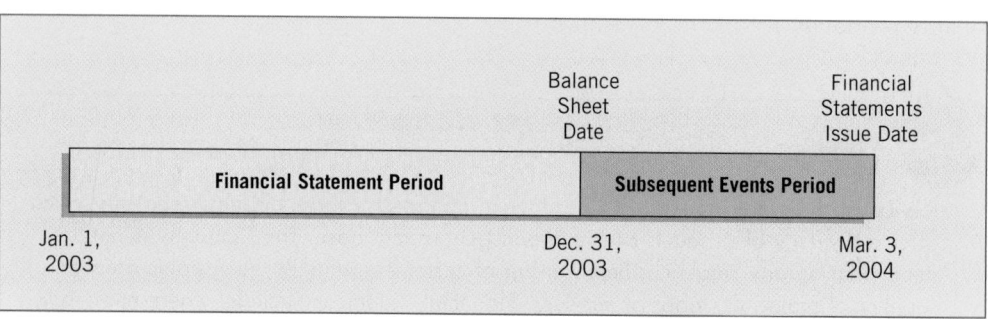

A period of several weeks, and sometimes months, may elapse after the end of the year before the financial statements are issued. Taking and pricing the inventory, reconciling subsidiary ledgers with controlling accounts, preparing necessary adjusting entries, assuring that all transactions for the period have been entered, obtaining an audit of the financial statements by independent certified public accountants, and printing the annual report all take time. During the period between the balance sheet date and its distribution to stockholders and creditors, important transactions or other events may occur that materially affect the company's financial position or operating situation.

Many who read a recent balance sheet believe the balance sheet condition is constant and project it into the future. However, readers must be told if the company has sold one of its plants, acquired a subsidiary, suffered extraordinary losses, settled significant litigation, or experienced any other important event in the post–balance-sheet period. Without an explanation in a note, the reader might be misled and draw inappropriate conclusions.

Two types of events or transactions occurring after the balance sheet date may have a material effect on the financial statements or may need to be considered to interpret these statements accurately:

① **Events that provide additional evidence about conditions that existed at the balance sheet date, affect the estimates used in preparing financial statements, and, therefore, result in needed adjustments.** All information available prior to the issuance of the financial statements is used to evaluate estimates previously made. To ignore these subsequent events is to pass up an opportunity to improve the accuracy of the financial statements. This first type encompasses information that would have been recorded in the accounts had it been known at the balance sheet date.

UNDERLYING
CONCEPTS

The periodicity or time period assumption implies that economic activities of an enterprise can be divided into artificial time periods for purpose of analysis.

For example, if a loss on an account receivable results from a customer's bankruptcy subsequent to the balance sheet date, the financial statements are adjusted before their issuance. The bankruptcy stems from the customer's poor financial health existing at the balance sheet date.

The same criterion applies to settlements of litigation. The financial statements must be adjusted if the events that gave rise to the litigation, such as personal injury or patent infringement, took place prior to the balance sheet date. If the event giving rise to the claim took place subsequent to the balance sheet date, no adjustment is necessary but disclosure is. To illustrate, a loss resulting from a customer's fire or flood after the balance sheet date is not indicative of conditions existing at that date. Thus, adjustment of the financial statements is not necessary.

② **Events that provide evidence about conditions that did not exist at the balance sheet date but arise subsequent to that date and do not require adjustment of the financial statements.** Some of these events may have to be disclosed to keep the financial statements from being misleading. These disclosures take the form of notes, supplemental schedules, or even pro forma "as if" financial data prepared as if the event had occurred on the balance sheet date. Below are examples of such events that require disclosure (but do not result in adjustment).

(a) Sale of bonds or capital stock; stock splits or stock dividends.
(b) Business combination pending or effected.
(c) Settlement of litigation when the event giving rise to the claim took place subsequent to the balance sheet date.
(d) Loss of plant or inventories from fire or flood.
(e) Losses on receivables resulting from conditions (such as customer's major casualty) arising subsequent to the balance sheet date.
(f) Gains or losses on certain marketable securities.[16]

---

[16]"Subsequent Events," *Statement on Auditing Standards No. 1* (New York: AICPA, 1973), pp. 123–124. *Accounting Trends and Techniques—2001* listed the following types of subsequent events and their frequency of occurrence among the 600 companies surveyed: debt incurred, reduced, or refinanced, 72; business combinations pending or effected, 63; discontinued operations, 33; litigation, 31; capital stock issued or repurchased, 16; employee benefit plans, 4; stock splits or dividends, stock rights, 7.

An example of subsequent events disclosure for **Boeing Company**, which has a December 31 year-end, is presented in Illustration 4-18.

Illustration 4-18
Disclosure of Subsequent Event

BOEING COMPANY

Note 4 (in part): Mergers and Accquistions

Proposed Acquisition of Hughes Space and Communications Business. On January 13, 2000, the Company announced an agreement to acquire the Hughes space and communications business and related operations for $3.75 billion. The transaction is subject to regulatory and government reviews and is expected to be finalized by the end of the second quarter of 2000. Hughes is a technological leader in space-based communications, reconnaissance, surveillance and imaging systems. It is also a leading manufacturer of commercial satellites. Under the definitive agreement, Boeing also will acquire Hughes Electron Dynamics, a supplier of electronic components for satellites, and Spectrolab, a provider of solar cells and panels for satellites.

Many subsequent events or developments are not likely to require either adjustment of or disclosure in the financial statements. Typically, these are nonaccounting events or conditions that managements normally communicate by other means. These events include legislation, product changes, management changes, strikes, unionization, marketing agreements, and loss of important customers.

Illustration 4-19
Disclosure of Financial Instrument Fair Values

INTEL CORP.

Fair values of financial instruments. The estimated fair values of financial instruments outstanding at fiscal year-end were as follows:

(in millions)	2000 Carrying amount	Estimated fair value
Cash and cash equivalents	$ 2,976	$ 2,976
Short-term investments	10,498	10,498
Trading assets	355	355
Marketable strategic equity securities	1,915	1,915
Other long-term investments	1,801	1,801
Non-marketable instruments	1,886	3,579
Swaps hedging investments in debt securities	12	12
Options hedging deferred compensation liabilities	(5)	(5)
Short-term debt	(378)	(378)
Long-term debt	(707)	(702)
Swaps hedging debt	—	(1)
Currency forward contracts	2	6

Fair Values

As discussed in Chapter 2, historical cost is the primary valuation basis in financial statements. However, fair value information is thought to be more useful for certain types of assets and liabilities. This is particularly so in the case of financial instruments.

Financial instruments are defined as cash, an ownership interest, or a contractual right to receive or obligation to deliver cash or another financial instrument. Such contractual rights to receive cash or other financial instruments are assets. Contractual obligations to pay are liabilities. Cash, investments, accounts receivable, and payables are examples of financial instruments.

Financial instruments are increasing both in use and variety. As a consequence of the increasing use, companies are required to disclose both the carrying value and the estimated fair values of their financial instruments. For example, **Intel** provides extensive disclosures of the fair value of its financial instrument assets and liabilities, as shown in Illustration 4-19 (next page). More extensive discussion of financial instrument accounting and reporting is provided in Chapters 7, 11, 13, and 16.

TECHNIQUES OF DISCLOSURE

The effect of various contingencies on financial condition, the methods of valuing assets, and the company's contracts and agreements should be disclosed as completely and as intelligently as possible. These methods of disclosing pertinent information are available: parenthetical explanations, notes, cross reference and contra items, and supporting schedules.

OBJECTIVE 5
Identify major disclosure techniques for the balance sheet.

Parenthetical Explanations

Additional information is often provided by parenthetical explanations following the item. For example, investments in available-for-sale securities are shown on the balance sheet under Investments as follows.

Investments in available-for-sale securities (cost, $330,586)—at fair value	$401,500

This device permits disclosure of additional pertinent balance sheet information that adds clarity and completeness. It has an advantage over a note because it brings the additional information into the body of the statement where it is less likely to be overlooked. Of course, lengthy parenthetical explanations that might distract the reader from the balance sheet information must be used with care.

UNDERLYING CONCEPTS

The user-specific quality of understandability requires accountants to be careful in describing transactions and events.

Notes

Notes are used if additional explanations cannot be shown conveniently as parenthetical explanations. For example, inventory costing methods are reported in **The Quaker Oats Company**'s accompanying notes as shown on the next page.

Illustration 4-20
Note Disclosure

THE QUAKER OATS COMPANY

Inventories (Note 1)

Finished goods	$326,000,000
Grain and raw materials	114,100,000
Packaging materials and supplies	39,000,000
Total inventories	479,100,000

Note 1: Inventories. Inventories are valued at the lower of cost or market, using various cost methods, and include the cost of raw materials, labor, and overhead. The percentage of year-end inventories valued using each of the methods is as follows:

Average quarterly cost	21%
Last-in, first-out (LIFO)	65%
First-in, first-out (FIFO)	14%

If the LIFO method of valuing certain inventories was not used, total inventories would have been $60,100,000 higher than reported.

Notes are commonly used to disclose the following: the existence and amount of any preferred stock dividends in arrears, the terms of or obligations imposed by purchase commitments, special financial arrangements and instruments, depreciation policies, any changes in the application of accounting principles, and the existence of contingencies.

Notes therefore must present all essential facts as completely and succinctly as possible. Careless wording may mislead rather than aid readers. Notes should add to the total information made available in the financial statements, not raise unanswered questions or contradict other portions of the statements. The following notes illustrate a common method of presenting such information.

Illustration 4-21
More Note Disclosures

CONSOLIDATED PAPERS, INC.

Note 7: Commitments. The company had capital expenditure purchase commitments outstanding of approximately $17 million.

ALBERTO-CULVER COMPANY

Note 3: Long-Term Debt. Various borrowing arrangements impose restrictions on such items as total debt, working capital, dividend payments, treasury stock purchases and interest expense. The company was in compliance with these arrangements and $68 million of consolidated retained earnings was not restricted as to the payment of dividends and purchases of treasury stock.

WILLAMETTE INDUSTRIES, INC.

Note 4: Property, Plant, and Equipment (partial). The company changed its accounting estimates relating to depreciation. The estimated service lives for most machinery and equipment were extended five years. The change was based upon a study performed by the company's engineering department, comparisons to typical industry practices, and the effect of the company's extensive capital investments which have resulted in a mix of assets with longer productive lives due to technological advances. As a result of the change, net income was increased $51,900, or $0.46 per diluted share.

Illustration 4-21
More Note Disclosures
(continued)

Cross Reference and Contra Items

A direct relationship between an asset and a liability is "cross referenced" on the balance sheet. For example, on December 31, 2003, the following might be shown among the current assets.

Cash on deposit with sinking fund trustee for redemption of bonds payable—see Current liabilities	$800,000

Included among the current liabilities is the amount of bonds payable to be redeemed within one year:

Bonds payable to be redeemed in 2004—see Current assets	$2,300,000

This cross reference points out that $2,300,000 of bonds payable are to be redeemed currently, for which only $800,000 in cash has been set aside. Therefore, the additional cash needed must come from unrestricted cash, from sales of investments, from profits, or from some other source. The same information can be shown parenthetically, if this technique is preferred.

Another common procedure is to establish contra or adjunct accounts. A **contra account** on a balance sheet is an item that reduces either an asset, liability, or owners' equity account. Examples include Accumulated Depreciation and Discount on Bonds Payable. Contra accounts provide some flexibility in presenting the financial information. With the use of the Accumulated Depreciation account, for example, a reader of the statement can see the original cost of the asset as well as the depreciation to date.

An **adjunct account**, on the other hand, increases either an asset, liability, or owners' equity account. An example is Premium on Bonds Payable, which, when added to the Bonds Payable account, describes the total bond liability of the enterprise.

Supporting Schedules

Often a separate schedule is needed to present more detailed information about certain assets or liabilities, because the balance sheet provides just a single summary item.

Property, plant, and equipment	
Land, buildings, equipment, and other fixed assets—net (see Schedule 3)	$643,300

Illustration 4-22
Disclosure through Use of
Supporting Schedules

A separate schedule then might be presented as follows.

	Total	Land	Buildings	Equip.	Other Fixed Assets
SCHEDULE 3 **LAND, BUILDINGS, EQUIPMENT, AND OTHER FIXED ASSETS**					
Balance January 1, 2004	$740,000	$46,000	$358,000	$260,000	$76,000
Additions in 2004	161,200		120,000	38,000	3,200
	901,200	46,000	478,000	298,000	79,200
Assets retired or sold in 2004	31,700			27,000	4,700
Balance December 31, 2004	869,500	46,000	478,000	271,000	74,500
Depreciation taken to January 1, 2004	196,000		102,000	78,000	16,000
Depreciation taken in 2004	56,000		28,000	24,000	4,000
	252,000		130,000	102,000	20,000
Depreciation on assets retired in 2004	25,800			22,000	3,800
Depreciation accumulated December 31, 2004	226,200		130,000	80,000	16,200
Book value of assets	$643,300	$46,000	$348,000	$191,000	$58,300

Terminology

The account titles in the general ledger do not necessarily represent the best terminology for balance sheet purposes. Account titles are often brief and include technical terms that are understood only by accountants. But balance sheets are examined by many persons who are not acquainted with the technical vocabulary of accounting. Thus, they should contain descriptions that will be generally understood and not be subject to misinterpretation.

For example, the profession has recommended that the word **reserve** be used only to describe an appropriation of retained earnings. This term had been used in several ways: to describe amounts deducted from assets (contra accounts such as accumulated depreciation and allowance for doubtful accounts), and as a part of the title of contingent or estimated liabilities. Because of the different meanings attached to this term, misinterpretation often resulted from its use. The use of "reserve" only to describe appropriated retained earnings has resulted in a better understanding of its significance when it appears in a balance sheet. However, the term "appropriated" appears more logical, and its use should be encouraged.

For years the profession has recommended that the use of the word **surplus** be discontinued in balance sheet presentations of owners' equity. The use of the terms capital surplus, paid-in surplus, and earned surplus is confusing. Although condemned by the profession, these terms appear all too frequently in current financial statements.

SUMMARY OF LEARNING OBJECTIVES

❶ Identify the uses and limitations of a balance sheet. The balance sheet provides information about the nature and amounts of investments in enterprise resources, obligations to creditors, and the owners' equity in net resources. The balance sheet contributes to financial reporting by providing a basis for (1) computing rates of return,

(2) evaluating the capital structure of the enterprise, and (3) assessing the liquidity, solvency, and financial flexibility of the enterprise.

The limitations of a balance sheet are: (1) The balance sheet does not reflect current value because accountants have adopted a historical cost basis in valuing and reporting assets and liabilities. (2) Judgments and estimates must be used in preparing a balance sheet. The collectibility of receivables, the salability of inventory, and the useful life of long-term tangible and intangible assets are difficult to determine. (3) The balance sheet omits many items that are of financial value to the business but cannot be recorded objectively, such as human resources, customer base, and reputation.

❷ Identify the major classifications of the balance sheet. The general elements of the balance sheet are assets, liabilities, and equity. The major classifications within the balance sheet on the asset side are current assets; long-term investments; property, plant, and equipment; intangible assets; and other assets. The major classifications of liabilities are current and long-term liabilities. In a corporation, owners' equity is generally classified as capital stock, additional paid-in capital, and retained earnings.

❸ Prepare a classified balance sheet using the report and account formats. The report form lists liabilities and stockholders' equity directly below assets on the same page. The account form lists assets by sections on the left side and liabilities and stockholders' equity by sections on the right side.

❹ Identify balance sheet information requiring supplemental disclosure. Five types of information normally are supplemental to account titles and amounts presented in the balance sheet: (1) *Contingencies:* Material events that have an uncertain outcome. (2) *Accounting policies:* Explanations of the valuation methods used or the basic assumptions made concerning inventory valuation, depreciation methods, investments in subsidiaries, etc. (3) *Contractual situations:* Explanations of certain restrictions or covenants attached to specific assets or, more likely, to liabilities. (4) *Post–balance-sheet events:* Events occurring after the balance date but before statements are issued. (5) *Fair values:* Disclosures related to fair values, particularly related to financial instruments.

❺ Identify major disclosure techniques for the balance sheet. There are four methods of disclosing pertinent information in the balance sheet: (1) *Parenthetical explanations:* Additional information or description is often provided by parenthetical explanations following the item. (2) *Notes:* Notes are used if additional explanations or descriptions cannot be shown conveniently as parenthetical explanations. (3) *Cross reference and contra items:* A direct relationship between an asset and a liability is "cross referenced" on the balance sheet. (4) *Supporting schedules:* Often a separate schedule is needed to present more detailed information about certain assets or liabilities, because the balance sheet provides just a single summary item.

KEY TERMS

account form, *136*
adjunct account, *145*
available-for-sale
  securities, *129*
balance sheet, *124*
contingency, *139*
contra account, *145*
current assets, *127*
current liabilities, *133*
financial flexibility, *125*
financial instruments, *142*
held-to-maturity
  securities, *129*
intangible assets, *132*
liquidity, *124*
long-term investments, *131*
long-term liabilities, *135*
owners' (stockholders')
  equity, *136*
post–balance-sheet
  events, *140*
property, plant, and
  equipment, *132*
report form, *136*
reserve, *146*
solvency, *125*
subsequent events, *140*
trading securities, *129*
working capital, *134*

REVIEW EXERCISE

Presented below is a condensed balance sheet of James Henry Corporation for the year 2004.

JAMES HENRY CORPORATION
BALANCE SHEET
DECEMBER 31, 2004

Current assets	$ 82,000	Current liabilities	$ 82,000
Long-term investments	124,000	Long-term liabilities	265,000
Property, plant, and equipment	301,000	Stockholder's equity	235,000
Intangibles	75,000		$582,000
	$582,000		

Additional information:

1. The current assets include: cash $50,000; accounts receivable $45,000, less $5,000 allowance for doubtful accounts; advances from customers $9,000; and prepaid insurance $1,000.

2. Investments include: investment in subsidiary $82,000; premium on bonds payable $4,000; patents $16,000; treasury stock at cost of $20,000; and available-for-sale securities, not to be sold in the near term at fair value $10,000.

3. Property, plant, and equipment consists of: buildings $180,000 less accumulated depreciation of $30,000; land held for speculation $75,000; equipment of $95,000 less accumulated depreciation of $25,000; and a refundable deposit on rental equipment of $6,000 on a lease that ends in 2 months.

4. Intangible assets include: goodwill $80,000; and an unrealized holding gain on available-for-sale securities $5,000.

5. Current liabilities include: accounts payable $47,000; and a note payable (due in 90 days) $35,000.

6. Long-term liabilities consist of: bonds payable $150,000; preferred stock, $100 par, $100,000; and cash dividends payable $15,000.

7. Stockholders' equity consists of: common stock, $1 par, $80,000; additional paid-in capital $40,000; and retained earnings $115,000.

Instructions

From the information provided, prepare a classified balance sheet at December 31, 2004, showing the details of each classification.

SOLUTION TO REVIEW EXERCISE

JAMES HENRY CORPORATION
BALANCE SHEET
DECEMBER 31, 2004

Assets

Current assets			
Cash		$50,000	
Accounts receivable	$ 45,000		
Less: Allowance for doubtful accounts	5,000	40,000	
Prepaid insurance		1,000	
Deposits		6,000	$ 97,000
Long-term investments			
Available for sale securities, at fair value	10,000		
Land held for speculation	75,000		
Investment in subsidiary	82,000		167,000
Property, plant, and equipment			
Building	180,000		
Less: Accumulated depreciation	30,000	150,000	
Equipment	95,000		
Less: Accumulated depreciation	25,000	70,000	220,000
Intangible assets			
Goodwill		80,000	
Patents		16,000	96,000
Total assets			$580,000

Liabilities and Stockholders' Equity		
Current liabilities		
Accounts payable	$ 47,000	
Advances from customers	9,000	
Notes payable	35,000	
Dividends payable	15,000	
Total current liabilities		$106,000
Long-term liabilities		
Bonds payable	150,000	
Plus: Premium on bonds	4,000	154,000
Total liabilities		260,000
Stockholders' equity		
Preferred stock, $100 par, 1,000 shares issued	100,000	
Common stock, $1 par, 80,000 shares issued	80,000	
Additional paid-in capital	40,000	220,000
Retained earnings		115,000
Accumulated other comprehensive income—Unrealized holding gain		5,000
Less: Treasury stock, at cost		(20,000)
Total stockholders' equity and liabilities		$580,000

QUESTIONS

1 How does information from the balance sheet help users of the financial statements?

2 What is meant by solvency? What information in the balance sheet can be used to assess a company's solvency?

3 A recent financial magazine indicated that a drug company had good financial flexibility. What is meant by financial flexibility, and why is it important?

4 Discuss at least two situations in which estimates could affect the usefulness of information in the balance sheet.

5 Jones Company reported an increase in inventories in the past year. Discuss the effect of this change on the current ratio (current assets ÷ current liabilities). What does this tell a statement user about Jones Company's liquidity?

6 What is meant by liquidity? Rank the following assets from one to five in order of liquidity.

(a) Goodwill.

(b) Inventories.

(c) Buildings.

(d) Short-term investments.

(e) Accounts receivable.

7 What are the major limitations of the balance sheet as a source of information?

8 Discuss at least two items that are important to the value of companies like Intel or IBM but that are not recorded in their balance sheets. What are some reasons why these items are not recorded in the balance sheet?

9 How does separating current assets from property, plant, and equipment in the balance sheet help analysts?

10 In its December 31, 2004, balance sheet Oakley Corporation reported as an asset, "Net notes and accounts receivable, $7,100,000." What other disclosures are necessary?

11 Should available-for-sale securities always be reported as a current asset? Explain.

12 What is the relationship between current assets and current liabilities?

13 The New York Knicks, Inc. sold 10,000 season tickets at $1,000 each. By December 31, 2004, 18 of the 40 home games had been played. What amount should be reported as a current liability at December 31, 2004?

14 What is working capital? How does working capital relate to the operating cycle?

15 In what section of the balance sheet should the following items appear, and what balance sheet terminology would you use?

(a) Treasury stock (recorded at cost).

(b) Checking account at bank.

(c) Land (held as an investment).

(d) Sinking fund.

(e) Unamortized premium on bonds payable.

(f) Copyrights.

(g) Pension fund assets.

(h) Premium on capital stock.

(i) Long-term investments (pledged against bank loans payable).

16 Where should the following items be shown on the balance sheet, if shown at all?

(a) Allowance for doubtful accounts receivable.

(b) Merchandise held on consignment.

(c) Advances received on sales contract.

(d) Cash surrender value of life insurance.

(e) Land.

(f) Merchandise out on consignment.

(g) Pension fund on deposit with a trustee (under a trust revocable at depositor's option).

(h) Franchises.

(i) Accumulated depreciation of plant and equipment.

(j) Materials in transit—purchased f.o.b. destination.

17 State the generally accepted accounting principle (standard) applicable to the balance sheet valuation of each of the following assets.

(a) Trade accounts receivable.

(b) Land.

(c) Inventories.

(d) Trading securities (common stock of other companies).

(e) Prepaid expenses.

18 Refer to the definition of assets on page 127. Discuss how a leased building might qualify as an asset of the lessee under this definition.

19 Christine Agazzi says, "Retained earnings should be reported as an asset, since it is earnings which are reinvested in the business." How would you respond to Agazzi?

20 The creditors of Nick Anderson Company agree to accept promissory notes for the amount of its indebtedness with a proviso that two-thirds of the annual profits must be applied to their liquidation. How should these notes be reported on the balance sheet of the issuing company? Give a reason for your answer.

21 What is the Altman Z-score? What balance sheet information is used in computing a Z-score?

22 What are the major types of subsequent events? Indicate how each of the following subsequent events would be reported.

(a) Collection of a note written off in a prior period.

(b) Issuance of a large preferred stock offering.

(c) Acquisition of a company in a different industry.

(d) Destruction of a major plant in a flood.

(e) Death of the company's chief executive officer (CEO).

(f) Settlement of a four-week strike at additional wage costs.

(g) Settlement of a federal income tax case at considerably more tax than anticipated at year-end.

(h) Change in the product mix from consumer goods to industrial goods.

23 What are some of the techniques of disclosure for the balance sheet?

24 What is a "Summary of Significant Accounting Policies"?

25 What types of contractual obligations must be disclosed in great detail in the notes to the balance sheet? Why do you think these detailed provisions should be disclosed?

26 What is the profession's recommendation in regard to the use of the term "surplus"? Explain.

BRIEF EXERCISES

BE4-1   La Bouche Corporation has the following accounts included in its December 31, 2004, trial balance: Accounts Receivable $110,000; Inventories $290,000; Allowance for Doubtful Accounts $8,000; Patents $72,000; Prepaid Insurance $9,500; Accounts Payable $77,000; Cash $27,000. Prepare the current assets section of the balance sheet listing the accounts in proper sequence.

BE4-2   Jodi Corporation's adjusted trial balance contained the following asset accounts at December 31, 2004: Cash $7,000; Land $40,000; Patents $12,500; Accounts Receivable $90,000; Prepaid Insurance $5,200; Inventory $34,000; Allowance for Doubtful Accounts $4,000; Trading Securities $11,000. Prepare the current assets section of the balance sheet, listing the accounts in proper sequence.

BE4-3   Included in Goo Goo Dolls Company's December 31, 2004, trial balance are the following accounts: Prepaid Rent $5,200; Held-to-Maturity Securities $61,000; Unearned Fees $17,000; Land Held for Investment $39,000; Long-term Receivables $42,000. Prepare the long-term investments section of the balance sheet.

BE4-4   Adam Ant Company's December 31, 2004, trial balance includes the following accounts: Inventories $120,000; Buildings $207,000; Accumulated Depreciation–Equipment $19,000; Equipment $190,000; Land Held for Investment $46,000; Accumulated Depreciation–Buildings $45,000; Land $61,000; Capital Leases $70,000. Prepare the property, plant, and equipment section of the balance sheet.

BE4-5   Mason Corporation has the following accounts included in its December 31, 2004, trial balance: Trading Securities $21,000; Goodwill $150,000; Prepaid Insurance $12,000; Patents $220,000; Franchises $110,000. Prepare the intangible assets section of the balance sheet.

BE4-6 Mickey Snyder Corporation's adjusted trial balance contained the following asset accounts at December 31, 2004: Prepaid Rent $12,000; Goodwill $40,000; Franchise Fees Receivable $2,000; Franchises $47,000; Patents $33,000; Trademarks $10,000. Prepare the intangible assets section of the balance sheet.

BE4-7 John Hawk Corporation's adjusted trial balance contained the following liability accounts at December 31, 2004: Bonds Payable (due in 3 years) $100,000; Accounts Payable $72,000; Notes Payable (due in 90 days) $12,500; Accrued Salaries $4,000; Income Taxes Payable $7,000. Prepare the current liabilities section of the balance sheet.

BE4-8 Included in Ewing Company's December 31, 2004, trial balance are the following accounts: Accounts Payable $240,000; Obligations under Capital Leases $375,000; Discount on Bonds Payable $24,000; Advances from Customers $41,000; Bonds Payable $400,000; Wages Payable $27,000; Interest Payable $12,000; Income Taxes Payable $29,000. Prepare the current liabilities section of the balance sheet.

BE4-9 Use the information presented in BE4-8 for Ewing Company to prepare the long-term liabilities section of the balance sheet.

BE4-10 Kevin Flynn Corporation's adjusted trial balance contained the following accounts at December 31, 2004: Retained Earnings $120,000; Common Stock $700,000; Bonds Payable $100,000; Additional Paid-in Capital $200,000; Goodwill $55,000; Accumulated Other Comprehensive Loss $150,000. Prepare the stockholders' equity section of the balance sheet.

BE4-11 Young Company's December 31, 2004, trial balance includes the following accounts: Investment in Common Stock $70,000; Retained Earnings $114,000; Trademarks $31,000; Preferred Stock $172,000; Common Stock $55,000; Deferred Income Taxes $88,000; Additional Paid-in Capital $174,000. Prepare the stockholders' equity section of the balance sheet.

EXERCISES

E4-1 **(Balance Sheet Classifications)** Presented below are a number of balance sheet accounts of Deep Blue Something, Inc.

(a) Investment in Preferred Stock.
(b) Treasury Stock.
(c) Common Stock Distributable.
(d) Cash Dividends Payable.
(e) Accumulated Depreciation.
(f) Warehouse in Process of Construction.
(g) Petty Cash.

(h) Accrued Interest on Notes Payable.
(i) Deficit.
(j) Trading Securities.
(k) Income Taxes Payable.
(l) Unearned Subscription Revenue.
(m) Work in Process.
(n) Accrued Vacation Pay.

Instructions
For each of the accounts above, indicate the proper balance sheet classification. In the case of borderline items, indicate the additional information that would be required to determine the proper classification.

E4-2 **(Classification of Balance Sheet Accounts)** Presented below are the captions of Faulk Company's balance sheet.

(a) Current assets
(b) Investments
(c) Property, plant, and equipment
(d) Intangible assets
(e) Other assets

(f) Current liabilities
(g) Noncurrent liabilities
(h) Capital stock
(i) Additional paid-in capital
(j) Retained earnings

Instructions
Indicate by letter where each of the following items would be classified.

1. Preferred stock.
2. Goodwill.
3. Wages payable.
4. Trade accounts payable.

5. Buildings.
6. Trading securities.
7. Current portion of long-term debt.
8. Premium on bonds payable.

9. Allowance for doubtful accounts.
10. Accounts receivable.
11. Cash surrender value of life insurance.
12. Notes payable (due next year).
13. Office supplies.
14. Common stock.
15. Land.
16. Bond sinking fund.
17. Merchandise inventory.
18. Prepaid insurance.
19. Bonds payable.
20. Taxes payable.

E4-3 **(Classification of Balance Sheet Accounts)** Assume that Fielder Enterprises uses the following headings on its balance sheet.

(a) Current assets
(b) Investments
(c) Property, plant, and equipment
(d) Intangible assets
(e) Other assets
(f) Current liabilities
(g) Long-term liabilities
(h) Capital stock
(i) Paid-in Capital in excess of par
(j) Retained earnings

Instructions

Indicate by letter how each of the following usually should be classified. If an item should appear in a note to the financial statements, use the letter "N" to indicate this fact. If an item need not be reported at all on the balance sheet, use the letter "X."

1. Unexpired insurance.
2. Stock owned in affiliated companies.
3. Unearned subscriptions revenue.
4. Advances to suppliers.
5. Unearned rent revenue.
6. Treasury stock.
7. Premium on preferred stock.
8. Copyrights.
9. Petty cash fund.
10. Sales tax payable.
11. Accrued interest on notes receivable.
12. Twenty-year issue of bonds payable that will mature within the next year. (No sinking fund exists, and refunding is not planned.)
13. Machinery retired from use and held for sale.
14. Fully depreciated machine still in use.
15. Accrued interest on bonds payable.
16. Salaries that company budget shows will be paid to employees within the next year.
17. Discount on bonds payable. (Assume related to bonds payable in No. 12.)
18. Accumulated depreciation.

E4-4 **(Preparation of a Classified Balance Sheet)** Assume that Denis Savard Inc. has the following accounts at the end of the current year.

1. Common Stock.
2. Discount on Bonds Payable.
3. Treasury Stock (at cost).
4. Note Payable, short-term.
5. Raw Materials.
6. Preferred Stock Investments—Long-term.
7. Unearned Rent Revenue.
8. Work in Process.
9. Copyrights.
10. Buildings.
11. Notes Receivable (short-term).
12. Cash.
13. Accrued Salaries Payable.
14. Accumulated Depreciation—Buildings.
15. Cash Restricted for Plant Expansion.
16. Land Held for Future Plant Site.
17. Allowance for Doubtful Accounts—Accounts Receivable.
18. Retained Earnings.
19. Premium on Common Stock.
20. Unearned Subscriptions Revenue.
21. Receivables—Officers (due in one year).
22. Finished Goods.
23. Accounts Receivable.
24. Bonds Payable (due in 4 years).

Instructions

Prepare a classified balance sheet in good form (no monetary amounts are necessary).

E4-5 **(Preparation of a Corrected Balance Sheet)** Uhura Company has decided to expand its operations. The bookkeeper recently completed the balance sheet presented below in order to obtain additional funds for expansion.

UHURA COMPANY
BALANCE SHEET
FOR THE YEAR ENDED 2004

Current assets	
Cash (net of bank overdraft of $30,000)	$200,000
Accounts receivable (net)	340,000
Inventories at lower of average cost or market	401,000
Trading securities—at cost (fair value $120,000)	140,000
Property, plant, and equipment	
Building (net)	570,000
Office equipment (net)	160,000
Land held for future use	175,000
Intangible assets	
Goodwill	80,000
Cash surrender value of life insurance	90,000
Prepaid expenses	12,000
Current liabilities	
Accounts payable	105,000
Notes payable (due next year)	125,000
Pension obligation	82,000
Rent payable	49,000
Premium on bonds payable	53,000
Long-term liabilities	
Bonds payable	500,000
Stockholders' equity	
Common stock, $1.00 par, authorized	
400,000 shares, issued 290,000	290,000
Additional paid-in capital	160,000
Retained earnings	?

Instructions

Prepare a revised balance sheet given the available information. Assume that the accumulated depreciation balance for the buildings is $160,000 and for the office equipment, $105,000. The allowance for doubtful accounts has a balance of $17,000. The pension obligation is considered a long-term liability.

E4-6 (Corrections of a Balance Sheet) The bookkeeper for Geronimo Company has prepared the following balance sheet as of July 31, 2004.

GERONIMO COMPANY
BALANCE SHEET
AS OF JULY 31, 2004

Cash	$ 69,000	Notes and accounts payable	$ 44,000
Accounts receivable (net)	40,500	Long-term liabilities	75,000
Inventories	60,000	Stockholders' equity	155,500
Equipment (net)	84,000		$274,500
Patents	21,000		
	$274,500		

The following additional information is provided.

1. Cash includes $1,200 in a petty cash fund and $15,000 in a bond sinking fund.
2. The net accounts receivable balance is comprised of the following three items: (a) accounts receivable—

debit balances $52,000; (b) accounts receivable—credit balances $8,000; (c) allowance for doubtful accounts $3,500.

3. Merchandise inventory costing $5,300 was shipped out on consignment on July 31, 2004. The ending inventory balance does not include the consigned goods. Receivables in the amount of $5,300 were recognized on these consigned goods.

4. Equipment had a cost of $112,000 and an accumulated depreciation balance of $28,000.

5. Taxes payable of $6,000 were accrued on July 31. Geronimo Company, however, had set up a cash fund to meet this obligation. This cash fund was not included in the cash balance, but was offset against the taxes payable amount.

Instructions

Prepare a corrected classified balance sheet as of July 31, 2004, from the available information, adjusting the account balances using the additional information.

E4-7 (Current Assets Section of the Balance Sheet) Presented below are selected accounts of Yasunari Kawabata Company at December 31, 2004.

Finished Goods	$ 52,000	Cost of Goods Sold	$2,100,000
Revenue Received in Advance	90,000	Notes Receivable	40,000
Bank Overdraft	8,000	Accounts Receivable	161,000
Equipment	253,000	Raw Materials	207,000
Work-in-Process	34,000	Supplies Expense	60,000
Cash	37,000	Allowance for Doubtful Accounts	12,000
Short-term Investments in Stock	31,000	Licenses	18,000
Customer Advances	36,000	Additional Paid-in Capital	88,000
Cash Restricted for Plant Expansion	50,000	Treasury Stock	22,000

The following additional information is available.

1. Inventories are valued at lower of cost or market using LIFO.
2. Equipment is recorded at cost. Accumulated depreciation, computed on a straight-line basis, is $50,600.
3. The short-term investments have a fair value of $29,000. (Assume they are trading securities.)
4. The notes receivable are due April 30, 2006, with interest receivable every April 30. The notes bear interest at 12%. (Hint: Accrue interest due on December 31, 2004.)
5. The allowance for doubtful accounts applies to the accounts receivable. Accounts receivable of $50,000 are pledged as collateral on a bank loan.
6. Licenses are recorded net of accumulated amortization of $14,000.
7. Treasury stock is recorded at cost.

Instructions

Prepare the current assets section of Yasunari Kawabata Company's December 31, 2004, balance sheet, with appropriate disclosures.

 **E4-8 (Current vs. Long-term Liabilities)** Frederic Chopin Corporation is preparing its December 31, 2004, balance sheet. The following items may be reported as either a current or long-term liability.

1. On December 15, 2004, Chopin declared a cash dividend of $2.50 per share to stockholders of record on December 31. The dividend is payable on January 15, 2005. Chopin has issued 1,000,000 shares of common stock, of which 50,000 shares are held in treasury.
2. Also on December 31, Chopin declared a 10% stock dividend to stockholders of record on January 15, 2005. The dividend will be distributed on January 31, 2005. Chopin's common stock has a par value of $10 per share and a market value of $38 per share.
3. At December 31, bonds payable of $100,000,000 are outstanding. The bonds pay 12% interest every September 30 and mature in installments of $25,000,000 every September 30, beginning September 30, 2005.
4. At December 31, 2003, customer advances were $12,000,000. During 2004, Chopin collected $30,000,000 of customer advances, and advances of $25,000,000 were earned.

Instructions

For each item above indicate the dollar amounts to be reported as a current liability and as a long-term liability, if any.

E4-9 (Current Assets and Current Liabilities) The current assets and liabilities sections of the balance sheet of Allessandro Scarlatti Company appear as follows.

ALLESSANDRO SCARLATTI COMPANY				
BALANCE SHEET (PARTIAL)				
DECEMBER 31, 2004				
Cash		$ 40,000	Accounts payable	$ 61,000
Accounts receivable	$89,000		Notes payable	67,000
Less: Allowance for				$128,000
doubtful accounts	7,000	82,000		
Inventories		171,000		
Prepaid expenses		9,000		
		$302,000		

The following errors in the corporation's accounting have been discovered:

1. January 2005 cash disbursements entered as of December 2004 included payments of accounts payable in the amount of $39,000, on which a cash discount of 2% was taken.
2. The inventory included $27,000 of merchandise that had been received at December 31 but for which no purchase invoices had been received or entered. Of this amount, $12,000 had been received on consignment; the remainder was purchased f.o.b. destination, terms 2/10, n/30.
3. Sales for the first four days in January 2005 in the amount of $30,000 were entered in the sales book as of December 31, 2004. Of these, $21,500 were sales on account and the remainder were cash sales.
4. Cash, not including cash sales, collected in January 2005 and entered as of December 31, 2004, totaled $35,324. Of this amount, $23,324 was received on account after cash discounts of 2% had been deducted; the remainder represented the proceeds of a bank loan.

Instructions

(a) Restate the current assets and liabilities sections of the balance sheet in accordance with good accounting practice. (Assume that both accounts receivable and accounts payable are recorded gross.)
(b) State the net effect of your adjustments on Allesandro Scarlatti Company's retained earnings balance.

E4-10 (Current Liabilities) Norma Smith is the controller of Baylor Corporation and is responsible for the preparation of the year-end financial statements. The following transactions occurred during the year.

(a) On December 20, 2004, an employee filed a legal action against Baylor for $100,000 for wrongful dismissal. Management believes the action to be frivolous and without merit. The likelihood of payment to the employee is remote.
(b) Bonuses to key employees based on net income for 2004 are estimated to be $150,000.
(c) On December 1, 2004, the company borrowed $600,000 at 8% per year. Interest is paid quarterly.
(d) Credit sales for the year amounted to $10,000,000. Baylor's expense provision for doubtful accounts is estimated to be 3% of credit sales.
(e) On December 15, 2004, the company declared a $2.00 per share dividend on the 40,000 shares of common stock outstanding, to be paid on January 5, 2005.
(f) During the year, customer advances of $160,000 were received; $50,000 of this amount was earned by December 31, 2004.

Instructions

For each item above, indicate the dollar amount to be reported as a current liability. If a liability is not reported, explain why.

E4-11 (Balance Sheet Preparation) Presented below is the adjusted trial balance of Kelly Corporation at December 31, 2004.

	Debits	Credits
Cash	$?	
Office Supplies	1,200	
Prepaid Insurance	1,000	
Equipment	48,000	
Accumulated Depreciation—Equipment		$ 4,000
Trademarks	950	
Accounts Payable		10,000
Wages Payable		500
Unearned Service Revenue		2,000
Bonds Payable, due 2011		9,000
Common Stock		10,000
Retained Earnings		25,000
Service Revenue		10,000
Wages Expense	9,000	
Insurance Expense	1,400	
Rent Expense	1,200	
Interest Expense	900	
Total	$?	$?

Additional information:

1. Net loss for the year was $2,500.
2. No dividends were declared during 2004.

Instructions

Prepare a classified balance sheet as of December 31, 2004.

E4-12 (Preparation of a Balance Sheet) Presented below is the trial balance of John Nalezny Corporation at December 31, 2004.

	Debits	Credits
Cash	$ 197,000	
Sales		$ 8,100,000
Trading Securities (at cost, $145,000)	153,000	
Cost of Goods Sold	4,800,000	
Long-term Investments in Bonds	299,000	
Long-term Investments in Stocks	277,000	
Short-term Notes Payable		90,000
Accounts Payable		455,000
Selling Expenses	2,000,000	
Investment Revenue		63,000
Land	260,000	
Buildings	1,040,000	
Dividends Payable		136,000
Accrued Liabilities		96,000
Accounts Receivable	435,000	
Accumulated Depreciation—Buildings		152,000

Allowance for Doubtful Accounts		25,000
Administrative Expenses	900,000	
Interest Expense	211,000	
Inventories	597,000	
Extraordinary Gain		80,000
Prior Period Adjustment—Depr. Error	140,000	
Long-term Notes Payable		900,000
Equipment	600,000	
Bonds Payable		1,000,000
Accumulated Depreciation—Equipment		60,000
Franchise (net of $80,000 amortization)	160,000	
Common Stock ($5 par)		1,000,000
Treasury Stock	191,000	
Patent (net of $30,000 amortization)	195,000	
Retained Earnings		218,000
Additional Paid-in Capital		80,000
Totals	$12,455,000	$12,455,000

Instructions

Prepare a balance sheet at December 31, 2004, for John Nalezny Corporation. Ignore income taxes.

E4-13 **(Post–Balance-Sheet Events)** Madrasah Corporation issued its financial statements for the year ended December 31, 2004, on March 10, 2005. The following events took place early in 2005.

(a) On January 10, 10,000 shares of $5 par value common stock were issued at $66 per share.
(b) On March 1, Madrasah determined after negotiations with the Internal Revenue Service that income taxes payable for 2004 should be $1,270,000. At December 31, 2004, income taxes payable were recorded at $1,100,000.

Instructions

Discuss how the preceding post–balance-sheet events should be reflected in the 2004 financial statements.

E4-14 **(Post–Balance-Sheet Events)** For each of the following subsequent (post–balance-sheet) events, in-dicate whether a company should **(a)** adjust the financial statements, **(b)** disclose in notes to the financial statements, or **(c)** neither adjust nor disclose.

_____ **1.** Settlement of federal tax case at a cost considerably in excess of the amount expected at year-end.
_____ **2.** Introduction of a new product line.
_____ **3.** Loss of assembly plant due to fire.
_____ **4.** Sale of a significant portion of the company's assets.
_____ **5.** Retirement of the company president.
_____ **6.** Prolonged employee strike.
_____ **7.** Loss of a significant customer.
_____ **8.** Issuance of a significant number of shares of common stock.
_____ **9.** Material loss on a year-end receivable because of a customer's bankruptcy.
_____ **10.** Hiring of a new president.
_____ **11.** Settlement of prior year's litigation against the company.
_____ **12.** Merger with another company of comparable size.

PROBLEMS

P4-1 **(Preparation of a Classified Balance Sheet, Periodic Inventory)** Presented below is a list of accounts in alphabetical order.

Accounts Receivable	Accumulated Depreciation—Buildings
Accrued Wages	Accumulated Depreciation—Equipment

Advances to Employees	Land for Future Plant Site
Advertising Expense	Loss from Flood
Allowance for Doubtful Accounts	Notes Payable
Bond Sinking Fund	Patent (net of amortization)
Bonds Payable	Pension Obligations
Building	Petty Cash
Cash in Bank	Preferred Stock
Cash on Hand	Premium on Bonds Payable
Cash Surrender Value of Life Insurance	Premium on Preferred Stock
Commission Expense	Prepaid Rent
Common Stock	Purchases
Copyright (net of amortization)	Purchase Returns and Allowances
Dividends Payable	Retained Earnings
Equipment	Sales
FICA Taxes Payable	Sales Discounts
Gain on Sale of Equipment	Sales Salaries
Interest Receivable	Trading Securities
Inventory—Beginning	Transportation-in
Inventory—Ending	Treasury Stock (at cost)
Land	Unearned Subscriptions Revenue

Instructions

Prepare a classified balance sheet in good form. (No monetary amounts are to be shown.)

P4-2 (Balance Sheet Preparation) Presented below are a number of balance sheet items for Letterman, Inc., for the current year, 2004.

Goodwill	$ 125,000	Accumulated depreciation—equipment	$ 292,000
Payroll taxes payable	177,591	Inventories	239,800
Bonds payable	300,000	Rent payable—short-term	45,000
Discount on bonds payable	15,000	Taxes payable	98,362
Cash	360,000	Long-term rental obligations	480,000
Land	480,000	Common stock, $1 par value	200,000
Notes receivable	545,700	Preferred stock, $10 par value	150,000
Notes payable to banks	265,000	Prepaid expenses	87,920
Accounts payable	590,000	Equipment	1,470,000
Retained earnings	?	Trading securities	121,000
Refundable federal and state income taxes	97,630	Accumulated depreciation—building	170,200
Unsecured notes payable (long-term)	1,600,000	Building	1,640,000

Instructions

Prepare a classified balance sheet in good form. Common stock authorized was 400,000 shares, and preferred stock authorized was 20,000 shares. Assume that notes receivable and notes payable are short-term, unless stated otherwise. Cost and fair value of marketable securities are the same.

P4-3 (Balance Sheet Adjustment and Preparation) The adjusted trial balance of Side Kicks Company and other related information for the year 2004 is presented below.

SIDE KICKS COMPANY
ADJUSTED TRIAL BALANCE
DECEMBER 31, 2004

	Debits	Credits
Cash	$ 41,000	
Accounts Receivable	163,500	
Allowance for Doubtful Accounts		$ 8,700

Prepaid Insurance	5,900	
Inventory	308,500	
Long-term Investments	339,000	
Land	85,000	
Construction Work in Progress	124,000	
Patents	36,000	
Equipment	400,000	
Accumulated Depreciation of Equipment		140,000
Unamortized Discount on Bonds Payable	20,000	
Accounts Payable		148,000
Accrued Expenses		49,200
Notes Payable		94,000
Bonds Payable		400,000
Capital Stock		500,000
Premium on Capital Stock		45,000
Retained Earnings		138,000
	$1,522,900	$1,522,900

Additional information:

1. The inventory has a replacement market value of $353,000. The LIFO method of inventory value is used.
2. The cost and fair value of the long-term investments that consist of stocks and bonds is the same.
3. The amount of the Construction Work in Progress account represents the costs expended to date on a building in the process of construction. (The company rents factory space at the present time.) The land on which the building is being constructed cost $85,000, as shown in the trial balance.
4. The patents were purchased by the company at a cost of $40,000 and are being amortized on a straight-line basis.
5. Of the unamortized discount on bonds payable, $2,000 will be amortized in 2005.
6. The notes payable represent bank loans that are secured by long-term investments carried at $120,000. These bank loans are due in 2005.
7. The bonds payable bear interest at 11% payable every December 31, and are due January 1, 2015.
8. Six hundred thousand shares of common stock of a par value of $1 were authorized, of which 500,000 shares were issued are outstanding.

Instructions

Prepare a balance sheet as of December 31, 2004, so that all important information is fully disclosed.

P4-4 **(Preparation of a Corrected Balance Sheet)** Presented below is the balance sheet of Russell Crowe Corporation as of December 31, 2004.

RUSSELL CROWE CORPORATION
BALANCE SHEET
DECEMBER 31, 2004

Assets

Goodwill (Note 2)	$ 120,000
Building (Note 1)	1,640,000
Inventories	312,100
Land	750,000
Accounts receivable	170,000
Treasury stock (50,000 shares, no par)	87,000
Cash on hand	175,900
Assets allocated to trustee for plant expansion	
Cash in bank	70,000
U.S. Treasury notes, at cost and fair value	138,000
	$3,463,000

Equities

Notes payable (Note 3)	$ 600,000
Common stock, authorized and issued, 1,000,000 shares, no par	1,150,000
Retained earnings	658,000
Appreciation capital (Note 1)	570,000
Federal income taxes payable	75,000
Reserve for depreciation of building	410,000
	$3,463,000

Note 1: Buildings are stated at cost, except for one building that was recorded at appraised value. The excess of appraisal value over cost was $570,000. Depreciation has been recorded based on cost.

Note 2: Goodwill in the amount of $120,000 was recognized because the company believed that book value was not an accurate representation of the fair market value of the company. The gain of $120,000 was credited to Retained Earnings.

Note 3: Notes payable are long-term except for the current installment due of $100,000.

Instructions

Prepare a corrected classified balance sheet in good form. The notes above are for information only.

P4-5 (Balance Sheet Adjustment and Preparation) Presented below is the balance sheet of Stephen King Corporation for the current year, 2004.

STEPHEN KING CORPORATION				
BALANCE SHEET				
DECEMBER 31, 2004				
Current assets	$ 435,000	Current liabilities	$ 330,000
Investments	640,000	Long-term liabilities	1,000,000
Property, plant, and equipment	1,720,000	Stockholders' equity	1,770,000
Intangible assets	305,000		$3,100,000
	$3,100,000		

The following information is presented.

1. The current assets section includes: cash $100,000, accounts receivable $170,000 less $10,000 for allowance for doubtful accounts, inventories $180,000, and unearned revenue $5,000. The cash balance is composed of $114,000, less a bank overdraft of $14,000. Inventories are stated on the lower of FIFO cost or market.

2. The investments section includes: the cash surrender value of a life insurance contract $40,000; investments in common stock, short-term (trading) $80,000 and long-term (available-for-sale) $270,000; and bond sinking fund $250,000. The cost and fair value of investments in common stock are the same.

3. Property, plant, and equipment includes: buildings $1,040,000 less accumulated depreciation $360,000; equipment $450,000 less accumulated depreciation $180,000; land $500,000; and land held for future use $270,000.

4. Intangible assets include: a franchise $165,000; goodwill $100,000; and discount on bonds payable $40,000.

5. Current liabilities include: accounts payable $90,000; notes payable—short-term $80,000 and long-term $120,000; and taxes payable $40,000.

6. Long-term liabilities are composed solely of 10% bonds payable due 2012.

7. Stockholders' equity has: preferred stock, no par value, authorized 200,000 shares, issued 70,000 shares for $450,000; and common stock, $1.00 par value, authorized 400,000 shares, issued 100,000 shares at an average price of $10. In addition, the corporation has retained earnings of $320,000.

Instructions

Prepare a balance sheet in good form, adjusting the amounts in each balance sheet classification as affected by the information given above.

 **P4-6 (Corrected Balance Sheet—Subsequent Events)** Your firm has been engaged to examine the financial statements of Will Smith Corporation for the year 2004. The bookkeeper who maintains the financial records has prepared all the unaudited financial statements for the corporation since its organization on January 2, 2000. The client provides you with the information below.

WILL SMITH CORPORATION
BALANCE SHEET
AS OF DECEMBER 31, 2004

Assets		Liabilities	
Current assets	$1,881,100	Current liabilities	$ 962,400
Other assets	5,171,400	Long-term liabilities	1,439,500
		Capital	4,650,600
	$7,052,500		$7,052,500

An analysis of current assets discloses the following:

Cash (restricted in the amount of $400,000 for plant expansion)	$ 571,000
Investments in land	185,000
Accounts receivable less allowance of $30,000	480,000
Inventories (LIFO flow assumption)	645,100
	$1,881,100

Other assets include:

Prepaid expenses	$ 47,400
Plant and equipment less accumulated depreciation of $1,430,000	4,130,000
Cash surrender value of life insurance policy	84,000
Unamortized bond discount	49,500
Notes receivable (short-term)	162,300
Goodwill	252,000
Land	446,200
	$5,171,400

Current liabilities include:

Accounts payable	$ 510,000
Notes payable (due 2006)	157,400
Estimated income taxes payable	145,000
Premium on common stock	150,000
	$ 962,400

Long-term liabilities include:

Unearned revenue	$ 489,500
Dividends payable (cash)	200,000
8% bonds payable (due May 1, 2009)	750,000
	$1,439,500

Capital includes:

Retained earnings	$2,810,600
Capital stock, par value $10; authorized 200,000 shares, 184,000 shares issued	1,840,000
	$4,650,600

The supplementary information below is also provided.

1. On May 1, 2004, the corporation issued at 93.4, $750,000 of bonds to finance plant expansion. The long-term bond agreement provided for the annual payment of interest every May 1. The existing plant was pledged as security for the loan. Use straight-line method for discount amortization.

2. The bookkeeper made the following mistakes.
   (a) In 2002, the ending inventory was overstated by $183,000. The ending inventories for 2003 and 2004 were correctly computed.
   (b) In 2004, accrued wages in the amount of $275,000 were omitted from the balance sheet and these expenses were not charged on the income statement.
   (c) In 2004, a gain of $175,000 (net of tax) on the sale of certain plant assets was credited directly to retained earnings.

3. A major competitor has introduced a line of products that will compete directly with Smith's primary line, now being produced in a specially designed new plant. Because of manufacturing innovations, the competitor's line will be of comparable quality but priced 50% below Smith's line. The competitor announced its new line on January 14, 2005. Smith indicates that the company will meet the lower prices that are high enough to cover variable manufacturing and selling expenses, but permit recovery of only a portion of fixed costs.

4. You learned on January 28, 2005, prior to completion of the audit, of heavy damage because of a recent fire to one of Smith's two plants; the loss will not be reimbursed by insurance. The newspapers described the event in detail.

Instructions

Analyze the above information to prepare a corrected balance sheet for Smith in accordance with proper accounting and reporting principles. Prepare a description of any notes that might need to be prepared. The books are closed and adjustments to income are to be made through retained earnings.

CONCEPTUAL CASES

C4-1 (Reporting the Financial Effects of Varied Transactions) In an examination of Juan Acevedo Corporation as of December 31, 2004, you have learned that the following situations exist. No entries have been made in the accounting records for these items.

1. The corporation erected its present factory building in 1989. Depreciation was calculated by the straight-line method, using an estimated life of 35 years. Early in 2004, the board of directors conducted a careful survey and estimated that the factory building had a remaining useful life of 25 years as of January 1, 2004.

2. An additional assessment of 2003 income taxes was levied and paid in 2004.

3. When calculating the accrual for officers' salaries at December 31, 2004, it was discovered that the accrual for officers' salaries for December 31, 2003, had been overstated.

4. On December 15, 2004, Acevedo Corporation declared a 1% common stock dividend on its common stock outstanding, payable February 1, 2005, to the common stockholders of record December 31, 2004.

Instructions

Describe fully how each of the items above should be reported in the financial statements of Acevedo Corporation for the year 2004.

C4-2 (Current Asset and Liability Classification) Below are the titles of a number of debit and credit accounts as they might appear on the balance sheet of Ethan Allen Corporation as of October 31, 2004.

Debits	Credits
Interest Accrued on U.S. Government Securities	Capital Stock—Preferred
Notes Receivable	11% First Mortgage Bonds, due in 2011
Petty Cash Fund	Preferred Cash Dividend, payable Nov. 1, 2004
U.S. Government Securities	Allowance for Doubtful Accounts Receivable
Treasury Stock	Federal Income Taxes Payable
Unamortized Bond Discount	Customers' Advances (on contracts to be completed next year)
Cash in Bank	Premium on Bonds Redeemable in 2004
Land	Officers' 2004 Bonus Accrued

Debits	Credits
Inventory of Operating Parts and Supplies	Accrued Payroll
Inventory of Raw Materials	Notes Payable
Patents	Accrued Interest on Bonds
Cash and U.S. Government Bonds Set Aside for Property Additions	Accumulated Depreciation
Investment in Subsidiary	Accounts Payable
Accounts Receivable	Capital in Excess of Par
U.S. Government Contracts	Accrued Interest on Notes Payable
Regular	8% First Mortgage Bonds, to be redeemed in 2002 out of current assets
Installments—Due Next Year	
Installments—Due After Next year	
Goodwill	
Inventory of Finished Goods	
Inventory of Work in Process	
Deficit	

Instructions

Select the current asset and current liability items from among these debits and credits. If there appear to be certain borderline cases that you are unable to classify without further information, mention them and explain your difficulty, or give your reasons for making questionable classifications, if any.

(AICPA adapted)

C4-3 (Identifying Balance Sheet Deficiencies) The assets of LaShon Johnson Corporation are presented below (000s omitted).

LASHON JOHNSON CORPORATION
BALANCE SHEET (PARTIAL)
DECEMBER 31, 2004

Assets

Current assets		
Cash		$ 100,000
Unclaimed payroll checks		27,500
Marketable securities (cost $30,000) at fair value		37,000
Accounts receivable (less bad debt reserve)		75,000
Inventories—at lower of cost (determined by the next-in, first-out method) or market		240,000
Total current assets		479,500
Tangible assets		
Land (less accumulated depreciation)		80,000
Buildings and equipment	$800,000	
Less: Accumulated depreciation	250,000	550,000
Net tangible assets		630,000
Long-term investments		
Stocks and bonds		100,000
Treasury stock		70,000
Total long-term investments		170,000
Other assets		
Discount on bonds payable		19,400
Sinking fund		975,000
Total other assets		994,400
Total assets		$2,273,900

Instructions
Indicate the deficiencies, if any, in the foregoing presentation of LaShon Johnson Corporation's assets. Marketable securities are considered trading securities.

C4-4 (Critique of Balance Sheet Format and Content) Presented below is the balance sheet of Bellemy Brothers Corporation (000s omitted).

BELLEMY BROTHERS CORPORATION
BALANCE SHEET
DECEMBER 31, 2004

Assets

Current assets		
Cash	$26,000	
Marketable securities	18,000	
Accounts receivable	25,000	
Merchandise inventory	20,000	
Supplies inventory	4,000	
Stock investment in Subsidiary Company	20,000	$113,000
Investments		
Treasury stock		25,000
Property, plant, and equipment		
Buildings and land	91,000	
Less: Reserve for depreciation	31,000	60,000
Other assets		
Cash surrender value of life insurance		19,000
		$217,000

Liabilities and Capital

Current liabilities		
Accounts payable	$22,000	
Reserve for income taxes	15,000	
Customers' accounts with credit balances	1	$ 37,001
Deferred credits		
Unamortized premium on bonds payable		2,000
Long-term liabilities		
Bonds payable		60,000
Total liabilities		99,001
Capital stock		
Capital stock, par $5	85,000	
Earned surplus	24,999	
Cash dividends declared	8,000	117,999
		$217,000

Instructions
Evaluate the balance sheet presented. State briefly the proper treatment of any item criticized.

C4-5 (Identifying Balance Sheet Deficiencies) The financial statement below was prepared by employees of your client, Walt Whitman Co. The statement is unaccompanied by notes.

WALT WHITMAN CO.
BALANCE SHEET
AS OF NOVEMBER 30, 2004

Current assets				
Cash			$ 100,000	
Accounts receivable (less allowance of $30,000 for doubtful accounts)			419,900	
Inventories			1,954,000	$2,473,900
Less: Current liabilities				
Accounts payable			306,400	
Accrued payroll			28,260	
Accrued interest on mortgage note			12,000	
Estimated taxes payable			66,000	412,660
Net working capital				2,061,240
Property, plant, and equipment (at cost)				

	Cost	Depreciation	Value	
Land and buildings	$ 983,300	$410,000	$ 573,300	
Machinery and equipment	1,135,700	568,699	567,001	
	$2,119,000	$978,699		1,140,301

Deferred charges				
Prepaid taxes and other expenses			23,700	
Unamortized discount on mortgage note			10,800	34,500
Total net working capital and noncurrent assets				3,236,041
Less: Deferred liabilities				
Mortgage note payable			300,000	
Unearned revenue			1,808,000	2,108,000
Total net assets				$1,128,041
Stockholders' equity				
10% Preferred stock at par value				$ 300,000
Common stock at par value				397,000
Paid-in surplus				210,000
Retained earnings				265,641
Treasury stock at cost (400 shares)				(44,600)
Total stockholders' equity				$1,128,041

Instructions

Indicate the deficiencies, if any, in the balance sheet above in regard to form, terminology, descriptions, content, and the like.

 **C4-6 (Presentation of Property, Plant, and Equipment)** Andrea Pafko, corporate comptroller for Nicholson Industries, is trying to decide how to present "Property, plant, and equipment" in the balance sheet. She realizes that the statement of cash flows will show that the company made a significant

investment in purchasing new equipment this year, but overall she knows the company's plant assets are rather old. She feels that she can disclose one figure titled "Property, plant, and equipment, net of depreciation," and the result will be a low figure. However, it will not disclose the age of the assets. If she chooses to show the cost less accumulated depreciation, the age of the assets will be apparent. She proposes the following.

Property, plant, and equipment, net of depreciation	$10,000,000
rather than	
Property, plant and equipment	$50,000,000
Less: Accumulated depreciation	(40,000,000)
Net book value	$10,000,000

Instructions
Answer the following questions.

(a) What are the ethical issues involved?
(b) What should Pafko do?

C4-7 **(Post–Balance-Sheet Events)** At December 31, 2003, Joni Brandt Corp. has assets of $10,000,000, liabilities of $6,000,000, common stock of $2,000,000 (representing 2,000,000 shares of $1.00 par common stock), and retained earnings of $2,000,000. Net sales for the year 2003 were $18,000,000, and net income was $800,000. As auditors of this company, you are making a review of subsequent events on February 13, 2004, and you find the following.

1. On February 3, 2004, one of Brandt's customers declared bankruptcy. At December 31, 2003, this company owed Brandt $300,000, of which $40,000 was paid in January, 2004.
2. On January 18, 2004, one of the three major plants of the client burned.
3. On January 23, 2004, a strike was called at one of Brandt's largest plants, which halted 30% of its production. As of today (February 13) the strike has not been settled.
4. A major electronics enterprise has introduced a line of products that would compete directly with Brandt's primary line, now being produced in a specially designed new plant. Because of manufacturing innovations, the competitor has been able to achieve quality similar to that of Brandt's products, but at a price 50% lower. Brandt officials say they will meet the lower prices, which are high enough to cover variable manufacturing and selling costs but which permit recovery of only a portion of fixed costs.
5. Merchandise traded in the open market is recorded in the company's records at $1.40 per unit on December 31, 2003. This price had prevailed for 2 weeks, after release of an official market report that predicted vastly enlarged supplies; however, no purchases were made at $1.40. The price throughout the preceding year had been about $2.00, which was the level experienced over several years. On January 18, 2004, the price returned to $2.00, after public disclosure of an error in the official calculations of the prior December, correction of which destroyed the expectations of excessive supplies. Inventory at December 31, 2003, was on a lower of cost or market basis.
6. On February 1, 2004, the board of directors adopted a resolution accepting the offer of an investment banker to guarantee the marketing of $1,200,000 of preferred stock.

Instructions
State in each case how the 2003 financial statements would be affected, if at all.

USING YOUR JUDGMENT

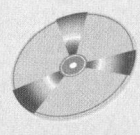

FINANCIAL REPORTING PROBLEM

3M COMPANY

The financial statements of **3M** were provided with your book or can be accessed on the Take Action! CD.

Instructions

Refer to 3M's financial statements and the accompanying notes to answer the following questions.

(a) What alternative formats could 3M have adopted for its balance sheet? Which format did it adopt?
(b) Identify the various techniques of disclosure 3M might have used to disclose additional pertinent financial information. Which technique does it use in its financials?
(c) In what classifications are 3M's investments reported? What valuation basis does 3M use to report its investments? How much working capital did 3M have on December 31, 2001? December 31, 2000?
(d) Does 3M report any subsequent event(s)? If so, what is the nature of the event(s) reported?

FINANCIAL STATEMENT ANALYSIS CASES

CASE 1: UNIROYAL TECHNOLOGY CORPORATION

Uniroyal Technology Corporation (UTC), with corporate offices in Sarasota, Florida, is organized into three operating segments. The high-performance plastics segment is responsible for research, development, and manufacture of a wide variety of products, including orthopedic braces, graffiti-resistant seats for buses and airplanes, and a static-resistant plastic used in the central processing units of microcomputers. The coated fabrics segment manufactures products such as automobile seating, door and instrument panels, and specialty items such as waterproof seats for personal watercraft and stain-resistant, easy-cleaning upholstery fabrics. The foams and adhesives segment develops and manufactures products used in commercial roofing applications.

The following items relate to operations in a recent year.

1. Serious pressure was placed on profitability by sharply increasing raw material prices. Some raw materials increased in price 50% during the past year. Cost containment programs were instituted and product prices were increased whenever possible, which resulted in profit margins actually improving over the course of the year.
2. The company entered into a revolving credit agreement, under which UTC may borrow the lesser of $15,000,000 or 80% of eligible accounts receivable. At the end of the year, approximately $4,000,000 was outstanding under this agreement. The company plans to use this line of credit in the upcoming year to finance operations and expansion.

Instructions

(a) Should investors be informed of raw materials price increases, such as described in item 1? Does the fact that the company successfully met the challenge of higher prices affect the answer? Explain.
(b) How should the information in item 2 be presented in the financial statements of UTC?

CASE 2: SHERWIN-WILLIAMS COMPANY

Sherwin-Williams, based in Cleveland, Ohio, manufactures a wide variety of paint and other coatings, which are marketed through its specialty stores and in other retail outlets. The company also manufactures paint for automobiles. The Automotive Division has had financial difficulty. During a recent year, five branch locations of the Automotive Division were closed, and new management was put in place for the branches remaining.

The following titles were shown on Sherwin-Williams' balance sheet for that year.

Accounts payable	Machinery and equipment
Accounts receivable, less allowance	Other accruals
Accrued taxes	Other capital
Buildings	Other current assets
Cash and cash equivalents	Other long-term liabilities
Common stock	Postretirement obligations other than pensions
Employee compensation payable	Retained earnings
Finished goods inventories	Short-term investments
Intangibles and other assets	Taxes payable
Land	Work in process and raw materials inventories
Long-term debt	

Instructions

(a) Organize the accounts in the general order in which they would have been presented in a classified balance sheet.

(b) When several of the branch locations of the Automotive Division were closed, what balance sheet accounts were most likely affected? Did the balance in those accounts decrease or increase?

COMPARATIVE ANALYSIS CASE

THE COCA-COLA COMPANY AND PEPSICO, INC.

Instructions

Go to the Take Action! CD and use information found there to answer the following questions related to **The Coca-Cola Company** and **PepsiCo, Inc.**

(a) What format(s) did these companies use to present their balance sheets?

(b) How much working capital did each of these companies have at the end of 2001? Speculate as to their rationale for the amount of working capital they maintain.

(c) What is the most significant difference in the asset structure of the two companies? What causes this difference?

(d) What are the companies' annual and 5-year (1997–2001) growth rates in total assets and long-term debt?

INTERNATIONAL REPORTING CASE

Presented below is the balance sheet for **Tomkins PLC**, a British company.

Instructions

(a) Identify at least three differences in balance sheet reporting between British and U.S. firms, as shown in Tomkins's balance sheet.

(b) Review Tomkins's balance sheet and identify how the format of this financial statement provides useful information, as illustrated in the chapter.

TOMKINS

TOMKINS PLC
Consolidated Balance Sheet
at 30 April 2001

	£ million
Capital employed	
Fixed assets	
Intangible assets	199.7
Tangible assets	903.0
Investments	12.2
	1,114.9
Current assets	
Stock	473.5
Debtors	741.1
Cash	400.4
	1,615.0
Current liabilities	
Creditors: amounts falling due within one year	(813.3)
Net current assets	801.7
Total assets less current liabilities	1,916.6
Creditors: amounts falling due after more than one year	(425.8)
Provisions for liabilities and charges	(405.4)
Net assets	1,085.4
Capital and reserves	
Called up share capital	
Ordinary shares	39.1
Convertible preference shares	337.2
Redeemable preference shares	426.7
	803.0
Share premium account	89.7
Capital redemption reserve	64.8
Profit and loss account	94.5
Shareholders' funds	1,052.0
Equity minority interest	33.4
	1,085.4

*Remember to check the **Take Action! CD**
and the book's **companion Web site**
to find additional resources for this chapter.*

INCOME STATEMENT AND RELATED INFORMATION

CHAPTER 5

WHICH INCOME NUMBER?

Recently, companies have been providing investors a choice in reported income numbers. In addition to income measured according to generally accepted accounting principles (GAAP), companies also are reporting an income measure that has been adjusted for certain items. Companies make these adjustments because they believe the items are not representative of operating results. In some cases these adjustments are quite large. As shown in the following table, in a recent quarter the reporting of such "pro forma" income measures put a very different spin on operating results. In some cases (JDS-Uniphase, PMC-Sierra, and Yahoo!), a loss under GAAP measurement rules became an operating profit after pro forma adjustments.

Earnings Per Share		
Company	Pro Forma	GAAP
JDS-Uniphase	$0.14	−$1.13
Checkfree	0.04	−1.17
Amazon.com	−0.22	−0.66
PMC-Sierra	0.02	−0.38
Corning	0.29	0.14
Qualcomm	0.29	0.18
Yahoo!	0.01	−0.02

Characteristic of pro forma reporting practices is Amazon.com, which made adjustments for items such as stock-based compensation, amortization of goodwill and intangibles, impairment charges, and equity in losses of investees. All of these adjustments make pro forma earnings higher than GAAP income. In its earnings announcement, Amazon defended its pro forma reporting, saying that it gives better insight into the fundamental operations of the business.

So what's wrong with focusing investors on the fundamentals of the business? According to Ed Jenkins, former chair of the FASB, one problem is that there are no standards for the reporting of pro forma numbers. As a result, investors will have a hard time comparing Amazon's pro forma measure with that reported by another company, which has a different idea of what is fundamental to its business. Also, there is concern that many companies use pro forma reporting to deflect investor attention from bad news.

Rather than relying on management's choice of the number to focus on, GAAP income numbers are subject to the same rules for all companies, are audited, and give investors a more complete picture of company profitability, not the story preferred by management.[1]

[1] Adapted from David Henry, "The Numbers Game," *Business Week* (May 14, 2001), pp. 100–110.

As shown in the opening story, investors need complete and comparable information on income and its components to make valid assessments of company profitability. The purpose of this chapter is to examine the many different types of revenues, expenses, gains, and losses that affect the income statement and related information. The content and organization of this chapter are as follows.

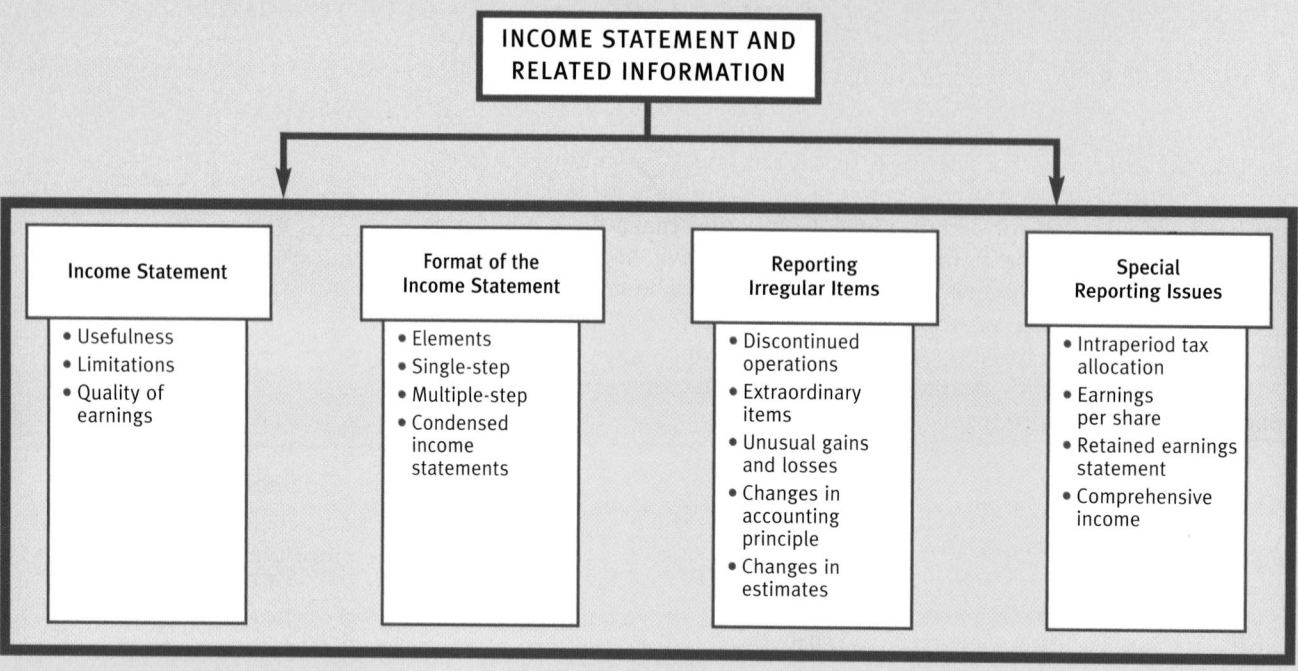

INCOME STATEMENT AND RELATED INFORMATION

Income Statement	Format of the Income Statement	Reporting Irregular Items	Special Reporting Issues
• Usefulness • Limitations • Quality of earnings	• Elements • Single-step • Multiple-step • Condensed income statements	• Discontinued operations • Extraordinary items • Unusual gains and losses • Changes in accounting principle • Changes in estimates	• Intraperiod tax allocation • Earnings per share • Retained earnings statement • Comprehensive income

INCOME STATEMENT

OBJECTIVE 1
Identify the uses and limitations of an income statement.

The **income statement**, often called the statement of income or statement of earnings,[2] is the report that measures the success of enterprise operations for a given period of time. The business and investment community uses this report to determine profitability, investment value, and credit worthiness. It provides investors and creditors with information that helps them predict the **amounts, timing, and uncertainty of future cash flows**.

Usefulness of the Income Statement

The income statement helps users of financial statements predict future cash flows in a number of ways. For example, investors and creditors can use the information in the income statement to:

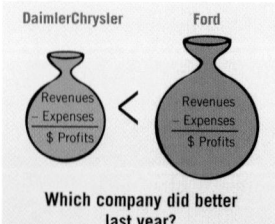

DaimlerChrysler   Ford

Revenues − Expenses $ Profits < Revenues − Expenses $ Profits

Which company did better last year?

① **Evaluate the past performance of the enterprise.** By examining revenues and expenses, you can tell how the company performed and compare its performance to its competitors. For example, the income data provided by **DaimlerChrysler** can be used to compare its performance to that of **Ford**.

② **Provide a basis for predicting future performance.** Information about past performance can be used to determine important trends that, if continued, provide

[2]*Accounting Trends and Techniques—2001* (New York: AICPA) indicates that for the 600 companies surveyed, the term *income* was employed in the title of 284 income statements. The term *operations* was second in acceptance with 198, and the term *earnings* was used by 108 companies.

information about future performance. For example, **General Electric** has reported consistent increases in revenues in recent years. Although success in the past does not necessarily mean the company will be successful in the future, predictions of future revenues, and hence earnings and cash flows, can be made with some confidence, if a reasonable correlation exists between past and future performance.

GE Profits

Hmm....Where am I headed?

③ **Help assess the risk or uncertainty of achieving future cash flows.** Information on the various components of income—revenues, expenses, gains, and losses—highlights the relationships among them and can be used to assess the risk of not achieving a particular level of cash flows in the future. For example, segregating **IBM**'s operating performance from other nonrecurring sources of income is useful because operations are usually the primary means by which revenues and cash are generated. Thus, results from continuing operations usually have greater significance for predicting future performance than do results from nonrecurring activities and events.

IBM Income for Year Ended 12/31/03	Recurring?
Revenues	
– Operating expenses	
Operating income	Yes
± Unusual or extraordinary items	No
$ Net Income	?

Recurring items are more certain in the future.

In summary, information in the income statement—revenues, expenses, gains, and losses—helps users evaluate past performance and provides insights into achieving a particular level of cash flows in the future.

Limitations of the Income Statement

Because net income is an estimate and reflects a number of assumptions, income statement users need to be aware of certain limitations associated with the information contained in the income statement. Some of these limitations include:

① **Items that cannot be measured reliably are not reported in the income statement.** Current practice prohibits recognition of certain items from the determination of income even though the effects of these items arguably affect the performance of an entity from one point in time to another. For example, unrealized gains and losses on certain investment securities may not be recorded in income when there is uncertainty that the changes in value will ever be realized. In addition, more and more companies, like **Cisco Systems** and **Microsoft**, have experienced increases in value due to brand recognition, customer service, and product quality. Presently, a common framework for identifying and reporting these types of values has not been developed.

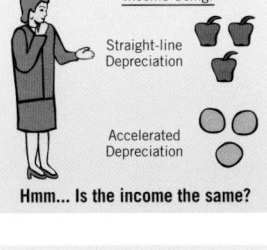

You left something out!

② **Income numbers are affected by the accounting methods employed.** For example, one company may choose to depreciate its plant assets on an accelerated basis; another chooses straight-line depreciation. Assuming all other factors are equal, the income for the first company will be lower, even though the companies are essentially the same. In effect, we are comparing apples to oranges.

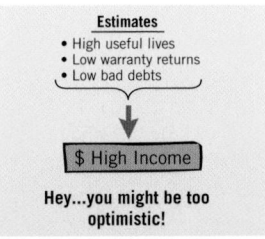

Income Using:

Straight-line Depreciation

Accelerated Depreciation

Hmm... Is the income the same?

③ **Income measurement involves judgment.** For example, one company in good faith may estimate the useful life of an asset to be 20 years while another company uses a 15-year estimate for the same type of asset. Similarly, some companies may make overly optimistic estimates of future warranty returns and bad debt write-offs, which results in lower expense and higher income.

Estimates
• High useful lives
• Low warranty returns
• Low bad debts

↓

$ High Income

Hey...you might be too optimistic!

In summary, several limitations of the income statement reduce the usefulness of this statement for predicting the amounts, timing, and uncertainty of future cash flows.

Quality of Earnings

Our discussion to this point has highlighted the importance of information in the income statement for investment and credit decisions, including the evaluation of the company and its managers.[3] Companies try to meet or beat Wall Street expectations so that the market price of their stock and the value of management's stock options increase. As a result, companies have incentives to manage income to meet earnings targets or to make earnings look less risky.

Recently, the SEC has expressed concern that the motivations to meet earnings targets may be overriding good business practices. As a result, the quality of earnings and the quality of financial reporting are eroding. As indicated by one SEC chairman, "Managing may be giving way to manipulation; integrity may be losing out to illusion."[4] Therefore the SEC has started to take decisive action to prevent the practice of earnings management.

What is **earnings management**? It is often defined as the planned timing of revenues, expenses, gains, and losses to smooth out bumps in earnings. In most cases, earnings management is used to increase income in the current year at the expense of income in future years. For example, companies prematurely recognize sales before they are complete in order to boost earnings. As one commentator noted, ". . . it's like popping a cork in a bottle of wine before it is ready."

Earnings management can also be used to decrease current earnings in order to increase income in the future. The classic case is the use of "cookie jar" reserves. These are established by using unrealistic assumptions to estimate liabilities for such items as sales returns, loan losses, and warranty returns. These reserves can then be reduced in the future to increase income.

Such earnings management has a negative effect on the **quality of earnings** if it distorts the information in a way that is less useful for predicting future earnings and cash flows. Markets are based on trust, and it is imperative that the bond between

WHAT DO THE NUMBERS MEAN?

MANAGE UP, MANAGE DOWN

The quality of earnings is adversely affected whether earnings are managed up or down. For example, **W.R. Grace** managed earnings down by taking excess "cookie jar" reserves in good earnings years. During the early 1990s, Grace was growing fast, with profits increasing 30 percent annually. Analysts' targets had Grace growing 24 percent each year. Worried that they could not continue to meet these growth expectations, management began stashing away excess profits in an all-purpose reserve. In 1995, when profits were not meeting expectations, Grace wanted to reduce this reserve and so increase income. The SEC objected, noting that generally accepted accounting principles would be violated if Grace were to do so.

More recently, **MicroStrategy** managed earnings up by booking revenue for future software upgrades, even though it had not yet delivered on the upgrades. And **Rent-Way, Inc.** managed its earnings up by understating some $65 million in expenses relating to such items as automobile maintenance and insurance payments.

Does the market value accounting quality? Well, each of these companies took a beating in the marketplace when its earnings management practices were uncovered. For example, Rent-Way's stock price plummeted from above $25 per share to below $10 per share when it announced restatements for its improper expense accounting. So, whether earnings are managed up or down, companies had better be prepared to pay the price for poor accounting quality.

---

[3]In support of the usefulness of income information, accounting researchers have documented that the market prices of companies change when income is reported to the market. See W.H. Beaver, "The Information Content of Annual Earnings Announcements," *Empirical Research in Accounting: Selected Studies, Journal of Accounting Research* (Supplement 1968), pp. 67–92.

[4]A. Levitt, the "Numbers Game." Remarks to NYU Center for Law and Business, September 28, 1998 (Securities and Exchange Commission, 1998).

shareholders and the company be strong. If investors or others lose faith in the numbers reported in the financial statements, U.S. capital markets will be damaged. As mentioned in the opening story, heightened scrutiny of income measurement and reporting is warranted to ensure the quality of earnings and investors' confidence in the income statement.

FORMAT OF THE INCOME STATEMENT

Elements of the Income Statement

Net income results from revenue, expense, gain, and loss transactions. These transactions are summarized in the income statement. This method of income measurement is called the **transaction approach** because it focuses on the income-related activities that have occurred during the period.[5] Income can be further classified by customer, product line, or function or by operating and nonoperating, continuing and discontinued, and regular and irregular categories.[6] More formal definitions of income-related items, referred to as the major elements of the income statement, are as follows.

ELEMENTS OF FINANCIAL STATEMENTS

REVENUES. Inflows or other enhancements of assets of an entity or settlements of its liabilities during a period from delivering or producing goods, rendering services, or other activities that constitute the entity's ongoing major or central operations.

EXPENSES. Outflows or other using-up of assets or incurrences of liabilities during a period from delivering or producing goods, rendering services, or carrying out other activities that constitute the entity's ongoing major or central operations.

GAINS. Increases in equity (net assets) from peripheral or incidental transactions of an entity except those that result from revenues or investments by owners.

LOSSES. Decreases in equity (net assets) from peripheral or incidental transactions of an entity except those that result from expenses or distributions to owners.[7]

Revenues take many forms, such as sales, fees, interest, dividends, and rents. Expenses also take many forms, such as cost of goods sold, depreciation, interest, rent, salaries and wages, and taxes. Gains and losses also are of many types, resulting from the sale of investments, sale of plant assets, settlement of liabilities, write-offs of assets due to obsolescence or casualty, and theft.

[5]The most common alternative to the transaction approach is the **capital maintenance approach** to income measurement. Under this approach, income for the period is determined based on the change in equity, after adjusting for capital contributions (e.g., investments by owners) or distributions (e.g., dividends). The main drawback associated with the capital maintenance approach is that the components of income are not evident in its measurement. The Internal Revenue Service uses the capital maintenance approach to identify unreported income and refers to this approach as the "net worth check."

[6]The term "irregular" encompasses transactions and other events that are derived from developments outside the normal operations of the business.

[7]"Elements of Financial Statements," *Statement of Financial Accounting Concepts No. 6* (Stamford, Conn.: FASB, 1985), pars. 78–89.

INTERNATIONAL INSIGHT

For some nations, financial reporting is prepared on the same basis as tax returns. In such cases, companies have incentives to minimize reported income.

The distinction between revenues and gains and the distinction between expenses and losses depend to a great extent on the typical activities of the enterprise. For example, when **McDonald's** sells a hamburger, the selling price is recorded as revenue. However, when McDonald's sells a french-fryer, any excess of the selling price over the book value would be recorded as a gain. This difference in treatment results because the sale of the hamburger is part of McDonald's regular operations while the sale of the french-fryer is not.

The importance of reporting these elements should not be underestimated. For most decision makers, the parts of a financial statement will often be more useful than the whole. As indicated earlier, investors and creditors are interested in predicting the amounts, timing, and uncertainty of future income and cash flows. Having income statement elements shown in some detail and in comparison form with prior years' data, decision makers are better able to assess future income and cash flows.

Single-Step Income Statements

In reporting revenues, gains, expenses, and losses, a format known as the **single-step income statement** is often used. In the single-step statement, just two groupings exist: revenues and expenses. Expenses are deducted from revenues to arrive at net income or loss. The expression "single-step" is derived from the single subtraction necessary to arrive at net income. Frequently income tax is reported separately as the last item before net income to indicate its relationship to income before income tax. Illustration 5-1 shows the single-step income statement of Dan Deines Company.

Illustration 5-1
Single-step Income Statement

OBJECTIVE **2**
Prepare a single-step income statement.

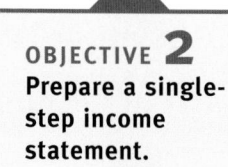

DAN DEINES COMPANY	
INCOME STATEMENT	
FOR THE YEAR ENDED DECEMBER 31, 2004	
Revenues	
Net sales	$2,972,413
Dividend revenue	98,500
Rental revenue	72,910
Total revenues	3,143,823
Expenses	
Cost of goods sold	1,982,541
Selling expenses	453,028
Administrative expenses	350,771
Interest expense	126,060
Income tax expense	66,934
Total expenses	2,979,334
Net income	$ 164,489
Earnings per common share	$1.74

Because of its simplicity, the single-step income statement is widely used in financial reporting. In recent years, though, the multiple-step form has become more popular.[8]
The primary advantage of the single-step format lies in the simplicity of presentation and the absence of any implication that one type of revenue or expense item has priority over another. Potential classification problems are thus eliminated.

[8]*Accounting Trends and Techniques—2001.* Of the 600 companies surveyed by the AICPA, 466 employed the multiple-step form, and 134 employed the single-step income statement format. This is a reversal from 1983, when 314 used the single-step form and 286 used the multiple-step form.

Multiple-Step Income Statements

Some contend that including other important revenue and expense classifications makes the income statement more useful. These further classifications include:

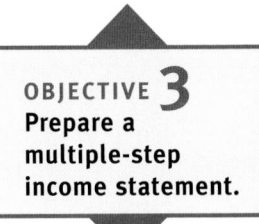

OBJECTIVE **3**
Prepare a
multiple-step
income statement.

① A separation of operating and nonoperating activities of the company. For example, enterprises often present an income from operations figure and then sections entitled "Other revenues and gains" and "Other expenses and losses." These other categories include interest revenue and expense, gains or losses from sales of miscellaneous items, and dividends received.

② A classification of expenses by functions, such as merchandising (cost of goods sold), selling, and administration. This permits immediate comparison with costs of previous years and with other departments in the same year.

A **multiple-step income statement** is used to recognize these additional relationships. This statement recognizes a separation of operating transactions from nonoperating transactions and matches costs and expenses with related revenues. It highlights certain intermediate components of income that are used for the computation of ratios used to assess the performance of the enterprise.

Intermediate Components of the Income Statement

When a multiple-step income statement is used, some or all of the following sections or subsections may be prepared.

INCOME STATEMENT SECTIONS

① **Operating Section.** A report of the revenues and expenses of the company's principal operations.
  (a) Sales or Revenue Section. A subsection presenting sales, discounts, allowances, returns, and other related information. Its purpose is to arrive at the net amount of sales revenue.
  (b) Cost of Goods Sold Section. A subsection that shows the cost of goods that were sold to produce the sales.
  (c) Selling Expenses. A subsection that lists expenses resulting from the company's efforts to make sales.
  (d) Administrative or General Expenses. A subsection reporting expenses of general administration.

② **Nonoperating Section.** A report of revenues and expenses resulting from secondary or auxiliary activities of the company. In addition, special gains and losses that are infrequent or unusual, but not both, are normally reported in this section. Generally these items break down into two main subsections:
  (a) Other Revenues and Gains. A list of the revenues earned or gains incurred, generally net of related expenses, from nonoperating transactions.
  (b) Other Expenses and Losses. A list of the expenses or losses incurred, generally net of any related incomes, from nonoperating transactions.

③ **Income Tax.** A short section reporting federal and state taxes levied on income from continuing operations.

④ **Discontinued Operations.** Material gains or losses resulting from the disposition of a segment of the business.

⑤ **Extraordinary Items.** Unusual and infrequent material gains and losses.

⑥ **Cumulative Effect of a Change in Accounting Principle.**

⑦ **Earnings Per Share.**

Although the content of the operating section is always the same, the organization of the material need not be as described above. The breakdown above uses a **natural expense classification**. It is commonly used for manufacturing concerns and for merchandising companies in the wholesale trade. Another classification of operating expenses, recommended for retail stores, uses a **functional expense classification** of administrative, occupancy, publicity, buying, and selling expenses.

Usually, financial statements that are provided to external users have less detail than internal management reports. The latter tend to have more expense categories—usually grouped along lines of responsibility. This detail allows top management to judge staff performance. Furthermore, irregular transactions such as discontinued operations, extraordinary items, and cumulative effect of changes in accounting principles should be reported separately, following income from continuing operations.

To illustrate the multiple-step income statement, Dan Deines Company's statement of income is presented in Illustration 5-2. Items 1, 2, 3, and 7 from the list on page 177 are shown in the statement.[9] Note that in arriving at net income, three subtotals are presented:

① net sales revenue

② gross profit

③ income from operations

The disclosure of net sales revenue is useful because regular revenues are reported as a separate item. Irregular or incidental revenues are disclosed elsewhere in the income statement. As a result, trends in revenue from continuing operations should be easier to understand and analyze.

Similarly, the reporting of gross profit provides a useful number for evaluating performance and assessing future earnings. A study of the trend in gross profits may show how successfully a company uses its resources; it may also be a basis for understanding how profit margins have changed as a result of competitive pressure.

Finally, disclosing income from operations highlights the difference between regular and irregular or incidental activities. This disclosure helps users recognize that incidental or irregular activities are unlikely to continue at the same level. Furthermore, disclosure of operating earnings may assist in comparing different companies and assessing operating efficiencies.

Condensed Income Statements

In some cases it is impossible to present in a single income statement of convenient size all the desired expense detail. This problem is solved by including only the totals of expense groups in the statement of income and preparing supplementary schedules to support the totals. With this format, the income statement itself may be reduced to a few lines on a single sheet. For this reason, readers who wish to study all the reported data on operations must give their attention to the supporting schedules. The income

---

[9]Earnings per share or net loss per share is required to be included on the face of the income statement.

DAN DEINES COMPANY
INCOME STATEMENT
FOR THE YEAR ENDED DECEMBER 31, 2004

Sales Revenue			
Sales			$3,053,081
Less: Sales discounts		$ 24,241	
Sales returns and allowances		56,427	80,668
Net sales revenue			2,972,413
Cost of Goods Sold			
Merchandise inventory, Jan. 1, 2004		461,219	
Purchases	$1,989,693		
Less: Purchase discounts	19,270		
Net purchases	1,970,423		
Freight and transportation-in	40,612	2,011,035	
Total merchandise available for sale		2,472,254	
Less: Merchandise inventory, Dec. 31, 2004		489,713	
Cost of goods sold			1,982,541
Gross profit on sales			989,872
Operating Expenses			
Selling expenses			
Sales salaries and commissions	202,644		
Sales office salaries	59,200		
Travel and entertainment	48,940		
Advertising expense	38,315		
Freight and transportation-out	41,209		
Shipping supplies and expense	24,712		
Postage and stationery	16,788		
Depreciation of sales equipment	9,005		
Telephone and Internet expense	12,215	453,028	
Administrative expenses			
Officers' salaries	186,000		
Office salaries	61,200		
Legal and professional services	23,721		
Utilities expense	23,275		
Insurance expense	17,029		
Depreciation of building	18,059		
Depreciation of office equipment	16,000		
Stationery, supplies, and postage	2,875		
Miscellaneous office expenses	2,612	350,771	803,799
Income from operations			186,073
Other Revenues and Gains			
Dividend revenue		98,500	
Rental revenue		72,910	171,410
			357,483
Other Expenses and Losses			
Interest on bonds and notes			126,060
Income before income tax			231,423
Income tax			66,934
Net income for the year			$ 164,489
Earnings per common share			$1.74

Illustration 5-2
Multiple-step Income
Statement

*Income Statements for
Real Companies*

statement shown in Illustration 5-3 for Dan Deines Company is a condensed version of the more detailed multiple-step statement presented earlier and is more representative of the type found in practice.

Illustration 5-3
Condensed Income
Statement

DAN DEINES COMPANY
INCOME STATEMENT
FOR THE YEAR ENDED DECEMBER 31, 2004

Net sales		$2,972,413
Cost of goods sold		1,982,541
Gross profit		989,872
Selling expenses (see Note D)	$453,028	
Administrative expenses	350,771	803,799
Income from operations		186,073
Other revenues and gains		171,410
		357,483
Other expenses and losses		126,060
Income before income tax		231,423
Income tax		66,934
Net income for the year		$ 164,489
Earnings per share		$1.74

An example of a supporting schedule, cross-referenced as Note D and detailing the selling expenses, is shown in Illustration 5-4.

Illustration 5-4
Sample Supporting
Schedule

Note D: Selling expenses

Sales salaries and commissions	$202,644
Sales office salaries	59,200
Travel and entertainment	48,940
Advertising expense	38,315
Freight and transportation-out	41,209
Shipping supplies and expense	24,712
Postage and stationery	16,788
Depreciation of sales equipment	9,005
Telephone and Internet expense	12,215
Total selling expenses	$453,028

How much detail to include in the income statement is always a problem. On the one hand, we want to present a simple, summarized statement so that a reader can readily discover important factors. On the other hand, we want to disclose the results of all activities and to provide more than just a skeleton report. Certain basic elements are always included, but as we'll see, they can be presented in various formats.

OBJECTIVE 4
Explain how irregular items are reported.

REPORTING IRREGULAR ITEMS

As illustrated through the use of a multiple-step or condensed income statement, flexibility in the presentation of the components of income is permitted. In two important areas, however, specific guidelines have been developed. These two areas relate to what is included in income and how certain unusual or irregular items are reported.

What should be included in net income has been a controversy for many years. For example, should irregular gains and losses, and corrections of revenues and expenses of prior years be closed directly to Retained Earnings and therefore not be reported in the income statement? Or should they first be presented in the income statement and then carried to Retained Earnings along with the net income or loss for the period? In general, **income measurement follows an all-inclusive approach. This approach indicates that most items, even irregular ones, are recorded in income.**[10]

One exception is errors in prior years' income measurement. Because these items have affected earnings already reported in a prior period, errors from prior periods are not included in current income. Rather, these items are recorded as adjustments to retained earnings.[11]

Currently there is growing debate concerning **how** irregular items that are part of current income should be reported within the income statement. This issue is extremely important, because the reporting of irregular items on the income statement is substantial. For example, Illustration 5-5 identifies the most common types and number of irregular items reported in a survey of 600 large companies. As indicated, restructuring charges, which many times contain write-offs and other one-time items, were reported by more than one-fourth of the surveyed firms. About 20 percent of the surveyed firms reported either an extraordinary item or a discontinued operation charge.[12]

INTERNATIONAL INSIGHT

In many countries the "modified all-inclusive" income statement approach does not parallel that of the U.S. For example, some gains and losses are not reported on the income statement. Rather, they are taken directly to owners' equity accounts.

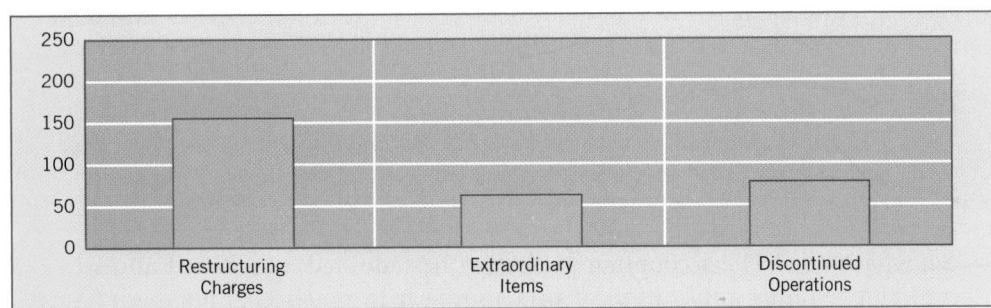

Illustration 5-5
Number of Irregular Items Reported in a Recent Year by 600 Large Companies

As discussed in the opening story, it is important to have consistent and comparable income reporting practices so that the information that companies disseminate is not too promotional. Developing a framework for reporting irregular items is important to ensure that financial statement users have reliable income information.[13]

Some users advocate a **current operating performance approach** to income reporting. These analysts argue that the most useful income measure will reflect only regular and recurring revenue and expense elements. Irregular items do not reflect an enterprise's future earning power. In contrast, others warn that a focus on operating income potentially misses important information about a firm's performance. Any gain or loss experienced by the firm, whether directly or indirectly related to operations, contributes to its

---

[10]As discussed later in this chapter, the FASB has issued a statement of concepts that offers some guidance on this topic—"Recognition and Measurement in Financial Statements of Business Enterprises," *Statement of Financial Accounting Concepts No. 5* (Stamford, Conn.: FASB, 1984).

[11]This is referred to as "prior period adjustments." Another example of items that bypass the income statement is the gains or losses arising from certain investment securities and pension adjustments. Both examples are cases where there is uncertainty about the realization of the gains or losses. These gains and losses are recorded in owners' equity until they are realized.

[12]*Accounting Trends and Techniques—2001* (New York: AICPA).

[13]The FASB and other international accounting standard setters continue to study the best way to report income. See *Reporting Financial Performance: A Proposed Approach* (Norwalk, Conn.: FASB, September 1999).

long-run profitability. As one analyst notes, "write-offs matter. . . . They speak to the volatility of (past) earnings."[14] As a result, some nonoperating items can be used to assess the riskiness of future earnings. Furthermore, determining which items are operating and which items are irregular requires judgment and could lead to differences in the treatment of irregular items and to possible manipulation of income measures.

What do the numbers mean?

Are one-time charges bugging you?

Which number, net income or income from operations, should an analyst use in evaluating companies that have unusual items? Some argue that operating income is better because it is more representative of what will happen in the future. Others note that special items are often no longer special. For example, one study noted that in 2001, companies in the Standard & Poors' 500 index wrote off items totaling $165 billion—more than in the prior five years combined. And one study by **Multex.com** and the *Wall Street Journal* indicates that these charges should not be ignored. Based on data for companies taking unusual charges from 1996–2001, the study documented that companies reporting the largest unusual charges had more negative stock price performance following the charge, compared to companies with smaller charges. Thus, rather than signaling that the bad times are behind, these unusual charges indicated poorer future earnings.

Rather than ignoring unusual charges, some analysts use these charges to weed out stocks that may be headed for a fall. Following the "cockroach theory," any charge indicating a problem raises the probability of more problems. Thus, investors should be wary of the increasing use of restructuring and other one-time charges, which may bury expenses that signal future performance declines.

Source: J. Weil and S. Liesman, "Stock Gurus Disregard Most Big Write-offs, But They Often Hold Vital Clues to Outlook," *Wall Street Journal* Electronic Edition (December 31, 2001).

So, what to do? The accounting profession has **adopted a modified all-inclusive concept and requires application of this approach in practice**. A number of subsequent pronouncements require **irregular items** to be highlighted so that the reader of financial statements can better determine the long-run earning power of the enterprise. These items fall into five general categories:

1. Discontinued operations.
2. Extraordinary items.
3. Unusual gains and losses.
4. Changes in accounting principle.
5. Changes in estimates.

Discontinued Operations

As indicated in Illustration 5-5, one of the most common types of irregular items is discontinued operations. A **discontinued operation** occurs when (a) the results of operations and cash flows of a component of a company have been (or will be) eliminated from the ongoing operations, and (b) there is no significant continuing involvement in that component after the disposal transaction. To illustrate a **component**, S.C. Johnson manufactures and sells consumer products and has several product groups, each with different product lines and brands. For S.C. Johnson, a product group is the lowest level at which operations and cash flows can be clearly distinguished from the rest of the company's operations. Therefore each product group is a component of the company, and if disposed of, would be classified as a discontinued operation.

[14]D. McDermott, "Latest Profit Data Stir Old Debate Between Net and Operating Income," *Wall Street Journal* (May 3, 1999).

Here is another example. Assume that Softso Inc. has experienced losses with certain brands in its beauty-care products group. As a result, Softso decides to sell the beauty-care business. It will not have any continuing involvement in the product group after it is sold. In this case, the operations and the cash flows of the product group are eliminated from the ongoing operations of Softso and are reported as a discontinued operation. On the other hand, assume Softso decides to remain in the beauty-care business but will discontinue the brands that experienced losses. Because the cash flows from the brands cannot be differentiated from the cash flows of the product group as a whole, the brands are not considered a component. As a result, any gain or loss on the sale of the brands is not classified as a discontinued operation.

Discontinued operations are generally reported in a separate income statement category for the gain or loss from **disposal of a component of a business**. In addition, the **results of operations of a component that has been or will be disposed of** are also reported separately from continuing operations. The effects of discontinued operations are shown net of tax as a separate category, after continuing operations but before extraordinary items.[15]

To illustrate, Multiplex Products, Inc., a highly diversified company, decides to discontinue its electronics division. During the current year, the electronics division lost $300,000 (net of tax) and was sold at the end of the year at a loss of $500,000 (net of tax). The information is shown on the current year's income statement as follows.

Income from continuing operations		$20,000,000
Discontinued operations		
Loss from operation of discontinued electronics division (net of tax)	$300,000	
Loss from disposal of electronics division (net of tax)	500,000	800,000
Net income		$19,200,000

Illustration 5-6
Income Statement
Presentation of
Discontinued Operations

Note that the phrase **"Income from continuing operations"** is used only when gains or losses on discontinued operations occur.

Extraordinary Items

Extraordinary items are defined as nonrecurring **material** items that differ significantly from the entity's typical business activities. The criteria for extraordinary items are as follows.

> Extraordinary items are events and transactions that are distinguished by their unusual nature **and** by the infrequency of their occurrence. **Both** of the following criteria must be met to classify an event or transaction as an extraordinary item:
>
> (a) **Unusual Nature.** The underlying event or transaction should possess a high degree of abnormality and be of a type clearly unrelated to, or only incidentally related to, the ordinary and typical activities of the entity, taking into account the environment in which the entity operates.
>
> (b) **Infrequency of Occurrence.** The underlying event or transaction should be of a type that would not reasonably be expected to recur in the foreseeable future, taking into account the environment in which the entity operates.[16]

---

[15]"Accounting for the Impairment or Disposal of Long-Lived Assets," *Statement of Financial Accounting Standards No. 144* (Norwalk, Conn.: FASB, 2001), par. 4. This recent standard requires discontinued operation reporting, even though the assets disposed of (i.e., component of the business) do not meet the definition of a business segment.

[16]"Reporting the Results of Operations," *Opinions of the Accounting Principles Board No. 30* (New York: AICPA, 1973), par. 20.

For further clarification, the APB specified that the following gains and losses are **not extraordinary items**.

(a) Write-down or write-off of receivables, inventories, equipment leased to others, deferred research and development costs, or other intangible assets.

(b) Gains or losses from exchange or translation of foreign currencies, including those relating to major devaluations and revaluations.

(c) Gains or losses on disposal of a component of an entity.

(d) Other gains or losses from sale or abandonment of property, plant, or equipment used in the business.

(e) Effects of a strike, including those against competitors and major suppliers.

(f) Adjustment of accruals on long-term contracts.[17]

The items listed above are not considered extraordinary "because they are usual in nature and may be expected to recur as a consequence of customary and continuing business activities."

Only rarely does an event or transaction clearly meet the criteria for an extraordinary item.[18] For example, gains or losses such as (a) and (d) above would be classified as extraordinary if they are a **direct result of a major casualty** (such as an earthquake), **an expropriation**, or **a prohibition under a newly enacted law or regulation**. Such circumstances would clearly meet the criteria of unusual and infrequent. A good example of an extraordinary item is the approximately $36 million loss incurred by **Weyerhaeuser Company** (forest and lumber) as a result of volcanic activity at Mount St. Helens. Standing timber, logs, buildings, equipment, and transportation systems covering 68,000 acres were destroyed by the volcanic eruption.

INTERNATIONAL INSIGHT

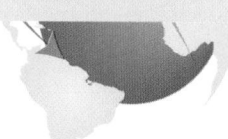

Classification of items as extraordinary differs across nations. Even in countries in which the criteria for identifying extraordinary items are similar, they are not interpreted identically. Thus, what is extraordinary in the U.S. is not necessarily extraordinary elsewhere.

In determining whether an item is extraordinary, **the environment in which the entity operates is of primary importance**. The environment includes such factors as industry characteristics, geographic location, and the nature and extent of governmental regulations. Thus, extraordinary item treatment is accorded the loss from hail damages to a tobacco grower's crops because severe damage from hailstorms in its locality is rare. On the other hand, frost damage to a citrus grower's crop in Florida does not qualify as extraordinary because frost damage is normally experienced every three or four years. In this environment, the criterion of infrequency is not met.

Similarly, when a company sells the only significant security investment it has ever owned, the gain or loss meets the criteria of an extraordinary item. Another company, however, that has a portfolio of securities acquired for investment purposes would not have an extraordinary item. Sale of such securities would be considered part of its ordinary and typical activities.

There are **exceptions** to the general rules provided above. The disposal of a component of an entity at a gain or loss [item (c) above], which is not an extraordinary item, requires special accounting treatment.[19]

---

[17]Ibid., par. 23, as amended by "Accounting for the Impairment or Disposal of Long-lived Assets," *Statement of Financial Accounting Standards No. 144* (Norwalk, Conn.: FASB, 2001).

[18]*Accounting Trends and Techniques—2001* (New York: AICPA) indicates that just 55 of the 600 companies surveyed reported an extraordinary item.

[19]Debt extinguishments had been the most common reason for companies reporting extraordinary items. In a recent four-year period, just 11 percent of surveyed companies reported an extraordinary item; over 90 percent of these were related to debt extinguishments (*Accounting Trends and Techniques—2001*, New York: AICPA). Recently the FASB eliminated extraordinary item treatment for these gains and losses ("Rescission of FASB Statements No. 4, 44, and 64 and Technical Corrections," *Statement of Financial Accounting Standards No. 145* (Norwalk, Conn.: FASB, 2002). Thus, reporting an extraordinary item is likely to become an even more rare event in the future.

In addition, considerable judgment must be exercised in determining whether an item should be reported as extraordinary. For example, some paper companies have had their forest lands condemned by the government for state or national parks or forests. Is such an event extraordinary, or is it part of normal operations? Such determination is not easy; much depends on the frequency of previous condemnations, the expectation of future condemnations, materiality, and the like.[20]

EXTRAORDINARY TIMES

WHAT DO THE NUMBERS MEAN?

No recent event better illustrates the difficulties of determining whether a transaction meets the definition of extraordinary than the financial impacts of the terrorist attacks on the World Trade Center on September 11, 2001. To many, this event, which resulted in the tragic loss of lives, jobs, and in some cases, entire businesses, clearly meets the criteria for unusual and infrequent. For example, in the wake of the terrorist attacks that destroyed the World Trade Center and turned much of lower Manhattan including Wall Street into a war zone, airlines, insurance companies, and other businesses recorded major losses due to property damage, business disruption, and suspension of airline travel and of securities trading. But, to the surprise of many, extraordinary item reporting was not permitted for losses arising from the terrorist attacks.

The reason? After much deliberation, the Emerging Issues Task Force (EITF) of the FASB decided that measurement of the possible loss was too difficult. Take the airline industry as an example: What portion of the airlines' losses after September 11 was related to the terrorist attack, and what portion was due to the ongoing recession? There also was concern that some companies would use the attacks as a reason for reporting as extraordinary some losses that had little direct relationship to the attacks. For example, shortly after the attacks, energy company **AES** and shoe retailer **Footstar**, who both were experiencing profit pressure before 9-11, put some of the blame for their poor performance on the attacks.

Source: J. Creswell, "Bad News Bearers Shift the Blame," *Fortune* (October 15, 2001), p. 44.

Extraordinary items are to be shown net of taxes in a separate section in the income statement, usually just before net income. After listing the usual revenues, costs and expenses, and income taxes, the remainder of the statement shows the following.

Income before extraordinary items
Extraordinary items (less applicable income tax of $_____)
Net income

Illustration 5-7
Income Statement Placement of Extraordinary Items

For example, the reporting of an extraordinary loss for **Keystone Consolidated Industries, Inc.** is shown in Illustration 5-8 on page 186.

Unusual Gains and Losses

Because of the restrictive criteria for extraordinary items, financial statement users must carefully examine the financial statements for items that are **unusual or infrequent but**

---

[20]It is often difficult to determine what is extraordinary, because assessing the materiality of individual items requires judgment. However, in making materiality judgments, extraordinary items should be considered individually, and not in the aggregate. "Reporting the Results of Operations," op. cit., par. 24.

Illustration 5-8
Income Statement
Presentation of
Extraordinary Items

KEYSTONE CONSOLIDATED INDUSTRIES, INC.

Income before extraordinary item	$11,638,000
Extraordinary item—flood loss (Note E)	1,216,000
Net income	$10,422,000

Note E: Extraordinary Item. The Keystone Steel and Wire Division's Steel Works experienced a flash flood on June 22. The extraordinary item represents the estimated cost, net of related income taxes of $1,279,000, to restore the steel works to full operation.

not both. As indicated earlier, items such as write-downs of inventories and transaction gains and losses from fluctuation of foreign exchange are not considered extraordinary items. Thus, these items are sometimes shown with the normal, recurring revenues, costs, and expenses. If they are not material in amount, they are combined with other items in the income statement. If they are material, they must be disclosed separately, but are shown **above** "Income (loss) before extraordinary items."

For example, **Pepsico, Inc.** presented an unusual charge in the following manner in its income statement.

Illustration 5-9
Income Statement
Presentation of Unusual
Charges

PEPSICO

PEPSICO, INC.
(in millions)

Net sales	$20,917
Costs and expenses, net	
Cost of sales	8,525
Selling, general, and administrative expenses	9,241
Amortization of intangible assets	199
Unusual items (Note 2)	290
Operating income	$ 2,662

Note 2 (Restructuring Charge)

Dispose and write down assets	$183
Improve productivity	94
Strengthen the international bottler structure	13
Net loss	$290

The net charge to strengthen the international bottler structure includes proceeds of $87 million associated with a settlement related to a previous Venezuelan bottler agreement, which were partially offset by related costs.

Restructuring charges, like the one reported by Pepsico, have been common in recent years. A **restructuring charge** relates to a major reorganization of company affairs, such as costs associated with employee layoffs, plant closing costs, write-offs of assets, and so on. There has been a tendency to **report unusual items in a separate section just above "Income from operations before income taxes" and "Extraordinary items,"** especially when there are multiple unusual items. A restructuring charge should not be reported as an extraordinary item, because these write-offs are considered part of a company's ordinary and typical activities.

For example, when **General Electric Company** experienced multiple unusual items in one year, it reported them in a separate "Unusual items" section of the income statement below "Income before unusual items and income taxes." When a multiple-step income statement is being prepared for homework purposes, unusual gains and losses should be reported in the "Other revenues and gains" or "Other expenses and losses" section unless you are instructed to prepare a separate unusual items section.[21]

In dealing with events that are either unusual or nonrecurring but not both, the profession attempted to prevent a practice that many believed was misleading. Companies often reported such transactions on a net-of-tax basis and prominently displayed the earnings per share effect of these items. Although not captioned extraordinary items, they are presented in the same manner. Some had referred to these as "first cousins" to extraordinary items. As a consequence, the Board specifically **prohibited a net-of-tax treatment for such items**, to ensure that users of financial statements can easily differentiate extraordinary items—which are reported net of tax—from material items that are unusual or infrequent, but not both.

Changes in Accounting Principle

Changes in accounting occur frequently in practice, because important events or conditions may be in dispute or uncertain at the statement date. One type of accounting change, therefore, comprises the normal recurring corrections and adjustments that are made by every business enterprise. Another accounting change results when an accounting principle is adopted that is different from the one previously used. Changes in accounting principle would include a change in the method of inventory pricing from FIFO to average cost or a change in depreciation from the double-declining to the straight-line method.[22]

Changes in accounting principle are recognized by including the cumulative effect as of the beginning of the year, net of tax in the current year's income statement. This amount is based on a retroactive computation of changing to a new accounting principle. **The effect on net income of adopting the new accounting principle should be disclosed as a separate item following extraordinary items in the income statement.**

To illustrate, Gaubert Inc. decided in March 2004 to change from an accelerated method of computing depreciation on its plant assets to the straight-line method. The assets originally cost $100,000 in 2002 and have a service life of four years. The data assumed for this illustration are as shown in Illustration 5-10.

UNDERLYING CONCEPTS

Companies can change principles, but it must be demonstrated that the newly adopted principle is preferable to the old one. Such changes mean that consistency from period to period is lost.

Year	Accelerated Depreciation	Straight-Line Depreciation	Excess of Accelerated over Straight-Line Method
2002	$40,000	$25,000	$15,000
2003	30,000	25,000	5,000
Total			$20,000

Illustration 5-10
Calculation of a Change in Accounting Principle

[21]Many companies are reporting "one-time items." However, some companies have taken restructuring charges practically every year. **Citicorp** (now **Citigroup**) took restructuring charges six years in a row, between 1988 and 1993; **Eastman Kodak Co.** did so five out of six years in 1989 to 1994. Recent research on the market reaction to income containing "one-time" items indicates that the market discounts the earnings of companies that report a series of "nonrecurring" items. Such evidence supports the contention that these elements reduce the quality of earnings. J. Elliott and D. Hanna, "Repeated Accounting Write-offs and the Information Content of Earnings," *Journal of Accounting Research* (Supplement, 1996).

[22]"Accounting Changes," *Opinions of the Accounting Principles Board No. 20* (New York: AICPA, 1971), par. 18. In Chapter 17, we examine in greater detail the problems related to accounting changes.

The information presented in the 2004 financial statements is shown in Illustration 5-11. (The tax rate was 30 percent.)

Income before extraordinary item and cumulative effect of a change in accounting principle	$120,000
Extraordinary item—casualty loss (net of $12,000 tax)	(28,000)
Cumulative effect on prior years of retroactive application of new depreciation method (net of $6,000 tax)	14,000
Net income	$106,000

Changes in Estimates

Estimates are inherent in the accounting process. Estimates are made, for example, of useful lives and salvage values of depreciable assets, of uncollectible receivables, of inventory obsolescence, and of the number of periods expected to benefit from a particular expenditure. Not infrequently, as time passes, as circumstances change, or as additional information is obtained, even estimates originally made in good faith must be changed. Such **changes in estimates** are accounted for in the period of change if they affect only that period, or in the period of change and future periods if the change affects both.

To illustrate a change in estimate that affects only the period of change, assume that DuPage Materials Corp. has consistently estimated its bad debt expense at 1 percent of credit sales. In 2003, however, DuPage's controller determines that the estimate of bad debts for the current year's credit sales must be revised upward to 2 percent, or double the prior years' percentage. Using 2 percent results in a bad debt charge of $240,000, or double the amount using the 1 percent estimate for prior years. The 2 percent rate is necessary to reduce accounts receivable to net realizable value. The provision is recorded at December 31, 2003, as follows.

Bad Debt Expense	240,000	
Allowance for Doubtful Accounts		240,000

UNDERLYING CONCEPTS

The AICPA Special Committee on Financial Reporting indicates a company's core activities—usual and recurring events—provide the best historical data from which users determine trends and relationships and make their predictions about the future. Therefore, the effects of core and non-core activities should be separately displayed.

The entire change in estimate is included in 2003 income because no future periods are affected by the change. **Changes in estimate are not handled retroactively**. That is, they are not carried back to adjust prior years. (Changes in estimate that affect both the current and future periods are examined in greater detail in Chapter 17.) **Changes in estimate are not considered errors (prior period adjustments) or extraordinary items.**

Summary of Irregular Items

The public accounting profession now tends to accept a modified all-inclusive income concept instead of the current operating performance concept. Except for a couple of items (discussed later in this chapter) that are charged or credited directly to retained earnings, all other irregular gains or losses or nonrecurring items are closed to Income Summary and are included in the income statement. Of these, **discontinued operations of a component** of a business is classified as a separate item in the income statement after continuing operations. The **unusual, material, nonrecurring items** that are significantly different from the typical or customary business activities are shown in a separate section for **"Extraordinary items"** below discontinued operations. Other items of a material amount that are of an **unusual or nonrecurring** nature and are **not consid-**

ered extraordinary are separately disclosed. In addition, the cumulative adjustment that occurs when a change in accounting principles develops is disclosed as a separate item just before net income.

Because of the numerous intermediate income figures that are created by the reporting of these irregular items, careful evaluation of earnings information reported by the financial press is needed. Illustration 5-12 summarizes the basic concepts previously discussed. Although the chart is simplified, it provides a useful framework for determining the treatment of special items affecting the income statement.

Illustration 5-12

Summary of Irregular Items in the Income Statement

Type of Situation[a]	Criteria	Examples	Placement on Financial Statements
Discontinued operations	Disposal of a component of a business for which the operations and cash flows can be clearly distinguished from the rest of the company's operations.	Sale by diversified company of major division that represents only activities in electronics industry. Food distributor that sells wholesale to supermarket chains and through fast-food restaurants decides to discontinue the division that sells to one of two classes of customers.	Shown in separate section of the income statement after continuing operations but before extraordinary items. (Shown net of tax.)
Extraordinary items	Material, and both unusual and infrequent (nonrecurring).	Gains or losses resulting from casualties, an expropriation, or a prohibition under a new law.	Separate section in the income statement entitled "Extraordinary items." (Shown net of tax.)
Unusual gains or losses, not considered extraordinary	Material; character typical of the customary business activities; unusual or infrequent but not both.	Write-downs of receivables, inventories; adjustments of accrued contract prices; gains or losses from fluctuations of foreign exchange; gains or losses from sales of assets used in business.	Separate section in income statement above income before extraordinary items. Often reported in "Other revenues and gains" or "Other expenses and losses" section. (Not shown net of tax.)
Changes in principle[b]	Change from one generally accepted principle to another.	Change in the basis of inventory pricing from FIFO to average cost; change in the method of depreciation from accelerated to straight-line.	Cumulative effect of the change is reflected in the income statement between the captions "Extraordinary items" and "Net income." (Shown net of tax.)
Changes in estimates	Normal, recurring corrections and adjustments.	Changes in the realizability of receivables and inventories; changes in estimated lives of equipment, intangible assets; changes in estimated liability for warranty costs, income taxes, and salary payments.	Change in income statement only in the account affected. (Not shown net of tax.)

[a]This summary provides only the general rules to be followed in accounting for the various situations described above. Exceptions do exist in some of these situations.

[b]The general rule per *APB Opinion No. 20* is to use the cumulative effect approach. However, recent FASB pronouncements require or permit the retroactive method whenever a new standard is adopted for the first time.

SPECIAL REPORTING ISSUES

Intraperiod Tax Allocation

OBJECTIVE **5**
Explain intraperiod tax allocation.

Intraperiod Tax Allocation

We noted that certain irregular items are shown on the income statement net of tax. Many believe that the resulting income tax effect should be directly associated with that event or item. In other words, the tax expense for the year should be related, where possible, to **specific items** on the income statement to provide a more informative disclosure to statement users. This procedure is called **intraperiod tax allocation**, that is, allocation within a period. Its main purpose is to relate the income tax expense of the fiscal period to the items that affect the amount of the tax provisions. Intraperiod tax allocation is used for the following items: (1) income from continuing operations, (2) discontinued operations, (3) extraordinary items, and (4) changes in accounting principle. The general concept is **"let the tax follow the income."**

The income tax expense attributable to "income from continuing operations" is computed by finding the income tax expense related to revenue and to expense transactions used in determining this income. In this tax computation, no effect is given to the tax consequences of the items excluded from the determination of "income from continuing operations." A separate tax effect is then associated with each irregular item.

Extraordinary Gains

In applying the concept of intraperiod tax allocation, assume that Schindler Co. has income before income tax and extraordinary item of $250,000 and an extraordinary gain from the sale of a single stock investment of $100,000. If the income tax rate is assumed to be 30 percent, the following information is presented on the income statement.

Illustration 5-13
Intraperiod Tax Allocation, Extraordinary Gain

Income before income tax and extraordinary item		$250,000
Income tax		75,000
Income before extraordinary item		175,000
Extraordinary gain—sale of investment	$100,000	
Less: Applicable income tax	30,000	70,000
Net income		$245,000

The income tax of $75,000 ($250,000 × 30%) attributable to "Income before income tax and extraordinary item" is determined from revenue and expense transactions related to this income. In this income tax computation, the tax consequences of items excluded from the determination of "Income before income tax and extraordinary item" are not considered. The "Extraordinary gain—sale of investment" then shows a separate tax effect of $30,000.

Extraordinary Losses

To illustrate the reporting of an extraordinary loss, assume that Schindler Co. has income before income tax and extraordinary item of $250,000 and an extraordinary loss from a major casualty of $100,000. Assuming a 30 percent tax rate, the presentation of income tax on the income statement would be as shown in Illustration 5-14. In this case, the loss provides a positive tax benefit of $30,000 and, therefore, is subtracted from the $100,000 loss.

Special Reporting Issues ◆ 191

Income before income tax and extraordinary item		$250,000
Income tax		75,000
Income before extraordinary item		175,000
Extraordinary item—loss from casualty	$100,000	
Less: Applicable income tax reduction	30,000	70,000
Net income		$105,000

Illustration 5-14
Intraperiod Tax
Allocation, Extraordinary
Loss

An extraordinary item may be reported "net of tax" with note disclosure, as illustrated below.

Income before income tax and extraordinary item	$250,000
Income tax	75,000
Income before extraordinary item	175,000
Extraordinary item, less applicable income tax reduction (Note 1)	70,000
Net income	$105,000

Note 1: During the year the Company suffered a major casualty loss of $70,000, net of applicable income tax reduction of $30,000.

Illustration 5-15
Note Disclosure of
Intraperiod Tax Allocation

Earnings per Share

The results of a company's operations are customarily summed up in one important figure: net income. As if this condensation were not enough of a simplification, the financial world has widely accepted an even more distilled and compact figure as its most significant business indicator—**earnings per share** (EPS).

The computation of earnings per share is usually straightforward. **Net income minus preferred dividends (income available to common stockholders) is divided by the weighted average of common shares outstanding to arrive at earnings per share.**[23] To illustrate, assume that Lancer, Inc. reports net income of $350,000 and declares and pays preferred dividends of $50,000 for the year. The weighted average number of common shares outstanding during the year is 100,000 shares. Earnings per share is $3.00, as computed in Illustration 5-16.

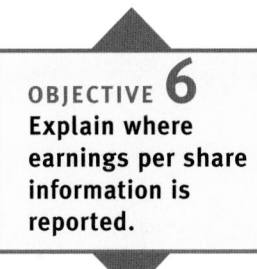

OBJECTIVE 6
Explain where earnings per share information is reported.

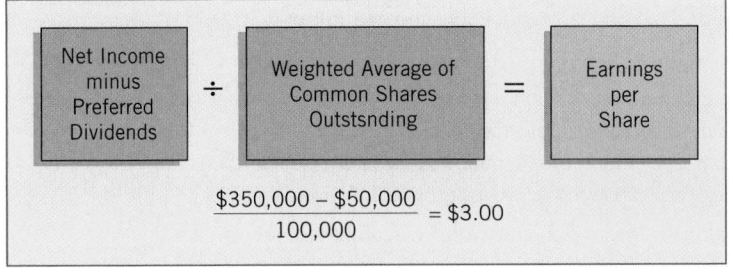

Illustration 5-16
Equation Illustrating
Computation of Earnings
per Share

Note that the EPS figure measures the number of dollars earned by each share of common stock—not the dollar amount paid to stockholders in the form of dividends.

[23]In the calculation of earnings per share, preferred dividends are deducted from net income if declared or if cumulative though not declared.

"Net income per share" or "earnings per share" is a ratio commonly used in prospectuses, proxy material, and annual reports to stockholders. It is also highlighted in the financial press, by statistical services like Standard & Poor's, and by Wall Street securities analysts. Because of its importance, **earnings per share is required to be disclosed on the face of the income statement**. A company that reports a discontinued operation, an extraordinary item, or the cumulative effect of a change in accounting principle, must report per share amounts for these line items either on the face of the income statement or in the notes to the financial statements.[24]

To illustrate the income statement order of presentation and the earnings per share data, we present an income statement for Poquito Industries Inc. in Illustration 5-17. Notice the order in which data are shown. In addition, per share information is shown

Illustration 5-17

Income Statement

POQUITO INDUSTRIES INC. INCOME STATEMENT FOR THE YEAR ENDED DECEMBER 31, 2003		
Sales revenue		$1,480,000
Cost of goods sold		600,000
Gross profit		880,000
Selling and administrative expenses		320,000
Income from operations		560,000
Other revenues and gains		
Interest revenue		10,000
Other expenses and losses		
Loss on disposal of part of Textile Division	$ (5,000)	
Unusual charge—loss on sale of investments	(45,000)	(50,000)
Income from continuing operations before income tax		520,000
Income tax		208,000
Income from continuing operations		312,000
Discontinued operations		
Income from operations of Pizza Division, less applicable income tax of $24,800	54,000	
Loss on disposal of Pizza Division, less applicable income tax of $41,000	(90,000)	(36,000)
Income before extraordinary item and cumulative effect of accounting change		276,000
Extraordinary item—loss from earthquake, less applicable income tax of $23,000		(45,000)
Cumulative effect on prior years of retroactive application of new depreciation method, less applicable income tax of $30,900		(60,000)
Net income		$ 171,000
Per share of common stock		
Income from continuing operations		$3.12
Income from operations of discontinued division, net of tax		0.54
Loss on disposal of discontinued operation, net of tax		(0.90)
Income before extraordinary item and cumulative effect		2.76
Extraordinary loss, net of tax		(0.45)
Cumulative effect of change in accounting principle, net of tax		(0.60)
Net income		$1.71

[24]"Earnings Per Share," *Statement of Financial Accounting Standards No. 128* (Norwalk, Conn.: FASB, 1996).

at the bottom. Assume that the company had 100,000 shares outstanding for the entire year. The Poquito Industries Inc. income statement, in Illustration 5-17, is highly condensed. Items such as "Unusual charge," "Discontinued operations," "Extraordinary item," and the "Change in accounting principle" would have to be described fully and appropriately in the statement or related notes.

Many corporations have simple capital structures that include only common stock. For these companies, a presentation such as "earnings per common share" is appropriate on the income statement. In many instances, however, companies' earnings per share are subject to dilution (reduction) in the future because existing contingencies permit the issuance of additional common shares.[25]

In summary, the simplicity and availability of figures for per share earnings lead inevitably to their widespread use. Because of the undue importance that the public, even the well-informed public, attaches to earnings per share, the EPS figure must be made as meaningful as possible.

Retained Earnings Statement

Net income increases retained earnings, and a net loss decreases retained earnings. Both cash and stock dividends decrease retained earnings. Prior period adjustments may either increase or decrease retained earnings. A **prior period adjustment** is a correction of an error in the financial statements of a prior period. Prior period adjustments (net of tax) are charged or credited to the opening balance of retained earnings, and thus excluded from the determination of net income for the current period.

Information related to retained earnings may be shown in different ways. For example, some companies prepare a separate retained earnings statement, as shown in Illustration 5-18.

OBJECTIVE 7
Prepare a retained earnings statement.

TIGER WOODS INC. RETAINED EARNINGS STATEMENT FOR THE YEAR ENDED DECEMBER 31, 2004		
Balance, January 1, as reported		$1,050,000
Correction for understatement of net income in prior period (inventory error)		50,000
Balance, January 1, as adjusted		1,100,000
Add: Net income		360,000
		1,460,000
Less: Cash dividends	$100,000	
Stock dividends	200,000	300,000
Balance, December 31		$1,160,000

Illustration 5-18
Retained Earnings Statement

The reconciliation of the beginning to the ending balance in retained earnings provides information about why net assets increased or decreased during the year. The association of dividend distributions with net income for the period indicates what management is doing with earnings: It may be "plowing back" into the business part or all of the earnings, distributing all current income, or distributing current income plus the accumulated earnings of prior years.

Restrictions of Retained Earnings

Retained earnings is often restricted in accordance with contractual requirements, board of directors' policy, or the apparent necessity of the moment. The amounts of retained

---

[25]Ibid. The computational problems involved in accounting for these dilutive securities in earnings per share computations are discussed in Chapter 17.

earnings restricted are generally disclosed in the notes to the financial statements. In some cases, the amount of retained earnings restricted is transferred to **Appropriated Retained Earnings**. The retained earnings section may therefore report two separate amounts—(1) retained earnings free (unrestricted) and (2) retained earnings appropriated (restricted). The total of these two amounts equals the total retained earnings.[26]

Comprehensive Income

As indicated earlier, the all-inclusive income concept is used in determining financial performance for a period of time. Under this concept, all revenues, expenses, and gains and losses recognized during the period are included in income. However, over time, specific exceptions to this general concept have developed. Certain items now bypass income and are reported directly in equity.

An example of one of these items is unrealized gains and losses on available-for-sale securities.[27] Why are these gains and losses on available-for-sale securities excluded from net income? Because disclosing them separately (1) reduces the volatility of net income due to fluctuations in fair value, yet (2) informs the financial statement user of the gain or loss that would be incurred if the securities were sold at fair value.

Items that bypass the income statement are included under the concept of comprehensive income. **Comprehensive income** includes all changes in equity during a period except those resulting from investments by owners and distributions to owners. Comprehensive income, therefore, includes all revenues and gains, expenses and losses reported in net income, and in addition it includes gains and losses that bypass net income but affect stockholders' equity. These items that bypass the income statement are referred to as **other comprehensive income**.

OBJECTIVE **8**
Explain how other comprehensive income is reported.

The FASB decided that the components of other comprehensive income must be displayed in one of three ways: **(1) a second income statement; (2) a combined income statement of comprehensive income; or (3) as a part of the statement of stockholders' equity.**[28] Regardless of the format used, net income must be added to other comprehensive income to arrive at comprehensive income. Earnings per share information related to comprehensive income is not required.

To illustrate these presentation formats, assume that V. Gill Inc. reports the following information for 2004: sales revenue $800,000, cost of goods sold $600,000, operating expenses $90,000, and an unrealized holding gain on available-for-sale securities of $30,000, net of tax.[29]

---

[26]*Accounting Trends and Techniques—2001* (New York: AICPA) indicates that most companies (577 of 600 surveyed) present changes in retained earnings either within the statement of stockholders' equity (534 firms) or in a separate statement of retained earnings. Only 10 of the 600 companies prepare a combined statement of income and retained earnings.

[27]Available-for-sale securities are further discussed in Chapter 13. Other examples of other comprehensive items are translation gains and losses on foreign currency, excess of additional pension liability over unrecognized prior service cost, and unrealized gains and losses on certain hedging transactions.

[28]"Reporting Comprehensive Income," *Statement of Financial Accounting Standards No. 130* (Norwalk, Conn.: FASB, June 1997). *Accounting Trends and Techniques—2001* (New York: AICPA) indicates that for the 600 companies surveyed, 519 report comprehensive income. Most companies (422 of 497) include comprehensive income as part of the statement of stockholders' equity.

[29]A company is required to display the components of other comprehensive income either (1) net of related tax effects or (2) before related tax effects with one amount shown for the aggregate amount of tax related to the total amount of other comprehensive income. Under either alternative, each component of other comprehensive income must be shown, net of related taxes either in the face of the statement or in the notes.

Second Income Statement

The two-income statement format is shown in Illustration 5-19 below. Reporting comprehensive income in a separate statement indicates that the gains and losses identified as other comprehensive income have the same status as traditional gains and losses. In addition, the relationship of the traditional income statement to the comprehensive income statement is apparent because net income is the starting point in the comprehensive income statement.

V. GILL INC.	
INCOME STATEMENT	
FOR THE YEAR ENDED DECEMBER 31, 2004	
Sales revenue	$800,000
Cost of goods sold	600,000
Gross profit	200,000
Operating expenses	90,000
Net income	$110,000

V. GILL INC.	
COMPREHENSIVE INCOME STATEMENT	
FOR THE YEAR ENDED DECEMBER 31, 2004	
Net income	$110,000
Other comprehensive income	
Unrealized holding gain, net of tax	30,000
Comprehensive income	$140,000

Illustration 5-19
Two-Statement Format:
Comprehensive Income

Combined Income Statement

The second approach provides a combined statement of comprehensive income in which the traditional net income would be a subtotal, with total comprehensive income shown as a final total. The combined statement has the advantage of not requiring the creation of a new financial statement. However, burying net income in a subtotal on the statement is a disadvantage.

Statement of Stockholders' Equity

A third approach is to report other comprehensive income items in a **statement of stockholders' equity** (often referred to as statement of changes in stockholders' equity). This statement reports the changes in each stockholder's equity account and in total stockholders' equity during the year. The statement of stockholders' equity is often **prepared in columnar form** with columns for each account and for total stockholders' equity.

To illustrate its presentation, assume the same information above related to V. Gill Inc. and that the company had the following stockholder equity account balances at the beginning of 2004: Common Stock $300,000; Retained Earnings $50,000; and Accumulated Other Comprehensive Income $60,000. No changes in the Common Stock account occurred during the year. A statement of stockholders' equity for V. Gill Inc. is shown in Illustration 5-20 on the next page.

Most companies use the statement of stockholders' equity approach to provide information related to the components of other comprehensive income. Because many companies already provide a statement of stockholders' equity, adding additional columns to display information related to comprehensive income is not costly.

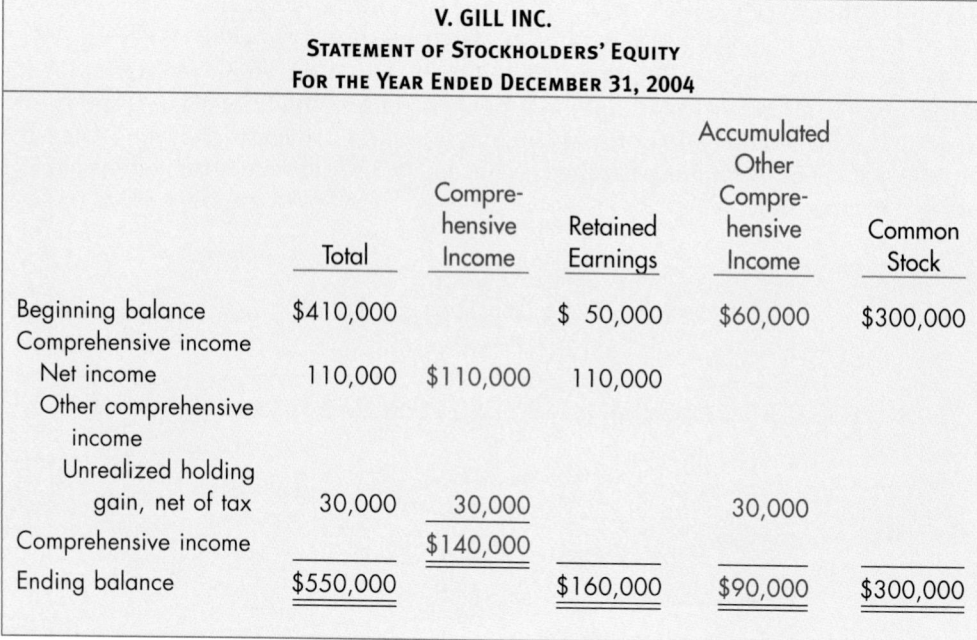

	Total	Compre-hensive Income	Retained Earnings	Accumulated Other Compre-hensive Income	Common Stock
Beginning balance	$410,000		$ 50,000	$60,000	$300,000
Comprehensive income					
Net income	110,000	$110,000	110,000		
Other comprehensive income					
Unrealized holding gain, net of tax	30,000	30,000		30,000	
Comprehensive income		$140,000			
Ending balance	$550,000		$160,000	$90,000	$300,000

V. GILL INC.
STATEMENT OF STOCKHOLDERS' EQUITY
FOR THE YEAR ENDED DECEMBER 31, 2004

*Examples of Comprehensive
Income Reporting*

Balance Sheet Presentation

Regardless of the display format used, the **accumulated other comprehensive income** of $90,000 is reported in the stockholders' equity section of the balance sheet of V. Gill Inc. as follows.

V. GILL INC.
BALANCE SHEET
AS OF DECEMBER 31, 2004
(STOCKHOLDERS' EQUITY SECTION)

Stockholders' equity	
Common stock	$300,000
Retained earnings	160,000
Accumulated other comprehensive income	90,000
Total stockholders' equity	$550,000

By providing information on the components of comprehensive income as well as total accumulated other comprehensive income, the firm communicates information about all changes in net assets.[30] With this information, users will be better able to understand the quality of the company's earnings. This information should help users predict the amounts, timing, and uncertainty of future cash flows.

SUMMARY OF LEARNING OBJECTIVES

❶ Identify the uses and limitations of an income statement. The income statement provides investors and creditors with information that helps them predict the amounts, timing, and uncertainty of future cash flows. Also, the income statement helps users

---

[30]Note that prior period adjustments and the cumulative effect of changes in accounting principle are not considered other comprehensive income items.

determine the risk (level of uncertainty) of not achieving particular cash flows. The limitations of an income statement are: (1) The statement does not include many items that contribute to general growth and well-being of an enterprise. (2) Income numbers are often affected by the accounting methods used. (3) Income measures are subject to estimates.

The *transaction approach* focuses on the activities that have occurred during a given period. Instead of presenting only a net change, it discloses the components of the change. The transaction approach to income measurement requires the use of revenue, expense, loss, and gain accounts.

② Prepare a single-step income statement. In a single-step income statement, just two groupings exist: revenues and expenses. Expenses are deducted from revenues to arrive at net income or loss—a single subtraction. Frequently, income tax is reported separately as the last item before net income to indicate its relationship to income before income tax.

③ Prepare a multiple-step income statement. A multiple-step income statement shows two further classifications: (1) a separation of operating results from those obtained through the subordinate or nonoperating activities of the company; and (2) a classification of expenses by functions, such as merchandising or manufacturing, selling, and administration.

④ Explain how irregular items are reported. Irregular gains or losses or nonrecurring items are generally closed to Income Summary and are included in the income statement. These are treated in the income statement as follows: (1) Discontinued operation of a component of a business is classified as a separate item, after continuing operations. (2) The unusual, material, nonrecurring items that are significantly different from the customary business activities are shown in a separate section for extraordinary items, below discontinued operations. (3) Other items of a material amount that are of an unusual or nonrecurring nature and are not considered extraordinary are separately disclosed. (4) The cumulative adjustment that occurs when a change in accounting principles develops is disclosed as a separate item, just before net income.

⑤ Explain intraperiod tax allocation. The tax expense for the year should be related, where possible, to specific items on the income statement, to provide a more informative disclosure to statement users. This procedure is called intraperiod tax allocation, that is, allocation within a period. Its main purpose is to relate the income tax expense for the fiscal period to the following items that affect the amount of the tax provisions: (1) income from continuing operations, (2) discontinued operations, (3) extraordinary items, and (4) changes in accounting principle.

⑥ Explain where earnings per share information is reported. Because of the inherent dangers of focusing attention solely on earnings per share, the profession concluded that earnings per share must be disclosed on the face of the income statement. A company that reports a discontinued operation, an extraordinary item, or the cumulative effect of a change in accounting principle must report per share amounts for these line items either on the face of the income statement or in the notes to the financial statements.

⑦ Prepare a retained earnings statement. The retained earnings statement should disclose net income (loss), dividends, prior period adjustments, and restrictions of retained earnings.

⑧ Explain how other comprehensive income is reported. The components of other comprehensive income are reported in a second statement, a combined income statement of comprehensive income, or in a statement of stockholders' equity.

KEY TERMS

accumulated other comprehensive income, *196*
all-inclusive approach, *181*
appropriated retained earnings, *194*
capital maintenance approach, *175*
changes in estimates, *188*
comprehensive income, *194*
current operating performance approach, *181*
discontinued operation, *182*
earnings management, *174*
earnings per share, *191*
extraordinary items, *183*
income statement, *172*
intraperiod tax allocation, *190*
irregular items, *182*
modified all-inclusive concept, *182*
multiple-step income statement, *177*
other comprehensive income, *194*
prior period adjustments, *193*
quality of earnings, *174*
single-step income statement, *176*
statement of stockholders' equity, *195*
transaction approach, *175*

REVIEW EXERCISE

Presented below are ten income statements items from Ritter Corporation for the year ended December 31, 2004.

Sales	$3,200,000
Cost of goods sold	1,650,000
Interest revenue	10,000
Loss from abandonment of plant assets	60,000
Gain from extinguishment of debt	100,000
Selling expenses	340,000
Administrative expenses	280,000
Effect of change from declining-balance to straight-line depreciation	50,000
Loss from earthquake (unusual and infrequent)	40,000
Gain on disposal of a component of Ritter's business	90,000

Instructions

Using the information above, prepare a condensed multiple-step income statement. Assume a tax rate of 30% and 100,000 shares of common stock outstanding during 2004.

SOLUTION TO REVIEW EXERCISE

RITTER CORPORATION
INCOME STATEMENT
FOR THE YEAR ENDED DECEMBER 31, 2004

Sales		$3,200,000
Cost of goods sold		1,650,000
Gross profit		1,550,000
Selling expenses	$340,000	
Administrative expenses	280,000	620,000
Income from operations		930,000
Other revenues and gains		
Interest revenue	10,000	
Gain on debt extinguishment	100,000	
Other expenses and losses		
Loss from plant abandonment	(60,000)	50,000
Income before income taxes		980,000
Income taxes (30%)		294,000
Income from continuing operations		686,000
Discontinued operations		
Gain from disposal of component of business	90,000	
Less: Applicable income tax	27,000	63,000
Income before extraordinary items and cumulative effect of a change in accounting principle		749,000
Extraordinary items		
Loss from earthquake	40,000	
Less: Applicable income tax	12,000	(28,000)

Cumulative effect on prior years of retroactive application of new depreciation method	50,000	
Less: Applicable income tax	15,000	35,000
Net income		$ 756,000

Per share of common stock	
Income from continuing operations	$6.86
Discontinued operations	0.63
Income before extraordinary items and cumulative effort of accounting change	7.49
Extraordinary item, loss from earthquake, net of tax	(0.28)
Change in accounting principle, net of tax	0.35
Net income	$7.56

QUESTIONS

1 What kinds of questions about future cash flows do investors and creditors attempt to answer with information in the income statement?

2 How can information based on past transactions be used to predict future cash flows?

3 Identify at least two situations in which important changes in value are not reported in the income statement.

4 Identify at least two situations in which application of different accounting methods or accounting estimates results in difficulties in comparing companies.

5 Explain the transaction approach to measuring income. Why is the transaction approach to income measurement preferable to other ways of measuring income?

6 What is earnings management?

7 How can earnings management affect the quality of earnings?

8 Why should caution be exercised in the use of the income figure derived in an income statement? What are the objectives of generally accepted accounting principles in their application to the income statement?

9 A *Wall Street Journal* article noted that **MicroStrategy** reported higher income than its competitors by using a more aggressive policy for recognizing revenue on future upgrades. Some contend that MicroStrategy's quality of earnings is low. What does the term"quality of earnings" mean?

10 What is the major distinction (a) between revenues and gains and (b) between expenses and losses?

11 What are the advantages and disadvantages of the single-step income statement?

12 What is the basis for distinguishing between operating and nonoperating items?

13 Distinguish between the all-inclusive income statement and the current operating performance income statement. According to present generally accepted accounting principles, which is recommended? Explain.

14 How should prior period adjustments be reported in the financial statements? Give an example of a prior period adjustment.

15 Discuss the appropriate treatment in the financial statements of each of the following.

   (a) An amount of $113,000 realized in excess of the cash surrender value of an insurance policy on the life of one of the founders of the company who died during the year.

   (b) A profit-sharing bonus to employees computed as a percentage of net income.

   (c) Additional depreciation on factory machinery because of an error in computing depreciation for the previous year.

   (d) Rent received from subletting a portion of the office space.

   (e) A patent infringement suit, brought 2 years ago against the company by another company, was settled this year by a cash payment of $725,000.

   (f) A reduction in the Allowance for Doubtful Accounts balance, because the account appears to be considerably in excess of the probable loss from uncollectible receivables.

16 Indicate where the following items would ordinarily appear on the financial statements of Allepo, Inc. for the year 2003.

   (a) The service life of certain equipment was changed from 8 to 5 years. If a 5-year life had been used previously, additional depreciation of $425,000 would have been charged.

(b) In 2003 a flood destroyed a warehouse that had a book value of $1,600,000. Floods are rare in this locality.

(c) In 2003 the company wrote off $1,000,000 of inventory that was considered obsolete.

(d) An income tax refund related to the 2000 tax year was received.

(e) In 2000, a supply warehouse with an expected useful life of 7 years was erroneously expensed.

(f) Allepo, Inc. changed its depreciation from double-declining to straight-line on machinery in 2003. The cumulative effect of the change was $925,000 (net of tax).

17 Give the section of a multiple-step income statement in which each of the following is shown.

(a) Loss on inventory write-down.

(b) Loss from strike.

(c) Bad debt expense.

(d) Loss on disposal of a component of the business.

(e) Gain on sale of machinery.

(f) Interest revenue.

(g) Depreciation expense.

(h) Material write-offs of notes receivable.

18 Barry Bonds Land Development, Inc. purchased land for $70,000 and spent $30,000 developing it. It then sold the land for $160,000. Tom Glavine Manufacturing purchased land for a future plant site for $100,000. Due to a change in plans, Glavine later sold the land for $160,000. Should these two companies report the land sales, both at gains of $60,000, in a similar manner?

19 You run into Rex Grossman at a party and begin discussing financial statements. Rex says, "I prefer the single-step income statement because the multiple-step format generally overstates income." How should you respond to Rex?

20 Federov Corporation has eight expense accounts in its general ledger which could be classified as selling expenses. Should Federov report these eight expenses separately in its income statement or simply report one total amount for selling expenses?

21 Jose DeLeon Investments reported an unusual gain from the sale of certain assets in its 2003 income statement. How does intraperiod tax allocation affect the reporting of this unusual gain?

22 What effect does intraperiod tax allocation have on reported net income?

23 Letterman Company computed earnings per share as follows.

$$\frac{\text{Net income}}{\text{Common shares outstanding at year end}}$$

Letterman has a simple capital structure. What possible errors might the company have made in the computation? Explain.

24 Maria Shriver Corporation reported 2003 earnings per share of $7.21. In 2004, Maria Shriver reported earnings per share as follows.

On income before extraordinary item	$6.40
On extraordinary item	1.88
On net income	$8.28

Is the increase in earnings per share from $7.21 to $8.28 a favorable trend?

25 What is meant by "tax allocation within a period"? What is the justification for such practice?

26 When does tax allocation within a period become necessary? How should this allocation be handled?

27 During 2003, Natsume Sozeki Company earned income of $1,000,000 before income taxes and realized a gain of $450,000 on a government-forced condemnation sale of a division plant facility. The income is subject to income taxation at the rate of 34%. The gain on the sale of the plant is taxed at 30%. Proper accounting suggests that the unusual gain be reported as an extraordinary item. Illustrate an appropriate presentation of these items in the income statement.

28 On January 30, 2003, a suit was filed against Pierogi Corporation under the Environmental Protection Act. On August 6, 2004, Pierogi Corporation agreed to settle the action and pay $920,000 in damages to certain current and former employees. How should this settlement be reported in the 2004 financial statements? Discuss.

29 Tiger Paper Company decided to close two small pulp mills in Conway, New Hampshire, and Corvallis, Oregon. Would these closings be reported in a separate section entitled "Discontinued operations after income from continuing operations"? Discuss.

30 What major types of items are reported in the retained earnings statement?

31 Generally accepted accounting principles usually require the use of accrual accounting to "fairly present" income. If the cash receipts and disbursements method of accounting will "clearly reflect" taxable income, why does this method not usually also "fairly present" income?

32 State some of the more serious problems encountered in seeking to achieve the ideal measurement of periodic net income. Explain what accountants do as a practical alternative.

33 What is meant by the terms components, elements, and items as they relate to the income statement? Why might items have to be disclosed in the income statement?

34 What are the three ways that other comprehensive income may be displayed (reported)?

35 How should the disposal of a component of a business be disclosed in the income statement?

BRIEF EXERCISES

BE5-1 Tim Allen Co. had sales revenue of $540,000 in 2003. Other items recorded during the year were:

Cost of goods sold	$320,000
Wage expense	120,000
Income tax expense	25,000
Increase in value of company reputation	15,000
Other operating expenses	10,000
Unrealized gain on value of patents	20,000

Prepare a single-step income statement for Allen for 2003. Allen has 100,000 shares of stock outstanding.

BE5-2 Turner Corporation had net sales of $2,400,000 and interest revenue of $31,000 during 2004. Expenses for 2004 were: cost of goods sold $1,250,000; administrative expenses $212,000; selling expenses $280,000; interest expense $45,000. Turner's tax rate is 30%. The corporation had 100,000 shares of common stock authorized and 70,000 shares issued and outstanding during 2004. Prepare a single-step income statement for the year ended December 31, 2004.

BE5-3 Using the information provided in BE5-2, prepare a condensed multiple-step income statement for Turner Corporation.

BE5-4 Green Day Corporation had income from continuing operations of $12,600,000 in 2004. During 2004, it disposed of its restaurant division at an after-tax loss of $189,000. Prior to disposal, the division operated at a loss of $315,000 (net of tax) in 2004. Green Day had 10,000,000 shares of common stock outstanding during 2004. Prepare a partial income statement for Green Day beginning with income from continuing operations.

BE5-5 Boyz II Men Corporation had income before income taxes for 2004 of $7,300,000. In addition, it suffered an unusual and infrequent pretax loss of $770,000 from a volcano eruption. The corporation's tax rate is 30%. Prepare a partial income statement for Boyz II Men beginning with income before income taxes. The corporation had 5,000,000 shares of common stock outstanding during 2004.

BE5-6 Shawn Bradley Company changed from straight-line depreciation to double-declining balance depreciation at the beginning of 2004. The plant assets originally cost $1,500,000 in 2002. Using straight-line depreciation, depreciation expense is $60,000 per year. Under the double-declining balance method, depreciation expense would be $120,000, $110,400, and $101,568 for 2002, 2003, and 2004. If Bradley's tax rate is 30%, by what amount would the cumulative effect of a change in accounting principle increase or decrease 2004 net income?

BE5-7 Jana Kingston Company has recorded bad debt expense in the past at a rate of $1\frac{1}{2}$% of net sales. In 2004, Kingston decides to increase its estimate to 2%. If the new rate had been used in prior years, cumulative bad debt expense would have been $380,000 instead of $285,000. In 2004, bad debt expense will be $120,000 instead of $90,000. If Kingston's tax rate is 30%, what amount should it report as the cumulative effect of changing the estimated bad debt rate?

BE5-8 In 2004, Kirby Puckett Corporation reported net income of $1,200,000. It declared and paid preferred stock dividends of $250,000. During 2004, Puckett had a weighted average of 190,000 common shares outstanding. Compute Puckett's 2004 earnings per share.

BE5-9 Lincoln Corporation has retained earnings of $675,000 at January 1, 2004. Net income during 2004 was $2,400,000, and cash dividends declared and paid during 2004 totaled $75,000. Prepare a retained earnings statement for the year ended December 31, 2004.

BE5-10 Using the information from BE5-9, prepare a retained earnings statement for the year ended December 31, 2004. Assume an error was discovered: land costing $80,000 (net of tax) was charged to repairs expense in 2001.

BE5-11 On January 1, 2003, Creative Works Inc. had cash and common stock of $60,000. At that date the company had no other asset, liability or equity balances. On January 2, 2003, it purchased for cash $20,000 of equity securities that it classified as available-for-sale. It received cash dividends of $3,000 during the year on these securities. In addition, it has an unrealized holding gain on these securities of $5,000 net of tax. Determine the following amounts for 2003: (a) net income; (b) comprehensive income; (c) other comprehensive income; and (d) accumulated other comprehensive income (end of 2003).

EXERCISES

E5-1 (Computation of Net Income) Presented below are changes in all the account balances of Fritz Reiner Furniture Co. during the current year, except for retained earnings.

	Increase (Decrease)		Increase (Decrease)
Cash	$ 79,000	Accounts Payable	$(51,000)
Accounts Receivable (net)	45,000	Bonds Payable	82,000
Inventory	127,000	Common Stock	125,000
Investments	(47,000)	Additional Paid-in Capital	13,000

Instructions

Compute the net income for the current year, assuming that there were no entries in the Retained Earnings account except for net income and a dividend declaration of $19,000 which was paid in the current year.

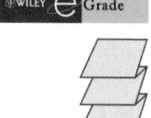

E5-2 (Income Statement Items) Presented below are certain account balances of Paczki Products Co.

Rental revenue	$ 6,500	Sales discounts	7,800
Interest expense	12,700	Selling expenses	99,400
Beginning retained earnings	114,400	Sales	390,000
Ending retained earnings	134,000	Income tax	31,000
Dividends revenue	71,000	Cost of goods sold	184,400
Sales returns	$ 12,400	Administrative expenses	82,500

Instructions

From the foregoing, compute the following: (a) total net revenue; (b) net income; (c) dividends declared during the current year.

E5-3 (Single-step Income Statement) The financial records of LeRoi Jones Inc. were destroyed by fire at the end of 2004. Fortunately the controller had kept certain statistical data related to the income statement as presented below.

1. The beginning merchandise inventory was $92,000 and decreased 20% during the current year.
2. Sales discounts amount to $17,000.
3. 20,000 shares of common stock were outstanding for the entire year.
4. Interest expense was $20,000.
5. The income tax rate is 30%.
6. Cost of goods sold amounts to $500,000.
7. Administrative expenses are 20% of cost of goods sold but only 8% of gross sales.
8. Four-fifths of the operating expenses relate to sales activities.

Instructions

From the foregoing information prepare an income statement for the year 2004 in single-step form.

E5-4 (Multiple-step and Single-step) Two accountants for the firm of Elwes and Wright are arguing about the merits of presenting an income statement in a multiple-step versus a single-step format. The discussion involves the following 2004 information related to P. Bride Company ($000 omitted).

Administrative expenses	
Officers' salaries	$ 4,900
Depreciation of office furniture and equipment	3,960
Cost of goods sold	60,570
Rental revenue	17,230
Selling expenses	
Transportation-out	2,690
Sales commissions	7,980
Depreciation of sales equipment	6,480

Sales	96,500
Income tax	9,070
Interest expense on bonds payable	1,860

Instructions

(a) Prepare an income statement for the year 2004 using the multiple-step form. Common shares outstanding for 2004 total 40,550 (000 omitted).

(b) Prepare an income statement for the year 2004 using the single-step form.

(c) Which one do you prefer? Discuss.

E5-5 (Multiple-step and Extraordinary Items) The following balances were taken from the books of Maria Conchita Alonzo Corp. on December 31, 2004.

Interest revenue	$ 86,000	Accumulated depreciation—equipment	$ 40,000
Cash	51,000	Accumulated depreciation—building	28,000
Sales	1,380,000	Notes receivable	155,000
Accounts receivable	150,000	Selling expenses	194,000
Prepaid insurance	20,000	Accounts payable	170,000
Sales returns and allowances	150,000	Bonds payable	100,000
Allowance for doubtful accounts	7,000	Administrative and general expenses	97,000
Sales discounts	45,000	Accrued liabilities	32,000
Land	100,000	Interest expense	60,000
Equipment	200,000	Notes payable	100,000
Building	140,000	Loss from earthquake damage (extraordinary item)	150,000
Cost of goods sold	621,000	Common stock	500,000
		Retained earnings	21,000

Assume the total effective tax rate on all items is 34%.

Instructions

Prepare a multiple-step income statement; 100,000 shares of common stock were outstanding during the year.

E5-6 (Multiple-step and Single-step) The accountant of Whitney Houston Shoe Co. has compiled the following information from the company's records as a basis for an income statement for the year ended December 31, 2004.

Rental revenue	$ 29,000
Interest on notes payable	18,000
Market appreciation on land above cost	31,000
Wages and salaries—sales	114,800
Materials and supplies—sales	17,600
Income tax	37,400
Wages and salaries—administrative	135,900
Other administrative expense	51,700
Cost of goods sold	496,000
Net sales	980,000
Depreciation on plant assets (70% selling, 30% administrative)	65,000
Dividends declared	16,000

There were 20,000 shares of common stock outstanding during the year.

Instructions

(a) Prepare a multiple-step income statement.

(b) Prepare a single-step income statement.

(c) Which format do you prefer? Discuss.

E5-7 **(Income Statement, EPS)** Presented below are selected ledger accounts of Tucker Corporation as of December 31, 2004.

Cash	$ 50,000
Administrative expenses	100,000
Selling expenses	80,000
Net sales	540,000
Cost of goods sold	210,000
Cash dividends declared (2004)	20,000
Cash dividends paid (2004)	15,000
Discontinued operations (loss before income taxes)	40,000
Depreciation expense, not recorded in 2003	30,000
Retained earnings, December 31, 2003	90,000
Effective tax rate 30%	

Instructions

(a) Compute net income for 2004.

(b) Prepare a partial income statement beginning with income from continuing operations before income tax, and including appropriate earnings per share information. Assume 10,000 shares of common stock were outstanding during 2004.

E5-8 **(Multiple-step Statement with Retained Earnings)** Presented below is information related to Ivan Calderon Corp. for the year 2004.

Net sales	$1,300,000	Write-off of inventory due to obsolescence	$ 80,000
Cost of goods sold	780,000	Depreciation expense omitted by accident in 2003	55,000
Selling expenses	65,000	Casualty loss (extraordinary item) before taxes	50,000
Administrative expenses	48,000	Dividends declared	45,000
Dividend revenue	20,000	Retained earnings at December 31, 2003	980,000
Interest revenue	7,000	Effective tax rate of 34% on all items	

Instructions

(a) Prepare a multiple-step income statement for 2004. Assume that 60,000 shares of common stock are outstanding.

(b) Prepare a separate retained earnings statement for 2004.

E5-9 **(Earnings Per Share)** The stockholders' equity section of Tkachuk Corporation appears below as of December 31, 2004.

8% cumulative preferred stock, $50 par value, authorized		
100,000 shares, outstanding 90,000 shares		$ 4,500,000
Common stock, $1.00 par, authorized and issued 10 million shares		10,000,000
Additional paid-in capital		20,500,000
Retained earnings	$134,000,000	
Net income	33,000,000	167,000,000
		$202,000,000

Net income for 2004 reflects a total effective tax rate of 34%. Included in the net income figure is a loss of $18,000,000 (before tax) as a result of a major casualty.

Instructions

Compute earnings per share data as it should appear on the financial statements of Tkachuk Corporation.

E5-10 (Condensed Income Statement—Periodic Inventory Method) Presented below are selected ledger accounts of Spock Corporation at December 31, 2004.

Cash	$ 185,000	Travel and entertainment	$ 69,000
Merchandise inventory	535,000	Accounting and legal services	33,000
Sales	4,275,000	Insurance expense	24,000
Advances from customers	117,000	Advertising	54,000
Purchases	2,786,000	Transportation-out	93,000
Sales discounts	34,000	Depreciation of office	48,000
Purchase discounts	27,000	Depreciation of sales equipment	36,000
Sales salaries	284,000	Telephone—sales	17,000
Office salaries	346,000	Utilities—office	32,000
Purchase returns	15,000	Miscellaneous office expenses	8,000
Sales returns	79,000	Rental revenue	240,000
Transportation-in	72,000	Extraordinary loss (before tax)	70,000
Accounts receivable	142,500	Interest expense	176,000
Sales commissions	83,000	Common stock ($10 par)	900,000

Spock's effective tax rate on all items is 34%. A physical inventory indicates that the ending inventory is $686,000.

Instructions
Prepare a condensed 2004 income statement for Spock Corporation.

E5-11 (Retained Earnings Statement) Eddie Zambrano Corporation began operations on January 1, 2001. During its first 3 years of operations, Zambrano reported net income and declared dividends as follows.

	Net income	Dividends declared
2001	$ 40,000	$-0-
2002	125,000	50,000
2003	160,000	50,000

The following information relates to 2004:

Income before income tax	$240,000
Prior period adjustment: understatement of 2002 depreciation expense (before taxes)	$ 25,000
Cumulative decrease in income from change in inventory methods (before taxes)	$ 35,000
Dividends declared (of this amount, $25,000 will be paid on Jan. 15, 2005)	$100,000
Effective tax rate	40%

Instructions
(a) Prepare a 2004 retained earnings statement for Eddie Zambrano Corporation.
(b) Assume Eddie Zambrano Corp. restricted retained earnings in the amount of $70,000 on December 31, 2004. After this action, what would Zambrano report as total retained earnings in its December 31, 2004, balance sheet?

E5-12 (Earnings per Share) At December 31, 2003, Shiga Naoya Corporation had the following stock outstanding.

10% cumulative preferred stock, $100 par, 107,500 shares	$10,750,000
Common stock, $5 par, 4,000,000 shares	20,000,000

During 2004, Shiga Naoya's only stock transaction was the issuance of 400,000 shares of common on April 1. The following also occurred during 2004.

Income from continuing operations before taxes	$23,650,000
Discontinued operations (loss before taxes)	$ 3,225,000
Preferred dividends declared	$ 1,075,000
Common dividends declared	$ 2,200,000
Effective tax rate	35%

Instructions

Compute earnings per share data as it should appear in the 2004 income statement of Shiga Naoya Corporation.

E5-13 (Change in Accounting Principle) Tom Kothe Company placed an asset in service on January 2, 2002. Its cost was $450,000 with an estimated service life of 6 years. Salvage value was estimated to be $30,000. Using the double-declining-balance method of depreciation, the depreciation for 2002, 2003, and 2004 would be $150,000, $100,000, and $66,667 respectively. During 2004 the company's management decided to change to the straight-line method of depreciation. Assume a 35% tax rate.

Instructions

(a) How much depreciation expense will be reported in the income from continuing operations of the company's income statement for 2004? (Hint: Use the new depreciation in the current year.)

(b) What amount will be reported as the cumulative effect of the change in accounting principle for 2004?

E5-14 (Comprehensive Income) Roxanne Carter Corporation reported the following for 2004: net sales $1,200,000; cost of goods sold $750,000; selling and administrative expenses $320,000; and an unrealized holding gain on available for sale securities $18,000.

Instructions

Prepare a statement of comprehensive income, using the two-income statement format. Ignore income taxes and earnings per share.

E5-15 (Comprehensive Income) C. Reither Co. reports the following information for 2004: sales revenue $700,000; cost of goods sold $500,000; operating expenses $80,000; and an unrealized holding loss on available-for-sale securities for 2004 of $60,000. It declared and paid a cash dividend of $10,000 in 2004.

C. Reither Co. has January 1, 2004, balances in common stock $350,000; accumulated other comprehensive income $80,000; and retained earnings $90,000. It issued no stock during 2004.

Instructions

Prepare a statement of stockholders' equity.

E5-16 (Various Reporting Formats) The following information was taken from the records of Roland Carlson Inc. for the year 2004. Income tax applicable to income from continuing operations $187,000; income tax applicable to loss on discontinued operations $25,500; income tax applicable to extraordinary gain $32,300; income tax applicable to extraordinary loss $20,400; and unrealized holding gain on available-for-sale securities $15,000.

Extraordinary gain	$ 95,000	Cash dividends declared	$ 150,000
Loss on discontinued operations	75,000	Retained earnings January 1, 2004	600,000
Administrative expenses	240,000	Cost of goods sold	850,000
Rent revenue	40,000	Selling expenses	300,000
Extraordinary loss	60,000	Sales	1,900,000

Shares outstanding during 2004 were 100,000.

Instructions

(a) Prepare a single-step income statement for 2004.

(b) Prepare a retained earnings statement for 2004.

(c) Show how comprehensive income is reported using the second income statement format.

PROBLEMS

P5-1 (Multi-step Income, Retained Earnings) Presented below is information related to American Horse Company for 2004.

Retained earnings balance, January 1, 2004	$ 980,000
Sales for the year	25,000,000
Cost of goods sold	17,000,000
Interest revenue	70,000
Selling and administrative expenses	4,700,000
Write-off of goodwill (not tax deductible)	820,000
Income taxes for 2004	905,000
Gain on the sale of investments (normal recurring)	110,000
Loss due to flood damage—extraordinary item (net of tax)	390,000
Loss on the disposition of the wholesale division (net of tax)	440,000
Loss on operations of the wholesale division (net of tax)	90,000
Dividends declared on common stock	250,000
Dividends declared on preferred stock	70,000

Instructions

Prepare a multi-step income statement and a retained earnings statement. American Horse Company decided to discontinue its entire wholesale operations and to retain its manufacturing operations. On September 15, American Horse sold the wholesale operations to Rogers Company. During 2004, there were 300,000 shares of common stock outstanding all year.

P5-2 (Single-step Income, Retained Earnings, Periodic Inventory) Presented below is the trial balance of Mary J. Blige Corporation at December 31, 2004.

MARY J. BLIGE CORPORATION
TRIAL BALANCE
YEAR ENDED DECEMBER 31, 2004

	Debits	Credits
Purchase Discounts		$ 10,000
Cash	$ 205,100	
Accounts Receivable	105,000	
Rent Revenue		18,000
Retained Earnings		260,000
Salaries Payable		18,000
Sales		1,000,000
Notes Receivable	110,000	
Accounts Payable		49,000
Accumulated Depreciation—Equipment		28,000
Sales Discounts	14,500	
Sales Returns	17,500	
Notes Payable		70,000
Selling Expenses	232,000	
Administrative Expenses	99,000	
Common Stock		300,000

Income Tax Expense	38,500	
Cash Dividends	45,000	
Allowance for Doubtful Accounts		5,000
Supplies	14,000	
Freight-in	20,000	
Land	70,000	
Equipment	140,000	
Bonds Payable		100,000
Gain on Sale of Land		30,000
Accumulated Depreciation—Building		19,600
Merchandise Inventory	89,000	
Building	98,000	
Purchases	610,000	
Totals	$1,907,600	$1,907,600

A physical count of inventory on December 31 resulted in an inventory amount of $124,000.

Instructions

Prepare a single-step income statement and a retained earnings statement. Assume that the only changes in the retained earnings during the current year were from net income and dividends. Thirty thousand shares of common stock were outstanding the entire year.

P5-3 (Irregular Items) Tony Rich Inc. reported income from continuing operations before taxes during 2004 of $790,000. Additional transactions occurring in 2004 but not considered in the $790,000 are as follows.

1. The corporation experienced an uninsured flood loss (extraordinary) in the amount of $80,000 during the year. The tax rate on this item is 46%.
2. At the beginning of 2002, the corporation purchased a machine for $54,000 (salvage value of $9,000) that had a useful life of 6 years. The bookkeeper used straight-line depreciation for 2002, 2003, and 2004 but failed to deduct the salvage value in computing the depreciation base.
3. Sale of securities held as a part of its portfolio resulted in a loss of $57,000 (pretax).
4. When its president died, the corporation realized $110,000 from an insurance policy. The cash surrender value of this policy had been carried on the books as an investment in the amount of $46,000 (the gain is nontaxable).
5. The corporation disposed of its recreational division at a loss of $115,000 before taxes. Assume that this transaction meets the criteria for discontinued operations.
6. The corporation decided to change its method of inventory pricing from average cost to the FIFO method. The effect of this change on prior years is to increase 2002 income by $60,000 and decrease 2003 income by $20,000 before taxes. The FIFO method has been used for 2004. The tax rate on these items is 40%.

Instructions

Prepare an income statement for the year 2004 starting with income from continuing operations before taxes. Compute earnings per share as it should be shown on the face of the income statement. Common shares outstanding for the year are 80,000 shares. (Assume a tax rate of 30% on all items, unless indicated otherwise.)

P5-4 (Multiple- and Single-step Income, Retained Earnings) The following account balances were included in the trial balance of J.R. Reid Corporation at June 30, 2004.

Sales	$1,678,500	Depreciation of office furniture	
Sales discounts	31,150	and equipment	$ 7,250
Cost of goods sold	896,770	Real estate and other local taxes	7,320
Sales salaries	56,260	Bad debt expense—selling	4,850
Sales commissions	97,600	Building expense—prorated	
Travel expense—salespersons	28,930	to administration	9,130
Freight-out	21,400	Miscellaneous office expenses	6,000
Entertainment expense	14,820	Sales returns	62,300

Telephone and Internet expense—sales	9,030	Dividends received	38,000
Depreciation of sales equipment	4,980	Bond interest expense	18,000
Building expense—prorated to sales	6,200	Income taxes	133,000
Miscellaneous selling expenses	4,715	Depreciation understatement due	
Office supplies used	3,450	to error—2001 (net of tax)	17,700
Telephone and Internet expense—		Dividends declared on	
administration	2,820	preferred stock	9,000
		Dividends declared on common	
		stock	32,000

The Retained Earnings account had a balance of $337,000 at June 30, 2004, before closing. There are 80,000 shares of common stock outstanding.

Instructions

(a) Using the multiple-step form, prepare an income statement and a retained earnings statement for the year ended June 30, 2004.

(b) Using the single-step form, prepare an income statement and a retained earnings statement for the year ended June 30, 2004.

P5-5 **(Irregular Items)** Presented below is a combined single-step income and retained earnings statement for Sandy Freewalt Company for 2003.

		(000 omitted)
Net sales		$640,000
Cost and expenses		
Cost of goods sold		500,000
Selling, general, and administrative expenses		66,000
Other, net		17,000
		583,000
Income before income tax		57,000
Income tax		19,400
Net income		37,600
Retained earnings at beginning of period, as previously reported	$141,000	
Adjustment required for correction of error	(7,000)	
Retained earnings at beginning of period, as restated		134,000
Dividends on common stock		(12,200)
Retained earnings at end of period		$159,400

Additional facts are as follows:

1. "Selling, general, and administrative expenses" for 2003 included a usual but infrequently occurring charge of $10,500,000.
2. "Other, net" for 2003 included an extraordinary item (charge) of $9,000,000. If the extraordinary item (charge) had not occurred, income taxes for 2003 would have been $22,400,000 instead of $19,400,000.
3. "Adjustment required for correction of an error" was a result of a change in estimate (useful life of certain assets reduced to 8 years and a catch-up adjustment made).
4. Sandy Freewalt Company disclosed earnings per common share for net income in the notes to the financial statements.

Instructions

Determine from these additional facts whether the presentation of the facts in the Sandy Freewalt Company income and retained earnings statement is appropriate. If the presentation is not appropriate, describe the appropriate presentation and discuss its theoretical rationale. (Do not prepare a revised statement.)

P5-6 (Retained Earnings Statement, Prior Period Adjustment) Below is the retained earnings account for the year 2004 for LeClair Corp.

Retained earnings, January 1, 2004		$257,600
Add:		
Gain on sale of investments (net of tax)	$41,200	
Net income	84,500	
Refund on litigation with government, related to the year 2001 (net of tax)	21,600	
Recognition of income earned in 2003, but omitted from income statement in that year (net of tax)	25,400	172,700
		430,300
Deduct:		
Loss on discontinued operations (net of tax)	25,000	
Write-off of goodwill (net of tax)	60,000	
Cumulative effect on income in changing from straight-line depreciation to accelerated depreciation in 2004 (net of tax)	18,200	
Cash dividends declared	32,000	135,200
Retained earnings, December 31, 2004		$295,100

Instructions

(a) Prepare a corrected retained earnings statement. LeClair Corp. normally sells investments of the type mentioned above.

(b) State where the items that do not appear in the corrected retained earnings statement should be shown.

P5-7 (Income Statement and Irregular Items) Rufino Tamayo Corporation commenced business on January 1, 2001. Recently the corporation has had several unusual accounting problems related to the presentation of its income statement for financial reporting purposes.

You have been the CPA for Rufino Tamayo Corporation for several years and have been asked to examine the following data.

RUFINO TAMAYO CORPORATION	
INCOME STATEMENT	
FOR THE YEAR ENDED DECEMBER 31, 2004	
Sales	$9,500,000
Cost of goods sold	5,900,000
Gross profit	3,600,000
Selling and administrative expense	1,300,000
Income before income tax	2,300,000
Income tax (30%)	690,000
Net income	$1,610,000

In addition, this information was provided:

1. The controller mentioned that the corporation has had difficulty in collecting on several of their receivables. For this reason, the bad debt write-off was increased from 1% to 2% of sales. The controller estimates that if this rate had been used in past periods, an additional $83,000 worth of expense would have been charged. The bad debt expense for the current period was calculated using the new rate and is part of selling and administrative expense.

2. Common shares outstanding at the end of 2004 totaled 400,000. No additional shares were purchased or sold during 2004.

3. Rufino Tamayo noted also that the following items were not included in the income statement.
   (a) Inventory in the amount of $72,000 was obsolete.
   (b) The major casualty loss suffered by the corporation was partially uninsured and cost $127,000, net of tax (extraordinary item).
4. Retained earnings as of January 1, 2004, was $2,800,000. Cash dividends of $700,000 were paid in 2004.
5. In January 2004, Rufino Tamayo Corporation changed its method of accounting for plant assets from the straight-line method to the accelerated method (double-declining balance). The controller has prepared a schedule indicating what depreciation expense would have been in previous periods if the double-declining method had been used. (The effective tax rate for 2001, 2002, and 2003 was 30%.)

	Depreciation Expense under Straight-Line	Depreciation Expense under Double-Declining	Difference
2001	$ 75,000	$150,000	$ 75,000
2002	75,000	112,500	37,500
2003	75,000	84,375	9,375
	$225,000	$346,875	$121,875

6. In 2004, Rufino Tamayo discovered that two errors were made in previous years. First, when it took a physical inventory at the end of 2001, one of the count sheets was apparently lost. The ending inventory for 2001 was therefore understated by $95,000. The inventory was correctly taken in 2002, 2003, and 2004. Also, the corporation found that in 2003 it had failed to record $40,000 as an expense for sales commissions. The effective tax rate for 2001, 2002, and 2003 was 30%. The sales commissions for 2003 are included in 2004 expenses.

Instructions
Prepare the income statement for Rufino Tamayo Corporation in accordance with professional pronouncements. Do not prepare notes to the financial statements.

P5-8 (Income Statement, Irregular Items) Rap Corp. has 100,000 shares of common stock outstanding. In 2004, the company reports income from continuing operations before taxes of $1,210,000. Additional transactions not considered in the $1,210,000 are as follows.

1. In 2004, Rap Corp. sold equipment for $40,000. The machine had originally cost $80,000 and had accumulated depreciation of $36,000. The gain or loss is considered ordinary.
2. The company discontinued operations of one of its subsidiaries during the current year at a loss of $190,000 before taxes. Assume that this transaction meets the criteria for discontinued operations. The loss on operations of the discontinued subsidiary was $90,000 before taxes; the loss from disposal of the subsidiary was $100,000 before taxes.
3. In 2004, the company reviewed its accounts receivable and determined that $26,000 of accounts receivable that had been carried for years appeared unlikely to be collected.
4. An internal audit discovered that amortization of intangible assets was understated by $35,000 (net of tax) in a prior period. The amount was charged against retained earnings.
5. The company sold its only investment in common stock during the year at a gain of $145,000. The gain is taxed at a total effective rate of 40%. Assume that the transaction meets the requirements of an extraordinary item.

Instructions
Analyze the above information and prepare an income statement for the year 2004, starting with income from continuing operations before income taxes. Compute earnings per share as it should be shown on the face of the income statement. (Assume a total effective tax rate of 38% on all items, unless otherwise indicated.)

CONCEPTUAL CASES

C5-1 (Identification of Income Statement Deficiencies) John Amos Corporation was incorporated and began business on January 1, 2003. It has been successful and now requires a bank loan for additional working capital to finance expansion. The bank has requested an audited income statement for the year 2003. The accountant for John Amos Corporation provides you with the following income statement which John Amos plans to submit to the bank.

JOHN AMOS CORPORATION
INCOME STATEMENT

Sales		$850,000
Dividends		32,300
Gain on recovery of insurance proceeds from		
earthquake loss (extraordinary)		38,500
		920,800
Less:		
Selling expenses	$101,100	
Cost of goods sold	510,000	
Advertising expense	13,700	
Loss on obsolescence of inventories	34,000	
Loss on discontinued operations	48,600	
Administrative expense	73,400	780,800
Income before income tax		140,000
Income tax		56,000
Net income		$ 84,000

Instructions

Indicate the deficiencies in the income statement presented above. Assume that the corporation desires a single-step income statement.

C5-2 (Income Reporting Deficiencies) The following represents a recent income statement for Boeing Company.

Sales	$21,924,000,000
Costs and expenses	20,773,000,000
Income from operations	1,151,000,000
Other income	122,000,000
Interest and debt expense	(130,000,000)
Earnings before income taxes	1,143,000,000
Income taxes	(287,000,000)
Net income	$ 856,000,000

It includes only *five* separate numbers (two of which are in billions of dollars), *two* subtotals, and the net earnings figure.

Instructions

(a) Indicate the deficiencies in the income statement.

(b) What recommendations would you make to Boeing to improve the usefulness of its income statement?

C5-3 (All-inclusive vs. Current Operating) Information concerning the operations of a corporation is presented in an income statement. Some believe that income statements should be prepared on a "current operating performance" basis (earning power concept), whereas others prefer an "all-inclusive" basis (historical concept). Proponents of the two types of income statements do not agree upon the proper treatment of material nonrecurring charges and credits.

Instructions

(a) Define "current operating performance" and "all-inclusive" as used above.

(b) Explain the differences in content and organization of a "current operating performance" income statement and an "all-inclusive" income statement. Include a discussion of the proper treatment of material nonrecurring charges and credits.

(c) Give the principal arguments for the use of each of the two statements, "all-inclusive" income statement or a "current operating performance" income statement.

(AICPA adapted)

C5-4 **(Extraordinary Items)** Jeff Foxworthy, vice-president of finance for Red Neck Company, has recently been asked to discuss with the company's division controllers the proper accounting for extraordinary items. Jeff Foxworthy prepared the factual situations presented below as a basis for discussion.

1. An earthquake destroys one of the oil refineries owned by a large multinational oil company. Earthquakes are rare in this geographical location.
2. A publicly held company has incurred a substantial loss in the unsuccessful registration of a bond issue.
3. A large portion of a cigarette manufacturer's tobacco crops are destroyed by a hailstorm. Severe damage from hailstorms is rare in this locality.
4. A large diversified company sells a block of shares from its portfolio of securities acquired for investment purposes.
5. A company sells a block of common stock of a publicly traded company. The block of shares, which represents less than 10% of the publicly held company, is the only security investment the company has ever owned.
6. A company that operates a chain of warehouses sells the excess land surrounding one of its warehouses. When the company buys property to establish a new warehouse, it usually buys more land than it expects to use for the warehouse with the expectation that the land will appreciate in value. Twice during the past 5 years the company sold excess land.
7. A company experiences a material loss in the repurchase of a large bond issue that has been outstanding for 3 years. The company regularly repurchases bonds of this nature.
8. A railroad experiences an unusual flood loss to part of its track system. Flood losses normally occur every 3 or 4 years.
9. A machine tool company sells the only land it owns. The land was acquired 10 years ago for future expansion, but shortly thereafter the company abandoned all plans for expansion but decided to hold the land for appreciation.

Instructions

Determine whether the foregoing items should be classified as extraordinary items. Present a rationale for your position.

C5-5 **(Earnings Management)** Grace Inc. has recently reported steadily increasing income. The company reported income of $20,000 in 2000, $25,000 in 2001, and $30,000 in 2002. A number of market analysts have recommended that investors buy the stock because they expect the steady growth in income to continue. Grace is approaching the end of its fiscal year in 2003, and it again appears to be a good year. However, it has not yet recorded warranty expense.

Based on prior experience, this year's warranty expense should be around $5,000, but some top management has approached the controller to suggest a larger, more conservative warranty expense should be recorded this year. Income before warranty expense is $43,000. Specifically, by recording an $8,000 warranty accrual this year, Grace could report an increase in income for this year and still be in a position to cover its warranty costs in future years.

Instructions
(a) What is earnings management?
(b) What is the effect of the proposed accounting in 2003? In 2004?
(c) What is the appropriate accounting in this situation?

C5-6 (Earnings Management) Arthur Miller, controller for the Salem Corporation, is preparing the company's income statement at year-end. He notes that the company lost a considerable sum on the sale of some equipment it had decided to replace. Since the company has sold equipment routinely in the past, Miller knows the losses cannot be reported as extraordinary. He also does not want to highlight it as a material loss since he feels that will reflect poorly on him and the company. He reasons that if the company had recorded more depreciation during the assets' lives, the losses would not be so great. Since depreciation is included among the company's operating expenses, he wants to report the losses along with the company's expenses, where he hopes it will not be noticed.

Instructions
(a) What are the ethical issues involved?
(b) What should Miller do?

C5-7 (Income Reporting Items) Woody Allen Corp. is an entertainment firm that derives approximately 30% of its income from the Casino Royale Division, which manages gambling facilities. As auditor for Woody Allen Corp., you have recently overheard the following discussion between the controller and financial vice-president.

VICE-PRESIDENT: If we sell the Casino Royale Division, it seems ridiculous to segregate the results of the sale in the income statement. Separate categories tend to be absurd and confusing to the stockholders. I believe that we should simply report the gain on the sale as other income or expense without detail.

CONTROLLER: Professional pronouncements would require that we disclose this information separately in the income statement. If a sale of this type is considered unusual and infrequent, it must be reported as an extraordinary item.

VICE-PRESIDENT: What about the walkout we had last month when our employees were upset about their commission income? Would this situation not also be an extraordinary item?

CONTROLLER: I am not sure whether this item would be reported as extraordinary or not.

VICE-PRESIDENT: Oh well, it doesn't make any difference because the net effect of all these items is immaterial, so no disclosure is necessary.

Instructions
(a) On the basis of the foregoing discussion, answer the following questions: Who is correct about handling the sale? What would be the income statement presentation for the sale of the Casino Royale Division?
(b) How should the walkout by the employees be reported?
(c) What do you think about the vice-president's observation on materiality?
(d) What are the earnings per share implications of these topics?

C5-8 (Identification of Extraordinary Items) Loni Anderson Company is a major manufacturer of foodstuffs whose products are sold in grocery and convenience stores throughout the United States. The company's name is well known and respected because its products have been marketed nationally for over 50 years.

In April 2003 the company was forced to recall one of its major products. A total of 35 persons in Oshkosh were treated for severe intestinal pain, and eventually 3 people died from complications. All of the people had consumed Anderson's product.

The product causing the problem was traced to one specific lot. Anderson keeps samples from all lots of foodstuffs. After thorough testing, Anderson and the legal authorities confirmed that the product had been tampered with after it had left the company's plant and was no longer under the company's control.

All of the product was recalled from the market—the only time an Anderson product has been recalled nationally and the only time for tampering. Persons who still had the product in their homes, even though it was not from the affected lot, were encouraged to return the product for credit or refund. A media campaign was designed and implemented by the company to explain what had happened and what the company was doing to minimize any chance of recurrence. Anderson decided to continue the product with the same trade name and same wholesale price. However, the packaging was redesigned completely to be tamper resistant and safety sealed. This required the purchase and installation of new equipment.

The corporate accounting staff recommended that the costs associated with the tampered product be treated as an extraordinary charge on the 2003 financial statements. Corporate accounting was asked to identify the various costs that could be associated with the tampered product and related recall. These costs ($000 omitted) are as follows.

1.	Credits and refunds to stores and consumers	$30,000
2.	Insurance to cover lost sales and idle plant costs for possible future recalls	5,000
3.	Transportation costs and off-site warehousing of returned product	2,000
4.	Future security measures for other Anderson products	4,000
5.	Testing of returned product and inventory	900
6.	Destruction of returned product and inventory	2,400
7.	Public relations program to reestablish brand credibility	4,200
8.	Communication program to inform customers, answer inquiries, prepare press releases, etc.	1,600
9.	Higher cost arising from new packaging	800
10.	Investigation of possible involvement of employees, former employees, competitors, etc.	500
11.	Packaging redesign and testing	2,000
12.	Purchase and installation of new packaging equipment	6,000
13.	Legal costs for defense against liability suits	750
14.	Lost sales revenue due to recall	32,000

Anderson's estimated earnings before income taxes and before consideration of any of the above items for the year ending December 31, 2003, are $225 million.

Instructions
(a) Loni Anderson Company plans to recognize the costs associated with the product tampering and recall as an extraordinary charge.
  (1) Explain why Anderson could classify this occurrence as an extraordinary charge.
  (2) Describe the placement and terminology used to present the extraordinary charge in the 2003 income statement.
(b) Refer to the 14 cost items identified by the corporate accounting staff of Anderson Company.
  (1) Identify the cost items by number that should be included in the extraordinary charge for 2003.
  (2) For any item that is not included in the extraordinary charge, explain why it would not be included in the extraordinary charge.

(CMA adapted)

C5-9 **(Identification of Income Statement Weaknesses)** The following financial statement was prepared by employees of Cynthia Taylor Corporation.

CYNTHIA TAYLOR CORPORATION
INCOME STATEMENT
YEAR ENDED DECEMBER 31, 2004

Revenues		
Gross sales, including sales taxes	$1,044,300	
Less: Returns, allowances, and cash discounts	56,200	
Net sales	988,100	
Dividends, interest, and purchase discounts	30,250	
Recoveries of accounts written off in prior years	13,850	
Total revenues	1,032,200	

Costs and expenses	
Cost of goods sold, including sales taxes	465,900
Salaries and related payroll expenses	60,500
Rent	19,100
Freight-in and freight-out	3,400
Bad debt expense	27,800
Total costs and expenses	576,700
Income before extraordinary items	455,500
Extraordinary items	
Loss on discontinued styles (Note 1)	71,500
Loss on sale of marketable securities (Note 2)	39,050
Loss on sale of warehouse (Note 3)	86,350
Total extraordinary items	196,900
Net income	$ 258,600
Net income per share of common stock	$2.30

Note 1: New styles and rapidly changing consumer preferences resulted in a $71,500 loss on the disposal of discontinued styles and related accessories.

Note 2: The corporation sold an investment in marketable securities at a loss of $39,050. The corporation normally sells securities of this nature.

Note 3: The corporation sold one of its warehouses at an $86,350 loss.

Instructions

Identify and discuss the weaknesses in classification and disclosure in the single-step income statement above. You should explain why these treatments are weaknesses and what the proper presentation of the items would be in accordance with recent professional pronouncements.

C5-10 (Classification of Income Statement Items) As audit partner for Noriyuki and Morita, you are in charge of reviewing the classification of unusual items that have occurred during the current year. The following material items have come to your attention.

1. A merchandising company incorrectly overstated its ending inventory 2 years ago by a material amount. Inventory for all other periods is correctly computed.
2. An automobile dealer sells for $137,000 an extremely rare 1930 S type Invicta which it purchased for $21,000 10 years ago. The Invicta is the only such display item the dealer owns.
3. A drilling company during the current year extended the estimated useful life of certain drilling equipment from 9 to 15 years. As a result, depreciation for the current year was materially lowered.
4. A retail outlet changed its computation for bad debt expense from 1% to ½ of 1% of sales because of changes in its customer clientele.
5. A mining concern sells a foreign subsidiary engaged in uranium mining, although it (the seller) continues to engage in uranium mining in other countries.
6. A steel company changes from straight-line depreciation to accelerated depreciation in accounting for its plant assets.
7. A construction company, at great expense, prepared a major proposal for a government loan. The loan is not approved.
8. A water pump manufacturer has had large losses resulting from a strike by its employees early in the year.
9. Depreciation for a prior period was incorrectly understated by $950,000. The error was discovered in the current year.
10. A large sheep rancher suffered a major loss because the state required that all sheep in the state be killed to halt the spread of a rare disease. Such a situation has not occurred in the state for 20 years.
11. A food distributor that sells wholesale to supermarket chains and to fast-food restaurants (two distinguishable classes of customers) decides to discontinue the division that sells to one of the two classes of customers.

Instructions

From the foregoing information, indicate in what section of the income statement or retained earnings statement these items should be classified. Provide a brief rationale for your position.

C5-11   (Comprehensive Income)   Ferguson Arthur, Jr., controller for Jenkins Corporation, is preparing the company's financial statements at year-end. Currently, he is focusing on the income statement and determining the format for reporting comprehensive income. During the year, the company earned net income of $400,000 and had unrealized gains on available-for-sale securities of $20,000. In the previous year net income was $410,000, and the company had no unrealized gains or losses.

Instructions

(a) Show how income and comprehensive income will be reported on a comparative basis for the current and prior years, using the two-income statement format.

(b) Show how income and comprehensive income will be reported on a comparative basis for the current and prior years, using the combined income statement format.

(c) Which format should Arthur recommend?

USING YOUR JUDGMENT

FINANCIAL REPORTING PROBLEM

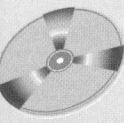

3M COMPANY

The financial statements of **3M** were provided with your book or can be accessed on the Take Action! CD.

Instructions

Refer to 3M's financial statements and the accompanying notes to answer the following questions.

(a) What type of income statement format does 3M use? Indicate why this format might be used to present income statement information.

(b) What are 3M's primary revenue sources?

(c) Compute 3M's gross profit for each of the years 1999–2001. Explain why profit margin declined in 2001.

(d) Why does 3M make a distinction between operating and nonoperating revenue?

(e) What financial ratios did 3M choose to report in its "Financial Summary" section covering the years 1991–2001.

FINANCIAL STATEMENT ANALYSIS CASES

CASE 1: BANKRUPTCY PREDICTION REVISITED

The Z-score bankruptcy prediction model was introduced in Chapter 4. Recall that the model uses balance sheet and income information to arrive at a Z-Score, which can be used to predict financial distress:

$$Z = \frac{\text{Working capital}}{\text{Total assets}} \times 1.2 + \frac{\text{Retained earnings}}{\text{Total assets}} \times 1.4 + \frac{\text{EBIT}}{\text{Total assets}} \times 3.3 + \frac{\text{Sales}}{\text{Total assets}} \times .99$$

$$+ \frac{\text{MV equity}}{\text{Total liabilities}} \times 0.6$$

EBIT is earnings before interest and taxes. MV Equity is the market value of common equity, which can be determined by multiplying stock price by shares outstanding.

Following extensive testing, Altman found that companies with Z-scores above 3.0 are unlikely to fail; those with Z-scores below 1.81 are very likely to fail. While the original model was developed for publicly held manufacturing companies, the model has been modified to apply to companies in various industries, emerging companies, and companies not traded in public markets.

Instructions

(a) Use information in the financial statements of a company like **PepsiCo** or **Coca-Cola** to compute the Z-score for the past 2 years.

(b) Interpret your result. Where does the company fall in the financial distress range?

(c) The Z-score uses EBIT as one of its elements. Why do you think this income measure is used?

CASE 2: DRESSER INDUSTRIES

Dresser Industries provides products and services to oil and natural gas exploration, production, transmission and processing companies. A recent income statement is reproduced below. Dollar amounts are in millions.

Sales	$2,697.0
Service revenues	1,933.9
Share of earnings of unconsolidated affiliates	92.4
Total revenues	4,723.3
Cost of sales	1,722.7
Cost of services	1,799.9
Total costs of sales and services	3,522.6
Gross earnings	1,200.7
Selling, engineering, administrative and general expenses	(919.8)
Special charges	(70.0)
Other income (deductions)	
Interest expense	(47.4)
Interest earned	19.1
Other, net	4.8
Earnings before income taxes and other items below	187.4
Income taxes	(79.4)
Minority interest	(10.3)
Earnings from continuing operations	97.7
Discontinued operations	(35.3)
Earnings before extraordinary items and accounting changes	62.4
Extraordinary items	(6.3)
Cumulative effect of accounting changes	(393.8)
Net earnings (loss)	$(337.7)

Instructions

Assume that 177,636,000 shares of stock were issued and outstanding. Prepare the per-share portion of the income statement. Remember to begin with "Income from continuing operations."

COMPARATIVE ANALYSIS CASE

THE COCA-COLA COMPANY AND PEPSICO, INC.

Instructions

Go to the Take Action! CD and use information found there to answer the following questions related to The Coca-Cola Company and PepsiCo, Inc.

(a) What type of income format(s) is used by these two companies? Identify any differences in income statement format between these two companies.

(b) What are the gross profits, operating profit, and net income for these two companies over the 3-year period 1999–2001? Which company has had better financial results over this period of time?

(c) Identify the irregular items reported by these two companies in their income statements over the 3-year period 1999–2001. Do these irregular items appear to be significant?

(d) Refer to PepsiCo's Management Analysis section under "Items Affecting Comparability:" Briefly discuss how these items affect the comparability and consistency of PepsiCo's income over 1999–2001.

INTERNATIONAL REPORTING CASE

Presented below is the income statement for a British company, Avon Rubber PLC.

AVON RUBBER PLC
Consolidated Profit and Loss Account
for the year ended 30 September 2000

	2000		
	Before exceptional items £'000	Exceptional items (note 5) £'000	Total £'000
Turnover	277,997	—	277,997
Cost of sales	(231,842)	(1,984)	(233,826)
Gross profit	46,155	(1,984)	44,171
Net operating expenses (including £623,000 goodwill amortisation)	(30,891)	(4,688)	(35,579)
Share of profits/(losses) of joint ventures and associates	161	—	161
Operating profit	15,425	(6,672)	8,753
Profit on disposal of fixed assets	—	25	25
Profit on ordinary activities before interest	15,425	(6,647)	8,778
Interest receivable	2,871	—	2,871
Interest payable	(5,911)	—	(5,911)
Profit on ordinary activities before taxation	12,385	(6,647)	5,738
Taxation	(4,360)	1,400	(2,960)
Profit on ordinary activities after taxation	8,025	(5,247)	2,778
Minority interests	717	—	717
Profit for the year	8,742	(5,247)	3,495
Dividends	(6,735)	—	(6,735)
(Loss)/retained profit for the year	2,007	(5,247)	(3,240)
Basic earnings per ordinary share			12.4p

Instructions

(a) Review the Avon Rubber income statement and identify at least three differences between the British income statement and an income statement of a U.S. company as presented in the chapter.

(b) Identify any irregular items reported by Avon Rubber. Is the reporting of these irregular items in Avon's income statement similar to reporting of these items in U.S. companies' income statements? Explain.

*Remember to check the **Take Action! CD**
and the book's **companion Web site**
to find additional resources for this chapter.*

REVENUES AND CASH FLOWS

BOEING BOUNCING BACK

In a press release, Boeing Co., the maker of planes, weapons, and rockets, indicated that it experienced a better-than-expected 42 percent increase in earnings for the fourth quarter. The aerospace company also boosted its projected profit margins for the next two years amid a continuing recovery in the commercial-jet unit.

Although sales for the last quarter slipped 11 percent, earnings per share increased $0.05 more than analysts expected. Revenues, operating margins, and free cash flows for the current period and the outlook for the future are shown below.

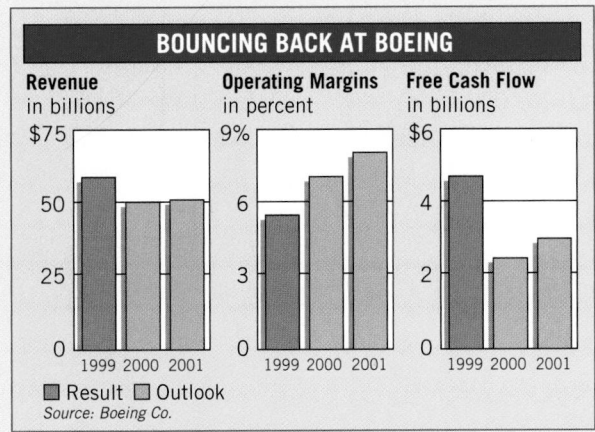

The rising performance and improved outlook at Boeing is attributable to improvements in many of the company's business lines and expansion in aircraft-related services. It is also credited to planning put in place a year earlier by Chief Financial Officer Deborah Hopkins, whose projections investors have come to see as reliable.

The commercial-jet unit, under a recovery plotted by President Alan Mulally, produced an operating-earnings margin of 7 percent for a recent quarter. The improvement, stemming partly from cost cutting and reduced overtime pay, compares with a return of less than half of 1 percent in the same period in the previous year.[1]

[1]Adapted from Jeff Cole, "Boeing Profit Rises 42%; Company Raises Projections for Profit Margins," *Wall Street Journal, Interactive Edition* (January 20, 2000).

LEARNING OBJECTIVES

After studying this chapter, you should be able to:

1. Apply the revenue recognition principle.

2. Describe accounting issues involved with revenue recognition at point of sale.

3. Apply the percentage-of-completion method for long-term contracts.

4. Apply the completed-contract method for long-term contracts.

5. Describe the installment-sales and cost-recovery methods of accounting.

6. Indicate the purpose of the statement of cash flows.

7. Identify the content of the statement of cash flows.

8. Prepare a statement of cash flows.

9. Understand the usefulness of the statement of cash flows.

As indicated in the opening story about **Boeing Co.**, investors look at many factors to assess a company's well-being, such as revenue growth, gross profit margins, and cash flow measures. Although bottom-line numbers such as net income or total assets are extremely important, they often do not tell the complete story. Information about the components of these bottom-line numbers, such as revenues, expenses, and cash flows, enable users to better predict future performance and understand the relative significance of each component. The purpose of this chapter is to discuss two key financial reporting elements—revenues from the income statement and the statement of cash flows, which shows the cash received and paid during the year.

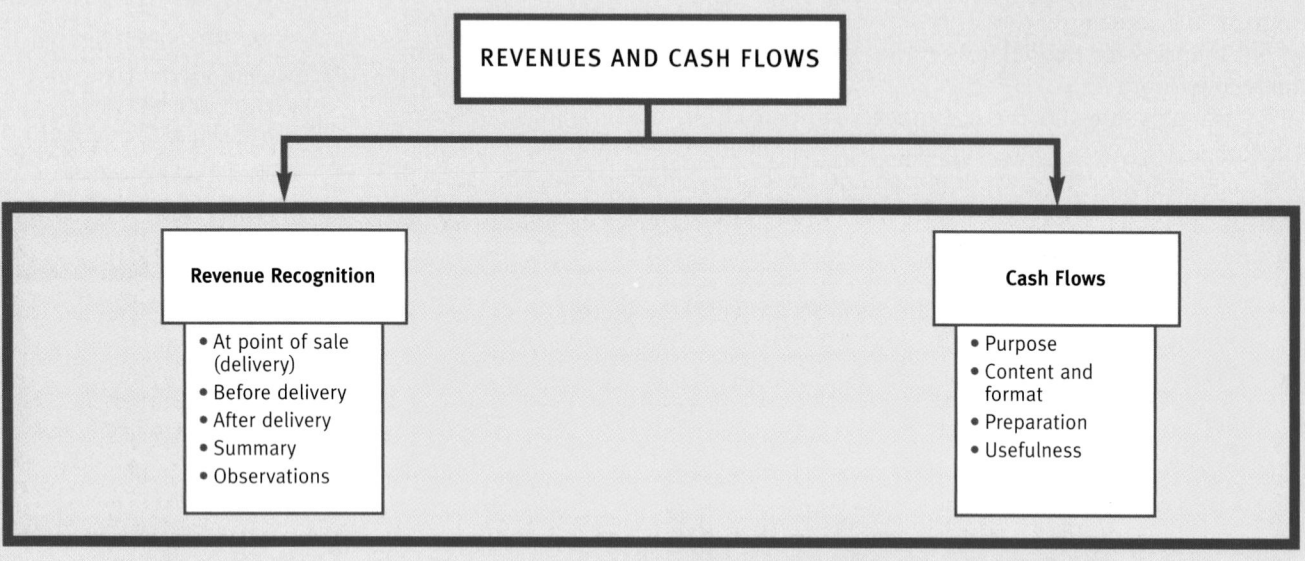

REVENUE RECOGNITION

OBJECTIVE 1
Apply the revenue recognition principle.

Although certain industries have very specific guidelines that provide additional insight into when revenue should be recognized, in general, the guidelines for revenue recognition are quite broad. The **revenue recognition principle** provides that revenue is recognized when (1) it is realized or realizable and (2) it is earned. Revenues are **realized** when goods and services are exchanged for cash or claims to cash (receivables). Revenues are **realizable** when assets received in exchange are readily convertible to known amounts of cash or claims to cash. Revenues are **earned** when the entity has substantially accomplished what it must do to be entitled to the benefits represented by the revenues, that is, when the earnings process is complete or virtually complete.

Four revenue transactions are recognized in accordance with this principle.

UNDERLYING CONCEPTS

Revenues are inflows of assets and/or settlements of liabilities from delivering or producing goods, rendering services, or other earning activities that constitute an enterprise's ongoing major or central operations during a period.

1. Revenue from **selling products** is recognized at the date of sale, usually interpreted to mean the date of delivery to customers.
2. Revenue from **services rendered** is recognized when services have been performed and are billable.
3. Revenue from **permitting others to use enterprise assets** (such as revenue from interest, rent, and royalties) is recognized as time passes or as the assets are used.
4. Revenue from **disposing of assets** other than products is recognized at the date of sale.

These revenue transactions are diagrammed in Illustration 6-1.

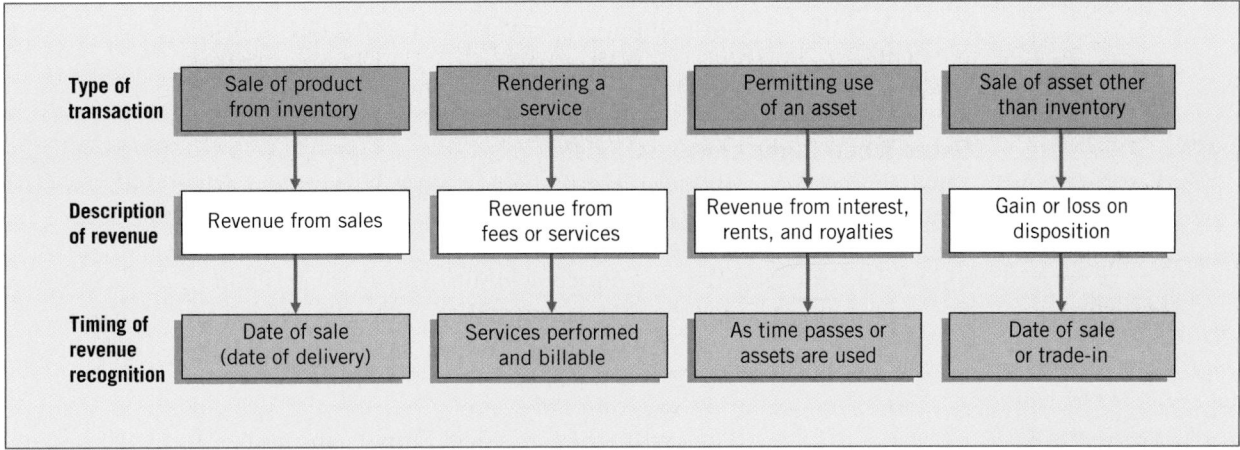

Illustration 6-1
Revenue Recognition
Classified by Nature of
Transaction

Our discussion of revenue recognition is devoted exclusively to two of the four general types of revenue transactions described above, namely, (1) selling products and (2) rendering services—both of which are **sales transactions**. The other two types of revenue transactions—(3) revenue from permitting others to use enterprise assets, and (4) revenue from disposing of assets other than products—are discussed in several other sections of the textbook. Our discussion of product sales transactions is organized around the following topics.

① Revenue recognition at point of sale (delivery).
② Revenue recognition before delivery.
③ Revenue recognition after delivery.

This organization of revenue recognition topics is depicted graphically in Illustration 6-2.

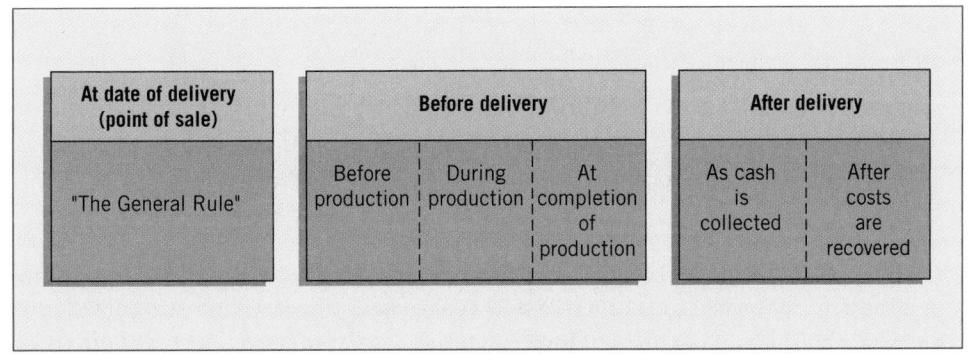

Illustration 6-2
Revenue Recognition
Alternatives

Revenue Recognition at Point of Sale (Delivery)

The two conditions for recognizing revenue (being realized or realizable and being earned) are usually met by the time the product or merchandise is delivered or services are rendered to customers.[2] Revenues from manufacturing and selling activities

OBJECTIVE **2**
**Describe
accounting issues
involved with
revenue recognition
at point of sale.**

[2]It should be noted that the SEC believes that revenue is realized or realizable and earned when all of the following criteria are met: (1) Persuasive evidence of an arrangement exists; (2) delivery has occurred or services have been rendered; (3) the seller's price to the buyer is fixed or determinable; and (4) collectibility is reasonably assured. See "Revenue Recognition in Financial Statements," *SEC Staff Accounting Bulletin No. 101* (December 3, 1999). The SEC provided more specific guidance because the general criteria were sometimes difficult to interpret.

are commonly recognized at **point of sale** (usually meaning delivery).[3] Problems of implementation, however, can arise. Two such situations are discussed below: (1) sales when right of return exists, and (2) trade loading and channel stuffing.

Sales When Right of Return Exists

Whether cash or credit sales are involved, a special problem arises with claims for returns and allowances. Certain companies experience such a **high rate of returns**— a high ratio of returned merchandise to sales—that they find it necessary to postpone reporting sales until the return privilege has substantially expired. For example, in the publishing industry the rate of return approaches 25 percent for hardcover books and 65 percent for some magazines. Other types of companies that experience high return rates are perishable food dealers, rack jobbers or distributors who sell to retail outlets, record and tape companies, and some toy and sporting goods manufacturers. Returns in these industries are frequently made either through a right of contract or as a matter of practice involving "guaranteed sales" agreements or consignments.

Three alternative revenue recognition methods are available when the seller is exposed to continued risks of ownership through return of the product. These are: (1) not recording a sale until all return privileges have expired; (2) recording the sale, but reducing sales by an estimate of future returns; and (3) recording the sale and accounting for the returns as they occur. The FASB concluded that if a company sells its product but gives the buyer the right to return it, then revenue from the sales transaction shall be recognized at the time of sale **only if all of the following** six conditions have been met.[4]

1. The seller's price to the buyer is substantially fixed or determinable at the date of sale.
2. The buyer has paid the seller, or the buyer is obligated to pay the seller and the obligation is not contingent on resale of the product.
3. The buyer's obligation to the seller would not be changed in the event of theft or physical destruction or damage of the product.
4. The buyer acquiring the product for resale has economic substance apart from that provided by the seller.
5. The seller does not have significant obligations for future performance to directly bring about resale of the product by the buyer.
6. The amount of future returns can be reasonably estimated.

What if revenue cannot be recognized at the time of sale because the six conditions are not met? In that case sales revenue and cost of sales that are not recognized at the time of sale should be recognized either when the return privilege has substantially expired or when those six conditions subsequently are met (whichever occurs first). Sales revenue and cost of sales reported in the income statement should be reduced by the amount of the estimated returns.

Trade Loading and Channel Stuffing

Some companies record revenues at date of delivery with neither buyback nor unlimited return provisions. Although they appear to be following acceptable point-of-sale revenue recognition practices, they are recognizing revenues and earnings prematurely. The domestic cigarette industry at one time engaged in a distribution practice known

---

[3]"Recognition and Measurement in Financial Statements of Business Enterprises," *Statement of Financial Accounting Concepts No. 5* (Stamford, Conn.: FASB, 1984), par. 84.

[4]"Revenue Recognition When Right of Return Exists," *Statement of Financial Accounting Standards No. 48* (Stamford, Conn.: FASB, 1981), par. 6.

as **trade loading**. "Trade loading is a crazy, uneconomic, insidious practice through which manufacturers—trying to show sales, profits, and market share they don't actually have—induce their wholesale customers, known as the trade, to buy more product than they can promptly resell."[5] In total, the cigarette industry appears to have exaggerated a couple years' operating profits by as much as $600 million by taking the profits from future years.

In the computer software industry this same practice is referred to as **channel stuffing**. When a software maker needed to make its financial results look good, it offered deep discounts to its distributors to overbuy and then recorded revenue when the software left the loading dock.[6] Of course, the distributors' inventories become bloated and the marketing channel gets stuffed, but the software maker's financials are improved—to the detriment of future periods' results, unless the process is repeated.

Trade loading and channel stuffing hype sales, distort operating results, and "window dress" financial statements. If used without an appropriate allowance for sales returns, channel stuffing is a classic example of booking tomorrow's revenue today. **The practices of trade loading and channel stuffing need to be discouraged.** Business managers need to be aware of the ethical dangers of misleading the financial community by engaging in such practices to improve their financial statements.

NO TAKE-BACKS, REVISITED

WHAT DO THE NUMBERS MEAN?

You may recall from an earlier discussion in Chapter 2 (page 37) that investors in **Lucent Technologies** were negatively affected when Lucent violated one of the fundamental criteria for revenue recognition—the "no take-back" rule, which holds that revenue should not be booked on inventory that is shipped if the customer can return it at some point in the future. In this particular case, Lucent agreed to take back shipped inventory from its distributors, if the distributors are unable to sell the items to their customers.

In essence, Lucent was "stuffing the channel." By booking sales when goods were shipped, even though it most likely would get them back, Lucent was able to report continued sales growth. However, Lucent investors got a nasty surprise when distributors returned those goods and Lucent was forced to restate its financial results. The restatement erased $679 million in revenues, turning an operating profit into a loss. In response to this bad news, Lucent's stock price declined $1.31 per share, or 8.5 percent. Lucent is not alone in this practice. **Sunbeam** got caught stuffing the sales channel with barbecue grills and other outdoor items, which contributed to its troubles when it was forced to restate its earnings.

Additional Disclosures of Revenue Recognition Policies

Investors can be tipped off to potential channel stuffing by carefully reviewing a company's revenue recognition policy for generous return policies and by watching inventory and receivable levels. When sales increase along with receivables, that's one sign that customers are not paying for goods shipped on credit. And growing inventory levels are an indicator that customers have all the goods they need. Both scenarios suggest a higher likelihood of goods being returned and revenues and income being restated. So remember, no take-backs!

Source: Adapted from S. Young, "Lucent Slashes First Quarter Outlook, Erases Revenue from Latest Quarter," *Wall Street Journal, Interactive Edition* (December 22, 2000), and Tracey Byrnes, "Too Many Thin Mints: Spotting the Practice of Channel Stuffing," *Wall Street Journal, Interactive Edition* (February 7, 2002).

---

[5]"The $600 Million Cigarette Scam," *Fortune* (December 4, 1989), p. 89.

[6]"Software's Dirty Little Secret," *Forbes* (May 15, 1989), p. 128.

Revenue Recognition Before Delivery

For the most part, recognition at the point of sale (delivery) is used because most of the uncertainties concerning the earning process are removed and the exchange price is known. Under certain circumstances, however, revenue is recognized prior to completion and delivery. The most notable example is long-term construction contract accounting where the percentage-of-completion method is applicable.

Long-term contracts such as construction-type contracts, development of military and commercial aircraft, weapons delivery systems, and space exploration hardware frequently provide that the seller (builder) may bill the purchaser at intervals, as various points in the project are reached. When the project consists of separable units such as a group of buildings or miles of roadway, passage of title and billing may take place at stated stages of completion, such as the completion of each building unit or every 10 miles of road. Such contract provisions provide for delivery in installments, and the accounting records should report this by recording sales when installments are "delivered."[7]

Two distinctly different methods of accounting for long-term construction contracts are recognized.[8] They are:

1. **Percentage-of-Completion Method.** Revenues and gross profit are recognized each period based upon the progress of the construction, that is, the percentage of completion.

2. **Completed-Contract Method.** Revenues and gross profit are recognized only when the contract is completed.

The rationale for using percentage-of-completion accounting is that under most of these contracts the buyer and seller have obtained enforceable rights. The buyer has the legal right to require specific performance on the contract. The seller has the right to require progress payments that provide evidence of the buyer's ownership interest. As a result, a continuous sale occurs as the work progresses, and revenue should be recognized accordingly.

The percentage-of-completion method must be used when estimates of progress toward completion, revenues, and costs are reasonably dependable and **all the following conditions** exist.[9]

1. The contract clearly specifies the enforceable rights regarding goods or services to be provided and received by the parties, the consideration to be exchanged, and the manner and terms of settlement.

2. The buyer can be expected to satisfy all obligations under the contract.

3. The contractor can be expected to perform the contractual obligations.

The completed-contract method should be used only (1) when an entity has primarily short-term contracts, or (2) when the conditions for using the percentage-of-completion method cannot be met, or (3) when there are inherent hazards in the contract beyond the normal, recurring business risks. The presumption is that **percentage-of-completion is the better method and that the completed-contract**

---

[7]*Statement of Financial Accounting Concepts No. 5*, par. 84, item c.

[8]*Accounting Trends and Techniques—2001* reports that, of the 95 of its 600 sample companies that referred to long-term construction contracts, 90 used the percentage-of-completion method and 5 used the completed-contract method.

[9]"Accounting for Performance of Construction-Type and Certain Production-Type Contracts," *Statement of Position 81-1* (New York: AICPA, 1981), par. 23.

method should be used only when the percentage-of-completion method is inappropriate.

Percentage-of-Completion Method

The **percentage-of-completion method** recognizes revenues, costs, and gross profit as progress is made toward completion on a long-term contract. To defer recognition of these items until completion of the entire contract is to misrepresent the efforts (costs) and accomplishments (revenues) of the interim accounting periods. In order to apply the percentage-of-completion method, one must have some basis or standard for measuring the progress toward completion at particular interim dates.

One of the common techniques used to determine the progress toward completion is the **cost-to-cost basis**. Under the cost-to-cost basis, the percentage of completion is measured by comparing costs incurred to date with the most recent estimate of the total costs to complete the contract, as shown in the following formula.

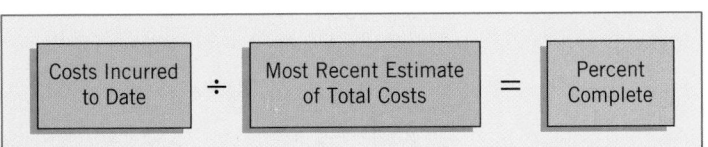

Illustration 6-3
Formula for Percentage of Completion, Cost-to-Cost Basis

The percentage that costs incurred bear to total estimated costs is applied to the total revenue or the estimated total gross profit on the contract in arriving at the revenue or the gross profit amounts to be recognized to date.

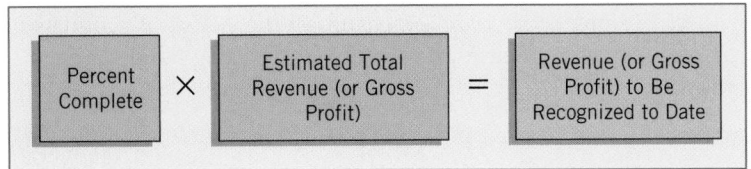

Illustration 6-4
Formula for Total Revenue to Be Recognized to Date

To find the amounts of revenue and gross profit recognized each period, we would need to subtract total revenue or gross profit recognized in prior periods, as shown in the following formula.

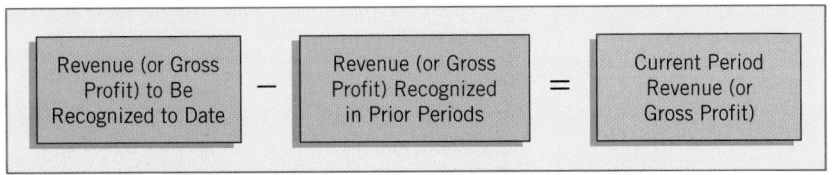

Illustration 6-5
Formula for Amount of Current Period Revenue, Cost-to-Cost Basis

Because **the profession specifically recommends the cost-to-cost method** (without excluding other bases for measuring progress toward completion), we have adopted it for use in our illustrations.[10]

Illustration of Percentage-of-Completion Method—Cost-to-Cost Basis. To illustrate the percentage-of-completion method, assume that Hardhat Construction Company has a contract starting July 2003, to construct a $4,500,000 bridge that is expected to be completed in October 2005, at an estimated cost of $4,000,000. The following data pertain to the construction period. (Note that by the end of 2004 the estimated total cost has increased from $4,000,000 to $4,050,000.)

---

[10]Committee on Accounting Procedure, "Long-Term Construction-Type Contracts," *Accounting Research Bulletin No. 45* (New York: AICPA, 1955), p. 7.

	2003	2004	2005
Costs to date	$1,000,000	$2,916,000	$4,050,000
Estimated costs to complete	3,000,000	1,134,000	—

The percentage complete would be computed as follows.

Illustration 6-6
Application of Percentage-of-Completion Method, Cost-to-Cost Basis

	2003	2004	2005
Contract price	$4,500,000	$4,500,000	$4,500,000
Less estimated cost			
Costs to date	1,000,000	2,916,000	4,050,000
Estimated costs to complete	3,000,000	1,134,000	—
Estimated total costs	4,000,000	4,050,000	4,050,000
Estimated total gross profit	$ 500,000	$ 450,000	$ 450,000
Percent complete	25%	72%	100%
	($1,000,000 / $4,000,000)	($2,916,000 / $4,050,000)	($4,050,000 / $4,050,000)

In this illustration, the costs incurred to date as a proportion of the estimated total costs to be incurred on the project are a measure of the extent of progress toward completion. The estimated revenue and gross profit to be recognized for each year are calculated as follows.

Illustration 6-7
Percentage-of-Completion, Revenue and Gross Profit, by Year

	2003	2004	2005
Revenue recognized in:			
2003 $4,500,000 × 25%	$1,125,000		
2004 $4,500,000 × 72%		$3,240,000	
Less: Revenue recognized in 2003		1,125,000	
Revenue in 2004		$2,115,000	
2005 $4,500,000 × 100%			$4,500,000
Less: Revenue recognized in 2003 and 2004			3,240,000
Revenue in 2005			$1,260,000
Gross profit recognized in:			
2003 $500,000 × 25%	$ 125,000		
2004 $450,000 × 72%		$ 324,000	
Less: Gross profit recognized in 2003		125,000	
Gross profit in 2004		$ 199,000	
2005 $450,000 × 100%			$ 450,000
Less: Gross profit recognized in 2003 and 2004			324,000
Gross profit in 2005			$ 126,000

Thus, in each year of the contract, new estimates of expected costs to complete the project are combined with realized costs, to determine the percentage of the project completed.

The Hardhat Construction Company illustration contained a **change in estimate** in the second year, 2004, when the estimated total costs increased from $4,000,000 to $4,050,000. The change in estimate is accounted for in a **cumulative catch-up manner**. This is done by adjusting the percent completed to the new estimate of total costs and then deducting the amount of revenues and gross profit recognized in prior periods from revenues and gross profit computed for progress to date. That is, the change in estimate is accounted for **in the period of change** so that the balance sheet at the end of the period of change and the accounting in subsequent periods are as they would have been if the revised estimate had been the original estimate.

Appendix 6B shows the journal entries that would be recorded in each year of the Hardhat contract.

UNDERLYING CONCEPTS

The completed-contract method does not violate the matching concept because the costs are also deferred until the completion of the contract.

Completed-Contract Method

Under the **completed-contract method**, revenue and gross profit are recognized only at point of sale, that is, when the contract is completed. Costs of long-term contracts in process are accumulated, but there are **no interim charges or credits to income statement accounts for revenues**, **costs**, **and gross profit**.

The principal advantage of the completed-contract method is that reported revenue is based on final results rather than on estimates of unperformed work. Its major disadvantage is that it does not reflect current performance when the period of a contract extends into more than one accounting period. Although operations may be fairly uniform during the period of the contract, revenue is not reported until the year of completion, creating a distortion of earnings.

Comparing the two methods in relation to the same bridge project, Hardhat Construction Company would have recognized gross profit as follows.

OBJECTIVE **4**
Apply the completed-contract method for long-term contracts.

	Percentage-of-Completion	Completed-Contract
2003	$125,000	$ 0
2004	199,000	0
2005	126,000	450,000

Illustration 6-8
Comparison of Gross Profit Recognized under Different Methods

Long-Term Contract Losses

Cost estimates at the end of the current period may indicate that a loss will result upon completion of the entire contract. Under both the percentage-of-completion and the completed-contract methods, **the entire expected contract loss must be recognized in the current period**. The treatment for unprofitable contracts is consistent with the accounting custom of anticipating foreseeable losses to avoid overstatement of current and future income (conservatism).

Illustration. To illustrate the accounting for an overall loss on a long-term contract, assume that at December 31, 2004, Hardhat Construction Company estimates the costs to complete the bridge contract at $1,640,250 instead of $1,134,000. Revised estimates relative to the bridge contract appear as follows.

Illustration 6-9
Computation of Loss
on Contract

	2003	2004
	Original Estimates	Revised Estimates
Contract price	$4,500,000	$4,500,000
Estimated total cost	4,000,000	4,556,250*
Estimated gross profit	$ 500,000	
Estimated loss		$ (56,250)

*($2,916,000 + $1,640,250)

Under the percentage-of-completion method, $125,000 of gross profit was recognized in 2003 (see Illustration 6-7). This $125,000 must be offset in 2004 because it is no longer expected to be realized. In addition, the total estimated loss of $56,250 must be recognized in 2004 since losses must be recognized as soon as estimable. Therefore, a total loss of $181,250 ($125,000 + $56,250) must be recognized in 2004.

Under the **completed-contract method**, the contract loss of $56,250 is also recognized in the year in which it first became evident. Because no previous income was recognized, the total loss reported in 2004 is $56,250.

Completion-of-Production Basis

In certain cases revenue is recognized at the completion of production even though no sale has been made. Examples of such situations involve precious metals or agricultural products with assured prices. Under the **completion-of-production basis**, revenue is recognized when these metals are mined or agricultural crops harvested because the sales price is reasonably assured, the units are interchangeable, and no significant costs are involved in distributing the product. When sale or cash receipt precedes production and delivery, as in the case of magazine subscriptions, revenues may be recognized as earned by production and delivery.[11]

Revenue Recognition After Delivery

In some cases, the collection of the sales price is not reasonably assured and revenue recognition is deferred. One of two methods is generally employed to defer revenue recognition until the cash is received: **the installment-sales method** or **the cost-recovery method**. In some situations cash is received prior to delivery or transfer of the property and is recorded as a deposit because the sale transaction is incomplete. This is referred to as the **deposit method**.

Installment-Sales Accounting Method

The installment-sales method **emphasizes collection rather than sale. It recognizes income in the periods of collection rather than in the period of sale.** This method is justified on the basis that when there is no reasonable approach for estimating the degree of collectibility, revenue should not be recognized until cash is collected.

The expression "installment sales" is generally used to describe any type of sale for which payment is required in periodic installments over an extended period of time. It is used in retailing where all types of farm and home equipment and furnishings are sold on an installment basis. It is also sometimes used in the heavy equipment indus-

UNDERLYING CONCEPTS

This is not an exception to the revenue recognition principle. At the completion of production, realization is virtually assured and the earning process is substantially completed.

OBJECTIVE 5
Describe the installment-sales and cost-recovery methods of accounting.

---

[11]Such revenue satisfies the criteria of *Concepts Statement No. 5* since the assets are readily realizable and the earning process is virtually complete (see par. 84, items b and c).

try in which machine installations are paid for over a long period. Another application of the method is in land development sales.

The installment-sales method is frequently justified on the grounds that the risk of not collecting an account receivable may be so great that the sale itself is not sufficient evidence that recognition should occur. In some cases this reasoning may be valid, but not in a majority of cases. The general approach is that if a sale has been completed, it should be recognized. If bad debts are expected, they should be recorded as separate estimates of uncollectibles. Although collection expenses, repossession expenses, and bad debts are an unavoidable part of installment sales, the incurrence of these costs and the collectibility of the receivables are reasonably predictable.

We study this topic in financial accounting because the method is acceptable in cases where a reasonable basis of estimating the degree of collectibility is deemed not to exist. In addition, weaknesses in the sales method of revenue recognition became very apparent when the franchise and land development booms of the 1960s and 1970s produced many failures and disillusioned investors. Application of the installment-sales method to **franchise and license operations** resulted in an abuse described as "front-end loading" (recognizing revenue prematurely, such as when the franchise is granted or the license issued rather than as it is earned or as the cash is received). Many **land development** ventures were susceptible to the same abuses. As a result, the FASB prescribes application of the installment-sales method of accounting for sales of real estate under certain circumstances.[12]

Expanded Discussion of the Accounting for Franchises

THE CHECK IS IN THE MAIL

Datapoint Corp. encouraged its customers to load up with large shipments at the end of the year, allowing Datapoint to report these shipments as revenues, even though payment hadn't been collected. Unfortunately, some of the customers either went broke or quit before paying for the equipment received. As a result, the company had to record substantial bad debts or in some cases reverse previously recorded sales. If Datapoint had used a less aggressive revenue recognition method, such as the installment-sales method, this revenue would not have been reported. As a result, revenue recognition practices that are cash-basis oriented, such as the installment-sales method, are becoming more acceptable as it becomes difficult to tell when a sale is a sale.

WHAT DO THE NUMBERS MEAN?

Illustration. Under the installment-sales method, each cash collection from a customer consists of (1) a partial recovery of the cost of the goods sold, and (2) partial gross profit from the sale. For example, if the gross profit rate at date of sale is 40 percent, each subsequent receipt consists of 60 percent recovery of cost of goods sold and 40 percent gross profit. The formula to recognize gross profit is as follows.

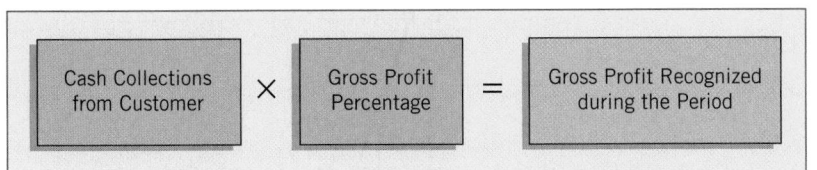

Illustration 6-10
Gross Profit Formula—
Installment-Sales Method

To illustrate, assume that an Iowa farm machinery dealer in the first year of operations had installment sales of $600,000 and a cost of goods sold on installment of $420,000. Total gross profit is, therefore, $180,000 ($600,000 − $420,000), and the gross

[12]"Accounting for Sales of Real Estate," *Statement of Financial Accounting Standards No. 66* (Norwalk, Conn.: FASB, 1982), pars. 45–47.

profit percentage is 30 percent ($180,000 ÷ $600,000). The collections on the installment sales were as follows: First year $280,000 (down payment plus monthly payments); second year $200,000; and, third year $120,000. The collections of cash and recognition of the gross profit are summarized in Illustration 6-11. (Interest charges are ignored in this illustration.)

Illustration 6-11

Gross Profit Recognized—Installment-Sales Method

Year	Cash Collected	×	Gross Profit Percentage	=	Gross Profit Recognized
2001	$280,000		30%		$ 84,000
2002	200,000		30%		60,000
2003	120,000		30%		36,000
Total	$600,000				$180,000

Under the installment-sales method of accounting, gross profit is therefore recognized **in the period in which the cash is collected**.

As indicated earlier, use of the installment-sales method is justified when the risk of not collecting an account receivable may be such that the sale is not sufficient evidence for revenue to be recognized.

To illustrate the installment-sales method in accounting for the sales of merchandise in a more complex situation, assume the following data.

Illustration 6-12

Installment-Sales Data

	2003	2004	2005
Installment sales	$200,000	$250,000	$240,000
Cost of installment sales	150,000	190,000	168,000
Gross profit	$ 50,000	$ 60,000	$ 72,000
Rate of gross profit on sales	25%[a]	24%[b]	30%[c]
Cash receipts			
2003 sales	$ 60,000	$100,000	$ 40,000
2004 sales		100,000	125,000
2005 sales			80,000

$$^a \frac{\$50,000}{\$200,000} \qquad ^b \frac{\$60,000}{\$250,000} \qquad ^c \frac{\$72,000}{\$240,000}$$

The realized gross profit is computed for the year 2003 as follows.

Illustration 6-13

Computation of Realized and Deferred Gross Profit, Year 1

2003	
Rate of gross profit current year	25%
Cash collected on current year's sales	$60,000
Realized gross profit (25% of $60,000)	15,000

The realized gross profit is computed for the year 2004 as follows.

Illustration 6-14
Computation of Realized and Deferred Gross Profit, Year 2

2004	
Current year's sales	
Rate of gross profit	24%
Cash collected on current year's sales	$100,000
Realized gross profit (24% of $100,000)	24,000
Prior year's sales	
Rate of gross profit—2003	25%
Cash collected on 2003 sales	$100,000
Gross profit realized in 2004 on 2003 sales (25% of $100,000)	25,000
Total gross profit realized in 2004	
Realized on collections of 2003 sales	$ 25,000
Realized on collections of 2004 sales	24,000
Total	$ 49,000

Note that the gross profit rate of each year's sales must be applied to cash collections of accounts receivable from that year's sales to arrive at the realized gross profit.

In 2005, the total gross profit realized would be $64,000, as shown by the following computations.

Illustration 6-15
Computation of Realized and Deferred Gross Profit, Year 3

2005	
Current year's sales	
Rate of gross profit	30%
Cash collected on current year's sales	$ 80,000
Gross profit realized on 2005 sales (30% of $80,000)	24,000
Prior years' sales	
2003 sales	
Rate of gross profit	25%
Cash collected	$ 40,000
Gross profit realized in 2005 on 2003 sales (25% of $40,000)	10,000
2004 sales	
Rate of gross profit	24%
Cash collected	$125,000
Gross profit realized in 2005 on 2004 sales (24% of $125,000)	30,000
Total gross profit realized in 2005	
Realized on collections of 2003 sales	$ 10,000
Realized on collections of 2004 sales	30,000
Realized on collections of 2005 sales	24,000
Total	$ 64,000

Expanded discussion of installment sales accounting, including journal entries, is presented in Appendix 6B.

Cost-Recovery Method

Under the cost-recovery method, no profit is recognized until cash payments by the buyer exceed the seller's cost of the merchandise sold. After all costs have been recovered, any additional cash collections are included in income. *APB Opinion No. 10* allows a seller to use the cost-recovery method to account for sales in which "there is no reasonable basis for estimating collectibility." This method is required under *FASB*

Statements No. 45 (franchises) and *No. 66* (real estate) where a high degree of uncertainty exists related to the collection of receivables.[13]

To illustrate the cost-recovery method, assume that early in 2003, Fesmire Manufacturing sells inventory with a cost of $25,000 to Higley Company for $36,000 with payments receivable of $18,000 in 2003, $12,000 in 2004, and $6,000 in 2005. If the cost-recovery method applies to this sale transaction and the cash is collected on schedule, the amount of gross profit recognized annually is shown below.

Illustration 6-16

Computation of Gross Profit—Cost-Recovery Method

Year	Cash Received	Original Cost Recovered	Balance of Unrecovered Cost	Gross Profit Realized
Beginning balance	—	—	$25,000	—
12/31/03	$18,000	$18,000	7,000	$ –0–
12/31/04	12,000	7,000	–0–	5,000
12/31/05	6,000	–0–	–0–	6,000

As shown, unlike the installment-sales method which recognizes income as cash is collected, the cost-recovery method recognizes profit only when cash collections exceed the total cost of the goods sold.

Deposit Method

In some cases, cash is received from the buyer before transfer of the goods or property; there is not sufficient transfer of the risks and rewards of ownership for a sale to be recorded. In such cases the seller has not performed under the contract and has no claim against the purchaser. The method of accounting for these incomplete transactions is the **deposit method**. Under the deposit method the seller reports the cash received from the buyer as a deposit on the contract and classifies it as a liability (refundable deposit or unearned revenue) on the balance sheet. The seller continues to report the property as an asset on its balance sheet, along with any related existing debt. Also, the seller continues to charge depreciation expense as a period cost for the property. **No revenue or income should be recognized until the sale is complete.**[14] At that time, the deposit account is closed and one of the revenue recognition methods discussed in this chapter is applied to the sale.

The **major difference between the installment-sales and cost-recovery methods and the deposit method** is that in the installment-sales and cost-recovery methods it is assumed that the seller has performed on the contract, but cash collection is highly uncertain. In the deposit method, the seller has not performed and no legitimate claim exists. The **deposit method** postpones recognizing a sale until a determination can be made as to whether a sale has occurred for accounting purposes. Revenue recognition is delayed until a future event occurs. If there has not been sufficient transfer of risks and rewards of ownership, even if a deposit has been received, recognition of the sale should be postponed until sufficient transfer has occurred. In that sense, the deposit method is not a revenue recognition method, whereas the installment-sales and cost-recovery methods are.

---

[13]"Omnibus Opinion—1966," *Opinions of the Accounting Principles Board No. 10* (New York: AICPA, 1969), footnote 8, page 149; "Accounting for Franchise Fee Revenue," *Statement of Financial Accounting Standards No. 45* (Stamford, Conn.: FASB, 1981), par. 6; "Accounting for Sales of Real Estate," *Statement of Financial Accounting Standards No. 66,* pars. 62 and 63.

[14]*Statement of Financial Accounting Standards No. 66,* par. 65.

Summary of Product Revenue Recognition Bases

The revenue recognition bases or methods, the criteria for their use, and the reasons for departing from the sale basis are summarized in Illustration 6-17.

Illustration 6-17
Revenue Recognition
Bases Other Than the Sale
Basis for Products[15]

Recognition Basis (or Method of Applying a Basis)	Criteria for Use	Reason(s) for Departing from Sale Basis
Percentage-of-completion method	Long-term construction of property; dependable estimates of extent of progress and cost to complete; reasonable assurance of collectibility of contract price; expectation that both contractor and buyer can meet obligations; and absence of inherent hazards that make estimates doubtful.	Availability of evidence of ultimate proceeds; better measure of periodic income; avoidance of fluctuations in revenues, expenses, and income; performance is a "continuous sale" and therefore not a departure from the sale basis.
Completed-contract method	Use on short-term contracts, and whenever percentage-of-completion cannot be used on long-term contracts.	Existence of inherent hazards in the contract beyond the normal, recurring business risks; conditions for using the percentage-of-completion method are absent.
Completion-of-production basis	Immediate marketability at quoted prices; unit interchangeability; difficulty of determining costs; and no significant distribution costs.	Known or determinable revenues; inability to determine costs and thereby defer expense recognition until sale.
Installment-sales method and cost-recovery method	Absence of reasonable basis for estimating degree of collectibility and costs of collection.	Collectibility of the receivable is so uncertain that gross profit (or income) is not recognized until cash is actually received.
Deposit method	Cash received before the sales transaction is completed.	No recognition of revenue and income because there is not sufficient transfer of the risks and rewards of ownership.

---

[15]Adapted from Henry R. Jaenicke, *Survey of Present Practices in Recognizing Revenues, Expenses, Gains, and Losses, A Research Report* (Stamford, Conn.: FASB, 1981), p. 11.

**WHAT DO THE
NUMBERS MEAN?**

NEW INDUSTRY, NEW RULES?

Inappropriate recognition of revenue can occur in any industry. Products that are sold to distributors for resale pose different risks than products or services that are sold directly to customers. Sales in high-technology industries, where rapid product obsolescence is a significant issue, pose different risks than sale of inventory with a longer life, such as farm or construction equipment, automobiles, trucks, and appliances.

Difficulties often occur with revenue recognition in new industries. For example, a number of dot-com companies, like **Ivillage**, **Salon.com**, and **Earthweb**, have turned themselves into virtual trading posts, swapping ad space with one another. In these situations, an equal amount of revenue and expense is reported, so there is no effect on cash flows and net income. But Internet stocks often trade on revenue multiples, not earning multiples. Therefore, reporting of higher revenue amounts may affect stock valuations. The SEC has expressed concern that dot-com companies like **Priceline** are increasing their revenue by including product sales in their revenue figures, even though they are acting only as the distributor (intermediary) on behalf of other companies. In other words, dot-com companies should be reporting only a distribution (brokerage) fee for selling another company's products.

Observations

As indicated earlier, the issue of the proper time to recognize revenue has received considerable attention over the last few years. A series of highly publicized cases of companies recognizing revenue prematurely has caused the SEC to increase its enforcement actions in this area. In some of these cases, significant adjustments to previously issued financial statements were made. As indicated by Lynn Turner, former chief accountant of the SEC, "When people cross over the boundaries of legitimate reporting, the Commission will take appropriate action to ensure the fairness and integrity that investors need and depend on every day." The SEC has made it clear that it will not tolerate abuses of the financial reporting process and that those who fail to adhere to "certain standards" will be prosecuted.

For our capital markets to be efficient, investors must have confidence that the financial information is both relevant and reliable. As a result, it is imperative that aggressive revenue recognition practices be eliminated. It is hoped that recent efforts by the SEC and the accounting profession will lead to higher-quality reporting in this area.

CASH FLOWS

**UNDERLYING
CONCEPTS**

The statement of cash flows meets one of the objectives of financial reporting—to help assess the amounts, timing, and uncertainty of future cash flows.

In Chapter 2, "assessing the amounts, timing, and uncertainty of cash flows" was presented as one of the three basic objectives of financial reporting. The balance sheet and the income statement present, to a limited extent, information about the cash flows of an enterprise during a period. For instance, comparative balance sheets might show what new assets have been acquired or disposed of and what liabilities have been incurred or liquidated. The income statement provides information about resources, but not exactly cash, provided by operations.

Indeed, the discussion in the first part of this chapter indicates that revenue recognition is based on certain criteria, which are not based on receipt of cash. And as discussed in Chapter 2, expenses are recorded according to matching or accrual principles rather than the payment of cash. While investors usually focus on net income measured on an accrual basis, information on cash flows can be important for assessing a company's liquidity, financial flexibility, and overall financial performance.

As shown in Illustration 6-18, **W.T. Grant** provides a classic example of the need to look not only at net income but also at cash flow from operations in evaluating financial performance.

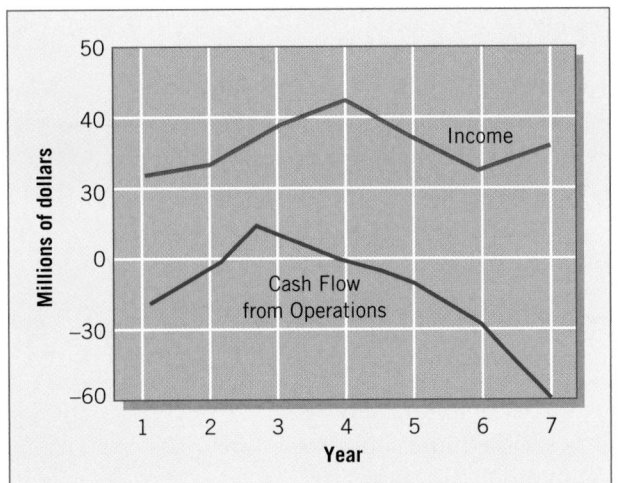

Illustration 6-18
Income and Cash Flow for
W.T. Grant.

Although W.T. Grant showed consistent profits and even some periods of earnings growth, its cash flow began to "go south." W.T. Grant filed for bankruptcy shortly after year 7. Analysis of cash flows would have provided an early-warning signal of W.T. Grant's problems.

Purpose of the Statement of Cash Flows

As indicated earlier, neither the balance sheet nor income statement presents a detailed summary of all the cash inflows and outflows or of the sources and uses of cash during the period. To fill this need, the FASB requires the **statement of cash flows** (also called the **cash flow statement**).[16]

The primary purpose of a statement of cash flows is to provide relevant information about the cash receipts and cash payments of an enterprise during a period. To achieve this purpose, the statement of cash flows reports (1) the cash effects of operations during a period, (2) investing transactions, (3) financing transactions, and (4) the net increase or decrease in cash during the period.[17]

Reporting the sources, uses, and net increase or decrease in cash helps investors, creditors, and others know what is happening to a company's most liquid resource. Most individuals maintain their checkbooks and prepare their tax returns on a cash basis. They thus can relate to the statement of cash flows and comprehend the causes and effects of cash inflows and outflows and the net increase or decrease in cash. The statement of cash flows provides answers to the following simple but important questions.

OBJECTIVE 6
Indicate the purpose of the statement of cash flows.

1. Where did the cash come from during the period?
2. What was the cash used for during the period?
3. What was the change in the cash balance during the period?

---

[16]"Statement of Cash Flows," *Statement of Financial Accounting Standards No. 95* (Stamford, Conn.: FASB, 1987).

[17]The basis recommended by the FASB is actually "cash and cash equivalents." Cash equivalents are short-term, highly liquid investments such as Treasury bills, commercial paper, and money market funds purchased with cash that is in excess of immediate needs.

Content and Format of the Statement of Cash Flows

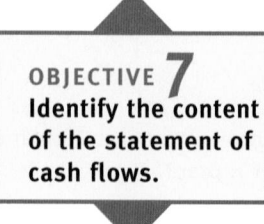

OBJECTIVE **7**
Identify the content of the statement of cash flows.

Cash receipts and cash payments during a period are classified in the statement of cash flows into three different activities—operating, investing, and financing activities. These classifications are defined as follows.

① **Operating activities** involve the cash effects of transactions that enter into the determination of net income.

② **Investing activities** include making and collecting loans and acquiring and disposing of investments (both debt and equity) and property, plant, and equipment.

③ **Financing activities** involve liability and owners' equity items. They include: (a) obtaining resources from owners and providing them with a return on (and a return of) their investment and (b) borrowing money from creditors and repaying the amounts borrowed.

With cash flows classified into those three categories, the statement of cash flows has assumed the following basic format.

Illustration 6-19

Basic Format of Cash Flow Statement

STATEMENT OF CASH FLOWS	
Cash flows from operating activities	$XXX
Cash flows from investing activities	XXX
Cash flows from financing activities	XXX
Net increase (decrease) in cash	XXX
Cash at beginning of year	XXX
Cash at end of year	$XXX

Illustration 6-20

Cash Inflows and Outflows

The inflows and outflows of cash classified by activity are shown in Illustration 6-20.

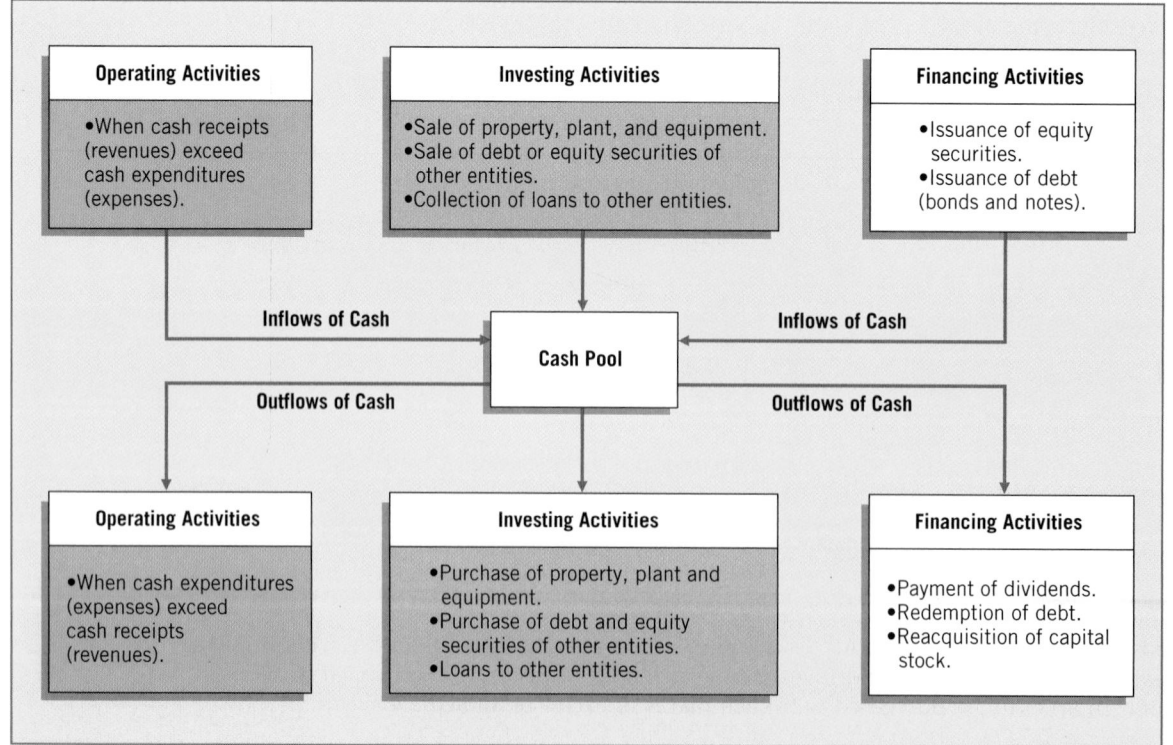

The statement's value is that it helps users evaluate liquidity, solvency, and financial flexibility. **Liquidity** refers to the "nearness to cash" of assets and liabilities. **Solvency** refers to the firms' ability to pay its debts as they mature. And **financial flexibility** refers to a firm's ability to respond and adapt to financial adversity and unexpected needs and opportunities.

Preparation of the Statement of Cash Flows

The information to prepare the statement of cash flows usually comes from (1) comparative balance sheets, (2) the current income statement, and (3) selected transaction data. Preparing the statement of cash flows from these sources involves four steps:

OBJECTIVE 8
Prepare a statement of cash flows.

1. Determine the cash provided by operations.
2. Determine the cash provided by or used in investing and financing activities.
3. Determine the change (increase or decrease) in cash during the period.
4. Reconcile the change in cash with the beginning and the ending cash balances.

The following simple illustration demonstrates how these steps are applied. On January 1, 2004, in its first year of operations, Telemarketing Inc. issued 50,000 shares of $1.00 par value common stock for $50,000 cash. The company rented its office space, furniture, and telecommunications equipment and performed surveys and marketing services throughout the first year. In June 2004 the company purchased land for $15,000. The comparative balance sheets at the beginning and end of the year 2004 and the income statement for the year ended 2004 are shown in Illustrations 6-21 and 6-22.

Illustration 6-21
Comparative Balance Sheets

TELEMARKETING INC.
BALANCE SHEETS

Assets	Dec. 31, 2004	Jan. 1, 2004	Increase/Decrease
Cash	$31,000	$ –0–	$31,000 Increase
Accounts receivable	41,000	–0–	41,000 Increase
Land	15,000	–0–	15,000 Increase
Total	$87,000	$ –0–	
Liabilities and Stockholders' Equity			
Accounts payable	$12,000	$ –0–	12,000 Increase
Common stock	50,000	–0–	50,000 Increase
Retained earnings	25,000	–0–	25,000 Increase
Total	$87,000	$ –0–	

Illustration 6-22
Income Statement Data

TELEMARKETING INC.
INCOME STATEMENT
FOR THE YEAR ENDED DECEMBER 31, 2004

Revenues	$172,000
Operating expenses	120,000
Income before income taxes	52,000
Income tax expense	13,000
Net income	$ 39,000

Additional information:
Dividends of $14,000 were paid during the year.

Cash provided by operations (the excess of cash receipts over cash payments) is determined by converting net income on an accrual basis to a cash basis. This is accomplished by adding to or deducting from net income those items in the income statement not affecting cash. This procedure requires an analysis not only of the current year's income statement but also of the comparative balance sheets and selected transaction data.

Analysis of Telemarketing's comparative balance sheets reveals two items that give rise to noncash credits or charges to the income statement: (1) The increase in accounts receivable reflects a noncash credit of $41,000 to revenues. (2) The increase in accounts payable reflects a noncash charge of $12,000 to expenses. **To arrive at cash provided by operations, the increase in accounts receivable must be deducted from net income, and the increase in accounts payable must be added back to net income.**

As a result of the accounts receivable and accounts payable adjustments, cash provided by operations is determined to be $10,000, computed as follows.

Illustration 6-23

Computation of Net Cash Provided by Operations

Net income		$ 39,000
Adjustments to reconcile net income		
to net cash provided by operating activities:		
Increase in accounts receivable	$(41,000)	
Increase in accounts payable	12,000	(29,000)
Net cash provided by operating activities		$ 10,000

The increase of $50,000 in common stock resulting from the issuance of 50,000 shares for cash is classified as a financing activity. Likewise, the payment of $14,000 cash in dividends is a financing activity. Telemarketing Inc.'s only investing activity was the land purchase. The statement of cash flows for Telemarketing Inc. for 2004 is as follows.

Illustration 6-24

Statement of Cash Flows

INTERNATIONAL INSIGHT

International Accounting Standard 7 requires a statement of cash flows. Both international standards and U.S. GAAP specify that the cash flows must be classified as operating, investing, or financing.

TELEMARKETING INC.		
STATEMENT OF CASH FLOWS		
FOR THE YEAR ENDED DECEMBER 31, 2004		
Cash flows from operating activities		
Net income		$39,000
Adjustments to reconcile net income to		
net cash provided by operating activities:		
Increase in accounts receivable	$(41,000)	
Increase in accounts payable	12,000	(29,000)
Net cash provided by operating activities		10,000
Cash flows from investing activities		
Purchase of land	(15,000)	
Net cash used by investing activities		(15,000)
Cash flows from financing activities		
Issuance of common stock	50,000	
Payment of cash dividends	(14,000)	
Net cash provided by financing activities		36,000
Net increase in cash		31,000
Cash at beginning of year		–0–
Cash at end of year		$31,000

The increase in cash of $31,000 reported in the statement of cash flows agrees with the increase of $31,000 in the Cash account calculated from the comparative balance sheets.

An illustration of a more comprehensive statement of cash flows is presented in Illustration 6-25.[18]

NESTOR COMPANY STATEMENT OF CASH FLOWS FOR THE YEAR ENDED DECEMBER 31, 2004		
Cash flows from operating activities		
Net income		$ 320,750
Adjustments to reconcile net income to net cash provided by operating activities:		
Depreciation expense	$88,400	
Amortization of intangibles	16,300	
Gain on sale of plant assets	(8,700)	
Increase in accounts receivable (net)	(11,000)	
Decrease in inventory	15,500	
Decrease in accounts payable	(9,500)	91,000
Net cash provided by operating activities		411,750
Cash flows from investing activities		
Sale of plant assets	90,500	
Purchase of equipment	(182,500)	
Purchase of land	(70,000)	
Net cash used by investing activities		(162,000)
Cash flows from financing activities		
Payment of cash dividend	(19,800)	
Issuance of common stock	100,000	
Redemption of bonds	(50,000)	
Net cash provided by financing activities		30,200
Net increase in cash		279,950
Cash at beginning of year		135,000
Cash at end of year		$ 414,950

Illustration 6-25
Comprehensive Statement of Cash Flows

INTERNATIONAL INSIGHT

Statements of cash flows are not required in all countries. Some nations require a statement reporting sources and applications of "funds" (often defined as working capital). Others have no requirement for either cash or funds flow statements.

Some significant non-cash transactions are reported either at the bottom of the statement or in a separate disclosure. Examples are (1) acquiring assets by issuing debt or equity securities, (2) exchanges of long-lived assets, and (3) issuance of equity securities to retire debt. For homework purposes, any significant non-cash transactions should not be reported on the statement of cash flows.

Usefulness of the Statement of Cash Flows

"Happiness is a positive cash flow" is certainly true. Although net income provides a long-term measure of a company's success or failure, cash is the lifeblood of a company. Without cash, a company will not survive.

Creditors examine the cash flow statement carefully because they are concerned about being paid. A good starting point in their examination is to find net cash provided by operating activities. A high amount of net cash provided by operating activities indicates that a company is able to generate sufficient cash internally from operations to pay its bills without further borrowing. Conversely, a low or negative amount

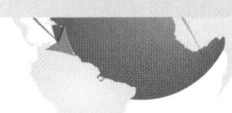

OBJECTIVE **9**
Understand the usefulness of the statement of cash flows.

[18]Chapter 17 presents an expanded discussion of preparation of the statement of cash flows.

of net cash provided by operating activities indicates that a company cannot generate enough cash internally from its operations and, therefore, must borrow or issue equity securities to acquire additional cash. Consequently, creditors look for answers to the following questions in the company's cash flow statements.

① How successful is the company in generating net cash provided by operating activities?

② What are the trends in net cash flow provided by operating activities over time?

③ What are the major reasons for the positive or negative net cash provided by operating activities?

You should recognize that companies can fail even though they are profitable. The difference between net income and net cash provided by operating activities can be substantial. Companies such as **W.T. Grant Company** and **Prime Motor Inn**, for example, reported high net income numbers but negative net cash provided by operating activities. Eventually both these companies filed for bankruptcy.

For W.T. Grant (see page 237), the reasons for the difference between a positive net income and a negative net cash provided by operating activities was substantial increases in receivables and/or inventory. To illustrate this problem more specifically, assume Ho Inc. in its first year of operations reported a net income of $80,000. Its net cash provided by operating activities, however, was a negative $95,000, as shown in Illustration 6-26.

Illustration 6-26
Negative Net Cash Provided by Operating Activities

HO INC.		
NET CASH FLOW FROM OPERATING ACTIVITIES		
Cash flows from operating activities		
Net income		$ 80,000
Adjustments to reconcile net income to net cash provided by operating activities:		
Increase in receivables	$(75,000)	
Increase in inventories	(100,000)	(175,000)
Net cash provided by operating activities		$ (95,000)

Note that the negative net cash provided by operating activities occurred for Ho even though it reported a positive net income. Ho could easily experience a "cash crunch" because it has tied up its cash in receivables and inventory. If problems in collecting receivables occur, or if inventory is slow moving or becomes obsolete, Ho's creditors may have difficulty collecting on their loans.

Financial Liquidity

One relationship (ratio) that is often used to assess liquidity is the **current cash debt coverage ratio**. It indicates whether the company can pay off its current liabilities in a given year from its operations. The formula for this ratio is:

Illustration 6-27
Formula for Current Cash Debt Coverage Ratio

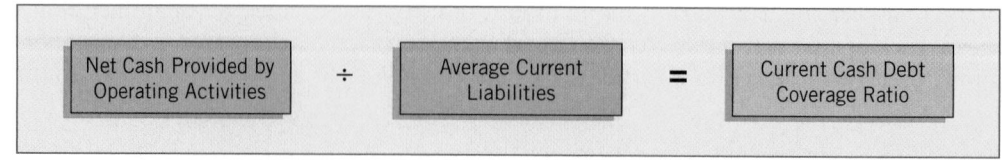

The higher this ratio, the less likely a company will have liquidity problems. For example, a ratio near 1:1 is good because it indicates that the company can meet all of its current obligations from internally generated cash flow.

Financial Flexibility

A more long-run measure which provides information on financial flexibility is the **cash debt coverage ratio**. This ratio indicates a company's ability to repay its liabilities from net cash provided by operating activities, without having to liquidate the assets employed in its operations. The formula for this ratio is:

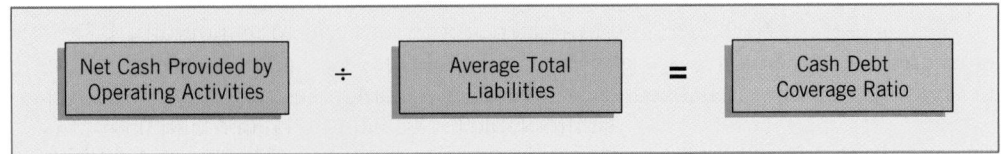

Net Cash Provided by Operating Activities	÷	Average Total Liabilities	=	Cash Debt Coverage Ratio

Illustration 6-28
Formula for Cash Debt
Coverage Ratio

The higher this ratio, the less likely the company will experience difficulty in meeting its obligations as they come due. As a result, it signals whether the company can pay its debts and survive if external sources of funds become limited or too expensive.

Free Cash Flow

A more sophisticated way to examine a company's financial flexibility is to develop a free cash flow analysis. This analysis starts with net cash provided by operating activities and ends with **free cash flow**, which is calculated as net cash provided by operating activities less capital expenditures and dividends.[19] Free cash flow is the amount of discretionary cash flow a company has for purchasing additional investments, retiring its debt, purchasing treasury stock, or simply adding to its liquidity.

This measure indicates a company's level of financial flexibility. Questions that a free cash flow analysis answers are:

1. Is the company able to pay its dividends without resorting to external financing?
2. If business operations decline, will the company be able to maintain its needed capital investment?
3. What is the free cash flow that can be used for additional investment, retirement of debt, purchase of treasury stock, or addition to liquidity?

Presented below is a free cash flow analysis using the cash flow statement for Nestor Company shown in Illustration 6-25 (page 241).

NESTOR COMPANY	
FREE CASH FLOW ANALYSIS	
Net cash provided by operating activities	$411,750
Less: Capital expenditures	(252,500)
Dividends	(19,800)
Free cash flow	$139,450

Illustration 6-29
Free Cash Flow
Computation

[19]In determining free cash flows, some companies do not subtract dividends because they believe these expenditures to be discretionary.

This analysis shows that Nestor has positive, and substantial, net cash provided by operating activities of $411,750. Nestor reports on its statement of cash flows that it purchased equipment of $182,500 and land of $70,000 for total capital spending of $252,500. This amount is subtracted from net cash provided by operating activities because without continued efforts to maintain and expand facilities it is unlikely that Nestor can continue to maintain its competitive position. Capital spending is deducted first on the free cash flow statement to indicate it is the least discretionary expenditure a company generally makes. Dividends are then deducted to arrive at free cash flow. Although a company can cut its dividend, it will usually do so only in a financial emergency. Nestor has more than sufficient cash flow to meet its capital spending and dividend payments and therefore has satisfactory financial flexibility.

Nestor used its free cash flow to redeem bonds and add to its liquidity. If it finds additional investments that are profitable, it can increase its spending without putting its dividend or basic capital spending in jeopardy. Companies that have strong financial flexibility can take advantage of profitable investments even in tough times. In addition, strong financial flexibility frees companies from worry about survival in poor economic times. In fact, those with strong financial flexibility often fare better in poor economic times because they can take advantage of opportunities that other companies cannot.

KEY TERMS

cash debt coverage
    ratio, *243*
completed-contract
    method, *229*
completion-of-production
    basis, *230*
cost-recovery method, *233*
cost-to-cost basis, *227*
current cash debt coverage
    ratio, *242*
deposit method, *234*
earned (revenues), *222*
financing activities, *238*
free cash flow, *243*
high rate of returns, *224*
installment-sales
    method, *230*
investing activities, *238*
operating activities, *238*
percentage-of-completion
    method, *227*
point of sale (delivery), *224*
realizable (revenues), *222*
realized (revenues), *222*
revenue recognition
    principle, *222*
statement of cash flows, *237*

SUMMARY OF LEARNING OBJECTIVES

❶ Apply the revenue recognition principle. The revenue recognition principle provides that revenue is recognized (1) when it is realized or realizable and (2) when it is earned. Revenues are realized when goods and services are exchanged for cash or claims to cash. Revenues are realizable when assets received in exchanges are readily convertible to known amounts of cash or claims to cash. Revenues are earned when the entity has substantially accomplished what it must do to be entitled to the benefits represented by the revenues, that is, when the earnings process is complete or virtually complete.

❷ Describe accounting issues involved with revenue recognition at point of sale. The two conditions for recognizing revenue are usually met by the time a product or merchandise is delivered or services are rendered to customers. Revenues from manufacturing and selling activities are commonly recognized at time of sale.

❸ Apply the percentage-of-completion method for long-term contracts. To apply the percentage-of-completion method to long-term contracts, one must have some basis for measuring the progress toward completion at particular interim dates. One of the most popular input measures used to determine the progress toward completion is the cost-to-cost basis. Using this basis, the percentage of completion is measured by comparing costs incurred to date with the most recent estimate of the total costs to complete the contract. The percentage that costs incurred bear to total estimated costs is applied to the total revenue or the estimated total gross profit on the contract in arriving at the revenue or the gross profit amounts to be recognized to date.

❹ Apply the completed-contract method for long-term contracts. Under this method, revenue and gross profit are recognized only at point of sale, that is, when the contract is completed. Under both the percentage-of-completion and the completed-contract methods, the entire expected contract loss must be recognized in the current period.

❺ Describe the installment-sales and cost-recovery methods of accounting. The *installment-sales method* recognizes income in the periods of collection rather than in the period of sale. The installment-sales method of accounting is justified on the basis that when there is no reasonable approach for estimating the degree of collectibility, revenue should not be recognized until cash is collected. Under the *cost-recovery method,* no profit is recognized until cash payments by the buyer exceed the seller's cost of the merchandise sold. After all costs have been recovered, any additional cash collections are included in income.

⑥ Indicate the purpose of the statement of cash flows. The primary purpose of a statement of cash flows is to provide relevant information about the cash receipts and cash payments of an enterprise during a period. Reporting the sources, uses, and net increase or decrease in cash enables investors, creditors, and others to know what is happening to a company's most liquid resource.

⑦ Identify the content of the statement of cash flows. Cash receipts and cash payments during a period are classified in the statement of cash flows into three different activities: (1) *Operating activities:* Involve the cash effects of transactions that enter into the determination of net income. (2) *Investing activities:* Include making and collecting loans and acquiring and disposing of investments (both debt and equity) and property, plant, and equipment. (3) *Financing activities:* Involve liability and owners' equity items and include (a) obtaining capital from owners and providing them with a return on their investment and (b) borrowing money from creditors and repaying the amounts borrowed.

⑧ Prepare a statement of cash flows. The information to prepare the statement of cash flows usually comes from (1) comparative balance sheets, (2) the current income statement, and (3) selected transaction data. Preparing the statement of cash flows from these sources involves the following steps: (1) determine the cash provided by operations; (2) determine the cash provided by or used in investing and financing activities; (3) determine the change (increase or decrease) in cash during the period; and (4) reconcile the change in cash with the beginning and the ending cash balances.

⑨ Understand the usefulness of the statement of cash flows. Creditors examine the cash flow statement carefully because they are concerned about being paid. The amount and trend of net cash flow provided by operating activities in relation to the company's liabilities is helpful in making this assessment. In addition, measures such as free cash flow provide creditors and stockholders with a better picture of the company's financial flexibility.

REVIEW EXERCISE

Diversified Products, Inc. operates in several lines of business including the construction and real estate industries. While the majority of its revenues are recognized at point of sale, Diversified appropriately recognizes revenue on long-term construction contracts using the percentage-of-completion method. It recognizes sales of some properties using the installment-sales approach. Income data for 2003 from operations other than construction and real estate are as follows.

Revenues	$9,500,000
Expenses	7,750,000

1. Diversified started a construction project during 2002. The total contract price is $1,000,000, and $200,000 in costs were incurred in 2003. Estimated costs to complete the project in 2004 are $400,000. In 2002 Diversified incurred $200,000 of costs and recognized $50,000 gross profit on this project.

2. During this year, Diversified sold real estate parcels at a price of $630,000. Gross profit at a 25% rate is recognized when cash is received. Diversified collected $500,000 during the year on these sales.

Instructions

(a) Determine net income for Diversified Products for 2003. Ignore taxes.

(b) Determine cash flow from operations for Diversified Products for 2003. In 2003 Diversified had depreciation expense of $175,000 and a net increase in working capital (changes in accounts receivable and accounts payable) of $250,000.

SOLUTION TO REVIEW EXERCISE

(a)

	Revenues	$9,500,000
	Expenses	7,750,000
		1,750,000
	Gross profit on construction contract*	50,000
	Gross profit on installment sales**	125,000
	Net income	$1,925,000

$$* \quad \frac{\$200,000 + \$200,000}{\$200,000 + \$200,000 + \$400,000} = 50\% \times (\$1,000,000 - \$800,000) = \$100,000$$

Less gross profit recognized in 2002	(50,000)
	$ 50,000

**$500,000 × 25% = $125,000

(b)

Net income	$1,925,000
Depreciation expense (non-cash expense)	175,000
Increase in working capital	(250,000)
Cash flow from operations	$1,850,000

RATIO ANALYSIS—A REFERENCE

USING RATIOS TO ANALYZE FINANCIAL PERFORMANCE

Qualitative information from financial statements can be gathered by examining relationships between items on the statements and identifying trends in these relationships. A useful starting point in developing this information is the application of ratio analysis.

A **ratio** expresses the mathematical relationship between one quantity and another. **Ratio analysis** expresses the relationship among selected financial statement data. The relationship is expressed in terms of either a percentage, a rate, or a simple proportion. To illustrate, recently **IBM Corporation** had current assets of $41,338 million and current liabilities of $29,226 million. The relationship is determined by dividing current assets by current liabilities. The alternative means of expression are:

> **Percentage:** Current assets are 141% of current liabilities.
> **Rate:** Current assets are 1.41 times as great as current liabilities.
> **Proportion:** The relationship of current assets to liabilities is 1.41:1.

For analysis of financial statements, ratios can be classified into four types, as follows.

<aside>
OBJECTIVE 10
After studying Appendix 6A, you should be able to: Identify the major types of financial ratios and what they measure.
</aside>

MAJOR TYPES OF RATIOS

LIQUIDITY RATIOS. Measures of the enterprise's short-run ability to pay its maturing obligations.

ACTIVITY RATIOS. Measures of how effectively the enterprise is using the assets employed.

PROFITABILITY RATIOS. Measures of the degree of success or failure of a given enterprise or division for a given period of time.

COVERAGE RATIOS. Measures of the degree of protection for long-term creditors and investors.

Expanded Discussion of Financial Statement Analysis

In Chapter 6 two ratios related to the statement of cash flows were discussed. Throughout the remainder of the textbook, ratios are provided to help you understand and interpret the information presented. In Illustration 6A-1 (on the next page) are the ratios that will be used throughout the text. You should find this chart helpful as you examine these ratios in more detail in the following chapters.

SUMMARY OF LEARNING OBJECTIVE FOR APPENDIX 6A

10 Identify the major types of financial ratios and what they measure. Ratios express the mathematical relationship between one quantity and another, in terms of either a percentage, a rate, or a proportion. *Liquidity ratios* measure the short-run ability to pay maturing obligations. *Activity ratios* measure the effectiveness of asset usage. *Profitability* ratios measure the success or failure of an enterprise. *Coverage ratios* measure the degree of protection for long-term creditors and investors.

<aside>
KEY TERMS

activity ratios, 247
coverage ratios, 247
liquidity ratios, 247
profitability ratios, 247
ratio analysis, 247
</aside>

Illustration 6A-1
A Summary of Financial Ratios

Ratio	Formula	Purpose or Use
I. Liquidity		
1. Current ratio	$\dfrac{\text{Current assets}}{\text{Current liabilities}}$	Measures short-term debt-paying ability
2. Quick or acid-test ratio	$\dfrac{\text{Cash, marketable securities, and receivables (net)}}{\text{Current liabilities}}$	Measures immediate short-term liquidity
3. Current cash debt coverage ratio	$\dfrac{\text{Net cash provided by operating activities}}{\text{Average current liabilities}}$	Measures a company's ability to pay off its current liabilities in a given year from its operations
II. Activity		
4. Receivable turnover	$\dfrac{\text{Net sales}}{\text{Average trade receivables (net)}}$	Measures liquidity of receivables
5. Inventory turnover	$\dfrac{\text{Cost of goods sold}}{\text{Average inventory}}$	Measures liquidity of inventory
6. Asset turnover	$\dfrac{\text{Net sales}}{\text{Average total assets}}$	Measures how efficiently assets are used to generate sales
III. Profitability		
7. Profit margin on sales	$\dfrac{\text{Net income}}{\text{Net sales}}$	Measures net income generated by each dollar of sales
8. Rate of return on assets	$\dfrac{\text{Net income}}{\text{Average total assets}}$	Measures overall profitability on assets
9. Rate of return on common stock equity	$\dfrac{\text{Net income minus preferred dividends}}{\text{Average common stockholders' equity}}$	Measures return on owners' investment
10. Earnings per share	$\dfrac{\text{Net income minus preferred dividends}}{\text{Weighted shares outstanding}}$	Measures net income earned on each share of common stock
11. Price-earnings ratio	$\dfrac{\text{Market price of stock}}{\text{Earnings per share}}$	Measures the ratio of the market price per share to earnings per share
12. Payout ratio	$\dfrac{\text{Cash dividends}}{\text{Net income}}$	Measures percentage of earnings distributed in the form of cash dividends
IV. Coverage		
13. Debt to total assets	$\dfrac{\text{Total debt}}{\text{Total assets or equities}}$	Measures the percentage of total assets provided by creditors
14. Times interest earned	$\dfrac{\text{Income before interest charges and taxes}}{\text{Interest charges}}$	Measures ability to meet interest payments as they come due
15. Cash debt coverage ratio	$\dfrac{\text{Net cash provided by operating activities}}{\text{Average total liabilities}}$	Measures a company's ability to repay its total liabilities in a given year from its operations
16. Book value per share	$\dfrac{\text{Common stockholders' equity}}{\text{Outstanding shares}}$	Measures the amount each share would receive if the company were liquidated at the amounts reported on the balance sheet

REVENUE RECOGNITION PROCEDURES

LONG-TERM CONTRACTS

To illustrate the percentage-of-completion method using journal entries, assume that Hardhat Construction Company has a contract starting July 2003, to construct a $4,500,000 bridge that is expected to be completed in October 2005, at an estimated cost of $4,000,000. The following data pertain to the construction period (note that by the end of 2004 the estimated total cost has increased from $4,000,000 to $4,050,000).

OBJECTIVE 11
After studying Appendix 6B, you should be able to: Prepare the journal entries to record long-terms contracts.

	2003	2004	2005
Costs to date	$1,000,000	$2,916,000	$4,050,000
Estimated costs to complete	3,000,000	1,134,000	—
Progress billings during the year	900,000	2,400,000	1,200,000
Cash collected during the year	750,000	1,750,000	2,000,000

The percent complete would be computed as follows.

	2003	2004	2005
Contract price	$4,500,000	$4,500,000	$4,500,000
Less estimated cost			
Costs to date	1,000,000	2,916,000	4,050,000
Estimated costs to complete	3,000,000	1,134,000	—
Estimated total costs	4,000,000	4,050,000	4,050,000
Estimated total gross profit	$ 500,000	$ 450,000	$ 450,000
Percent complete	25%	72%	100%
	$\left(\dfrac{\$1,000,000}{\$4,000,000}\right)$	$\left(\dfrac{\$2,916,000}{\$4,050,000}\right)$	$\left(\dfrac{\$4,050,000}{\$4,050,000}\right)$

Illustration 6B-1
Application of Percentage-of-Completion Method, Cost-to-Cost Basis

On the basis of the data above, the following entries would be prepared to record (1) the costs of construction, (2) progress billings, and (3) collections. These entries

Illustration 6B-2
Journal Entries— Percentage-of-Completion Method, Cost-to-Cost Basis

	2003		2004		2005	
To record costs of construction:						
Construction in Process	1,000,000		1,916,000		1,134,000	
Materials, Cash, Payables, etc.		1,000,000		1,916,000		1,134,000
To record progress billings:						
Accounts Receivable	900,000		2,400,000		1,200,000	
Billings on Construction in Process		900,000		2,400,000		1,200,000
To record collections:						
Cash	750,000		1,750,000		2,000,000	
Accounts Receivable		750,000		1,750,000		2,000,000

appear as summaries of the many transactions that would be entered individually as they occur during the year.

In this illustration, the costs incurred to date as a proportion of the estimated total costs to be incurred on the project are a measure of the extent of progress toward completion. The estimated revenue and gross profit to be recognized for each year are calculated as follows.

Illustration 6B-3
Percentage-of-Completion, Revenue and Gross Profit by Year

		2003	2004	2005
Revenue recognized in:				
2003	$4,500,000 × 25%	$1,125,000		
2004	$4,500,000 × 72%		$3,240,000	
	Less: Revenue recognized in 2003		1,125,000	
	Revenue in 2004		$2,115,000	
2005	$4,500,000 × 100%			$4,500,000
	Less: Revenue recognized in 2003 and 2004			3,240,000
	Revenue in 2005			$1,260,000
Gross profit recognized in:				
2003	$500,000 × 25%	$ 125,000		
2004	$450,000 × 72%		$ 324,000	
	Less: Gross profit recognized in 2003		125,000	
	Gross profit in 2004		$ 199,000	
2005	$450,000 × 100%			$ 450,000
	Less: Gross profit recognized in 2003 and 2004			324,000
	Gross profit in 2005			$ 126,000

Illustration 6B-4
Journal Entries to Recognize Revenue and Gross Profit and to Record Contract Completion—Percentage-of-Completion Method, Cost-to-Cost Basis

The entries to recognize revenue and gross profit each year and to record completion and final approval of the contract are shown below.

	2003		2004		2005	
To recognize revenue and gross profit:						
Construction in Process (gross profit)	125,000		199,000		126,000	
Construction Expenses	1,000,000		1,916,000		1,134,000	
Revenue from Long-Term Contract		1,125,000		2,115,000		1,260,000
To record completion of the contract:						
Billings on Construction in Process					4,500,000	
Construction in Process						4,500,000

Note that gross profit as computed in Illustration 6B-3 is debited to Construction in Process, and Revenue from Long-Term Contract is credited for the amounts as computed above. The difference between the amounts recognized each year for revenue and gross profit is debited to a nominal account, Construction Expenses. Similar to cost of goods sold in a manufacturing enterprise, this account is reported in the income statement and represents the actual cost of construction incurred in that period. For example, in the Hardhat Construction Company cost-to-cost illustration, the actual costs of $1,000,000 in 2003 are used to compute both the gross profit of $125,000 and the percent complete (25%).

Costs must continue to be accumulated in the Construction in Process account to maintain a record of total costs incurred (plus recognized profit) to date. Although theoretically a series of "sales" takes place using the percentage-of-completion method, the inventory cost cannot be removed until the construction is completed and transferred to the new owner. The Construction in Process account would include the following summarized entries over the term of the construction project.

	CONSTRUCTION IN PROCESS				
2003	construction costs	$1,000,000	12/31/05	to close	
2003	recognized gross profit	125,000		completed	
2004	construction costs	1,916,000		project	$4,500,000
2004	recognized gross profit	199,000			•
2005	construction costs	1,134,000			
2005	recognized gross profit	126,000			
	Total	$4,500,000	Total		$4,500,000

The Hardhat Construction Company illustration contained a **change in estimate** in the second year, 2004, when the estimated total costs increased from $4,000,000 to $4,050,000. The procedure used is to adjust the percent completed to the new estimate of total costs and then deduct the amount of revenues and gross profit recognized in prior periods from revenues and gross profit computed for progress to date. In this way, the change in estimate is accounted for in a **cumulative catch-up manner** (see year 2004 in Illustration 6B-1), **in the period of change**. Therefore the balance sheet at the end of the period of change and the accounting in subsequent periods are as they would have been if the revised estimate had been the original estimate.

Financial Statement Presentation—Percentage of Completion

Generally when a receivable from a sale is recorded, the Inventory account is reduced. In this case, however, both the receivable and the inventory continue to be carried. Subtracting the balance in the **Billings** account from Construction in Process avoids double-counting the inventory. During the life of the contract, the difference between the Construction in Process and the Billings on Construction in Process accounts is reported in the balance sheet **as a current asset if a debit, and as a current liability if a credit**.

When the costs incurred plus the gross profit recognized to date (the balance in Construction in Process) exceed the billings, this excess is reported as a current asset entitled "Cost and recognized profit in excess of billings." The unbilled portion of revenue recognized to date can be calculated at any time by subtracting the billings to date from the revenue recognized to date for 2003 for Hardhat Construction, as shown in Illustration 6B-6 (next page).

When the billings exceed costs incurred and gross profit to date, this excess is reported as a current liability entitled "Billings in excess of costs and recognized profit."

When a company has a number of projects, and costs exceed billings on some contracts and billings exceed costs on others, the contracts should be segregated. The asset side should include only those contracts on which costs and recognized profit exceed billings. The liability side includes only those on which billings exceed costs and

Contract revenue recognized to date: $4,500,000 \times \dfrac{\$1,000,000}{\$4,000,000} =$	$1,125,000
Billings to date	900,000
Unbilled revenue	$ 225,000

recognized profit. Separate disclosures of the dollar volume of billings and costs are preferable to a summary presentation of the net difference.

Using data from the previous illustration, Hardhat Construction Company would report the status and results of its long-term construction activities under the percentage-of-completion method as follows.

HARDHAT CONSTRUCTION COMPANY

	2003	2004	2005
Income Statement			
Revenue from long-term contracts	$1,125,000	$2,115,000	$1,260,000
Costs of construction	1,000,000	1,916,000	1,134,000
Gross profit	$ 125,000	$ 199,000	$ 126,000

Balance Sheet (12/31)

Current assets			
Accounts receivable		$ 150,000	$ 800,000
Inventories			
Construction in process	$1,125,000		
Less: Billings	900,000		
Costs and recognized profit in excess of billings		$ 225,000	
Current liabilities			
Billings ($3,300,000) in excess of costs and recognized profit ($3,240,000)			$ 60,000

Note 1. Summary of Significant Accounting Policies
Long-term construction contracts. The company recognizes revenues and reports profits from long-term construction contracts, its principal business, under the percentage-of-completion method of accounting. These contracts generally extend for periods in excess of one year. The amounts of revenues and profits recognized each year are based on the ratio of costs incurred to the total estimated costs. Costs included in construction in process include direct materials, direct labor, and project-related overhead. Corporate general and administrative expenses are charged to the periods as incurred and are not allocated to construction contracts.

Completed-Contract Method

The **annual entries** to record costs of construction, progress billings, and collections from customers would be identical to those illustrated under the percentage-of-completion method with the significant exclusion of the recognition of revenue and gross profit. For the bridge project of Hardhat Construction Company illustrated on the preceding pages, the following entries are made in 2005 under the completed-contract method to recognize revenue and costs and to close out the inventory and billing accounts.

2005

Billings on Construction in Process	4,500,000	
Revenue from Long-Term Contracts		4,500,000
Costs of Construction	4,050,000	
Construction in Process		4,050,000

Comparing the two methods in relation to the same bridge project, Hardhat Construction Company would have recognized gross profit as follows.

	Percentage-of-Completion	Completed-Contract
2003	$125,000	$ 0
2004	199,000	0
2005	126,000	450,000

Illustration 6B-8
Comparison of Gross Profit Recognized under Different Methods

Hardhat Construction would report its long-term construction activities as follows.

Illustration 6B-9
Financial Statement Presentation—Completed Contract Method

HARDHAT CONSTRUCTION COMPANY			
	2003	2004	2005
Income Statement			
Revenue from long-term contracts	—	—	$4,500,000
Costs of construction	—	—	4,050,000
Gross profit	—	—	$ 450,000

Balance Sheet (12/31)			
Current assets			
Accounts receivable		$150,000	$800,000
Inventories			
Construction in process	$1,000,000		
Less: Billings	900,000		
Unbilled contract costs		$100,000	
Current liabilities			
Billings ($3,300,000) in excess of contract			
costs ($2,916,000)			$384,000

Note 1. Summary of Significant Accounting Policies
Long-term construction contracts. The company recognizes revenues and reports profits from long-term construction contracts, its principal business, under the completed-contract method. These contracts generally extend for periods in excess of one year. Contract costs and billings are accumulated during the periods of construction, but no revenues or profits are recognized until completion of the contract. Costs included in construction in process include direct material, direct labor, and project-related overhead. Corporate general and administrative expenses are charged to the periods as incurred.

INSTALLMENT SALES

The steps to record installment sales are as follows.

For the sales in any one year:

① During the year, record both sales and cost of sales in the regular way, using the special accounts described later, and compute the rate of gross profit on installment-sales transactions.

OBJECTIVE **12**
Prepare the journal entries to record installment sales.

② At the end of the year, apply the rate of gross profit to the cash collections of the current year's installment sales to arrive at the realized gross profit.

③ The gross profit not realized should be deferred to future years.

For sales made in prior years:

① The gross profit rate of each year's sales must be applied against cash collections of accounts receivable resulting from that year's sales to arrive at the realized gross profit.

From the preceding discussion of the general practice followed in taking up income from installment sales, it is apparent that special accounts must be used. These accounts provide certain special information required to determine the realized and unrealized gross profit in each year of operations. The requirements for special accounts are as follows.

① Installment-sales transactions must be kept separate in the accounts from all other sales.

② Gross profit on sales sold on installment must be determinable.

③ The amount of cash collected on installment-sales accounts receivable must be known, and, further, the total collected on the current year's sales and on each preceding year's sales must be determinable.

④ Provision must be made for carrying forward each year's deferred gross profit.

In each year, ordinary operating expenses are charged to expense accounts and are closed to the Income Summary account as under customary accounting procedure. Thus, the only peculiarity in computing net income under the installment-sales method as generally applied is **the deferral of gross profit until realized by accounts receivable collection**.

To illustrate the installment-sales method in accounting for the sales of merchandise, assume the following data.

	2003	2004	2005
Installment sales	$200,000	$250,000	$240,000
Cost of installment sales	150,000	190,000	168,000
Gross profit	$ 50,000	$ 60,000	$ 72,000
Rate of gross profit on sales	25%[a]	24%[b]	30%[c]
Cash receipts			
2003 sales	$ 60,000	$100,000	$ 40,000
2004 sales		100,000	125,000
2005 sales			80,000

$$ ^a\ \frac{\$50,000}{\$200,000} \qquad ^b\ \frac{\$60,000}{\$250,000} \qquad ^c\ \frac{\$72,000}{\$240,000} $$

To simplify the illustration, interest charges have been excluded. Summary entries in general journal form for year 2003 are shown at the top of the next page.

2003

Installment Accounts Receivable, 2003	200,000	
Installment Sales		200,000
(To record sales made on installment in 2003)		
Cash	60,000	
Installment Accounts Receivable, 2003		60,000
(To record cash collected on installment receivables)		
Cost of Installment Sales	150,000	
Inventory (or Purchases)		150,000
(To record cost of goods sold on installment in 2003 on		
either a perpetual or a periodic inventory basis)		
Installment Sales	200,000	
Cost of Installment Sales		150,000
Deferred Gross Profit, 2003		50,000
(To close installment sales and cost of installment sales		
for the year)		
Deferred Gross Profit, 2003	15,000	
Realized Gross Profit on Installment Sales		15,000
(To remove from deferred gross profit the profit realized		
through cash collections; $60,000 \times 25\%$)		
Realized Gross Profit on Installment Sales	15,000	
Income Summary		15,000
(To close profits realized by collections)		

The realized and deferred gross profit is computed for the year 2003 as follows.

2003	
Rate of gross profit current year	25%
Cash collected on current year's sales	$60,000
Realized gross profit (25% of $60,000)	15,000
Gross profit to be deferred ($50,000 − $15,000)	35,000

Illustration 6B-10
Computation of Realized and Deferred Gross Profit, Year 1

Summary entries in journal form for year 2 (2004) are shown below.

2004

Installment Accounts Receivable, 2004	250,000	
Installment Sales		250,000
(To record sales made on installment in 2004)		
Cash	200,000	
Installment Accounts Receivable, 2003		100,000
Installment Accounts Receivable, 2004		100,000
(To record cash collected on installment receivables)		
Cost of Installment Sales	190,000	
Inventory (or Purchases)		190,000
(To record cost of goods sold on installment in 2004)		
Installment Sales	250,000	
Cost of Installment Sales		190,000
Deferred Gross Profit, 2004		60,000
(To close installment sales and cost of installment sales		
for the year)		

Deferred Gross Profit, 2003 ($100,000 × 25%)	25,000	
Deferred Gross Profit, 2004 ($100,000 × 24%)	24,000	
Realized Gross Profit on Installment Sales		49,000
(To remove from deferred gross profit the profit realized		
through collections)		
Realized Gross Profit on Installment Sales	49,000	
Income Summary		49,000
(To close profits realized by collections)		

The realized and deferred gross profit is computed for the year 2004 as follows.

Illustration 6B-11

Computation of Realized and Deferred Gross Profit, Year 2

2004

Current year's sales

Rate of gross profit	24%
Cash collected on current year's sales	$100,000
Realized gross profit (24% of $100,000)	24,000
Gross profit to be deferred ($60,000 − $24,000)	36,000

Prior year's sales

Rate of gross profit—2003	25%
Cash collected on 2003 sales	$100,000
Gross profit realized in 2004 on 2003 sales (25% of $100,000)	25,000

Total gross profit realized in 2004

Realized on collections of 2003 sales	$ 25,000
Realized on collections of 2004 sales	24,000
Total	$ 49,000

The entries in 2005 would be similar to those of 2004, and the total gross profit taken up or realized would be $64,000, as shown by the following computations.

Illustration 6B-12

Computation of Realized and Deferred Gross Profit, Year 3

2005

Current year's sales

Rate of gross profit	30%
Cash collected on current year's sales	$ 80,000
Gross profit realized on 2005 sales (30% of $80,000)	24,000
Gross profit to be deferred ($72,000 − $24,000)	48,000

Prior years' sales

2003 sales

Rate of gross profit	25%
Cash collected	$ 40,000
Gross profit realized in 2005 on 2003 sales (25% of $40,000)	10,000

2004 sales

Rate of gross profit	24%
Cash collected	$125,000
Gross profit realized in 2005 on 2004 sales (24% of $125,000)	30,000

Total gross profit realized in 2005

Realized on collections of 2003 sales	$ 10,000
Realized on collections of 2004 sales	30,000
Realized on collections of 2005 sales	24,000
Total	$ 64,000

Additional Problems of Installment-Sales Accounting

In addition to computing realized and deferred gross profit currently, other problems are involved in accounting for installment-sales transactions. These problems are related to:

1 Interest on installment contracts.
2 Uncollectible accounts.
3 Defaults and repossessions.

Interest on Installment Contracts

Because the collection of installment receivables is spread over a long period, it is customary to charge the buyer interest on the unpaid balance. A schedule of equal payments consisting of interest and principal is set up. Each successive payment is attributable to a smaller amount of interest and a correspondingly larger amount attributable to principal, as shown in Illustration 6B-13. This illustration assumes that an asset costing $2,400 is sold for $3,000 with interest of 8 percent included in the three installments of $1,164.10.

Date	Cash (Debit)	Interest Earned (Credit)	Installment Receivables (Credit)	Installment Unpaid Balance	Realized Gross Profit (20%)
1/2/03	—	—	—	$3,000.00	—
1/2/04	$1,164.10[a]	$240.00[b]	$ 924.10[c]	2,075.90[d]	$184.82[e]
1/2/05	1,164.10	166.07	998.03	1,077.87	199.61
1/2/06	1,164.10	86.23	1,077.87	–0–	215.57
					$600.00

[a]Periodic payment = Original unpaid balance ÷ PV of an annuity of $1.00 for three periods at 8% (Appendix A, Table 4); $1,164.10 = $3,000 ÷ 2.57710.
[b]$3,000.00 × .08 = $240.
[c]$1,164.10 − $240.00 = $924.10.
[d]$3,000.00 − $924.10 = $2,075.90.
[e]$924.10 × .20 = $184.82.

Illustration 6B-13
Installment Payment Schedule

Interest should be accounted for separately from the gross profit recognized on the installment-sales collections during the period. It is recognized as interest revenue at the time of the cash receipt.

Uncollectible Accounts

The problem of bad debts or uncollectible accounts receivable is somewhat different for concerns selling on an installment basis because of a repossession feature commonly incorporated in the sales agreement. This feature gives the selling company an opportunity to recoup any uncollectible accounts through repossession and resale of repossessed merchandise. If the experience of the company indicates that repossessions do not, as a rule, compensate for uncollectible balances, it may be advisable to provide for such losses through charges to a special bad debt expense account just as is done for other credit sales.

Defaults and Repossessions

Depending on the terms of the sales contract and the policy of the credit department, the seller can repossess merchandise sold under an installment arrangement if the purchaser fails to meet payment requirements. Repossessed merchandise may be reconditioned before being offered for sale. It may be resold for cash or installment payments.

The accounting for **repossessions** recognizes that the related installment receivable account is not collectible and that it should be written off. Along with the account receivable, the applicable deferred gross profit must be removed from the ledger using the following entry:

Repossessed Merchandise (an inventory account)	xx	
Deferred Gross Profit	xx	
Installment Accounts Receivable		xx

The entry above assumes that the repossessed merchandise is to be recorded on the books at exactly the amount of the uncollected account less the deferred gross profit applicable. This assumption may or may not be proper. The condition of the merchandise repossessed, the cost of reconditioning, and the market for second-hand merchandise of that particular type must all be considered. **The objective should be to put any asset acquired on the books at its fair value or, when fair value is not ascertainable, at the best possible approximation of fair value.** If the fair value of the merchandise repossessed is less than the uncollected balance less the deferred gross profit, a "loss on repossession" should be recorded at the date of repossession.

Some contend that repossessed merchandise should be entered at a valuation that will permit the company to make its regular rate of gross profit on resale. If it is entered at its approximated cost to purchase, the regular rate of gross profit could be provided for upon its ultimate sale, but that is completely a secondary consideration. It is more important that the asset acquired by repossession be recorded at fair value in accordance with the general practice of carrying assets at acquisition price as represented by the fair market value at the date of acquisition.

To illustrate the required entry, assume that a refrigerator was sold to Marilyn Hunt for $500 on September 1, 2003. Terms require a down payment of $200 and $20 on the first of every month for 15 months, starting October 1, 2003. It is further assumed that the refrigerator cost $300 and that it is sold to provide a 40 percent rate of gross profit on selling price. At the year-end, December 31, 2003, a total of $60 should have been collected in addition to the original down payment.

If Hunt makes her January and February payments in 2004 and then defaults, the account balances applicable to Hunt at time of default would be:

Installment Account Receivable ($500 − $200 − $20 − $20 − $20 − $20 − $20)	200 (dr.)
Deferred Gross Profit [40% × ($500 − $200 − $20 − $20 − $20)]	96 (cr.)

The deferred gross profit applicable to the Hunt account still has the December 31, 2003, balance because no entry has yet been made to take up gross profit realized by 2004 cash collections. The regular entry at the end of 2004, however, will take up the gross profit realized by all cash collections including amounts received from Hunt. Hence, the balance of deferred gross profit applicable to Hunt's account may be computed by applying the gross profit rate for the year of sale to the 2004 balance of Hunt's account receivable, 40 percent of $200, or $80. The account balances should therefore be considered as:

Installment Account Receivable (Hunt)	200 (dr.)
Deferred Gross Profit (applicable to Hunt after recognition of $8 of profit in both January and February)	80 (cr.)

If the estimated fair value of the article repossessed is set at $70, the following entry would be required to record the repossession:

Deferred Gross Profit	80	
Repossessed Merchandise	70	
Loss on Repossession	50	
Installment Account Receivable (Hunt)		200

The amount of the loss is determined by the following two steps: (1) Subtract the deferred gross profit from the amount of the account receivable, to determine the unrecovered cost (or book value) of the merchandise repossessed. (2) Subtract the estimated fair value of the merchandise repossessed from the unrecovered cost to get the amount of the loss on repossession. The loss on the refrigerator in our example is computed as shown in Illustration 6B-14.

Balance of account receivable (representing uncollected selling price)	$200
Less: Deferred gross profit	80
Unrecovered cost	120
Less: Estimated fair value of merchandise repossessed	70
Loss (Gain) on repossession	$ 50

Illustration 6B-14
Computation of Loss on Repossession

As pointed out earlier, the loss on repossession may be charged to Allowance for Doubtful Accounts if such an account is carried.

Financial Statement Presentation of Installment-Sales Transactions

If installment-sales transactions represent a significant part of total sales, full disclosure of installment sales, the cost of installment sales, and any expenses allocable to installment sales is desirable. If, however, installment sales constitute an insignificant part of total sales, it may be satisfactory to include only the realized gross profit in the income statement as a special item following the gross profit on sales, as shown below.

HEALTH MACHINE COMPANY	
STATEMENT OF INCOME	
FOR THE YEAR ENDED DECEMBER 31, 2004	
Sales	$620,000
Cost of goods sold	490,000
Gross profit on sales	130,000
Gross profit realized on installment sales	51,000
Total gross profit on sales	$181,000

Illustration 6B-15
Disclosure of Installment-Sales Transactions—Insignificant Amount

If more complete disclosure of installment-sales transactions is desired, a presentation similar to that shown in Illustration 6B-16 (next page) may be used.

The apparent awkwardness of this method of presentation is difficult to avoid if full disclosure of installment-sales transactions is to be provided in the income statement. One solution, of course, is to prepare a separate schedule showing installment-sales transactions, with only the final figure carried into the income statement.

Illustration 6B-16

Disclosure of Installment-Sales Transactions— Significant Amount

	Installment Sales	Other Sales	Total
HEALTH MACHINE COMPANY STATEMENT OF INCOME FOR THE YEAR ENDED DECEMBER 31, 2004			
Sales	$248,000	$620,000	$868,000
Cost of goods sold	182,000	490,000	672,000
Gross profit on sales	66,000	130,000	196,000
Less: Deferred gross profit on installment sales of this year	47,000		47,000
Realized gross profit on this year's sales	19,000	130,000	149,000
Add: Gross profit realized on installment sales of prior years	32,000		32,000
Gross profit realized this year	$ 51,000	$130,000	$181,000

In the balance sheet it is generally considered desirable to classify installment accounts receivable by year of collectibility. There is some question as to whether installment accounts that are not collectible for two or more years should be included in current assets. If installment sales are part of normal operations, they may be considered as current assets because they are collectible within the operating cycle of the business. Little confusion should result from this practice if maturity dates are fully disclosed, as illustrated in the following example.

Illustration 6B-17

Disclosure of Installment Accounts Receivable, by Year

Current assets		
Notes and accounts receivable		
Trade customers	$78,800	
Less: Allowance for doubtful accounts	3,700	
	75,100	
Installment accounts collectible in 2004	22,600	
Installment accounts collectible in 2005	47,200	$144,900

On the other hand, receivables from an installment contract (or contracts), resulting from a transaction not related to normal operations should be reported in the other assets section if due beyond one year.

Repossessed merchandise is a part of inventory and should be included as such in the current assets section of the balance sheet. Any gain or loss on repossessions should be included in the income statement in the "Other revenues and gains" or "Other expenses and losses" section.

Deferred gross profit on installment sales is generally treated as unearned revenue and is classified as a current liability. Theoretically, deferred gross profit consists of three elements: (1) income tax liability to be paid when the sales are reported as realized revenue (current liability); (2) allowance for collection expense, bad debts, and repossession losses (deduction from installment accounts receivable); and (3) net income (retained earnings, restricted as to dividend availability). Because of the difficulty in allocating deferred gross profit among these three elements, however, the whole amount is frequently reported as unearned revenue.

Summary of Learning Objectives for Appendix 6B

① Prepare the journal entries to record long-term contracts. Entries are necessary to record (1) costs of construction, (2) progress billings, and (3) collections. At the end of the period, revenue and gross profit are also recorded. The annual entries to record costs of construction, progress billings, and collections from customers under the completed-contract method would be identical to those for the percentage-of-completion method, with the significant exclusion of the recognition of revenue and gross profit.

② Prepare the journal entries to record installment sales. During the year, record both sales and cost of sales in the regular way. At the end of the year, apply the rate of gross profit to the cash collections of the current year's installment sales to arrive at the realized gross profit. The gross profit not realized should be deferred to future years.

Note: All **asterisked** Questions, Exercises, Problems, and Conceptual Cases relate to material contained in the appendixes to the chapter.

QUESTIONS

1 When is revenue conventionally recognized? What conditions should exist for the recognition at date of sale of all or part of the revenue and income of any sale transaction?

2 When is revenue recognized in the following situations: (a) Revenue from selling products? (b) Revenue from services rendered? (c) Revenue from permitting others to use enterprise assets? (d) Revenue from disposing of assets other than products?

3 Identify several types of sales transactions and indicate the types of business for which that type of transaction is common.

4 Barnaby Inc. is exposed to continued risks of a high rate of return of its products sold. Under what conditions may Barnaby recognize sales transactions as current revenue?

5 What are the two basic methods of accounting for long-term construction contracts? Indicate the circumstances that determine when one or the other of these methods should be used.

6 F. Scott Fitzgerald Construction Co. has a $60 million contract to construct a highway overpass and cloverleaf. The total estimated cost for the project is $50 million. Costs incurred in the first year of the project are $9 million. F. Scott Fitzgerald Construction Co. appropriately uses the percentage-of-completion method. How much revenue and gross profit should F. Scott Fitzgerald recognize in the first year of the project?

7 For what reasons should the percentage-of-completion method be used over the completed-contract method whenever possible?

8 What is a common input technique that is used to determine the extent of progress in long-term construction projects?

9 How are losses on the total long-term contracts accounted for?

10 Describe the installment-sales method of accounting.

11 Explain the differences between the installment-sales method and the cost-recovery method.

12 Identify and briefly describe the two methods generally employed to account for the cash received in situations where the collection of the sales price is not reasonably assured.

13 What is the deposit method and when might it be applied?

14 What is the nature of an installment sale? How do installment sales differ from ordinary credit sales?

15 Jack London sold his condominium for $500,000 on September 14, 2002; he had paid $310,000 for it in 1994. London collected the selling price as follows: 2002, $80,000; 2003, $320,000; and 2004, $100,000. London appropriately uses the installment-sales method. Prepare a schedule to determine the gross profit for 2002, 2003, and 2004 from the installment sale.

16 When is revenue recognized under the cost-recovery method?

17 When is revenue recognized under the deposit method? How does the deposit method differ from the installment-sales and cost-recovery methods?

18 What is the purpose of a statement of cash flows? How does it differ from a balance sheet and an income statement?

19 The net income for the year for Won Long, Inc. is $750,000, but the statement of cash flows reports that the cash provided by operating activities is $640,000. What might account for the difference?

20 Net income for the year for Jenkins, Inc. was $750,000, but the statement of cash flows reports that cash provided by operating activities was $860,000. What might account for the difference?

21 Differentiate between operating activities, investing activities, and financing activities.

22 Each of the following items must be considered in preparing a statement of cash flows. Indicate where each item is to be reported in the statement, if at all. Assume that net income is reported as $90,000.

(a) Accounts receivable increased from $32,000 to $39,000 from the beginning to the end of the year.

(b) During the year, 10,000 shares of preferred stock with a par value of $100 a share were issued at $115 per share.

(c) Depreciation expense amounted to $14,000, and bond premium amortization amounted to $5,000.

(d) Land increased from $10,000 to $30,000.

23 Marker Co. has net cash provided by operating activities of $900,000. Its average current liabilities for the period are $1,000,000, and its average total liabilities are $1,500,000. Comment on the company's liquidity and financial flexibility, given this information.

24 Net income for the year for Hatfield, Inc. was $750,000, but the statement of cash flows reports that cash provided by operating activities was $860,000. Hatfield also reported capital expenditures of $75,000 and paid dividends in the amount of $20,000. Compute Hatfield's free cash flow.

25 What is the purpose of a free cash flow analysis?

*26 Under the percentage-of-completion method, how are the Construction in Process and the Billings on Construction in Process accounts reported in the balance sheet?

BRIEF EXERCISES

BE6-1 Scooby Doo Music sold CDs to retailers and recorded sales revenue of $800,000. During 2002, retailers returned CDs to Scooby Doo and were granted credit of $78,000. Past experience indicates that the normal return rate is 15%. Prepare Scooby Doo's entries to record (a) the $78,000 of returns and (b) estimated returns at December 31, 2002.

BE6-2 Shock Wave, Inc. began work on a $7,000,000 contract in 2004 to construct an office building. During 2004, Shock Wave, Inc. incurred costs of $1,715,000. At December 31, 2004, the estimated future costs to complete the project total $3,185,000. Compute the estimated revenue and gross profit to be recognized in 2004.

BE6-3 Use the information from BE6-2, but assume Shock Wave uses the completed-contract method. Compute the estimated revenue and gross profit to be recognized in 2004.

BE6-4 Shaq Fu Construction Company began work on a $420,000 construction contract in 2004. During 2004, Shaq Fu incurred costs of $288,000, billed its customer for $215,000, and collected $175,000. At December 31, 2004, the estimated future costs to complete the project total $162,000. Determine Shaq Fu's profit or loss for 2002 using (a) the percentage-of-completion method and (b) the completed contract method, if any.

BE6-5 Thunder Paradise Corporation began selling goods on an installment basis on January 1, 2004. During 2004, Thunder Paradise had installment sales of $150,000; cash collections of $54,000; cost of installment sales of $105,000. Determine the gross profit recognized, using the installment-sales method.

BE6-6 Yogi Bear Corporation sold equipment to Magilla Company for $20,000. The equipment is on Yogi's books at a net amount of $14,000. Yogi collected $10,000 in 2003, $5,000 in 2004, and $5,000 in 2005. If Yogi uses the installment-sales method, what amount of gross profit will be recognized in each year?

BE6-7 Use the information from BE6-6. If Yogi uses the cost-recovery method, what amount of gross profit will be recognized in each year?

BE6-8 Midwest Beverage Company reported the following items in the most recent year.

Net income	$40,000
Dividends paid	5,000
Increase in accounts receivable	10,000
Increase in accounts payable	5,000
Purchase of equipment (capital expenditure)	8,000
Depreciation expense	4,000
Issue of notes payable	20,000

Compute cash flow provided by operations, the net change in cash during the year, and free cash flow.

BE6-9 Kes Company reported 2004 net income of $151,000. During 2004, accounts receivable increased by $13,000 and accounts payable increased by $9,500. Depreciation expense was $39,000. Prepare the cash flows from operating activities section of the statement of cash flows.

BE6-10 Yorkis Perez Corporation engaged in the following cash transactions during 2004.

Sale of land and building	$181,000
Purchase of treasury stock	40,000
Purchase of land	37,000
Payment of cash dividend	85,000
Purchase of equipment	53,000
Issuance of common stock	147,000
Retirement of bonds	100,000

Compute the net cash provided (used) by investing activities.

BE6-11 Use the information presented in BE6-10 for Yorkis Perez Corporation to compute the net cash used (provided) by financing activities.

BE6-12 Using the information in BE6-10, determine Yorkis Perez's free cash flow, assuming that it reported net cash provided by operating activities of $400,000.

*__BE6-13__ Using the information from BE6-2, prepare Shock Wave's 2004 journal entries using the percentage-of-completion method.

*__BE6-14__ Using the information from BE6-2, prepare Shock Wave's 2004 journal entries using the completed-contract method.

*__BE6-15__ Using the information in BE6-5, prepare Thunder Paradise's entries to record installment sales, cash collected, cost of installment sales, deferral of gross profit, and gross profit recognized.

EXERCISES

E6-1 (Recognition of Profit on Long-Term Contracts) During 2003 Pierson Company started a construction job with a contract price of $1,500,000. The job was completed in 2005. The following information is available.

	2003	2004	2005
Costs incurred to date	$400,000	$935,000	$1,070,000
Estimated costs to complete	600,000	165,000	–0–

Instructions

(a) Compute the amount of gross profit to be recognized each year assuming the percentage-of-completion method is used.

(b) Compute the amount of gross profit to be recognized each year assuming the completed-contract method is used.

(AICPA adapted)

E6-2 (Gross Profit on Uncompleted Contract) On April 1, 2003, Brad Bridgewater Inc. entered into a cost-plus-fixed-fee contract to construct an electric generator for Tom Dolan Corporation. At the contract date, Bridgewater estimated that it would take 2 years to complete the project at a cost of $2,000,000. The fixed fee stipulated in the contract is $450,000. Bridgewater appropriately accounts for this contract under the percentage-of-completion method. During 2003 Bridgewater incurred costs of $700,000 related to the project. The estimated cost at December 31, 2003, to complete the contract is $1,300,000. Dolan was billed $600,000 under the contract.

Instructions

Prepare a schedule to compute the amount of gross profit to be recognized by Bridgewater under the contract for the year ended December 31, 2003. Show supporting computations in good form.

(AICPA adapted)

E6-3 (Recognition of Profit, Percentage-of-Completion) In 2003 Jeff Rouse Construction Company agreed to construct an apartment building at a price of $1,000,000. The information relating to the costs and billings for this contract is as follows.

	2003	2004	2005
Costs incurred to date	$280,000	$600,000	$ 785,000
Estimated costs yet to be incurred	520,000	200,000	–0–
Customer billings to date	150,000	400,000	1,000,000
Collection of billings to date	120,000	320,000	940,000

Instructions

Assuming that the percentage-of-completion method is used, compute the amount of gross profit to be recognized in 2003, and 2004.

E6-4 (Recognition of Revenue on Long-Term Contract) Amy Van Dyken Construction Company uses the percentage-of-completion method of accounting. In 2003, Van Dyken began work under contract #E2-D2, which provided for a contract price of $2,200,000. Other details follow:

	2003	2004
Costs incurred during the year	$ 480,000	$1,425,000
Estimated costs to complete, as of December 31	1,120,000	–0–
Billings during the year	420,000	1,680,000

Instructions

(a) What portion of the total contract price would be recognized as revenue in 2003? In 2004?
(b) Assuming the same facts as those above except that Van Dyken uses the completed-contract method of accounting, what portion of the total contract price would be recognized as revenue in 2004?

E6-5 (Recognition of Profit for Long-Term Contracts) Andre Agassi Construction Company began operations January 1, 2003. During the year, Andre Agassi Construction entered into a contract with Lindsey Davenport Corp. to construct a manufacturing facility. At that time, Agassi estimated that it would take 5 years to complete the facility at a total cost of $4,500,000. The total contract price for construction of the facility is $6,300,000. During the year, Agassi incurred $1,185,800 in construction costs related to the construction project. The estimated cost to complete the contract is $4,204,200. Lindsey Davenport Corp. was billed and paid 30% of the contract price.

Instructions

Prepare schedules to compute the amount of gross profit to be recognized for the year ended December 31, 2003, under each of the following methods.

(a) Completed-contract method.
(b) Percentage-of-completion method.

Show supporting computations in good form.

(AICPA adapted)

E6-6 (Long-Term Contract Reporting) Derrick Adkins Construction Company began operations in 2003. Construction activity for the first year is shown below. All contracts are with different customers, and any work remaining at December 31, 2003, is expected to be completed in 2004.

Project	Total Contract Price	Billings through 12/31/03	Cash Collections through 12/31/03	Contract Costs Incurred through 12/31/03	Estimated Additional Costs to Complete
1	$ 560,000	$ 360,000	$340,000	$450,000	$140,000
2	670,000	220,000	210,000	126,000	504,000
3	500,000	500,000	440,000	330,000	–0–
	$1,730,000	$1,080,000	$990,000	$906,000	$644,000

Instructions

Derrick Adkins Construction Company uses the completed-contract method. Determine the amount of income or loss to be reported for each of the three projects in 2003.

E6-7 **(Installment-Sales Method Calculations)** Austin Corporation appropriately uses the installment-sales method of accounting to recognize income in its financial statements. The following information is available for 2003 and 2004.

	2003	2004
Installment sales	$900,000	$1,000,000
Cost of installment sales	630,000	680,000
Cash collections on 2003 sales	370,000	350,000
Cash collections on 2004 sales	–0–	475,000

Instructions

Compute the amount of realized gross profit recognized in each year.

(AICPA adapted)

E6-8 **(Installment-Sales and Cost-Recovery Methods)** Kenny Harrison Corp., a capital goods manufacturing business that started on January 4, 2003, and operates on a calendar-year basis, uses the installment-sales method of profit recognition in accounting for all its sales. The following data were taken from the 2003 and 2004 records.

	2003	2004
Installment sales	$480,000	$620,000
Gross profit as a percent of costs	25%	28%
Cash collections on sales of 2003	$140,000	$240,000
Cash collections on sales of 2004	–0–	$180,000

The amounts given for cash collections exclude amounts collected for interest charges.

Instructions

(a) Compute the amount of realized gross profit to be recognized on the 2004 income statement, using the installment-sales method.

(b) Compute the amount of realized gross profit to be recognized on the income statement, using the cost-recovery method.

(CIA adapted)

E6-9 **(Installment-Sales Method and Cost-Recovery Method)** On January 1, 2003, Barkley Company sold property for $200,000. The sale price will be collected as follows: $100,000 in 2003, $60,000 in 2004, and $40,000 in 2005. The property had cost Barkley $150,000 when it was purchased in 2001.

Instructions

(a) Compute the amount of gross profit realized each year assuming Barkley uses the cost-recovery method.

(b) Compute the amount of gross profit realized each year assuming Barkley uses the installment-sales method.

E6-10 **(Cost-Recovery Method)** On January 1, 2004, Tom Brands sells 200 acres of farmland for $600,000. Tom Brands purchased the farmland in 1989 at a cost of $500,000. The sale price will be paid in three installments of $200,000 each on December 31, 2004, 2005, and 2006. Collectibility of the payments is uncertain; Tom, therefore, uses the cost-recovery method.

Instructions

Determine the realized gross profit that Tom should recognize on December 31, 2004, 2005, and 2006.

E6-11 (Statement of Cash Flows—Classifications) The major classifications of activities reported in the statement of cash flows are operating, investing, and financing. Classify each of the transactions listed below as:

1. Operating activity—add to net income.
2. Operating activity—deduct from net income.
3. Investing activity.
4. Financing activity.
5. Not reported as a cash flow.

The transactions are as follows.

(a) Issuance of capital stock.
(b) Purchase of land and building.
(c) Redemption of bonds.
(d) Sale of equipment.
(e) Depreciation of machinery.
(f) Amortization of patent.
(g) Issuance of bonds for plant assets.

(h) Payment of cash dividends.
(i) Exchange of furniture for office equipment.
(j) Purchase of treasury stock.
(k) Loss on sale of equipment.
(l) Increase in accounts receivable during the year.
(m) Decrease in accounts payable during the year.

E6-12 (Preparation of a Statement of Cash Flows) The comparative balance sheets of Constantine Cavamanlis Inc. at the beginning and the end of the year 2004 appear below.

CONSTANTINE CAVAMANLIS INC.
BALANCE SHEETS

Assets	Dec. 31, 2004	Jan. 1, 2004	Inc./Dec.
Cash	$ 45,000	$ 13,000	$32,000 Inc.
Accounts receivable	91,000	88,000	3,000 Inc.
Equipment	39,000	22,000	17,000 Inc.
Less: Accumulated depreciation	(17,000)	(11,000)	6,000 Inc.
Total	$158,000	$112,000	
Liabilities and Stockholders' Equity			
Accounts payable	$ 20,000	$ 15,000	5,000 Inc.
Common stock	100,000	80,000	20,000 Inc.
Retained earnings	38,000	17,000	21,000 Inc.
Total	$158,000	$112,000	

Net income of $44,000 was reported and dividends of $23,000 were paid in 2004. New equipment was purchased and none was sold.

Instructions
Prepare a statement of cash flows for the year 2004.

E6-13 (Preparation of a Statement of Cash Flows) Presented below is a condensed version of the comparative balance sheets for Zubin Mehta Corporation for the last two years at December 31.

	2004	2003
Cash	$ 177,000	$ 78,000
Accounts receivable	180,000	185,000
Investments	52,000	74,000
Equipment	298,000	240,000
Less: Accumulated depreciation	(106,000)	(89,000)
Current liabilities	134,000	151,000
Capital stock	160,000	160,000
Retained earnings	307,000	177,000

Additional information:
Investments were sold at a loss (not extraordinary) of $10,000; no equipment was sold; cash dividends paid were $30,000; and net income was $160,000.

Instructions

(a) Prepare a statement of cash flows for 2004 for Zubin Mehta Corporation.
(b) Determine Zubin Mehta Corporation's free cash flow.

E6-14   (Preparation of a Statement of Cash Flows)   A comparative balance sheet for Shabbona Corporation is presented below.

	December 31	
Assets	2004	2003
Cash	$ 73,000	$ 22,000
Accounts receivable	82,000	66,000
Inventories	180,000	189,000
Land	71,000	110,000
Equipment	260,000	200,000
Accumulated depreciation—equipment	(69,000)	(42,000)
Total	$597,000	$545,000
Liabilities and Stockholders' Equity		
Accounts payable	$ 34,000	$ 47,000
Bonds payable	150,000	200,000
Common stock ($1 par)	214,000	164,000
Retained earnings	199,000	134,000
Total	$597,000	$545,000

Additional information:

1. Net income for 2004 was $125,000.
2. Cash dividends of $60,000 were declared and paid.
3. Bonds payable amounting to $50,000 were retired through issuance of common stock.

Instructions

(a) Prepare a statement of cash flows for 2004 for Shabbona Corporation.
(b) Determine Shabbona Corporation's current cash debt coverage ratio, cash debt coverage ratio, and free cash flow. Comment on its liquidity and financial flexibility.

E6-15   (Preparation of a Statement of Cash Flows and a Balance Sheet)   Grant Wood Corporation's balance sheet at the end of 2003 included the following items.

Current assets	$235,000	Current liabilities	$150,000
Land	30,000	Bonds payable	100,000
Building	120,000	Common stock	180,000
Equipment	90,000	Retained earnings	44,000
Accum. depr.—build.	(30,000)	Total	$474,000
Accum. depr.—equip.	(11,000)		
Patents	40,000		
Total	$474,000		

The following information is available for 2004.

1. Net income was $55,000.
2. Equipment (cost $20,000 and accumulated depreciation, $8,000) was sold for $10,000.
3. Depreciation expense was $4,000 on the building and $9,000 on equipment.

4. Patent amortization was $2,500.
5. Current assets other than cash increased by $29,000. Current liabilities increased by $13,000.
6. An addition to the building was completed at a cost of $27,000.
7. A long-term investment in stock was purchased for $16,000.
8. Bonds payable of $50,000 were issued.
9. Cash dividends of $30,000 were declared and paid.
10. Treasury stock was purchased at a cost of $11,000.

Instructions

(a) Prepare a statement of cash flows for 2004.
(b) Prepare a balance sheet at December 31, 2004.

E6-16 (Preparation of a Statement of Cash Flows, Analysis) The comparative balance sheets of Madrasah Corporation at the beginning and end of the year 2004 appear below.

MADRASAH CORPORATION
BALANCE SHEETS

Assets	Dec. 31, 2004	Jan. 1, 2004	Inc./Dec.
Cash	$ 20,000	$ 13,000	$ 7,000 Inc.
Accounts receivable	106,000	88,000	18,000 Inc.
Equipment	39,000	22,000	17,000 Inc.
Less: Accumulated depreciation	(17,000)	(11,000)	6,000 Inc.
Total	$148,000	$112,000	
Liabilities and Stockholders' Equity			
Accounts payable	$ 20,000	$ 15,000	5,000 Inc.
Common stock	100,000	80,000	20,000 Inc.
Retained earnings	28,000	17,000	11,000 Inc.
Total	$148,000	$112,000	

Net income of $44,000 was reported and dividends of $33,000 were paid in 2004. New equipment was purchased and none was sold.

Instructions

(a) Prepare a statement of cash flows for the year 2004.
*(b) Compute the current ratio as of January 1, 2004, and December 31, 2004, and compute free cash flow for the year 2004.
(c) In light of the analysis in (b), comment on Madrasah's liquidity and financial flexibility.

E6-17 (Preparation of a Statement of Cash Flows, Analysis) A comparative balance sheet for Nicholson Industries Inc. is presented below.

NICHOLSON INDUSTRIES INC.
BALANCE SHEETS

	December 31	
Assets	2004	2003
Cash	$ 13,000	$ 22,000
Accounts receivable	112,000	66,000
Inventories	220,000	189,000
Land	71,000	110,000

Equipment	260,000	200,000
Accumulated depreciation—equipment	(69,000)	(42,000)
Total	$607,000	$545,000
Liabilities and Stockholders' Equity		
Accounts payable	$ 44,000	$ 47,000
Bonds payable	150,000	200,000
Common stock ($1 par)	214,000	164,000
Retained earnings	199,000	134,000
Total	$607,000	$545,000

Additional information:

1. Net income for 2004 was $125,000.
2. Cash dividends of $60,000 were declared and paid.
3. Bonds payable amounting to $50,000 were retired through issuance of common stock.

Instructions

(a) Prepare a statement of cash flows for the year 2004 for Nicholson.
*(b) Compute the current and acid-test ratios for 2003 and 2004.
*(c) Compute Nicholson's free cash flow and the current cash debt coverage ratio for 2004.
(d) Based on the analyses in (b) and (c), comment on Nicholson's liquidity and financial flexibility.

*E6-18 **(Entries for Long-Term Contracts)** Assume the same information as in E6-4. Prepare a complete set of journal entries for Amy Van Dyken Construction for 2003, using the percentage-of-completion method.

*E6-19 **(Entries for Installment Sales)** Assume the same information as in E6-7. Prepare all journal entries required for Austin Corporation in 2004.

*E6-20 **(Analysis of Percentage-of-Completion Financial Statements)** In 2003, Beth Botsford Construction Corp. began construction work under a 3-year contract. The contract price was $1,000,000. Beth Botsford uses the percentage-of-completion method for financial accounting purposes. The income to be recognized each year is based on the proportion of cost incurred to total estimated costs for completing the contract. The financial statement presentations relating to this contract at December 31, 2003, follow.

Balance Sheet

Accounts receivable—construction contract billings		$21,500
Construction in progress	$65,000	
Less contract billings	61,500	
Cost of uncompleted contract in excess of billings		3,500

Income Statement

Income (before tax) on the contract recognized in 2003	$18,200

Instructions

(a) How much cash was collected in 2003 on this contract?
(b) What was the initial estimated total income before tax on this contract?

(AICPA adapted)

*E6-21 **(Gross Profit Calculations and Repossessed Merchandise)** Randy Barnes Corporation, which began business on January 1, 2003, appropriately uses the installment-sales method of accounting. The following data were obtained for the years 2003 and 2004.

	2003	2004
Installment sales	$750,000	$840,000
Cost of installment sales	525,000	604,800
General & administrative expenses	70,000	84,000
Cash collections on sales of 2003	310,000	300,000
Cash collections on sales of 2004	–0–	400,000

Instructions

(a) Compute the balance in the deferred gross profit accounts on December 31, 2003, and on December 31, 2004.

(b) A 2003 sale resulted in default in 2005. At the date of default, the balance on the installment receivable was $12,000, and the repossessed merchandise had a fair value of $8,000. Prepare the entry to record the repossession.

(AICPA adapted)

*E6-22 (Interest Revenue from Installment Sale) Gail Devers Corporation sells farm machinery on the installment plan. On July 1, 2003, Devers entered into an installment sale contract with Gwen Torrence Inc. for a 10-year period. Equal annual payments under the installment sale are $100,000 and are due on July 1. The first payment was made on July 1, 2003.

Additional information

1. The amount that would be realized on an outright sale of similar farm machinery is $676,000.
2. The cost of the farm machinery sold to Gwen Torrence Inc. is $500,000.
3. The finance charges relating to the installment period are $324,000 based on a stated interest rate of 10%, which is appropriate.
4. Circumstances are such that the collection of the installments due under the contract is reasonably assured.

Instructions

What income or loss before income taxes should Devers record for the year ended December 31, 2003, as a result of the transaction above?

(AICPA adapted)

PROBLEMS

P6-1 (Comprehensive Two-Part Revenue Recognition) Simona Amanar Industries has two operating divisions—Gina Construction Division and Chorkina Securities Division. Each division maintains its own accounting system and method of revenue recognition.

Gina Construction Division

During the fiscal year ended November 30, 2003, Gina Construction Division had one construction project in process. A $30,000,000 contract for construction of a civic center was granted on June 19, 2003, and construction began on August 1, 2003. Estimated costs of completion at the contract date were $25,000,000 over a 2-year time period from the date of the contract. On November 30, 2003, construction costs of $7,800,000 had been incurred and progress billings of $9,500,000 had been made. The construction costs to complete the remainder of the project were reviewed on November 30, 2003, and were estimated to amount to only $16,200,000 because of an expected decline in raw materials costs. Revenue recognition is based upon a percentage-of-completion method.

Chorkina Securities Division

Chorkina Securities Division works through manufacturers' agents in various cities. Orders for alarm systems and down payments are forwarded from agents, and the division ships the goods f.o.b. factory directly to customers (usually police departments and security guard companies). Customers are billed directly for the balance due plus actual shipping costs. The company received orders for $6,000,000 of goods during the fiscal year ended November 30, 2003. Down payments of $600,000 were received and $5,200,000 of goods were billed and shipped. Actual freight costs of $100,000 were also billed. Commissions of 10% on product price are paid to manufacturing agents after goods are shipped to customers. Such goods are warranted for 90 days after shipment, and warranty returns have been about 1% of sales. Revenue is recognized at the point of sale by this division.

Instructions

(a) There are a variety of methods of revenue recognition. Define and describe each of the following methods of revenue recognition and indicate whether each is in accordance with generally accepted accounting principles.

    (1) Point of sale.

    (2) Completion-of-production.

    (3) Percentage-of-completion.

    (4) Installment-sales.

(b) Compute the revenue to be recognized in fiscal year 2003 for the two operating divisions of Simona Amanar Industries in accordance with generally accepted accounting principles.

P6-2 **(Recognition of Profit on Long-Term Contract)** Jenny Thompson Construction Company has entered into a contract beginning January 1, 2003, to build a parking complex. It has been estimated that the complex will cost $600,000 and will take 3 years to construct. The complex will be billed to the purchasing company at $900,000. The following data pertain to the construction period.

	2003	2004	2005
Costs to date	$270,000	$420,000	$600,000
Estimated costs to complete	330,000	180,000	–0–
Progress billings to date	270,000	550,000	900,000
Cash collected to date	240,000	500,000	900,000

Instructions

(a) Using the percentage-of-completion method, compute the estimated gross profit that would be recognized during each year of the construction period.

(b) Using the completed-contract method, compute the estimated gross profit that would be recognized during each year of the construction period.

P6-3 **(Recognition of Profit on Long-Term Contract)** On March 1, 2003, Winter Company entered into a contract to build an apartment building. It is estimated that the building will cost $2,000,000 and will take 3 years to complete. The contract price was $3,000,000. The following information pertains to the construction period.

	2003	2004	2005
Costs to date	$ 600,000	$1,560,000	$2,100,000
Estimated costs to complete	1,400,000	390,000	–0–
Progress billings to date	1,050,000	2,100,000	3,000,000
Cash collected to date	950,000	1,950,000	2,750,000

Instructions

Compute the amount of gross profit to be recognized each year assuming the percentage-of-completion method is used.

P6-4 **(Recognition of Profit, Percentage-of-Completion)** On February 1, 2003, Amanda Beard Construction Company obtained a contract to build an athletic stadium. The stadium was to be built at a total cost of $5,400,000 and was scheduled for completion by September 1, 2005. One clause of the contract stated that Beard was to deduct $15,000 from the $6,600,000 billing price for each week that completion was delayed. Completion was delayed 6 weeks, which resulted in a $90,000 penalty. Below are the data pertaining to the construction period.

	2003	2004	2005
Costs to date	$1,782,000	$3,850,000	$5,500,000
Estimated costs to complete	3,618,000	1,650,000	–0–
Progress billings to date	1,200,000	3,100,000	6,510,000
Cash collected to date	1,000,000	2,800,000	6,510,000

Instructions

Using the percentage-of-completion method, compute the estimated gross profit recognized in the years 2003–2005.

P6-5 (Long-Term Contract with an Overall Loss) On July 1, 2003, Kim Kyung-wook Construction Company Inc. contracted to build an office building for Fu Mingxia Corp. for a total contract price of $1,950,000. On July 1, Kyung-wook estimated that it would take between 2 and 3 years to complete the building. On December 31, 2005, the building was deemed substantially completed. Following are accumulated contract costs incurred, estimated costs to complete the contract, and accumulated billings to Mingxia for 2003, 2004, and 2005.

	At 12/31/03	At 12/31/04	At 12/31/05
Contract costs incurred to date	$ 150,000	$1,200,000	$2,100,000
Estimated costs to complete the contract	1,350,000	800,000	–0–
Billings to Mingxia	300,000	1,100,000	1,850,000

Instructions

(a) Using the percentage-of-completion method, prepare schedules to compute the profit or loss to be recognized as a result of this contract for the years ended December 31, 2003, 2004, and 2005. (Ignore income taxes.)

(b) Using the completed-contract method, prepare schedules to compute the profit or loss to be recognized as a result of this contract for the years ended December 2003, 2004, and 2005. (Ignore income taxes.)

P6-6 (Installment Sales Computations) Presented below is summarized information for Deng Yaping Co., which sells merchandise on the installment basis.

	2003	2004	2005
Sales (on installment plan)	$250,000	$260,000	$280,000
Cost of sales	150,000	163,800	182,000
Gross profit	$100,000	$ 96,200	$ 98,000
Collections from customers on:			
2003 installment sales	$ 75,000	$100,000	$ 50,000
2004 installment sales		100,000	120,000
2005 installment sales			110,000

Instructions

Compute the realized gross profit for each of the years 2003, 2004, and 2005.

P6-7 (Installment Sales Income Statements) Laura Flessel Stores sells merchandise on open account as well as on installment terms.

	2003	2004	2005
Sales on account	$385,000	$426,000	$525,000
Installment sales	320,000	275,000	380,000
Collections on installment sales			
Made in 2003	110,000	90,000	40,000
Made in 2004		110,000	140,000
Made in 2005			125,000
Cost of sales			
Sold on account	270,000	277,000	341,000
Sold on installment	214,400	167,750	224,200
Selling expenses	77,000	87,000	92,000
Administrative expenses	50,000	51,000	52,000

Instructions

From the data above, which cover the 3 years since Laura Flessel Stores commenced operations, determine the net income for each year, applying the installment-sales method of accounting.

P6-8 (Completed-Contract Method) Renata Mauer Construction Company, Inc., entered into a firm fixed-price contract with Giovanna Trillini Clinic on July 1, 2001, to construct a four-story office building. At that time, Mauer estimated that it would take between 2 and 3 years to complete the project. The total contract price for construction of the building is $4,500,000. Mauer appropriately accounts for this contract under the completed-contract method in its financial statements and for income tax reporting. The building was deemed substantially completed on December 31, 2003. Estimated percentage of completion, accumulated contract costs incurred, estimated costs to complete the contract, and accumulated billings to the Trillini Clinic under the contract were as follows.

	At December 31, 2001	At December 31, 2002	At December 31, 2003
Percentage of completion	30%	65%	100%
Contract costs incurred	$1,140,000	$3,055,000	$4,800,000
Estimated costs to complete the contract	$2,660,000	$1,645,000	–0–
Billings to Trillini Clinic	$1,500,000	$2,500,000	$4,300,000

Instructions

Prepare schedules to compute the profit or loss to be recognized as a result of this contract for the years ended December 31, 2002, 2003, and 2004. Ignore income taxes. Show supporting computations in good form.

(AICPA adapted)

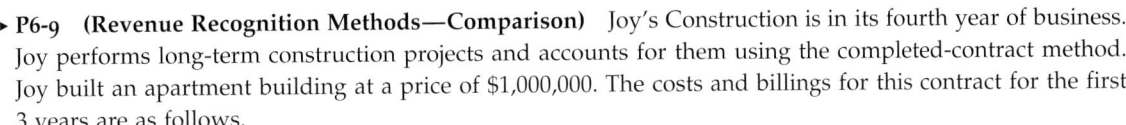 **P6-9 (Revenue Recognition Methods—Comparison)** Joy's Construction is in its fourth year of business. Joy performs long-term construction projects and accounts for them using the completed-contract method. Joy built an apartment building at a price of $1,000,000. The costs and billings for this contract for the first 3 years are as follows.

	2002	2003	2004
Costs incurred to date	$320,000	$600,000	$ 790,000
Estimated costs yet to be incurred	480,000	200,000	–0–
Customer billings to date	150,000	410,000	1,000,000
Collection of billings to date	120,000	340,000	950,000

Joy has contacted you, a certified public accountant, about the following concern. She would like to attract some investors, but she believes that in order to recognize revenue she must first "deliver" the product. Therefore, on her income statement she did not recognize any gross profits from the above contract until 2004, when she recognized the entire $210,000. That looked good for 2004, but the preceding years looked grim by comparison. She wants to know about an alternative to this completed-contract revenue recognition.

Instructions

Draft a letter to Joy, telling her about the percentage-of-completion method of recognizing revenue. Compare it to the completed-contract method. Explain the idea behind the percentage-of-completion method. In addition, illustrate how much revenue she could have recognized in 2002, 2003, and 2004 if she had used this method.

 **P6-10 (Comprehensive Problem—Long-Term Contracts)** You have been engaged by Rich Mathre Construction Company to advise it concerning the proper accounting for a series of long-term contracts. Rich Mathre Construction Company commenced doing business on January 1, 2003. Construction activities for the first year of operations are shown below. All contract costs are with different customers, and any work remaining at December 31, 2003, is expected to be completed in 2004.

Project	Total Contract Price	Billings Through 12/31/03	Cash Collections Through 12/31/03	Contract Costs Incurred Through 12/31/03	Estimated Additional Costs to Complete
A	$ 300,000	$200,000	$180,000	$248,000	$ 67,000
B	350,000	110,000	105,000	67,800	271,200
C	280,000	280,000	255,000	186,000	–0–
D	200,000	35,000	25,000	123,000	87,000
E	240,000	205,000	200,000	185,000	15,000
	$1,370,000	$830,000	$765,000	$809,800	$440,200

Instructions

(a) Prepare a schedule to compute gross profit (loss) to be reported, using the percentage-of-completion method.

(b) Repeat the requirements for part (a) assuming Rich Mathre uses the completed-contract method.

(c) Using the responses above for illustrative purposes, prepare a brief report comparing the conceptual merits (both positive and negative) of the two revenue recognition approaches.

P6-11 **(Preparation of a Statement of Cash Flows and a Balance Sheet)** Alistair Cooke Inc. had the following balance sheet at the end of operations for 2003.

ALISTAIR COOKE INC.
BALANCE SHEET
DECEMBER 31, 2003

Cash	$ 20,000	Accounts payable	$ 30,000
Accounts receivable	21,200	Long-term notes payable	41,000
Investments (trading)	32,000	Capital stock	100,000
Plant assets (net)	81,000	Retained earnings	23,200
Land	40,000		$194,200
	$194,200		

During 2004 the following occurred.

1. Alistair Cooke Inc. sold part of its investment portfolio for $17,000. This transaction resulted in a gain of $3,400 for the firm. The company often sells and buys securities of this nature.
2. A tract of land was purchased for $18,000 cash.
3. Long-term notes payable in the amount of $16,000 were retired before maturity by paying $16,000 cash.
4. An additional $24,000 in capital stock was issued at par.
5. Dividends totalling $8,200 were declared and paid to stockholders.
6. Net income for 2004 was $32,000 after allowing for depreciation of $12,000.
7. Land was purchased through the issuance of $30,000 in bonds.
8. At December 31, 2004, Cash was $39,000, Accounts Receivable was $41,600, and Accounts Payable remained at $30,000.

Instructions

(a) Prepare a statement of cash flows for 2004.

(b) Prepare the balance sheet as it would appear at December 31, 2004.

(c) How might the statement of cash flows help the user of the financial statements? Compute two cash flow ratios.

P6-12 **(Preparation of a Statement of Cash Flows and Balance Sheet)** Roger Mudd Inc. had the following balance sheet at the end of operations for 2003.

ROGER MUDD INC.
BALANCE SHEET
DECEMBER 31, 2003

Cash	$ 20,000	Accounts payable	$ 30,000
Accounts receivable	21,200	Bonds payable	41,000
Investments (trading)	32,000	Capital stock	100,000
Plant assets (net)	81,000	Retained earnings	23,200
Land	40,000		$194,200
	$194,200		

During 2004 the following occurred.

1. Mudd liquidated its investment portfolio at a loss of $3,000.
2. A tract of land was purchased for $38,000.
3. An additional $26,000 in common stock was issued at par.
4. Dividends totaling $10,000 were declared and paid to stockholders.
5. Net income for 2004 was $35,000, including $12,000 in depreciation expense.
6. Land was purchased through the issuance of $30,000 in additional bonds.
7. At December 31, 2004, Cash was $66,200, Accounts Receivable was $42,000, and Accounts Payable was $40,000.

Instructions

(a) Prepare a statement of cash flows for the year 2004 for Mudd.
(b) Prepare the balance sheet as it would appear at December 31, 2004.
(c) Compute the current and acid-test ratios for 2003 and 2004.
(d) Compute Mudd's free cash flow and the current cash debt coverage ratio for 2004.
(e) Use the analysis of Mudd to illustrate how information in the balance sheet and statement of cash flows helps the user of the financial statements.

*P6-13 **(Entries for Long-Term Contract)** Assume the same information as P6-3. (a) Prepare all necessary journal entries for Winter Company for 2005. (b) Prepare a partial balance sheet for December 31, 2004, showing the balances in the receivables and inventory accounts.

*P6-14 **(Installment Sales Entries)** Assume the same information as P6-6. Prepare the journal entries required by Deng Yaping Co. in 2005, applying the installment-sales method of accounting. (Ignore interest charges.)

*P6-15 **(Installment Sales Computations and Entries)** Isabell Werth Stores sell appliances for cash and also on the installment plan. Entries to record cost of sales are made monthly.

ISABELL WERTH STORES
TRIAL BALANCE
DECEMBER 31, 2005

	Dr.	Cr.
Cash	$153,000	
Installment Accounts Receivable, 2004	48,000	
Installment Accounts Receivable, 2005	91,000	
Inventory—New Merchandise	123,200	
Inventory—Repossessed Merchandise	24,000	
Accounts Payable		$ 98,500
Deferred Gross Profit, 2004		45,600
Capital Stock		170,000
Retained Earnings		93,900
Sales		343,000
Installment Sales		200,000

Cost of Sales	255,000	
Cost of Installment Sales	128,000	
Gain or Loss on Repossessions	800	
Selling and Administrative Expenses	128,000	
	$951,000	$951,000

The accounting department has prepared the following analysis of cash receipts for the year.

Cash sales (including repossessed merchandise)	$424,000
Installment accounts receivable, 2004	104,000
Installment accounts receivable, 2005	109,000
Other	36,000
Total	$673,000

Repossessions recorded during the year are summarized as follows.

	2004
Uncollected balance	$8,000
Loss on repossession	800
Repossessed merchandise	4,800

Instructions

From the trial balance and accompanying information:

(a) Compute the rate of gross profit for 2004 and 2005.
(b) Prepare closing entries as of December 31, 2005, under the installment-sales method of accounting.
(c) Prepare an income statement for the year ended December 31, 2005. Include only the realized gross profit in the income statement.

*P6-16 (Installment-Sales Entries) The following summarized information relates to the installment-sales activity of Lisa Jacob Stores Inc. for the year 2003.

Installment sales during 2003	$500,000
Costs of goods sold on installment basis	330,000
Collections from customers	200,000
Unpaid balances on merchandise repossessed	24,000
Estimated value of merchandise repossessed	9,200

Instructions

(a) Prepare journal entries at the end of 2003 to record on the books of Lisa Jacob Stores, Inc. the summarized data above.
(b) Prepare the entry to record the gross profit realized during 2003.

CONCEPTUAL CASES

C6-1 (Revenue Recognition—Alternative Methods) Alexsandra Isosev Industries has three operating divisions—Falilat Mining, Mourning Paperbacks, and Osygus Protection Devices. Each division maintains its own accounting system and method of revenue recognition.

Falilat Mining

Falilat Mining specializes in the extraction of precious metals such as silver, gold, and platinum. During the fiscal year ended November 30, 2003, Falilat entered into contracts worth $2,250,000 and shipped metals worth $2,000,000. A quarter of the shipments were made from inventories on hand at the beginning of the fiscal year, and the remainder were made from metals that were mined during the year. Mining totals for the year, valued at market prices, were: silver at $750,000, gold at $1,300,000, and platinum at $490,000. Falilat uses the completion-of-production method to recognize revenue, because its operations meet the specified criteria (i.e., reasonably assured sales prices, interchangeable units, and insignificant distribution costs).

Mourning Paperbacks

Mourning Paperbacks sells large quantities of novels to a few book distributors that in turn sell to several national chains of bookstores. Mourning allows distributors to return up to 30% of sales, and distributors give the same terms to bookstores. While returns from individual titles fluctuate greatly, the returns from distributors have averaged 20% in each of the past 5 years. A total of $8,000,000 of paperback novel sales were made to distributors during the fiscal year. On November 30, 2003, $3,200,000 of fiscal 2003 sales were still subject to return privileges over the next 6 months. The remaining $4,800,000 of fiscal 2003 sales had actual returns of 21%. Sales from fiscal 2003 totaling $2,500,000 were collected in fiscal 2003, with less than 18% of sales returned. Mourning records revenue according to the method referred to as revenue recognition when the right of return exits, because all applicable criteria for use of this method are met by Mourning's operations.

Osygus Protection Devices

Osygus Protection Devices works through manufacturers' agents in various cities. Orders for alarm systems and down payments are forwarded from agents, and Osygus ships the goods f.o.b. shipping point. Customers are billed for the balance due plus actual shipping costs. The firm received orders for $6,000,000 of goods during the fiscal year ended November 30, 2003. Down payments of $600,000 were received, and $5,000,000 of goods were billed and shipped. Actual freight costs of $100,000 were also billed. Commissions of 10% on product price were paid to manufacturers' agents after the goods were shipped to customers. Such goods are warranted for 90 days after shipment, and warranty returns have been about 1% of sales. Revenue is recognized at the point of sale by Osygus.

Instructions

(a) There are a variety of methods for revenue recognition. Define and describe each of the following methods of revenue recognition, and indicate whether each is in accordance with generally accepted accounting principles.
   (1) Completion-of-production method.
   (2) Percentage-of-completion method.
   (3) Installment-sales method.
(b) Compute the revenue to be recognized in the fiscal year ended November 30, 2003, for:
   (1) Falilat Mining.
   (2) Mourning Paperbacks.
   (3) Osygus Protection Devices.

(CMA adapted)

C6-2 **(Recognition of Revenue—Theory)** Revenue is usually recognized at the point of sale. Under special circumstances, however, bases other than the point of sale are used for the timing of revenue recognition.

Instructions

(a) Why is the point of sale usually used as the basis for the timing of revenue recognition?
(b) Disregarding the special circumstances when bases other than the point of sale are used, discuss the merits of each of the following objections to the sales basis of revenue recognition.
   (1) It is too conservative because revenue is earned throughout the entire process of production.
   (2) It is not conservative enough because accounts receivable do not represent disposable funds, sales returns and allowances may be made, and collection and bad debt expenses may be incurred in a later period.
(c) Revenue may also be recognized (1) during production and (2) when cash is received. For each of these two bases of timing revenue recognition, give an example of the circumstances in which it is properly used and discuss the accounting merits of its use in lieu of the sales basis.

(AICPA adapted)

C6-3 **(Recognition of Revenue—Theory)** The earning of revenue by a business enterprise is recognized for accounting purposes when the transaction is recorded. In some situations, revenue is recognized approximately as it is earned in the economic sense. In other situations, however, accountants have developed guidelines for recognizing revenue by other criteria, such as at the point of sale.

Instructions

(Ignore income taxes.)

(a) Explain and justify why revenue is often recognized as earned at time of sale.

(b) Explain in what situations it would be appropriate to recognize revenue as the productive activity takes place.

(c) At what times, other than those included in (a) and (b) above, may it be appropriate to recognize revenue? Explain.

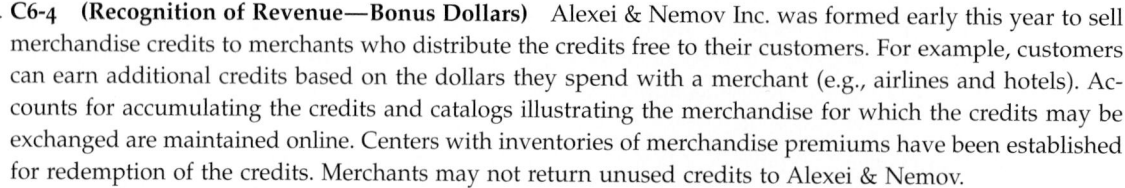

C6-4 (Recognition of Revenue—Bonus Dollars) Alexei & Nemov Inc. was formed early this year to sell merchandise credits to merchants who distribute the credits free to their customers. For example, customers can earn additional credits based on the dollars they spend with a merchant (e.g., airlines and hotels). Accounts for accumulating the credits and catalogs illustrating the merchandise for which the credits may be exchanged are maintained online. Centers with inventories of merchandise premiums have been established for redemption of the credits. Merchants may not return unused credits to Alexei & Nemov.

The following schedule expresses Alexei & Nemov's expectations as to percentages of a normal month's activity that will be attained. For this purpose, a "normal month's activity" is defined as the level of operations expected when expansion of activities ceases or tapers off to a stable rate. The company expects that this level will be attained in the third year and that sales of credits will average $6,000,000 per month throughout the third year.

Month	Actual Credit Sales Percent	Merchandise Premium Purchases Percent	Credit Redemptions Percent
6th	30%	40%	10%
12th	60	60	45
18th	80	80	70
24th	90	90	80
30th	100	100	95

Alexei & Nemov plans to adopt an annual closing date at the end of each 12 months of operation.

Instructions

(a) Discuss the factors to be considered in determining when revenue should be recognized in measuring the income of a business enterprise.

(b) Discuss the accounting alternatives that should be considered by Alexei & Nemov Inc. for the recognition of its revenues and related expenses.

(c) For each accounting alternative discussed in (b), give balance sheet accounts that should be used and indicate how each should be classified.

(AICPA adapted)

C6-5 (Recognition of Revenue from Subscriptions) *Cutting Edge* is a monthly magazine that has been on the market for 18 months. It currently has a circulation of 1.4 million copies. Currently negotiations are underway to obtain a bank loan in order to update their facilities. They are producing close to capacity and expect to grow at an average of 20% per year over the next 3 years.

After reviewing the financial statements of *Cutting Edge*, Gary Hall, the bank loan officer, had indicated that a loan could be offered to *Cutting Edge* only if it could increase its current ratio and decrease its debt to equity ratio to a specified level.

Alexander Popov, the marketing manager of *Cutting Edge,* has devised a plan to meet these requirements. Popov indicates that an advertising campaign can be initiated to immediately increase circulation. The potential customers would be contacted after the purchase of another magazine's mailing list. The campaign would include:

1. An offer to subscribe to *Cutting Edge* at three-fourths the normal price.

2. A special offer to all new subscribers to receive the most current world atlas whenever requested at a guaranteed price of $2.00.

3. An unconditional guarantee that any subscriber will receive a full refund if dissatisfied with the magazine.

Although the offer of a full refund is risky, Popov claims that few people will ask for a refund after receiving half of their subscription issues. Popov notes that other magazine companies have tried this sales promotion technique and experienced great success. Their average cancellation rate was 25%. On the average, each company increased its initial circulation threefold and in the long run had increased circulation to twice that which existed before the promotion. In addition, 60% of the new subscribers are expected to take advantage of the atlas premium. Popov feels confident that the increased subscriptions from the advertising campaign will increase the current ratio and decrease the debt to equity ratio.

You are the controller of *Cutting Edge* and must give your opinion of the proposed plan.

Instructions
(a) When should revenue from the new subscriptions be recognized?
(b) How would you classify the estimated sales returns stemming from the unconditional guarantee?
(c) How should the atlas premium be recorded? Is the estimated premium claims a liability? Explain.
(d) Does the proposed plan achieve the goals of increasing the current ratio and decreasing the debt to equity ratio?

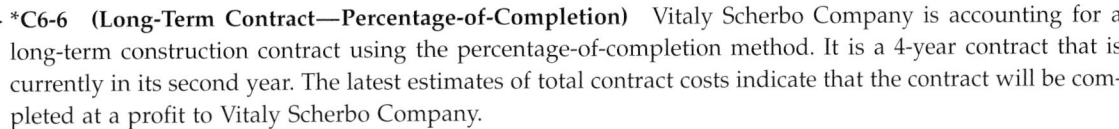 ***C6-6 (Long-Term Contract—Percentage-of-Completion)** Vitaly Scherbo Company is accounting for a long-term construction contract using the percentage-of-completion method. It is a 4-year contract that is currently in its second year. The latest estimates of total contract costs indicate that the contract will be completed at a profit to Vitaly Scherbo Company.

Instructions
(a) What theoretical justification is there for Vitaly Scherbo Company's use of the percentage-of-completion method?
(b) How would progress billings be accounted for? Include in your discussion the classification of progress billings in Vitaly Scherbo Company financial statements.
(c) How would the income recognized in the second year of the 4-year contract be determined using the cost-to-cost method of determining percentage of completion?
(d) What would be the effect on earnings per share in the second year of the 4-year contract of using the percentage-of-completion method instead of the completed-contract method? Discuss.

(AICPA adapted)

*C6-7 (Revenue Recognition—Real Estate Development) Pankratov Lakes is a new recreational real estate development which consists of 500 lake-front and lake-view lots. As a special incentive to the first 100 buyers of lake-view lots, the developer is offering 3 years of free financing on 10-year, 12% notes, no down payment, and one week at a nearby established resort—"a $1,200 value." The normal price per lot is $12,000. The cost per lake-view lot to the developer is an estimated average of $2,000. The development costs continue to be incurred; the actual average cost per lot is not known at this time. The resort promotion cost is $700 per lot. The notes are held by Davis Corp., a wholly owned subsidiary.

Instructions
(a) Discuss the revenue recognition and gross profit measurement issues raised by this situation.
(b) How would the developer's past financial and business experience influence your decision concerning the recording of these transactions?
(c) Assume 50 persons have accepted the offer, signed 10-year notes, and have stayed at the local resort. Prepare the journal entries that you believe are proper.
(d) What should be disclosed in the notes to the financial statements?

 **C6-8 (Membership Fees)** Midwest Health Club (MHC) offers one-year memberships. Membership fees are due in full at the beginning of the individual membership period. As an incentive to new customers, MHC advertised that any customers not satisfied for any reason can receive a refund of the remaining portion of unused membership fees. As a result of this policy, Stanley Hack, corporate controller, recognized revenue ratably over the life of the membership.

MHC is in the process of preparing its year-end financial statements. Phyllis Cavaretta, MHC's treasurer, is concerned about the company's lackluster performance this year. She reviews the financial statements Hack prepared and tells Hack to recognize membership revenue when the fees are received.

Instructions
Answer the following questions.

(a) What are the ethical issues involved?
(b) What should Hack do?

C6-9 **(Cash Flow Analysis)** The partner in charge of the James Spencer Corporation audit comes by your desk and leaves a letter he has started to the CEO and a copy of the cash flow statement for the year ended December 31, 2003. Because he must leave on an emergency, he asks you to finish the letter by explaining: (1) the disparity between net income and cash flow; (2) the importance of operating cash flow; (3) the renewable source(s) of cash flow; and (4) possible suggestions to improve the cash position.

JAMES SPENCER CORPORATION
STATEMENT OF CASH FLOWS
FOR THE YEAR ENDED DECEMBER 31, 2003

Cash flows from operating activities		
Net income		$100,000
Adjustments to reconcile net income to net cash provided by		
operating activities:		
Depreciation expense	$ 10,000	
Amortization expense	1,000	
Loss on sale of fixed assets	5,000	
Increase in accounts receivable (net)	(40,000)	
Increase in inventory	(35,000)	
Decrease in accounts payable	(41,000)	(100,000)
Net cash provided by operating activities		–0–
Cash flows from investing activities		
Sale of plant assets	$ 25,000	
Purchase of equipment	(100,000)	
Purchase of land	(200,000)	
Net cash used by investing activities		(275,000)
Cash flows from financing activities		
Payment of dividends	$ (10,000)	
Redemption of bonds	(100,000)	
Net cash used by financing activities		(110,000)
Net decrease in cash		(385,000)
Cash balance, January 1, 2003		400,000
Cash balance, December 31, 2003		$ 15,000

Date

James Spencer, III, CEO
James Spencer Corporation
125 Wall Street
Middleton, Kansas 67458

Dear Mr. Spencer:

I have good news and bad news about the financial statements for the year ended December 31, 2003. The good news is that net income of $100,000 is close to what we predicted in the strategic plan last year, indicating strong performance this year. The bad news is that the cash balance is seriously low. Enclosed is the Statement of Cash Flows, which best illustrates how both of these situations occurred simultaneously. . . .

Instructions
Complete the letter to the CEO, including the four components requested by your boss.

USING YOUR JUDGMENT

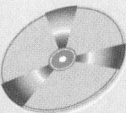

FINANCIAL REPORTING PROBLEM

3M COMPANY
The financial statements of **3M** were provided with your book or can be accessed on the Take Action! CD.

Instructions
Refer to 3M's financial statements and the accompanying notes to answer the following questions.

(a) What were 3M's sales for 2001?
(b) What was the percentage of increase in 3M's sales from 2000 to 2001? From 1999 to 2001? From 1996 to 2001?
(c) In its notes to the financial statements, what criteria does 3M use to recognize revenue?
(d) What were 3M's cash flows from its operating, investing, and financing activities for 2001? What were its trends in net cash provided by operating activities over the period 1999 to 2001? Explain why the change in accounts payable and other current liabilities is deducted from net income to arrive at net cash provided by operating activities.
(e) Compute 3M's (1) current cash debt coverage ratio, (2) cash debt coverage ratio, and (3) free cash flow for 2001. What do these ratios indicate about Kodak's financial condition?

FINANCIAL STATEMENT ANALYSIS CASE

WESTINGHOUSE ELECTRIC CORPORATION
The following note appears in the "Summary of Significant Accounting Policies" section of the Annual Report of **Westinghouse Electric Corporation**.

> **Note 1 (in part): Revenue Recognition.** Sales are primarily recorded as products are shipped and services are rendered. The percentage-of-completion method of accounting is used for nuclear steam supply system orders with delivery schedules generally in excess of five years and for certain construction projects where this method of accounting is consistent with industry practice.
>
> WFSI revenues are generally recognized on the accrual method. When accounts become delinquent for more than two payment periods, usually 60 days, income is recognized only as payments are received. Such delinquent accounts for which no payments are received in the current month, and other accounts on which income is not being recognized because the receipt of either principal or interest is questionable, are classified as nonearning receivables.

Instructions
(a) Identify the revenue recognition methods used by Westinghouse Electric as discussed in its note on significant accounting policies.
(b) Under what conditions are the revenue recognition methods identified in the first paragraph of Westinghouse's note above acceptable?
(c) From the information provided in the second paragraph of Westinghouse's note, identify the type of operation being described and defend the acceptability of the revenue recognition method.

COMPARATIVE ANALYSIS CASE

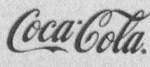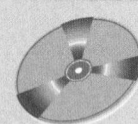 THE COCA-COLA COMPANY AND PEPSICO, INC.

Instructions

Go to the Take Action! CD and use information found there to answer the following questions related to **The Coca-Cola Company** and **PepsiCo, Inc.**

(a) What were Coca-Cola's and PepsiCo's net revenues (sales) for the year 2001? Which company increased its revenues more (dollars and percentage) from 2000 to 2001?

(b) In which foreign countries (geographic areas) did Coca-Cola and PepsiCo experience significant revenues in 2001? Compare the amounts of foreign revenues to U.S. revenues for both Coca-Cola and PepsiCo.

(c) What were these two companies' trends in net cash provided by operating activities over the period 1999 to 2001?

(d) Compute both companies' (1) current cash debt coverage ratio, (2) cash debt coverage ratio, and (3) free cash flow. What do these ratios indicate about the financial condition of the two companies?

(e) What ratios do each of these companies use in the Management's Discussion and Analysis section of the Annual Report to explain their financial condition related to debt financing?

INTERNATIONAL REPORTING CASE

As noted in the chapter, there is international diversity in the preparation of the statement of cash flows. For example, under International Accounting Standards, companies may choose how to classify dividends and interest in the cash flow statement. In some countries, like Brazil, a cash flow statement is not required. **Embraer**, a Brazilian aircraft manufacturer, prepared a statement of changes in financial position, rather than a statement of cash flows.

Instructions

Refer to Embraer's Statement of Changes in Financial Position on the next page to answer the following questions.

(a) Briefly discuss at least two similarities between Embraer's statement of changes in financial position and a statement of cash flows prepared according to U.S. GAAP.

(b) Briefly discuss at least two differences between Embraer's statement of changes in financial position and a statement of cash flows prepared according to U.S. GAAP.

EMBRAER
Consolidated Statement of Changes in Financial Position
for the Year Ended December 31, 2000
(in thousands of Brazilian reals)

Sources of Funds	2000
Provided by operations	
Net income	645,179
Items not affecting working capital—Depreciation,	
amortization, gains and losses	214,996
Long-term deferred income and social contribution taxes	9,751
Provision for contingencies	15,471
Funds provided by operations	885,397
From shareholders	
Capital increase	439,824
From third parties	
Increase in long-term liabilities	444,991
Transfer to current assets	52,194
Increase in minority interest	10,690
Funds provided by third parties	507,875
Total sources	1,833,096
Applications of Funds	
Increase in noncurrent assets	17,903
Increase in permanent assets	
Investments; property plant and equipment; other	301,798
Transfer to current liabilities	308,608
Dividends	187,042
Interest on capital	100,698
Total applications	916,049
Increase in working capital	917,047
Working capital—end of year	
Current assets	4,053,088
Current liabilities	2,668,783
	1,384,305
Working capital—beginning of year	467,258
Increase in working capital	917,047

*Remember to check the **Take Action! CD**
and the book's **companion Web site**
to find additional resources for this chapter.*

CASH AND RECEIVABLES

UGLY DUCKLING OR SWAN?

LEARNING
OBJECTIVES

After studying this chapter, you should be able to:

1. Identify items considered cash.
2. Indicate how cash and related items are reported.
3. Define receivables and identify the different types of receivables.
4. Explain accounting issues related to recognition of accounts receivable.
5. Explain accounting issues related to valuation of accounts receivable.
6. Explain accounting issues related to recognition of notes receivable.
7. Explain accounting issues related to valuation of notes receivable.
8. Explain accounting issues related to disposition of accounts and notes receivable.
9. Explain how receivables are reported and analyzed.

Ugly Duckling Corporation is a used car dealer that has carved out a niche by selling cars to customers with questionable credit histories. Ugly Duckling and other "sub-prime lenders" attempt to make a profit by loaning money to riskier borrowers so they can purchase automobiles or homes. To compensate for the higher probability of default of these customers, sub-prime lenders charge higher rates of interest on these high-risk loans.

In theory, this strategy should work. Although some borrowers will not be able to repay their loans, Ugly Duckling plans to make up these losses based on the higher interest payments received from borrowers who do not default and who continue to pay on their loans. Furthermore, in many instances these companies are able to package their sub-prime loans and sell them as securities (a process called securitization). If they receive more for the securities than the amount at which the loans are recorded on the books, they record a gain on the sale of the asset. Recognition of these gains at the time of sale is appropriate if Ugly Duckling can arrive at a reasonable estimate of the proportion of the loans that will not be repaid.

However, estimating the proportion of these high-risk loans that are likely to default is difficult. If rates are not set high enough to cover unexpected higher rates of default, Ugly Duckling and other sub-prime lenders will be in a severe cash squeeze. In addition, if too many of the loans that were sold default, Ugly Duckling will have to take them back, thereby eliminating any gain they recorded on the original sale. Indeed, in 1999, **ContiFinancial** had to write off over $654 million in sub-prime loans. Similarly, **Superior Bank FSB**, which specialized in sub-prime loans, was taken over by bank regulators because it overestimated the value of its sub-prime loans.

Thus, the sub-prime lending business is a risky one. Depending on default and interest rate assumptions on these receivables, companies like Ugly Duckling may not survive to grow into lending swans.

PREVIEW OF CHAPTER 7

As the opening story indicates, difficulties associated with estimating the collectibility of accounts receivable resulted in significant write-downs and restatements of earnings for businesses that rely on credit sales. The purpose of this chapter is to discuss two assets that are of importance to companies such as **Ugly Duckling**, **ContiFinancial**, and **Superior Bank FSB**—cash and receivables. The content and organization of the chapter are as follows.

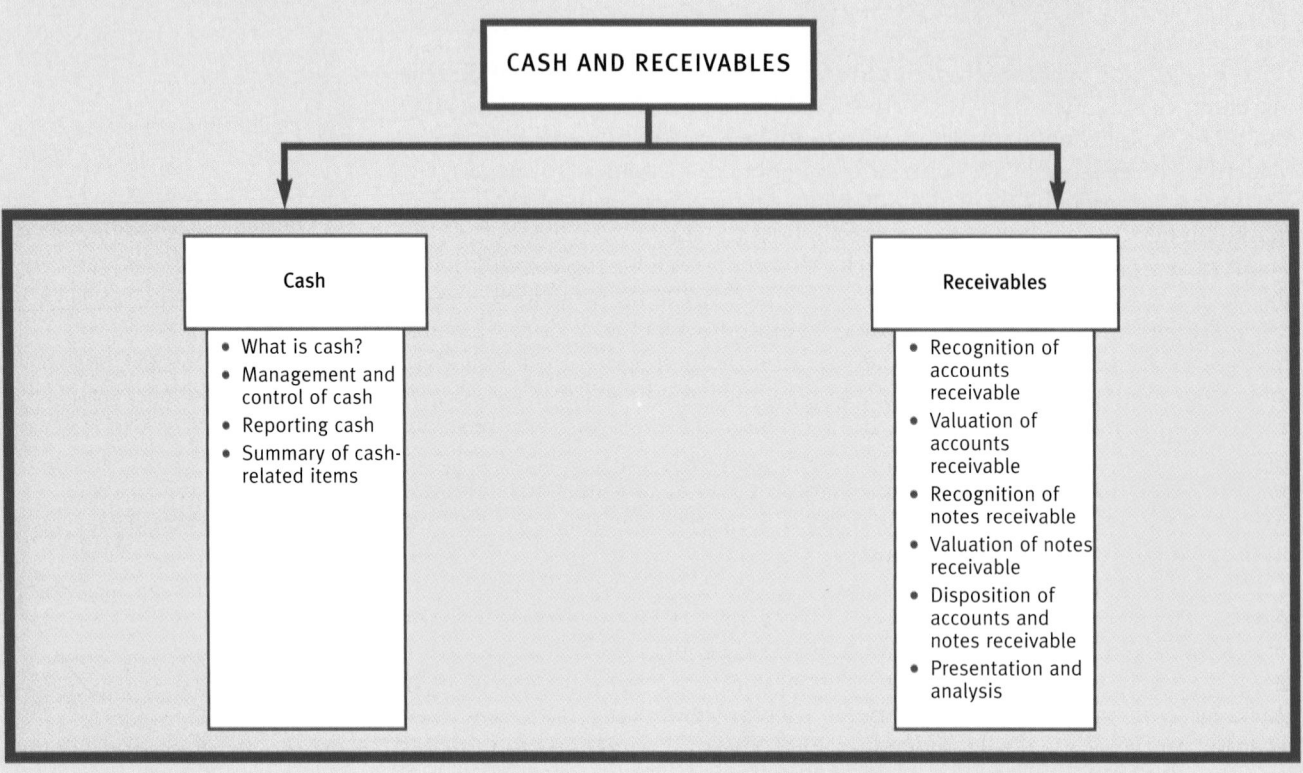

CASH AND RECEIVABLES

Cash
- What is cash?
- Management and control of cash
- Reporting cash
- Summary of cash-related items

Receivables
- Recognition of accounts receivable
- Valuation of accounts receivable
- Recognition of notes receivable
- Valuation of notes receivable
- Disposition of accounts and notes receivable
- Presentation and analysis

SECTION 1 | *CASH*

WHAT IS CASH?

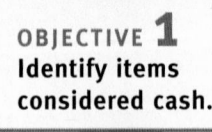

OBJECTIVE 1
Identify items considered cash.

Cash, the most liquid of assets, is the standard medium of exchange and the basis for measuring and accounting for all other items. It is generally classified as a current asset. To be reported as **cash**, it must be readily available for the payment of current obligations, and it must be free from any contractual restriction that limits its use in satisfying debts.

Cash consists of coin, currency, and available funds on deposit at the bank. Negotiable instruments such as money orders, certified checks, cashier's checks, personal checks, and bank drafts are also viewed as cash. Savings accounts are usually classified as cash, although the bank has the legal right to demand notice before withdrawal. But, because prior notice is rarely demanded by banks, savings accounts are considered cash.

Money market funds, money market savings certificates, certificates of deposit (CDs), and similar types of deposits and "short-term paper"[1] that provide small investors with an opportunity to earn high rates of interest are more appropriately classified as temporary investments than as cash. The reason is that these securities usually contain restrictions or penalties on their conversion to cash. Money market funds that provide checking account privileges, however, are usually classified as cash.

Certain items present classification problems: **Postdated checks and I.O.U.s** are treated as receivables. **Travel advances** are properly treated as receivables if the advances are to be collected from the employees or deducted from their salaries. Otherwise, classification of the travel advance as a prepaid expense is more appropriate. **Postage stamps on hand** are classified as part of office supplies inventory or as a prepaid expense. **Petty cash funds and change funds** are included in current assets as cash because these funds are used to meet current operating expenses and to liquidate current liabilities.

MANAGEMENT AND CONTROL OF CASH

Cash is the asset most susceptible to improper diversion and use. Two problems of accounting for cash transactions face management: (1) Proper controls must be established to ensure that no unauthorized transactions are entered into by officers or employees. (2) Information necessary to the proper management of cash on hand and cash transactions must be provided. Yet even with sophisticated control devices errors can and do happen. The *Wall Street Journal* ran a story entitled "A $7.8 Million Error Has a Happy Ending for a Horrified Bank," which described how **Manufacturers Hanover Trust Co.** mailed about $7.8 million too much in cash dividends to its stockholders. As implied in the headline, most of the monies were subsequently returned.

To safeguard cash and to ensure the accuracy of the accounting records for cash, effective **internal control** over cash is imperative. There are new challenges to maintaining control over liquid assets as more and more transactions are conducted with the swipe of a debit or credit card. For example, over 25 percent of bill payments in the United States are now being made through the use of digital cash (credit cards, debit cards, and electronic transfers).[2] In addition, electronic commerce conducted over the Internet continues to grow. Estimated holiday sales over the Internet in 2001 were $9.6 billion, a 15 percent increase over the previous year. Each of these trends contributes to the shift from cold cash to digital cash and poses new challenges for the con-

---

[1]A variety of "short-term paper" is available for investment. For example, **certificates of deposit** (CDs) represent formal evidence of indebtedness, issued by a bank, subject to withdrawal under the specific terms of the instrument. Issued in $10,000 and $100,000 denominations, they mature in 30 to 360 days and generally pay interest at the short-term interest rate in effect at the date of issuance. **Money market savings certificates** are issued by banks and savings and loan associations in denominations of $10,000 or more for 6-month periods (6 to 48 months). The interest rate is tied to the 26-week Treasury bill rate. In **money market funds,** a variation of the mutual fund, the yield is determined by the mix of Treasury bills and commercial paper making up the fund's portfolio. Most money market funds require an initial minimum investment of $5,000; many allow withdrawal by check or wire transfer. **Treasury bills** are U.S. government obligations generally having 91- and 182-day maturities; they are sold in $10,000 denominations at weekly government auctions. **Commercial paper** is a short-term note (30 to 270 days) issued by corporations with good credit ratings. Issued in $5,000 and $10,000 denominations, these notes generally yield a higher rate than Treasury bills.

[2]Non-U.S. consumers are even bigger users of digital cash than U.S. consumers. For example, non-check payments in Japan and Europe comprise over 70 percent of all payment transactions. U.S. consumers' continued use of checks and cash for payment raises other fraud concerns, though, as duplication technology makes it easier for crooks to forge checks and currency.

trol of cash. The appendix to this chapter discusses some of the basic control procedures used to ensure that cash is reported correctly.

WHAT DO THE NUMBERS MEAN?

LOSING CONTROL

The U.S. Federal Reserve (the Fed) also has an interest in controlling cash. The Fed relies on management of reserves on cash and checking account deposits held by banks as one of its tools for managing the money supply and interest rates. Thus, when Alan Greenspan wants to slow down the economy a bit, he can raise the required reserve ratio and keep more of the money in the bank, rather than allowing those dollars to circulate in the economy. However, as more transactions are executed through the use of stored-value cards or other forms of electronic cash, fewer funds are held by the banks. And as the cash disappears, the Fed is losing control of one of its monetary policy tools.

OBJECTIVE 2
Indicate how cash and related items are reported.

REPORTING CASH

Although the reporting of cash is relatively straightforward, there are a number of issues that merit special attention. These issues relate to the reporting of:

1. Restricted cash.
2. Bank overdrafts.
3. Cash equivalents.

Restricted Cash

Petty cash, payroll, and dividend funds are examples of cash set aside for a particular purpose. In most situations, these fund balances are not material and therefore are not segregated from cash when reported in the financial statements. When material in amount, restricted cash is segregated from "regular" cash for reporting purposes. The **restricted cash** is classified either in the current assets or in the long-term assets section, depending on the date of availability or disbursement. Classification in the current section is appropriate if the cash is to be used (within a year or the operating cycle, whichever is longer) for payment of existing or maturing obligations. On the other hand, if the cash is to be held for a longer period of time, the restricted cash is shown in the long-term section of the balance sheet.

Cash classified in the long-term section is frequently set aside for plant expansion, retirement of long-term debt or, in the case of **International Thoroughbred Breeders**, for entry fee deposits.

Illustration 7-1
Disclosure of Restricted Cash

INTERNATIONAL THOROUGHBRED BREEDERS

Restricted cash and investments (See Note) $3,730,000

Note: Restricted Cash. At year-end, the Company had approximately $3,730,000, which was classified as restricted cash and investments. These funds are primarily cash received from horsemen for nomination and entry fees to be applied to upcoming racing meets, purse winnings held in trust for horsemen, and amounts held for unclaimed ticketholder winnings.

Banks and other lending institutions often require customers to whom they lend money to maintain minimum cash balances in checking or savings accounts. These minimum balances, called **compensating balances**, are defined by the SEC as "that portion of any demand deposit (or any time deposit or certificate of deposit) maintained by a corporation which constitutes support for existing borrowing arrangements of the corporation with a lending institution. Such arrangements would include both outstanding borrowings and the assurance of future credit availability."[3]

To ensure that investors are not misled about the amount of cash available to meet recurring obligations, the SEC recommends that **legally restricted deposits** held as compensating balances against **short-term** borrowing arrangements be stated separately among the "Cash and cash equivalent items" in current assets. Restricted deposits held as compensating balances against **long-term** borrowing arrangements should be separately classified as noncurrent assets in either the investments or other assets sections, using a caption such as "Cash on deposit maintained as compensating balance." In cases where compensating balance arrangements exist without agreements that restrict the use of cash amounts shown on the balance sheet, the arrangements and the amounts involved should be described in the notes.

INTERNATIONAL INSIGHT

Among other potential restrictions, companies need to determine whether any of the cash in accounts outside the U.S. is restricted by regulations against exportation of currency.

Bank Overdrafts

Bank overdrafts occur when a check is written for more than the amount in the cash account. They should be reported in the current liabilities section and are usually added to the amount reported as accounts payable. If material, these items should be separately disclosed either on the face of the balance sheet or in the related notes.[4]

Bank overdrafts are generally not offset against the cash account. A major exception is when available cash is present in another account in the same bank on which the overdraft occurred. Offsetting in this case is required.

Cash Equivalents

A current classification that has become popular is "Cash and cash equivalents."[5] **Cash equivalents** are short-term, highly liquid investments that are both (a) readily convertible to known amounts of cash, and (b) so near their maturity that they present insignificant risk of changes in interest rates. Generally only investments with original maturities of three months or less qualify under these definitions. Examples of cash equivalents are Treasury bills, commercial paper, and money market funds. Some companies combine cash with temporary investments on the balance sheet. In these cases, the amount of the temporary investments is described either parenthetically or in the notes.

Additional Disclosures of Restricted Cash

[3]*Accounting Series Release No. 148,* "Amendments to Regulations S-X and Related Interpretations and Guidelines Regarding the Disclosure of Compensating Balances and Short-Term Borrowing Arrangements," Securities and Exchange Commission (November 13, 1973). The SEC defines 15 percent of liquid assets (current cash balances, whether restricted or not, plus marketable securities) as being material.

[4]Bank overdrafts usually occur because of a simple oversight by the company writing the check. Banks often expect companies to have overdrafts from time to time and therefore negotiate a fee as payment for this possible occurrence. However, in the early 1980s, **E. F. Hutton** (a large brokerage firm) intentionally began overdrawing its accounts by astronomical amounts—on some days exceeding $1 billion—thus obtaining interest-free loans which it could invest. Because the amounts were so large and fees were not negotiated in advance, E. F. Hutton came under criminal investigation for its actions.

[5]*Accounting Trends and Techniques—2001,* indicates that approximately 9 percent of the companies surveyed use the caption "Cash," 85 percent use "Cash and cash equivalents," and 5 percent use a caption such as "Cash and marketable securities" or similar terminology.

SUMMARY OF CASH-RELATED ITEMS

Cash and cash equivalents include the medium of exchange and most negotiable instruments. If the item cannot be converted to coin or currency on short notice, it is separately classified as an investment, as a receivable, or as a prepaid expense. Cash that is not available for payment of currently maturing liabilities is segregated and classified in the long-term assets section. Illustration 7-2 summarizes the classification of cash-related items.

Illustration 7-2
Classification of
Cash-Related Items

CLASSIFICATION OF CASH, CASH EQUIVALENTS, AND NONCASH ITEMS		
Item	Classification	Comment
Cash	Cash	If unrestricted, report as cash. If restricted, identify and classify as current and noncurrent assets.
Petty cash and change funds	Cash	Report as cash.
Short-term paper	Cash equivalents	Investments with maturity of less than 3 months, often combined with cash.
Short-term paper	Temporary investments	Investments with maturity of 3 to 12 months.
Postdated checks and IOU's	Receivables	Assumed to be collectible.
Travel advances	Receivables	Assumed to be collected from employees or deducted from their salaries.
Postage on hand (as stamps or in postage meters)	Prepaid expenses	May also be classified as office supplies inventory.
Bank overdrafts	Current liability	If right of offset exists, reduce cash.
Compensating balances	Cash separately classified as a deposit maintained as compensating balance	Classify as current or noncurrent in the balance sheet. Disclose separately in notes details of the arrangement.

SECTION 2 | *RECEIVABLES*

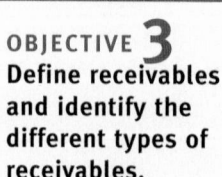

OBJECTIVE **3**
Define receivables and identify the different types of receivables.

Receivables are claims held against customers and others for money, goods, or services. For financial statement purposes, receivables are classified as either **current** (short-term) or **noncurrent** (long-term). **Current receivables** are expected to be collected within a year or during the current operating cycle, whichever is longer. All other receivables are classified as **noncurrent**. Receivables are further classified in the balance sheet as either trade or nontrade receivables.

Trade receivables are amounts owed by customers for goods sold and services rendered as part of normal business operations. Trade receivables, usually the most significant an enterprise possesses, may be subclassified into accounts receivable and notes receivable. **Accounts receivable** are oral promises of the purchaser to pay for goods and services sold. They are normally collectible within 30 to 60 days and represent "open accounts" resulting from short-term extensions of credit. **Notes receivable** are written promises to pay a certain sum of money on a specified future date. They may arise from sales, financing, or other transactions. Notes may be short-term or long-term.

Nontrade receivables arise from a variety of transactions and can be written promises either to pay or to deliver. Some examples of nontrade receivables are:

1. Advances to officers and employees.
2. Advances to subsidiaries.
3. Deposits to cover potential damages or losses.
4. Deposits as a guarantee of performance or payment.
5. Dividends and interest receivable.
6. Claims against:

    (a) Insurance companies for casualties sustained.
    (b) Defendants under suit.
    (c) Governmental bodies for tax refunds.
    (d) Common carriers for damaged or lost goods.
    (e) Creditors for returned, damaged, or lost goods.
    (f) Customers for returnable items (crates, containers, etc.).

Because of the peculiar nature of nontrade receivables, they are generally classified and reported as separate items in the balance sheet. Illustration 7-3 shows the reporting of trade and non-trade receivables in the balance sheets of **Adolph Coors Company** and **Seaboard Corporation**.

Illustration 7-3
Receivables Balance Sheet Presentations

ADOLPH COORS COMPANY (in thousands)		
Current assets		
Cash and cash equivalents		$160,038
Short-term investments		96,190
Accounts and notes receivable		
Trade, less allowance for doubtful accounts of $299		106,962
Subsidiaries		11,896
Other, less allowance for certain claims of $584		7,751
Inventories		102,660
Other supplies, less allowance for obsolete supplies of $3,968		27,729
Prepaid expenses and other assets		12,848
Deferred tax asset		22,917
Total current assets		$548,991

SEABOARD CORPORATION (in thousands)		
Current assets		
Cash and cash equivalents		$ 19,760
Short-term investments		91,375
Receivables		
Trade	$194,966	
Due from foreign affiliates	36,662	
Other	41,816	
	273,444	
Allowance for doubtful receivables	(29,801)	
Net receivables		243,643
Inventories		218,030
Deferred income taxes		14,132
Prepaid expenses and deposits		23,760
Current assets of discontinued operations		–
Total current assets		$610,700

The basic issues in accounting for accounts and notes receivable are the same: **recognition**, **valuation**, and **disposition**. We will discuss these basic issues of accounts and notes receivable in the following sequence.

1. Recognition and valuation of accounts receivable.
2. Recognition and valuation of notes receivable.
3. Disposition of accounts and notes receivable.

RECOGNITION OF ACCOUNTS RECEIVABLE

OBJECTIVE **4**
Explain accounting issues related to recognition of accounts receivable.

In most receivables transactions, the amount to be recognized is the exchange price between the two parties. **The exchange price is the amount due from the debtor** (a customer or a borrower). It is generally evidenced by some type of business document, often an invoice. Two factors that may complicate the measurement of the exchange price are (1) the availability of discounts (trade and cash discounts), and (2) the length of time between the sale and the due date of payments (the interest element).

Trade Discounts

Customers are often quoted prices on the basis of list or catalog prices that may be subject to a trade or quantity discount. Such **trade discounts** are used to avoid frequent changes in catalogs, to quote different prices for different quantities purchased, or to hide the true invoice price from competitors.

Trade discounts are commonly quoted in percentages. For example, if your textbook has a list price of $90.00 and the publisher sells it to college bookstores for list less a 30 percent trade discount, the receivable recorded by the publisher is $63.00 per textbook. The normal practice is simply to deduct the trade discount from the list price and bill the customer net.

As another example, Maxwell House at one time sold a 10 oz. jar of its instant coffee listing at $4.65 to supermarkets for $3.90, a trade discount of approximately 16 percent. The supermarkets in turn sold the instant coffee for $3.99 per jar. Maxwell House records the receivable and related sales revenue at $3.90 per jar, not $4.65.

Cash Discounts (Sales Discounts)

Cash discounts (sales discounts) are offered as an inducement for prompt payment. They are communicated in terms that read, for example, 2/10, n/30 (2 percent if paid within 10 days, gross amount due in 30 days), or 2/10, E.O.M. (2 percent if paid within 10 days of the end of the month).

Companies that fail to take sales discounts are usually not using their money advantageously. An enterprise that receives a 1 percent reduction in the sales price for payment within 10 days, total payment due within 30 days, is effectively earning 18.25 percent (.01 ÷ [20/365]), or at least avoiding that rate of interest cost. For this reason, companies usually take the discount unless their cash is severely limited.

The easiest and most commonly used method of recording sales and related sales discount transactions is to enter the receivable and sale at the gross amount. Under this method, sales discounts are recognized in the accounts only when payment is received within the discount period. Sales discounts would then be shown in the income statement as a deduction from sales to arrive at net sales.

Some contend that sales discounts not taken reflect penalties added to an established price to encourage prompt payment. That is, the seller offers sales on account at a slightly higher price than if selling for cash, and the increase is offset by the cash discount offered. Thus, customers who pay within the discount period purchase at the cash price. Those who pay after expiration of the discount period are penalized because they must pay an amount in excess of the cash price. If this reasoning is used, sales and receivables are recorded net, and any discounts not taken are subsequently debited to Accounts Receivable and credited to Sales Discounts Forfeited. The entries in Illustration 7-4 on the next page show the difference between the gross and net methods.

If the gross method is employed, sales discounts are reported as a deduction from sales in the income statement. Proper matching would dictate that a reasonable estimate of material amounts of expected discounts to be taken also should be charged

Gross Method			Net Method		
Sales of $10,000, terms 2/10, n/30					
Accounts Receivable	10,000		Accounts Receivable	9,800	
Sales		10,000	Sales		9,800
Payment of $4,000 received within discount period					
Cash	3,920		Cash	3,920	
Sales Discounts	80		Accounts Receivable		3,920
Accounts Receivable		4,000			
Payment of $6,000 received after discount period					
Cash	6,000		Accounts Receivable	120	
Accounts Receivable		6,000	Sales Discounts Forfeited		120
			Cash	6,000	
			Accounts Receivable		6,000

Illustration 7-4
Entries under Gross and Net Methods of Recording Cash (Sales) Discounts

against sales. If the net method is used, Sales Discounts Forfeited are considered as an "Other revenue" item.[6]

Theoretically, the recognition of Sales Discounts Forfeited is correct because the receivable is stated closer to its realizable value and the net sales figure measures the revenue earned from the sale. As a practical matter, however, the net method is seldom used because it requires additional analysis and bookkeeping. For one thing, the net method requires adjusting entries to record sales discounts forfeited on accounts receivable that have passed the discount period.

Nonrecognition of Interest Element

Ideally, receivables should be measured in terms of their present value, that is, the discounted value of the cash to be received in the future. When expected cash receipts require a waiting period, the receivable face amount is not worth the amount that is ultimately received.

To illustrate, assume that a company makes a sale on account for $1,000 with payment due in 4 months. The applicable annual rate of interest is 12 percent, and payment is made at the end of 4 months. The present value of that receivable is not $1,000 but $961.54 ($1,000 × .96154).[7] In other words, $1,000 to be received 4 months from now is not the same as $1,000 received today.

Theoretically, any revenue after the period of sale is interest revenue. In practice, interest revenue related to accounts receivable is ignored because the amount of the discount is not usually material in relation to the net income for the period. The profession specifically excludes from the present value considerations "receivables arising from transactions with customers in the normal course of business which are due in customary trade terms not exceeding approximately one year."[8]

UNDERLYING CONCEPTS

Materiality means it must make a difference to a decision maker. The FASB believes that present value concepts can be ignored for short-term receivables.

[6]To the extent that discounts not taken reflect a short-term financing, some argue that an interest revenue account could be used to record these amounts.

[7]The number .96154 is the present value of 1 interest factor for 1 period at 4 percent, as shown in Table 2 in Appendix A (Time Value of Money) at the back of the book. If you need to brush up on your understanding of time value of money concepts and techniques, consult Appendix A.

[8]"Interest on Receivables and Payables," *Opinions of the Accounting Principles Board No. 21* (New York: AICPA, 1971), par. 3(a).

VALUATION OF ACCOUNTS RECEIVABLE

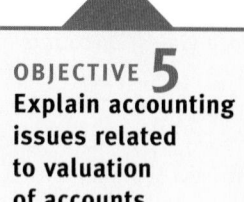

OBJECTIVE **5**
Explain accounting issues related to valuation of accounts receivable.

Reporting of receivables involves (1) classification and (2) valuation on the balance sheet. Classification involves determining the length of time each receivable will be outstanding. Receivables intended to be collected within a year or the operating cycle, whichever is longer, are classified as current; all other receivables are classified as long-term.

Short-term receivables are valued and reported at net realizable value—**the net amount expected to be received in cash.** Determining net realizable value requires an estimation of both uncollectible receivables and any returns or allowances to be granted.

Uncollectible Accounts Receivable

As one accountant so aptly noted, the credit manager's idea of heaven probably would be a place where everyone (eventually) paid his or her debts.[9] The recent experience of **Sears**, as shown in Illustration 7-5, indicates the importance of credit sales for many companies. Note that while credit cards represent the largest source of Sears' profits, its increased bad debt expense has led to a lower stock price.

Illustration 7-5
Sears' Credit Card Growth and Stock Performance

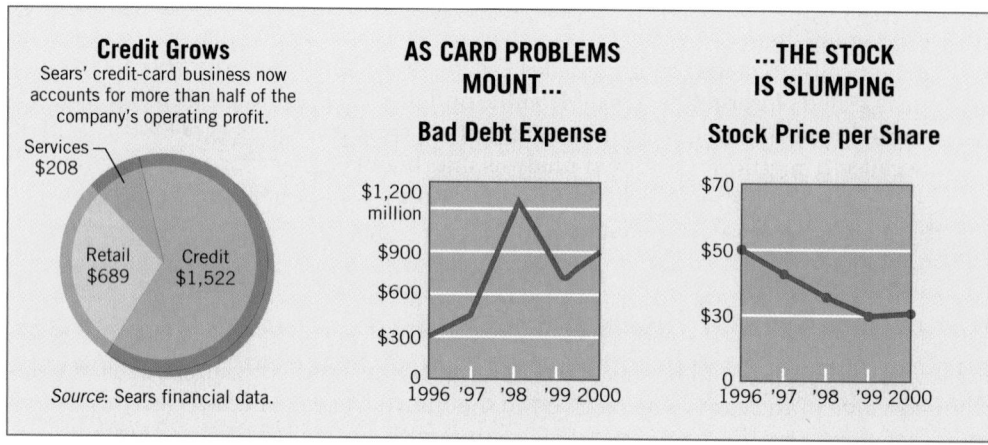

Sales on any basis other than cash make possible the subsequent failure to collect the account. An uncollectible account receivable is a loss of revenue that requires, through proper entry in the accounts, a decrease in the asset accounts receivable and a related decrease in income and stockholders' equity. The loss in revenue and the decrease in income are recognized by recording bad debt expense.

Two procedures are used to record uncollectible accounts:

METHODS FOR RECORDING UNCOLLECTIBLES

1. *Direct Write-Off Method.* No entry is made until a specific account has definitely been established as uncollectible. Then the loss is recorded by crediting Accounts Receivable and debiting Bad Debt Expense.

2. *Allowance Method.* An estimate is made of the expected uncollectible accounts from all sales made on account or from the total of outstanding receivables. This estimate is entered as an expense and an indirect reduction in accounts receivable (via an increase in the allowance account) in the period in which the sale is recorded.

---

[9]William J. Vatter, *Managerial Accounting* (Englewood Cliffs, N.J.: Prentice-Hall, 1950), p. 60.

The **direct write-off method** records the bad debt in the year in which it is determined that a specific receivable cannot be collected. In contrast, the **allowance method** enters the expense on an estimated basis in the accounting period in which the sales on account are made.

Supporters of the **direct write-off method** contend that facts, not estimates, are recorded. It assumes that a good account receivable resulted from each sale, and that later events proved certain accounts to be uncollectible and worthless. From a practical standpoint this method is simple and convenient to apply, although receivables do not generally become worthless at an identifiable moment of time. But the direct write-off method is theoretically deficient because it usually does not match costs with revenues of the period, nor does it result in receivables being stated at estimated realizable value on the balance sheet. **As a result, its use is not considered appropriate, except when the amount uncollectible is immaterial.**

Advocates of the **allowance method** believe that bad debt expense should be recorded in the same period as the sale, to obtain a proper matching of expenses and revenues and to achieve a proper carrying value for accounts receivable. They support the position that although estimates are involved, the percentage of receivables that will not be collected can be predicted from past experiences, present market conditions, and an analysis of the outstanding balances. Many companies set their credit policies to provide for a certain percentage of uncollectible accounts. (In fact, many feel that failure to reach that percentage means that sales are being lost by credit policies that are too restrictive.)

Because the collectibility of receivables is considered a loss contingency, the allowance method is appropriate in situations where it is probable that an asset has been impaired and that the amount of the loss can be reasonably estimated.[10]

A receivable is a prospective cash inflow, and the probability of its collection must be considered in valuing cash flows. These estimates normally are made either on (1) the basis of percentage of sales or (2) the basis of outstanding receivables.

Percentage-of-Sales (Income Statement) Approach

If there is a fairly stable relationship between previous years' credit sales and bad debts, then that relationship can be turned into a percentage and used to determine this year's bad debt expense.

The **percentage-of-sales approach** matches costs with revenues because it relates the charge to the period in which the sale is recorded. To illustrate, assume that Chad Shumway Corp. estimates from past experience that about 2 percent of credit sales become uncollectible. If Shumway Corp. has credit sales of $400,000 in 2003, the entry to record bad debt expense using the percentage-of-sales method is as follows.

Bad Debt Expense	8,000	
Allowance for Doubtful Accounts		8,000

The Allowance for Doubtful Accounts is a valuation account (i.e., a contra asset) and is subtracted from trade receivables on the balance sheet.[11] The amount of bad debt expense and the related credit to the allowance account are unaffected by any balance currently existing in the allowance account. Because the bad debt expense estimate is related to a nominal account (Sales), and any balance in the allowance is ignored, this

UNDERLYING CONCEPTS

The percentage-of-sales method is a good illustration of the use of the matching principle, which relates expenses to revenues earned.

[10]"Accounting for Contingencies," *Statement of Financial Accounting Standards No. 5* (Stamford, Conn.: FASB, 1975), par. 8.

[11]The account description employed for the allowance account is usually Allowance for Doubtful Accounts or simply Allowance. *Accounting Trends and Techniques—2001*, for example, indicates that approximately 78 percent of the companies surveyed used "allowance" in their description.

method is frequently referred to as the **income statement approach**. A proper matching of cost and revenues is therefore achieved.

Percentage-of-Receivables (Balance Sheet) Approach

Using past experience, a company can estimate the percentage of its outstanding receivables that will become uncollectible, without identifying specific accounts. This procedure provides a reasonably accurate estimate of the receivables' realizable value, but does not fit the concept of matching cost and revenues. Rather, its objective is to report receivables in the balance sheet at net realizable values. Hence it is referred to as the **percentage-of-receivables** (or **balance sheet**) **approach**.

The percentage of receivables may be applied using one **composite rate** that reflects an estimate of the uncollectible receivables. Another approach that is more sensitive to the actual status of the accounts receivable sets up an **aging schedule** and applies a different percentage based on past experience to the various age categories. An aging schedule is frequently used in practice. It indicates which accounts require special attention by providing the age of such accounts receivable. The following schedule of Wilson & Co. is an example.

Illustration 7-6
Accounts Receivable
Aging Schedule

WILSON & CO.
AGING SCHEDULE

Name of Customer	Balance Dec. 31	Under 60 days	61–90 days	91–120 days	Over 120 days
Western Stainless Steel Corp.	$ 98,000	$ 80,000	$18,000		
Brockway Steel Company	320,000	320,000			
Freeport Sheet & Tube Co.	55,000				$55,000
Allegheny Iron Works	74,000	60,000		$14,000	
	$547,000	$460,000	$18,000	$14,000	$55,000

Summary

Age	Amount	Percentage Estimated to be Uncollectible	Required Balance in Allowance
Under 60 days old	$460,000	4%	$18,400
61–90 days old	18,000	15%	2,700
91–120 days old	14,000	20%	2,800
Over 120 days	55,000	25%	13,750
Year-end balance of allowance for doubtful accounts			$37,650

The amount $37,650 would be the bad debt expense to be reported for this year, assuming that no balance existed in the allowance account.

To change the illustration slightly, **assume that the allowance account had a credit balance of $800 before adjustment**. In this case, the amount to be added to the allowance account is $36,850 ($37,650 − $800), and the following entry is made.

Bad Debt Expense	36,850	
Allowance for Doubtful Accounts		36,850

The balance in the Allowance account is therefore stated at $37,650. **If the Allowance balance before adjustment had a debit balance of $200**, then the amount to be recorded for bad debt expense would be $37,850 ($37,650 desired balance + $200 debit balance).

In the percentage-of-receivables method, the balance in the allowance account **cannot be ignored**, because the percentage is related to a real account (Accounts Receivable).

An aging schedule is usually not prepared to determine the bad debt expense. Rather, it is prepared as a control device to determine the composition of receivables and to identify delinquent accounts. The estimated loss percentage developed for each category is based on previous loss experience and the advice of credit department personnel. Regardless of whether a composite rate or an aging schedule is employed, the primary objective of the percentage of outstanding receivables method for financial statement purposes is to report receivables in the balance sheet at net realizable value. However, it is deficient in that it may not match the bad debt expense to the period in which the sale takes place.

The allowance for doubtful accounts as a percentage of receivables will vary, depending upon the industry and the economic climate. Companies such as **Eastman Kodak**, **General Electric**, and **Monsanto** have recorded allowances ranging from $3.00 to $6.00 per $100 of accounts receivable. Others such as **CPC International** ($1.48), **Texaco** ($1.23), and **USX Corp.** ($0.78) are examples of large enterprises that have had bad debt allowances of less than $1.50 per $100. At the other extreme are hospitals that allow for $15.00 to $20.00 per $100.00 of accounts receivable.[12]

In summary, the percentage-of-receivables method results in a more accurate valuation of receivables on the balance sheet. From a matching viewpoint, the percentage-of-sales approach provides the better results. The following diagram relates these methods to the basic theory.

Tutorial on Recording Uncollectible Accounts

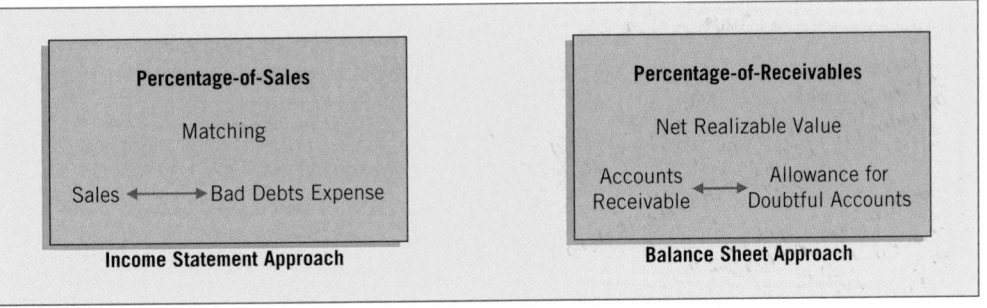

Illustration 7-7
Comparison of Methods for Estimating Uncollectibles

The account title employed for the allowance account is usually Allowance for Doubtful Accounts or simply Allowance.

Regardless of the method chosen, determining the expense associated with uncollectible accounts is an area of accounting that is subject to a large degree of judgment. Recently there has been concern that some banks are using this judgment to manage earnings. By overestimating the amounts of uncollectible loans in a good earnings year, the bank can "save for a rainy day" in a future period. In future (less profitable) periods, the overly conservative allowance for loan loss account can be reduced to increase earnings. In this regard, the SEC brought action against **Suntrust Banks**, requiring a

INTERNATIONAL INSIGHT

The U.S. has been critical of some countries' use of excess reserves to manage income. These same countries would argue that Suntrust Banks' accounting for loan losses is a similar practice.

---

[12]A U.S. Department of Commerce study indicated, as a general rule, the following relationships between the age of accounts receivable and their uncollectibility.

30 days or less	4% uncollectible
31–60 days	10% uncollectible
61–90 days	17% uncollectible
91–120 days	26% uncollectible

After 120 days, an approximate 3–4 percent increase in uncollectibles for every 30 days outstanding occurs for the remainder of the first year.

reversal of $100 million of bad debt expense. This reversal increased aftertax profit by $61 million.[13]

Collection of Accounts Receivable Written Off

When a particular account receivable is determined to be uncollectible, the balance is removed from the books by debiting Allowance for Doubtful Accounts and crediting Accounts Receivable. If a collection is eventually made on a receivable that was previously written off, the procedure is first to reestablish the receivable by debiting Accounts Receivable and crediting Allowance for Doubtful Accounts. An entry is then made to debit Cash and credit the customer's account for the amount received.

If the direct write-off approach is employed, the amount collected is debited to Cash and credited to a revenue account entitled Uncollectible Amounts Recovered, with proper notation in the customer's account.

WHAT DO THE NUMBERS MEAN?

COLLECTION IS A CLICK AWAY

What do lenders do when they determine that receivables are uncollectible? After they record bad debts on their books, the next step is to try to collect what they can from the deadbeat customers. Some lenders auction their bad loans in the market for distressed debt, usually paying a fee of 5–15 percent to a distressed debt broker, who arranges the sale. Recently, several Web sites have sprung up to provide a meeting place for lenders with bad loans and collectors who are willing to make a bid on the bad loans and then try to collect on them. These sites are sort of an "eBay of deadbeats." For example, **Bank One Corp.** listed $211 million of unpaid credit card receivables on **DebtforSale.com**. While the lendors generally recover less than 10 percent of the face value of the receivables in an auction, by going online they are able to reduce the costs of their bad debts. Online services charge just 0.5–1 percent for their auction services.

Source: Adapted from P. Gogoi, "An eBay of Deadbeats," *Business Week* (September 18, 2000), p. 124.

RECOGNITION OF NOTES RECEIVABLE

A note receivable is supported by a formal **promissory note**, a written promise to pay a certain sum of money at a specific future date. Such a note is a negotiable instrument that is signed by a **maker** in favor of a designated **payee** who may legally and readily sell or otherwise transfer the note to others. Although notes contain an interest element because of the time value of money, notes are classified as interest-bearing or non-interest-bearing. **Interest-bearing notes** have a stated rate of interest. **Zero-interest-bearing notes** (noninterest-bearing) include interest as part of their face amount instead of stating it explicitly. Notes receivable are considered fairly liquid, even if long-term, because they may be easily converted to cash.

Notes receivable are frequently accepted from customers who need to extend the payment period of an outstanding receivable. Notes are also sometimes required of high-risk or new customers. In addition, notes are often used in loans to employees and subsidiaries and in the sales of property, plant, and equipment. In some industries (e.g., the pleasure and sport boat industry) all credit sales are supported by notes. The majority of notes, however, originate from lending transactions. The basic issues in accounting for notes receivable are the same as those for accounts receivable: recognition, valuation, and disposition.

Short-term notes are generally recorded at face value (less allowances) because the interest implicit in the maturity value is immaterial. A general rule is that notes treated

[13]Recall from the earnings management discussion in Chapter 5 that increasing or decreasing income through management manipulation can reduce the quality of financial reports.

as cash equivalents (maturities of 3 months or less) are not subject to premium or discount amortization.

Long-term notes receivable, however, should be recorded and reported at the **present value of the cash expected to be collected**. When the interest stated on an interest-bearing note is equal to the effective (market) rate of interest, the note sells at face value.[14] When the stated rate is different from the market rate, the cash exchanged (present value) is different from the face value of the note. The difference between the face value and the cash exchanged, either a discount or a premium, is then recorded and amortized over the life of a note to approximate the effective (market) interest rate. This illustrates one of the many situations in which time value of money concepts are applied to accounting measurement.[15]

> **OBJECTIVE 6**
> Explain accounting issues related to recognition of notes receivable.

Note Issued at Face Value

To illustrate the discounting of a note issued at face value, assume that Bigelow Corp. lends Scandinavian Imports $10,000 in exchange for a $10,000, 3-year note bearing interest at 10 percent annually. The market rate of interest for a note of similar risk is also 10 percent. This time diagram depicting both cash flows is shown below.

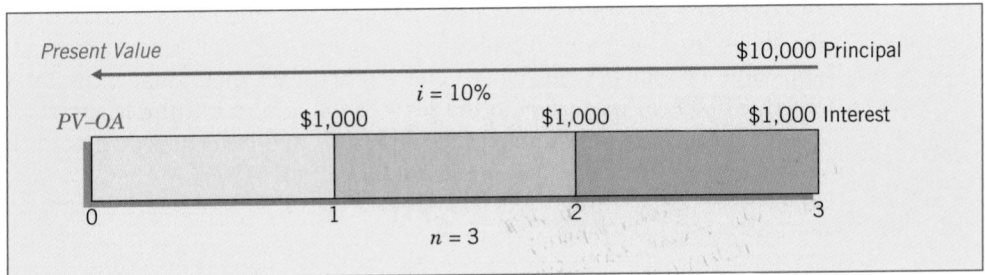

The present value or exchange price of the note is computed as follows.

Face value of the note		$10,000
Present value of the principal:		
$10,000 ($PVF_{3,10\%}$) = $10,000 (.75132)	$7,513	
Present value of the interest:		
$1,000 ($PVF\text{-}OA_{3,10\%}$) = $1,000 (2.48685)	2,487	
Present value of the note		10,000
Difference		$ –0–

Illustration 7-8
Present Value of Note—
Stated and Market Rates
the Same

[14]The **stated interest rate**, also referred to as the face rate or the coupon rate, is the rate contracted as part of the note. The **effective interest rate**, also referred to as the market rate or the effective yield, is the rate used in the market to determine the value of the note—that is, the discount rate used to determine present value.

[15]In the illustrations and formulas that follow in the next sections, you will see the abbreviations *PVF* and *PVF-OA*. They refer to the present value factor of a single sum (*PVF*) and to the factor for the present value of an ordinary annuity (*PVF-OA*). Remember that an *ordinary annuity* is a stream of equal periodic cash flows. Calculation of the present value of a stream of equal periodic cash flows uses the interest factors for the present value of an ordinary annuity (*PVF-OA*). Calculation of the present value of a single sum, such as the principal on a note or loan, uses the interest factors for a single sum (*PVF*). For an in-depth discussion of the time value of money techniques, see Appendix A at the end of the book.

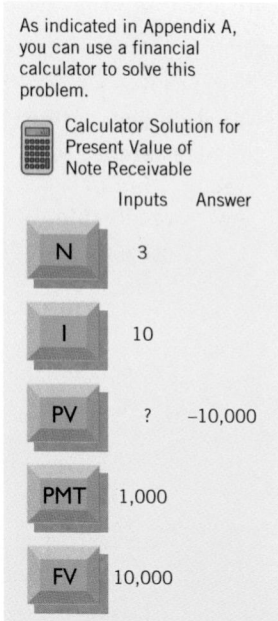

As indicated in Appendix A, you can use a financial calculator to solve this problem.

Calculator Solution for Present Value of Note Receivable

	Inputs	Answer
N	3	
I	10	
PV	?	−10,000
PMT	1,000	
FV	10,000	

In this case, the present value of the note and its face value are the same, that is, $10,000, because the effective and stated rates of interest are also the same. The receipt of the note is recorded by Bigelow Corp. as follows.

Notes Receivable	10,000	
Cash		10,000

Bigelow Corp. would recognize the interest earned each year as follows.

Cash	1,000	
Interest Revenue		1,000

Note Not Issued at Face Value

Zero-Interest-Bearing Notes

If a zero-interest-bearing note is received solely for cash, its present value is the cash paid to the issuer. Because both the future amount and the present value of the note are known, the interest rate can be computed (i.e., it is implied). The **implicit interest rate** is the rate that equates the cash paid with the amounts receivable in the future. The difference between the future (face) amount and the present value (cash paid) is recorded as a discount and amortized to interest revenue over the life of the note.

To illustrate, Jeremiah Company receives a 3-year, $10,000 zero-interest-bearing note, the present value of which is $7,721.80. The implicit rate that equates the total cash to be received ($10,000 at maturity) to the present value of the future cash flows ($7,721.80) is 9 percent (the present value of 1 for 3 periods at 9 percent is .77218). The time diagram depicting the one cash flow is shown below.

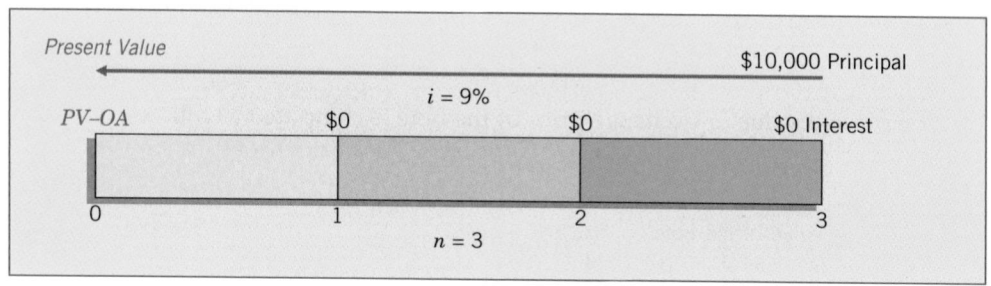

The entry to record the transaction is as follows:

Notes Receivable	10,000.00	
Discount on Notes Receivable ($10,000 − $7,721.80)		2,278.20
Cash		7,721.80

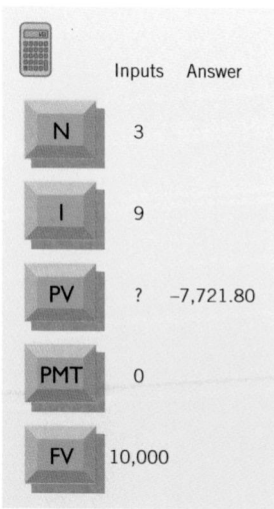

	Inputs	Answer
N	3	
I	9	
PV	?	−7,721.80
PMT	0	
FV	10,000	

The Discount on Notes Receivable is a valuation account. It is reported on the balance sheet as a contra-asset account to notes receivable. The discount is then amortized, and interest revenue is recognized annually using the **effective interest method**. The 3-year discount amortization and interest revenue schedule is shown in Illustration 7-9 on the next page.

Interest revenue at the end of the first year using the effective interest method is recorded as follows.

Discount on Notes Receivable	694.96	
Interest Revenue ($7,721.80 × 9%)		694.96

The amount of the discount, $2,278.20 in this case, represents the interest revenue to be received from the note over the 3 years.

	Cash Received	Interest Revenue	Discount Amortized	Carrying Amount of Note
Date of issue				$ 7,721.80
End of year 1	$-0-	$ 694.96ᵃ	$ 694.96ᵇ	8,416.76ᶜ
End of year 2	-0-	757.51	757.51	9,174.27
End of year 3	-0-	825.73ᵈ	825.73	10,000.00
	$-0-	$2,278.20	$2,278.20	

SCHEDULE OF NOTE DISCOUNT AMORTIZATION
EFFECTIVE INTEREST METHOD
0% NOTE DISCOUNTED AT 9%

ᵃ$7,721.80 × .09 = $694.96 ᶜ$7,721.80 + $694.96 = $8,416.76
ᵇ$694.96 − 0 = $694.96 ᵈ5¢ adjustment to compensate for rounding

Illustration 7-9
Discount Amortization
Schedule—Effective
Interest Method

Interest-Bearing Notes

Often the stated rate and the effective rate are different. The zero-interest-bearing case above is one example of such a situation.

To illustrate a more common situation, assume that Morgan Corp. made a loan to Marie Co. and received in exchange a 3-year, $10,000 note bearing interest at 10 percent annually. The market rate of interest for a note of similar risk is 12 percent. The time diagram depicting both cash flows is shown below.

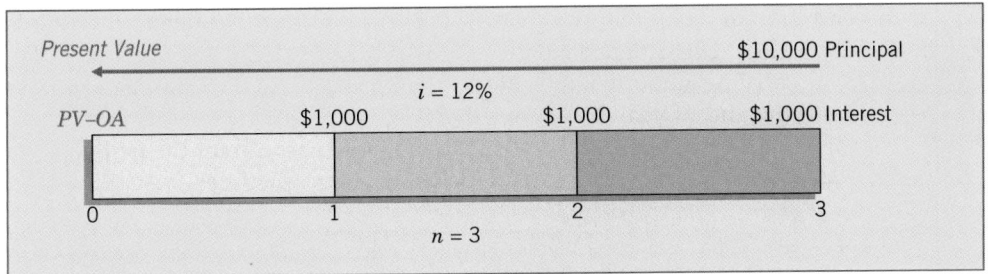

The present value of the two cash flows is computed as follows.

Face value of the note		$10,000
Present value of the principal:		
$10,000 (PVF₃,₁₂%) = $10,000 (.71178)	$7,118	
Present value of the interest:		
$1,000 (PVF-OA₃,₁₂%) = $1,000 (2.40183)	2,402	
Present value of the note		9,520
Difference (Discount)		$ 480

Illustration 7-10
Computation of Present
Value—Effective Rate
Different from Stated
Rate

In this case, because the effective rate of interest (12 percent) is greater than the stated rate (10 percent), the present value of the note is less than the face value. That is, the note was exchanged at a **discount**. The receipt of the note at a discount is recorded by Morgan as follows.

Notes Receivable	10,000	
Discount on Notes Receivable		480
Cash		9,520

The discount is then amortized and interest revenue is recognized annually using the **effective interest method**. The 3-year discount amortization and interest revenue schedule is shown below.

Illustration 7-11
Discount Amortization
Schedule—Effective
Interest Method

	Cash Received	Interest Revenue	Discount Amortized	Carrying Amount of Note
SCHEDULE OF NOTE DISCOUNT AMORTIZATION				
EFFECTIVE INTEREST METHOD				
10% NOTE DISCOUNTED AT 12%				
Date of issue				$ 9,520
End of year 1	$1,000[a]	$1,142[b]	$142[c]	9,662[d]
End of year 2	1,000	1,159	159	9,821
End of year 3	1,000	1,179	179	10,000
	$3,000	$3,480	$480	

[a]$10,000 × 10% = $1,000   [c]$1,142 − $1,000 = $142
[b]$9,520 × 12% = $1,142   [d]$9,520 + $142 = $9,662

On the date of issue, the note has a present value of $9,520. Its unamortized discount—additional interest revenue to be spread over the 3-year life of the note—is $480.

At the end of year 1, Morgan receives $1,000 in cash. But its interest revenue is $1,142 ($9,520 × 12%). The difference between $1,000 and $1,142 is the amortized discount, $142. The carrying amount of the note is now $9,662 ($9,520 + $142). This process is repeated until the end of year 3.

Receipt of the annual interest and amortization of the discount for the first year are recorded by Morgan as follows (amounts per amortization schedule).

Cash	1,000	
Discount on Notes Receivable	142	
Interest Revenue		1,142

When the present value exceeds the face value, the note is exchanged at a premium. The premium on a note receivable is recorded as a debit and amortized using the effective interest method over the life of the note as annual reductions in the amount of interest revenue recognized.

Notes Received for Property, Goods, or Services

When a **note is received in exchange for property, goods, or services** in a bargained transaction entered into at arm's length, the stated interest rate is presumed to be fair unless:

1. No interest rate is stated, or
2. The stated interest rate is unreasonable, or
3. The face amount of the note is materially different from the current cash sales price for the same or similar items or from the current market value of the debt instrument.[16]

---

[16]"Interest on Receivables and Payables," *Opinions of the Accounting Principles Board No. 21* (New York: AICPA, 1971), par. 12.

In these circumstances, the present value of the note is measured by the fair value of the property, goods, or services or by an amount that reasonably approximates the market value of the note.

To illustrate, Oasis Development Co. sold a corner lot to Rusty Pelican as a restaurant site and accepted in exchange a 5-year note having a maturity value of $35,247 and no stated interest rate. The land originally cost Oasis $14,000 and at the date of sale had an appraised fair value of $20,000. Given the criterion above, it is acceptable to use the fair market value of the land, $20,000, as the present value of the note. The entry to record the sale therefore is:

Notes Receivable	35,247	
Discount on Notes Receivable ($35,247 − $20,000)		15,247
Land		14,000
Gain on Sale of Land ($20,000 − $14,000)		6,000

The discount is amortized to interest revenue over the 5-year life of the note using the effective interest method.

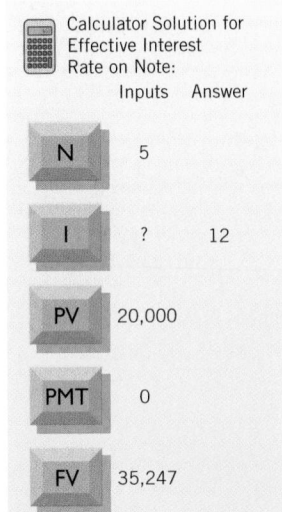

Calculator Solution for Effective Interest Rate on Note:

	Inputs	Answer
N	5	
I	?	12
PV	20,000	
PMT	0	
FV	35,247	

Choice of Interest Rate

In note transactions, the effective or real interest rate is either evident or determinable by other factors involved in the exchange, such as the fair market value of what is given or received. But, if the fair value of the property, goods, services, or other rights is not determinable, and if the note has no ready market, the problem of determining the present value of the note is more difficult. To estimate the present value of a note under such circumstances, an applicable interest rate that may differ from the stated interest rate must be approximated. This process of interest-rate approximation is called **imputation**, and the resulting interest rate is called an **imputed interest rate**.

The choice of a rate is affected by the prevailing rates for similar instruments of issuers with similar credit ratings. It is also affected specifically by restrictive covenants, collateral, payment schedule, the existing prime interest rate, etc. Determination of the imputed interest rate is made when the note is received; any subsequent changes in prevailing interest rates are ignored.

VALUATION OF NOTES RECEIVABLE

> **OBJECTIVE 7**
> Explain accounting issues related to valuation of notes receivable.

Like accounts receivable, short-term notes receivable are recorded and reported at their net realizable value—that is, at their face amount less all necessary allowances. The primary notes receivable allowance account is Allowance for Doubtful Accounts. The computations and estimations involved in valuing short-term notes receivable and in recording bad debt expense and the related allowance are **exactly the same as for trade accounts receivable**. Either a percentage of sales revenue or an analysis of the receivables can be used to estimate the amount of uncollectibles.

Long-term notes receivable, however, pose additional estimation problems. For evidence, we need only look at the problems our financial institutions, most notably money-center banks, have had in collecting receivables from energy loans, real estate loans, and loans to less-developed countries.[17]

A note receivable is considered **impaired** when it is probable that the creditor will be unable to collect all amounts due (both principal and interest) according to the contractual terms of the loan. Impairments, as well as restructurings, of receivables and

[17]A wise person once said that a bank lending money to a Third World country is like lending money to one's children: You should never expect to get the interest, let alone the principal.

debts are discussed and illustrated in considerable detail in Appendix F at the end of the book.

WHAT DO THE NUMBERS MEAN?

PUTTING THE SQUEEZE ON

When the economy slows, lenders, such as **J.P. Morgan** and **First Chicago**, get stingier in granting new loans or renewing loans to existing customers. This tightening of loans is referred to as a "credit squeeze." However, it is sometimes difficult for banks to cut back on lending when the economy goes from good times to bad. When times are good and banks are competing for lending business, lenders often grant business customers "lines of credit" as a sweetener in order to close a loan. In contrast to a term loan that is supported by a note, a line of credit allows borrowing on a day-to-day basis.

When times turn bad, the bank can cut back on loans via notes receivable, but it still must honor the lines of credit, even to weak customers. For example, **Xerox Inc.** got a $7 billion line of credit before it hit the skids during 2000. Although, Xerox has not been able to access the traditional loan markets, it has been able to draw on its line of credit to make ends meet. Thus, what seemed like of good competitive tool in good times has put the squeeze on *lenders* when times have turned bad.

Source: Adapted from H. Timmons and D. Sparks, "Feeling a Credit Squeeze," *Business Week* (December 4, 2000), pp. 148–149.

DISPOSITION OF ACCOUNTS AND NOTES RECEIVABLE

OBJECTIVE 8
Explain accounting issues related to disposition of accounts and notes receivable.

In the normal course of events, accounts and notes receivable are collected when due and removed from the books. However, as credit sales and receivables have grown in size and significance, this "normal course of events" has evolved. **In order to accelerate the receipt of cash from receivables, the owner may transfer accounts or notes receivable to another company for cash.**

There are various reasons for this early transfer. First, for competitive reasons, providing sales financing for customers is virtually mandatory in many industries. In the sale of durable goods, such as automobiles, trucks, industrial and farm equipment, computers, and appliances, a large majority of sales are on an installment contract basis. Many major companies in these industries have created wholly-owned subsidiaries specializing in receivables financing. **General Motors Corp.** has **General Motors Acceptance Corp. (GMAC)**, and **Sears** has **Sears Roebuck Acceptance Corp. (SRAC)**.

Second, the **holder** may sell receivables because money is tight and access to normal credit is not available or is prohibitively expensive. Also, a firm may have to sell its receivables, instead of borrowing, to avoid violating existing lending agreements.

Finally, billing and collection of receivables are often time-consuming and costly. Credit card companies such as **MasterCard, VISA, American Express, Diners Club, Discover**, and others take over the collection process and provide merchants with immediate cash.

Conversely, some **purchasers** of receivables buy them to obtain the legal protection of ownership rights afforded a purchaser of assets versus the lesser rights afforded a secured creditor. In addition, banks and other lending institutions may be forced to purchase receivables because of legal lending limits. That is, they cannot make any additional loans but they can buy receivables and charge a fee for this service.

The transfer of receivables to a third party for cash is accomplished in one of two ways:

1. Secured borrowing.
2. Sales of receivables.

Secured Borrowing

Receivables are often used as collateral in a borrowing transaction. A creditor often requires that the debtor designate (assign) or pledge[18] receivables as security for the loan. If the loan is not paid when due, the creditor has the right to convert the collateral to cash—that is, to collect the receivables.

To illustrate, on March 1, 2003, Howat Mills, Inc. provides (assigns) $700,000 of its accounts receivable to Citizens Bank as collateral for a $500,000 note. Howat Mills will continue to collect the accounts receivable; the account debtors are not notified of the arrangement. Citizens Bank assesses a finance charge of 1 percent of the accounts receivable and interest on the note of 12 percent. Settlement by Howat Mills to the bank is made monthly for all cash collected on the receivables.

Illustration 7-12

Entries for Transfer of Receivables—Secured Borrowing

Howat Mills, Inc.			Citizens Bank		
Transfer of accounts receivable and issuance of note on March 1, 2003					
Cash	493,000		Notes Receivable	500,000	
Finance Charge	7,000*		Finance Revenue		7,000*
Notes Payable		500,000	Cash		493,000
*(1% × $700,000)					
Collection in March of $440,000 of accounts less cash discounts of $6,000 plus receipt of $14,000 sales returns					
Cash	434,000				
Sales Discounts	6,000				
Sales Returns	14,000		(No entry)		
Accounts Receivable		454,000			
($440,000 + $14,000 = $454,000)					
Remitted March collections plus accrued interest to the bank on April 1					
Interest Expense	5,000*		Cash	439,000	
Notes Payable	434,000		Interest Revenue		5,000*
Cash		439,000	Notes Receivable		434,000
*($500,000 × .12 × 1/12)					
Collection in April of the balance of accounts less $2,000 written off as uncollectible					
Cash	244,000				
Allowance for Doubtful Accounts	2,000		(No entry)		
Accounts Receivable		246,000*			
*($700,000 − $454,000)					
Remitted the balance due of $66,000 ($500,000 − $434,000) on the note plus interest on May 1					
Interest Expense	660*		Cash	66,660	
Notes Payable	66,000		Interest Revenue		660*
Cash		66,660	Notes Receivable		66,000
*($66,000 × .12 × 1/12)					

In addition to recording the collection of receivables, all discounts, returns and allowances, and bad debts must be recognized. Each month the proceeds from the collection of the accounts receivable are used to retire the note obligation. In addition, interest on the note is paid.[19]

---

[18]If the receivables are transferred to the transferee for custodial purposes, the custodial arrangement is often referred to as a **pledge**.

[19]What happens if Citizens Bank collected the transferred accounts receivable rather than Howat Mills? Citizens Bank would simply remit the cash proceeds to Howat Mills, and Howat Mills would make the same entries shown in Illustration 7-12. As a result, the receivables used as collateral are reported as an asset on the transferor's balance sheet.

Sales of Receivables

Sales of receivables have increased substantially in recent years. A common type is a sale to a factor. **Factors** are finance companies or banks that buy receivables from businesses for a fee and then collect the remittances directly from the customers. **Factoring receivables** is traditionally associated with the textile, apparel, footwear, furniture, and home furnishing industries.[20] An illustration of a factoring arrangement is shown below.

Illustration 7-13

Basic Procedures in Factoring

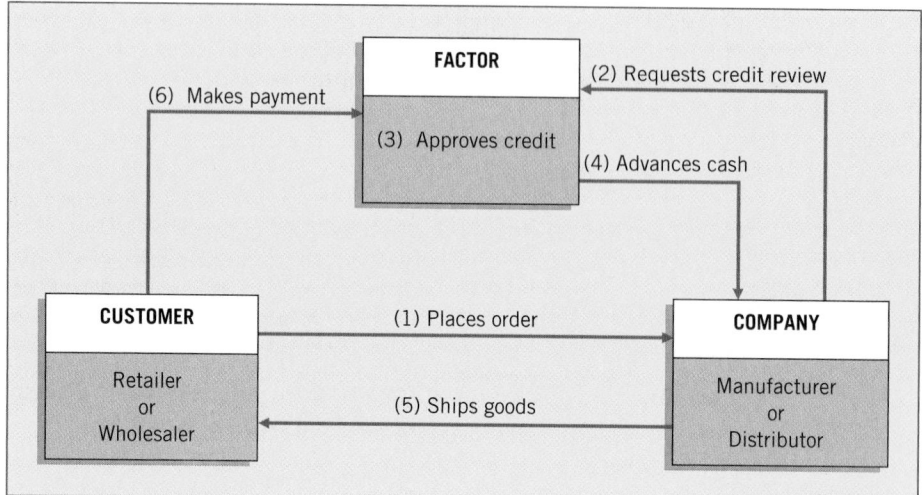

As indicated in the opening story, a recent phenomenon in the sale (transfer) of receivables is securitization. **Securitization** takes a pool of assets such as credit card receivables, mortgage receivables, or car loan receivables and sells shares in these pools of interest and principal payments (in effect, creating securities backed by these pools of assets). Virtually every asset with a payment stream and a long-term payment history is a candidate for securitization.

What are the differences between factoring and securitization? Factoring usually involves sale to only one company, fees are high, the quality of the receivables is low, and the seller afterward does not service the receivables. In a securitization, many investors are involved, margins are tight, the receivables are of higher quality, and the seller usually continues to service the receivables.

In either a factoring or a securitization transaction, receivables are sold on either a **without recourse** or a **with recourse** basis.[21]

Sale without Recourse

When receivables are sold **without recourse**, the purchaser assumes the risk of collectibility and absorbs any credit losses. The transfer of accounts receivable in a non-recourse transaction is an outright sale of the receivables both in form (transfer of title) and substance (transfer of control). In nonrecourse transactions, as in any sale of assets, Cash is debited for the proceeds; Accounts Receivable is credited for the face

---

[20]Credit cards like **MasterCard** and **VISA** are a type of factoring arrangement. Typically the purchaser of the receivable charges a $3/4$–$1\frac{1}{2}$ percent commission of the receivables purchased (the commission is 4–5 percent for credit card factoring).

[21]**Recourse** is the right of a transferee of receivables to receive payment from the transferor of those receivables for (1) failure of the debtors to pay when due, (2) the effects of prepayments, or (3) adjustments resulting from defects in the eligibility of the transferred receivables. See "Accounting for Transfers and Servicing of Financial Assets and Extinguishments of Liabilities," *Statement of Financial Accounting Standards No. 140* (Stamford, Conn.: FASB, 2000), p. 155.

value of the receivables. The difference, reduced by any provision for probable adjustments (discounts, returns, allowances, etc.), is recognized as a Loss on the Sale of Receivables. The seller uses a Due from Factor account (reported as a receivable) to account for the proceeds retained by the factor to cover probable sales discounts, sales returns, and sales allowances.

To illustrate, Crest Textiles, Inc. factors $500,000 of accounts receivable with Commercial Factors, Inc., on a **without recourse** basis. The receivable records are transferred to Commercial Factors, Inc., which will receive the collections. Commercial Factors assesses a finance charge of 3 percent of the amount of accounts receivable and retains an amount equal to 5 percent of the accounts receivable. The journal entries for both Crest Textiles and Commercial Factors for the receivables transferred without recourse are as follows.

Comprehensive Illustration of Sale Without Recourse

Illustration 7-14
Entries for Sale of Receivables Without Recourse

Crest Textiles, Inc.			Commercial Factors, Inc.		
Cash	460,000		Accounts (Notes) Receivable	500,000	
Due from Factor	25,000*		Due to Crest Textiles		25,000
Loss on Sale of Receivables	15,000**		Financing Revenue		15,000
Accounts (Notes) Receivable		500,000	Cash		460,000
*(5% × $500,000)					
**(3% × $500,000)					

In recognition of the sale of receivables, Crest Textiles records a loss of $15,000. The factor's net income will be the difference between the financing revenue of $15,000 and the amount of any uncollectible receivables.

Sale with Recourse

If receivables are sold **with recourse**, the seller guarantees payment to the purchaser in the event the debtor fails to pay. To record this type of transaction, a **financial components approach** is used, because the seller has a continuing involvement with the receivable.[22] In this approach, each party to the sale recognizes the assets and liabilities that it controls after the sale and no longer recognizes the assets and liabilities that were sold or extinguished.

To illustrate, assume the same information as in Illustration 7-14 for Crest Textiles and for Commercial Factors except that the receivables are sold on a with recourse basis. It is determined that this recourse obligation has a fair value of $6,000. To determine the loss on the sale of the receivables by Crest Textiles, the net proceeds from the sale are computed as follows.

Illustration 7-15
Net Proceeds Computation

Cash received	$460,000	
Due from factor	25,000	$485,000
Less: Recourse obligation		6,000
Net proceeds		$479,000

[22]Previous accounting standards generally required that the transferor account for financial assets transferred as an inseparable unit that had been entirely sold or entirely retained. Those standards were difficult to apply and produced inconsistent and arbitrary results. Values are now assigned to such components as the recourse provision, servicing rights, and agreement to reacquire.

Net proceeds are cash or other assets received in a sale less any liabilities incurred. The loss is then computed as follows.

Illustration 7-16
Loss on Sale Computation

Carrying (book) value	$500,000
Net proceeds	479,000
Loss on sale of receivables	$ 21,000

The journal entries for both Crest Textiles and Commercial Factors for the receivables sold with recourse are as follows.

Illustration 7-17
Entries for Sale of Receivables with Recourse

Crest Textiles, Inc.			Commercial Factors, Inc.		
Cash	460,000		Accounts Receivable	500,000	
Due from Factor	25,000		Due to Crest Textiles		25,000
Loss on Sale of			Financing Revenue		15,000
Receivables	21,000		Cash		460,000
Accounts (Notes)					
Receivable		500,000			
Recourse Liability		6,000			

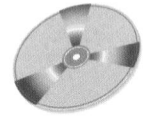

Tutorial on the Disposition of Receivables

In this case, Crest Textiles recognizes a loss of $21,000. In addition, a liability of $6,000 is recorded to indicate the probable payment to Commercial Factors for uncollectible receivables. If all the receivables are collected, Crest Textiles would eliminate its recourse liability and increase income. Commercial Factors' net income is the financing revenue of $15,000 because it will have no bad debts related to these receivables.

Secured Borrowing versus Sale

The FASB concluded that a sale occurs only if the seller surrenders control of the receivables to the buyer. The following three conditions must be met before a sale can be recorded:

INTERNATIONAL INSIGHT

The IASC has a similar conceptual approach to the sale of receivables, although it provides more flexibility in implementation.

① The transferred asset has been isolated from the transferor (put beyond reach of the transferor and its creditors).

② The transferees have obtained the right to pledge or exchange either the transferred assets or beneficial interests in the transferred assets.

③ The transferor does not maintain effective control over the transferred assets through an agreement to repurchase or redeem them before their maturity.

If the three conditions are met, a sale occurs. Otherwise, the transferor should record the transfer as a secured borrowing. If sale accounting is appropriate, it is still necessary to consider assets obtained and liabilities incurred in the transaction. The rules of accounting for transfers of receivables are shown in Illustration 7-18 on the next page.

Illustration 7-18 shows that if there is continuing involvement in a sale transaction, the assets obtained and liabilities incurred must be recorded.

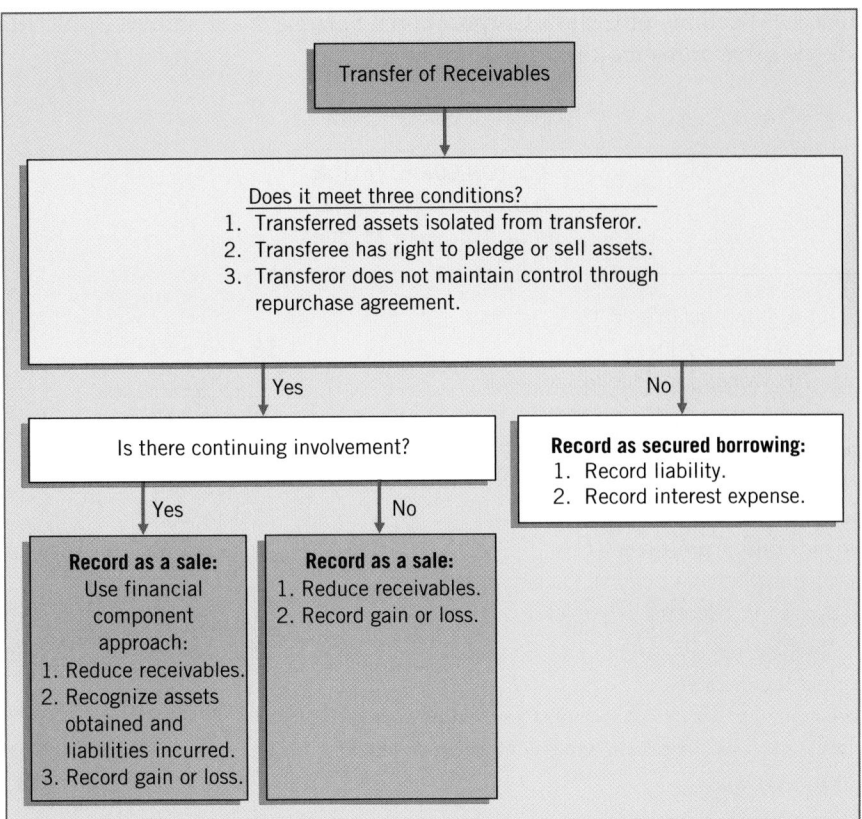

Illustration 7-18
Accounting for Transfers
of Receivables

PRESENTATION AND ANALYSIS

Presentation of Receivables

The general rules in classifying receivables are:

① Segregate the different types of receivables that an enterprise possesses, if material.

② Ensure that the valuation accounts are appropriately offset against the proper receivable accounts.

③ Determine that receivables classified in the current assets section will be converted into cash within the year or the operating cycle, whichever is longer.

④ Disclose any loss contingencies that exist on the receivables.

⑤ Disclose any receivables designated or pledged as collateral.

⑥ Disclose all significant concentrations of credit risk arising from receivables.[23]

OBJECTIVE **9**
**Explain how
receivables are
reported and
analyzed.**

---

[23]Concentrations of credit risk exist when receivables have common characteristics that may affect their collection. These common characteristics might be companies in the same industry or same region of the country. For example, financial statements users want to know if a substantial amount of receivables are with defense contractors or with companies in the volatile parts of the world. No numerical guidelines are provided as to what is meant by a "concentration of credit risk." When a concentration is identified, three items should be disclosed: (1) information on the characteristic that determines the concentration, (2) the amount of loss that could occur upon nonperformance, and (3) information on any collateral related to the receivable. "Disclosures about Fair Value of Financial Instruments," *Statement of Financial Accounting Standards No. 107* (Norwalk, Conn.: FASB, 1991), par. 15.

The assets sections of Colton Corporation's balance sheet shown below illustrate many of the disclosures required for receivables.

Illustration 7-19
Disclosure of Receivables

Additional Disclosures of Receivables

Holding receivables that will be paid in a foreign currency represents risk that the exchange rate may move against the company, causing a decrease in the amount collected in terms of U.S. dollars. Companies engaged in cross-border transactions often "hedge" these receivables by buying contracts to exchange currencies at specified amounts at future dates.

COLTON CORPORATION BALANCE SHEET (PARTIAL) AS OF DECEMBER 31, 2003		
Current assets		
Cash and cash equivalents		$ 1,870,250
Accounts receivable (Note 2)	$8,977,673	
Less: Allowance for doubtful accounts	500,226	
	8,477,447	
Advances to subsidiaries due 9/30/04	2,090,000	
Notes receivable—trade (Note 2)	1,532,000	
Federal income taxes refundable	146,704	
Dividends and interest receivable	75,500	
Other receivables and claims (including debit balances in accounts payable)	174,620	12,496,271
Total current assets		14,366,521
Noncurrent receivables		
Notes receivable from officers and key employees		376,090
Claims receivable (litigation settlement to be collected over four years)		585,000

Note 2: Accounts and Notes Receivable. In November 2003, the Company arranged with a finance company to refinance a part of its indebtedness. The loan is evidenced by a 12% note payable. The note is payable on demand and is secured by substantially all the accounts receivable.

Analysis of Receivables

Financial ratios are frequently computed to evaluate the liquidity of a company's accounts receivable. The ratio used to assess the liquidity of the receivables is the **receivables turnover ratio**. This ratio measures the number of times, on average, receivables are collected during the period. The ratio is computed by dividing net sales by average (net) receivables outstanding during the year. Theoretically, the numerator should include only net credit sales. This information is frequently not available, however, and if the relative amounts of credit and cash sales remain fairly constant, the trend indicated by the ratio will still be valid. Unless seasonal factors are significant, average receivables outstanding can be computed from the beginning and ending balances of net trade receivables.

To illustrate, **Gateway** reported 2001 net sales of $6,080 million, its beginning and ending accounts receivable balances were $545 million and $220 million, respectively. Its accounts receivables turnover ratio is computed in Illustration 7-20.

Illustration 7-20
Computation of Accounts Receivable Turnover

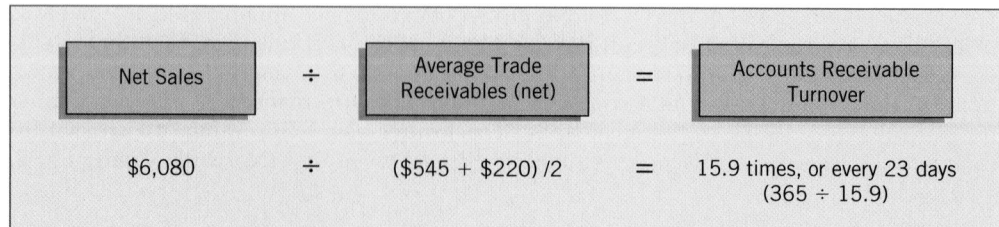

This information provides some indication of the quality of the receivables, and also an idea of how successful the firm is in collecting its outstanding receivables. If possible, an aging schedule should also be prepared to determine how long receivables have been outstanding. It is possible that a satisfactory receivables turnover may have resulted because certain receivables were collected quickly though others have been outstanding for a relatively long period. An aging schedule would reveal such patterns.[24]

UNDERLYING CONCEPTS

Providing information that will help users assess an enterprises's current liquidity and prospective cash flows is a primary objective of accounting.

SUMMARY OF LEARNING OBJECTIVES

❶ Identify items considered cash. To be reported as "cash," an asset must be readily available for the payment of current obligations and free from contractual restrictions that limit its use in satisfying debts. Cash consists of coin, currency, and available funds on deposit at the bank. Negotiable instruments such as money orders, certified checks, cashier's checks, personal checks, and bank drafts are also viewed as cash. Savings accounts are usually classified as cash.

❷ Indicate how cash and related items are reported. Cash is reported as a current asset in the balance sheet. The reporting of other related items are: (1) *Restricted cash:* The SEC recommends that legally restricted deposits held as compensating balances against short-term borrowing be stated separately among the "Cash and cash equivalent items" in current assets. Restricted deposits held against long-term borrowing arrangements should be separately classified as noncurrent assets in either the investments or other assets sections. (2) *Bank overdrafts:* They should be reported in the current liabilities section and are usually added to the amount reported as accounts payable. If material, these items should be separately disclosed either on the face of the balance sheet or in the related notes. (3) *Cash equivalents:* This item is often reported together with cash as "Cash and cash equivalents."

❸ Define receivables and identify the different types of receivables. Receivables are claims held against customers and others for money, goods, or services. The receivables are classified into three types: (1) current or noncurrent, (2) trade or nontrade, (3) accounts receivable or notes receivable.

❹ Explain accounting issues related to recognition of accounts receivable. Two issues that may complicate the measurement of accounts receivable are: (1) The availability of discounts (trade and cash discounts), and (2) the length of time between the sale and the payment due dates (the interest element).

Ideally, receivables should be measured in terms of their present value—that is, the discounted value of the cash to be received in the future. The profession specifically excludes from the present-value considerations receivables arising from normal business transactions that are due in customary trade terms within approximately one year.

❺ Explain accounting issues related to valuation of accounts receivable. Short-term receivables are valued and reported at net realizable value—the net amount expected to be received in cash, which is not necessarily the amount legally receivable. Determining net realizable value requires an estimation of uncollectible receivables.

❻ Explain accounting issues related to recognition of notes receivable. Short-term notes are recorded at face value. Long-term notes receivable are recorded at the present value of the cash expected to be collected. When the interest stated on an interest-

KEY TERMS

accounts receivable, *290*
aging schedule, *296*
allowance method, *295*
bank overdrafts, *289*
cash, *286*
cash discounts, *292*
cash equivalents, *289*
compensating balances, *289*
direct write-off method, *295*
factoring receivables, *306*
financial components
     approach, *307*
imputed interest rate, *303*
net realizable value, *294*
nontrade receivables, *291*
notes receivable, *291*
percentage-of-receivables
     approach, *296*
percentage-of-sales
     approach, *295*
promissory note, *298*
receivables, *290*
receivables turnover
     ratio, *310*
restricted cash, *288*
sales discounts, *292*
securitization, 306
trade discounts, *292*
trade receivables, *290*
with recourse, *307*
without recourse, *306*
zero-interest-bearing
     notes, *298*

---

[24]Often the receivables turnover is transformed to **days to collect accounts receivable** or days outstanding—an average collection period. In this case, 15.9 is divided into 365 days to obtain 23 days. Several figures other than 365 could be used here. A most common alternative is 360 days because it is divisible by 30 (days) and 12 (months). Use 365 days in any homework computations.

bearing note is equal to the effective (market) rate of interest, the note sells at face value. When the stated rate is different from the effective rate, either a discount or premium is recorded.

⑦ **Explain accounting issues related to valuation of notes receivable.** Like accounts receivable, short-term notes receivable are recorded and reported at their net realizable value. The same is also true of long-term receivables. Special issues relate to uncollectibles and impairments.

⑧ **Explain accounting issues related to disposition of accounts and notes receivable.** To accelerate the receipt of cash from receivables, the owner may transfer the receivables to another company for cash. The transfer of receivables to a third party for cash may be accomplished in one of two ways: (1) *Secured borrowing:* A creditor often requires that the debtor designate or pledge receivables as security for the loan. (2) *Sales (factoring) of receivables:* Factors are finance companies or banks that buy receivables from businesses and then collect the remittances directly from the customers. In many cases, transferors may have some continuing involvement with the receivable sold. A financial components approach is used to record this type of transaction.

⑨ **Explain how receivables are reported and analyzed.** Disclosure of receivables requires that valuation accounts be appropriately offset against receivables, receivables be appropriately classified as current or noncurrent, pledged or designated receivables be identified, and concentrations of risks arising from receivables be identified. Receivables may be analyzed based on turnover and the days outstanding.

REVIEW EXERCISE

Mike Horn Corporation manufactures sweatshirts for sale to athletic-wear retailers. The following information was available for Horn for the year ended December 31, 2003 and 2004.

	December 31, 2003	December 31, 2004
Cash	$ 20,000	$ 15,000
Trade accounts receivable	40,000	?
Allowance for doubtful accounts	5,500	?
Inventories	85,000	80,000
Current liabilities	80,000	86,000
Total credit sales	480,000	550,000
Collections on trade accounts receivable	440,000	500,000

During 2004, Horn had the following transactions.

1. On June 30, sales of $50,000 to a major customer were settled, with Horn accepting a 1-year $50,000 note bearing 11% interest, payable at maturity.

2. Horn factors some accounts receivable at the end of the year. Accounts totaling $40,000 are transferred to First Factors, Inc. with recourse. First Factors will receive the collections from Horn's customers and retain 6% of the balances. Horn is assessed a finance charge of 4% on this transfer. The fair value of the recourse obligation is $4,000.

3. On the basis of the latest available information, the 2004 provision for bad debts is estimated to be 0.8% of credit sales. Horn charged off as uncollectible, accounts with balances of $2,300.

Instructions

(a) Based on the above transactions, determine the balance for Trade Accounts Receivable and the Allowance for Doubtful Accounts at December 31, 2004.

(b) Prepare the current assets section of Horn's balance sheet at December 31, 2004. The cash balance at December 31, 2004, reflects the following items: checking account $4,000; postage stamps $1,100; petty cash $300; currency $3,000; customers' checks (post-dated) $2,000.

(c) Compute the current ratio and the receivables turnover ratio for Horn at December 31, 2004. Use these measures to analyze Horn's liquidity. The receivables turnover ratio in 2003 was 10.37.

(d) Discuss how the analysis in part (c) would be affected if Horn had transferred the receivables in a secured borrowing transaction.

SOLUTION TO THE REVIEW EXERCISE

(a)

TRADE ACCOUNTS RECEIVABLE		ALLOWANCE FOR DOUBTFUL ACCOUNTS	
Beginning balance	$ 40,000	Beginning balance	$5,500
Credit sales during 2004	550,000	Charge-offs	(2,300)
Collections during 2004	(500,000)	2004 provision (0.8% × $550,000)	4,400
Factored receivables	(40,000)	Ending balance	$7,600
Ending balance	$ 50,000		

(b)

Current assets		
Cash*		$ 11,900
Trade accounts receivable	$50,000	
Allowance for doubtful accounts	(7,600)	42,400
Customer receivable		2,000
Interest receivable**		2,750
Due from factor***		2,400
Note receivable		50,000
Inventories		80,000
Prepaid postage		1,100
Total current assets		$192,550

*($15,000 − $2,000 − $1,100)
**($50,000 × 11% × ½)
***($40,000 × 6%)

(c) Liquidity analysis

2003	2004
Current ratio = ($139,500 ÷ $80,000) = 1.74	($192,550 ÷ $86,000) = 2.24
Receivables turnover = 10.37 times	$\dfrac{\$550,000}{(\$34,500 + \$42,400)/2} = 14.3$ times

Both ratios indicate that Horn's liquidity has improved relative to the prior year.

(d) With a secured borrowing, the receivables would stay on Horn's books and Horn would record a note payable. This would reduce the current ratio and receivables turnover ratio.

CASH CONTROLS

As indicated in Chapter 7, cash creates many management and control problems. The purpose of this appendix is to discuss some of the basic control issues related to cash.

USING BANK ACCOUNTS

A company can vary the number and location of banks and the types of bank accounts to obtain desired control objectives. For large companies operating in multiple locations, the location of bank accounts can be important. Establishing collection accounts in strategic locations can accelerate the flow of cash into the company by shortening the time between a customer's mailing of a payment and the company's use of the cash. Multiple collection centers generally are used to reduce the size of a company's **collection float**, which is the difference between the amount on deposit according to the company's records and the amount of collected cash according to the bank record.

The **general checking account** is the principal bank account in most companies and frequently the only bank account in small businesses. Cash is deposited in and disbursed from this account as all transactions are cycled through it. Deposits from and disbursements to all other bank accounts are made through the general checking account.

Imprest bank accounts are used to make a specific amount of cash available for a limited purpose. The account acts as a clearing account for a large volume of checks or for a specific type of check. The specific and intended amount to be cleared through the imprest account is deposited by transferring that amount from the general checking account or other source. Imprest bank accounts are often used for disbursing payroll checks, dividends, commissions, bonuses, confidential expenses (e.g., officers' salaries), and travel expenses.

Lockbox accounts are frequently used by large, multilocation companies to make collections in cities within areas of heaviest customer billing. The company rents a local post office box and authorizes a local bank to pick up the remittances mailed to that box number. The bank empties the box at least once a day and immediately credits the company's account for collections. The greatest advantage of a lockbox is that it accelerates the availability of collected cash. Generally, in a lockbox arrangement the bank microfilms the checks for record purposes and provides the company with a deposit slip, a list of collections, and any customer correspondence. If the control over cash is improved and if the income generated from accelerating the receipt of funds exceeds the cost of the lockbox system, then it is considered a worthwhile undertaking.

THE IMPREST PETTY CASH SYSTEM

Almost every company finds it necessary to pay small amounts for a great many things such as taxi fares, minor office supplies, employee's lunches, and other miscellaneous expenses. It is frequently impractical to require that such disbursements be made by check, yet some control over them is important. A simple method of obtaining reasonable control, while adhering to the rule of disbursement by check, is the **imprest system for petty cash** disbursements. This is how the system works:

① Someone is designated petty cash custodian and given a small amount of currency from which to make small payments. The transfer of funds to petty cash is recorded as:

Petty Cash	300	
Cash		300

② As disbursements are made, the petty cash custodian obtains signed receipts from each individual to whom cash is paid. If possible, evidence of the disbursement should be attached to the petty cash receipt. Petty cash transactions are not recorded until the fund is reimbursed, and then such entries are recorded by someone other than the petty cash custodian.

③ When the supply of cash runs low, the custodian presents to the general cashier a request for reimbursement supported by the petty cash receipts and other disbursement evidence. The custodian receives a company check to replenish the fund. At this point, transactions are recorded based on petty cash receipts.

Office Supplies Expense	42	
Postage Expense	53	
Entertainment Expense	76	
Cash Over and Short	2	
Cash		173

④ If it is decided that the amount of cash in the petty cash fund is excessive, an adjustment may be made as follows (lowering the fund balance from $300 to $250).

Cash	50	
Petty Cash		50

Entries are made to the Petty Cash account only to increase or decrease the size of the fund.

A **Cash Over and Short** account is used when the petty cash fund fails to prove out. When this occurs, it is usually due to an error (failure to provide correct change, overpayment of expense, lost receipt, etc.). If cash proves out **short** (i.e., the sum of the receipts and cash in the fund is less than the imprest amount), the shortage is debited to the Cash Over and Short account. If cash proves out **over**, the overage is credited to Cash Over and Short. This account is left open until the end of the year, when it is closed. It is generally shown on the income statement as an "Other expense or revenue."

There are usually expense items in the fund except immediately after reimbursement. Therefore, if accurate financial statements are desired, the funds must be reimbursed at the end of each accounting period and also when nearly depleted.

Under the imprest system the petty cash custodian is responsible at all times for the amount of the fund on hand either as cash or in the form of signed receipts. These receipts provide the evidence required by the disbursing officer to issue a reimbursement check. Two additional procedures are followed to obtain more complete control over the petty cash fund:

① Surprise counts of the fund are made from time to time by a superior of the petty cash custodian to determine that the fund is being accounted for satisfactorily.

② Petty cash receipts are canceled or mutilated after they have been submitted for reimbursement, so that they cannot be used to secure a second reimbursement.

PHYSICAL PROTECTION OF CASH BALANCES

Not only must cash receipts and cash disbursements be safeguarded through internal control measures, but also the cash on hand and in banks must be protected. Because receipts become cash on hand and disbursements are made from cash in banks, adequate control of receipts and disbursements is a part of the protection of cash balances. Certain other procedures, however, should be given some consideration.

Physical protection of cash is so elementary a necessity that it requires little discussion. Every effort should be made to minimize the cash on hand in the office. A petty cash fund, the current day's receipts, and perhaps funds for making change should be all that is on hand at any one time. Insofar as possible, these funds should be kept in a vault, safe, or locked cash drawer. Each day's receipts should be transmitted intact to the bank as soon as practicable. Accurately stating the amount of available cash both in internal management reports and in external financial statements is also extremely important.

Every company has a record of cash received, disbursed, and the balance. Because of the many cash transactions, however, errors or omissions may be made in keeping this record. Therefore, it is necessary periodically to prove the balance shown in the general ledger. Cash actually present in the office—petty cash, change funds, and undeposited receipts—can be counted, for comparison with the company records. Cash on deposit is not available for count and is proved by preparing a bank reconciliation—a reconciliation of the company's record and the bank's record of the company's cash.

RECONCILIATION OF BANK BALANCES

At the end of each calendar month the bank supplies each customer with a **bank statement** (a copy of the bank's account with the customer) together with the customer's checks that have been paid by the bank during the month.[1] If no errors were made by the bank or the customer, if all deposits made and all checks drawn by the customer reached the bank within the same month, and if no unusual transactions occurred that affected either the company's or the bank's record of cash, the balance of cash reported by the bank to the customer would be the same as that shown in the customer's own records. This condition seldom occurs for one or more of the reconciling items presented at the top of the next page. Hence, differences between the depositor's record of cash and the bank's record are usual and expected. Therefore, the two must be reconciled to determine the nature of the differences between the two amounts.

A **bank reconciliation** is a schedule explaining any differences between the bank's and the company's records of cash. If the difference results only from transactions not yet recorded by the bank, the company's record of cash is considered correct. But, if some part of the difference arises from other items, the bank's records or the company's records must be adjusted.

Two forms of bank reconciliation may be prepared. One form reconciles from the bank statement balance to the book balance or vice versa. The other form reconciles

---

[1]As mentioned in Chapter 7, use of paper checks continues to be a popular means of payment. However, ready availability of desktop publishing software and hardware has created new opportunities for check fraud in the form of duplicate, altered, and forged checks. At the same time, new fraud-fighting technologies, such as ultraviolet imaging, high-capacity barcodes, and biometrics are being developed. These technologies convert paper documents into document files that are processed electronically, thereby reducing the risk of fraud.

RECONCILING ITEMS

1 *Deposits in Transit.* End-of-month deposits of cash recorded on the depositor's books in one month are received and recorded by the bank in the following month.

2 *Outstanding Checks.* Checks written by the depositor are recorded when written but may not be recorded by (may not "clear") the bank until the next month.

3 *Bank Charges.* Charges recorded by the bank against the depositor's balance for such items as bank services, printing checks, **not-sufficient-funds (NSF) checks**, and safe-deposit box rentals. The depositor may not be aware of these charges until the receipt of the bank statement.

4 *Bank Credits.* Collections or deposits by the bank for the benefit of the depositor that may be unknown to the depositor until receipt of the bank statement. Examples are note collection for the depositor and interest earned on interest-bearing checking accounts.

5 *Bank or Depositor Errors.* Errors on either the part of the bank or the part of the depositor cause the bank balance to disagree with the depositor's book balance.

both the bank balance and the book balance to a correct cash balance. This latter form is more widely used. A sample of that form and its common reconciling items are shown in Illustration 7A-1.

Balance per bank statement (end of period)		$$$
Add: Deposits in transit	$$	
Undeposited receipts (cash on hand)	$$	
Bank errors that understate the bank statement balance	$$	$$
Deduct: Outstanding checks	$$	$$$
Bank errors that overstate the bank statement balance	$$	$$
Correct cash balance		$$$
Balance per depositor's books		$$$
Add: Bank credits and collections not yet recorded in the books	$$	
Book errors that understate the book balance	$$	$$
		$$$
Deduct: Bank charges not yet recorded in the books	$$	
Book errors that overstate the book balance	$$	$$
Correct cash balance		$$$

Illustration 7A-1
Bank Reconciliation Form and Content

This form of reconciliation consists of two sections: (1) "Balance per bank statement" and (2) "Balance per depositor's books." Both sections end with the same "Correct cash balance." The correct cash balance is the amount to which the books must be adjusted and is the amount reported on the balance sheet. **Adjusting journal entries are prepared for all the addition and deduction items appearing in the "Balance per depositor's books" section.** Any errors attributable to the bank should be called to the bank's attention immediately.

To illustrate, Nugget Mining Company's books show a cash balance at the Denver National Bank on November 30, 2003, of $20,502. The bank statement covering the month of November shows an ending balance of $22,190. An examination of Nugget's accounting records and November bank statement identified the following reconciling items.

① A deposit of $3,680 was mailed November 30 but does not appear on the bank statement.

② Checks written in November but not charged to the November bank statement are:

Check #7327	$ 150
#7348	4,820
#7349	31

③ Nugget has not yet recorded the $600 of interest collected by the bank November 20 on Sequoia Co. bonds held by the bank for Nugget.

④ Bank service charges of $18 are not yet recorded on Nugget's books.

⑤ One of Nugget's customer's checks for $220 was returned with the bank statement and marked "NSF." The bank treated this bad check as a disbursement.

⑥ Nugget discovered that check #7322, written in November for $131 in payment of an account payable, had been incorrectly recorded in its books as $311.

⑦ A check for Nugent Oil Co. in the amount of $175 that had been incorrectly charged to Nugget Mining accompanied the bank statement.

The reconciliation of bank and book balances to the correct cash balance of $21,044 would appear as follows.

Illustration 7A-2

Sample Bank Reconciliation

NUGGET MINING COMPANY			
BANK RECONCILIATION			
Denver National Bank, November 30, 2003			
Balance per bank statement (end of period)			$22,190
Add: Deposit in transit	(1)	$3,680	
Bank error—incorrect check charged to account by bank	(7)	175	3,855
			26,045
Deduct: Outstanding checks	(2)		5,001
Correct cash balance			$21,044
Balance per books			$20,502
Add: Interest collected by the bank	(3)	$ 600	
Error in recording check #7322	(6)	180	780
			21,282
Deduct: Bank service charges	(4)	18	
NSF check returned	(5)	220	238
Correct cash balance			$21,044

The journal entries required to adjust and correct Nugget Mining's books in early December 2003 are taken from the items in the "Balance per books" section and are as follows.

Cash	600	
Interest Revenue		600
(To record interest on Sequoia Co. bonds, collected by bank)		
Cash	180	
Accounts Payable		180
(To correct error in recording amount of check #7322)		
Office Expense—Bank Charges	18	
Cash		18
(To record bank service charges for November)		
Accounts Receivable	220	
Cash		220
(To record customer's check returned NSF)		

Expanded Discussion of a Four-Column Bank Reconciliation

When the entries are posted, Nugget's cash account will have a balance of $21,044. Nugget should return the Nugent Oil Co. check to Denver National Bank, informing the bank of the error.

SUMMARY OF LEARNING OBJECTIVE FOR APPENDIX 7A

⑩ Explain common techniques employed to control cash. The common techniques employed to control cash are: (1) *Using bank accounts:* A company can vary the number and location of banks and the types of accounts to obtain desired control objectives. (2) *The imprest petty cash system:* It may be impractical to require small amounts of various expenses be paid by check, yet some control over them is important. (3) *Physical protection of cash balances:* Adequate control of receipts and disbursements is a part of the protection of cash balances. Every effort should be made to minimize the cash on hand in the office. (4) *Reconciliation of bank balances:* Cash on deposit is not available for count and is proved by preparing a bank reconciliation.

KEY TERMS

bank reconciliation, *316*
imprest system for petty cash, *314*
not-sufficient-funds (NSF) checks, *317*

Note: All **asterisked** Questions, Brief Exercises, Exercises, Problems, and Conceptual Cases relate to material covered in the appendix to the chapter.

QUESTIONS

1 What may be included under the heading of "cash"?

2 In what accounts should the following items be classified?

  (a) Coins and currency.

  (b) U.S. Treasury (government) bonds.

  (c) Certificate of deposit.

  (d) Cash in a bank that is in receivership.

  (e) NSF check (returned with bank statement).

  (f) Deposit in foreign bank (exchangeability limited).

  (g) Postdated checks.

  (h) Cash (to be used for retirement of long-term bonds).

  (i) Deposits in transit.

  (j) 100 shares of America Online stock (intention is to sell in one year or less).

  (k) Savings and checking accounts.

  (l) Petty cash.

  (m) Stamps.

  (n) Travel advances.

3 Define a "compensating balance." How should a compensating balance be reported?

4 Michael Tilsen Thomas Inc. reported in a recent annual report "Restricted cash for debt redemption." What section of the balance sheet would report this item?

5 What are the reasons that a company gives trade discounts? Why are trade discounts not recorded in the accounts like cash discounts?

6 What are two methods of recording accounts receivable transactions when a cash discount situation is involved? Which is more theoretically correct? Which is used in practice more of the time? Why?

7 What are the basic problems that occur in the valuation of accounts receivable?

8 What is the theoretical justification of the allowance method as contrasted with the direct write-off method of accounting for bad debts?

9 Indicate how well the percentage-of-sales method and the aging method accomplish the objectives of the allowance method of accounting for bad debts.

10 Of what merit is the contention that the allowance method lacks the objectivity of the direct write-off method? Discuss in terms of accounting's measurement function.

11 Explain how the accounting for bad debts can be used for earnings management.

12 Because of calamitous earthquake losses, Kishwaukee Company, one of your client's oldest and largest customers, suddenly and unexpectedly became bankrupt. Approximately 30% of your client's total sales have been made to Kishwaukee Company during each of the past several years. The amount due from Kishwaukee Company—none of which is collectible—equals 22% of total accounts receivable, an amount that is considerably in excess of what was determined to be an adequate provision for doubtful accounts at the close of the preceding year. How would your client record the write-off of the Kishwaukee Company receivable if it is using the allowance method of accounting for bad debts? Justify your suggested treatment.

13 What is the normal procedure for handling the collection of accounts receivable previously written off using the direct write-off method? The allowance method?

14 On January 1, 2003, John Singer Co. sells property for which it had paid $690,000 to Sargent Company, receiving in return Sargent's zero-interest-bearing note for $1,000,000 payable in 5 years. What entry would John Singer make to record the sale, assuming that John Singer frequently sells similar items of property for a cash sales price of $620,000?

15 What is "imputed interest"? In what situations is it necessary to impute an interest rate for notes receivable? What are the considerations in imputing an appropriate interest rate?

16 Indicate three reasons why a company might sell its receivables to another company.

17 When is the financial components approach to recording the transfers of receivables used? When should a transfer of receivables be recorded as a sale?

18 Hale Hardware is planning to factor some of its receivables. The cash received will be used to pay for inventory purchases. The factor has indicated that it will require "recourse" on the sold receivables. Explain to the controller of Hale Hardware what "recourse" is and how the recourse will be reflected in Hale's financial statements after the sale of the receivables.

19 Morley Safer Company includes in its trial balance for December 31 an item for Accounts Receivable, $769,000. This balance consists of the following items.

Due from regular customers	$523,000
Refund receivable on prior year's income taxes (an established claim)	15,500
Loans to officers	22,000
Loan to wholly owned subsidiary	45,500
Advances to creditors for goods ordered	61,000
Accounts receivable assigned as security for loans payable	75,000
Notes receivable past due plus interest on these notes	27,000
Total	$769,000

Illustrate how these items should be shown in the balance sheet as of December 31.

20 What is the accounts receivable turnover ratio, and what type of information does it provide?

21 You are evaluating Hawthorn Downs Racetrack for a potential loan. An examination of the notes to the financial statements indicates restricted cash at year-end amounts to $100,000. Explain how you would use this information in evaluating Hawthorn's liquidity.

*22 Distinguish among the following: (1) a general checking account, (2) an imprest bank account, and (3) a lockbox account.

BRIEF EXERCISES

BE7-1 Stowe Enterprises owns the following assets at December 31, 2004.

Cash in bank—savings account	63,000	Checking account balance	17,000
Cash on hand	9,300	Postdated checks	750
Cash refund due from IRS	31,400	Certificates of deposit (180-day)	90,000

What amount should be reported as cash?

BE7-2 Montoya Co. uses the gross method to record sales made on credit. On June 1, 2004, it made sales of $40,000 with terms 3/15, n/45. On June 12, 2004, Montoya received full payment for the June 1 sale. Prepare the required journal entries for Montoya Co.

BE7-3 Use the information from BE7-2, assuming Montoya Co. uses the net method to account for cash discounts. Prepare the required journal entries for Montoya Co.

BE7-4   Battle Tank, Inc. had net sales in 2003 of $1,200,000. At December 31, 2003, before adjusting entries, the balances in selected accounts were: Accounts Receivable $250,000 debit, and Allowance for Doubtful Accounts $2,100 credit. If Battle Tank estimates that 2% of its net sales will prove to be uncollectible, prepare the December 31, 2003, journal entry to record bad debt expense.

BE7-5   Use the information presented in BE7-4 for Battle Tank, Inc.

(a) Instead of estimating the uncollectibles at 2% of net sales, assume that 10% of accounts receivable will prove to be uncollectible. Prepare the entry to record bad debts expense.

(b) Instead of estimating uncollectibles at 2% of net sales, assume Battle Tank prepares an aging schedule that estimates total uncollectible accounts at $24,600. Prepare the entry to record bad debts expense.

BE7-6   Addams Family Importers sold goods to Acme Decorators for $20,000 on November 1, 2003, accepting Acme's $20,000, 6-month, 12% note. Prepare Addams' November 1 entry, December 31 annual adjusting entry, and May 1 entry for the collection of the note and interest.

BE7-7   Aero Acrobats lent $15,944 to Afterburner, Inc., accepting Afterburner's 2-year, $20,000, zero-interest-bearing note. The implied interest is 12%. Prepare Aero's journal entries for the initial transaction, recognition of interest each year, and the collection of $20,000 at maturity.

BE7-8   On October 1, 2003, Akira, Inc. assigns $1,000,000 of its accounts receivable to Alisia National Bank as collateral for a $700,000 note. The bank assesses a finance charge of 2% of the receivables assigned and interest on the note of 13%. Prepare the October 1 journal entries for both Akira and Alisia.

BE7-9   CRC Incorporated factored $100,000 of accounts receivable with Fredrick Factors Inc. on a without recourse basis. Fredrick assesses a 2% finance charge of the amount of accounts receivable and retains an amount equal to 6% of accounts receivable for possible adjustments. Prepare the journal entry for CRC Incorporated and Fredrick Factors to record the factoring of the accounts receivable to Fredrick.

BE7-10   Use the information in BE7-9 for CRC. Assume that the receivables are sold with recourse. Prepare the journal entry for CRC to record the sale, assuming that the recourse obligation has a fair value of $7,500.

BE7-11   Keyser Woodcrafters sells $200,000 of receivables to Commercial Factors, Inc. on a recourse basis. Commercial assesses a finance charge of 5% and retains an amount equal to 4% of accounts receivable. Keyser estimates the fair value of the recourse obligation to be $8,000. Prepare the journal entry for Keyser to record the sale.

BE7-12   Use the information presented in BE7-11 for Keyser Woodcrafters but assume that the recourse obligation has a fair value of $4,000, instead of $8,000. Discuss the effects of this change in the value of the recourse obligation on Keyser's balance sheet and income statement.

BE7-13   The financial statements of **General Mills, Inc.** report net sales of $5,416,000,000. Accounts receivable are $277,300,000 at the beginning of the year and $337,800,000 at the end of the year. Compute General Mills's accounts receivable turnover ratio. Compute General Mills's average collection period for accounts receivable in days.

*BE7-14   Genesis Company designated Alex Kidd as petty cash custodian and established a petty cash fund of $200. The fund is reimbursed when the cash in the fund is at $17. Petty cash receipts indicate funds were disbursed for office supplies $94, and miscellaneous expense $87. Prepare journal entries for the establishment of the fund and the reimbursement.

*BE7-15   Jaguar Corporation is preparing a bank reconciliation and has identified the following potential reconciling items. For each item, indicate if it is (1) added to balance per bank statement, (2) deducted from balance per bank statement, (3) added to balance per books, or (4) deducted from balance per books.

(a) Deposit in transit $5,500.

(b) Interest credited to Jaguar's account $31.

(c) Bank service charges $25.

(d) Outstanding checks $7,422.

(e) NSF check returned $377.

*BE7-16   Use the information presented in BE7-15 for Jaguar Corporation. Prepare any entries necessary to make Jaguar's accounting records correct and complete.

EXERCISES

E7-1 (Determining Cash Balance) The controller for Clint Eastwood Co. is attempting to determine the amount of cash to be reported on its December 31, 2003, balance sheet. The following information is provided.

1. Commercial savings account of $600,000 and a commercial checking account balance of $900,000 are held at First National Bank of Yojimbo.
2. Money market fund account held at Volonte Co. (a mutual fund organization) permits Eastwood to write checks on this balance, $5,000,000.
3. Travel advances of $180,000 for executive travel for the first quarter of next year (employee to reimburse through salary reduction).
4. A separate cash fund in the amount of $1,500,000 is restricted for the retirement of long-term debt.
5. Petty cash fund of $1,000.
6. An I.O.U. from Marianne Koch, a company officer, in the amount of $190,000.
7. A bank overdraft of $110,000 has occurred at one of the banks the company uses to deposit its cash receipts. At the present time, the company has no deposits at this bank.
8. The company has two certificates of deposit, each totaling $500,000. These CDs have a maturity of 120 days.
9. Eastwood has received a check that is dated January 12, 2004, in the amount of $125,000.
10. Eastwood has agreed to maintain a cash balance of $500,000 at all times at First National Bank of Yojimbo to ensure future credit availability.
11. Eastwood has purchased $2,100,000 of commercial paper of Sergio Leone Co. which is due in 60 days.
12. Currency and coin on hand amounted to $7,700.

Instructions

(a) Compute the amount of cash to be reported on Eastwood Co.'s balance sheet at December 31, 2003.

(b) Indicate the proper reporting for items that are not reported as cash on the December 31, 2003, balance sheet.

E7-2 (Determine Cash Balance) Presented below are a number of independent situations.

Instructions

For each individual situation, determine the amount that should be reported as cash. If the item(s) is not reported as cash, explain the rationale.

1. Checking account balance $925,000; certificate of deposit $1,400,000; cash advance to subsidiary of $980,000; utility deposit paid to gas company $180.
2. Checking account balance $600,000; an overdraft in special checking account at same bank as normal checking account of $17,000; cash held in a bond sinking fund $200,000; petty cash fund $300; coins and currency on hand $1,350.
3. Checking account balance $590,000; postdated check from customer $11,000; cash restricted due to maintaining compensating balance requirement of $100,000; certified check from customer $9,800; postage stamps on hand $620.
4. Checking account balance at bank $37,000; money market balance at mutual fund (has checking privileges) $48,000; NSF check received from customer $800.
5. Checking account balance $700,000; cash restricted for future plant expansion $500,000; short-term Treasury bills $180,000; cash advance received from customer $900 (not included in checking account balance); cash advance of $7,000 to company executive, payable on demand; refundable deposit of $26,000 paid to federal government to guarantee performance on construction contract.

E7-3 (Financial Statement Presentation of Receivables) Jack Gleason Company shows a balance of $181,140 in the Accounts Receivable account on December 31, 2003. The balance consists of the following.

Installment accounts due in 2004	$23,000
Installment accounts due after 2004	34,000
Overpayments to creditors	2,640

Due from regular customers, of which $40,000 represents	
accounts pledged as security for a bank loan	79,000
Advances to employees	1,500
Advance to subsidiary company (made in 1998)	81,000

Instructions

Illustrate how the information above should be shown on the balance sheet of Jack Gleason Company on December 31, 2003.

E7-4 **(Determine Ending Accounts Receivable)** Your accounts receivable clerk, Ms. Mitra Adams, to whom you pay a salary of $1,500 per month, has just purchased a new Cadillac. You decided to test the accuracy of the accounts receivable balance of $82,000 as shown in the ledger.

The following information is available for your *first year* in business.

(1) Collections from customers	$198,000
(2) Merchandise purchased	320,000
(3) Ending merchandise inventory	90,000
(4) Goods are marked to sell at 40% above cost	

Instructions

Compute an estimate of the ending balance of accounts receivable from customers that should appear in the ledger and any apparent shortages. Assume that all sales are made on account.

E7-5 **(Record Sales Gross and Net)** On June 3, Benedict Arnold Company sold to Chester Arthur merchandise having a sale price of $3,000 with terms of 2/10, n/60, f.o.b. shipping point. An invoice totaling $90, terms n/30, was received by Chester on June 8 from the John Booth Transport Service for the freight cost. On June 12, the company received a check for the balance due from Chester Arthur.

Instructions

(a) Prepare journal entries on the Benedict Arnold Company books to record all the events noted above under each of the following bases.
   (1) Sales and receivables are entered at gross selling price.
   (2) Sales and receivables are entered at net of cash discounts.
(b) Prepare the journal entry under basis 2, assuming that Chester Arthur did not remit payment until July 29.

E7-6 **(Recording Sales Transactions)** Presented below is information from Perez Computers Incorporated.

July 1 Sold $20,000 of computers to Robertson Company with terms 3/15, n/60. Perez uses the gross method to record cash discounts.
10 Perez received payment from Robertson for the full amount owed from the July transactions.
17 Sold $200,000 in computers and peripherals to The Clark Store with terms of 2/10, n/30.
30 The Clark Store paid Perez for its purchase of July 17.

Instructions

Prepare the necessary journal entries for Perez Computers.

E7-7 **(Recording Bad Debts)** Shaquille Company reports the following financial information before adjustments.

	Dr.	Cr.
Accounts Receivable	$100,000	
Allowance for Doubtful Accounts		$ 2,000
Sales (all on credit)		900,000
Sales Returns and Allowances	50,000	

Instructions

Prepare the journal entry to record Bad Debt Expense assuming Shaquille Company estimates bad debts at (a) 1% of net sales and (b) 5% of accounts receivable.

E7-8 (Recording Bad Debts) At the end of 2004 Juarez Company has accounts receivable of $800,000 and an allowance for doubtful accounts of $40,000. On January 16, 2005, Juarez Company determined that its receivable from Maximillan Company of $6,000 will not be collected, and management authorized its write-off.

Instructions

(a) Prepare the journal entry for Juarez Company to write off the Maximillan receivable.

(b) What is the net realizable value of Juarez Company's accounts receivable before the write-off of the Maximillan receivable?

(c) What is the net realizable value of Juarez Company's accounts receivable after the write-off of the Maximillan receivable?

E7-9 (Computing Bad Debts and Preparing Journal Entries) The trial balance before adjustment of Patsy Cline Inc. shows the following balances.

	Dr.	Cr.
Accounts Receivable	$90,000	
Allowance for Doubtful Accounts	1,750	
Sales (all on credit)		$680,000

Instructions

Give the entry for estimated bad debts assuming that the allowance is to provide for doubtful accounts on the basis of (a) 4% of gross accounts receivable and (b) 1% of net sales.

E7-10 (Bad Debt Reporting) The chief accountant for Emily Dickinson Corporation provides you with the following list of accounts receivable written off in the current year.

Date	Customer	Amount
March 31	E. L. Masters Company	$7,800
June 30	Stephen Crane Associates	6,700
September 30	Amy Lowell's Dress Shop	7,000
December 31	R. Frost, Inc.	9,830

Emily Dickinson Corporation follows the policy of debiting Bad Debt Expense as accounts are written off. The chief accountant maintains that this procedure is appropriate for financial statement purposes because the Internal Revenue Service will not accept other methods for recognizing bad debts.

All of Emily Dickinson Corporation's sales are on a 30-day credit basis. Sales for the current year total $2,200,000, and research has determined that bad debt losses approximate 2% of sales.

Instructions

(a) Do you agree or disagree with Emily Dickinson Corporation policy concerning recognition of bad debt expense? Why or why not?

(b) By what amount would net income differ if bad debt expense was computed using the percentage-of-sales approach?

E7-11 (Bad Debts—Aging) Gerard Manley, Inc. includes the following account among its trade receivables.

		Hopkins Co.			
1/1	Balance forward	700	1/28	Cash (#1710)	1,100
1/20	Invoice #1710	1,100	4/2	Cash (#2116)	1,350
3/14	Invoice #2116	1,350	4/10	Cash (1/1 Balance)	155
4/12	Invoice #2412	1,710	4/30	Cash (#2412)	1,000
9/5	Invoice #3614	490	9/20	Cash (#3614 and	
10/17	Invoice #4912	860		part of #2412)	790
11/18	Invoice #5681	2,000	10/31	Cash (#4912)	860
12/20	Invoice #6347	800	12/1	Cash (#5681)	1,250
			12/29	Cash (#6347)	800

Instructions

Age the balance and specify any items that apparently require particular attention at year-end.

E7-12 (Journalizing Various Receivable Transactions) Presented below is information related to James Garfield Corp.

July 1 James Garfield Corp. sold to Warren Harding Co. merchandise having a sales price of $8,000 with terms 2/10, net/60. Garfield records its sales and receivables net.

5 Accounts receivable of $9,000 (gross) are factored with Andrew Jackson Credit Corp. without recourse at a financing charge of 9%. Cash is received for the proceeds; collections are handled by the finance company. (These accounts were all past the discount period.)

9 Specific accounts receivable of $9,000 (gross) are pledged to Alf Landon Credit Corp. as security for a loan of $6,000 at a finance charge of 6% of the amount of the loan. The finance company will make the collections. (All the accounts receivable are past the discount period.)

Dec. 29 Warren Harding Co. notifies Garfield that it is bankrupt and will pay only 10% of its account. Give the entry to write off the uncollectible balance using the allowance method. (Note: First record the increase in the receivable on July 11 when the discount period passed.)

Instructions

Prepare all necessary entries in general journal form for Garfield Corp.

E7-13 (Assigning Accounts Receivable) On April 1, 2004, Rasheed Company assigns $400,000 of its accounts receivable to the Third National Bank as collateral for a $200,000 loan due July 1, 2004. The assignment agreement calls for Rasheed Company to continue to collect the receivables. Third National Bank assesses a finance charge of 2% of the accounts receivable, and interest on the loan is 10% (a realistic rate of interest for a note of this type).

Instructions

(a) Prepare the April 1, 2004, journal entry for Rasheed Company.
(b) Prepare the journal entry for Rasheed's collection of $350,000 of the accounts receivable during the period from April 1, 2004, through June 30, 2004.
(c) On July 1, 2004, Rasheed paid Third National all that was due from the loan it secured on April 1, 2004.

E7-14 (Journalizing Various Receivable Transactions) The trial balance before adjustment for Judy Collins Company shows the following balances.

	Dr.	Cr.
Accounts Receivable	$82,000	
Allowance for Doubtful Accounts	2,120	
Sales		$430,000

Instructions

Using the data above, give the journal entries required to record each of the following cases. (Each situation is independent.)

1. To obtain additional cash, Collins factors without recourse $25,000 of accounts receivable with Stills Finance. The finance charge is 10% of the amount factored.
2. To obtain a one-year loan of $55,000, Collins assigns $65,000 of specific receivable accounts to Crosby Financial. The finance charge is 8% of the loan; the cash is received and the accounts turned over to Crosby Financial.
3. The company wants to maintain the Allowance for Doubtful Accounts at 5% of gross accounts receivable.
4. The company wishes to increase the allowance by 1½% of net sales.

E7-15 **(Transfer of Receivables with Recourse)** Ames Quartet Inc. factors receivables with a carrying amount of $200,000 to Joffrey Company for $160,000 on a with recourse basis.

Instructions

The recourse provision has a fair value of $1,000. This transaction should be recorded as a sale. Prepare the appropriate journal entry to record this transaction on the books of Ames Quartet Inc.

E7-16 **(Transfer of Receivables with Recourse)** Whitney Houston Corporation factors $175,000 of accounts receivable with Kathleen Battle Financing, Inc. on a with recourse basis. Kathleen Battle Financing will collect the receivables. The receivable records are transferred to Kathleen Battle Financing on August 15, 2003. Kathleen Battle Financing assesses a finance charge of 2% of the amount of accounts receivable and also reserves an amount equal to 4% of accounts receivable to cover probable adjustments.

Instructions

(a) What conditions must be met for a transfer of receivables with recourse to be accounted for as a sale?
(b) Assume the conditions from part (a) are met. Prepare the journal entry on August 15, 2003, for Whitney Houston to record the sale of receivables, assuming the recourse obligation has a fair value of $2,000.

E7-17 **(Transfer of Receivables Without Recourse)** JFK Corp. factors $300,000 of accounts receivable with LBJ Finance Corporation on a without recourse basis on July 1, 2003. The receivable records are transferred to LBJ Finance, which will receive the collections. LBJ Finance assesses a finance charge of 1½% of the amount of accounts receivable and retains an amount equal to 4% of accounts receivable to cover sales discounts, returns, and allowances. The transaction is to be recorded as a sale.

Instructions

(a) Prepare the journal entry on July 1, 2003, for JFK Corp. to record the sale of receivables without recourse.
(b) Prepare the journal entry on July 1, 2003, for LBJ Finance Corporation to record the purchase of receivables without recourse.

E7-18 **(Note Transactions at Unrealistic Interest Rates)** On July 1, 2004. Agincourt Inc. made two sales.

1. It sold land having a fair market value of $700,000 in exchange for a 4-year non-interest-bearing promissory note in the face amount of $1,101,460. The land is carried on Agincourt's books at a cost of $590,000.
2. It rendered services in exchange for a 3%, 8-year promissory note having a face value of $400,000 (interest payable annually).

Agincourt Inc. recently had to pay 8% interest for money that it borrowed from British National Bank. The customers in these two transactions have credit ratings that require them to borrow money at 12% interest.

Instructions

Record the two journal entries that should be recorded by Agincourt Inc. for the sales transactions above that took place on July 1, 2004.

E7-19 **(Notes Receivable with Unrealistic Interest Rate)** On December 31, 2002, Ed Abbey Co. performed environmental consulting services for Hayduke Co. Hayduke was short of cash, and Abbey Co. agreed to accept a $200,000 non-interest-bearing note due December 31, 2004, as payment in full. Hayduke is somewhat of a credit risk and typically borrows funds at a rate of 15%. Abbey is much more creditworthy and has various lines of credit at 6%.

Instructions
(a) Prepare the journal entry to record the transaction of December 31, 2002, for the Ed Abbey Co.
(b) Assuming Ed Abbey Co.'s fiscal year-end is December 31, prepare the journal entry for December 31, 2003.
(c) Assuming Ed Abbey Co.'s fiscal year-end is December 31, prepare the journal entry for December 31, 2304.

E7-20 (Analysis of Receivables) Presented below is information for Jones Company.

1. Beginning-of-the-year Accounts Receivable balance was $15,000.
2. Net sales for the year were $185,000. (Credit sales were $100,000 of the total sales.) Jones does not offer cash discounts.
3. Collections on accounts receivable during the year were $70,000.

Instructions
(a) Prepare (summary) journal entries to record the items noted above.
(b) Compute Jones' accounts receivable turnover ratio for the year.
(c) Use the turnover ratio computed in (b) to analyze Jones' liquidity. The turnover ratio last year was 13.65.

E7-21 (Transfer of Receivables) Use the information for Jones Company as presented in E7-20. Jones is planning to factor some accounts receivable at the end of the year. Accounts totaling $25,000 will be transferred to Credit Factors, Inc. with recourse. Credit Factors will retain 5% of the balances and assesses a finance charge of 4%. The fair value of the recourse obligation is $1,200.

Instructions
(a) Prepare the journal entry to record the sale of receivables.
(b) Compute Jones' accounts receivables turnover ratio for the year, assuming the receivables are sold, and discuss how factoring of receivables affects the turnover ratio.

*E7-22 **(Petty Cash)** Carolyn Keene, Inc. decided to establish a petty cash fund to help ensure internal control over its small cash expenditures. The following information is available for the month of April.

1. On April 1, it established a petty cash fund in the amount of $200.
2. A summary of the petty cash expenditures made by the petty cash custodian as of April 10 is as follows.

Delivery charges paid on merchandise purchased	$60.00
Supplies purchased and used	25.00
Postage expense	33.00
I.O.U. from employees	17.00
Miscellaneous expense	36.00

The petty cash fund was replenished on April 10. The balance in the fund was $27.
3. The petty cash fund balance was increased $100 to $300 on April 20.

Instructions
Prepare the journal entries to record transactions related to petty cash for the month of April.

*E7-23 **(Petty Cash)** The petty cash fund of Fonzarelli's Auto Repair Service, a sole proprietorship, contains the following.

1. Coins and currency		$ 15.20
2. Postage stamps		2.90
3. An I.O.U. from Richie Cunningham, an employee, for cash advance		40.00
4. Check payable to Fonzarelli's Auto Repair from		
Pottsie Weber, an employee, marked NSF		34.00
5. Vouchers for the following:		
Stamps	$ 20.00	
Two Rose Bowl tickets for Nick Fonzarelli	170.00	
Printer cartridge	14.35	204.35
		$296.45

The general ledger account Petty Cash has a balance of $300.00.

Instructions

Prepare the journal entry to record the reimbursement of the petty cash fund.

*E7-24 **(Bank Reconciliation and Adjusting Entries)** Angela Lansbury Company deposits all receipts and makes all payments by check. The following information is available from the cash records.

June 30 Bank Reconciliation

Balance per bank	$7,000
Add: Deposits in transit	1,540
Deduct: Outstanding checks	(2,000)
Balance per books	$6,540

Month of July Results

	Per Bank	Per Books
Balance July 31	$8,650	$9,250
July deposits	5,000	5,810
July checks	4,000	3,100
July note collected (not included in July deposits)	1,000	—
July bank service charge	15	—
July NSF check from a customer, returned by the bank (recorded by bank as a charge)	335	—

Instructions

(a) Prepare a bank reconciliation going from balance per bank and balance per book to correct cash balance.
(b) Prepare the general journal entry or entries to correct the Cash account.

*E7-25 **(Bank Reconciliation and Adjusting Entries)** Logan Bruno Company has just received the August 31, 2003, bank statement, which is summarized below.

County National Bank	Disbursements	Receipts	Balance
Balance, August 1			$ 9,369
Deposits during August		$32,200	41,569
Note collected for depositor, including $40 interest		1,040	42,609
Checks cleared during August	$34,500		8,109
Bank service charges	20		8,089
Balance, August 31			8,089

The general ledger Cash account contained the following entries for the month of August.

Cash			
Balance, August 1	10,050	Disbursements in August	34,903
Receipts during August	35,000		

Deposits in transit at August 31 are $3,800, and checks outstanding at August 31 total $1,050. Cash on hand at August 31 is $310. The bookkeeper improperly entered one check in the books at $146.50 which was written for $164.50 for supplies (expense); it cleared the bank during the month of August.

Instructions

(a) Prepare a bank reconciliation dated August 31, 2003, proceeding to a correct balance.
(b) Prepare any entries necessary to make the books correct and complete.
(c) What amount of cash should be reported in the August 31 balance sheet?

PROBLEMS

P7-1 **(Determine Proper Cash Balance)** Dumaine Equipment Co. closes its books regularly on December 31, but at the end of 2003 it held its cash book open so that a more favorable balance sheet could be prepared for credit purposes. Cash receipts and disbursements for the first 10 days of January were recorded as December transactions. The following information is given.

1. January cash receipts recorded in the December cash book totaled $39,640, of which $22,000 represents cash sales, and $17,640 represents collections on account for which cash discounts of $360 were given.
2. January cash disbursements recorded in the December check register liquidated accounts payable of $26,450 on which discounts of $250 were taken.
3. The ledger has not been closed for 2003.
4. The amount shown as inventory was determined by physical count on December 31, 2003.

Instructions

(a) Prepare any entries you consider necessary to correct Dumaine's accounts at December 31.
(b) To what extent was Dumaine Equipment Co. able to show a more favorable balance sheet at December 31 by holding its cash book open? (Use ratio analysis.) Assume that the balance sheet that was prepared by the company showed the following amounts:

	Dr.	Cr.
Cash	$39,000	
Receivables	42,000	
Inventories	67,000	
Accounts payable		$45,000
Other current liabilities		14,200

P7-2 **(Bad Debt Reporting)** Presented below are a series of unrelated situations.

1. Spock Company's unadjusted trial balance at December 31, 2003, included the following accounts.

	Debit	Credit
Allowance for doubtful accounts	$4,000	
Net sales		$1,500,000

Spock Company estimates its bad debt expense to be 1½% of net sales. Determine its bad debt expense for 2003.

2. An analysis and aging of Scotty Corp. accounts receivable at December 31, 2003, disclosed the following.

Amounts estimated to be uncollectible	$ 180,000
Accounts receivable	1,750,000
Allowance for doubtful accounts (per books)	125,000

What is the net realizable value of Scotty's receivables at December 31, 2003?

3. Uhura Co. provides for doubtful accounts based on 3% of credit sales. The following data are available for 2003.

Credit sales during 2003	$2,100,000
Allowance for doubtful accounts 1/1/03	17,000
Collection of accounts written off in prior years (customer credit was reestablished)	8,000
Customer accounts written off as uncollectible during 2003	30,000

What is the balance in the Allowance for Doubtful Accounts at December 31, 2003?

4. At the end of its first year of operations, December 31, 2003, Chekov Inc. reported the following information.

Accounts receivable, net of allowance for doubtful accounts	$950,000
Customer accounts written off as uncollectible during 2003	24,000
Bad debt expense for 2003	84,000

What should be the balance in accounts receivable at December 31, 2003, before subtracting the allowance for doubtful accounts?

5. The following accounts were taken from Chappel Inc.'s balance sheet at December 31, 2003.

	Debit	Credit
Net credit sales		$750,000
Allowance for doubtful accounts	$ 14,000	
Accounts receivable	410,000	

If doubtful accounts are 3% of accounts receivable, determine the bad debt expense to be reported for 2003.

Instructions

Answer the questions relating to each of the five independent situations as requested.

P7-3 (Bad Debt Reporting—Aging) Ignace Paderewski Corporation operates in an industry that has a high rate of bad debts. Before any year-end adjustments, the balance in Paderewski's Accounts Receivable account was $555,000 and the Allowance for Doubtful Accounts had a credit balance of $35,000. The year-end balance reported in the balance sheet for the Allowance for Doubtful Accounts will be based on the aging schedule shown below.

Days Account Outstanding	Amount	Probability of Collection
Less than 16 days	$300,000	.98
Between 16 and 30 days	100,000	.90
Between 31 and 45 days	80,000	.85
Between 46 and 60 days	40,000	.75
Between 61 and 75 days	20,000	.40
Over 75 days	15,000	.00

Instructions

(a) What is the appropriate balance for the Allowance for Doubtful Accounts at year-end?
(b) Show how accounts receivable would be presented on the balance sheet.
(c) What is the dollar effect of the year-end bad debt adjustment on the before-tax income?

(CMA adapted)

P7-4 (Bad Debt Reporting) From inception of operations to December 31, 2004, Blaise Pascal Corporation provided for uncollectible accounts receivable under the allowance method: provisions were made monthly at 2% of credit sales; bad debts written off were charged to the allowance account; recoveries of bad debts previously written off were credited to the allowance account; and no year-end adjustments to the allowance account were made. Pascal's usual credit terms are net 30 days.

The balance in the Allowance for Doubtful Accounts was $154,000 at January 1, 2004. During 2004 credit sales totaled $9,000,000, interim provisions for doubtful accounts were made at 2% of credit sales, $95,000 of bad debts were written off, and recoveries of accounts previously written off amounted to $15,000. Pascal installed a computer facility in November 2004, and an aging of accounts receivable was prepared for the first time as of December 31, 2004. A summary of the aging is as follows.

Classification by Month of Sale	Balance in Each Category	Estimated % Uncollectible
November–December 2004	$1,080,000	2%
July–October	650,000	10%
January–June	420,000	25%
Prior to 1/1/04	150,000	70%
	$2,300,000	

Based on the review of collectibility of the account balances in the "prior to 1/1/04" aging category, additional receivables totaling $60,000 were written off as of December 31, 2004. The 70% uncollectible estimate applies to the remaining $90,000 in the category. Effective with the year ended December 31, 2004, Pascal adopted a new accounting method for estimating the allowance for doubtful accounts at the amount indicated by the year-end aging analysis of accounts receivable.

Instructions

(a) Prepare a schedule analyzing the changes in the Allowance for Doubtful Accounts for the year ended December 31, 2004. Show supporting computations in good form. (*Hint:* In computing the 12/31/04 allowance, subtract the $60,000 write-off).

(b) Prepare the journal entry for the year-end adjustment to the Allowance for Doubtful Accounts balance as of December 31, 2004.

(AICPA adapted)

P7-5 **(Bad Debt Reporting)** Presented below is information related to the Accounts Receivable accounts of Gulistan Inc. during the current year 2004.

1. An aging schedule of the accounts receivable as of December 31, 2004, is as follows.

Age	Net Debit Balance	% to Be Applied after Correction Is Made
Under 60 days	$172,342	1%
61–90 days	136,490	3%
91–120 days	39,924*	6%
Over 120 days	23,644	$4,200 definitely
	$372,400	uncollectible; estimated remainder uncollectible is 25%

*The $2,740 write-off of receivables is related to the 91-to-120 day category.

2. The Accounts Receivable control account has a debit balance of $372,400 on December 31, 2004.

3. Two entries were made in the Bad Debt Expense account during the year: (1) a debit on December 31 for the amount credited to Allowance for Doubtful Accounts, and (2) a credit for $2,740 on November 3, 2004, and a debit to Allowance for Doubtful Accounts because of a bankruptcy.

4. The Allowance for Doubtful Accounts is as follows for 2004:

	Allowance for Doubtful Accounts				
Nov. 3	Uncollectible accounts written off	2,740	Jan. 1	Beginning balance	8,750
			Dec. 31	5% of $372,400	18,620

5. A credit balance exists in the Accounts Receivable (61–90 days) of $4,840, which represents an advance on a sales contract.

Instructions

Assuming that the books have not been closed for 2004, make the necessary correcting entries.

P7-6 (Journalize Various Account and Notes Receivable Transactions) The balance sheet of Antonio Vivaldi Company at December 31, 2003, includes the following.

Notes receivable	$ 36,000	
Accounts receivable	182,100	
Less: Allowance for doubtful accounts	17,300	200,800

Transactions in 2004 include the following.

1. Accounts receivable of $138,000 were collected including accounts of $40,000 on which 2% sales discounts were allowed.
2. $6,300 was received in payment of an account which was written off the books as worthless in 2000. (*Hint:* Reestablish the receivable account.)
3. Customer accounts of $17,500 were written off during the year.
4. At year-end the Allowance for Doubtful Accounts was estimated to need a balance of $20,000. This estimate is based on an analysis of aged accounts receivable.

Instructions

Prepare all journal entries necessary to reflect the transactions above.

P7-7 (Assigned Accounts Receivable—Journal Entries) Nikos Company finances some of its current operations by assigning accounts receivable to a finance company. On July 1, 2004, it assigned, under guarantee, specific accounts amounting to $100,000. The finance company advanced to Nikos 80% of the accounts assigned (20% of the total to be withheld until the finance company has made its full recovery), less a finance charge of ½% of the total accounts assigned.

On July 31 Nikos Company received a statement that the finance company had collected $55,000 of these accounts and had made an additional charge of ½% of the total accounts outstanding as of July 31. This charge is to be deducted at the time of the first remittance due Nikos Company from the finance company. (*Hint:* Make entries at this time.) On August 31, 2004, Nikos Company received a second statement from the finance company, together with a check for the amount due. The statement indicated that the finance company had collected an additional $30,000 and had made a further charge of ½% of the balance outstanding as of August 31.

Instructions

Make all entries on the books of Nikos Company that are involved in the transactions above.

(AICPA adapted)

P7-8 (Notes Receivable with Realistic Interest Rate) On October 1, 2004, Jeppo Farm Equipment Company sold a pecan-harvesting machine to Lujan Brothers Farm, Inc. In lieu of a cash payment Lujan Brothers Farm gave Jeppo a 2-year, $100,000, 12% note (a realistic rate of interest for a note of this type). The note required interest to be paid annually on October 1. Jeppo's financial statements are prepared on a calendar-year basis.

Instructions

Assuming Lujan Brothers Farm fulfills all the terms of the note, prepare the necessary journal entries for Jeppo Farm Equipment Company for the entire term of the note.

P7-9 (Notes Receivable Journal Entries) On December 31, 2004, Menachem Inc. rendered services to Begin Corporation at an agreed price of $91,844.10, accepting $36,000 down and agreeing to accept the balance in four equal installments of $18,000 receivable each December 31. An assumed interest rate of 11% is imputed.

Instructions

Prepare the entries that would be recorded by Menachem Inc. for the sale and for the receipts and interest on the following dates. (Assume that the effective interest method is used for amortization purposes).

(a) December 31, 2004.   **(c)** December 31, 2006.   **(e)** December 31, 2008.

(b) December 31, 2005.   **(d)** December 31, 2007.

P7-10 (Comprehensive Accounts Receivable) Jair Lynch Supply produces paints and related products for sale to the construction industry throughout the southwest United States. While sales have remained relatively stable despite a decline in the amount of new construction, there has been a noticeable change in the timeliness with which Lynch's customers are paying their bills.

Lynch sells its products on payment terms of 2/10, n/30. In the past, over 75% of the credit customers have taken advantage of the discount by paying within 10 days of the invoice date. During the fiscal year ended November 30, 2003, the number of customers taking the full 30 days to pay has increased. Current indications are that less than 60% of the customers are now taking the discount. Uncollectible accounts as a percentage of total credit sales have risen from the 1.5% provided in past years to 4.0% in the current year.

In response to a request for more information on the deterioration of accounts receivable collections, Lynch's controller has prepared the following report.

JAIR LYNCH SUPPLY
ACCOUNTS RECEIVABLE COLLECTIONS
NOVEMBER 30, 2003

The fact that some credit accounts will prove uncollectible is normal, and annual bad debt write-offs had been 1.5% of total credit sales for many years. However, during the 2002–03 fiscal year, this percentage increased to 4.0%. The current accounts receivable balance is $1,500,000, and the condition of this balance in terms of age and probability of collection is shown below.

Proportion of Total	Age Categories	Probability of Collection
64.0%	1 to 10 days	99.0%
18.0	11 to 30 days	97.5
8.0	Past due 31 to 60 days	95.0
5.0	Past due 61 to 120 days	80.0
3.0	Past due 121 to 180 days	65.0
2.0	Past due over 180 days	20.0

At the beginning of the fiscal year, December 1, 2002, the Allowance for Doubtful Accounts had a credit balance of $27,300. Lynch has provided for a monthly bad debt expense accrual during the fiscal year just ended based on the assumption that 4% of total credit sales will be uncollectible. Total credit sales for the 2002–03 fiscal year amounted to $8,000,000, and write-offs of uncollectible accounts during the year totaled $292,500.

Instructions

(a) Prepare an accounts receivable aging schedule at November 30, 2003, for Jair Lynch Supply using the age categories identified in the controller's report showing:
  (1) the amount of accounts receivable outstanding for each age category and in total.
  (2) the estimated amount that is uncollectible for each category and in total.
(b) Compute the amount of the year-end adjustment necessary to bring Jair Lynch Supply's Allowance for Doubtful Accounts to the balance indicated by the aging analysis.
(c) Calculate the net realizable value of Jair Lynch Supply's accounts receivable at November 30, 2003. Ignore any discounts that may be applicable to the accounts not yet due.
(d) Describe the accounting to be performed for subsequent collections of previously written-off accounts receivable.

                                                               (CMA adapted)

P7-11 **(Comprehensive Receivables Problem)** Connecticut Inc. had the following long-term receivable account balances at December 31, 2003.

Note receivable from sale of division	$1,800,000
Note receivable from officer	400,000

Transactions during 2004 and other information relating to Connecticut's long-term receivables were as follows.

1. The $1,800,000 note receivable is dated May 1, 2003, bears interest at 9%, and represents the balance of the consideration received from the sale of Connecticut's electronics division to New York Company. Principal payments of $600,000 plus appropriate interest are due on May 1, 2004, 2005, and 2006. The first principal and interest payment was made on May 1, 2004. Collection of the note installments is reasonably assured.

2. The $400,000 note receivable is dated December 31, 2003, bears interest at 8%, and is due on December 31, 2006. The note is due from Marcus Camby, president of Connecticut Inc. and is collateralized by 10,000 shares of Connecticut's common stock. Interest is payable annually on December 31, and all interest payments were paid on their due dates through December 31, 2004. The quoted market price of Connecticut's common stock was $45 per share on December 31, 2004.

3. On April 1, 2004, Connecticut sold a patent to Pennsylvania Company in exchange for a $200,000 non-interest-bearing note due on April 1, 2006. There was no established exchange price for the patent, and the note had no ready market. The prevailing rate of interest for a note of this type at April 1, 2004, was 12%. The present value of $1 for two periods at 12% is 0.797 (use this factor). The patent had a carrying value of $40,000 at January 1, 2004, and the amortization for the year ended December 31, 2004, would have been $8,000. The collection of the note receivable from Pennsylvania is reasonably assured.

4. On July 1, 2004, Connecticut sold a parcel of land to Harrisburg Company for $200,000 under an installment sale contract. Harrisburg made a $60,000 cash down payment on July 1, 2004, and signed a 4-year 11% note for the $140,000 balance. The equal annual payments of principal and interest on the note will be $45,125 payable on July 1, 2005, through July 1, 2008. The land could have been sold at an established cash price of $200,000. The cost of the land to Connecticut was $150,000. Circumstances are such that the collection of the installments on the note is reasonably assured.

Instructions
(a) Prepare the long-term receivables section of Connecticut's balance sheet at December 31, 2004.
(b) Prepare a schedule showing the current portion of the long-term receivables and accrued interest receivable that would appear in Connecticut's balance sheet at December 31, 2004.
(c) Prepare a schedule showing interest revenue from the long-term receivables that would appear on Connecticut's income statement for the year ended December 31, 2004.

P7-12 **(Income Effects of Receivables Transactions)** Radisson Company requires additional cash for its business. Radisson has decided to use its accounts receivable to raise the additional cash and has asked you to determine the income statement effects of the following contemplated transactions.

1. On July 1, 2003, Radisson assigned $400,000 of accounts receivable to Stickum Finance Company. Radisson received an advance from Stickum of 85% of the assigned accounts receivable less a commission of 3% on the advance. Prior to December 31, 2003, Radisson collected $220,000 on the assigned accounts receivable, and remitted $232,720 to Stickum, $12,720 of which represented interest on the advance from Stickum.

2. On December 1, 2003, Radisson sold $300,000 of net accounts receivable to Wunsch Company for $250,000. The receivables were sold outright on a without recourse basis.

3. On December 31, 2003, an advance of $120,000 was received from First Bank by pledging $160,000 of Radisson's accounts receivable. Radisson's first payment to First Bank is due on January 30, 2004.

Instructions
Prepare a schedule showing the income statement effects for the year ended December 31, 2003, as a result of the above facts.

*P7-13 (Petty Cash, Bank Reconciliation) Bill Howe is reviewing the cash accounting for Kappeler, Inc., a local mailing service. Howe's review will focus on the petty cash account and the bank reconciliation for the month ended May 31, 2003. He has collected the following information from Kappeler's bookkeeper for this task.

Petty Cash

1. The petty cash fund was established on May 10, 2003, in the amount of $250.00.
2. Expenditures from the fund by the custodian as of May 31, 2003, were evidenced by approved receipts for the following.

Postage expense	$33.00
Mailing labels and other supplies	75.00
I.O.U. from employees	30.00
Shipping charges	57.45
Newspaper advertising	22.80
Miscellaneous expense	15.35

On May 31, 2003, the petty cash fund was replenished and increased to $300.00; currency and coin in the fund at that time totaled $16.40.

Bank Reconciliation

THIRD NATIONAL BANK BANK STATEMENT			
	Disbursements	Receipts	Balance
Balance, May 1, 2003			$8,769
Deposits		$28,000	
Note payment direct from customer (interest of $30)		930	
Checks cleared during May	$31,150		
Bank service charges	27		
Balance, May 31, 2003			6,522

Kappeler's Cash Account

Balance, May 1, 2003	$ 9,150
Deposits during May 2003	31,000
Checks written during May 2003	(31,835)

Deposits in transit are determined to be $3,000, and checks outstanding at May 31 total $550. Cash on hand (besides petty cash) at May 31, 2003, is $246.

Instructions

(a) Prepare the journal entries to record the transactions related to the petty cash fund for May.
(b) Prepare a bank reconciliation dated May 31, 2003, proceeding to a correct balance, and prepare the journal entries necessary to make the books correct and complete.
(c) What amount of cash should be reported in the May 31, 2003, balance sheet?

*P7-14 (Bank Reconciliation and Adjusting Entries) The cash account of Jose Orozco Co. showed a ledger balance of $3,969.85 on June 30, 2003. The bank statement as of that date showed a balance of $4,150. Upon comparing the statement with the cash records, the following facts were determined.

1. There were bank service charges for June of $25.00.
2. A bank memo stated that Bao Dai's note for $900 and interest of $36 had been collected on June 29, and the bank had made a charge of $5.50 on the collection. (No entry had been made on Orozco's books when Bao Dai's note was sent to the bank for collection.)

3. Receipts for June 30 for $2,890 were not deposited until July 2.
4. Checks outstanding on June 30 totaled $2,136.05.
5. The bank had charged the Orozco Co.'s account for a customer's uncollectible check amounting to $453.20 on June 29.
6. A customer's check for $90 had been entered as $60 in the cash receipts journal by Orozco on June 15.
7. Check no. 742 in the amount of $491 had been entered in the cashbook as $419, and check no. 747 in the amount of $58.20 had been entered as $582. Both checks had been issued to pay for purchases of equipment.

Instructions
(a) Prepare a bank reconciliation dated June 30, 2003, proceeding to a correct cash balance.
(b) Prepare any entries necessary to make the books correct and complete.

*P7-15 (Bank Reconciliation and Adjusting Entries) Presented below is information related to Tanizaki Inc.

Balance per books at October 31, $41,847.85; receipts $173,523.91; disbursements $166,193.54. Balance per bank statement November 30, $56,274.20.

The following checks were outstanding at November 30.

1224	$1,635.29
1230	2,468.30
1232	3,625.15
1233	482.17

Included with the November bank statement and not recorded by the company were a bank debit memo for $27.40 covering bank charges for the month, a debit memo for $572.13 for a customer's check returned and marked NSF, and a credit memo for $1,400 representing bond interest collected by the bank in the name of Tanizaki Inc. Cash on hand at November 30 recorded and awaiting deposit amounted to $1,915.40.

Instructions
(a) Prepare a bank reconciliation (to the correct balance) at November 30, 2003, for Tanizaki Inc. from the information above.
(b) Prepare any journal entries required to adjust the cash account at November 30.

*P7-16 (Bank Reconciliation) Presented below is information related to Junichiro Industries.

JUNICHIRO INDUSTRIES		
BANK RECONCILIATION		
MAY 31, 2003		
Balance per bank statement		$30,928.46
Less: Outstanding checks		
No. 6124	$2,125.00	
No. 6138	932.65	
No. 6139	960.57	
No. 6140	1,420.00	5,438.22
		25,490.24
Add deposit in transit		4,710.56
Balance per books (correct balance)		$30,200.80

CHECK REGISTER—JUNE

Date	Payee	No.	Invoice Amount	Discount	Cash
June 1	Ren Mfg.	6141	$ 237.50		$ 237.50
1	Stimpy Mfg.	6142	915.00	$ 9.15	905.85
8	Rugrats Co., Inc.	6143	122.90	2.45	120.45
9	Ren Mfg.	6144	306.40		306.40
10	Petty Cash	6145	89.93		89.93
17	Muppet Babies Photo	6146	706.00	14.12	691.88
22	Hey Dude Publishing	6147	447.50		447.50
23	Payroll Account	6148	4,130.00		4,130.00
25	Dragnet Tools, Inc.	6149	390.75	3.91	386.84
28	Double Dare Insurance Agency	6150	1,050.00		1,050.00
28	Get Smart Construction	6151	2,250.00		2,250.00
29	MMT, Inc.	6152	750.00		750.00
30	Lassie Co.	6153	400.00	8.00	392.00
			$11,795.98	$37.63	$11,758.35

NICKELODEON STATE BANK
BANK STATEMENT
GENERAL CHECKING ACCOUNT OF JUNICHIRO INDUSTRIES—JUNE 2003

Debits			Date	Credits	Balance
					$30,928.46
$2,125.00	$ 237.50	$ 905.85	June 1	$4,710.56	32,370.67
932.65	120.45		12	1,507.06	32,824.63
1,420.00	447.50	306.40	23	1,458.55	32,109.28
4,130.00		11.05 (BC)	26		27,968.23
89.93	2,250.00	1,050.00	28	4,157.48	28,735.78

Cash received June 29 and 30 and deposited in the mail for the general checking account June 30 amounted to $4,607.96. Because the cash account balance at June 30 is not given, it must be calculated from other information in the problem.

Instructions

From the information above, prepare a bank reconciliation (to the correct balance) as of June 30, 2003, for Junichiro Industries.

CONCEPTUAL CASES

C7-1 (Bad Debt Accounting) Ariel Company has significant amounts of trade accounts receivable. Ariel uses the allowance method to estimate bad debts instead of the direct write-off method. During the year, some specific accounts were written off as uncollectible, and some that were previously written off as uncollectible were collected.

Instructions

(a) What are the deficiencies of the direct write-off method?

(b) What are the two basic allowance methods used to estimate bad debts, and what is the theoretical justification for each?

(c) How should Ariel account for the collection of the specific accounts previously written off as uncollectible?

C7-2 (Various Receivable Accounting Issues) Anne Archer Company uses the net method of accounting for sales discounts. Anne Archer also offers trade discounts to various groups of buyers.

On August 1, 2003, Archer sold some accounts receivable on a without recourse basis. Archer incurred a finance charge.

Archer also has some notes receivable bearing an appropriate rate of interest. The principal and total interest are due at maturity. The notes were received on October 1, 2003, and mature on September 30, 2005. Archer's operating cycle is less than one year.

Instructions

(a) **(1)** Using the net method, how should Archer account for the sales discounts at the date of sale? What is the rationale for the amount recorded as sales under the net method?

   (2) Using the net method, what is the effect on Archer's sales revenues and net income when customers do not take the sales discounts?

(b) What is the effect of trade discounts on sales revenues and accounts receivable? Why?

(c) How should Archer account for the accounts receivable factored on August 1, 2003? Why?

(d) How should Archer account for the note receivable and the related interest on December 31, 2003? Why?

C7-3 (Bad Debt Reporting Issues) Ben Gazarra conducts a wholesale merchandising business that sells approximately 5,000 items per month with a total monthly average sales value of $250,000. Its annual bad debt ratio has been approximately 1½% of sales. In recent discussions with his bookkeeper, Mr. Gazarra has become confused by all the alternatives apparently available in handling the Allowance for Doubtful Accounts balance. The following information has been shown.

1. An allowance can be set up (a) on the basis of a percentage of sales or (b) on the basis of a valuation of all past due or otherwise questionable accounts receivable. Those considered uncollectible can be charged to such allowance at the close of the accounting period, or specific items can be charged off directly against (1) Gross Sales or to (2) Bad Debt Expense in the year in which they are determined to be uncollectible.

2. Collection agency and legal fees, and so on, incurred in connection with the attempted recovery of bad debts can be charged to (a) Bad Debt Expense, (b) Allowance for Doubtful Accounts, (c) Legal Expense, or (d) General Expense.

3. Debts previously written off in whole or in part but currently recovered can be credited to (a) Other Revenue, (b) Bad Debt Expense, or (c) Allowance for Doubtful Accounts.

Instructions

Which of the foregoing methods would you recommend to Mr. Gazarra in regard to (1) allowances and charge-offs, (2) collection expenses, and (3) recoveries? State briefly and clearly the reasons supporting your recommendations.

C7-4 (Basic Note and Accounts Receivable Transactions)

Part 1

On July 1, 2004, Eve Arden Company, a calendar-year company, sold special-order merchandise on credit and received in return an interest-bearing note receivable from the customer. Eve Arden Company will receive interest at the prevailing rate for a note of this type. Both the principal and interest are due in one lump sum on June 30, 2005.

Instructions

When should Eve Arden Company report interest income from the note receivable? Discuss the rationale for your answer.

Part 2

On December 31, 2004, Eve Arden Company had significant amounts of accounts receivable as a result of credit sales to its customers. Eve Arden Company uses the allowance method based on credit sales to estimate bad debts. Past experience indicates that 2% of credit sales normally will not be collected. This pattern is expected to continue.

Instructions

(a) Discuss the rationale for using the allowance method based on credit sales to estimate bad debts. Contrast this method with the allowance method based on the balance in the trade receivables accounts.

(b) How should Eve Arden Company report the allowance for bad debts account on its balance sheet at December 31, 2004? Also, describe the alternatives, if any, for presentation of bad debt expense in Eve Arden Company's 2004 income statement.

(AICPA adapted)

C7-5 **(Bad Debt Reporting Issues)** Rosita Arenas Company sells office equipment and supplies to many organizations in the city and surrounding area on contract terms of 2/10, n/30. In the past, over 75% of the credit customers have taken advantage of the discount by paying within 10 days of the invoice date.

The number of customers taking the full 30 days to pay has increased within the last year. Current indications are that less than 60% of the customers are now taking the discount. Bad debts as a percentage of gross credit sales have risen from the 1.5% provided in past years to about 4% in the current year.

The controller has responded to a request for more information on the deterioration in collections of accounts receivable with the report reproduced below.

ROSITA ARENAS COMPANY

FINANCE COMMITTEE REPORT—ACCOUNTS RECEIVABLE COLLECTIONS

MAY 31, 2004

The fact that some credit accounts will prove uncollectible is normal. Annual bad debt write-offs have been 1.5% of gross credit sales over the past five years. During the last fiscal year, this percentage increased to slightly less than 4%. The current Accounts Receivable balance is $1,600,000. The condition of this balance in terms of age and probability of collection is as follows.

Proportion of Total	Age Categories	Probability of Collection
68%	not yet due	99%
15%	less than 30 days past due	96½%
8%	30 to 60 days past due	95%
5%	61 to 120 days past due	91%
2½%	121 to 180 days past due	70%
1½%	over 180 days past due	20%

The Allowance for Doubtful Accounts had a credit balance of $43,300 on June 1, 2003. Rosita Arenas Company has provided for a monthly bad debts expense accrual during the current fiscal year based on the assumption that 4% of gross credit sales will be uncollectible. Total gross credit sales for the 2003–04 fiscal year amounted to $4,000,000. Write-offs of bad accounts during the year totaled $145,000.

Instructions

(a) Prepare an accounts receivable aging schedule for Rosita Arenas Company using the age categories identified in the controller's report to the finance committee showing:

(1) The amount of accounts receivable outstanding for each age category and in total.

(2) The estimated amount that is uncollectible for each category and in total.

(b) Compute the amount of the year-end adjustment necessary to bring Allowance for Doubtful Accounts to the balance indicated by the age analysis. Then prepare the necessary journal entry to adjust the accounting records.

(c) In a recessionary environment with tight credit and high interest rates:

(1) Identify steps Rosita Arenas Company might consider to improve the accounts receivable situation.

(2) Then evaluate each step identified in terms of the risks and costs involved.

(CMA adapted)

C7-6 **(Sale of Notes Receivable)** Sergey Luzov Wholesalers Co. sells industrial equipment for a standard 3-year note receivable. Revenue is recognized at time of sale. Each note is secured by a lien on the equipment and has a face amount equal to the equipment's list price. Each note's stated interest rate is below the customer's market rate at date of sale. All notes are to be collected in three equal annual installments beginning one year after sale. Some of the notes are subsequently sold to a bank with recourse, some are subsequently sold without recourse, and some are retained by Luzov. At year end, Luzov evaluates all outstanding notes receivable and provides for estimated losses arising from defaults.

Instructions

(a) What is the appropriate valuation basis for Luzov's notes receivable at the date it sells equipment?

(b) How should Luzov account for the sale, without recourse, of a February 1, 2003, note receivable sold on May 1, 2003? Why is it appropriate to account for it in this way?

(c) At December 31, 2003, how should Luzov measure and account for the impact of estimated losses resulting from notes receivable that it

    (1) Retained and did **not** sell?

    (2) Sold to bank with recourse?

(AICPA adapted)

C7-7 **(Non-Interest-Bearing Note Receivable)** On September 30, 2003, Tiger Machinery Co. sold a machine and accepted the customer's non-interest-bearing note. Tiger normally makes sales on a cash basis. Since the machine was unique, its sales price was not determinable using Tiger's normal pricing practices.

After receiving the first of two equal annual installments on September 30, 2004, Tiger immediately sold the note with recourse. On October 9, 2005, Tiger received notice that the note was dishonored, and it paid all amounts due. At all times prior to default, the note was reasonably expected to be paid in full.

Instructions

(a) **(1)** How should Tiger determine the sales price of the machine?

    (2) How should Tiger report the effects of the non-interest-bearing note on its income statement for the year ended December 31, 2003? Why is this accounting presentation appropriate?

(b) What are the effects of the sale of the note receivable with recourse on Tiger's income statement for the year ended December 31, 2004, and its balance sheet at December 31, 2004?

(c) How should Tiger account for the effects of the note being dishonored?

C7-8 **(Reporting of Notes Receivable, Interest, and Sale of Receivables)** On July 1, 2004, Gale Sondergaard Company sold special-order merchandise on credit and received in return an interest-bearing note receivable from the customer. Sondergaard will receive interest at the prevailing rate for a note of this type. Both the principal and interest are due in one lump sum on June 30, 2005.

On September 1, 2004, Sondergaard sold special-order merchandise on credit and received in return a non-interest-bearing note receivable from the customer. The prevailing rate of interest for a note of this type is determinable. The note receivable is due in one lump sum on August 31, 2006.

Sondergaard also has significant amounts of trade accounts receivable as a result of credit sales to its customers. On October 1, 2004, some trade accounts receivable were assigned to Irene Dunne Finance Company on a non-notification (Sondergaard handles collections) basis for an advance of 75% of their amount at an interest charge of 12% on the balance outstanding.

On November 1, 2004, other trade accounts receivable were sold on a without recourse basis. The factor withheld 5% of the trade accounts receivable factored as protection against sales returns and allowances and charged a finance charge of 3%.

Instructions

(a) How should Sondergaard determine the interest income for 2004 on the:

    (1) Interest-bearing note receivable? Why?

    (2) Noninterest-bearing note receivable? Why?

(b) How should Sondergaard report the interest-bearing note receivable and the noninterest-bearing note receivable on its balance sheet at December 31, 2004?

(c) How should Sondergaard account for subsequent collections on the trade accounts receivable assigned on October 1, 2004, and the payments to Irene Dunne Finance? Why?

(d) How should Sondergaard account for the trade accounts receivable factored on November 1, 2004? Why?

(AICPA adapted)

C7-9 (Accounting for Non-interest-Bearing Note) Soon after beginning the year-end audit work on March 10 at Engone Company, the auditor has the following conversation with the controller.

CONTROLLER: The year ended March 31st should be our most profitable in history and, as a consequence, the board of directors has just awarded the officers generous bonuses.

AUDITOR: I thought profits were down this year in the industry, according to your latest interim report.

CONTROLLER: Well, they were down, but 10 days ago we closed a deal that will give us a substantial increase for the year.

AUDITOR: Oh, what was it?

CONTROLLER: Well, you remember a few years ago our former president bought stock in Rocketeer Enterprises because he had those grandiose ideas about becoming a conglomerate. For 6 years we have not been able to sell this stock, which cost us $3,000,000 and has not paid a nickel in dividends. Thursday we sold this stock to Campbell Inc. for $4,000,000. So, we will have a gain of $700,000 ($1,000,000 pretax) which will increase our net income for the year to $4,000,000, compared with last year's $3,800,000. As far as I know, we'll be the only company in the industry to register an increase in net income this year. That should help the market value of the stock!

AUDITOR: Do you expect to receive the $4,000,000 in cash by March 31st, your fiscal year-end?

CONTROLLER: No. Although Campbell Inc. is an excellent company, they are a little tight for cash because of their rapid growth. Consequently, they are going to give us a $4,000,000 non-interest-bearing note due $400,000 per year for the next 10 years. The first payment is due on March 31 of next year.

AUDITOR: Why is the note non-interest-bearing?

CONTROLLER: Because that's what everybody agreed to. Since we don't have any interest-bearing debt, the funds invested in the note do not cost us anything and besides, we were not getting any dividends on the Rocketeer Enterprises stock.

Instructions

Do you agree with the way the controller has accounted for the transaction? If not, how should the transaction be accounted for?

C7-10 (Receivables Management) As the manager of the accounts receivable department for Vicki Maher Leather Goods, Ltd., you recently noticed that Percy Shelley, your accounts receivable clerk who is paid $1,200 per month, has been wearing unusually tasteful and expensive clothing. (This is Vicki Maher's first year in business.) This morning, Shelley drove up to work in a brand new Lexus.

Naturally suspicious by nature, you decide to test the accuracy of the accounts receivable balance of $132,000 as shown in the ledger. The following information is available for your first year (precisely 9 months ended September 30, 2003) in business.

(1) Collections from customers	$198,000
(2) Merchandise purchased	360,000
(3) Ending merchandise inventory	90,000
(4) Goods are marked to sell at 40% above cost.	

Instructions

Assuming all sales were made on account, compute the ending accounts receivable balance that should appear in the ledger, noting any apparent shortage. Then, draft a memo dated October 3, 2003, to John Castle, the branch manager, explaining the facts in this situation. Remember that this problem is serious, and you do not want to make hasty accusations.

C7-11 (Bad Debt Reporting) Rudolph Company is a subsidiary of Hundley Corp. The controller believes that the yearly allowance for doubtful accounts for Rudolph should be 2% of net credit sales. The president, nervous that the parent company might expect the subsidiary to sustain its 10% growth rate, suggests that the controller increase the allowance for doubtful accounts to 3% yearly. The supervisor thinks that the lower net income, which reflects a 6% growth rate, will be a more sustainable rate for Rudolph Company.

Instructions

(a) Should the controller be concerned with Rudolph Company's growth rate in estimating the allowance? Explain your answer.

(b) Does the president's request pose an ethical dilemma for the controller? Give your reasons.

USING YOUR JUDGMENT

FINANCIAL REPORTING PROBLEM

3M COMPANY

The financial statements of 3M were provided with your book or can be accessed on the Take Action! CD.

Instructions

Refer to 3M's financial statements and the accompanying notes to answer the following questions.

(a) What criteria does 3M use to classify "Cash and cash equivalents" as reported in its balance sheet?

(b) As of December 31, 2001, what balances did 3M have in cash and cash equivalents? What were the major uses of cash during the year?

(c) In recent years the accounting profession has encouraged companies to disclose any concentration of risk not apparent in their financial statements. What risks relative to accounts receivable does 3M disclose in its Notes to Consolidated Financial Statements?

COMPARATIVE ANALYSIS CASE

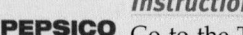

THE COCA-COLA COMPANY AND PEPSICO, INC.

Instructions

Go to the Take Action! CD and use the information found there to answer the following questions related to The Coca-Cola Company and PepsiCo, Inc.

(a) What were the cash and cash equivalents reported by Coca-Cola and PepsiCo at the end of 2001? What does each company classify as cash equivalents?

(b) What were the accounts receivable (net) for Coca-Cola and PepsiCo at the end of 2001? Which company reports the greater allowance for doubtful accounts receivable (amount and percentage of gross receivable) at the end of 2001?

(c) Assuming that all "net operating revenues" (Coca-Cola) and all "net sales" (PepsiCo) were net *credit* sales, compute the receivables turnover ratio for 2001 for Coca-Cola and PepsiCo; also compute the days outstanding for receivables. What is your evaluation of the difference?

FINANCIAL STATEMENT ANALYSIS CASE

OCCIDENTAL PETROLEUM CORPORATION

Occidental Petroleum Corporation reported the following information in its 2000 Annual Report.

OCCIDENTAL PETROLEUM CORPORATION Consolidated Balance Sheets (in millions)		
Assets at December 31,	2000	1999
Current assets		
Cash and cash equivalents	$ 97	$ 214
Trade receivables, net of allowances	809	559
Receivables from joint ventures, partnerships and other	517	215
Inventories	485	503
Prepaid expenses and other	159	197
Total current assets	2,067	1,688
Long-term receivables, net	2,119	168

Notes to Consolidated Financial Statements

Cash and Cash Equivalents. Cash equivalents consist of highly liquid money-market mutual funds and bank deposits with initial maturities of three months or less. Cash equivalents totaled approximately $46 million and $162 million at December 31, 2000 and 1999, respectively.

Trade Receivables. In 1992, Occidental entered into a new agreement to sell, under a revolving sale program, an undivided percentage ownership interest in a designated pool of trade receivables, with limited recourse. Under this program, Occidental serves as the collection agent with respect to the receivables sold. An interest in new receivables is sold as collections are made from customers. As of December 31, 2000, Occidental had received net cash proceeds totaling $360 million.

Instructions
(a) What items other than coin and currency may be included in "cash"?
(b) What items may be included in "cash equivalents"?
(c) What are compensating balance arrangements, and how should they be reported in financial statements?
(d) What are the possible differences between cash equivalents and short-term (temporary) investments?
(e) Occidental has sold some of its receivables. How much cash did it receive under this agreement in 2000?
(f) Assuming that the sale agreement meets the criteria for sale accounting, the carrying value of the receivables sold was $375 million, the finance charge was 1% of the balances sold, and the fair value of the limited recourse was $15 million, what was the effect on income from the sale of receivables?
(g) Briefly discuss the impact of the transaction in (f) on Occidental's liquidity.

*Remember to check the **Take Action! CD**
and the book's **companion Web site**
to find additional resources for this chapter.*

ACCOUNTING FOR INVENTORIES

INVENTORIES IN THE CRYSTAL BALL

Policy makers, economists, and investors all want to know where the economy is headed. For example, if the economy is headed for a slow-down, it might be prudent on the part of the Federal Reserve to cut interest rates or for Congress to consider a tax cut to head off an economic downturn. Information on inventories is a key input into various decision makers' economic prediction models. For example, every month the U.S. Commerce Department reports data on inventory levels and sales. As shown in the table below, in a recent month these data indicated an increasing level of inventories.

November Inventory and Sales
(billions of dollars, seasonally adjusted)

	1999	2000	Percent Change
Total business inventories	$1,145	$1,221	+6.64%
Total business sales	$ 862	$ 896	+3.94%
Inventory/Sales ratio	1.33	1.36	

More importantly, not only were inventories rising, but they were rising at a faster rate than sales. These data raised some warnings about future economic growth, because rising inventory levels relative to sales indicate that consumers are trimming spending faster than companies can slow production.[1]

These data also raised warning flags for investors in individual companies. As one analyst remarked, "When inventory grows faster than sales, profits drop." That is, when companies face slowing sales and growing inventory, then markdowns in prices are usually not far behind. These markdowns, in turn, lead to lower sales revenue and income, as profit margins on sales are squeezed.[2]

Research supporting these observations has found that increases in retailers' inventory translate into lower prices and lower net income.[3] Interestingly, the same research found that for manufacturers, only increases in finished goods inventory lead to future profit decline. Increases in raw materials and work-in-process inventories provide a signal that the company is building its inventory to meet increased demand, and therefore future sales and income will be higher. These research results reinforce the usefulness of the GAAP requirement that a manufacturer's inventory components should be disclosed on the balance sheet or in related notes.

After studying this chapter, you should be able to:

1. Identify major classifications of inventory.
2. Distinguish between perpetual and periodic inventory systems.
3. Identify the items that should be included as inventory cost.
4. Describe and compare the cost flow assumptions used in accounting for inventories.
5. Explain the significance and use of a LIFO reserve.
6. Explain the effect of LIFO liquidations.
7. Explain the dollar-value LIFO method.
8. Identify the major advantages and disadvantages of LIFO.
9. Explain and apply the lower of cost or market rule.
10. Explain how inventory is reported and analyzed.

[1]N. Kulish, "Business Inventories Rose for November, Possibly Adding Evidence of Slowdown," *Wall Street Journal, Interactive Edition* (January 17, 2001).

[2]S. Pulliam, "Heard on the Street," *Wall Street Journal* (May 21, 1997), p. C1.

[3]Victor Bernard and J. Noel, "Do Inventory Disclosures Predict Sales and Earnings?" *Journal of Accounting, Auditing, and Finance* (March 1991), pp. 145–182.

As indicated in the opening story, information on inventories and changes in inventory is relevant to predicting financial performance. The purpose of this chapter is to discuss the basic issues related to accounting and reporting for the costs of inventory. The content and organization of the chapter are as follows.

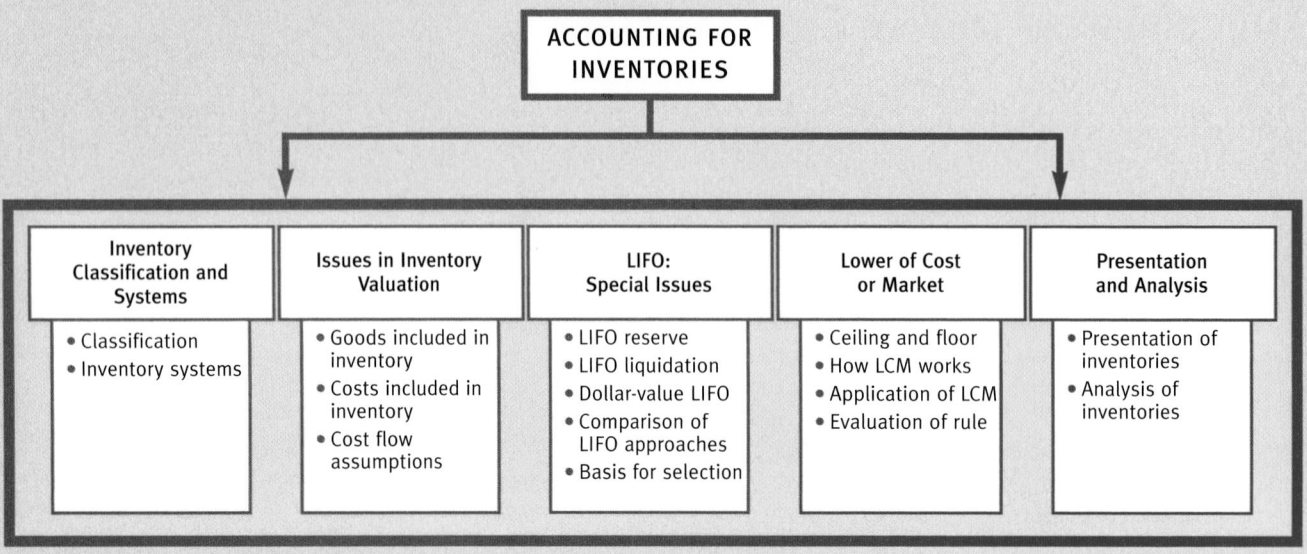

ACCOUNTING FOR INVENTORIES				
Inventory Classification and Systems	**Issues in Inventory Valuation**	**LIFO: Special Issues**	**Lower of Cost or Market**	**Presentation and Analysis**
• Classification • Inventory systems	• Goods included in inventory • Costs included in inventory • Cost flow assumptions	• LIFO reserve • LIFO liquidation • Dollar-value LIFO • Comparison of LIFO approaches • Basis for selection	• Ceiling and floor • How LCM works • Application of LCM • Evaluation of rule	• Presentation of inventories • Analysis of inventories

INVENTORY CLASSIFICATION AND SYSTEMS

Classification

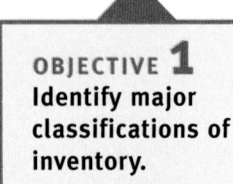

OBJECTIVE **1**
Identify major classifications of inventory.

Additional Inventory Disclosures

Inventories are asset items held for sale in the ordinary course of business or goods that will be used or consumed in the production of goods to be sold. The description and measurement of inventory require careful attention because the investment in inventories is frequently the largest current asset of merchandising (retail) and manufacturing businesses.

A **merchandising concern**, such as **Wal-Mart**, ordinarily purchases its merchandise in a form ready for sale. It reports the cost assigned to unsold units left on hand as **merchandise inventory**. Only one inventory account, Merchandise Inventory, appears in the financial statements.

Manufacturing concerns, on the other hand, produce goods to be sold to the merchandising firms. Many of the largest U.S. businesses are manufacturers—**Boeing, IBM, Exxon Mobil, Procter & Gamble, Ford, Motorola**, to name only a few. Although the products they produce may be quite different, manufacturers normally have three inventory accounts—Raw Materials, Work in Process, and Finished Goods.

The cost assigned to goods and materials on hand but not yet placed into production is reported as **raw materials inventory**. Raw materials include the wood to make a baseball bat or the steel to make a car. These materials ultimately can be traced directly to the end product.

At any point in a continuous production process some units are not completely processed. The cost of the raw material on which production has been started but not completed, plus the direct labor cost applied specifically to this material and a ratable share of manufacturing overhead costs, constitute the **work in process inventory**.

The costs identified with the completed but unsold units on hand at the end of the fiscal period are reported as **finished goods inventory**. The current assets sections presented in Illustration 8-1 contrast the financial statement presentation of inventories of a merchandising company and those of a manufacturing company. The remainder of the balance sheet is essentially similar for the two types of companies.

Merchandising Company WAL-MART Balance Sheet January 31, 2000	
Current assets (in millions)	
Cash and cash equivalents	$ 1,856
Receivables	1,341
Inventories at LIFO cost	19,793
Prepaid expenses and other	1,366
Total current assets	$24,356

Manufacturing Company ADOLPH COORS COMPANY Balance Sheet December 26, 1999		
Current assets (in millions)		
Cash and cash equivalents		$164
Short-term investments		113
Accounts and notes receivable (net)		160
Inventories		
Finished	$44	
In process	19	
Raw materials	34	
Packaging materials	10	
Total inventories		107
Prepaid expenses and other		69
Total current assets		$613

Illustration 8-1
Comparison of Current Assets Presentation for Merchandising and Manufacturing Companies

Inventory Systems

Whether a company is involved in manufacturing or merchandising, an accurate accounting system with up-to-date records is essential. Sales and customers may be lost if products ordered by customers are not available in the desired style, quality, and quantity. Also, businesses must monitor inventory levels carefully to limit the financing costs of carrying large amounts of inventory. Companies use one of two types of systems for maintaining accurate inventory records—the perpetual system or the periodic system.

Perpetual System

Under a **perpetual inventory system**, a continuous record of changes in inventory is maintained in the Inventory account. That is, all purchases and sales (issues) of goods are recorded directly in the Inventory account **as they occur**. The accounting features of a perpetual inventory system are as follows.

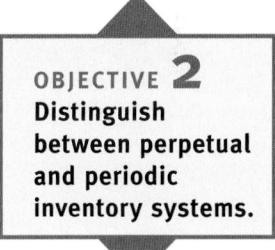

OBJECTIVE **2**
Distinguish between perpetual and periodic inventory systems.

1. Purchases of merchandise for resale or raw materials for production are debited to Inventory rather than to Purchases.
2. Freight-in, purchase returns and allowances, and purchase discounts are recorded in Inventory rather than in separate accounts.
3. Cost of goods sold is recognized for each sale by debiting the account, Cost of Goods Sold, and crediting Inventory.
4. Inventory is a control account that is supported by a subsidiary ledger of individual inventory records. The subsidiary records show the quantity and cost of each type of inventory on hand.

The perpetual inventory system provides a continuous record of the balances in both the Inventory account and the Cost of Goods Sold account.

Under a computerized recordkeeping system, additions to and issuances from inventory can be recorded nearly instantaneously. The popularity and affordability of computerized accounting software have made the perpetual system cost-effective for many kinds of businesses. Recording sales with optical scanners at the cash register has been incorporated into perpetual inventory systems at many retail stores.

WHAT DO THE NUMBERS MEAN?

STAYING LEAN

With the introduction and use of "just-in-time" (JIT) inventory order systems and better supplier relationships, inventory levels have become leaner for many companies.

Wal-Mart provides a classic example of the use of tight inventory controls. Department managers use a scanner that when placed over the bar code corresponding to a particular item, will tell them how many items were sold yesterday, last week, and over the same period last year. It will tell them how many of those items are in stock, how many are on the way, and how many the neighboring Wal-Marts are carrying (in case one store runs out). Such practices have helped Wal-Mart become one of the top-ranked companies on the Fortune 500 in terms of sales.

Periodic System

Under a **periodic inventory system**, the quantity of inventory on hand is determined only periodically, as its name implies. All acquisitions of inventory during the accounting period are recorded by debits to a Purchases account. The total in the Purchases account at the end of the accounting period is added to the cost of the inventory on hand at the beginning of the period, to determine the total cost of the goods available for sale during the period. To compute the cost of goods sold, ending inventory is subtracted from the cost of goods available for sale. Note that under a periodic inventory system, the cost of goods sold is a residual amount that is dependent upon a physically counted ending inventory.

No matter what type of inventory records are in use or how well organized the procedures for recording purchases and requisitions, the danger of loss and error is always present. Waste, breakage, theft, improper entry, failure to prepare or record requisitions, and any number of similar possibilities may cause the inventory records to differ from the actual inventory on hand. This requires periodic verification of the inventory records by actual count, weight, or measurement. These counts are compared with the detailed inventory records. The records are corrected to agree with the quantities actually on hand.

Insofar as possible, the physical inventory should be taken near the end of a company's fiscal year so that correct inventory quantities are available in preparing annual accounting reports. Because this is not always possible, however, physical inventories taken within two or three months of the year's end are satisfactory, if the detailed inventory records are maintained with a fair degree of accuracy.[4]

---

[4]In recent years, some companies have developed methods of determining inventories, including statistical sampling, that are sufficiently reliable to make unnecessary an annual physical count of each item of inventory. However, most companies need more current information regarding their inventory levels to protect against stockouts or overpurchasing and to aid in the preparation of monthly or quarterly financial data. As a consequence, many companies use a **modified perpetual inventory system** in which increases and decreases in quantities only—not dollar amounts—are kept in a detailed inventory record. It is merely a memorandum device outside the double-entry system, which helps in determining the level of inventory at any point in time.

To illustrate the difference between a perpetual and a periodic system, assume that Fesmire Company had the following transactions during the current year.

Beginning inventory	100 units at $ 6 = $ 600
Purchases	900 units at $ 6 = $5,400
Sales	600 units at $12 = $7,200
Ending inventory	400 units at $ 6 = $2,400

The entries to record these transactions during the current year are shown in Illustration 8-2.

PERPETUAL INVENTORY SYSTEM		PERIODIC INVENTORY SYSTEM	
1. Beginning inventory, 100 units at $6:			
The inventory account shows the inventory on hand at $600.		The inventory account shows the inventory on hand at $600.	
2. Purchase 900 units at $6:			
Inventory	5,400	Purchases	5,400
Accounts Payable	5,400	Accounts Payable	5,400
3. Sale of $600 units at $12:			
Accounts Receivable	7,200	Accounts Receivable	7,200
Sales	7,200	Sales	7,200
Cost of Goods Sold	3,600	(No entry)	
(600 at $6)			
Inventory	3,600		
4. End-of-period entries for inventory accounts, 400 units at $6:			
No entry necessary.		Inventory (ending, by count)	2,400
The account, Inventory, shows the ending		Cost of Goods Sold	3,600
balance of $2,400		Purchases	5,400
($600 + $5,400 − $3,600).		Inventory (beginning)	600

Illustration 8-2
Comparative Entries—
Perpetual vs. Periodic

When a perpetual inventory system is used and a difference exists between the perpetual inventory balance and the physical inventory count, a separate entry is needed to adjust the perpetual inventory account. To illustrate, assume that at the end of the reporting period, the perpetual inventory account reported an inventory balance of $4,000, but a physical count indicated $3,800 was actually on hand. The entry to record the necessary writedown is as follows.

Inventory Over and Short	200	
Inventory		200

Perpetual inventory overages and shortages generally represent a misstatement of cost of goods sold. The difference is a result of normal and expected shrinkage, breakage, shoplifting, incorrect record keeping, and the like. Inventory Over and Short would therefore be an adjustment of Cost of Goods Sold. In practice, the account Inventory Over and Short is sometimes reported in the "Other revenues and gains" or "Other expenses and losses" section of the income statement, depending on its balance. Note that in a periodic inventory system the account Inventory Over and Short does not arise; there are no accounting records available against which to compare the physical count. Thus, inventory overages and shortages are buried in cost of goods sold.

BASIC ISSUES IN INVENTORY VALUATION

The valuation of inventories can be a complex process that requires determining the following.

① The physical goods to be included in inventory (who owns the goods?—goods in transit, consigned goods, special sales agreements).

② The costs to be included in inventory (product vs. period costs).

③ The cost flow assumption to be adopted (specific identification, average cost, FIFO, LIFO, retail, etc.).

We will explore these basic issues in the next three sections.

Physical Goods Included in Inventory

Technically, purchases should be recorded when legal title to the goods passes to the buyer. General practice, however, is to record acquisitions when the goods are received, because it is difficult for the buyer to determine the exact time of legal passage of title for every purchase. In addition, no material error is likely to result from such a practice if it is consistently applied. Exceptions to the general rule can arise for goods in transit and consigned goods.

Goods in Transit

Sometimes purchased merchandise is in transit—not yet received—at the end of a fiscal period. The accounting for these shipped goods depends on who owns them. That can be determined by application of the "passage of title" rule. If the goods are shipped **f.o.b. shipping point**, title passes to the buyer when the seller delivers the goods to the common carrier, who acts as an agent for the buyer. (The abbreviation f.o.b. stands for free on board.) If the goods are shipped **f.o.b. destination**, title does not pass until the buyer receives the goods from the common carrier. "Shipping point" and "destination" are often designated by a particular location, for example, f.o.b. Denver.

The accounting rule is that goods to which legal title has passed should be recorded as purchases of the fiscal period. Goods shipped f.o.b. shipping point that are in transit at the end of the period belong to the buyer and should be shown in the buyer's records. Legal title to these goods passed to the buyer when the goods were shipped. To disregard such purchases would result in an understatement of inventories and accounts payable in the balance sheet and an understatement of purchases and ending inventories in the income statement.

Consigned Goods

A specialized method of marketing certain products uses a device known as a **consignment** shipment. Under this arrangement, one party (the consignor) ships merchandise to another (the consignee), who acts as the consignor's agent in selling the **consigned goods**. The consignee agrees to accept the goods without any liability, except to exercise due care and reasonable protection from loss or damage, until the goods are sold to a third party. When the consignee sells the goods, the revenue less a selling commission and expenses incurred in accomplishing the sale is remitted to the consignor.

Goods out on consignment remain the property of the consignor and are included in the consignor's inventory at purchase price or production cost. Occasionally, the inventory out on consignment is shown as a separate item, but unless the amount is large there is little need for this. Sometimes the inventory on consignment is reported in the notes to the financial statements. For example, **Eagle Clothes, Inc.** reported the following related to consigned goods: "Inventories consist of finished goods shipped on consignment to customers of the Company's subsidiary **April-Marcus, Inc.**"

The consignee makes no entry to the inventory account for goods received because they are the property of the consignor. The consignee should be extremely careful *not* to include any of the goods consigned as a part of inventory.

Costs Included in Inventory

One of the most important problems in dealing with inventories concerns the dollar amount at which the inventory should be carried in the accounts. **The acquisition of inventories, like other assets, is generally accounted for on a basis of cost.**

Product Costs

Product costs are those costs that "attach" to the inventory and are recorded in the inventory account. These costs are directly connected with the bringing of goods to the place of business of the buyer and converting such goods to a salable condition. Such charges would include freight charges on goods purchased, other direct costs of acquisition, and labor and other production costs incurred in processing the goods up to the time of sale.

It would seem proper also to allocate to inventories a share of any buying costs or expenses of a purchasing department, storage costs, and other costs incurred in storing or handling the goods before they are sold. However, because of the practical difficulties involved in allocating such costs and expenses, these items are not ordinarily included in valuing inventories.

For a manufacturing company, costs include direct materials, direct labor, and manufacturing overhead costs. Manufacturing overhead costs include indirect materials, indirect labor, and such items as depreciation, taxes, insurance, and heat and electricity incurred in the manufacturing process.

Period Costs

Selling expenses and, under ordinary circumstances, **general and administrative expenses** are not considered to be directly related to the acquisition or production of goods and, therefore, are not considered to be a part of inventories. Such costs are **period costs**.

Conceptually, these expenses are as much a cost of the product as the initial purchase price and related freight charges attached to the product. Why then are these costs not considered inventoriable items? Selling expenses are generally considered as more directly related to the cost of goods sold than to the unsold inventory. In most cases, though, the costs, especially administrative expenses, are so unrelated or indirectly related to the immediate production process that any allocation is purely arbitrary.

Interest costs associated with getting inventories ready for sale usually are expensed as incurred. A major argument for this approach is that interest costs are really a cost of financing. Others have argued, however, that interest costs incurred to finance activities associated with making inventories ready for sale are as much a cost of the asset as materials, labor, and overhead, and therefore should be capitalized.[5] **The FASB has ruled that interest costs related to assets constructed for internal use or assets produced as discrete projects (such as ships or real estate projects) for sale or lease should be capitalized.**[6] The FASB emphasized that these discrete projects should take considerable time, entail substantial expenditures, and be likely to involve significant amounts of interest cost. Interest costs should not be capitalized for inventories that are routinely manufactured or otherwise produced

Discussion of Inventory Errors

UNDERLYING CONCEPTS

In capitalizing interest, both constraints—materiality and cost/benefit—are applied.

---

[5]The reporting rules related to interest cost capitalization have their greatest impact in accounting for long-term assets and, therefore, are discussed in Chapter 9.

[6]"Capitalization of Interest Cost," *Statement of Financial Accounting Standards No. 34* (Stamford, Conn.: FASB, 1979).

in large quantities on a repetitive basis, because the informational benefit does not justify the cost.

Illustration 8-3 summarizes the guidelines for determining the physical goods and costs to be included in inventory.

Illustration 8-3

Goods and Costs Included in Inventory

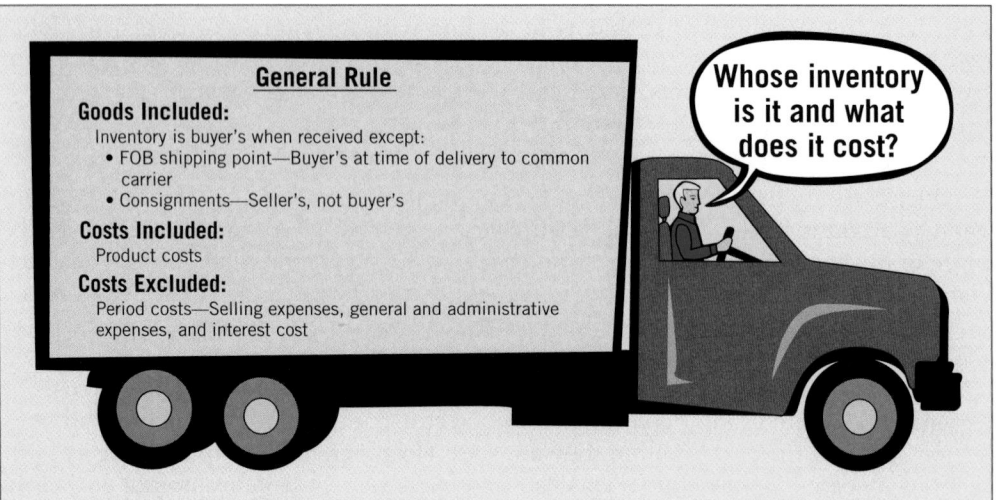

General Rule

Goods Included:
Inventory is buyer's when received except:
• FOB shipping point—Buyer's at time of delivery to common carrier
• Consignments—Seller's, not buyer's

Costs Included:
Product costs

Costs Excluded:
Period costs—Selling expenses, general and administrative expenses, and interest cost

Whose inventory is it and what does it cost?

WHAT DO THE NUMBERS MEAN?

YOU MAY NEED A MAP

Does it really matter where companies report certain costs in their income statements? As long as all the costs are included in expenses in the computation of income, why should the "geography" matter?

For e-tailers, such as **Amazon.com** or **Drugstore.com**, *where* certain selling costs are reported does appear to be important. Contrary to well-established retailer practices, these companies insist on reporting some selling costs—fulfillment costs related to inventory shipping and warehousing—as part of administrative expenses, instead of as cost of goods sold. While the practice doesn't affect the bottom line, it does make the e-tailers' gross margins look better. For example, in a recent quarter Amazon.com reported $265 million in these costs. Some experts thought those charges should be included in costs of goods sold, which would make Amazon's gross profit substantially lower based on traditional retailer accounting practices, as shown below.

(in millions)	E-tailer Reporting	Traditional Reporting
Sales	$2,795	$2,795
Cost of goods sold	2,132	2,397
Gross profit	$ 663	$ 398
Gross margin%	24%	14%

Similarly, if **Drugstore.com** and **eToys.com** were to make a similar adjustment, their gross margins would go from positive to negative.

Thus, if you want to be able to compare the operating results of e-tailers to other traditional retailers, it might be a good idea to have a good accounting map in order to navigate their income statements and how they report certain selling costs.

Source: Adapted from P. Elstrom, "The End of Fuzzy Math?" *Business Week*, e.Biz–Net Worth (December 11, 2000).

What Cost Flow Assumption Should Be Adopted?

During any given fiscal period it is very likely that merchandise will be purchased at several different prices. If inventories are to be priced at cost and numerous purchases have been made at different unit costs, which of the various cost prices should be used? Conceptually, a specific identification of the given items sold and unsold seems optimal, but this measure is often not only expensive but impossible to achieve. Consequently, one of several systematic inventory **cost flow assumptions** is used. Indeed, the actual physical flow of goods and the cost flow assumption are often quite different. **There is no requirement that the cost flow assumption adopted be consistent with the physical movement of goods.** The major objective in selecting a method should be to choose the one that, under the circumstances, most clearly reflects periodic income.[7]

To illustrate, assume that Call-Mart Inc. had the following transactions in its first month of operations.

Date	Purchases	Sold or Issued	Balance
March 2	2,000 @ $4.00		2,000 units
March 15	6,000 @ $4.40		8,000 units
March 19		4,000 units	4,000 units
March 30	2,000 @ $4.75		6,000 units

From this information, we can compute the ending inventory of 6,000 units and the cost of goods available for sale (beginning inventory + purchases) of $43,900 [(2,000 @ $4.00) + (6,000 @ $4.40) + (2,000 @ $4.75)]. The question is, which price or prices should be assigned to the 6,000 units of ending inventory? The answer depends on which cost flow assumption is employed.

Specific Identification

Specific identification calls for identifying each item sold and each item in inventory. The costs of the specific items sold are included in the cost of goods sold, and the costs of the specific items on hand are included in the inventory. This method may be used only in instances where it is practical to separate physically the different purchases made. It can be successfully applied in situations where a relatively small number of costly, easily distinguishable items are handled. In the retail trade this includes some types of jewelry, fur coats, automobiles, and some furniture. In manufacturing it includes special orders and many products manufactured under a job cost system.

To illustrate the specific identification method, assume that Call-Mart Inc.'s 6,000 units of inventory is composed of 1,000 units from the March 2 purchase, 3,000 from the March 15 purchase, and 2,000 from the March 30 purchase. The ending inventory and cost of goods sold would be computed as shown in Illustration 8-4 (page 354).

Conceptually, this method appears ideal because actual costs are matched against actual revenue, and ending inventory is reported at actual cost. In other words, **under specific identification the cost flow matches the physical flow of the goods.** On closer observation, however, this method has certain deficiencies.

One argument against specific identification is that it makes it possible to manipulate net income. For example, assume that a wholesaler purchases otherwise identical plywood early in the year at three different prices. When the plywood is sold, the wholesaler can select either the lowest or the highest price to charge to expense simply by selecting the plywood from a specific lot for delivery to the customer. A busi-

[7]"Restatement and Revision of Accounting Research Bulletins," *Accounting Research Bulletin No. 43* (New York: AICPA, 1953), Ch. 4, Statement 4.

Illustration 8-4
Specific Identification
Method

Date	No. of Units	Unit Cost	Total Cost
March 2	1,000	$4.00	$ 4,000
March 15	3,000	4.40	13,200
March 30	2,000	4.75	9,500
Ending inventory	6,000		$26,700

Cost of goods available for sale (computed in previous section)	$43,900
Deduct: Ending inventory	26,700
Cost of goods sold	$17,200

ness manager, therefore, can manipulate net income simply by delivering to the customer the higher- or lower-priced item, depending on whether higher or lower reported earnings is desired for the period.

Another problem relates to the arbitrary allocation of costs that sometimes occurs with specific inventory items. In certain circumstances, it is difficult to relate adequately, for example, shipping charges, storage costs, and discounts directly to a given inventory item. The alternative, then, is to allocate these costs somewhat arbitrarily, which leads to a "breakdown" in the precision of the specific identification method.[8]

Average Cost

As the name implies, the **average cost method** prices items in the inventory on the basis of the average cost of all similar goods available during the period. To illustrate, assuming that Call-Mart Inc. used the periodic inventory method, the ending inventory and cost of goods sold would be computed as follows using a **weighted-average method**.

Illustration 8-5
Weighted-Average
Method—Periodic
Inventory

Date of Invoice	No. Units	Unit Cost	Total Cost
March 2	2,000	$4.00	$ 8,000
March 15	6,000	4.40	26,400
March 30	2,000	4.75	9,500
Total goods available	10,000		$43,900

Weighted-average cost per unit $\frac{\$43,900}{10,000} = \$4.39$

Inventory in units 6,000 units
Ending inventory 6,000 × $4.39 = $26,340

Cost of goods available for sale	$43,900
Deduct: Ending inventory	26,340
Cost of goods sold	$17,560

[8]A good illustration of the cost allocation problem arises in the motion picture industry. Often actors receive a percentage of net income for a given movie or television program. Some actors who had these arrangements have alleged that their programs have been extremely profitable to the motion picture studios but they have received little in the way of profit sharing. Actors contend that the studios allocate additional costs to successful projects to ensure that there will be no profits to share.

A beginning inventory, if any, is included both in the total units available and in the total cost of goods available in computing the average cost per unit.

Another average cost method is the **moving-average method**, which is used with perpetual inventory records. The application of the average cost method for perpetual records is shown in Illustration 8-6.

Date	Purchased		Sold or Issued		Balance		
March 2	(2,000 @ $4.00)	$ 8,000			(2,000 @ $4.00)	$ 8,000	
March 15	(6,000 @ 4.40)	26,400			(8,000 @ 4.30)	34,400	
March 19			(4,000 @ $4.30)				
				$17,200	(4,000 @ 4.30)	17,200	
March 30	(2,000 @ 4.75)	9,500			(6,000 @ 4.45)	26,700	

Illustration 8-6
Moving-Average
Method—Perpetual
Inventory

In this method, a new average unit cost is computed each time a purchase is made. On March 15, after 6,000 units are purchased for $26,400, 8,000 units costing $34,400 ($8,000 plus $26,400) are on hand. The average unit cost is $34,400 divided by 8,000, or $4.30. This unit cost is used in costing withdrawals until another purchase is made, when a new average unit cost is computed. Accordingly, the cost of the 4,000 units withdrawn on March 19 is shown at $4.30, a total cost of goods sold of $17,200. On March 30, following the purchase of 2,000 units for $9,500, a new unit cost of $4.45 is determined for an ending inventory of $26,700.

The use of the average cost methods is usually justified on the basis of practical rather than conceptual reasons. These methods are simple to apply and objective. They are not as subject to income manipulation as some of the other inventory pricing methods. In addition, proponents of the average cost methods argue that it is often impossible to measure a specific physical flow of inventory and therefore it is better to cost items on an average-price basis. This argument is particularly persuasive when the inventory involved is relatively homogeneous in nature.

First-In, First-Out (FIFO)

The **FIFO method** assumes that goods are used in the order in which they are purchased. In other words, it assumes that **the first goods purchased are the first used** (in a manufacturing concern) **or sold** (in a merchandising concern). The inventory remaining must therefore represent the most recent purchases.

To illustrate, assume that Call-Mart Inc. uses the periodic inventory system (amount of inventory computed only at the end of the month). The cost of the ending inventory is computed by taking the cost of the most recent purchase and working back until all units in the inventory are accounted for. The ending inventory and cost of goods sold are determined as shown in Illustration 8-7.

Date	No. Units	Unit Cost	Total Cost
March 30	2,000	$4.75	$ 9,500
March 15	4,000	4.40	17,600
Ending inventory	6,000		$27,100
Cost of goods available for sale		$43,900	
Deduct: Ending inventory		27,100	
Cost of goods sold		$16,800	

Illustration 8-7
FIFO Method—Periodic
Inventory

If a perpetual inventory system in quantities and dollars is used, a cost figure is attached to each withdrawal. Then the cost of the 4,000 units removed on March 19 would be made up of the items purchased on March 2 and March 15. The inventory on a FIFO basis perpetual system for Call-Mart Inc. is shown in Illustration 8-8.

Illustration 8-8
FIFO Method—Perpetual Inventory

Date	Purchased		Sold or Issued	Balance	
March 2	(2,000 @ $4.00)	$ 8,000		2,000 @ $4.00	$ 8,000
March 15	(6,000 @ 4.40)	26,400		2,000 @ 4.00 ⎱ 6,000 @ 4.40 ⎰	34,400
March 19			2,000 @ $4.00 ⎱ 2,000 @ 4.40 ⎰ ($16,800)	4,000 @ 4.40	17,600
March 30	(2,000 @ 4.75)	9,500		4,000 @ 4.40 ⎱ 2,000 @ 4.75 ⎰	27,100

The ending inventory in this situation is $27,100, and the cost of goods sold is $16,800 [(2,000 @ 4.00) + (2,000 @ $4.40)].

Notice that in these two FIFO examples, the cost of goods sold ($16,800) and ending inventory ($27,100) are the same. **In all cases where FIFO is used, the inventory and cost of goods sold would be the same at the end of the month whether a perpetual or periodic system is used.** This is true because the same costs will always be first in and, therefore, first out. This is true whether cost of goods sold is computed as goods are sold throughout the accounting period (the perpetual system) or as a residual at the end of the accounting period (the periodic system).

One objective of FIFO is to approximate the physical flow of goods. When the physical flow of goods is actually first-in, first-out, the FIFO method closely approximates specific identification. At the same time, it does not permit manipulation of income because the enterprise is not free to pick a certain cost item to be charged to expense.

Another advantage of the FIFO method is that the ending inventory is close to current cost. Because the first goods in are the first goods out, the ending inventory amount will be composed of the most recent purchases. This is particularly true where the inventory turnover is rapid. This approach generally provides a reasonable approximation of replacement cost on the balance sheet when price changes have not occurred since the most recent purchases.

The basic disadvantage of the FIFO method is that current costs are not matched against current revenues on the income statement. The oldest costs are charged against the more current revenue, which can lead to distortions in gross profit and net income.

INTERNATIONAL INSIGHT

Until recently, LIFO was typically used only in the United States. However, LIFO is acceptable under the Directives of the European Union, and its use has now spread in some degree to other countries. Nonetheless, LIFO is still used primarily in the United States and is still prohibited in some countries.

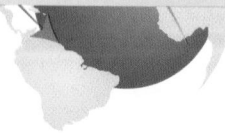

Last-In, First-Out (LIFO)

The **LIFO method** first matches against revenue the cost of the last goods purchased. If a periodic inventory is used, then it would be assumed that **the cost of the total quantity sold or issued during the month would have come from the most recent purchases**. The ending inventory would be priced by using the total units as a basis of computation and disregarding the exact dates of sales or issuances. Illustration 8-9 assumes that the cost of the 4,000 units withdrawn absorbed the 2,000 units purchased on March 30 and 2,000 of the 6,000 units purchased on March 15. The inventory and related cost of goods sold would then be computed.

Date of Invoice	No. Units	Unit Cost	Total Cost
March 2	2,000	$4.00	$ 8,000
March 15	4,000	4.40	17,600
Ending inventory	6,000		$25,600

Goods available for sale	$43,900	
Deduct: Ending inventory	25,600	
Cost of goods sold	$18,300	

Illustration 8-9
LIFO Method—Periodic Inventory

If a perpetual inventory record is kept in quantities and dollars, compared to the periodic record, application of the last-in, first-out method will result in **different ending inventory and cost of goods sold amounts**, as shown in Illustration 8-10.

Date	Purchased		Sold or Issued	Balance	
March 2	(2,000 @ $4.00)	$ 8,000		2,000 @ $4.00	$ 8,000
March 15	(6,000 @ 4.40)	26,400		2,000 @ 4.00 6,000 @ 4.40	34,400
March 19			(4,000 @ $4.40) $17,600	2,000 @ 4.00 2,000 @ 4.40	16,800
March 30	(2,000 @ 4.75)	9,500		2,000 @ 4.00 2,000 @ 4.40 2,000 @ 4.75	26,300

Illustration 8-10
LIFO Method—Perpetual Inventory

The month-end periodic inventory computation presented in Illustration 8-9 (inventory $25,600 and cost of goods sold $18,300) shows a different amount from the perpetual inventory computation (inventory $26,300 and cost of goods sold $17,600). The periodic system matches the total withdrawals for the month with the total purchases for the month in applying the last-in, first-out method. In contrast, the perpetual system matches each withdrawal with the immediately preceding purchases. In effect, the periodic computation assumed that the cost of the goods that were purchased on March 30 were included in the sale or issue on March 19.

Tutorial on Inventory Methods

SPECIAL ISSUES RELATED TO LIFO

LIFO Reserve

Many companies use LIFO for tax and external reporting purposes, but maintain a FIFO, average cost, or standard cost system for internal reporting purposes. There are several reasons to do so: (1) Companies often base their pricing decisions on a FIFO, average, or standard cost assumption, rather than on a LIFO basis. (2) Record keeping on some other basis is easier because the LIFO assumption usually does not approximate the physical flow of the product. (3) Profit-sharing and other bonus arrangements are often not based on a LIFO inventory assumption. Finally, (4) the use of a pure LIFO system is troublesome for interim periods, for which estimates must be made of year-end quantities and prices.

The difference between the inventory method used for internal reporting purposes and LIFO is referred to as the Allowance to Reduce Inventory to LIFO or the **LIFO reserve**. The change in the allowance balance from one period to the next is called the **LIFO effect**. The LIFO effect is the adjustment that must be made to the accounting records in a given year.

OBJECTIVE 5
Explain the significance and use of a LIFO reserve.

To illustrate, assume that Acme Boot Company uses the FIFO method for internal reporting purposes and LIFO for external reporting purposes. At January 1, 2004, the Allowance to Reduce Inventory to LIFO balance was $20,000, and the ending balance should be $50,000. The LIFO effect is therefore $30,000, and the following entry is made at year-end.

Cost of Goods Sold	30,000	
Allowance to Reduce Inventory to LIFO		30,000

The Allowance to Reduce Inventory to LIFO would be deducted from inventory to ensure that the inventory is stated on a LIFO basis at year-end.

The AICPA Task Force on LIFO Inventory Problems concluded that either the LIFO reserve or the replacement cost of the inventory should be disclosed.[9] An example of this kind of disclosure is shown below.

Illustration 8-11

Note Disclosure of LIFO Reserve

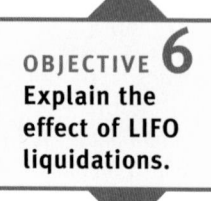

Additional LIFO Reserve Disclosures

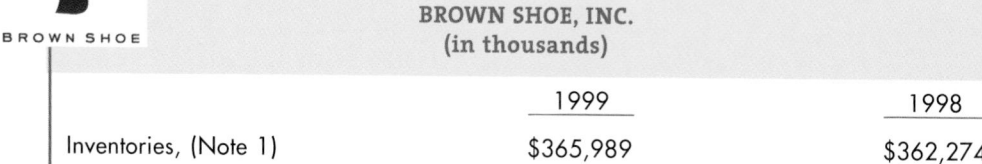

	1999	1998
Inventories, (Note 1)	$365,989	$362,274

Note 1 (partial): Inventories. Inventories are valued at the lower of cost or market determined principally by the last-in, first-out (LIFO) method. If the first-in, first-out (FIFO) cost method had been used, inventories would have been $11,709 higher in 1999 and $13,424 higher in 1998.

BROWN SHOE, INC.
(in thousands)

LIFO Liquidation

OBJECTIVE 6
Explain the effect of LIFO liquidations.

Up to this point, we have emphasized a **specific goods approach** to costing LIFO inventories (also called traditional LIFO or unit LIFO). This approach is often unrealistic for two reasons:

1. When a company has many different inventory items, the accounting cost of keeping track of each inventory item is expensive.
2. Erosion of the LIFO inventory can easily occur. Referred to as **LIFO liquidation**, this often leads to distortions of net income and substantial tax payments.

To understand the LIFO liquidation problem, assume that Basler Co. has 30,000 pounds of steel in its inventory on December 31, 2004, costed on a specific goods LIFO approach.

ENDING INVENTORY (2004)			
	Pounds	Unit Cost	LIFO Cost
2001	8,000	$ 4	$ 32,000
2002	10,000	6	60,000
2003	7,000	9	63,000
2004	5,000	10	50,000
	30,000		$205,000

[9]The AICPA Task Force on LIFO Inventory Problems, *Issues Paper* (New York: AICPA, November 30, 1984), par. 2–24. The SEC has endorsed this issues paper, and therefore it has authoritative status for GAAP purposes.

As indicated, the ending 2004 inventory for Basler Co. comprises costs from past periods. These costs are called **layers** (increases from period to period). The first layer is identified as the base layer. The layers for Basler are shown in Illustration 8-12.

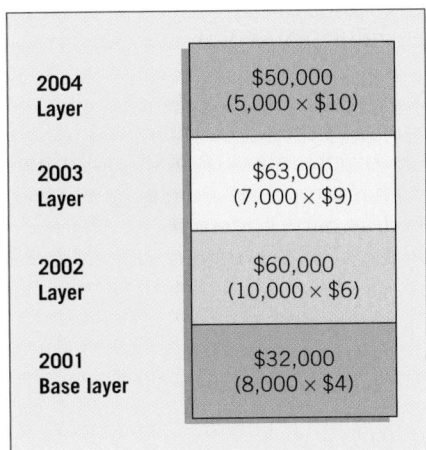

Illustration 8-12
Layers of LIFO Inventory

The price of steel has increased over the 4-year period. In 2005, Basler Co. experienced metal shortages and had to liquidate much of its inventory (a LIFO liquidation). At the end of 2005, only 6,000 pounds of steel remained in inventory. Because the company is using LIFO, the most recent layer, 2004, is liquidated first, followed by the 2003 layer, and so on. The result: Costs from preceding periods are matched against sales revenues reported in current dollars. This leads to a distortion in net income and a substantial tax bill in the current period. These effects are shown in Illustration 8-13. Unfortunately LIFO liquidations can occur frequently when a specific goods LIFO approach is employed.

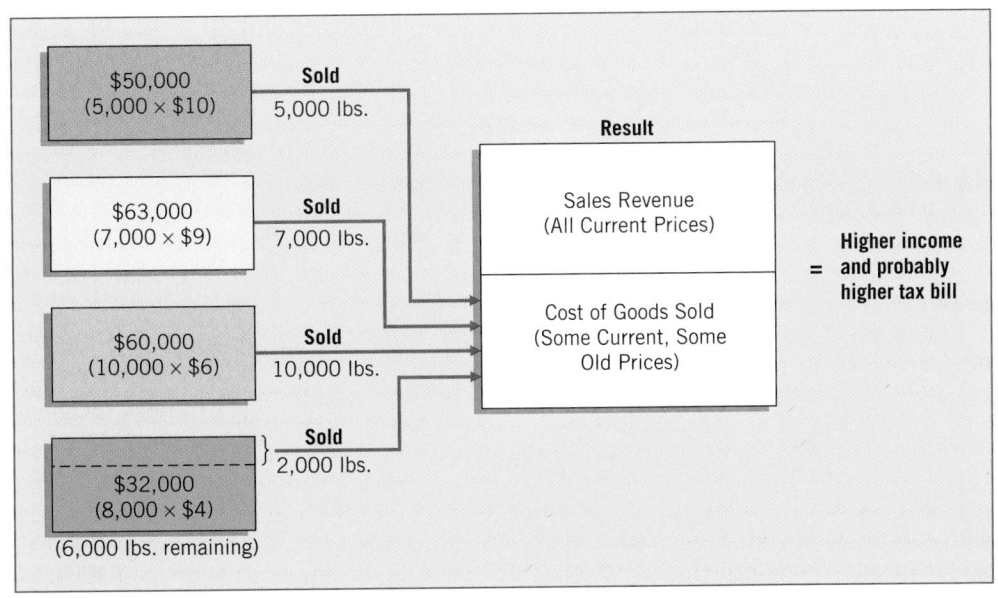

Illustration 8-13
LIFO Liquidation

To alleviate the LIFO liquidation problems and to simplify the accounting, goods can be combined into pools. A **pool** is defined as a group of items of a similar nature. Thus, instead of only identical units, a number of similar units or products are combined and accounted for together. This method is referred to as the **specific goods pooled LIFO approach**. With the specific goods pooled LIFO approach, LIFO liquidations are less likely to happen because the reduction of one quantity in the pool may be offset by an increase in another.

The specific goods pooled LIFO approach eliminates some of the disadvantages of the specific goods (traditional) accounting for LIFO inventories. This pooled approach, using quantities as its measurement basis, however, creates other problems.

First, most companies are continually changing the mix of their products, materials, and production methods. If a pooled approach using quantities is employed, such changes mean that the pools must be continually redefined; this can be time consuming and costly.

Second, even when such an approach is practical, an erosion ("LIFO liquidation") of the layers often results, and much of the LIFO costing benefit is lost. An erosion of the layers results because a specific good or material in the pool may be replaced by another good or material either temporarily or permanently. The new item may not be similar enough to be treated as part of the old pool. Therefore any inflationary profit deferred on the old goods may have to be recognized as the old goods are replaced.

Dollar-Value LIFO

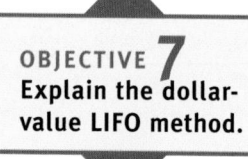

OBJECTIVE **7**
Explain the dollar-value LIFO method.

To overcome the problems of redefining pools and eroding layers, the dollar-value LIFO method was developed. **An important feature of the dollar-value LIFO method is that increases and decreases in a pool are determined and measured in terms of total dollar value, not the physical quantity of the goods in the inventory pool.**

Such an approach has two important advantages over the specific goods pooled approach. First, a broader range of goods may be included in a dollar-value LIFO pool. Second, in a dollar-value LIFO pool, replacement is permitted if it is a similar material, or similar in use, or interchangeable. (In contrast, in a specific goods LIFO pool, an item may be replaced only with an item that is substantially identical.)

Thus, dollar-value LIFO techniques help protect LIFO layers from erosion. Because of this advantage, the dollar-value LIFO method is frequently used in practice.[10] The more traditional LIFO approaches would be used only in situations where few goods are employed and little change in product mix is predicted.

Under the dollar-value LIFO method, it is possible to have the entire inventory in only one pool, although several pools are commonly employed.[11] In general, the more goods included in a pool, the more likely that decreases in the quantities of some goods will be offset by increases in the quantities of other goods in the same pool. Thus liquidation of the LIFO layers is avoided. It follows that having fewer pools means less cost and less chance of a reduction of a LIFO layer.

Dollar-Value LIFO Illustration

To illustrate how the dollar-value LIFO method works, assume that dollar-value LIFO was first adopted (base period) on December 31, 2003. The inventory at current prices on that date was $20,000, and the inventory on December 31, 2004, at current prices is $26,400.

We should not conclude that the quantity has increased 32 percent during the year ($26,400 ÷ $20,000 = 132%). First, we need to ask: What is the value of the ending inventory in terms of beginning-of-the-year prices? Assuming that prices have increased 20 percent during the year, the ending inventory at beginning-of-the-year prices

---

[10]A study by James M. Reeve and Keith G. Stanga disclosed that the vast majority of respondent companies applying LIFO use the dollar-value method or the dollar-value retail method to apply LIFO. Only a small minority of companies use the specific goods (unit LIFO) approach or the specific goods pooling approach. See J.M. Reeve and K.G. Stanga, "The LIFO Pooling Decision," *Accounting Horizons* (June 1987), p. 27.

[11]The Reeve and Stanga study (ibid.) reports that most companies have only a few pools—the median is six for retailers and three for nonretailers. But the distributions are highly skewed; some companies have 100 or more pools. Retailers that use LIFO have significantly more pools than nonretailers. About a third of the nonretailers (mostly manufacturers) use a single pool for their entire LIFO inventory.

amounts to $22,000 ($26,400 ÷ 120%). Therefore, the inventory quantity has increased 10 percent, or from $20,000 to $22,000 in terms of beginning-of-the-year prices.

The next step is to price this real-dollar quantity increase. This real-dollar quantity increase of $2,000 valued at year-end prices is $2,400 (120% × $2,000). This increment (layer) of $2,400, when added to the beginning inventory of $20,000, gives a total of $22,400 for the December 31, 2004, inventory, as shown below.

First layer—(beginning inventory) in terms of 100	$20,000
Second layer—(2004 increase) in terms of 120	2,400
Dollar-value LIFO inventory, December 31, 2004	$22,400

It should be emphasized that **a layer is formed only when the ending inventory at base-year prices exceeds the beginning inventory at base-year prices**. And only when a new layer is formed must a new index be computed.

Comprehensive Dollar-Value LIFO Illustration

To illustrate the use of the dollar-value LIFO method in a more complex situation, assume that Bismark Company develops the following information.

December 31	Inventory at End-of-Year Prices	÷ Price Index (percentage)	= End-of-Year Inventory at Base-Year Prices
(Base year) 2001	$200,000	100	$200,000
2002	299,000	115	260,000
2003	300,000	120	250,000
2004	351,000	130	270,000

At December 31, 2001, the ending inventory under dollar-value LIFO is simply the $200,000 computed as shown in Illustration 8-14.

Ending Inventory at Base-Year Prices	Layer at Base-Year Prices	Price Index (percentage)	Ending Inventory at LIFO Cost
$200,000	$200,000 ×	100 =	$200,000

Illustration 8-14
Computation of 2001 Inventory at LIFO Cost

At December 31, 2002, a comparison of the ending inventory at base-year prices ($260,000) with the beginning inventory at base-year prices ($200,000), indicates that the quantity of goods has increased $60,000 ($260,000 − $200,000). This increment (layer) is then priced at the 2002 index of 115 percent to arrive at a new layer of $69,000. Ending inventory for 2002 is $269,000, composed of the beginning inventory of $200,000 and the new layer of $69,000. The computations are in Illustration 8-15 (page 362).

At December 31, 2003, a comparison of the ending inventory at base-year prices ($250,000) with the beginning inventory at base-year prices ($260,000) indicates that the quantity of goods has decreased $10,000 ($250,000 − $260,000). If the ending inventory at base-year prices is less than the beginning inventory at base-year prices, **the decrease must be subtracted from the most recently added layer. When a decrease occurs, previous layers must be "peeled off" at the prices in existence when the layers were added.** In Bismark Company's situation, this means that $10,000 in base-year prices

Illustration 8-15
Computation of 2002
Inventory at LIFO Cost

Ending Inventory at Base-Year Prices	Layers at Base-Year Prices		Price Index (percentage)		Ending Inventory at LIFO Cost
$260,000	2001 $200,000	×	100	=	$200,000
	2002 60,000	×	115	=	69,000
	$260,000				$269,000

must be removed from the 2002 layer of $60,000 at base-year prices. The balance of $50,000 ($60,000 − $10,000) at base-year prices must be valued at the 2002 price index of 115 percent, so this 2002 layer now is valued at $57,500 ($50,000 × 115%). The ending inventory is therefore computed at $257,500, consisting of the beginning inventory of $200,000 and the second layer, $57,500. The computations for 2003 are shown in Illustration 8-16.

Illustration 8-16
Computation of 2003
Inventory at LIFO Cost

Ending Inventory at Base-Year Prices	Layers at Base-Year Prices		Price Index (percentage)		Ending Inventory at LIFO Cost
$250,000	2001 $200,000	×	100	=	$200,000
	2002 50,000	×	115	=	57,500
	$250,000				$257,500

Note that if a layer or base (or portion thereof) has been eliminated, it cannot be rebuilt in future periods. That is, it is gone forever.

At December 31, 2004, a comparison of the ending inventory at base-year prices ($270,000) with the beginning inventory at base-year prices ($250,000) indicates that the dollar quantity of goods has increased $20,000 ($270,000 − $250,000) in terms of base-year prices. After converting the $20,000 increase to the 2004 price index, the ending inventory is $283,500, composed of the beginning layer of $200,000, a 2002 layer of $57,500, and a 2004 layer of $26,000 ($20,000 × 130%). This computation is shown in Illustration 8-17.

Illustration 8-17
Computation of 2004
Inventory at LIFO Cost

Ending Inventory at Base-Year Prices	Layers at Base-Year Prices		Price Index (percentage)		Ending Inventory at LIFO Cost
$270,000	2001 $200,000	×	100	=	$200,000
	2002 50,000	×	115	=	57,500
	2003 20,000	×	130	=	26,000
	$270,000				$283,500

The ending inventory at base-year prices must always equal the total of the layers at base-year prices. Checking that this situation exists will help to ensure that the dollar-value computation is made correctly.

Comparison of LIFO Approaches

Three different approaches to computing LIFO inventories are presented in this chapter—specific goods LIFO, specific goods pooled LIFO, and dollar-value LIFO. As indicated earlier, the use of the specific goods LIFO is unrealistic because most enterprises have numerous goods in inventory at the end of a period, and costing (pricing) them on a unit basis is extremely expensive and time consuming.

The specific goods pooled LIFO approach is better in that it reduces record keeping and clerical costs. In addition, it is more difficult to erode the layers because the reduction of one quantity in the pool may be offset by an increase in another. Nonetheless, the pooled approach using quantities as its measurement basis can lead to untimely LIFO liquidations.

As a result, **dollar-value LIFO is the method employed by most companies that currently use a LIFO system**. Although the approach appears complex, the logic and the computations are actually quite simple, once an appropriate index is determined.

This is not to suggest that problems do not exist with the dollar-value LIFO method. The selection of the items to be put in a pool can be subjective.[12] Such a determination, however, is extremely important because manipulation of the items in a pool without conceptual justification can affect reported net income. For example, the SEC noted that some companies have set up pools that are easy to liquidate. As a result, when the company wants to increase its income, it decreases inventory, thereby matching low-cost inventory items to current revenues.

To curb this practice, the SEC has taken a much harder line on the number of pools that companies may establish. In the well-publicized **Stauffer Chemical Company** case, Stauffer had increased the number of LIFO pools from 8 to 280, boosting its net income by $16,515,000 or approximately 13 percent.[13] Stauffer justified the change in its Annual Report on the basis of "achieving a better matching of cost and revenue." The SEC required Stauffer to reduce the number of its inventory pools, contending that some pools were inappropriate and alleging income manipulation.

Tutorial on LIFO Inventory Issues

Basis for Selection of Inventory Method

How does one choose among the various inventory methods? Although no absolute rules can be stated, preferability for LIFO can ordinarily be established in either of the following circumstances: (1) if selling prices and revenues have been increasing faster than costs, thereby distorting income, and (2) in situations where LIFO has been traditional, such as department stores and industries where a fairly constant "base stock" is present (such as refining, chemicals, and glass).[14]

Conversely, LIFO would probably not be appropriate: (1) where prices tend to lag behind costs; (2) in situations where specific identification is traditional, such as in the sale of automobiles, farm equipment, art, and antique jewelry; or (3) where unit costs tend to decrease as production increases, thereby nullifying the tax benefit that LIFO might provide.[15]

Major Advantages of LIFO

One obvious advantage of LIFO approaches is that in certain situations the LIFO cost flow actually approximates the physical flow of the goods in and out of inventory. For instance, in the case of a coal pile, the last coal in is the first coal out because it is on the top of the pile. The coal remover is not going to take the coal from the bot-

OBJECTIVE **8**
Identify the major advantages and disadvantages of LIFO.

---

[12]It is suggested that companies analyze how inventory purchases are affected by price changes, how goods are stocked, how goods are used, and if future liquidations are likely. See William R. Cron and Randall Hayes, "The Dollar Value LIFO Pooling Decision: The Conventional Wisdom Is Too General," *Accounting Horizons* (December 1989), p. 57.

[13]Commerce Clearing House, *SEC Accounting Rules* (Chicago: CCH, 1983), par. 4035.

[14]*Accounting Trends and Techniques—2001* reports that of 887 inventory method disclosures, 283 used LIFO, 386 used FIFO, 180 used average cost, and 38 used other methods.

[15]See Barry E. Cushing and Marc J. LeClere, "Evidence on the Determinants of Inventory Accounting Policy Choice," *The Accounting Review* (April 1992), pp. 355–366, Table 4, p. 363, for a list of factors hypothesized to affect FIFO–LIFO choices.

tom of the pile! The coal that is going to be taken first is the coal that was placed on the pile last.

However, the coal pile situation is one of only a few situations where the actual physical flow corresponds to LIFO. Therefore most adherents of LIFO use other arguments for its widespread employment, as follows.

Matching   In LIFO, the more recent costs are matched against current revenues to provide a better measure of current earnings. During periods of inflation, many challenge the quality of non-LIFO earnings, noting that by failing to match current costs against current revenues, **transitory or "paper" profits ("inventory profits") are created**. Inventory profits occur when the inventory costs matched against sales are less than the inventory replacement cost. The cost of goods sold therefore is understated and profit is overstated. Using LIFO (rather than a method such as FIFO), current costs are matched against revenues and inventory profits are thereby reduced.

Tax Benefits/Improved Cash Flow   Tax benefits are the major reason why LIFO has become popular. As long as the price level increases and inventory quantities do not decrease, a deferral of income tax occurs, because the items most recently purchased at the higher price level are matched against revenues. For example, when **Fuqua Industries** decided to switch to LIFO, it had a resultant tax savings of about $4 million. Even if the price level decreases later, the company has been given a temporary deferral of its income taxes. Thus, use of LIFO in such situations improves a company's cash flow.[16]

The tax law requires that if a company uses LIFO for tax purposes, it must also use LIFO for financial accounting purposes[17] (although neither tax law nor GAAP requires a company to pool its inventories in the same manner for book and tax purposes). This requirement is often referred to as the **LIFO conformity rule**. Other inventory valuation methods do not have this requirement.

Major Disadvantages of LIFO Approaches
Despite its advantages, LIFO has the following drawbacks.

Reduced Earnings   Many corporate managers view the lower profits reported under the LIFO method in inflationary times as a distinct disadvantage. They would rather have higher reported profits than lower taxes. Some fear that an accounting change to LIFO may be misunderstood by investors and that, as a result of the lower profits, the price of the company's stock will fall. In fact, though, there is some evidence to refute this contention.

It is questionable whether companies should switch from LIFO to FIFO for the sole purpose of increasing reported earnings.[18] Intuitively one would assume that

---

[16]In periods of rising prices, the use of fewer pools will translate into greater income tax benefits through the use of LIFO. The use of fewer pools allows inventory reductions of some items to be offset by inventory increases in others. In contrast, the use of more pools increases the likelihood that old, low-cost inventory layers will be liquidated and tax consequences will be negative. See Reeve and Stanga, ibid., pp. 28–29.

[17]Management often selects an accounting procedure because a lower tax results from its use, instead of an accounting method that is conceptually more appealing. Throughout this textbook, an effort has been made to identify accounting procedures that provide income tax benefits to the user.

[18]Because of steady or falling raw materials costs and costs savings from electronic data interchange and just-in-time technologies in recent years, many businesses using LIFO are no longer experiencing substantial tax benefits from LIFO. Even some companies for which LIFO is creating a benefit are finding that the administrative costs associated with LIFO are higher than the LIFO benefit obtained. As a result, some companies are deciding to move to FIFO or average cost.

companies with higher reported earnings would have a higher share (common stock price) valuation. Some studies have indicated, however, that the users of financial data exhibit a much higher sophistication than might be expected. Share prices are the same and, in some cases, even higher under LIFO in spite of lower reported earnings.[19]

The concern about reduced income resulting from adoption of LIFO has even less substance now because the IRS has relaxed the LIFO conformity rule which required a company that employed LIFO for tax purposes to use it for book purposes as well. The IRS has relaxed restrictions against providing non-LIFO income numbers as supplementary information. As a result, the profession now permits supplemental non-LIFO disclosures. The supplemental disclosure, while not intended to override the basic LIFO method adopted for financial reporting, may be useful in comparing operating income and working capital with companies not on LIFO.

Inventory Understated LIFO may have a distorting effect on a company's balance sheet. The inventory valuation is normally outdated because the oldest costs remain in inventory. This understatement makes the working capital position of the company appear worse than it really is.

The magnitude and direction of this variation between the carrying amount of inventory and its current price depend on the degree and direction of the price changes and the amount of inventory turnover. The combined effect of rising product prices and avoidance of inventory liquidations increases the difference between the inventory carrying value at LIFO and current prices of that inventory, thereby magnifying the balance sheet distortion attributed to the use of LIFO.

COMPARING APPLES TO APPLES

WHAT DO THE NUMBERS MEAN?

A common ratio used by investors to evaluate a company's liquidity is the current ratio, which is computed as current assets divided by current liabilities. A higher current ratio indicates that a company is better able to meet its current obligations when they come due. However, it is not meaningful to compare the current ratio for a company using LIFO to one for a company using FIFO. It would be like comparing apples to oranges, since inventory (and cost of goods sold) would be measured differently for the two companies.

The LIFO reserve can be used to make the current ratio comparable on an apples to apples basis. To make the LIFO company comparable to the FIFO company, the following adjustments should do the trick:

> Inventory Adjustment: LIFO inventory + LIFO reserve = FIFO inventory

(For cost of goods sold, the *change* in the LIFO reserve is added to LIFO cost of goods sold to yield the comparable FIFO amount.)

For **Brown Shoe, Inc.** (see Illustration 8-11), with current assets of $487.8 million and current liabilities of $217.8 million, the current ratio using LIFO is: $487.8 ÷ $217.8 = 2.2. After adjusting for the LIFO effect, Brown's current ratio under FIFO would be: ($487.8 + $11.7) ÷ $217.8 = 2.3.

Thus, without the LIFO adjustment, the Brown Shoe current ratio is understated.

---

[19]See, for example, Shyam Sunder, "Relationship Between Accounting Changes and Stock Prices: Problems of Measurement and Some Empirical Evidence," *Empirical Research in Accounting: Selected Studies, 1973* (Chicago: University of Chicago), pp. 1–40. But see Robert Moren Brown, "Short-Range Market Reaction to Changes to LIFO Accounting Using Preliminary Earnings Announcement Dates," *The Journal of Accounting Research* (Spring 1980), which found that companies that do change to LIFO suffer a short-run decline in the price of their stock.

Physical Flow LIFO does not approximate the physical flow of the items except in peculiar situations (such as the coal pile). Originally LIFO could be used only in certain circumstances. This situation has changed over the years to the point where physical flow characteristics no longer play an important role in determining whether LIFO may be employed.

Involuntary Liquidation/Poor Buying Habits If the base or layers of old costs are eliminated, strange results can occur because old, irrelevant costs can be matched against current revenues. A distortion in reported income for a given period may result, as well as consequences that are detrimental from an income tax point of view.[20]

Because of the liquidation problem, LIFO may cause poor buying habits. A company may simply purchase more goods and match these goods against revenue to ensure that the old costs are not charged to expense. Furthermore, the possibility always exists with LIFO that a company will attempt to manipulate its net income at the end of the year simply by altering its pattern of purchases.[21]

One survey uncovered the following reasons why companies reject LIFO.[22]

Illustration 8-18
Why Do Companies Reject LIFO? Summary of Responses

INTERNATIONAL
INSIGHT

Despite an effort to eliminate it, LIFO remains acceptable under international accounting standards.

Reasons to Reject LIFO	Number	% of Total*
No expected tax benefits		
No required tax payment	34	16%
Declining prices	31	15
Rapid inventory turnover	30	14
Immaterial inventory	26	12
Miscellaneous tax related	38	17
	159	74%
Regulatory or other restrictions	26	12%
Excessive cost		
High administrative costs	29	14%
LIFO liquidation–related costs	12	6
	41	20%
Other adverse consequences		
Lower reported earnings	18	8%
Bad accounting	7	3
	25	11%

*Percentage totals more than 100% as some companies offered more than one explanation.

Often the inventory methods are used in combination with other methods. For example, most companies never use LIFO totally, but rather use it in combination with other valuation approaches. One reason is that certain product lines can be highly susceptible to deflation instead of inflation. In addition, if the level of inventory is unstable, unwanted involuntary liquidations may result in certain product lines if LIFO is used. Finally, where inventory turnover in certain product lines is high, the additional

---

[20]The AICPA Task Force on LIFO Inventory Problems recommends that the effects on income of LIFO inventory liquidations be disclosed in the notes to the financial statements, but that the effects not receive special treatment in the income statement. *Issues Paper* (New York: AICPA, 1984), pp. 36–37.

[21]For example, one reason why **General Tire and Rubber** at one time accelerated raw material purchases at the end of the year was to minimize the book profit from a liquidation of LIFO inventories and to minimize income taxes for the year.

[22]Michael H. Granof and Daniel Short, "Why Do Companies Reject LIFO?" *Journal of Accounting, Auditing, and Finance* (Summer 1984), pp. 323–333, Table 1, p. 327.

recordkeeping and expense are not justified by LIFO. Average cost is often used in such cases because it is easy to compute.[23]

This variety of inventory methods has been devised to assist in accurate computation of net income rather than to permit manipulation of reported income. Hence, it is recommended that the pricing method most suitable to a company be selected and, once selected, be applied consistently thereafter. If conditions indicate that the inventory pricing method in use is unsuitable, serious consideration should be given to all other possibilities before selecting another method. Any change should be clearly explained and its effect disclosed in the financial statements.

To improve comparability of its LIFO inventory amounts, **JC Penney, Inc.** presented the following information in its Annual Report.

JC PENNEY, INC.

Some companies in the retail industry use the FIFO method in valuing part or all of their inventories. Had JC Penney used the FIFO method and made no other assumptions with respect to changes in income resulting therefrom, income and income per share from continuing operations would have been:

Income from continuing operations (in millions)	$325
Income from continuing operations per share	$4.63

Illustration 8-19
Supplemental Non-LIFO Disclosure

LOWER OF COST OR MARKET

Inventories are recorded at their cost. However, a major departure from the historical cost principle is made in the area of inventory valuation if inventory declines in value below its original cost. Whatever the reason for a decline—obsolescence, price-level changes, damaged goods, and so forth—the inventory should be written down to reflect this loss. **The general rule is that the historical cost principle is abandoned when the future utility (revenue-producing ability) of the asset is no longer as great as its original cost.**

Inventories that experience a decline in utility are valued therefore on the basis of the lower of cost or market, instead of on an original cost basis. **Cost** is the acquisition price of inventory computed using one of the historical cost-based methods—specific identification, average cost, FIFO, or LIFO. The term **market** in the phrase "the lower of cost or market" (LCM) generally means the cost to replace the item by purchase or reproduction. In a retailing business the term "market" refers to the market in which goods were purchased, not the market in which they are sold. In manufacturing, the term "market" refers to the cost to reproduce. Thus the rule really means that **goods are to be valued at cost or cost to replace, whichever is lower.** For example, a **Casio** calculator wristwatch that costs a retailer $30.00 when purchased, that can be sold for $48.95, and that can be replaced for $25.00 should be valued at $25.00 for inventory purposes under the lower of cost or market rule. The lower of cost or market rule of valuation can be used after any of the cost flow methods discussed above have been applied to determine the inventory cost.

A departure from cost is justified because **a loss of utility should be charged against revenues in the period in which the loss occurs**, not in the period in which it is sold.

OBJECTIVE 9
Explain and apply the lower of cost or market rule.

UNDERLYING CONCEPTS

The use of the lower of cost or market rule is an excellent example of the conservatism constraint.

---

[23]For an interesting discussion of the reasons for and against the use of FIFO and average cost, see Michael H. Granof and Daniel G. Short "For Some Companies, FIFO Accounting Makes Sense," *Wall Street Journal* (August 30, 1982), and the subsequent rebuttal by Gary C. Biddle "Taking Stock of Inventory Accounting Choices," *Wall Street Journal* (September 15, 1982).

In addition, the lower of cost or market method is **a conservative approach to inventory valuation**. That is, when doubt exists about the value of an asset, it is preferable to undervalue rather than to overvalue it.

Lower of Cost or Market—Ceiling and Floor

Why use replacement cost to represent market value? The reason is that a decline in the replacement cost of an item usually reflects or predicts a decline in selling price. Using replacement cost allows a company to maintain a consistent rate of gross profit on sales (normal profit margin). Sometimes, however, a reduction in the replacement cost of an item does not indicate a corresponding reduction in its utility. Then, two additional valuation limitations are used to value ending inventory—net realizable value and net realizable value less a normal profit margin.

Net realizable value (NRV) is defined as the estimated selling price in the ordinary course of business less reasonably predictable costs of completion and disposal. A normal profit margin is subtracted from that amount to arrive at **net realizable value less a normal profit margin**.

To illustrate, assume that Jerry Mander Corp. has unfinished inventory with a sales value of $1,000, estimated cost of completion of $300, and a normal profit margin of 10 percent of sales. The following net realizable value can be determined.

Illustration 8-20
Computation of Net Realizable Value

Inventory—sales value	$1,000
Less: Estimated cost of completion and disposal	300
Net realizable value	700
Less: Allowance for normal profit margin (10% of sales)	100
Net realizable value less a normal profit margin	$ 600

The general rule of lower of cost or market is: Inventory is valued at the lower of cost or market, with market limited to an amount that is not more than net realizable value or less than net realizable value less a normal profit margin.[24]

What is the rationale for these two limitations? The **upper (ceiling)** and **lower (floor) limits** for the value of the inventory are intended to prevent the inventory from being reported at an amount in excess of the net selling price or at an amount less than the net selling price less a normal profit margin. The maximum limitation, **not to exceed the net realizable value (ceiling)**, covers obsolete, damaged, or shopworn material and prevents overstatement of inventories and understatement of the loss in the current period. That is, if the replacement cost of an item is greater than its net realizable value, inventory should not be reported at replacement cost because the company can receive only the selling price less cost of disposal. To report the inventory at replacement cost would result in an overstatement of inventory and an understated loss in the current period.

To illustrate, assume that **Staples** paid $1,000 for a laser printer that can now be replaced for $900 and whose net realizable value is $700. At what amount should the laser printer be reported in the financial statements? To report the replacement cost of $900 overstates the ending inventory and understates the loss for the period. The printer should, therefore, be reported at $700.

The minimum limitation is **not to be less than net realizable value reduced by an allowance for an approximately normal profit margin (floor)**. This deters understatement of inventory and overstatement of the loss in the current period. It establishes a floor below which the inventory should not be priced regardless of replace-

[24]"Restatement and Revision of Accounting Research Bulletins," *Accounting Research Bulletin No. 43* (New York: AICPA, 1953), Ch. 4, par. 8.

ment cost. It makes no sense to price inventory below net realizable value less a normal margin because this minimum amount (floor) measures what the company can receive for the inventory and still earn a normal profit. These guidelines are illustrated graphically in Illustration 8-21.

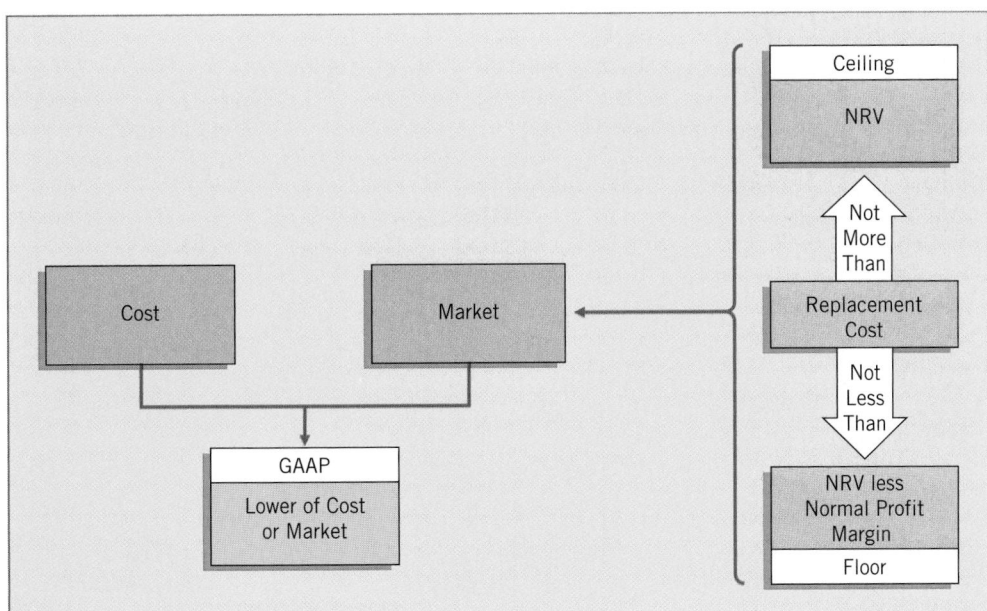

Illustration 8-21
Inventory Valuation—
Lower of Cost or Market

How Lower of Cost or Market Works

The amount that is compared to cost, often referred to as **designated market value**, is **always the middle value of three amounts**: replacement cost, net realizable value, and net realizable value less a normal profit margin. To illustrate how designated market value is computed, assume the following information relative to the inventory of Regner Foods, Inc.

Illustration 8-22
Computation of
Designated Market Value

Food	Replacement Cost	Net Realizable Value (Ceiling)	Net Realizable Value Less a Normal Profit Margin (Floor)	Designated Market Value
Spinach	$ 88,000	$120,000	$104,000	$104,000
Carrots	90,000	100,000	70,000	90,000
Cut beans	45,000	40,000	27,500	40,000
Peas	36,000	72,000	48,000	48,000
Mixed vegetables	105,000	92,000	80,000	92,000

Designated Market Value Decision:

Spinach	Net realizable value less a normal profit margin is selected because it is the middle value.
Carrots	Replacement cost is selected because it is the middle value.
Cut beans	Net realizable value is selected because it is the middle value.
Peas	Net realizable value less a normal profit margin is selected because it is the middle value.
Mixed vegetables	Net realizable value is selected because it is the middle value.

Designated market value is then compared to cost to determine the lower of cost or market. To illustrate, the final inventory value for Regner Foods is determined as follows.

Illustration 8-23
Determining Final Inventory Value

Food	Cost	Replace-ment Cost	Net Realizable Value (Ceiling)	Net Realizable Value Less a Normal Profit Margin (Floor)	Designated Market Value	Final Inventory Value
Spinach	$ 80,000	$ 88,000	$120,000	$104,000	$104,000	$ 80,000
Carrots	100,000	90,000	100,000	70,000	90,000	90,000
Cut beans	50,000	45,000	40,000	27,500	40,000	40,000
Peas	90,000	36,000	72,000	48,000	48,000	48,000
Mixed vegetables	95,000	105,000	92,000	80,000	92,000	92,000
						$350,000

Final Inventory Value:

Spinach	Cost ($80,000) is selected because it is lower than designated market value (net realizable value less a normal profit margin).
Carrots	Designated market value (replacement cost, $90,000) is selected because it is lower than cost.
Cut beans	Designated market value (net realizable value, $40,000) is selected because it is lower than cost.
Peas	Designated market value (net realizable value less a normal profit margin, $48,000) is selected because it is lower than cost.
Mixed vegetables	Designated market value (net realizable value, $92,000) is selected because it is lower than cost.

The application of the lower of cost or market rule incorporates only losses in value that occur in the normal course of business from such causes as style changes, shift in demand, or regular shop wear. Damaged or deteriorated goods are reduced to net realizable value. When material, such goods may be carried in separate inventory accounts.

Methods of Applying Lower of Cost or Market

In the Regner Foods illustration, we assumed that the lower of cost or market rule was applied to each individual type of food. However, the lower of cost or market rule may be applied either directly to each item, to each category, or to the total of the inventory. Increases in market prices tend to offset decreases in market prices, if a major category or total inventory approach is followed in applying the lower of cost or market rule. To illustrate, assume that Regner Foods separates its food products into two major categories, frozen and canned, as shown in Illustration 8-24 (next page).

If the lower of cost or market rule is applied to individual items, the amount of inventory is $350,000. If the rule is applied to major categories, it is $370,000. If LCM is applied to the total inventory, it is $374,000. The reason for the difference is that market values higher than cost are offset against market values lower than cost when the major categories or total inventory approach is adopted. For Regner Foods, the high market value for spinach is partially offset when the major categories approach is adopted, and it is totally offset when the total inventory approach is used.

The most common practice is to price the inventory on an item-by-item basis. For one thing, tax rules require that an individual-item basis be used unless doing so in-

	Cost	Designated Market	**Lower of Cost or Market By:**		
			Individual Items	Major Categories	Total Inventory
Frozen					
Spinach	$ 80,000	$104,000	$ 80,000		
Carrots	100,000	90,000	90,000		
Cut beans	50,000	40,000	40,000		
Total frozen	230,000	234,000		$230,000	
Canned					
Peas	90,000	48,000	48,000		
Mixed vegetables	95,000	92,000	92,000		
Total canned	185,000	140,000		140,000	
Total	$415,000	$374,000	$350,000	$370,000	$374,000

Illustration 8-24
Alternative Applications of Lower of Cost or Market

volves practical difficulties. In addition, the individual-item approach gives the most conservative valuation for balance sheet purposes.[25] Inventory is often priced on a total-inventory basis when there is only one end product (comprised of many different raw materials), because the main concern is the pricing of the final inventory. If several end products are produced, a category approach might be used. The method selected should be the one that most clearly reflects income. **Whichever method is selected, it should be applied consistently from one period to another.**[26]

Evaluation of the Lower of Cost or Market Rule

The lower of cost or market rule suffers some conceptual deficiencies:

1. Decreases in the value of the asset and the charge to expense are recognized in the period in which the loss in utility occurs—not in the period of sale. On the other hand, increases in the value of the asset are recognized only at the point of sale. This treatment is inconsistent and can lead to distortions in income data.

2. Application of the rule results in inconsistency because the inventory of a company may be valued at cost in one year and at market in the next year.

3. Lower of cost or market values the inventory in the balance sheet conservatively, but its effect on the income statement may or may not be conservative. Net income for the year in which the loss is taken is definitely lower. Net income of the subsequent period may be higher than normal if the expected reductions in sales price do not materialize.

4. Application of the lower of cost or market rule uses a "normal profit" in determining inventory values. Since "normal profit" is an estimated figure based

UNDERLYING CONCEPTS

The inconsistency in the presentation of inventory is an example of the trade-off between *relevancy* and *reliability*. Market is more relevant than cost, and cost is more reliable than market. Apparently, relevance takes precedence in a down market, and reliability is more important than relevancy in an up market.

[25]If a company uses dollar-value LIFO, determining the LIFO cost of an individual item may be more difficult. The company might decide that it is more appropriate to apply the lower of cost or market rule to the total amount of each pool. The AICPA Task Force on LIFO Inventory Problems concluded that the most reasonable approach to applying the lower of cost or market provisions to LIFO inventories is to base the determination on reasonable groupings of items and that a pool constitutes a reasonable grouping.

[26]Inventory accounting for financial statement purposes can be different from income tax purposes. For example, the lower of cost or market rule cannot be used with LIFO for tax purposes. There is nothing, however, to prevent the use of the lower of cost or market and LIFO for financial accounting purposes.

upon past experience (and might not be attained in the future), it is not objective in nature and presents an opportunity for income manipulation.

Many financial statement users appreciate the lower of cost or market rule because they at least know that the inventory is not overstated. In addition, recognizing all losses but anticipating no gains generally results in lower income.

WHAT DO THE NUMBERS MEAN?

ALL ITS BERRIES IN ONE BASKET

The latest quarter has not been very good for **Northland Cranberries**. The Wisconsin cranberry producer reported lower sales compared to the same quarter in the prior year and an operating loss:

	Current Quarter	Same Quarter, Prior Year
Revenues	$61,206,000	$76,609,000
Net income	(79,846,000)	3,577,000

Things are so bad that Northland is in violation of several debt covenants and looking to sell assets in order to generate cash for paying it debts.

What is behind these dismal numbers? Northland cites declining market prices for cranberries which have led the company to take an inventory write-down of $30.4 million in the current quarter. All companies in this industry are affected by declining market prices for cranberries, but Northland is particularly vulnerable because so much of its business is concentrated in the cranberry market. What's more, Northland is a small competitor in a cranberry and juice market dominated by major producers, such as **Ocean Spray**, **Tropicana** (owned by **PepsiCo**), and **Minute-Maid** (owned by **Coca-Cola**). These large producers are able to withstand market pressures in the cranberry market with sales in other juices and beverages. Northland must take its lumps in the cranberry market with inventory write-downs and operating losses.

PRESENTATION AND ANALYSIS

Presentation of Inventories

OBJECTIVE 10
Explain how inventory is reported and analyzed.

Accounting standards require financial statement disclosure of the composition of the inventory, inventory financing arrangements, and the inventory costing methods employed. The standards also require the consistent application of costing methods from one period to another.

Manufacturers should report the inventory composition either in the balance sheet or in a separate schedule in the notes. The relative mix of raw materials, work in process, and finished goods is important in assessing liquidity and in computing the stage of inventory completion.

Significant or unusual financing arrangements relating to inventories may require note disclosure. Examples are: transactions with related parties, product financing arrangements, firm purchase commitments, involuntary liquidation of LIFO inventories, and pledging of inventories as collateral. Inventories pledged as collateral for a loan should be presented in the current assets section rather than as an offset to the liability.

The basis upon which inventory amounts are stated (lower of cost or market) and the method used in determining cost (LIFO, FIFO, average cost, etc.) should also be reported. For example, the annual report of **Mumford of Wyoming** contains the following disclosures.

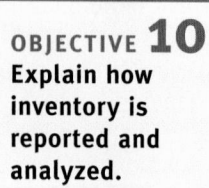

Additional Inventory Disclosures

MUMFORD OF WYOMING

Note A: Significant Accounting Policies

Live feeder cattle and feed—last-in, first-out (LIFO) cost, which is below approximate market	$854,800
Live range cattle—lower of principally identified cost or market	$1,240,500
Live sheep and supplies—lower of first-in, first-out (FIFO) cost or market	$674,000
Dressed meat and by-products—principally at market less allowances for distribution and selling expenses	$362,630

Illustration 8-25
Disclosure of Inventory Methods

The preceding illustration shows that a company can use different pricing methods for different elements of its inventory. If Mumford changes the method of pricing any of its inventory elements, a change in accounting principle must be reported. For example, if Mumford changes its method of accounting for live sheep from FIFO to average cost, this change, along with the effect on income, should be separately reported in the financial statements. Changes in accounting principle require an explanatory paragraph in the auditor's report describing the change in method.

Fortune Brands, Inc. reported its inventories in its Annual Report as follows (note the "trade practice" followed in classifying inventories among the current assets).

FORTUNE BRANDS, INC.

Current assets	
Inventories (Note 2)	
Leaf tobacco	$ 563,424,000
Bulk whiskey	232,759,000
Other raw materials, supplies and work in process	238,906,000
Finished products	658,326,000
	1,693,415,000

Note 2: Inventories
Inventories are priced at the lower of cost (average; first-in, first-out; and minor amounts at last-in, first-out) or market. In accordance with generally recognized trade practice, the leaf tobacco and bulk whiskey inventories are classified as current assets, although part of such inventories due to the duration of the aging process, ordinarily will not be sold within one year.

Illustration 8-26
Disclosure of Trade Practice in Valuing Inventories

Analysis of Inventories

As illustrated in the opening story, the amount of inventory that a company carries can have significant economic consequences. As a result, inventories must be managed. But, inventory management is a double-edged sword that requires constant attention. On the one hand, management wants to have a great variety and quantity on hand so customers have the greatest selection and always find what they want in stock. However, such an inventory policy may incur excessive carrying costs (e.g., investment, storage, insurance, taxes, obsolescence, and damage). On the other hand, low inventory levels lead to stockouts, lost sales, and disgruntled customers. Financial ratios can be used to help chart a middle course between these two dangers. Common ratios used in the management and evaluation of inventory levels are inventory turnover and a related measure, average days to sell the inventory.

The **inventory turnover ratio** measures the number of times on average the inventory was sold during the period. Its purpose is to measure the liquidity of the inventory. The inventory turnover is computed by dividing the cost of goods sold by the average inventory on hand during the period. Unless seasonal factors are significant, average inventory can be computed from the beginning and ending inventory balances. For example, in its 2001 annual report **Kellogg Company** reported a beginning inventory of $443.8 million, an ending inventory of $574.5 million, and cost of goods sold of $4,129 million for the year. The inventory turnover formula and Kellogg Company's 2001 ratio computation are shown below.

Illustration 8-27
Inventory Turnover Ratio

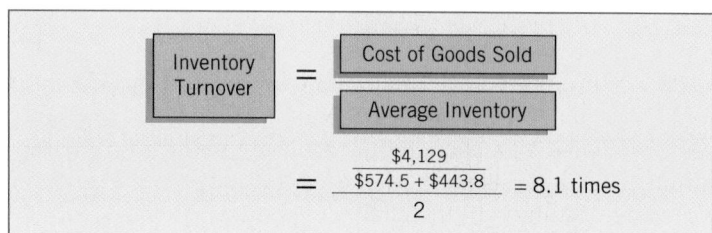

A variant of the inventory turnover ratio is the **average days to sell inventory**. This measure represents the average number of days' sales for which inventory is on hand. For example, the inventory turnover for Kellogg Company of 8.1 times divided into 365 is approximately 45.1 days.

There are typical levels of inventory in every industry. However, companies that are able to keep their inventory at lower levels with higher turnovers than those of their competitors, and still satisfy customer needs, are the most successful.

SUMMARY OF LEARNING OBJECTIVES

KEY TERMS

average cost method, *354*
average days to sell
    inventory, *374*
consigned goods, *350*
cost flow assumptions, *353*
designated market value,
    369
dollar-value LIFO, *360*
finished goods inventory,
    346
first-in, first-out (FIFO)
    method, *355*
f.o.b. destination, *350*
f.o.b. shipping point, *350*
inventories, *346*
inventory turnover ratio, *374*
last-in, first-out (LIFO)
    method, *356*
LIFO effect, *357*
LIFO liquidation, *358*
LIFO reserve, *357*

❶ Identify major classifications of inventory. Only one inventory account, Merchandise Inventory, appears in the financial statements of a merchandising concern. A manufacturer normally has three inventory accounts: Raw Materials, Work in Process, and Finished Goods. The cost assigned to goods and materials on hand but not yet placed into production is reported as raw materials inventory. The cost of the raw materials on which production has been started but not completed, plus the direct labor cost applied specifically to this material and a ratable share of manufacturing overhead costs, constitute the work in process inventory. The costs identified with the completed but unsold units on hand at the end of the fiscal period are reported as finished goods inventory.

❷ Distinguish between perpetual and periodic inventory systems. Under a perpetual inventory system, a continuous record of changes in inventory is maintained in the Inventory account. That is, all purchases and sales (issues) of goods are recorded directly in the Inventory account as they occur. Under a periodic inventory system, the quantity of inventory on hand is determined only periodically. The Inventory account remains the same and a Purchases account is debited. Cost of goods sold is determined at the end of the period using a formula. Ending inventory is ascertained by physical count.

❸ Identify the items that should be included as inventory cost. Product costs are directly connected with the bringing of goods to the place of business of the buyer and converting such goods to a salable condition. Such charges would include freight charges on goods purchased, other direct costs of acquisition, and labor and other production costs incurred in processing the goods up to the time of sale. Manufacturing overhead costs are also allocated to inventory. These costs include indirect materials, indirect labor, and such items as depreciation, taxes, insurance, heat, and electricity incurred in the manufacturing process.

④ Describe and compare the cost flow assumptions used in accounting for inventories. (1) *Average cost* prices items in the inventory on the basis of the average cost of all similar goods available during the period. (2) *First-in, first-out (FIFO)* assumes that goods are used in the order in which they are purchased. The inventory remaining must therefore represent the most recent purchases. (3) *Last-in, first-out (LIFO)* matches the cost of the last goods purchased against revenue.

⑤ Explain the significance and use of a LIFO reserve. The difference between the inventory method used for internal reporting purposes and LIFO is referred to as the Allowance to Reduce Inventory to LIFO, or the LIFO reserve. Either the LIFO reserve or the replacement cost of the inventory should be disclosed in the financial statements.

⑥ Explain the effect of LIFO liquidations. The effect of LIFO liquidations is that costs from preceding periods are matched against sales revenues reported in current dollars. This leads to a distortion in net income and a substantial tax bill in the current period. LIFO liquidations can occur frequently when a specific goods LIFO approach is employed.

⑦ Explain the dollar-value LIFO method. An important feature of the dollar-value LIFO method is that increases and decreases in a pool are determined and measured in terms of total dollar value, not the physical quantity of the goods in the inventory pool.

⑧ Identify the major advantages and disadvantages of LIFO. The major advantages of LIFO are the following: (1) Recent costs are matched against current revenues to provide a better measure of current earnings. (2) As long as the price level increases and inventory quantities do not decrease, a deferral of income tax occurs in LIFO. (3) Because of the deferral of income tax, there is improvement of cash flow. Major disadvantages are: (1) reduced earnings, (2) understated inventory, and (3) no approximated physical flow of the items except in peculiar situations.

⑨ Explain and apply the lower of cost or market rule. If inventory declines in value below its original cost for whatever reason, the inventory should be written down to reflect this loss. The general rule is that the historical cost principle is abandoned when the future utility (revenue-producing ability) of the asset is no longer as great as its original cost.

⑩ Explain how inventory is reported and analyzed. Accounting standards require financial statement disclosure of: (1) the composition of the inventory (in the balance sheet or a separate schedule in the notes); (2) significant or unusual inventory financing arrangements; and (3) inventory costing methods employed (which may differ for different elements of inventory). Accounting standards also require the consistent application of costing methods from one period to another. Common ratios used in the management and evaluation of inventory levels are inventory turnover and a related measure, average days to sell the inventory.

lower (floor) limit, *368*
lower of cost or market (LCM), *368*
market (for LCM), *367*
merchandise inventory, *346*
moving-average method, *355*
net realizable value (NRV), *368*
net realizable value less a normal profit margin, *368*
period costs, *351*
periodic inventory system, *348*
perpetual inventory system, *347*
product costs, *351*
raw materials inventory, *346*
specific goods pooled LIFO approach, *359*
specific identification, *353*
upper (ceiling) limit, *368*
weighted-average method, *354*
work in process inventory, *346*

REVIEW EXERCISE

Norwel Company makes miniature circuit boards that are components of wireless phones and personal organizers. The company has experienced strong growth, and you are especially interested in how well Norwel is managing its inventory balances. You have collected the following information for the current year.

Inventory at the beginning of year	$125.5 million
Inventory at the end of year, before any adjustments	$116.7 million
Total cost of goods sold, before any adjustments	$1,776.4 million

The company values inventory at lower of cost (using LIFO cost flow assumption) or market.

Instructions

(a) Compute Norwel's inventory turnover ratio.

(b) Recompute the inventory turnover ratio after adjusting Norwel's inventory information for the following items.

1. During the year, Norwel recorded sales and costs of goods sold on $2 million of units shipped to various wholesalers on consignment. At year-end, none of these units have been sold by wholesalers.

2. Shipping contracts changed 2 months ago from f.o.b. shipping point to f.o.b. destination point. At the end of the year, $5 million of products are en route to China (and will not arrive until after financial statements are released). Current inventory balances do not reflect this change in policy.

3. At the end of the year, a certain section of inventory with an historical cost of $12 million was determined to have a replacement cost of $10.8 million; net realizable value of $10.0 million; and net realizable value less a normal profit margin of $9.4 million.

4. To be more consistent with industry inventory valuation practices, Norwel changed from LIFO to FIFO for its inventory of high-speed circuit boards. This inventory is currently carried at $724 million (cost of goods sold, $941 million). Data for this item of inventory for the year are as follows.

Month	Units purchased	Inventory sold	Price per unit	Units balance
January 1	100		$3.10	100
April 10	150		3.20	250
October 20		130		120
November 20	250		3.50	370
December 15		150		220

SOLUTION TO REVIEW EXERCISE

(a) $\dfrac{\$1,776.4}{(\$125.5 + \$116.7)/2} = 14.7$ times

(b) Adjustments to ending inventory

Item	Adjustment to Ending Inventory ($000,000)	Explanation
1. Consigned goods	$2	Norwel should count the goods it has consigned in other stores.
2. Goods in transit	$5	Goods officially change hands at the point of destination. Norwel should still show these goods in inventory (no cost of goods sold), until they reach the destination.

Item	Adjustment to Ending Inventory ($000,000)	Explanation
3. Lower of cost or market	$(2)	The correct valuation is $10.0 million since the market designation of $10.0 million is less than the original cost.
4. Change to FIFO	$46[a]	

[a]Circuit board ending inventory under LIFO: $724
  Circuit board ending inventory under FIFO: 220 @ $3.50 = $770
    Difference: $46 ($770 − $724)

$$\text{Adjusted inventory turnover ratio:} = \frac{\$1{,}725.4^{b}}{(\$125.5 + \$167.7)^{c}/2}$$

$$= 11.8 \text{ times}$$

[b]Cost of goods sold: $1,776.40 − $2 − $5 + $2 − $46 = $1,725.40
[c]Ending inventory: $116.7 + $2 + $5 − $2 + $46 = $167.7

GROSS PROFIT METHOD

OBJECTIVE 11

After studying Appendix 8A, you should be able to: Determine ending inventory by applying the gross profit method.

The basic purpose of taking a physical inventory is to verify the accuracy of the perpetual inventory records or, if no records exist, to arrive at an inventory amount. Sometimes, taking a physical inventory is impractical. In such cases, substitute measures are used to approximate inventory on hand. One substitute method of verifying or determining the inventory amount is called the gross profit method (also called the gross margin method).[1] This method is widely used by auditors in situations where only an estimate of the company's inventory is needed (e.g., interim reports). It is also used where either inventory or inventory records have been destroyed by fire or other catastrophe.

The **gross profit method** is based on three assumptions: (1) The beginning inventory plus purchases equal total goods to be accounted for. (2) Goods not sold must be on hand. And (3) if the sales, reduced to cost, are deducted from the sum of the opening inventory plus purchases, the result is the ending inventory.

To illustrate, assume that Cetus Corp. has a beginning inventory of $60,000 and purchases of $200,000, both at cost. Sales at selling price amount to $280,000. The gross profit on selling price is 30 percent. The gross margin method is applied as follows.

Illustration 8A-1

Application of Gross Profit Method

Beginning inventory (at cost)		$ 60,000
Purchases (at cost)		200,000
Goods available (at cost)		260,000
Sales (at selling price)	$280,000	
Less: Gross profit (30% of $280,000)	84,000	
Sales (at cost)		196,000
Approximate inventory (at cost)		$ 64,000

All the information needed to compute Cetus's inventory at cost, except for the gross profit percentage, is available in the current period's records. The gross profit percentage is determined by reviewing company policies or prior period records. In some cases, this percentage must be adjusted if prior periods are not considered representative of the current period.[2]

[1] An estimation method used in the retail industry, the retail method, is discussed in Appendix C at the end of the book.

[2] An alternative method of estimating inventory using the gross profit percentage, considered by some to be less complicated than the traditional method, uses the standard income statement format as follows. (Assume the same data as in the Cetus illustration above.)

Sales		$280,000		$280,000
Cost of sales				
Beginning inventory	$ 60,000		$ 60,000	
Purchases	200,000		200,000	
Goods available for sale	260,000		260,000	
Ending inventory	(3) ?		(3) 64,000 Est.	
Cost of goods sold		(2) ?		(2)196,000 Est.
Gross profit on sales (30%)		(1) ?		(1) 84,000 Est.

(footnote continues on next page)

COMPUTATION OF GROSS PROFIT PERCENTAGE

In most situations, the **gross profit percentage** is given as a percentage of selling price. The previous illustration, for example, used a 30 percent gross profit on sales. Gross profit on selling price is the common method for quoting the profit for several reasons: (1) Most goods are stated on a retail basis, not a cost basis. (2) A profit quoted on selling price is lower than one based on cost, and this lower rate gives a favorable impression to the consumer. (3) The gross profit based on selling price can never exceed 100 percent.[3]

In Illustration 8A-1, the gross profit was a given. But how was that figure derived? To see how a gross profit percentage is computed, assume that an article cost $15 and sells for $20, a gross profit of $5. This markup is ¼ or 25 percent of retail and ⅓ or 33⅓ percent of cost.

$$\frac{\text{Markup}}{\text{Retail}} = \frac{\$5}{\$20} = 25\% \text{ at retail} \qquad \frac{\text{Markup}}{\text{Cost}} = \frac{\$5}{\$15} = 33\tfrac{1}{3}\% \text{ on cost}$$

Illustration 8A-2
Computation of Gross Profit Percentage

Although it is normal to compute the gross profit on the basis of selling price, you should understand the basic relationship between markup on cost and markup on selling price.

For example, assume that you were told that the markup on cost for a given item is 25 percent. What, then, is the **gross profit on selling price**? To find the answer, assume that the selling price of the item is $1.00. In this case, the following formula applies.

$$
\begin{aligned}
\text{Cost} + \text{Gross profit} &= \text{Selling price} \\
C + .25C &= SP \\
(1 + .25)C &= SP \\
1.25C &= \$1.00 \\
C &= \$0.80
\end{aligned}
$$

The gross profit equals $0.20 ($1.00 − $0.80), and the rate of gross profit on selling price is therefore 20 percent ($0.20/$1.00).

Conversely, assume that you were told that the gross profit on selling price is 20 percent. What is the **markup on cost**? To find the answer, again assume that the selling price is $1.00. Again, the same formula holds:

Compute the unknowns as follows: first the gross profit amount, then cost of goods sold, and then the ending inventory, as shown below.

(1) $280,000 × 30% = $84,000 (gross profit on sales).
(2) $280,000 − $84,000 = $196,000 (cost of goods sold).
(3) $260,000 − $196,000 = $64,000 (ending inventory).

[3]The terms "gross margin percentage," "rate of gross profit," and "percentage markup" are synonymous, although "markup" is more commonly used in reference to cost and "gross profit" in reference to sales.

$$\text{Cost} + \text{Gross profit} = \text{Selling price}$$
$$C + .20SP = SP$$
$$C = (1 - .20)SP$$
$$C = .80SP$$
$$C = .80(\$1.00)$$
$$C = \$0.80$$

Here, as in the previous example, the markup equals $0.20 ($1.00 − $0.80), and the markup on cost is 25 percent ($0.20/$0.80).

Retailers use the following formulas to express these relationships:

Illustration 8A-3

Formulas Relating to Gross Profit

1. Gross profit on selling price $= \dfrac{\text{Percentage markup on cost}}{100\% + \text{Percentage markup on cost}}$

2. Percentage markup on cost $= \dfrac{\text{Gross profit on selling price}}{100\% - \text{Gross profit on selling price}}$

To understand how these formulas are employed, consider the following calculations.

Illustration 8A-4

Application of Gross Profit Formulas

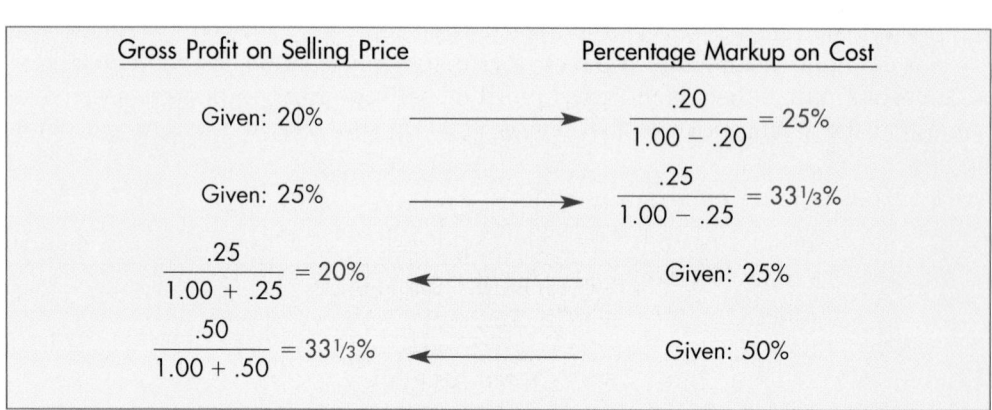

Because selling price is greater than cost, and with the gross profit amount the same for both, **gross profit on selling price will always be less than the related percentage based on cost**. It should be emphasized that sales may not be multiplied by a cost-based markup percentage; the gross profit percentage must be converted to a percentage based on selling price.

Gross profits are closely followed by managements and analysts. A small change in the gross profit rate can have a significant effect on the bottom line. In 1993, **Apple Computer** suffered a textbook case of shrinking gross profits. In response to pricing wars in the personal computer market, Apple was forced to quickly reduce the price of its signature Macintosh computers—reducing prices more quickly than it could reduce its costs. As a result its gross profit rate fell from 44 percent in 1992 to 40 percent in 1993. Though the drop of 4 percent may appear small, its impact on the bottom line caused Apple's stock price to drop from $57 per share on June 1, 1993, to $27.50 by mid-July 1993. A similar effect (a 40 percent plummet in stock price) occurred when **Woolworth Corp.** disclosed a "correction of gross profits" due to a reporting of inaccurate gross profits in at least three of the company's quarterly reports during the fiscal year ended January 29, 1994.[4]

[4]"Two Top Woolworth Officers Step Down Amid Probe of Accounting Irregularities," *Wall Street Journal* (April 4, 1994), p. A3.

EVALUATION OF GROSS PROFIT METHOD

What are the major disadvantages of the gross profit method? One major disadvantage is that **it provides an estimate**. As a result, a physical inventory must be taken once a year to verify the inventory that is actually on hand. Second, the gross profit method **uses past percentages** in determining the markup. Although the past can often provide answers to the future, a current rate is more appropriate. It is important to emphasize that whenever significant fluctuations occur, the percentage should be adjusted as appropriate. Third, **care must be taken in applying a blanket gross profit rate**. Frequently, a store or department handles merchandise with widely varying rates of gross profit. In these situations, the gross profit method may have to be applied by subsections, lines of merchandise, or a similar basis that classifies merchandise according to their respective rates of gross profit.

The gross profit method is not normally acceptable for financial reporting purposes because it provides only an estimate. A physical inventory is needed as additional verification that the inventory indicated in the records is actually on hand. Nevertheless, the gross profit method is permitted to determine ending inventory for interim (generally quarterly) reporting purposes, provided the use of this method is disclosed. Note that the gross profit method will follow closely the inventory method used (FIFO, LIFO, average cost) because it is based on historical records.

SUMMARY OF LEARNING OBJECTIVE FOR APPENDIX 8A

KEY TERMS

gross profit method, *378*
gross profit percentage, *379*

🔹 **Determine ending inventory by applying the gross profit method.** The steps to determine ending inventory by applying the gross profit method are as follows: (1) Compute the gross profit percentage on selling price. (2) Compute gross profit by multiplying net sales by the gross profit percentage. (3) Compute cost of goods sold by subtracting gross profit from net sales. (4) Compute ending inventory by subtracting cost of goods sold from total goods available for sale.

Note: All **asterisked** Questions, Brief Exercises, Exercises, Problems, and Conceptual Cases relate to material covered in the appendix to the chapter.

QUESTIONS

1 In what ways are the inventory accounts of a retailing concern different from those of a manufacturing enterprise?

2 Why should inventories be included in (a) a statement of financial position and (b) the computation of net income?

3 What is the difference between a perpetual inventory and a physical inventory? If a company maintains a perpetual inventory, should its physical inventory at any date be equal to the amount indicated by the perpetual inventory records? Why?

4 Mariah Carey Inc. indicated in a recent annual report that approximately $19 million of merchandise was received on consignment. Should Mariah Carey Inc. report this amount on its balance sheet? Explain.

5 Where, if at all, should the following items be classified on a balance sheet?

    (a) Goods out on approval to customers.

    (b) Goods in transit that were recently purchased f.o.b. destination.

    (c) Land held by a realty firm for sale.

    (d) Raw materials.

    (e) Goods received on consignment.

    (f) Manufacturing supplies.

6 Define "cost" as applied to the valuation of inventories.

7 Specific identification is sometimes said to be the ideal method of assigning cost to inventory and to cost of goods sold. Briefly indicate the arguments for and against this method of inventory valuation.

8 First-in, first-out; weighted average; and last-in, first-out methods are often used instead of specific identification for inventory valuation purposes. Compare these methods with the specific identification method, discussing the theoretical propriety of each method in the determination of income and asset valuation.

9 As compared with the FIFO method of costing inventories, does the LIFO method result in a larger or smaller net income in a period of rising prices? What is the comparative effect on net income in a period of falling prices?

10 What is the dollar-value method of LIFO inventory valuation? What advantage does the dollar-value method have over the specific goods approach of LIFO inventory valuation? Why will the traditional LIFO inventory costing method and the dollar-value LIFO inventory costing method produce different inventory valuations if the composition of the inventory base changes?

11 Explain the following terms:

(a) LIFO layer.

(b) LIFO reserve.

(c) LIFO effect.

12 On December 31, 2003, the inventory of Mario Lemieux Company amounts to $800,000. During 2004, the company decides to use the dollar-value LIFO method of costing inventories. On December 31, 2004, the inventory is $1,026,000 at December 31, 2004, prices. Using the December 31, 2003, price level of 100 and the December 31, 2004, price level of 108, compute the inventory value at December 31, 2004, under the dollar-value LIFO method.

13 In an article that appeared in the *Wall Street Journal*, the phrases "phantom (paper) profits" and "high LIFO profits" through involuntary liquidation were used. Explain these phrases.

14 Where there is evidence that the utility of inventory goods, as part of their disposal in the ordinary course of business, will be less than cost, what is the proper accounting treatment?

15 Explain the rationale for the ceiling and floor in the lower of cost or market method of valuing inventories.

16 What approaches may be employed in applying the lower of cost or market procedure? Which approach is normally used and why?

17 In some instances accounting principles require a departure from valuing inventories at cost alone. Determine the proper unit inventory price in the following cases.

	Cases				
	1	2	3	4	5
Cost	$15.90	$16.10	$15.90	$15.90	$15.90
Net realizable value	14.30	19.20	15.20	10.40	16.40
Net realizable value less normal profit	12.80	17.60	13.75	8.80	14.80
Market (replacement cost)	14.80	17.20	12.80	9.70	16.80

18 Bodeans Company reported inventory in its balance sheet as follows:

> Inventories $115,756,800

What additional disclosures might be necessary to present the inventory fairly?

19 Of what significance is inventory turnover to a retail store?

*20 What are the major uses of the gross profit method?

*21 A fire destroys all of the merchandise of Rosanna Arquette Company on February 10, 2004. Presented below is information compiled up to the date of the fire.

Inventory, January 1, 2004	$ 400,000
Sales to February 10, 2004	1,750,000
Purchases to February 10, 2004	1,140,000
Freight-in to February 10, 2004	60,000
Rate of gross profit on selling price	40%

What is the approximate inventory on February 10, 2004?

BRIEF EXERCISES

BE8-1 Included in the December 31 trial balance of Billie Joel Company are the following assets.

Cash	$ 190,000	Work in process	$200,000
Equipment (net)	1,100,000	Receivables (net)	400,000
Prepaid insurance	41,000	Patents	110,000
Raw materials	335,000	Finished goods	150,000

Prepare the current assets section of the December 31 balance sheet.

BE8-2 Alanis Morrissette Company uses a perpetual inventory system. Its beginning inventory consists of 50 units that cost $30 each. During June, the company purchased 150 units at $30 each, returned 6 units for credit, and sold 125 units at $50 each. Journalize the June transactions.

BE8-3 Mayberry Company took a physical inventory on December 31 and determined that goods costing $200,000 were on hand. Not included in the physical count were $15,000 of goods purchased from Taylor Corporation, f.o.b. shipping point; and $22,000 of goods sold to Mount Pilot Company for $30,000, f.o.b. destination. Both the Taylor purchase and the Mount Pilot sale were in transit at year-end. What amount should Mayberry report as its December 31 inventory?

BE8-4 Jose Zorilla Company uses a periodic inventory system. For April, when the company sold 700 units, the following information is available.

	Units	Unit Cost	Total Cost
April 1 inventory	250	$10	$ 2,500
April 15 purchase	400	12	4,800
April 23 purchase	350	13	4,550
	1,000		$11,850

Compute the April 30 inventory and the April cost of goods sold using the average cost method.

BE8-5 Data for Jose Zorilla Company are presented in BE8-4. Compute the April 30 inventory and the April cost of goods sold using the FIFO method.

BE8-6 Data for Jose Zorilla Company are presented in BE8-4. Compute the April 30 inventory and the April cost of goods sold using the LIFO method.

BE8-7 Easy-E Company had ending inventory at end-of-year prices of $100,000 at December 31, 2002; $123,200 at December 31, 2003; and $134,560 at December 31, 2004. The year-end price indexes were 100 for 2002; 110 for 2003; and 116 for 2004. Compute the ending inventory for Easy-E Company for 2002 through 2004 using the dollar-value LIFO method.

BE8-8 Wingers uses the dollar-value LIFO method of computing its inventory. Data for the past 3 years follow. Compute the value of the 2002 and 2003 inventories using the dollar-value LIFO method.

Year Ended December 31	Inventory at Current-year Cost	Price Index
2001	$19,750	100
2002	21,708	108
2003	25,935	114

BE8-9 Presented below is information related to Alstott Inc.'s inventory.

(per unit)	Skis	Boots	Parkas
Historical cost	$190.00	$106.00	$53.00
Selling price	217.00	145.00	73.75
Cost to distribute	19.00	8.00	2.50
Current replacement cost	203.00	105.00	51.00
Normal profit margin	32.00	29.00	21.25

Determine the following: (a) the two limits to market value (i.e., the ceiling and the floor) that should be used in the lower of cost or market computation for skis; (b) the cost amount that should be used in the lower of cost or market comparison of boots; and (c) the market amount that should be used to value parkas on the basis of the lower of cost or market.

BE8-10 Robin Corporation has the following four items in its ending inventory.

Item	Cost	Replacement Cost	Net Realizable Value (NRV)	NRV Less Normal Profit Margin
Jokers	$2,000	$1,900	$2,100	$1,600
Penguins	5,000	5,100	4,950	4,100
Riddlers	4,400	4,550	4,625	3,700
Scarecrows	3,200	2,990	3,830	3,070

Determine the final lower of cost of market inventory value for each item.

BE8-11 In its 2000 Annual Report, **Deere and Company** reported inventory of $1,552.9 million on October 31, 2000, and $1,294.3 million on October 31, 1999, cost of goods sold of $8,936.1 million for fiscal year 2000, and net sales of $11,168.6 million. Compute Deere and Company's inventory turnover and the average days to sell inventory for the fiscal year 2000.

*BE8-12 Big Hurt Corporation's April 30 inventory was destroyed by fire. January 1 inventory was $150,000, and purchases for January through April totaled $500,000. Sales for the same period were $700,000. Big Hurt's normal gross profit percentage is 31%. Using the gross profit method, estimate Big Hurt's April 30 inventory that was destroyed by fire.

EXERCISES

E8-1 (Inventoriable Costs) Presented below is a list of items that may or may not be reported as inventory in a company's December 31 balance sheet.

1. Goods out on consignment at another company's store.
2. Goods sold on an installment basis.
3. Goods purchased f.o.b. shipping point that are in transit at December 31.
4. Goods purchased f.o.b. destination that are in transit at December 31.
5. Goods sold to another company, for which our company has signed an agreement to repurchase at a set price that covers all costs related to the inventory.
6. Goods sold f.o.b. shipping point that are in transit at December 31.
7. Freight charges on goods purchased.
8. Factory labor costs incurred on goods still unsold.
9. Interest costs incurred for inventories that are routinely manufactured.
10. Costs incurred to advertise goods held for resale.
11. Materials on hand not yet placed into production by a manufacturing firm.
12. Office supplies.
13. Raw materials on which a manufacturing firm has started production, but which are not completely processed.
14. Factory supplies.
15. Goods held on consignment from another company.
16. Costs identified with units completed by a manufacturing firm, but not yet sold.
17. Goods sold f.o.b. destination that are in transit at December 31.
18. Temporary investments in stocks and bonds that will be resold in the near future.

Instructions
Indicate which of these items would typically be reported as inventory in the financial statements. If an item should **not** be reported as inventory, indicate how it should be reported in the financial statements.

E8-2 (Inventoriable Costs) In your audit of Jose Oliva Company, you find that a physical inventory on December 31, 2002, showed merchandise with a cost of $441,000 was on hand at that date. You also discover the following items were all excluded from the $441,000.

1. Merchandise of $61,000 which is held by Oliva on consignment. The consignor is the Max Suzuki Company.
2. Merchandise costing $38,000 which was shipped by Oliva f.o.b. destination to a customer on December 31, 2002. The customer was expected to receive the merchandise on January 6, 2003.
3. Merchandise costing $46,000 which was shipped by Oliva f.o.b. shipping point to a customer on December 29, 2002. The customer was scheduled to receive the merchandise on January 2, 2003.
4. Merchandise costing $83,000 shipped by a vendor f.o.b. destination on December 30, 2002, and received by Oliva on January 4, 2003.
5. Merchandise costing $51,000 shipped by a vendor f.o.b. seller on December 31, 2002, and received by Oliva on January 5, 2003.

Instructions
Based on the above information, calculate the amount that should appear on Oliva's balance sheet at December 31, 2002, for inventory.

E8-3 **(Inventoriable Costs)** In an annual audit of Jan Matejko Company at December 31, 2004, you find the following transactions near the closing date.

1. A special machine, fabricated to order for a customer, was finished and specifically segregated in the back part of the shipping room on December 31, 2004. The customer was billed on that date and the machine excluded from inventory although it was shipped on January 4, 2005.

2. Merchandise costing $2,800 was received on January 3, 2005, and the related purchase invoice recorded January 5. The invoice showed the shipment was made on December 29, 2004, f.o.b. destination.

3. A packing case containing a product costing $3,400 was standing in the shipping room when the physical inventory was taken. It was not included in the inventory because it was marked "Hold for shipping instructions." Your investigation revealed that the customer's order was dated December 18, 2004, but that the case was shipped and the customer billed on January 10, 2005. The product was a stock item of your client.

4. Merchandise received on January 6, 2005, costing $680 was entered in the purchase journal on January 7, 2005. The invoice showed shipment was made f.o.b. supplier's warehouse on December 31, 2004. Because it was not on hand at December 31, it was not included in inventory.

5. Merchandise costing $720 was received on December 28, 2004, and the invoice was not recorded. You located it in the hands of the purchasing agent; it was marked "on consignment."

Instructions

Assuming that each of the amounts is material, state whether the merchandise should be included in the client's inventory. Give your reason for your decision on each item.

E8-4 **(Inventoriable Costs—Perpetual)** Colin Davis Machine Company maintains a general ledger account for each class of inventory, debiting such accounts for increases during the period and crediting them for decreases. The transactions below relate to the Raw Materials inventory account, which is debited for materials purchased and credited for materials requisitioned for use.

1. An invoice for $8,100, terms f.o.b. destination, was received and entered January 2, 2004. The receiving report shows that the materials were received December 28, 2003.

2. Materials costing $28,000, shipped f.o.b. destination, were not entered by December 31, 2003, "because they were in a railroad car on the company's siding on that date and had not been unloaded."

3. Materials costing $7,300 were returned to the creditor on December 29, 2003, and were shipped f.o.b. shipping point. The return was entered on that date, even though the materials are not expected to reach the creditor's place of business until January 6, 2004.

4. An invoice for $7,500, terms f.o.b. shipping point, was received and entered December 30, 2003. The receiving report shows that the materials were received January 4, 2004, and the bill of lading shows that they were shipped January 2, 2004.

5. Materials costing $19,800 were received December 30, 2003, but no entry was made for them because "they were ordered with a specified delivery of no earlier than January 10, 2004."

Instructions

Prepare correcting general journal entries required at December 31, 2003, assuming that the books have not been closed.

E8-5 **(Determining Merchandise Amounts—Periodic)** Two or more items are omitted in each of the following tabulations of income statement data. Fill in the amounts that are missing.

	2002	2003	2004
Sales	$290,000	$?	$410,000
Sales returns	11,000	13,000	?
Net sales	?	347,000	?
Beginning inventory	20,000	32,000	?
Ending inventory	?	?	?
Purchases	?	260,000	298,000
Purchase returns and allowances	5,000	8,000	10,000
Transportation-in	8,000	9,000	12,000
Cost of goods sold	233,000	?	293,000
Gross profit on sales	46,000	91,000	97,000

E8-6 (Financial Statement Presentation of Manufacturing Amounts—Periodic) Navajo Company is a manufacturing firm. Presented below is selected information from its 2003 accounting records.

Raw materials inventory, 1/1/03	$ 30,800	Transportation-out	$ 8,000
Raw materials inventory, 12/31/03	37,400	Selling expenses	300,000
Work in process inventory, 1/1/03	72,600	Administrative expenses	180,000
Work in process inventory, 12/31/03	61,600	Purchase discounts	10,640
Finished goods inventory, 1/1/03	35,200	Purchase returns and allowances	6,460
Finished goods inventory, 12/31/03	22,000	Interest expense	15,000
Purchases	278,600	Direct labor	440,000
Transportation-in	6,600	Manufacturing overhead	330,000

Instructions
(a) Compute raw materials used.
(b) Compute the cost of goods manufactured.
(c) Compute cost of goods sold.
(d) Indicate how inventories would be reported in the December 31, 2003, balance sheet.

E8-7 (Periodic versus Perpetual Entries) The Fong Sai-Yuk Company sells one product. Presented below is information for January for the Fong Sai-Yuk Company.

Jan.	2 Inventory	100 units at $5 each
	4 Sale	80 units at $8 each
	11 Purchase	150 units at $6 each
	13 Sale	120 units at $8.75 each
	20 Purchase	160 units at $7 each
	27 Sale	100 units at $9 each

Fong Sai-Yuk uses the FIFO cost flow assumption. All purchases and sales are on account.

Instructions
(a) Assume Fong Sai-Yuk uses a periodic system. Prepare all necessary journal entries, including the end-of-month closing entry to record cost of goods sold. A physical count indicates that the ending inventory for January is 110 units.
(b) Compute gross profit using the periodic system.
(c) Assume Fong Sai-Yuk uses a perpetual system. Prepare all necessary journal entries.
(d) Compute gross profit using the perpetual system.

E8-8 (FIFO and LIFO—Periodic and Perpetual) Inventory information for Part 311 of Monique Aaron Corp. discloses the following information for the month of June.

June	1 Balance	300 units @ $10	June 10 Sold	200 units @ $24
	11 Purchased	800 units @ $12	15 Sold	500 units @ $25
	20 Purchased	500 units @ $13	27 Sold	300 units @ $27

Instructions
(a) Assuming that the periodic inventory method is used, compute the cost of goods sold and ending inventory under (1) LIFO and (2) FIFO.
(b) Assuming that the perpetual inventory record is kept in dollars and costs are computed at the time of each withdrawal, what is the value of the ending inventory at LIFO?
(c) Assuming that the perpetual inventory record is kept in dollars and costs are computed at the time of each withdrawal, what is the gross profit if the inventory is valued at FIFO?
(d) Why is it stated that LIFO usually produces a lower gross profit than FIFO?

E8-9 (FIFO, LIFO and Average Cost Determination) John Adams Company's record of transactions for the month of April was as follows.

	Purchases			Sales	
April 1 (balance on hand)	600 @ $6.00		April 3	500 @ $10.00	
4	1,500 @ 6.08		9	1,400 @ 10.00	
8	800 @ 6.40		11	600 @ 11.00	
13	1,200 @ 6.50		23	1,200 @ 11.00	
21	700 @ 6.60		27	900 @ 12.00	
29	500 @ 6.79			4,600	
	5,300				

Instructions

(a) Assuming that perpetual inventory records are kept in units only, compute the inventory at April 30 using (1) LIFO and (2) average cost.

(b) Assuming that perpetual inventory records are kept in dollars, determine the inventory using (1) FIFO and (2) LIFO.

(c) Compute cost of goods sold assuming periodic inventory procedures and inventory priced at FIFO.

(d) In an inflationary period, which inventory method—FIFO, LIFO, average cost—will show the highest net income?

E8-10 (FIFO, LIFO, Average Cost Inventory) Shania Twain Company was formed on December 1, 2002. The following information is available from Twain's inventory records for Product BAP.

	Units	Unit Cost
January 1, 2003 (beginning inventory)	600	$ 8.00
Purchases in 2003		
January 5	1,200	9.00
January 25	1,300	10.00
February 16	800	11.00
March 26	600	12.00

A physical inventory on March 31, 2003, shows 1,600 units on hand.

Instructions

Prepare schedules to compute the ending inventory at March 31, 2003, under each of the following inventory methods.

(a) FIFO.   **(b)** LIFO.   **(c)** Weighted average.

E8-11 (Compute FIFO, LIFO, Average Cost—Periodic) Presented below is information related to Blowfish radios for Hootie Company for the month of July.

Date	Transaction	Units In	Unit Cost	Total	Units Sold	Selling Price	Total
July 1	Balance	100	$4.10	$ 410			
6	Purchase	800	4.20	3,360			
7	Sale				300	$7.00	$ 2,100
10	Sale				300	7.30	2,190
12	Purchase	400	4.50	1,800			
15	Sale				200	7.40	1,480
18	Purchase	300	4.60	1,380			
22	Sale				400	7.40	2,960
25	Purchase	500	4.58	2,290			
30	Sale				200	7.50	1,500
	Totals	2,100		$9,240	1,400		$10,230

Instructions
(a) Assuming that the periodic inventory method is used, compute the inventory cost at July 31 under each of the following cost flow assumptions.
   (1) FIFO.
   (2) LIFO.
   (3) Weighted-average. (Round the weighted-average unit cost to the nearest one-tenth of one cent.)
(b) Answer the following questions.
   (1) Which of the methods used above will yield the lowest figure for gross profit for the income statement? Explain why.
   (2) Which of the methods used above will yield the lowest figure for ending inventory for the balance sheet? Explain why.

E8-12 (FIFO and LIFO—Periodic and Perpetual) The following is a record of Pervis Ellison Company's transactions for Boston teapots for the month of May 2004.

May 1	Balance 400 units @ $20	May 10	Sale 300 units @ $38
12	Purchase 600 units @ $25	20	Sale 540 units @ $38
28	Purchase 400 units @ $30		

Instructions
(a) Assuming that perpetual inventories are **not** maintained and that a physical count at the end of the month shows 560 units on hand, what is the cost of the ending inventory using (1) FIFO and (2) LIFO?
(b) Assuming that perpetual records are maintained and they tie into the general ledger, calculate the ending inventory using (1) FIFO and (2) LIFO.

E8-13 (FIFO and LIFO; Income Statement Presentation) The board of directors of Deion Sanders Corporation is considering whether or not it should instruct the accounting department to shift from a first-in, first-out (FIFO) basis of pricing inventories to a last-in, first-out (LIFO) basis. The following information is available.

Sales	21,000 units @ $50
Inventory, January 1	6,000 units @ 20
Purchases	6,000 units @ 22
	10,000 units @ 25
	7,000 units @ 30
Inventory, December 31	8,000 units @ ?
Operating expenses	$200,000

Instructions
Prepare a condensed income statement for the year on both bases for comparative purposes.

E8-14 (FIFO and LIFO Effects) You are the vice-president of finance of Sandy Alomar Corporation, a retail company. The company prepared two different schedules of gross margin for the first quarter ended March 31, 2004. These schedules appear below.

	Sales ($5 per unit)	Cost of Goods Sold	Gross Margin
Schedule 1	$150,000	$124,900	$25,100
Schedule 2	150,000	129,400	20,600

The computation of cost of goods sold in each schedule is based on the following data.

	Units	Cost per Unit	Total Cost
Beginning inventory, January 1	10,000	$4.00	$40,000
Purchase, January 10	8,000	4.20	33,600
Purchase, January 30	6,000	4.25	25,500
Purchase, February 11	9,000	4.30	38,700
Purchase, March 17	11,000	4.40	48,400

Jane Torville, the president of the corporation, cannot understand how two different gross margins can be computed from the same set of data. As the vice-president of finance you have explained to Ms. Torville that the two schedules are based on different assumptions concerning the flow of inventory costs, i.e., first-in, first-out, and last-in, first-out. Schedules 1 and 2 were not necessarily prepared in this sequence of cost flow assumptions.

Instructions

Prepare two separate schedules computing cost of goods sold and supporting schedules showing the composition of the ending inventory under both cost flow assumptions.

E8-15 (FIFO and LIFO—Periodic) Howie Long Shop began operations on January 2, 2004. The following stock record card for footballs was taken from the records at the end of the year.

Date	Voucher	Terms	Units Received	Unit Invoice Cost	Gross Invoice Amount
1/15	10624	Net 30	50	$20.00	$1,000.00
3/15	11437	1/5, net 30	65	16.00	1,040.00
6/20	21332	1/10, net 30	90	15.00	1,350.00
9/12	27644	1/10, net 30	84	12.00	1,008.00
11/24	31269	1/10, net 30	76	11.00	836.00
	Totals		365		$5,234.00

A physical inventory on December 31, 2004, reveals that 100 footballs were in stock. The bookkeeper informs you that all the discounts were taken. Assume that Howie Long Shop uses the invoice price less discount for recording purchases.

Instructions

(a) Compute the December 31, 2004, inventory using the FIFO method.
(b) Compute the 2004 cost of goods sold using the LIFO method.
(c) What method would you recommend to the owner to minimize income taxes in 2004, using the inventory information for footballs as a guide?

E8-16 (LIFO Effect) The following example was provided to encourage the use of the LIFO method.

In a nutshell, LIFO subtracts inflation from inventory costs, deducts it from taxable income, and records it in a LIFO reserve account on the books. The LIFO benefit grows as inflation widens the gap between current-year and past-year (minus inflation) inventory costs. This gap is:

	With LIFO	Without LIFO
Revenue	$3,200,000	$3,200,000
Cost of goods sold	2,800,000	2,800,000
Operating expenses	150,000	150,000
Operating income	250,000	250,000
LIFO adjustment	40,000	0
Taxable income	$210,000	$250,000
Income taxes @ 36%	$ 75,600	$ 90,000
Cash flow	$174,400	$160,000
Extra cash	$ 14,400	0
Increased cash flow	9%	0%

Instructions

(a) Explain what is meant by the LIFO reserve account.

(b) How does LIFO subtract inflation from inventory costs?

(c) Explain how the cash flow of $174,400 in this example was computed. Explain why this amount may not be correct.

(d) Why does a company that uses LIFO have extra cash? Explain whether this situation will always exist.

E8-17 (Alternative Inventory Methods—Comprehensive) Tori Amos Corporation began operations on December 1, 2003. The only inventory transaction in 2003 was the purchase of inventory on December 10, 2003, at a cost of $20 per unit. None of this inventory was sold in 2003. Relevant information is as follows.

Ending inventory units		
December 31, 2003		100
December 31, 2004, by purchase date		
December 2, 2004	100	
July 20, 2004	50	150

During the year the following purchases and sales were made.

Purchases		Sales	
March 15	300 units at $24	April 10	200
July 20	300 units at 25	August 20	300
September 4	200 units at 28	November 18	150
December 2	100 units at 30	December 12	200

The company uses the periodic inventory method.

Instructions

(a) Determine ending inventory under (1) specific identification, (2) FIFO, (3) LIFO periodic, and (4) average cost.

(b) Determine ending inventory using dollar-value LIFO. Assume that the December 2, 2004, purchase cost is the current cost of inventory. (*Hint*: The beginning inventory is the base layer priced at $20 per unit; the relevant price index is 1.4667.)

E8-18 (Dollar-Value LIFO) Oasis Company has used the dollar-value LIFO method for inventory cost determination for many years. The following data were extracted from Oasis's records.

Date	Price Index	Ending Inventory at Base Prices	Ending Inventory at Dollar-Value LIFO
December 31, 2002	105	$92,000	$92,600
December 31, 2003	?	97,000	98,350

Instructions

Calculate the index used for 2003 that yielded the above results.

E8-19 (Dollar-Value LIFO) The dollar-value LIFO method was adopted by Enya Corp. on January 1, 2004. Its inventory on that date was $160,000. On December 31, 2004, the inventory at prices existing on that date amounted to $140,000. The price level at January 1, 2004, was 100, and the price level at December 31, 2004, was 112.

Instructions

(a) Compute the amount of the inventory at December 31, 2004, under the dollar-value LIFO method.

(b) On December 31, 2005, the inventory at prices existing on that date was $172,500, and the price level was 115. Compute the inventory on that date under the dollar-value LIFO method.

E8-20 **(Dollar-Value LIFO)** Presented below is information related to Dino Radja Company.

Date	Ending Inventory (End-of-Year Prices)	Price Index
December 31, 2001	$ 80,000	100
December 31, 2002	115,500	105
December 31, 2003	108,000	120
December 31, 2004	122,200	130
December 31, 2005	154,000	140
December 31, 2006	176,900	145

Instructions

Compute the ending inventory for Dino Radja Company for 2001 through 2006 using the dollar-value LIFO method.

E8-21 **(Lower of Cost or Market)** The inventory of 3T Company on December 31, 2004, consists of these items.

Part No.	Quantity	Cost per Unit	Cost to Replace per Unit
110	600	$ 90	$100
111	1,000	60	52
112	500	80	76
113	200	170	180
120	400	205	208
121ᵃ	1,600	16	14
122	300	240	235

ᵃPart No. 121 is obsolete and has a realizable value of $0.20 each as scrap.

Instructions

(a) Determine the inventory as of December 31, 2004, by the lower of cost or market method, applying this method directly to each item.
(b) Determine the inventory by the lower of cost or market method, applying the method to the total of the inventory.

E8-22 **(Lower of Cost or Market)** Smashing Pumpkins Company uses the lower of cost or market method, on an individual-item basis, in pricing its inventory items. The inventory at December 31, 2004, consists of products D, E, F, G, H, and I. Relevant per-unit data for these products appear below.

	Item D	Item E	Item F	Item G	Item H	Item I
Estimated selling price	$120	$110	$95	$90	$110	$90
Cost	75	80	80	80	50	36
Replacement cost	120	72	70	30	70	30
Estimated selling expense	30	30	30	25	30	30
Normal profit	20	20	20	20	20	20

Instructions

Using the lower of cost or market rule, determine the proper unit value for balance sheet reporting purposes at December 31, 2004, for each of the inventory items above.

E8-23 **(Lower of Cost or Market)** Michael Bolton Company follows the practice of pricing its inventory at the lower of cost or market, on an individual-item basis.

Item No.	Quantity	Cost per Unit	Cost to Replace	Estimated Selling Price	Cost of Completion and Disposal	Normal Profit
1320	1,200	$3.20	$3.00	$4.50	$.35	$1.25
1333	900	2.70	2.30	3.50	.50	.50
1426	800	4.50	3.70	5.00	.40	1.00
1437	1,000	3.60	3.10	3.20	.25	.90
1510	700	2.25	2.00	3.25	.80	.60
1522	500	3.00	2.70	3.80	.40	.50
1573	3,000	1.80	1.60	2.50	.75	.50
1626	1,000	4.70	5.20	6.00	.50	1.00

Instructions

From the information above, determine the amount of Bolton Company inventory.

E8-24 (Analysis of Inventories) The financial statements of **General Mills, Inc's.** 2000 Annual Report disclose the following information.

(in millions)	May 28, 2000	May 30, 1999	May 31, 1998
Inventories	$510.5	$426.7	$389.7

	Fiscal Year	
	2000	1999
Sales	$6,700.2	$6,246.1
Cost of goods sold	2,697.6	2,593.1
Net income	614.4	534.5

Instructions

Compute General Mills' **(a)** inventory turnover, and **(b)** the average days to sell inventory for 2000 and 1999.

*E8-25 (Gross Profit Method) Rasheed Wallace Company lost most of its inventory in a fire in December just before the year-end physical inventory was taken. The corporation's books disclosed the following.

Beginning inventory	$170,000	Sales	$650,000
Purchases for the year	390,000	Sales returns	24,000
Purchase returns	30,000	Rate of gross margin on sales	40%

Merchandise with a selling price of $21,000 remained undamaged after the fire. Damaged merchandise with an original selling price of $15,000 had a net realizable value of $5,300.

Instructions

Compute the amount of the loss as a result of the fire, assuming that the corporation had no insurance coverage.

PROBLEMS

P8-1 (Various Inventory Issues) The following independent situations relate to inventory accounting.

1. Jag Co. purchased goods with a list price of $150,000, subject to trade discounts of 20% and 10% with no cash discounts allowable. How much should Jag Co. record as the cost of these goods?

2. Francis Company's inventory of $1,100,000 at December 31, 2003, was based on a physical count of goods priced at cost and before any year-end adjustments relating to the following items.
   a. Goods shipped f.o.b. shipping point on December 24, 2003, from a vendor at an invoice cost of $69,000 to Francis Company were received on January 4, 2004.
   b. The physical count included $29,000 of goods billed to Sakic Corp. f.o.b. shipping point on December 31, 2003. The carrier picked up these goods on January 3, 2004.
   What amount should Francis report as inventory on its balance sheet?

3. Mark Messier Corp. had 1,500 units of part M.O. on hand May 1, 2003, costing $21 each. Purchases of part M.O. during May were as follows.

	Units	Unit Cost
May 9	2,000	$22.00
17	3,500	23.00
26	1,000	24.00

A physical count on May 31, 2003, shows 2,100 units of part M.O. on hand. Using the FIFO method, what is the cost of part M.O. inventory at May 31, 2003? Using the LIFO method, what is the inventory cost? Using the average cost method, what is the inventory cost?

4. Forsberg Company adopted the dollar-value LIFO method on January 1, 2003 (using internal price indexes and multiple pools). The following data are available for inventory pool A for the 2 years following adoption of LIFO.

Inventory	At Base-Year Cost	At Current-Year Cost	Price Index
1/1/03	$200,000	$200,000	100
12/31/03	240,000	252,000	105
12/31/04	256,000	286,720	112

Using the dollar-value LIFO method, at what amount should the inventory be reported at December 31, 2004?

5. Eric Lindros Inc., a retail store chain, had the following information in its general ledger for the year 2004.

Merchandise purchased for resale	$909,400
Interest on notes payable to vendors	8,700
Purchase returns	16,500
Freight-in	22,000
Freight-out	17,100

What is Lindros' inventoriable cost for 2004?

Instructions

Answer each of the questions above about inventories and explain your answers.

P8-2 (Compute FIFO, LIFO, and Average Cost—Periodic and Perpetual) Taos Company's record of transactions concerning part X for the month of April was as follows.

Purchases		Sales	
April 1 (balance on hand)	100 @ $5.00	April 5	300
4	400 @ 5.10	12	200
11	300 @ 5.30	27	800
18	200 @ 5.35	28	100
26	500 @ 5.60		
30	200 @ 5.80		

Instructions

(a) Compute the inventory at April 30 on each of the following bases. Assume that perpetual inventory records are kept in units only. Carry unit costs to the nearest cent.
   (1) First-in, first-out (FIFO).
   (2) Last-in, first-out (LIFO).
   (3) Average cost.
(b) If the perpetual inventory record is kept in dollars, and costs are computed at the time of each withdrawal, what amount would be shown as ending inventory in 1, 2, and 3 above? Carry average unit costs to four decimal places.

P8-3 (Compute FIFO, LIFO and Average Cost—Periodic and Perpetual) Some of the information found on a detail inventory card for David Letterman Inc. for the first month of operations is as follows.

	Received		Issued,	Balance,
Date	No. of Units	Unit Cost	No. of Units	No. of Units
January 2	1,200	$3.00		1,200
7			700	500
10	600	3.20		1,100
13			500	600
18	1,000	3.30	300	1,300
20			1,100	200
23	1,300	3.40		1,500
26			800	700
28	1,500	3.60		2,200
31			1,300	900

Instructions

(a) From these data compute the ending inventory on each of the following bases. Assume that perpetual inventory records are kept in units only. Carry unit costs to the nearest cent and ending inventory to the nearest dollar.

(1) First-in, first-out (FIFO).
(2) Last-in, first-out (LIFO).
(3) Average cost.

(b) If the perpetual inventory record is kept in dollars, and costs are computed at the time of each withdrawal, would the amounts shown as ending inventory in 1, 2, and 3 above be the same? Explain and compute.

P8-4 (Compute FIFO, LIFO, Average Cost—Periodic and Perpetual) Iowa Company is a multi-product firm. Presented below is information concerning one of its products, the Hawkeye.

Date	Transaction	Quantity	Price/Cost
1/1	Beginning inventory	1,000	$12
2/4	Purchase	2,000	18
2/20	Sale	2,500	30
4/2	Purchase	3,000	23
11/4	Sale	2,000	33

Instructions

Compute cost of goods sold, assuming Iowa uses:

(a) Periodic system, FIFO cost flow. ⎫ same answer
(b) Perpetual system, FIFO cost flow. ⎭
(c) Periodic system, LIFO cost flow.
(d) Perpetual system, LIFO cost flow.
(e) Periodic system, weighted-average cost flow.
(f) Perpetual system, moving-average cost flow.

P8-5 (Financial Statement Effects of FIFO and LIFO) The management of Maine Company has asked its accounting department to describe the effect upon the company's financial position and its income statements of accounting for inventories on the LIFO rather than the FIFO basis during 2004 and 2005. The accounting department is to assume that the change to LIFO would have been effective on January 1, 2004, and that the initial LIFO base would have been the inventory value on December 31, 2003. Presented below are the company's financial statements and other data for the years 2004 and 2005 when the FIFO method was employed.

	Financial Position as of		
	12/31/03	12/31/04	12/31/05
Cash	$ 90,000	$130,000	$ 141,600
Accounts receivable	80,000	100,000	120,000
Inventory	120,000	140,000	180,000
Other assets	160,000	170,000	200,000
Total assets	$450,000	$540,000	$ 641,600
Accounts payable	$ 40,000	$ 60,000	$ 80,000
Other liabilities	70,000	80,000	110,000
Common stock	200,000	200,000	200,000
Retained earnings	140,000	200,000	251,600
Total equities	$450,000	$540,000	$ 641,600

	Income for Years Ended	
	12/31/04	12/31/05
Sales	$900,000	$1,350,000
Less: Cost of goods sold	505,000	770,000
Other expenses	205,000	304,000
	710,000	1,074,000
Net income before income taxes	190,000	276,000
Income taxes (40%)	76,000	110,400
Net income	$114,000	$ 165,600

Other data:

1. Inventory on hand at 12/31/03 consisted of 40,000 units valued at $3.00 each.
2. Sales (all units sold at the same price in a given year):

   2004—150,000 units @ $6.00 each   2005—180,000 units @ $7.50 each

3. Purchases (all units purchased at the same price in given year):

   2004—150,000 units @ $3.50 each   2005—180,000 units @ $4.50 each

4. Income taxes at the effective rate of 40% are paid on December 31 each year.

Instructions

Name the account(s) presented in the financial statements that would have different amounts for 2005 if LIFO rather than FIFO had been used, and state the new amount for each account that is named. Show computations.

(CMA adapted)

P8-6 (Dollar-Value LIFO) Falcon's Televisions produces television sets in three categories: portable, midsize, and console. On January 1, 2003, Falcon adopted dollar-value LIFO and decided to use a single inventory pool. The company's January 1 inventory consists of:

Category	Quantity	Cost per Unit	Total Cost
Portable	6,000	$100	$ 600,000
Midsize	8,000	250	2,000,000
Console	3,000	400	1,200,000
	17,000		$3,800,000

During 2003, the company had the following purchases and sales.

Category	Quantity Purchased	Cost per Unit	Quantity Sold	Selling Price per Unit
Portable	15,000	$120	14,000	$150
Midsize	20,000	300	24,000	405
Console	10,000	460	6,000	600
	45,000		44,000	

Instructions

(Round to four decimals.)

(a) Compute ending inventory, cost of goods sold, and gross profit.
(b) Assume the company uses three inventory pools instead of one. Repeat instruction (a).

P8-7 (LIFO Effect on Income) Michelle Kwan Inc. sells two products: figure skates and speed skates. At December 31, 2004, Kwan used the first-in, first-out (FIFO) inventory method. Effective January 1, 2005, Kwan changed to the last-in, first-out (LIFO) inventory method. The cumulative effect of this change is not determinable and, as a result, the ending inventory of 2004 for which the FIFO method was used is also the beginning inventory for 2005 for the LIFO method. Any layers added during 2005 should be costed by reference to the first acquisitions of 2005 and any layers liquidated during 2005 should be considered a permanent liquidation.

The following information was available from Kwan's inventory records for the 2 most recent years.

	Figure Skates		Speed Skates	
	Units	Unit Cost	Units	Unit Cost
2004 purchases				
January 7	7,000	$40.00	22,000	$20.00
April 16	12,000	45.00		
November 8	17,000	54.00	18,500	34.00
December 13	9,000	62.00		
2005 purchases				
February 11	3,000	66.00	23,000	36.00
May 20	8,000	75.00		
October 15	20,000	81.00		
December 23			15,500	42.00
Units on hand				
December 31, 2004	15,100		15,000	
December 31, 2005	18,000		13,200	

Instructions

Compute the effect on income before income taxes for the year ended December 31, 2005, resulting from the change from the FIFO to the LIFO inventory method.

(AICPA adapted)

P8-8 (Dollar-Value LIFO) Warren Dunn Company cans a variety of vegetable-type soups. Recently, the company decided to value its inventories using dollar-value LIFO pools. The clerk who accounts for inventories does not understand how to value the inventory pools using this new method, so, as a private consultant, you have been asked to teach him how this new method works.

He has provided you with the following information about purchases made over a 6-year period.

Date	Ending Inventory (End-of-Year Prices)	Price Index
Dec. 31, 1998	$ 80,000	100
Dec. 31, 1999	115,500	105
Dec. 31, 2000	108,000	120
Dec. 31, 2001	131,300	130
Dec. 31, 2002	154,000	140
Dec. 31, 2003	174,000	145

You have already explained to him how this inventory method is maintained, but he would feel better about it if you were to leave him detailed instructions explaining how these calculations are done and why he needs to put all inventories at a base-year value.

Instructions

(a) Compute the ending inventory for Warren Dunn Company for 1998 through 2003 using dollar-value LIFO.

(b) Using your computation schedules as your illustration, write a step-by-step set of instructions explaining how the calculations are done. Begin your explanation by briefly explaining the theory behind this inventory method, including the purpose of putting all amounts into base-year price levels.

P8-9   (Lower of Cost or Market)   Grant Wood Company manufactures desks. Most of the company's desks are standard models and are sold on the basis of catalog prices. At December 31, 2004, the following finished desks appear in the company's inventory.

Finished Desks	A	B	C	D
2004 catalog selling price	$450	$480	$900	$1,050
FIFO cost per inventory list 12/31/04	470	450	830	960
Estimated current cost to manufacture (at December 31, 2004, and early 2005)	460	440	610	1,000
Sales commissions and estimated other costs of disposal	45	60	90	130
2005 catalog selling price	500	540	900	1,200

The 2004 catalog was in effect through November 2004, and the 2005 catalog is effective as of December 1, 2004. All catalog prices are net of the usual discounts. Generally, the company attempts to obtain a 20% gross margin on selling price and has usually been successful in doing so.

Instructions

At what amount should each of the four desks appear in the company's December 31, 2004, inventory, assuming that the company has adopted a lower of FIFO cost or market approach for valuation of inventories on an individual-item basis?

P8-10   (Lower of Cost or Market)   Jonathan Brandis Company is a food wholesaler that supplies independent grocery stores in the immediate region. The company has a perpetual inventory system for all of its food products. The first-in, first-out (FIFO) method of inventory valuation is used to determine the cost of the inventory at the end of each month. Transactions and other related information regarding two of the items (instant coffee and sugar) carried by Brandis are given below for October 2003, the last month of Brandis' fiscal year.

	Instant Coffee	Sugar
Standard unit of packaging	Case containing 24, one-pound jars.	Baler containing 12, five-pound bags.
Inventory, 10/1/03	1,000 cases @ $60.20 per case	500 balers @ $6.50 per baler
Purchases	1. 10/10/03—1,600 cases @ $62.10 per case plus freight of $480.	1. 10/5/03—850 balers @ $5.76 per baler plus freight of $320.
	2. 10/20/03—2,400 cases @ $64.00 per case plus freight of $480.	2. 10/16/03—640 balers @ $6.00 per baler plus freight of $320.
		3. 10/24/03—600 balers @ $6.20 per baler plus freight of $360.

Purchase terms	2/10, net/30, f.o.b. shipping point	Net 30 days, f.o.b. shipping point
October sales	3,600 cases @ $76.00 per case	1,950 balers @ $8.00 per baler
Returns and allowances	A customer returned 50 cases that had been shipped in error. The customer's account was credited for $3,800.	As the October 16 purchase was unloaded, 20 balers were discovered damaged. A representative of the trucking firm confirmed the damage and the balers were discarded. Credit of $120 for the merchandise and $10 for the freight was received by Brandis.
Inventory values 10/31/03		
Net realizable value	$66.00 per case	$6.60 per baler
Net realizable value less a normal profit of 15% of net realizable value	$56.10 per case	$5.61 per baler

Brandis' sales terms are 1/10, net/30, f.o.b. shipping point. Brandis records all purchases net of purchase discounts and takes all purchase discounts. The most recent quoted price for coffee is $60 per case and for sugar $6.10 per baler, before freight and purchase discounts.

Instructions

(a) Calculate the number of units in inventory and the FIFO unit cost for instant coffee and sugar as of October 31, 2003.

(b) Brandis Company applies the lower of cost or market rule in valuing its year-end inventory. Calculate the total dollar amount of the inventory for instant coffee and sugar applying the lower of cost or market rule on an individual-product basis.

(c) Could Brandis Company apply the lower of cost or market rule to groups of products or the inventory as a whole rather than on an individual-product basis? Explain your answer.

(CMA adapted)

P8-11 (Statement and Note Disclosure, and LCM) Garth Brooks Specialty Company, a division of Fresh Horses Inc., manufactures three models of gear shift components for bicycles that are sold to bicycle manufacturers, retailers, and catalog outlets. Since beginning operations in 1971, Brooks has assumed a first-in, first-out cost flow in its perpetual inventory system. Except for overhead, manufacturing costs are accumulated using actual costs. Overhead is applied to production using predetermined overhead rates. The balances of the inventory accounts at the end of Brooks's fiscal year, November 30, 2003, are shown below. The inventories are stated at cost before any year-end adjustments.

Finished goods	$647,000
Work-in-process	112,500
Raw materials	240,000
Factory supplies	69,000

The following information relates to Brooks' inventory and operations.

1. The finished goods inventory consists of the items analyzed below.

	Cost	Market
Down tube shifter		
Standard model	$ 67,500	$ 67,000
Click adjustment model	94,500	87,000
Deluxe model	108,000	110,000
Total down tube shifters	270,000	264,000

Bar end shifter		
Standard model	83,000	90,050
Click adjustment model	99,000	97,550
Total bar end shifters	182,000	187,600
Head tube shifter		
Standard model	78,000	77,650
Click adjustment model	117,000	119,300
Total head tube shifters	195,000	196,950
Total finished goods	$647,000	$648,550

2. One-half of the head tube shifter finished goods inventory is held by catalog outlets on consignment.
3. Three-quarters of the bar end shifter finished goods inventory has been pledged as collateral for a bank loan.
4. One-half of the raw materials balance represents derailleurs acquired at a contracted price 20 percent above the current market price. The market value of the rest of the raw materials is $127,400.
5. The total market value of the work-in-process inventory is $108,700.
6. Included in the cost of factory supplies are obsolete items with an historical cost of $4,200. The market value of the remaining factory supplies is $65,900.
7. Brooks applies the lower of cost or market method to each of the three types of shifters in finished goods inventory. For each of the other three inventory accounts, Brooks applies the lower of cost or market method to the total of each inventory account.
8. Consider all amounts presented above to be material in relation to Brooks' financial statements taken as a whole.

Instructions
(a) Prepare the inventory section of Brooks's statement of financial position as of November 30, 2003, including any required note(s).
(b) Without prejudice to your answer to requirement (a), assume that the market value of Brooks's inventories is less than cost. Explain how this decline would be presented in Brooks's income statement for the fiscal year ended November 30, 2003.

(CMA adapted)

*P8-12 (Gross Profit Method) David Hasselholf Company lost most of its inventory in a fire in December just before the year-end physical inventory was taken. Corporate records disclose the following.

Inventory (beginning)	$ 80,000	Sales	$415,000
Purchases	280,000	Sales returns	21,000
Purchase returns	28,000	Gross profit % based on selling price	34%

Merchandise with a selling price of $30,000 remained undamaged after the fire, and damaged merchandise has a salvage value of $7,150. The company does not carry fire insurance on its inventory.

Instructions
Prepare a formal labeled schedule computing the fire loss incurred, using the gross profit method.

CONCEPTUAL CASES

C8-1 (Inventoriable Costs) You are asked to travel to Milwaukee to observe and verify the inventory of the Milwaukee branch of one of your clients. You arrive on Thursday, December 30, and find that the inventory procedures have just been started. You spot a railway car on the sidetrack at the unloading door and ask the warehouse superintendent Predrag Danilovic how he plans to inventory the contents of the car. He responds, "We are not going to include the contents in the inventory."

Later in the day, you ask the bookkeeper for the invoice on the carload and the related freight bill. The invoice lists the various items, prices, and extensions of the goods in the car. You note that the carload was shipped December 24 from Albuquerque, f.o.b. Albuquerque, and that the total invoice price of the goods in the car was $35,300. The freight bill called for a payment of $1,500. Terms were net 30 days. The bookkeeper affirms the fact that this invoice is to be held for recording in January.

Instructions

(a) Does your client have a liability that should be recorded at December 31? Discuss.

(b) Prepare a journal entry(ies), if required, to reflect any accounting adjustment required. Assume a perpetual inventory system is used by your client.

(c) For what possible reason(s) might your client wish to postpone recording the transaction?

C8-2 (Inventoriable Costs) Alonzo Spellman, an inventory control specialist, is interested in better understanding the accounting for inventories. Although Alonzo understands the more sophisticated computer inventory control systems, he has little knowledge of how inventory cost is determined. In studying the records of Ditka Enterprises, which sells normal brand-name goods from its own store and on consignment through Wannstedt Inc., he asks you to answer the following questions.

Instructions

(a) Should Ditka Enterprises include in its inventory normal brand-name goods purchased from its suppliers but not yet received if the terms of purchase are f.o.b. shipping point (manufacturer's plant)? Why?

(b) Should Ditka Enterprises include freight-in expenditures as an inventory cost? Why?

(c) What are products on consignment? How should they be reported in the financial statements?

(AICPA adapted)

C8-3 (Inventoriable Costs) Jack McDowell, the controller for McDowell Lumber Company, has recently hired you as assistant controller. He wishes to determine your expertise in the area of inventory accounting and therefore asks you to answer the following unrelated questions.

(a) A company is involved in the wholesaling and retailing of automobile tires for foreign cars. Most of the inventory is imported, and it is valued on the company's records at the actual inventory cost plus freight-in. At year-end, the warehousing costs are prorated over cost of goods sold and ending inventory. Are warehousing costs considered a product cost or a period cost?

(b) A certain portion of a company's "inventory" is composed of obsolete items. Should obsolete items that are not currently consumed in the production of "goods or services to be available for sale" be classified as part of inventory?

(c) A company purchases airplanes for sale to others. However, until they are sold, the company charters and services the planes. What is the proper way to report these airplanes in the company's financial statements?

C8-4 (General Inventory Issues) In January 2004, Wesley Crusher Inc. requested and secured permission from the commissioner of the Internal Revenue Service to compute inventories under the last-in, first-out (LIFO) method and elected to determine inventory cost under the dollar-value method. Crusher Inc. satisfied the commissioner that cost could be accurately determined by use of an index number computed from a representative sample selected from the company's single inventory pool.

Instructions

(a) Why should inventories be included in (1) a balance sheet and (2) the computation of net income?

(b) The Internal Revenue Code allows some accountable events to be considered differently for income tax reporting purposes and financial accounting purposes, while other accountable events must be reported the same for both purposes. Discuss why it might be desirable to report some accountable events differently for financial accounting purposes than for income tax reporting purposes.

(c) Discuss the ways and conditions under which the FIFO and LIFO inventory costing methods produce different inventory valuations. Do not discuss procedures for computing inventory cost.

(AICPA adapted)

C8-5   (LIFO Inventory Advantages)   Jean Honore, president of Fragonard Co., recently read an article that claimed that at least 100 of the country's largest 500 companies were either adopting or considering adopting the last-in, first-out (LIFO) method for valuing inventories. The article stated that the firms were switching to LIFO to (1) neutralize the effect of inflation in their financial statements, (2) eliminate inventory profits, and (3) reduce income taxes. Ms. Honore wonders if the switch would benefit her company.

Fragonard currently uses the first-in, first-out (FIFO) method of inventory valuation in its periodic inventory system. The company has a high inventory turnover rate, and inventories represent a significant proportion of the assets.

Ms. Honore has been told that the LIFO system is more costly to operate and will provide little benefit to companies with high turnover. She intends to use the inventory method that is best for the company in the long run rather than selecting a method just because it is the current fad.

Instructions

(a) Explain to Ms. Honore what "inventory profits" are and how the LIFO method of inventory valuation could reduce them.

(b) Explain to Ms. Honore the conditions that must exist for Fragonard Co. to receive tax benefits from a switch to the LIFO method.

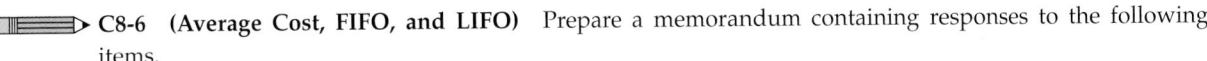

C8-6   (Average Cost, FIFO, and LIFO)   Prepare a memorandum containing responses to the following items.

(a) Describe the cost flow assumptions used in average cost, FIFO, and LIFO methods of inventory valuation.

(b) Distinguish between weighted average cost and moving average cost for inventory costing purposes.

(c) Identify the effects on both the balance sheet and the income statement of using the LIFO method instead of the FIFO method for inventory costing purposes over a substantial time period when purchase prices of inventoriable items are rising. State why these effects take place.

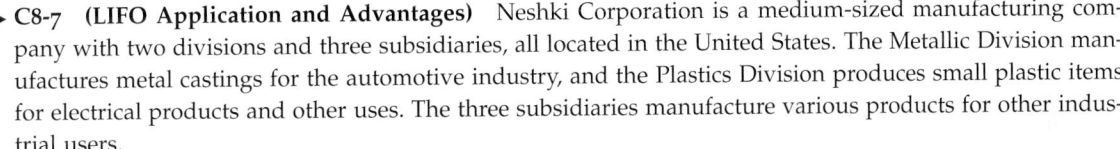

C8-7   (LIFO Application and Advantages)   Neshki Corporation is a medium-sized manufacturing company with two divisions and three subsidiaries, all located in the United States. The Metallic Division manufactures metal castings for the automotive industry, and the Plastics Division produces small plastic items for electrical products and other uses. The three subsidiaries manufacture various products for other industrial users.

Neshki Corporation plans to change from the lower of first-in, first-out (FIFO) cost or market method of inventory valuation to the last-in, first-out (LIFO) method of inventory valuation to obtain tax benefits. To make the method acceptable for tax purposes, the change also will be made for its annual financial statements.

Instructions

(a) Describe the establishment of and subsequent pricing procedures for each of the following LIFO inventory methods.

  (1) LIFO applied to units of product when the periodic inventory system is used.

  (2) Application of the dollar-value method to LIFO units of product.

(b) Discuss the specific advantages and disadvantages of using the dollar-value LIFO application as compared to specific goods LIFO (unit LIFO). Ignore income tax considerations.

(c) Discuss the general advantages and disadvantages claimed for LIFO methods.

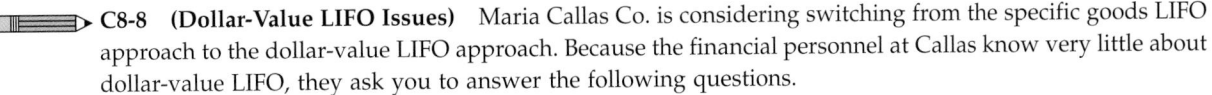

C8-8   (Dollar-Value LIFO Issues)   Maria Callas Co. is considering switching from the specific goods LIFO approach to the dollar-value LIFO approach. Because the financial personnel at Callas know very little about dollar-value LIFO, they ask you to answer the following questions.

(a) What is a LIFO pool?

(b) Is it possible to use a LIFO pool concept and not use dollar-value LIFO? Explain.

(c) What is a LIFO liquidation?

(d) How are price indexes used in the dollar-value LIFO method?

(e) What are the advantages of dollar-value LIFO over specific goods LIFO?

C8-9 (FIFO and LIFO) Günter Grass Company is considering changing its inventory valuation method from FIFO to LIFO because of the potential tax savings. However, the management wishes to consider all of the effects on the company, including its reported performance, before making the final decision.

The inventory account, currently valued on the FIFO basis, consists of 1,000,000 units at $7 per unit on January 1, 2004. There are 1,000,000 shares of common stock outstanding as of January 1, 2004, and the cash balance is $400,000.

The company has made the following forecasts for the period 2004–2006.

	2004	2005	2006
Unit sales (in millions of units)	1.1	1.0	1.3
Sales price per unit	$10	$10	$12
Unit purchases (in millions of units)	1.0	1.1	1.2
Purchase price per unit	$7	$8	$9
Annual depreciation (in thousands of dollars)	$300	$300	$300
Cash dividends per share	$0.15	$0.15	$0.15
Cash payments for additions to and replacement of plant and equipment (in thousands of dollars)	$350	$350	$350
Income tax rate	40%	40%	40%
Operating expense (exclusive of depreciation) as a percent of sales	15%	15%	15%
Common shares outstanding (in millions)	1	1	1

Instructions

(a) Prepare a schedule that illustrates and compares the following data for Günter Grass Company under the FIFO and the LIFO inventory method for 2004–2006. Assume the company would begin LIFO at the beginning of 2004.
   (1) Year-end inventory balances.
   (2) Annual net income after taxes.
   (3) Earnings per share.
   (4) Cash balance.
   Assume all sales are collected in the year of sale and all purchases, operating expenses, and taxes are paid during the year incurred.

(b) Using the data above, your answer to (a), and any additional issues you believe need to be considered, prepare a report that recommends whether or not Günter Grass Company should change to the LIFO inventory method. Support your conclusions with appropriate arguments.

(CMA adapted)

C8-10 (Lower of Cost or Market) You have been asked by the financial vice president to develop a short presentation on the lower of cost or market method for inventory purposes. The financial VP needs to explain this method to the president, because it appears that a portion of the company's inventory has declined in value.

Instructions

The financial VP asks you to answer the following questions.

(a) What is the purpose of the lower of cost or market method?

(b) What is meant by market? (*Hint*: Discuss the ceiling and floor constraints.)

(c) Do you apply the lower of cost or market method to each individual item, to a category, or to the total of the inventory? Explain.

(d) What are the potential disadvantages of the lower of cost or market method?

C8-11 (LIFO Method) Gamble Company uses the LIFO method for inventory costing. In an effort to lower net income, company president Oscar Gamble tells the plant accountant to take the unusual step of recommending to the purchasing department a large purchase of inventory at year-end. The price of the item to be purchased has nearly doubled during the year, and the item represents a major portion of inventory value.

Instructions

Answer the following questions.

(a) Identify the major stakeholders. If the plant accountant recommends the purchase, what are the consequences?

(b) If Gamble Company were using the FIFO method of inventory costing, would Oscar Gamble give the same order? Why or why not?

*C8-12 (Gross Profit Method) Presented below is information related to Joey Harrington Corporation for the current year.

Beginning inventory	$ 600,000	
Purchases	1,500,000	
Total goods available for sale		$2,100,000
Sales		2,500,000

Instructions

(a) Compute the ending inventory, assuming that (1) gross profit is 45% of sales; (2) gross profit is 60% of cost; (3) gross profit is 35% of sales; and (4) gross profit is 25% of cost.

(b) Harrington would like to use the gross profit method to value its inventories for financial reporting purposes. Prepare a brief memorandum to Harrington explaining why use of the gross profit method would not be permitted for financial reporting.

USING YOUR JUDGMENT

FINANCIAL REPORTING PROBLEM

3M COMPANY

The financial statements of **3M** were provided with your book or can be accessed on the Take Action! CD.

Instructions

Refer to 3M's financial statements and the accompanying notes to answer the following questions.

(a) How does 3M value its inventories? Which inventory costing method does 3M use as a basis for reporting its inventories?

(b) How does 3M report its inventories in the balance sheet? In the notes to its financial statements, what three descriptions are used to classify its inventories?

(c) What was 3M's inventory turnover ratio in 2001? What is its gross profit percentage? Evaluate 3M's inventory turnover ratio and gross profit percentage.

FINANCIAL STATEMENT ANALYSIS CASES

CASE 1 SONIC, INC.

Sonic, Inc. reported the following information regarding 2001–2002 inventory.

SONIC, INC.

	2002	2001
Current assets		
Cash	$ 153,010	$ 538,489
Accounts receivable, net of allowance for doubtful accounts		
of $46,000 in 2002 and $160,000 in 2001	1,627,980	2,596,291
Inventories (Note 2)	1,340,494	1,734,873
Other current assets	123,388	90,592
Assets of discontinued operations	—	32,815
Total current assets	3,244,872	4,993,060

Notes to Consolidated Financial Statements

Note 1 (in part): Nature of Business and Significant Accounting Policies

Inventories—Inventories are stated at the lower of cost or market. Cost is determined by the last-in, first-out (LIFO) method by the parent company and by the first-in, first-out (FIFO) method by its subsidiaries.

Note 2: Inventories

Inventories consist of the following:

	2002	2001
Raw materials	$1,264,646	$2,321,178
Work in process	240,988	171,222
Finished goods and display units	129,406	711,252
Total inventories	1,635,040	3,203,652
Less: Amount classified as long-term	294,546	1,468,779
Current portion	$1,340,494	$1,734,873

Inventories are stated at the lower of cost determined by the LIFO method or market for Sonic, Inc. Inventories for the two wholly-owned subsidiaries, Sonic Command, Inc. (U.S.) and Sonic Limited (U.K.) are stated on the FIFO method which amounted to $566,000 at October 31, 2001. No inventory is stated on the FIFO method at October 31, 2002. Included in inventory stated at FIFO cost was $32,815 at October 31, 2001, of Sonic Command inventory classified as an asset from discontinued operations (see Note 14). If the FIFO method had been used for the entire consolidated group, inventories after an adjustment to the lower of cost or market, would have been approximately $2,000,000 and $3,800,000 at October 31, 2002 and 2001, respectively.

Inventory has been written down to estimated net realizable value, and results of operations for 2002, 2001, and 2000 include a corresponding charge of approximately $868,000, $960,000, and $273,000, respectively, which represents the excess of LIFO cost over market.

Inventory of $294,546 and $1,468,779 at October 31, 2002 and 2001, respectively, shown on the balance sheet as a noncurrent asset represents that portion of the inventory that is not expected to be sold currently.

Reduction in inventory quantities during the years ended October 31, 2002, 2001, and 2000 resulted in liquidation of LIFO inventory quantities carried at a lower cost prevailing in prior years as compared with the cost of fiscal 2000 purchases. The effect of these reductions was to decrease the net loss by approximately $24,000, $157,000 and $90,000 at October 31, 2002, 2001, and 2000, respectively.

Instructions

(a) Why might Sonic, Inc. use two different methods for valuing inventory?

(b) Comment on why Sonic, Inc. might disclose how its LIFO inventories would be valued under FIFO.

(c) Why does the LIFO liquidation reduce operating costs?

(d) Comment on whether Sonic would report more or less income if it had been on a FIFO basis for all its inventory.

CASE 2 BARRICK GOLD CORPORATION

Barrick Gold Corporation, with headquarters in Toronto, Canada, is the world's most profitable and largest gold mining company outside South Africa. Part of the key to Barrick's success has been due to its ability to maintain cash flow while improving production and increasing its reserves of gold-containing property. During 2000, Barrick achieved record growth in cash flow, production, and reserves.

The company maintains an aggressive policy of developing previously identified target areas that have the possibility of a large amount of gold ore, and that have not been previously developed. Barrick limits the riskiness of this development by choosing only properties that are located in politically stable regions, and by the company's use of internally generated funds, rather than debt, to finance growth.

Barrick's inventories are as follows:

Inventories (in millions, US dollars)

Current	
Gold in process	$ 85
Mine operating supplies	43
	$128
Non-current (included in property, plant, and equipment)	
Ore in stockpiles	$202

Instructions

(a) Why do you think that there are no finished goods inventories? Why do you think the raw material, ore in stockpiles, is considered to be a non-current asset?

(b) Consider that Barrick has no finished goods inventories. What journal entries are made to record a sale?

(c) Suppose that gold bullion that cost $1.8 million to produce was sold for $2.4 million. The journal entry was made to record the sale, but no entry was made to remove the gold from the gold in process inventory. How would this error affect the following?

Balance Sheet		Income Statement	
Inventory	?	Cost of goods sold	?
Retained earnings	?	Net income	?
Accounts payable	?		
Working capital	?		
Current ratio	?		

COMPARATIVE ANALYSIS CASE

THE COCA-COLA COMPANY AND PEPSICO, INC.

Instructions

Go to the Take Action! CD and use information found there to answer the following questions related to The Coca-Cola Company and PepsiCo, Inc.

(a) What is the amount of inventory reported by Coca-Cola at December 31, 2001, and by PepsiCo at December 31, 2001? What percent of total assets is invested in inventory by each company?

(b) What inventory costing methods are used by Coca-Cola and PepsiCo? How does each company value its inventories?

(c) In the notes, what classifications (description) are used by Coca-Cola and PepsiCo to categorize their inventories?

(d) Compute and compare the inventory turnover ratios and days to sell inventory for 2001 for Coca-Cola and PepsiCo. Indicate why there might be a significant difference between the two companies.

*Remember to check the **Take Action! CD**
and the book's **companion Web site**
to find additional resources for this chapter.*

ACCOUNTING FOR PROPERTY, PLANT, AND EQUIPMENT

CHAPTER 9

WHERE HAVE ALL THE ASSETS GONE?

Investments in long-lived assets, such as property, plant, and equipment, are important elements in many companies' balance sheets. As indicated in the chart below, major companies, such as **General Mills**, **Wal-Mart**, and **Southwest Airlines** recently reported property, plant, and equipment (PP&E) as a percent of total assets ranging from 30 percent up to nearly 90 percent.

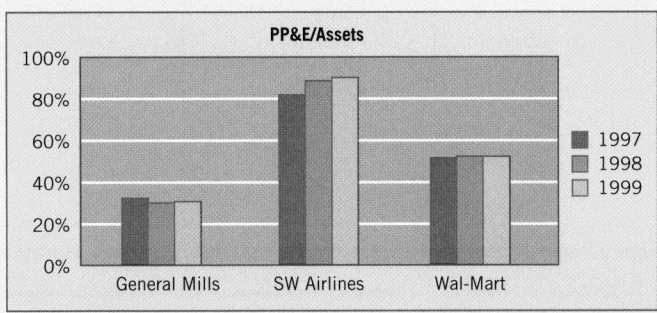

However, for various strategic reasons, a number of companies are now shedding property, plant, and equipment. They are using the proceeds to pay other companies to perform manufacturing and assembly functions—functions that were previously performed in company-owned facilities. As a result, some companies such as **Cisco**, **Lucent**, and **Nortel** do not need to invest as much in long-lived assets, as indicated in the following chart.

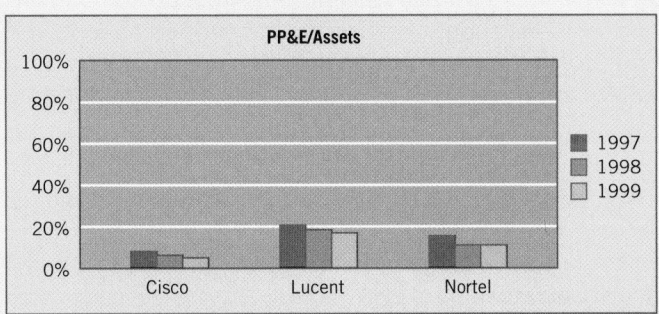

Nortel is a good example of the specifics of this strategy. The company is in the midst of a 36-month plan to sell and outsource certain facilities in order to reduce Nortel's direct manufacturing activities and costs. Nortel also sold its training and headset businesses and plans to more aggressively outsource other operations to reduce costs. Reductions in these areas will enable Nortel to concentrate on its core operations. The market seems to approve of this strategy. As measured by price/earnings (P/E) ratios early in 2000, Nortel's P/E ratio was well above that of competitors not pursuing aggressive outsourcing strategies.[1]

[1] Adapted from Chapter 1 in Grady Means and David Schneider, *MetaCapitalism: The e-Business Revolution and the Design of 21st-Century Companies and Markets.* (New York: John Wiley and Sons, 2000).

LEARNING OBJECTIVES

After studying this chapter, you should be able to:

1. Describe property, plant, and equipment and costs included in its initial valuation.
2. Describe the accounting problems associated with interest capitalization.
3. Understand accounting issues related to acquiring and valuing plant assets.
4. Describe the accounting treatment for costs subsequent to acquisition.
5. Explain the concept of depreciation.
6. Identify the factors involved in the depreciation process.
7. Compare activity, straight-line, and decreasing-charge methods of depreciation.
8. Describe the accounting treatment for the disposal of property, plant, and equipment.
9. Explain how property, plant, and equipment are reported and analyzed.

As indicated in the opening story, a company like **Southwest Airlines** has a substantial investment in property, plant, and equipment. Conversely, other companies, such as **Nortel**, have a minor investment in these types of assets. The purpose of this chapter is to discuss the proper accounting for the acquisition, use, and disposition of property, plant, and equipment. The content and organization of the chapter are as follows.

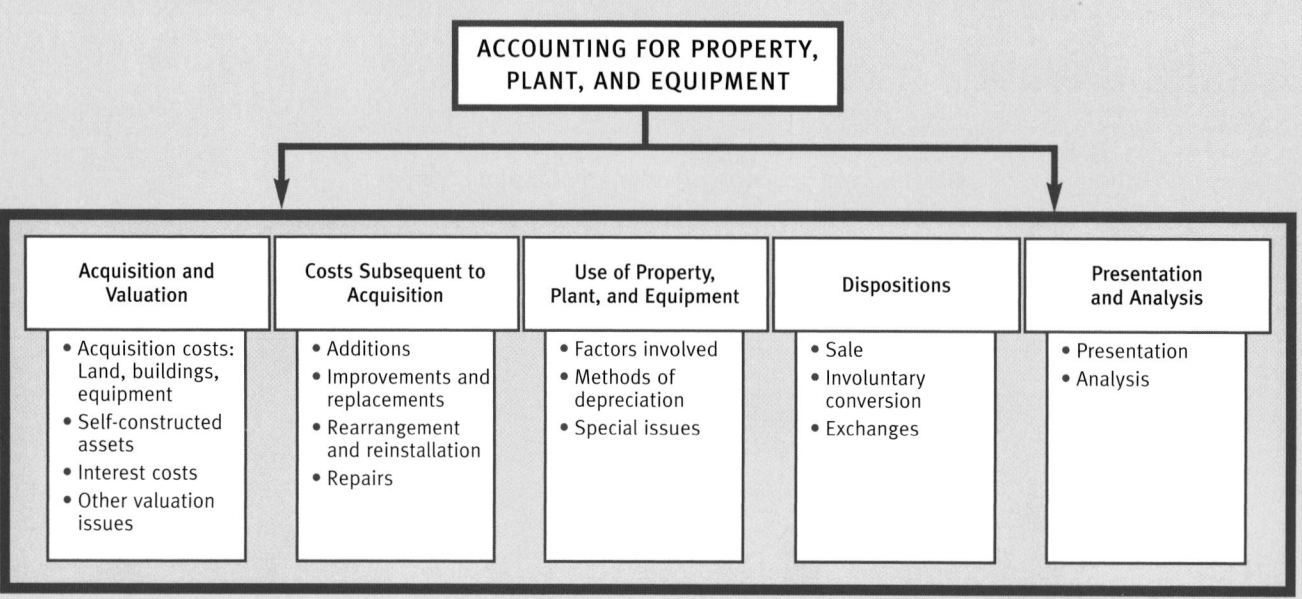

ACCOUNTING FOR PROPERTY, PLANT, AND EQUIPMENT				
Acquisition and Valuation	**Costs Subsequent to Acquisition**	**Use of Property, Plant, and Equipment**	**Dispositions**	**Presentation and Analysis**
• Acquisition costs: Land, buildings, equipment • Self-constructed assets • Interest costs • Other valuation issues	• Additions • Improvements and replacements • Rearrangement and reinstallation • Repairs	• Factors involved • Methods of depreciation • Special issues	• Sale • Involuntary conversion • Exchanges	• Presentation • Analysis

OBJECTIVE 1
Describe property, plant, and equipment and costs included in its initial valuation.

Property, plant, and equipment; plant assets; or **fixed assets** include land, building structures (offices, factories, warehouses), and equipment (machinery, furniture, tools). These terms are used interchangeably throughout this textbook. The major characteristics of property, plant, and equipment are as follows.

1. **They are acquired for use in operations and not for resale.** Only assets used in normal business operations should be classified as property, plant, and equipment. An idle building is more appropriately classified separately as an investment. Land held by land developers or subdividers is classified as inventory.

2. **They are long-term in nature and usually subject to depreciation.** Property, plant, and equipment yield services over a number of years. The investment in these assets is assigned to future periods through periodic depreciation charges. The exception is land, which is not depreciated unless a material decrease in value occurs, such as a loss in fertility of agricultural land because of poor crop rotation, drought, or soil erosion.

3. **They possess physical substance.** Property, plant, and equipment are tangible assets characterized by physical existence or substance and thus are differentiated from intangible assets, such as patents or goodwill. Unlike raw material, however, property, plant, and equipment do not physically become part of a product held for resale.

ACQUISITION AND VALUATION OF PROPERTY, PLANT, AND EQUIPMENT

Historical cost is the usual basis for valuing property, plant, and equipment. **Historical cost is measured by the cash or cash equivalent price of obtaining the asset and bringing it to the location and condition necessary for its intended use.** The purchase price, freight costs, sales taxes, and installation costs of a productive asset are considered part of the asset's cost. These costs are allocated to future periods through depreciation. Any related costs incurred **after the asset's acquisition**, such as additions, improvements, or replacements, are **added to the asset's cost if they provide future service potential**. Otherwise they are expensed immediately.

Cost of Land

All expenditures made to acquire land and to ready it for use are considered part of the land cost. Thus, when **Wal-Mart** or **Home Depot** purchases land on which to build a new store, its land costs typically include (1) the purchase price; (2) closing costs, such as title to the land, attorney's fees, and recording fees; (3) costs incurred in getting the land in condition for its intended use, such as grading, filling, draining, and clearing; (4) assumption of any liens, mortgages, or encumbrances on the property; and (5) any additional land improvements that have an indefinite life.

When land has been purchased for the purpose of constructing a building, all costs incurred up to the excavation for the new building are considered land costs. **Removal of old buildings—clearing, grading, and filling—are considered land costs because these costs are necessary to get the land in condition for its intended purpose.** Any proceeds obtained in the process of getting the land ready for its intended use, such as salvage receipts on the demolition of an old building or the sale of cleared timber, are treated as **reductions in the price of the land**.

In some cases, the purchaser of land has to assume certain obligations on the land such as back taxes or liens. In such situations, the cost of the land is the cash paid for it, plus the encumbrances. In other words, if the purchase price of the land is $50,000 cash, but accrued property taxes of $5,000 and liens of $10,000 are assumed, the cost of the land is $65,000.

Special assessments for local improvements, such as pavements, street lights, sewers, and drainage systems, are usually charged to the Land account because they are relatively permanent in nature and are maintained and replaced by the local government body. In addition, permanent improvements made by the owner, such as landscaping, are properly chargeable to the Land account. **Improvements with limited lives**, such as private driveways, walks, fences, and parking lots, are recorded separately as Land Improvements so that they can be depreciated over their estimated lives.

Generally, land is part of property, plant, and equipment. However, if the major purpose of acquiring and holding land is speculative, land is more appropriately classified as an **investment**. If the land is held by a real estate concern for resale, it should be classified as **inventory**.

In cases where land is held as an investment, what accounting treatment should be given taxes, insurance, and other direct costs incurred while holding the land? Many believe these costs should be capitalized because the revenue from the investment still has not been received. This approach is reasonable and seems justified except in cases where the asset is currently producing revenue (such as rental property).

Cost of Buildings

The cost of buildings should include all expenditures related directly to their acquisition or construction. These costs include (1) materials, labor, and overhead costs incurred during construction and (2) professional fees and building permits. Generally, companies contract to have their buildings constructed. All costs incurred, from excavation to completion, are considered part of the building costs.

One accounting problem is deciding what to do about an old building that is on the site of a newly proposed building. Is the cost of removal of the old building a cost of the land or a cost of the new building? The answer is that **if land is purchased with an old building on it, then the cost of demolition less its salvage value is a cost of getting the land ready for its intended use and relates to the land rather than to the new**

building. As indicated earlier, all costs of getting an asset ready for its intended use are costs of that asset.

Cost of Equipment

The term "equipment" in accounting includes delivery equipment, office equipment, machinery, furniture and fixtures, furnishings, factory equipment, and similar fixed assets. The cost of such assets includes the purchase price, freight and handling charges incurred, insurance on the equipment while in transit, cost of special foundations if required, assembling and installation costs, and costs of conducting trial runs. Costs thus include all expenditures incurred in acquiring the equipment and preparing it for use.

Self-Constructed Assets

Occasionally companies construct their own assets. Determining the cost of such machinery and other fixed assets can be a problem. Without a purchase price or contract price, the company must allocate costs and expenses to arrive at the cost of the **self-constructed asset.** Materials and direct labor used in construction pose no problem; these costs can be traced directly to work and material orders related to the fixed assets constructed.

However, the assignment of indirect costs of manufacturing creates special problems. These indirect costs, called **overhead** or burden, include power, heat, light, insurance, property taxes on factory buildings and equipment, factory supervisory labor, depreciation of fixed assets, and supplies.

The approach followed for overhead is to assign a portion of all overhead to the construction process. The reason: These costs are attached to all products and assets manufactured or constructed. Failure to allocate overhead costs understates the initial cost of the asset and results in an inaccurate future allocation.

If the allocated overhead results in recording construction costs in excess of the costs that would be charged by an outside independent producer, the excess overhead should be recorded as a period loss rather than be capitalized, to avoid capitalizing the asset at more than its probable market value.

OBJECTIVE 2
Describe the accounting problems associated with interest capitalization.

Interest Costs During Construction

The proper accounting for interest costs has been a long-standing controversy. Some argue that no interest should be charged to construction costs. They contend that if a company had used stock (equity) financing rather than debt, this cost would not have been recorded. Others argue that all costs of funds, whether identifiable or not, should be recorded. Interest, whether actual or imputed, is a cost of the building and should be recorded as such. Illustration 9-1 indicates how interest costs might be added to the cost of the asset.

Illustration 9-1
Capitalization of Interest Costs

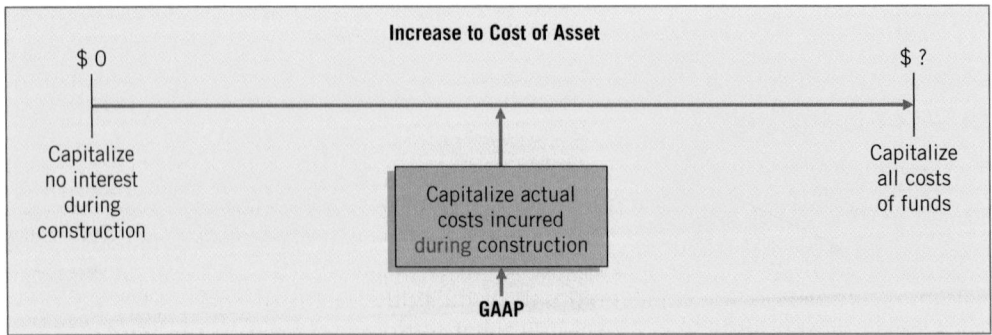

Capitalizing actual interest (with modification) is the approach required under GAAP. This method is in accordance with the concept that the **historical cost of ac-**

quiring an asset includes all costs (including interest) incurred to bring the asset to the condition and location necessary for its intended use. The rationale for this approach is that during construction the asset is not generating revenues, and therefore interest costs should be deferred (capitalized).[2] Once construction is completed, the asset is ready for its intended use and revenues can be earned. At this point interest should be reported as an expense and matched to these revenues. It follows that any interest cost incurred in purchasing an asset that is ready for its intended use should be expensed.

To illustrate the impact of interest capitalization on financial statements, assume that Richards Company begins construction on a building early in 2002 and completes construction by the end of the year. Richards incurred total interest costs on borrowing during 2002 in the amount of $325,000. It determined that $165,000 of these total interest costs is attributable to expenditures on the new building. (A comprehensive illustration of the procedures for determining the amount of capitalized interest is presented in Appendix 9A.) The following summary journal entry shows how capitalized interest and interest expense would be recorded by Richards in 2002.

Building (Capitalized Interest)	165,000	
Interest Expense	160,000	
Cash		325,000

At December 31, 2002, Richards would disclose the amount of interest capitalized, either as part of the nonoperating section of the income statement or in the notes accompanying the financial statements. Both forms of disclosure are illustrated below.

Income from operations		XXXX
Other expenses and losses		
Interest expense	$325,000	
Less: Capitalized interest	165,000	160,000
Income before taxes on income		XXXX
Income taxes		XXX
Net income		XXXX

Illustration 9-2
Capitalized Interest Reported in the Income Statement

Note 1: Accounting Policies. *Capitalized Interest.* During 2002 total interest cost was $325,000, of which $165,000 was capitalized and $160,000 was charged to expense.

Illustration 9-3
Capitalized Interest Disclosed in a Note

Special Issues Related to Interest Capitalization

Two issues related to interest capitalization merit special attention:

⟨**1**⟩ Expenditures for land.
⟨**2**⟩ Interest revenue.

Expenditures for Land. When land is purchased with the intention of developing it for a particular use, interest costs associated with those expenditures qualify for interest capitalization. If land is purchased as a site for a structure (such as a plant site), interest costs capitalized during the period of construction are part of the cost of the plant, not the land. Conversely, if land is being developed for lot sales, any capitalized interest cost should be part of the acquisition cost of the developed land. However,

[2]"Capitalization of Interest Cost," *Statement of Financial Accounting Standards No. 34* (Stamford, Conn.: FASB, 1979).

interest costs involved in purchasing land held **for speculation** should **not** be capitalized because the asset is ready for its intended use.

Interest Revenue. Companies frequently borrow money to finance construction of assets and temporarily invest the excess borrowed funds in interest-bearing securities until the funds are needed to pay for construction. During the early stages of construction, interest revenue earned may exceed the interest cost incurred on the borrowed funds.

The question is whether it is appropriate to offset interest revenue against interest cost when determining the amount of interest to be capitalized as a part of the construction cost of assets. In general, **interest revenue should not be netted or offset against interest cost**. Temporary or short-term investment decisions are not related to the interest incurred as part of the acquisition cost of assets. Therefore, the interest incurred on qualifying assets should be capitalized whether or not excess funds are temporarily invested in short-term securities. Some are critical of this accounting because a company can defer the interest cost but report the interest revenue in the current period.

WHAT DO THE NUMBERS MEAN?

INTERNATIONAL INSIGHT

Under international accounting standards *(IAS No. 23)*, capitalization of interest is allowed, but it is not the preferred treatment. Thus, the financial statements of U.S. and IAS companies may not be comparable if capitalized interest costs are significant and the IAS company uses the preferred treatment. An analyst can use the information disclosed by the U.S. company to convert the U.S. GAAP numbers to be comparable to the IAS company.

WHAT'S IN YOUR INTEREST?

The requirement to capitalize interest can have a significant impact on financial statements. For example, when earnings of building manufacturer **Jim Walter's Corporation** dropped from $1.51 to $1.17 per share, the company was able to offset 11 cents per share of the decline by capitalizing the interest on coal mining projects and several plants under construction.

How can statement users determine the impact of interest capitalization on a company's bottom line? They can examine the notes to the financial statements. Companies with material interest capitalization are required to disclose the amounts of capitalized interest relative to total interest costs. For example, **Anadarko Petroleum Corporation** capitalized nearly 30 percent of its total interest costs in a recent year and provided the following footnote related to capitalized interest.

Financial Footnotes

Total interest costs incurred during the year were $82,415,000. Of this amount, the Company capitalized $24,716,000. Capitalized interest is included as part of the cost of oil and gas properties. The capitalization rates are based on the Company's weighted-average cost of borrowings used to finance the expenditures.

Other Valuation Issues

Like other assets, **property, plant, and equipment should be recorded at the fair market value of what is given up or the fair value of the asset received, whichever is more clearly evident**. Fair market value, however, is sometimes obscured by the process through which the asset is acquired. As an example, assume that land and buildings are bought together for one price. How are separate values for the land and building determined? A number of accounting problems of this nature are examined in the following sections.

Cash Discounts

When plant assets are purchased subject to cash discounts for prompt payment, how should the discount be reported? If the discount is taken, it should be considered a reduction in the purchase price of the asset. What is not clear, however, is whether a reduction in the asset cost should occur even if the discount is not taken.

Two points of view exist on this matter. Under one approach, the discount, whether taken or not, is considered a reduction in the cost of the asset. The rationale for this approach is that the real cost of the asset is the cash or cash equivalent price of the asset. In addition, some argue that the terms of cash discounts are so attractive that failure to take them indicates management error or inefficiency. Proponents of the other approach argue that failure to take the discount should not always be considered a loss because the terms may be unfavorable or because it might not be prudent for the company to take the discount. At present, both methods are employed in practice. The former method is generally preferred.

OBJECTIVE **3**
Understand accounting issues related to acquiring and valuing plant assets.

Lump Sum Purchase

A special problem of pricing fixed assets arises when a group of plant assets is purchased at a single **lump sum price**. When such a situation occurs, which is not at all unusual, the practice is to allocate the total cost among the various assets on the basis of their relative fair market values. The assumption is that costs will vary in direct proportion to sales value. This is the same principle that is applied to allocate a lump sum cost among different inventory items.

To determine fair market value, any of the following might be used: an appraisal for insurance purposes, the assessed valuation for property taxes, or simply an independent appraisal by an engineer or other appraiser.

To illustrate, Norduct Homes, Inc. decides to purchase several assets of a small heating concern, Comfort Heating, for $80,000. Comfort Heating is in the process of liquidation, and its assets sold are:

	Book Value	Fair Market Value
Inventory	$30,000	$ 25,000
Land	20,000	25,000
Building	35,000	50,000
	$85,000	$100,000

The $80,000 purchase price would be allocated on the basis of the relative fair market values (assuming specific identification of costs is not practicable) in the following manner.

Inventory	$\dfrac{\$25,000}{\$100,000} \times \$80,000 = \$20,000$	
Land	$\dfrac{\$25,000}{\$100,000} \times \$80,000 = \$20,000$	
Building	$\dfrac{\$50,000}{\$100,000} \times \$80,000 = \$40,000$	

Illustration 9-4
Allocation of Purchase Price—Relative Fair Market Value Basis

Issuance of Stock

When property is acquired by issuance of securities, such as common stock, the cost of the property is not properly measured by the par or stated value of such stock. If the stock is being actively traded, **the market value of the stock issued is a fair indication of the cost of the property acquired because the stock is a good measure of the current cash equivalent price**.

For example, Upgrade Living Co. decides to purchase some adjacent land for expansion of its cabinet operation. In lieu of paying cash for the land, the company issues to Deedland Company 5,000 shares of common stock (par value $10) that have a fair market value of $12 per share. Upgrade Living Co. would make the following entry.

Land (5,000 × $12)	60,000	
Common Stock		50,000
Additional Paid-In Capital		10,000

If the market value of the common stock exchanged is not determinable, the market value of the property should be established and used as the basis for recording the asset and issuance of the common stock.[3]

Accounting for Contributions

Companies sometimes receive or make contributions (donations or gifts). Such contributions are referred to as **nonreciprocal transfers** because they are transfers of assets in one direction. A contribution is often some type of asset (such as cash, securities, land, buildings, or use of facilities), but it also could be the forgiveness of a debt.

In general, contributions received should be recognized as revenues in the period received.[4] Contributions would be measured at the fair value of the assets received.[5] To illustrate, Max Wayer Meat Packing, Inc. has recently accepted a donation of land with a fair value of $150,000 from the Memphis Industrial Development Corp. in return for a promise to build a packing plant in Memphis. Max Wayer's entry is:

Land	150,000	
Contribution Revenue		150,000

When a nonmonetary asset is contributed, the amount of the donation should be recorded as an expense at the fair value of the donated asset. If a difference exists between the fair value of the asset and its book value, a gain or loss should be recognized. To illustrate, Kline Industries donates land to the city of Los Angeles for a city park. The land cost $80,000 and has a fair market value of $110,000. The entry to record this donation would be:

Contribution Expense	110,000	
Land		80,000
Gain on Disposal of Land		30,000

In some cases, companies will promise to give (pledge) some type of asset in the future. The question is whether this promise should be recorded immediately or at the time the assets are given. If the promise is **unconditional** (depends only on the passage of time or on demand by the recipient for performance), the contribution expense

---

[3]When the fair market value of the stock is used as the basis of valuation, careful consideration must be given to the effect that the issuance of additional shares will have on the existing market price. Where the effect on market price appears significant, an independent appraisal of the asset received should be made. This valuation should be employed as the basis for valuation of the asset as well as for the stock issued. In the unusual case where the fair market value of the stock or the fair market value of the asset cannot be determined objectively, the board of directors of the corporation may set the value.

[4]"Accounting for Contributions Received and Contributions Made," *Statement of Financial Accounting Standards No. 116* (Norwalk, Conn.: FASB, 1993). Transfers of assets from governmental units to business enterprises are excluded from the scope of this standard. However, we believe that the basic requirements should hold also for these types of contributions, and therefore all assets should be recorded at fair value and all credits should be recorded as revenue.

[5]"Accounting for Nonmonetary Transactions," op. cit., par. 18. Also, *FASB No. 116* indicates that expenses on contributions made should be recorded at the fair value of the assets given up.

and related payable should be reported. If the promise is **conditional**, the expense is recognized in the period benefited by the contribution, which is generally when the asset is transferred.

Summary

In summary, historical cost is generally used as the basis for recording the acquisition of property, plant, and equipment. Historical cost is measured by the cash or cash-equivalent price of obtaining an asset and bringing it to the location and condition for its intended use. Modifications to the general rule arise in a number of special situations, as summarized in Illustration 9-5.

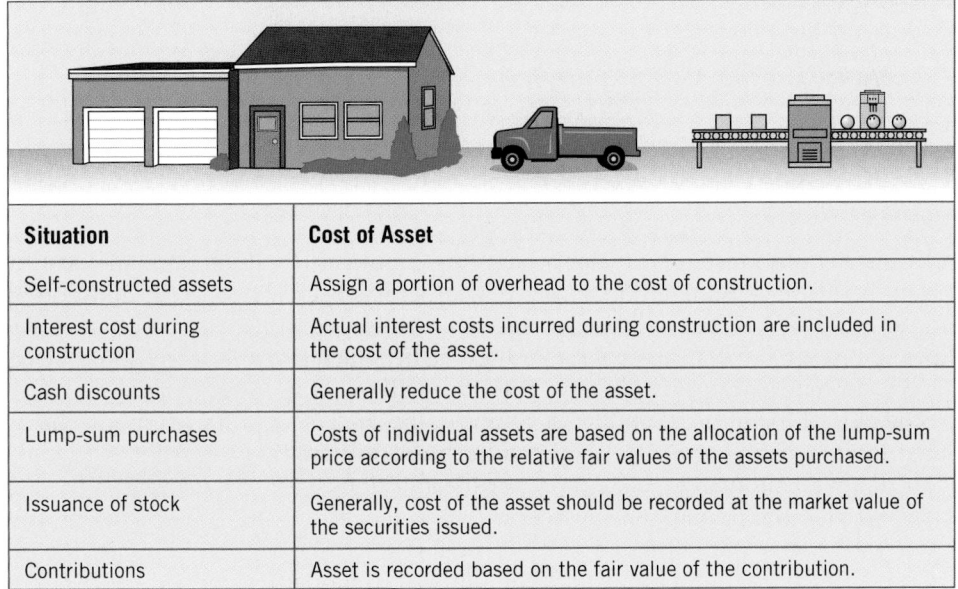

Situation	Cost of Asset
Self-constructed assets	Assign a portion of overhead to the cost of construction.
Interest cost during construction	Actual interest costs incurred during construction are included in the cost of the asset.
Cash discounts	Generally reduce the cost of the asset.
Lump-sum purchases	Costs of individual assets are based on the allocation of the lump-sum price according to the relative fair values of the assets purchased.
Issuance of stock	Generally, cost of the asset should be recorded at the market value of the securities issued.
Contributions	Asset is recorded based on the fair value of the contribution.

Illustration 9-5
Accounting for Acquisition of Property, Plant, and Equipment in Special Situations

INTERNATIONAL INSIGHT

In many nations, such as Great Britain and Brazil, companies are allowed to revalue their fixed assets at amounts above historical cost. These revaluations may be at appraisal values or at amounts linked to a specified index. Other nations, such as Japan and Germany, do not allow such revaluations.

COSTS SUBSEQUENT TO ACQUISITION

After plant assets are installed and ready for use, additional costs are incurred that range from ordinary repairs to significant additions. The major problem is allocating these costs to the proper time periods. **In general, costs incurred to achieve greater future benefits should be capitalized, whereas expenditures that simply maintain a given level of services should be expensed.** In order for costs to be capitalized, one of three conditions must be present:

① The useful life of the asset must be increased.
② The quantity of units produced from the asset must be increased.
③ The quality of the units produced must be enhanced.

Expenditures that do not increase an asset's future benefits should be expensed. Ordinary repairs are expenditures that maintain the existing condition of the asset or restore it to normal operating efficiency and should be expensed immediately.

Most expenditures below an established arbitrary minimum amount are expensed rather than capitalized. Many enterprises have adopted the rule that expenditures below, say, $100 or $500, should always be expensed. Although conceptually this treatment may not be correct, expediency demands it. Otherwise, depreciation schedules would have to be set up for such items as wastepaper baskets and ash trays.

OBJECTIVE **4**
Describe the accounting treatment for costs subsequent to acquisition.

Although the distinction between a **capital (asset) expenditure** and a **revenue (expense) expenditure** is not always clear-cut, in most cases, **consistent application of a capital/expense policy** is more important than attempting to provide general theoretical guidelines for each transaction. Generally, four major types of expenditures are incurred relative to existing assets.

MAJOR TYPES OF EXPENDITURES

ADDITIONS. Increase or extension of existing assets.

IMPROVEMENTS AND REPLACEMENTS. Substitution of an improved asset for an existing one.

REARRANGEMENT AND REINSTALLATION. Movement of assets from one location to another.

REPAIRS. Expenditures that maintain assets in condition for operation.

Additions

Additions should present no major accounting problems. By definition, **any addition to plant assets is capitalized** because a new asset has been created. The addition of a wing to a hospital or the addition of an air conditioning system to an office, for example, increases the service potential of that facility. Such expenditures should be capitalized and matched against the revenues that will result in future periods.

The most difficult problem that develops in this area is accounting for any changes related to the existing structure as a result of the addition. Is the cost that is incurred to tear down an old wall to make room for the addition a cost of the addition or an expense or loss of the period? The answer is that it depends on the original intent. If the company had anticipated that an addition was going to be added later, then this cost of removal is a proper cost of the addition. But if the company had not anticipated this development, it should properly be reported as a loss in the current period on the basis that the company was inefficient in its planning. Normally, the carrying amount of the old wall remains in the accounts, although theoretically it should be removed.

Improvements and Replacements

Improvements (often referred to as **betterments**) and **replacements** are substitutions of one asset for another. What is the difference between an improvement and a replacement? An improvement is the substitution of a **better asset** for the one currently used (say, a concrete floor for a wooden floor). A replacement, on the other hand, is the substitution of a **similar asset** (a wooden floor for a wooden floor).

Many times improvements and replacements result from a general policy to modernize or rehabilitate an older building or piece of equipment. The problem is differentiating these types of expenditure from normal repairs. Does the expenditure increase the **future service potential** of the asset? Or does it merely **maintain the existing level** of service? Frequently, the answer is not clear-cut, and good judgment must be used in order to classify these expenditures.

If it is determined that the expenditure increases the future service potential of the asset and, therefore, should be capitalized, the accounting is handled according to the **substitution approach.** Conceptually, the substitution approach is the correct procedure if the carrying amount of the old asset is available. If the carrying amount of the old asset can be determined, it is a simple matter to remove the cost of the old asset and replace it with the cost of the new asset.

To illustrate, Instinct Enterprises decides to replace the pipes in its plumbing system. A plumber suggests that in place of the cast iron pipes and copper tubing, a newly developed plastic tubing be used. The old pipe and tubing have a book value of $15,000 (cost of $150,000 less accumulated depreciation of $135,000), and a scrap value of $1,000. The plastic tubing system has a cost of $125,000. Assuming that Instinct has to pay $124,000 for the new tubing after exchanging the old tubing, the entry is:

Plumbing System	125,000	
Accumulated Depreciation	135,000	
Loss on Disposal of Plant Assets	14,000	
Plumbing System		150,000
Cash ($125,000 − $1,000)		124,000

The problem is determining the book value of the old asset. Generally, the components of a given asset depreciate at different rates, but no separate accounting is made. For example, the tires, motor, and body of a truck depreciate at different rates, but most companies use one rate for the entire truck. Separate depreciation rates could be set for each component, but it would be impractical. If the carrying amount of the old asset cannot be determined, one of two other approaches is adopted.

One approach is to capitalize the improvement and not remove the carrying amount of the old asset from the accounts, because sufficient depreciation was taken on the item to reduce the carrying amount almost to zero. Although this assumption may not be true in every case, the differences are not often significant. Improvements are usually handled in this manner.

In cases when the quantity or quality of the asset itself has not been improved, but its useful life has been extended, the expenditure may be debited to Accumulated Depreciation rather than to an asset account. The theory behind this approach is that the replacement extends the useful life of the asset and thereby recaptures some or all of the past depreciation. The net carrying amount of the asset is the same whether the asset is debited or the accumulated depreciation is debited.

Rearrangement and Reinstallation

Rearrangement and reinstallation costs, which are expenditures intended to benefit future periods, are different from additions, replacements, and improvements. An example is the rearrangement and reinstallation of machines to facilitate future production. If the original installation cost and the accumulated depreciation to date can be determined or estimated, the rearrangement and reinstallation cost is handled as a replacement. If not, which is generally the case, the new costs (if material in amount) should be capitalized as an asset to be amortized over future periods expected to benefit. If these costs are not material, if they cannot be separated from other operating expenses, or if their future benefit is questionable, they should be immediately expensed.

Repairs

Ordinary repairs are expenditures made to maintain plant assets in operating condition. They are charged to an expense account in the period in which they are incurred on the basis that **it is the primary period benefited**. Replacing minor parts, lubricating and adjusting equipment, repainting, and cleaning are examples of maintenance charges that occur regularly and are treated as ordinary operating expenses.

It is often difficult to distinguish a repair from an improvement or replacement. The major consideration is whether the expenditure benefits more than one year or one operating cycle, whichever is longer. If a **major repair** (such as an overhaul) occurs, several periods will benefit and the cost should be handled as an addition, improvement, or replacement.[6]

---

[6]If income statements are prepared for short periods of time, say, monthly or quarterly, the same principles apply. Ordinary repairs and other regular maintenance charges for an annual period may benefit several quarters, and allocation of the cost among the periods concerned might be required.

Some advocate accruing estimated repair costs beyond one year on the assumption that depreciation does not take into consideration the incurrence of repair costs. For example, in open hearth furnace rebuilding, companies may wish to establish an allowance for repairs because the amount of repairs can be estimated with a high degree of certainty. Although conceptually appealing, it is difficult to justify the Allowance for Repairs account as a liability because one might ask, "To whom do you owe the liability?" Placement in the stockholders' equity section is also illogical because no addition to the stockholders' investment has taken place. Thus, companies may not anticipate repairs and maintenance expenses (and record liabilities) until they arise.[7]

Summary of Costs Subsequent to Acquisition

The following schedule summarizes the accounting treatment for various costs incurred subsequent to the acquisition of capitalized assets.

Illustration 9-6

Summary of Costs Subsequent to Acquisition of Property, Plant, and Equipment

Type of Expenditure	Normal Accounting Treatment
Additions	Capitalize cost of addition to asset account.
Improvements and replacements	(a) **Carrying value known:** Remove cost of and accumulated depreciation on old asset, recognizing any gain or loss. Capitalize cost of improvement/replacement. (b) **Carrying value unknown:** 1. If the asset's useful life is extended, debit accumulated depreciation for cost of improvement/replacement. 2. If the quantity or quality of the asset's productivity is increased, capitalize cost of improvement/replacement to asset account.
Rearrangement and reinstallation	(a) If original installation cost is **known**, account for cost of rearrangement/reinstallation as a replacement (carrying value known). (b) If original installation cost is **unknown** and rearrangement/reinstallation cost is **material** in amount and benefits future periods, capitalize as an asset. (c) If original installation cost is **unknown** and rearrangement/reinstallation cost is **not material or future benefit is questionable**, expense the cost when incurred.
Repairs	(a) **Ordinary:** Expense cost of repairs when incurred. (b) **Major:** As appropriate, treat as an addition, improvement, or replacement.

USE OF PROPERTY, PLANT, AND EQUIPMENT

OBJECTIVE 5
Explain the concept of depreciation.

Depreciation is the accounting process of allocating the cost of tangible assets to expense in a systematic and rational manner to those periods expected to benefit from the use of the asset. Assets are not depreciated on the basis of a decline in their fair market value, but on the basis of systematic charges to expense.

[7]SEC announcement at the March 2000 meeting of the Emerging Issues Task Force. The only exception to this treatment is the airline industry, presumably because these companies have unique substantial repairs and maintenance programs. The AICPA is working on a project to address diversity in practice in the accounting for subsequent costs. *Proposed Statement of Position*, "Accounting for Certain Costs and Activities Related to Property, Plant, and Equipment" (New York: AICPA, June 29, 2001).

This approach is employed because the value of the asset may fluctuate between the time the asset is purchased and the time it is sold or junked. Attempts to measure these interim value changes have not been well received because values are difficult to measure objectively. Therefore, the asset's cost is charged to depreciation expense over its estimated life, making no attempts to value the asset at fair market value between acquisition and disposition. The cost allocation approach is used because a matching of costs with revenues occurs and because fluctuations in market value are tenuous and difficult to measure.

Factors Involved in the Depreciation Process

Before a pattern of charges to revenue can be established, three basic questions must be answered:

1. What depreciable base is to be used for the asset?
2. What is the asset's useful life?
3. What method of cost apportionment is best for this asset?

OBJECTIVE **6**
Identify the factors involved in the depreciation process.

The answers to these questions involve the distillation of several estimates into one single figure. The calculations on which depreciation is based assume perfect knowledge of the future, which is never attainable.

Depreciable Base for the Asset

The base established for depreciation is a function of two factors: the original cost, and salvage or disposal value. We discussed historical cost earlier in this chapter. **Salvage value** is the estimated amount that will be received at the time the asset is sold or removed from service. It is the amount to which the asset must be written down or depreciated during its useful life. If an asset has a cost of $10,000 and a salvage value of $1,000, its **depreciation base** is $9,000.

Original cost	$10,000
Less: Salvage value	1,000
Depreciation base	$ 9,000

Illustration 9-7
Computation of Depreciation Base

From a practical standpoint, salvage value is often considered to be zero because its valuation is small. Some long-lived assets, however, have substantial salvage values.

Estimation of Service Lives

The service life of an asset and its physical life are often not the same. A piece of machinery may be physically capable of producing a given product for many years beyond its service life. But the equipment is not used for all of those years because the cost of producing the product in later years may be too high. For example, the old Slater cotton mill in Pawtucket, Rhode Island, is preserved in remarkable physical condition as an historic landmark in U.S. industrial development, although its service life was terminated many years ago.[8]

Assets are retired for two reasons: **physical factors** (such as casualty or expiration of physical life) and **economic factors** (obsolescence). Physical factors are the wear and tear, decay, and casualties that make it difficult for the asset to perform indefinitely. These physical factors set the outside limit for the service life of an asset.

[8]Taken from J. D. Coughlan and W. K. Strand, *Depreciation Accounting, Taxes and Business Decisions* (New York: The Ronald Press, 1969), pp. 10–12.

To illustrate the concepts of physical and economic factors, consider a new nuclear power plant. Which do you think would be more important in determining the useful life of a nuclear power plant—physical factors or economic factors? The limiting factors seem to be (1) ecological considerations, (2) competition from other power sources, and (3) safety concerns. Physical life does not appear to be the primary factor affecting useful life. Although the plant's physical life may be far from over, the plant may become obsolete in 10 years.

For a house, physical factors undoubtedly are more important than the economic or functional factors relative to useful life. Whenever the physical nature of the asset is the primary determinant of useful life, maintenance plays an extremely vital role. The better the maintenance, the longer the life of the asset.[9]

In some cases, arbitrary service lives are selected. In others, sophisticated statistical methods are employed to establish a useful life for accounting purposes. In many cases, the primary basis for estimating the useful life of an asset is the enterprise's past experience with the same or similar assets. In a highly industrial economy such as that of the United States, where research and innovation are so prominent, technological factors have as much effect, if not more, on service lives of tangible plant assets as physical factors do.

Methods of Depreciation

The third factor involved in the depreciation process is the **method** of cost apportionment. The profession requires that the depreciation method employed be "systematic and rational."

A number of depreciation methods are used. They may be classified as follows.

UNDERLYING CONCEPTS

Depreciation is an attempt to match the cost of an asset to the periods that benefit from the use of that asset.

(1) Activity method (units of use or production).
(2) Straight-line method.
(3) Decreasing charge methods (accelerated):

  (a) Sum-of-the-years'-digits.
  (b) Declining-balance method.[10]

To illustrate these depreciation methods, assume that Stanley Coal Mines recently purchased an additional crane for digging purposes. Pertinent data concerning the purchase of the crane are as follows.

Illustration 9-8
Data Used to Illustrate Depreciation Methods

Cost of crane	$500,000
Estimated useful life	5 years
Estimated salvage value	$ 50,000
Productive life in hours	30,000 hours

[9]The airline industry also illustrates the type of problem involved in estimation. In the past, aircraft were assumed not to wear out—they just became obsolete. However, some jets have been in service as long as 20 years, and maintenance of these aircraft has become increasingly expensive. In addition, the public's concern about worn-out aircraft has been heightened by some recent air disasters. As a result, some airlines are finding it necessary to replace aircraft not because of obsolescence but because of physical deterioration.

[10]*Accounting Trends and Techniques—2001* reports that of its 600 surveyed companies, various depreciation methods were used for financial reporting purposes: straight-line, 576; declining-balance, 22; sum-of-the-years'-digits, 7; accelerated method (not specified), 53; units of production, 34.

Activity Method

The **activity method** (also called the variable-charge approach) assumes that depreciation is **a function of use or productivity, instead of the passage of time**. The life of the asset is considered in terms of either the **output** it provides (units it produces), or an **input** measure such as the number of hours it works. Conceptually, the proper cost association is established in terms of output instead of hours used, but often the output is not easily measurable. In such cases, an input measure such as machine hours is a more appropriate method of measuring the dollar amount of depreciation charges for a given accounting period.

Stanley's crane poses no particular problem because the usage (hours) is relatively easy to measure. If the crane is used 4,000 hours the first year, the depreciation charge is:

OBJECTIVE **7**
Compare activity, straight-line, and decreasing-charge methods of depreciation.

$$\frac{\boxed{\text{Cost less salvage}} \times \boxed{\text{Hours this year}}}{\boxed{\text{Total estimated hours}}} = \boxed{\text{Depreciation charge}}$$

$$\frac{(\$500{,}000 - \$50{,}000) \times 4{,}000}{30{,}000} = \$60{,}000$$

Illustration 9-9
Depreciation Calculation, Activity Method—Crane Example

The major limitation of this method is that it is not appropriate in situations in which depreciation is a function of time instead of activity. For example, a building is subject to a great deal of steady deterioration from the elements (time) regardless of its use. In addition, where an asset is subject to economic or functional factors, independent of its use, the activity method loses much of its significance. For example, if a company is expanding rapidly, a particular building may soon become obsolete for its intended purposes. In both cases, activity is irrelevant. Another problem in using an activity method is that an estimate of units of output or service hours received is often difficult to determine.

Where loss of services is a result of activity or productivity, the activity method will best match costs and revenues. Companies that desire low depreciation during periods of low productivity and high depreciation during high productivity either adopt or switch to an activity method. In this way, a plant running at 40 percent of capacity generates 60 percent lower depreciation charges. **Inland Steel**, for example, switched to units-of-production depreciation at one time and reduced its losses by $43 million, or $1.20 per share.

Straight-Line Method

The **straight-line method** considers depreciation a **function of time rather than a function of usage**. This method is widely employed in practice because of its simplicity. The straight-line procedure is often the most conceptually appropriate, too. When creeping obsolescence is the primary reason for a limited service life, the decline in usefulness may be constant from period to period. The depreciation charge for the crane is computed as follows.

★ **UNDERLYING CONCEPTS**

If benefits flow on a "straight-line" basis, then justification exists for matching the cost of the asset on a straight-line basis with these benefits.

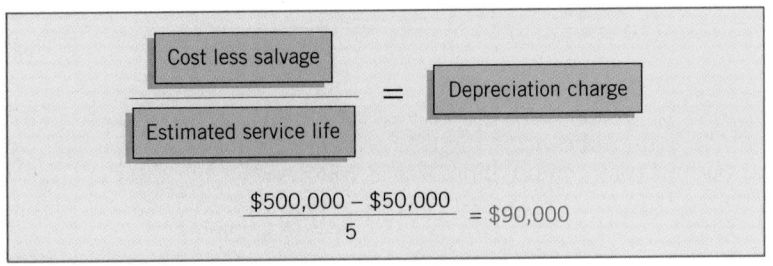

$$\frac{\boxed{\text{Cost less salvage}}}{\boxed{\text{Estimated service life}}} = \boxed{\text{Depreciation charge}}$$

$$\frac{\$500{,}000 - \$50{,}000}{5} = \$90{,}000$$

Illustration 9-10
Depreciation Calculation, Straight-Line Method— Crane Example

The major objection to the straight-line method is that it rests on two unrealistic assumptions: (1) The asset's economic usefulness is the same each year, and (2) the repair and maintenance expense is essentially the same each period.

One additional problem that occurs in using straight-line—as well as some others—is that distortions in the rate of return analysis (income/assets) develop. Illustration 9-11 indicates how the rate of return increases, given constant revenue flows, because the asset's book value decreases.

Illustration 9-11
Depreciation and Rate of Return Analysis—Crane Example

Year	Depreciation Expense	Undepreciated Asset Balance (book value)	Income (after depreciation expense)	Rate of Return (Income ÷ Assets)
0		$500,000		
1	$90,000	410,000	$100,000	24.4%
2	90,000	320,000	100,000	31.2%
3	90,000	230,000	100,000	43.5%
4	90,000	140,000	100,000	71.4%
5	90,000	50,000	100,000	200.0%

UNDERLYING CONCEPTS

The matching concept does not justify a constant charge to income. If the benefits from the asset decline as the asset gets older, then a decreasing charge to income would better match cost to benefits.

Decreasing-Charge Methods

The **decreasing-charge methods**—often called **accelerated depreciation methods**—provide for a higher depreciation cost in the earlier years and lower charges in later periods. The main justification for this approach is that more depreciation should be charged in earlier years because the asset suffers its greatest loss of services in those years. Another argument presented is that the accelerated methods provide a constant cost because the depreciation charge is lower in the later periods, at the time when the repair and maintenance costs are often higher. Generally, one of two decreasing-charge methods is employed: the sum-of-the-years'-digits method, or the declining-balance method.

Sum-of-the-Years'-Digits. The **sum-of-the-years'-digits method** results in a decreasing depreciation charge based on a decreasing fraction of depreciable cost (original cost less salvage value). Each fraction uses the sum of the years as a denominator (5 + 4 + 3 + 2 + 1 = 15) and the number of years of estimated life remaining as of the beginning of the year as a numerator. In this method, the numerator decreases year by year and the denominator remains constant (5/15, 4/15, 3/15, 2/15, and 1/15). At the end of the asset's useful life, the balance remaining should be equal to the salvage value. This method of computation is shown in Illustration 9-12 on page 423.[11]

Declining-Balance Method. Another decreasing charge method is the **declining-balance method**, which utilizes a depreciation rate (expressed as a percentage) that is some multiple of the straight-line method. For example, the double-declining rate for a 10-year asset would be 20 percent (double the straight-line rate, which is 1/10 or 10 percent). The declining-balance rate remains constant and is applied to the book value each year. Unlike other methods, in the declining-balance method **the salvage value is not deducted** in computing the depreciation base. The declining-balance rate is multiplied by the book value of the asset at the beginning of each period. Since the book

INTERNATIONAL INSIGHT

German companies depreciate their fixed assets at a much faster rate than U.S. companies because German tax laws permit accelerated depreciation of up to triple the straight-line rate.

---

[11]What happens if the estimated service life of the asset is, let us say, 51 years? How would you calculate the sum-of-the-years'-digits? Fortunately mathematicians have developed a formula that permits easy computation. It is as follows:

$$\frac{n(n+1)}{2} = \frac{51(51+1)}{2} = 1,326$$

Year	Depreciation Base	Remaining Life in Years	Depreciation Fraction	Depreciation Expense	Book Value, End of Year
1	$450,000	5	5/15	$150,000	$350,000
2	450,000	4	4/15	120,000	230,000
3	450,000	3	3/15	90,000	140,000
4	450,000	2	2/15	60,000	80,000
5	450,000	1	1/15	30,000	50,000[a]
		15	15/15	$450,000	

[a]Salvage value.

Illustration 9-12
Sum-of-the-Years'-Digits Depreciation Schedule— Crane Example

value of the asset is reduced each period by the depreciation charge, the constant-declining-balance rate is applied to a successively lower book value which results in lower depreciation charges each year. This process continues until the book value of the asset is reduced to its estimated salvage value, at which time depreciation is discontinued.

Various multiples are used in practice, such as twice (200 percent) the straight-line rate (**double-declining-balance method**) and 150 percent of the straight-line rate. Using the double-declining approach in the crane example, Stanley Coal Mines would have the depreciation charges shown in Illustration 9-13 below.

Year	Book Value of Asset First of Year	Rate on Declining Balance[a]	Depreciation Expense	Balance Accumulated Depreciation	Book Value, End of Year
1	$500,000	40%	$200,000	$200,000	$300,000
2	300,000	40%	120,000	320,000	180,000
3	180,000	40%	72,000	392,000	108,000
4	108,000	40%	43,200	435,200	64,800
5	64,800	40%	14,800[b]	450,000	50,000

[a]Based on twice the straight-line rate of 20% ($90,000/$450,000 = 20%; 20% × 2 = 40%).
[b]Limited to $14,800 because book value should not be less than salvage value.

Illustration 9-13
Double-Declining Depreciation Schedule— Crane Example

Enterprises often switch from the declining-balance method to the straight-line method near the end of the asset's useful life to ensure that the asset is depreciated only to its salvage value.[12]

[12]A pure form of the declining-balance method (sometimes appropriately called the "fixed percentage of book value method") has also been suggested as a possibility. This approach finds a rate that depreciates the asset exactly to salvage value at the end of its expected useful life. The formula for determination of this rate is as follows:

$$\text{Depreciation rate} = 1 - \sqrt[n]{\frac{\text{Salvage value}}{\text{Acquisition cost}}}$$

The life in years is n. Once the depreciation rate is computed, it is applied on the declining book value of the asset from period to period, which means that depreciation expense will be successively lower. This method is not used extensively in practice because the computations are cumbersome and it is not permitted for tax purposes.

**WHAT DO THE
NUMBERS MEAN?**

*Tutorial on
Depreciation*

DECELERATING DEPRECIATION

Which depreciation method should management select? Many believe that the method that best matches revenues with expenses should be used. For example, if revenues generated by the asset are constant over its useful life, straight-line depreciation should be selected. On the other hand, if revenues are higher (or lower) at the beginning of the asset's life, then a decreasing (or increasing) method should be used. Thus, if revenues from the asset can be reliably estimated, selecting a depreciation method that best matches costs with those revenues would seem to provide the most useful information to investors and creditors for assessing the future cash flows from the asset.

Managers in the real estate industry face a different challenge when considering depreciation choices. Real estate managers are frustrated with depreciation accounting because in their view, real estate often does not decline in value. In addition, because real estate is highly debt-financed, most real estate concerns report losses in earlier years of operations when the sum of depreciation and interest exceeds the revenue from the real estate project. As a result, real estate companies, like **Kimco Realty**, argue for some form of **increasing-charge** method of depreciation (lower depreciation at the beginning and higher depreciation at the end). With such a method, higher total assets and net income would be reported in the earlier years of the project.[13]

Special Depreciation Issues

Two special issues related to depreciation remain to be discussed. The major issues are:

① How should depreciation be computed for partial periods?
② How are revisions in depreciation rates handled?

Depreciation and Partial Periods

Plant assets are seldom purchased on the first day of a fiscal period or disposed of on the last day of a fiscal period. A practical question is: How much depreciation should be charged for the partial periods involved?

In computing depreciation expense for partial periods, it is necessary to determine the depreciation expense for the full year and then to prorate this depreciation expense between the two periods involved. This process should continue throughout the useful life of the asset.

Assume, for example, that an automated drill machine with a 5-year life is purchased by Steeltex Company for $45,000 (no salvage value) on June 1, 2002. The company's fiscal year ends December 31, and depreciation is charged for 7 months during that year. The total depreciation for a full year (assuming straight-line depreciation) is $9,000 ($45,000/5), and the depreciation for the first, partial year is:

$$\frac{7}{12} \times \$9,000 = \$5,250$$

[13]In this regard, real estate investment trusts (REITs) often report (in addition to net income) an earnings measure, funds from operations (FFO), that adjusts income for depreciation expense and other noncash expenses. This method is not GAAP, and there is mixed empirical evidence about whether FFO or GAAP income is more useful to real estate investment trust investors. See, for example, Richard Gore and David Stott, "Toward a More Informative Measure of Operating Performance in the REIT Industry: Net Income vs. FFO," *Accounting Horizons* (December 1998); and Linda Vincent, "The Information Content of FFO for REITs," *Journal of Accounting and Economics* (January 1999).

Sometimes the process of allocating costs to a partial period is modified to handle acquisitions and disposals of plant assets more simply. Depreciation may be computed for the full period on the opening balance in the asset account and no depreciation is charged on acquisitions during the year. Other variations charge a full year's depreciation on assets used for a full year, or charge one-half year's depreciation in the year of acquisition and in the year of disposal (referred to as the "half-year" convention), or charge a full year in the year of acquisition and none in the year of disposal.

A company is at liberty to adopt any one of these several fractional-year policies in allocating cost to the first and last years of an asset's life so long as the method is applied consistently. However, **unless otherwise stipulated, depreciation is normally computed on the basis of the nearest full month**. Illustration 9-14 shows depreciation allocated under five different fractional-year policies using the straight-line method on the $45,000 automated drill machine purchased by Steeltex Company on June 1, 2002, discussed earlier.

Machine Cost = $45,000	Depreciation Allocated per Period Over 5-Year Life*					
Fractional-Year Policy	2002	2003	2004	2005	2006	2007
1. Nearest full month	5,250[a]	9,000	9,000	9,000	9,000	3,750[b]
2. Half year in period of acquisition and disposal	4,500	9,000	9,000	9,000	9,000	4,500
3. Full year in period of acquisition, none in period of disposal	9,000	9,000	9,000	9,000	9,000	–0–
4. None in period of acquisition, full year in period of disposal	–0–	9,000	9,000	9,000	9,000	9,000

[a]7/12 ($9,000)   [b]5/12 ($9,000)
*Rounded to nearest dollar.

Illustration 9-14
Fractional-Year Depreciation Policies

Revision of Depreciation Rates

When a plant asset is purchased, depreciation rates are carefully determined based on past experience with similar assets and other pertinent information. The provisions for depreciation are only estimates, however, and it may be necessary to revise them during the life of the asset. Unexpected physical deterioration or unforeseen obsolescence may make the useful life of the asset less than originally estimated. Improved maintenance procedures, revision of operating procedures, or similar developments may prolong the life of the asset beyond the expected period.[14]

For example, assume that machinery originally costing $90,000 is estimated to have a 20-year life with no salvage value. However, during year 11 it is estimated that the machine will be used an additional 20 years. Its total life, therefore, will be 30 years instead of 20. Depreciation has been recorded at the rate of 1/20 of $90,000, or $4,500 per year by the straight-line method. On the basis of a 30-year life, depreciation should have been 1/30 of $90,000, or $3,000 per year. Depreciation, therefore, has been overestimated, and net income has been understated by $1,500 for each of

---

[14]As an example of a change in operating procedures, **General Motors** (GM) used to write off its tools—such as dies and equipment used to manufacture car bodies—over the life of the body type. Through this procedure, it expensed tools twice as fast as **Ford** and three times as fast as **DaimlerChrysler**. However, it slowed the depreciation process on these tools and lengthened the lives on its plant and equipment. These revisions had the effect of reducing depreciation and amortization charges by approximately $1.23 billion, or $2.55 per share, in the year of the change.

the past 10 years, or a total amount of $15,000. The amount of the difference can be computed as shown below.

Illustration 9-15
Computation of Accumulated Difference Due to Revisions

	Per Year	For 10 Years
Depreciation charged per books (1/20 × $90,000)	$4,500	$45,000
Depreciation based on a 30-year life (1/30 × $90,000)	3,000	30,000
Excess depreciation charged	$1,500	$15,000

Changes in estimate should be handled in the current and prospective periods. No changes should be made in previously reported results. Opening balances are not adjusted, and no attempt is made to "catch up" for prior periods. The reason is that changes in estimates are a continual and inherent part of any estimation process, and continual restatement of prior periods would occur for revisions of estimates unless they are handled prospectively. Therefore, no entry is made at the time the change in estimate occurs. Charges for depreciation in subsequent periods (assuming use of the straight-line method) are based on **dividing the remaining book value less any salvage value by the remaining estimated life**.

Illustration 9-16
Computing Depreciation after Revision of Estimated Life

Machinery	$90,000
Less: Accumulated depreciation	45,000
Book value of machinery at end of 10th year	$45,000

Depreciation (future periods) = $45,000 book value ÷ 20 years remaining life = $2,250

The entry to record depreciation for each of the remaining 20 years is:

Depreciation Expense	2,250	
Accumulated Depreciation—Machinery		2,250

DEPRECIATION CHOICES

WHAT DO THE NUMBERS MEAN?

The amount of depreciation expense recorded depends on both the depreciation method used and estimates of service lives and salvage values of the assets. Differences in these choices and estimates can have a significant impact on a company's reported results and can make it difficult to compare the depreciation numbers of different companies. For example, when **DuPont** switched its depreciation method from accelerated to straight-line, it reported a $250 million decrease in depreciation expense (and an increase in income) in the year of the change. And when **Willamette Industries** extended by 5 years the estimated service lives of its machinery and equipment, the effect on income was an increase of nearly $54 million.

An analyst can determine the impact of these management choices and judgments on the amount of depreciation expense by examining the notes to financial statements. For example, Willamette Industries provided the following note to its financial statements to explain the rationale for the change in estimated useful lives and to provide information that can be used to compare the useful lives of its assets to those of other companies.

Note 4: Property, Plant, and Equipment (partial)

	Range of useful lives
Land	—
Buildings	15–35
Machinery & equipment	5–25
Furniture & fixtures	3–15

In 1999, the estimated service lives for most machinery and equipment were extended five years. The change was based upon a study performed by the company's engineering department, comparisons to typical industry practices, and the effect of the company's extensive capital investments which have resulted in a mix of assets with longer productive lives due to technological advances. As a result of the change, 1999 net income was increased by $54,000,000.

*Expanded Discussion—
Special Depreciation
Methods*

DISPOSITIONS OF PLANT ASSETS

Plant assets may be retired voluntarily or disposed of by sale, exchange, involuntary conversion, or abandonment. Regardless of the time of disposal, depreciation must be taken up to the date of disposition, and then all accounts related to the retired asset should be removed. Ideally, the book value of the specific plant asset would be equal to its disposal value. But this is generally not the case. As a result, a gain or loss develops. The reason: Depreciation is an estimate of cost allocation and not a process of valuation. **The gain or loss is really a correction of net income** for the years during which the fixed asset was used. If it had been possible at the time of acquisition to forecast the exact date of disposal and the amount to be realized at disposition, then a more accurate estimate of depreciation could have been recorded and no gain or loss would be incurred.

OBJECTIVE **8**
Describe the accounting treatment for the disposal of property, plant, and equipment.

Gains or losses on the retirement of plant assets should be shown in the income statement along with other items that arise from customary business activities. If, however, the "operations of a component of a business" are sold, abandoned, spun off, or otherwise disposed of, then the results of "continuing operations" should be reported separately from "discontinued operations." Any gain or loss from disposal of a component of a business should be reported with the related results of discontinued operations and not as an extraordinary item.

Sale of Plant Assets

Depreciation must be recorded for the period of time between the date of the last depreciation entry and the date of sale. To illustrate, assume that depreciation on a machine costing $18,000 has been recorded for 9 years at the rate of $1,200 per year. If the machine is sold in the middle of the tenth year for $7,000, the entry to record depreciation to the date of sale is:

Depreciation Expense	600	
Accumulated Depreciation—Machinery		600

This separate entry ordinarily is not made because most companies enter all depreciation, including this amount, in one entry at the end of the year. In either case the entry for the sale of the asset is:

Cash	7,000	
Accumulated Depreciation—Machinery	11,400	
[($1,200 × 9) + $600]		
Machinery		18,000
Gain on Disposal of Machinery		400

The book value of the machinery at the time of the sale is $6,600 ($18,000 − $11,400). Because the machinery is sold for $7,000, the amount of the gain on the sale is $400.

Involuntary Conversion

Sometimes an asset's service is terminated through some type of **involuntary conversion** such as fire, flood, theft, or condemnation. The gains or losses are treated no differently from those in any other type of disposition except that **they are often reported in the extraordinary items section of the income statement**.

To illustrate, Camel Transport Corp. was forced to sell a plant located on company property that stood directly in the path of an interstate highway. For a number of years the state had sought to purchase the land on which the plant stood, but the company resisted. The state ultimately exercised its right of eminent domain and was upheld by the courts. In settlement, Camel received $500,000, which was substantially in excess of the $200,000 book value of the plant and land (cost of $400,000 less accumulated depreciation of $200,000). The following entry was made.

Cash	500,000	
Accumulated Depreciation—Plant Assets	200,000	
Plant Assets		400,000
Gain on Disposal of Plant Assets		300,000

The gain or loss that develops on these types of unusual, nonrecurring transactions should be shown as an extraordinary item. Similar treatment is given to other types of involuntary conversions such as those resulting from a major casualty (such as an earthquake) or an expropriation, assuming that it meets other conditions for extraordinary item treatment. The difference between the amount recovered (condemnation award or insurance recovery), if any, and the asset's book value is reported as a gain or loss.

Exchanges

The proper accounting for exchanges of nonmonetary assets, such as property, plant, and equipment, is controversial.[15] Some argue that the accounting for these types of exchanges should be based on the fair value of the asset given up or the fair value of the asset received, with a gain or loss recognized. Others believe that the accounting should be based on the recorded amount (book value) of the asset given up, with no gain or loss recognized. Still others favor an approach that would recognize losses in all cases, but defer gains in special situations.

Ordinarily accounting for the exchange of **nonmonetary assets** like property, plant, and equipment should be based on **the fair value of the asset given up or the fair value of the asset received, whichever is clearly more evident.**[16] Thus, any gains or

---

[15]Nonmonetary assets are items whose price in terms of the monetary unit may change over time, whereas monetary assets—cash and short- or long-term accounts and notes receivable—are fixed in terms of units of currency by contract or otherwise.

[16]"Accounting for Nonmonetary Transactions," *Opinions of the Accounting Principles Board No. 29* (New York: AICPA, 1973), par 18.

losses on the exchange **should be recognized immediately**. The rationale for such immediate recognition is that the earnings process related to these assets is completed and, therefore, a gain or loss should be recognized. This approach is always employed when the assets are **dissimilar** in nature, such as the exchange of computers for a truck, or the exchange of equipment for inventory. If the fair value of either asset is not reasonably determinable, the book value of the asset given up is usually used as the basis for recording the nonmonetary exchange.

The general rule of immediate recognition is modified when exchanges of **similar** nonmonetary assets occur for gain situations. For example, when a company exchanges its inventory items with inventory of another company because of color, size, etc. to facilitate sale to an outside customer, the earnings process is not considered completed and a **gain** should not be recognized. Likewise if a company trades **similar productive assets**, such as land for land or equipment for equipment, the earnings process is not considered complete and, therefore, **a gain should not be recognized**. However, if the exchange transaction involving **similar assets** would result in a loss, **the loss is recognized immediately**.

In certain situations, gains on exchange of similar nonmonetary assets may be recognized when **monetary consideration (boot)** is received. When monetary consideration such as cash is received in addition to the nonmonetary asset, it is assumed that a portion of the earnings process is completed and, therefore, a partial gain is recognized.[17] The alternative exchange situations are summarized in Illustration 9-17.

Type of Exchange	Accounting Guidance	Rationale
Dissimilar assets	Recognize gains and losses immediately.	Earnings process is complete.
Similar assets — No cash received	Defer gains; recognize losses immediately.	Earnings process is not complete.

Illustration 9-17
Accounting for Exchanges

To illustrate the accounting for these different types of transactions, we will look at the following situations.

⟨**1**⟩ Accounting for dissimilar assets.
⟨**2**⟩ Accounting for similar assets—gain or loss situations.

Dissimilar Assets

The cost of a nonmonetary asset acquired in exchange for a **dissimilar nonmonetary asset** is usually recorded at the **fair value of the asset given up**, and a gain or loss is recognized. The **fair value of the asset received** should be used only if it is more clearly evident than the fair value of the asset given up.

To illustrate, Interstate Transportation Company exchanged a number of used trucks plus cash for vacant land that might be used for a future plant site. The trucks

---

[17]When the monetary consideration is significant, i.e., **25 percent or more** of the fair value of the exchange, the transaction is considered a **monetary exchange** by both parties. In such "monetary" exchanges the fair values are used to measure the gains or losses that are recognized in their entirety. *EITF Issue No. 86-29*, "Nonmonetary Transactions: Magnitude of Boot and the Exception to the Use of Fair Value," *Emerging Issues Task Force Abstracts* (October 1, 1987).

have a combined book value of $42,000 (cost $64,000 less $22,000 accumulated depreciation). Interstate's purchasing agent, who has had previous dealings in the second-hand market, indicates that the trucks have a fair market value of $49,000. In addition to the trucks, Interstate must pay $17,000 cash for the land. The cost of the land to Interstate is $66,000 computed as follows.

Illustration 9-18
Computation of Land Cost

Fair value of trucks exchanged	$49,000
Cash paid	17,000
Cost of land	$66,000

The journal entry to record the exchange transaction is:

Land	66,000	
Accumulated Depreciation—Trucks	22,000	
Trucks		64,000
Gain on Disposal of Trucks		7,000
Cash		17,000

The gain is the difference between the fair value of the trucks and their book value. It is verified as follows.

Illustration 9-19
Computation of Gain on Disposal of Used Trucks

Fair value of trucks		$49,000
Cost of trucks	$64,000	
Less: Accumulated depreciation	22,000	
Book value of trucks		42,000
Gain on disposal of used trucks		$ 7,000

It follows that if the fair value of the trucks was $39,000 instead of $49,000, a loss on the exchange of $3,000 ($42,000 − $39,000) would be reported. In either case, as a result of the exchange of dissimilar assets, the earnings process on the used trucks has been completed and **a gain or loss should be recognized**.

Similar Assets—Loss Situation

Similar nonmonetary assets are those that are of the same general type, or that perform the same function, or that are employed in the same line of business. When similar nonmonetary assets are exchanged and a loss results, the loss should be recognized immediately. For example, Information Processing, Inc. trades its used machine for a new model. The machine given up has a book value of $8,000 (original cost $12,000 less $4,000 accumulated depreciation) and a fair value of $6,000. It is traded for a new model that has a list price of $16,000. In negotiations with the seller, a trade-in allowance of $9,000 is finally agreed on for the used machine. The cash payment that must be made for the new asset and the cost of the new machine are computed as follows.

Illustration 9-20
Computation of Cost of New Machine

List price of new machine	$16,000
Less: Trade-in allowance for used machine	9,000
Cash payment due	7,000
Fair value of used machine	6,000
Cost of new machine	$13,000

The journal entry to record this transaction is:

Equipment	13,000	
Accumulated Depreciation—Equipment	4,000	
Loss on Disposal of Equipment	2,000	
Equipment		12,000
Cash		7,000

The loss on the disposal of the used machine can be verified as follows:

Fair value of used machine	$6,000
Book value of used machine	8,000
Loss on disposal of used machine	$2,000

Illustration 9-21
Computation of Loss on Disposal of Used Machine

Why was the trade-in allowance or the book value of the old asset not used as a basis for the new equipment? The trade-in allowance is not used because it included a price concession (similar to a price discount) to the purchaser. Few individuals pay list price for a new car. Trade-in allowances on the used car are often inflated so that actual selling prices are below list prices. To record the car at list price would state it at an amount in excess of its cash equivalent price because the new car's list price is usually inflated. Use of book value in this situation would overstate the value of the new machine by $2,000. Because assets should not be valued at more than their cash equivalent price, the loss should be recognized immediately rather than added to the cost of the newly acquired asset.

Similar Assets—Gain Situation

The accounting treatment for exchanges of **similar** nonmonetary assets when a gain develops is more complex. If the exchange does not complete the earnings process, then **any gain should be deferred**.

The real estate industry provides a good example of why the accounting profession decided not to recognize gains on exchanges of similar nonmonetary assets. In this industry, it is common to "swap" real estate holdings. Assume that Landmark Company and Hillfarm, Inc. each had undeveloped land on which they intended to build shopping centers. Appraisals indicated that the land of both companies had increased significantly in value. The companies decided to exchange (swap) their undeveloped land, record a gain, and report their new parcels of land at current fair values. But, should gains be recognized at this point? No: The earnings process is not completed because the companies remain in the same economic position after the swap as before. Therefore, the asset acquired should be recorded at book value with no gain recognized. In contrast, had book value exceeded fair value, a loss would be recognized immediately.

In another exchange of similar nonmonetary assets with a gain, assume Davis Rent-A-Car has a rental fleet of automobiles consisting primarily of Ford Motor Company products. Davis' management is interested in increasing the variety of automobiles in its rental fleet by adding numerous General Motors models. Davis arranges with Nertz Rent-A-Car to exchange a group of Ford automobiles with a fair value of $160,000 and a book value of $135,000 (cost $150,000 less accumulated depreciation $15,000) for a number of Chevy and Pontiac models with a fair value of $170,000. Davis pays $10,000 in cash in addition to the Ford automobiles exchanged. The total gain to Davis Rent-A-Car is computed as shown in Illustration 9-22.

Fair value of Ford automobiles exchanged	$160,000
Book value of Ford automobiles exchanged	135,000
Total gain (unrecognized)	$ 25,000

Illustration 9-22
Computation of Gain (Unrecognized)

But the earnings process is not considered completed in this transaction. The company still has a fleet of cars, although different models. Therefore, the total gain is deferred, and the basis of the General Motors automobiles is reduced via two different but acceptable computations as shown below.

Illustration 9-23

Basis of New Automobiles—Fair Value vs. Book Value

Fair value of GM automobiles	$170,000		Book value of Ford automobiles	$135,000
Less: Gain deferred	(25,000)	OR	Cash paid	10,000
Basis of GM automobiles	$145,000		Basis of GM automobiles	$145,000

The entry by Davis to record this transaction is as follows:

Automobiles (GM)	145,000	
Accumulated Depreciation—Automobiles	15,000	
Automobiles (Ford)		150,000
Cash		10,000

The gain that reduced the basis of the new automobiles will be recognized when those automobiles are sold to an outside party. While these automobiles are held, depreciation charges will be lower and net income will be higher in subsequent periods because of the reduced basis.

Presented below in summary form are the accounting requirements for recognizing gains and losses on exchanges of nonmonetary assets.[18]

Illustration 9-24

Summary of Gain and Loss Recognition on Exchanges of Nonmonetary Assets

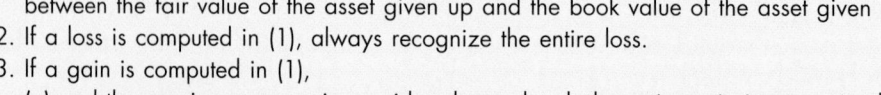

1. Compute the total gain or loss on the transaction, which is equal to the difference between the fair value of the asset given up and the book value of the asset given up.
2. If a loss is computed in (1), always recognize the entire loss.
3. If a gain is computed in (1),
    (a) and the earnings process is considered completed, the entire gain is recognized (dissimilar assets).
    (b) and the earnings process is not considered completed (similar assets),
        (1) and no cash is involved, no gain is recognized.
        (2) and some cash is given, no gain is recognized.

Expanded Discussion of Gains on Exchanges of Similar Assets

An enterprise that engages in one or more nonmonetary exchanges during a period should disclose in financial statements for the period the nature of the transactions, the method of accounting for the assets transferred, and gains or losses recognized on transfers.[19]

PRESENTATION AND ANALYSIS

Presentation of Property, Plant, and Equipment

OBJECTIVE 9
Explain how property, plant, and equipment are reported and analyzed.

The basis of valuation—usually historical cost—for property, plant, and equipment should be disclosed along with pledges, liens, and other commitments related to these assets. Any liability secured by property, plant, and equipment should not be offset

[18]Adapted from an article by Robert Capettini and Thomas E. King, "Exchanges of Nonmonetary Assets: Some Changes," *The Accounting Review* (January 1976).

[19]"Accounting for Nonmonetary Transactions," op. cit., par. 28.

against these assets, but should be reported in the liabilities section. Property, plant, and equipment not currently employed as producing assets in the business (such as idle facilities or land held as an investment) should be segregated from assets used in operations.

When assets are depreciated, a valuation account normally called Accumulated Depreciation is credited. The employment of an Accumulated Depreciation account permits the user of the financial statements to see the original cost of the asset and the amount of depreciation that has been charged to expense in past years.

Because of the significant impact on the financial statements of the depreciation method(s) used, the following disclosures should be made.

a. Depreciation expense for the period.

b. Balances of major classes of depreciable assets, by nature and function.

c. Accumulated depreciation, either by major classes of depreciable assets or in total.

d. A general description of the method or methods used in computing depreciation with respect to major classes of depreciable assets.[20]

The 2001 Annual Report of **Micron Technology** in Illustration 9-26, on page 434, illustrates an acceptable disclosure using condensed balance sheet data supplemented with details and policies in notes to the financial statements.

Analysis of Property, Plant, Equipment

Assets may be analyzed relative to activity (turnover) and profitability. How efficiently a company uses its assets to generate sales is measured by the **asset turnover ratio**. This ratio is determined by dividing net sales by average total assets for the period. The resulting number is the dollars of sales produced by each dollar invested in assets. To illustrate, we will use the following data from **Tootsie Roll Industries** 2001 annual report.

TOOTSIE ROLL INDUSTRIES

	(in millions)
Net sales	$423.5
Total assets, 12/31/01	618.7
Total assets, 12/31/00	562.4
Net income	65.6

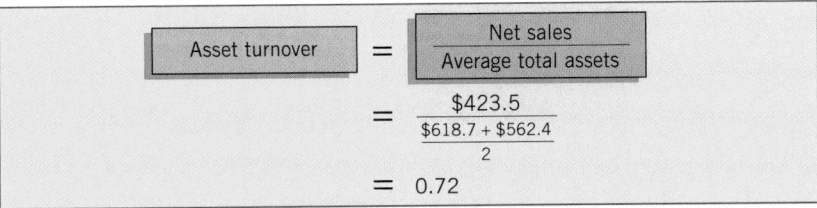

Illustration 9-25
Asset Turnover Ratio

The asset turnover ratio shows that Tootsie Roll generated sales of $0.72 per dollar of assets in the year ended December 31, 2001.

---

[20]"Omnibus Opinion–1967," *Opinions of the Accounting Principles Board No. 12* (New York: AICPA, 1967), par. 5. Some believe that the average useful life of the assets or the range of years for asset life is significant information that should be disclosed.

*Additional Property, Plant,
and Equipment Disclosures*

MICRON TECHNOLOGY, INC.
(amounts in millions except par value amounts)
Consolidated Balance Sheets

	August 30, 2001	August 31, 2000
Total current assets	$3,137.7	$4,720.1
Product and process technology, net	198.4	213.0
Property, plant, and equipment, net	4,704.1	4,171.7
Other assets	323.0	287.1
Total assets	$8,363.2	$9,391.9

Notes to Consolidated Financial Statements (partial)

Property, plant, and equipment. Property, plant, and equipment are stated at cost. Depreciation is computed using the straight-line method over the estimated useful lives of 5 to 30 years for buildings, 2 to 20 years for equipment, and 2 to 5 years for software. When property or equipment is retired or otherwise disposed of, the net book value of the asset is removed from the Company's accounts and the net gain or loss is included in the determination of income.

The Company capitalizes interest on borrowings during the active construction period of major capital projects. Capitalized interest is added to the cost of the underlying assets and is amortized over the useful lives of the assets. The Company capitalized interest costs of $9.8 million, $6.4 million, and $1.3 million in 2001, 2000, and 1999, respectively, in connection with various capital projects.

	2001	2000
Land	$ 94.7	$ 46.3
Buildings	1,815.1	1,360.6
Equipment	5,721.3	4,793.5
Construction in progress	402.3	611.1
Software	165.5	140.2
	8,198.9	6,951.7
Accumulated depreciation	(3,494.8)	(2,780.0)
	$ 4,704.1	$ 4,171.7

In 2001, the Company capitalized $420.4 million of costs relating to the Company's semiconductor manufacturing facility in Lehi, Utah. As of August 30, 2001, construction in progress included costs of $194.1 million related to idle facilities in Lehi which are not ready for their intended use and are not being depreciated.

Depreciation expense was $1,049.6 million, $902.0 million, and $753.9 million for 2001, 2000, and 1999, respectively.

Asset turnover ratios vary considerably among industries. For example, a large utility company like **Union Electric Company** (now **Ameren UE**) has a ratio of 0.36 times, and a large grocery chain like **Atlantic and Pacific Tea (A&P)** has a ratio of 3.6 times.

Use of the **profit margin on sales ratio** (rate of return on sales) in conjunction with the asset turnover ratio offers an interplay that leads to a **rate of return on total assets**. By using the Tootsie Roll Industries data shown above, the profit margin on sales ratio and the rate of return on total assets are computed as follows.

$$\boxed{\text{Profit margin on sales}} = \frac{\text{Net income}}{\text{Net sales}}$$

$$= \frac{\$65.6}{\$423.5}$$

$$= 15.4\%$$

$$\boxed{\begin{array}{c}\text{Rate of return}\\\text{on total assets}\end{array}} = \boxed{\text{Profit margin on sales}} \times \boxed{\text{Asset turnover}}$$

$$= 15.4\% \times 0.72$$

$$= 11.1\%$$

Illustration 9-27
Profit Margin on Sales

The profit margin on sales does not answer the question of how profitably a company uses its assets. But by relating the profit margin on sales to the asset turnover during a period of time, it is possible to ascertain how profitably the assets were used during that period of time.

The **rate of return on assets (ROA)** can be directly computed by dividing net income by average total assets. By using Tootsie Roll's data, the ratio is computed as follows.

$$\boxed{\begin{array}{c}\text{Rate of return}\\\text{on assets}\end{array}} = \boxed{\frac{\text{Net income}}{\text{Average total assets}}}$$

$$= \frac{\$65.6}{\dfrac{\$618.7 + \$562.4}{2}}$$

$$= 11.1\%$$

Illustration 9-28
Rate of Return on Assets

The 11.1 percent rate of return computed in this manner is identical to the 11.1 percent rate computed by multiplying the profit margin on sales by the asset turnover (except for rounding). The rate of return on assets is a good measure of profitability because it combines the effects of profit margin and asset turnover.

SUMMARY OF LEARNING OBJECTIVES

1 Describe property, plant, and equipment and costs included in its initial valuation. The major characteristics of property, plant, and equipment are: (1) They are acquired for use in operations and not for resale. (2) They are long-term in nature and usually subject to depreciation. And (3) they possess physical substance. The costs included in initial valuation of property, plant, and equipment are as follows:

Cost of land: Includes all expenditures made to acquire land and to ready it for use. Land costs typically include (1) the purchase price; (2) closing costs, such as title to the land, attorney's fees, and recording fees; (3) costs incurred in getting the land in condition for its intended use, such as grading, filling, draining, and clearing; (4) assumption of any liens, mortgages, or encumbrances on the property; and (5) any additional land improvements that have an indefinite life.

Cost of buildings: Includes all expenditures related directly to their acquisition or construction. These costs include (1) materials, labor, and overhead costs incurred during construction, and (2) professional fees and building permits.

KEY TERMS

accelerated-depreciation
  method, *422*
activity method, *421*
additions, *416*
asset turnover ratio, *433*
betterments, *416*
capital expenditure, *416*
declining-balance
  method, *422*
decreasing-charge
  method, *422*
depreciation, *418*
depreciation base, *419*
dissimilar nonmonetary
  assets, *429*
double-declining-balance
  method, *423*
fixed assets, *408*
historical cost, *408*

improvements
(betterments), *416*

involuntary conversion, *428*

lump sum price, *413*

major repairs, *417*

nonmonetary assets, *428*

nonreciprocal transfers, *414*

ordinary repairs, *417*

plant assets, *408*

profit margin on sales
ratio, *434*

property, plant, and
equipment, *408*

rate of return on assets
(ROA), *435*

rearrangement and
reinstallation costs, *417*

replacements, *416*

revenue expenditure, *416*

salvage value, *419*

self-constructed asset, *410*

similar nonmonetary
assets, *430*

straight-line method, *421*

substitution approach, *416*

sum-of-the-years'-digits
method, *422*

Cost of equipment: Includes the purchase price, freight and handling charges incurred, insurance on the equipment while in transit, cost of special foundations if required, assembling and installation costs, and costs of conducting trial runs.

② **Describe the accounting problems associated with interest capitalization.**   Only actual interest (with modifications) should be capitalized. The rationale for this approach is that during construction, the asset is not generating revenue and therefore interest cost should be deferred (capitalized). Once construction is completed, the asset is ready for its intended use and revenues can be earned. Any interest cost incurred in purchasing an asset that is ready for its intended use should be expensed.

③ **Understand accounting issues related to acquiring and valuing plant assets.**   The following issues relate to acquiring and valuing plant assets: (1) *Cash discounts:* Whether taken or not, they are generally considered a reduction in the cost of the asset; the real cost of the asset is the cash or cash equivalent price of the asset. (2) *Lump sum purchase:* Allocate the total cost among the various assets on the basis of their relative fair market values. (3) *Issuance of stock:* If the stock is actively traded, the market value of the stock issued is a fair indication of the cost of the property acquired. If the market value of the common stock exchanged is not determinable, the value of the property should be established and used as the basis for recording the asset and issuance of the common stock. (4) *Contributions:* Should be recorded at the fair value of the asset received and a related credit should be made to revenue for the same amount.

④ **Describe the accounting treatment for costs subsequent to acquisition.**   See Illustration 9-6 for a summary of how to account for costs subsequent to acquisition.

⑤ **Explain the concept of depreciation.**   Depreciation is the accounting process of allocating the cost of tangible assets to expense in a systematic and rational manner to those periods expected to benefit from the use of the asset.

⑥ **Identify the factors involved in the depreciation process.**   Three factors involved in the depreciation process are: (1) determining the depreciation base for the asset, (2) estimating service lives, and (3) selecting a method of cost apportionment (depreciation).

⑦ **Compare activity, straight-line, and decreasing-charge methods of depreciation.** (1) *Activity method:* Assumes that depreciation is a function of use or productivity instead of the passage of time. The life of the asset is considered in terms of either the output it provides, or an input measure such as the number of hours it works. (2) *Straight-line method:* Considers depreciation a function of time instead of a function of usage. This method is widely employed in practice because of its simplicity. The straight-line procedure is often the most conceptually appropriate when the decline in usefulness is constant from period to period. (3) *Decreasing-charge methods:* Provide for a higher depreciation cost in the earlier years and lower charges in later periods. The main justification for this approach is that the asset suffers the greatest loss of services in its early years.

⑧ **Describe the accounting treatment for the disposal of property, plant, and equipment.**   Regardless of the time of disposal, depreciation must be taken up to the date of disposition, and then all accounts related to the retired asset should be removed. Gains or losses on the retirement of plant assets should be shown in the income statement along with other items that arise from customary business activities. Gains or losses on involuntary conversions should be reported as extraordinary items. Illustrations 9-17 and 9-24 contain summaries of how to account for disposals through exchange.

⑨ **Explain how property, plant, and equipment are reported and analyzed.**   The basis of valuation for property, plant, and equipment should be disclosed along with pledges, liens, and other commitments related to these assets. Any liability secured by property, plant, and equipment should not be offset against these assets, but should be reported in the liabilities section. When assets are depreciated, a valuation account normally called Accumulated Depreciation is credited. Analysis may be performed to evaluate the asset turnover ratio, profit margin on sales, and rate of return on assets.

REVIEW EXERCISE

Norwel Company (as discussed in the Review Exercise in Chapter 8) manufactures miniature circuit boards used in wireless phones and personal organizers. On June 5, 2003, Norwel purchased a circuit board stamping machine at a retail price of $12,000. Norwel paid 5% sales tax on this purchase. Norwel paid a contractor $1,400 for a specially wired platform for the machine, to ensure non-interrupted power to the machine. Norwel estimates the machine will have a 4-year useful life, with a salvage value of $2,000 at the end of 4 years. Norwel uses straight-line depreciation and employs the "half-year" convention in accounting for partial-year depreciation. Norwel's fiscal year ends on December 31.

Instructions

(a) At what amount should Norwel record the acquisition cost of the machine?

(b) How much depreciation expense should Norwel record in 2003 and in 2004?

(c) At what amount will the machine be reported in Norwel's balance sheet at December 31, 2004?

(d) On July 1, 2005, Norwel decides to outsource its circuit board operations to Boards-R-Us Inc. As part of this plan, Norwel sells the machine (and the platform) to Boards-R-Us for $7,000. What is the impact of this disposal on Norwel's 2005 income before taxes?

SOLUTION TO REVIEW EXERCISE

(a) Historical cost is measured by the cash or cash-equivalent price of obtaining the asset and bringing it to the location and condition for its intended use. For Norwel, this is:

Price	$12,000
Tax ($12,000 × .05)	600
Platform	1,400
Total	$14,000

(b) Depreciable base: ($14,000 − $2,000) = $12,000

Depreciation expense: $12,000 ÷ 4 = $3,000 per year

2003: $\frac{1}{2}$ year = $3,000 × .50 = $1,500

2004: full year = $3,000

(c) The amount reported on the balance sheet is the cost of the asset less accumulated depreciation:

Machine	$14,000
Accumulated depreciation	(4,500)
Book value	$ 9,500

(d) The income effect is a gain or loss, determined by comparing the book value of the asset to the disposal value:

Book value	
Cost	$14,000
Accumulated depreciation ($1,500 + $3,000 + $1,500)	6,000
Book value	8,000
Cash received for machine and platform	7,000
Pretax loss	$ 1,000

INTEREST CAPITALIZATION PROCEDURES

INTEREST CAPITALIZATION

In this appendix, we illustrate the specific steps for determining the amount of interest capitalization, under the approach recognized as GAAP. To implement this general approach, three items must be considered:

1. Qualifying assets.
2. Capitalization period.
3. Amount to capitalize.

OBJECTIVE **10**
After studying Appendix 9A, you should be able to: Understand the procedures for determining capitalized interest amounts.

Qualifying Assets

To qualify for interest capitalization, assets must require a period of time to get them ready for their intended use. Interest costs are capitalized starting with the first expenditure related to the asset, and capitalization continues until the asset is substantially completed and ready for its intended use.

Assets that qualify for interest cost capitalization include assets under construction for an enterprise's own use (including buildings, plants, and large machinery) and assets intended for sale or lease that are constructed or otherwise produced as discrete projects (e.g., ships or real estate developments).

Examples of assets that do not qualify for interest capitalization are (1) assets that are in use or ready for their intended use, and (2) assets that are not being used in the earnings activities of the enterprise and that are not undergoing the activities necessary to get them ready for use. Examples of this second type would be land that is not being developed and assets not being used because of obsolescence, excess capacity, or need for repair.

Capitalization Period

The **capitalization period** is the period of time during which interest must be capitalized. It begins when three conditions are present:

1. Expenditures for the asset have been made.
2. Activities that are necessary to get the asset ready for its intended use are in progress.
3. Interest cost is being incurred.

INTERNATIONAL INSIGHT

Under international accounting standards, capitalization of interest is allowed, but it is not the preferred treatment. The benchmark treatment is to expense interest in the period incurred.

Interest capitalization **continues as long as these three conditions are present**. The capitalization period ends when the asset is substantially complete and ready for its intended use.

Amount to Capitalize

The amount of interest to be capitalized is limited to the lower of actual interest cost incurred during the period or avoidable interest. **Avoidable interest** is the amount of interest cost during the period that theoretically could have been avoided if expenditures for the asset had not been made. If the actual interest cost for the period is $90,000 and the avoidable interest is $80,000, only $80,000 is capitalized. Or, if the actual interest cost is $80,000 and the avoidable interest is $90,000, only $80,000 is capitalized. In no situation should interest cost include a cost of capital charge for stockholders' equity. And, interest capitalization is required for a qualifying asset only if its effect, compared with the effect of expensing interest, is material.[1]

To apply the avoidable interest concept, the potential amount of interest that may be capitalized during an accounting period is determined by multiplying the interest rate(s) by the **weighted-average accumulated expenditures** for qualifying assets during the period.

Weighted-Average Accumulated Expenditures

In computing the weighted-average accumulated expenditures, the construction expenditures are weighted by the amount of time (fraction of a year or accounting period) that interest cost could be incurred on the expenditure. To illustrate, assume a 17-month bridge construction project with current-year payments to the contractor of $240,000 on March 1, $480,000 on July 1, and $360,000 on November 1. The weighted-average accumulated expenditures for the year ended December 31 are computed as follows.

Illustration 9A-1

Computation of Weighted-Average Accumulated Expenditures

Expenditures			Capitalization		Weighted-Average
Date	Amount	×	Period*	=	Accumulated Expenditures
March 1	$ 240,000		10/12		$200,000
July 1	480,000		6/12		240,000
November 1	360,000		2/12		60,000
	$1,080,000				$500,000

*Months between date of expenditure and date interest capitalization stops or end of year, whichever comes first (in this case, December 31).

To compute the weighted-average accumulated expenditures, we weight the expenditures by the amount of time that interest cost could be incurred on each one. For the March 1 expenditure, 10 months' interest cost can be associated with the expenditure. For the expenditure on July 1, only 6 months' interest costs can be incurred, and for the expenditure made on November 1, only 2 months of interest cost is incurred.

Interest Rates

The principles to be used in selecting the appropriate interest rates to be applied to the weighted-average accumulated expenditures are:

① For the portion of weighted-average accumulated expenditures that is less than or equal to any amounts borrowed specifically to finance construction of the assets, **use the interest rate incurred on the specific borrowings**.

② For the portion of weighted-average accumulated expenditures that is greater than any debt incurred specifically to finance construction of the assets, **use a**

---

[1]"Capitalization of Interest Cost," *Statement of Financial Accounting Standards No. 34* (Stamford, Conn.: FASB, 1979).

weighted average of interest rates incurred on all other outstanding debt during the period.[2]

An illustration of the computation of a weighted-average interest rate for debt greater than the amount incurred specifically to finance construction of the assets is shown in Illustration 9A-2.

	Principal	Interest
12%, 2-year note	$ 600,000	$ 72,000
9%, 10-year bonds	2,000,000	180,000
7.5%, 20-year bonds	5,000,000	375,000
	$7,600,000	$627,000

$$\text{Weighted-average interest rate} = \frac{\text{Total interest}}{\text{Total principal}} = \frac{\$627,000}{\$7,600,000} = 8.25\%$$

Illustration 9A-2
Computation of Weighted-Average Interest Rate

Comprehensive Illustration of Interest Capitalization

To illustrate the issues related to interest capitalization, assume that on November 1, 2002, Shalla Company contracted with Pfeifer Construction Co. to have a building constructed for $1,400,000 on land costing $100,000 (purchased from the contractor and included in the first payment). Shalla made the following payments to the construction company during 2003.

Tutorial on Interest Capitalization

January 1	March 1	May 1	December 31	Total
$210,000	$300,000	$540,000	$450,000	$1,500,000

Construction was completed and the building was ready for occupancy on December 31, 2003. Shalla Company had the following debt outstanding at December 31, 2003.

Specific Construction Debt

1. 15%, 3-year note to finance purchase of land and construction of the building, dated December 31, 2002, with interest payable annually on December 31 $750,000

Other Debt

2. 10%, 5-year note payable, dated December 31, 1999, with interest payable annually on December 31 $550,000
3. 12%, 10-year bonds issued December 31, 1998, with interest payable annually on December 31 $600,000

---

[2]The interest rate to be used may be based exclusively on an average rate of all the borrowings, if desired. For our purposes, we will use the specific borrowing rate followed by the average interest rate because we believe it to be more conceptually consistent. Either method can be used; *FASB Statement No. 34* does not provide explicit guidance on this measurement. For a discussion of this issue and others related to interest capitalization, see Kathryn M. Means and Paul M. Kazenski, "SFAS 34: Recipe for Diversity," *Accounting Horizons* (September 1988); and Wendy A. Duffy, "A Graphical Analysis of Interest Capitalization," *Journal of Accounting Education* (Fall 1990).

The weighted-average accumulated expenditures during 2003 are computed as follows.

Illustration 9A-3

Computation of Weighted-Average Accumulated Expenditures

Expenditures			Current Year Capitalization		Weighted-Average
Date	Amount	×	Period*	=	Accumulated Expenditures
January 1	$ 210,000		12/12		$210,000
March 1	300,000		10/12		250,000
May 1	540,000		8/12		360,000
December 31	450,000		0		0
	$1,500,000				$820,000

Note that the expenditure made on December 31, the last day of the year, does not have any interest cost.

The avoidable interest is computed as follows.

Illustration 9A-4

Computation of Avoidable Interest

Weighted-Average Accumulated Expenditures	×	Interest Rate	=	Avoidable Interest
$750,000		.15 (construction note)		$112,500
70,000^a		.1104 (weighted average		7,728
$820,000		of other debt)^b		$120,228

^{a}The amount by which the weighted-average accumulated expenditures exceeds the specific construction loan.

^{b}Weighted-average interest rate computation:

	Principal	Interest
10%, 5-year note	$ 550,000	$ 55,000
12%, 10-year bonds	600,000	72,000
	$1,150,000	$127,000

$$\text{Weighted-average interest rate} = \frac{\text{Total interest}}{\text{Total principal}} = \frac{\$127,000}{\$1,150,000} = 11.04\%$$

The actual interest cost, which represents the maximum amount of interest that may be capitalized during 2003, is computed as shown below.

Illustration 9A-5

Computation of Actual Interest Cost

Construction note	$750,000 × .15	=	$112,500
5-year note	$550,000 × .10	=	55,000
10-year bonds	$600,000 × .12	=	72,000
Actual interest			$239,500

The interest cost to be capitalized is the lesser of $120,228 (avoidable interest) or $239,500 (actual interest), which is $120,228.

The journal entries made by Shalla Company during 2003 would be as follows.

January 1

Land	100,000	
Building (or Construction in Process)	110,000	
Cash		210,000

March 1

Building	300,000	
Cash		300,000

May 1

Building	540,000	
Cash		540,000

December 31

Building	450,000	
Cash		450,000

Building (Capitalized Interest)	120,228	
Interest Expense ($239,500 − $120,228)	119,272	
Cash ($112,500 + $55,000 + $72,000)		239,500

Capitalized interest cost should be written off as part of depreciation over the useful life of the assets involved and not over the term of the debt. The total interest cost incurred during the period should be disclosed, with the portion charged to expense and the portion capitalized indicated.

At December 31, 2003, Shalla would disclose the amount of interest capitalized either as part of the nonoperating section of the income statement or in the notes accompanying the financial statements. Both forms of disclosure are illustrated below.

Income from operations		XXXX
Other expenses and losses:		
Interest expense	$239,500	
Less: Capitalized interest	120,228	119,272
Income before taxes on income		XXXX
Income taxes		XXX
Net income		XXXX

Illustration 9A-6
Capitalized Interest Reported in the Income Statement

Note 1: Accounting Policies. *Capitalized Interest.* During 2003 total interest cost was $239,500, of which $120,228 was capitalized and $119,272 was charged to expense.

Illustration 9A-7
Capitalized Interest Disclosed in a Note

SUMMARY OF LEARNING OBJECTIVE FOR APPENDIX 9A

⑩ Understand the procedures for determining capitalized interest amounts. The amount of avoidable interest is determined by applying interest rates (either on specific construction borrowing or rates on other outstanding debt) to weighted-average accumulated expenditures. Weights on expenditures are based on the amount of time during the period that interest cost could be incurred on the expenditure. The amount capitalized in the cost of the asset is the lower of the avoidable or actual interest.

Note: All **asterisked** Questions, Exercises, Problems, and Conceptual Cases relate to material contained in the appendix to the chapter.

KEY TERMS

avoidable interest, *440*
capitalization period, *439*
weighted-average
   accumulated
   expenditures, *440*

QUESTIONS

1 What are the major characteristics of plant assets?

2 Esplanade Inc. owns land that it purchased on January 1, 1996, for $420,000. At December 31, 2003, its current value is $770,000 as determined by appraisal. At what amount

should Esplanade report this asset on its December 31, 2003, balance sheet? Explain.

3 Name the items, in addition to the amount paid to the former owner or contractor, that may properly be included as part of the acquisition cost of the following plant assets.

(a) Land.

(b) Machinery and equipment.

(c) Buildings.

4 Indicate where the following items would be shown on a balance sheet.

(a) A lien that was attached to the land when purchased.

(b) Landscaping costs.

(c) Attorney's fees and recording fees related to purchasing land.

(d) A parking lot servicing employees in the building.

(e) Cost of temporary building for workers during construction of building.

(f) Interest expense on bonds payable incurred during construction of a building.

(g) Assessments for sidewalks that are maintained by the city.

(h) The cost of demolishing an old building that was on the land when purchased.

5 What is the rationale for assigning a portion of overhead to the cost of an asset?

6 The Buildings account of Diego Rivera Inc. includes the following items that were used in determining the basis for depreciating the cost of a building.

(a) Architect's fees.

(b) Interest and taxes during construction.

(c) Commission paid on the sale of capital stock.

(d) Bond discount.

Do you agree with these charges? If not, how would you deal with each of the items above in the corporation's books and in its annual financial statements?

7 Jones Company has purchased two tracts of land. One tract will be the site of its new manufacturing plant. The other is being purchased with the hope that it will be sold in the next year at a profit. How should these two tracts of land be reported in the balance sheet?

8 One financial accounting issue encountered when a company constructs its own plant is whether the interest cost on funds borrowed to finance construction should be capitalized and then amortized over the life of the assets constructed. What is a common accounting justification for capitalizing such interest?

9 How should the amount of interest capitalized be disclosed in the footnotes to the financial statements? How should interest revenue from temporarily invested excess funds borrowed to finance the construction of assets be accounted for?

10 Discuss the basic accounting problem that arises in handling each of the following situations.

(a) Assets purchased by issuance of capital stock.

(b) Acquisition of plant assets by gift or donation.

(c) Purchase of a plant asset subject to a cash discount.

(d) Assets purchased on a long-term credit basis.

(e) A group of assets acquired for a lump sum.

(f) An asset traded in or exchanged for another asset.

11 Yukio Mishima Industries acquired equipment this year to be used in its operations. The equipment was delivered by the suppliers, installed by Mishima, and placed into operation. Some of it was purchased for cash with discounts available for prompt payment. What costs should Mishima capitalize for the new equipment purchased this year? Explain.

12 Adam Mickiewicz Co. purchased for $2,200,000 property that included both land and a building to be used in operations. The seller's book value was $300,000 for the land and $900,000 for the building. By appraisal, the fair market value was estimated to be $500,000 for the land and $2,000,000 for the building. At what amount should Mickiewicz report the land and the building at the end of the year?

13 Richardson Co. acquires machinery by paying $10,000 cash. Richardson purchased a similar machine last month for $13,500. At what cost should the new equipment be recorded?

14 Ron Dayne is evaluating two recent transactions involving exchanges of equipment. In one case, similar assets were exchanged; in the second situation, dissimilar assets were exchanged. Explain to Ron the differences in accounting for these two situations.

15 Identify the factors that are relevant in determining the annual depreciation charge, and explain whether these factors are determined objectively or whether they are based on judgment.

16 Some believe that accounting depreciation measures the decline in the value of fixed assets. Do you agree? Explain.

17 Explain how estimation of service lives can result in unrealistically high valuations of fixed assets.

18 The plant manager of a manufacturing firm suggested in a conference of the company's executives that accountants should speed up depreciation on the machinery in the finishing department because improvements were rapidly making those machines obsolete and a depreciation fund big enough to cover their replacement is needed. Discuss the accounting concept of depreciation and the effect on a business concern of the depreciation recorded for plant assets, paying particular attention to the issues raised by the plant manager.

19 Elizabeth Ashley Company purchased a machine on January 2, 2003, for $600,000. The machine has an estimated useful life of 5 years and a salvage value of $100,000. Depreciation was computed by the 150%

declining-balance method. What is the amount of accumulated depreciation at the end of December 31, 2004?

20 Linda Blair Company purchased machinery for $120,000 on January 1, 2003. It is estimated that the machinery will have a useful life of 20 years, scrap value of $15,000, production of 84,000 units, and working hours of 42,000. During 2003 the company uses the machinery for 14,300 hours, and the machinery produces 20,000 units. Compute depreciation under the straight-line, units-of-output, working-hours, sum-of-the-years'-digits, and declining-balance (use 10% as the annual rate) methods.

21 A building that was purchased December 31, 1978, for $2,400,000 was originally estimated to have a life of 50 years with no salvage value at the end of that time. Depreciation has been recorded through 2002. During 2003 an examination of the building by an engineering firm discloses that its estimated useful life is 15 years after 2002. What should be the amount of depreciation for 2003?

22 Melanie Mayron purchased a computer for $6,000 on July 1, 2003. She intends to depreciate it over 4 years using the double-declining balance method. Salvage value is $1,000. Compute depreciation for 2004.

23 Saadi Company purchased a heavy-duty truck on July 1, 2000, for $30,000. It was estimated that it would have a useful life of 10 years and then would have a trade-in value of $6,000. It was traded on August 1, 2004, for a similar truck costing $39,000; $13,000 was allowed as trade-in value (also fair value) on the old truck and $26,000 was paid in cash. What is the entry to record the trade-in? The company uses the straight-line method.

24 Once equipment has been installed and placed in operation, subsequent expenditures relating to this equipment are frequently thought of as repairs or general maintenance and, hence, chargeable to operations in the period in which the expenditure is made. Actually, determination of whether such an expenditure should be charged to operations or capitalized involves a much more careful analysis of the character of the expenditure. What are the factors that should be considered in making such a decision? Discuss fully.

25 What accounting treatment is normally given to the following items in accounting for plant assets?

(a) Additions.

(b) Major repairs.

(c) Improvements and replacements.

26 New machinery, which replaced a number of employees, was installed and put in operation in the last month of the fiscal year. The employees had been dismissed after payment of an extra month's wages, and this amount was added to the cost of the machinery. Discuss the propriety of the charge and, if it was improper, describe the proper treatment.

27 To what extent do you consider the following items to be proper costs of the fixed asset? Give reasons for your opinions.

(a) Overhead of a business that builds its own equipment.

(b) Cost of constructing new models of machinery.

(c) Cash discounts on purchases of equipment.

(d) Interest paid during construction of a building.

(e) Cost of a safety device installed on a machine.

(f) Freight on equipment returned before installation, for replacement by other equipment of greater capacity.

(g) Cost of plywood partitions erected as part of the remodeling of the office.

(h) Replastering of a section of the building.

(i) Cost of a new motor for one of the trucks.

28 Recently, Michelangelo Manufacturing Co. presented the account "Allowance for Repairs" in the long-term liabilities section. Evaluate this procedure.

29 What are the general rules for how gains or losses on retirement of plant assets should be reported in income?

*30 What interest rate should be used in determining the amount of interest to be capitalized? How should the amount to be capitalized be determined?

BRIEF EXERCISES

BE9-1 Bonanza Brothers Inc. purchased land at a price of $27,000. Closing costs were $1,400. An old building was removed at a cost of $12,200. What amount should be recorded as the cost of the land?

BE9-2 Chavez Corporation purchased a truck by issuing an $80,000, 4-year, noninterest-bearing note to Equinox Inc. The market rate of interest for obligations of this nature is 12%. Prepare the journal entry to record the purchase of this truck. (*Hint:* Present value factors may be found in Appendix A.)

BE9-3   Cool Spot Inc. purchased land, building, and equipment from Pinball Wizard Corporation for a cash payment of $306,000. The estimated fair values of the assets are land $60,000; building $220,000; and equipment $80,000. At what amounts should each of the three assets be recorded?

BE9-4   Dark Wizard Company obtained land by issuing 2,000 shares of its $10 par value common stock. The land was recently appraised at $85,000. The common stock is actively traded at $41 per share. Prepare the journal entry to record the acquisition of the land.

BE9-5   Strider Corporation traded a used truck (cost $20,000, accumulated depreciation $18,000) for a small computer worth $3,700. Strider also paid $1,000 in the transaction. Prepare the journal entry to record the exchange.

BE9-6   Sloan Company traded a used welding machine (cost $9,000, accumulated depreciation $3,000) for office equipment with an estimated fair value of $5,000. Sloan also paid $2,000 cash in the transaction. Prepare the journal entry to record the exchange.

BE9-7   Bubey Company traded a used truck for a new truck. The used truck cost $30,000 and has accumulated depreciation of $27,000. The new truck is worth $35,000. Bubey also made a cash payment of $33,000. Prepare Bubey's entry to record the exchange.

BE9-8   Buck Rogers Corporation traded a used truck for a new truck. The used truck cost $20,000 and has accumulated depreciation of $17,000. The new truck is worth $35,000. Rogers also made a cash payment of $33,000. Prepare Rogers' entry to record the exchange.

BE9-9   Indicate which of the following costs should be expensed when incurred.

(a) $13,000 paid to rearrange and reinstall machinery.
(b) $200 paid for tune-up and oil change on delivery truck.
(c) $200,000 paid for addition to building.
(d) $7,000 paid to replace a wooden floor with a concrete floor.
(e) $2,000 paid for a major overhaul on a truck, which extends useful life.

BE9-10   Cheetah Company purchased machinery on January 1, 2003, for $60,000. The machinery is estimated to have a salvage value of $6,000 after a useful life of 8 years. (a) Compute 2003 depreciation expense using the straight-line method. (b) Compute 2003 depreciation expense using the straight-line method assuming the machinery was purchased on September 1, 2003.

BE9-11   Use the information for Cheetah Company given in BE9-10. (a) Compute 2003 depreciation expense using the sum-of-the-years'-digits method. (b) Compute 2003 depreciation expense using the sum-of-the-years'-digits method assuming the machinery was purchased on April 1, 2003.

BE9-12   Use the information for Cheetah Company given in BE9-10. (a) Compute 2003 depreciation expense using the double-declining balance method. (b) Compute 2003 depreciation expense using the double-declining balance method assuming the machinery was purchased on October 1, 2003.

BE9-13   Garfield Company purchased a machine on July 1, 2003, for $25,000. Garfield paid $200 in title fees and county property tax of $125 on the machine. In addition, Garfield paid $500 shipping charges for delivery, and paid $475 to a local contractor to build and wire a platform for the machine on the plant floor. The machine has an estimated useful life of 6 years with a scrap value of $3,000. Determine the depreciation base of Garfield's new machine. Garfield uses straight-line depreciation.

BE9-14   Myst Company purchased a computer for $7,000 on January 1, 2002. Straight-line depreciation is used, based on a 5-year life and a $1,000 salvage value. In 2004, the estimates are revised. Myst now feels the computer will be used until December 31, 2005, when it can be sold for $500. Compute the 2004 depreciation.

BE9-15   Sim City Corporation owns machinery that cost $20,000 when purchased on January 1, 2000. Depreciation has been recorded at a rate of $3,000 per year, resulting in a balance in accumulated depreciation of $9,000 at December 31, 2002. The machinery is sold on September 1, 2003, for $10,500. Prepare journal entries to (a) update depreciation for 2003 and (b) record the sale.

BE9-16   Use the information presented for Sim City Corporation in BE9-15, but assume the machinery is sold for $5,200 instead of $10,500. Prepare journal entries to (a) update depreciation for 2003 and (b) record the sale.

Exercises

E9-1 (Acquisition Costs of Realty) The following expenditures and receipts are related to land, land improvements, and buildings acquired for use in a business enterprise. The receipts are enclosed in parentheses.

(a)	Money borrowed to pay building contractor (signed a note)	$(275,000)
(b)	Payment for construction from note proceeds	275,000
(c)	Cost of land fill and clearing	8,000
(d)	Delinquent real estate taxes on property assumed by purchaser	7,000
(e)	Premium on 6-month insurance policy during construction	6,000
(f)	Refund of 1-month insurance premium because construction completed early	(1,000)
(g)	Architect's fee on building	22,000
(h)	Cost of real estate purchased as a plant site (land $200,000 and building $50,000)	250,000
(i)	Commission fee paid to real estate agency	9,000
(j)	Installation of fences around property	4,000
(k)	Cost of razing and removing building	11,000
(l)	Proceeds from salvage of demolished building	(5,000)
(m)	Interest paid during construction on money borrowed for construction	13,000
(n)	Cost of parking lots and driveways	19,000
(o)	Cost of trees and shrubbery planted (permanent in nature)	14,000
(p)	Excavation costs for new building	3,000

Instructions

Identify each item by letter and list the items in columnar form, as shown below. All receipt amounts should be reported in parentheses. For any amounts entered in the Other Accounts column also indicate the account title.

				Other
Item	Land	Land Improvements	Building	Accounts

E9-2 (Acquisition Costs of Realty) Martin Buber Co. purchased land as a factory site for $400,000. The process of tearing down two old buildings on the site and constructing the factory required 6 months.

The company paid $42,000 to raze the old buildings and sold salvaged lumber and brick for $6,300. Legal fees of $1,850 were paid for title investigation and drawing the purchase contract. Payment to an engineering firm was made for a land survey, $2,200, and for drawing the factory plans, $68,000. The land survey had to be made before definitive plans could be drawn. Title insurance on the property cost $1,500, and a liability insurance premium paid during construction was $900. The contractor's charge for construction was $2,740,000. The company paid the contractor in two installments: $1,200,000 at the end of 3 months and $1,540,000 upon completion. Interest costs of $170,000 were incurred to finance the construction.

Instructions

Determine the cost of the land and the cost of the building as they should be recorded on the books of Martin Buber Co. Assume that the land survey was for the building.

E9-3 (Acquisition Costs of Trucks) Alexei Urmanov Corporation operates a retail computer store. To improve delivery services to customers, the company purchases three new trucks on April 1, 2003. The terms of acquisition for each truck are described below.

1. Truck #1 has a list price of $15,000 and is acquired for a cash payment of $13,900.
2. Truck #2 has a list price of $16,000. It is acquired in exchange for a computer system that Urmanov carries in inventory. The computer system cost $12,000 and is normally sold by Urmanov for $15,200. Urmanov uses a perpetual inventory system.
3. Truck #3 has a list price of $14,000. It is acquired in exchange for 1,000 shares of common stock in Urmanov Corporation. The stock has a par value per share of $10 and a market value of $13 per share.

Instructions

Prepare the appropriate journal entries for the foregoing transactions for Urmanov Corporation.

 E9-4 (Treatment of Various Costs) Ben Sisko Supply Company, a newly formed corporation, incurred the following expenditures related to Land, to Buildings, and to Machinery and Equipment.

Abstract company's fee for title search		$ 520
Architect's fees		2,800
Cash paid for land and dilapidated building thereon		87,000
Removal of old building	$20,000	
Less: Salvage	5,500	14,500
Surveying before construction		370
Interest on short-term loans during construction		7,400
Excavation before construction for basement		19,000
Machinery purchased (subject to 2% cash discount, which was not taken)		55,000
Freight on machinery purchased		1,340
Storage charges on machinery, necessitated by noncompletion of building when machinery was delivered		2,180
New building constructed (building construction took 6 months from date of purchase of land and old building)		485,000
Assessment by city for drainage project		1,600
Hauling charges for delivery of machinery from storage to new building		620
Installation of machinery		2,000
Trees, shrubs, and other landscaping after completion of building (permanent in nature)		5,400

Instructions

Determine the amounts that should be debited to Land, to Buildings, and to Machinery and Equipment. Assume the benefits of capitalizing interest during construction exceed the cost of implementation. Indicate how any costs not debited to these accounts should be recorded.

E9-5 (Correction of Improper Cost Entries) Plant acquisitions for selected companies are as follows.

1. Belanna Industries Inc. acquired land, buildings, and equipment from a bankrupt company, Torres Co., for a lump sum price of $700,000. At the time of purchase, Torres assets had the following book and appraisal values.

	Book Values	Appraisal Values
Land	$200,000	$150,000
Buildings	250,000	350,000
Equipment	300,000	300,000

To be conservative, the company decided to take the lower of the two values for each asset acquired. The following entry was made.

Land	150,000	
Buildings	250,000	
Equipment	300,000	
Cash		700,000

2. Harry Enterprises purchased store equipment by making a $2,000 cash down payment and signing a 1-year, $23,000, 10% note payable. The purchase was recorded as follows.

Store Equipment	27,300	
Cash		2,000
Note Payable		23,000
Interest Payable		2,300

3. Kim Company purchased office equipment for $20,000, terms 2/10, n/30. Because the company intended to take the discount, it made no entry until it paid for the acquisition. The entry was:

Office Equipment	20,000	
Cash		19,600
Purchase Discounts		400

4. Kaisson Inc. recently received at zero cost land from the Village of Cardassia as an inducement to locate its business in the Village. The appraised value of the land is $27,000. The company made no entry to record the land because it had no cost basis.

5. Zimmerman Company built a warehouse for $600,000. It could have purchased the building for $740,000. The controller made the following entry.

Warehouse	740,000	
Cash		600,000
Profit on Construction		140,000

Instructions

Prepare the entry that should have been made at the date of each acquisition.

E9-6 (Entries for Equipment Acquisitions) Jane Geddes Engineering Corporation purchased conveyor equipment with a list price of $10,000. The vendor's credit terms were 2/10, n/30. Presented below are two independent cases related to the equipment. Assume that the purchases of equipment are recorded gross. (Round to nearest dollar.)

(a) Geddes paid cash for the equipment 8 days after the purchase.

(b) Geddes traded in equipment with a book value of $2,000 (initial cost $8,000), and paid $9,500 in cash one month after the purchase. The old equipment could have been sold for $400 at the date of trade (assume similar equipment).

Instructions

Prepare the general journal entries required to record the acquisition and payment in each of the independent cases above. Round to the nearest dollar.

E9-7 (Entries for Asset Acquisition, Including Self-Construction) Below are transactions related to Fred Couples Company.

(a) The City of Pebble Beach gives the company 5 acres of land as a plant site. The market value of this land is determined to be $81,000.

(b) 13,000 shares of common stock with a par value of $50 per share are issued in exchange for land and buildings. The property has been appraised at a fair market value of $810,000, of which $180,000 has been allocated to land and $630,000 to buildings. The stock of Fred Couples Company is not listed on any exchange, but a block of 100 shares was sold by a stockholder 12 months ago at $65 per share, and a block of 200 shares was sold by another stockholder 18 months ago at $58 per share.

(c) No entry has been made to remove from the accounts for Materials, Direct Labor, and Overhead the amounts properly chargeable to plant asset accounts for machinery constructed during the year. The following information is given relative to costs of the machinery constructed.

Materials used	$12,500
Factory supplies used	900
Direct labor incurred	15,000
Additional overhead (over regular) caused by construction of machinery, excluding factory supplies used	2,700
Fixed overhead rate applied to regular manufacturing operations	60% of direct labor cost
Cost of similar machinery if it had been purchased from outside suppliers	44,000

Instructions

Prepare journal entries on the books of Fred Couples Company to record these transactions.

E9-8 **(Entries for Acquisition of Assets)** Presented below is information related to Zonker Company.

1. On July 6 Zonker Company acquired the plant assets of Doonesbury Company, which had discontinued operations. The appraised value of the property is:

Land	$ 400,000
Building	1,200,000
Machinery and equipment	800,000
Total	$2,400,000

   Zonker Company gave 12,500 shares of its $100 par value common stock in exchange. The stock had a market value of $168 per share on the date of the purchase of the property.

2. Zonker Company expended the following amounts in cash between July 6 and December 15, the date when it first occupied the building.

Repairs to building	$105,000
Construction of bases for machinery to be installed later	135,000
Driveways and parking lots	122,000
Remodeling of office space in building, including new partitions and walls	161,000
Special assessment by city on land	18,000

3. On December 20, the company paid cash for machinery, $260,000, subject to a 2% cash discount, and freight on machinery of $10,500.

Instructions

Prepare entries on the books of Zonker Company for these transactions.

E9-9 **(Analysis of Subsequent Expenditures)** King Donovan Resources Group has been in its plant facility for 15 years. Although the plant is quite functional, numerous repair costs are incurred to maintain it in sound working order. The company's plant asset book value is currently $800,000, as indicated below.

Original cost	$1,200,000
Accumulated depreciation	400,000
	$ 800,000

During the current year, the following expenditures were made to the plant facility.

(a) Because of increased demands for its product, the company increased its plant capacity by building a new addition at a cost of $270,000.

(b) The entire plant was repainted at a cost of $23,000.

(c) The roof was an asbestos cement slate. For safety purposes it was removed and replaced with a wood shingle roof at a cost of $61,000. Book value of the old roof was $41,000.

(d) The electrical system was completely updated at a cost of $22,000. The cost of the old electrical system was not known. It is estimated that the useful life of the building will not change as a result of this updating.

(e) A series of major repairs were made at a cost of $47,000, because parts of the wood structure were rotting. The cost of the old wood structure was not known. These extensive repairs are estimated to increase the useful life of the building.

Instructions

Indicate how each of these transactions would be recorded in the accounting records.

E9-10 **(Analysis of Subsequent Expenditures)** The following transactions occurred during 2004. Assume that depreciation of 10% per year is charged on all machinery and 5% per year on buildings, on a straight-line basis, with no estimated salvage value. Depreciation is charged for a full year on all fixed assets acquired during the year, and no depreciation is charged on fixed assets disposed of during the year.

Jan. 30   A building that cost $132,000 in 1987 is torn down to make room for a new building. The wrecking contractor was paid $5,100 and was permitted to keep all materials salvaged.

Mar. 10   Machinery that was purchased in 1997 for $16,000 is sold for $2,900 cash, f.o.b. purchaser's plant. Freight of $300 is paid on this machinery.

Mar. 20   A gear breaks on a machine that cost $9,000 in 1999, and is replaced at a cost of $385. The replacement does not extend the useful life of the machine.

May 18   A special base installed for a machine in 1998 when the machine was purchased has to be replaced at a cost of $5,500 because of defective workmanship on the original base. The cost of the machinery was $14,200 in 1998. The cost of the base was $3,500, and this amount was charged to the Machinery account in 1998.

June 23   One of the buildings is repainted at a cost of $6,900. It had not been painted since it was constructed in 2000.

Instructions

Prepare general journal entries for the transactions. (Round to nearest dollar.)

E9-11   (Analysis of Subsequent Expenditures)   Plant assets often require expenditures subsequent to acquisition. It is important that they be accounted for properly. Any errors will affect both the balance sheets and income statements for a number of years.

Instructions

For each of the following items, indicate whether the expenditure should be capitalized (C) or expensed (E) in the period incurred.

(a)   _____   Improvement.

(b)   _____   Replacement of a minor broken part on a machine.

(c)   _____   Expenditure that increases the useful life of an existing asset.

(d)   _____   Expenditure that increases the efficiency and effectiveness of a productive asset but does not increase its salvage value.

(e)   _____   Expenditure that increases the efficiency and effectiveness of a productive asset and increases the asset's salvage value.

(f)   _____   Expenditure that increases the quality of the output of the productive asset.

(g)   _____   Improvement to a machine that increased its fair market value and its production capacity by 30% without extending the machine's useful life.

(h)   _____   Ordinary repairs.

(i)   _____   Addition.

(j)   _____   Interest on borrowing necessary to finance a major overhaul of machinery. The overhaul extended the life of the machinery.

E9-12   (Depreciation Computations—SL, SYD, DDB)   Deluxe Ezra Company purchases equipment on January 1, year 1, at a cost of $469,000. The asset is expected to have a service life of 12 years and a salvage value of $40,000.

Instructions

(a) Compute the amount of depreciation for each of years 1 through 3 using the straight-line depreciation method.

(b) Compute the amount of depreciation for each of years 1 through 3 using the sum-of-the-years'-digits method.

(c) Compute the amount of depreciation for each of years 1 through 3 using the double-declining balance method. (In performing your calculations, round constant percentage to the nearest one-hundredth of a point and round answers to the nearest dollar.)

E9-13   (Depreciation—Conceptual Understanding)   Rembrandt Company acquired a plant asset at the beginning of year 1. The asset has an estimated service life of 5 years. An employee has prepared depreciation schedules for this asset using three different methods to compare the results of using one method with the results of using other methods. You are to assume that the following schedules have been correctly prepared for this asset using (1) the straight-line method, (2) the sum-of-the-years'-digits method, and (3) the double-declining balance method.

Year	Straight-line	Sum-of-the-Years'-Digits	Double-declining Balance
1	$ 9,000	$15,000	$20,000
2	9,000	12,000	12,000
3	9,000	9,000	7,200
4	9,000	6,000	4,320
5	9,000	3,000	1,480
Total	$45,000	$45,000	$45,000

Instructions
Answer the following questions.

(a) What is the cost of the asset being depreciated?
(b) What amount, if any, was used in the depreciation calculations for the salvage value for this asset?
(c) Which method will produce the highest charge to income in year 1?
(d) Which method will produce the highest charge to income in year 4?
(e) Which method will produce the highest book value for the asset at the end of year 3?
(f) If the asset is sold at the end of year 3, which method would yield the highest gain (or lowest loss) on disposal of the asset?

E9-14 **(Depreciation Computations—SYD, DDB—Partial Periods)** Judds Company purchased a new plant asset on April 1, 2003, at a cost of $711,000. It was estimated to have a service life of 20 years and a salvage value of $60,000. Judds' accounting period is the calendar year.

Instructions
(a) Compute the depreciation for this asset for 2003 and 2004 using the sum-of-the-years'-digits method.
(b) Compute the depreciation for this asset for 2003 and 2004 using the double-declining balance method.

E9-15 **(Depreciation Computations—Five Methods)** Jon Seceda Furnace Corp. purchased machinery for $315,000 on May 1, 2003. It is estimated that it will have a useful life of 10 years, scrap value of $15,000, production of 240,000 units, and working hours of 25,000. During 2004 Seceda Corp. uses the machinery for 2,650 hours, and the machinery produces 25,500 units.

Instructions
From the information given, compute the depreciation charge for 2004 under each of the following methods (round to three decimal places).

(a) Straight-line.   **(c)** Working hours.   **(e)** Declining-balance
(b) Units-of-output.   **(d)** Sum-of-the-years'-digits.   (use 20% as the annual rate).

E9-16 **(Depreciation Computations—Four Methods)** Robert Parish Corporation purchased a new machine for its assembly process on August 1, 2003. The cost of this machine was $117,900. The company estimated that the machine would have a trade-in value of $12,900 at the end of its service life. Its life is estimated at 5 years and its working hours are estimated at 21,000 hours. Year-end is December 31.

Instructions
Compute the depreciation expense under the following methods: **(a)** straight-line depreciation for 2003, **(b)** activity method for 2003, assuming that machine usage was 800 hours, **(c)** sum-of-the-years'-digits for 2004, and **(d)** double-declining balance for 2004. Each of the foregoing should be considered unrelated.

E9-17 (Depreciation Computations—Five Methods, Partial Periods) Muggsy Bogues Company purchased equipment for $212,000 on October 1, 2003. It is estimated that the equipment will have a useful life of 8 years and a salvage value of $12,000. Estimated production is 40,000 units and estimated working hours 20,000. During 2003, Bogues uses the equipment for 525 hours and the equipment produces 1,000 units.

Instructions

Compute depreciation expense under each of the following methods. Bogues is on a calendar-year basis ending December 31.

(a) Straight-line method for 2003.

(b) Activity method (units of output) for 2003.

(c) Activity method (working hours) for 2003.

(d) Sum-of-the-years'-digits method for 2005.

(e) Double-declining balance method for 2004.

E9-18 (Different Methods of Depreciation) Jackel Industries presents you with the following information.

Description	Date Purchased	Cost	Salvage Value	Life in Years	Depreciation Method	Accumulated Depreciation to 12/31/03	Depreciation for 2004
Machine A	2/12/02	$142,500	$16,000	10	(a)	$33,350	(b)
Machine B	8/15/01	(c)	21,000	5	SL	29,000	(d)
Machine C	7/21/00	75,400	23,500	8	DDB	(e)	(f)
Machine D	10/12/(g)	219,000	69,000	5	SYD	70,000	(h)

Instructions

Complete the table for the year ended December 31, 2004. The company depreciates all assets using the half-year convention.

E9-19 (Depreciation Computation—Addition, Change in Estimate) In 1976, Herman Moore Company completed the construction of a building at a cost of $2,000,000 and first occupied it in January 1977. It was estimated that the building will have a useful life of 40 years, and a salvage value of $60,000 at the end of that time.

Early in 1987, an addition to the building was constructed at a cost of $500,000. At that time it was estimated that the remaining life of the building would be, as originally estimated, an additional 30 years, and that the addition would have a life of 30 years, and a salvage value of $20,000.

In 2005, it is determined that the probable life of the building and addition will extend to the end of 2036 or 20 years beyond the original estimate.

Instructions

(a) Using the straight-line method, compute the annual depreciation that would have been charged from 1977 through 1986.

(b) Compute the annual depreciation that would have been charged from 1987 through 2004.

(c) Prepare the entry, if necessary, to adjust the account balances because of the revision of the estimated life in 2005.

(d) Compute the annual depreciation to be charged beginning with 2005.

E9-20 (Depreciation—Replacement, Change in Estimate) Randy Johnson Company constructed a building at a cost of $2,200,000 and occupied it beginning in January 1984. It was estimated at that time that its life would be 40 years, with no salvage value.

In January 2004, a new roof was installed at a cost of $300,000, and it was estimated then that the building would have a useful life of 25 years from that date. The cost of the old roof was $160,000.

Instructions

(a) What amount of depreciation should have been charged annually from the years 1984 to 2003? (Assume straight-line depreciation.)

(b) What entry should be made in 2004 to record the replacement of the roof?

(c) Prepare the entry in January 2004 to record the revision in the estimated life of the building, if necessary.

(d) What amount of depreciation should be charged for the year 2004?

E9-21 (Nonmonetary Exchange with Boot) Busytown Corporation, which manufactures shoes, hired a recent college graduate to work in its accounting department. On the first day of work, the accountant was assigned to total a batch of invoices with the use of an adding machine. Before long, the accountant, who had never before seen such a machine, managed to break the machine. Busytown Corporation gave the machine plus $340 to Dick Tracy Business Machine Company (dealer) in exchange for a new machine. Assume the following information about the machines.

	Busytown Corp. (Old Machine)	Dick Tracy Co. (New Machine)
Machine cost	$290	$270
Accumulated depreciation	140	–0–
Fair value	85	425

Instructions

For each company, prepare the necessary journal entry to record the exchange.

E9-22 (Nonmonetary Exchange with Boot) Carlos Arruza Company exchanged equipment used in its manufacturing operations plus $3,000 in cash for similar equipment used in the operations of Tony LoBianco Company. The following information pertains to the exchange.

	Carlos Arruza Co.	Tony LoBianco Co.
Equipment (cost)	$28,000	$28,000
Accumulated depreciation	19,000	10,000
Fair value of equipment	12,500	15,500
Cash given up	3,000	

Instructions

Prepare the journal entries to record the exchange on the books of both companies.

E9-23 (Nonmonetary Exchange with Boot) Dana Ashbrook Inc. has negotiated the purchase of a new piece of automatic equipment at a price of $8,000 plus trade-in, f.o.b. factory. Dana Ashbrook Inc. paid $8,000 cash and traded in used equipment. The used equipment had originally cost $62,000. It had a book value of $42,000 and a secondhand market value of $47,800, as indicated by recent transactions involving similar equipment. Freight and installation charges for the new equipment required a cash payment of $1,100.

Instructions

(a) Prepare the general journal entry to record this transaction, assuming that the assets Dana Ashbrook Inc. exchanged are similar in nature.

(b) Assuming the same facts as in (a) except that the assets exchanged are dissimilar in nature, prepare the general journal entry to record this transaction.

E9-24 (Entries for Disposition of Assets) On December 31, 2003, Travis Tritt Inc. has a machine with a book value of $940,000. The original cost and related accumulated depreciation at this date are as follows.

Machine	$1,300,000
Accumulated depreciation	360,000
	$ 940,000

Depreciation is computed at $60,000 per year on a straight-line basis.

Instructions

Presented below is a set of independent situations. For each independent situation, indicate the journal entry to be made to record the transaction. Make sure that depreciation entries are made to update the book value of the machine prior to its disposal.

(a) A fire completely destroys the machine on August 31, 2004. An insurance settlement of $430,000 was received for this casualty. Assume the settlement was received immediately.

(b) On April 1, 2004, Tritt sold the machine for $1,040,000 to Dwight Yoakam Company.

(c) On July 31, 2004, the company donated this machine to the Mountain King City Council. The fair market value of the machine at the time of the donation was estimated to be $1,100,000.

E9-25 (Disposition of Assets) On April 1, 2003, Gloria Estefan Company received a condemnation award of $430,000 cash as compensation for the forced sale of the company's land and building, which stood in the path of a new state highway. The land and building cost $60,000 and $280,000, respectively, when they were acquired. At April 1, 2003, the accumulated depreciation relating to the building amounted to $160,000. On August 1, 2003, Estafan purchased a piece of replacement property for cash. The new land cost $90,000, and the new building cost $400,000.

Instructions

Prepare the journal entries to record the transactions on April 1 and August 1, 2003.

*E9-26 (Capitalization of Interest) Harrisburg Furniture Company started construction of a combination office and warehouse building for its own use at an estimated cost of $5,000,000 on January 1, 2003. Harrisburg expected to complete the building by December 31, 2003. Harrisburg has the following debt obligations outstanding during the construction period.

Construction loan—12% interest, payable semiannually, issued December 31, 2002	$2,000,000
Short-term loan—10% interest, payable monthly, and principal payable at maturity on May 30, 2004	1,400,000
Long-term loan—11% interest, payable on January 1 of each year. Principal payable on January 1, 2007	1,000,000

Instructions

(Carry all computations to two decimal places.)

(a) Assume that Harrisburg completed the office and warehouse building on December 31, 2003, as planned, at a total cost of $5,200,000. The weighted average of accumulated expenditures was $3,600,000. Compute the avoidable interest on this project.

(b) Compute the depreciation expense for the year ended December 31, 2004. Harrisburg elected to depreciate the building on a straight-line basis and determined that the asset has a useful life of 30 years and a salvage value of $300,000.

*E9-27 (Capitalization of Interest) On December 31, 2002, Alma-Ata Inc. borrowed $3,000,000 at 12% payable annually to finance the construction of a new building. In 2003, the company made the following expenditures related to this building: March 1, $360,000; June 1, $600,000; July 1, $1,500,000; December 1, $1,500,000. Additional information is provided as follows.

1. Other debt outstanding

10-year, 13% bond, December 31, 1996, interest payable annually	$4,000,000
6-year, 10% note, dated December 31, 2000, interest payable annually	$1,600,000

2. March 1, 2003, expenditure included land costs of $150,000

3. Interest revenue earned in 2003 $ 49,000

Instructions

(a) Determine the amount of interest to be capitalized in 2003 in relation to the construction of the building.

(b) Prepare the journal entry to record the capitalization of interest and the recognition of interest expense, if any, at December 31, 2003.

PROBLEMS

P9-1 (Classification of Acquisition Costs) Selected accounts included in the property, plant, and equipment section of Spud Webb Corporation's balance sheet at December 31, 2002, had the following balances.

Land	$ 300,000
Land improvements	140,000
Buildings	1,100,000
Machinery and equipment	960,000

During 2003 the following transactions occurred.

1. A tract of land was acquired for $150,000 as a potential future building site.
2. A plant facility consisting of land and building was acquired from Ken Norman Company in exchange for 20,000 shares of Webb's common stock. On the acquisition date, Webb's stock had a closing market price of $37 per share on a national stock exchange. The plant facility was carried on Norman's books at $110,000 for land and $320,000 for the building at the exchange date. Current appraised values for the land and building, respectively, are $230,000 and $690,000.
3. Items of machinery and equipment were purchased at a total cost of $400,000. Additional costs were incurred as follows.

Freight and unloading	$13,000
Sales taxes	20,000
Installation	26,000

4. Expenditures totaling $95,000 were made for new parking lots, streets, and sidewalks at the corporation's various plant locations. These expenditures had an estimated useful life of 15 years.
5. A machine costing $80,000 on January 1, 1995, was scrapped on June 30, 2003. Double-declining-balance depreciation has been recorded on the basis of a 10-year life.
6. A machine was sold for $20,000 on July 1, 2003. Original cost of the machine was $44,000 on January 1, 2000, and it was depreciated on the straight-line basis over an estimated useful life of 7 years and a salvage value of $2,000.

Instructions

(a) Prepare a detailed analysis of the changes in each of the following balance sheet accounts for 2003.

Land
Land improvements
Buildings
Machinery and equipment

(*Hint:* Disregard the related accumulated depreciation accounts.)

(b) List the items in the fact situation that were not used to determine the answer to (a), showing the pertinent amounts and supporting computations in good form for each item. In addition, indicate where, or if, these items should be included in Spud Webb's financial statements.

(AICPA adapted)

P9-2 (Classification of Land and Building Costs) Lenny Wilkins Company was incorporated on January 2, 2004, but was unable to begin manufacturing activities until July 1, 2004, because new factory facilities were not completed until that date.

The Land and Building account at December 31, 2004, was as follows.

January 31, 2004	Land and building	$160,000
February 28, 2004	Cost of removal of building	9,800
May 1, 2004	Partial payment of new construction	60,000
May 1, 2004	Legal fees paid	3,770
June 1, 2004	Second payment on new construction	40,000
June 1, 2004	Insurance premium	2,280
June 1, 2004	Special tax assessment	4,000
June 30, 2004	General expenses	36,300
July 1, 2004	Final payment on new construction	40,000
December 31, 2004	Asset write-up	43,800
		399,950
December 31, 2004	Depreciation—2004 at 1%	4,000
	Account balance	$395,950

The following additional information is to be considered.

1. To acquire land and building the company paid $80,000 cash and 800 shares of its 8% cumulative preferred stock, par value $100 per share. Fair market value of the stock is $107 per share.
2. Cost of removal of old buildings amounted to $9,800, and the demolition company retained all materials of the building.
3. Legal fees covered the following.

Examination of title covering purchase of land	$1,910
Legal work in connection with construction contract	1,860
	$3,770

4. Insurance premium covered the building for a 2-year term beginning May 1, 2004.
5. The special tax assessment covered street improvements that are permanent in nature.
6. General expenses covered the following for the period from January 2, 2004, to June 30, 2004.

President's salary	$32,100
Plant superintendent covering supervision of new building	4,200
	$36,300

7. Because of a general increase in construction costs after entering into the building contract, the board of directors increased the value of the building $43,800, believing that such an increase was justified to reflect the current market at the time the building was completed. Retained earnings was credited for this amount.
8. Estimated life of building—50 years.
   Writeoff for 2004—1% of asset value (1% of $400,000, or $4,000).

Instructions

(a) Prepare entries to reflect correct land, building, and depreciation allowance accounts at December 31, 2004.

(b) Show the proper presentation of land, building, and depreciation on the balance sheet at December 31, 2004.

(AICPA adapted)

P9-3 (Costs of Self-Constructed Assets) George Fayne Mining Co. received a $760,000 low bid from a reputable manufacturer for the construction of special production equipment needed by Fayne in an expansion program. Because the company's own plant was not operating at capacity, Fayne decided to construct the equipment there and recorded the following production costs related to the construction.

Services of consulting engineer	$ 40,000
Work subcontracted	31,000
Materials	300,000
Plant labor normally assigned to production	114,000
Plant labor normally assigned to maintenance	160,000
Total	$645,000

Management prefers to record the cost of the equipment under the incremental cost method. Approximately 40% of the company's production is devoted to government supply contracts which are all based in some way on cost. The contracts require that any self-constructed equipment be allocated its full share of all costs related to the construction.

The following information is also available.

1. The production labor was for partial fabrication of the equipment in the plant. Skilled personnel were required and were assigned from other projects. The maintenance labor would have been idle time of nonproduction plant employees who would have been retained on the payroll whether or not their services were utilized.

2. Payroll taxes and employee fringe benefits are approximately 35% of labor cost and are included in manufacturing overhead cost. Total manufacturing overhead for the year was $6,084,000, including the $160,000 maintenance labor used to construct the equipment.

3. Manufacturing overhead is approximately 60% variable and is applied on the basis of production labor cost. Production labor cost for the year for the corporation's normal products totaled $8,286,000.

4. General and administrative expenses include $27,000 of allocated executive salary cost and $13,750 of postage, telephone, supplies, and miscellaneous expenses identifiable with this equipment construction.

Instructions

(a) Prepare a schedule computing the amount that should be reported as the full cost of the constructed equipment to meet the requirements of the government contracts. Any supporting computations should be in good form.

(b) Prepare a schedule computing the incremental cost of the constructed equipment.

(c) What is the greatest amount that should be capitalized as the cost of the equipment? Why?

(AICPA adapted)

P9-4 (Purchases by Deferred Payment, Lump-sum, and Nonmonetary Exchanges) Kent Adamson Company is a manufacturer of ballet shoes and is experiencing a period of sustained growth. In an effort to expand its production capacity to meet the increased demand for its product, the company recently made several acquisitions of plant and equipment. Tod Mullinger, newly hired in the position of fixed-assets accountant, requested that Watt Kaster, Adamson's controller, review the following transactions.

Transaction 1

On June 1, 2003, Adamson Company purchased equipment from Venghaus Corporation. Adamson issued a $20,000, 4-year, non-interest-bearing note to Venghaus for the new equipment. Adamson will pay off the note in four equal installments due at the end of each of the next 4 years. At the date of the transaction, the prevailing market rate of interest for obligations of this nature was 10%. Freight costs of $425 and installation costs of $500 were incurred in completing this transaction. The appropriate factors for the time value of money at a 10% rate of interest are given below. (See Appendix A for an additional discussion of present value concepts.)

Future value of $1 for 4 periods	1.46
Future value of an ordinary annuity for 4 periods	4.64
Present value of $1 for 4 periods	0.68
Present value of an ordinary annuity for 4 periods	3.17

Transaction 2

On December 1, 2003, Adamson Company purchased several assets of Haukap Shoes Inc., a small shoe manufacturer whose owner was retiring. The purchase amounted to $210,000 and included the assets listed below. Adamson Company engaged the services of Tennyson Appraisal Inc., an independent appraiser, to determine the fair market values of the assets which are also presented below.

	Haukap Book Value	Fair Market Value
Inventory	$ 60,000	$ 50,000
Land	40,000	80,000
Building	70,000	120,000
	$170,000	$250,000

During its fiscal year ended May 31, 2004, Adamson incurred $8,000 for interest expense in connection with the financing of these assets.

Transaction 3

On March 1, 2004, Adamson Company exchanged a number of used trucks plus cash for vacant land adjacent to its plant site. Adamson intends to use the land for a parking lot. The trucks had a combined book value of $35,000, as Adamson had recorded $20,000 of accumulated depreciation against these assets. Adamson's purchasing agent, who has had previous dealings in the second-hand market, indicated that the trucks had a fair market value of $46,000 at the time of the transaction. In addition to the trucks, Adamson Company paid $19,000 cash for the land.

Instructions

(a) Plant assets such as land, buildings, and equipment receive special accounting treatment. Describe the major characteristics of these assets that differentiate them from other types of assets.

(b) For each of the three transactions described above, determine the value at which Adamson Company should record the acquired assets. Support your calculations with an explanation of the underlying rationale.

(c) The books of Adamson Company show the following additional transactions for the fiscal year ended May 31, 2004.
   1. Acquisition of a building for speculative purposes.
   2. Purchase of a 2-year insurance policy covering plant equipment.
   3. Purchase of the rights for the exclusive use of a process used in the manufacture of ballet shoes. For each of these transactions, indicate whether the asset should be classified as a plant asset. If it is a plant asset, explain why it is. If it is not a plant asset, explain why not, and identify the proper classification.

(CMA adapted)

 **P9-5 (Depreciation for Partial Period—SL, SYD, and DDB)** Onassis Company purchased Machine #201 on May 1, 2003. The following information relating to Machine #201 was gathered at the end of May.

Price	$73,500
Credit terms	2/10, n/30
Freight-in costs	$ 970
Preparation and installation costs	$ 3,800
Labor costs during regular production operations	$10,500

It was expected that the machine could be used for 10 years, after which the salvage value would be zero. Onassis intends to use the machine for only 8 years, however, after which it expects to be able to sell it for $1,200. The invoice for Machine #201 was paid May 5, 2003. Onassis uses the calendar year as the basis for the preparation of financial statements.

Instructions

(a) Compute the depreciation expense for the years indicated using the following methods. (Round to the nearest dollar.)
   (1) Straight-line method for 2003.

(2) Sum-of-the-years'-digits method for 2004.

(3) Double-declining balance method for 2003.

(b) Suppose Jackie Ari, the president of Onassis, tells you that because the company is a new organization, she expects it will be several years before production and sales reach optimum levels. She asks you to recommend a depreciation method that will allocate less of the company's depreciation expense to the early years and more to later years of the assets' lives. What method would you recommend?

P9-6 (Depreciation—Partial Periods, Machinery) Goran Tool Company records depreciation annually at the end of the year. Its policy is to take a full year's depreciation on all assets used throughout the year, and depreciation for one-half a year on all machines acquired or disposed of during the year. The depreciation rate for the machinery is 10% applied on a straight-line basis, with no estimated scrap value.

The balance of the Machinery account at the beginning of 2004 was $172,300; the Accumulated Depreciation on Machinery account had a balance of $72,900. The following transactions affecting the machinery accounts took place during the year.

Jan. 15	Machine No. 38, which cost $9,600 when acquired June 3, 1997, was retired and sold as scrap metal for $600.
Feb. 27	Machine No. 81 was purchased. The fair market value of this machine was $12,500. It replaces Machines No. 12 and No. 27, which were traded in on the new machine. Machine No. 12 was acquired Feb. 4, 1992, at a cost of $5,500 and is still carried in the accounts although fully depreciated and not in use. Machine No. 27 was acquired June 11, 1997, at a cost of $8,200. In addition to these two used machines, $9,000 was paid in cash. (Assume exchange of similar assets.)
Apr. 7	Machine No. 54 was equipped with electric control equipment at a cost of $940. This machine, originally equipped with simple hand controls, was purchased Dec. 11, 2000, for $1,800. The new electric controls can be attached to any one of several machines in the shop.
12	Machine No. 24 was repaired at a cost of $720 after a fire caused by a short circuit in the wiring burned out the motor and damaged certain essential parts.
July 22	Machines No. 25, 26, and 41 are sold for $3,100 cash. The purchase dates and cost of these machines are:

No. 25	$4,000	May 8, 1996
No. 26	3,200	May 8, 1996
No. 41	2,800	June 1, 1998

Instructions

(a) Record each transaction in general journal entry form.

(b) Compute and record depreciation for the year. No machines now included in the balance of the account were acquired before January 1, 1995.

P9-7 (Depreciation—SYD, Act., SL, and DDB) The following data relate to the Plant Assets account of Arthur Fiedler, Inc. at December 31, 2003.

	Plant Assets			
	A	B	C	D
Original cost	$35,000	$51,000	$80,000	$80,000
Year purchased	1998	1999	2000	2002
Useful life	10 years	15,000 hours	15 years	10 years
Salvage value	$ 3,100	$ 3,000	$ 5,000	$ 5,000
Depreciation method	Sum-of-the-years'-digits	Activity	Straight-line	Double-declining balance
Accum. Depr. through 2003[a]	$23,200	$35,200	$15,000	$16,000

[a]In the year an asset is purchased, Fiedler, Inc. does not record any depreciation expense on the asset.

In the year an asset is retired or traded in, Fiedler, Inc. takes a full year's depreciation on the asset.

The following transactions occurred during 2004.

(a) On May 5, Asset A was sold for $13,000 cash. The company's bookkeeper recorded this retirement in the following manner in the cash receipts journal:

Cash	13,000	
Asset A		13,000

(b) On December 31, it was determined that Asset B had been used 2,100 hours during 2004.

(c) On December 31, before computing depreciation expense on Asset C, the management of Fiedler, Inc. decided the useful life remaining from 1/1/04 was 10 years.

(d) On December 31, it was discovered that a plant asset purchased in 2003 had been expensed completely in that year. This asset cost $22,000 and has a useful life of 10 years and no salvage value. Management has decided to use the double-declining balance method for this asset, which can be referred to as "Asset E."

Instructions

Prepare the necessary correcting entries for the year 2004. Record the appropriate depreciation expense on the above-mentioned assets.

P9-8 (Nonmonetary Exchanges with Boot) Susquehanna Corporation wishes to exchange a machine used in its operations. Susquehanna has received the following offers from other companies in the industry:

1. Choctaw Company offered to exchange a similar machine plus $23,000.
2. Powhatan Company offered to exchange a similar machine.

In addition, Susquehanna contacted Seminole Corporation, a dealer in machines. To obtain a new machine, Susquehanna must pay $93,000 in addition to trading in its old machine.

	Susquehanna	Choctaw	Powhatan	Seminole
Machine cost	$160,000	$120,000	$147,000	$130,000
Accumulated depreciation	50,000	45,000	71,000	–0–
Fair value	92,000	69,000	92,000	185,000

Instructions

For each of the three independent situations, prepare the journal entries to record the exchange on the books of each company. (Round to nearest dollar.)

P9-9 (Nonmonetary Exchanges with Boot) During the current year, Garrison Construction trades an old crane that has a book value of $80,000 (original cost $140,000 less accumulated depreciation $60,000) for a new crane from Keillor Manufacturing Co. The new crane cost Keillor $165,000 to manufacture and is classified as inventory. The following information is also available.

	Garrison Const.	Keillor Mfg. Co.
Fair market value of old crane	$ 72,000	
Fair market value of new crane		$190,000
Cash paid	118,000	
Cash received		118,000

Instructions

(a) Assuming that this exchange is considered to involve dissimilar assets, prepare the journal entries on the books of (1) Garrison Construction and (2) Keillor Manufacturing.

(b) Assuming that this exchange is considered to involve similar assets, prepare the journal entries on the books of (1) Garrison Construction and (2) Keillor Manufacturing.

(c) Assuming the same facts as those in (a), except that the fair market value of the old crane is $98,000 and the cash paid is $92,000, prepare the journal entries on the books of (1) Garrison Construction and (2) Keillor Manufacturing.

P9-10 **(Dispositions, Including Condemnation, and Demolition)** Presented below is a schedule of property dispositions for Frank Thomas Co.

	Cost	Accumulated Depreciation	Cash Proceeds	Fair Market Value	Nature of Disposition
		SCHEDULE OF PROPERTY DISPOSITIONS			
Land	$40,000	—	$31,000	$31,000	Condemnation
Building	15,000	—	3,600	—	Demolition
Warehouse	70,000	$11,000	74,000	74,000	Destruction by fire
Furniture	10,000	7,850	—	3,100	Contribution
Automobile	8,000	3,460	2,960	2,960	Sale

The following additional information is available.

Land

On February 15, a condemnation award was received as consideration for unimproved land held primarily as an investment, and on March 31, another parcel of unimproved land to be held as an investment was purchased at a cost of $35,000.

Building

On April 2, land and building were purchased at a total cost of $75,000, of which 20% was allocated to the building on the corporate books. The real estate was acquired with the intention of demolishing the building, and this was accomplished during the month of November. Cash proceeds received in November represent the net proceeds from demolition of the building.

Warehouse

On June 30, the warehouse was destroyed by fire. The warehouse was purchased January 2, 1990, and had depreciated $11,000. On December 27, the insurance proceeds and other funds were used to purchase a replacement warehouse at a cost of $90,000.

Furniture

On August 15, furniture was contributed to a qualified charitable organization. No other contributions were made or pledged during the year.

Automobile

On November 3, the automobile was sold to Ozzie Guillen, a stockholder.

Instructions

Indicate how these items would be reported on the income statement of Frank Thomas Co.

(AICPA adapted)

*P9-11 **(Comprehensive Fixed Asset Problem)** Selig Sporting Goods Inc. has been experiencing growth in the demand for its products over the last several years. The last two Olympic Games greatly increased the popularity of basketball around the world. As a result, a European sports retailing consortium entered into an agreement with Selig's Roundball Division to purchase basketballs and other accessories on an increasing basis over the next 5 years.

To be able to meet the quantity commitments of this agreement, Selig had to obtain additional manufacturing capacity. A real estate firm located an available factory in close proximity to Selig's Roundball manufacturing facility, and Selig agreed to purchase the factory and used machinery from Starks Athletic Equipment Company on October 1, 2002. Renovations were necessary to convert the factory for Selig's manufacturing use.

The terms of the agreement required Selig to pay Starks $50,000 when renovations started on January 1, 2003, with the balance to be paid as renovations were completed. The overall purchase price for the factory and machinery was $400,000. The building renovations were contracted to Malone Construction at $100,000. The payments made, as renovations progressed during 2003, are shown below. The factory was placed in service on January 1, 2004.

	1/1	4/1	10/1	12/31
Starks	$50,000	$100,000	$100,000	$150,000
Malone		30,000	30,000	40,000

On January 1, 2003, Selig secured a $500,000 line-of-credit with a 12% interest rate to finance the purchase cost of the factory and machinery, and the renovation costs. Selig drew down on the line-of-credit to meet the payment schedule shown above; this was Selig's only outstanding loan during 2003.

Rob Stewart, Selig's controller, will capitalize the maximum allowable interest costs for this project. Selig's policy regarding purchases of this nature is to use the appraisal value of the land for book purposes and prorate the balance of the purchase price over the remaining items. The building had originally cost Starks $300,000 and had a net book value of $50,000. The machinery originally cost $125,000 and had a net book value of $40,000 on the date of sale. The land was recorded on Starks' books at $40,000. An appraisal conducted by independent appraisers at the time of acquisition valued the land at $280,000, the building at $105,000, and the machinery at $45,000.

Linda Safford, chief engineer, estimated that the renovated plant would be used for 15 years, with an estimated salvage value of $30,000. Safford estimated that the productive machinery would have a remaining useful life of 5 years and a salvage value of $3,000. Selig's depreciation policy specifies the 200% declining-balance method for machinery and the 150% declining-balance method for the plant. One-half year's depreciation is taken in the year the plant is placed in service and one-half year is allowed when the property is disposed of or retired. Selig uses a 360-day year for calculating interest costs.

Instructions

(a) Determine the amounts to be recorded on the books of Selig Sporting Goods Inc. as of December 31, 2003, for each of the following properties acquired from Starks Athletic Equipment Company.

   (1) Land.   **(2)** Building.   **(3)** Machinery.

(b) Calculate Selig Sporting Goods Inc.'s 2004 depreciation expense, for book purposes, for each of the properties acquired from Starks Athletic Equipment Company.

(c) Discuss the arguments for and against the capitalization of interest costs.

(CMA adapted)

*P9-12 **(Interest During Construction)** Jerry Landscaping began construction of a new plant on December 1, 2003. On this date the company purchased a parcel of land for $142,000 in cash. In addition, it paid $2,000 in surveying costs and $4,000 for a title insurance policy. An old dwelling on the premises was demolished at a cost of $3,000, with $1,000 being received from the sale of materials.

Architectural plans were also formalized on December 1, 2003, when the architect was paid $30,000. The necessary building permits costing $3,000 were obtained from the city and paid for on December 1 as well. The excavation work began during the first week in December with payments made to the contractor as follows.

Date of Payment	Amount of Payment
March 1	$240,000
May 1	360,000
July 1	60,000

The building was completed on July 1, 2004.

To finance construction of this plant, Jerry borrowed $600,000 from the bank on December 1, 2003. Jerry had no other borrowings. The $600,000 was a 10-year loan bearing interest at 8%.

Instructions

Compute the balance in each of the following accounts at December 31, 2003, and December 31, 2004.

(a) Land.

(b) Buildings.

(c) Interest Expense.

*P9-13   (Capitalization of Interest)   Wordcrafters Inc. is a book distributor that had been operating in its original facility since 1978. The increase in certification programs and continuing education requirements in several professions has contributed to an annual growth rate of 15% for Wordcrafters since 1998. Wordcrafters' original facility became obsolete by early 2003 because of the increased sales volume and the fact that Wordcrafters now carries tapes and disks in addition to books.

On June 1, 2003, Wordcrafters contracted with Favre Construction to have a new building constructed for $5,000,000 on land owned by Wordcrafters. The payments made by Wordcrafters to Favre Construction are shown in the schedule below.

Date	Amount
July 30, 2003	$1,200,000
January 30, 2004	1,500,000
May 30, 2004	1,300,000
Total payments	$4,000,000

Construction was completed and the building was ready for occupancy on May 27, 2004. Wordcrafters had no new borrowings directly associated with the new building but had the following debt outstanding at May 31, 2004, the end of its fiscal year.

14 ½%, 5-year note payable of $2,000,000, dated April 1, 2000, with interest payable annually on April 1.
12%, 10-year bond issue of $3,000,000 sold at par on June 30, 1996, with interest payable annually on June 30.

The new building qualifies for interest capitalization. The effect of capitalizing the interest on the new building, compared with the effect of expensing the interest, is material.

Instructions
(a) Compute the weighted average accumulated expenditures on Wordcrafters' new building during the capitalization period.
(b) Compute the avoidable interest on Wordcrafters' new building.
(c) Some interest cost of Wordcrafters Inc. is capitalized for the year ended May 31, 2004.
   (1) Identify the items relating to interest costs that must be disclosed in Wordcrafters' financial statements.
   (2) Compute the amount of each of the items that must be disclosed.

(CMA adapted)

CONCEPTUAL CASES

C9-1   (Options to Purchase Property)   Your client, Salvador Plastics Co., found three suitable sites, each having certain unique advantages, for a new plant facility. In order to thoroughly investigate the advantages and disadvantages of each site, 1-year options were purchased for an amount equal to 6% of the contract price of each site. The costs of the options cannot be applied against the contracts. Before the options expired, one of the sites was purchased at the contract price of $400,000. The option on this site had cost $24,000. The two options not exercised had cost $16,000 each.

Instructions
Present arguments in support of recording the cost of the land at each of the following amounts.

(a) $400,000.
(b) $424,000.
(c) $456,000.

(AICPA adapted)

C9-2   (Acquisition, Improvements, and Sale of Realty)   William Bradford Company purchased land for use as its corporate headquarters. A small factory that was on the land when it was purchased was torn down before construction of the office building began. Furthermore, a substantial amount of rock blasting and removal had to be done to the site before construction of the building foundation began. Because the office building was set back on the land far from the public road, Bradford Company had the contractor construct a paved road that led from the public road to the parking lot of the office building.

Three years after the office building was occupied, Bradford Company added four stories to the office building. The four stories had an estimated useful life of 5 years more than the remaining estimated useful life of the original office building.

Ten years later the land and building were sold at an amount more than their net book value, and Bradford Company had a new office building constructed in another state for use as its new corporate headquarters.

Instructions

(a) Which of the expenditures above should be capitalized? How should each be depreciated or amortized? Discuss the rationale for your answers.

(b) How would the sale of the land and building be accounted for? Include in your answer an explanation of how to determine the net book value at the date of sale. Discuss the rationale for your answer.

C9-3 (Accounting for Self-Constructed Assets) Shanette Medical Labs, Inc. began operations 5 years ago producing stetrics, a new type of instrument it hoped to sell to doctors, dentists, and hospitals. The demand for stetrics far exceeded initial expectations, and the company was unable to produce enough stetrics to meet demand.

The company was manufacturing its product on equipment that it built at the start of its operations. To meet demand, more efficient equipment was needed. The company decided to design and build the equipment, because the equipment currently available on the market was unsuitable for producing stetrics.

In 2003, a section of the plant was devoted to development of the new equipment and a special staff was hired. Within 6 months a machine developed at a cost of $714,000 increased production dramatically and reduced labor costs substantially. Elated by the success of the new machine, the company built three more machines of the same type at a cost of $441,000 each.

Instructions

(a) In general, what costs should be capitalized for self-constructed equipment?

(b) Discuss the propriety of including in the capitalized cost of self-constructed assets:

  (1) The increase in overhead caused by the self-construction of fixed assets.

  (2) A proportionate share of overhead on the same basis as that applied to goods manufactured for sale.

(c) Discuss the proper accounting treatment of the $273,000 ($714,000 − $441,000) by which the cost of the first machine exceeded the cost of the subsequent machines. This additional cost should not be considered research and development costs.

C9-4 (Depreciation Basic Concepts) Prophet Manufacturing Company was organized January 1, 2004. During 2004 it has used in its reports to management the straight-line method of depreciating its plant assets.

On November 8 you are having a conference with Prophet's officers to discuss the depreciation method to be used for income tax and stockholder reporting. Frank Peretti, president of Prophet, has suggested the use of a new method, which he feels is more suitable than the straight-line method for the needs of the company during the period of rapid expansion of production and capacity that he foresees. Following is an example in which the proposed method is applied to a fixed asset with an original cost of $248,000, an estimated useful life of 5 years, and a scrap value of approximately $8,000.

Year	Years of Life Used	Fraction Rate	Depreciation Expense	Accumulated Depreciation at End of Year	Book Value at End of Year
1	1	1/15	$16,000	$ 16,000	$232,000
2	2	2/15	32,000	48,000	200,000
3	3	3/15	48,000	96,000	152,000
4	4	4/15	64,000	160,000	88,000
5	5	5/15	80,000	240,000	8,000

The president favors the new method because he has heard that:

1. It will increase the funds recovered during the years near the end of the assets' useful lives when maintenance and replacement disbursements are high.
2. It will result in increased write-offs in later years and thereby will reduce taxes.

Instructions

(a) What is the purpose of accounting for depreciation?

(b) Is the president's proposal within the scope of generally accepted accounting principles? In making your decision discuss the circumstances, if any, under which use of the method would be reasonable and those, if any, under which it would not be reasonable.

(c) The president wants your advice on the following questions.

   (1) Do depreciation charges recover or create funds? Explain.

   (2) Assume that the Internal Revenue Service accepts the proposed depreciation method in this case. If the proposed method were used for stockholder and tax reporting purposes, how would it affect the availability of funds generated by operations?

C9-5 **(Depreciation Concepts)** As a cost accountant for San Francisco Cannery, you have been approached by Merton Miller, canning room supervisor, about the 2003 costs charged to his department. In particular, he is concerned about the line item "depreciation." Miller is very proud of the excellent condition of his canning room equipment. He has always been vigilant about keeping all equipment serviced and well oiled. He is sure that the huge charge to depreciation is a mistake; it does not at all reflect the cost of minimal wear and tear that the machines have experienced over the last year. He believes that the charge should be considerably lower.

The machines being depreciated are six automatic canning machines. All were put into use on January 1, 2003. Each cost $469,000, having a salvage value of $40,000 and a useful life of 12 years. San Francisco depreciates this and similar assets using double-declining balance. Miller has also pointed out that if you used straight-line depreciation the charge to his department would not be so great.

Instructions

Write a memo to Merton Miller to clear up his misunderstanding of the term "depreciation." Also, calculate year-1 depreciation on all machines using both methods. Explain the theoretical justification for double-declining balance and why, in the long run, the aggregate charge to depreciation will be the same under both methods.

C9-6 **(Nonmonetary Exchanges)** You have two clients who are considering trading machinery with each other. Although the machines are different from each other, you believe that they are "similar" for the purposes of recording a nonmonetary exchange. Your clients would prefer that the machines be considered dissimilar, to allow them to record gains. Here are the facts.

	Client A	Client B
Original cost	$100,000	$150,000
Accumulated depreciation	40,000	80,000
Market value	90,000	120,000
Cash received (paid)	(30,000)	30,000

Instructions

(a) Record the entry on Client B's books assuming the assets are dissimilar.

(b) Record the entry on Client B's books assuming the assets are similar.

(c) Record the trade-in on Client A's books assuming the assets are dissimilar.

(d) Record the trade-in on Client A's books assuming the assets are similar.

(e) Write a memo to the controller of Company A indicating and explaining the dollar impact on current and future statements of treating the assets as "similar" versus "dissimilar."

C9-7 (Assets Acquired through Issuance of Stock) You have been engaged to examine the financial statements of Richard Corporation for the year ending December 31, 2003. Richard was organized in January 2003 by Messrs. Dean and Anderson, original owners of options to acquire oil leases on 5,000 acres of land for $1,200,000. They expected that (1) the oil leases would be acquired by the corporation and (2) subsequently 180,000 shares of the corporation's common stock would be sold to the public at $20 per share. In February 2004, they exchanged their options, $400,000 cash, and $200,000 of other assets for 75,000 shares of common stock of the corporation. The corporation's board of directors appraised the leases at $2,100,000, basing its appraisal on the price of other acreage recently leased in the same area. The options were, therefore, recorded at $900,000 ($2,100,000 − $1,200,000 option price).

The options were exercised by the corporation in March 2004, prior to the sale of common stock to the public in April 2004. Leases on approximately 500 acres of land were abandoned as worthless during the year.

Instructions

(a) Why is the valuation of assets acquired by a corporation in exchange for its own common stock sometimes difficult?

(b) (1) What reasoning might Richard Corporation use to support valuing the leases at $2,100,000, the amount of the appraisal by the board of directors?

   (2) Assuming that the board's appraisal was sincere, what steps might Richard Corporation have taken to strengthen its position to use the $2,100,000 value and to provide additional information if questions were raised about possible overvaluation of the leases?

(c) Discuss the propriety of charging one-tenth of the recorded value of the leases to expense at December 31, 2004, because leases on 500 acres of land were abandoned during the year.

(AICPA adapted)

C9-8 (Costs of Acquisition) The invoice price of a machine is $40,000. Various other costs relating to the acquisition and installation of the machine including transportation, electrical wiring, special base, and so on amount to $7,500. The machine has an estimated life of 10 years, with no residual value at the end of that period.

The owner of the business suggests that the incidental costs of $7,500 be charged to expense immediately for the following reasons.

1. If the machine should be sold, these costs cannot be recovered in the sales price.
2. The inclusion of the $7,500 in the machinery account on the books will not necessarily result in a closer approximation of the market price of this asset over the years, because of the possibility of changing demand and supply levels.
3. Charging the $7,500 to expense immediately will reduce federal income taxes.

Instructions

Discuss each of the points raised by the owner of the business.

(AICPA adapted)

C9-9 (Cost Allocation) Field Company purchased a warehouse in a downtown district where land values are rapidly increasing. Adolph Phillips, controller, and Wilma Smith, financial vice president, are trying to allocate the cost of the purchase between the land and the building. Phillips, noting that depreciation can be taken only on the building, favors placing a very high proportion of the cost on the warehouse itself, thus reducing taxable income and income taxes. Smith, his supervisor, argues that the allocation should recognize the increasing value of the land, regardless of the depreciation potential of the warehouse. Besides, she says, net income is negatively impacted by additional depreciation and will cause the company's stock price to go down.

Instructions

(a) What stakeholder interests are in conflict?
(b) What ethical issues does Phillips face?
(c) How should these costs be allocated?

USING YOUR JUDGMENT

FINANCIAL REPORTING PROBLEM

3M COMPANY

The financial statements of 3M were provided with your book or can be accessed on the Take Action! CD.

Instructions

Refer to 3M's financial statements and the accompanying notes to answer the following questions.

(a) What descriptions are used by 3M in its balance sheet to classify its property, plant, and equipment?
(b) What method or methods of depreciation does 3M use to depreciate its property, plant, and equipment?
(c) Over what estimated useful lives does 3M depreciate its property, plant, and equipment?
(d) What amounts for depreciation expense did 3M charge to its income statement in 2001, 2000, and 1999?
(e) What were the additions to property, plant, and equipment made by 3M in 2001, 2000, and 1999?

COMPARATIVE ANALYSIS CASE

THE COCA-COLA COMPANY VERSUS PEPSICO. INC.

Instructions

Go to the Take Action! CD and use information found there to answer the following questions related to The Coca-Cola Company and PepsiCo, Inc.

(a) What amount is reported in the balance sheets as property, plant, and equipment (net) of Coca-Cola at December 31, 2001, and of PepsiCo at December 30, 2001? What percentage of total assets is invested in property, plant, and equipment by each company?
(b) What depreciation methods are used by Coca-Cola and PepsiCo for property, plant, and equipment? How much depreciation was reported by Coca-Cola and PepsiCo in 2001, 2000, and 1999?
(c) Compute and compare the following ratios for Coca-Cola and PepsiCo for 2001.
   (1) Asset turnover.
   (2) Profit margin on sales.
   (3) Ratio of return on assets.
(d) What amount was spent in 2001 for capital expenditures by Coca-Cola and PepsiCo? What amount of interest was capitalized in 2001?

FINANCIAL STATEMENT ANALYSIS CASE
MCDONALD'S CORPORATION

McDonald's is the largest and best-known global food service retailer, with more than 30,000 restaurants in 121 countries. On any day, McDonald's serves approximately 1 percent of the world's population. Presented on the next page is information related to McDonald's property and equipment.

Instructions

(a) What method of depreciation does McDonald's use?
(b) Does depreciation and amortization expense cause cash flow from operations to increase? Explain.
(c) What does the schedule of cash flow measures indicate?

MCDONALD'S CORPORATION
Summary of Significant Accounting Policies Section

Property and Equipment. Property and equipment are stated at cost, with depreciation and amortization provided on the straight-line method over the following estimated useful lives: buildings—up to 40 years; leasehold improvements—lesser of useful lives of assets or lease terms including option periods; and equipment—3 to 12 years.

[In the notes to the financial statements:]

Property and Equipment

(in millions)	December 31, 2000	1999
Land	$ 3,932.7	$ 3,838.6
Buildings and improvements on owned land	8,250.0	7,953.6
Buildings and improvements on leased land	7,513.3	7,076.6
Equipment, signs, and seating	3,172.2	2,906.6
Other	700.8	675.4
	23,569.0	22,450.8
Accumulated depreciation and amortization	(6,521.4)	(6,126.3)
Net property and equipment	$17,047.6	$16,324.5

Depreciation and amortization expense was (in millions):
2000—$900.9; 1999—$858.1; 1998—$808.0.

[In the management discussion and analysis section, the following schedule is provided:]

Cash Provided by Operations

(in millions)	2000	1999	1998
Cash provided by operations	$2,751	$3,009	$2,766
Free cash flow	806	1,141	887
Cash provided by operations as a percent of capital expenditures	141%	161%	147%
Cash provided by operations as a percent of average total debt	35	42	41

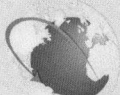

INTERNATIONAL REPORTING CASE

Companies following international accounting standards are permitted to revalue fixed assets above the assets' historical costs. Such revaluations are allowed under various countries' standards and the standards issued by the International Accounting Standards Board (IASB). **Nestlé SA**, headquartered in Switzerland, follows IASB standards. In a recent year, Nestlé disclosed information on revaluations of its tangible fixed assets as shown on the next page. The revaluation reserve measures the amount by which tangible fixed assets are recorded above historical cost and is reported in Nestlé's stockholders' equity.

NESTLÉ SA

Tangible fixed assets

The revaluation reserve included in the carrying value of net tangible fixed assets at net replacement value is as follows.

(in millions of Swiss francs)	Land and Buildings	Machinery and Equipment	Tools, Furniture, and Other Equipment	Vehicles	Total
Net replacement value	9,492	10,727	1,571	378	22,168
Net book value	7,474	8,724	1,659	328	18,185
Revaluation reserve	2,018	2,003	(88)	50	3,983

The following additional data were reported by Nestlé. Amounts for Tootsie Roll in the same year are provided for comparison.

	Nestlé (Swiss francs, in millions)	Tootsie Roll ($, in thousands)
Total revenues	69,998	375,594
Average total assets	52,857	413,924
Net income	4,005	60,682

Instructions

(a) Compute the following ratios for Nestlé and Tootsie Roll.
  - **(1)** Return on assets.
  - **(2)** Profit margin.
  - **(3)** Asset turnover.

  How do these companies compare on these performance measures?

(b) Nestlé reports a revaluation reserve of 3,983 Swiss francs. Assume that 1,550 of this amount arose from an increase in the net replacement value of land and buildings during the year. Prepare the journal entry to record this increase. (*Hint:* Credit the Revaluation Reserve account.)

(c) Under IASB standards, are Nestlé's assets and equity overstated? If so, why? When comparing Nestlé to U.S. companies, like Tootsie Roll, what adjustments would you need to make in order to have valid comparisons of ratios such as those computed in (a) above?

www.wiley.com/college/kieso

Remember to check the **Take Action! CD**
and the book's **companion Web site**
to find additional resources for this chapter.

INTANGIBLE ASSETS

TRYING TO GRASP THE INTANGIBLE

In 1494, a mathematically minded Venetian monk named Luca Pacioli published his *Summa de Arithmetica, Geometrica*, the first accounting textbook. It illustrated double-entry accounting, a system that makes the modern corporation manageable, even possible. Today, half a millennium later, Pacioli's process, still pretty much intact, is being challenged like never before.

Pacioli's accounting system lets businesses keep track of changes in their assets. But this system deals primarily with *tangible assets* such as cash, inventory, investments, receivables, and property, plant, and equipment. What go unrecorded are *intangible assets* such as quality of management, customer loyalty, information infrastructure, trade secrets, patents, goodwill, research, and, considered by some the ultimate intangible, *knowledge*—a company's intellectual capital. As former FASB chairman Edmund Jenkins attests, "The components of cost in a product today are largely R & D, intellectual assets, and services. The old accounting system, which tells us the cost of material and labor, isn't applicable." Argues Professor James Quinn of Dartmouth College, "Even in manufacturing, perhaps three-fourths of the value added derives from knowledge."[1]

This refrain is echoed by the managing editor of *Fortune* magazine, Walter Kiechel, who says, "To be sure, there are still industries in which the factory confers a competitive advantage. But this is changing fast, as more and more companies realize that their edge derives less from their machines, bricks, and mortar than from what we used to think of as the intangibles, like the brainpower resident in the corporation."[2]

In this emerging economy of knowledge, even some banks have concluded that "soft" assets (like computer programming know-how and information infrastructure) can be a better credit risk than "hard" assets (like buildings). But how should the "soft assets" be valued? Accountants get little solace from former FASB chairman Donald Kirk, who acknowledges, "There are arguments that balance sheets ignore certain intangibles, but the reporting issues of trying to recognize them are, in my mind, insurmountable."[3] It appears that the assets that really count are the ones accountants can't count—yet.

After studying this chapter, you should be able to:

1. Describe the characteristics of intangible assets.
2. Identify the costs included in the initial valuation of intangible assets.
3. Explain the procedure for amortizing intangible assets.
4. Identify the categories of intangible assets.
5. Explain the conceptual issues related to goodwill.
6. Describe the accounting procedures for recording goodwill.
7. Explain the accounting issues related to impairments.
8. Identify the conceptual issues related to research and development costs.
9. Describe the accounting procedures for research and development costs and for other similar costs.
10. Indicate the presentation of intangible assets and related items.

[1]Thomas Stewart, "Your Company's Most Valuable Asset: Intellectual Capital," *Fortune* (October 3, 1994), p. 68.

[2]"Searching for Nonfiction in Financial Statements," *Fortune* (December 23, 1996), p. 38.

[3]Ibid.

PREVIEW OF CHAPTER 10

As the opening story indicates, the accounting and reporting of intangibles is taking on increasing importance in this information age. The purpose of this chapter is to explain the basic conceptual and reporting issues related to intangible assets. The content and organization of the chapter are as follows:

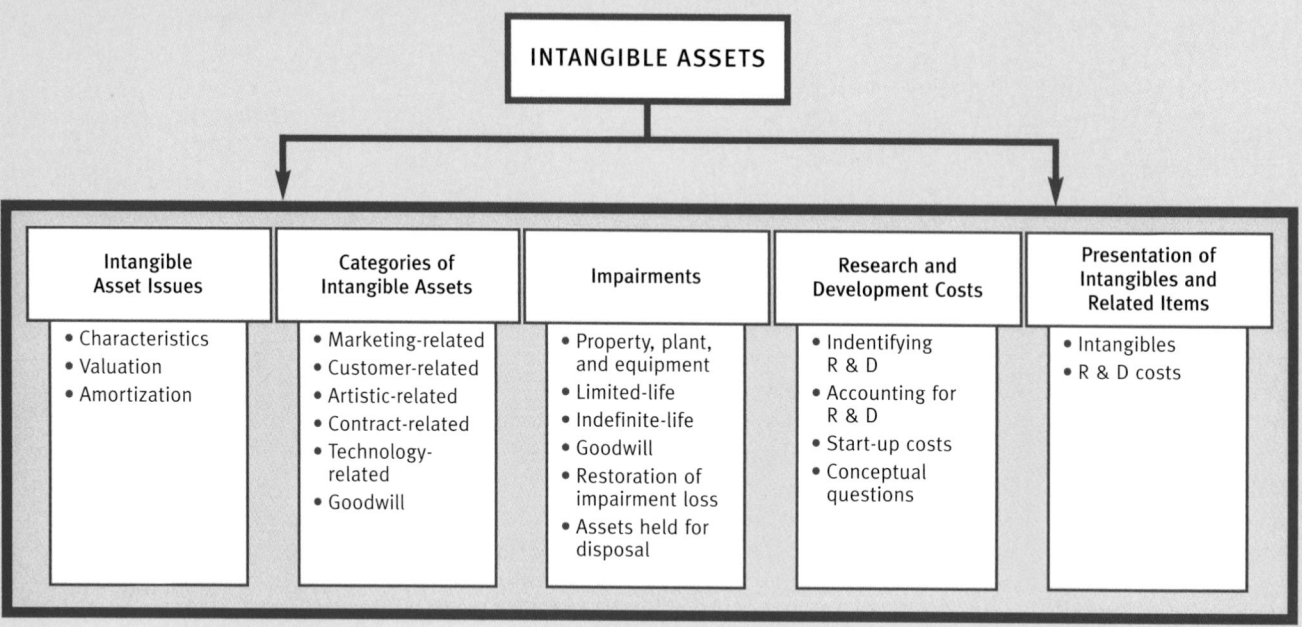

INTANGIBLE ASSET ISSUES

Characteristics

OBJECTIVE 1
Describe the characteristics of intangible assets.

Gap Inc.'s most important asset is not store fixtures—brand image is. The major asset of **Coca-Cola** is not its plant facilities—its secret formula for making Coke is. **America Online**'s most important asset is not its Internet connection equipment—its subscriber base is. As these examples show, we have an economy dominated today by information and service providers, and their major assets are often intangible in nature. Accounting for these intangibles is difficult, and as a result many intangibles are presently not reported on a company's balance sheet. **Intangible assets** have two main characteristics.[4]

1. **They lack physical existence.** Unlike tangible assets such as property, plant, and equipment, intangible assets derive their value from the rights and privileges granted to the company using them.

2. **They are not financial instruments.** Assets such as bank deposits, accounts receivable, and long-term investments in bonds and stocks lack physical substance, but are not classified as intangible assets. These assets are financial instruments and derive their value from the right (claim) to receive cash or cash equivalents in the future.

In most cases, intangible assets provide services over a period of years. As a result, they are normally classified as long-term assets. The most common types of in-

---

[4]"Goodwill and Other Intangible Assets," *Statement of Financial Accounting Standards No. 142* (Norwalk, Conn.: FASB, 2001).

tangibles are patents, copyrights, franchises or licenses, trademarks or trade names, and goodwill.

Valuation

Purchased Intangibles
Intangibles purchased from another party are **recorded at cost**. Cost includes all costs of acquisition and expenditures necessary to make the intangible asset ready for its intended use—for example, purchase price, legal fees, and other incidental expenses.

If intangibles are acquired for stock or in exchange for other assets, **the cost of the intangible is the fair value of the consideration given or the fair value of the intangible received, whichever is more clearly evident**. When several intangibles, or a combination of intangibles and tangibles, are bought in a "basket purchase," the cost should be allocated on the basis of fair values. Essentially the accounting treatment for purchased intangibles closely parallels that followed for purchased tangible assets.

OBJECTIVE 2
Identify the costs included in the initial valuation of intangible assets.

Internally-Created Intangibles
Costs incurred internally to create intangibles are generally expensed as incurred. Thus, even though a company may incur substantial research and development costs to create an intangible, these costs are expensed. Various reasons are given for this approach. Some argue that the costs incurred internally to create intangibles bear no relationship to their real value; therefore, expensing these costs is appropriate. Others note that with a purchased intangible, a reliable number for the cost of the intangible can be determined; with internally developed intangibles, it is difficult to associate costs with specific intangible assets. And others argue that due to the underlying subjectivity related to intangibles, a conservative approach should be followed—that is, expense as incurred. As a result, the **only internal costs capitalized are direct costs** incurred in obtaining the intangible, such as legal costs.

UNDERLYING CONCEPTS

The basic attributes of intangibles, their uncertainty as to future benefits, and their uniqueness, have discouraged valuation in excess of cost.

Amortization of Intangibles

Intangibles have either a limited (finite) useful life or an indefinite useful life. An intangible asset with a **limited life is amortized**; an intangible asset with an **indefinite life is not amortized**.

OBJECTIVE 3
Explain the procedure for amortizing intangible assets.

Limited-Life Intangibles
The expiration of intangible assets is called **amortization**. Limited-life intangibles should be amortized by systematic charges to expense over their useful life. The useful life should reflect the periods over which these assets will contribute to cash flows. Factors considered in determining useful life are:

1. The expected use of the asset by the entity.
2. The expected useful life of another asset or a group of assets to which the useful life of the intangible asset may relate (such as mineral rights to depleting assets).
3. Any legal, regulatory, or contractual provisions that may limit the useful life.
4. Any legal, regulatory, or contractual provisions that enable renewal or extension of the asset's legal or contractual life without substantial cost. This factor assumes that there is evidence to support renewal or extension and that renewal or extension can be accomplished without material modifications of the existing terms and conditions.
5. The effects of obsolescence, demand, competition, and other economic factors. Examples include the stability of the industry, known technological advances,

legislative action that results in an uncertain or changing regulatory environment, and expected changes in distribution channels.

⑥ The level of maintenance expenditure required to obtain the expected future cash flows from the asset. For example, a material level of required maintenance in relation to the carrying amount of the asset may suggest a very limited useful life.[5]

The amount of amortization expense for a limited-life intangible asset should reflect the pattern in which the asset is consumed or used up, if that pattern can be reliably determined. For example, assume that Second Wave, Inc. has purchased a license to provide a limited quantity of a gene product, called Mega. The cost of the license should be amortized following the pattern of use of Mega. If the pattern of production or consumption cannot be determined, the straight-line method of amortization should be used. (For homework problems, assume the use of the straight-line method unless stated otherwise.)

When intangible assets are amortized the charges should be shown as expenses, and the credits should be made either to the appropriate asset accounts or to separate accumulated amortization accounts.

The amount of an intangible asset to be amortized should be its cost less residual value. The residual value is assumed to be zero unless at the end of its useful life the intangible asset has value to another entity. For example, if U2D Co. has a commitment from Hardy Co. to purchase its intangible asset at the end of its useful life, U2D Co. should reduce the cost of its intangible asset by the residual value. Similarly, if market values for residual values can be reliably determined, market values should be considered.

What happens if the life of a limited-life intangible asset is changed? In that case the remaining carrying amount should be amortized over the revised remaining useful life.

Indefinite-Life Intangibles

If no legal, regulatory, contractual, competitive, or other factors limit the useful life of an intangible asset, the useful life is considered indefinite. **Indefinite** means that there is no foreseeable limit on the period of time over which the intangible asset is expected to provide cash flows. An intangible asset with an indefinite life is not amortized.

To illustrate, assume that Double Clik, Inc. acquired a trademark that is used to distinguish a leading consumer product. The trademark is renewable every 10 years at minimal cost. All evidence indicates that this trademark product will generate cash flows for an indefinite period of time. In this case, the trademark has an indefinite life because it is expected to contribute to cash flows indefinitely; therefore, no amortization is recorded.

In summary, the accounting treatment for intangible assets is shown in Illustration 10-1.

Illustration 10-1
Accounting Treatment for
Intangibles

Type of Intangible	MANNER ACQUIRED		Amortization
	Purchased	Internally Created	
Limited-life intangibles	Capitalize	Expense*	Over useful life
Indefinite-life intangibles	Capitalize	Expense*	Do not amortize

*Except for direct costs, such as legal costs.

[5]Ibid, par. 11.

CATEGORIES OF INTANGIBLE ASSETS

As indicated, the accounting for intangible assets depends on whether the intangible has a limited or an indefinite life. There are many different types of intangibles, and they are often classified into the following six major categories.[6]

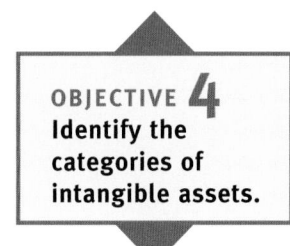

OBJECTIVE **4**
Identify the categories of intangible assets.

◇**1**◇ Marketing-related intangible assets.

◇**2**◇ Customer-related intangible assets.

◇**3**◇ Artistic-related intangible assets.

◇**4**◇ Contract-related intangible assets.

◇**5**◇ Technology-related intangible assets.

◇**6**◇ Goodwill.

Marketing-Related Intangible Assets

Marketing-related intangible assets are those assets primarily used in the marketing or promotion of products or services. Examples are trademarks or trade names, newspaper mastheads, Internet domain names, and noncompetition agreements.

A very common form of a marketing-related intangible asset is a trademark or trade name. A **trademark** or **trade name** is a word, phrase, or symbol that distinguishes or identifies a particular enterprise or product. Under common law, the right to use a trademark or trade name, whether it is registered or not, rests exclusively with the original user as long as the original user continues to use it. Registration with the U.S. Patent and Trademark Office provides legal protection for an **indefinite number of renewals for periods of 10 years each**. Therefore a business that uses an established trademark or trade name may properly consider it to have an indefinite life. Trade names like Kleenex, Pepsi-Cola, Oldsmobile, Excedrin, Wheaties, and Sunkist create immediate product identification in our minds, thereby enhancing marketability.

If a trademark or trade name is acquired, its capitalizable cost is the purchase price. If a trademark or trade name is developed by the enterprise itself, the capitalizable cost includes attorney fees, registration fees, design costs, consulting fees, successful legal defense costs, and other expenditures directly related to securing it (excluding research and development costs). When the total cost of a trademark or trade name is insignificant, it can be expensed rather than capitalized. In most cases, the life of a trademark or trade name is indefinite, and therefore its cost is not amortized.

The value of a marketing-related intangible can be substantial. Consider Internet domain names as an example. The name **Drugs.com** recently sold for $800,000, and the bidding for the name **Loans.com** approached $500,000.

Company names themselves identify qualities and characteristics that the companies have worked hard and spent much to develop. In a recent year an estimated 1,230 companies took on new names in an attempt to forge new identities and paid over $250 million to corporate-identity consultants. Among these were **Primerica** (formerly American Can), **Navistar** (formerly International Harvester), **Nissan** (formerly Datsun), and **USX** (U.S. Steel).[7]

---

[6]This classification framework has been adapted from "Business Combinations," *Statement of Financial Accounting Standards No. 141* (Norwalk, Conn.: FASB, 2001).

[7]To illustrate how various intangibles might arise from a given product, consider what the creators of the highly successful game, Trivial Pursuit, did to protect their creation. First, they copyrighted the 6,000 questions that are at the heart of the game. Then they shielded the Trivial Pursuit name by applying for a registered trademark. As a third mode of protection, the creators obtained a design patent on the playing board's design because it represents a unique graphic creation.

Customer-Related Intangible Assets

Customer-related intangible assets occur as a result of interactions with outside parties. Examples are customer lists, order or production backlogs, and both contractual and noncontractual customer relationships.

To illustrate, assume that We-Market Inc. acquired the customer list of a large newspaper for $6,000,000 on January 1, 2003. The customer list is a database that includes name, contact information, order history, and demographic information for a list of customers. We-Market expects to benefit from the information on the acquired list for 3 years, and it believes that these benefits will be spread evenly over the 3 years. In this case, the customer list is a limited-life intangible that should be amortized on a straight-line basis over the 3-year period.

The entry to record the purchase of the customer list and the amortization of the customer list at the end of each year is as follows.

January 1, 2003

Customer List	6,000,000	
Cash		6,000,000
(To record purchase of customer list)		

December 31, 2003, 2004, 2005

Customer List Amortization Expense	2,000,000	
Customer List (or Accumulated Customer		
List Amortization)		2,000,000
(To record amortization expense)		

In the preceding example it was assumed that the customer list had no residual value. But what if We-Market determines that it can sell the list for $60,000 to another company at the end of 3 years? In that case this residual value should be subtracted from the cost in order to determine the proper amortization expense for each year. Amortization expense would therefore be $1,980,000, as shown below.

<table>
<tr><td>Illustration 10-2
Calculation of
Amortization Expense
with Residual Value</td><td>

Cost	$6,000,000
Residual value	60,000
Amortization base	$5,940,000

Amortization expense per period: $1,980,000 ($5,940,000 ÷ 3)

</td></tr>
</table>

The residual value should be assumed to be zero unless the asset's useful life is less than the economic life and reliable evidence is available concerning the residual value.[8]

Artistic-Related Intangible Assets

Artistic-related intangible assets involve ownership rights to plays, literary works, musical works, pictures, photographs, and video and audiovisual material. These ownership rights are protected by copyrights.

A **copyright** is a federally granted right that all authors, painters, musicians, sculptors, and other artists have in their creations and expressions. A copyright is granted

---

[8]"Goodwill and Other Intangible Assets," *Statement of Financial Accounting Standards No. 142* (Norwalk, Conn.: FASB, 2001), par. B55.

for the **life of the creator plus 50 years**. It gives the owner, or heirs, the exclusive right to reproduce and sell an artistic or published work. Copyrights are not renewable. The costs of acquiring and defending a copyright may be capitalized, but the research and development costs involved must be expensed as incurred.

Generally, the useful life of the copyright is less than its legal life (life in being plus 50 years). The costs of the copyright should be allocated to the years in which the benefits are expected to be received. The difficulty of determining the number of years over which benefits will be received normally encourages the company to write these costs off over a fairly short period of time.

Copyrights can be valuable. **Really Useful Group** is a company that consists of copyrights on the musicals of Andrew Lloyd Webber—*Cats, Phantom of the Opera, Jesus Christ-Superstar,* and others. It has little in the way of hard assets, yet it has been valued at $300 million. The **Walt Disney Company** is facing loss of its copyright on Mickey Mouse on January 1, 2004, which may affect sales of billions of dollars of Mickey-related goods and services (including theme parks). Although Disney may be able to use its trademarks on Mickey (which may be renewed indefinitely) to protect itself, many big entertainment companies, Disney included, are quietly pushing Congress for a copyright extension.

INTERNATIONAL INSIGHT

Copyrights in Europe last for the author's life plus 70 years. Those in the United States who want to see the copyright period extended are arguing for the extension, in part, on the basis of the fairness a global standard would provide.

Contract-Related Intangible Assets

Contract-related intangible assets represent the value of rights that arise from contractual arrangements. Examples are franchise and licensing agreements, construction permits, broadcast rights, and service or supply contracts. A very common form of contract-based intangible asset is a franchise.

A **franchise** is a contractual arrangement under which the franchisor grants the franchisee the right to sell certain products or services, to use certain trademarks or trade names, or to perform certain functions, usually within a designated geographical area. For example, when you drive down the street in an automobile purchased from a **Toyota** dealer, fill your tank at the corner **ChevronTexaco** station, eat lunch at **McDonald's**, cool off with one of **Baskin-Robbins'** 31 flavors, work at a **Coca-Cola** bottling plant, live in a home purchased through a **Century 21** real estate broker, or vacation at a **Holiday Inn** resort, you are dealing with franchises.

The franchisor, having developed a unique concept or product, protects its concept or product through a patent, copyright, or trademark or trade name. The franchisee acquires the right to exploit the franchisor's idea or product by signing a franchise agreement.

Another type of franchise is the arrangement commonly entered into by a municipality (or other governmental body) and a business enterprise that uses public property. In such cases, a privately owned enterprise is permitted to use public property in performing its services. Examples are the use of public waterways for a ferry service, the use of public land for telephone or electric lines, the use of phone lines for cable TV, the use of city streets for a bus line, or the use of the airwaves for radio or TV broadcasting. Such operating rights, obtained through agreements with governmental units or agencies, are frequently referred to as **licenses** or **permits**.

Franchises and licenses may be for a definite period of time, for an indefinite period of time, or perpetual. The enterprise securing the franchise or license carries an intangible asset account entitled Franchise or License on its books only when there are costs (such as a lump sum payment in advance or legal fees and other expenditures) that are identified with the acquisition of the operating right. **The cost of a franchise (or license) with a limited life should be amortized as operating expense over the life of the franchise.** A franchise with an indefinite life, or a perpetual franchise, should be carried at cost and not be amortized.

Annual payments made under a franchise agreement should be entered as operating expenses in the period in which they are incurred. They do not represent an asset to the concern since they do not relate to future rights to use public property.

Technology-Related Intangible Assets

Technology-related intangible assets relate to innovations or technological advances. Examples are patented technology and trade secrets. To illustrate, patents are granted by the U.S. Patent and Trademark Office. A **patent** gives the holder exclusive right to use, manufacture, and sell a product or process **for a period of 20 years** without interference or infringement by others. With this exclusive right, fortunes can be made. For example, companies such as **Merck**, **Polaroid**, and **Xerox** were founded on patents.[9] The two principal kinds of patents are **product patents**, which cover actual physical products, and **process patents**, which govern the process by which products are made.

If a patent is purchased from an inventor (or other owner), the purchase price represents its cost. Other costs incurred in connection with securing a patent, as well as attorneys' fees and other unrecovered costs of a successful legal suit to protect the patent, can be capitalized as part of the patent cost. Research and development costs related to the **development** of the product, process, or idea that is subsequently patented **must be expensed as incurred**, however. See pages 492 and 494 for a more complete presentation of accounting for research and development costs.

The cost of a patent should be amortized over its legal life or its useful life (the period benefits are received), whichever is **shorter**. If a patent is owned from the date it is granted, and it is expected to be useful during its entire legal life, it should be amortized over 20 years. If it appears that the patent will be useful for a shorter period of time, say, for 5 years, its cost should be amortized to expense over 5 years. Changing demand, new inventions superseding old ones, inadequacy, and other factors often limit the useful life of a patent to less than the legal life. For example, the useful life of patents in the pharmaceutical and drug industry is frequently less than the legal life because of the testing and approval period that follows their issuance. A typical drug patent has 5 to 11 years knocked off its 20-year legal life because 1 to 4 years must be spent on tests on animals, 4 to 6 years on human tests, and 2 to 3 years for the Food and Drug Administration to review the tests—all after the patent is issued but before the product goes on a pharmacist's shelves.

WHAT DO THE NUMBERS MEAN?

PATENT BATTLES

From bioengineering to software design to the Internet, battles over patents are heating up as global competition intensifies. For example, Priceline.com filed suit against Microsoft for launching Hotel Price Matcher, a service that operates pretty much like the name-your-own-price-system pioneered by Priceline. And Amazon.com filed a complaint against Barnesandnoble.com, its bitter rival in the Web-retailing wars. The suit alleges that Barnesandnoble.com is infringing on Amazon.com's patent for one-click shopping and asks the court to stop Barnesandnoble.com from using its own quick-checkout system, called ExpressLane.

Source: Adapted from "Battle over Patents Threatens to Damp Web's Innovative Spirit," *Wall Street Journal* (November 8, 1999).

Legal fees and other costs incurred in successfully defending a patent suit are debited to Patents, an asset account, because such a suit establishes the legal rights of the holder of the patent. Such costs should be amortized along with acquisition cost over the remaining useful life of the patent.

[9]Consider the opposite result: Sir Alexander Fleming, who discovered penicillin, decided not to use a patent to protect his discovery. He hoped that companies would produce it more quickly to help save sufferers. Companies, however, refused to develop it because they did not have the patent shield and, therefore, were afraid to make the investment.

Amortization expense should reflect the pattern in which the patent is used up, if that pattern can be reliably determined. Amortization of patents may be credited directly to the Patents account, or it may be credited to an Accumulated Patent Amortization account. To illustrate, assume that Harcott Co. incurs $180,000 in legal costs on January 1, 2003, to successfully defend a patent. The patent has a useful life of 20 years, and is amortized on a straight-line basis. The entries to record the legal fees and the amortization at the end of each year are as follows.

January 1, 2003

Patents	180,000	
Cash		180,000
(To record legal fees related to patent)		

December 31, 2003

Patent Amortization Expense	9,000	
Patents (or Accumulated Patent Amortization)		9,000
(To record amortization of patent)		

Amortization on a units-of-production basis would be computed in a manner similar to that described for depreciation on property, plant, and equipment in Chapter 9, page 421.

THE VALUE OF A SECRET FORMULA

WHAT DO THE NUMBERS MEAN?

While the nuclear secrets contained within the Los Alamos nuclear lab seem easier to check out than a library book, **Coca-Cola** has managed to keep the recipe for the world's best-selling soft drink under wraps for more than 100 years. How has it done so?

Coca-Cola offers almost no information about its lifeblood. The only written copy of the formula resides in a SunTrust Bank vault in Atlanta. This handwritten sheet isn't available to anyone except by vote of the Coca-Cola board of directors.

Why can't science offer some clues? Coke contains 17 to 18 ingredients. That includes the usual caramel color and corn syrup, as well as a blend of oils known as 7X (rumored to be a mix of orange, lemon, cinnamon, and others). Distilling natural products like these is complicated, since they're made of thousands of compounds. One ingredient you won't find is cocaine. Although the original formula contained trace amounts, today's Coke doesn't. When was it removed? That is a secret too.

Some experts indicate that the power of this formula and related brand image account for almost 95 percent of Coke's $150 billion stock value.

Source: Adapted from Reed Tucker, "How Has Coke's Formula Stayed a Secret?" *Fortune* (July 24, 2000), p. 42.

Goodwill

OBJECTIVE 5
Explain the conceptual issues related to goodwill.

Although companies are permitted to capitalize certain costs to develop specifically identifiable assets such as patents and copyrights, the amounts capitalized are generally not significant. But material amounts of intangible assets are recorded when companies purchase intangible assets, particularly in situations involving the purchase of another business (often referred to as a business combination).

In a business combination, the cost (purchase price) is assigned where possible to the identifiable tangible and intangible net assets, and the remainder is recorded in an intangible asset account called **Goodwill**. Goodwill is often referred to as the most intangible of intangible assets, because it can only be identified with the business as a whole. The only way it can be sold is to sell the business.

The problem of determining the proper cost to allocate to intangible assets in a business combination is complex because of the many different types of intangibles that might be considered. Many of these types of intangibles have been discussed earlier. It is extremely difficult not only to identify certain types of intangibles but also to assign a value to them in a business combination. As a result, the approach followed is to record identifiable intangible assets that can be reliably measured. Other intangible assets that are difficult to identify or measure are recorded as goodwill.[10]

Recording Goodwill

Internally Created Goodwill. **Goodwill generated internally should not be capitalized in the accounts.** The reason: Measuring the components of goodwill is simply too complex, and associating any costs with future benefits too difficult. The future benefits of goodwill may have no relationship to the costs incurred in the development of that goodwill. To add to the mystery, goodwill may even exist in the absence of specific costs to develop it. In addition, because no objective transaction with outside parties has taken place, a great deal of subjectivity—even misrepresentation—might be involved.

Purchased Goodwill. Goodwill is recorded only when an entire business is purchased, because goodwill is a "going concern" valuation and cannot be separated from the business as a whole. To record goodwill, the fair market value of the net tangible and identifiable intangible assets are compared with the purchase price of the acquired business. The difference is considered goodwill. This is why goodwill is sometimes referred to as a "plug," or "gap filler," or "**master valuation**" account. **Goodwill is the residual—the excess of cost over fair value of the identifiable net assets acquired.**

To illustrate, Multi-Diversified, Inc. decides that it needs a parts division to supplement its existing tractor distributorship. The president of Multi-Diversified is interested in buying a small concern in Chicago (Tractorling Company) that has an established reputation and is seeking a merger candidate. The balance sheet of Tractorling Company is presented in Illustration 10-3.

OBJECTIVE 6
Describe the accounting procedures for recording goodwill.

UNDERLYING CONCEPTS

Capitalizing goodwill only when it is purchased in an arm's-length transaction and not capitalizing any goodwill generated internally is another example of reliability winning out over relevance.

Illustration 10-3
Tractorling Balance Sheet

TRACTORLING CO. BALANCE SHEET AS OF DECEMBER 31, 2002			
Assets		**Equities**	
Cash	$ 25,000	Current liabilities	$ 55,000
Receivables	35,000	Capital stock	100,000
Inventories	42,000	Retained earnings	100,000
Property, plant, and equipment, net	153,000		
Total assets	$255,000	Total equities	$255,000

After considerable negotiation, Tractorling Company decides to accept Multi-Diversified's offer of $400,000. What, then, is the value of the goodwill, if any?

The answer is not obvious. The fair market values of Tractorling's identifiable assets are not disclosed in its historical cost-based balance sheet. Suppose, though, that as

[10]The new business combination standard provides detailed guidance regarding the recognition of identifiable intangible assets in a business combination. Using this guidance, the expectation is that more identifiable intangible assets will be recognized in the financial statements as a result of business combinations. If this situation occurs, less goodwill will be recognized.

the negotiations progress, Multi-Diversified conducts an investigation of the underlying assets of Tractorling to determine the fair market value of the assets. Such an investigation may be accomplished either through a purchase audit undertaken by Multi-Diversified's auditors in order to estimate the values of the seller's assets, or by an independent appraisal from some other source. The following valuations are determined.

Illustration 10-4
Fair Market Value of
Tractorling's Net Assets

Fair Market Values	
Cash	$ 25,000
Receivables	35,000
Inventories	122,000
Property, plant, and equipment, net	205,000
Patents	18,000
Liabilities	(55,000)
Fair market value of net assets	$350,000

Normally, differences between current fair market value and book value are more common among long-term assets, although significant differences can also develop in the current assets category. Cash obviously poses no problems as to value. And receivables normally are fairly close to current valuation, although at times certain adjustments need to be made because of inadequate bad debt provisions. Liabilities usually are stated at book value, although if interest rates have changed since the liabilities were incurred, a different valuation (such as present value) might be appropriate. Careful analysis must be made to determine that no unrecorded liabilities are present.

The $80,000 difference in Tractorling's inventories ($122,000 − $42,000) could result from a number of factors, the most likely being that the company uses LIFO. Recall that during periods of inflation, LIFO better matches expenses against revenues, but in doing so creates a balance sheet distortion. Ending inventory is comprised of older layers costed at lower valuations.

In many cases, the values of long-term assets such as property, plant, and equipment, and intangibles may have increased substantially over the years. This difference could be due to inaccurate estimates of useful lives, continual expensing of small expenditures (say, less than $300), inaccurate estimates of salvage values, and the discovery of some unrecorded assets (as in Tractorling's case where Patents are discovered to have a fair value of $18,000). Or, replacement costs may have substantially increased.

Since the fair market value of net assets is now determined to be $350,000, why would Multi-Diversified pay $400,000? Undoubtedly, the seller pointed to an established reputation, good credit rating, top management team, well-trained employees, and so on, as factors that make the value of the business greater than $350,000. At the same time, Multi-Diversified placed a premium on the future earning power of these attributes as well as the basic asset structure of the enterprise today. At this point in the negotiations, price can be a function of many factors; the most important is probably sheer skill at the bargaining table.

The difference between the purchase price of $400,000 and the fair market value of $350,000 is labeled goodwill. Goodwill is viewed as one or a group of unidentifiable values (intangible assets) the cost of which "is measured by the difference between the cost of the group of assets or enterprise acquired and the sum of the assigned costs of individual tangible and identifiable intangible assets acquired less liabilities assumed."[11] This procedure for valuation is referred to as a **master valuation approach**

---

[11]The FASB expressed concern about measuring goodwill as a residual, but noted that there is no real measurement alternative since goodwill is not separable from the enterprise as a whole. "Business Combinations," *Statement of Financial Accounting Standards No. 141* (Norwalk, Conn.: FASB, 2001), par. B145.

because goodwill is assumed to cover all the values that cannot be specifically identified with any identifiable tangible or intangible asset. This approach is shown in Illustration 10-5.

Illustration 10-5

Determination of Goodwill—Master Valuation Approach

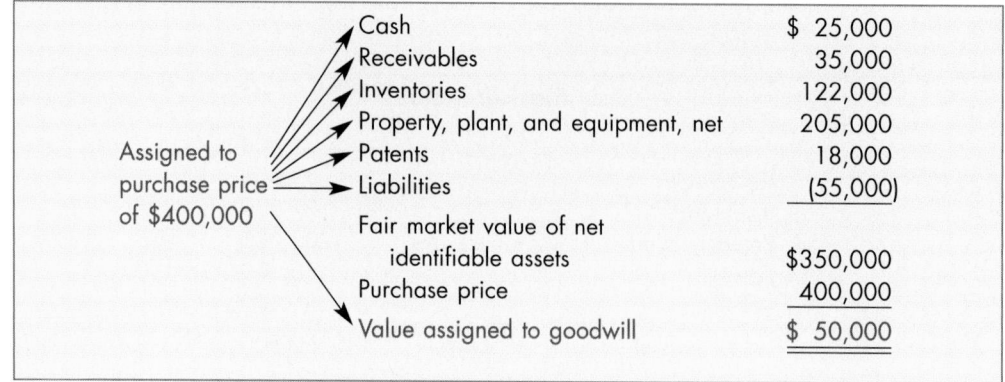

Cash	$ 25,000	
Receivables	35,000	
Inventories	122,000	
Property, plant, and equipment, net	205,000	
Patents	18,000	
Liabilities	(55,000)	
Fair market value of net identifiable assets	$350,000	
Purchase price	400,000	
Value assigned to goodwill	$ 50,000	

Assigned to purchase price of $400,000

Expanded Discussion— Valuing Goodwill

The entry to record this transaction would be as follows.

Cash	25,000	
Receivables	35,000	
Inventories	122,000	
Property, Plant, and Equipment	205,000	
Patents	18,000	
Goodwill	50,000	
Liabilities		55,000
Cash		400,000

Goodwill is often identified on the balance sheet as the **excess of cost over the fair value** of the net assets acquired.

Goodwill Write-off

Goodwill acquired in a business combination **is considered to have an indefinite life and therefore should not be amortized**. The Board's position is that investors find the amortization charge of little use in evaluating financial performance. In addition, although goodwill may decrease over time, predicting the actual life of goodwill and an appropriate pattern of amortization is extremely difficult.

On the other hand, knowing the amount invested in goodwill is important to the investment community. Therefore, **income statements are not charged unless goodwill has been impaired**. This approach will have a significant impact on the income statements of some companies because goodwill often is the largest intangible asset on a company's balance sheet.

Prior to the new FASB standard, companies were required to amortize this intangible. For example, it was estimated that as a result of the new rules, earnings per share in 2001 would increase 21 percent for **International Paper**, 16 percent for **Johnson Controls**, and 30 percent for **Pepsi Bottling Group**.

Some believe that goodwill's value eventually disappears and therefore that goodwill should be charged to expense over the periods affected. Amortizing goodwill, they argue, provides a better matching of expense with revenues. Others note that the accounting treatment for purchased goodwill and goodwill created internally should be consistent. Goodwill created internally is immediately expensed and does not appear as an asset; the same treatment, they argue, should be accorded purchased goodwill. Even though these arguments may have some merit, the FASB decided that nonamortization of goodwill combined with an adequate impairment test provides the most useful financial information to the investment community.

Companies will use 2002 to take massive write-offs that will cut earnings by 15 percent to 20 percent, says Goldman Sachs Group Inc. Chief Investment Strategist Abby Joseph Cohen. "Simply stated, many companies are writing off not only the kitchen sink but the bathtub as well," Ms. Cohen wrote. For instance, **AOL Time Warner Inc.** plans a goodwill write-down in the first quarter that—by itself—will reduce S&P 500 earnings by $2 to $4 on an after-tax basis, Ms. Cohen said.

WHAT DO THE NUMBERS MEAN?

Ms. Cohen attributes companies' massive write-downs to "the air," or implied or real impacts from the September 11, 2001, terrorist attacks, the official announcement that the country is in a recession, and new rules for the write-down of goodwill. She also says that when all is said and done, 2002 will have seen write-offs that cut into S&P earnings by 35 percent to 40 percent.

Still, Ms. Cohen isn't backing off estimates of 7 percent to 8 percent long-term earnings growth, saying that the hits will be tough to swallow in the quarter during which they are taken, but that they won't be of lasting impact psychologically or operationally. "The quarter in which the write-offs are recorded typically bears the statistical brunt, but may not be reflective of performance in future quarters," according to Ms. Cohen.

Negative Goodwill—Badwill

Negative goodwill arises when the fair value of the assets acquired is higher than the purchase price of the assets. This situation is a result of market imperfection; the seller would have been better off to sell the assets individually than in total. However, situations do occur in which the purchase price is less than the value of the net identifiable assets and so a credit develops. This credit is referred to as **negative goodwill** or, alternatively, as **excess of fair value over the cost acquired**, **badwill**, or **bargain purchase**.

The FASB requires that this remaining excess be recognized as an extraordinary gain. The Board noted that extraordinary gain treatment is appropriate in order to highlight the fact that an excess exists, and to reflect the unusual nature and infrequent occurrence of the item. Some disagree with the approach, as it results in a gain at the time of the purchase. However, it appears that the Board took a practical approach, given that this transaction rarely occurs.

IMPAIRMENTS

As discussed, in some cases, the carrying amount of a long-lived asset (property, plant, and equipment or intangible assets) is not recoverable, and therefore a write-off is needed. This write-off is referred to as an **impairment**. The reporting rules for impairments are as follows.

Type of Long-Lived Asset	Impairment Test
Property, plant, and equipment	Recoverability test, then fair value test
Limited-life intangible	Recoverability test, then fair value test
Indefinite-life intangible other than goodwill	Fair value test
Goodwill	Fair value test on reporting unit, then fair value test on implied goodwill

Illustration 10-6
Impairment Tests

As indicated in Illustration 10-6, a recoverability test is first performed to determine whether an impairment has occurred for property, plant, and equipment and for limited-life intangibles. If the asset's cost is not recoverable, a fair value test is then used to measure the impairment loss. For indefinite-life intangibles other than goodwill, only the fair value test is employed. For goodwill, a more complex fair value test is used.

In the following sections, we look at impairments of the various types of long-lived assets shown in Illustration 10-6.

Impairment of Property, Plant, and Equipment

If events or changes in circumstances indicate that the carrying amount of property, plant, or equipment may not be recoverable, a **recoverability test** is used to determine whether an impairment has occurred. To apply the first step of the recoverability test, you estimate the future net cash flows expected from the **use of that asset and its eventual disposition**. If the sum of the expected future net cash flows (undiscounted) is **less than the carrying amount** of the asset, the asset is considered impaired. Conversely, if the sum of the expected future net cash flows (undiscounted) is **equal to or greater than the carrying amount** of the asset, no impairment has occurred.[12]

The recoverability test is a screening device to determine whether an impairment has occurred. For example, if the expected future net cash flows from an asset are $400,000 and its carrying amount is $350,000, no impairment has occurred. However, if its expected future net cash flows are $300,000, an impairment has occurred. The rationale for the recoverability test is the basic presumption that a balance sheet should report long-lived assets at no more than the carrying amounts that are recoverable.

If the recoverability test indicates that an impairment has occurred, a loss is computed. **The impairment loss is the amount by which the carrying amount of the asset exceeds its fair value.** The fair value of an asset is measured by its market value if an active market for it exists. If no active market exists, the **present value of expected future net cash flows** should be used. The company's market rate of interest should be used in discounting to present value. To summarize, the process of determining an impairment loss is as follows.

① Review events or changes in circumstances for possible impairment.[13]

② If the review indicates impairment, apply the recoverability test. If the sum of the expected future net cash flows from the long-lived asset is less than the carrying amount of the asset, an impairment has occurred.

③ Assuming an impairment, the impairment loss is the amount by which the carrying amount of the asset is greater than the fair value of the asset. The fair value is the market value or the present value.

Illustration One: No Impairment

M. Alou Inc. has equipment that, due to changes in its use, is reviewed for possible impairment. The asset's carrying amount is $600,000 ($800,000 cost less $200,000 accu-

---

[12]"Accounting for the Impairment or Disposal of Long-lived Assets," *Statement of Financial Accounting Standards No. 144* (Norwalk, Conn.: 2001).

[13]Examples of various events or changes in circumstances are:

a. A significant decrease in the market value of an asset.

b. A significant change in the extent or manner in which an asset is used.

c. A significant adverse change in legal factors or in the business climate that affects the value of an asset.

d. An accumulation of costs significantly in excess of the amount originally expected to acquire or construct an asset.

e. A projection or forecast that demonstrates continuing losses associated with an asset.

mulated depreciation). The expected future net cash flows (undiscounted) from the use of the asset and its eventual disposition are determined to be $650,000.

The recoverability test indicates that the $650,000 of expected future net cash flows from the asset's use exceed its carrying amount of $600,000. As a result, no impairment is assumed to have occurred. The undiscounted future net cash flows must be less than the carrying amount for an asset to be deemed impaired and for the impairment loss to be measured. Therefore, M. Alou Inc. will not recognize an impairment loss in this case.

Illustration Two: With Impairment

Assume the same facts as Illustration One, except that the expected future net cash flows from Alou's equipment are $580,000 (instead of $650,000). The recoverability test indicates that the expected future net cash flows of $580,000 from the use of the asset are less than its carrying amount of $600,000. Therefore an impairment has occurred.

The difference between the carrying amount of Alou's asset and its fair value is the **impairment loss**. This asset has a market value of $525,000. The computation of the loss is:

Carrying amount of the equipment	$600,000
Fair value of equipment (market value)	525,000
Loss on impairment	$ 75,000

Illustration 10-7
Computation of Impairment Loss

The entry to record the impairment loss is as follows.

Loss on Impairment	75,000	
Accumulated Depreciation		75,000

The impairment loss is reported as part of income from continuing operations, generally in the "Other expenses and losses" section. This loss should **not be reported as an extraordinary item**. Costs associated with an impairment loss are the same costs that would flow through operations and be reported as part of continuing operations. These assets will continue to be used in operations and, therefore, the loss should not be reported below "Income from continuing operations."

A company that recognizes an impairment loss should disclose the asset(s) impaired, the events leading to the impairment, the amount of the loss, and how fair value was determined (disclosing the interest rate used, if appropriate).

Impairment of Limited-Life Intangibles

The rules that apply to impairments of property, plant, and equipment also apply to limited-life intangibles. To illustrate, assume that Lerch, Inc. has a patent on how to extract oil from shale rock. Unfortunately, reduced oil prices have made the shale oil technology somewhat unprofitable, and the patent has provided little income to date. As a result, a **recoverability test** is performed. It is found that the expected net future cash flows from this patent are $35 million, and Lerch's patent has a carrying amount of $60 million. Because the expected future net cash flows of $35 million are less than the carrying amount of $60 million, an impairment loss must be measured.

Discounting the expected net future cash flows at its market rate of interest, Lerch determines the fair value of its patent to be $20 million. The impairment loss computation (fair value test) is shown in Illustration 10-8 on the next page.

Illustration 10-8
Computation of Loss on
Impairment of Patent

Carrying amount of patent	$60,000,000
Fair value (based on present value computation)	20,000,000
Loss on impairment	$40,000,000

The journal entry to record this loss is:

Loss on Impairment	40,000,000	
Patents		40,000,000

After the impairment is recognized, the reduced carrying amount of the patents is its new cost basis. The patent's new cost should be amortized over its useful life or legal life, whichever is shorter. Even if oil prices increase in subsequent periods, and the value of the patent increases, **restoration of the previously recognized impairment loss is not permitted**.

Impairment of Indefinite-Life Intangibles Other Than Goodwill

Indefinite-life intangibles other than goodwill should be tested for impairment at least annually. The impairment test for an indefinite-life asset other than goodwill is a **fair value test**. This test compares the fair value of the intangible asset with the asset's carrying amount. If the fair value of the intangible asset is less than the carrying amount, impairment is recognized. This one-step test is used because it would be relatively easy for many indefinite-life assets to meet the recoverability test (because cash flows may extend many years into the future). **As a result, the recoverability test is not used.**

To illustrate, assume that Arcon Radio purchased a broadcast license for $2,000,000. The license is renewable every 10 years if the company provides appropriate service and does not violate Federal Communications Commission (FCC) rules and procedures. The license has been renewed with the FCC twice, at a minimal cost. Cash flows were expected to last indefinitely, and therefore Arcon reported the license as an indefinite-life intangible asset. Recently the FCC decided to no longer renew broadcast licenses, but to auction these licenses to the highest bidder. Arcon's existing license has 2 years remaining, and cash flows are expected for these 2 years. Arcon performs an impairment test and determines that the fair value of the intangible asset is $1,500,000. It therefore reports an impairment loss of $500,000, computed as follows.

Illustration 10-9
Computation of Loss on
Impairment of Broadcast
License

Carrying amount of broadcast license	$2,000,000
Fair value of broadcast license	1,500,000
Loss on impairment	$ 500,000

The license would now be reported at $1,500,000, its fair value. Even if the value of the license increases in the remaining 2 years, restoration of the previously recognized impairment loss is not permitted.

Impairment of Goodwill

The impairment rule for goodwill is a two-step process. First, the fair value of the reporting unit should be compared to its carrying amount including goodwill. If the fair value of the reporting unit is greater than the carrying amount, goodwill is considered not to be impaired, and the company does not have to do anything else.

To illustrate, assume that Kohlbuy Corporation has three divisions in its company. One division, Pritt Products, was purchased 4 years ago for $2 million. Unfortunately, it has experienced operating losses over the last 3 quarters, and management is reviewing the division for purposes of recognizing an impairment. The Pritt Division's net assets, including the associated goodwill of $900,000 from purchase, are listed in Illustration 10-10.

Cash	$ 200,000
Receivables	300,000
Inventory	700,000
Property, plant, and equipment (net)	800,000
Goodwill	900,000
Less: Accounts and notes payable	(500,000)
Net assets	$2,400,000

Illustration 10-10
Net Assets of Pritt Division, Including Goodwill

It is determined that the fair value of Pritt Division is $2,800,000. **As a result, no impairment is recognized, because the fair value of the division is greater than the carrying amount of the net assets.**

However, if the fair value of Pritt Division is less than the carrying amount of the net assets, then a second step must be performed to determine whether impairment has occurred. In the second step, the fair value of the goodwill must be determined (implied value of goodwill) and compared to its carrying amount. To illustrate, assume that the fair value of Pritt's Division was $1,900,000 instead of $2,800,000. The implied value of the goodwill in this case is computed in Illustration 10-11.[14]

Fair value of Pritt Division	$1,900,000
Net identifiable assets (excluding goodwill) ($2,400,000 − $900,000)	1,500,000
Implied value of goodwill	$ 400,000

Illustration 10-11
Determination of Implied Value of Goodwill

The implied value of the goodwill is then compared to the recorded goodwill to determine whether an impairment has occurred, as shown in Illustration 10-12.

Carrying amount of goodwill	$900,000
Implied value of goodwill	400,000
Loss on impairment	$500,000

Illustration 10-12
Measurement of Goodwill Impairment

Restoration of Impairment Loss

Once an impairment loss is recorded, the reduced carrying amount of an asset held for use becomes its new cost basis. As a result, the new cost basis is not changed except for depreciation or amortization in future periods or for additional impairments.

To illustrate, assume that Ortiz Company at December 31, 2002, has a patent with a carrying amount of $500,000, which is impaired and is written down to its fair value

---

[14]Illustration 10-11 assumes that the carrying amount and the fair value of net identifiable assets (excluding goodwill) are the same. If different, the fair value of the net identifiable assets (excluding goodwill) is used to determine the implied goodwill.

of $400,000. At the end of 2003, assume that the fair value of this asset is $480,000. The carrying amount of the patent should not change in 2003 except for the amortization taken in 2003. **The impairment loss may not be restored for an asset held for use.** The rationale for not writing the asset up in value is that the new cost basis puts the impaired asset on an equal basis with other assets that are not impaired.

Impairment of Assets to Be Disposed Of

What happens if the impaired asset is intended to be disposed of instead of held for use? In this case, the impaired asset is reported at the lower of cost or net realizable value (fair value less cost to sell). Because the asset is intended to be disposed of in a short period of time, net realizable value is used in order to provide a better measure of the net cash flows that will be received from this asset.

Assets that are being held for disposal are not depreciated or amortized during the period they are held. The rationale is that depreciation is inconsistent with the notion of assets to be disposed of and with the use of the lower of cost or net realizable value. In other words, **assets held for disposal are like inventory and should be reported at the lower of cost or net realizable value**.

Because assets held for disposal will be recovered through sale rather than through operations, they are continually revalued. Each period they are reported at the lower of cost or net realizable value. Thus **an asset held for disposal can be written up or down in future periods**, as long as the value after the write-up is never greater than the carrying amount of the asset before the impairment. Losses or gains related to these impaired assets should be reported as part of **income from continuing operations**.

RESEARCH AND DEVELOPMENT COSTS

OBJECTIVE 8
Identify the conceptual issues related to research and development costs.

Research and development (R & D) costs are not in themselves intangible assets. The accounting for R & D costs is presented here, however, because research and development activities frequently result in the development of something that is patented or copyrighted (such as a new product, process, idea, formula, composition, or literary work).

Many businesses spend considerable sums of money on research and development to create new products or processes, to improve present products, and to discover new knowledge that may be valuable at some future date. The following schedule shows the outlays for R & D made by selected U.S. companies.

Illustration 10-13
R & D Outlays, as a Percentage of Sales and Profits

Company	R & D Dollars	% of Sales	% of Profits
Deere & Co.	$ 444,400,000	3.73%	43.51%
Dell Computer	272,000,000	1.49%	18.63%
General Mills	70,000,000	1.12%	13.10%
Johnson & Johnson	2,269,000,000	9.59%	74.17%
Kellogg	121,900,000	1.80%	24.25%
Merck	1,821,100,000	6.77%	34.70%

The difficulties in accounting for these research and development (R & D) expenditures are: (1) identifying the costs associated with particular activities, projects, or achievements, and (2) determining the magnitude of the future benefits and length of time over which such benefits may be realized. Because of these latter uncertainties, the accounting practice in this area has been simplified by requiring that **all research and development costs be charged to expense when incurred**.[15]

Identifying R & D Activities

To differentiate research and development costs from similar costs, the following definitions are used for **research activities** and **development activities**.[16]

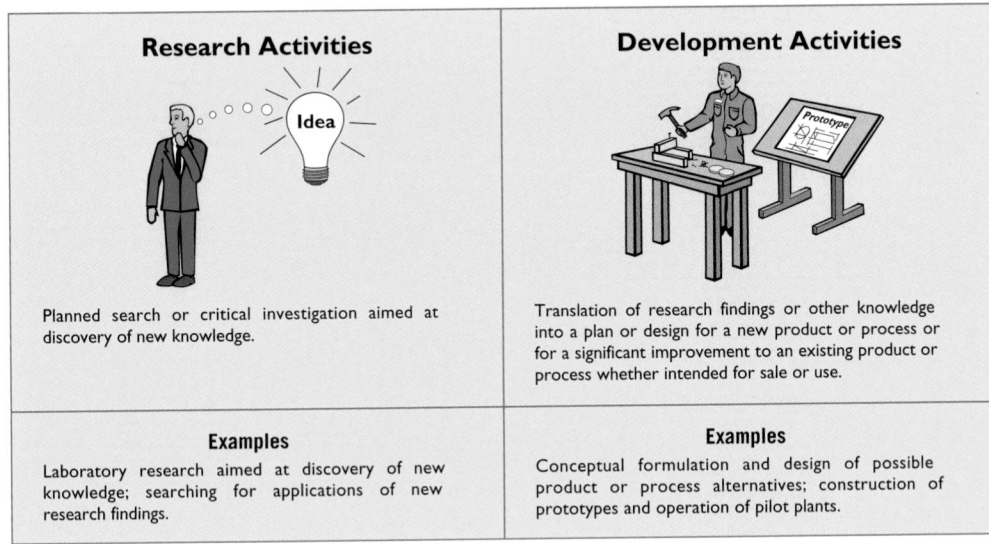

Illustration 10-14
R & D Activities

Research Activities	Development Activities
Planned search or critical investigation aimed at discovery of new knowledge.	Translation of research findings or other knowledge into a plan or design for a new product or process or for a significant improvement to an existing product or process whether intended for sale or use.
Examples	**Examples**
Laboratory research aimed at discovery of new knowledge; searching for applications of new research findings.	Conceptual formulation and design of possible product or process alternatives; construction of prototypes and operation of pilot plants.

It should be emphasized that R & D activities do not include routine or periodic alterations to existing products, production lines, manufacturing processes, and other ongoing operations, even though these alterations may represent improvements. For example, routine ongoing efforts to refine, enrich, or improve the qualities of an existing product are not considered R & D activities.

OBJECTIVE **9**
Describe the accounting procedures for research and development costs and for other similar costs.

Accounting for R & D Activities

The costs associated with R & D activities and the accounting treatment accorded them are as follows.

1. *Materials, Equipment, and Facilities.* Expense the entire costs, **unless the items have alternative future uses** (in other R & D projects or otherwise), in which case carry as inventory and allocate as consumed; or capitalize and depreciate as used.

2. *Personnel.* Salaries, wages, and other related costs of personnel engaged in R & D should be expensed as incurred.

3. *Purchased Intangibles.* Expense the entire cost, **unless the items have alternative future uses** (in other R & D projects or otherwise), in which case capitalize and amortize.

4. *Contract Services.* The costs of services performed by others in connection with the reporting company's R & D should be expensed as incurred.

INTERNATIONAL INSIGHT

International accounting standards require the capitalization of appropriate development expenditures. This conflicts with U.S. GAAP.

[15]"Accounting for Research and Development Costs," *Statement of Financial Accounting Standards No. 2* (Stamford, Conn.: FASB, 1974), par. 12.

[16]Ibid., par. 8.

⟨5⟩ *Indirect Costs.* A reasonable allocation of indirect costs shall be included in R & D costs, except for general and administrative cost, which must be clearly related in order to be included and expensed.[17]

Consistent with item 1 above, if an enterprise owns a research facility consisting of buildings, laboratories, and equipment that conducts R & D activities and that has alternative future uses (in other R & D projects or otherwise), the facility should be accounted for as a capitalized operational asset. The depreciation and other costs related to such research facilities are accounted for as R & D expenses.

To illustrate the identification of R & D activities and the accounting treatment of related costs, assume that Next Century Incorporated develops, produces, and markets laser machines for medical, industrial, and defense uses. The types of expenditures related to its laser machine activities, along with the recommended accounting treatment, are listed in Illustration 10-15.

Illustration 10-15

Sample R & D Expenditures and Their Accounting Treatment

NEXT CENTURY INCORPORATED	
Type of Expenditure	Accounting Treatment
1. Construction of long-range research facility for use in current and future projects (three-story, 400,000-square-foot building).	Capitalize and depreciate as R & D expense.
2. Acquisition of R & D equipment for use on current project only.	Expense immediately as R & D.
3. Acquisition of machinery to be used on current and future R & D projects.	Capitalize and depreciate as R & D expense.
4. Purchase of materials to be used on current and future R & D projects.	Allocate to R & D projects; expense as consumed.
5. Salaries of research staff designing new laser bone scanner.	Expense immediately as R & D.
6. Research costs incurred under contract with New Horizon, Inc., and billable monthly.	Record as a receivable (reimbursable expenses).
7. Material, labor, and overhead costs of prototype laser scanner.	Expense immediately as R & D.
8. Costs of testing prototype and design modifications.	Expense immediately as R & D.
9. Legal fees to obtain patent on new laser scanner.	Capitalize as patent and amortize to overhead as part of cost of goods manufactured.
10. Executive salaries.	Expense as operating expense (general and administrative).
11. Cost of marketing research to promote new laser scanner.	Expense as operating expense (selling).
12. Engineering costs incurred to advance the laser scanner to full production stage.	Expense immediately as R & D.
13. Costs of successfully defending patent on laser scanner.	Capitalize as patent and amortize to overhead as part of cost of goods manufactured.
14. Commissions to sales staff marketing new laser scanner.	Expense as operating expense (selling).

[17]Ibid., par. 11.

Start-Up Costs

Many costs have characteristics similar to research and development costs. For the most part **these costs are expensed as incurred**. A brief explanation for these start-up costs is shown in Illustration 10-16.

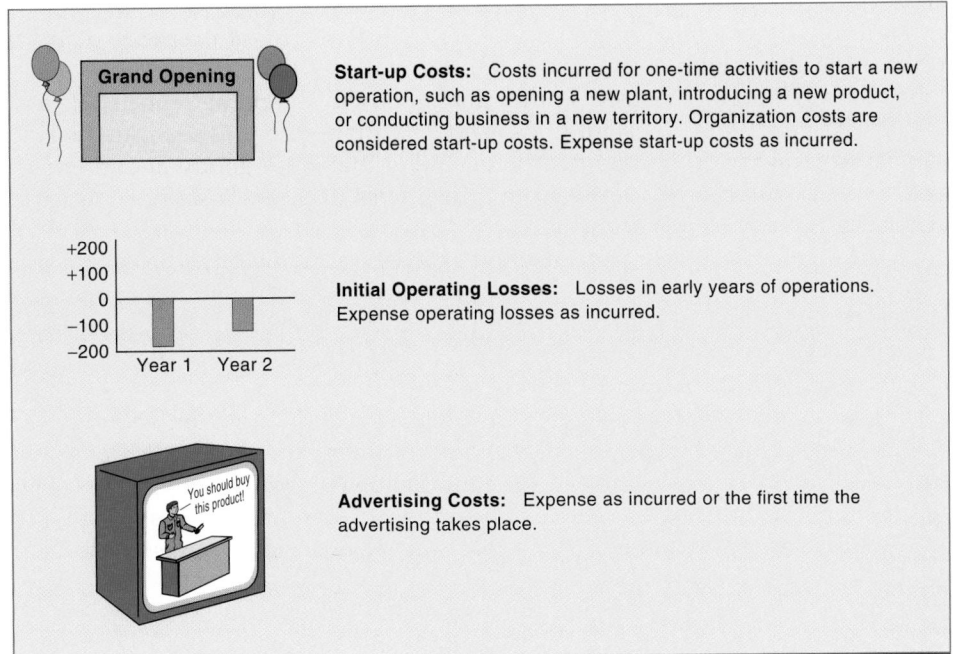

Illustration 10-16
Accounting for Start-up Costs

Note that it is not uncommon for start-up activities to occur at the same time as other activities, such as the acquisition or development of assets. For example, in opening a new plant, the cost of the plant is an asset and should be depreciated using appropriate GAAP reporting guidelines. Similarly, tangible assets used in advertising, such as billboards or blimps, are recorded as assets because they have alternative future uses.[18]

Conceptual Questions

The requirement that all R & D costs (as well as start-up costs) incurred internally be expensed immediately is a conservative, practical solution that ensures consistency in practice and uniformity among companies. But the practice of immediately writing off expenditures made in the expectation of benefiting future periods cannot be justified on the grounds that it is good accounting theory.

Proponents of immediate expensing contend that from an income statement standpoint, long-run application of this standard frequently makes little difference. They contend that because of the ongoing nature of most companies' R & D activities, the amount of R & D cost charged to expense each accounting period would be about the same whether there is immediate expensing or capitalization and subsequent amortization. Critics of this practice argue that the balance sheet should report an intangible asset related to expenditures that have future benefit. To preclude capitalization of all R & D expenditures removes from the balance sheet what may be a company's most valuable

UNDERLYING CONCEPTS

The requirement that all R & D costs be expensed as incurred is an example of the conflict between relevance and reliability, with this requirement leaning strongly in support of reliability, as well as conservatism, consistency, and comparability. No attempt is made to match costs and revenues.

[18]"Reporting on the Costs of Start-up Activities," *Statement of Position 98-5* (New York: AICPA, 1998).

asset. This standard represents one of the many trade-offs made among relevance, reliability, and cost-benefit considerations.[19]

PRESENTATION OF INTANGIBLES AND RELATED ITEMS

Intangible Assets

OBJECTIVE **10**
Indicate the presentation of Intangible assets and related items.

The reporting of intangible assets differs from the reporting of property, plant, and equipment in that contra accounts are not normally shown for intangibles. On the balance sheet, all intangible assets other than goodwill should be reported as a separate item. If goodwill is present, it also should be reported as a separate item. The Financial Accounting Standards Board concluded that since goodwill and other intangible assets differ significantly from other types of assets, users of the balance sheet will benefit from this disclosure.

On the income statement, amortization expense and impairment losses for intangible assets other than goodwill should be presented as part of continuing operations. Goodwill impairment losses should also be presented as a separate line item in the continuing operations section, unless the goodwill impairment is associated with a discontinued operation.

The notes to the financial statements should include information about acquired intangible assets, including the aggregate amortization expense for each of the succeeding 5 years. The notes should include information about changes in the carrying amount of goodwill during the period. Illustration 10-17 on page 493 shows the type of disclosure made related to intangible assets in the financial statements and related notes for Harbaugh Company.

Research and Development Costs

Acceptable accounting practice requires that disclosure be made in the financial statements (generally in the notes) of the total R & D costs charged to expense each period for which an income statement is presented. **Merck & Co., Inc.**, a global research pharmaceutical company, reported both internal and acquired research and development in its recent income statement, as shown in Illustration 10-18 on page 494.

In addition, Merck provides a discussion about R & D expenditures in its annual report, as shown in Illustration 10-19 on page 494.

---

[19]Recent research suggests that capitalizing research and development costs may be helpful to investors. For example, one study showed that a significant relationship exists between R & D outlays and subsequent benefits in the form of increased productivity, earnings, and shareholder value for R & D–intensive companies. Baruch Lev and Theodore Sougiannis,"The Capitalization, Amortization, and Value-Relevance of R & D," *Journal of Accounting and Economics* (February 1996). In another study, it was found that there was a significant decline in earnings usefulness for companies that were forced to switch from capitalizing to expensing R & D costs, and that the decline appears to persist over time. Martha L. Loudder and Bruce K. Behn,"Alternative Income Determination Rules and Earnings Usefulness: The Case of R & D Costs," *Contemporary Accounting Research* (Fall 1995).

Illustration 10-17

Intangible Asset
Disclosures

HARBAUGH COMPANY (in thousands)
Balance Sheet (partial)

Intangible assets (Note C)	$3,840
Goodwill (Note D)	2,575

Income Statement (partial)

as part of Continuing operations

Amortization expense	$380
Impairment losses (goodwill)	46

Note C: Acquired Intangible Assets

	As of December 31, 2003	
	Gross Carrying Amount	Accumulated Amortization
Amortized intangible assets		
Trademark	$2,000	$(100)
Customer list	500	(310)
Other	60	(10)
Total	$2,560	$(420)
Unamortized intangible assets		
Licenses	$1,300	
Trademark	400	
Total	$1,700	

Aggregate Amortization Expense

For year ended 12/31/03	$380

Estimated Amortization Expense

For year ended 12/31/04	$200
For year ended 12/31/05	$ 90
For year ended 12/31/06	$ 70
For year ended 12/31/07	$ 60
For year ended 12/31/08	$ 50

Note D: Goodwill

The changes in the carrying amount of goodwill for 2003 are as follows:

($000s)	Technology Segment	Communications Segment	Total
Balance as of January 1, 2003	$1,413	$904	$2,317
Goodwill acquired during year	189	115	304
Impairment losses	—	(46)	(46)
Balance as of December 31, 2003	$1,602	$973	$2,575

The Communications segment is tested for impairment in the third quarter. Due to an increase in competition in the cable industry, operating profits and cash flows were lower than expected in the fourth quarter of 2002 and the first and second quarters of 2003. Based on that trend, the earnings forecast was revised. In September 2003, a goodwill impairment loss of $46 was recognized in the Communications reporting unit. The fair value of that reporting unit was estimated using the expected present value of future cash flows.

Illustration 10-18
Income Statement
Disclosure of R & D Costs

Additional Disclosures of Intangibles and R & D Costs

❖ MERCK

MERCK & CO., INC.
(in millions)

	Years Ended December 31		
	1998	**1997**	**1996**
Sales	$26,898.2	$23,636.9	$19,828.7
Costs, expenses, and other			
Materials and production	13,925.4	11,790.3	9,319.2
Marketing and administrative	4,511.4	4,299.2	3,841.3
Research and development	1,821.1	1,683.7	1,487.3
Acquired research	1,039.5	—	—
Equity income from affiliates	(884.3)	(727.9)	(600.7)
Gains on sales of businesses	(2,147.7)	(213.4)	—
Other (income) expense, net	499.7	342.7	240.8
	$18,765.1	$17,174.6	$14,287.9

Illustration 10-19
Merck's R & D Disclosure

MERCK & CO., INC.

Research and development in the pharmaceutical industry is inherently a long-term process. The following data show an unbroken trend of year-to-year increases in research and development spending. For the period to 1989 to 1998, the compounded annual growth rate in research and development was 11%. Research and development expenses for 1999 are estimated to approximate $2.1 billion.

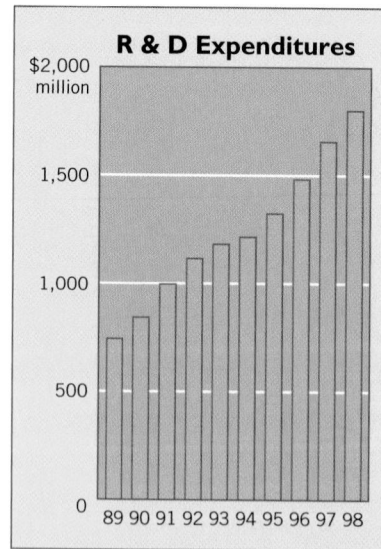

    In 1998, in connection with the restructuring of AMI, the Company recorded a $1.04 billion charge for acquired research associated with 10 product candidates in Phase II or later stages of development and U.S. rights to future Astra products which have not yet entered Phase II, for which, at the acquisition date, commercial viability had not been established.

SUMMARY OF LEARNING OBJECTIVES

❶ Describe the characteristics of intangible assets. Intangible assets have two main characteristics: (1) They lack physical existence, and (2) they are not financial instruments. In most cases, intangible assets provide services over a period of years. As a result, they are normally classified as long-term assets.

❷ Identify the costs included in the initial valuation of intangible assets. Intangibles are recorded at cost. Cost includes all costs of acquisition and expenditures necessary to make the intangible asset ready for its intended use. If intangibles are acquired for stock or in exchange for other assets, the cost of the intangible is the fair value of the consideration given or the fair value of the intangible received, whichever is more clearly evident. When several intangibles, or a combination of intangibles and tangibles, are bought in a "basket purchase," the cost should be allocated on the basis of fair values.

❸ Explain the procedure for amortizing intangible assets. Intangibles have either a limited useful life or an indefinite useful life. An intangible asset with a limited life is amortized. An intangible asset with an indefinite life is not amortized. Limited-life intangibles should be amortized by systematic charges to expense over their useful life. The useful life should reflect the period over which these assets will contribute to cash flows. The amount to report for amortization expense should reflect the pattern in which the asset is consumed or used up if that pattern can be reliably determined. Otherwise a straight-line approach should be used.

❹ Identify the categories of intangible assets. Major categories of intangibles are: (1) marketing-related intangibles which are used in the marketing or promotion of products or services; (2) customer-related intangibles which are a result of interactions with outside parties; (3) artistic-related intangibles which involve ownership rights to such items as plays and literary works; (4) contract-related intangibles which represent the value of rights that arise from contractual arrangements; (5) technology-related intangible assets which relate to innovations or technological advances; and (6) goodwill which arises in business combinations.

❺ Explain the conceptual issues related to goodwill. Goodwill is unique because unlike receivables, inventories, and patents that can be sold or exchanged individually in the marketplace, goodwill can be identified only with the business as a whole. Goodwill is a "going concern" valuation and is recorded only when an entire business is purchased. Goodwill generated internally should not be capitalized in the accounts, because measuring the components of goodwill is too complex and associating any costs with future benefits too difficult. The future benefits of goodwill may have no relationship to the costs incurred in the development of that goodwill. Goodwill may exist even in the absence of specific costs to develop it.

❻ Describe the accounting procedures for recording goodwill. To record goodwill, the fair market value of the net tangible and identifiable intangible assets are compared with the purchase price of the acquired business. The difference is considered goodwill. Goodwill is the residual—the excess of cost over fair value of the identifiable net assets acquired. Goodwill is often identified on the balance sheet as the excess of cost over the fair value of the net assets acquired.

❼ Explain the accounting issues related to impairments. Impairment of a long-lived asset occurs when the carrying amount of the asset is not recoverable. Impairments for property, plant, and equipment and for limited-life intangible assets are based on a recoverability test and a fair value test. Indefinite-life intangibles use only a fair value test. Goodwill impairments use a two-step process: First, test the fair value of the reporting unit, then do the fair value test on implied goodwill.

❽ Identify the conceptual issues related to research and development costs. R & D costs are not in themselves intangible assets, but research and development activities

KEY TERMS

amortization, 473
badwill, 483
copyright, 476
development activities, 489
fair value test, 486
franchise, 477
goodwill, 479
impairment, 483
indefinite-life
    intangibles, 473
intangible assets, 472
license (permit), 477
limited-life intangibles, 473
master valuation
    approach, 481
negative goodwill
    (badwill), 483
patent, 478
recoverability test, 484
research activities, 489
research and development
    (R & D) costs, 488
start-up costs, 491
trademark, trade name, 475

frequently result in the development of something that is patented or copyrighted. The difficulties in accounting for R & D expenditures are: (1) identifying the costs associated with particular activities, projects, or achievements, and (2) determining the magnitude of the future benefits and length of time over which such benefits may be realized. Because of these latter uncertainties, the FASB has standardized and simplified accounting practice by requiring that all research and development costs be charged to expense when incurred.

⑨ **Describe the accounting procedures for research and development costs and for other similar costs.** The costs associated with R & D activities and the accounting treatment accorded them are as shown on pages 489–490. A reasonable allocation of indirect costs shall be included in R & D costs, except for general and administrative costs, which must be related to be included and expensed. Many costs have characteristics similar to R & D costs. Examples are start-up costs, initial operating losses, and advertising costs. For the most part, these costs are expensed as incurred, similar to the accounting for R & D costs.

⑩ **Indicate the presentation of intangible assets and related items.** The reporting of intangibles differs from the reporting of property, plant, and equipment in that contra accounts are not normally shown. On the balance sheet, all intangible assets other than goodwill should be reported as a separate item. If goodwill is present, it too should be reported as a separate item. On the income statement, amortization expense and impairment losses should normally be reported in continuing operations. The notes to the financial statements have additional detailed information. Disclosure must be made in the financial statements for the total R & D costs charged to expense each period for which an income statement is presented.

REVIEW EXERCISE

Argot Co., organized in 2003, provided you with the following information.

1. Purchased a franchise for $42,000 on July 1, 2003. The rights to the franchise will expire on July 1, 2011.
2. Incurred a net loss of $33,000 in 2003, including a state incorporation fee of $2,000 and related legal fees of organizing, $5,000. (All fees were incurred in 2003.)
3. Purchased a patent on January 2, 2004, for $80,000. It is estimated to have a 10-year life.
4. Costs incurred to develop a secret formula as of March 1, 2004, were $90,000. The secret formula has an indefinite life.
5. On April 1, 2004, Argot Co. purchased a small manufacturing concern for $700,000. Goodwill recorded in the transaction was $180,000.
6. On July 1, 2004, legal fees for successful defense of the patent purchased on January 2, 2004, were $11,400.
7. Research and development costs incurred as of September 1, 2004, were $110,000.

Instructions
(a) Prepare the journal entries to record all the entries related to the patent during 2004.
(b) At December 31, 2004, an impairment test is performed on the franchise purchased in 2003. It is estimated that the net cash flows to be received from the franchise will be $25,000, and its fair value is $13,000. Compute the amount of impairment, if any, to be recorded on December 31, 2004.
(c) What is the amount to be reported for intangible assets on the balance sheet at December 31, 2003? At December 31, 2004?

SOLUTION TO REVIEW EXERCISE

(a)

January 2, 2004

Patents	80,000	
Cash		80,000

July 1, 2004

Patents	11,400	
Cash		11,400

December 31, 2004

Patent Expense	8,600	
Patents		8,600

Computation of patent expense:

$80,000 \times 12/120 =$	$8,000
$11,400 \times 6/114 =$	600
Total	$8,600

(b) Computation of impairment loss:

Cost	$42,000
Less: Accumulated amortization	7,875*
Book value	$34,125

*$42,000 \times 18/96 = $7,875$

Book value of $34,125 is greater than net cash flows of $25,000. Therefore the franchise is impaired. The impairment loss is computed as follows.

Book value	$34,125
Fair value	13,000
Loss on impairment	$21,125

(c) Intangible assets as of December 31, 2003:

Franchise	$39,375*
*Cost	$42,000
Less: Accumulated amortization	2,625**
Total	$39,375

**$42,000 \times 6/96 = $2,625$

Note that the net loss and all organization costs are charged in 2003.

Intangible assets as of December 31, 2004:

Franchise	$ 13,000	
Patents	$ 82,800	($80,000 + $11,400 − $8,600)
Goodwill	$180,000	

Note that all the costs to develop the secret formula and the research and development costs are expensed as incurred.

QUESTIONS

1 What are the two main characteristics of intangible assets?

2 If intangibles are acquired for stock, how is the cost of the intangible determined?

3 Intangibles have either an unlimited life or an indefinite useful life. How should these two different types of intangibles be amortized?

4 Why does the accounting profession make a distinction between internally created intangibles and purchased intangibles?

5 In 2003, Sheila Wright Corp. spent $420,000 for "goodwill" visits by sales personnel to key customers. The purpose of these visits was to build a solid, friendly relationship for the future and to gain insight into the problems and needs of the companies served. How should this expenditure be reported?

6 What are factors to be considered in estimating the useful life of an intangible asset?

7 What should be the pattern of amortization for a limited-life intangible?

8 Marcy Co. acquired a trademark that is helpful in distinguishing one of its new products. The trademark is renewable every 10 years at minimal cost. All evidence indicates that this trademark product will generate cash flows for an indefinite period of time. How should this trademark be amortized?

9 Alonzo Mourning Company spent $190,000 developing a new process, $45,000 in legal fees to obtain a patent, and $91,000 to market the process that was patented, all in the year 2003. How should these costs be accounted for in 2003?

10 Yellow 3 purchased a patent for $450,000. The patent has an estimated useful life of 10 years. Its pattern of use or consumption cannot be reliably determined. Prepare the entry to record the amortization of the patent in its first year of use.

11 Explain the difference between artistic-related intangible assets and contract-related intangible assets.

12 What is goodwill? What is negative goodwill?

13 Under what circumstances is it appropriate to record goodwill in the accounts? How should goodwill, properly recorded on the books, be written off in order to conform with generally accepted accounting principles?

14 In examining financial statements, financial analysts often write off goodwill immediately. Evaluate this procedure.

15 Astaire Inc. is considering the write-down of its long-term plant because of a lack of profitability. Explain to the management of Astaire how to determine whether a write-off is permitted.

16 Assume the same information as question 15, except that a limited-life intangible is being considered for write-off. How would this situation be reported?

17 Last year Wilde Company recorded an impairment on an intangible asset held for use. Recent appraisals indicate that the asset has increased in value. Should Wilde record this recovery in value?

18 Kuga Co. has equipment with a carrying amount of $700,000. The expected future net cash flows from the equipment is $705,000, and its fair value is $590,000. The equipment is expected to be used in operations in the future. What amount (if any) should Kuga report as an impairment to its equipment?

19 Explain how gains and losses on impaired assets should be reported in income.

20 Logan Company determines that its goodwill is impaired. It finds that its implied goodwill is $380,000, and its recorded goodwill is $400,000. The fair value of its identifiable assets is $1,450,000. What is the amount of goodwill impaired?

21 What is the nature of research and development costs?

22 Research and development activities may include (a) personnel costs, (b) materials and equipment costs, and (c) indirect costs. What is the recommended accounting treatment for these three types of R & D costs?

23 Which of the following activities should be expensed currently as R & D costs?

(a) Testing in search for or evaluation of product or process alternatives.

(b) Engineering follow-through in an early phase of commercial production.

(c) Legal work in connection with patent applications or litigation, and the sale or licensing of patents.

24 Indicate the proper accounting for the following items.

(a) Organization costs.

(b) Advertising costs.

(c) Operating losses.

25 In 2002, Cassie Logan Corporation developed a new product that will be marketed in 2003. In connection with the development of this product, the following costs were incurred in 2002: research and development costs $420,000; materials and supplies consumed $60,000; compensation paid to research consultants $125,000. It is anticipated that these costs will be recovered in 2005. What is the amount of research and development costs that Cassie Logan should record in 2002 as a charge to expense?

26 Recently, a group of university students decided to incorporate for the purposes of selling a process to recycle the waste product from manufacturing cheese. Some of the initial costs involved were legal fees and office expenses incurred in starting the business, state incorporation fees, and stamp taxes. One student wishes to charge these costs against revenue in the current period; another wishes to defer these costs and amortize them in the future. Which student is correct?

27 An intangible asset with an estimated useful life of 30 years was acquired on January 1, 1993, for $450,000. On January 1, 2003, a review was made of intangible assets and their expected service lives, and it was determined that this asset had an estimated useful life of 25 more years from the date of the review. What is the amount of amortization for this intangible in 2003?

BRIEF EXERCISES

BE10-1 Doom Troopers Corporation purchases a patent from Judge Dredd Company on January 1, 2004, for $64,000. The patent has a remaining legal life of 16 years. Doom Troopers feels the patent will be useful for 10 years. Prepare Doom Troopers' journal entries to record the purchase of the patent and 2004 amortization.

BE10-2 Use the information provided in BE10-1. Assume that at January 1, 2006, the carrying amount of the patent on Doom Troopers' books is $51,200. In January, Doom Troopers spends $24,000 successfully defending a patent suit. Doom Troopers still feels the patent will be useful until the end of 2013. Prepare the journal entries to record the $24,000 expenditure and 2006 amortization.

BE10-3 Dr. Robotnik's, Inc. spent $60,000 in attorney fees while developing the trade name of its new product, the Mean Bean Machine. Prepare the journal entries to record the $60,000 expenditure and the first year's amortization, using an 8-year life.

BE10-4 Incredible Hulk Corporation commenced operations in early 2004. The corporation incurred $70,000 of costs such as fees to underwriters, legal fees, state fees, and promotional expenditures during its formation. Prepare journal entries to record the $70,000 expenditure and 2004 amortization, if any. Assume amortization (if any) is based on a 5-year life.

BE10-5 Knuckles Corporation obtained a franchise from Sonic Hedgehog Inc. for a cash payment of $100,000 on April 1, 2004. The franchise grants knuckles the right to sell certain products and services for a period of 8 years. Prepare Knuckles' April 1 journal entry and December 31 adjusting entry.

BE10-6 On September 1, 2004, Dungeon Corporation acquired Dragon Enterprises for a cash payment of $750,000. At the time of purchase, Dragon's balance sheet showed assets of $620,000, liabilities of $200,000, and owners' equity of $420,000. The fair value of Dragon's assets is estimated to be $800,000. Compute the amount of goodwill acquired by Dungeon.

BE10-7 Nobunaga Corporation owns a patent that has a carrying amount of $330,000. Nobunaga expects future net cash flows from this patent to total $190,000. The fair value of the patent is $110,000. Prepare Nobunaga's journal entry, if necessary, to record the loss on impairment.

BE10-8 Kinoland Company owns machinery that cost $900,000 and has accumulated depreciation of $360,000. The expected future net cash flows from the use of this asset are expected to be $500,000. The fair value of the equipment is $400,000. Prepare the journal entry, if any, to record the impairment loss.

BE10-9 Evander Corporation purchased Holyfield Company 3 years ago and at that time recorded goodwill of $400,000. The Holyfield Division's net assets, excluding goodwill, have a carrying amount and a fair value of $790,000. Evander expects net future cash flows of $700,000 from the Holyfield Division. The fair value of the division is estimated to be $1,200,000. Prepare Evander's journal entry, if necessary, to record impairment of the goodwill.

BE10-10 Dorsett Corporation incurred the following costs in 2004.

Cost of laboratory research aimed at discovery of new knowledge	$140,000
Cost of testing in search for product alternatives	100,000
Cost of engineering activity required to advance the design of a product to the manufacturing stage	210,000
	$450,000

Prepare the necessary 2004 journal entry or entries for Dorsett.

BE10-11 Indicate whether the following items are capitalized or expensed in the current year.

(a) Purchase cost of a patent from a competitor.

(b) Research and development costs.

(c) Organizational costs.

(d) Costs incurred internally to create goodwill.

BE10-12 Langer Industries had one patent recorded on its books as of January 1, 2004. This patent had a book value of $240,000 and a remaining useful life of 8 years. During 2004, Langer incurred research and development costs of $96,000 and brought a patent infringement suit against a competitor. On December 1, 2004, Langer received the good news that its patent was valid and that its competitor could not use the process Langer had patented. The company incurred $85,000 to defend this patent. At what amount should patent(s) be reported on the December 31, 2004, balance sheet, assuming monthly amortization of patents?

BE10-13 Wiggens Industries acquired two copyrights during 2004. One copyright related to a textbook that was developed internally at a cost of $9,900. This textbook is estimated to have a useful life of 3 years from September 1, 2004, the date it was published. The second copyright (a history research textbook) was purchased from University Press on December 1, 2004, for $19,200. This textbook has an indefinite useful life. How should these two copyrights be reported on Wiggens' balance sheet as of December 31, 2004?

EXERCISES

E10-1 **(Classification Issues—Intangibles)** Presented below is a list of items that could be included in the intangible assets section of the balance sheet.

1. Investment in a subsidiary company.
2. Timberland.
3. Cost of engineering activity required to advance the design of a product to the manufacturing stage.
4. Lease prepayment (6 months' rent paid in advance).
5. Cost of equipment obtained.
6. Cost of searching for applications of new research findings.
7. Costs incurred in the formation of a corporation.
8. Operating losses incurred in the start-up of a business.
9. Training costs incurred in the start-up of new operation.
10. Purchase cost of a franchise.
11. Goodwill generated internally.
12. Cost of testing in search for product alternatives.
13. Goodwill acquired in the purchase of a business.
14. Cost of developing a patent.
15. Cost of purchasing a patent from an inventor.
16. Legal costs incurred in securing a patent.
17. Unrecovered costs of a successful legal suit to protect the patent.
18. Cost of conceptual formulation of possible product alternatives.
19. Cost of purchasing a copyright.
20. Research and development costs.
21. Long-term receivables.
22. Cost of developing a trademark.
23. Cost of purchasing a trademark.

Instructions

(a) Indicate which items on the list above would generally be reported as intangible assets in the balance sheet.

(b) Indicate how, if at all, the items not reportable as intangible assets would be reported in the financial statements.

E10-2 (Classification Issues—Intangibles) Presented below is selected account information related to Martin Burke Inc. as of December 21, 2003. All these accounts have debit balances.

Cable television franchises	Film contract rights
Music copyrights	Customer lists
Research and development costs	Prepaid expenses
Goodwill	Covenants not to compete
Cash	Brand names
Discount on notes payable	Notes receivable
Accounts receivable	Investments in affiliated companies
Property, plant, and equipment	Organization cost
Internet domain name	Land

Instructions

Identify which items should be classified as an intangible asset. For those items not classified as an intangible asset, indicate where they would be reported in the financial statements.

E10-3 (Classification Issues—Intangible Asset) Joni Hyde Inc. has the following amounts included in its general ledger at December 31, 2003.

Organization costs	$24,000
Trademarks	15,000
Discount on bonds payable	35,000
Deposits with advertising agency for ads to promote goodwill of company	10,000
Excess of cost over fair value of net identifiable assets of acquired subsidiary	75,000
Cost of equipment acquired for research and development projects; the equipment has an alternative future use	90,000
Costs of developing a secret formula for a product that is expected to be marketed for at least 20 years	80,000

Instructions

(a) On the basis of the information above, compute the total amount to be reported by Hyde for intangible assets on its balance sheet at December 31, 2003.

(b) If an item is not to be included in intangible assets, explain its proper treatment for reporting purposes.

E10-4 (Intangible Amortization) Presented below is selected information for Alatorre Company. Answer each of the factual situations.

1. Alatorre purchased a patent from Vania Co. for $1,000,000 on January 1, 2002. The patent is being amortized over its remaining legal life of 10 years, expiring on January 1, 2012. During 2004, Alatorre determined that the economic benefits of the patent would not last longer than 6 years from the date of acquisition. What amount should be reported in the balance sheet for the patent, net of accumulated amortization, at December 31, 2004?

2. Alatorre bought a franchise from Alexander Co. on January 1, 2003, for $400,000. The carrying amount of the franchise on Alexander's books on January 1, 2003, was $500,000. The franchise agreement had an estimated useful life of 30 years. Because Alatorre must enter a competitive bidding at the end of 2012, it is unlikely that the franchise will be retained beyond 2012. What amount should be amortized for the year ended December 31, 2004?

3. On January 1, 2000, Alatorre incurred organization costs of $275,000. Amortization of these costs (if any) would be over 5 years. What amount, if any, should be reported as unamortized organization costs as of December 31, 2004?

4. Alatorre purchased the license for distribution of a popular consumer product on January 1, 2004, for $150,000. It is expected that this product will generate cash flows for an indefinite period of time. The license has an initial term of 5 years but by paying a nominal fee, Alatorre can renew the license indefinitely for successive 5-year terms. What amount should be amortized for the year ended December 31, 2004?

E10-5 (Correct Intangible Asset Account) As the recently appointed auditor for William J. Bryan Corporation, you have been asked to examine selected accounts before the 6-month financial statements of June 30, 2003, are prepared. The controller for William J. Bryan Corporation mentions that only one account (shown below) is kept for Intangible Assets.

Intangible Assets

		Debit	Credit	Balance
January 4	Research and development costs	940,000		940,000
January 5	Legal costs to obtain patent	75,000		1,015,000
January 31	Payment of 7 months' rent on property leased by Bryan	91,000		1,106,000
February 11	Premium on common stock		250,000	856,000
March 31	Unamortized bond discount on bonds due March 31, 2023	84,000		940,000
April 30	Promotional expenses related to start-up of business	207,000		1,147,000
June 30	Operating losses for first 6 months	241,000		1,388,000

Instructions

Prepare the entry or entries necessary to correct this account. Assume that the patent has a useful life of 10 years.

E10-6 (Recording and Amortization of Intangibles) Rolanda Marshall Company, organized in 2003, has set up a single account for all intangible assets. The following summary discloses the debit entries that have been recorded during 2004.

1/2/04	Purchased patent (8-year life)	$ 350,000
4/1/04	Purchased goodwill	360,000
7/1/04	Purchased franchise with 10-year life; expiration date 7/1/14	450,000
8/1/04	Payment of copyright (5-year life)	156,000
9/1/04	Research and development costs	215,000
		$1,531,000

Instructions

Prepare the necessary entries to clear the Intangible Assets account and to set up separate accounts for distinct types of intangibles. Make the entries as of December 31, 2004, recording any necessary amortization and reflecting all balances accurately as of that date (straight-line amortization).

E10-7 (Accounting for Trade Name) In early January 2003, Gayle Crystal Corporation applied for a trade name, incurring legal costs of $16,000. In January 2004, Gayle Crystal incurred $7,800 of legal fees in a successful defense of its trade name.

Instructions

(a) Compute 2003 amortization, 12/31/03 book value, 2004 amortization, and 12/31/04 book value if the company amortizes the trade name over 10 years.

(b) Compute the 2004 amortization and the 12/31/04 book value, assuming that at the beginning of 2004, Crystal determines that the trade name will provide no future benefits beyond December 31, 2007.

(c) Ignoring the response for part (b), compute the 2005 amortization and the 12/31/05 book value, assuming that at the beginning of 2005, based on new market research, Crystal determines that the fair value of the trade name is $15,000. Estimated future net cash flow from the trade name is $16,000 on January 3, 2005.

E10-8 **(Accounting for Organization Costs)** Horace Greeley Corporation was organized in 2002 and began operations at the beginning of 2003. The company is involved in interior design consulting services. The following costs were incurred prior to the start of operations.

Attorney's fees in connection with organization of the company	$15,000
Purchase of drafting and design equipment	10,000
Costs of meetings of incorporators to discuss organizational activities	7,000
State filing fees to incorporate	1,000
	$33,000

Instructions
(a) Compute the total amount of organization costs incurred by Greeley.
(b) Prepare the journal entry to record organization costs for 2003.

E10-9 **(Accounting for Patents, Franchises, and R & D)** Jimmy Carter Company has provided information on intangible assets as follows:

A patent was purchased from Gerald Ford Company for $2,000,000 on January 1, 2003. Carter estimated the remaining useful life of the patent to be 10 years. The patent was carried in Ford's accounting records at a net book value of $2,000,000 when Ford sold it to Carter.

During 2004, a franchise was purchased from the Ronald Reagan Company for $480,000. In addition, 5% of revenue from the franchise must be paid to Reagan. Revenue from the franchise for 2004 was $2,500,000. Carter estimates the useful life of the franchise to be 10 years and takes a full year's amortization in the year of purchase.

Carter incurred research and development costs in 2004 as follows.

Materials and equipment	$142,000
Personnel	189,000
Indirect costs	102,000
	$433,000

Carter estimates that these costs will be recouped by December 31, 2007. The materials and equipment purchased have no alternative uses.

On January 1, 2004, because of recent events in the field, Carter estimates that the remaining life of the patent purchased on January 1, 2003, is only 5 years from January 1, 2004.

Instructions
(a) Prepare a schedule showing the intangibles section of Carter's balance sheet at December 31, 2004. Show supporting computations in good form.
(b) Prepare a schedule showing the income statement effect for the year ended December 31, 2004, as a result of the facts above. Show supporting computations in good form.

(AICPA adapted)

E10-10 **(Accounting for Patents)** During 2000, George Winston Corporation spent $170,000 in research and development costs. As a result, a new product called the New Age Piano was patented. The patent was obtained on October 1, 2000, and had a legal life of 20 years and a useful life of 10 years. Legal costs of $18,000 related to the patent were incurred as of October 1, 2000.

Instructions
(a) Prepare all journal entries required in 2000 and 2001 as a result of the transactions above.
(b) On June 1, 2002, Winston spent $9,480 to successfully prosecute a patent infringement. As a result, the estimate of useful life was extended to 12 years from June 1, 2002. Prepare all journal entries required in 2002 and 2003.

(c) In 2004, Winston determined that a competitor's product would make the New Age Piano obsolete and the patent worthless by December 31, 2005. Prepare all journal entries required in 2004 and 2005.

E10-11 (Accounting for Patents) Tones Industries has the following patents on its December 31, 2003, balance sheet.

Patent Item	Initial Cost	Date Acquired	Useful Life at Date Acquired
Patent A	$30,600	3/1/00	17 years
Patent B	$15,000	7/1/01	10 years
Patent C	$14,400	9/1/02	4 years

The following events occurred during the year ended December 31, 2004.

1. Research and development costs of $245,700 were incurred during the year.
2. Patent D was purchased on July 1 for $36,480. This patent has a remaining useful life of 9½ years.
3. As a result of reduced demands for certain products protected by Patent B, a possible impairment of Patent B's value may have occurred at December 31, 2004. The controller for Tones estimates the future cash flows from Patent B will be as follows.

For the Year Ended	Future Cash Flows
December 31, 2005	$2,000
December 31, 2006	2,000
December 31, 2007	2,000

The proper discount rate to be used for these flows is 8%. (Assume that the cash flows occur at the end of the year.)

Instructions
(a) Compute the total carrying amount of Tones' patents on its December 31, 2003, balance sheet.
(b) Compute the total carrying amount of Tones' patents on its December 31, 2004, balance sheet.

E10-12 (Accounting for Goodwill) Fred Moss, owner of Moss Interiors, is negotiating for the purchase of Zweifel Galleries. The condensed balance sheet of Zweifel is given below.

ZWEIFEL GALLERIES				
BALANCE SHEET				
AS OF DECEMBER 31, 2003				
Assets		**Liabilities and Stockholders' Equity**		
Cash	$100,000	Accounts payable		$ 50,000
Land	70,000	Long-term notes payable		300,000
Building (net)	200,000	Total liabilities		350,000
Equipment (net)	175,000	Common stock	$200,000	
Copyright (net)	30,000	Retained earnings	25,000	225,000
Total assets	$575,000	Total liabilities and stockholders' equity		$575,000

Moss and Zweifel agree that:

1. Land is undervalued by $30,000.
2. Equipment is overvalued by $5,000.

Zweifel agrees to sell the gallery to Moss for $350,000.

Instructions

Prepare the entry to record the purchase of Zweifel Galleries on Moss's books.

E10-13 (Accounting for Goodwill) On July 1, 2003, Brigham Corporation purchased Young Company by paying $250,000 cash and issuing a $100,000 note payable to Steve Young. At July 1, 2003, the balance sheet of Young Company was as follows.

Cash	$ 50,000	Accounts payable	$200,000
Receivables	90,000	Young, capital	235,000
Inventory	100,000		$435,000
Land	40,000		
Buildings (net)	75,000		
Equipment (net)	70,000		
Trademarks	10,000		
	$435,000		

The recorded amounts all approximate current values except for land (worth $60,000), inventory (worth $125,000), and trademarks (worth $15,000).

Instructions

(a) Prepare the July 1 entry for Brigham Corporation to record the purchase.
(b) Prepare the December 31 entry for Brigham Corporation to record amortization of intangibles. The trademark has an estimated useful life of 4 years with a residual value of $3,000.

E10-14 (Impairment) Presented below is information related to equipment owned by Suarez Company at December 31, 2003.

Cost	$9,000,000
Accumulated depreciation to date	1,000,000
Expected future net cash flows	7,000,000
Fair value	4,800,000

Assume that Suarez will continue to use this asset in the future. As of December 31, 2003, the equipment has a remaining useful life of 4 years.

Instructions

(a) Prepare the journal entry (if any) to record the impairment of the asset at December 31, 2003.
(b) Prepare the journal entry to record depreciation expense for 2004.
(c) The fair value of the equipment at December 31, 2004, is $5,100,000. Prepare the journal entry (if any) necessary to record this increase in fair value.

E10-15 (Impairment) Assume the same information as E10-14, except that Suarez intends to dispose of the equipment in the coming year. It is expected that the cost of disposal will be $20,000.

Instructions

(a) Prepare the journal entry (if any) to record the impairment of the asset at December 31, 2003.
(b) Prepare the journal entry (if any) to record depreciation expense for 2004.
(c) The asset was not sold by December 31, 2004. The fair value of the equipment on that date is $5,300,000. Prepare the journal entry (if any) necessary to record this increase in fair value. It is expected that the cost of disposal is still $20,000.

E10-16 (Impairment) The management of Luis Andujar Inc. was discussing whether certain equipment should be written off as a charge to current operations because of obsolescence. This equipment has a cost of $900,000, with depreciation to date of $400,000 as of December 31, 2003. On December 31, 2003, management projected its future net cash flows from this equipment to be $300,000 and its fair value to be $230,000. The company intends to use this equipment in the future.

Instructions

(a) Prepare the journal entry (if any) to record the impairment at December 31, 2003.

(b) Where should the gain or loss (if any) on the write-down be reported in the income statement?

(c) At December 31, 2004, the equipment's fair value increased to $260,000. Prepare the journal entry (if any) to record this increase in fair value.

(d) What accounting issues did management face in accounting for this impairment?

E10-17 (Intangible Impairment) Presented below is information related to copyrights owned by Walter de la Mare Company at December 31, 2003.

Cost	$8,600,000
Carrying amount	4,300,000
Expected future net cash flows	4,000,000
Fair value	3,200,000

Assume that Walter de la Mare Company will continue to use this copyright in the future. As of December 31, 2003, the copyright is estimated to have a remaining useful life of 10 years.

Instructions

(a) Prepare the journal entry (if any) to record the impairment of the asset at December 31, 2003. The company does not use accumulated amortization accounts.

(b) Prepare the journal entry to record amortization expense for 2004 related to the copyrights.

(c) The fair value of the copyright at December 31, 2004, is $3,400,000. Prepare the journal entry (if any) necessary to record the increase in fair value.

E10-18 (Goodwill Impairment) Presented below is net asset information (including associated goodwill of $200 million) related to the Carlos Division of Santana, Inc.

CARLOS DIVISION **NET ASSETS** **AS OF DECEMBER 31, 2003** **(IN MILLIONS)**	
Cash	$ 50
Receivables	200
Property, plant, and equipment (net)	2,600
Goodwill	200
Less: Notes payable	(2,700)
Net assets	$ 350

The purpose of this division is to develop a nuclear-powered aircraft. If successful, traveling delays associated with refueling could be substantially reduced. Many other benefits would also occur. To date, management has not had much success and is deciding whether a write-down at this time is appropriate. Management estimated its future net cash flows from the project to be $400 million. Management has also received an offer to purchase the division for $335 million. All identifiable assets' and liabilities' book and fair value amounts are the same.

Instructions

(a) Prepare the journal entry (if any) to record the impairment at December 31, 2003.

(b) At December 31, 2004, it is estimated that the division's fair value increased to $345 million. Prepare the journal entry (if any) to record this increase in fair value.

E10-19 (Accounting for R & D Costs) Leontyne Price Company from time to time embarks on a research program when a special project seems to offer possibilities. In 2003 the company expends $325,000 on a research project, but by the end of 2003 it is impossible to determine whether any benefit will be derived from it.

Instructions

(a) What account should be charged for the $325,000, and how should it be shown in the financial statements?

(b) The project is completed in 2004, and a successful patent is obtained. The R & D costs to complete the project are $110,000. The administrative and legal expenses incurred in obtaining patent number 472-1001-84 in 2004 total $16,000. The patent has an expected useful life of 5 years. Record these costs in journal entry form. Also, record patent amortization (full year) in 2004.

(c) In 2005, the company successfully defends the patent in extended litigation at a cost of $47,200, thereby extending the patent life to 12/31/12. What is the proper way to account for this cost? Also, record patent amortization (full year) in 2005.

(d) Additional engineering and consulting costs incurred in 2005 required to advance the design of a product to the manufacturing stage total $60,000. These costs enhance the design of the product considerably. Discuss the proper accounting treatment for this cost.

E10-20 (Accounting for R & D Costs) Thomas More Company incurred the following costs during 2003 in connection with its research and development activities.

Cost of equipment acquired that will have alternative uses in future research and development projects over the next 5 years (uses straight-line depreciation)	$280,000
Materials consumed in research and development projects	59,000
Consulting fees paid to outsiders for research and development projects	100,000
Personnel costs of persons involved in research and development projects	128,000
Indirect costs reasonably allocable to research and development projects	50,000
Materials purchased for future research and development projects	34,000

Instructions

Compute the amount to be reported as research and development expense by More on its income statement for 2003. Assume equipment is purchased at beginning of year.

PROBLEMS

P10-1 (Correct Intangible Asset Account) Esplanade Co., organized in 2002, has set up a single account for all intangible assets. The following summary discloses the debit entries that have been recorded during 2002 and 2003.

Intangible Assets

7/1/02	8-year franchise; expiration date 6/30/10	$ 42,000
10/1/02	Advance payment on laboratory space (2-year lease)	28,000
12/31/02	Net loss for 2002 including state incorporation fee, $1,000, and	
	related legal fees of organizing, $5,000 (all fees incurred in 2002)	16,000
1/2/03	Patent purchased (10-year life)	74,000
3/1/03	Cost of developing a secret formula (indefinite life)	75,000
4/1/03	Goodwill purchased (indefinite life)	278,400
6/1/03	Legal fee for successful defense of patent purchased above	12,650
9/1/03	Research and development costs	160,000

Instructions

Prepare the necessary entries to clear the Intangible Assets account and to set up separate accounts for distinct types of intangibles. Make the entries as of December 31, 2003, recording any necessary amortization and reflecting all balances accurately as of that date. (Ignore income tax effects.)

P10-2 (Accounting for Patents) Ankara Laboratories holds a valuable patent (No. 758-6002-1A) on a precipitator that prevents certain types of air pollution. Ankara does not manufacture or sell the products and processes it develops. It conducts research and develops products and processes which it patents, and then assigns the patents to manufacturers on a royalty basis. Occasionally it sells a patent. The history of Ankara patent number 758-6002-1A is as follows.

Date	Activity	Cost
1993–1994	Research conducted to develop precipitator	$384,000
Jan. 1995	Design and construction of a prototype	87,600
March 1995	Testing of models	42,000
Jan. 1996	Fees paid engineers and lawyers to prepare patent application; patent granted July 1, 1996	62,050
Nov. 1997	Engineering activity necessary to advance the design of the precipitator to the manufacturing stage	81,500
Dec. 1998	Legal fees paid to successfully defend precipitator patent	35,700
April 1999	Research aimed at modifying the design of the patented precipitator	43,000
July 2003	Legal fees paid in unsuccessful patent infringement suit against a competitor	34,000

Ankara assumed a useful life of 17 years when it received the initial precipitator patent. On January 1, 2001, it revised its useful life estimate downward to 5 remaining years. Amortization is computed for a full year if the cost is incurred prior to July 1, and no amortization for the year if the cost is incurred after June 30. The company's year ends December 31.

Instructions

Compute the carrying value of patent No. 758-6002-1A on each of the following dates.

(a) December 31, 1996.
(b) December 31, 2000.
(c) December 31, 2003.

P10-3 **(Accounting for Franchise, Patents, and Trade Name)** Information concerning Haerhpin Corporation's intangible assets is as follows.

1. On January 1, 2003, Haerhpin signed an agreement to operate as a franchisee of Hsian Copy Service, Inc. for an initial franchise fee of $75,000. Of this amount, $15,000 was paid when the agreement was signed, and the balance is payable in 4 annual payments of $15,000 each, beginning January 1, 2004. The agreement provides that the down payment is not refundable and no future services are required of the franchisor. The present value at January 1, 2003, of the 4 annual payments discounted at 14% (the implicit rate for a loan of this type) is $43,700. The agreement also provides that 5% of the revenue from the franchise must be paid to the franchisor annually. Haerhpin's revenue from the franchise for 2003 was $950,000. Haerhpin estimates the useful life of the franchise to be 10 years.
2. Haerhpin incurred $65,000 of experimental and development costs in its laboratory to develop a patent which was granted on January 2, 2003. Legal fees and other costs associated with registration of the patent totaled $13,600. Haerhpin estimates that the useful life of the patent will be 8 years.
3. A trademark was purchased from Shanghai Company for $32,000 on July 1, 2000. Expenditures for successful litigation in defense of the trademark totaling $8,160 were paid on July 1, 2003. Haerhpin estimates that the useful life of the trademark will be 20 years from the date of acquisition.

Instructions

(a) Prepare a schedule showing the intangible assets section of Haerhpin's balance sheet at December 31, 2003. Show supporting computations in good form.
(b) Prepare a schedule showing all expenses resulting from the transactions that would appear on Haerhpin's income statement for the year ended December 31, 2003. Show supporting computations in good form.

(AICPA adapted)

 **P10-4 (Accounting for R & D Costs)** During 2001, Florence Nightingale Tool Company purchased a building site for its proposed research and development laboratory at a cost of $60,000. Construction of the building was started in 2001. The building was completed on December 31, 2002, at a cost of $280,000 and was placed in service on January 2, 2003. The estimated useful life of the building for depreciation purposes was 20 years; the straight-line method of depreciation was to be employed and there was no estimated net salvage value.

Management estimates that about 50% of the projects of the research and development group will result in long-term benefits (i.e., at least 10 years) to the corporation. The remaining projects either benefit the current period or are abandoned before completion. A summary of the number of projects and the direct costs incurred in conjunction with the research and development activities for 2003 appears below.

Upon recommendation of the research and development group, Florence Nightingale Tool Company acquired a patent for manufacturing rights at a cost of $80,000. The patent was acquired on April 1, 2002, and has an economic life of 10 years.

	Number of Projects	Salaries and Employee Benefits	Other Expenses (excluding Building Depreciation Charges)
Completed projects with long-term benefits	15	$ 90,000	$50,000
Abandoned projects or projects that benefit the current period	10	65,000	15,000
Projects in process—results indeterminate	5	40,000	12,000
Total	30	$195,000	$77,000

Instructions

If generally accepted accounting principles were followed, how would the items above relating to research and development activities be reported on the company's

(a) Income statement for 2003?
(b) Balance sheet as of December 31, 2003?

Be sure to give account titles and amounts, and briefly justify your presentation.

(CMA adapted)

P10-5 (Goodwill, Impairment) On July 31, 2003, Postera Company paid $3,000,000 to acquire all of the common stock of Mendota Incorporated, which became a division of Postera. Mendota reported the following balance sheet at the time of the acquisition.

Current assets	$ 800,000	Current liabilities	$ 600,000
Noncurrent assets	2,700,000	Long-term liabilities	500,000
		Stockholders' equity	2,400,000
		Total liabilities and	
Total assets	$3,500,000	stockholders' equity	$3,500,000

It was determined at the date of the purchase that the fair value of the identifiable net assets of Mendota was $2,650,000. Over the next 6 months of operations, the newly purchased division experienced operating losses. In addition, it now appears that it will generate substantial losses for the foreseeable future. At December 31, 2003, Mendota reports the following balance sheet information.

Current assets	$ 450,000
Noncurrent assets (including goodwill recognized in purchase)	2,400,000
Current liabilities	(700,000)
Long-term liabilities	(500,000)
Net assets	$1,650,000

It is determined that the fair value of the Mendota Division is $1,850,000. The recorded amount for Mendota's net assets (excluding goodwill) is the same as fair value, except for property, plant, and equipment, which has a fair value $150,000 above the carrying value.

Instructions

(a) Compute the amount of goodwill recognized, if any, on July 31, 2003.

(b) Determine the impairment loss, if any, to be recorded on December 31, 2003.

(c) Assume that fair value of the Mendota Division is $1,500,000 instead of $1,850,000. Determine the impairment loss, if any, to be recorded on December 31, 2003.

(d) Prepare the journal entry to record the impairment loss, if any, and indicate where the loss would be reported in the income statement.

CONCEPTUAL CASES

C10-1 (Accounting for Intangible-Type Expenditures) Missie McGeorge, Inc. is a large, publicly held corporation. Listed below are four selected expenditures made by the company during the current fiscal year ended April 30, 2004. The proper accounting treatment of these transactions must be determined in order that McGeorge's annual financial statements will be prepared in accordance with generally accepted accounting principles.

1. McGeorge, Inc. spent $3,000,000 on a program designed to improve relations with its dealers. This project was favorably received by the dealers and McGeorge's management believes that significant future benefits should be received from this program. The program was conducted during the fourth quarter of the current fiscal year.

2. A pilot plant was constructed during 2003–04 at a cost of $5,500,000 to test a new production process. The plant will be operated for approximately 5 years. At that time, the company will make a decision regarding the economic value of the process. The pilot plant is too small for commercial production, so it will be dismantled when the test is over.

3. McGeorge, Inc. purchased Eagle Company for $6,000,000 in cash in early August 2003. The fair market value of the identifiable assets of Eagle was $5,200,000.

4. During the first six months of the 2003–04 fiscal year, $400,000 was expended for legal work in connection with a successful patent application. The patent became effective November 1, 2003. The legal life of the patent is 20 years and the economic life of the patent is expected to be approximately 10 years.

Instructions

For each of the four expenditures presented, determine and justify:

(a) The amount, if any, that should be capitalized and be included on McGeorge's statement of financial position prepared as of April 30, 2004.

(b) The amount that should be included in McGeorge's statement of income for the year ended April 30, 2004.

(CMA adapted)

C10-2 (Accounting for Pollution Expenditure) Phil Mickelson Company operates several plants at which limestone is processed into quicklime and hydrated lime. The Eagle Ridge plant, where most of the equipment was installed many years ago, continually deposits a dusty white substance over the surrounding countryside. Citing the unsanitary condition of the neighboring community of Scales Mound, the pollution of the Galena River, and the high incidence of lung disease among workers at Eagle Ridge, the state's Pollution Control Agency has ordered the installation of air pollution control equipment. Also, the Agency has assessed a substantial penalty, which will be used to clean up Scales Mound. After considering the costs involved (which could not have been reasonably estimated prior to the Agency's action), Phil Mickelson Company decides to comply with the Agency's orders, the alternative being to cease operations at Eagle Ridge at the end of the current fiscal year. The officers of Mickelson agree that the air pollution control equipment should be capitalized and depreciated over its useful life, but they disagree over the period(s) to which the penalty should be charged.

Instructions

Discuss the conceptual merits and reporting requirements of accounting for the penalty as a:

(a) Charge to the current period.
(b) Correction of prior periods.
(c) Capitalizable item to be amortized over future periods.

(AICPA adapted)

C10-3 (Accounting for Pre-Opening Costs) After securing lease commitments from several major stores, Lobo Shopping Center, Inc. was organized and built a shopping center in a growing suburb.

The shopping center would have opened on schedule on January 1, 2003, if it had not been struck by a severe tornado in December; it opened for business on October 1, 2003. All of the additional construction costs that were incurred as a result of the tornado were covered by insurance.

In July 2002, in anticipation of the scheduled January opening, a permanent staff had been hired to promote the shopping center, obtain tenants for the uncommitted space, and manage the property.

A summary of some of the costs incurred in 2002 and the first 9 months of 2003 follows.

	2002	January 1, 2003 through September 30, 2003
Interest on mortgage bonds	$720,000	$540,000
Cost of obtaining tenants	300,000	360,000
Promotional advertising	540,000	557,000

The promotional advertising campaign was designed to familiarize shoppers with the center. Had it been known in time that the center would not open until October 2003, the 2002 expenditure for promotional advertising would not have been made. The advertising had to be repeated in 2003.

All of the tenants who had leased space in the shipping center at the time of the tornado accepted the October occupancy date on condition that the monthly rental charges for the first 9 months of 2003 be canceled.

Instructions

Explain how each of the costs for 2002 and the first 9 months of 2003 should be treated in the accounts of the shopping center corporation. Give the reasons for each treatment.

(AICPA adapted)

C10-4 (Accounting for Patents) On June 30, 2003, your client, Bearcat Company, was granted two patents covering plastic cartons that it had been producing and marketing profitably for the past 3 years. One patent covers the manufacturing process and the other covers the related products.

Bearcat executives tell you that these patents represent the most significant breakthrough in the industry in the past 30 years. The products have been marketed under the registered trademarks Evertight, Duratainer, and Sealrite. Licenses under the patents have already been granted by your client to other manufacturers in the United States and abroad and are producing substantial royalties.

On July 1, Bearcat commenced patent infringement actions against several companies whose names you recognize as those of substantial and prominent competitors. Bearcat's management is optimistic that these suits will result in a permanent injunction against the manufacture and sale of the infringing products and collection of damages for loss of profits caused by the alleged infringement.

The financial vice president has suggested that the patents be recorded at the discounted value of expected net royalty receipts.

Instructions

(a) What is the meaning of "discounted value of expected net receipts"? Explain.
(b) How would such a value be calculated for net royalty receipts?
(c) What basis of valuation for Bearcat's patents would be generally accepted in accounting? Give supporting reasons for this basis.
(d) Assuming no practical problems of implementation and ignoring generally accepted accounting principles, what is the preferable basis of valuation for patents? Explain.

(e) What would be the preferable theoretical basis of amortization? Explain.

(f) What recognition, if any, should be made of the infringement litigation in the financial statements for the year ending September 30, 2003? Discuss.

(AICPA adapted)

 **C10-5** **(Accounting for Research and Development Costs)** Indiana Jones Co. is in the process of developing a revolutionary new product. A new division of the company was formed to develop, manufacture, and market this new product. As of year-end (December 31, 2003) the new product has not been manufactured for resale; however, a prototype unit was built and is in operation.

Throughout 2003 the new division incurred certain costs. These costs include design and engineering studies, prototype manufacturing costs, administrative expenses (including salaries of administrative personnel), and market research costs. In addition, approximately $900,000 in equipment (estimated useful life—10 years) was purchased for use in developing and manufacturing the new product. Approximately $315,000 of this equipment was built specifically for the design development of the new product. The remaining $585,000 of equipment was used to manufacture the pre-production prototype and will be used to manufacture the new product once it is in commercial production.

Instructions

(a) How are "research" and "development" defined in *Statement of Financial Accounting Standards No. 2?*

(b) Briefly indicate the practical and conceptual reasons for the conclusion reached by the Financial Accounting Standards Board on accounting and reporting practices for research and development costs.

(c) In accordance with *Statement of Financial Accounting Standards No. 2,* how should the various costs of Indiana Jones described above be recorded on the financial statements for the year ended December 31, 2003?

(AICPA adapted)

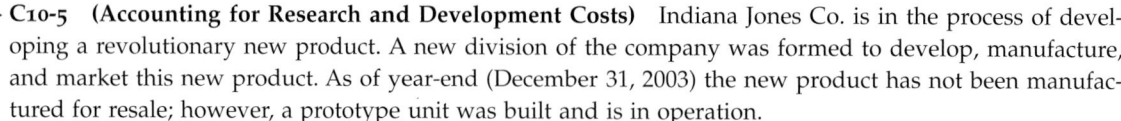

USING YOUR JUDGMENT

FINANCIAL REPORTING PROBLEM

3M COMPANY

The financial statements of 3M were provided with your book or can be accessed on the Take Action! CD.

Instructions

Refer to 3M's financial statements and the accompanying notes to answer the following questions.

(a) Does 3M report any intangible assets, especially goodwill, in its 2001 financial statements and accompanying notes?

(b) How much research and development (R&D) cost was expensed by 3M in 2001 and 2000? What percentage of sales revenue and net income did 3M spend on R&D in 2001 and 2000? How much does 3M expect to spend on R&D in 2002?

FINANCIAL STATEMENT ANALYSIS CASE

 ### MERCK AND JOHNSON & JOHNSON

Merck & Co., Inc. and Johnson & Johnson are two leading producers of health care products. Each has considerable assets, and each expends considerable funds each year toward the development of new products. The development of a new health care product is often very expensive, and risky. New products frequently must undergo considerable testing before approval for distribution to the public. For example, it took Johnson & Johnson 4 years and $200 million to develop its 1-DAY ACUVUE contact lenses. Below are some basic data compiled from the financial statements of these two companies.

(all dollars in millions)	Johnson & Johnson	Merck
Total assets	$15,668	$21,857
Total revenue	15,734	14,970
Net income	2,006	2,997
Research and development expense	1,278	1,230
Intangible assets	2,403	7,212

Instructions

(a) What kinds of intangible assets might a health care products company have? Does the composition of these intangibles matter to investors—that is, would it be perceived differently if all of Merck's intangibles were goodwill, than if all of its intangibles were patents?

(b) Suppose the president of Merck has come to you for advice. He has noted that by eliminating research and development expenditures the company could have reported $1.3 billion more in net income. He is frustrated because much of the research never results in a product, or the products take years to develop. He says shareholders are eager for higher returns, so he is considering eliminating research and development expenditures for at least a couple of years. What would you advise?

(c) The notes to Merck's financial statements note that Merck has goodwill of $4.1 billion. Where does recorded goodwill come from? Is it necessarily a good thing to have a lot of goodwill on your books?

COMPARATIVE ANALYSIS CASE

THE COCA-COLA COMPANY AND PEPSICO, INC.

Instructions

Go to the Take Action! CD and use information found there to answer the following questions related to **The Coca-Cola Company** and **PepsiCo. Inc.**

(a) **(1)** What amounts for intangible assets were reported in their respective balance sheets by Coca-Cola and PepsiCo?

(2) What percentage of total assets is each of these reported amounts?

(3) What was the change in the amount of intangibles from 2000 to 2001 for Coca-Cola and PepsiCo?

(b) **(1)** On what basis and over what periods of time did Coca-Cola and PepsiCo amortize their intangible assets?

(2) What were the amounts of accumulated amortization reported by Coca-Cola and PepsiCo at the end of 2001 and 2000?

(3) What was the composition of identifiable and unidentifiable intangible assets reported by Coca-Cola and PepsiCo at the end of 2001?

(c) What caused the significant increase in Coca-Cola's intangible assets in 2001?

INTERNATIONAL REPORTING CASE

BAYER AND SMITHKLINE BEECHAM

Presented below are data and accounting policy notes for the goodwill of three international drug companies. **Bayer**, a German company, prepares its statements in accordance with International Accounting Standards (IAS); **Smithkline Beecham** follows United Kingdom (U.K.) rules; and **Merck**, a U.S. company, prepares its financial statements in accordance with U.S. GAAP.

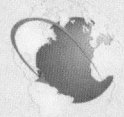

Related Information	Bayer (DM millions)	Smithkline Beecham (£ millions)	Merck ($ millions)
Amortization expense	136	69	0
Net income	3,157	606	5,248
Accumulated goodwill amortization	306	313	0
Stockholders' equity	24,991	1,747	31,853

The following accounting policy notes related to goodwill appeared with the companies' financial statements.

Bayer

Intangible assets that have been acquired are recognized at cost and amortized over their estimated useful lives. Goodwill, including that resulting from capital consolidation, is capitalized in accordance with *IAS 22* (Business Combinations) and normally is amortized over a period of 5 or at most 20 years.

Smithkline Beecham

Goodwill, representing the excess of the purchase consideration over the fair value of the net separable assets acquired, is capitalised and amortised over an appropriate period not exceeding 20 years.

Merck

Goodwill represents the excess of acquisition costs over the fair value of net assets of businesses purchased and is not amortized.

Instructions

(a) Compute the return on equity for each of these companies, and use this analysis to briefly discuss the relative profitability of the three companies.

(b) Assume that each of the companies uses the maximum allowable amortization period for goodwill. Discuss how these companies' goodwill amortization policies affect your ability to compare their amortization expense and income.

(c) Some analysts believe that the only valid way to compare companies that follow different goodwill accounting practices is to treat all goodwill as an asset and record expense only if the goodwill is impaired.[20] Using the data above, make these adjustments as appropriate, and compare the profitability of the three drug companies, comparing this information to your analysis in (a).

Remember to check the **Take Action! CD**
and the book's **companion Web site**
to find additional resources for this chapter.

---

[20]Trevor Harris, *Apples to Apples: Accounting for Value in World Markets* (New York: Morgan Stanley Dean Witter, February 1998).

ACCOUNTING FOR LIABILITIES

CHAPTER 11

YOUR DEBT IS KILLING MY STOCK

Traditionally, investors in the stock and bond markets operate in their own separate worlds. However, in recent volatile markets, even quiet murmurs in the bond market have been amplified into (usually negative) movements in stock prices. At one extreme, these gyrations heralded the demise of a company well before the investors could sniff out the problem.

The swift decline of **Enron** in late 2001 provided the ultimate lesson that a company with no credit is no company at all. As one analyst remarked, "You can no longer have an opinion on a company's stock without having an appreciation for its credit rating." Other energy companies, such as **Calpine**, **NRG Energy**, and **AES Corp.**, also felt the effect of Enron contagion as lenders tightened or closed down the credit supply and raised interest rates on already-high levels of debt. The result? Stock prices took a hit.

Other industries are not immune from the negative stock price effects of credit problems. Industrial conglomerate **Tyco International** felt these effects when questions about its merger accounting turned into concerns over its debt levels and liquidity. Equity investors headed for the exits, driving down the Tyco share price, even as management was reassuring them that the company was not in danger of default. Tyco investors were reluctant to believe the reassurances, given the company's high level of debt taken on to finance its growth through acquisition. This was yet another example of stock prices taking a hit due to concerns about credit quality. Thus, even if your investment tastes are in stocks, keep an eye on the liabilities.[1]

LEARNING OBJECTIVES

After studying this chapter, you should be able to:

1. Describe the nature, type, and valuation of current liabilities.

2. Identify various types of bond issues.

3. Describe the accounting valuation for bonds at date of issuance.

4. Describe the accounting procedures for the extinguishment of debt.

5. Identify the criteria used to account for and disclose gain and loss contingencies.

6. Explain the accounting for different types of loss contingencies.

7. Explain the reporting of off-balance-sheet financing arrangements.

8. Indicate how liabilities and contingencies are presented and analyzed.

[1]Adapted from Steven Vames, "Credit Quality, Stock Investing Seem to Go Hand in Hand," *Wall Street Journal* (April 1, 2002), p. R4.

As the opening story indicates, investors are paying considerable attention to a company's liabilities. Companies with high debt levels and the related impact of higher interest costs on income performance are being severely punished in the stock market. The purpose of this chapter is to explain the accounting issues related to liabilities. The content and organization of the chapter are as follows.

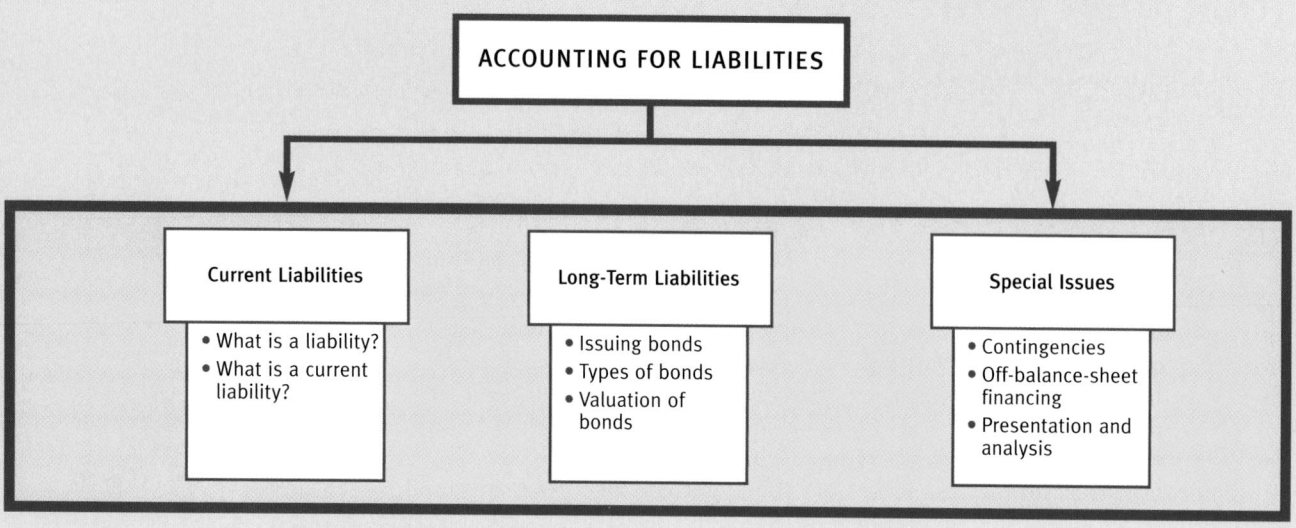

ACCOUNTING FOR LIABILITIES		
Current Liabilities	**Long-Term Liabilities**	**Special Issues**
• What is a liability? • What is a current liability?	• Issuing bonds • Types of bonds • Valuation of bonds	• Contingencies • Off-balance-sheet financing • Presentation and analysis

SECTION 1 | *CURRENT LIABILITIES*

WHAT IS A LIABILITY?

The question, "What is a liability?" is not easy to answer. For example, one might ask whether preferred stock is a liability or an ownership claim. The first reaction is to say that preferred stock is in fact an ownership claim and should be reported as part of stockholders' equity. In fact, preferred stock has many elements of debt as well.[2] The issuer (and in some cases the holder) often has the right to call the stock within a specific period of time—making it similar to a repayment of principal. The dividend is in many cases almost guaranteed (cumulative provision)—making it look like interest. And preferred stock is but one of many financial instruments that are difficult to classify.[3]

To help resolve some of these controversies, the FASB, as part of its conceptual framework study, defined **liabilities** as **"probable future sacrifices of economic benefits arising from present obligations of a particular entity to transfer assets or pro-**

---

[2]This illustration is not just a theoretical exercise. In practice, there are a number of preferred stock issues that have all the characteristics of a debt instrument, except that they are called and legally classified preferred stock. In some cases, the IRS has even permitted the dividend payments to be treated as interest expense for tax purposes.

[3]The FASB is considering a new standard for addressing these issues. See "Exposure Draft: Accounting for Financial Instruments with Characteristics of Liabilities, Equity, or Both," *Proposed Statement of Financial Accounting Standards* (Norwalk, Conn.: FASB, October 27, 2000).

vide services to other entities in the future as a result of past transactions or events."[4] In other words, a liability has three essential characteristics:

① It is a present obligation that entails settlement by probable future transfer or use of cash, goods, or services.

② It is an unavoidable obligation.

③ The transaction or other event creating the obligation has already occurred.

Because liabilities involve future disbursements of assets or services, one of their most important features is the date on which they are payable. Currently maturing obligations must be satisfied promptly and in the ordinary course of business if operations are to be continued. Liabilities with a more distant due date do not, as a rule, represent a claim on the enterprise's current resources and are therefore in a slightly different category. This feature gives rise to the basic division of liabilities into (1) current liabilities and (2) long-term debt.

WHAT IS A CURRENT LIABILITY?

Current assets are cash or other assets that can reasonably be expected to be converted into cash, sold, or consumed in operations within a single operating cycle or within a year if more than one cycle is completed each year. **Current liabilities are "obligations whose liquidation is reasonably expected to require use of existing resources properly classified as current assets, or the creation of other current liabilities."[5]** This definition has gained wide acceptance because it recognizes operating cycles of varying lengths in different industries and takes into consideration the important relationship between current assets and current liabilities.

The **operating cycle** is the period of time elapsing between the acquisition of goods and services involved in the manufacturing process and the final cash realization resulting from sales and subsequent collections. Industries that manufacture products requiring an aging process and certain capital-intensive industries have an operating cycle of considerably more than one year. On the other hand, most retail and service establishments have several operating cycles within a year.

Here are some typical current liabilities:

① Accounts payable.

② Notes payable.

③ Current maturities of long-term debt.

④ Dividends payable.

⑤ Unearned revenues.

⑥ Sales taxes payable.

⑦ Income taxes payable (discussed in Chapter 14).

⑧ Employee-related liabilities (discussed in Chapter 15).

OBJECTIVE 1
Describe the nature, type, and valuation of current liabilities.

In practice, current liabilities are usually recorded in accounting records and reported in financial statements at their full maturity value. Because of the short time periods involved, frequently less than one year, the difference between the present value of a current liability and the maturity value is not usually large. The slight overstate-

---

[4]"Elements of Financial Statements of Business Enterprises," *Statement of Financial Accounting Concepts No. 6* (Stamford, Conn.: FASB, 1980).

[5]Committee on Accounting Procedure, American Institute of Certified Public Accountants, "Accounting Research and Terminology Bulletins," Final Edition (New York: AICPA, 1961), p. 21.

ment of liabilities that results from carrying current liabilities at maturity value is accepted as immaterial.[6]

Accounts Payable

Accounts payable, or **trade accounts payable**, are balances owed to others for goods, supplies, or services purchased on open account. Accounts payable arise because of the time lag between the receipt of services or acquisition of title to assets and the payment for them. This period of extended credit is usually found in the terms of the sale (e.g., 2/10, n/30 or 1/10, E.O.M.) and is commonly 30 to 60 days.

Most accounting systems are designed to record liabilities for purchases of goods when the goods are received or, practically, when the invoices are received. Frequently there is some delay in recording the goods and the related liability on the books. If title has passed to the purchaser before the goods are received, the transaction should be recorded at the time of title passage. Attention must be paid to transactions occurring near the end of one accounting period and at the beginning of the next to ascertain that the record of goods received (the inventory) is in agreement with the liability (accounts payable) and that both are recorded in the proper period.

Measuring the amount of an account payable poses no particular difficulty because the invoice received from the creditor specifies the due date and the exact outlay in money that is necessary to settle the account. The only calculation that may be necessary concerns the amount of cash discount. See Chapter 8 for illustrations of entries related to accounts payable and purchase discounts.

Notes Payable

Notes payable are written promises to pay a certain sum of money on a specified future date and may arise from purchases, financing, or other transactions. In some industries, notes (often referred to as **trade notes payable**) are required as part of the sales/purchases transaction in lieu of the normal extension of open account credit. Notes payable to banks or loan companies generally arise from cash loans. Notes may be classified as short-term or long-term, depending upon the payment due date. Notes may also be interest-bearing or zero-interest-bearing.

Interest-Bearing Note Issued

Assume that Castle National Bank agrees to lend $100,000 on March 1, 2003, to Landscape Co. if Landscape Co. signs a $100,000, 12 percent, 4-month note. The entry to record the cash received by Landscape Co. on March 1 is:

March 1

Cash	100,000	
Notes Payable		100,000
(To record issuance of 12%, 4-month note to Castle National Bank)		

If Landscape Co. prepares financial statements semiannually, an adjusting entry is required to recognize interest expense and interest payable of $4,000 ($100,000 × 12% × 4/12) at June 30. The adjusting entry is:

[6]*APB Opinion No. 21,* "Interest on Receivables and Payables," specifically exempts from present value measurements those payables arising from transactions with suppliers in the normal course of business that do not exceed approximately one year.

June 30

Interest Expense	4,000	
Interest Payable		4,000
(To accrue interest for 4 months on Castle National		
Bank note)		

If Landscape prepared financial statements monthly, the adjusting entry at the end of each month would have been $1,000 ($100,000 × 12% × 1/12).

At maturity (July 1), Landscape Co. must pay the face value of the note ($100,000) plus $4,000 interest ($100,000 × 12% × 4/12).

The entry to record payment of the note and accrued interest is as follows.

July 1

Notes Payable	100,000	
Interest Payable	4,000	
Cash		104,000
(To record payment of Castle National Bank interest-		
bearing note and accrued interest at maturity)		

Zero-Interest-Bearing Note Issued

A zero-interest-bearing note may be issued instead of an interest-bearing note. A zero-interest-bearing note does not explicitly state an interest rate on the face of the note. **Interest is still charged**, however, because the borrower is required at maturity to pay back an amount greater than the cash received at the issuance date. In other words, the borrower receives in cash the present value of the note. The present value equals the face value of the note at maturity minus the interest or discount charged by the lender for the term of the note. In essence, the bank takes its fee "up front" rather than on the date the note matures.

To illustrate, assume that Landscape Co. issues a $104,000, 4-month, zero-interest-bearing note to Castle National Bank. The present value of the note is $100,000.[7] The entry to record this transaction for Landscape Co. is as follows.

March 1

Cash	100,000	
Discount on Notes Payable	4,000	
Notes Payable		104,000
(To record issuance of 4-month, zero-interest-bearing		
note to Castle National Bank)		

The Notes Payable account is credited for the face value of the note, which is $4,000 more than the actual cash received. The difference between the cash received and the face value of the note is debited to Discount on Notes Payable. **Discount on Notes Payable is a contra account to Notes Payable, and therefore is subtracted from Notes Payable on the balance sheet.** The balance sheet presentation on March 1 is as follows.

Current liabilities		
Notes payable	104,000	
Less: Discount on notes payable	4,000	100,000

Illustration 11-1
Balance Sheet
Presentation of Discount

[7]The bank discount rate used in this example to find the present value is 11.538 percent.

The amount of the discount, $4,000 in this case, represents the cost of borrowing $100,000 for 4 months. Accordingly, the discount is charged to interest expense over the life of the note. That is, the Discount on Notes Payable balance **represents interest expense chargeable to future periods.** Thus, it would be incorrect to debit Interest Expense for $4,000 at the time the loan is obtained.

Current Maturities of Long-Term Debt

The portion of bonds, mortgage notes, and other long-term indebtedness that matures within the next fiscal year—**current maturities of long-term debt**—is reported as a current liability. When only a part of a long-term debt is to be paid within the next 12 months, as in the case of serial bonds that are to be retired through a series of annual installments, **the maturing portion of long-term debt is reported as a current liability,** and the balance as a long-term debt.

Long-term debts maturing currently should not be included as current liabilities if they are to be:

1 retired by assets accumulated for this purpose that properly have not been shown as current assets,

2 refinanced, or retired from the proceeds of a new debt issue, or

3 converted into capital stock.

In these situations, the use of current assets or the creation of other current liabilities does not occur. Therefore, classification as a current liability is inappropriate. The plan for liquidation of such a debt should be disclosed either parenthetically or by a note to the financial statements.

However, a liability that is **due on demand** (callable by the creditor) or will be due on demand within a year (or operating cycle, if longer) should be classified as a current liability. Liabilities often become callable by the creditor when there is a violation of the debt agreement. For example, most debt agreements specify a given level of equity to debt be maintained, or specify that working capital be of a minimum amount. If an agreement is violated, classification of the debt as current is required because it is a reasonable expectation that existing working capital will be used to satisfy the debt. Only if it can be shown that it is **probable** that the violation will be cured (satisfied) within the grace period usually given in these agreements can the debt be classified as noncurrent.[8]

UNDERLYING CONCEPTS

Preferred dividends in arrears do represent a probable future economic sacrifice, but the expected sacrifice does not result from a past transaction or past event. The sacrifice will result from a future event (declaration by the board of directors). Note disclosure improves the predictive value of the financial statements.

Dividends Payable

A **cash dividend payable** is an amount owed by a corporation to its stockholders as a result of board of directors' authorization. At the date of declaration the corporation assumes a liability that places the stockholders in the position of creditors in the amount of dividends declared. Because cash dividends are always paid within one year of declaration (generally within 3 months), they are classified as current liabilities.

Accumulated but undeclared dividends on cumulative preferred stock are not a recognized liability because **preferred dividends in arrears** are not an obligation until formal action is taken by the board of directors authorizing the distribution of earnings. Nevertheless, the amount of cumulative dividends unpaid should be disclosed in a note, or it may be shown parenthetically in the capital stock section.

Dividends payable in the form of additional shares of stock are not recognized as a liability. Such **stock dividends** (as discussed in Chapter 12) do not require future outlays of assets or services and are revocable by the board of directors at any time prior

---

[8]"Classification of Obligations That Are Callable by the Creditor," *Statement of Financial Accounting Standards No. 78* (Stamford, Conn.: FASB, 1983).

to issuance. Even so, such undistributed stock dividends are generally reported in the stockholders' equity section because they represent retained earnings in the process of transfer to paid-in capital.

Unearned Revenues

A magazine publisher such as **Golf Digest** may receive a customer's check when magazines are ordered, and an airline company, such as **American Airlines**, often sells tickets for future flights. Restaurants may issue meal tickets that can be exchanged or used for future meals. Who hasn't received or given a **McDonald's** gift certificate? And software companies, like **Microsoft**, issue coupons that allow customers to upgrade to the next version of their software. How do these companies account for **unearned revenues** that are received before goods are delivered or services are rendered?

① When the advance is received, Cash is debited, and a current liability account identifying the source of the unearned revenue is credited.

② When the revenue is earned, the unearned revenue account is debited, and an earned revenue account is credited.

To illustrate, assume that Allstate University sells 10,000 season football tickets at $50 each for its five-game home schedule. The entry for the sales of season tickets is:

August 6

Cash	500,000	
Unearned Football Ticket Revenue		500,000
(To record sale of 10,000 season tickets)		

As each game is completed, the following entry is made.

September 7

Unearned Football Ticket Revenue	100,000	
Football Ticket Revenue		100,000
(To record football ticket revenues earned)		

Unearned Football Ticket Revenue is, therefore, unearned revenue and is reported as a current liability in the balance sheet. As revenue is earned, a transfer from unearned revenue to earned revenue occurs. Unearned revenue is material for some companies: In the airline industry, tickets sold for future flights represent almost 50 percent of total current liabilities. At **United Air Lines**, unearned ticket revenue is the largest current liability, recently amounting to over $1.4 billion.

Illustration 11-2 shows specific unearned and earned revenue accounts used in selected types of businesses.

Type of Business	Account Title	
	Unearned Revenue	Earned Revenue
Airline	Unearned Passenger Ticket Revenue	Passenger Revenue
Magazine publisher	Unearned Subscription Revenue	Subscription Revenue
Hotel	Unearned Rental Revenue	Rental Revenue
Auto dealer	Unearned Warranty Revenue	Warranty Revenue

Illustration 11-2
Unearned and Earned Revenue Accounts

The balance sheet should report obligations for any commitments that are redeemable in goods and services. The income statement should report revenues earned during the period.

WHAT DO THE NUMBERS MEAN?

WHAT ABOUT THAT SHORT-TERM DEBT?

The evaluation of credit quality involves more than simply assessing a company's ability to repay loans. Credit analysts also evaluate debt management strategies. Management decisions that are viewed as prudent will be rewarded with liquidity, lower debt service costs, and a higher stock price. The wrong decisions can bring higher debt costs and lower stock prices.

General Electric Capital Corp., a subsidiary of General Electric, recently experienced the negative effects of market scrutiny of its debt management policies when analysts complained that GE had been slow to refinance its mountains of short-term debt. GE had issued these current obligations, with maturities of 270 days or less, when interest rates were low. However, in light of expectations that the Fed would raise interest rates, analysts began to worry about the higher interest costs GE would pay when these loans were refinanced. Some analysts recommended that it was time to reduce dependence on short-term credit. The reasoning goes that a shift to more dependable long-term debt, thereby locking in slightly higher rates for the long-term, is the better way to go.

Thus, scrutiny of GE debt strategies led to analysts' concerns about GE's earnings prospects. Investors took the analysis to heart, and GE experienced a 2-day 6 percent drop in its stock price.

Source: Adapted from Steven Vames, "Credit Quality, Stock Investing Seem to Go Hand in Hand," *Wall Street Journal* (April 1, 2002), p. R4.

SECTION 2 | *LONG-TERM LIABILITIES*

Long-term debt consists of probable future sacrifices of economic benefits arising from present obligations that are not payable within a year or the operating cycle of the business, whichever is longer. Bonds payable, long-term notes payable, mortgages payable, pension liabilities, and lease liabilities are examples of long-term liabilities.

Incurring long-term debt is often accompanied by considerable formality. For example, the bylaws of corporations usually require approval by the board of directors and the stockholders before bonds can be issued or other long-term debt arrangements can be contracted.

Generally, long-term debt has various **covenants** or **restrictions** for the protection of both lenders and borrowers. The covenants and other terms of the agreement between the borrower and the lender are stated in the bond indenture or note agreement. Items often mentioned in the indenture or agreement include the amounts authorized to be issued, interest rate, due date(s), call provisions, property pledged as security, sinking fund requirements, working capital and dividend restrictions, and limitations concerning the assumption of additional debt. Whenever these stipulations are important for a complete understanding of the financial position and the results of operations, they should be described in the body of the financial statements or the notes.[9]

ISSUING BONDS

Bonds are the most common type of long-term debt reported on a company's balance sheet. The main purpose of bonds is to borrow for the long term when the amount of capital needed is too large for one lender to supply. By issuing bonds in $100, $1,000, or $10,000 denominations, a large amount of long-term indebtedness can be divided into many small investing units, thus enabling more than one lender to participate in the loan.

A bond arises from a contract known as a **bond indenture** and represents a promise to pay: (1) a sum of money at a designated maturity rate, plus (2) periodic interest at a specified rate on the maturity amount (face value). Individual bonds are evidenced by a paper certificate and typically have a $1,000 face value. Bond interest payments usually are made semiannually, although the interest rate is generally expressed as an annual rate.

An entire bond issue may be sold to an investment banker who acts as a selling agent in the process of marketing the bonds. In such arrangements, investment bankers may either underwrite the entire issue by guaranteeing a certain sum to the corporation, thus taking the risk of selling the bonds for whatever price they can get (firm underwriting), or they may sell the bond issue for a commission to be deducted from the proceeds of the sale (best efforts underwriting). Alternatively, the issuing company may choose to place privately a bond issue by selling the bonds directly to a large institution, financial or otherwise, without the aid of an underwriter (private placement).

TYPES OF BONDS

Some of the more common types of bonds found in practice are defined below.

> **OBJECTIVE 2**
> **Identify various types of bond issues.**

TYPES OF BONDS

SECURED AND UNSECURED BONDS. Secured bonds are backed by a pledge of some sort of collateral. Mortgage bonds are secured by a claim on real estate. Collateral trust bonds are secured by stocks and bonds of other corporations. Bonds not backed by collateral are **unsecured**. A **debenture bond** is unsecured. A "junk bond" is unsecured and also very risky, and therefore pays a high interest rate. These bonds are often used to finance leveraged buyouts.

---

[9]Although it would seem that these covenants provide adequate protection to the long-term debt holder, many bondholders suffer considerable losses when additional debt is added to the capital structure. Consider what can happen to bondholders in leveraged buyouts (LBOs), which are usually led by management. In an LBO of **RJR Nabisco**, for example, solidly rated 9⅜ percent bonds due in 2016 plunged 20 percent in value when management announced the leveraged buyout. Such a loss in value occurs because the additional debt added to the capital structure increases the likehood of default. Although bondholders have covenants to protect them, they often are written in a manner that can be interpreted in a number of different ways.

TERM, SERIAL BONDS, AND CALLABLE BONDS. Bond issues that mature on a single date are called **term bonds**, and issues that mature in installments are called **serial bonds**. Serially maturing bonds are frequently used by school or sanitary districts, municipalities, or other local taxing bodies that receive money through a special levy. **Callable bonds** give the issuer the right to call and retire the bonds prior to maturity.

CONVERTIBLE, COMMODITY-BACKED, AND DEEP DISCOUNT BONDS. If bonds are convertible into other securities of the corporation for a specified time after issuance, they are **convertible bonds**.

Two types of bonds have been developed in an attempt to attract capital in a tight money market—commodity-backed bonds and deep discount bonds. **Commodity-backed bonds** (also called **asset-linked bonds**) are redeemable in measures of a commodity, such as barrels of oil, tons of coal, or ounces of rare metal. To illustrate, Sunshine Mining, a silver mining producer, sold two issues of bonds redeemable with either $1,000 in cash or 50 ounces of silver, whichever is greater at maturity, and that have a stated interest rate of 8½ percent. The accounting problem is one of projecting the maturity value, especially since silver has fluctuated between $4 and $40 an ounce since issuance.

J. C. Penney Company sold the first publicly marketed long-term debt securities in the United States that do not bear interest. These **deep discount bonds**, also referred to as **zero-interest debenture bonds**, are sold at a discount that provides the buyer's total interest payoff at maturity.

REGISTERED AND BEARER (COUPON) BONDS. Bonds issued in the name of the owner are **registered bonds** and require surrender of the certificate and issuance of a new certificate to complete a sale. A **bearer** or **coupon bond**, however, is not recorded in the name of the owner and may be transferred from one owner to another by mere delivery.

INCOME AND REVENUE BONDS. Income bonds pay no interest unless the issuing company is profitable. **Revenue bonds**, so called because the interest on them is paid from specified revenue sources, are most frequently issued by airports, school districts, counties, toll-road authorities, and governmental bodies.

VALUATION OF BONDS PAYABLE—DISCOUNT AND PREMIUM

OBJECTIVE 3
Describe the accounting valuation for bonds at date of issuance.

The selling price of a bond issue is set by the supply and demand of buyers and sellers, relative risk, market conditions, and the state of the economy. The investment community values a bond at the present value of its future cash flows, which consist of (1) interest and (2) principal. The rate used to compute the present value of these cash flows is the interest rate that provides an acceptable return on an investment commensurate with the issuer's risk characteristics.

The interest rate written in the terms of the bond indenture (and ordinarily printed on the bond certificate) is known as the **stated, coupon,** or **nominal rate**. This rate, which is set by the issuer of the bonds, is expressed as a percentage of the **face value**, also called the **par value, principal amount,** or **maturity value,** of the bonds. If the rate employed by the investment community (buyers) differs from the stated rate, the present value of the bonds computed by the buyers (and the current purchase price) will differ from the face value of the bonds. The difference between the face value and the present value of the bonds is either a discount or premium.[10] If the bonds sell for less than face value, they are sold at a **discount**. If the bonds sell for more than face value, they are sold at a **premium**.

The rate of interest actually earned by the bondholders is called the **effective yield**, or **market rate**. If bonds sell at a discount, the effective yield is higher than the stated rate. Conversely, if bonds sell at a premium, the effective yield is lower than the stated rate. While the bond is outstanding, its price is affected by several variables, most notably the market rate of interest. There is an inverse relationship between the market interest rate and the price of the bond.

HOW'S MY RATING?

WHAT DO THE NUMBERS MEAN?

Two major publication companies, **Moody's Investors Service** and **Standard & Poor's Corporation** issue quality ratings on every public debt issue. The following table summarizes the ratings issued by Standard & Poor's, along with historical default rates on bonds with different ratings. As expected, bonds receiving the highest quality rating of AAA have the lowest historical default rates. And bonds rated below BBB, which are considered below investment grade ("junk bonds") experience default rates ranging from 20 to 50 percent.

Original Rating	Default Rate*
AAA	0.52%
AA	1.31
A	2.32
BBB	6.64
BB	19.52
B	35.76
CCC	54.38

*Percentage of defaults by issuers rated by Standard & Poor's over the past 15 years, based on rating they were initially assigned.
Data: Standard & Poor's Corp.

Because debt ratings reflect credit quality, they are closely monitored by the market when determining the required yield and pricing of bonds at issuance. For example, in late 2001, the spreads in the required yields between corporate investment grade and junk bonds ranged from 6 to 8 percent. For a company such as **WorldCom**, which issued over $11 billion in debt in 2001, every 1 percent of yield it saves by maintaining a higher credit rating translates into over $100 million dollars of reduced interest expense. Thus, it is not surprising that companies also keep a close watch on their credit rating.

Source: A. Borrus, M. McNamee, and H. Timmons, "The Credit Raters: How They Work and How They Might Work Better," *Business Week* (April 8, 2002), pp. 38–40.

---

[10]Until the 1950s it was common for corporations to issue bonds with low, even-percentage coupons (such as 4 percent) to demonstrate their financial solidity. Frequently, the result was large discounts. More recently, it has become acceptable to set the stated rate of interest on bonds in rather precise fractions (such as $10\frac{7}{8}$ percent). Companies usually attempt to align the stated rate as closely as possible with the market or effective rate at the time of issue.

To illustrate the computation of the **present value of a bond issue**, consider ServiceMaster which issues $100,000 in bonds, due in 5 years with 9 percent interest payable annually at year-end. At the time of issue, the market rate for such bonds is 11 percent. The following time diagram depicts both the interest and the principal cash flows.

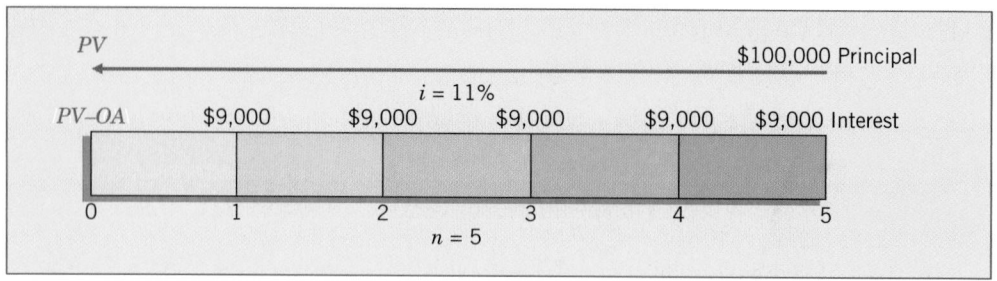

The actual principal and interest cash flows are discounted at an 11 percent rate for 5 periods as follows.

Illustration 11-3
Present Value
Computation of Bond
Selling at a Discount

Present value of the principal:	
$100,000 × .59345 (Appendix A, Table 2)	$59,345.00
Present value of the interest payments:	
$9,000 × 3.69590 (Appendix A, Table 4)	33,263.10
Present value (selling price) of the bonds	$92,608.10

By paying $92,608.10 at the date of issue, the investors will realize an effective rate or yield of 11 percent over the 5-year term of the bonds. These bonds would sell at a discount of $7,391.90 ($100,000 − $92,608.10). The price at which the bonds sell is typically stated as a percentage of the face or par value of the bonds. For example, the Service-Master bonds sold for 92.6 (92.6% of par). If ServiceMaster had received $102,000, we would say the bonds sold for 102 (102% of par).

When bonds sell below face value, it means that investors demand a rate of interest **higher** than the stated rate. The investors are not satisfied with the stated rate because they can earn a greater rate on alternative investments of equal risk. They cannot change the stated rate, so they refuse to pay face value for the bonds. Thus, by changing the amount invested, they alter the effective rate of return. The investors receive interest at the stated rate computed on the face value, but they are earning at **an effective rate that is higher than the stated rate because they paid less than face value for the bonds**.

Bonds Issued at Par on Interest Date

When bonds are issued on an interest payment date at par (face value), no interest has accrued, and no premium or discount exists. The accounting entry is made simply for the cash proceeds and the face value of the bonds. To illustrate, if 10-year term bonds with a par value of $800,000, dated January 1, 2003, and bearing interest at an annual rate of 10 percent payable semiannually on January 1 and July 1, are issued on January 1 at par, the entry on the books of the issuing corporation would be:

Cash	800,000	
Bonds Payable		800,000

The entry to record the first semiannual interest payment of $40,000 ($800,000 × .10 × 1/2) on July 1, 2003, would be as follows.

Bond Interest Expense	40,000	
Cash		40,000

The entry to record accrued interest expense at December 31, 2003 (year-end) would be as follows.

Bond Interest Expense	40,000	
Bond Interest Payable		40,000

Bonds Issued at Discount or Premium on Interest Date

If the $800,000 of bonds illustrated above were issued on January 1, 2003, at 97 (meaning 97% of par), the issuance would be recorded as follows.

Cash ($800,000 × .97)	776,000	
Discount on Bonds Payable	24,000	
Bonds Payable		800,000

Because of its relation to interest, as previously discussed, **the discount is amortized and charged to interest expense over the period of time that the bonds are outstanding**. The methods used to amortize the discount or premium are shown in Appendix 11A.

Classification of Discount and Premium

Discount on bonds payable is **not an asset** because it does not provide any future economic benefit. The enterprise has the use of the borrowed funds, but for that use it must pay interest. A bond discount means that the company borrowed less than the face or maturity value of the bond and therefore is faced with an actual (effective) interest rate higher than the stated (nominal) rate. Conceptually, discount on bonds payable is a liability valuation account; that is, it is a reduction of the face or maturity amount of the related liability. This account is referred to as a **contra account**.

Premium on bonds payable has no existence apart from the related debt. The lower interest cost results because the proceeds of borrowing exceed the face or maturity amount of the debt. Conceptually, premium on bonds payable is a liability valuation account; that is, it is an addition to the face or maturity amount of the related liability. This account is referred to as an **adjunct account**. As a result, **bond discount and bond premium are reported as a direct deduction from or addition to the face amount of the bond**.

Costs of Issuing Bonds

The issuance of bonds involves engraving and printing costs, legal and accounting fees, commissions, promotion costs, and other similar charges. According to *APB Opinion No. 21*, these items should be debited to a **deferred charge account** (asset) for Unamortized Bond Issue Costs and amortized over the life of the debt, in a manner similar to that used for discount on bonds.

The FASB, however, in *Concepts Statement No. 3* takes the position that debt issue cost can be treated as either an expense or a reduction of the related debt liability. Debt issue cost is not considered an asset because it provides no future economic benefit. The cost of issuing bonds, in effect, reduces the proceeds of the bonds issued and increases the effective interest rate. It thus may be accounted for the same as the unamortized discount.

There is an obvious difference between GAAP and *Concepts Statement No. 3*'s view of debt issue costs. Until a standard is issued to supersede *Opinion No. 21,* however, **acceptable GAAP for debt issue costs is to treat them as a deferred charge and amortize them over the life of the debt**.

To illustrate the accounting for costs of issuing bonds, assume that Microchip Corporation sold $20,000,000 of 10-year debenture bonds for $20,795,000 on January 1, 2004 (also the date of the bonds). Costs of issuing the bonds were $245,000. The entry at January 1, 2004, for issuance of the bonds would be as follows.

January 1, 2004

Cash	20,550,000	
Unamortized Bond Issue Costs	245,000	
Premium on Bonds Payable		795,000
Bonds Payable		20,000,000
(To record issuance of bonds)		

The bond issue costs are amortized over the life of the bonds.

Extinguishment of Debt

OBJECTIVE **4**
Describe the accounting procedures for the extinguishment of debt.

How is the payment of debt—often referred to as **extinguishment of debt**—recorded? If the bonds (or any other form of debt security) are held to maturity, the answer is straightforward: No gain or loss is computed. Any premium or discount and any issue costs will be fully amortized at the date the bonds mature. As a result, the carrying amount will be equal to the maturity (face) value of the bond. As the maturity or face value is also equal to the bond's market value at that time, no gain or loss exists.

In some cases, debt is extinguished before its maturity date. The amount paid on extinguishment or redemption before maturity, including any call premium and expense of reacquisition, is called the **reacquisition price**. On any specified date, the **net carrying amount** of the bonds is the amount payable at maturity, adjusted for unamortized premium or discount, and cost of issuance. Any excess of the net carrying amount over the reacquisition price is a **gain from extinguishment**, whereas the excess of the reacquisition price over the net carrying amount is a **loss from extinguishment**. At the time of reacquisition, **the unamortized premium or discount, and any costs of issue applicable to the bonds, must be amortized up to the reacquisition date**.

To illustrate, assume that on January 1, 1993, General Bell Corp. issued at 97 bonds with a par value of $800,000, due in 20 years. Bond issue costs totaling $16,000 were incurred. Eight years after the issue date, the entire issue is called at 101 and canceled.[11] At that time, the unamortized discount balance is $14,400, and the unamortized issue cost balance is $9,600. Illustration 11-4 indicates how the loss on redemption (extinguishment) is computed.

[11]The issuer of callable bonds is generally required to exercise the call on an interest date. Therefore, the amortization of any discount or premium will be up to date, and there will be no accrued interest. However, early extinguishments through purchases of bonds in the open market are more likely to be on other than an interest date. If the purchase is not made on an interest date, the discount or premium must be amortized, and the interest payable must be accrued from the last interest date to the date of purchase.

Illustration 11-4
Computation of Loss on
Redemption of Bonds

Reacquisition price ($800,000 × 1.01)		$808,000
Net carrying amount of bonds redeemed:		
Face value	$800,000	
Unamortized discount	(14,400)	
Unamortized issue costs	(9,600)	776,000
Loss on redemption		$ 32,000

*[$800,000 × (1 − .97)]

The entry to record the reacquisition and cancellation of the bonds is:

Bonds Payable	800,000	
Loss on Redemption of Bonds	32,000	
Discount on Bonds Payable		14,400
Unamortized Bond Issue Costs		9,600
Cash		808,000

Note that it is often advantageous for the issuing corporation to acquire the **entire** outstanding bond issue and replace it with a new bond issue bearing a lower rate of interest. The replacement of an existing issuance with a new one is called **refunding**. Whether the early redemption or other extinguishment of outstanding bonds is a non-refunding or a refunding situation, the difference (gain or loss) between the reacquisition price and the net carrying amount of the redeemed bonds should be recognized currently in income of the period of redemption.

MORE DEBT, PLEASE

WHAT DO THE NUMBERS MEAN?

As shown in the following charts, growth of U.S. corporate and consumer debt is outpacing the growth in assets. This increase in debt levels is sparking some concern for stock prices, with corporate debt exceeding $4.9 trillion and consumer debt exceeding $7.5 trillion in 2001—both are more than twice their 1989 levels.

Growth Rates for Corporate and Consumer Debt and Assets

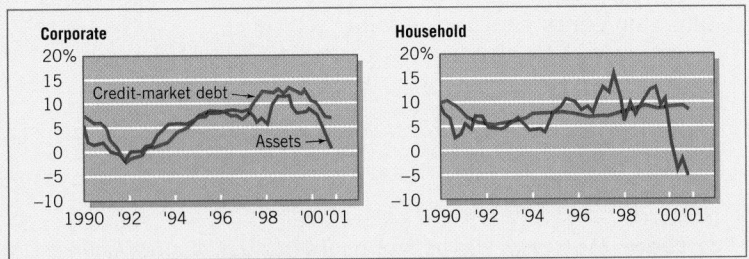

Increasing debt levels can be good indicators of the vibrancy of the economy, especially when the borrowed money is used to expand productive capacity or communications networks to better serve growing customer demand. Unfortunately, a substantial amount of the money borrowed by corporations in the recent debt run-up was used in share buybacks, some of which were used to compensate management via stock option plans.

Source: Adapted from Gregory Zuckerman, "Climb of Corporate Debt Trips Analysts' Alarm," *Wall Street Journal* (December 31, 2001), p. C1.

| SECTION 3 | *SPECIAL ISSUES* |

Presented in this section are three important issues related to liability accounting and presentation. These issues are as follows.

①. Contingencies.
②. Off-balance-sheet financing.
③. Presentation and analysis.

CONTINGENCIES

A **contingency** is defined as "an existing condition, situation, or set of circumstances involving uncertainty as to possible gain (**gain contingency**) or loss (**loss contingency**) to an enterprise that will ultimately be resolved when one or more future events occur or fail to occur."[12]

Gain Contingencies

OBJECTIVE 5
Identify the criteria used to account for and disclose gain and loss contingencies.

Gain contingencies are claims or rights to receive assets (or have a liability reduced) whose existence is uncertain but which may become valid eventually. The typical gain contingencies are:

①. Possible receipts of monies from gifts, donations, bonuses, and so on.
②. Possible refunds from the government in tax disputes.
③. Pending court cases where the probable outcome is favorable.
④. Tax loss carryforwards (discussed in Chapter 14).

A conservative policy is followed in this area. Gain contingencies are not recorded. They are disclosed in the notes only when the probabilities are high that a gain contingency will become a reality. As a result, it is unusual to find information about contingent gains in the financial statements and the accompanying notes. An example of a disclosure of a gain contingency is as follows.

Illustration 11-5
Disclosure of Gain
Contingency

BMC INDUSTRIES, INC.

Note 13: Legal Matters. In the first quarter, a U.S. District Court in Miami, Florida, awarded the Company a $5.1 million judgment against Barth Industries (Barth) of Cleveland, Ohio and its parent, Nesco Holdings, Inc. (Nesco). The judgment relates to an agreement under which Barth and Nesco were to help automate the plastic lens production plant in Fort Lauderdale, Florida. The Company has not recorded any income relating to this judgment because Barth and Nesco have filed an appeal.

[12]"Accounting for Contingencies," *Statement of Financial Accounting Standards No. 5* (Stamford, Conn.: FASB, 1975), par. 1.

Loss Contingencies

Loss contingencies are situations involving uncertainty as to possible loss. A liability incurred as a result of a loss contingency is by definition a **contingent liability**. Contingent liabilities are obligations that depend upon the occurrence of one or more future events to confirm either the amount payable, the payee, the date payable, or its existence. That is, these factors depend upon a contingency.

When a loss contingency exists, the likelihood that the future event or events will confirm the incurrence of a liability can range from probable to remote. The FASB uses the terms **probable**, **reasonably possible**, and **remote** to identify three areas within that range and assigns the following meanings.

Probable. The future event or events are likely to occur.

Reasonably possible. The chance of the future event or events occurring is more than remote but less than likely.

Remote. The chance of the future event or events occurring is slight.

An estimated loss from a loss contingency should be accrued by a charge to expense and a liability recorded only if **both** of the following conditions are met.[13]

1. Information available prior to the issuance of the financial statements indicates that it is **probable that a liability has been incurred** at the date of the financial statements.

2. The amount of the loss can be **reasonably estimated**.

Neither the exact payee nor the exact date payable need be known to record a liability. **What must be known is whether it is probable that a liability has been incurred.**

The second criterion indicates that an amount for the liability can be reasonably determined. Otherwise, it should not be accrued as a liability. Evidence to determine a reasonable estimate of the liability may be based on the company's own experience, experience of other companies in the industry, engineering or research studies, legal advice, or educated guesses by personnel in the best position to know.

Use of the terms probable, reasonably possible, and remote to classify contingencies involves judgment and subjectivity. The items in Illustration 11-6 (on page 532) are examples of loss contingencies and the general accounting treatment accorded them.

Practicing accountants express concern over the diversity that now exists in the interpretation of "probable," "reasonably possible," and "remote." Current practice relies heavily on the exact language used in responses received from lawyers (such language is necessarily biased and protective rather than predictive). As a result, accruals and disclosures of contingencies vary considerably in practice. Some of the more common loss contingencies are:[14]

1. Litigation, claims, and assessments.
2. Guarantee and warranty costs.
3. Environmental liabilities.
4. Self-insurance risks.

---

[13]Loss contingencies that result in the incurrence of a liability are discussed in this chapter. Loss contingencies that result in the impairment of an asset (e.g., collectibility of receivables or threat of expropriation of assets) are discussed in other sections of this textbook.

[14]*Accounting Trends and Techniques—2001* reports that of the 600 companies surveyed, loss contingencies were reported as follows: litigation, 468; environmental, 249; insurance, 58; possible tax assessments, 47; governmental investigation, 45; and others, 47.

Illustration 11-6
Accounting Treatment of
Loss Contingencies

Loss Related to	Usually Accrued	Not Accrued	May be Accrued*
1. Collectibility of receivables	X		
2. Obligations related to product warranties and product defects	X		
3. Premiums offered to customers	X		
4. Risk of loss or damage of enterprise property by fire, explosion, or other hazards		X	
5. General or unspecified business risks		X	
6. Risk of loss from catastrophes assumed by property and casualty insurance companies, including reinsurance companies		X	
7. Threat of expropriation of assets			X
8. Pending or threatened litigation			X
9. Actual or possible claims and assessments**			X
10. Guarantees of indebtedness of others			X
11. Obligations of commercial banks under "standby letters of credit"			X
12. Agreements to repurchase receivables (or the related property) that have been sold			X

*Should be accrued when both criteria are met (probable and reasonably estimable).

**Estimated amounts of losses incurred prior to the balance sheet date but settled subsequently should be accrued as of the balance sheet date.

Note that general risk contingencies that are inherent in business operations, such as the possibility of war, strike, uninsurable catastrophes, or a business recession, are not reported in the notes to the financial statements.

Litigation, Claims, and Assessments

The following factors, among others, must be considered in determining whether a liability should be recorded with respect to **pending or threatened litigation** and actual or possible **claims** and **assessments**.

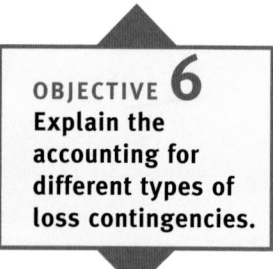

OBJECTIVE 6
Explain the accounting for different types of loss contingencies.

① The **time period** in which the underlying cause of action occurred.

② The **probability** of an unfavorable outcome.

③ The ability to make a **reasonable estimate** of the amount of loss.

To report a loss and a liability in the financial statements, **the cause for litigation must have occurred on or before the date of the financial statements**. It does not matter that the company did not become aware of the existence or possibility of the lawsuit or claims until after the date of the financial statements but before they are issued. To evaluate the probability of an unfavorable outcome, consider the following: the nature of the litigation; the progress of the case; the opinion of legal counsel; the experience of your company and others in similar cases; and any management response to the lawsuit.

The outcome of pending litigation, however, can seldom be predicted with any assurance. And, even if the evidence available at the balance sheet date does not favor the defendant, it is hardly reasonable to expect the company to publish in its financial statements a dollar estimate of the probable negative outcome. Such specific disclosures could weaken the company's position in the dispute and encourage the plaintiff to intensify its efforts. A typical example of the wording of such a disclosure is the note to the financial statements of **Apple Computer, Inc.**, relating to its litigation concerning repetitive stress injuries, as shown in Illustration 11-7.

APPLE COMPUTER, INC.

"Repetitive Stress Injury" Litigation. The Company is named in numerous lawsuits (fewer than 100) alleging that the plaintiff incurred so-called "repetitive stress injury" to the upper extremities as a result of using keyboards and/or mouse input devices sold by the Company. On October 4, in a trial of one of these cases (*Dorsey v. Apple*) in the United States District Court for the Eastern District of New York, the jury rendered a verdict in favor of the Company, and final judgment in favor of the Company has been entered. The other cases are in various stages of pretrial activity. These suits are similar to those filed against other major suppliers of personal computers. Ultimate resolution of the litigation against the Company may depend on progress in resolving this type of litigation in the industry overall.

Illustration 11-7
Disclosure of Litigation

With respect to **unfiled suits** and **unasserted claims and assessments**, a company must determine (1) the degree of **probability** that a suit may be filed or a claim or assessment may be asserted, and (2) the **probability** of an unfavorable outcome. For example, assume that Nawtee Company is being investigated by the Federal Trade Commission for restraint of trade, and enforcement proceedings have been instituted. Such proceedings are often followed by private claims of triple damages for redress. In this case, Nawtee Company must determine the probability of the claims being asserted **and** the probability of triple damages being awarded. If both are probable, if the loss is reasonably estimable, and if the cause for action is dated on or before the date of the financial statements, then the liability should be accrued.[15]

Guarantee and Warranty Costs

A **warranty (product guarantee)** is a promise made by a seller to a buyer to make good on a deficiency of quantity, quality, or performance in a product. It is commonly used by manufacturers as a sales promotion technique. Automakers, for instance, "hyped" their sales by extending their new-car warranty to 7 years or 100,000 miles. For a specified period of time following the date of sale to the consumer, the manufacturer may promise to bear all or part of the cost of replacing defective parts, to perform any necessary repairs or servicing without charge, to refund the purchase price, or even to "double your money back."

Warranties and guarantees entail future costs. These frequently are significant additional costs, which are sometimes called "after costs" or "post-sale costs." Although the future cost is indefinite as to amount, due date, and even customer, a liability is probable in most cases and should be recognized in the accounts if it can be reasonably estimated. The amount of the liability is an estimate of all the costs that will be incurred after sale and delivery and that are incident to the correction of defects or deficiencies required under the warranty provisions. Warranty costs are a classic example of a loss contingency.

---

[15]Contingencies involving an unasserted claim or assessment need not be disclosed when no claimant has come forward unless (1) it is considered probable that a claim will be asserted, and (2) there is a reasonable possibility that the outcome will be unfavorable.

There are two basic methods of accounting for warranty costs: (1) the cash basis method and (2) the accrual method.

Cash Basis Under the **cash basis method**, warranty costs are charged to expense as they are incurred. In other words, **warranty costs are charged to the period in which the seller or manufacturer complies with the warranty**. No liability is recorded for future costs arising from warranties, nor is the period in which the sale is recorded necessarily charged with the costs of making good on outstanding warranties. Use of this method, the only one recognized for income tax purposes, is frequently justified for accounting on the basis of expediency when warranty costs are immaterial or when the warranty period is relatively short. The cash basis method is required when a warranty liability is not accrued in the year of sale either because

⟨**1**⟩ it is not probable that a liability has been incurred, or
⟨**2**⟩ the amount of the liability cannot be reasonably estimated.

Accrual Basis If it is probable that customers will make claims under warranties relating to goods or services that have been sold and a reasonable estimate of the costs involved can be made, the accrual method must be used. Under the **accrual method**, warranty costs are charged to operating expense **in the year of sale**. It is the generally accepted method and should be used whenever the warranty is an integral and inseparable part of the sale and is viewed as a loss contingency. We refer to this approach as the **expense warranty approach**.

Illustration of Expense Warranty Approach. To illustrate the expense warranty method, assume that Denson Machinery Company begins production on a new machine in July 2003, and sells 100 units at $5,000 each by its year-end, December 31, 2003. Each machine is under warranty for one year. The company has estimated, based on past experience with a similar machine, that the warranty cost will probably average $200 per unit. Further, as a result of parts replacements and services rendered in compliance with machinery warranties, the company incurs $4,000 in warranty costs in 2003 and $16,000 in 2004.

⟨**1**⟩ Sale of 100 machines at $5,000 each, July through December 2003:

Cash or Accounts Receivable	500,000	
Sales		500,000

⟨**2**⟩ Recognition of warranty expense, July through December 2003:

Warranty Expense	4,000	
Cash, Inventory, Accrued Payroll		4,000
(Warranty costs incurred)		
Warranty Expense	16,000	
Estimated Liability under Warranties		16,000
(To accrue estimated warranty costs)		

The December 31, 2003, balance sheet would report Estimated Liability Under Warranties as a current liability of $16,000, and the income statement for 2003 would report Warranty Expense of $20,000.

⟨3⟩ Recognition of warranty costs incurred in 2004 (on 2003 machinery sales):

Estimated Liability under Warranties	16,000	
Cash, Inventory, or Accrued Payroll		16,000
(Warranty costs incurred)		

If the cash basis method were applied to the facts in the Denson Machinery Company example, $4,000 would be recorded as warranty expense in 2003 and $16,000 as warranty expense in 2004, with all of the sale price being recorded as revenue in 2003. In many instances, application of the cash basis method does not match the warranty costs relating to the products sold during a given period with the revenues derived from such products. In such instances, **it violates the matching principle**. Where ongoing warranty policies exist year after year, the differences between the cash and the expense warranty basis probably would not be so great.

Sales Warranty Approach.   A warranty is sometimes **sold separately from the product**. For example, when you purchase a television set or VCR, you will be entitled to the manufacturer's warranty. You also will undoubtedly be offered an extended warranty on the product at an additional cost.[16]

In this case, the seller should recognize separately the sale of the television or VCR with the manufacturer's warranty and the sale of the extended warranty.[17] This approach is referred to as the **sales warranty approach**. **Revenue on the sale of the extended warranty is deferred** and is generally recognized on a straight-line basis over the life of the contract. Revenue is deferred because the seller of the warranty has an obligation to perform services over the life of the contract. Only costs that vary with and are directly related to the sale of the contracts (mainly commissions) should be deferred and amortized. Costs such as employees' salaries, advertising, and general and administrative expenses that would have been incurred even if no contract were sold should be expensed as incurred.

To illustrate, assume you have just purchased a new automobile from Hanlin Auto for $20,000. In addition to the regular warranty on the auto (all repairs will be paid by the manufacturer for the first 36,000 miles or 3 years, whichever comes first), you purchase at a cost of $600 an extended warranty that protects you for an additional 3 years or 36,000 miles. The entry to record the sale of the automobile (with the regular warranty) and the sale of the extended warranty on January 2, 2003, on Hanlin Auto's books is:

Cash	20,600	
Sales		20,000
Unearned Warranty Revenue		600

The entry to recognize revenue at the end of the fourth year (using straight-line amortization) would be as follows.

Unearned Warranty Revenue	200	
Warranty Revenue		200

UNDERLYING CONCEPTS

Warranties are loss contingencies that satisfy the conditions necessary for a liability. Regarding the income statement, the *matching principle* requires that the related expense be reported in the period in which the sale occurs.

---

[16]A contract is separately priced **if the customer has the option to purchase** the services provided under the contract for an expressly stated amount separate from the price of the product. An extended warranty or product maintenance contract usually meets these conditions.

[17]"Accounting for Separately Extended Warranty and Product Maintenance Contracts," *FASB Technical Bulletin No. 90–1* (Stamford, Conn.: FASB, 1990).

Because the extended warranty contract does not start until after the regular warranty expires, revenue is not recognized until the fourth year. If the costs of performing services under the extended warranty contract are incurred on other than a straight-line basis (as historical evidence might indicate), revenue should be recognized over the contract period in proportion to the costs expected to be incurred in performing services under the contract.[18]

WHAT DO THE NUMBERS MEAN?

FREQUENT BUYERS

Numerous companies offer premiums to customers in the form of a promise of future goods or services as an incentive for purchases today. Premium plans that have widespread adoption are the **frequent-flyer programs** used by all major airlines. On the basis of mileage accumulated, frequent-flyer members are awarded discounted or free airline tickets. Airline customers can earn miles toward free travel by making long-distance phone calls, staying in hotels, and charging gasoline and groceries on a credit card. Those free tickets represent an enormous potential liability because people using them may displace paying passengers.

When airlines first started offering frequent-flyer bonuses, everyone assumed that they could accommodate the free-ticket holders with otherwise-empty seats. That made the additional cost of the program so minimal that airlines didn't accrue it or report the small liability. But, as more and more paying passengers have been crowded off flights by frequent-flyer awardees, the loss of revenues has grown enormously. For example, United Airlines recently reported a liability of $1.4 billion for advance ticket sales, some of which pertains to free frequent-flyer tickets.

Although the accounting for this transaction has been studied by the profession, no authoritative guidelines have been issued.

Environmental Liabilities

Estimates to clean up existing toxic waste sites run to upward of $752 billion over a 30-year period. In addition, the cost of cleaning up our air and preventing future deterioration of the environment is estimated to cost even more. The average environmental cost per firm in various industries at one time was: high-tech firms, $2 million (6.1% of revenues); utilities, $340 million (6.1% of revenues); steel and metals, $50 million (2.9% of revenues), and oil companies, $430 million (1.9% of revenues). Given that the average pretax profit of the 500 largest U.S. manufacturing companies recently was 7.7 percent of sales, these figures are staggering!

These costs will only grow when one considers "Superfund legislation." This federal legislation provides not only a government-supported fund to clean up pollution, but also a mandate to clean up existing waste sites. Further, it provided the Environmental Protection Agency (EPA) with the power to clean up waste sites and charge the clean-up costs to parties the EPA deems responsible for contaminating the site. These potentially responsible parties have an onerous liability. The EPA estimates that it will likely cost an average of $25 million to clean up each polluted site. For the most troublesome sites, the cost could easily reach $100 million or more.

In many industries, the construction and operation of long-lived assets involves obligations associated with the retirement of those assets. For example, when a mining company opens up a strip mine, it may also make a commitment to restore the land on which the mine is located once the mining activity is completed. Similarly, when an oil company erects an offshore drilling platform, it may be legally obligated to dismantle and remove the platform at the end of its useful life.

Accounting Recognition of Asset Retirement Obligations A company must recognize an **asset retirement obligation (ARO)** when the company has an existing legal obligation

[18]Ibid, par. 3.

associated with the retirement of a long-lived asset and when the amount of the liability can be reasonably estimated. The ARO should be recorded at fair value.[19]

Obligating Events.   Examples of existing legal obligations, which would require recognition of a liability include, but are not limited to:

- decommissioning nuclear facilities,
- dismantling, restoring, and reclamation of oil and gas properties,
- certain closure, reclamation, and removal costs of mining facilities,
- closure and post-closure costs of landfills.

In order to capture the benefits of these long-lived assets, **the company is generally legally obligated for the costs associated with retirement of the asset, whether the company hires another party to perform the retirement activities or performs the activities with its own workforce and equipment.** AROs give rise to various recognition patterns. For example, the obligation may arise at the outset of the asset's use (e.g., erection of an oil-rig), or it may build over time (e.g., a landfill that expands over time).

Measurement.   An ARO is initially measured at fair value, which is defined as the amount that the company would be required to pay in an active market to settle the ARO. While active markets do not exist for many AROs, an estimate of fair value should be based on the best information available. Such information could include market prices of similar liabilities, if available. Alternatively, fair value can be estimated based on present value techniques.

Recognition and Allocation.   To record an ARO in the financial statements, the cost associated with the ARO is included in the carrying amount of the related long-lived asset, and a liability is recorded for the same amount. An asset retirement cost is recorded as part of the related asset because these costs are considered a cost of operating the asset and are necessary to prepare the asset for its intended use. Therefore, the specific asset (e.g., mine, drilling platform, nuclear power plant) should be increased because the future economic benefit comes from the use of this productive asset. **The capitalized asset retirement costs should not be recorded in a separate account because there is no future economic benefit that can be associated with these costs alone.**

   In subsequent periods, the cost of the ARO is allocated to expense over the period of the related asset's useful life. While the straight-line method is acceptable for this allocation, other systematic and rational allocations also are permitted.

Illustration of ARO Accounting Provisions.   To illustrate the accounting for AROs, assume that on January 1, 2003, Wildcat Oil Company erected an oil platform in the Gulf of Mexico. Wildcat is legally required to dismantle and remove the platform at the end of its useful life, which is estimated to be 5 years. It is estimated that the total cost of dismantling and removal will be $1,000,000. Based on a 10 percent discount rate, the present value of the asset retirement obligation is $620,920 ($1,000,000 ×.62092). Wildcat would make the following journal entry to record this ARO.

January 1, 2003

Drilling Platform	620,920	
Asset Retirement Obligation		620,920

During the life of the asset, the asset retirement cost is allocated to expense. Using the straight-line method, Wildcat would make the following entries to record this expense.

---

[19]"Accounting for Asset Retirement Obligations," *Statement of Financial Accounting Standards No. 143* (Norwalk, Conn.: FASB, 2001).

December 31, 2003, 2004, 2005, 2006, 2007

Depreciation Expense ($620,920 ÷ 5)	124,184	
Accumulated Depreciation		124,184

In addition, interest expense must be accrued each period. The entry at December 31, 2003, to record interest expense and the related increase in the asset retirement obligation is as follows.

December 31, 2003

Interest Expense ($620,920 × 10%)	62,092	
Asset Retirement Obligation		62,092

On January 10, 2008, Wildcat contracts with Rig Reclaimers, Inc. to dismantle the platform at a contract price of $995,000. Wildcat would make the following journal entry to record settlement of the ARO.

January 10, 2008

Asset Retirement Obligation	1,000,000	
Gain on Settlement of ARO		5,000
Cash		995,000

UNDERLYING CONCEPTS

Even if the amount of losses is estimable with a high degree of certainty, the losses are not liabilities because they result from a future event and not from a past event.

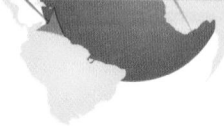

INTERNATIONAL INSIGHT

In Switzerland, companies may make provisions for general (non-specified) contingencies to the extent allowed by tax regulations.

More extensive disclosure is needed regarding environmental liabilities. In addition, more of these liabilities should be recorded. The SEC believes that managements should not delay recognition of a liability due to significant uncertainty. The SEC argues that if the liability is within a range and no amount within the range is the best estimate, then management should recognize the minimum amount of the range; that treatment is in accordance with *FASB Interpretation No. 14*, "Reasonable Estimation of the Amount of a Loss." The SEC also believes that environmental liabilities should be reported in the balance sheet independent of recoveries from third parties. Thus, possible insurance recoveries are not permitted to be netted against liabilities but must be shown separately. Because there is much litigation regarding recovery of insurance proceeds, these "assets" appear to be gain contingencies and, therefore, companies will not be reporting these on the balance sheet.[20]

Self-Insurance

A company may insure against many contingencies such as fire, flood, storm, and accident by taking out insurance policies and paying premiums to insurance companies. Some contingencies are, however, not insurable, or the insurance rates are prohibitive (e.g., earthquakes and riots). For such contingencies, even though insurance may be available, some businesses adopt a policy of self-insurance.

Despite its name, **self-insurance** is **not insurance**, **but risk assumption**. Any company that assumes its own risks puts itself in the position of incurring expenses or losses as they occur. There is little theoretical justification for the establishment of a liability based on a hypothetical charge to insurance expense. This is "as if" accounting. The conditions for accrual stated in *FASB Statement No. 5* are not satisfied prior to the occurrence of the event; until that time there is no diminution in the value of the prop-

---

[20]As indicated earlier, the FASB pronouncements on this topic require that, when some amount within the range appears at the time to be a better estimate than any other amount within the range, that amount is accrued. When no amount within the range is a better estimate than any other amount, the dollar amount at the low end of the range is **accrued** and the dollar amount at the high end of the range is **disclosed**. See *FASB Interpretation No. 14*, "Reasonable Estimation of the Amount of a Loss" (Stamford, Conn.: FASB, 1976), par. 3, and *FASB Statement No. 5*, "Accounting for Contingencies" (Stamford, Conn.: FASB, 1975).

erty. And unlike an insurance company, which has contractual obligations to reimburse policyholders for losses, a company can have no such obligation to itself and, hence, no liability either before or after the occurrence of damage.[21]

The following note from the annual report of **Adolph Coors Company** is typical of the self-insurance disclosure.

ADOLPH COORS COMPANY

Notes to Financial Statements

Note 4: Commitments and Contingencies. It is generally the policy of the Company to act as a self-insurer for certain insurable risks consisting primarily of physical loss to corporate property, business interruption resulting from such loss, employee health insurance programs, and workers' compensation. Losses and claims are accrued as incurred.

Illustration 11-8
Disclosure of Self-Insurance

Exposure to **risks of loss resulting from uninsured past injury to others**, however, is an existing condition involving uncertainty about the amount and timing of losses that may develop. In such a case, a contingency exists. A company with a fleet of vehicles for example, would have to accrue uninsured losses resulting from injury to others or damage to the property of others that took place prior to the date of the financial statements (if the experience of the company or other information enables it to make a reasonable estimate of the liability). However, it should not establish a liability for **expected future injury** to others or damage to the property of others, even if the amount of losses is reasonably estimable.

OFF-BALANCE-SHEET FINANCING

What do **Krispy Kreme, Cisco, Enron,** and **Aldephi Communications** have in common? They all have been accused of using off-balance-sheet financing to minimize the reporting of debt on their balance sheets. **Off-balance-sheet financing** is an attempt to borrow monies is such a way that the obligations are not recorded. It has become an issue of extreme importance because many allege that Enron, in one of the largest corporate failures on record, hid a considerable amount of its debt off the balance sheet. As a result, any company that uses off-balance-sheet financing today is taking the risk that investors (given their concerns about what happened at Enron) will dump their stock, and share price will suffer. Nevertheless, a considerable amount of off-balance-sheet financing will continue to exist. As one writer noted, "The basic drives of humans are few: to get enough food, to find shelter, and to keep debt off the balance sheet."

OBJECTIVE 7
Explain the reporting of off-balance-sheet financing arrangements.

Different Forms

Off-balance-sheet financing can take many different forms. Here are a few examples:

1. **Non-Consolidated Subsidiary:** Under present GAAP, a parent company does not have to consolidate a subsidiary company that is less than 50 percent owned. In such cases, the parent therefore does not report the assets and liabilities of the

[21]"Accounting for Contingencies," *FASB Statement No. 5*, op. cit., par. 28. A commentary in *Forbes* (June 15, 1974), p. 42, stated its position on this matter quite succinctly: "The simple and unquestionable fact of life is this: Business is cyclical and full of unexpected surprises. Is it the role of accounting to disguise this unpleasant fact and create a fairyland of smoothly rising earnings? Or, should accounting reflect reality, warts and all—floods, expropriations and all manner of rude shocks?"

subsidiary. All the parent reports on its balance sheet is the investment in the subsidiary. As a result, users of the financial statements may not understand that the subsidiary has considerable debt for which the parent may ultimately be liable if the subsidiary runs into financial difficulty.

② **Special Purpose Entity (SPE):** A **special purpose entity** is an entity created by a company to perform a special project. To illustrate, assume that Clarke Company has decided to build a new factory. In determining whether to build the new factory, an important variable in the decision is that management does not want to report on its balance sheet the borrowing used to fund the construction. It therefore creates an SPE whose sole purpose is to build the plant. The SPE finances and builds the plant, and then Clarke Company guarantees that all the products produced by the plant will be purchased, either by Clarke Company or some outside party. (Some refer to this as a **take-or-pay contract**). As a result, Clarke Company does not report the asset or liability on its books. It should be emphasized that the accounting rules in this area are complex, but a company can achieve this objective with relative ease.

③ **Operating Leases:** Another way that companies keep debt of the balance sheet is by leasing. Instead of owning the assets, companies lease them. Again, by meeting certain conditions, the company has to report only rent expense each period and to provide note disclosure of the transaction. It should be noted that SPEs often use leases to accomplish off-balance-sheet treatment. Accounting for lease transactions is discussed extensively in Chapter 16.

Rationale

Why do companies engage in off-balance-sheet financing? A major reason is that many believe that **removing debt enhances the quality of the balance sheet** and permits credit to be obtained more readily and at less cost.

Second, loan covenants often impose a limitation on the amount of debt a company may have. As a result, off-balance-sheet financing is used, because **these types of commitments might not be considered in computing the debt limitation**.

Third, it is argued by some that the asset side of the balance sheet is severely understated. For example, companies that use LIFO costing for inventories and depreciate assets on an accelerated basis will often have carrying amounts for inventories and property, plant, and equipment that are much lower than their current values. As an offset to these lower values, some managements believe that part of the debt does not have to be reported. In other words, **if assets were reported at current values**, less pressure would undoubtedly exist for off-balance-sheet financing arrangements.

Whether the arguments above have merit is debatable. The general idea "out of sight, out of mind" may not be true in accounting. Many users of financial statements indicate that they factor these off-balance-sheet financing arrangements into their computations when assessing debt to equity relationships. Similarly, many loan covenants also attempt to take these complex arrangements into account. Nevertheless, many companies still believe that benefits will accrue if certain obligations are not reported on the balance sheet.

The FASB response to off-balance-sheet financing arrangements has been increased disclosure (note) requirements. This response is consistent with an "efficient markets" philosophy: the important question is not whether the presentation is off-balance-sheet or not, but whether the items are disclosed at all.[22] The authors believe that financial reporting would be enhanced if more obligations were recorded on the balance sheet

---

[22]It is unlikely that the FASB will be able to stop all types of off-balance-sheet transactions. Financial information is the Holy Grail of Wall Street. Developing new financial instruments and arrangements to sell and market to customers is not only profitable, but also adds to the prestige of the investment firms that create them. Thus, new financial products will continue to appear that will test the ability of the FASB to develop appropriate accounting standards for them.

instead of merely described in the notes to the financial statements. Given the problems with companies such as **Enron, Dynergy, Williams Company, Adelphia Communications**, and **Calpine**, our expectation is that less off-balance-sheet financing will occur in the future.

PRESENTATION AND ANALYSIS

Presentation of Current Liabilities

The current liabilities accounts are commonly presented as the first classification in the liabilities and stockholders' equity section of the balance sheet. Within the current liabilities section the accounts may be listed in order of maturity, in descending order of amount, or in order of liquidation preference.

Detail and supplemental information concerning current liabilities should be sufficient to meet the requirement of full disclosure. Secured liabilities should be identified clearly, and the related assets pledged as collateral indicated. If the due date of any liability can be extended, the details should be disclosed. Current liabilities should not be offset against assets that are to be applied to their liquidation.

OBJECTIVE 8
Indicate how liabilities and contingencies are presented and analyzed.

Additional Disclosures of Current Liabilities

Presentation of Long-Term Debt

Companies that have large amounts and numerous issues of long-term debt frequently report only one amount in the balance sheet and support this with comments and schedules in the accompanying notes. Long-term debt that **matures within one year** should be reported as a current liability, unless retirement is to be accomplished with other than current assets. If the debt is to be refinanced, converted into stock, or is to be retired from a bond retirement fund, it should continue to be reported as noncurrent and accompanied with a note explaining the method to be used in its liquidation.

Note disclosures generally indicate the nature of the liabilities, maturity dates, interest rates, call provisions, conversion privileges, restrictions imposed by the creditors, and assets designated or pledged as security. Any assets pledged as security for the debt should be shown in the assets section of the balance sheet. The fair value of the long-term debt should also be disclosed if it is practical to estimate fair value. Finally, disclosure is required of future payments for sinking fund requirements and maturity amounts of long-term debt during each of the next 5 years. The purpose of these disclosures is to aid financial statement users in evaluating the amounts and timing of future cash flows. An example of the type of information provided is shown in Illustration 11-9 (on page 542) for **Best Buy Co.** Note that if the company has any off-balance-sheet financing, extensive note disclosure must be provided.

Presentation of Contingencies

A loss contingency and a liability is recorded if the loss is both probable and estimable. But, if the loss is **either probable or estimable but not both**, and if there is at least a **reasonable possibility** that a liability may have been incurred, the following disclosure in the notes is required.

INTERNATIONAL INSIGHT

U.S. GAAP provides more guidance on the content of disclosures about contingencies than do IASC standards.

1. The nature of the contingency.
2. An estimate of the possible loss or range of loss or a statement that an estimate cannot be made.

Certain other contingent liabilities that should be disclosed even though the possibility of loss may be remote are the following.

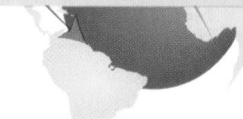

1. Guarantees of indebtedness of others.
2. Obligations of commercial banks under "stand-by letters of credit."

Illustration 11-9
Liability and Contingency Disclosure

BEST BUY CO.
(dollars in thousands)

	March 3, 2001	Feb. 26, 2000
Current assets		
Cash and cash equivalents	$ 746,879	$ 750,723
Receivables	209,031	189,301
Recoverable costs from developed properties	103,846	72,770
Merchandise inventories	1,766,934	1,183,681
Other current assets	101,973	41,985
Total current assets	2,928,663	2,238,460
Current liabilities		
Accounts payable	$1,772,722	$1,313,940
Accrued compensation and related expenses	154,159	102,065
Accrued liabilities	545,590	287,888
Accrued income taxes	127,287	65,366
Current portion of long-term debt	114,940	15,790
Total current liabilities	2,714,698	1,785,049
Long-term liabilities	121,952	99,448
Long-term debt (Note 3.)	181,009	14,860

Note 3. Debt (in part)

	March 3, 2001	Feb. 26, 2000
Senior subordinated notes, face amount $109,500, unsecured, due 2003, interest rate 9.0%, effective rate 8.9%	$ 110,471	$ —
Senior subordinated notes, face amount $150,000, unsecured, due 2008, interest rate 9.9%, effective rate 8.5%	160,574	—
Mortgage and other debt, interest rates ranging from 5.3% to 9.4%	24,904	30,650
Total debt	295,949	30,650
Less current portion	(114,940)	(15,790)
Long-term debt	$ 181,009	$ 14,860

The mortgage and other debt are secured by certain property and equipment with a net book value of $43,500 and $35,600 at March 3, 2001, and February 26, 2000, respectively.

During fiscal 2001, 2000, and 1999, interest paid totaled $7,000, $5,300, and $23,800, respectively.

During fiscal 2001, 2000, and 1999, interest expense totaled $6,900, $5,100, and $19,400, respectively, and is included in net interest income. The fair value of long-term debt approximates the carrying value.

The future maturities of long-term debt consist of the following:

Fiscal Year	
2002	$114,940
2003	2,036
2004	895
2005	745
2006	810
Thereafter	176,523
	$295,949

Note 9. Legal Proceedings
The Company is involved in various legal proceedings arising during the normal course of conducting business. Management believes that the resolution of these proceedings, either individually or in the aggregate, will not have a significant adverse impact on the Company's consolidated financial statements.

③ Guarantees to repurchase receivables (or any related property) that have been sold or assigned.

Disclosure should include the nature and amount of the guarantee and, if estimable, the amount that could be recovered from outside parties.

Analysis of Current Liabilities

The distinction between current liabilities and long-term debt is important because it provides information about the liquidity of the company. Liquidity regarding a liability is the time that is expected to elapse until a liability has to be paid. In other words, a liability soon to be paid is a current liability. A liquid company is better able to withstand a financial downturn. Also, it has a better chance of taking advantage of investment opportunities that develop.

Certain basic ratios such as net cash flow provided by operating activities to current liabilities, and the turnover ratios for receivables and inventory, are used to assess liquidity. Two other ratios used to examine liquidity are the current ratio and the acid-test ratio.

The **current ratio** is the ratio of total current assets to total current liabilities. The formula is shown below.

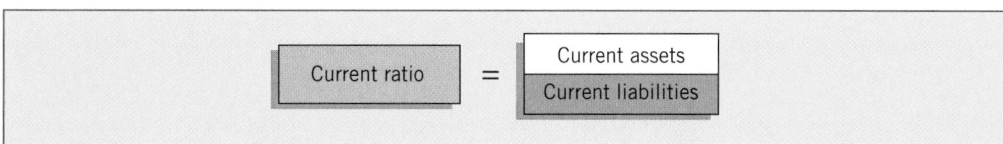

Illustration 11-10
Formula for Current Ratio

It is frequently expressed as a coverage of so many times. Sometimes it is called the **working capital ratio** because working capital is the excess of current assets over current liabilities.

A satisfactory current ratio does not disclose that a portion of the current assets may be tied up in slow-moving inventories. With inventories, especially raw materials and work in process, there is a question of how long it will take to transform them into the finished product and what ultimately will be realized in the sale of the merchandise. Elimination of the inventories, along with any prepaid expenses from the current assets, might provide better information for the short-term creditors. Many analysts favor an **acid-test** or **quick ratio** that relates total current liabilities to cash, marketable securities, and receivables. The formula for this ratio is shown below.

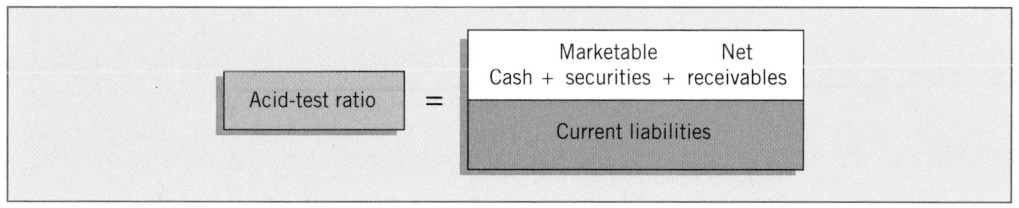

Illustration 11-11
Formula for Acid-Test Ratio

To illustrate the computation of these two ratios, we use the information for **Best Buy Co.**, reported in Illustration 11-9. The computation of the current and acid-test ratios for Best Buy are shown in Illustration 11-12 (on page 544).

From this information, it appears that Best Buy's current position is adequate. The acid-test ratio is well below 1, and a comparison to another retailer, **Circuit City**, whose acid-test ratio is 0.80, indicates that Best Buy may be carrying more inventory than its industry counterparts.

Illustration 11-12
Computation of Current
and Acid-Test Ratios for
Best Buy

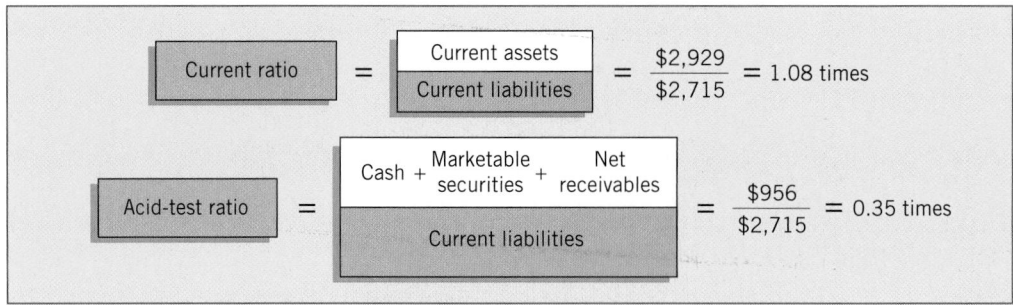

Analysis of Long-Term Debt

Long-term creditors and stockholders are interested in a company's long-run solvency, particularly its ability to pay interest as it comes due and to repay the face value of the debt at maturity. Debt to total assets and times interest earned are two ratios that provide information about debt-paying ability and long-run solvency.

The **debt to total assets ratio** measures the percentage of the total assets provided by creditors. It is computed as shown in the following formula by dividing total debt (both current and long-term liabilities) by total assets.

Illustration 11-13
Computation of Debt to
Total Assets Ratio

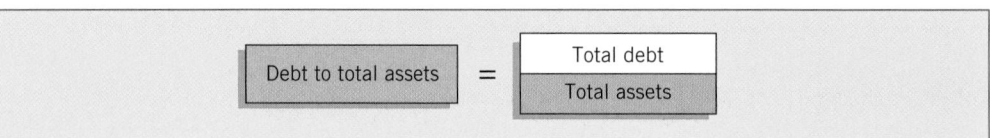

The higher the percentage of debt to total assets, the greater the risk that the company may be unable to meet its maturing obligations.

The **times interest earned ratio** indicates the company's ability to meet interest payments as they come due. It is computed by dividing income before interest expense and income taxes by interest expense.

Illustration 11-14
Computation of Times
Interest Earned Ratio

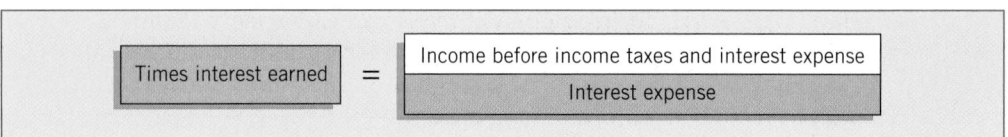

To illustrate these ratios, we will use data from **Best Buy**'s 2001 Annual Report, which disclosed total liabilities of $3,018 million, total assets of $4,840 million, interest expense of $6.9 million, income taxes of $246 million, and net income of $396 million. Best Buy's debt to total assets and times interest earned ratios are computed as follows.

Illustration 11-15
Computation of Long-
Term Debt Ratios for
Best Buy

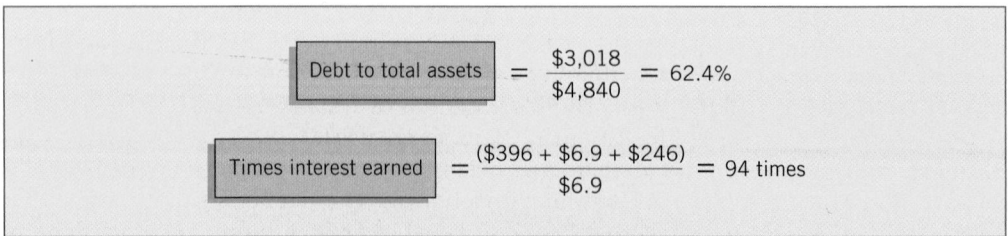

Even though Best Buy has a relatively high debt to total assets percentage of 62.4 percent, its interest coverage of 94 times indicates it can easily meet its interest payments as they come due.

SUMMARY OF LEARNING OBJECTIVES

❶ Describe the nature, type, and valuation of current liabilities. Current liabilities are obligations whose liquidation is reasonably expected to require the use of current assets or the creation of other current liabilities. Theoretically, liabilities should be measured by the present value of the future outlay of cash required to liquidate them. In practice, current liabilities are usually recorded in accounting records and reported in financial statements at their full maturity value.

There are several types of liabilities, such as: (1) accounts payable, (2) notes payable, (3) current maturities of long-term debt, (4) dividends payable, (5) unearned revenues, (6) taxes payable, and (7) employee-related liabilities.

❷ Identify various types of bond issues. Various types of bond issues are: (1) *Secured and unsecured bonds.* (2) *Term, serial bonds, and callable bonds.* (3) *Convertible, commodity-backed, and deep discount bonds.* (4) *Registered and bearer (coupon) bonds.* (5) *Income and revenue bonds.* The variety in the types of bonds is a result of attempts to attract capital from different investors and risk takers and to satisfy the cash flow needs of the issuers.

❸ Describe the accounting valuation for bonds at date of issuance. The investment community values a bond at the present value of its future cash flows, which consist of interest and principal. The rate used to compute the present value of these cash flows is the interest rate that provides an acceptable return on an investment commensurate with the issuer's risk characteristics. The interest rate written in the terms of the bond indenture and ordinarily appearing on the bond certificate is the stated, coupon, or nominal rate. This rate, which is set by the issuer of the bonds, is expressed as a percentage of the face value (also called the par value, principal amount, or maturity value) of the bonds. If the rate employed by the buyers differs from the stated rate, the present value of the bonds computed by the buyers will differ from the face value of the bonds. The difference between the face value and the present value of the bonds is either a discount or premium.

❹ Describe the accounting procedures for the extinguishment of debt. At the time of reacquisition, the unamortized premium or discount and any costs of issue applicable to the debt must be amortized up to the reacquisition date. The amount paid on extinguishment or redemption before maturity, including any call premium and expense of reacquisition, is the reacquisition price. On any specified date, the net carrying amount of the debt is the amount payable at maturity, adjusted for unamortized premium or discount, and cost of issuance. Any excess of the net carrying amount over the reacquisition price is a gain from extinguishment, whereas the excess of the reacquisition price over the net carrying amount is a loss from extinguishment. Gains and losses on extinguishments are recognized currently in income.

❺ Identify the criteria used to account for and disclose gain and loss contingencies. Gain contingencies are not recorded. They are disclosed in the notes only when the probabilities are high that a gain contingency will become a reality. An estimated loss from a loss contingency should be accrued by a charge to expense and a liability recorded only if both of the following conditions are met: (1) Information available prior to the issuance of the financial statements indicates that it is probable that a liability has been incurred at the date of the financial statements, and (2) the amount of the loss can be reasonably estimated.

❻ Explain the accounting for different types of loss contingencies. (1) The following factors must be considered in determining whether a liability should be recorded with

KEY TERMS

acid-test (quick) ratio, *543*
asset retirement obligation (ARO), *536*
bearer (coupon) bonds, *524*
bond discount, *525*
bond indenture, *523*
bond premium, *525*
callable bonds, *524*
cash dividend payable, *520*
commodity-backed bonds, *524*
contingency, *530*
contingent liabilities, *531*
convertible bonds, *524*
current liabilities, *517*
current maturities of long-term debt, *520*
current ratio, *543*
debenture bonds, *523*
debt to total assets ratio, *544*
deep discount (zero-interest) debenture bonds, *524*
effective yield, or market rate, *525*
expense warranty approach, *534*
extinguishment of debt, *528*
face, par, principal or maturity value, *524*
gain contingencies, *530*
income bonds, *524*
liabilities, *516*
litigation, claims, and assessments, *532*
long-term debt, *522*
loss contingencies, *531*
notes payable (trade notes payable), *518*
off-balance-sheet financing, *539*
operating cycle, *517*
preferred dividends in arrears, *520*
present value of a bond issue, *526*
probable (contingency), *531*
reasonably possible (contingency), *531*

refunding, *529*
registered bonds, *524*
remote (contingency), *531*
revenue bonds, *524*
sales warranty
    approach, *535*
secured bonds, *523*
self-insurance, *538*
serial bonds, *524*
special purpose entity
    (SPE), *540*
stated, coupon, or nominal
    rate, *524*
take-or-pay contract, *540*
term bonds, *524*
times interest earned
    ratio, *544*
trade accounts payable, *518*
trade notes payable, *518*
unearned revenues, *521*
warranty, *533*
zero-interest debenture
    bonds, *524*

respect to pending or threatened litigation and actual or possible claims and assessments: (a) the time period in which the underlying cause for action occurred; (b) the probability of an unfavorable outcome; and (c) the ability to make a reasonable estimate of the amount of loss.

(2) If it is probable that customers will make claims under warranties relating to goods or services that have been sold and a reasonable estimate of the costs involved can be made, the accrual method must be used. Warranty costs under the accrual basis are charged to operating expense in the year of sale.

(3) Asset retirement obligations must be recognized when a company has an existing legal obligation related to the retirement of a long-lived asset and the amount can be reasonably estimated.

7 Explain the reporting of off-balance-sheet financing arrangements. Off-balance-sheet financing is an attempt to borrow funds in such a way that the obligations are not recorded. Examples of off-balance-sheet arrangements are (1) non-consolidated subsidiaries, (2) special purpose entities, and (3) operating leases.

8 Indicate how liabilities and contingencies are presented and analyzed. The current liability accounts are commonly presented as the first classification in the liabilities and stockholders' equity section of the balance sheet. Within the current liabilities section the accounts may be listed in order of maturity, in descending order of amount, or in order of liquidation preference. Detail and supplemental information concerning current liabilities should be sufficient to meet the requirement of full disclosure. If the loss is either probable or estimable but not both, and if there is at least a reasonable possibility that a liability may have been incurred, disclosure should be made in the notes of the nature of the contingency and an estimate given of the possible loss. Two ratios used to analyze liquidity are the current and acid-test ratios.

Companies that have large amounts and numerous issues of long-term debt frequently report only one amount in the balance sheet and support this with comments and schedules in the accompanying notes. Any assets pledged as security for the debt should be shown in the assets section of the balance sheet. Long-term debt that matures within one year should be reported as a current liability, unless retirement is to be accomplished with other than current assets. If the debt is to be refinanced, converted into stock, or is to be retired from a bond retirement fund, it should continue to be reported as noncurrent and accompanied with a note explaining the method to be used in its liquidation. Disclosure is required of future payments for sinking fund requirements and maturity amounts of long-term debt during each of the next 5 years. Debt to total assets and times interest earned are two ratios that provide information about debt-paying ability and long-run solvency.

REVIEW EXERCISE

Honoré de Balzac Inc. has been producing quality children's apparel for more than 25 years. The company's fiscal year runs from April 1 to March 31. The following information relates to the obligations of Balzac as of March 31, 2002.

Bonds Payable

Balzac issued $5,000,000 of 11% bonds on July 1, 1996, at par. The bonds will mature on July 1, 2006. Interest is paid semiannually on July 1 and January 1.

Notes Payable

Balzac has signed several long-term notes with financial institutions and insurance companies. The maturities of these notes are given in the schedule below. The total unpaid interest for all of these notes amounts to $210,000 on March 31, 2002.

Due Date	Amount Due
April 1, 2002	$ 200,000
July 1, 2002	300,000
October 1, 2002	150,000
January 1, 2003	150,000
April 1, 2003 – March 31, 2004	600,000
April 1, 2004 – March 31, 2005	500,000
	$1,900,000

Estimated Warranties

Balzac has a one-year product warranty on some selected items in its product line. The estimated warranty liability on sales made during the 2000–01 fiscal year and still outstanding as of March 31, 2001, amounted to $84,000. The warranty costs on sales made from April 1, 2001, through March 31, 2002, are estimated at $210,000. The actual warranty costs incurred during the current 2001–02 fiscal year are as follows.

Warranty claims honored on 2000–01 sales	$ 84,000
Warranty claims honored on 2001–02 sales	95,000
Total warranty claims honored	$179,000

Other Information

1. *Trade payables.* Accounts payable for supplies, goods, and services purchased on open account amount to $370,000 as of March 31, 2002.

2. *Miscellaneous accruals.* Other accruals not separately classified amount to $75,000 as of March 31, 2002.

3. *Dividends.* On March 15, 2002, Balzac's board of directors declared a cash dividend of $0.40 per common share and a 10% common stock dividend. Both dividends were to be distributed on April 12, 2002, to the common stockholders of record at the close of business on March 31, 2002. Data regarding Balzac common stock are as follows.

Par value	$5 per share
Number of shares issued and outstanding	3,000,000 shares
Market values of common stock:	
March 15, 2002	$22.00 per share
March 31, 2002	21.50 per share
April 12, 2002	22.50 per share

4. Balzac purchased a warehouse in 1998 for $300,000. In February 2002, due to the passage of a new wetlands restoration law, Balzac will be required to restore the wetlands surrounding the warehouse site when the warehouse is abandoned in 2006. Balzac has estimated that the present value of the cost to restore the site is $35,000.

Instructions

Prepare the liabilities section of the balance sheet and appropriate notes to the statement for Balzac Inc. as of March 31, 2002, as they should appear in its annual report to the stockholders.

SOLUTION TO REVIEW EXERCISE

BALZAC INC.
BALANCE SHEET AS OF MARCH 31, 2002

Current liabilities		
Notes payable ($200,000 + $300,000 + $150,000 + $150,000)		$ 800,000
Accounts payable to trade creditors		370,000
Estimated warranty payables ($84,000 + $210,000 − $179,000)		115,000
Cash dividends payable (3,000,000 × $0.40) (Note A)		1,200,000
Accrued interest [($5,000,000 × .11 × ¼) + $210,000]		347,500
Miscellaneous accruals		75,000
Total current liabilities		2,907,500
Long-term liabilities		
11% bonds payable (Note B)	$5,000,000	
Asset retirement obligation, warehouse site	35,000	
Notes payable (Note C)	1,100,000	
Total long-term liabilities		6,135,000
Total liabilities		$9,042,500

NOTES TO THE FINANCIAL STATEMENTS

Note A—Cash Dividends On March 15, 2002, the Board of Directors declared a cash dividend of $0.40 per common share to common stockholders of record on March 31, 2002. The dividend is payable on April 12, 2002.

Note B—Bonds The 11% bonds call for semiannual interest payments on each January 1 and July 1. The bonds mature on July 1, 2006.

Note C—Notes Payable The current liabilities include current maturities of several notes payable. The long-term notes payable mature as follows.

DUE DATE	AMOUNT DUE
April 1, 2003–March 31, 2004	$600,000
April 1, 2004–March 31, 2005	500,000

EFFECTIVE INTEREST AMORTIZATION

The preferred procedure for amortization of a discount or premium is the **effective interest method** (also called **present value amortization**). Under the effective interest method:

1. Bond interest expense is computed first by multiplying the **carrying value**[1] of the bonds at the beginning of the period by the effective interest rate.

2. The bond discount or premium amortization is then determined by comparing the bond interest expense with the interest to be paid.

The computation of the amortization is depicted graphically as follows.

> **OBJECTIVE 9**
> After studying Appendix 11A, you should be able to: Compute amortization of bond discount and premium using the effective interest method.

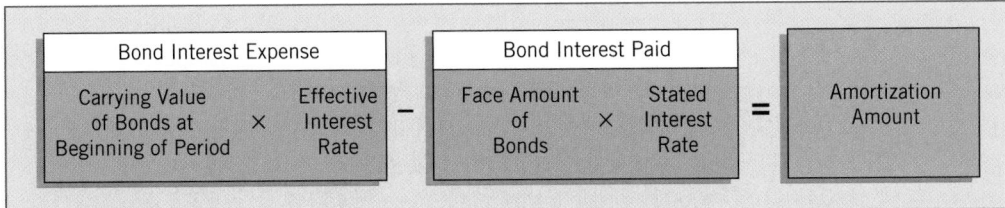

Illustration 11A-1
Bond Discount and Premium Amortization Computation

The effective interest method produces a periodic interest expense equal to **a constant percentage of the carrying value of the bonds**. Since the percentage is the effective rate of interest incurred by the borrower at the time of issuance, the effective interest method results in a better matching of expenses with revenues than the straight-line method. **Bond interest expense is increased by amortization of a discount and decreased by amortization of a premium.**

Some bonds are callable by the issuer after a certain date at a stated price, so that the issuing corporation may have the opportunity to reduce its bonded indebtedness or take advantage of lower interest rates. **Whether callable or not, any premium or discount must be amortized over the life to maturity date because early redemption (call of the bond) is not a certainty.**

BONDS ISSUED AT A DISCOUNT

To illustrate amortization of a discount, Evermaster Corporation issued $100,000 of 8 percent term bonds on January 1, 2003, due on January 1, 2008, with interest payable each July 1 and January 1. Because the investors required an effective interest rate of 10 percent, they paid $92,278 for the $100,000 of bonds, creating a $7,722 discount. The $7,722 discount is computed as follows.[2]

---

[1]The **book value**, also called the **carrying value**, equals the face amount minus any unamortized discount or plus any unamortized premium.

[2]Because interest is paid semiannually, the interest rate used is 5% ($10\% \times \frac{6}{12}$). The number of periods is 10 (5 years $\times$ 2).

Illustration 11A-2

Computation of Discount on Bonds Payable

Maturity value of bonds payable	$100,000
Present value of $100,000 due in 5 years at 10%, interest payable semiannually (Appendix A, Table 2); $FV(PVF_{10,5\%})$; ($100,000 × .61391)	$61,391
Present value of $4,000 interest payable semiannually for 5 years at 10% annually (Appendix A, Table 4); $R(PVF\text{-}OA_{10,5\%})$; ($4,000 × 7.72173)	30,887
Proceeds from sale of bonds	92,278
Discount on bonds payable	$ 7,722

The 5-year amortization schedule appears below.

Illustration 11A-3

Bond Discount Amortization Schedule

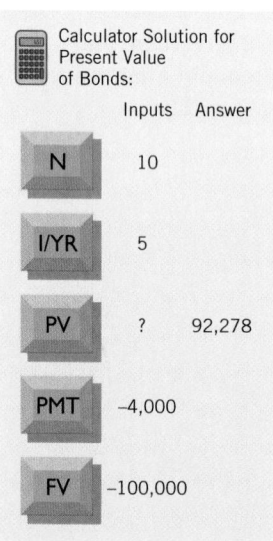

Calculator Solution for Present Value of Bonds:

	Inputs	Answer
N	10	
I/YR	5	
PV	?	92,278
PMT	–4,000	
FV	–100,000	

Schedule of Bond Discount Amortization
Effective Interest Method—Semiannual Interest Payments
5-Year, 8% Bonds Sold to Yield 10%

Date	Cash Paid	Interest Expense	Discount Amortized	Carrying Amount of Bonds
1/1/03				$ 92,278
7/1/03	$ 4,000[a]	$ 4,614[b]	$ 614[c]	92,892[d]
1/1/04	4,000	4,645	645	93,537
7/1/04	4,000	4,677	677	94,214
1/1/05	4,000	4,711	711	94,925
7/1/05	4,000	4,746	746	95,671
1/1/06	4,000	4,783	783	96,454
7/1/06	4,000	4,823	823	97,277
1/1/07	4,000	4,864	864	98,141
7/1/07	4,000	4,907	907	99,048
1/1/08	4,000	4,952	952	100,000
	$40,000	$47,722	$7,722	

[a]$4,000 = $100,000 × .08 × 6/12   [c]$614 = $4,614 − $4,000
[b]$4,614 = $92,278 × .10 × 6/12   [d]$92,892 = $92,278 + $614

The entry to record the issuance of Evermaster Corporation's bonds at a discount on January 1, 2003, is:

Cash	92,278	
Discount on Bonds Payable	7,722	
Bonds Payable		100,000

The journal entry to record the first interest payment on July 1, 2003, and amortization of the discount is:

Bond Interest Expense	4,614	
Discount on Bonds Payable		614
Cash		4,000

The journal entry to record the interest expense accrued at December 31, 2003 (year-end) and amortization of the discount is:

Bond Interest Expense	4,645	
Bond Interest Payable		4,000
Discount on Bonds Payable		645

BONDS ISSUED AT A PREMIUM

If the market had been such that the investors were willing to accept an effective interest rate of 6 percent on the bond issue described above, they would have paid $108,530 or a premium of $8,530, computed as follows.

Maturity value of bonds payable		$100,000
Present value of $100,000 due in 5 years at 6%, interest payable semiannually (Appendix A, Table 2); $FV(PVF_{10,3\%})$; ($100,000 × .74409)	$74,409	
Present value of $4,000 interest payable semiannually for 5 years at 6% annually (Appendix A, Table 4); $R(PVF\text{-}OA_{10,3\%})$; ($4,000 × 8.53020)	34,121	
Proceeds from sale of bonds		108,530
Premium on bonds payable		$ 8,530

illustration 11A-4
Computation of Premium on Bonds Payable

The 5-year amortization schedule appears below.

illustration 11A-5
Bond Premium Amortization Schedule

Schedule of Bond Premium Amortization
Effective Interest Method—Semiannual Interest Payments
5-Year, 8% Bonds Sold to Yield 6%

Date	Cash Paid	Interest Expense	Premium Amortized	Carrying Amount of Bonds
1/1/03				$108,530
7/1/03	$ 4,000[a]	$ 3,256[b]	$ 744[c]	107,786[d]
1/1/04	4,000	3,234	766	107,020
7/1/04	4,000	3,211	789	106,231
1/1/05	4,000	3,187	813	105,418
7/1/05	4,000	3,162	838	104,580
1/1/06	4,000	3,137	863	103,717
7/1/06	4,000	3,112	888	102,829
1/1/07	4,000	3,085	915	101,914
7/1/07	4,000	3,057	943	100,971
1/1/08	4,000	3,029	971	100,000
	$40,000	$31,470	$8,530	

[a]$4,000 = $100,000 × .08 × 6/12
[b]$3,256 = $108,530 × .06 × 6/12
[c]$744 = $4,000 − $3,256
[d]$107,786 = $108,530 − $744

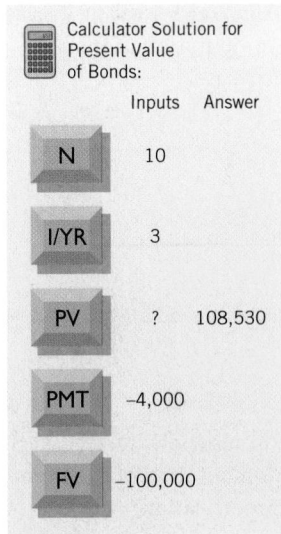

Calculator Solution for Present Value of Bonds:

	Inputs	Answer
N	10	
I/YR	3	
PV	?	108,530
PMT	−4,000	
FV	−100,000	

The entry to record the issuance of Evermaster bonds at a premium on January 1, 2003, is:

Cash	108,530	
Premium on Bonds Payable		8,530
Bonds Payable		100,000

The journal entry to record the first interest payment on July 1, 2003, and amortization of the premium is:

Bond Interest Expense	3,256	
Premium on Bonds Payable	744	
Cash		4,000

The discount or premium should be amortized as an adjustment to interest expense over the life of the bond in such a way as to result in a **constant rate of interest** when applied to the carrying amount of debt outstanding at the beginning of any given period.[3] Although the effective interest method is recommended, a **straight-line method** is permitted if the results obtained are not materially different from those produced by the effective interest method. Under the straight-line method, the amount amortized each year is a constant amount.

The journal entry to record the first interest payment on the Evermaster bonds issued at a premium, using straight-line amortization, is:

July 1, 2003

Bond Interest Expense	3,147	
Premium on Bonds Payable ($8,530 ÷ 10)	853	
Cash		4,000

ACCRUING INTEREST

In our previous examples, the interest payment dates and the date the financial statements were issued were the same. For example, when Evermaster sold bonds at a premium (page 551), the two interest payment dates coincided with the financial reporting dates. However, what happens if Evermaster wishes to report financial statements at the end of February 2003? In this case, the premium is prorated by the appropriate number of months, to arrive at the proper interest expense as follows.

Illustration 11A-6
Computation of Interest Expense

Interest accrual ($4,000 × ⅔)	$1,333.33
Premium amortized ($744 × ⅔)	(248.00)
Interest expense (Jan.–Feb.)	$1,085.33

The journal entry to record this accrual is as follows.

Bond Interest Expense	1,085.33	
Premium on Bonds Payable	248.00	
Bond Interest Payable		1,333.33

If the company prepares financial statements 6 months later, the same procedure is followed; that is, the premium amortized would be as follows.

Illustration 11A-7
Computation of Premium Amortization

Premium amortized (March–June) ($744 × ⅔)	$496.00
Premium amortized (July–August) ($766 × ⅔)	255.33
Premium amortized (March–August, 2003)	$751.33

[3]"Interest on Receivables and Payables," *Opinions of the Accounting Principles Board No. 21* (New York: AICPA, 1971), par. 16.

SUMMARY OF LEARNING OBJECTIVE FOR APPENDIX 11A

KEY TERMS

carrying value, 549
effective interest method of
    amortization, 549
straight-line method of
    amortization, 552

⑨ Compute amortization of bond discount and premium using the effective interest method. The discount (premium) is amortized and charged (credited) to interest expense over the period of time that the bonds are outstanding. Bond interest expense is increased by amortization of a discount and decreased by amortization of a premium. The preferred procedure for amortization of a discount or premium is the effective interest method. Under the effective interest method, (1) bond interest expense is computed by multiplying the carrying value of the bonds at the beginning of the period by the effective interest rate, and (2) the bond discount or premium amortization is then determined by comparing the bond interest expense with the interest to be paid.

QUESTIONS

1 Distinguish between a current liability and a long-term debt.

2 Assume that your friend Greg Jonas, who is a music major, asks you to define and discuss the nature of a liability. Assist him by preparing a definition of a liability and by explaining to him what you believe are the elements or factors inherent in the concept of a liability.

3 Why is the liability section of the balance sheet of primary significance to bankers?

4 How are current liabilities related by definition to current assets? How are current liabilities related to a company's operating cycle?

5 Jon Bryant, a newly hired loan analyst, is examining the current liabilities of a corporate loan applicant. He observes that unearned revenues have declined in the current year compared to the prior year. Is this a positive indicator about the client's liquidity? Explain.

6 How is present value related to the concept of a liability?

7 What is the nature of a "discount" on notes payable?

8 How should a debt callable by the creditor be reported in the debtor's financial statements?

9 Discuss the accounting treatment or disclosure that should be accorded a declared but unpaid cash dividend; an accumulated but undeclared dividend on cumulative preferred stock; a stock dividend distributable.

10 How does unearned revenue arise? Why can it be classified properly as a current liability? Give several examples of business activities that result in unearned revenues.

11 (a) From what sources might a corporation obtain funds through long-term debt? (b) What is a bond indenture? What does it contain? (c) What is a mortgage?

12 Differentiate between term bonds, mortgage bonds, collateral trust bonds, debenture bonds, income bonds, callable bonds, registered bonds, bearer or coupon bonds, convertible bonds, commodity-backed bonds, and deep discount bonds.

13 Distinguish between the following interest rates for bonds payable:

(a) yield rate   (d) market rate

(b) nominal rate   (e) effective rate

(c) stated rate

14 Distinguish between the following values relative to bonds payable:

(a) maturity value   (c) market value

(b) face value   (d) par value

15 Under what conditions of bond issuance does a discount on bonds payable arise? Under what conditions of bond issuance does a premium on bonds payable arise?

16 How should discount on bonds payable be reported on the financial statements? Premium on bonds payable?

17 How should the costs of issuing bonds be accounted for and classified in the financial statements?

18 Why would a company wish to reduce its bond indebtedness before its bonds reach maturity? Indicate how this can be done and the correct accounting treatment for such a transaction.

19 Define (a) a contingency and (b) a contingent liability.

20 Under what conditions should a contingent liability be recorded?

21 Distinguish between a current liability and a contingent liability. Give two examples of each type.

22 How are the terms probable, reasonably possible, and remote related to contingent liabilities?

23 Contrast the cash basis method and the accrual method of accounting for warranty costs.

24 How does the expense warranty approach differ from the sales warranty approach?

25 Should a liability be recorded for risk of loss due to lack of insurance coverage? Discuss.

26 What factors must be considered in determining whether or not to record a liability for pending litigation? For threatened litigation?

27 What is off-balance-sheet financing? Why might a company be interested in off-balance-sheet financing?

28 What disclosures are required relative to long-term debt and sinking fund requirements?

29 Within the current liabilities section, how do you believe the accounts should be listed? Defend your position.

30 How does the acid-test ratio differ from the current ratio? How are they similar?

31 When should liabilities for each of the following items be recorded on the books of an ordinary business corporation?

(a) Acquisition of goods by purchase on credit.

(b) Officers' salaries.

(c) Special bonus to employees.

(d) Dividends.

*32 Zeno Company sells its bonds at a premium and applies the effective interest method in amortizing the premium. Will the annual interest expense increase or decrease over the life of the bonds? Explain.

BRIEF EXERCISES

BE11-1 Congo Corporation uses a periodic inventory system and the gross method of accounting for purchase discounts. On July 1, Congo purchased $40,000 of inventory, terms 2/10, n/30, FOB shipping point. Congo paid freight costs of $1,200. On July 3, Congo returned damaged goods and received credit of $6,000. On July 10, Congo paid for the goods. Prepare all necessary journal entries for Congo.

BE11-2 Desert Storm Company borrowed $50,000 on November 1, 2003, by signing a $50,000, 9%, 3-month note. Prepare Desert Storm's November 1, 2003, entry; the December 31, 2003, annual adjusting entry; and the February 1, 2004, entry.

BE11-3 Kawasaki Corporation borrowed $50,000 on November 1, 2003, by signing a $51,125, 3-month, zero-interest-bearing note. Prepare Kawasaki's November 1, 2003, entry; the December 31, 2003, annual adjusting entry; and the February 1, 2004, entry.

BE11-4 Game Pro Magazine sold 10,000 annual subscriptions on August 1, 2003, for $18 each. Prepare Game Pro's August 1, 2003, journal entry and the December 31, 2003, annual adjusting entry.

BE11-5 Ghostbusters Corporation issues $300,000 of 9% bonds, due in 10 years, with interest payable semi-annually. At the time of issue, the market rate for such bonds is 10%. Compute the issue price of the bonds.

BE11-6 The Goofy Company issued $200,000 of 10% bonds on January 1, 2004. The bonds are due January 1, 2009, with interest payable each July 1 and January 1. The bonds are issued at face value. Prepare Goofy's journal entries for (a) the January issuance, (b) the July 1 interest payment, and (c) the December 31 adjusting entry.

BE11-7 Assume the bonds in BE11-6 were issued at 98. Prepare the journal entry at January 1, 2004.

BE11-8 Assume the bonds in BE11-6 were issued at 103. Prepare the journal entry at January 1, 2004.

BE11-9 At December 31, 2004, Treasure Land Corporation has the following account balances.

Bonds payable, due January 1, 2012	$2,000,000
Discount on bonds payable	98,000
Bond interest payable	80,000

Show how the above accounts should be presented on the December 31, 2004, balance sheet, including the proper classifications.

BE11-10 On January 1, 2004, Uncharted Waters Corporation retired $600,000 of bonds at 99. At the time of retirement, the unamortized premium was $15,000 and unamortized bond issue costs were $5,250. Prepare the corporation's journal entry to record the reacquisition of the bonds.

BE11-11 Justice League Inc. is involved in a lawsuit at December 31, 2003. (a) Prepare the December 31 entry assuming it is probable that Justice League will be liable for $700,000 as a result of this suit. (b) Prepare the December 31 entry, if any, assuming it is *not* probable that Justice League will be liable for any payment as a result of this suit.

BE11-12 Kohlbeck Company recently was sued by a competitor for patent infringement. Attorneys have determined that it is probable that Kohlbeck will lose the case and that a reasonable estimate of damages to be paid by Kohlbeck is $200,000. In light of this case, Kohlbeck is considering establishing a $100,000 self-insurance allowance. What entry(ies), if any, should Kohlbeck record to recognize this loss contingency?

BE11-13 Frantic Factory provides a 2-year warranty with one of its products which was first sold in 2003. In that year, Frantic spent $70,000 servicing warranty claims. At year-end, Frantic estimates that an additional $500,000 will be spent in the future to service warranty claims related to 2003 sales. Prepare Frantic's journal entry to record the $70,000 expenditure, and the December 31 adjusting entry.

BE11-14 Herzog Zwei Corporation sells VCRs. The corporation also offers its customers a 2-year warranty contract. During 2003, Herzog Zwei sold 15,000 warranty contracts at $99 each. The corporation spent $180,000 servicing warranties during 2003, and it estimates that an additional $900,000 will be spent in the future to service the warranties. Prepare Herzog Zwei's journal entries for (a) the sale of contracts, (b) the cost of servicing the warranties, and (c) the recognition of warranty revenue.

BE11-15 Darby's Drillers erects and places into service an off-shore oil platform on January 1, 2003, at a cost of $10,000,000. Darby is legally required to dismantle and remove the platform at the end of its useful life in 10 years. The estimated present value of the dismantling and removal costs at January 1, 2003, is $500,000. Prepare the entry to record the asset retirement obligation.

*BE11-16 On January 1, 2004, Qix Corporation issued $400,000 of 7% bonds, due in 10 years. The bonds were issued for $372,816, and pay interest each July 1 and January 1. Qix uses the effective interest method. Prepare the company's journal entries for (a) the January 1 issuance, (b) the July 1 interest payment, and (c) the December 31 adjusting entry. Assume an effective interest rate of 8%.

*BE11-17 Assume the bonds in BE11-16 were issued for $429,757 and the effective interest rate is 6%. Prepare the company's journal entries for (a) the January 1 issuance, (b) the July 1 interest payment, and (c) the December 31 adjusting entry.

*BE11-18 Izzy Corporation issued $400,000 of 7% bonds on November 1, 2004, for $429,757. The bonds were dated November 1, 2004, and mature in 10 years, with interest payable each May 1 and November 1. Izzy uses the effective interest method with an effective rate of 6%. Prepare Izzy's December 31, 2004, adjusting entry.

EXERCISES

E11-1 (Balance Sheet Classification of Various Liabilities) How would each of the following items be reported on the balance sheet?

(a) Accrued vacation pay.
(b) Estimated taxes payable.
(c) Service warranties on appliance sales.
(d) Bank overdraft.
(e) Employee payroll deductions unremitted.
(f) Unpaid bonus to officers.
(g) Deposit received from customer to guarantee performance of a contract.

(h) Sales taxes payable.
(i) Gift certificates sold to customers but not yet redeemed.
(j) Premium offers outstanding.
(k) Discount on notes payable.
(l) Personal injury claim pending.
(m) Current maturities of long-term debts to be paid from current assets.
(n) Cash dividends declared but unpaid.
(o) Dividends in arrears on preferred stock.
(p) Loans from officers.

E11-2 (Accounts and Notes Payable) The following are selected 2003 transactions of Sean Astin Corporation.

Sept. 1 Purchased inventory from Encino Company on account for $50,000. Astin records purchases gross and uses a periodic inventory system.
Oct. 1 Issued a $50,000, 12-month, 12% note to Encino in payment of account.
Oct. 1 Borrowed $50,000 from the Shore Bank by signing a 12-month, noninterest-bearing $56,000 note.

Instructions
(a) Prepare journal entries for the selected transactions above.
(b) Prepare adjusting entries at December 31.
(c) Compute the total net liability to be reported on the December 31 balance sheet for:
  (1) the interest-bearing note.
  (2) the noninterest-bearing note.

E11-3 **(Classification of Liabilities)**   Presented below are various account balances of K.D. Lang Inc.

(a) Unamortized premium on bonds payable, of which $3,000 will be amortized during the next year.

(b) Bank loans payable of a winery, due March 10, 2007. (The product requires aging for 5 years before sale.)

(c) Serial bonds payable, $1,000,000, of which $200,000 are due each July 31.

(d) Amounts withheld from employees' wages for income taxes.

(e) Notes payable due January 15, 2006.

(f) Credit balances in customers' accounts arising from returns and allowances after collection in full of account.

(g) Bonds payable of $2,000,000 maturing June 30, 2005.

(h) Overdraft of $1,000 in a bank account. (No other balances are carried at this bank.)

(i) Deposits made by customers who have ordered goods.

Instructions

Indicate whether each of the items above should be classified on December 31, 2004, as a current liability, a long-term liability, or under some other classification. Consider each one independently from all others; that is, do not assume that all of them relate to one particular business. If the classification of some of the items is doubtful, explain why in each case.

E11-4 **(Classification)**   The following items are found in the financial statements.

(a) Discount on bonds payable

(b) Unamortized bond issue costs

(c) Gain on repurchase of debt

(d) Mortgage payable (payable in equal amounts over next 3 years)

(e) Debenture bonds payable (maturing in 5 years)

(f) Notes payable (due in 4 years)

(g) Premium on bonds payable

(h) Income bonds payable (due in 3 years)

Instructions

Indicate how each of these items should be classified in the financial statements.

E11-5 **(Entries for Bond Transactions)**   Presented below are two independent situations.

1. On January 1, 2003, Paul Simon Company issued $200,000 of 9%, 10-year bonds at par. Interest is payable quarterly on April 1, July 1, October 1, and January 1.

2. On June 1, 2001, Graceland Company issued $100,000 of 12%, 10-year bonds dated January 1 at par plus accrued interest. Interest is payable semiannually on July 1 and January 1.

Instructions

For each of these two independent situations, prepare journal entries to record:

(a) The issuance of the bonds.

(b) The payment of interest on July 1.

(c) The accrual of interest on December 31.

E11-6 **(Warranties)**   Soundgarden Company sold 200 copymaking machines in 2003 for $4,000 apiece, together with a one-year warranty. Maintenance on each machine during the warranty period averages $330.

Instructions

(a) Prepare entries to record the sale of the machines and the related warranty costs, assuming that the accrual method is used. Actual warranty costs incurred in 2003 were $17,000.

(b) On the basis of the data above, prepare the appropriate entries, assuming that the cash basis method is used.

E11-7 **(Warranties)**   Sheryl Crow Equipment Company sold 500 Rollomatics during 2003 at $6,000 each. During 2003, Crow spent $20,000 servicing the 2-year warranties that accompany the Rollomatic. All applicable transactions are on a cash basis.

Instructions

(a) Prepare 2003 entries for Crow using the expense warranty approach. Assume that Crow estimates the total cost of servicing the warranties will be $120,000 for 2 years.

(b) Prepare 2003 entries for Crow assuming that the warranties are not an integral part of the sale. Assume that of the sales total, $150,000 relates to sales of warranty contracts. Crow estimates the total cost of servicing the warranties will be $120,000 for 2 years. Estimate revenues earned on the basis of costs incurred and estimated costs.

E11-8 (Entry for Retirement of Bond; Bond Issue Costs) On January 2, 1998, Banno Corporation issued $1,500,000 of 10% bonds at 97 due December 31, 2007. Legal and other costs of $24,000 were incurred in connection with the issue. Interest on the bonds is payable annually each December 31. The $24,000 issue costs are being deferred and amortized. The discount on the bonds is also being amortized.

The bonds are callable at 101 (i.e., at 101% of face amount), and on January 2, 2003, Banno called $900,000 face amount of the bonds and retired them. Unamortized bond discount at retirement was $13,500, and unamortized bond issue cost was $7,200.

Instructions

Ignoring income taxes, compute the amount of loss, if any, to be recognized by Banno as a result of retiring the $900,000 of bonds in 2003, and prepare the journal entry to record the retirement.

(AICPA adapted)

E11-9 (Entries for Retirement and Issuance of Bonds) Larry Hagman, Inc. had outstanding $6,000,000 of 11% bonds (interest payable July 31 and January 31) due in 10 years. On July 1, it issued $9,000,000 of 10%, 15-year bonds (interest payable July 1 and January 1) at 98. A portion of the proceeds was used to call the 11% bonds at 102 on August 1. Unamortized bond discount and issue cost applicable to the 11% bonds were $120,000 and $30,000, respectively.

Instructions

Prepare the journal entries necessary to record issuance of the new bonds and the refunding of the bonds.

E11-10 (Entries for Retirement and Issuance of Bonds) Linda Day George Company had bonds outstanding with a maturity value of $300,000. On April 30, 2004, when these bonds had an unamortized discount of $10,000, they were called in at 104. To pay for these bonds, George had issued other bonds a month earlier bearing a lower interest rate. The newly issued bonds had a life of 10 years. The new bonds were issued at 103 (face value $300,000). Issue costs related to the new bonds were $3,000.

Instructions

Ignoring interest, compute the gain or loss and record this refunding transaction.

(AICPA adapted)

E11-11 (Contingencies) Presented below are three independent situations. Answer the question at the end of each situation.

1. During 2003, Salt-n-Pepa Inc. became involved in a tax dispute with the IRS. Salt-n-Pepa's attorneys have indicated that they believe it is probable that Salt-n-Pepa will lose this dispute. They also believe that Salt-n-Pepa will have to pay the IRS between $900,000 and $1,400,000. After the 2003 financial statements were issued, the case was settled with the IRS for $1,200,000. What amount, if any, should be reported as a liability for this contingency as of December 31, 2003?

2. On October 1, 2003, Alan Jackson Chemical was identified as a potentially responsible party by the Environmental Protection Agency. Jackson's management along with its counsel have concluded that it is probable that Jackson will be responsible for damages, and a reasonable estimate of these damages is $5,000,000. Jackson's insurance policy of $9,000,000 has a deductible clause of $500,000. How should Alan Jackson Chemical report this information in its financial statements at December 31, 2003?

3. Melissa Etheridge Inc. had a manufacturing plant in Bosnia, which was destroyed in the civil war. It is not certain who will compensate Etheridge for this destruction, but Etheridge has been assured by governmental officials that it will receive a definite amount for this plant. The amount of the compensation will be less than the fair value of the plant, but more than its book value. How should the contingency be reported in the financial statements of Etheridge Inc.?

E11-12 **(Asset Retirement Obligation)** Oil Products Company purchases an oil tanker depot on January 1, 2004, at a cost of $600,000. Oil Products expects to operate the depot for 10 years, at which time it is legally required to dismantle the depot and remove the underground storage tanks. It is estimated that it will cost $75,000 to dismantle the depot and remove the tanks at the end of the depot's useful life.

Instructions

(a) Prepare the journal entries to record the depot and the asset retirement obligation for the depot on January 1, 2004. Based on an effective interest rate of 6%, the present value of the asset retirement obligation on January 1, 2004, is $41,879.

(b) Prepare any journal entries required for the depot and the asset retirement obligation at December 31, 2004. Oil Products uses straight-line depreciation; the estimated residual value for the depot is zero.

(c) On December 31, 2013, Oil Products pays a demolition firm to dismantle the depot and remove the tanks at a price of $80,000. Prepare the journal entry for the settlement of the asset retirement obligation.

E11-13 **(Financial Statement Impact of Liability Transactions)** Presented below is a list of possible transactions.

1. Purchased inventory for $80,000 on account (assume perpetual system is used).
2. Issued an $80,000 note payable in payment on account (see item 1 above).
3. Recorded accrued interest on the note from item 2 above.
4. Borrowed $100,000 from the bank by signing a 6-month, $112,000, noninterest-bearing note.
5. Recognized 4 months' interest expense on the note from item 4 above.
6. Recorded cash sales of $75,260, which includes 6% sales tax.
7. Recorded accrued property taxes payable.
8. Recorded bonuses due to employees.
9. Recorded a contingent loss on a lawsuit that the company will probably lose.
10. Accrued warranty expense (assume expense warranty approach).
11. Paid warranty costs that were accrued in item 10 above.
12. Recorded sales of product and related warranties (assume sales warranty approach).
13. Paid warranty costs under contracts from item 12 above.
14. Recognized warranty revenue (see item 12 above).

Instructions

Set up a table using the format shown below and analyze the effect of the 14 transactions on the financial statement categories indicated.

#	Assets	Liabilities	Owners' Equity	Net Income
1				

Use the following code:

I: Increase   D: Decrease   NE: No net effect

E11-14 **(Ratio Computations and Discussion)** Sprague Company has been operating for several years, and on December 31, 2003, presented the following balance sheet.

SPRAGUE COMPANY			
Balance Sheet			
December 31, 2003			
Cash	$ 40,000	Accounts payable	$ 80,000
Receivables	75,000	Mortgage payable	140,000
Inventories	95,000	Common stock ($1.00 par)	150,000
Plant assets (net)	220,000	Retained earnings	60,000
	$430,000		$430,000

The net income for 2003 was $25,000. Assume that total assets are the same in 2002 and 2003.

Instructions

Compute each of the following ratios. For each of the four indicate the manner in which it is computed and its significance as a tool in the analysis of the financial soundness of the company.

(a) Current ratio.
(b) Acid-test ratio.
(c) Debt to total assets.
(d) Rate of return on assets.

E11-15 (Long-Term Debt Disclosure) At December 31, 2002, Helen Reddy Company has outstanding three long-term debt issues. The first is a $2,000,000 note payable which matures June 30, 2005. The second is a $6,000,000 bond issue which matures September 30, 2006. The third is a $17,500,000 sinking fund debenture with annual sinking fund payments of $3,500,000 in each of the years 2004 through 2008.

Instructions

Prepare the note disclosure required by *FASB Statement No. 47,* "Disclosure of Long-term Obligations," for the long-term debt at December 31, 2002.

E11-16 (Ratio Computations and Analysis) Hood Company's condensed financial statements provide the following information.

HOOD COMPANY Balance Sheet		
	Dec. 31, 2003	Dec. 31, 2002
Cash	$ 52,000	$ 60,000
Accounts receivable (net)	198,000	80,000
Marketable securities (short-term)	80,000	40,000
Inventories	440,000	360,000
Prepaid expenses	3,000	7,000
Total current assets	$ 773,000	$ 547,000
Property, plant, and equipment (net)	857,000	853,000
Total assets	$1,630,000	$1,400,000
Current liabilities	240,000	160,000
Bonds payable	400,000	400,000
Common stockholders' equity	990,000	840,000
Total liabilities and stockholders' equity	$1,630,000	$1,400,000

Income Statement For the Year Ended 2003	
Sales	$1,640,000
Cost of goods sold	(800,000)
Gross profit	840,000
Selling and administrative expense	(440,000)
Interest expense	(40,000)
Net income	$ 360,000

Instructions

(a) Determine the following:
   (1) Current ratio at December 31, 2003.
   (2) Acid-test ratio at December 31, 2003.
   (3) Accounts receivable turnover for 2003.
   (4) Inventory turnover for 2003.
   (5) Rate of return on assets for 2003.
   (6) Profit margin on sales.
(b) Prepare a brief evaluation of the financial condition of Hood Company and of the adequacy of its profits.

E11-17 **(Ratio Computations and Effect of Transactions)** Presented below is information related to Carver Inc.

CARVER INC. Balance Sheet December 31, 2003				
Cash		$ 45,000	Notes payable (short-term)	$ 50,000
Receivables	$110,000		Accounts payable	32,000
Less: Allowance	15,000	95,000	Accrued liabilities	5,000
Inventories		170,000	Capital stock (par $5)	260,000
Prepaid insurance		8,000	Retained earnings	141,000
Land		20,000		$488,000
Equipment (net)		150,000		
		$488,000		

Income Statement For the Year Ended December 31, 2003		
Sales		$1,400,000
Cost of goods sold		
Inventory, Jan. 1, 2003	$200,000	
Purchases	790,000	
Cost of goods available for sale	990,000	
Inventory, Dec. 31, 2003	170,000	
Cost of goods sold		820,000
Gross profit on sales		580,000
Operating expenses		170,000
Net income		$ 410,000

Instructions

(a) Compute the following ratios or relationships of Carver Inc. Assume that the ending account balances are representative unless the information provided indicates differently.
   (1) Current ratio.
   (2) Inventory turnover.
   (3) Receivables turnover.
   (4) Earnings per share.
   (5) Profit margin on sales.
   (6) Rate of return on assets on December 31, 2003.

(b) Indicate for each of the following transactions whether the transaction would improve, weaken, or have no effect on the current ratio of Carver Inc. at December 31, 2003.
   (1) Write off an uncollectible account receivable, $2,200.
   (2) Purchase additional capital stock for cash.
   (3) Pay $40,000 on notes payable (short-term).
   (4) Collect $23,000 on accounts receivable.
   (5) Buy equipment on account.
   (6) Give an existing creditor a short-term note in settlement of account.

*E11-18 Celine Dion Company issued $600,000 of 10%, 20-year bonds on January 1, 2004, at 102. Interest is payable semiannually on July 1 and January 1. Dion Company uses the effective interest method of amortization for bond premium or discount. Assume an effective yield of 9.75%.

Instructions
Prepare the journal entries to record the following. (Round to the nearest dollar.)

(a) The issuance of the bonds.
(b) The payment of interest and related amortization on July 1, 2004.
(c) The accrual of interest and the related amortization on December 31, 2004.

*E11-19 (Amortization Schedules—Straight-line Interest) Dan Majerle Company sells 10% bonds having a maturity value of $2,000,000 for $1,855,816. The bonds are dated January 1, 2003, and mature January 1, 2008. Interest is payable annually on January 1.

Instructions
Set up a schedule of interest expense and discount amortization under the straight-line method.

*E11-20 (Determine Proper Amounts in Account Balances) Presented below are two independent situations.

(a) CeCe Winans Corporation incurred the following costs in connection with the issuance of bonds: (1) printing and engraving costs, $12,000; (2) legal fees, $49,000, and (3) commissions paid to underwriter, $60,000. What amount should be reported as Unamortized Bond Issue Costs, and where should this amount be reported on the balance sheet?
(b) Ron Kenoly Inc. issued $600,000 of 9%, 10-year bonds on June 30, 2003, for $562,500. This price provided a yield of 10% on the bonds. Interest is payable semiannually on December 31 and June 30. If Kenoly uses the effective interest method, determine the amount of interest expense to record if financial statements are issued on October 31, 2003.

*E11-21 (Entries and Questions for Bond Transactions) On June 30, 2004, Mischa Auer Company issued $4,000,000 face value of 13%, 20-year bonds at $4,300,920, a yield of 12%. Auer uses the effective interest method to amortize bond premium or discount. The bonds pay semiannual interest on June 30 and December 31.

Instructions
(a) Prepare the journal entries to record the following transactions.
  (1) The issuance of the bonds on June 30, 2004.
  (2) The payment of interest and the amortization of the premium on December 31, 2004.
  (3) The payment of interest and the amortization of the premium on June 30, 2005.
  (4) The payment of interest and the amortization of the premium on December 31, 2005.
(b) Show the proper balance sheet presentation for the liability for bonds payable on the December 31, 2005, balance sheet.
(c) Provide the answers to the following questions.
  (1) What amount of interest expense is reported for 2005?
  (2) Will the bond interest expense reported in 2005 be the same as, greater than, or less than the amount that would be reported if the straight-line method of amortization were used?
  (3) Determine the total cost of borrowing over the life of the bond.
  (4) Will the total bond interest expense for the life of the bond be greater than, the same as, or less than the total interest expense if the straight-line method of amortization were used?

*E11-22 (Entries for Bond Transactions) On January 1, 2003, Aumont Company sold 12% bonds having a maturity value of $500,000 for $537,907.37, which provides the bondholders with a 10% yield. The bonds are dated January 1, 2003, and mature January 1, 2008, with interest payable December 31 of each year. Aumont Company allocates interest and unamortized discount or premium on the effective interest basis.

Instructions
(a) Prepare the journal entry at the date of the bond issuance.
(b) Prepare a schedule of interest expense and bond amortization for 2003–2005.
(c) Prepare the journal entry to record the interest payment and the amortization for 2003.
(d) Prepare the journal entry to record the interest payment and the amortization for 2005.

*E11-23 **(Information Related to Various Bond Issues)** Karen Austin Inc. has issued three types of debt on January 1, 2003, the start of the company's fiscal year.

(a) $10 million, 10-year, 15% unsecured bonds, interest payable quarterly. Bonds were priced to yield 12%.
(b) $25 million par of 10-year, zero-coupon bonds at a price to yield 12% per year.
(c) $20 million, 10-year, 10% mortgage bonds, interest payable annually to yield 12%.

Instructions

Prepare a schedule that identifies the following items for each bond: (1) maturity value, (2) number of interest periods over life of bond, (3) stated rate per each interest period, (4) effective interest rate per each interest period, (5) payment amount per period, and (6) present value of bonds at date of issue.

PROBLEMS

P11-1 (Current Liability Entries and Adjustments) Described below are certain transactions of James Edwards Corporation.

1. On February 2, the corporation purchased goods from Jack Haley Company for $50,000 subject to cash discount terms of 2/10, n/30. Purchases and accounts payable are recorded by the corporation at net amounts after cash discounts. The invoice was paid on February 26.
2. On April 1, the corporation bought a truck for $40,000 from General Motors Company, paying $4,000 in cash and signing a one-year, 12% note for the balance of the purchase price.
3. On May 1, the corporation borrowed $80,000 from Chicago National Bank by signing a $92,000 non-interest-bearing note due one year from May 1.
4. On August 1, the board of directors declared a $300,000 cash dividend that was payable on September 10 to stockholders of record on August 31.

Instructions

(a) Make all the journal entries necessary to record the transactions above using appropriate dates.
(b) James Edwards Corporation's year-end is December 31. Assuming that no adjusting entries relative to the transactions above have been recorded, prepare any adjusting journal entries concerning interest that are necessary to present fair financial statements at December 31. Assume straight-line amortization of discounts.

P11-2 (Comprehensive Problem; Issuance, Classification, Reporting) Presented below are four independent situations.

(a) On March 1, 2004, Heide Co. issued at 103 plus accrued interest $3,000,000, 9% bonds. The bonds are dated January 1, 2004, and pay interest semiannually on July 1 and January 1. In addition, Heide Co. incurred $27,000 of bond issuance costs. Compute the net amount of cash received by Heide Co. as a result of the issuance of these bonds.
(b) On January 1, 2003, Reymont Co. issued 9% bonds with a face value of $500,000 for $469,280 to yield 10%. The bonds are dated January 1, 2003, and pay interest annually. What amount is reported as bond discount on the issue date?
(c) Czeslaw Building Co. has a number of long-term bonds outstanding at December 31, 2004. These long-term bonds have the following sinking fund requirements and maturities for the next 6 years.

	Sinking Fund	Maturities
2005	$300,000	$100,000
2006	100,000	250,000
2007	100,000	100,000
2008	200,000	—
2009	200,000	150,000
2010	200,000	100,000

Indicate how this information should be reported in the financial statements at December 31, 2004.

(d) In the long-term debt structure of Marie Curie Inc., the following three bonds were reported: mortgage bonds payable $10,000,000; collateral trust bonds $5,000,000; bonds maturing in installments, secured by plant equipment $4,000,000. Determine the total amount, if any, of debenture bonds outstanding.

P11-3 (Warranties, Accrual, and Cash Basis) Davey Lopes Corporation sells portable computers under a 2-year warranty contract that requires the corporation to replace defective parts and to provide the necessary repair labor. During 2003 the corporation sells for cash 300 computers at a unit price of $3,500. On the basis of past experience, the 2-year warranty costs are estimated to be $155 for parts and $185 for labor per unit. (For simplicity, assume that all sales occurred on December 31, 2003.) The warranty is not sold separately from the computer.

Instructions
(a) Record any necessary journal entries in 2003, applying the cash basis method.
(b) Record any necessary journal entries in 2003, applying the expense warranty accrual method.
(c) What liability relative to these transactions would appear on the December 31, 2003, balance sheet, and how would it be classified if the cash basis method is applied?
(d) What liability relative to these transactions would appear on the December 31, 2003, balance sheet, and how would it be classified if the expense warranty accrual method is applied?

In 2004 the actual warranty costs to Davey Lopes Corporation were $21,400 for parts and $24,900 for labor.

(e) Record any necessary journal entries in 2004, applying the cash basis method.
(f) Record any necessary journal entries in 2004, applying the expense warranty accrual method.

P11-4 (Warranties, Accrual, and Cash Basis) Albert Belle Company sells a machine for $7,400 under a 12-month warranty agreement that requires the company to replace all defective parts and to provide the repair labor at no cost to the customers. With sales being made evenly throughout the year, the company sells 650 machines in 2004 (warranty expense is incurred half in 2004 and half in 2005). As a result of product testing, the company estimates that the warranty cost is $370 per machine ($170 parts and $200 labor).

Instructions
Assuming that actual warranty costs are incurred exactly as estimated, what journal entries would be made relative to these facts.

(a) Under application of the expense warranty accrual method for:
  (1) Sale of machinery in 2004?
  (2) Warranty costs incurred in 2004?
  (3) Warranty expense charged against 2004 revenues?
  (4) Warranty costs incurred in 2005?
(b) Under application of the cash basis method for:
  (1) Sale of machinery in 2004?
  (2) Warranty costs incurred in 2004?
  (3) Warranty expense charged against 2004 revenues?
  (4) Warranty costs incurred in 2005?
(c) What amount, if any, is disclosed in the balance sheet as a liability for future warranty costs as of December 31, 2004, under each method?
(d) Which method best reflects the income in 2004 and 2005 of Albert Belle Company? Why?

P11-5 (Loss Contingencies: Entries and Essay) On November 24, 2003, 26 passengers on Tom Paris Airlines Flight No. 901 were injured upon landing when the plane skidded off the runway. Personal injury suits for damages totaling $5,000,000 were filed on January 11, 2004, against the airline by 18 injured passengers. The airline carries no insurance. Legal counsel has studied each suit and advised Paris that it can reasonably expect to pay 60% of the damages claimed. The financial statements for the year ended December 31, 2003, were issued February 27, 2004.

Instructions
(a) Prepare any disclosures and journal entries required by the airline in preparation of the December 31, 2003, financial statements.

(b) Ignoring the Nov. 24, 2003, accident, what liability due to the risk of loss from lack of insurance coverage should Tom Paris Airlines record or disclose? During the past decade the company has experienced at least one accident per year and incurred average damages of $3,200,000. Discuss fully.

P11-6 **(Loss Contingencies: Entries and Essays)** Shoyo Corporation, in preparation of its December 31, 2003, financial statements, is attempting to determine the proper accounting treatment for each of the following situations.

1. As a result of uninsured accidents during the year, personal injury suits for $350,000 and $60,000 have been filed against the company. It is the judgment of Shoyo's legal counsel that an unfavorable outcome is unlikely in the $60,000 case but that an unfavorable verdict approximating $225,000 will probably result in the $350,000 case.

2. Shoyo Corporation owns a subsidiary in a foreign country that has a book value of $5,725,000 and an estimated fair value of $8,700,000. The foreign government has communicated to Shoyo its intention to expropriate the assets and business of all foreign investors. On the basis of settlements other firms have received from this same country, Shoyo expects to receive 40% of the fair value of its properties as final settlement.

3. Shoyo's chemical product division consisting of five plants is uninsurable because of the special risk of injury to employees and losses due to fire and explosion. The year 2003 is considered one of the safest (luckiest) in the division's history because no loss due to injury or casualty was suffered. Having suffered an average of three casualties a year during the rest of the past decade (ranging from $60,000 to $700,000), management is certain that next year the company will probably not be so fortunate.

Instructions
(a) Prepare the journal entries that should be recorded as of December 31, 2003, to recognize each of the situations above.

(b) Indicate what should be reported relative to each situation in the financial statements and accompanying notes. Explain why.

P11-7 **(Liability Errors)** You are the independent auditor engaged to audit Christine Agazzi Corporation's December 31, 2002, financial statements. Christine Agazzi manufactures household appliances. During the course of your audit, you discovered the following contingent liabilities.

1. Christine Agazzi began production on a new dishwasher in June 2002 and, by December 31, 2002, sold 100,000 to various retailers for $500 each. Each dishwasher is under a one-year warranty. The company estimates that its warranty expense per dishwasher will amount to $25. At year-end, the company had already paid out $1,000,000 in warranty expenses. Christine Agazzi's income statement shows warranty expenses of $1,000,000 for 2002. Agazzi accounts for warranty costs on the accrual basis.

2. In response to your attorney's letter, Robert Sklodowski, Esq., has informed you that Agazzi has been cited for dumping toxic waste into the Kishwaukee River. Clean-up costs and fines amount to $3,330,000. Although the case is still being contested, Sklodowski is certain that Agazzi will most probably have to pay the fine and clean-up costs. No disclosure of this situation was found in the financial statements.

3. Christine Agazzi is the defendant in a patent infringement lawsuit by Heidi Goldman over Agazzi's use of a hydraulic compressor in several of its products. Sklodowski claims that, if the suit goes against Agazzi, the loss may be as much as $5,000,000; however, Sklodowski believes the loss of this suit to be only reasonably possible. Again, no mention of this suit occurs in the financial statements.

As presented, these contingencies are not reported in accordance with GAAP which may create problems in issuing a clean audit report. You feel the need to note these problems in the work papers.

Instructions
Heading each page with the name of the company, balance sheet date, and a brief description of the problem, write a brief narrative for each of the above issues in the form of **a memorandum** to be incorporated in the audit work papers. Explain what led to the discovery of each problem, what the problem really is,

and what you advised your client to do (along with any appropriate journal entries) in order to bring these contingencies in accordance with GAAP.

P11-8 (Various Current Liabilities) Alex Rodriguez Inc., a publishing company, is preparing its December 31, 2002, financial statements and must determine the proper accounting treatment for the following situations; they have retained your group to assist them in this task.

(a) Rodriguez sells subscriptions to several magazines for a 1-year, 2-year, or 3-year period. Cash receipts from subscribers are credited to magazine subscriptions collected in advance, and this account had a balance of $2,300,000 at December 31, 2002. Outstanding subscriptions at December 31, 2002, expire as follows.

During 2003—$600,000
During 2004— 500,000
During 2005— 800,000

(b) On January 2, 2002, Rodriguez discontinued collision, fire, and theft coverage on its delivery vehicles and became self-insured for these risks. Actual losses of $50,000 during 2002 were charged to delivery expense. The 2001 premium for the discontinued coverage amounted to $80,000 and the controller wants to set up a reserve for self-insurance by a debit to delivery expense of $30,000 and a credit to the reserve for self-insurance of $30,000.

(c) A suit for breach of contract seeking damages of $1,000,000 was filed by an author against Rodriguez on July 1, 2002. The company's legal counsel believes that an unfavorable outcome is probable. A reasonable estimate of the court's award to the plaintiff is in the range between $300,000 and $700,000. No amount within this range is a better estimate of potential damages than any other amount.

(d) During December 2002, a competitor company filed suit against Rodriguez for industrial espionage claiming $1,500,000 in damages. In the opinion of management and company counsel, it is reasonably possible that damages will be awarded to the plaintiff. However, the amount of potential damages awarded to the plaintiff cannot be reasonably estimated.

Instructions

For each of the above situations, provide the journal entry that should be recorded as of December 31, 2002, or explain why an entry should not be recorded.

(AICPA adapted)

*P11-9 (Comprehensive Bond Problem) In each of the following independent cases the company closes its books on December 31.

1. Danny Ferry Co. sells $250,000 of 10% bonds on March 1, 2003. The bonds pay interest on September 1 and March 1. The due date of the bonds is September 1, 2006. The bonds yield 12%. Give entries through December 31, 2004.

2. Brad Dougherty Co. sells $600,000 of 12% bonds on June 1, 2003. The bonds pay interest on December 1 and June 1. The due date of the bonds is June 1, 2007. The bonds yield 10%. On October 1, 2004, Dougherty buys back $120,000 worth of bonds for $126,000 (includes accrued interest). Give entries through December 1, 2005.

Instructions

(Round to the nearest dollar.)

For the two cases above prepare all of the relevant journal entries from the time of sale until the date indicated. Use the effective interest method for discount and premium amortization (construct amortization tables where applicable). Amortize premium or discount on interest dates and at year-end. (Assume that no reversing entries were made.)

*P11-10 (Analysis of Amortization Schedule and Interest Entries) The following amortization and interest schedule reflects the issuance of 10-year bonds by Terrel Brandon Corporation on January 1, 1996, and the subsequent interest payments and charges. The company's year-end is December 31, and financial statements are prepared once yearly.

AMORTIZATION SCHEDULE				
Year	Cash	Interest	Amount Unamortized	Book Value
1/1/96			$5,651	$ 94,349
1996	$11,000	$11,322	5,329	94,671
1997	11,000	11,361	4,968	95,032
1998	11,000	11,404	4,564	95,436
1999	11,000	11,452	4,112	95,888
2000	11,000	11,507	3,605	96,395
2001	11,000	11,567	3,038	96,962
2002	11,000	11,635	2,403	97,597
2003	11,000	11,712	1,691	98,309
2004	11,000	11,797	894	99,106
2005	11,000	11,894		100,000

Instructions

(a) Indicate whether the bonds were issued at a premium or a discount and how you can determine this fact from the schedule.

(b) Indicate whether the amortization schedule is based on the straight-line method or the effective interest method and how you can determine which method is used.

(c) Determine the stated interest rate and the effective interest rate.

(d) On the basis of the schedule above, prepare the journal entry to record the issuance of the bonds on January 1, 1996.

(e) On the basis of the schedule above, prepare the journal entry or entries to reflect the bond transactions and accruals for 1996. (Interest is paid January 1.)

(f) On the basis of the schedule above, prepare the journal entry or entries to reflect the bond transactions and accruals for 2003. Brandon Corporation does not use reversing entries.

CONCEPTUAL CASES

C11-1 **(Nature of Liabilities)** Presented below is the current liabilities section of Nizami Corporation.

	($000)	
	2002	2001
Current liabilities		
Notes payable	$ 68,713	$ 7,700
Accounts payable	179,496	101,379
Compensation to employees	60,312	31,649
Accrued liabilities	158,198	77,621
Income taxes payable	10,486	26,491
Current maturities of long-term debt	16,592	6,649
Total current liabilities	$493,797	$251,489

Instructions

Answer the following questions.

(a) What are the essential characteristics that make an item a liability?

(b) How does one distinguish between a current liability and a long-term liability?

(c) What are accrued liabilities? Give three examples of accrued liabilities that Nizami might have.

(d) What is the theoretically correct way to value liabilities? How are current liabilities usually valued?

(e) Why are notes payable reported first in the current liability section?

C11-2 **(Current versus Noncurrent Classification)** D'Annunzio Corporation includes the following items in its liabilities at December 31, 2003.

1. Notes payable, $25,000,000, due June 30, 2004.
2. Deposits from customers on equipment ordered by them from D'Annunzio, $6,250,000.
3. Salaries payable, $3,750,000, due January 14, 2004.

Instructions

Indicate in what circumstances, if any, each of the three liabilities above would be excluded from current liabilities.

C11-3 **(Current versus Noncurrent Classification)** The following items are listed as liabilities on the balance sheet of Eleutherios Company on December 31, 2003.

Accounts payable	$ 420,000
Notes payable	750,000
Bonds payable	2,250,000

The accounts payable represent obligations to suppliers that are due in January 2004. The notes payable mature on various dates during 2004. The bonds payable mature on July 1, 2004.

These liabilities must be reported on the balance sheet in accordance with generally accepted accounting principles governing the classification of liabilities as current and noncurrent.

Instructions

(a) What is the general rule for determining whether a liability is classified as current or noncurrent?
(b) Under what conditions may any of Eleutherios Company's liabilities be classified as noncurrent? Explain your answer.

(CMA adapted)

C11-4 **(Bond Theory: Balance Sheet Presentations, Interest Rate, Premium)** On January 1, 2004, Branagh Company issued for $1,075,230 its 20-year, 13% bonds that have a maturity value of $1,000,000 and pay interest semiannually on January 1 and July 1. Bond issue costs were not material in amount. Below are three presentations of the long-term liability section of the balance sheet that might be used for these bonds at the issue date.

1. Bonds payable (maturing January 1, 2024)	$1,000,000
Unamortized premium on bonds payable	75,230
Total bond liability	$1,075,230
2. Bonds payable—principal (face value $1,000,000 maturing January 1, 2024)	$ 97,220[a]
Bonds payable—interest (semiannual payment $65,000)	978,010[b]
Total bond liability	$1,075,230
3. Bonds payable—principal (maturing January 1, 2024)	$1,000,000
Bonds payable—interest ($65,000 per period for 40 periods)	2,600,000
Total bond liability	$3,600,000

[a]The present value of $1,000,000 due at the end of 40 (6-month) periods at the yield rate of 6% per period.
[b]The present value of $65,000 per period for 40 (6-month) periods at the yield rate of 6% per period.

Instructions

(a) Discuss the conceptual merit(s) of each of the date-of-issue balance sheet presentations shown above for these bonds.
(b) Explain why investors would pay $1,075,230 for bonds that have a maturity value of only $1,000,000.
(c) Assuming that a discount rate is needed to compute the carrying value of the obligations arising from a bond issue at any date during the life of the bonds, discuss the conceptual merit(s) of using for this purpose:
   (1) The coupon or nominal rate.
   (2) The effective or yield rate at date of issue.

(d) If the obligations arising from these bonds are to be carried at their present value computed by means of the current market rate of interest, how would the bond valuation at dates subsequent to the date of issue be affected by an increase or a decrease in the market rate of interest?

(AICPA adapted)

C11-5 (Various Long-Term Liability Conceptual Issues) Emma Thompson Company has completed a number of transactions during 2003. In January the company purchased under contract a machine at a total price of $1,200,000, payable over 5 years with installments of $240,000 per year. The seller has considered the transaction as an installment sale with the title transferring to Thompson at the time of the final payment.

On March 1, 2003, Thompson issued $10 million of general revenue bonds priced at 99 with a coupon of 10% payable July 1 and January 1 of each of the next 10 years. The July 1 interest was paid and on December 30 the company transferred $1,000,000 to the trustee, Hollywood Trust Company, for payment of the January 1, 2001, interest.

Due to the depressed market for the company's stock, Thompson purchased $500,000 par value of their 6% convertible bonds for a price of $455,000. It expects to resell the bonds when the price of its stock has recovered.

As the accountant for Emma Thompson Company, you have prepared the balance sheet as of December 31, 2003, and have presented it to the president of the company. You are asked the following questions about it.

1. Why has depreciation been charged on equipment being purchased under contract? Title has not passed to the company as yet and, therefore, they are not our assets. Why should the company not show on the left side of the balance sheet only the amount paid to date instead of showing the full contract price on the left side and the unpaid portion on the right side? After all, the seller considers the transaction an installment sale.
2. What is bond discount? As a debit balance, why is it not classified among the assets?
3. Bond interest is shown as a current liability. Did we not pay our trustee, Hollywood Trust Company, the full amount of interest due this period?

Instructions
Outline your answers to these questions by writing a brief paragraph that will justify your treatment.

C11-6 (Loss Contingencies) Animaniacs Company is a manufacturer of toys. During the year, the following situations arose.

1. A safety hazard related to one of its toy products was discovered. It is considered probable that liabilities have been incurred. On the basis of past experience, a reasonable estimate of the amount of loss can be made.
2. One of its small warehouses is located on the bank of a river and could no longer be insured against flood losses. No flood losses have occurred after the date that the insurance became unavailable.
3. This year, Animaniacs began promoting a new toy by including a coupon, redeemable for a movie ticket, in each toy's carton. The movie ticket, which cost Animaniacs $3, is purchased in advance and then mailed to the customer when the coupon is received by Animaniacs. Animaniacs estimated, based on past experience, that 60% of the coupons would be redeemed. Forty-five percent of the coupons were actually redeemed this year, and the remaining 15% of the coupons are expected to be redeemed next year.

Instructions
(a) How should Animaniacs report the safety hazard? Why? Do not discuss deferred income tax implications.
(b) How should Animaniacs report the noninsurable flood risk? Why?
(c) How should Animaniacs account for the toy promotion campaign in this year?

C11-7 (Loss Contingencies) On February 1, 2003, one of the huge storage tanks of Paunee Manufacturing Company exploded. Windows in houses and other buildings within a one-mile radius of the explosion were severely damaged, and a number of people were injured. As of February 15, 2003 (when the December 31, 2002, financial statements were completed and sent to the publisher for printing and public distribution), no suits had been filed or claims asserted against the company as a consequence of the explosion. The company fully anticipates that suits will be filed and claims asserted for injuries and damages. Because the casualty was uninsured and the company considered at fault, Paunee Manufacturing will have to cover the damages from its own resources.

Instructions

Discuss fully the accounting treatment and disclosures that should be accorded the casualty and related contingent losses in the financial statements dated December 31, 2002.

C11-8 (Loss Contingency) Presented below is a note disclosure for Ralph Ellison Corporation.

Litigation and Environmental: The Company has been notified, or is a named or a potentially responsible party in a number of governmental (federal, state and local) and private actions associated with environmental matters, such as those relating to hazardous wastes, including certain sites which are on the United States EPA National Priorities List ("Superfund"). These actions seek cleanup costs, penalties and/or damages for personal injury or to property or natural resources.

In 2001, the Company recorded a pre-tax charge of $56,229,000, included in the "Other Expense (Income)—Net" caption of the Company's Consolidated Statements of Income, as an additional provision for environmental matters. These expenditures are expected to take place over the next several years and are indicative of the Company's commitment to improve and maintain the environment in which it operates. At December 31, 2001, environmental accruals amounted to $69,931,000, of which $61,535,000 are considered noncurrent and are included in the "Deferred Credits and Other Liabilities" caption of the Company's Consolidated Balance Sheets.

While it is impossible at this time to determine with certainty the ultimate outcome of environmental matters, it is management's opinion, based in part on the advice of independent counsel (after taking into account accruals and insurance coverage applicable to such actions) that when the costs are finally determined they will not have a material adverse effect on the financial position of the Company.

Instructions

Answer the following questions.

(a) What conditions must exist before a loss contingency can be recorded in the accounts?
(b) Suppose that Ralph Ellison Corporation could not reasonably estimate the amount of the loss, although it could establish with a high degree of probability the minimum and maximum loss possible. How should this information be reported in the financial statements?
(c) If the amount of the loss is uncertain, how would the loss contingency be reported in the financial statements?

C11-9 (Loss Contingencies) The following three independent sets of facts relate to (1) the possible accrual or (2) the possible disclosure of a loss contingency.

Situation I

Subsequent to the date of a set of financial statements, but prior to the issuance of the financial statements, a company enters into a contract that will probably result in a significant loss to the company. The amount of the loss can be reasonably estimated.

Situation II

A company offers a one-year warranty for the product that it manufactures. A history of warranty claims has been compiled and the probable amount of claims related to sales for a given period can be determined.

Situation III

A company has adopted a policy of recording self-insurance for any possible losses resulting from injury to others by the company's vehicles. The premium for an insurance policy for the same risk from an independent insurance company would have an annual cost of $4,000. During the period covered by the financial statements, there were no accidents involving the company's vehicles that resulted in injury to others.

Instructions

Discuss the accrual or type of disclosure necessary (if any) and the reason(s) why such disclosure is appropriate for each of the three independent sets of facts above.

(AICPA adapted)

C11-10 (Debt Issue) Roland Carlson is the president, founder, and majority owner of Thebeau Medical Corporation, an emerging medical technology products company. Thebeau is in dire need of additional capital to keep operating and to bring several promising products to final development, testing, and production. Roland, as owner of 51% of the outstanding stock, manages the company's operations. He places heavy emphasis on research and development and long-term growth. The other principal stockholder is Jana Kingston who, as a nonemployee investor, owns 40% of the stock. Jana would like to deemphasize the R & D functions and emphasize the marketing function to maximize short-run sales and profits from existing products. She believes this strategy would raise the market price of Thebeau's stock.

All of Roland's personal capital and borrowing power is tied up in his 51% stock ownership. He knows that any offering of additional shares of stock will dilute his controlling interest because he won't be able to participate in such an issuance. But, Jana has money and would likely buy enough shares to gain control of Thebeau. She then would dictate the company's future direction, even if it meant replacing Roland as president and CEO.

The company already has considerable debt. Raising additional debt will be costly, will adversely affect Thebeau's credit rating, and will increase the company's reported losses due to the growth in interest expense. Jana and the other minority stockholders express opposition to the assumption of additional debt, fearing the company will be pushed to the brink of bankruptcy. Wanting to maintain his control and to preserve the direction of "his" company, Roland is doing everything to avoid a stock issuance and is contemplating a large issuance of bonds, even if it means the bonds are issued with a high effective-interest rate.

Instructions

(a) Who are the stakeholders in this situation?

(b) What are the ethical issues in this case?

(c) What would you do if you were Roland?

Using Your Judgment

Financial Reporting Problem

3M Company

The financial statements of 3M were provided with your book or can be accessed on the Take Action! CD.

Instructions

Refer to these financial statements and the accompanying notes to answer the following questions.

(a) What was 3M's short-term debt and related weighted average interest rate in this debt?

(b) What was 3M's working capital, acid-test ratio, and current ratio? Comment on 3M's liquidity.

(c) What types of commitments and contingencies has 3M reported in its financial statements? What is management's reaction to these contingencies?

(d) What cash outflow obligations related to the repayment of long-term debt does 3M have over the next 5 years?

(e) 3M indicates that it believes that it has the ability to meet business requirements in the foreseeable future. Prepare an assessment of its solvency and financial flexibility using ratio analysis.

Financial Statement Analysis Cases

Case 1: Northland Cranberries

Despite being a publicly traded company only since 1987, **Northland Cranberries** of Wisconsin Rapids, Wisconsin, is one of the world's largest cranberry growers. Despite its short life as a publicly traded corporation, it has engaged in an aggressive growth strategy. As a consequence, the company has taken on significant amounts of both short-term and long-term debt. The following information is taken from recent annual reports of the company.

	Current Year	Prior Year
Current assets	$ 6,745,759	$ 5,598,054
Total assets	107,744,751	83,074,339
Current liabilities	10,168,685	4,484,687
Total liabilities	73,118,204	49,948,787
Stockholders' equity	34,626,547	33,125,552
Net sales	21,783,966	18,051,355
Cost of goods sold	13,057,275	8,751,220
Interest expense	3,654,006	2,393,792
Income tax expense	1,051,000	1,917,000
Net income	1,581,707	2,942,954

Instructions

(a) Evaluate the company's liquidity by calculating and analyzing working capital and the current ratio.

(b) The following discussion of the company's liquidity was provided by the company in the Management Discussion and Analysis section of the company's annual report. Comment on whether you agree with management's statements, and what might be done to remedy the situation.

The lower comparative current ratio in the current year was due to $3 million of short-term borrowing then outstanding which was incurred to fund the Yellow River Marsh acquisitions last year. As a result of the extreme seasonality of its business, the company does not believe that its current ratio or its underlying stated working capital at the current, fiscal year-end is a meaningful indication of the Company's liquidity. As of March 31 of each fiscal year, the Company has historically carried no significant amounts of inventories and by such date all of the Company's accounts receivable from its crop sold for processing under the supply agreements have been paid in cash, with the resulting cash received from such payments used to reduce indebtedness. The Company utilizes its revolving bank credit facility, together with cash generated from operations, to fund its working capital requirements throughout its growing season.

CASE 2: COMMONWEALTH EDISON CO.

The following article appeared in the *Wall Street Journal*.

Bond Markets

Giant Commonwealth Edison Issue Hits Resale Market With $70 Million Left Over

NEW YORK—**Commonwealth Edison Co.**'s slow-selling new 9¼% bonds were tossed onto the resale market at a reduced price with about $70 million still available from the $200 million offered Thursday, dealers said.

The Chicago utility's bonds, rated double-A by Moody's and double-A-minus by Standard & Poor's, originally had been priced at 99.803, to yield 9.3% in 5 years. They were marked down yesterday the equivalent of about $5.50 for each $1,000 face amount, to about 99.25, where their yield jumped to 9.45%.

Instructions

(a) How will the development above affect the accounting for Commonwealth Edison's bond issue?

(b) Provide several possible explanations for the markdown and the slow sale of Commonwealth Edison's bonds.

COMPARATIVE ANALYSIS CASE

THE COCA-COLA COMPANY AND PEPSICO INC.

Instructions

Go to the Take Action! CD and use information found there to answer the following questions related to The Coca-Cola Company and PepsiCo, Inc.

(a) How much working capital does each of these companies have at the end of 2001? Comment on the appropriateness of the working capital they maintain.

(b) Compute both company's (a) current cash debt coverage ratio, (b) cash debt coverage ratio, (c) current ratio, (d) acid-test ratio, (e) receivable turnover ratio and (f) inventory turnover ratio for 2001. Comment on each company's overall liquidity.

(c) What types of loss or gain contingencies do these two companies have at December 31, 2001?

(d) Compute the debt to total assets ratio and the times interest earned ratio for these two companies. Comment on the quality of these two ratios for both Coca-Cola and PepsiCo.

(e) What is the difference between the fair value and the historical cost (carrying amount) of each company's debt at year-end 2001? Why might a difference exist in these two amounts?

(f) Both companies have debt issued in foreign countries. Speculate as to why these companies may use foreign debt to finance their operations. What risks are involved in this strategy, and how might they adjust for this risk?

INTERNATIONAL REPORTING CASE

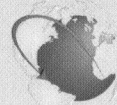

An important difference between U.S. and international accounting standards is the accounting for liabilities related to provisions. Due in part to differences in tax laws, accounting standards in some countries and the standards issued by the International Accounting Standards Board (IASB) allow recognition of liabilities for items that would not meet the definition of a liability under U.S. GAAP. The following note disclosure for liabilities related to provisions was provided by **Hoechst A.G.**, a leading German drug company, in a recent annual report. Hoechst prepares its statements in accordance with IASB standards.

Other provisions

	Current Year	Prior Year
	(in DM millions)	
Taxes	2,350	2,349
Restructuring	709	1,109
Damage and product liability claims	795	553
Environmental protection	869	814
Self insurance loss provisions	631	870
Employee-related commitments	1,123	1,243
Other	2,274	2,538
Total	8,751	9,476
Current portion thereof	(5,013)	(5,679)

Hoechst reported the following additional items in its annual report. Data for **Merck & Co.**, a U.S. drug company, are provided for comparison.

	Hoechst (DM millions)	Merck ($ millions)
Current assets	20,528	10,229
Average current liabilities	5,346	5,819
Liquid assets	391	3,356
Receivables (net)	14,362	3,374
Cash flow from operations	4,628	5,328

Instructions

(a) Compute the following ratios for Hoechst and Merck: current ratio, acid-test ratio, and the current cash debt coverage ratio. Compare the liquidity of these two drug companies based on these ratios.

(b) Identify items in Hoechst's provision disclosure that likely would not be recognized as liabilities under U.S. GAAP. (*Hint:* Refer to Illustration 11-6 in the chapter.)

(c) Discuss how the items identified in (b) would affect the comparative analysis in part (a). What adjustments would you make in your analysis? Assume that 75% of the provisions for restructuring and self-insurance are current liabilities.

Remember to check the **Take Action! CD**
and the book's **companion Web site**
to find additional resources for this chapter.

STOCKHOLDERS' EQUITY

CHAPTER 12

STOCKING UP

Quick—how did the market do yesterday? If asked this question, you probably responded that the market increased or decreased, based on the change in the Dow Jones Industrial Average. And just what is the Dow Jones Industrial Average (DJIA)? It is the average of 30 U.S. "blue-chip" (high-quality) stocks which represent the various sectors of the U.S. economy and have broad public ownership. **AT&T, American Express, Coca-Cola, Exxon Mobil, General Electric, Merck,** and **McDonald's** are examples of the type of companies found in this index.

The DJIA and other stock market indexes are becoming of increasing importance to most Americans. The reason: More and more of the country's wealth is tied up in the stock market. For example, the following chart shows the increase of stock as a percentage of U.S. household net worth over time.

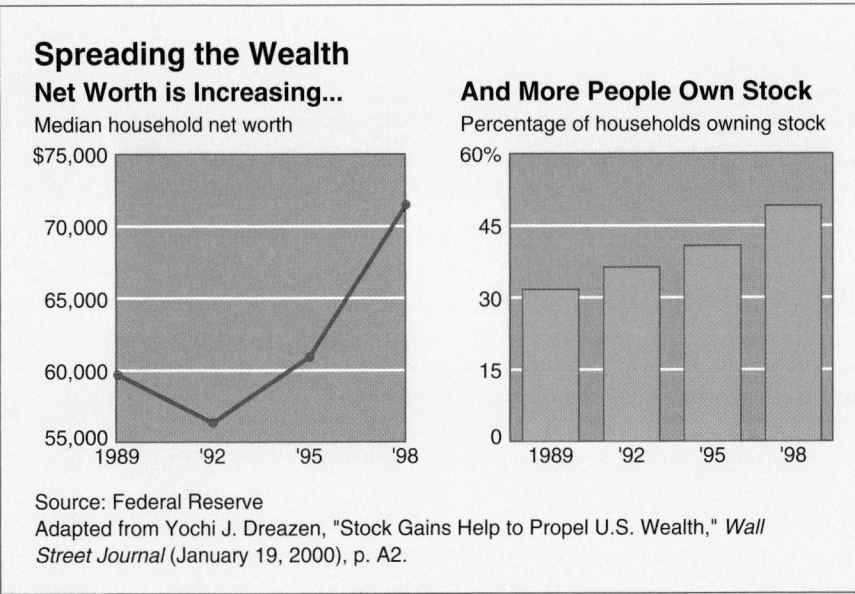

Spreading the Wealth

Net Worth is Increasing...

Median household net worth

And More People Own Stock

Percentage of households owning stock

Source: Federal Reserve
Adapted from Yochi J. Dreazen, "Stock Gains Help to Propel U.S. Wealth," *Wall Street Journal* (January 19, 2000), p. A2.

Fueled by stock-market gains, America's wealth grew at a strong pace in the latter half of the 1990s. At the same time, a record number of Americans at all income levels now own stock, intertwining their financial well-being with the stock market like never before. When the next data on household finances are reported in 2003, we will find out if Americans are staying in stocks following the recent market downturns.

As indicated from the opening story, more and more people are investing in the stock market. A public debate even has begun about whether some portion of Social Security funds should be invested in stocks. The stock market is of substantial importance in any economy that functions on private ownership. It provides a market where prices are established to serve as signals and incentives to guide the allocation of the economy's financial resources. The purpose of this chapter is to explain the various accounting issues for various transactions related to the stockholders' equity of a corporation. The content and organization of this chapter are as follows.

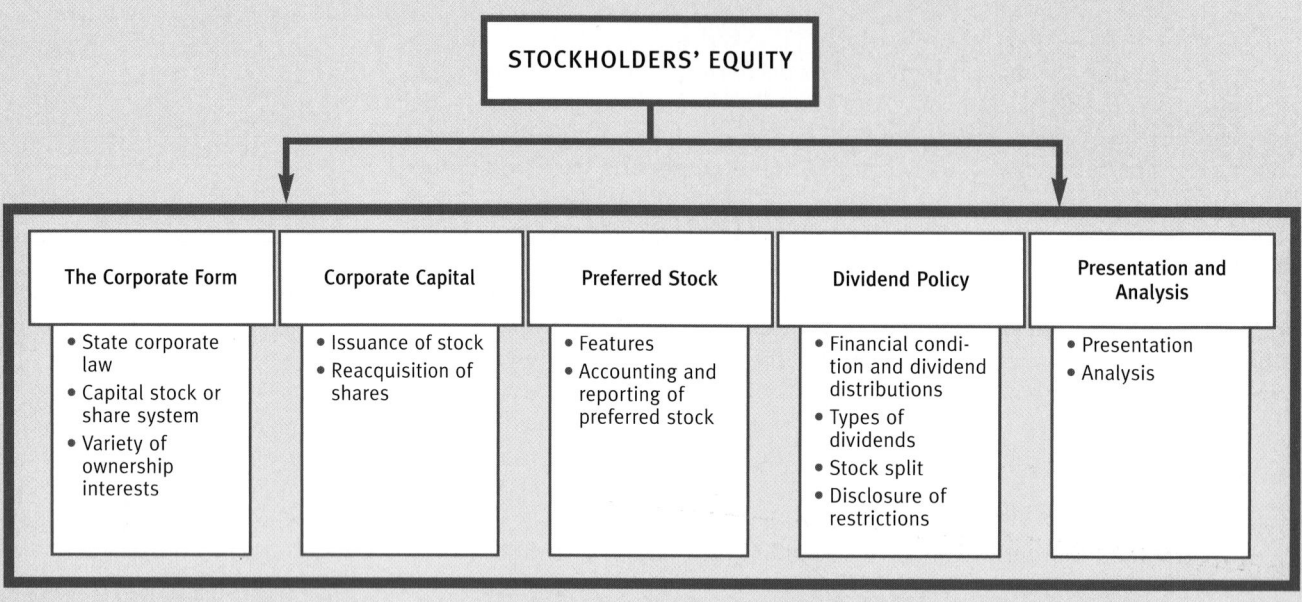

THE CORPORATE FORM

OBJECTIVE 1
Discuss the characteristics of the corporate form of organization.

Of the three **primary forms of business organization—the proprietorship, the partnership, and the corporation—**the dominant form of business is the corporate form. In terms of the aggregate amount of resources controlled, goods and services produced, and people employed, the corporation is by far the leader. All of the "Fortune 500" largest industrial firms are corporations. Although the corporate form has a number of advantages (as well as disadvantages) over the other two forms, its principal advantage is its facility for attracting and accumulating large amounts of capital.

Among the special characteristics of the corporate form that affect accounting are:

1. Influence of state corporate law.
2. Use of the capital stock or share system.
3. Development of a variety of ownership interests.

State Corporate Law

Anyone who wishes to establish a corporation must submit **articles of incorporation** to the state in which incorporation is desired. Assuming the requirements are properly fulfilled, the corporation charter is issued, and the corporation is recognized as a legal entity subject to state law. Regardless of the number of states in which a corporation has operating divisions, it is incorporated in only one state.

It is to the company's advantage to incorporate in a state whose laws are favorable to the corporate form of business organization. **General Motors**, for example, is incorporated in Delaware; **USX Corp.** is a New Jersey corporation. Some corporations have increasingly been incorporating in states with laws favorable to existing management. For example, to thwart possible unfriendly takeovers, **Gulf Oil** changed its state of incorporation to Delaware. There, certain tactics against takeovers can be approved by the board of directors alone, without a vote of the shareholders.

Each state has its own business incorporation act, and the accounting for stockholders' equity follows the provisions of this act. In many cases states have adopted the principles contained in the Model Business Corporate Act prepared by the American Bar Association. State laws are complex and vary both in their provisions and in their definitions of certain terms. Some laws fail to define technical terms, and so terms often mean one thing in one state and another thing in a different state. These problems may be further compounded because legal authorities often interpret the effects and restrictions of the laws differently.

Capital Stock or Share System

Stockholders' equity in a corporation is generally made up of a large number of units or shares. Within a given class of stock each share is exactly equal to every other share. Each owner's interest is determined by the number of shares he or she possesses. If a company has but one class of stock divided into 1,000 shares, a person owning 500 shares controls one-half of the ownership interest of the corporation; one holding 10 shares has a one-hundredth interest.

Each share of stock has certain rights and privileges that can be restricted only by special contract at the time the shares are issued. One must examine the articles of incorporation, stock certificates, and the provisions of the state law to ascertain such restrictions on or variations from the standard rights and privileges. In the absence of restrictive provisions, each share carries the following rights:

1. To share proportionately in profits and losses.
2. To share proportionately in management (the right to vote for directors).
3. To share proportionately in corporate assets upon liquidation.
4. To share proportionately in any new issues of stock of the same class—called the **preemptive right**.[1]

The first three rights are to be expected in the ownership of any business. The last may be used in a corporation to protect each stockholder's proportional interest in the enterprise. **The preemptive right protects an existing stockholder from involuntary dilution of ownership interest.** Without this right, stockholders with a given percentage interest might find their interest reduced by the issuance of additional stock without their knowledge and at prices that were not favorable to them. The preemptive right that attaches to existing shares has been eliminated by many corporations. The reason is that this right makes it inconvenient for corporations to make large issuances of additional stock, as they frequently do in acquiring other companies.

The great advantage of the share system is the ease with which an interest in the business may be transferred from one individual to another. **Individuals owning shares in a corporation may sell them to others at any time and at any price without obtaining the consent of the company or other stockholders.** Each share is personal property of the owner and may be disposed of at will. All that is required of the corporation is that it maintain a list or subsidiary ledger of stockholders as a guide to dividend payments, issuance of stock rights, voting proxies, and the like. Because shares are

---

[1]This privilege is referred to as a **stock right** or **warrant.** The warrants issued in these situations are of short duration, unlike the warrants issued with other securities.

**INTERNATIONAL
INSIGHT**

The American and British systems of corporate governance
and finance depend to a large
extent on equity financing and
the widely dispersed ownership
of shares traded in highly liquid
markets. The German and
Japanese systems have relied
more on debt financing, inter-
locking stock ownership,
banker/directors, and
worker/shareholder rights.

freely and frequently transferred, it is necessary for the corporation to revise the subsidiary ledger of stockholders periodically, generally in advance of every dividend payment or stockholders' meeting. Also, the major stock exchanges require controls that the typical corporation finds uneconomic to provide. Thus **registrars and transfer agents** who specialize in providing services for recording and transferring stock are usually used. The negotiability of stock certificates is governed by the Uniform Stock Transfer Act and the Uniform Commercial Code.

Variety of Ownership Interests

In every corporation one class of stock must represent the basic ownership interest. That class is called common stock. **Common stock** is the residual corporate interest that bears the ultimate risks of loss and receives the benefits of success. It is guaranteed neither dividends nor assets upon dissolution. But common stockholders generally control the management of the corporation and tend to profit most if the company is successful. In the event that a corporation has only one authorized issue of capital stock, that issue is by definition common stock, whether so designated in the charter or not.

In an effort to appeal to all types of investors, corporations may offer two or more classes of stock, each with different rights or privileges. The preceding section pointed out that each share of stock of a given issue has the same rights as other shares of the same issue and that there are four rights inherent in every share. By special stock contracts between the corporation and its stockholders, certain of these rights may be sacrificed by the stockholder in return for other special rights or privileges. Thus special classes of stock are created. Because they have certain preferential rights, they are usually called **preferred stock**. In return for any special preference, the preferred stockholder is always called on to sacrifice some of the inherent rights of capital stock interests.

A common type of preference is to give the preferred stockholders a prior claim on earnings. They are assured a dividend, usually at a stated rate, before any amount may be distributed to the common stockholders. In return for this preference the preferred stock may sacrifice its right to a voice in management or its right to share in profits beyond the stated rate.

***WHAT DO THE
NUMBERS MEAN?***

CLASSY STOCK

Some companies grant preferences to different shareholders by issuing different classes of common stock. And sometimes these different classes of shares trade at dramatically different prices. For example, **Molex** has issued both common shares and Class A common stock, with the common shares trading at up to a 15 percent premium over the Class A shares. Why the difference in price? The most common explanation is voting rights. In the Molex case, the common shareholders get one vote per share; Class A shares don't get to vote.

For most retail investors, voting rights are not that important. But for family-controlled companies, issuing newer classes of lower or non-voting stock is an effective way to create currency for acquisitions, increase liquidity, or put a public value on the company without diluting the family's voting control. Thus, investors must be careful when comparing the apparent bargain prices for some classes of stock—they may end up as second-class citizens with no voting rights.

Source: Adapted from Lauren Rublin, "Separate but Equal," *Barons On-Line* (August 16, 1999).

CORPORATE CAPITAL

Owner's equity in a corporation is defined as stockholders' equity, shareholders' equity, or corporate capital. The following three categories normally appear as part of stockholders' equity:

①⟩ Capital stock.

②⟩ Additional paid-in capital.

③⟩ Retained earnings.

The first two categories, capital stock and additional paid-in capital, constitute contributed (paid-in) capital. **Retained earnings** represents the earned capital of the enterprise. **Contributed capital (paid-in capital)** is the total amount paid in on capital stock—the amount provided by stockholders to the corporation for use in the business. Contributed capital includes items such as the par value of all outstanding stock and premiums less discounts on issuance. **Earned capital** is the capital that develops if the business operates profitably; it consists of all undistributed income that remains invested in the enterprise.

Stockholders' equity is the difference between the assets and the liabilities of the enterprise. **Therefore, the owners' or stockholders' interest in a business enterprise is a residual interest.**[2] **Stockholders' (owners') equity** represents the cumulative net contributions by stockholders plus earnings that have been retained. As a residual interest, stockholders' equity has no existence apart from the assets and liabilities of the enterprise—stockholders' equity equals net assets. Stockholders' equity is not a claim to specific assets but a claim against a portion of the total assets. Its amount is not specified or fixed; it depends on the enterprise's profitability. Stockholders' equity grows if the enterprise is profitable. It shrinks, or may disappear entirely, if the enterprise is unprofitable.

> OBJECTIVE **2**
> Explain the key components of stockholders' equity.

Issuance of Stock

In issuing stock, the following procedures are followed: First, the stock must be authorized by the state, generally in a certificate of incorporation or charter. Next, shares are offered for sale, and contracts to sell stock are entered into. Then, amounts to be received for the stock are collected and the shares issued.

The accounting problems involved in the issuance of stock are discussed under the following topics.

> OBJECTIVE **3**
> Explain the accounting procedures for issuing shares of stock.

①⟩ Accounting for par value stock.

②⟩ Accounting for no-par stock.

③⟩ Accounting for stock issued in combination with other securities (lump-sum sales).

④⟩ Accounting for stock issued in noncash transactions.

⑤⟩ Accounting for costs of issuing stock.

Par Value Stock

The par value of a stock has no relationship to its fair market value. At present, the par value associated with most capital stock issuances is very low ($1, $5, $10). Such values contrast dramatically with the situation in the early 1900s, when practically all stock

---

[2]"Elements of Financial Statements," *Statement of Financial Accounting Concepts No. 6* (Stamford, Conn.: FASB, 1985), par. 60.

issued had a par value of $100. The reason for this change is to permit the original sale of stock at low amounts per share and to avoid the contingent liability associated with stock sold below par.[3]

To show the required information for issuance of par value stock, accounts must be kept for each class of stock as follows.

① *Preferred Stock or Common Stock.* Reflects the par value of the corporation's issued shares. These accounts are credited when the shares are originally issued. No additional entries are made in these accounts unless additional shares are issued or shares are retired.

② *Paid-in Capital in Excess of Par* or *Additional Paid-in Capital.* Indicates any excess over par value paid in by stockholders in return for the shares issued to them. Once paid in, the excess over par becomes a part of the corporation's additional paid-in capital, and the individual stockholder has no greater claim on the excess paid in than all other holders of the same class of shares.

No entry is generally made in the general ledger accounts at the time the corporation receives its stock authorization from the state of incorporation.

No-Par Stock

Many states permit the issuance of capital stock without par value. **No-par stock** is shares issued with no per-share amount printed on the stock certificate. The reasons for issuance of no-par stock are twofold: First, issuance of no-par stock **avoids the contingent liability** that might occur if par value stock were issued at a discount. Second, some confusion exists over the relationship (or rather the absence of a relationship) between the par value and fair market value. If shares have no par value, **the questionable treatment of using par value as a basis for fair value never arises**. This circumstance is particularly advantageous whenever stock is issued for property items such as tangible or intangible fixed assets. The major disadvantages of no-par stock are that some states levy a high tax on these issues, and the total may be considered legal capital.

No-par shares, like par value shares, are sold for whatever price they will bring, but unlike par value shares, they are issued without a premium or a discount. The exact amount received represents the credit to common or preferred stock. For example, Video Electronics Corporation is organized with authorized common stock of 10,000 shares without par value. No entry, other than a memorandum entry, need be made for the authorization, inasmuch as no amount is involved. If 500 shares are then issued for cash at $10 per share, the entry should be:

Cash	5,000	
Common Stock—No-Par Value		5,000

If another 500 shares are issued for $11 per share, the entry should be:

Cash	5,500	
Common Stock—No-Par Value		5,500

---

[3]Stock with a low par value is rarely, if ever, issued below par value. If stock is issued below par, the discount is recorded as a debit to Additional Paid-in Capital. In addition, the original purchaser or the current holder of the shares issued below par may be called on to pay in the amount of the discount to prevent creditors from sustaining a loss upon liquidation of the corporation.

True no-par stock should be carried in the accounts at issue price without any complications due to additional paid-in capital or discount. But some states permit the issuance of no-par stock and then either require or, in some cases, permit such stock to have a **stated value**, that is, a minimum value below which it cannot be issued. Thus, instead of becoming no-par stock, it becomes, in effect, stock with a very low par value, open to all the criticism and abuses that first encouraged the development of no-par stock.[4]

If no-par stock is required to have a minimum issue price of $5 per share and no provision is made as to how amounts in excess of $5 per share are to be handled, the board of directors usually declares all such amounts to be additional paid-in capital, which in many states is fully or partially available for dividends. Thus, no-par value stock with either a minimum stated value or a stated value assigned by the board of directors permits a new corporation to commence its operations with additional paid-in capital that may be in excess of its stated capital. For example, if 1,000 of the shares with a $5 stated value were issued at $15 per share for cash, the entry could be either

Cash	15,000	
Common Stock		15,000

or

Cash	15,000	
Common Stock		5,000
Paid-in Capital in Excess of Stated Value		10,000

In most instances the obvious advantages to the corporation of setting up an initial Additional Paid-in Capital account will influence the board of directors to require the latter entry. Whether for this or for other reasons, the prevailing tendency is to account for no-par stock with stated value as if it were par value stock with par equal to the stated value.

Stock Issued with Other Securities (Lump-Sum Sales)

Generally, corporations sell classes of stock separately from one another so that the proceeds relative to each class, and ordinarily even relative to each lot, are known. Occasionally, two or more classes of securities are issued for a single payment or lump sum. It is not uncommon, for example, for more than one type or class of security to be issued in the acquisition of another company. The accounting problem in such **lump-sum sales** is the allocation of the proceeds among the several classes of securities. The two methods of allocation available are (1) the proportional method and (2) the incremental method.

Proportional Method. If the fair market value or other sound basis for determining relative value is available for each class of security, **the lump sum received is allocated among the classes of securities on a proportional basis**, that is, the ratio that each is to the total. For instance, if 1,000 shares of $10 stated value common stock having a market value of $20 a share, and 1,000 shares of $10 par value preferred stock having a market value of $12 a share are issued for a lump sum of $30,000, the allocation of the $30,000 to the two classes would be as shown in Illustration 12-1.

---

[4]*Accounting Trends and Techniques—2001* indicates that its 600 surveyed companies reported 644 issues of outstanding common stock, 561 par value issues, and 57 no-par issues; 7 of the no-par issues were shown at their stated (assigned) values.

Illustration 12-1
Allocation in Lump-Sum
Securities Issuance—
Proportional Method

Fair market value of common (1,000 × $20) =	$20,000
Fair market value of preferred (1,000 × $12) =	12,000
Aggregate fair market value	$32,000
Allocated to common: $\frac{\$20,000}{\$32,000} \times \$30,000 =$	$18,750
Allocated to preferred: $\frac{\$12,000}{\$32,000} \times \$30,000 =$	11,250
Total allocation	$30,000

Incremental Method. In instances where the fair market value of all classes of securities is not determinable, the incremental method may be used. The market value of the securities is used as a basis for those classes that are known, and the remainder of the lump sum is allocated to the class for which the market value is not known. For instance, if 1,000 shares of $10 stated value common stock having a market value of $20, and 1,000 shares of $10 par value preferred stock having no established market value are issued for a lump sum of $30,000, the allocation of the $30,000 to the two classes would be as follows.

Illustration 12-2
Allocation in Lump-Sum
Securities Issuance—
Incremental Method

Lump-sum receipt	$30,000
Allocated to common (1,000 × $20)	20,000
Balance allocated to preferred	$10,000

If no fair value is determinable for any of the classes of stock involved in a lump-sum exchange, the allocation may have to be arbitrary. An expert's appraisal may be used. Or, if it is known that one or more of the classes of securities issued will have a determinable market value in the near future, the arbitrary basis may be used with the intent to make an adjustment when the future market value is established.

Stock Issued in Noncash Transactions

Accounting for the issuance of shares of stock for property or services involves an issue of valuation. **The general rule is: Stock issued for services or property other than cash should be recorded at either the fair value of the stock issued or the fair value of the noncash consideration received, whichever is more clearly determinable.**

If both are readily determinable and the transaction is the result of an arm's-length exchange, there will probably be little difference in their fair values. In such cases it should not matter which value is regarded as the basis for valuing the exchange.

If the fair value of the stock being issued and the property or services being received are not readily determinable, the value to be assigned is generally established by the board of directors or management at an amount they consider fair and that is not controverted by available evidence. Independent appraisals usually serve as dependable bases. The use of the book, par, or stated values as a basis of valuation for these transactions should be avoided.

Unissued stock or treasury stock (issued shares that have been reacquired but not retired) may be exchanged for the property or services. If treasury shares are used, their cost should not be regarded as the decisive factor in establishing the fair value of the property or services. Instead, the fair value of the treasury stock, if known, should be used to value the property or services. If the fair value of the treasury stock is not known, the fair value of the property or services should be used, if determinable.

The following series of transactions illustrates the procedure for recording the issuance of 10,000 shares of $10 par value common stock for a patent, in various circumstances.

① The fair value of the patent is not readily determinable, but the fair value of the stock is known to be $140,000.

Patent	140,000	
Common Stock (10,000 shares × $10 per share)		100,000
Paid-in Capital in Excess of Par		40,000

② The fair value of the stock is not readily determinable, but the fair value of the patent is determined to be $150,000.

Patent	150,000	
Common Stock (10,000 shares × $10 per share)		100,000
Paid-in Capital in Excess of Par		50,000

③ Neither the fair value of the stock nor the fair value of the patent is readily determinable. An independent consultant values the patent at $125,000, and the board of directors agrees with that valuation.

Patent	125,000	
Common Stock (10,000 shares × $10 share)		100,000
Paid-in Capital in Excess of Par		25,000

In corporate law, the board of directors is granted the power to set the value of noncash transactions. This power has been abused. The issuance of stock for property or services has resulted in cases of overstated corporate capital through intentional overvaluation of the property or services received. The overvaluation of the stockholders' equity resulting from inflated asset values creates what is referred to as **watered stock**. The "water" can be eliminated from the corporate structure by simply writing down the overvalued assets.

If as a result of the issuance of stock for property or services the recorded assets are undervalued, **secret reserves** are created. An understated corporate structure or secret reserve may also be achieved by other methods: excessive depreciation or amortization charges, expensing capital expenditures, excessive write-downs of inventories or receivables, or any other understatement of assets or overstatement of liabilities. An example of a liability overstatement is an excessive provision for estimated product warranties that ultimately results in an understatement of owners' equity, thereby creating a secret reserve.

Costs of Issuing Stock

Direct costs incurred to sell stock, such as underwriting costs, accounting and legal fees, printing costs, and taxes, should be reported as a reduction of the amounts paid in. Issue costs are therefore debited to Additional Paid-in Capital because they are unrelated to corporate operations. In effect, **issue costs are a cost of financing** and should reduce the proceeds received from the sale of the stock.

Management salaries and other indirect costs related to the stock issue should be expensed as incurred because it is difficult to establish a relationship between these costs and the proceeds received upon sale. In addition, corporations annually incur costs for maintaining the stockholders' records and handling ownership transfers. These recurring costs, primarily registrar and transfer agents' fees, are normally charged to expense in the period in which incurred.

Reacquisition of Shares

OBJECTIVE 4
Explain the accounting for treasury stock.

It is not unusual for companies to buy back their own shares. In fact, share buybacks now exceed dividends as a form of distribution to stockholders.[5] **Merrill Lynch & Co.** estimated that in a recent year more than 1,400 corporations announced buyback programs totaling over $80 billion and 2.4 billion shares. Two of the biggest stock buyback programs were **General Motors'** purchase of 20 percent (64 million shares) of its stock for $4.8 billion, and **Santa Fe Southern Pacific's** buyback of 38 percent (60 million shares) of its stock for $3.4 billion in the mid-1990s. Data on recent corporate buybacks indicate that companies are continuing to spend millions of dollars to repurchase shares. For example, during one week in 2001, over 70 companies announced buybacks of as much as $12 billion of their own shares. As a result of buybacks, **Boeing** reduced its shares outstanding by 11 percent, and outstanding shares of **Rex Stores** declined by 24 percent during 2001.

The reasons corporations purchase their outstanding stock are varied. Some major reasons are:

1. *To provide tax efficient distributions of excess cash to shareholders.* Capital gain rates on sales of stock to the company by the stockholders are approximately half of what ordinary tax rates are. As a result, most stockholders will pay less tax if they receive cash in a buyback versus receiving a cash dividend.

2. *To increase earnings per share and return on equity.* By reducing shares outstanding and by reducing stockholders' equity, certain performance ratios often are enhanced.

3. *To provide stock for employee stock compensation contracts or to meet potential merger needs.* **Honeywell Inc.** reported that part of its purchase of one million common shares was to be used for employee stock option contracts. Other companies acquire shares to have them available for business acquisitions.

4. *To thwart takeover attempts or to reduce the number of stockholders.* By reducing the number of shares held by the public, existing owners and managements can keep "outsiders" from gaining control or significant influence. When Ted Turner attempted to acquire **CBS**, CBS started a substantial buyback of its stock. Stock purchases may also be used to eliminate dissident stockholders.

5. *To make a market in the stock.* As one company executive noted, "Our company is trying to establish a floor for the stock." By purchasing stock in the marketplace, a demand is created which may stabilize the stock price or, in fact, increase it.

Some publicly held corporations have chosen to "go private," that is, to eliminate public (outside) ownership entirely by purchasing all of their outstanding stock. Such a procedure is often accomplished through a **leveraged buyout (LBO)**, as discussed in Chapter 11.

---

[5]At the beginning of the 1990s the situation was just the opposite; that is, share buybacks were less than half the level of dividends. Companies are extremely reluctant to reduce or eliminate their dividends, because they believe that this action would be viewed negatively by the market. On the other hand, many companies are no longer raising their dividends per share at the same percentage rate as increases in earnings per share, thus effectively reducing the dividend payout over time.

Once shares are reacquired, they may either be retired or held in the treasury for reissue. If not retired, such shares are referred to as **treasury shares** or **treasury stock**. Technically, treasury stock is a corporation's own stock that has been reacquired after having been issued and fully paid.

Treasury stock is not an asset. When treasury stock is purchased, a reduction occurs in both assets and stockholders' equity. It is inappropriate to imply that a corporation can own a part of itself. Treasury stock may be sold to obtain funds, but that possibility does not make treasury stock a balance sheet asset. When a corporation buys back some of its own outstanding stock, it has reduced its capitalization, but it has not acquired an asset. The possession of treasury stock does not give the corporation the right to vote, to exercise preemptive rights as a stockholder, to receive cash dividends, or to receive assets upon corporate liquidation. **Treasury stock is essentially the same as unissued capital stock**, and no one advocates classifying unissued capital stock as an asset in the balance sheet.[6]

UNDERLYING CONCEPTS

As indicated in Chapter 2, an asset should have probable future economic benefits. Treasury stock simply reduces common stock outstanding.

SIGNALS TO BUY?

WHAT DO THE NUMBERS MEAN?

Market analysts sometimes look to stock buybacks as a buy signal for a stock. That strategy is not that surprising if you look at the performance of companies that did buybacks. For example, in one study, buyback companies outperformed similar companies without buybacks by an average of 23 percent. In 2001, companies followed by **Buybackletter.com** over a 3-year period were up 16.4 percent, while the S&P 500 Stock Index was up just 7.1 percent in that period. Why the premium? Well, the conventional wisdom is that companies who buy back shares believe their shares are undervalued. Thus, the buyback announcement is viewed as an important piece of inside information about future company prospects.

One warning for traders following buybacks: Research shows that the biggest market gains accrue to companies that report the biggest reduction in shares outstanding following the buyback. Thus, you want to be certain that an announced buyback actually results in a net reduction in shares outstanding. For example, when companies, such as **Microsoft**, bought back shares to meet share demands for stock option exercises, net shares outstanding actually increased, when the repurchased shares were re-issued to the option holders upon exercise. In this case the buyback was not a signal to buy, but an indication that share ownership in the buyback company will be further diluted.

Source: Adapted from Ann Tergesen, "When Buybacks Are Signals to Buy," *Business Week Online* (October 1, 2001).

Purchase of Treasury Stock

Two general methods of handling treasury stock in the accounts are the cost method and the par value method. Both methods are generally acceptable. The **cost method** enjoys more widespread use.[7] It results in debiting the Treasury Stock account for the reacquisition cost and in reporting this account as a deduction from the total paid-in capital **and** retained earnings on the balance sheet. The **par** or **stated value method** records all transactions in treasury shares at their par value and reports the treasury stock as a deduction from capital stock only. No matter which method is used, the cost

---

[6]The possible justification for classifying these shares as assets is that they will be used to liquidate a specific liability that appears on the balance sheet. *Accounting Trends and Techniques—2001* reported that out of 600 companies surveyed, 410 disclosed treasury stock, but none classified it as an asset.

[7]*Accounting Trends and Techniques—2001* indicates that of its selected list of 600 companies, 384 carried common stock in treasury at cost and only 23 at par or stated value; 3 companies carried preferred stock in treasury at cost and 1 at par or stated value.

of the treasury shares acquired is considered a restriction on retained earnings in most states.

The cost method is generally used in accounting for treasury stock. This method derives its name from the fact that the Treasury Stock account is maintained at the cost of the shares purchased.[8] Under the cost method, the Treasury Stock account is debited for the cost of the shares acquired and upon reissuance of the shares is credited for this same cost. The price received for the stock when it was originally issued does not affect the entries to record the acquisition and reissuance of the treasury stock.

To illustrate, assume that Ho Company has issued 100,000 shares of $1 par value common stock at a price of $10 per share. In addition, it has retained earnings of $300,000. The stockholders' equity section on December 31, 2003, before purchase of treasury stock is as follows.

Illustration 12-3

Stockholders' Equity with No Treasury Stock

Stockholders' equity		
Paid-in capital		
Common stock, $1 par value, 100,000 shares		
issued and outstanding		$ 100,000
Additional paid-in capital		900,000
Total paid-in capital		1,000,000
Retained earnings		300,000
Total stockholders' equity		$1,300,000

On January 20, 2004, Ho Company acquires 10,000 shares of its stock at $11 per share. The entry to record the reacquisition is:

January 20, 2004

Treasury Stock	110,000	
Cash		110,000

Note that Treasury Stock is debited for the cost of the shares purchased. The original paid-in capital account, Common Stock, is not affected because the number of issued shares does not change. The same is true for the Additional Paid-in Capital account. Treasury stock is deducted from total paid-in capital and retained earnings in the stockholders' equity section.

The stockholders' equity section for Ho Company after purchase of the treasury stock is as follows.

Illustration 12-4

Stockholders' Equity with Treasury Stock

Stockholders' equity		
Paid-in capital		
Common stock, $1 par value, 100,000 shares		
issued and 90,000 outstanding		$ 100,000
Additional paid-in capital		900,000
Total paid-in capital		1,000,000
Retained earnings		300,000
Total paid-in capital and retained earnings		1,300,000
Less: Cost of treasury stock (10,000 shares)		110,000
Total stockholders' equity		$1,190,000

[8]If numerous acquisitions of blocks of treasury shares are made at different prices, inventory costing methods—such as specific identification, average, or FIFO—may be used to identify the cost at date of reissuance.

The cost of the treasury stock is subtracted from the total of common stock, additional paid-in capital, and retained earnings. It therefore reduces stockholders' equity. Many states require a corporation to restrict retained earnings for the cost of treasury stock purchased. The restriction serves to keep intact the corporation's legal capital that is temporarily being held as treasury stock. When treasury stock is sold, the restriction is lifted.

Both the number of shares issued (100,000) and the number in the treasury (10,000) are disclosed. The difference is the number of shares of stock outstanding (90,000). The term **outstanding stock** means the number of shares of issued stock that are being held by stockholders.

Sale of Treasury Stock

Treasury stock is usually sold or retired. When treasury shares are sold, the accounting for the sale depends on the price. If the selling price of the treasury stock is equal to cost, the sale of the shares is recorded by a debit to Cash and a credit to Treasury Stock. In cases where the selling price of the treasury stock is not equal to cost, then accounting for treasury stock sold **above cost** differs from the accounting for treasury stock sold **below cost**. However, the sale of treasury stock either above or below cost increases both total assets and stockholders' equity.

Sale of Treasury Stock above Cost. When the selling price of shares of treasury stock is greater than cost, the difference is credited to Paid-in Capital from Treasury Stock. To illustrate, assume that 1,000 shares of treasury stock of Ho Company previously acquired at $11 per share are sold at $15 per share on March 10. The entry is as follows.

March 10, 2004

Cash	15,000	
Treasury Stock		11,000
Paid-in Capital from Treasury Stock		4,000

There are two reasons why the $4,000 credit in the entry would not be made to Gain on Sale of Treasury Stock: (1) Gains on sales occur when **assets** are sold, and treasury stock is not an asset. (2) A corporation does not realize a gain or suffer a loss from stock transactions with its own stockholders. Thus, paid-in capital arising from the sale of treasury stock should not be included in the measurement of net income. Paid-in capital from treasury stock is listed separately on the balance sheet as a part of paid-in capital.

Sale of Treasury Stock below Cost. When treasury stock is sold below its cost, the excess of the cost over selling price is usually debited to Paid-in Capital from Treasury Stock. Thus, if Ho Company sells an additional 1,000 shares of treasury stock on March 21 at $8 per share, the entry is as follows.

March 21, 2004

Cash	8,000	
Paid-in Capital from Treasury Stock	3,000	
Treasury Stock		11,000

Observe from the two sale entries (sale above cost and sale below cost) that (1) Treasury Stock is credited at cost in each entry, (2) Paid-in Capital from Treasury Stock is used for the difference between the cost and the resale price of the shares, and (3) the original paid-in capital account, Common Stock, is not affected.

When the credit balance in Paid-in Capital from Treasury Stock is eliminated, any additional excess of cost over selling price is debited to Retained Earnings. To illustrate, assume that Ho Company sells an additional 1,000 shares at $8 per share on April 10. The balance in the Paid-in Capital from Treasury Stock account is:

Illustration 12-5
Treasury Stock
Transactions in Paid-in
Capital Account

Paid-in Capital from Treasury Stock			
Mar. 21	3,000	Mar. 10	4,000
		Balance	1,000

In this case, $1,000 of the excess is debited to Paid-in Capital from Treasury Stock, and the remainder is debited to Retained Earnings. The entry is:

April 10, 2004

Cash	8,000	
Paid-in Capital from Treasury Stock	1,000	
Retained Earnings	2,000	
Treasury Stock		11,000

Retiring Treasury Stock

The board of directors may approve the retirement of treasury shares. This decision results in cancellation of the treasury stock and a reduction in the number of shares of issued stock. Retired treasury shares have the status of authorized and unissued shares. The accounting effects are similar to the sale of treasury stock except that debits are made to the **paid-in capital accounts applicable to the retired shares** instead of to cash. For example, if the shares are originally sold at par, Common Stock is debited for the par value per share. If the shares are originally sold at $3 above par value, a debit to Paid-in Capital in Excess of Par Value for $3 per share is also required.

PREFERRED STOCK

OBJECTIVE 5
Explain the accounting for and reporting of preferred stock.

Preferred stock is a special class of shares that is designated "preferred" because it possesses certain preferences or features not possessed by the common stock.[9] The following features are those most often associated with preferred stock issues.

1. Preference as to dividends.
2. Preference as to assets in the event of liquidation.
3. Convertible into common stock.
4. Callable at the option of the corporation.
5. Nonvoting.

The features that distinguish preferred from common stock may be of a more restrictive and negative nature than preferences. For example, the preferred stock may be nonvoting, noncumulative, and nonparticipating.

[9]*Accounting Trends and Techniques—2001* reports that of its 600 surveyed companies, 86 had preferred stock outstanding; 71 had one class of preferred, and 10 had two classes.

Preferred stock is usually issued with a par value, and the dividend preference is expressed as a **percentage of the par value**. Thus, holders of 8 percent preferred stock with a $100 par value are entitled to an annual dividend of $8 per share. This stock is commonly referred to as 8 percent preferred stock. In the case of no-par preferred stock, a dividend preference is expressed as a **specific dollar amount** per share, for example, $7 per share. This stock is commonly referred to as $7 preferred stock.

A preference as to dividends is not assurance that dividends will be paid. It is merely assurance that the stated dividend rate or amount applicable to the preferred stock must be paid before any dividends can be paid on the common stock.

Features of Preferred Stock

A corporation may attach whatever preferences or restrictions in whatever combination it desires to a preferred stock issue, so long as it does not specifically violate its state incorporation law. Also, it may issue more than one class of preferred stock. The most common features attributed to preferred stock are discussed below.

1. *Cumulative Preferred Stock.* Dividends not paid in any year must be made up in a later year before any profits can be distributed to common stockholders. If the directors fail to declare a dividend at the normal date for dividend action, the dividend is said to have been "passed." Any passed dividend on cumulative preferred stock constitutes a **dividend in arrears**. Because no liability exists until the board of directors declares a dividend, a dividend in arrears is not recorded as a liability but is disclosed in a note to the financial statements. Noncumulative preferred stock is seldom issued because a passed dividend is lost forever to the preferred stockholder, and so this stock issue would be less marketable.

2. *Participating Preferred Stock.* Holders of participating preferred stock share ratably with the common stockholders in any profit distributions beyond the prescribed rate. That is, 5 percent preferred stock, if fully participating, will receive not only its 5 percent return, but also dividends at the same rates as those paid to common stockholders if amounts in excess of 5 percent of par or stated value are paid to common stockholders. Also, participating preferred stock may not always be fully participating, but may be partially participating. Although participating preferreds are not used extensively (unlike the cumulative provision), examples of companies that have used participating preferreds are **LTV Corporation**, **Southern California Edison**, and **Allied Products Corporation**.

3. *Convertible Preferred Stock.* The stockholders may at their option exchange preferred shares for common stock at a predetermined ratio. The convertible preferred stockholder not only enjoys a preferred claim on dividends but also has the option of converting into a common stockholder with unlimited participation in earnings.

4. *Callable Preferred Stock.* The issuing corporation at its option can call or redeem the outstanding preferred shares at specified future dates and at stipulated prices. Many preferred issues are callable. The call or redemption price is ordinarily set slightly above the original issuance price and is commonly stated in terms related to the par value. The callable feature permits the corporation to use the capital obtained through the issuance of such stock until the need has passed or it is no longer advantageous. The existence of a call price or prices tends to set a ceiling on the market value of the preferred shares unless they are convertible into common stock. When a preferred stock is called for redemption, any dividends in arrears must be paid.

Preferred stock is often issued (instead of debt) because a company's debt-to-equity ratio has become too high. In other instances, issuances are made through private placements with other corporations at a lower-than-market dividend rate because the acquiring corporation receives dividends that are largely tax free (owing to the IRS's 70 percent or 80 percent dividends received deduction).[10]

Accounting for and Reporting of Preferred Stock

The accounting for preferred stock at issuance is similar to that for common stock, with proceeds allocated between the par value of the preferred stock and additional paid-in capital. To illustrate, assume that Bishop Co. issues 10,000 shares of $10 par value preferred stock for $12 cash per share. The entry to record the issuance is:

Cash	120,000	
Preferred Stock		100,000
Paid-in Capital in Excess of Par		20,000

Thus, separate accounts are maintained for these different classes of shares.

Convertible preferred stock (in contrast to convertible bonds which are recorded as a liability on the date of issue) also is considered a part of stockholders' equity. In addition, when convertible preferred stocks are exercised, there is no theoretical justification for recognition of a gain or loss. No gain or loss is recognized when the entity deals with stockholders in their capacity as business owners. The **book value method is employed**: Preferred Stock, along with any related Additional Paid-in Capital, is debited; Common Stock and Additional Paid-in Capital (if an excess exists) are credited.

Preferred stock generally has no maturity date, and therefore no legal obligation exists to pay the preferred stockholder. As a result, preferred stock is classified as part of stockholders' equity. Preferred stock is generally reported at par value as the first item in the stockholders' equity section. Any excess over par value is reported as part of additional paid-in capital. Dividends on preferred stock are considered a distribution of income and not an expense of the corporation. Companies must disclose the pertinent rights of the preferred stock outstanding.[11]

OBJECTIVE **6**
Describe the policies used in distributing dividends.

DIVIDEND POLICY

Determining the proper amount of dividends to pay is a difficult financial management decision. Companies that are paying dividends are extremely reluctant to reduce or eliminate their dividend, because they believe that this action could be viewed negatively by the securities market. As a consequence, companies that have been paying cash dividends will make every effort to continue to do so. In addition, the type of shareholder the company has (taxable or nontaxable, retail investor or institutional investor) plays a large role in determining dividend policy. For example, a nontaxable

[10]Recently, more and more issuances of preferred stock have features that make the security more like debt (legal obligation to pay) than an equity instrument. For example, **redeemable preferred stock** is preferred stock that has a mandatory redemption period or a redemption feature that is outside the control of the issuer. Under current accounting standards, most companies report redeemable preferred stock between debt and equity classifications (the so-called **mezzanine**). Under a proposed accounting standard "Exposure Draft: Accounting for Financial Instruments with Characteristics of Liabilities, Equity, or Both," *Proposed Statement of Financial Accounting Standards* (Norwalk, Conn: FASB, October 27, 2000), companies will be required to report redeemable preferred stock as debt. Appendix 12A discusses two financial instruments that have characteristics of both debt and equity.

[11]"Disclosure of Information about Capital Structure," *Statement of Financial Accounting Standards No. 129* (Norwalk, Conn.: FASB, 1997).

entity will probably prefer cash dividends rather than a share buyback because tax considerations are not as important. As indicated earlier, more companies are becoming involved in share buyback programs and are either not starting or not increasing their present dividend program significantly.

Very few companies pay dividends in amounts equal to their legally available retained earnings. The major reasons are as follows.

1. Agreements (bond covenants) with specific creditors to retain all or a portion of the earnings, in the form of assets, to build up additional protection against possible loss.

2. Some state corporation laws require that earnings equivalent to the cost of treasury shares purchased be restricted against dividend declarations.

3. Desire to retain assets that would otherwise be paid out as dividends, to finance growth or expansion. This is sometimes called internal financing, reinvesting earnings, or "plowing" the profits back into the business.

4. Desire to smooth out dividend payments from year to year by accumulating earnings in good years and using such accumulated earnings as a basis for dividends in bad years.

5. Desire to build up a cushion or buffer against possible losses or errors in the calculation of profits.

The reasons above are probably self-explanatory except for the second. The laws of some states require that the corporation's legal capital be restricted from distribution to stockholders so that it may serve as a protection against loss for creditors.[12] The legality of a dividend can be determined only by reviewing the applicable state law.

Financial Condition and Dividend Distributions

Good management of a business requires attention to more than the legality of dividend distributions. Consideration must be given to economic conditions, most importantly, liquidity. Assume an extreme situation as follows.

BALANCE SHEET			
Plant assets	$500,000	Capital stock	$400,000
	$500,000	Retained earnings	100,000
			$500,000

Illustration 12-6
Balance Sheet, Showing a Lack of Liquidity

The depicted company has a retained earnings credit balance and generally, unless it is restricted, can declare a dividend of $100,000. But because all its assets are plant assets and used in operations, payment of a cash dividend of $100,000 would require the sale of plant assets or borrowing.

---

[12]If the corporation buys its own outstanding stock, it has reduced its legal capital and distributed assets to stockholders. If this were permitted, the corporation could, by purchasing treasury stock at any price desired, return to the stockholders their investments and leave creditors with little or no protection against loss.

Even if we assume a balance sheet showing current assets, the question remains as to whether those cash assets are needed for other purposes.

Balance Sheet, Showing
Cash but Minimal
Working Capital

BALANCE SHEET				
Cash	$100,000	Current liabilities		$ 60,000
Plant assets	460,000	Capital stock	$400,000	
	$560,000	Retained earnings	100,000	500,000
				$560,000

The existence of current liabilities implies very strongly that some of the cash is needed to meet current debts as they mature. In addition, day-by-day cash requirements for payrolls and other expenditures not included in current liabilities also require cash.

Thus, before a dividend is declared, management must consider **availability of funds to pay the dividend**. Other demands for cash should perhaps be investigated by preparing a cash forecast. A dividend should not be paid unless both the present and future financial position appear to warrant the distribution.

The SEC encourages companies to disclose their dividend policy in their annual report. Those that (1) have earnings but fail to pay dividends, or (2) do not expect to pay dividends in the forseeable future are encouraged to report this information. In addition, companies that have had a consistent pattern of paying dividends are encouraged to indicate whether they intend to continue this practice in the future.

Types of Dividends

OBJECTIVE **7**
Identify the various forms of dividend distributions.

Dividend distributions generally are based either on accumulated profits (that is, retained earnings) or on some other capital item such as additional paid-in capital. The natural expectation of any stockholder who receives a dividend is that the corporation has operated successfully and that he or she is receiving a share of its profits. A **liquidating dividend**—that is, a dividend not based on retained earnings—should be adequately described in the accompanying message to the stockholders so that there will be no misunderstanding about its source. Dividends are of the following types.

① Cash dividends.
② Property dividends.
③ Liquidating dividends.
④ Stock dividends.

Dividends are commonly paid in cash but occasionally are paid in stock or some other asset.[13] **All dividends, except for stock dividends, reduce the total stockholders' equity in the corporation**, because the equity is reduced either through an immediate or promised future distribution of assets. When a stock dividend is declared, the corporation does not pay out assets or incur a liability. It issues additional shares of stock to each stockholder and nothing more.

[13]*Accounting Trends and Techniques—2001* reported that of its 600 surveyed companies, 403 paid a cash dividend on common stock, 69 paid a cash dividend on preferred stock, 12 issued stock dividends, and 7 issued or paid dividends in kind. Some companies declare more than one type of dividend in a given year.

Cash Dividends

The board of directors votes on the declaration of **cash dividends**, and if the resolution is properly approved, the dividend is declared. Before it is paid, a current list of stockholders must be prepared. For this reason there is usually a time lag between declaration and payment. A resolution approved at the January 10 (**date of declaration**) meeting of the board of directors might be declared payable February 5 (**date of payment**) to all stockholders of record January 25 (**date of record**).[14]

In this example, the period from January 10 to January 25 gives time for any transfers in process to be completed and registered with the transfer agent. The time from January 25 to February 5 provides an opportunity for the transfer agent or accounting department, depending on who does this work, to prepare a list of stockholders as of January 25 and to prepare and mail dividend checks.

A declared cash dividend is a liability, and because payment is generally required very soon, is usually a current liability. The following entries are required to record the declaration and payment of an ordinary dividend payable in cash. For example, Roadway Freight Corp. on June 10 declared a cash dividend of 50 cents a share on 1.8 million shares payable July 16 to all stockholders of record June 24.

At date of declaration (June 10)

Retained Earnings (Cash Dividends Declared)	900,000	
Dividends Payable		900,000

At date of record (June 24)

No entry

At date of payment (July 16)

Dividends Payable	900,000	
Cash		900,000

To set up a ledger account that shows the amount of dividends declared during the year, Cash Dividends Declared might be debited instead of Retained Earnings at the time of declaration. This account is then closed to Retained Earnings at year-end.

Dividends may be declared either as a certain percent of par, such as a 6 percent dividend on preferred stock, or as an amount per share, such as 60 cents per share on no-par common stock. In the first case, the rate is multiplied by the par value of outstanding shares to get the total dividend. In the second, the amount per share is multiplied by the number of shares outstanding. **Cash dividends are not declared and paid on treasury stock.**

Dividend policies vary among corporations. Some older, well-established firms take pride in a long, unbroken string of quarterly dividend payments. They would lower or pass the dividend only if forced to do so by a sustained decline in earnings or a critical shortage of cash.

"Growth" companies, on the other hand, pay little or no cash dividends because their policy is to expand as rapidly as internal and external financing permit. Neither **Quest Medical, Inc.,** a small growth company, nor **Federal Express Corporation,** a large

INTERNATIONAL INSIGHT

As a less preferred but still allowable treatment, international accounting standards permit firms to reduce equity by the amount of proposed dividends prior to their legal declaration.

---

[14]Theoretically, the ex-dividend date is the day after the date of record. However, to allow time for transfer of the shares, the stock exchanges generally advance the ex-dividend date 2 to 4 days. Therefore, the party who owns the stock on the day prior to the expressed ex-dividend date receives the dividends, and the party who buys the stock on and after the ex-dividend date does not receive the dividend. Between the declaration date and the ex-dividend date, the market price of the stock includes the dividend.

growth company, has ever paid cash dividends to their common stockholders. These investors hope that the price of their shares will appreciate in value and that they will realize a profit when they sell their shares. As indicated earlier, many companies are less concerned with dividend payout, and more focused on increasing share price, stock repurchase programs, and corporate earnings.

Property Dividends

Dividends payable in assets of the corporation other than cash are called **property dividends** or **dividends in kind**. Property dividends may be merchandise, real estate, or investments, or whatever form the board of directors designates. **Ranchers Exploration and Development Corp.** reported one year that it would pay a fourth-quarter dividend in gold bars instead of cash. Because of the obvious difficulties of divisibility of units and delivery to stockholders, the usual property dividend is in the form of securities of other companies that the distributing corporation holds as an investment.

For example, when **DuPont**'s 23 percent stock interest in **General Motors** was held by the Supreme Court to be in violation of antitrust laws, DuPont was ordered to divest itself of the GM stock within 10 years. The stock represented 63 million shares of GM's 281 million shares then outstanding. DuPont couldn't sell the shares in one block of 63 million, nor could it sell 6 million shares annually for the next 10 years without severely depressing the value of the GM stock. At that time the entire yearly trading volume in GM stock did not exceed 6 million shares. DuPont solved its problem by declaring a property dividend and distributing the GM shares as a dividend to its own stockholders.

When the property dividend is declared, the corporation should **restate at fair value the property to be distributed**, **recognizing any gain or loss** as the difference between the property's fair value and carrying value at date of declaration. The declared dividend may then be recorded as a debit to Retained Earnings (or Property Dividends Declared) and a credit to Property Dividends Payable, at an amount equal to the fair value of the property to be distributed. Upon distribution of the dividend, Property Dividends Payable is debited, and the account containing the distributed asset (restated at fair value) is credited.

For example, Trendler, Inc. transferred to stockholders some of its investments in marketable securities costing $1,250,000 by declaring a property dividend on December 28, 2002, to be distributed on January 30, 2003, to stockholders of record on January 15, 2003. At the date of declaration the securities have a market value of $2,000,000. The entries are as follows.

At date of declaration (December 28, 2002)

Investments in Securities	750,000	
Gain on Appreciation of Securities		750,000
Retained Earnings (Property Dividends Declared)	2,000,000	
Property Dividends Payable		2,000,000

At date of distribution (January 30, 2003)

Property Dividends Payable	2,000,000	
Investments in Securities		2,000,000

Liquidating Dividends

Some corporations use paid-in capital as a basis for dividends. Without proper disclosure of this fact, stockholders may erroneously believe the corporation has been operating at a profit. A further result could be subsequent sale of additional shares at a higher price than is warranted. This type of deception, intentional or unintentional, can be avoided by requiring that a clear statement of the source of every dividend accompany the dividend check.

Dividends based on other than retained earnings are sometimes described as **liquidating dividends**, thus implying that they are a return of the stockholder's investment rather than of profits. In other words, **any dividend not based on earnings is a reduction of corporate paid-in capital and to that extent, it is a liquidating dividend**. Companies in the extractive industries may pay dividends equal to the total of accumulated income and depletion. The portion of these dividends in excess of accumulated income represents a return of part of the stockholder's investment.

For example, McChesney Mines Inc. issued a "dividend" to its common stockholders of $1,200,000. The cash dividend announcement noted that $900,000 should be considered income and the remainder a return of capital. The entries are:

At date of declaration

Retained Earnings	900,000	
Additional Paid-in Capital	300,000	
Dividends Payable		1,200,000

At date of payment

Dividends Payable	1,200,000	
Cash		1,200,000

In some cases, management may simply decide to cease business and declare a liquidating dividend. In these cases, liquidation may take place over a number of years to ensure an orderly and fair sale of assets. For example, when Overseas National Airways was dissolved, it agreed to pay a liquidating dividend to its stockholders over a period of years equivalent to $8.60 per share. Each liquidating dividend payment in such cases reduces paid-in capital.

Stock Dividends

If the management wishes to "capitalize" part of the earnings (i.e., reclassify amounts from earned to contributed capital), and thus retain earnings in the business on a permanent basis, it may issue a stock dividend. In this case, **no assets are distributed**, and each stockholder has exactly the same proportionate interest in the corporation and the same total book value after the stock dividend was issued as before it was declared. Of course, the book value per share is lower because an increased number of shares is held.

A **stock dividend** therefore is the nonreciprocal issuance by a corporation of its own stock to its stockholders on a pro rata basis. In recording a stock dividend, some believe that the **par value** of the stock issued as a dividend should be transferred from retained earnings to capital stock. Others believe that the **fair value** of the stock issued—its market value at the declaration date—should be transferred from retained earnings to capital stock and additional paid-in capital.

The fair value position was originally adopted in this country, at least in part, in order to influence the stock dividend policies of corporations. Evidently in 1941 both the New York Stock Exchange and a majority of the Committee on Accounting Procedure (CAP) regarded periodic stock dividends as objectionable. The CAP therefore acted to make it more difficult for corporations to sustain a series of such stock dividends

UNDERLYING CONCEPTS

If, by requiring fair value, the intent of the CAP was to punish companies that used stock dividends, it violated the neutrality concept (that is, that standards-setting should be even-handed).

OBJECTIVE **8**
Explain the
accounting for
small and large
stock dividends,
and for stock splits.

out of their accumulated earnings, by requiring the use of fair market value when it was substantially in excess of book value.[15]

When the stock dividend is less than 20–25 percent of the common shares outstanding at the time of the dividend declaration, the accounting profession requires that the **fair market value** of the stock issued be transferred from retained earnings. Stock dividends of less than 20–25 percent are often referred to as **small (ordinary) stock dividends**. This method of handling stock dividends is justified on the grounds that "many recipients of stock dividends look upon them as distributions of corporate earnings and usually in an amount equivalent to the fair value of the additional shares received."[16] We do not consider this a convincing argument. It is generally agreed that stock dividends are not income to the recipients, and therefore sound accounting should not recommend procedures simply because some recipients think they are income.

To illustrate a small stock dividend, assume that a corporation has outstanding 1,000 shares of $100 par value capital stock and retained earnings of $50,000. If the corporation declares a 10 percent stock dividend, it issues 100 additional shares to current stockholders. If it is assumed that the fair value of the stock at the time of the stock dividend is $130 per share, the entry is:

At date of declaration

Retained Earnings (Stock Dividend Declared)	13,000	
Common Stock Dividend Distributable		10,000
Paid-in Capital in Excess of Par		3,000

Note that no asset or liability has been affected. The entry merely reflects a reclassification of stockholders' equity. If a balance sheet is prepared between the dates of declaration and distribution, the common stock dividend distributable should be shown in the stockholders' equity section as an addition to capital stock (whereas cash or property dividends payable are shown as current liabilities).

When the stock is issued, the entry is:

At date of distribution

Common Stock Dividend Distributable	10,000	
Common Stock		10,000

No matter what the fair value is at the time of the stock dividend, each stockholder retains the same proportionate interest in the corporation.

Some state statutes specifically prohibit the issuance of stock dividends on treasury stock. In those states that permit treasury shares to participate in the distribution accompanying a stock dividend or stock split, practice is influenced by the planned use

---

[15]This was perhaps the earliest instance of an accounting pronouncement being affected by "economic consequences," because the Committee on Accounting Procedure described its action as required by "proper accounting and corporate policy." See Stephen A. Zeff, "The Rise of 'Economic Consequences,'" *The Journal of Accountancy* (December 1978), pp. 53–66.

[16]American Institute of Certified Public Accountants, *Accounting Research and Terminology Bulletins,* No. 43 (New York: AICPA, 1961), Ch. 7, par. 10. One study concluded that *small* stock dividends do not always produce significant amounts of extra value on the date after issuance (ex date) and that *large* stock dividends almost always fail to generate extra value on the ex-dividend date. Taylor W. Foster III and Don Vickrey, "The Information Content of Stock Dividend Announcements," *The Accounting Review,* Vol. LIII, No. 2 (April 1978), pp. 360–370.

of the treasury shares. For example, if the treasury shares are intended for issuance in connection with employee stock options, the treasury shares may participate in the distribution because the number of shares under option is usually adjusted for any stock dividends or splits. But unless there are specific uses for the treasury stock, no useful purpose is served by issuing additional shares to the treasury stock since they are essentially equivalent to authorized but unissued shares.

To continue with our example of the effect of the small stock dividend, note in Illustration 12-8 that the total stockholders' equity has not changed as a result of the stock dividend. Also note that the proportion of the total shares outstanding held by each stockholder is unchanged.

Before dividend	
Capital stock, 1,000 shares of $100 par	$100,000
Retained earnings	50,000
Total stockholders' equity	$150,000
Stockholders' interests:	
A. 400 shares, 40% interest, book value	$ 60,000
B. 500 shares, 50% interest, book value	75,000
C. 100 shares, 10% interest, book value	15,000
	$150,000
After declaration but before distribution of 10% stock dividend	
If fair value ($130) is used as basis for entry:	
Capital stock, 1,000 shares at $100 par	$100,000
Common stock distributable, 100 shares at $100 par	10,000
Paid-in capital in excess of par	3,000
Retained earnings ($50,000 − $13,000)	37,000
Total stockholders' equity	$150,000
After declaration and distribution of 10% stock dividend	
If fair value ($130) is used as basis for entry:	
Capital stock, 1,100 shares at $100 par	$110,000
Paid-in capital in excess of par	3,000
Retained earnings ($50,000 − $13,000)	37,000
Total stockholders' equity	$150,000
Stockholders' interest:	
A. 440 shares, 40% interest, book value	$ 60,000
B. 550 shares, 50% interest, book value	75,000
C. 110 shares, 10% interest, book value	15,000
	$150,000

Illustration 12-8
Effects of a Small (10%)
Stock Dividend

Stock Split

If a company has undistributed earnings over several years and a sizable balance in retained earnings has accumulated, the market value of its outstanding shares is likely to increase. Stock that was issued at prices less than $50 a share can easily attain a market value in excess of $200 a share. The higher the market price of a stock, the less readily it can be purchased by some investors.

The managements of many corporations believe that for better public relations, wider ownership of the corporation stock is desirable. They wish, therefore, to have a market price sufficiently low to be within range of the majority of potential investors.

To reduce the market value of shares, the common device of a **stock split** is employed. For example, after its stock price increased by 25-fold during 1999, Qualcomm Inc. split its stock 4-for-1. Qualcomm's stock had risen above $500 per share, raising concerns that Qualcomm could not meet an analyst target of $1,000 per share. The split reduced the analysts' target to $250, which could better be met with wider distribution of shares at lower trading prices.

From an accounting standpoint, **no entry is recorded for a stock split.** A memorandum note, however, is made to indicate that the par value of the shares has changed, and that the number of shares has increased. The lack of change in stockholders' equity is portrayed in Illustration 12-9 of a 2-for-1 stock split on 1,000 shares of $100 par value stock with the par being halved upon issuance of the additional shares.

Illustration 12-9
Effects of a Stock Split

Stockholders' Equity before 2-for-1 Split		Stockholders' Equity after 2-for-1 Split	
Common stock, 1,000 shares at $100 par	$100,000	Common stock, 2,000 shares at $50 par	$100,000
Retained earnings	50,000	Retained earnings	50,000
	$150,000		$150,000

WHAT DO THE NUMBERS MEAN?

SPLITSVILLE

Stock splits were all the rage in the booming stock market of the 1990s. Of major companies on the New York Stock Exchange, fewer than 80 companies split shares in 1990; by 1998, with stock prices soaring, over 200 companies split shares. Although the split does not increase a stockholder's proportionate ownership of the company, studies have shown that split shares usually outperform those that don't split, as well as the market as a whole, for several years after the split. In addition, the splits help the company keep the shares in more attractive price ranges.

What about when the market "turns south"? A number of companies who split their shares in the boom markets of the 1990s have since then seen their share prices decline to the point that they are considered too low. For example, since Ameritrade's 12-for-1 split in 1999, its stock price has declined over 74 percent, so that it was trading around $6 per share in March 2002. And Lucent is trading at less than $5 a share following a 4-for-1 split. For some investors, these low price stocks are unattractive because some brokerage commissions are based on the number of shares traded, not the dollar amount. Others are concerned that low-priced shares are easier for would-be scamsters to manipulate.

Some companies are considering reverse stock splits in which, say, 5 shares are consolidated into one. Thus, a stock previously trading at $5 per share would be part of an unsplit share trading at $25. By unsplitting, some of the negative consequences of a low trading price can be avoided. The downside to this strategy is that reverse splits might be viewed as additional bad news about the direction of the stock price. For example, Webvan, a failed Internet grocer, did a 1-for-25 reverse split just before it entered bankruptcy.

Source: Adapted from David Henry, "Stocks: The Case for Unsplitting," *BusinessWeek Online* (April 1, 2002).

Stock Split and Stock Dividend Differentiated

From a legal standpoint, a stock split is distinguished from a stock dividend because a stock split results in an increase in the number of shares outstanding and a corresponding decrease in the par or stated value per share. **A stock dividend, although it results in an increase in the number of shares outstanding, does not decrease the par value; thus it increases the total par value of outstanding shares.**

The reasons for issuing a stock dividend are numerous and varied. Stock dividends can be primarily a publicity gesture, **because they are considered by many as dividends**. Consequently, the corporation is not criticized for retention of profits. More defensible perhaps, the corporation may simply wish to retain profits in the business by capitalizing a part of retained earnings. In such a situation, a transfer is made on declaration of a stock dividend from earned capital to contributed or permanent capital.

A stock dividend, like a stock split, also may be used to increase the marketability of the stock, although marketability is often a secondary consideration. If the stock dividend is large, it has the same effect on market price as a stock split. The profession has taken the position that **whenever additional shares are issued for the purpose of reducing the unit market price, then the distribution more closely resembles a stock split than a stock dividend. This effect usually results only if the number of shares issued is more than 20–25 percent of the number of shares previously outstanding.**[17] A stock dividend of more than 20–25 percent of the number of shares previously outstanding is called a **large stock dividend**.[18] The profession also recommends that such a distribution not be called a stock dividend, but it might properly be called "a split-up effected in the form of a dividend" or "stock split."

Also, since the par value of the outstanding shares is not altered, the transfer from retained earnings is only in the amount required by statute. Ordinarily this means a transfer from retained earnings to capital stock **for the par value of the stock issued**, as opposed to a transfer of the market value of the shares issued as in the case of a small stock dividend.[19] For example, **Brown Group, Inc.** at one time authorized a 2-for-1 split, effected in the form of a stock dividend. As a result of this authorization, approximately 10.5 million shares were distributed, and more than $39 million representing the par value of the shares issued was transferred from Retained Earnings to the Common Stock account.

To illustrate a large stock dividend (stock split-up effected in the form of a dividend), Rockland Steel, Inc. declared a 30 percent stock dividend on November 20, payable December 29 to stockholders of record December 12. At the date of declaration, 1,000,000 shares, par value $10, are outstanding and with a fair market value of $200 per share. The entries are:

At date of declaration (November 20)

Retained Earnings	3,000,000	
Common Stock Dividend Distributable		3,000,000

Computation: 1,000,000 shares		300,000 Additional shares	
× 30%		× $10 Par value	
300,000		$3,000,000	

At date of distribution (December 29)

Common Stock Dividend Distributable	3,000,000	
Common Stock		3,000,000

---

[17]*Accounting Research and Terminology Bulletin No. 43*, par. 13.

[18]The SEC has added more precision to the 20–25 percent rule. Specifically, the SEC indicates that distributions of 25 percent or more should be considered a "split-up effected in the form of a dividend." Distributions of less than 25 percent should be accounted for as a stock dividend. The SEC more precisely defined GAAP here, and as a result the SEC rule is followed by public companies.

[19]Often, a split-up effected in the form of a dividend is debited to Paid-in Capital instead of Retained Earnings to indicate that this transaction should affect only paid-in capital accounts. No reduction of retained earnings is required except as indicated by legal requirements. For homework purposes, assume that the debit is to Retained Earnings. See, for example, Taylor W. Foster III and Edmund Scribner, "Accounting for Stock Dividends and Stock Splits: Corrections to Textbook Coverage," *Issues in Accounting Education* (February 1998).

Illustration 12-10 summarizes and compares the effects of various types of dividends and stock splits on various elements of the financial statements.

Illustration 12-10

Effects of Dividends and Stock Splits on Financial Statement Elements

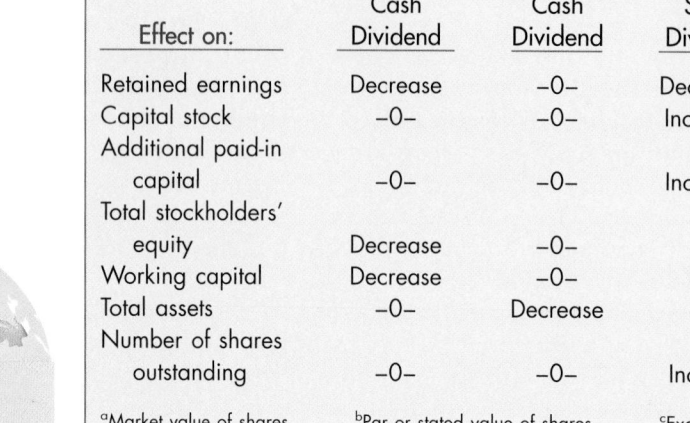

Effect on:	Declaration of Cash Dividend	Payment of Cash Dividend	Declaration and Distribution of		
			Small Stock Dividend	Large Stock Dividend	Stock Split
Retained earnings	Decrease	–0–	Decrease[a]	Decrease[b]	–0–
Capital stock	–0–	–0–	Increase[b]	Increase[b]	–0–
Additional paid-in capital	–0–	–0–	Increase[c]	–0–	–0–
Total stockholders' equity	Decrease	–0–	–0–	–0–	–0–
Working capital	Decrease	–0–	–0–	–0–	–0–
Total assets	–0–	Decrease	–0–	–0–	–0–
Number of shares outstanding	–0–	–0–	Increase	Increase	Increase

[a]Market value of shares. [b]Par or stated value of shares. [c]Excess of market value over par.

INTERNATIONAL INSIGHT

In Switzerland, companies are allowed to create income reserves. That is, they reduce income in years with good profits by allocating it to reserves on the balance sheet. In less profitable years, they are able to reallocate from the reserves to improve income. This "smoothes" income across years.

Disclosure of Restrictions on Retained Earnings

In many corporations restrictions on retained earnings or dividends exist, but no formal journal entries are made. Such restrictions are **best disclosed by note**. Parenthetical notations are sometimes used, but restrictions imposed by bond indentures and loan agreements commonly require an extended explanation. Notes provide a medium for more complete explanations and free the financial statements from abbreviated notations. The note disclosure should reveal the source of the restriction, pertinent provisions, and the amount of retained earnings subject to restriction, or the amount not restricted.

Restrictions may be based on the retention of a certain retained earnings balance, the corporation's ability to observe certain working capital requirements, additional borrowing, and on other considerations. The following example from the annual report of **Alberto-Culver Company** illustrates a note disclosing potential restrictions on retained earnings and dividends.

Illustration 12-11

Disclosure of Restrictions on Retained Earnings and Dividends

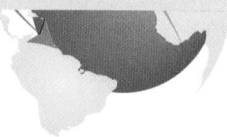

ALBERTO-CULVER COMPANY

Note 3 (in part): The $200 million revolving credit facility, the term note due September 2000, and the receivables agreement impose restrictions on such items as total debt, working capital, dividend payments, treasury stock purchases, and interest expense. At September 30, 1998, the company was in compliance with these arrangements, and $220 million of consolidated retained earnings was not restricted as to the payment of dividends.

OBJECTIVE 9
Indicate how stockholders' equity is presented and analyzed.

PRESENTATION AND ANALYSIS OF STOCKHOLDERS' EQUITY

Presentation

Balance Sheet

Illustration 12-12 shows a comprehensive stockholders' equity section from a balance sheet that includes most of the equity items discussed in this chapter.

Illustration 12-12
Comprehensive
Stockholders' Equity
Presentation

FROST CORPORATION STOCKHOLDERS' EQUITY DECEMBER 31, 2002		
Capital stock		

Preferred stock, $100 par value, 7% cumulative,
  100,000 shares authorized, 30,000 shares
  issued and outstanding
		$ 3,000,000

Common stock, no par, stated value $10 per share, 500,000 shares authorized, 400,000 shares issued		4,000,000
Common stock dividend distributable, 20,000 shares		200,000
Total capital stock		7,200,000
Additional paid-in capital[20]		
Excess over par—preferred	$ 150,000	
Excess over stated value—common	840,000	990,000
Total paid-in capital		8,190,000
Retained earnings		4,360,000
Total paid-in capital and retained earnings		12,550,000
Less: Cost of treasury stock (2,000 shares, common)		(190,000)
Accumulated other comprehensive loss[21]		(360,000)
Total stockholders' equity		$12,000,000

A company should disclose the pertinent rights and privileges of the various securities outstanding. For example, all of the following must be disclosed: dividend and liquidation preferences, participation rights, call prices and dates, conversion or exercise prices and pertinent dates, sinking fund requirements, unusual voting rights, and significant terms of contracts to issue additional shares. The disclosure related to liquidation preferences should be made in the equity section of the balance sheet, rather than in the notes to the financial statements, to emphasize the possible effect of this restriction on future cash flows.[22]

[20]*Accounting Trends and Techniques—2001* reports that of its 600 surveyed companies, 522 had additional paid-in capital; 281 used the caption "Additional paid-in capital"; 123 used "Capital in excess of par or stated value" as the caption; 86 used "Paid-in capital" or "Additional capital"; and 32 used other captions.

[21]A number of items may be included in the "Accumulated other comprehensive loss." Among these items are "Foreign currency translation adjustments" (covered in advanced accounting), "Unrealized holding gains and losses for available-for-sale securities" (covered in Chapter 13), "Excess of additional pension liability over unrecognized prior service cost" (covered in Chapter 15), "Guarantees of employee stock option plan (ESOP) debt," "Unearned or deferred compensation related to employee stock award plans," and others.

Accounting Trends and Techniques—2001 reports that of its 600 surveyed companies reporting other items in the equity section, 93 reported cumulative translation adjustments, 31 reported minimum pension liability adjustments, 38 reported unrealized losses/gains on certain investments, 145 reported unearned compensation, and 37 reported guarantees of ESOP debt. A number of companies had more than one item.

[22]"Disclosure of Information about Capital Structure," *Statement of Financial Accounting Standards No. 129* (Norwalk, Conn.: FASB, February 1997), par. 4.

Reporting of Stockholders' Equity in Real Company Annual Reports

Statement of Stockholders' Equity

Statements of stockholders' equity are frequently presented in the following basic format.

① Balance at the beginning of the period.
② Additions.
③ Deductions.
④ Balance at the end of the period.

The disclosure of changes in the separate accounts comprising stockholders' equity is required to make the financial statements sufficiently informative.[23] Disclosure of such changes may take the form of separate statements or may be made in the basic financial statements or notes thereto.[24]

A **columnar format** for the presentation of changes in stockholders' equity items in published annual reports is gaining in popularity. An example is **Goodyear Tire Company**'s statement of stockholders' equity shown in Illustration 12-14.

Analysis

Several ratios use stockholders' equity related amounts to evaluate a company's profitability and long-term solvency. The following three ratios are discussed and illustrated below.

① Rate of return on common stock equity.
② Payout ratio.
③ Book value per share.

Financial Analysis Primer

Rate of Return on Common Stock Equity

A widely used ratio that measures profitability from the common stockholders' viewpoint is **rate of return on common stock equity**. This ratio shows how many dollars of net income were earned for each dollar invested by the owners. It is computed by dividing net income less preferred dividends by average common stockholders' equity. For example, assume that Gerber's Inc. had net income of $360,000, declared and paid preferred dividends of $54,000, and average common stockholders' equity of $2,550,000. Gerber's ratio is computed as shown in Illustration 12-13.

As shown in Illustration 12-13, when preferred stock is present, preferred dividends are deducted from net income to compute income available to common stockholders. Similarly, the par value of preferred stock is deducted from total stockholders' equity to arrive at the amount of common stock equity used in this ratio.

---

[23]If a company has other comprehensive income, and total comprehensive income is computed only in the statement of stockholders' equity, the statement of stockholders' equity must be displayed with the same prominence as other financial statements. "Reporting Comprehensive Income," *Statement of Financial Accounting Standards No. 130* (Norwalk, Conn.: FASB, June 1997).

[24]*Accounting Trends and Techniques—2001* reports that of the 600 companies surveyed, 577 presented statements of stockholders' equity, 7 presented separate statements of retained earnings only, 10 presented combined statements of income and retained earnings, and 6 presented changes in equity items in the notes only.

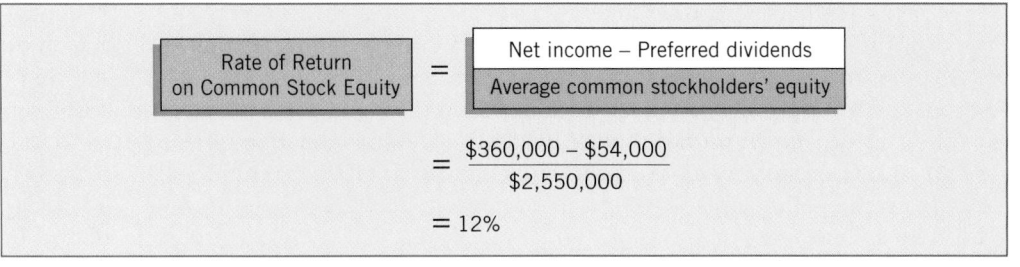

Illustration 12-13
Computation of Rate of Return on Common Stock Equity

$$= \frac{\$360,000 - \$54,000}{\$2,550,000}$$

$$= 12\%$$

Illustration 12-14
Columnar Format for Statement of Stockholders' Equity

GOODYEAR TIRE COMPANY
Statement of Stockholders' Equity

(dollars in millions, except per share)	Common Stock Shares	Common Stock Amount	Additional Paid-in Capital	Retained Earnings	Accumulated Other Comprehensive Income	Total Shareholders' Equity
Balance at December 31, 1999 (after deducting 39,343,548 treasury shares)	156,335,120	$156.3	$1,029.6	$3,706.9	$(1,100.2)	$3,792.6
Comprehensive income						
Net income				40.3		
Foreign currency translation					(201.7)	
Minimum pension liability (net of tax of $4.1)					(6.7)	
Unrealized investment gain (net of tax of $1.7)					2.8	
Total comprehensive income (loss)						(165.3)
Cash dividends— $1.20 per share				(188.4)		(188.4)
Common stock issued from treasury:						
Conversion of 1.2% convertible note payable	1,138,030	1.1	58.8			59.9
Stock compensation plans	130,812	.2	4.0			4.2
Balance at December 31, 2000 (after deducting 38,074,706 treasury shares)	157,603,962	$157.6	$1,092.4	$3,558.8	$(1,305.8)	$3,503.0

When the rate of return on total assets is lower than the rate of return on the common stockholders investment, the company is said to be trading on the equity at a gain. **Trading on the equity** describes the practice of using borrowed money at fixed interest rates or issuing preferred stock with constant dividend rates in hopes of obtaining a higher rate of return on the money used. These issues must be given a prior claim on some or all of the corporate assets. Thus, the advantage to common stockholders of trading on the equity must come from borrowing at a lower rate of interest than the rate of return obtained on the assets borrowed. If this can be done, the capital obtained from bondholders or preferred stockholders earns enough to pay the interest or preferred dividends and to leave a margin for the common stockholders. When this condition exists, trading on the equity is profitable.

Payout Ratio

Another measure of profitability is the **payout ratio**, which is the ratio of cash dividends to net income. If preferred stock is outstanding, this ratio is computed for common stockholders by dividing cash dividends paid to common stockholders by net income available to common stockholders. Assuming that Troy Co. has cash dividends of $100,000 and net income of $500,000, and no preferred stock outstanding, the payout ratio is computed in the following manner.

Illustration 12-15

Computation of Payout Ratio

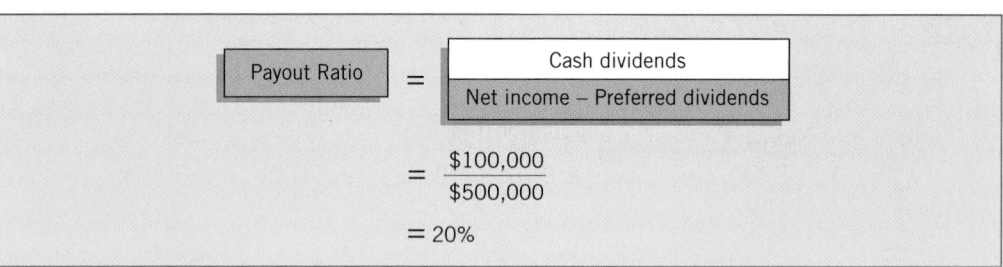

It is important to some investors that the payout be sufficiently high to provide a good yield on the stock.[25] However, payout ratios have declined for many companies because many investors view appreciation in the value of the stock as more important than the amount of the dividend.

Book Value Per Share

A much-used basis for evaluating net worth is found in the **book value** or **equity value per share** of stock. Book value per share of stock is the amount each share would receive if the company were liquidated **on the basis of amounts reported on the balance sheet**. However, the figure loses much of its relevance if the valuations on the balance sheet do not approximate fair market value of the assets. **Book value per share** is computed by dividing common stockholders' equity by outstanding common shares. Assuming that Chen Corporation's common stockholders' equity is $1,000,000 and it has 100,000 shares of common stock outstanding, its book value per share is computed as follows.

Illustration 12-16

Computation of Book Value Per Share

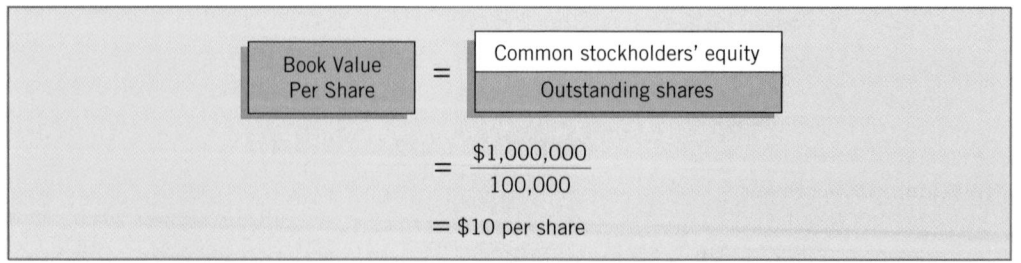

[25]Another closely watched ratio is the **dividend yield**—the cash dividend per share divided by the market price of the stock. This ratio affords investors some idea of the rate of return that will be received in cash dividends from their investment.

SUMMARY OF LEARNING OBJECTIVES

❶ Discuss the characteristics of the corporate form of organization. Among the specific characteristics of the corporate form that affect accounting are: (1) influence of state corporate law; (2) use of the capital stock or share system; and (3) development of a variety of ownership interests. In the absence of restrictive provisions, each share of stock carries the following rights: (1) to share proportionately in profits and losses; (2) to share proportionately in management (the right to vote for directors); (3) to share proportionately in corporate assets upon liquidation; (4) to share proportionately in any new issues of stock of the same class (called the preemptive right).

❷ Explain the key components of stockholders' equity. Stockholders' or owners' equity is classified into two categories: contributed capital, and earned capital. Contributed capital (paid-in capital) is the term used to describe the total amount paid in on capital stock. Put another way, it is the amount advanced by stockholders to the corporation for use in the business. Contributed capital includes items such as the par value of all outstanding capital stock and premiums less any discounts on issuance. Earned capital is the capital that develops if the business operates profitably; it consists of all undistributed income that remains invested in the enterprise.

❸ Explain the accounting procedures for issuing shares of stock. Accounts required to be kept for different types of stock are: *Par value stock:* (a) preferred stock or common stock; (b) paid-in capital in excess of par or additional paid-in capital; and (c) discount on stock. *No-par stock:* common stock or common stock and additional paid-in capital, if stated value used. *Stock issued in combination with other securities (lump-sum sales):* The two methods of allocation available are (a) the proportional method; and (b) the incremental method. *Stock issued in noncash transactions:* When stock is issued for services or property other than cash, the property or services should be recorded at either the fair market value of the stock issued, or the fair market value of the noncash consideration received, whichever is more clearly determinable.

❹ Explain the accounting for treasury stock. The cost method is generally used in accounting for treasury stock. This method derives its name from the fact that the Treasury Stock account is maintained at the cost of the shares purchased. Under the cost method, the Treasury Stock account is debited for the cost of the shares acquired and is credited for this same cost upon reissuance. The price received for the stock when originally issued does not affect the entries to record the acquisition and reissuance of the treasury stock.

❺ Explain the accounting for and reporting of preferred stock. Preferred stock is a special class of shares that possesses certain preferences or features not possessed by the common stock. The features that are most often associated with preferred stock issues are: (1) preference as to dividends; (2) preference as to assets in the event of liquidation; (3) convertible into common stock; (4) callable at the option of the corporation; (5) nonvoting. At issuance, the accounting for preferred stock is similar to that for common stock. When convertible preferred stock is converted, the book value method is employed: Preferred Stock, along with any related Additional Paid-in Capital, is debited, and Common Stock and Additional Paid-in Capital (if an excess exists) are credited.

❻ Describe the policies used in distributing dividends. The state incorporation laws normally provide information concerning the legal restrictions related to the payment of dividends. Corporations rarely pay dividends in an amount equal to the legal limit. This is due, in part, to the fact that assets represented by undistributed earnings are used to finance future operations of the business. If a company is considering declaring a dividend, two preliminary questions must be asked: (1) Is the condition of the corporation such that the dividend is **legally permissible**? (2) Is the condition of the corporation such that a dividend is **economically sound**?

❼ Identify the various forms of dividend distributions. Dividends are of the following types: (1) cash dividends, (2) property dividends, (3) liquidating dividends (dividends

KEY TERMS

additional paid-in capital, 580
book value per share, 604
callable preferred stock, 589
cash dividends, 593
common stock, 578
contributed (paid-in) capital, 579
convertible preferred stock, 589
cost method, 585
cumulative preferred stock, 589
earned capital, 579
large stock dividend, 599
leveraged buyout, 584
liquidating dividends, 595
lump-sum sales, 581
no-par stock, 580
par (stated) value method, 585
participating preferred stock, 589
payout ratio, 604
preemptive right, 577
preferred stock, 578
property dividends, 594
rate of return on common stock equity, 602
redeemable preferred stock, 590
residual interest, 579
retained earnings, 579
small (ordinary) stock dividends, 596
stated value, 581
statement of stockholders' equity, 602
stock dividends, 595
stock split, 598
stockholders' (owners') equity, 579
trading on the equity, 604
treasury stock, 585

based on other than retained earnings), (4) stock dividends (the nonreciprocal issuance by a corporation of its own stock to its stockholders on a pro rata basis).

Expanded Discussion of Quasi-Reorganization

⑧ Explain the accounting for small and large stock dividends, and for stock splits. Generally accepted accounting principles require that the accounting for small stock dividends (less than 20 or 25%) be based on the fair market value of the stock issued. When a stock dividend is declared, Retained Earnings is debited at the fair market value of the stock to be distributed. The entry includes a credit to Common Stock Dividend Distributable at par value times the number of shares, with any excess credited to Paid-in Capital in Excess of Par. If the number of shares issued exceeds 20 or 25% of the shares outstanding (large stock dividend), Retained Earnings is debited at par value, and there is no additional paid-in capital.

A stock dividend is a capitalization of retained earnings that results in a reduction in retained earnings and a corresponding increase in certain contributed capital accounts. The par value and total stockholders' equity remain unchanged with a stock dividend, and all stockholders retain their same proportionate share of ownership. A stock split results in an increase or decrease in the number of shares outstanding, with a corresponding decrease or increase in the par or stated value per share. No accounting entry is required for a stock split.

⑨ Indicate how stockholders' equity is presented and analyzed. The stockholders' equity section of a balance sheet includes capital stock, additional paid-in capital, and retained earnings. Additional items that might also be presented are treasury stock and accumulated other comprehensive income. A statement of stockholders' equity is often provided. Common ratios that use stockholders' equity amounts are: rate of return on common stock equity, payout ratio, and book value per share.

REVIEW EXERCISE

Galbraith Company was formed on July 1, 2000. It was authorized to issue 500,000 shares of $10 par value common stock and 100,000 shares of 8%, $25 par value, cumulative and nonparticipating preferred stock. Galbraith Company has a July 1–June 30 fiscal year. The following information relates to the stockholders' equity accounts of Galbraith Company.

Common Stock
Prior to the 2002–03 fiscal year, Galbraith Company had 110,000 shares of outstanding common stock issued as follows.

1. 95,000 shares were issued for cash on July 1, 2000, at $31 per share.

2. On July 24, 2000, 5,000 shares were exchanged for a plot of land which cost the seller $70,000 in 1994 and had an estimated market value of $220,000 on July 24, 2000.

3. 10,000 shares were issued on March 1, 2002, for $42 per share.

During the 2002–2003 fiscal year, the following transactions regarding common stock took place.

November 30, 2002	Galbraith purchased 2,000 shares of its own stock on the open market at $39 per share. Galbraith uses the cost method for treasury stock.
December 15, 2002	Galbraith declared a 5% stock dividend for stockholders of record on January 15, 2003, to be issued on January 31, 2003. Galbraith was having a liquidity problem and could not afford a cash dividend at the time. Galbraith's common stock was selling at $52 per share on December 15, 2002.
June 20, 2003	Galbraith sold 500 shares of its own common stock that it had purchased on November 30, 2002, for $21,000.

Preferred Stock
Galbraith issued 100,000 shares of preferred stock at $44 per share on July 1, 2001.

Cash Dividends

Galbraith has followed a schedule of declaring cash dividends in December and June, with payment being made to stockholders of record in the following month. The cash dividends which have been declared since inception of the company through June 30, 2003, are shown below.

Declaration Date	Common Stock	Preferred Stock
12/15/01	$0.30 per share	$1.00 per share
6/15/02	$0.30 per share	$1.00 per share
12/15/02	—	$1.00 per share

No cash dividends were declared during June 2003 due to the company's liquidity problems.

Retained Earnings

As of June 30, 2002, Galbraith's retained earnings account had a balance of $650,000. For the fiscal year ending June 30, 2003, Galbraith reported net income of $80,000.

Instructions

Prepare the stockholders' equity section of the balance sheet, including appropriate notes, for Galbraith Company as of June 30, 2003, as it should appear in its annual report to the shareholders.

SOLUTION TO REVIEW EXERCISE

Galbraith Company
Stockholders' Equity
June 30, 2003

Capital stock		
8% preferred stock, $25 par value, cumulative and nonparticipating, 100,000 shares authorized, 100,000 shares issued and outstanding — Note A		$2,500,000
Common stock, $10 par value, 500,000 shares authorized, 115,400 shares issued, with 1,500 shares held in the treasury		1,154,000
Additional paid-in capital		
On preferred stock	$1,900,000	
On common stock	2,716,000*	
On treasury stock	1,500	4,617,500
Total paid-in capital		8,272,500
Retained earnings		344,000**
Total capital and retained earnings		8,616,500
Less: Treasury stock, 1,500 shares at cost		58,500
Total stockholders' equity		$8,558,000

Note A: Galbraith Company is in arrears on the preferred stock in the amount of $100,000.

*Premium on Common Stock:

Issue of 95,000 shares × ($31 − $10)	$1,995,000
Issue of 5,000 shares for plot of land ($220,000 − $50,000)	170,000
10,000 shares issued (3/1/00) [10,000 × ($42 − $10)]	320,000
5,400 shares as dividend [5,500 × ($52 − $10)]	226,600
	$2,716,600

**Retained Earnings:

Beginning Balance		Income		Stock Dividend		Preferred Dividend		Ret. Earnings, Ending Balance
$650,000	+	$80,000	−	$286,800	−	$100,000	=	$344,000
								349,200

ACCOUNTING FOR FINANCIAL INSTRUMENTS WITH BOTH DEBT AND EQUITY CHARACTERISTICS

As indicated in both the liability and stockholders' equity chapters, it is sometimes difficult to determine whether a financial instrument is debt or equity, or a combination of both. As a result, the FASB has issued an exposure draft on this subject.[1] The purpose of this appendix is to discuss the accounting for two financial instruments that have both debt and equity characteristics. They are:

① Convertible debt.
② Stock warrants issued with other securities.

CONVERTIBLE DEBT

OBJECTIVE 10
After studying Appendix 12A, you should be able to: Understand the accounting issues related to financial instruments with both debt and equity characteristics.

If bonds can be converted into other corporate securities during some specified period of time after issuance, they are called **convertible bonds**. **A convertible bond combines the benefits of a bond with the privilege of exchanging it for stock at the holder's option.** It is purchased by investors who desire the security of a bond holding—guaranteed interest—plus the added option of conversion if the value of the stock appreciates significantly.

Corporations issue convertibles for two main reasons. One is the desire to raise equity capital without giving up more ownership control than necessary. A second reason is to obtain debt financing at cheaper rates. Many enterprises could issue debt only at high interest rates unless a convertible covenant were attached. The conversion privilege entices the investor to accept a lower interest rate than would normally be the case on a straight debt issue.[2]

[1]"Exposure Draft: Accounting for Financial Instruments with Characteristics of Liabilities, Equity, or Both," *Proposed Statement of Financial Accounting Standards* (Norwalk, Conn.: FASB, October 27, 2000).

[2]As with any investment, a buyer has to be careful. For example, **Wherehouse Entertainment Inc**, which had 6¼ percent convertibles outstanding, was taken private in a leveraged buyout. As a result, the convertible was suddenly as risky as a junk bond of a highly leveraged company with a coupon of only 6¼ percent. As one holder of the convertibles noted, "What's even worse is that the company will be so loaded down with debt that it probably won't have enough cash flow to make its interest payments. And the convertible debt we hold is subordinated to the rest of Wherehouse's debt." These types of situations have made convertibles less attractive and have led to the introduction of takeover protection covenants in some convertible bond offerings.

At Time of Issuance

Presently, the method for recording convertible bonds **at the date of issue follows the method used to record straight debt issues** (with none of the proceeds recorded as equity). Any discount or premium that results from the issuance of convertible bonds is amortized to its maturity date because it is difficult to predict when, if at all, conversion will occur.

At Time of Conversion

If bonds are converted into other securities, the book value method of recording the conversion is used. The book value method records the securities exchanged for the bond at the carrying amount (book value) of the bond. To illustrate, assume that Hilton, Inc. has a $1,000 bond that is convertible into 10 shares of common stock (par value $10). At the time of conversion, the unamortized premium is $50. The entry for the conversion of the Hilton, Inc. bonds would be:

Bonds Payable	1,000	
Premium on Bonds Payable	50	
Common Stock		100
Paid-in Capital in Excess of Par		950

If the bonds are retired rather than converted, a gain or loss on the transaction is reported if the book value differs from cash paid.

STOCK WARRANTS ISSUED WITH OTHER SECURITIES

Warrants issued with other securities are basically long-term options to buy common stock at a fixed price. Although some perpetual warrants are traded, generally their life is 5 years, occasionally 10.

A warrant works like this: **Tenneco, Inc.** offered a unit comprising one share of stock and one detachable warrant exercisable at $24.25 per share and good for 5 years. The unit sold for 22.75 ($22.75). Since the price of the common the day before the sale was 19.88 ($19.88), the difference suggests a price of 2.87 ($2.87) for the warrants.

In this situation, the warrants had an apparent value of 2.87 ($2.87), even though it would not be profitable at present for the purchaser to exercise the warrant and buy the stock, because the price of the stock was much below the exercise price of $24.25.[3] The investor pays for the warrant in order to receive a possible future call on the stock at a fixed price when the price has risen significantly. For example, if the price of the stock rises to $30, the investor has gained $2.88 ($30 − $24.25 − $2.87) on an investment of $2.87, a 100 percent increase! But, if the price never rises, the investor loses the full $2.87.[4]

The proceeds from the sale of debt with **detachable stock warrants** should be allocated between the two securities.[5] The profession takes the position that two separable instruments are involved, that is, (1) a bond and (2) a warrant giving the holder the right to purchase common stock at a certain price. Warrants that are detachable can

[3]Later in this discussion it will be shown that the value of the warrant is normally determined on the basis of a relative market value approach because of the difficulty of imputing a warrant value in any other manner.

[4]From the illustration, it is apparent that buying warrants can be an "all or nothing" proposition.

[5]A detachable warrant means that the warrant can sell separately from the bond. *APB Opinion No. 14* makes a distinction between detachable and nondetachable warrants because nondetachable warrants must be sold with the security as a complete package; thus, no allocation is permitted.

be traded separately from the debt, and therefore a market value can be determined. The two methods of allocation available are:

① The proportional method.
② The incremental method.

Proportional Method

AT&T's offering of detachable 5-year warrants to buy one share of common stock (par value $5) at $25 (at a time when a share was selling for approximately $50) enabled it to price its offering of bonds at par with a moderate 8¾ percent yield. To place a value on the two securities, one would determine (1) the value of the bonds without the warrants, and (2) the value of the warrants. For example, assume that AT&T's bonds (par $1,000) sold for 99 without the warrants soon after they were issued. The market value of the warrants at that time was $30. (Prior to sale the warrants will not have a market value.) The allocation is based on an estimate of market value, generally as established by an investment banker, or on the relative market value of the bonds and the warrants soon after they are issued and traded. The price paid for 10,000, $1,000 bonds with the warrants attached was par, or $10,000,000. The allocation between the bonds and warrants would be made in this manner:

Illustration 12A-1
Proportional Allocation of Proceeds between Bonds and Warrants

Fair market value of bonds (without warrants) ($10,000,000 × .99)	= $ 9,900,000
Fair market value of warrants (10,000 × $30)	= 300,000
Aggregate fair market value	$10,200,000
Allocated to bonds: $\frac{\$9,900,000}{\$10,200,000}$ × $10,000,000 =	$ 9,705,882
Allocated to warrants: $\frac{\$300,000}{\$10,200,000}$ × $10,000,000 =	294,118
Total allocation	$10,000,000

In this situation the bonds sell at a discount and are recorded as follows.

Cash	9,705,882	
Discount on Bonds Payable	294,118	
Bonds Payable		10,000,000

In addition, the company sells warrants that are credited to paid-in capital. The entry is as follows.

Cash	294,118	
Paid-in Capital—Stock Warrants		294,118

The entries may be combined if desired; they are shown separately here to indicate that the purchaser of the bond is buying not only a bond, but also a possible future claim on common stock.

Assuming that all 10,000 warrants are exercised (one warrant per one share of stock), the following entry would be made.

Cash (10,000 × $25)	250,000	
Paid-in Capital—Stock Warrants	294,118	
Common Stock (10,000 × $5)		50,000
Paid-in Capital in Excess of Par		494,118

What if the warrants are not exercised? In that case, Paid-in Capital — Stock Warrants is debited for $294,118, and Paid-in Capital from Expired Warrants is credited for a like amount. The additional paid-in capital reverts to the former stockholders.

Incremental Method

In instances where the fair value of either the warrants or the bonds is not determinable, the incremental method used in lump-sum security purchases (as explained on page 582) may be used. That is, the security for which the market value is determinable is used, and the remainder of the purchase price is allocated to the security for which the market value is not known. Assume that the market price of the AT&T warrants was known to be $300,000, but the market price of the bonds without the warrants could not be determined. In this case, the amount allocated to the warrants and the stock would be as follows.

Lump-sum receipt	$10,000,000
Allocated to the warrants	300,000
Balance allocated to bonds	$ 9,700,000

Illustration 12A-2
Incremental Allocation of Proceeds between Bonds and Warrants

CONCEPTUAL QUESTIONS

The question arises whether the allocation of value to the warrants is consistent with the handling accorded convertible debt, in which no value is allocated to the conversion privilege. The Board stated that the features of a convertible security are **inseparable** in the sense that choices are mutually exclusive: The holder either converts or redeems the bonds for cash, but cannot do both. No basis, therefore, exists for recognizing the conversion value in the accounts. The Board, however, indicated that the issuance of bonds with **detachable warrants** involves two securities, one a debt security, which will remain outstanding until maturity, and the other a warrant to purchase common stock. At the time of issuance, separable instruments exist, and therefore separate treatment is justified. **Nondetachable warrants**, however, **do not require an allocation of the proceeds between the bonds and the warrants**. The entire proceeds are recorded as debt.

Many argue that the conversion feature is not significantly different in nature from the call represented by a warrant. The question is whether, although the legal forms are different, sufficient similarities of substance exist to support the same accounting treatment. Some contend that inseparability per se is not a sufficient basis for restricting allocation between identifiable components of a transaction. Examples of allocation between assets of value in a single transaction are not uncommon, such as allocation of values in basket purchases and separation of principal and interest in capitalizing long-term leases. Critics of the current accounting for convertibles say that to deny recognition of value to the conversion feature merely looks to the form of the instrument and does not deal with the substance of the transaction.

In its recent exposure draft on this subject, the FASB now indicates that the debt and equity components of these securities (such as convertible debt or bonds issued with nondetachable warrants) should be separated. However, until the profession officially reverses its stand in this area, convertible debt and bonds issued with nondetachable warrants will continue to be reported solely as debt.

UNDERLYING CONCEPTS

Reporting a convertible bond solely as debt is not representationally faithful. However, the cost-benefit constraint is used to justify the failure to allocate between debt and equity.

INTERNATIONAL INSIGHT

International accounting standards require that the issuer of convertible debt record the liability and equity components separately.

SUMMARY OF LEARNING OBJECTIVE FOR APPENDIX 12A

⟨10⟩ **Understand the accounting issues related to financial instruments with both debt and equity characteristics.** Two securities that have both debt and equity characteristics are convertible debt and debt issued with stock warrants. The present accounting is to

KEY TERMS

convertible bond, *608*
detachable stock warrants, *609*

account for convertible debt and debt issued with nondetachable warrants as debt. Debt issued with detachable warrants is separated into debt and equity, using either the proportional method or the incremental method. It appears likely that the FASB will soon require that these types of securities with both debt and equity characteristics be separated into their debt and equity components.

Note: All **asterisked** Questions, Brief Exercises, Problems, and Conceptual Cases relate to material contained in the appendixes to the chapter.

QUESTIONS

1 In the absence of restrictive provisions, what are the basic rights of stockholders of a corporation?

2 Why is a preemptive right important?

3 Distinguish between common and preferred stock.

4 Why is the distinction between paid-in capital and retained earnings important?

5 Explain each of the following terms: authorized capital stock, unissued capital stock, issued capital stock, outstanding capital stock, and treasury stock.

6 What is meant by par value, and what is its significance to stockholders?

7 Describe the accounting for the issuance for cash of no-par value common stock at a price in excess of the stated value of the common stock.

8 Explain the difference between the proportional method and the incremental method of allocating the proceeds of lump sum sales of capital stock.

9 What are the different bases for stock valuation when assets other than cash are received for issued shares of stock?

10 Explain how underwriting costs and accounting and legal fees associated with the issuance of stock should be recorded.

11 For what reasons might a corporation purchase its own stock?

12 Discuss the propriety of showing:

(a) Treasury stock as an asset.

(b) "Gain" or "loss" on sale of treasury stock as additions to or deductions from income.

(c) Dividends received on treasury stock as income.

13 What features or rights may alter the character of preferred stock?

14 Little Texas Inc. recently noted that its 4% preferred stock and 4% participating second preferred stock, which are both cumulative, have priority as to dividends up to 4% of their par value. Its participating preferred stock participates equally with the common stock in any dividends in excess of 4%. What is meant by the term participating? Cumulative?

15 Where in the financial statements is preferred stock normally reported?

16 List possible sources of additional paid-in capital.

17 Goo Goo Dolls Inc. purchases 10,000 shares of its own previously issued $10 par common stock for $290,000. Assuming the shares are held in the treasury with intent to reissue, what effect does this transaction have on (a) net income, (b) total assets, (c) total paid-in capital, and (d) total stockholders' equity?

18 Indicate how each of the following accounts should be classified in the stockholders' equity section.

(a) Common Stock

(b) Retained Earnings

(c) Paid-in Capital in Excess of Par Value

(d) Treasury Stock

(e) Paid-in Capital from Treasury Stock

(f) Paid-in Capital in Excess of Stated Value

(g) Preferred Stock

19 What factors influence the dividend policy of a company?

20 What are the characteristics of state incorporation laws relative to the legality of dividend payments?

21 What are the principal considerations of a board of directors in making decisions involving dividend declarations? Discuss briefly.

22 Dividends are sometimes said to have been paid "out of retained earnings." What is the error in that statement?

23 Distinguish among: cash dividends, property dividends, liquidating dividends, and stock dividends.

24 Describe the accounting entry for a stock dividend, if any. Describe the accounting entry for a stock split, if any.

25 Stock splits and stock dividends may be used by a corporation to change the number of shares of its stock outstanding.

(a) What is meant by a stock split effected in the form of a dividend?

(b) From an accounting viewpoint, explain how the stock split effected in the form of a dividend differs from an ordinary stock dividend.

(c) How should a stock dividend that has been declared but not yet issued be classified in a statement of financial position? Why?

26 The following comment appeared in the notes of Belinda Alvarado Corporation's annual report: "Such distributions, representing proceeds from the sale of James Buchanan, Inc. were paid in the form of partial liquidating dividends and were in lieu of a portion of the Company's ordinary cash dividends." How would a partial liquidating dividend be accounted for in the financial records?

27 This comment appeared in the annual report of Rodriguez Lopez Inc.: "The Company could pay cash or property dividends on the Class A common stock without paying cash or property dividends on the Class B common stock. But if the Company pays any cash or property dividends on the Class B common stock, it would be required to pay at least the same dividend on the Class A common stock." How is a property dividend accounted for in the financial records?

28 For what reasons might a company restrict a portion of its retained earnings?

29 How are restrictions of retained earnings reported?

*30 On July 1, 2003, Roberts Corporation issued $3,000,000 of 9% bonds payable in 20 years. The bonds include detachable warrants giving the bondholder the right to purchase for $30 one share of $1 par value common stock at any time during the next 10 years. The bonds were sold for $3,000,000. The value of the warrants at the time of issuance was $200,000. Prepare the journal entry to record this transaction.

BRIEF EXERCISES

BE12-1 Lost Vikings Corporation issued 300 shares of $10 par value common stock for $4,100. Prepare Lost Vikings' journal entry.

BE12-2 Shinobi Corporation issued 600 shares of no-par common stock for $10,200. Prepare Shinobi's journal entry if (a) the stock has no stated value, and (b) the stock has a stated value of $2 per share.

BE12-3 Lufia Corporation has the following account balances at December 31, 2003.

Common stock, $5 par value	$ 210,000
Treasury stock	90,000
Retained earnings	2,340,000
Paid-in capital in excess of par	1,320,000

Prepare Lufia's December 31, 2003, stockholders' equity section.

BE12-4 Primal Rage Corporation issued 300 shares of $10 par value common stock and 100 shares of $50 par value preferred stock for a lump sum of $14,200. The common stock has a market value of $20 per share, and the preferred stock has a market value of $90 per share. Prepare the journal entry to record the issuance.

BE12-5 On February 1, 2003, Mario Andretti Corporation issued 2,000 shares of its $5 par value common stock for land worth $31,000. Prepare the February 1, 2003, journal entry.

BE12-6 Powerdrive Corporation issued 2,000 shares of its $10 par value common stock for $70,000. Powerdrive also incurred $1,500 of costs associated with issuing the stock. Prepare Powerdrive's journal entry to record the issuance of the company's stock.

BE12-7 Maverick Inc. has outstanding 10,000 shares of $10 par value common stock. On July 1, 2003, Maverick reacquired 100 shares at $85 per share. On September 1, Maverick reissued 60 shares at $90 per share. On November 1, Maverick reissued 40 shares at $83 per share. Prepare Maverick's journal entries to record these transactions using the cost method.

BE12-8 Power Rangers Corporation has outstanding 20,000 shares of $5 par value common stock. On August 1, 2003, Power Rangers reacquired 200 shares at $75 per share. On November 1, Power Rangers reissued the 200 shares at $70 per share. Power Rangers had no previous treasury stock transactions. Prepare Power Rangers' journal entries to record these transactions using the cost method.

BE12-9 Popeye Corporation issued 450 shares of $100 par value preferred stock for $61,500. Prepare Popeye's journal entry.

BE12-10 Micro Machines Inc. declared a cash dividend of $1.50 per share on its 2 million outstanding shares. The dividend was declared on August 1, payable on September 9 to all stockholders of record on August 15. Prepare all journal entries necessary on those three dates.

BE12-11 Ren Inc. owns shares of Stimpy Corporation stock classified as available-for-sale securities. At December 31, 2003, the available-for-sale securities were carried in Ren's accounting records at their cost of $875,000, which equals their market value. On September 21, 2004, when the market value of the securities was $1,400,000, Ren declared a property dividend whereby the Stimpy securities are to be distributed on October 23, 2004, to stockholders of record on October 8, 2004. Prepare all journal entries necessary on those three dates.

BE12-12 Radical Rex Mining Company declared, on April 20, a dividend of $700,000 payable on June 1. Of this amount, $125,000 is a return of capital. Prepare the April 20 and June 1 entries for Radical Rex.

BE12-13 Mike Holmgren Football Corporation has outstanding 200,000 shares of $10 par value common stock. The corporation declares a 5% stock dividend when the fair value of the stock is $65 per share. Prepare the journal entries for Mike Holmgren Football Corporation for both the date of declaration and the date of distribution.

BE12-14 Use the information from BE12-13, but assume Mike Holmgren Football Corporation declared a 100% stock dividend rather than a 5% stock dividend. Prepare the journal entries for both the date of declaration and the date of distribution.

*__BE12-15__ Divac Corporation issued 1,000 $1,000 bonds at 101. Each bond was issued with one detachable stock warrant. After issuance, the bonds were selling in the market at 98, and the warrants had a market value of $40. Use the proportional method to record the issuance of the bonds and warrants.

*__BE12-16__ Ceballos Corporation issued 1,000 $1,000 bonds at 101. Each bond was issued with one detachable stock warrant. After issuance, the bonds were selling separately at 98. The market price of the warrants without the bonds cannot be determined. Use the incremental method to record the issuance of the bonds and warrants.

*__BE12-17__ Malik Sealy Corporation issued 2,000 shares of $10 par value common stock upon conversion of 1,000 shares of $50 par value preferred stock. The preferred stock was originally issued at $55 per share. The common stock is trading at $26 per share at the time of conversion. Record the conversion of the preferred stock.

EXERCISES

E12-1 (Recording the Issuances of Common Stock) During its first year of operations, Collin Raye Corporation had the following transactions pertaining to its common stock.

Jan.	10	Issued 80,000 shares for cash at $6 per share.
Mar.	1	Issued 5,000 shares to attorneys in payment of a bill for $35,000 for services rendered in helping the company to incorporate.
July	1	Issued 30,000 shares for cash at $8 per share.
Sept.	1	Issued 60,000 shares for cash at $10 per share.

Instructions

(a) Prepare the journal entries for these transactions, assuming that the common stock has a par value of $5 per share.

(b) Prepare the journal entries for these transactions, assuming that the common stock is no par with a stated value of $3 per share.

E12-2 (Recording the Issuance of Common and Preferred Stock) Kathleen Battle Corporation was organized on January 1, 2003. It is authorized to issue 10,000 shares of 8%, $100 par value preferred stock, and 500,000 shares of no par common stock with a stated value of $1 per share. The following stock transactions were completed during the first year.

Jan.	10	Issued 80,000 shares of common stock for cash at $5 per share.
Mar.	1	Issued 5,000 shares of preferred stock for cash at $108 per share.
Apr.	1	Issued 24,000 shares of common stock for land. The asking price of the land was $90,000; the fair market value of the land was $80,000.

May	1	Issued 80,000 shares of common stock for cash at $7 per share.
Aug.	1	Issued 10,000 shares of common stock to attorneys in payment of their bill of $50,000 for services rendered in helping the company organize.
Sept.	1	Issued 10,000 shares of common stock for cash at $9 per share.
Nov.	1	Issued 1,000 shares of preferred stock for cash at $112 per share.

Instructions

Prepare the journal entries to record the above transactions.

E12-3 (Stock Issued for Land)   Twenty-five thousand shares reacquired by Elixir Corporation for $53 per share were exchanged for undeveloped land that has an appraised value of $1,700,000. At the time of the exchange the common stock was trading at $62 per share on an organized exchange.

Instructions

(a) Prepare the journal entry to record the acquisition of land assuming the stock was originally recorded on the cost method.

(b) Briefly identify the possible alternatives (including those that are totally unacceptable) for quantifying the cost of the land and briefly support your choice.

E12-4 (Lump Sum Sale of Stock with Bonds)   Faith Evans Corporation is a regional company which is an SEC registrant. The corporation's securities are thinly traded through the NASDAQ (National Association of Securities Dealers Quotes). Faith Evans Corp. has issued 10,000 units. Each unit consists of a $500 par, 12% subordinated debenture and 10 shares of $5 par common stock. The investment banker has retained 400 units as the underwriting fee. The other 9,600 units were sold to outside investors for cash at $880 per unit. Prior to this sale the 2-week ask price of common stock was $40 per share. Twelve percent is a reasonable market yield for the debentures.

Instructions

(a) Prepare the journal entry to record the previous transaction, under the following conditions.

  (1) Employing the incremental method, assuming the interest rate on the debentures is the best market measure.

  (2) Employing the proportional method, using the recent price quotes on the common stock.

(b) Briefly explain which method is, in your opinion, the better method.

E12-5 (Lump Sum Sales of Stock with Preferred Stock)   Dave Matthew Inc. issues 500 shares of $10 par value common stock and 100 shares of $100 par value preferred stock for a lump sum of $100,000.

Instructions

(a) Prepare the journal entry for the issuance when the market value of the common shares is $165 each and market value of the preferred is $230 each.

(b) Prepare the journal entry for the issuance when only the market value of the common stock is known and it is $170 per share.

E12-6 (Stock Issuances and Repurchase)   Lindsey Hunter Corporation is authorized to issue 50,000 shares of $5 par value common stock. During 2003, Lindsey Hunter took part in the following selected transactions.

1. Issued 5,000 shares of stock at $45 per share, less costs related to the issuance of the stock totaling $7,000.

2. Issued 1,000 shares of stock for land appraised at $50,000. The stock was actively traded on a national stock exchange at approximately $46 per share on the date of issuance.

3. Purchased 500 shares of treasury stock at $43 per share. The treasury shares purchased were issued in 2000 at $40 per share.

Instructions

(a) Prepare the journal entry to record item 1.

(b) Prepare the journal entry to record item 2.

(c) Prepare the journal entry to record item 3 using the cost method.

E12-7 **(Effect of Treasury Stock Transactions on Financials)** Joe Dumars Company has outstanding 40,000 shares of $5 par common stock which had been issued at $30 per share. Joe Dumars then entered into the following transactions.

1. Purchased 5,000 treasury shares at $45 per share.
2. Resold 2,000 of the treasury shares at $49 per share.
3. Resold 500 of the treasury shares at $40 per share.

Instructions

Use the following code to indicate the effect each of the four transactions has on the financial statement categories listed in the table below, assuming Joe Dumars Company uses the cost method: (I = Increase; D = Decrease; NE = No effect).

#	Assets	Liabilities	Stockholders' Equity	Paid-in Capital	Retained Earnings	Net Income
1						
2						
3						

E12-8 **(Preferred Stock Entries and Dividends)** Otis Thorpe Corporation has 10,000 shares of $100 par value, 8%, preferred stock and 50,000 shares of $10 par value common stock outstanding at December 31, 2003.

Instructions

Answer the questions in each of the following independent situations.

(a) If the preferred stock is cumulative and dividends were last paid on the preferred stock on December 31, 2000, what are the dividends in arrears that should be reported on the December 31, 2003, balance sheet? How should these dividends be reported?

(b) If the preferred stock is convertible into seven shares of $10 par value common stock and 4,000 shares are converted, what entry is required for the conversion assuming the preferred stock was issued at par value?

(c) If the preferred stock was issued at $107 per share, how should the preferred stock be reported in the stockholders' equity section?

E12-9 **(Correcting Entries for Equity Transactions)** Pistons Inc. recently hired a new accountant with extensive experience in accounting for partnerships. Because of the pressure of the new job, the accountant was unable to review what he had learned earlier about corporation accounting. During the first month, he made the following entries for the corporation's capital stock.

May	2	Cash	192,000	
		Capital Stock		192,000
		(Issued 12,000 shares of $5 par value common stock at $16 per share)		
	10	Cash	600,000	
		Capital Stock		600,000
		(Issued 10,000 shares of $30 par value preferred stock at $60 per share)		
	15	Capital Stock	15,000	
		Cash		15,000
		(Purchased 1,000 shares of common stock for the treasury at $15 per share)		
	31	Cash	8,500	
		Capital Stock		5,000
		Gain on Sale of Stock		3,500
		(Sold 500 shares of treasury stock at $17 per share)		

Exercises ◆ **617**

Instructions

On the basis of the explanation for each entry, prepare the entries that should have been made for the capital stock transactions.

E12-10   (Analysis of Equity Data and Equity Section Preparation)   For a recent 2-year period, the balance sheet of Santana Dotson Company showed the following stockholders' equity data in millions.

	2004	2003
Additional paid-in capital	$ 931	$ 817
Common stock—par	545	540
Retained earnings	7,167	5,226
Treasury stock	1,564	918
Total stockholders' equity	$7,079	$5,665
Common stock shares issued	218	216
Common stock shares authorized	500	500
Treasury stock shares	34	27

Instructions

(a)   Answer the following questions.

    (1)   What is the par value of the common stock?

    (2)   Was the cost per share of acquiring treasury stock higher in 2004 or in 2003?

(b)   Prepare the stockholders' equity section for 2004.

E12-11   (Equity Items on the Balance Sheet)   The following are selected transactions that may affect stockholders' equity.

1. Recorded accrued interest earned on a note receivable.
2. Declared a cash dividend.
3. Declared and distributed a stock split.
4. Recorded a retained earnings restriction.
5. Recorded the expiration of insurance coverage that was previously recorded as prepaid insurance.
6. Paid the cash dividend declared in item 2 above.
7. Recorded accrued interest expense on a note payable.
8. Declared a stock dividend.
9. Distributed the stock dividend declared in item 9.

Instructions

In the table below, indicate the effect each of the nine transactions has on the financial statement elements listed. Use the following code:

I = Increase   D = Decrease   NE = No effect

Item	Assets	Liabilities	Stockholders' Equity	Paid-in Capital	Retained Earnings	Net Income

E12-12 (Cash Dividend and Liquidating Dividend) Lotoya Davis Corporation has ten million shares of common stock issued and outstanding. On June 1 the board of directors voted an 80 cents per share cash dividend to stockholders of record as of June 14, payable June 30.

Instructions

(a) Prepare the journal entry for each of the dates above assuming the dividend represents a distribution of earnings.

(b) How would the entry differ if the dividend were a liquidating dividend?

(c) Assume Lotoya Davis Corporation holds 300,000 common shares in the treasury and as a matter of administrative convenience dividends are paid on treasury shares. How should this cash receipt be recorded?

E12-13 (Stock Split and Stock Dividend) The common stock of Alexander Hamilton Inc. is currently selling at $120 per share. The directors wish to reduce the share price and increase share volume prior to a new issue. The per share par value is $10; book value is $70 per share. Nine million shares are issued and outstanding.

Instructions

Prepare the necessary journal entries assuming the following.

(a) The board votes a 2-for-1 stock split.

(b) The board votes a 100% stock dividend.

(c) Briefly discuss the accounting and securities market differences between these two methods of increasing the number of shares outstanding.

E12-14 (Entries for Stock Dividends and Stock Splits) The stockholders' equity accounts of G.K. Chesterton Company have the following balances on December 31, 2004.

Common stock, $10 par, 300,000 shares issued and outstanding	$3,000,000
Paid-in capital in excess of par	1,200,000
Retained earnings	5,600,000

Shares of G.K. Chesterton Company stock are currently selling on the Midwest Stock Exchange at $37.

Instructions

Prepare the appropriate journal entries for each of the following cases.

(a) A stock dividend of 5% is declared and issued.

(b) A stock dividend of 100% is declared and issued.

(c) A 2-for-1 stock split is declared and issued.

E12-15 (Dividend Entries) The following data were taken from the balance sheet accounts of John Masefield Corporation on December 31, 2003.

Current assets	$540,000
Investments	624,000
Common stock (par value $10)	500,000
Paid-in capital in excess of par	150,000
Retained earnings	840,000

Instructions

Prepare the required journal entries for the following unrelated items.

(a) A 5% stock dividend is declared and distributed at a time when the market value of the shares is $39 per share.

(b) The par value of the capital stock is reduced to $2 with a 5-for-1 stock split.

(c) A dividend is declared January 5, 2004, and paid January 25, 2004, in bonds held as an investment. The bonds have a book value of $100,000 and a fair market value of $135,000.

E12-16 **(Computation of Retained Earnings)** The following information has been taken from the ledger accounts of Isaac Stern Corporation.

Total income since incorporation	$317,000
Total cash dividends paid	60,000
Proceeds from sale of donated stock	40,000
Total value of stock dividends distributed	30,000
Gains on treasury stock transactions	18,000
Unamortized discount on bonds payable	32,000

Instructions

Determine the current balance of retained earnings.

E12-17 **(Stockholders' Equity Section)** Bruno Corporation's post-closing trial balance at December 31, 2003, was as follows.

BRUNO CORPORATION Post-Closing Trial Balance December 31, 2003		
	Dr.	Cr.
Accounts payable		$ 310,000
Accounts receivable	$ 480,000	
Accumulated depreciation—building and equipment		185,000
Additional paid-in capital—common		
In excess of par value		1,300,000
From sale of treasury stock		160,000
Allowance for doubtful accounts		30,000
Bonds payable		300,000
Building and equipment	1,450,000	
Cash	190,000	
Common stock ($1 par value)		200,000
Dividends payable on preferred stock—cash		4,000
Inventories	560,000	
Land	400,000	
Preferred stock ($50 par value)		500,000
Prepaid expenses	40,000	
Retained earnings		301,000
Treasury stock—common at cost	170,000	
Totals	$3,290,000	$3,290,000

At December 31, 2003, Bruno had the following number of common and preferred shares:

	Common	Preferred
Authorized	600,000	60,000
Issued	200,000	10,000
Outstanding	190,000	10,000

The dividends on preferred stock are $4 cumulative. In addition, the preferred stock has a preference in liquidation of $50 per share.

Instructions

Prepare the stockholders' equity section of Bruno's balance sheet at December 31, 2003.

(AICPA adapted)

E12-18 (Dividends and Stockholders' Equity Section)   Anne Cleves Company reported the following amounts in the stockholders' equity section of its December 31, 2002, balance sheet.

Preferred stock, 10%, $100 par (10,000 shares authorized, 2,000 shares issued)	$200,000
Common stock, $5 par (100,000 shares authorized, 20,000 shares issued)	100,000
Additional paid-in capital	125,000
Retained earnings	450,000
Total	$875,000

During 2003, Cleves took part in the following transactions concerning stockholders' equity.

1. Paid the annual 2002 $10 per share dividend on preferred stock and a $2 per share dividend on common stock. These dividends had been declared on December 31, 2002.
2. Purchased 1,700 shares of its own outstanding common stock for $40 per share. Cleves uses the cost method.
3. Reissued 700 treasury shares for land valued at $30,000.
4. Issued 500 shares of preferred stock at $105 per share.
5. Declared a 10% stock dividend on the outstanding common stock when the stock is selling for $45 per share.
6. Issued the stock dividend.
7. Declared the annual 2003 $10 per share dividend on preferred stock and the $2 par share dividend on common stock. These dividends are payable in 2004.

Instructions
(a) Prepare journal entries to record the transactions described above.
(b) Prepare the December 31, 2003, stockholders' equity section. Assume 2003 net income was $330,000.

E12-19 (Comparison of Alternative Forms of Financing)   Shown below is the liabilities and stockholders' equity section of the balance sheet for Jana Kingston Company and Mary Ann Benson Company. Each has assets totaling $4,200,000.

Jana Kingston Co.		Mary Ann Benson Co.	
Current liabilities	$ 300,000	Current liabilities	$ 600,000
Long-term debt, 10%	1,200,000	Common stock ($20 par)	2,900,000
Common stock ($20 par)	2,000,000	Retained earnings (Cash	
Retained earnings (Cash		dividends, $328,000)	700,000
dividends, $220,000)	700,000		
	$4,200,000		$4,200,000

For the year each company has earned the same income before interest and taxes.

	Jana Kingston Co.	Mary Ann Benson Co.
Income before interest and taxes	$1,200,000	$1,200,000
Interest expense	120,000	–0–
	1,080,000	1,200,000
Income taxes (45%)	486,000	540,000
Net income	$ 594,000	$ 660,000

At year end, the market price of Kingston's stock was $101 per share, and Benson's was $63.50.

Instructions

(a) Which company is more profitable in terms of return on total assets?

(b) Which company is more profitable in terms of return on stockholders' equity?

(c) Which company has the greater net income per share of stock? Neither company issued or reacquired shares during the year.

(d) From the point of view of income, is it advantageous to the stockholders of Jana Kingston Co. to have the long-term debt outstanding? Why?

(e) What is the book value per share for each company?

E12-20 (Trading on the Equity Analysis) Presented below is information from the annual report of Emporia Plastics, Inc.

Operating income	$ 532,150
Bond interest expense	135,000
	397,150
Income taxes	183,432
Net income	$ 213,718
Bonds payable	$1,000,000
Common stock	875,000
Retained earnings	375,000

Instructions

Is Emporia Plastics Inc. trading on the equity successfully? Explain.

*E12-21 (Issuance of Bonds with Detachable Warrants) On September 1, 2003, Sands Company sold at 104 (plus accrued interest) 4,000 of its 9%, 10-year, $1,000 face value, nonconvertible bonds with detachable stock warrants. Each bond carried two detachable warrants; each warrant was for one share of common stock at a specified option price of $15 per share. Shortly after issuance, the warrants were quoted on the market for $3 each. No market value can be determined for the bonds above. Interest is payable on December 1 and June 1. Bond issue costs of $30,000 were incurred.

Instructions

Prepare in general journal format the entry to record the issuance of the bonds.

(AICPA adapted)

*E12-22 (Issuance of Bonds with Stock Warrants) On May 1, 2003, Friendly Company issued 2,000 $1,000 bonds at 102. Each bond was issued with one detachable stock warrant. Shortly after issuance, the bonds were selling at 98, but the market value of the warrants cannot be determined.

Instructions

(a) Prepare the entry to record the issuance of the bonds and warrants.

(b) Assume the same facts as part (a), except that the warrants had a fair value of $30. Prepare the entry to record the issuance of the bonds and warrants.

*E12-23 (Issuance and Conversion of Bonds) For each of the unrelated transactions described below, present the entry(ies) required to record each transaction.

1. Grand Corp. issued $20,000,000 par value 10% convertible bonds at 99. If the bonds had not been convertible, the company's investment banker estimates they would have been sold at 95. Expenses of issuing the bonds were $70,000.

2. Hoosier Company issued $20,000,000 par value 10% bonds at 98. One detachable stock purchase warrant was issued with each $100 par value bond. At the time of issuance, the warrants were selling for $4.

3. On July 1, 2001, Trady Company called its 11% convertible debentures for conversion. The $10,000,000 par value bonds were converted into 1,000,000 shares of $1 par value common stock. On July 1, there

was $55,000 of unamortized discount applicable to the bonds, and the company paid an additional $75,000 to the bondholders to induce conversion of all the bonds. The company records the conversion using the book value method.

*E12-24 **(Conversion of Bonds)** Vargo Company has bonds payable outstanding in the amount of $500,000, and the Premium on Bonds Payable account has a balance of $7,500. Each $1,000 bond is convertible into 20 shares of preferred stock of par value of $50 per share. All bonds are converted into preferred stock.

Instructions

(a) Assuming that the book value method was used, what entry would be made?

(b) Assuming that the bonds are quoted on the market at 102, make the entry to record the conversion of the bonds to preferred stock, using the market value of the bonds to record the amount credited to capital.

PROBLEMS

P12-1 (Equity Transactions and Statement Preparation) On January 5, 2003, Drabek Corporation received a charter granting the right to issue 5,000 shares of $100 par value, 8% cumulative and nonparticipating preferred stock, and 50,000 shares of $5 par value common stock. It then completed these transactions.

Jan. 11   Issued 20,000 shares of common stock at $16 per share.
Feb. 1   Issued Robb Nen Corp. 4,000 shares of preferred stock for the following assets: machinery with a fair market value of $50,000; a factory building with a fair market value of $110,000; and land with an appraised value of $270,000.
July 29   Purchased 1,800 shares of common stock at $19 per share, (Use cost method.)
Aug. 10   Sold the 1,800 treasury shares at $14 per share.
Dec. 31   Declared a $0.25 per share cash dividend on the common stock and declared the preferred dividend.
Dec. 31   Closed the Income Summary account. There was a $175,700 net income.

Instructions

(a) Record the journal entries for the transactions listed above.

(b) Prepare the stockholders' equity section of Drabek Corporation's balance sheet as of December 31, 2003.

P12-2 (Treasury Stock Transactions and Presentation) Jodz Company had the following stockholders' equity as of January 1, 2004.

Common stock, $5 par value, 20,000 shares issued	$100,000
Paid-in capital in excess of par	300,000
Retained earnings	320,000
Total stockholders' equity	$720,000

During 2004, the following transactions occurred.

Feb. 1   Jodz repurchased 2,000 shares of treasury stock at a price of $18 per share.
Mar. 1   800 shares of treasury stock repurchased above were reissued at $17 per share.
Mar. 18   500 shares of treasury stock repurchased above were reissued at $14 per share.
Apr. 22   600 shares of treasury stock repurchased above were reissued at $20 per share.

Instructions

(a) Prepare the journal entries to record the treasury stock transactions in 2004, assuming Jodz uses the cost method.

(b) Prepare the stockholders' equity section as of April 30, 2004. Net income for the first 4 months of 2004 was $110,000.

P12-3 (Equity Transactions and Statement Preparation)   Amado Company has two classes of capital stock outstanding: 8%, $20 par preferred and $5 par common. At December 31, 2002, the following accounts were included in stockholders' equity.

Preferred Stock, 150,000 shares	$ 3,000,000
Common Stock, 2,000,000 shares	10,000,000
Paid-in Capital in Excess of Par—Preferred	200,000
Paid-in Capital in Excess of Par—Common	27,000,000
Retained Earnings	4,500,000

The following transactions affected stockholders' equity during 2003.

Jan.	1	25,000 shares of preferred stock issued at $22 per share.
Feb.	1	40,000 shares of common stock issued at $20 per share.
June	1	2-for-1 stock split (par value reduced to $2.50).
July	1	30,000 shares of common treasury stock purchased at $9 per share. Amado uses the cost method.
Sept.	15	10,000 shares of treasury stock reissued at $11 per share.
Dec.	31	Net income is $2,100,000.
Dec.	31	The preferred dividend is declared, and a common dividend of 50¢ per share is declared.

Instructions

Prepare the stockholders' equity section for Amado Company at December 31, 2003. Show all supporting computations.

P12-4 (Stock Transactions—Assessment and Lump Sum)   Shikai Corporation's charter authorized issuance of 100,000 shares of $10 par value common stock and 50,000 shares of $50 preferred stock. The following transactions involving the issuance of shares of stock were completed. Each transaction is independent of the others.

1. Issued a $10,000, 9% bond payable at par and gave as a bonus one share of preferred stock, which at that time was selling for $106 a share.
2. Issued 500 shares of common stock for machinery. The machinery had been appraised at $7,100; the seller's book value was $6,200. The most recent market price of the common stock is $15 a share.
3. Issued 375 shares of common and 100 shares of preferred for a lump sum amounting to $11,300. The common had been selling at $14 and the preferred at $65.
4. Issued 200 shares of common and 50 shares of preferred for furniture and fixtures. The common had a fair market value of $16 per share and the furniture and fixtures were appraised at $6,200.

Instructions
Record the transactions listed above in journal entry form.

P12-5 (Treasury Stock—Cost Method)   Before Polska Corporation engages in the treasury stock transactions listed below, its general ledger reflects, among others, the following account balances (par value of its stock is $30 per share).

Paid-in Capital in Excess of Par	Common Stock	Retained Earnings
Balance $99,000	Balance $270,000	Balance $80,000

Instructions
Record the treasury stock transactions (given below) under the cost method of handling treasury stock; use the FIFO method for purchase-sale purposes.

(a) Bought 380 shares of treasury stock at $39 per share.
(b) Bought 300 shares of treasury stock at $43 per share.
(c) Sold 350 shares of treasury stock at $42 per share.
(d) Sold 120 shares of treasury stock at $38 per share.

P12-6 **(Treasury Stock—Cost Method—Equity Section Preparation)**   Constantine Company has the following owners' equity accounts at December 31, 2002.

Common Stock—$100 par value, authorized 8,000 shares	$480,000
Retained Earnings	294,000

Instructions

(a) Prepare entries in journal form to record the following transactions, which took place during 2003.

(1) 240 shares of outstanding stock were purchased at 97. (These are to be accounted for using the cost method.)

(2) A $20 per share cash dividend was declared.

(3) The dividend declared in No. 2 above was paid.

(4) The treasury shares purchased in No. 1 above were resold at 102.

(5) 500 shares of outstanding stock were purchased at 103.

(6) 330 of the shares purchased in No. 5 above were resold at 96.

(b) Prepare the stockholders' equity section of Constantine Company's balance sheet after giving effect to these transactions, assuming that the net income for 2003 was $94,000.

P12-7 **(Cash Dividend Entries)**   The books of John Dos Passos Corporation carried the following account balances as of December 31, 2003.

Cash	$ 195,000
Preferred stock, 6% cumulative, nonparticipating, $50 par	750,000
Common stock, no par value, 300,000 shares issued	1,500,000
Paid-in capital in excess of par (preferred)	150,000
Treasury stock (common 4,200 shares at cost)	33,600
Retained earnings	105,000

The preferred stock has dividends in arrears for the past year (2003)—to be settled by issuance of preferred stock.

The board of directors, at their annual meeting on December 21, 2004, declared the following: "The current year dividends shall be 6% on the preferred and $.30 per share on the common. The dividends in arrears shall be paid by issuing one share of treasury stock for each ten shares of preferred held."

The preferred is currently selling at $80 per share, and the common at $8 per share. Net income for 2004 is estimated at $77,000.

Instructions

(a) Prepare the journal entries required for the dividend declaration and payment, assuming that they occur simultaneously.

(b) Could John Dos Passos Corporation give the preferred stockholders 2 years' dividends and common stockholders a 30 cents per share dividend, all in cash?

P12-8 **(Dividends and splits)**   Gutsy Company provides you with the following condensed balance sheet information.

Assets		Liabilities and Stockholders' Equity		
Current assets	$ 40,000	Current and long-term liabilities		$100,000
Investments in ABC stock		Stockholders' equity		
(10,000 shares at cost)	60,000	Common stock ($2 par)	$ 20,000	
Equipment (net)	250,000	Paid-in capital in excess of par	110,000	
Intangibles	60,000	Retained earnings	180,000	310,000
Total assets	$410,000	Total liabilities and		
		stockholders' equity		$410,000

Instructions

For each transaction below, indicate the dollar impact (if any) on the following five items: (1) total assets, (2) common stock, (3) paid-in capital in excess of par, (4) retained earnings, and (5) stockholders' equity. (Each situation is independent.)

(a) Gutsy declares and pays a $0.50 per share dividend.
(b) Gutsy declares and issues a 10% stock dividend when the market price of the stock is $14 per share.
(c) Gutsy declares and issues a 40% stock dividend when the market price of the stock is $15 per share.
(d) Gutsy declares and distributes a property dividend. Gutsy gives one share of ABC stock for every two shares of Gutsy Company stock held. ABC is selling for $10 per share on the date the property dividend is declared.
(e) Gutsy declares a 2-for-1 stock split and issues new shares.

P12-9 (Stockholders' Equity Section of Balance Sheet) The following is a summary of all relevant transactions of Jadzia Dax Corporation since it was organized in 2001.

In 2001, 15,000 shares were authorized and 7,000 shares of common stock ($50 par value) were issued at a price of $57. In 2002, 1,000 shares were issued as a stock dividend when the stock was selling for $62. Three hundred shares of common stock were bought in 2003 at a cost of $66 per share. These 300 shares are still in the company treasury.

In 2002, 10,000 preferred shares were authorized and the company issued 4,000 of them ($100 par value) at $113. Some of the preferred stock was reacquired by the company and later reissued for $4,700 more than it cost the company.

The corporation has earned a total of $610,000 in net income after income taxes and paid out a total of $312,600 in cash dividends since incorporation.

Instructions

Prepare the stockholders' equity section of the balance sheet in proper form for Jadzia Dax Corporation as of December 31, 2003. Account for treasury stock using the cost method.

P12-10 (Stock Dividends and Stock Split) Jenny Durdil Inc. $10 par common stock is selling for $120 per share. Five million shares are currently issued and outstanding. The board of directors wishes to stimulate interest in Jenny Durdil common stock before a forthcoming stock issue but does not wish to distribute capital at this time. The board also believes that too many adjustments to the stockholders' equity section, especially retained earnings, might discourage potential investors.

The board has considered three options for stimulating interest in the stock:

1. A 20% stock dividend.
2. A 100% stock dividend.
3. A 2-for-1 stock split.

Instructions

Acting as financial advisor to the board, you have been asked to report briefly on each option and, considering the board's wishes, make a recommendation. Discuss the effects of each of the foregoing options.

P12-11 (Stock and Cash Dividends) Gul Ducat Corporation has outstanding 2,000,000 shares of common stock of a par value of $10 each. The balance in its retained earnings account at January 1, 2003, was $24,000,000, and it then had Additional Paid-in Capital of $5,000,000. During 2003, the company's net income was $5,700,000. A cash dividend of $0.60 a share was paid June 30, 2003, and a 6% stock dividend was distributed to stockholders of record at the close of business on December 31, 2003. You have been asked to advise on the proper accounting treatment of the stock dividend.

The existing stock of the company is quoted on a national stock exchange. The market price of the stock has been as follows.

October 31, 2003	$31
November 30, 2003	$33
December 31, 2003	$38
Average price over the 2-month period	$35

Instructions

(a) Prepare the journal entry to record the cash dividend.

(b) Prepare the journal entry to record the stock dividend.

(c) Prepare the stockholders' equity section (including schedules of retained earnings and additional paid-in capital) of the balance sheet of Gul Ducat Corporation for the year 2003 on the basis of the foregoing information. Draft a note to the financial statements setting forth the basis of the accounting for the stock dividend, and add separately appropriate comments or explanations regarding the basis chosen.

P12-12 **(Analysis and Classification of Equity Transactions)** Ohio Company was formed on July 1, 2000. It was authorized to issue 300,000 shares of $10 par value common stock and 100,000 shares of 8% $25 par value, cumulative and nonparticipating preferred stock. Ohio Company has a July 1–June 30 fiscal year.

The following information relates to the stockholders' equity accounts of Ohio Company.

Common Stock

Prior to the 2002–03 fiscal year, Ohio Company had 110,000 shares of outstanding common stock issued as follows.

1. 95,000 shares were issued for cash on July 1, 2000, at $31 per share.
2. On July 24, 2000, 5,000 shares were exchanged for a plot of land which cost the seller $70,000 in 1994 and had an estimated market value of $220,000 on July 24, 2000.
3. 10,000 shares were issued on March 1, 2000, for $42 per share.

During the 2002–03 fiscal year, the following transactions regarding common stock took place.

November 30, 2002	Ohio purchased 2,000 shares of its own stock on the open market at $39 per share. Ohio uses the cost method for treasury stock.
December 15, 2002	Ohio declared a 5% stock dividend for stockholders of record on January 15, 2001, to be issued on January 31, 2003. Ohio was having a liquidity problem and could not afford a cash dividend at the time. Ohio's common stock was selling at $52 per share on December 15, 2002.
June 20, 2003	Ohio sold 500 shares of its own common stock that it had purchased on November 30, 2002, for $21,000.

Preferred Stock

Ohio issued 50,000 shares of preferred stock at $44 per share on July 1, 2001.

Cash Dividends

Ohio has followed a schedule of declaring cash dividends in December and June, with payment being made to stockholders of record in the following month. The cash dividends which have been declared since inception of the company through June 30, 2003, are shown below.

Declaration Date	Common Stock	Preferred Stock
12/15/01	$0.30 per share	$1.00 per share
6/15/02	$0.30 per share	$1.00 per share
12/15/02	—	$1.00 per share

No cash dividends were declared during June 2003 due to the company's liquidity problems.

Retained Earnings

As of June 30, 2002, Ohio's retained earnings account had a balance of $690,000. For the fiscal year ending June 30, 2003, Ohio reported net income of $40,000.

Instructions

Prepare the stockholders' equity section of the balance sheet, including appropriate notes, for Ohio Company as of June 30, 2003, as it should appear in its annual report to the shareholders.

(CMA adapted)

*P12-13 **(Entries for Various Dilutive Securities)** The stockholders' equity section of McLean Inc. at the beginning of the current year appears below.

Common stock, $10 par value, authorized 1,000,000 shares, 300,000 shares issued and outstanding	$3,000,000
Paid-in capital in excess of par	600,000
Retained earnings	570,000

During the current year the following transactions occurred.

1. The company sold to the public a $200,000, 10% bond issue at par. The company also issued with each $100 bond one detachable stock purchase warrant, which provided for the purchase of common stock at $30 per share. Shortly after issuance, similar bonds without warrants were selling at 96 and the warrants at $8.
2. At the end of the year, 80% of the warrants in (2) had been exercised, and the remaining were outstanding and in good standing.

Instructions

(a) Prepare general journal entries for the current year to record the transactions listed above.
(b) Prepare the stockholders' equity section of the balance sheet at the end of the current year. Assume that retained earnings at the end of the current year is $750,000.

*P12-14 **(Entries for Conversion, Amortization, and Interest of Bonds)** Counter Inc. issued $1,500,000 of convertible 10-year bonds on July 1, 2003. The bonds provide for 12% interest payable semiannually on January 1 and July 1. The discount in connection with the issue was $34,000, which is being amortized monthly on a straight-line basis.

The bonds are convertible after one year into 8 shares of Counter Inc.'s $100 par value common stock for each $1,000 of bonds.

On August 1, 2004, $150,000 of bonds were turned in for conversion into common. Interest has been accrued monthly and paid as due. At the time of conversion any accrued interest on bonds being converted is paid in cash. Unamortized discount on the converted bonds is $3,032.

Instructions

Prepare the journal entries to record the conversion, amortization, and interest in connection with the bonds as of the following dates.

(a) July 1, 2003.
(b) August 1, 2004. (Assume the book value method is used.)

(AICPA adapted)

CONCEPTUAL CASES

C12-1 **(Preemptive Rights and Dilution of Ownership)** Alvarado Computer Company is a small, closely held corporation. Eighty percent of the stock is held by Eduardo Alvarado, president. Of the remainder, 10% is held by members of his family and 10% by Shaunda Jones, a former officer who is now retired. The balance sheet of the company at June 30, 2003, was substantially as shown below.

Assets		Liabilities and Stockholders' Equity	
Cash	$ 22,000	Current liabilities	$ 50,000
Other	450,000	Capital stock	250,000
	$472,000	Retained earnings	172,000
			$472,000

Additional authorized capital stock of $300,000 par value had never been issued. To strengthen the cash position of the company, Eduardo Alvarado issued capital stock with a par value of $100,000 to himself at par for cash. At the next stockholders' meeting, Jones objected and claimed that her interests had been injured.

Instructions

(a) Which stockholder's right was ignored in the issue of shares to Eduardo Alvarado?

(b) How may the damage to Jones' interests be repaired most simply?

(c) If Eduardo Alvarado offered Jones a personal cash settlement and they agreed to employ you as an impartial arbitrator to determine the amount, what settlement would you propose? Present your calculations with sufficient explanation to satisfy both parties.

C12-2 (Issuance of Stock for Land) Hopee Corporation is planning to issue 3,000 shares of its own $10 par value common stock for 2 acres of land to be used as a building site.

Instructions

(a) What general rule should be applied to determine the amount at which the land should be recorded?

(b) Under what circumstances should this transaction be recorded at the fair market value of the land?

(c) Under what circumstances should this transaction be recorded at the fair market value of the stock issued?

(d) Assume Hopee intentionally records this transaction at an amount greater than the fair market value of the land and the stock. Discuss this situation.

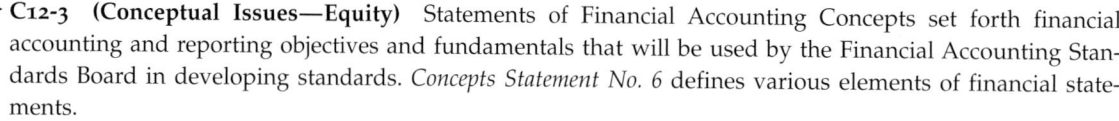 **C12-3 (Conceptual Issues—Equity)** Statements of Financial Accounting Concepts set forth financial accounting and reporting objectives and fundamentals that will be used by the Financial Accounting Standards Board in developing standards. *Concepts Statement No. 6* defines various elements of financial statements.

Instructions

Answer the following questions based on *SFAC No. 6*.

(a) Define and discuss the term "equity."

(b) What transactions or events change owners' equity?

(c) Define "investments by owners" and provide examples of this type of transaction. What financial statement element other than equity is typically affected by owner investments?

(d) Define "distributions to owners" and provide examples of this type of transaction. What financial statement element other than equity is typically affected by distributions?

(e) What are examples of changes within owners' equity that do not change the total amount of owners' equity?

C12-4 (Stock Dividends and Splits) The directors of Amman Corporation are considering the issuance of a stock dividend. They have asked you to discuss the proposed action by answering the following questions.

Instructions

(a) What is a stock dividend? How is a stock dividend distinguished from a stock split (1) from a legal standpoint, and (2) from an accounting standpoint?

(b) For what reasons does a corporation usually declare a stock dividend? A stock split?

(c) Discuss the amount, if any, of retained earnings to be capitalized in connection with a stock dividend.

(AICPA adapted)

C12-5 (Stock Dividends) Kitakyushu Inc., a client, is considering the authorization of a 10% common stock dividend to common stockholders. The financial vice president of Kitakyushu wishes to discuss the accounting implications of such an authorization with you before the next meeting of the board of directors.

Instructions

(a) The first topic the vice president wishes to discuss is the nature of the stock dividend to the recipient. Discuss the case against considering the stock dividend as income to the recipient.

(b) The other topic for discussion is the propriety of issuing the stock dividend to all "stockholders of record" or to "stockholders of record exclusive of shares held in the name of the corporation as treasury stock." Discuss the case against issuing stock dividends on treasury shares.

(AICPA adapted)

C12-6 **(Stock Dividend, Cash Dividend, and Treasury Stock)** Hsuchou Company has 30,000 shares of $10 par value common stock authorized and 20,000 shares issued and outstanding. On August 15, 2003, Hsuchou purchased 1,000 shares of treasury stock for $16 per share. Hsuchou uses the cost method to account for treasury stock. On September 14, 2003, Hsuchou sold 500 shares of the treasury stock for $20 per share.

In October 2003, Hsuchou declared and distributed 1,950 shares as a stock dividend from unissued shares when the market value of the common stock was $21 per share.

On December 20, 2003, Hsuchou declared a $1 per share cash dividend, payable on January 10, 2004, to shareholders of record on December 31, 2003.

Instructions

(a) How should Hsuchou account for the purchase and sale of the treasury stock, and how should the treasury stock be presented in the balance sheet at December 31, 2003?

(b) How should Hsuchou account for the stock dividend, and how would it affect the stockholders' equity at December 31, 2003? Why?

(c) How should Hsuchou account for the cash dividend, and how would it affect the balance sheet at December 31, 2003? Why?

(AICPA adapted)

C12-7 **(Treasury Stock)** Jean Loptien, president of Sycamore Corporation, is concerned about several large stockholders who have been very vocal lately in their criticisms of her leadership. She thinks they might mount a campaign to have her removed as the corporation's CEO. She decides that buying them out by purchasing their shares could eliminate them as opponents, and she is confident they would accept a "good" offer. Loptien knows the corporation's cash position is decent, so it has the cash to complete the transaction. She also knows the purchase of these shares will increase earnings per share, which should make other investors quite happy. (Earnings per share is calculated by dividing net income available for the common shareholders by the weighted average number of shares outstanding. Therefore, if the number of shares outstanding is decreased by purchasing treasury shares, earnings per share increases.)

Instructions

Answer the following questions.

(a) Who are the stakeholders in this situation?

(b) What are the ethical issues involved?

(c) Should Loptien authorize the transaction?

USING YOUR JUDGMENT

FINANCIAL REPORTING PROBLEM

3M COMPANY

The financial statements of **3M** were provided with your book or can be accessed on the Take Action! CD.

Instructions

Refer to these financial statements and the accompanying notes to answer the following questions.

(a) What is the par or stated value of 3M's preferred stock?

(b) What is the par or stated value of 3M's common stock?

(c) What percentage of 3M's authorized common stock was issued at December 31, 2001?

(d) How many shares of common stock were outstanding at December 31, 2001, and December 31, 2000?

(e) What amount of cash dividends per share was declared by 3M in 2001? What was the dollar amount effect of the cash dividends on 3M stockholders' equity?

(f) What is 3M's rate of return on common stock equity for 2001 and 2000?

(g) What is 3M's payout ratio for 2001 and 2000?

(h) What was the market price range (high/low) of 3M's common stock during the quarter ended December 31, 2001?

FINANCIAL STATEMENT ANALYSIS CASE

CASE 1: KELLOGG CORPORATION

Kellogg Corporation is the world's leading producer of ready-to-eat cereal products. In recent years the company has taken numerous steps aimed at improving its profitability and earnings per share. Presented below are some basic facts for the Kellogg Corporation.

(all dollars in millions)	2001	2000
Net sales	$8,853	$6,955
Net earnings	474	588
Total assets	10,369	4,886
Total liabilities	9,497	4,349
Common stock, $0.25 par value	104	104
Capital in excess of par value	92	102
Retained earnings	1,565	1,501
Treasury stock, at cost	337	374
Number of shares outstanding (in millions)	406	406

Instructions

(a) What are some of the reasons that management purchases its own stock?

(b) Explain how earnings per share might be affected by treasury stock transactions.

(c) Calculate the ratio of debt to total assets for 2000 and 2001, and discuss the implications of the change.

CASE 2: WIEBOLD, INCORPORATED

The following note related to stockholders' equity was reported in Wiebold's annual report.

> On February 1, 2000, the Board of Directors declared a 3-for-2 stock split, distributed on February 22, 2000, to shareholders of record on February 10, 2000. Accordingly, all numbers of common shares, except unissued shares and treasury shares, and all per share data have been restated to reflect this stock split in addition to the 3-for-2 stock split declared on January 27, 1999, distributed on February 26, 1999, to shareholders of record on February 10, 1999.
>
> On the basis of amounts declared and paid, the annualized quarterly dividends per share were $0.80 in 1999, $0.75 in 1998, and $0.71 in 1997.

Instructions

(a) What is the significance of the date of record and the date of distribution?

(b) Why might Weibold have declared a 3-for-2 for stock split?

(c) What impact does Wiebold's stock split have on (1) total stockholders' equity, (2) total par value, (3) outstanding shares, and (4) book value per share?

COMPARATIVE ANALYSIS CASE

THE COCA-COLA COMPANY AND PEPSICO, INC.

Instructions

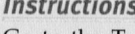

Go to the Take Action! CD and use information found there to answer the following questions related to The Coca-Cola Company and PepsiCo, Inc.

(a) What is the par or stated value of Coca-Cola's and PepsiCo's common or capital stock?

(b) What percentage of authorized shares was issued by Coca-Cola at December 31, 2001, and by PepsiCo at December 29, 2001?

(c) How many shares are held as treasury stock by Coca-Cola at December 31, 2001, and by PepsiCo at December 29, 2001?

(d) How many Coca-Cola common shares are outstanding at December 31, 2001? How many PepsiCo shares of capital stock are outstanding at December 29, 2001?

(e) What amounts of cash dividends per share were declared by Coca-Cola and PepsiCo in 2001? What were the dollar amount effects of the cash dividends on each company's stockholders' equity?

(f) What are Coca-Cola's and PepsiCo's rate of return on common/capital stock equity for 2001 and 2000? Which company gets the higher return on the equity of its shareholders?

(g) What are Coca-Cola's and PepsiCo's payout ratios for 2001?

(h) What was the market price range (high/low) for Coca-Cola's common stock and PepsiCo's capital stock during the fourth quarter of 2001? Which company's (Coca-Cola's or PepsiCo's) stock price increased more (%) during 2001?

*Remember to check the **Take Action! CD**
and the book's **companion Web site**
to find additional resources for this chapter.*

INVESTMENTS

IS COKE IN CONTROL HERE?

The Coca-Cola Company (Coke) owns 42 percent of the shares of **Coca-Cola Enterprises** (a U.S. bottling business) and 43 percent of **Coca-Cola Amatil** (a European and Asian bottling business). These bottling businesses are very important to The Coca-Cola Company, because they are the primary distributors of Coca-Cola products. Furthermore, these companies are very dependent on Coca-Cola, which provides significant marketing and distribution development support. Indeed, an argument can be made that the bottling companies are controlled by Coca-Cola, because they would not exist without its support.

However, because The Coca-Cola Company does not own more than 50 percent of the shares in these companies, it does not prepare consolidated financial statements. Instead, Coca-Cola accounts for these investments using the equity method. Under the equity method, Coca-Cola reports a single income item for its profits from the bottlers, and only the net amount of its investment is reported in the balance sheet.

Equity method accounting gives Coca-Cola a pristine balance sheet and income statement, by keeping the assets and liabilities and the profit margins of these bottlers separate from its beverage-making business. What's more, as summarized in the following table, many countries allow proportional consolidation, an accounting method that includes part of the assets, liabilities, and income of investees in the financial statements of the investor company.

After studying this chapter, you should be able to:

1 Identify the three categories of debt securities and describe the accounting and reporting treatment for each category.

2 Identify the categories of equity securities and describe the accounting and reporting treatment for each category.

3 Explain the equity method of accounting and compare it to the fair value method for equity securities.

4 Describe the disclosure requirements for investments in debt and equity securities.

5 Discuss the accounting for impairments of debt and equity investments.

6 Describe the accounting for transfer of investment securities between categories.

International Reporting of Less than 50% Equity Investments

Countries/Standards	Method(s) Allowed
U.S. GAAP: United Kingdom, Brazil, Mexico	Equity
IASC: France, Germany, Netherlands, Italy, Japan	Proportional consolidation or equity

This variation in practice makes it difficult to compare Coca-Cola to other international beverage companies and is part of the reason why U.S. and international accounting standards-setters are studying the accounting rules for equity investments like Coca-Cola's.[1]

---

[1]Based on Morgan Stanley Dean Witter, "Apples to Apples, Global Beverage: Thirst for Knowledge" (May 25, 1999).

As indicated in the opening story, the measurement, recognition, and disclosure for certain investments are under study by U.S. and international standards-setters. This chapter addresses the accounting for debt and equity investments. The appendix to this chapter covers the effective-interest method for bond amortization. The content and organization of this chapter are as follows.

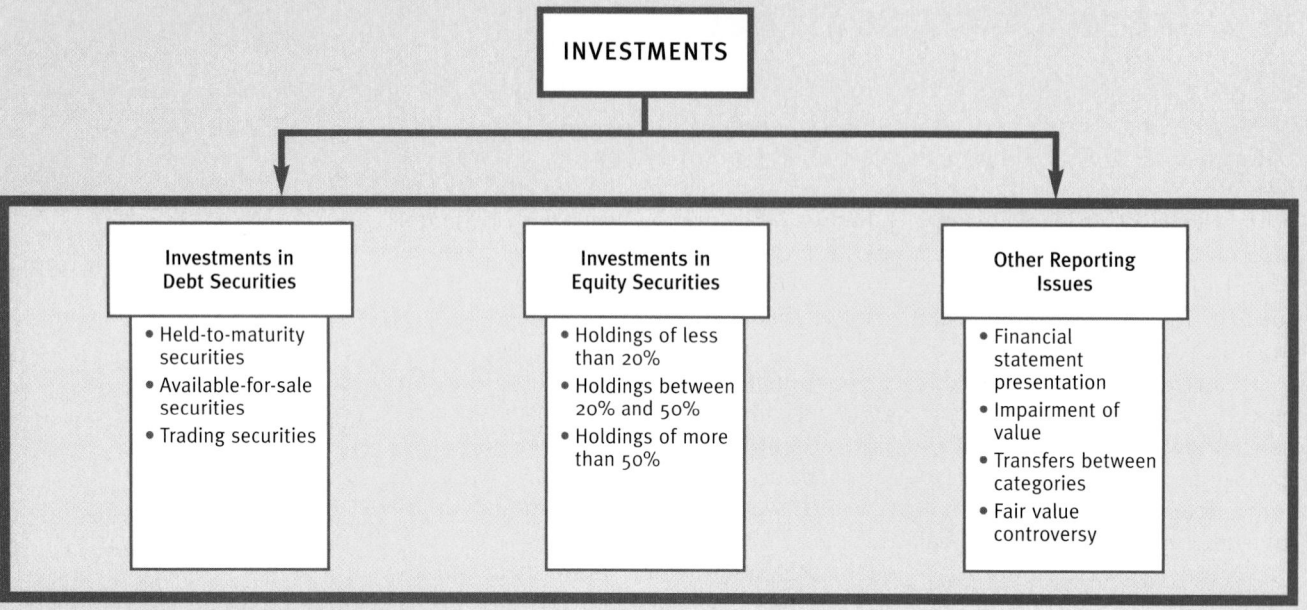

Companies have different motivations for investing in securities issued by other companies.[2] **One motivation is to earn a high rate of return.** A company can receive interest revenue from a debt investment or dividend revenue from an equity investment. In addition, capital gains on both types of securities can be realized. **Another motivation for investing (in equity securities) is to secure certain operating or financing arrangements with another company.** As in the opening story, **Coca-Cola** is able to exercise some control over bottler companies based on its significant (but not controlling) equity investment.

To provide useful information, the accounting for investments is based on the type of security (debt or equity) and management's intent with respect to the investment. As indicated in Illustration 13-1, our study of investments is organized by type of security. Within each section, we explain how the accounting for investments in debt and equity securities varies according to management intent.

---

[2]A **security** is a share, participation, or other interest in property or in an enterprise of the issuer or an obligation of the issuer that: (a) either is represented by an instrument issued in bearer or registered form or, if not represented by an instrument, is registered in books maintained to record transfers by or on behalf of the issuer; (b) is of a type commonly dealt in on securities exchanges or markets or, when represented by an instrument, is commonly recognized in any area in which it is issued or dealt in as a medium for investment; and (c) either is one of a class or series or by its terms is divisible into a class or series of shares, participations, interests, or obligations. From "Accounting for Certain Investments in Debt and Equity Securities," *Statement of Financial Accounting Standards No. 115* (Norwalk, Conn.: FASB, 1993), p. 48, par. 137.

Types of Security	Management Intent	Valuation Approach
Debt (Section 1)	No plans to sell	Amortized cost
	Plan to sell	Fair value
Equity (Section 2)	Plan to sell	Fair value
	Exercise some control	Equity method

Illustration 13-1
Summary of Investment Accounting Approaches

INVESTMENTS IN DEBT SECURITIES | SECTION 1

Debt securities are instruments representing a creditor relationship with an enterprise. Debt securities include U.S. government securities, municipal securities, corporate bonds, convertible debt, commercial paper, and all securitized debt instruments. Trade accounts receivable and loans receivable are not debt securities because they do not meet the definition of a security.

Investments in debt securities are grouped into three separate categories for accounting and reporting purposes. These categories are as follows:

Held-to-maturity: Debt securities that the enterprise has the positive intent and ability to hold to maturity.

Trading: Debt securities bought and held primarily for sale in the near term to generate income on short-term price differences.

Available-for-sale: Debt securities not classified as held-to-maturity or trading securities.

OBJECTIVE **1**
Identify the three categories of debt securities and describe the accounting and reporting treatment for each category.

Illustration 13-2 identifies these categories, along with the accounting and reporting treatments required for each.

Category	Valuation	Unrealized Holding Gains or Losses	Other Income Effects
Held-to-maturity	Amortized cost	Not recognized	Interest when earned; gains and losses from sale.
Trading securities	Fair value	Recognized in net income	Interest when earned; gains and losses from sale.
Available-for-sale	Fair value	Recognized as other comprehensive income and as separate component of stockholders' equity	Interest when earned; gains and losses from sale.

Illustration 13-2
Accounting for Debt Securities by Category

Amortized cost is the acquisition cost adjusted for the amortization of discount or premium, if appropriate. **Fair value** is the amount at which a financial instrument could be exchanged in a current transaction between willing parties, other than in a forced or liquidation sale.[3]

HELD-TO-MATURITY SECURITIES

Only debt securities can be classified as held-to-maturity because, by definition, equity securities have no maturity date. A debt security should be classified as **held-to-maturity** only if the reporting entity has **both (1) the positive intent** and **(2) the ability to hold those securities to maturity**. A company should not classify a debt security as held-to-maturity if the company intends to hold the security for an indefinite period of time. Likewise, if the enterprise anticipates that a sale may be necessary due to changes in interest rates, foreign currency risk, liquidity needs, or other asset-liability management reasons, the security should not be classified as held-to-maturity.[4]

Held-to-maturity securities are accounted for **at amortized cost**, not fair value. If management intends to hold certain investment securities to maturity and has no plans to sell them, fair values (selling prices) are not relevant for measuring and evaluating the cash flows associated with these securities. Finally, because held-to-maturity securities are not adjusted to fair value, they do not increase the volatility of either reported earnings or reported capital as do trading securities and available-for-sale securities.

To illustrate the accounting for held-to-maturity debt securities, assume that Robinson Company purchased $100,000 of 8% bonds of Evermaster Corporation on January 1, 2003, at par, paying $100,000. The bonds mature January 1, 2008; interest is payable each July 1 and January 1. The entry to record the investment is:

January 1, 2003

Held-to-Maturity Securities	100,000	
Cash		100,000

A Held-to-Maturity Securities account is used to indicate the type of debt security purchased. Discounts and premiums on long-term investments in bonds are amortized in a manner similar to discounts and premiums on bonds payable, discussed in Appendix 11A. Appendix 13A discusses in detail the amortization of bond discount and premium and its impact on interest revenue.

The journal entry to record the receipt of the first semiannual interest payment on July 1, 2003 is:

July 1, 2003

Cash	4,000	
Interest Revenue		4,000

---

[3]Ibid., pp. 47–48. The fair value is **readily determinable** if its sale price or other quotations are available on SEC registered exchanges, or, for over-the-counter securities, are published by recognized national publication systems.

[4]The FASB defines situations where, even though a security is sold before maturity, it has constructively been held to maturity, and thus does not represent a violation of the held-to-maturity requirement. These include selling a security close enough to maturity (such as 3 months) so that interest rate risk is no longer an important pricing factor.

Because Robinson Company is on a calendar-year basis, it accrues interest December 31, 2003, as follows.

December 31, 2003

Interest Receivable	4,000	
Interest Revenue		4,000

Robinson Company would report the following items related to its investment in Evermaster bonds in its December 31, 2003, financial statements.

Balance Sheet	
Current assets	
Interest receivable	$ 4,000
Long-term investments	
Held-to-maturity securities, at amortized cost	$100,000
Income Statement	
Other revenues and gains	
Interest revenue	$ 8,000

Illustration 13-3
Reporting of Held-to-Maturity Securities

The entry to record the redemption of the bond investment at maturity is:

January 1, 2008

Cash	104,000	
Interest Revenue		4,000
Held-to-Maturity Securities		100,000

AVAILABLE-FOR-SALE SECURITIES

Investments in debt securities that are in the **available-for-sale** category are reported at fair value. The unrealized gains and losses related to changes in the fair value of available-for-sale debt securities are recorded in an unrealized holding gain or loss account. This account is reported as other comprehensive income and as a separate component of stockholders' equity until realized. Thus, **changes in fair value are not reported as part of net income until the security is sold**. This approach reduces the volatility of net income.

UNDERLYING CONCEPTS

Recognizing unrealized gains and losses is an application of the concept of comprehensive income.

Illustration: Single Security

To illustrate the accounting for available-for-sale securities, assume that Graff Corporation purchases $100,000, 10%, 5-year bonds on January 1, 2003, with interest payable on July 1 and January 1. The bonds sell for $108,111 which results in a bond premium of $8,111 and an effective-interest rate of 8%.

The entry to record the purchase of the bonds is as follows.[5]

Calculator Solution for
Bond Price

	Inputs	Answer
N	10	
I	4	
PV	?	-108,111
PMT	5,000	
FV	100,000	

January 1, 2003

Available-for-Sale Securities	108,111	
Cash		108,111

To apply the fair value method to these debt securities, assume that at year-end the fair value of the bonds is $105,000 and that the carrying amount of the investments is $106,732. Comparing this fair value with the carrying amount (amortized cost) of the bonds at December 31, 2003, Graff recognizes an unrealized holding loss of $1,732 ($106,732 − $105,000). This loss is reported as other comprehensive income and as a separate component of stockholders' equity. The entry is as follows.

December 31, 2003

Unrealized Holding Gain or Loss—Equity	1,732	
Securities Fair Value Adjustment (Available-for-Sale)		1,732

A valuation account is used instead of crediting the Available-for-Sale Securities account. The use of the **Securities Fair Value Adjustment (Available-for-Sale) account** enables the company to maintain a record of its amortized cost. Because the adjustment account has a credit balance in this case, it is subtracted from the balance of the Available-for-Sale Securities account to arrive at fair value. The fair value is the amount reported on the balance sheet. At each reporting date, the bonds would be reported at fair value with an adjustment to the Unrealized Holding Gain or Loss—Equity account.

Illustration: Portfolio of Securities

To illustrate the accounting for a portfolio of securities, assume that Webb Corporation has two debt securities that are classified as available-for-sale. Illustration 13-4 provides information on amortized cost, fair value, and the amount of the unrealized gain or loss.

Illustration 13-4
Computation of Securities Fair Value Adjustment—Available-for-Sale Securities (2004)

AVAILABLE-FOR-SALE DEBT SECURITY PORTFOLIO DECEMBER 31, 2004			
Investments	Amortized Cost	Fair Value	Unrealized Gain (Loss)
Watson Corporation 8% bonds	$ 93,537	$103,600	$ 10,063
Anacomp Corporation 10% bonds	200,000	180,400	(19,600)
Total of portfolio	$293,537	$284,000	(9,537)
Previous securities fair value adjustment balance			0
Securities fair value adjustment—Cr.			$ (9,537)

[5]Investments acquired at par, at a discount, or at a premium are generally recorded in the accounts at cost, including brokerage and other fees but excluding the accrued interest; generally they are not recorded at maturity value. The use of a separate discount or premium account as a valuation account is acceptable procedure for investments, but in practice it has not been widely used.

The total fair value of Webb's available-for-sale portfolio is $284,000. The gross unrealized gains are $10,063, and the gross unrealized losses are $19,600, resulting in a net unrealized loss of $9,537. That is, the fair value of available-for-sale securities is $9,537 lower than its amortized cost. An adjusting entry is made to a valuation allowance to record the decrease in value and to record the loss as follows.

December 31, 2004

Unrealized Holding Gain or Loss—Equity	9,537	
Securities Fair Value Adjustment (Available-for-Sale)		9,537

The unrealized holding loss of $9,537 is reported as other comprehensive income and a reduction of stockholders' equity. As indicated earlier, unrealized holding gains and losses related to investments that are classified in the available-for-sale category are not included in net income.

Sale of Available-for-Sale Securities

If bonds carried as investments in available-for-sale securities are sold before the maturity date, entries must be made to remove from the Available-for-Sale Securities account the amortized cost of bonds sold. To illustrate, assume that Webb Corporation sold the Watson bonds (from Illustration 13-4) on July 1, 2005, for $90,000, at which time it had an amortized cost of $94,214. The computation of the realized loss is as follows.

Amortized cost (Watson bonds)	$94,214
Less: Selling price of bonds	90,000
Loss on sale of bonds	$ 4,214

Illustration 13-5
Computation of Loss on Sale of Bonds

The entry to record the sale of the Watson bonds is as follows.

July 1, 2005

Cash	90,000	
Loss on Sale of Securities	4,214	
Available-for-Sale Securities		94,214

This realized loss is reported in the "Other expenses and losses" section of the income statement. Assuming no other purchases and sales of bonds in 2005, Webb Corporation on December 31, 2005, prepares the information shown in Illustration 13-6.

As shown in Illustration 13-6 on page 640, Webb Corporation has an unrealized holding loss of $5,000. However, the Securities Fair Value Adjustment account already has a credit balance of $9,537. To reduce the adjustment account balance to $5,000, it is debited for $4,537, as follows.

December 31, 2005

Securities Fair Value Adjustment (Available-for-Sale)	4,537	
Unrealized Holding Gain or Loss—Equity		4,537

Illustration 13-6
Computation of Securities
Fair Value Adjustment—
Available-for-Sale (2005)

AVAILABLE-FOR-SALE DEBT SECURITY PORTFOLIO DECEMBER 31, 2005			
Investments	Amortized Cost	Fair Value	Unrealized Gain (Loss)
Anacomp Corporation 10% bonds (total portfolio)	$200,000	$195,000	$(5,000)
Previous securities fair value adjustment balance—Cr.			(9,537)
Securities fair value adjustment—Dr.			$ 4,537

Financial Statement Presentation

Webb Corporation's December 31, 2005, balance sheet and the 2005 income statement would contain the following items and amounts (the Anacomp bonds are long-term investments but are not intended to be held to maturity).

Illustration 13-7
Reporting of Available-for-Sale Securities

Balance Sheet	
Current assets	
Interest receivable	$ xxx
Investments	
Available-for-sale securities, at fair value	$195,000
Stockholders' equity	
Accumulated other comprehensive loss	$ 5,000
Income Statement	
Other revenues and gains	
Interest revenue	$ xxx
Other expenses and losses	
Loss on sale of securities	$ 4,214

Some favor including the unrealized holding gain or loss in net income rather than showing it as other comprehensive income.[6] However, some companies, particularly financial institutions, noted that recognizing gains and losses on assets, but not liabilities, would introduce substantial volatility in net income. They argued that often hedges exist between assets and liabilities so that gains in assets are offset by losses in liabilities, and vice versa. In short, to recognize gains and losses only on the asset side is unfair and not representative of the economic activities of the company.

This argument was convincing to the FASB. As a result, these unrealized gains and losses are **not included in net income**. However, even this approach does not solve some of the problems, because volatility of capital still results. This is of concern to financial institutions because regulators restrict financial institutions' operations based upon their level of capital. In addition, companies can still manage their net income by engaging in **gains trading** (i.e., selling the winners and holding the losers).

---

[6]In Chapter 5, we discussed the reporting of other comprehensive income and the concept of comprehensive income. "Reporting Comprehensive Income," *Statement of Financial Accounting Standards No. 130* (Norwalk, Conn.: FASB, 1997).

MARK-TO-MARKET EVERYWHERE

While many companies, particularly banks, opposed implementation of fair value accounting for investments, other companies have embraced the use of mark-to-market accounting. Energy companies, such as **Dynergy**, **Williams Companies**, and **Enron** use fair value methods to account for energy contracts, a type of derivative whose value depends on expected energy prices. (The accounting for derivative instruments is discussed in Appendix G, at the end of the book.)

However, there is concern that use of fair value methods for energy contracts may not be appropriate.[7] This is because determining fair value of these contracts requires estimation of energy prices 15 to 20 years in the future, based on changes in current market prices. If current prices increase, companies can record gains on the contract; under mark-to-market accounting these gains are recorded in income. Whether energy companies use unreasonable assumptions in their valuation models in order to book paper gains is subject to debate. However, most agree that companies need to disclose the models used to value energy contracts so that investors can compare the results of energy company trading operations.

WHAT DO THE NUMBERS MEAN?

TRADING SECURITIES

Trading securities are held with the intention of selling them in a short period of time. "Trading" in this context means frequent buying and selling, and trading securities are used to generate profits from short-term differences in price. The holding period for these securities is generally less than 3 months, and more probably is measured in days or hours. **These securities are reported at fair value, with unrealized holding gains and losses reported as part of net income. Any discount or premium is not amortized.** A **holding gain or loss** is the net change in the fair value of a security from one period to another, exclusive of dividend or interest revenue recognized but not received. In short, the FASB says to adjust the trading securities to fair value, at each reporting date. In addition, the change in value is reported as part of net income, not other comprehensive income.

To illustrate, assume that on December 31, 2004, Western Publishing Corporation determined its trading securities portfolio to be as shown in Illustration 13-8. (Assume that 2004 is the first year that Western Publishing held trading securities.) At the date of acquisition, these trading securities were recorded at cost, including brokerage commissions and taxes, in the account entitled Trading Securities. This is the first valuation of this recently purchased portfolio.

TRADING DEBT SECURITY PORTFOLIO DECEMBER 31, 2004			
Investments	Cost	Fair Value	Unrealized Gain (Loss)
Burlington Northern 10% bonds	$ 43,860	$ 51,500	$7,640
Chrysler Corporation 11% bonds	184,230	175,200	(9,030)
Time Warner 8% bonds	86,360	91,500	5,140
Total of portfolio	$314,450	$318,200	3,750
Previous securities fair value adjustment balance			0
Securities fair value adjustment—Dr.			$3,750

Illustration 13-8

Computation of Securities Fair Value Adjustment— Trading Securities Portfolio (2004)

[7]C. Cummins, "Williams: Enron's Game But Played with Caution," *Wall Street Journal Online* (January 23, 2002).

The total cost of Western's trading portfolio is $314,450. The gross unrealized gains are $12,780 ($7,640 + $5,140), and the gross unrealized losses are $9,030, resulting in a net unrealized gain of $3,750. The fair value of trading securities is $3,750 greater than its cost.

At December 31, an adjusting entry is made to a valuation allowance, referred to as Securities Fair Value Adjustment (Trading), to record the increase in value and to record the unrealized holding gain.

December 31, 2004

Securities Fair Value Adjustment (Trading)	3,750	
Unrealized Holding Gain or Loss—Income		3,750

Because the Securities Fair Value Adjustment account balance is a debit, it is added to the cost of the Trading Securities account to arrive at a fair value for the trading securities. The fair value of the securities is the amount reported on the balance sheet.

When securities are actively traded, the FASB believes that financial reporting is improved when the economic events affecting the company (changes in fair value) and related unrealized gains and losses are reported in the same period. Including changes in fair value in income provides more relevant information to current stockholders whose composition may be different next period.

SECTION 2 *INVESTMENTS IN EQUITY SECURITIES*

OBJECTIVE **2**
Identify the categories of equity securities and describe the accounting and reporting treatment for each category.

Equity securities are securities representing ownership interests such as common, preferred, or other capital stock. They also include rights to acquire or dispose of ownership interests at an agreed-upon or determinable price, such as in warrants, rights, and call or put options. Convertible debt securities and redeemable preferred stocks are not treated as equity securities. When equity securities are purchased, their cost includes the purchase price of the security plus broker's commissions and other fees incidental to the purchase.

The degree to which one corporation (**investor**) acquires an interest in the common stock of another corporation (**investee**) generally determines the accounting treatment for the investment subsequent to acquisition. Investments by one corporation in the common stock of another can be classified according to the percentage of the voting stock of the investee held by the investor:

① Holdings of less than 20% (fair value method)—investor has passive interest.

② Holdings between 20% and 50% (equity method)—investor has significant influence.

③ Holdings of more than 50% (consolidated statements)—investor has controlling interest.

These levels of interest or influence and the corresponding valuation and reporting method that must be applied to the investment are graphically displayed in Illustration 13-9.

Percentage of Ownership	0% ←————→ 20% ←————→ 50% ←————————→ 100%		
Level of Influence	Little or None	Significant	Control
Valuation Method	Fair Value Method	Equity Method	Consolidation

Illustration 13-9
Levels of Influence Determine Accounting Methods

The accounting and reporting for equity securities therefore depends upon the level of influence and the type of security involved, as shown in Illustration 13-10.

Category	Valuation	Unrealized Holding Gains or Losses	Other Income Effects
Holdings less than 20%			
1. Available-for-sale	Fair value	Recognized in "Other comprehensive income" and as separate component of stockholders' equity	Dividends declared; gains and losses from sale.
2. Trading	Fair value	Recognized in net income	Dividends declared; gains and losses from sale.
Holdings between 20% and 50%	Equity	Not recognized	Proportionate shares of investee's net income
Holdings more than 50%	Consolidation	Not recognized	Not applicable

Illustration 13-10
Accounting and Reporting for Equity Securities by Category

HOLDINGS OF LESS THAN 20%

As mentioned earlier, equity securities are recorded at cost. In some cases, cost is difficult to determine. For example, equity securities acquired in **exchange for noncash consideration** (property or services) should be recorded at (1) the fair value of the consideration given, or (2) the fair value of the security received, whichever is more clearly determinable. The absence of clearly determinable values for the property or services or a market price for the security acquired may require the use of appraisals or estimates to arrive at a cost.

If market prices are not available at the date of acquisition of several securities, it may be necessary to defer cost apportionment until evidence of at least one value becomes available. In some instances cost apportionment may have to wait until one of the securities is sold. In such cases, the proceeds from the sale of the one security may be subtracted from the lump sum cost, leaving the residual cost to be assigned as the cost of the other.[8]

---

[8]Accounting for numerous purchases of securities requires that information regarding the cost of individual purchases be preserved, as well as the dates of purchases and sales. If **specific identification** is not possible, the use of an **average cost** may be used for multiple purchases of the same class of security. The **first-in, first-out method** of assigning costs to investments at the time of sale is also acceptable and is normally employed.

When an investor has an interest of less than 20%, it is presumed that the investor has little or no influence over the investee. In such cases, if market prices are available, the investment is valued and reported subsequent to acquisition using the **fair value method**.[9] The fair value method requires that companies classify equity securities at acquisition as **available-for-sale securities** or **trading securities**. Because equity securities have no maturity date, they cannot be classified as held-to-maturity.

Available-for-Sale Securities

Available-for-sale securities when acquired are recorded at cost. To illustrate, assume that on November 3, 2004, Republic Corporation purchased common stock of three companies, each investment representing less than a 20% interest.

	Cost
Northwest Industries, Inc.	$259,700
Campbell Soup Co.	317,500
St. Regis Pulp Co.	141,350
Total cost	$718,550

These investments would be recorded as follows.

November 3, 2004

| Available-for-Sale Securities | 718,550 | |
| Cash | | 718,550 |

On December 6, 2004, Republic receives a cash dividend of $4,200 on its investment in the common stock of Campbell Soup Co. The cash dividend is recorded as follows.

December 6, 2004

| Cash | 4,200 | |
| Dividend Revenue | | 4,200 |

All three of the investee companies reported net income for the year, but only Campbell Soup declared and paid a dividend to Republic. But, as indicated before, when an investor owns less than 20% of the common stock of another corporation, it is presumed that the investor has relatively little influence on the investee. As a result, **net income earned by the investee is not considered a proper basis for recognizing income from the investment by the investor**. The reason is that the investee may choose to retain for use in the business increased net assets resulting from profitable operations. Therefore, **net income is not considered earned by the investor until cash dividends are declared by the investee**.

[9]When market prices are not available, the investment is valued and reported at cost in periods subsequent to acquisition. This approach is often referred to as the **cost method**. Dividends are recognized as dividend revenue when received, and the portfolio is valued and reported at acquisition cost. No gains or losses are recognized until the securities are sold.

At December 31, 2004, Republic's available-for-sale equity security portfolio has the following cost and fair value.

AVAILABLE-FOR-SALE EQUITY SECURITY PORTFOLIO DECEMBER 31, 2004			
Investments	Cost	Fair Value	Unrealized Gain (Loss)
Northwest Industries, Inc.	$259,700	$275,000	$ 15,300
Campbell Soup Co.	317,500	304,000	(13,500)
St. Regis Pulp Co.	141,350	104,000	(37,350)
Total of portfolio	$718,550	$683,000	(35,550)
Previous securities fair value adjustment balance			0
Securities fair value adjustment—Cr.			$ (35,550)

For Republic's available-for-sale equity securities portfolio, the gross unrealized gains are $15,300, and the gross unrealized losses are $50,850 ($13,500 + $37,350), resulting in a net unrealized loss of $35,550. The fair value of the available-for-sale securities portfolio is $35,550 less than its cost. As with available-for-sale **debt** securities, the net unrealized gains and losses related to changes in the fair value of available-for-sale **equity** securities are recorded in an Unrealized Holding Gain or Loss—Equity account that is reported as a **part of other comprehensive income and as a component of stockholders' equity until realized**. In this case, Republic prepares an adjusting entry debiting the Unrealized Holding Gain or Loss—Equity account and crediting the Securities Fair Value Adjustment account to record the decrease in fair value and to record the loss as follows.

December 31, 2004

Unrealized Holding Gain or Loss—Equity	35,550	
Securities Fair Value Adjustment (Available-for-Sale)		35,550

On January 23, 2005, Republic sold all of its Northwest Industries, Inc. common stock receiving net proceeds of $287,220. The realized gain on the sale is computed as follows.

Illustration 13-12
Computation of Gain on Sale of Stock

Net proceeds from sale	$287,220
Cost of Northwest shares	259,700
Gain on sale of stock	$ 27,520

The sale is recorded as follows.

January 23, 2005

Cash	287,220	
Available-for-Sale Securities		259,700
Gain on Sale of Stock		27,520

In addition, assume that on February 10, 2005, Republic purchased 20,000 shares of Continental Trucking at a market price of $12.75 per share plus brokerage commissions of $1,850 (total cost, $256,850).

On December 31, 2005, Republic's portfolio of available-for-sale securities is as follows.

Illustration 13-13
Computation of Securities Fair Value Adjustment—Available-for-Sale Equity Security Portfolio (2005)

AVAILABLE-FOR-SALE EQUITY SECURITY PORTFOLIO DECEMBER 31, 2005			
Investments	Cost	Fair Value	Unrealized Gain (Loss)
Continental Trucking	$256,850	$278,350	$21,500
Campbell Soup Co.	317,500	362,550	45,050
St. Regis Pulp Co.	141,350	139,050	(2,300)
Total of portfolio	$715,700	$779,950	64,250
Previous securities fair value adjustment balance—Cr.			(35,550)
Securities fair value adjustment—Dr.			$99,800

At December 31, 2005, the fair value of Republic's available-for-sale equity securities portfolio exceeds cost by $64,250 (unrealized gain). The Securities Fair Value Adjustment account had a credit balance of $35,550 at December 31, 2004. To adjust Republic's December 31, 2005, available-for-sale portfolio to fair value requires that the Securities Fair Value Adjustment account be debited for $99,800 ($35,550 + $64,250). The entry to record this adjustment is as follows.

December 31, 2005

Securities Fair Value Adjustment (Available-for-Sale)	99,800	
Unrealized Holding Gain or Loss—Equity		99,800

Trading Securities

The accounting entries to record trading equity securities are the same as for available-for-sale equity securities, except for recording the unrealized holding gain or loss. For trading equity securities, the unrealized holding gain or loss is **reported as part of net income**. Thus, the account title Unrealized Holding Gain or Loss—Income is used. When a sale is made, the remainder of the gain or loss is recognized in income.

HOLDINGS BETWEEN 20% AND 50%

An investor corporation may hold an interest of less than 50% in an investee corporation and thus not possess legal control. However, as shown in the opening story about Coca-Cola, an investment in voting stock of less than 50% can still give Coke (the investor) the ability to exercise significant influence over the operating and financial policies of its bottlers.[10] To provide a guide for accounting for investors when 50% or less of the common voting stock is held and to develop an operational definition of "sig-

[10]"The Equity Method of Accounting for Investments in Common Stock," *Opinions of the Accounting Principles Board No. 18* (New York: AICPA, 1971), par. 17.

nificant influence," the APB in *Opinion No. 18* noted that ability to exercise influence may be indicated in several ways. Examples would be: representation on the board of directors, participation in policy-making processes, material intercompany transactions, interchange of managerial personnel, or technological dependency. Another important consideration is the extent of ownership by an investor in relation to the concentration of other shareholdings. To achieve a reasonable degree of uniformity in application of the "significant influence" criterion, the profession concluded that an investment (direct or indirect) of 20 percent or more of the voting stock of an investee should lead to a presumption that in the absence of evidence to the contrary, an investor has the ability to exercise significant influence over an investee.[11]

In instances of "significant influence" (generally an investment of 20% or more), the investor is required to account for the investment using the **equity method**.

WHAT'S IN IT FOR ME?

WHAT DO THE NUMBERS MEAN?

The extent of control or influence for an equity investor, given a level of investment, can vary internationally. This was illustrated recently when **DaimlerChrysler** made a 33.4 % investment in **Mitsubishi Motors**. Under Japanese commercial law, that level of investment gives DaimlerChrysler regular seats on the board and gives it the power to veto board decisions. Whether this is a good deal for Mitsubishi will depend on whether and how DaimlerChrysler exercises its control over Mitsubishi operations. Mitsubishi is said to have pushed for assurances that DaimlerChrysler would not push for job cuts, but may have been willing to give DaimlerChrysler more control in exchange for the financial boost it provided and for access to the German-American carmaker's engineering and production expertise.

Source: S. Miller, and N. Shirouzu, "DaimlerChrysler to Acquire a Stake in Mitsubishi Motors for $1.94 Billion," *Wall Street Journal Interactive Edition* (March 27, 2000).

Equity Method

Under the **equity method** a substantive economic relationship is acknowledged between the investor and the investee. The investment is originally recorded at the cost of the shares acquired but is subsequently adjusted each period for changes in the net assets of the investee. That is, the **investment's carrying amount is periodically increased (decreased) by the investor's proportionate share of the earnings (losses) of the investee and decreased by all dividends received by the investor from the investee.** The equity method recognizes that investee's earnings increase investee's net assets, and that investee's losses and dividends decrease these net assets.

To illustrate the equity method and compare it with the fair value method, assume that Maxi Company purchases a 20% interest in Mini Company. To apply the fair value

OBJECTIVE 3
Explain the equity method of accounting and compare it to the fair value method for equity securities.

[11]Examples of cases in which an investment of 20% or more might not enable an investor to exercise significant influence are:

(1) The investee opposes the investor's acquisition of its stock.

(2) The investor and investee sign an agreement under which the investor surrenders significant shareholder rights.

(3) The investor's ownership share does not result in "significant influence" because majority ownership of the investee is concentrated among a small group of shareholders who operate the investee without regard to the views of the investor.

(4) The investor tries and fails to obtain representation on the investee's board of directors.

"Criteria for Applying the Equity Method of Accounting for Investments in Common Stock," *Interpretations of the Financial Accounting Standards Board No. 35* (Stamford, Conn.: FASB, 1981).

method in this example, assume that Maxi does not have the ability to exercise significant influence and the securities are classified as available-for-sale. Where the equity method is applied in this example, assume that the 20% interest permits Maxi to exercise significant influence. The entries are shown in Illustration 13-14.

Illustration 13-14
Comparison of Fair Value Method and Equity Method

ENTRIES BY MAXI COMPANY

Fair Value Method		Equity Method	

On January 2, 2004, Maxi Company acquired 48,000 shares (20% of Mini Company common stock) at a cost of $10 a share.

Available-for-Sale-Securities	480,000		Investment in Mini Stock	480,000	
Cash		480,000	Cash		480,000

For the year 2004, Mini Company reported net income of $200,000; Maxi Company's share is 20%, or $40,000.

No entry		Investment in Mini Stock	40,000	
		Revenue from Investment		40,000

At December 31, 2004, the 48,000 shares of Mini Company have a fair value (market price) of $12 a share, or $576,000.

Securities Fair Value Adjustment			No entry
(Available-for-Sale)	96,000		
Unrealized Holding Gain			
or Loss—Equity		96,000	

On January 28, 2005, Mini Company announced and paid a cash dividend of $100,000; Maxi Company received 20%, or $20,000.

Cash	20,000		Cash	20,000	
Dividend Revenue		20,000	Investment in Mini Stock		20,000

For the year 2005, Mini reported a net loss of $50,000; Maxi Company's share is 20%, or $10,000.

No entry		Loss on Investment	10,000	
		Investment in Mini Stock		10,000

At December 31, 2005, the Mini Company 48,000 shares have a fair value (market price) of $11 a share, or $528,000.

Unrealized Holding Gain			
or Loss—Equity	48,000		No entry
Securities Fair Value Adjustment			
(Available-for-Sale)		48,000	

Note that under the fair value method only the cash dividends received from Mini Company are reported as revenue by Maxi Company. **The earning of net income by the investee is not considered a proper basis for recognition of income from the investment by the investor.** The reason is that increased net assets resulting from the investee's profitable operation may be permanently retained in the business by the investee. Therefore, revenue is not considered earned by the investor until dividends are received from the investee.

Under the equity method, Maxi Company reports as revenue its share of the net income reported by Mini Company; the cash dividends received from Mini Company are recorded as a decrease in the investment carrying value. As a result, the investor records its share of the net income of the investee in the year when it is earned. In this case, the investor can ensure that any net asset increases of the investee resulting from net income will be paid in dividends if desired. To wait until a dividend is received ignores the fact that the investor is better off if the investee has earned income.

Using dividends as a basis for recognizing income poses an additional problem. For example, assume that the investee reports a net loss, but the investor exerts influence to force a dividend payment from the investee. In this case, the investor reports income, even though the investee is experiencing a loss. **In other words, if dividends are used as a basis for recognizing income, the economics of the situation are not properly reported.**

Investee Losses Exceed Carrying Amount

If an investor's share of the investee's losses exceeds the carrying amount of the investment, should the investor recognize additional losses? Ordinarily the investor should discontinue applying the equity method and not recognize additional losses.

If the investor's potential loss is not limited to the amount of its original investment (by guarantee of the investee's obligations or other commitment to provide further financial support), or if imminent return to profitable operations by the investee appears to be assured, it is appropriate for the investor to recognize additional losses.[12]

FROM BAD TO WORSE

WHAT DO THE NUMBERS MEAN?

Amazon.com, the pioneer of Internet retailing, has struggled to turn a profit. Furthermore, some of Amazon's equity investments have resulted in Amazon's recent earnings performance going from bad to worse. In 2001, Amazon.com disclosed equity stakes is such companies as **Altera International, Basis Technology, drugstore.com,** and **Eziba.com.** Apparently, these companies are not faring any better than Amazon, as indicated in Amazon's income statement.

(in thousands)	2001	2000	1999
Net income (loss)	$(567,227)	$(1,411,273)	$(719,968)
Equity in losses of equity method investees	30,327	304,596	76,769
% of total loss	5.3	21.6	10.7

Because these companies operate in the same depressed Internet economy as Amazon, under the equity method of accounting, their negative results can make Amazon's already bad bottom line even worse.

HOLDINGS OF MORE THAN 50%

INTERNATIONAL INSIGHT

In contrast to U.S. firms, financial statements of non-U.S. companies often include both consolidated (group) statements and parent company financial statements.

When one corporation acquires a voting interest of more than 50%—**controlling interest**—in another corporation, the investor corporation is referred to as the **parent** and the investee corporation as the **subsidiary.** The investment in the common stock of the subsidiary is presented as a long-term investment on the separate financial statements of the parent.

When the parent treats the subsidiary as an investment, **consolidated financial statements** are generally prepared instead of separate financial statements for the parent and the subsidiary. Consolidated financial statements disregard the distinction between separate legal entities and treat the parent and subsidiary corporations as a single economic entity. The subject of when and how to prepare consolidated financial statements is discussed extensively in advanced accounting. Whether or not consolidated financial statements are prepared, the investment in the subsidiary is generally

---

[12]"The Equity Method of Accounting for Investments in Common Stock," op. cit., par. 19(i).

accounted for on the parent's books **using the equity method** as explained in this chapter.

WHAT DO THE NUMBERS MEAN?

WHO'S IN CONTROL?

Presently the rules for consolidation seem very straightforward: If a company owns more than 50% of another company, it generally should be consolidated. If it owns less than 50%, it is generally not consolidated. However the FASB recognizes that the present test is too artificial, and determination of who really has control is often based on factors other than stock ownership.

In fact, specific guidelines have been developed that force consolidation even though stock ownership is not above 50% in certain limited situations. For example, Enron's failure to consolidate three special purpose entities that were effectively controlled by Enron led to an overstatement of income of $569 million and overstatement of equity of $1.2 billion. In each of these three cases, the GAAP answer would have led to consolidation. That is, the following factors indicate that consolidation should have occurred: the majority owner of the special purpose entity (SPE) made only a modest investment, the activities of the SPE were virtually to benefit Enron, and the substantive risks and rewards related to the assets or debt of the SPE rested directly or indirectly with Enron.

The FASB now indicates it will issue new guidelines related to SPEs, given all the reporting problems that have surfaced related to SPEs as a result of the Enron bankruptcy.

SECTION 3 | *OTHER REPORTING ISSUES*

We have identified the basic issues involved in accounting for investments in debt and equity securities. In addition, the following issues relate to both of these types of securities.

① Financial statement presentation
② Impairment of value
③ Transfers between categories
④ Fair value controversy

FINANCIAL STATEMENT PRESENTATION OF INVESTMENTS

OBJECTIVE 4
Describe the disclosure requirements for investments in debt and equity securities.

Companies are required to present individual amounts for the three categories of investments either on the balance sheet or in the related notes. Trading securities should be reported at aggregate fair value as current assets. Individual held-to-maturity and available-for-sale securities are classified as current or noncurrent depending upon the circumstances.

Held-to-maturity securities should be classified as current or noncurrent, based on the maturity date of the individual securities. Debt securities identified as available-for-sale should be classified as current or noncurrent, based on maturities and expectations as to sales and redemptions in the following year. Equity securities identified as available-for-sale should be classified as current if these securities are available for use in current operations. Thus, if the invested cash used to purchase the equity securities is considered a contingency fund to be used whenever a need arises, then the securities should be classified as current.

For securities classified as available-for-sale and separately for securities classified as held-to-maturity, a company should describe:

1. Aggregate fair value, gross unrealized holding gains, gross unrealized losses, and amortized cost basis by major security type (debt and equity).

2. Information about the contractual maturities of debt securities. Maturity information may be combined in appropriate groupings such as (a) within 1 year, (b) after 1 year through 5 years, (c) after 5 years through 10 years, and (d) after 10 years.

In classifying investments, management's expressed intent should be supported by evidence, such as the history of the company's investment activities, events subsequent to the balance sheet date, and the nature and purpose of the investment.

Companies have to be extremely careful with debt securities held to maturity. If a debt security in this category is sold prematurely, the sale may "taint" the entire held-to-maturity portfolio. That is, a management's statement regarding "intent" is no longer as credible, and therefore the securities might have to be reclassified. This could lead to unfortunate consequences. An interesting by-product of this situation is that companies that wish to retire their debt securities early are finding it difficult to do so; the holder will not sell because the securities are classified as held-to-maturity.

Disclosures Required Under the Equity Method

The significance of an investment to the investor's financial position and operating results should determine the extent of disclosures. The following disclosures in the investor's financial statements generally apply to the equity method.

1. The name of each investee and the percentage of ownership of common stock.
2. The accounting policies of the investor with respect to investments in common stock.
3. The difference, if any, between the amount in the investment account and the amount of underlying equity in the net assets of the investee.
4. The aggregate value of each identified investment based on quoted market price (if available).
5. When investments of 20% or more interest are, in the aggregate, material in relation to the financial position and operating results of an investor, it may be necessary to present summarized information concerning assets, liabilities, and results of operations of the investees, either individually or in groups, as appropriate.

⭐ **UNDERLYING CONCEPTS**

The consolidation of financial results of different companies follows the economic entity assumption and disregards legal entities. The key objective is to provide useful information to financial statement users.

In addition, the investor is expected to disclose the reasons for **not** using the equity method in cases of 20% or more ownership interest and **for** using the equity method in cases of less than 20% ownership interest.

Reclassification Adjustments

As indicated in Chapter 5, changes in unrealized holding gains and losses related to available-for-sale securities are reported as part of other comprehensive income. Companies have the option to display the components of other comprehensive income in one of three ways: (1) in a combined statement of income and comprehensive income, (2) in a separate statement of comprehensive income that begins with net income, or (3) in a statement of stockholders' equity.

The reporting of changes in unrealized gains or losses in comprehensive income is straightforward unless securities are sold during the year. In that case, double counting results when realized gains or losses are reported as part of net income but also are shown as part of other comprehensive income in the current period or in previous periods.

To ensure that gains and losses are not counted twice when a sale occurs, a **reclassification adjustment** is necessary. To illustrate, assume that Open Company has the following two available-for-sale securities in its portfolio at the end of 2003 (its first year of operations).

Illustration 13-15
Available-for-Sale
Security Portfolio (2003)

Investments	Cost	Fair Value	Unrealized Holding Gain (Loss)
Lehman Inc. common stocks	$ 80,000	$105,000	$25,000
Woods Co. common stocks	120,000	135,000	15,000
Total of portfolio	$200,000	$240,000	40,000
Previous securities fair value adjustment balance			–0–
Securities fair value adjustment—Dr.			$40,000

If Open Company reports net income in 2003 of $350,000, a statement of comprehensive income would be reported as follows.

Illustration 13-16
Statement of
Comprehensive
Income (2003)

OPEN CO. STATEMENT OF COMPREHENSIVE INCOME FOR THE YEAR ENDED DECEMBER 31, 2003	
Net income	$350,000
Other comprehensive income	
Holding gains arising during period	40,000
Comprehensive income	$390,000

During 2004, Open Company sold the Lehman Inc. common stock for $105,000 and realized a gain on the sale of $25,000 ($105,000 − $80,000). At the end of 2004, the fair value of the Woods Co. common stock increased an additional $20,000, to $155,000. The computation of the change in the securities fair value adjustment account is computed as follows.

Illustration 13-17
Available-for-Sale
Security Portfolio (2004)

Investments	Cost	Fair Value	Unrealized Holding Gain (Loss)
Woods Co. common stocks	$120,000	$155,000	$35,000
Previous securities fair value adjustment balance—Dr.			(40,000)
Securities fair value adjustment—Cr.			$ (5,000)

Illustration 13-17 indicates that an unrealized holding loss of $5,000 should be reported in comprehensive income in 2004. In addition, Open Company realized a gain of $25,000 on the sale of the Lehman common stock. Comprehensive income includes both realized and unrealized components, and therefore the total holding gain (loss) recognized in 2004 is $20,000, computed as follows.

Unrealized holding gain (loss)	$ (5,000)
Realized holding gain	25,000
Total holding gain recognized	$20,000

Illustration 13-18
Computation of Total Holding Gain (Loss)

Open Company reports net income of $720,000 in 2004, which includes the realized gain on sale of the Lehman securities. A statement of comprehensive income for 2004 is shown in Illustration 13-19, indicating how the components of holding gains (losses) are reported.

OPEN COMPANY		
STATEMENT OF COMPREHENSIVE INCOME		
FOR THE YEAR ENDED DECEMBER 31, 2004		
Net income (includes $25,000 realized gain on Lehman shares)		$720,000
Other comprehensive income		
Holding gains arising during period ($155,000 − $135,000)	$20,000	
Less: Reclassification adjustment for gains included in net income	(25,000)	(5,000)
Comprehensive income		$715,000

Illustration 13-19
Statement of Comprehensive Income (2004)

In 2003, the unrealized gain on the Lehman Co. common stock was included in comprehensive income. In 2004, it was sold and the realized gain reported in net income which increases comprehensive income again. To avoid double counting this gain, a reclassification adjustment is made to eliminate the realized gain from the computation of comprehensive income.

A company has the option to display reclassification adjustments on the face of the financial statement in which comprehensive income is reported, or it may disclose these reclassification adjustments in the notes to the financial statements.

Comprehensive Illustration

To illustrate the reporting of investment securities and related gain or loss on available-for-sale securities, assume that on January 1, 2003, Hinges Co. had cash and common stock of $50,000.[13] At that date the company had no other asset, liability, or equity bal-

---

[13]This example adapted from Dennis R. Beresford, L. Todd Johnson, and Cheri L. Reither, "Is a Second Income Statement Needed?" *Journal of Accountancy* (April 1996), p. 71.

ance. On January 2, Hinges Co. purchased for cash $50,000 of equity securities that are classified as available-for-sale. On June 30, Hinges Co. sold part of the available-for-sale security portfolio, realizing a gain as follows.

Illustration 13-20
Computation of Realized Gain

Fair value of securities sold	$22,000
Less: Cost of securities sold	20,000
Realized gain	$ 2,000

Hinges Co. did not purchase or sell any other securities during 2003. It received $3,000 in dividends during the year. At December 31, 2003, the remaining portfolio is:

Illustration 13-21
Computation of Unrealized Gain

Fair value of portfolio	$34,000
Less: Cost of portfolio	30,000
Unrealized gain	$ 4,000

The company's income statement for 2003 is shown in Illustration 13-22.

Illustration 13-22
Income Statement

HINGES CO.
INCOME STATEMENT
FOR THE YEAR ENDED DECEMBER 31, 2003

Dividend revenue	$3,000
Realized gains on investment in securities	2,000
Net income	$5,000

The company decides to report its change in the unrealized holding gain in a statement of comprehensive income as follows.

Illustration 13-23
Statement of Comprehensive Income

HINGES CO.
STATEMENT OF COMPREHENSIVE INCOME
FOR THE YEAR ENDED DECEMBER 31, 2003

Net income		$5,000
Other comprehensive income:		
Holding gains arising during the period	$6,000	
Less: Reclassification adjustment for gains included in net income	2,000	4,000
Comprehensive income		$9,000

Its statement of stockholders' equity would show the following.

Illustration 13-24
Statement of
Stockholders' Equity

HINGES CO. STATEMENT OF STOCKHOLDERS' EQUITY FOR THE YEAR ENDED DECEMBER 31, 2003				
	Common Stock	Retained Earnings	Accumulated Other Comprehensive Income	Total
Beginning balance	$50,000	$–0–	$–0–	$50,000
Add: Net income		5,000		5,000
Other comprehensive income			4,000	4,000
Ending balance	$50,000	$5,000	$4,000	$59,000

A comparative balance sheet is shown below.

Illustration 13-25
Comparative Balance
Sheet

HINGES CO. COMPARATIVE BALANCE SHEET		
	1/1/03	12/31/03
Assets		
Cash	$50,000	$25,000
Available-for-sale securities		34,000
Total assets	$50,000	$59,000
Stockholders' equity		
Common stock	$50,000	$50,000
Retained earnings		5,000
Accumulated other comprehensive income		4,000
Total stockholders' equity	$50,000	$59,000

This example indicates how an unrealized gain or loss on available-for-sale securities affects all the financial statements. It should be noted that the components that comprise accumulated comprehensive income must be disclosed.

IMPAIRMENT OF VALUE

OBJECTIVE **5**
Discuss the
accounting for
impairments of
debt and equity
investments.

Every investment should be evaluated at each reporting date to determine if it has suffered **impairment**—a loss in value that is other than temporary. A bankruptcy or a significant liquidity crisis being experienced by an investee are examples of situations in which a loss in value to the investor may be permanent. **If the decline is judged to be other than temporary, the cost basis of the individual security is written down to a**

new cost basis. The amount of the write-down is accounted for as a realized loss and, therefore, included in net income.

For debt securities, the impairment test is to determine whether "it is probable that the investor will be unable to collect all amounts due according to the contractual terms." **For equity securities,** the guideline is less precise. Any time realizable value is lower than the carrying amount of the investment, an impairment must be considered. Factors involved are the following: the length of time and the extent to which the fair value has been less than cost; the financial condition and near-term prospects of the issuer; and the intent and ability of the investor company to retain its investment to allow for any anticipated recovery in fair value.

To illustrate an impairment, assume that Strickler Company holds available-for-sale bond securities with a par value and amortized cost of $1 million. The fair value of these securities is $800,000. Strickler has previously reported an unrealized loss on these securities of $200,000 as part of other comprehensive income. In evaluating the securities, Strickler now determines it probable that it will not be able to collect all amounts due. In this case, the unrealized loss of $200,000 will be reported as a loss on impairment of $200,000 and included in income, with the bonds stated at their new cost basis. The journal entry to record this impairment would be as follows.

Loss on Impairment	200,000	
Securities Fair Value Adjustment (Available-for-Sale)	200,000	
Unrealized Holding Gain or Loss—Equity		200,000
Available-for-Sale Securities		200,000

The new cost basis of the investment in debt securities is $800,000. Subsequent increases and decreases in the fair value of impaired available-for-sale securities are included as other comprehensive income.[14]

The impairment test used for debt and equity securities is based on a fair value test. This test is slightly different from the impairment test for loans discussed in Appendix F at the end of the book. The FASB rejected the discounted cash flow alternative for securities because of the availability of market price information.

TRANSFERS BETWEEN CATEGORIES

OBJECTIVE 6
Describe the accounting for transfer of investment securities between categories.

Transfers between any of the categories are accounted for at fair value. Thus, if available-for-sale securities are transferred to held-to-maturity investments, the new investment (held-to-maturity) is recorded at the date of transfer at **fair value** in the new category. Similarly, if held-to-maturity investments are transferred to available-for-sale investments, the new investments (available-for-sale) are recorded at **fair value.** This **fair value** rule assures that a company cannot escape recognition of fair value simply by transferring securities to the held-to-maturity category. Illustration 13-26 summarizes the accounting treatment for transfers. **This illustration assumes that adjusting entries to report changes in fair value for the current period are not yet recorded.**

---

[14]Amortization of any discount related to the debt securities is not permitted after recording the impairment. The new cost basis of impaired held-to-maturity securities would not change unless additional impairment occurred.

Illustration 13-26
Accounting for Transfers

Type of Transfer	Measurement Basis	Impact of Transfer on Stockholders' Equity	Impact of Transfer on Net Income
Transfer from trading to available-for-sale	Security transferred at fair value at the date of transfer, which is the new cost basis of the security.	The unrealized gain or loss at the date of transfer increases or decreases stockholders' equity.	The unrealized gain or loss at the date of transfer is recognized in income.
Transfer from available-for-sale to trading	Security transferred at fair value at the date of transfer, which is the new cost basis of the security.	The unrealized gain or loss at the date of transfer increases or decreases stockholders' equity.	The unrealized gain or loss at the date of transfer is recognized in income.
Transfer from held-to-maturity to available-for-sale*	Security transferred at fair value at the date of transfer.	The separate component of stockholders' equity is increased or decreased by the unrealized gain or loss at the date of transfer.	None
Transfer from available-for-sale to held-to-maturity	Security transferred at fair value at the date of transfer.	The unrealized gain or loss at the date of transfer carried as a separate component of stockholders' equity is amortized over the remaining life of the security.	None

*Statement No. 115 states that these types of transfers should be rare.

Examples of the Entries for Recording Transfers Between Categories

FAIR VALUE CONTROVERSY

FASB Statement No. 115 leaves many issues unresolved. Many parties are dissatisfied with its results: some think it goes too far, others think it does not go far enough. In this section we look at some of the major unresolved issues.

Measurement Based on Intent

Debt securities can be classified as held-to-maturity, available-for-sale, or trading. As a result, three identical debt securities could be reported in three different ways in the financial statements. Some argue such treatment is confusing. Furthermore, the held-to-maturity category is based solely on intent, which is a subjective evaluation. What is not subjective is the market price of the debt instrument, which is observable in the marketplace. In other words, the three classifications are subjective, and therefore arbitrary classifications will result.

Gains Trading

Certain debt securities can be classified as held-to-maturity and therefore reported at amortized cost. Other debt and equity securities can be classified as available-for-sale and reported at fair value with the unrealized gain or loss reported as other comprehensive income. In either case, a company can become involved in "gains trading" (also referred to as "cherry picking"). In **gains trading**, companies sell their "winners," reporting the gains in income, and hold on to the losers.

Liabilities Not Fairly Valued

Many argue that if investment securities are going to be reported at fair value, so also should liabilities. They note that by recognizing changes in value on only one side of the balance sheet (the asset side), a high degree of volatility can occur in the income and stockholders' equity amounts. It is further argued that financial institutions are involved in asset and liability management (not just asset management) and that viewing only one side may lead managers to make uneconomic decisions as a result of the accounting. Although the Board was sympathetic with this view, it noted that certain debt securities were still reported at amortized cost and that other types of securities were excluded from the scope of this standard. In addition, serious valuation issues arose in relation to some types of liabilities. As a result, liabilities were excluded from consideration.[15]

Subjectivity of Fair Values

Some people question the relevance of fair value measures for investments in securities, arguing in favor of reporting based on amortized cost. They believe that amortized cost provides relevant information: it focuses on the decision to acquire the asset, the earning effects of that decision that will be realized over time, and the ultimate recoverable value of the asset. They argue that fair value ignores those concepts. Instead, fair value focuses on the effects of transactions and events that do not involve the enterprise, reflecting opportunity gains and losses whose recognition in the financial statements is, in their view, not appropriate until they are realized.

SUMMARY

The major debt and equity securities and their reporting treatment are summarized in Illustration 13-27.

---

[15]In a recent preliminary report concerning valuation of financial instruments, the FASB indicated its support for valuing liabilities at fair value. "Reporting Financial Instruments and Certain Related Assets and Liabilities at Fair Value," *FASB Preliminary Views* (Norwalk, Conn.: FASB, 1999).

Category	Balance Sheet	Income Statement
Trading (debt and equity securities)	Investments shown at fair value. Current assets.	Interest and dividends are recognized as revenue. Unrealized holding gains and losses are included in net income.
Available-for-sale (debt and equity securities)	Investments shown at fair value. Current or long-term assets. Unrealized holding gains and losses are a separate component of stockholders' equity.	Interest and dividends are recognized as revenue. Unrealized holding gains and losses are **not** included in net income but in other comprehensive income.
Held-to-maturity (debt securities)	Investments shown at amortized cost. Current or long-term assets.	Interest is recognized as revenue.
Equity method and/or consolidation (equity securities)	Investments originally are carried at cost, are periodically adjusted by the investor's share of the investee's earnings or losses, and are decreased by all dividends received from the investee. Classified long term.	Revenue is recognized to the extent of the investee's earnings or losses reported subsequent to the date of investment.

Illustration 13-27
Summary of Treatment of Major Debt and Equity Securities

SUMMARY OF LEARNING OBJECTIVES

① Identify the three categories of debt securities and describe the accounting and reporting treatment for each category. (1) *Held-to-maturity debt securities* are carried and reported at amortized cost. (2) *Trading debt securities* are valued for reporting purposes at fair value, with unrealized holding gains or losses included in net income. (3) *Available-for-sale debt securities* are valued for reporting purposes at fair value, with unrealized holding gains or losses reported as other comprehensive income and as a separate component of stockholders' equity.

② Identify the categories of equity securities and describe the accounting and reporting treatment for each category. The degree to which one corporation (investor) acquires an interest in the common stock of another corporation (investee) generally determines the accounting treatment for the investment. Long-term investments by one corporation in the common stock of another can be classified according to the percentage of the voting stock of the investee held by the investor.

③ Explain the equity method of accounting and compare it to the fair value method for equity securities. Under the equity method a substantive economic relationship is acknowledged between the investor and the investee. The investment is originally recorded at cost but is subsequently adjusted each period for changes in the net assets of the investee. That is, the investment's carrying amount is periodically increased (decreased) by the investor's proportionate share of the earnings (losses) of the investee, and is decreased by all dividends received by the investor from the investee. Under the fair value method the equity investment is reported by the investor at fair value each reporting period irrespective of the investee's earnings or dividends paid to the

KEY TERMS

amortized cost, *636*
available-for-sale securities, *637*
consolidated financial statements, *649*
controlling interest, *649*
debt securities, *635*
equity method, *647*
equity securities, *642*
exchange for noncash consideration, *643*
fair value, *636*
fair value method, *644*
gains trading, *658*
held-to-maturity securities, *636*
holding gain or loss, *641*
impairment, *655*
investee, *642*
investor, *642*
parent, *649*
reclassification adjustment, *652*
Securities Fair Value Adjustment account, *638*
security, *634* (*n*)
significant influence, *647*
subsidiary, *649*
trading securities, *641*

investor. The equity method is applied to investment holdings between 20% and 50% of ownership. The fair value method is applied to holdings below 20%.

④ Describe the disclosure requirements for investments in debt and equity securities. Trading securities should be reported at aggregate fair value as current assets. Individual held-to-maturity and available-for-sale securities are classified as current or non-current depending upon the circumstances. For available-for-sale and held-to-maturity securities, a company should describe: aggregate fair value, gross unrealized holding gains, gross unrealized losses, amortized cost basis by type (debt and equity), and information about the contractual maturity of debt securities. A reclassification adjustment is necessary when realized gains or losses are reported as part of net income but also are shown as part of other comprehensive income in the current or in previous periods. Unrealized holding gains or losses related to available-for-sale securities should be reported in other comprehensive income and the aggregate balance as accumulated comprehensive income on the balance sheet.

⑤ Discuss the accounting for impairments of debt and equity investments. Impairments of debt and equity securities are losses in value that are determined to be other than temporary, are based on a fair value test, and are charged to income.

⑥ Describe the accounting for transfer of investment securities between categories. Transfers of securities between categories of investments are accounted for at fair value, with unrealized holding gains or losses treated in accordance with the nature of the transfer.

Discussion of Special Issues Related to Investments

REVIEW EXERCISE

Powerpuff Corp. carries an account in its general ledger called Investments, which contained the following debits for investment purchases and no credits.

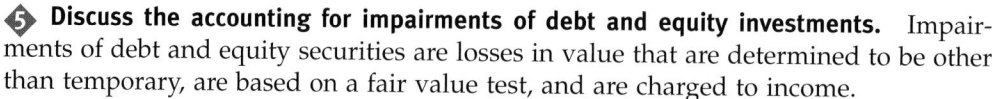
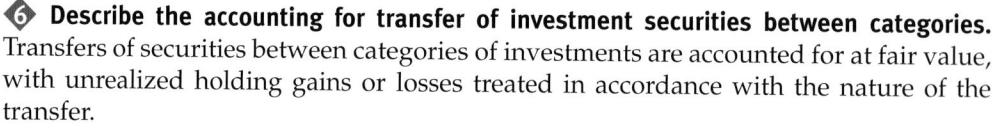

Feb. 1, 2003	Blossom Company common stock, $100 par 200 shares	$ 37,400
April 1	U.S. Government bonds, 11%, due April 1, 2013, interest payable April 1 and October 1, 100 bonds of $1,000 per each	100,000
July 1	Buttercup Company 12% bonds, par $50,000, dated March 1, 2003 purchased at par plus accrued interest, interest payable annually on March 1, due March 1, 2023	52,000

Instructions

(a) Prepare entries necessary to classify the amounts into proper accounts, assuming that all the securities are classified as available-for-sale.

(b) Prepare the entry to record the accrued interest on December 31, 2003.

(c) The fair values of the securities on December 31, 2003, were:

Blossom Company common stock	$ 33,800 (1% interest)
U.S. government bonds	124,700
Buttercup Company bonds	58,600

What entry or entries, if any, would you recommend be made?

(d) The U.S. government bonds were sold on July 1, 2004, for $119,200 plus accrued interest. Give the proper entry.

(e) Now assume Powerpuff's investment in Blossom Company represents 30% of Blossom's shares. Prepare the 2003 entries for the investment in Blossom stock. In 2003, Blossom declared and paid dividends of $9,000 (on September 30) and reported net income of $30,000.

SOLUTION TO REVIEW EXERCISE

(a)

Available-for-Sale Securities	187,400*	
Interest Revenue ($50,000 × .12 × 4/12)	2,000	
Investments		189,400
*($37,400 + $100,000 + $50,000)		

(b)

December 31, 2003

Interest Receivable	7,750	
Interest Revenue		7,750**

**[Accrued interest: $50,000 × .12 × 10/12 = $5,000

Accrued interest: $100,000 × .11 × 3/12 = 2,750

$7,750

(c)

Available-for-Sale Portfolio
December 31, 2003

Securities	Cost	Fair Value	Unrealized Gain (Loss)
Blossom Company stock	$ 37,400	$ 33,800	$ (3,600)
U.S. government bonds	100,000	124,700	24,700
Buttercup Company bonds	50,000	58,600	8,600
Total	$187,400	$217,100	29,700
Previous securities fair value adjustment balance			0
Securities fair value adjustment—Dr.			$29,700

Securities Fair Value Adjustment (Available-for-Sale)	29,700	
Unrealized Holding Gain or Loss—Equity		29,700

(d)

July 1, 2004

Cash ($119,200 + $2,750)	121,950	
Available-for-Sale Securities		100,000
Interest Revenue		2,750
($100,000 × .11 × 3/12)		
Gain on Sale of Securities		19,200

(e)

Investment in Blossom stock	37,400	
Investments		37,400

September 30, 2003

Cash	2,700	
Investment in Blossom stock		2,700
(30% × $9,000)		

December 31, 2003

Investment in Blossom stock	9,000	
Revenue from Investment		9,000
(30% × $30,000)		

DISCOUNT AND PREMIUM AMORTIZATION ON BOND INVESTMENTS

OBJECTIVE 7
After studying Appendix 13A, you should be able to: Understand the procedures for discount and premium amortization on bond investments.

In this appendix, we illustrate the procedures for amortizing discount and premium on bond investments. As indicated in Chapter 11, the effective-interest method is required to amortize premium or discount unless some other method—such as the straight-line method—yields a similar result. The effective-interest method is applied to bond investments in a fashion similar to that described for bonds payable. The effective-interest rate or yield is computed at the time of investment and is applied to its beginning carrying amount (book value) for each interest period to compute interest revenue. The investment carrying amount is increased by the amortized discount or decreased by the amortized premium in each period.

DISCOUNT AMORTIZATION

To illustrate discount amortization for held-to-maturity debt securities, assume that Robinson Company purchased $100,000 of 8% bonds of Evermaster Corporation on January 1, 2003, paying $92,278. The bonds mature January 1, 2008; interest is payable each July 1 and January 1. The discount of $7,722 ($100,000 − $92,278) provided an effective interest yield of 10%. The entry to record the investment is:

January 1, 2003

Held-to-Maturity Securities	92,278	
Cash		92,278

A Held-to-Maturity Securities account is used to indicate the type of debt security purchased. Illustration 13A-1 on page 663 shows the effect of the discount amortization on the interest revenue recorded each period for the investment in Evermaster Corporation bonds.

The journal entry to record the receipt of the first semiannual interest payment on July 1, 2003 (using the data in Illustration 13A-1), is:

July 1, 2003

Cash	4,000	
Held-to-Maturity Securities	614	
Interest Revenue		4,614

Calculator Solution for Bond Price

	Inputs	Answer
N	10	
I	5	
PV	?	−92,278
PMT	4,000	
FV	100,000	

			Bond	Carrying
	Cash	Interest	Discount	Amount
Date	Received	Revenue	Amortization	of Bonds
1/1/03				$ 92,278
7/1/03	$ 4,000ᵃ	$ 4,614ᵇ	$ 614ᶜ	92,892ᵈ
1/1/04	4,000	4,645	645	93,537
7/1/04	4,000	4,677	677	94,214
1/1/05	4,000	4,711	711	94,925
7/1/05	4,000	4,746	746	95,671
1/1/06	4,000	4,783	783	96,454
7/1/06	4,000	4,823	823	97,277
1/1/07	4,000	4,864	864	98,141
7/1/07	4,000	4,907	907	99,048
1/1/08	4,000	4,952	952	100,000
	$40,000	$47,722	$7,722	

8% Bonds Purchased to Yield 10%

ᵃ$4,000 = $100,000 × .08 × 6/12
ᵇ$4,614 = $92,278 × .10 × 6/12
ᶜ$614 = $4,614 − $4,000
ᵈ$92,892 = $92,278 + $614

Because Robinson Company is on a calendar-year basis, it accrues interest and amortizes the discount at December 31, 2003, as follows.

December 31, 2003

Interest Receivable	4,000
Held-to-Maturity Securities	645
Interest Revenue	4,645

Again, the interest and amortization amounts are provided in Illustration 13A-1.

The sale of a held-to-maturity debt security close enough to its maturity date that a change in the market interest rates would not significantly affect the security's fair value may be considered a sale at maturity. If Robinson Company sells its investment in Evermaster bonds on November 1, 2007, for example, at 99¾ plus accrued interest, the following computations and entries would be made. The discount amortization from July 1, 2007, to November 1, 2007, is $635 (4/6 × $952). The entry to record this discount amortization is as follows.

November 1, 2007

Held-to-Maturity Securities	635
Interest Revenue	635

The computation of the realized gain on the sale is shown in Illustration 13A-2.

Selling price of bonds (exclusive of accrued interest)		$99,750
Less: Book value of bonds on November 1, 2007:		
Amortized cost, July 1, 2007	$99,048	
Add: Discount amortized for the period July 1, 2007,		
to November 1, 2007	635	
		99,683
Gain on sale of bonds		$ 67

The entry to record the sale of the bonds is:

November 1, 2007

Cash	102,417	
Interest Revenue (4/6 × $4,000)		2,667
Held-to-Maturity Securities		99,683
Gain on Sale of Securities		67

The credit to Interest Revenue represents accrued interest for 4 months, for which the purchaser pays cash. The debit to Cash represents the selling price of the bonds, $99,750, plus accrued interest of $2,667. The credit to the Held-to-Maturity Securities account represents the book value of the bonds on the date of sale. The credit to Gain on Sale of Securities represents the excess of the selling price over the book value of the bonds.

PREMIUM AMORTIZATION

To illustrate premium amortization, assume that Graff Corporation purchases $100,000, 10%, 5-year bonds on January 1, 2003, with interest payable on July 1 and January 1. The bonds sell for $108,111, which results in a bond premium of $8,111 and an effective-interest rate of 8%. Graff classifies these securities as available-for-sale.

The entry to record the purchase of the bonds is as follows.

January 1, 2003

Available-for-Sale Securities	108,111	
Cash		108,111

Illustration 13A-3 discloses the effect of the premium amortization on the interest revenue recorded each period using the effective-interest method.

Illustration 13A-3
Schedule of Interest
Revenue and Bond
Premium Amortization—
Effective Interest Method

Calculator Solution for Bond Price

	Inputs	Answer
N	10	
I	4	
PV	?	−108,111
PMT	5,000	
FV	100,000	

10% BONDS PURCHASED TO YIELD 8%				
Date	Cash Received	Interest Revenue	Bond Premium Amortization	Carrying Amount of Bonds
1/1/03				$108,111
7/1/03	$ 5,000^a	$ 4,324^b	$ 676^c	107,435^d
1/1/04	5,000	4,297	703	106,732
7/1/04	5,000	4,269	731	106,001
1/1/05	5,000	4,240	760	105,241
7/1/05	5,000	4,210	790	104,451
1/1/06	5,000	4,178	822	103,629
7/1/06	5,000	4,145	855	102,774
1/1/07	5,000	4,111	889	101,885
7/1/07	5,000	4,075	925	100,960
1/1/08	5,000	4,040	960	100,000
	$50,000	$41,889	$8,111	

^{a}$5,000 = $100,000 × .10 × 6/12
^{b}$4,324 = $108,111 × .08 × 6/12
^{c}$676 = $5,000 − $4,324
^{d}$107,435 = $108,111 − $676

The entry to record interest revenue on July 1, 2003, would be as follows.

July 1, 2003

Cash	5,000	
Available-for-Sale Securities		676
Interest Revenue		4,324

At December 31, 2003, Graff would make the following entry to recognize interest revenue.

December 31, 2003

Interest Receivable	5,000	
Available-for-Sale Securities		703
Interest Revenue		4,297

As a result, Graff would report interest revenue for 2003 of $8,621 ($4,324 + $4,297).

UNDERLYING CONCEPTS

The use of some simpler method which yields results similar to the effective-interest method is an application of the materiality concept.

SUMMARY OF LEARNING OBJECTIVE FOR APPENDIX 13A

KEY TERM

effective-interest method, 662

⑦ Understand the procedures for discount and premium amortization on bond investments. Similar to bonds payable, discount or premium on bond investments should be amortized using the effective-interest method. The effective interest rate or yield is applied to the beginning carrying value of the investment for each interest period in order to compute interest revenue.

Note: All **asterisked** Questions, Exercises, Problems, and Conceptual Cases relate to material contained in the appendix to the chapter.

QUESTIONS

1 Distinguish between a debt security and an equity security.

2 What purpose does the variety in bond features (types and characteristics) serve?

3 What is the cost of a long-term investment in bonds?

4 Identify and explain the three types of classifications for investments in debt securities.

5 When should a debt security be classified as held-to-maturity?

6 Explain how trading securities are accounted for and reported.

7 At what amount should trading, available-for-sale, and held-to-maturity securities be reported on the balance sheet?

8 Indicate how unrealized holding gains and losses should be reported for investment securities classified as trading, available-for-sale, and held-to-maturity.

9 (a) Assuming no Securities Fair Value Adjustment (Available-for-Sale) account balance at the beginning of the year, prepare the adjusting entry at the end of the year if Laura Company has an unrealized holding loss of $70,000 on its available-for-sale securities. (b) Assume the same information as part (a), except that Laura Company has a debit balance in its Securities Fair Value Adjustment (Available-for-Sale) account of $10,000 at the beginning of the year. Prepare the adjusting entry at year-end.

10 How is the premium or discount handled relative to a trading debt security?

11 On what basis should stock acquired or exchanged for noncash consideration be recorded?

12 Identify and explain the different types of classifications for investment in equity securities.

13 Why are held-to-maturity investments applicable only to debt securities?

14 Emily Company sold 10,000 shares of Dickinson Co. common stock for $27.50 per share, incurring $1,770 in brokerage commissions. These securities were classified as trading and originally cost $250,000. Prepare the entry to record the sale of these securities.

15 Distinguish between the accounting treatment for available-for-sale equity securities and trading equity securities.

16 What constitutes "significant influence" when an investor's financial interest is below the 50% level?

17 Explain how the investment account is affected by investee activities under the equity method.

18 When the equity method is applied, what disclosures should be made in the investor's financial statements?

19 Molly Pitcher Co. uses the equity method to account for investments in common stock. What accounting should be made for dividends received in excess of Pitcher's share of investee's earnings subsequent to the date of investment?

20 Elizabeth Corp. has an investment carrying value (equity method) on its books of $170,000 representing a 40% interest in Dole Company, which suffered a $620,000 loss this year. How should Elizabeth Corp. handle its proportionate share of Dole's loss?

21 Where on the asset side of the balance sheet are trading securities, available-for-sale securities, and held-to-maturity securities reported? Explain.

22 Explain why reclassification adjustments are necessary.

23 Briefly discuss how a transfer of securities from the available-for-sale category to the trading category affects stockholders' equity and income.

24 When is a debt security considered impaired? Explain how to account for the impairment of an available-for-sale debt security.

*25 On July 1, 2004, Ingalls Company purchased $2,000,000 of Wilder Company's 8% bonds, due on July 1, 2011. The bonds, which pay interest semiannually on January 1 and July 1, were purchased for $1,750,000 to yield 10%. Determine the amount of interest revenue Ingalls should report on its income statement for year ended December 31, 2004.

*26 If the bonds in question 25 are classified as available-for-sale and they have a fair value at December 31, 2004, of $1,802,000, prepare the journal entry (if any) at December 31, 2004, to record this transaction.

Brief Exercises

BE13-1 Mask Corporation purchased, as a held-to-maturity investment, $40,000 of the 8%, 5-year bonds of Phantasy Star, Inc. at par. The bonds pay interest semiannually. Prepare Mask's journal entries for (a) the purchase of the investment, and (b) the receipt of semiannual interest.

BE13-2 Use the information from BE13-1, but assume the bonds are purchased as an available-for-sale security. Prepare Mask's journal entries for (a) the purchase of the investment, (b) the receipt of semiannual interest, and (c) the year-end fair value adjustment. Assume the first interest payment is received on December 31, when the fair value of the bonds is $42,900.

BE13-3 Pete Sampras Corporation purchased for $22,500 as a trading investment bonds with a face value of $20,000. At December 31, Sampras received annual interest of $2,000, and the fair value of the bonds was $20,900. Prepare Sampras' journal entries for (a) the purchase of the investment, (b) the interest received, and (c) the fair value adjustment.

BE13-4 Pacman Corporation purchased 300 shares of Galaga Inc. common stock as an available-for-sale investment for $9,900. During the year, Galaga paid a cash dividend of $3.25 per share. At year-end, Galaga stock was selling for $34.50 per share. Prepare Pacman's journal entries to record (a) the purchase of the investment, (b) the dividends received, and (c) the fair value adjustment.

BE13-5 Use the information from BE13-4, but assume the stock was purchased as a trading security. Prepare Pacman's journal entries to record (a) the purchase of the investment, (b) the dividends received, and (c) the fair value adjustment.

BE13-6 Penn Corporation purchased for $300,000 a 25% interest in Teller, Inc. This investment enables Penn to exert significant influence over Teller. During the year Teller earned net income of $180,000 and paid dividends of $60,000. Prepare Penn's journal entries related to this investment.

BE13-7 Swartentruber Company has a stock portfolio valued at $4,000. Its cost was $3,500. If the Securities Fair Value Adjustment (Available-for-Sale) has a debit balance of $200, prepare the journal entry at year-end.

BE13-8 The following information relates to Cargill Co. for 2003: net income $800,000; unrealized holding gain of $20,000 related to available-for-sale securities during the year; accumulated other comprehensive income of $60,000 on January 1, 2003. Determine (a) other comprehensive income for 2003, (b) comprehensive income for 2003, and (c) accumulated other comprehensive income at December 31, 2003.

*BE13-9   Moonwalker Company purchased, as a held-to-maturity investment, $50,000 of the 9%, 5-year bonds of Prime Time Corporation for $46,304, which provides an 11% return. Prepare Moonwalker's journal entries for (a) the purchase of the investment, and (b) the receipt of annual interest and discount amortization. Assume effective interest amortization is used.

*BE13-10   Use the information from BE13-9, but assume the bonds are purchased as an available-for-sale security. Prepare Moonwalker's journal entries for (a) the purchase of the investment, (b) the receipt of annual interest and discount amortization, and (c) the year-end fair value adjustment. The bonds have a year-end fair value of $47,200.

*BE13-11   Mask Corporation purchased, as a held-to-maturity investment, $40,000 of the 8%, 5-year bonds of Phantasy Star, Inc. for $43,412, which provides a 6% return. The bonds pay interest semiannually. Prepare Mask's journal entries for (a) the purchase of the investment, and (b) the receipt of semiannual interest and premium amortization. Assume effective-interest amortization is used.

EXERCISES

E13-1   (Investment Classifications)   For the following investments identify whether they are:

1.   Trading Securities
2.   Available-for-Sale Securities
3.   Held-to-Maturity Securities

Each case is independent of the other.

(a)   A bond that will mature in 4 years was bought 1 month ago when the price dropped. As soon as the value increases, which is expected next month, it will be sold.
(b)   10% of the outstanding stock of Farm-Co was purchased. The company is planning on eventually getting a total of 30% of its outstanding stock.
(c)   10-year bonds were purchased this year. The bonds mature at the first of next year.
(d)   Bonds that will mature in 5 years are purchased. The company would like to hold them until they mature, but money has been tight recently and they may need to be sold.
(e)   Preferred stock was purchased for its constant dividend. The company is planning to hold the preferred stock for a long time.
(f)   A bond that matures in 10 years was purchased. The company is investing money set aside for an expansion project planned 10 years from now.

E13-2   (Entries for Held-to-Maturity Securities)   On January 1, 2003, Dagwood Company purchased at par 12% bonds, having a maturity value of $300,000. They are dated January 1, 2003, and mature January 1, 2008, with interest receivable December 31 of each year. The bonds are classified in the held-to-maturity category.

Instructions
(a)   Prepare the journal entry at the date of the bond purchase.
(b)   Prepare the journal entry to record the interest received for 2003.
(c)   Prepare the journal entry to record the interest received for 2004.

E13-3   (Entries for Available-for-Sale and Trading Securities)   The following information is available for Barkley Company at December 31, 2003, regarding its investments.

Securities	Cost	Fair Value
3,000 shares of Myers Corporation common stock	$40,000	$48,000
1,000 shares of Cole Incorporated preferred stock	25,000	22,000
	$65,000	$70,000

Instructions

(a) Prepare the adjusting entry (if any) for 2003, assuming the securities are classified as trading.

(b) Prepare the adjusting entry (if any) for 2003, assuming the securities are classified as available-for-sale.

(c) Discuss how the amounts reported in the financial statements are affected by the entries in (a) and (b).

E13-4 **(Trading Securities Entries)** On December 21, 2003, Tiger Company provided you with the following information regarding its trading securities.

December 31, 2003

Investments (Trading)	Cost	Fair Value	Unrealized Gain (Loss)
Clemson Corp. stock	$20,000	$19,000	$(1,000)
Colorado Co. stock	10,000	9,000	(1,000)
Buffaloes Co. stock	20,000	20,600	600
Total of portfolio	$50,000	$48,600	(1,400)
Previous securities fair value adjustment balance			–0–
Securities fair value adjustment—Cr.			$(1,400)

During 2004, Colorado Company stock was sold for $9,400. The fair value of the stock on December 31, 2004, was: Clemson Corp. stock—$19,100; Buffaloes Co. stock—$20,500.

Instructions

(a) Prepare the adjusting journal entry needed on December 31, 2003.

(b) Prepare the journal entry to record the sale of the Colorado Company stock during 2004.

(c) Prepare the adjusting journal entry needed on December 31, 2004.

E13-5 **(Available-for-Sale Securities Entries and Reporting)** Rams Corporation purchases equity securities costing $73,000 and classifies them as available-for-sale securities. At December 31, the fair value of the portfolio is $65,000.

Instructions

Prepare the adjusting entry to report the securities properly. Indicate the statement presentation of the accounts in your entry.

E13-6 **(Available-for-Sale Securities Entries and Financial Statement Presentation)** At December 31, 2003, the available-for-sale equity portfolio for Steffi Graf, Inc. is as follows.

Security	Cost	Fair Value	Unrealized Gain (Loss)
A	$17,500	$15,000	($2,500)
B	12,500	14,000	1,500
C	23,000	25,500	2,500
Total	$53,000	$54,500	1,500
Previous securities fair value adjustment balance—Dr.			400
Securities fair value adjustment—Dr.			$1,100

On January 20, 2004, Steffi Graf, Inc. sold security A for $15,100. The sale proceeds are net of brokerage fees.

Instructions

(a) Prepare the adjusting entry at December 31, 2003, to report the portfolio at fair value.

(b) Show the balance sheet presentation of the investment related accounts at December 31, 2002. (Ignore notes presentation.)

(c) Prepare the journal entry for the 2004 sale of security A.

E13-7 (Comprehensive Income Disclosure) Assume the same information as E13-6 and that Steffi Graf Inc. reports net income in 2003 of $120,000 and in 2004 of $140,000. Total unrealized holding gains (including any realized holding gain or loss) arising during 2004 totals $40,000.

Instructions
(a) Prepare a statement of comprehensive income for 2003 starting with net income.
(b) Prepare a statement of comprehensive income for 2004 starting with net income.

E13-8 (Equity Securities Entries) Arantxa Corporation made the following cash purchases of securities during 2003, which is the first year in which Arantxa invested in securities.

1. On January 15, purchased 10,000 shares of Sanchez Company's common stock at $33.50 per share plus commission $1,980.
2. On April 1, purchased 5,000 shares of Vicario Co.'s common stock at $52.00 per share plus commission $3,370.
3. On September 10, purchased 7,000 shares of WTA Co.'s preferred stock at $26.50 per share plus commission $4,910.

On May 20, 2003, Arantxa sold 4,000 shares of Sanchez Company's common stock at a market price of $35 per share less brokerage commissions, taxes, and fees of $3,850. The year-end fair values per share were: Sanchez $30, Vicario $55, and WTA $28. In addition, the chief accountant of Arantxa told you that Arantxa Corporation holds these securities with the intention of selling them in order to earn profits from appreciation in prices.

Instructions
(a) Prepare the journal entries to record the above three security purchases.
(b) Prepare the journal entry for the security sale on May 20.
(c) Compute the unrealized gains or losses and prepare the adjusting entries for Arantxa on December 31, 2003.

E13-9 (Journal Entries for Fair Value and Equity Methods) Presented below are two independent situations.

Situation 1
Conchita Cosmetics acquired 10% of the 200,000 shares of common stock of Martinez Fashion at a total cost of $13 per share on March 18, 2003. On June 30, Martinez declared and paid a $75,000 cash dividend. On December 31, Martinez reported net income of $122,000 for the year. At December 31, the market price of Martinez Fashion was $15 per share. The securities are classified as available-for-sale.

Situation 2
Monica, Inc. obtained significant influence over Seles Corporation by buying 30% of Seles's 30,000 outstanding shares of common stock at a total cost of $9 per share on January 1, 2003. On June 15, Seles declared and paid a cash dividend of $36,000. On December 31, Seles reported a net income of $85,000 for the year.

Instructions
Prepare all necessary journal entries in 2003 for both situations.

E13-10 (Equity Method) Parent Co. invested $1,000,000 in Sub Co. for 25% of its outstanding stock. At the time of the purchase, Sub Co. had a book value of $3,200,000. Sub Co. pays out 40% of net income in dividends each year.

Instructions
Use the information in the following T-account for the investment in Sub to answer the following questions.

Investment in Sub Co.	
1,000,000	
110,000	
	44,000

(a) How much was Parent Co.'s share of Sub Co.'s net income for the year?
(b) How much was Parent Co.'s share of Sub Co.'s dividends for the year?
(c) What was Sub Co.'s total net income for the year?
(d) What was Sub Co.'s total dividends for the year?

E13-11 (Equity Investment—Trading) Oregon Co. had purchased 200 shares of Washington Co. for $40 each this year and classified the investment as a trading security. Oregon Co. sold 100 shares of the stock for $45 each. At year end the price per share of Washington Co. had dropped to $35.

Instructions
Prepare the journal entries for these transactions.

E13-12 (Securities Entries—Buy and Sell) Buddy Lazier Company has the following securities in its trading portfolio of securities on December 31, 2003.

Investments (Trading)	Cost	Fair Value
1,500 shares of Davy Jones, Inc., common	$ 73,500	$ 69,000
5,000 shares of Richie Hearn Corp., common	180,000	175,000
400 shares of Alessandro Zampedri, Inc., preferred	60,000	61,600
	$313,500	$305,600

All of the securities were purchased in 2003.
In 2004, Lazier completed the following securities transactions.

March 1	Sold the 1,500 shares of Davy Jones, Inc., Common, @ $45 less fees of $1,200.
April 1	Bought 700 shares of Roberto Guerrero Corp., Common, @ $75 plus fees of $1,300.

Lazier Company's portfolio of trading securities appeared as follows on December 31, 2004.

Investments (Trading)	Cost	Fair Value
5,000 shares of Richie Hearn Corp., common	$180,000	$175,000
700 shares of Guerrero Corp., common	53,800	50,400
400 shares of Zampedri preferred	60,000	58,000
	$293,800	$283,400

Instructions
Prepare the general journal entries for Lazier Company for:

(a) The 2003 adjusting entry.
(b) The sale of the Davy Jones stock.
(c) The purchase of the Roberto Guerrero stock.
(d) The 2004 adjusting entry for the trading portfolio.

E13-13 (Fair Value and Equity Method Compared) Jaycie Phelps Inc. acquired 20% of the outstanding common stock of Theresa Kulikowski Inc. on December 31, 2002. The purchase price was $1,200,000 for 50,000 shares. Kulikowski Inc. declared and paid an $0.85 per share cash dividend on June 30 and on December 31, 2003. Kulikowski reported net income of $730,000 for 2003. The fair value of Kulikowski's stock was $27 per share at December 31, 2003.

Instructions
(a) Prepare the journal entries for Jaycie Phelps Inc. for 2003, assuming that Phelps cannot exercise significant influence over Kulikowski. The securities should be classified as available-for-sale.
(b) Prepare the journal entries for Jaycie Phelps Inc. for 2003, assuming that Phelps can exercise significant influence over Kulikowski.
(c) At what amount is the investment in securities reported on the balance sheet under each of these methods at December 31, 2003? What is the total net income reported in 2003 under each of these methods?

E13-14 (Equity Method) On January 1, 2003, Warner Corporation purchased 30% of the common shares of Martz Company for $180,000. During the year, Martz earned net income of $80,000 and paid dividends of $20,000.

Instructions
Prepare the entries for Warner to record the purchase and any additional entries related to this investment in Martz Company in 2003.

E13-15 (Impairment of Debt Securities) Dominique Moceanu Corporation has municipal bonds classified as available-for-sale at December 31, 2003. These bonds have a par value of $800,000, an amortized cost of $800,000, and a fair value of $720,000. The unrealized loss of $80,000 previously recognized as other comprehensive income and as a separate component of stockholders' equity is now determined to be other than temporary. That is, the company believes that impairment accounting is now appropriate for these bonds.

Instructions
(a) Prepare the journal entry to recognize the impairment.
(b) What is the new cost basis of the municipal bonds? Given that the maturity value of the bonds is $800,000, should Moceanu Corporation accrete the difference between the carrying amount and the maturity value over the life of the bonds?
(c) At December 31, 2004, the fair value of the municipal bonds is $760,000. Prepare the entry (if any) to record this information.

*E13-16 (Entries for Held-to-Maturity Securities) On January 1, 2003, Hi and Lois Company purchased 12% bonds, having a maturity value of $300,000, for $322,744.44. The bonds provide the bondholders with a 10% yield. They are dated January 1, 2003, and mature January 1, 2008, with interest receivable December 31 of each year. Hi and Lois Company uses the effective-interest method to allocate unamortized discount or premium. The bonds are classified in the held-to-maturity category.

Instructions
(a) Prepare the journal entry at the date of the bond purchase.
(b) Prepare a bond amortization schedule.
(c) Prepare the journal entry to record the interest received and the amortization for 2003.
(d) Prepare the journal entry to record the interest received and the amortization for 2004.

*E13-17 (Entries for Available-for-Sale Securities) Assume the same information as in E13-16 except that the securities are classified as available-for-sale. The fair value of the bonds at December 31 of each year-end is as follows.

2003	$320,500	2006	$310,000
2004	$309,000	2007	$300,000
2005	$308,000		

Instructions
(a) Prepare the journal entry at the date of the bond purchase.
(b) Prepare the journal entries to record the interest received and recognition of fair value for 2003.
(c) Prepare the journal entry to record the recognition of fair value for 2004.

*E13-18 (Effective-Interest versus Straight-Line Bond Amortization) On January 1, 2003, Phantom Company acquires $200,000 of Spiderman Products, Inc., 9% bonds at a price of $185,589. The interest is payable each December 31, and the bonds mature December 31, 2005. The investment will provide Phantom Company a 12% yield. The bonds are classified as held-to-maturity.

Instructions
(a) Prepare a 3-year schedule of interest revenue and bond discount amortization, applying the straight-line method.
(b) Prepare a 3-year schedule of interest revenue and bond discount amortization, applying the effective-interest method.
(c) Prepare the journal entry for the interest receipt of December 31, 2004, and the discount amortization under the straight-line method.

(d) Prepare the journal entry for the interest receipt of December 31, 2004, and the discount amortization under the effective-interest method.

PROBLEMS

P13-1 (Debt Securities Available-for-Sale) On January 1, 2004, Bon Jovi Company purchased $200,000, 8% bonds of Mercury Co. at par. Interest is payable semiannually on July 1 and January 1. The bonds mature on January 1, 2009. On January 1, 2006, Bon Jovi Company sold the bonds for $185,363 after receiving interest to meet its liquidity needs.

Instructions
(a) Prepare the journal entry to record the purchase of bonds on January 1. Assume that the bonds are classified as available-for-sale.
(b) Prepare the journal entries to record the semiannual interest on July 1, 2004, and December 31, 2004.
(c) If the fair value of Mercury bonds is $186,363 on December 31, 2005, prepare the necessary adjusting entry. (Assume the securities fair value adjustment balance on January 1, 2005, is a debit of $3,375.)
(d) Prepare the journal entry to record the sale of the bonds on January 1, 2006.

P13-2 (Available-for-Sale Debt Securities) Presented below is information taken from a bond investment amortization schedule with related fair values provided. These bonds are classified as available-for-sale.

	12/31/03	12/31/04	12/31/05
Amortized cost	$491,150	$519,442	$550,000
Fair value	$499,000	$506,000	$550,000

Instructions
(a) Indicate whether the bonds were purchased at a discount or at a premium.
(b) Prepare the adjusting entry to record the bonds at fair value at December 31, 2003. The Securities Fair Value Adjustment account has a debit balance of $1,000 prior to adjustment.
(c) Prepare the adjusting entry to record the bonds at fair value at December 31, 2004.

P13-3 (Equity Securities Entries and Disclosures) Incognito Company has the following securities in its investment portfolio on December 31, 2003 (all securities were purchased in 2003): (1) 3,000 shares of Bush Co. common stock which cost $58,500, (2) 10,000 shares of David Sanborn Ltd. common stock which cost $580,000, and (3) 6,000 shares of Abba Company preferred stock which cost $255,000. The Securities Fair Value Adjustment account shows a credit of $10,100 at the end of 2003.

In 2004, Incognito completed the following securities transactions.

1. On January 15, sold 3,000 shares of Bush's common stock at $23 per share less fees of $2,150.
2. On April 17, purchased 1,000 shares of Tractors' common stock at $31.50 per share plus fees of $1,980.

On December 31, 2004, the market values per share of these securities were: Bush $20, Sanborn $62, Abba $40, and Tractors $29. In addition, the accounting supervisor of Incognito told you that, even though all these securities have readily determinable fair values, Incognito will not actively trade these securities because the top management intends to hold them for more than one year.

Instructions
(a) Prepare the entry for the security sale on January 15, 2004.
(b) Prepare the journal entry to record the security purchase on April 17, 2004.
(c) Compute the unrealized gains or losses and prepare the adjusting entry for Incognito on December 31, 2004.
(d) How should the unrealized gains or losses be reported on Incognito's balance sheet?

P13-4 (Trading and Available-for-Sale Securities Entries) Gypsy Kings Company has the following portfolio of investment securities at September 30, 2003, its last reporting date.

Trading Securities	Cost	Fair Value
Dan Fogelberg, Inc. common (5,000 shares)	$225,000	$200,000
Petra, Inc. preferred (3,500 shares)	133,000	140,000
Tim Weisberg Corp. common (1,000 shares)	180,000	179,000

On October 10, 2003, the Fogelberg shares were sold at a price of $54 per share. In addition, 3,000 shares of Los Tigres common stock were acquired at $59.50 per share on November 2, 2003. The December 31, 2003, fair values were: Petra $96,000, Los Tigres $132,000, and the Weisberg common $193,000. All the securities are classified as trading.

Instructions

(a) Prepare the journal entries to record the sale, purchase, and adjusting entries related to the trading securities in the last quarter of 2003.

(b) How would the entries in part (a) change if the securities were classified as available-for-sale?

P13-5 (Available-for-Sale and Held-to-Maturity Debt Securities Entries) The following information relates to the debt securities investments of the Yellowjackets Company.

1. On February 1, the company purchased 12% bonds of Vanessa Williams Co. having a par value of $500,000 at 100 plus accrued interest. Interest is payable April 1 and October 1.
2. On April 1, semiannual interest is received.
3. On July 1, 9% bonds of Chieftains, Inc. were purchased. These bonds with a par value of $200,000 were purchased at 100 plus accrued interest. Interest dates are June 1 and December 1.
4. On September 1, bonds with a par value of $100,000, purchased on February 1, are sold at 99 plus accrued interest.
5. On October 1, semiannual interest is received.
6. On December 1, semiannual interest is received.
7. On December 31, the fair value of the bonds purchased February 1 and July 1 are 95 and 93, respectively.

Instructions

(a) Prepare any journal entries you consider necessary, including year-end entries (December 31), assuming these are available-for-sale securities.

(b) If Yellowjackets classified these as held-to-maturity securities, explain how the journal entries would differ from those in part (a).

P13-6 (Applying Fair Value Method) Pacers Corp. is a medium-sized corporation specializing in quarrying stone for building construction. The company has long dominated the market, at one time achieving a 70% market penetration. During prosperous years, the company's profits, coupled with a conservative dividend policy, resulted in funds available for outside investment. Over the years, Pacers has had a policy of investing idle cash in equity securities. In particular, Pacers has made periodic investments in the company's principal supplier, Ricky Pierce Industries. Although the firm currently owns 12% of the outstanding common stock of Pierce Industries, Pacers does not have significant influence over the operations of Pierce Industries.

Cheryl Miller has recently joined Pacers as assistant controller, and her first assignment is to prepare the 2004 year-end adjusting entries for the accounts that are valued by the "fair value" rule for financial reporting purposes. Miller has gathered the following information about Pacers' pertinent accounts.

1. Pacers has trading securities related to Dale Davis Motors and Rik Smits Electric. During this fiscal year, Pacers purchased 100,000 shares of Davis Motors for $1,400,000; these shares currently have a market value of $1,600,000. Pacers' investment in Smits Electric has not been a profitable; the company acquired 50,000 shares of Smits in April 2004 at $20 per share, a purchase that currently has a value of $620,000.
2. Prior to 2004, Pacers invested $22,500,000 in Ricky Pierce Industries and has not changed its holdings this year. This investment in Ricky Pierce Industries was valued at $21,500,000 on December 31, 2003. Pacers' 12% ownership of Ricky Pierce Industries has a current market value of $22,275,000.

Instructions

(a) Prepare the appropriate adjusting entries for Pacers as of December 31, 2004, to reflect the application of the "fair value" rule for both classes of securities described above.

(b) For both classes of securities presented above, describe how the results of the valuation adjustments made in (a) would be reflected in the body of and/or notes to Pacers' 2004 financial statements.

P13-7 (Financial Statement Presentation of Available-for-Sale Investments) Woolford Company has the following portfolio of available-for-sale securities at December 31, 2003.

| | | Percent | Per Share | |
Security	Quantity	Interest	Cost	Market
Favre, Inc.	2,000 shares	8%	$11	$16
Walsh Corp.	5,000 shares	14%	23	17
Dilfer Company	4,000 shares	2%	31	24

Instructions

(a) What should be reported on Woolford's December 31, 2003, balance sheet relative to these long-term available-for-sale securities?

On December 31, 2004, Woolford's portfolio of available-for-sale securities consisted of the following common stocks.

| | | Percent | Per Share | |
Security	Quantity	Interest	Cost	Market
Walsh Corp.	5,000 shares	14%	$23	$30
Dilfer Company	4,000 shares	2%	31	23
Dilfer Company	2,000 shares	1%	25	23

At the end of year 2004, Woolford Company changed its intent relative to its investment in Favre, Inc. and reclassified the shares to trading securities status when the shares were selling for $9 per share.

(b) What should be reported on the face of Woolford's December 31, 2004, balance sheet relative to available-for-sale securities investments? What should be reported to reflect the transactions above in Woolford's 2004 income statement?

(c) Assuming that comparative financial statements for 2003 and 2004 are presented, draft the footnote necessary for full disclosure of Woolford's transactions and position in equity securities.

P13-8 (Gain on Sale of Securities and Comprehensive Income) On January 1, 2003, Enid Inc. had the following balance sheet.

| ENID INC. |
| **BALANCE SHEET** |
| **AS OF JANUARY 1, 2003** |

Assets		Equity	
Cash	$ 50,000	Common stock	$250,000
Available-for-sale securities	240,000	Accumulated other comprehensive income	40,000
Total	$290,000	Total	$290,000

The accumulated other comprehensive income related to unrealized holding gains on available-for-sale securities. The fair value of Enid Inc.'s available-for-sale securities at December 31, 2003, was $190,000; its cost was $120,000. No securities were purchased during the year. Enid Inc.'s income statement for 2003 was as follows. (Ignore income taxes.)

ENID INC. INCOME STATEMENT FOR THE YEAR ENDED DECEMBER 31, 2003	
Dividend revenue	$15,000
Gain on sale of available-for-sale securities	20,000
Net income	$35,000

Instructions

(Assume all transactions during the year were for cash.)

(a) Prepare the journal entry to record the sale of the available-for-sale securities in 2003.
(b) Prepare a statement of comprehensive income for 2003.
(c) Prepare a balance sheet as of December 31, 2003.

P13-9 **(Equity Investments—Available for Sale)** Big Brother Holdings, Inc. had the following available-for-sale investment portfolio at January 1, 2002.

Earl Company	1,000 shares @ $15 each	$15,000
Josie Company	900 shares @ $20 each	18,000
David Company	500 shares @ $9 each	4,500
Available-for-sale securities @ cost		37,500
Less: Securities fair value adjustment—Available- for-sale		7,500
Available-for-sale securities @ fair value		$30,000

During 2002, the following transactions took place.

1. On March 1, Josie Company paid a $2 per share dividend.
2. On April 30, Big Brother Holdings, Inc. sold 300 shares of David Company for $10 per share.
3. On May 15, Big Brother Holdings, Inc. purchased 50 more shares of Earl Co. stock at $16 per share.
4. At December 31, 2002, the stocks had the following price per share values: Earl $17, Josie $19, and David $8.

During 2003, the following transactions took place.

5. On February 1, Big Brother Holdings, Inc. sold the remaining David shares for $7 per share.
6. On March 1, Josie Company paid a $2 per share dividend.
7. On December 21, Earl Company declared a cash dividend of $3 per share to be paid in the next month.
8. At December 31, 2003, the stocks had the following price per shares values: Earl $19 and Josie $21.

Instructions

(a) Prepare journal entries for each of the above transactions.
(b) Prepare a partial balance sheet showing the Investments account at December 31, 2002 and 2003.

P13-10 **(Available-for-Sale Securities—Statement Presentation)** Maryam Alvarez Corp. invested its excess cash in available-for-sale securities during 2002. As of December 31, 2002, the portfolio of available-for-sale securities consisted of the following common stocks.

Security	Quantity	Cost	Fair Value
Keesha Jones, Inc.	1,000 shares	$ 15,000	$ 21,000
Eola Corp.	2,000 shares	50,000	42,000
Yevette Aircraft	2,000 shares	72,000	60,000
	Totals	$137,000	$123,000

Instructions

(a) What should be reported on Alvarez's December 31, 2002, balance sheet relative to these securities? What should be reported on Alvarez's 2002 income statement?

On December 31, 2003, Alvarez's portfolio of available-for-sale securities consisted of the following common stocks.

Security	Quantity	Cost	Fair Value
Keesha Jones, Inc.	1,000 shares	$ 15,000	$20,000
Keesha Jones, Inc.	2,000 shares	38,000	40,000
King Company	1,000 shares	16,000	12,000
Yevette Aircraft	2,000 shares	72,000	22,000
		Totals $141,000	$94,000

During the year 2003, Alvarez Corp. sold 2,000 shares of Eola Corp. for $38,200 and purchased 2,000 more shares of Keesha Jones, Inc. and 1,000 shares of King Company.

(b) What should be reported on Alvarez's December 31, 2003, balance sheet? What should be reported on Alvarez's 2003 income statement?

On December 31, 2004, Alvarez's portfolio of available-for-sale securities consisted of the following common stocks.

Security	Quantity	Cost	Fair Value
Yevette Aircraft	2,000 shares	$72,000	$82,000
King Company	2,500 shares	8,000	6,000
		Totals $80,000	$88,000

During the year 2004, Alvarez Corp. sold 3,000 shares of Keesha Jones, Inc. for $39,900 and 500 shares of King Company at a loss of $2,700.

(c) What should be reported on the face of Alvarez's December 31, 2004, balance sheet? What should be reported on Alvarez's 2004 income statement?

(d) What would be reported in a statement of comprehensive income at (1) December 31, 2002, and (2) December 31, 2003?

*P13-11 **(Debt Securities)** Presented below is an amortization schedule related to Kathy Baker Company's 5-year, $100,000 bond with a 7% interest rate and a 5% yield, purchased on December 31, 2001, for $108,660.

Date	Cash Received	Interest Revenue	Bond Premium Amortization	Carry Amount of Bonds
12/31/01				$108,660
12/31/02	$7,000	$5,433	$1,567	107,093
12/31/03	7,000	5,354	1,646	105,447
12/31/04	7,000	5,272	1,728	103,719
12/31/05	7,000	5,186	1,814	101,905
12/31/06	7,000	5,095	1,905	100,000

The following schedule presents a comparison of the amortized cost and fair value of the bonds at year-end.

	12/31/02	12/31/03	12/31/04	12/31/05	12/31/06
Amortized cost	$107,093	$105,447	$103,719	$101,905	$100,000
Fair value	$106,500	$107,500	$105,650	$103,000	$100,000

Instructions

(a) Prepare the journal entry to record the purchase of these bonds on December 31, 2001, assuming the bonds are classified as held-to-maturity securities.

(b) Prepare the journal entry(ies) related to the held-to-maturity bonds for 2002.

(c) Prepare the journal entry(ies) related to the held-to-maturity bonds for 2004.

(d) Prepare the journal entry(ies) to record the purchase of these bonds, assuming they are classified as available-for-sale.

(e) Prepare the journal entry(ies) related to the available-for-sale bonds for 2002.

(f) Prepare the journal entry(ies) related to the available-for-sale bonds for 2004.

*P13-12 (Debt Securities Available-for-Sale) On January 1, 2004, Bon Jovi Company purchased $200,000, 8% bonds of Mercury Co. for $184,557. The bonds were purchased to yield 10% interest. Interest is payable semiannually on July 1 and January 1. The bonds mature on January 1, 2009. Bon Jovi Company uses the effective interest method to amortize discount or premium. On January 1, 2006, Bon Jovi Company sold the bonds for $185,363 after receiving interest to meet its liquidity needs.

Instructions

(a) Prepare the journal entry to record the purchase of bonds on January 1. Assume that the bonds are classified as available-for-sale.

(b) Prepare the amortization schedule for the bonds.

(c) Prepare the journal entries to record the semiannual interest on July 1, 2004, and December 31, 2004.

(d) If the fair value of Mercury bonds is $186,363 on December 31, 2005, prepare the necessary adjusting entry. (Assume the securities fair value adjustment balance on January 1, 2005, is a debit of $3,375.)

(e) Prepare the journal entry to record the sale of the bonds on January 1, 2006.

*P13-13 (Entries for Long-Term Investments) Octavio Paz Corp. carries an account in its general ledger called Investments, which contained the following debits for investment purchases, and no credits.

Feb. 1, 2003	Chiang Kai-Shek Company common stock, $100 par, 200 shares	$ 37,400
April 1	U.S. government bonds, 11%, due April 1, 2013, interest payable April 1 and October 1, 100 bonds of $1,000 par each	100,000
July 1	Claude Monet Company 12% bonds, par $50,000, dated March 1, 2003 purchased at 104 plus accrued interest, interest payable annually on March 1, due March 1, 2023	54,000

Instructions

(a) Prepare entries necessary to classify the amounts into proper accounts, assuming that all the securities are classified as available-for-sale.

(b) Prepare the entry to record the accrued interest and the amortization of premium on December 31, 2003, using the straight-line method.

(c) The fair values of the securities on December 31, 2003, were:

Chiang Kai-shek Company common stock	$ 33,800
U.S. government bonds	124,700
Claude Monet Company bonds	58,600

What entry or entries, if any, would you recommend be made?

(d) The U.S. government bonds were sold on July 1, 2004, for $119,200 plus accrued interest. Give the proper entry.

CONCEPTUAL CASES

C13-1 (Issues Raised about Investment Securities) You have just started work for Andre Love Co. as part of the controller's group involved in current financial reporting problems. Jackie Franklin, controller for Love, is interested in your accounting background because the company has experienced a series of financial reporting surprises over the last few years. Recently, the controller has learned from the company's auditors that an FASB *Statement* may apply to its investment in securities. She assumes that you are familiar with this pronouncement and asks how the following situations should be reported in the financial statements.

Situation 1

Trading securities in the current assets section have a fair value of $4,200 lower than cost.

Situation 2

A trading security whose fair value is currently less than cost is transferred to the available-for-sale category.

Situation 3

An available-for-sale security whose fair value is currently less than cost is classified as noncurrent but is to be reclassified as current.

Situation 4

A company's portfolio of available-for-sale securities consists of the common stock of one company. At the end of the prior year the fair value of the security was 50% of original cost, and this reduction in market value was reported as an other than temporary impairment. However, at the end of the current year the fair value of the security had appreciated to twice the original cost.

Situation 5

The company has purchased some convertible debentures that it plans to hold for less than a year. The fair value of the convertible debenture is $7,700 below its cost.

Instructions

What is the effect upon carrying value and earnings for each of the situations above? Assume that these situations are unrelated.

C13-2 (Equity Securities) James Joyce Co. has the following available-for-sale securities outstanding on December 31, 2002 (its first year of operations).

	Cost	Fair Value
Anna Wickham Corp. stock	$20,000	$19,000
D. H. Lawrence Company stock	10,000	8,800
Edith Sitwell Company stock	20,000	20,600
	$50,000	$48,400

During 2003 D. H. Lawrence Company stock was sold for $9,200, the difference between the $9,200 and the "fair value" of $8,800 being recorded as a "Gain on Sale of Securities." The market price of the stock on December 31, 2003, was: Anna Wickham Corp. stock $19,900; Edith Sitwell Company stock $20,500.

Instructions

(a) What justification is there for valuing available-for-sale securities at fair value and reporting the unrealized gain or loss as part of stockholders' equity?

(b) How should James Joyce Company apply this rule on December 31, 2002? Explain.

(c) Did James Joyce Company properly account for the sale of the D. H. Lawrence Company stock? Explain.

(d) Are there any additional entries necessary for James Joyce Company at December 31, 2003, to reflect the facts on the financial statements in accordance with generally accepted accounting principles? Explain.

(AICPA adapted)

C13-3 (Financial Statement Effect of Equity Securities) Presented below are three unrelated situations involving equity securities.

Situation 1

An equity security, whose market value is currently less than cost, is classified as available-for-sale but is to be reclassified as trading.

Situation 2

A noncurrent portfolio with an aggregate market value in excess of cost includes one particular security whose market value has declined to less than one-half of the original cost. The decline in value is considered to be other than temporary.

Situation 3

The portfolio of trading securities has a cost in excess of fair value of $13,500. The available-for-sale portfolio has a fair value in excess of cost of $28,600.

Instructions

What is the effect upon carrying value and earnings for each of the situations above? Complete your response to each situation before proceeding to the next situation.

C13-4 (Equity Securities) The Financial Accounting Standards Board issued its *Statement No. 115* to clarify accounting methods and procedures with respect to certain debt and all equity securities. An important part of the statement concerns the distinction between held-to-maturity, available-for-sale, and trading securities.

Instructions

(a) Why does a company maintain an investment portfolio of held-to-maturity, available-for-sale, and trading securities?

(b) What factors should be considered in determining whether investments in securities should be classified as held-to-maturity, available-for-sale, and trading? How do these factors affect the accounting treatment for unrealized losses?

C13-5 (Investment Accounted for under the Equity Method) On July 1, 2004, Sylvia Warner Company purchased for cash 40% of the outstanding capital stock of Robert Graves Company. Both Sylvia Warner Company and Robert Graves Company have a December 31 year-end. Graves Company, whose common stock is actively traded in the over-the-counter market, reported its total net income for the year to Warner Company and also paid cash dividends on November 15, 2004, to Warner Company and its other stockholders.

Instructions

How should Warner Company report the above facts in its December 31, 2004, balance sheet and its income statement for the year then ended? Discuss the rationale for your answer.

(AICPA adapted)

 C13-6 (Equity Method) On July 1, 2003, Cheryl Munns Company purchased for cash 40% of the outstanding capital stock of Huber Corporation. Both Munns and Huber have a December 31 year-end. Huber Corporation, whose common stock is actively traded on the American Stock Exchange, paid a cash dividend on November 15, 2003, to Munns Company and its other stockholders. It also reported its total net income for the year of $920,000 to Munns Company.

Instructions

Prepare a one-page memorandum of instructions on how Cheryl Munns Company should report the above facts in its December 31, 2003, balance sheet and its 2003 income statement. In your memo, identify and describe the method of valuation you recommend. Provide rationale where you can. Address your memo to the chief accountant at Cheryl Munns Company.

 **C13-7 (Fair Value)** Addison Manufacturing holds a large portfolio of debt and equity securities as an investment. The fair value of the portfolio is greater than its original cost, even though some securities have decreased in value. Ted Abernathy, the financial vice president, and Donna Nottebart, the controller, are near year-end in the process of classifying for the first time this securities portfolio in accordance with *FASB Statement No. 115*. Abernathy wants to classify those securities that have increased in value during the period as trading securities in order to increase net income this year. He wants to classify all the securities that have decreased in value as available-for-sale (the equity securities) and as held-to-maturity (the debt securities).

Nottebart disagrees. She wants to classify those securities that have decreased in value as trading securities and those that have increased in value as available-for-sale (equity) and held-to-maturity (debt). She contends that the company is having a good earnings year and that recognizing the losses will help to smooth the income this year. As a result, the company will have built-in gains for future periods when the company may not be as profitable.

Instructions
Answer the following questions.

(a) Will classifying the portfolio as each proposes actually have the effect on earnings that each says it will?

(b) Is there anything unethical in what each of them proposes? Who are the stakeholders affected by their proposals?

(c) Assume that Abernathy and Nottebart properly classify the entire portfolio into trading, available-for-sale, and held-to-maturity categories. But then each proposes to sell just before year-end the securities with gains or with losses, as the case may be, to accomplish their effect on earnings. Is this unethical?

USING YOUR JUDGMENT

FINANCIAL REPORTING PROBLEM
3M COMPANY

The financial statements of **3M** were provided with your book or can be accessed on the Take Action! CD.

Instructions
Refer to 3M's financial statements and the accompanying notes to answer the following questions.

(a) What investments does 3M report in 2001, and where are these investments reported in its financial statements?

(b) How are 3M's investments valued? How does 3M determine fair value?

FINANCIAL STATEMENT ANALYSIS CASE

UNION PLANTERS

Union Planters is a Tennessee bank holding company. (That is, it is a corporation that owns banks.) It manages $32 billion in assets, the largest of which is its loan portfolio of $19 billion. In addition to its loan portfolio, however, like other banks it has significant debt and stock investments. The nature of these investments varies from short-term in nature to long-term in nature. As a consequence, consistent with the requirements of accounting rules, Union Planters reports its investments in two different categories—trading and available-for-sale. The following facts were found in a recent Union Planters' Annual Report.

(all dollars in millions)	Amortized Cost	Gross Unrealized Gains	Gross Unrealized Losses	Fair Value
Trading account assets	$ 275	—	—	$ 275
Securities available for sale	8,209	$108	$15	8,302
Net income				224
Net securities gains (losses)				(9)

Instructions

(a) Why do you suppose Union Planters purchases investments, rather than simply making loans? Why does it purchase investments that vary in nature both in terms of their maturities and in type (debt versus stock)?

(b) How must Union Planters account for its investments in each of the two categories?

(c) In what ways does classifying investments into two different categories assist investors in evaluating the profitability of a company like Union Planters?

(d) Suppose that the management of Union Planters was not happy with its net income for the year. What step could it have taken with its investment portfolio that would have definitely increased reported profit? How much could it have increased reported profit? Why do you suppose it chose not to do this?

COMPARATIVE ANALYSIS CASE

THE COCA-COLA COMPANY AND PEPSICO, INC.

Instructions

Go to the Take Action! CD and use information found there to answer the following questions related to **The Coca-Cola Company** and **PepsiCo, Inc.**

(a) Based on the information contained in these financial statements, determine each of the following for each company.

    (1) Cash used in (for) investing activities during 2001 (from the Statement of Cash Flows).

    (2) Cash used for acquisitions and investments in unconsolidated affiliates (or principally bottling companies) during 2001.

    (3) Total investment in unconsolidated affiliates (or investments and other assets) at December 31, 2001.

    (4) What conclusions concerning the management of investments can be drawn from these data?

(b) (1) Briefly identify from Coca-Cola's December 31, 2001, balance sheet the investments it reported as being accounted for under the equity method. (2) What is the amount of investments Coca-Cola reported in its 2001 balance sheet as "cost method investments," and what is the nature of these investments?

(c) In its note number 8 on Financial Instruments, what total amounts did Coca-Cola report at December 31, 2001, as: (1) trading securities, (2) available-for-sale securities, and (3) held-to-maturity securities?

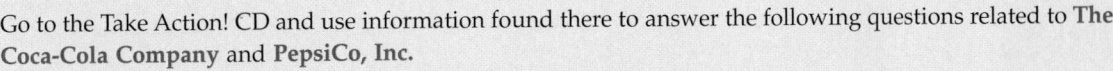

*Remember to check the **Take Action! CD**
and the book's **companion Web site**
to find additional resources for this chapter.*

ACCOUNTING FOR INCOME TAXES

CHAPTER 14

USE IT, BUT DON'T ABUSE IT

As part of prudent management, companies are expected to manage all costs in order to maximize shareholder value. For example, good managers look for the best prices for raw materials and supplies that go into making their products, and they are expected to be savvy bargainers in negotiating labor and other service contracts to minimize the overall cost of doing business.

Another set of costs that companies manage are those related to taxes. For example, by using accelerated depreciation methods for fixed assets, companies reduce their tax bills. With faster tax write-offs on fixed assets, companies report lower taxable income and pay lower taxes in the early years of the assets' lives, thereby managing tax costs.

What happens when companies cross the line from prudent tax management to abusive tax avoidance? Recently more companies appear to be crossing that line. As indicated in the following chart, corporate taxes as a share of profits dropped from 26.6 percent in 1994 to just 21.8 percent in 1999.

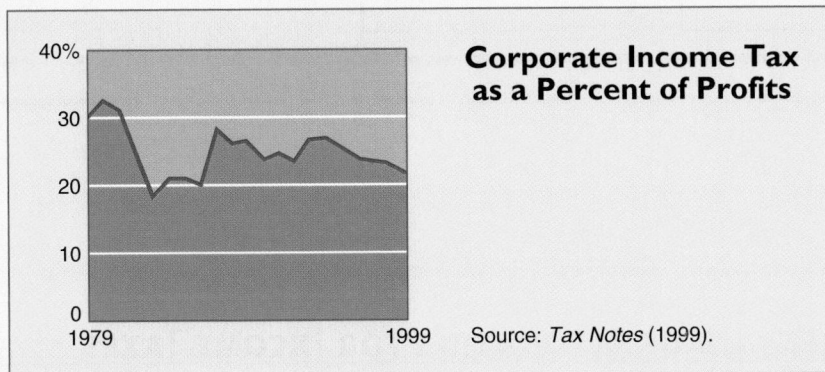

Source: *Tax Notes* (1999).

However, the IRS has been increasing its scrutiny of transactions that are done only to avoid taxes and that do not serve any legitimate business purpose. For example, in one recent case a company purchased and sold the same securities within an hour's time, simply to benefit from a multimillion dollar foreign tax credit. The tax judge in this case not only denied the credit but also imposed a 20 percent penalty. Thus, companies can manage their tax costs as long as they do not abuse the tax code.[1]

LEARNING OBJECTIVES

After studying this chapter, you should be able to:

1. Identify differences between pretax financial income and taxable income.
2. Describe a temporary difference that results in future taxable amounts.
3. Describe a temporary difference that results in future deductible amounts.
4. Explain the purpose of a deferred tax asset valuation allowance.
5. Describe the presentation of income tax expense in the income statement.
6. Describe various temporary and permanent differences.
7. Explain the effect of various tax rates and tax rate changes on deferred income taxes.
8. Apply accounting procedures for a loss carryback and a loss carryforward.
9. Describe the presentation of deferred income taxes in financial statements.
10. Indicate the basic principles of the asset-liability method.

---

[1]Based on Howard Gleckman and Lorraine Woellert, "Kiss the Tax Shelter Goodbye? The Courts Crack Down on Egregious Corporate Tax Avoidance," *Business Week* (November 15, 1999), p. 50.

Income taxes are a major cost of business to most corporations. As a result, as the opening story indicates, companies spend a considerable amount of time and effort to minimize their tax payments. The purpose of this chapter is to discuss the basic guidelines that companies must follow in reporting income taxes. The content and organization of the chapter are as follows.

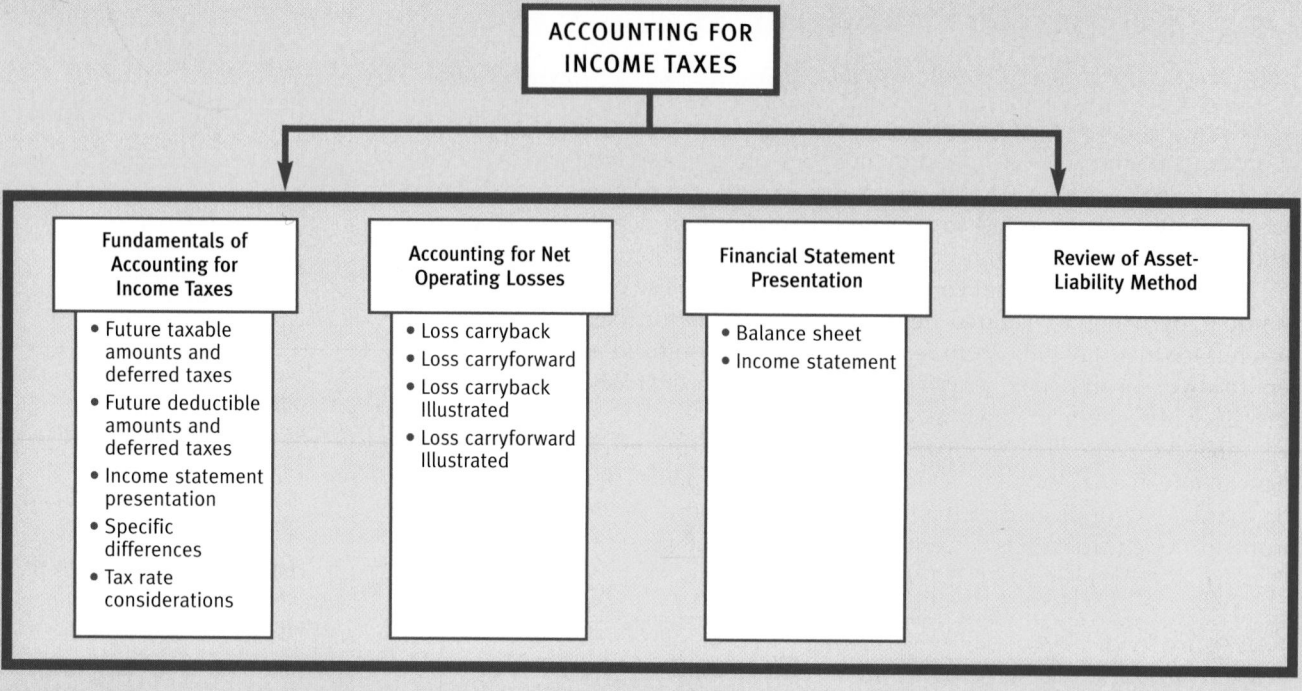

FUNDAMENTALS OF ACCOUNTING FOR INCOME TAXES

OBJECTIVE 1
Identify differences between pretax financial income and taxable income.

Up to this point, you have learned the basic guidelines that corporations use to report information to investors and creditors. Corporations also must file income tax returns following the guidelines developed by the Internal Revenue Service (IRS). Because GAAP and tax regulations are different in a number of ways, pretax financial income and taxable income frequently differ. Consequently, the amount that a company reports as tax expense will differ from the amount of taxes payable to the IRS. Illustration 14-1 (on page 685) highlights these differences.

Pretax financial income is a financial reporting term often referred to as income before taxes, income for financial reporting purposes, or income for book purposes. Pretax financial income is determined according to GAAP and is measured with the objective of providing useful information to investors and creditors. **Taxable income** (income for tax purposes) is a tax accounting term used to indicate the amount upon which income tax payable is computed. Taxable income is determined according to the Internal Revenue Code (the tax code), which is designed to raise money to support government operations.

To illustrate how differences in GAAP and IRS rules affect financial reporting and taxable income, assume that Chelsea Inc. reported revenues of $130,000 and expenses of $60,000 in each of its first 3 years of operations. Illustration 14-2 (on page 685) shows the (partial) income statement over these 3 years.

Illustration 14-1
Fundamental Differences between Financial and Tax Reporting

INTERNATIONAL INSIGHT

In some countries, taxable income and pretax financial income are the same. As a consequence, accounting for differences between tax and book income is not significant.

Illustration 14-2
Financial Reporting Income

CHELSEA INC. GAAP REPORTING				
	2004	2005	2006	Total
Revenues	$130,000	$130,000	$130,000	
Expenses	60,000	60,000	60,000	
Pretax financial income	$ 70,000	$ 70,000	$ 70,000	$ 210,000
Income tax expense (40%)	$ 28,000	$ 28,000	$ 28,000	$ 84,000

For tax purposes (following the tax code), Chelsea reported the same expenses to the IRS in each of the years. But taxable revenues were $100,000 in 2004, $150,000 in 2005, and $140,000 in 2006 as shown in Illustration 14-3.

Illustration 14-3
Tax Reporting Income

CHELSEA INC. TAX REPORTING				
	2004	2005	2006	Total
Revenues	$100,000	$150,000	$140,000	
Expenses	60,000	60,000	60,000	
Taxable income	$ 40,000	$ 90,000	$ 80,000	$ 210,000
Income tax payable (40%)	$ 16,000	$ 36,000	$ 32,000	$ 84,000

Income tax expense and income tax payable differ over the 3 years, but **in total** they are the same, as shown in Illustration 14-4.

Illustration 14-4

Comparison of Income Tax Expense to Income Tax Payable

		CHELSEA INC. INCOME TAX EXPENSE AND INCOME TAX PAYABLE			
		2004	2005	2006	Total
Income tax expense		$28,000	$28,000	$28,000	$84,000
Income tax payable		16,000	36,000	32,000	84,000
Difference		$12,000	$(8,000)	$(4,000)	$ –0–

The differences between income tax expense and income tax payable arise for a simple reason: For financial reporting, the full accrual method is used to report revenues, whereas for tax purposes a modified cash basis is used. As a result, Chelsea reports pretax financial income of $70,000 and income tax expense of $28,000 for each of the 3 years. However, taxable income fluctuates. For example, in 2004 taxable income is only $40,000, which means that just $16,000 is owed to the IRS that year. The income tax payable is classified as a current liability on the balance sheet.

As indicated in Illustration 14-4, for Chelsea the $12,000 ($28,000 − $16,000) difference between income tax expense and income tax payable in 2004 reflects taxes that will be paid in future periods. This $12,000 difference is often referred to as a **deferred tax amount**. In this case it is a **deferred tax liability**. In cases where taxes will be lower in the future, Chelsea would record a **deferred tax asset**. We explain the measurement and accounting for deferred tax liabilities and assets in the following two sections.

Future Taxable Amounts and Deferred Taxes

OBJECTIVE 2
Describe a temporary difference that results in future taxable amounts.

The example summarized in Illustration 14-4 shows how income tax payable can differ from income tax expense. One way that this can happen is when there are temporary differences between the amounts reported for tax purposes and those reported for book purposes. A **temporary difference** is the difference between the tax basis of an asset or liability and its reported (carrying or book) amount in the financial statements that will result in taxable amounts or deductible amounts in future years. **Taxable amounts** increase taxable income in future years, and **deductible amounts** decrease taxable income in future years.

In Chelsea Inc.'s situation, the only difference between the book basis and tax basis of the assets and liabilities relates to accounts receivable that arose from revenue recognized for book purposes. Illustration 14-5 indicates that accounts receivable are reported at $30,000 in the December 31, 2004, GAAP-basis balance sheet, but the receivables have a zero tax basis.

Illustration 14-5

Temporary Difference, Sales Revenue

Per Books	12/31/04	Per Tax Return	12/31/04
Accounts receivable	$30,000	Accounts receivable	$–0–

What will happen to this $30,000 temporary difference that originated in 2004 for Chelsea Inc.? Assuming that Chelsea expects to collect $20,000 of the receivables in 2005 and $10,000 in 2006, this collection will result in future taxable amounts of $20,000 in

2005 and $10,000 in 2006. These future taxable amounts will cause taxable income to exceed pretax financial income in both 2005 and 2006.

An assumption inherent in a company's GAAP balance sheet is that the assets and liabilities will be recovered and settled at their reported amounts (carrying amounts). This assumption creates a requirement under accrual accounting to recognize currently the deferred tax consequences of temporary differences—that is, the amount of income taxes that would be payable (or refundable) when the reported amounts of the assets are recovered and the liabilities are settled, respectively. The following diagram illustrates the reversal or turn-around of the temporary difference described in Illustration 14-5 and the resulting taxable amounts in future periods.

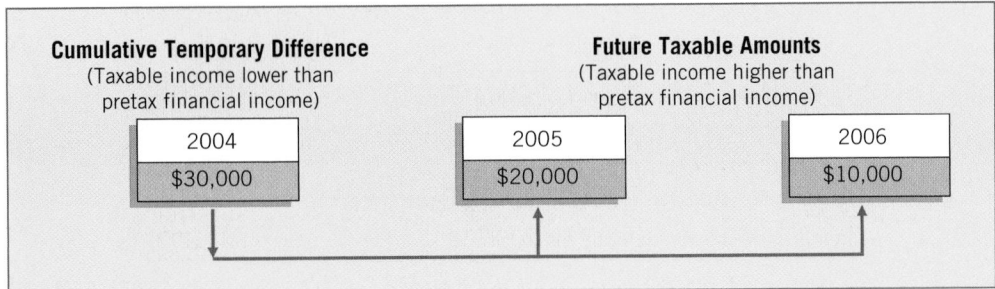

Illustration 14-6
Reversal of Temporary
Difference, Chelsea Inc.

We have assumed that Chelsea will collect the accounts receivable and report the $30,000 collection as taxable revenues in future tax returns. A payment of income tax in both 2005 and 2006 will therefore occur. We therefore should record in Chelsea's books in 2004 the deferred tax consequences of the revenue and related receivables reflected in the 2004 financial statements. This necessitates the recording of a deferred tax liability.

Deferred Tax Liability

A **deferred tax liability** is the deferred tax consequences attributable to taxable temporary differences. In other words, **a deferred tax liability represents the increase in taxes payable in future years as a result of taxable temporary differences existing at the end of the current year**. Recall from the Chelsea example that income tax payable is $16,000 ($40,000 × 40%) in 2004 (Illustration 14-4). In addition, a temporary difference exists at year-end because the revenue and related accounts receivable are reported differently for book and tax purposes. The book basis of accounts receivable is $30,000, and the tax basis is zero. Thus, the total deferred tax liability at the end of 2004 is $12,000, computed as follows.

Book basis of accounts receivable	$30,000
Tax basis of accounts receivable	–0–
Cumulative temporary difference at the end of 2004	30,000
Tax rate	40%
Deferred tax liability at the end of 2004	$12,000

Illustration 14-7
Computation of Deferred
Tax Liability, End of 2004

Another way to compute the deferred tax liability is to prepare a schedule that indicates the taxable amounts scheduled for the future as a result of existing temporary differences. Such a schedule (see Illustration 14-8, page 688) is particularly useful when the computations become more complex.

Illustration 14-8
Schedule of Future
Taxable Amounts

	Future Years		
	2005	2006	Total
Future taxable amounts	$20,000	$10,000	$30,000
Tax rate	40%	40%	
Deferred tax liability at the end of 2004	$ 8,000	$ 4,000	$12,000

Because it is the first year of operations for Chelsea, there is no deferred tax liability at the beginning of the year. The income tax expense for 2004 is computed as follows.

Illustration 14-9
Computation of Income
Tax Expense, 2004

Deferred tax liability at end of 2004	$12,000
Deferred tax liability at beginning of 2004	–0–
Deferred tax expense for 2004	12,000
Current tax expense for 2004 (Income tax payable)	16,000
Income tax expense (total) for 2004	$28,000

This computation indicates that income tax expense has two components—current tax expense (which is the amount of income tax payable for the period) and deferred tax expense. **Deferred tax expense** is the increase in the deferred tax liability balance from the beginning to the end of the accounting period.

Taxes due and payable are credited to Income Tax Payable, and the increase in deferred taxes is credited to Deferred Tax Liability. The sum of those two items is debited to Income Tax Expense. For Chelsea Inc. the following entry is made at the end of 2004.

Income Tax Expense	28,000	
Income Tax Payable		16,000
Deferred Tax Liability		12,000

At the end of 2005 (the second year), the difference between the book basis and the tax basis of the accounts receivable is $10,000. This difference is multiplied by the applicable tax rate to arrive at the deferred tax liability of $4,000 ($10,000 × 40%) to be reported at the end of 2005. Income tax payable for 2005 is $36,000 (Illustration 14-3), and the income tax expense for 2005 is as follows.

Illustration 14-10
Computation of Income
Tax Expense, 2005

Deferred tax liability at end of 2005	$ 4,000
Deferred tax liability at beginning of 2005	12,000
Deferred tax expense (benefit) for 2005	(8,000)
Current tax expense for 2005 (Income tax payable)	36,000
Income tax expense (total) for 2005	$28,000

The journal entry to record income tax expense, the change in the deferred tax liability, and income tax payable for 2005 is shown on the next page.

Income Tax Expense	28,000	
Deferred Tax Liability	8,000	
Income Tax Payable		36,000

In the entry to record income taxes at the end of 2006, the Deferred Tax Liability is reduced by $4,000. The Deferred Tax Liability account appears as follows at the end of 2006.

Deferred Tax Liability

| 2005 | 8,000 | 2004 | 12,000 |
| 2006 | 4,000 | | |

Illustration 14-11
Deferred Tax Liability
Account after Reversals

The Deferred Tax Liability account has a zero balance at the end of 2006.

"REAL LIABILITIES"

WHAT DO THE NUMBERS MEAN?

Some analysts dismiss deferred tax liabilities when assessing the financial strength of a company. But the FASB indicates that the deferred tax liability meets the definition of a liability established in *Statement of Financial Accounting Concepts No. 6*, "Elements of Financial Statements" because:

1. *It results from a past transaction.* In the Chelsea example, services were performed for customers and revenue was recognized in 2004 for financial reporting purposes but was deferred for tax purposes.

2. *It is a present obligation.* Taxable income in future periods will be higher than pretax financial income as a result of this temporary difference. Thus, a present obligation exists.

3. *It represents a future sacrifice.* Taxable income and taxes due in future periods will result from events that have already occurred. The payment of these taxes when they come due is the future sacrifice.

A study by B. Ayers[2] indicates that the market views deferred tax assets and liabilities similarly to other assets and liabilities, and that *SFAS No. 109* increased the usefulness of deferred tax amounts in financial statements.

Summary of Income Tax Accounting Objectives

One objective of accounting for income taxes is to recognize the amount of taxes payable or refundable for the current year. In Chelsea's case, income tax payable is $16,000 for 2004.

A **second objective** is to recognize deferred tax liabilities and assets for the future tax consequences of events that have already been recognized in the financial statements or tax returns. Chelsea sold services to customers that resulted in accounts receivable of $30,000 in 2004. That amount was reported on the 2004 income statement, but it was not reported on the tax return as income. It will appear on future tax returns as income for the period **when it is collected**. As a result, a $30,000 temporary difference exists at the end of 2004, which will cause future taxable amounts. A deferred tax liability of $12,000 is reported on the balance sheet at the end of 2004, which represents

[2]B. Ayers, "Deferred Tax Accounting Under *SFAS No. 109*: An Empirical Investigation of Its Incremental Value-Relevance Relative to *APB No. 11*," *The Accounting Review* (April 1998).

the increase in taxes payable in future years ($8,000 in 2005 and $4,000 in 2006) as a result of a temporary difference existing at the end of the current year. The related deferred tax liability is reduced by $8,000 at the end of 2005 and by another $4,000 at the end of 2006.

In addition to affecting the balance sheet, deferred taxes have an impact on income tax expense in each of the 3 years affected. In 2004, taxable income ($40,000) is less than pretax financial income ($70,000). Income tax payable for 2004 is therefore $16,000 (based on taxable income). Deferred tax expense of $12,000 is caused by the increase in the Deferred Tax Liability account on the balance sheet. Income tax expense is then $28,000 for 2004.

In 2005 and 2006, however, taxable income will be more than pretax financial income, due to the reversal of the temporary difference ($20,000 in 2005 and $10,000 in 2006). Income tax payable will therefore be higher than income tax expense in 2005 and 2006. The Deferred Tax Liability account will be debited for $8,000 in 2005 and $4,000 in 2006. Credits for these amounts are recorded in Income Tax Expense (often referred to as a **deferred tax benefit**).

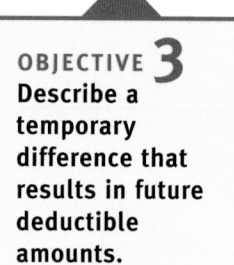

OBJECTIVE **3**
Describe a temporary difference that results in future deductible amounts.

Future Deductible Amounts and Deferred Taxes

Assume that during 2004, Cunningham Inc. estimated its warranty costs related to the sale of microwave ovens to be $500,000, paid evenly over the next 2 years. For book purposes, in 2004 Cunningham reported warranty expense and a related estimated liability for warranties of $500,000 in its financial statements. For tax purposes, **the warranty tax deduction is not allowed until paid**. Therefore, no warranty liability is recognized on a tax-basis balance sheet. Thus, the balance sheet difference at the end of 2004 is as follows.

Illustration 14-12
Temporary Difference,
Warranty Liability

Per Books	12/31/04	Per Tax Return	12/31/04
Estimated liability for warranties	$500,000	Estimated liability for warranties	$–0–

When the warranty liability is paid, an expense (deductible amount) will be reported for tax purposes. Because of this temporary difference, Cunningham Inc. should recognize in 2004 the tax benefits (positive tax consequences) for the tax deductions that will result from the future settlement of the liability. This future tax benefit is reported in the December 31, 2004, balance sheet as a **deferred tax asset**.

Another way to think about this situation is as follows: Deductible amounts will occur in future tax returns. These **future deductible amounts** will cause taxable income to be less than pretax financial income in the future as a result of an existing temporary difference. Cunningham's temporary difference originates (arises) in one period (2004) and reverses over two periods (2005 and 2006). This situation is diagrammed as follows.

Illustration 14-13
Reversal of Temporary
Difference,
Cunningham Inc.

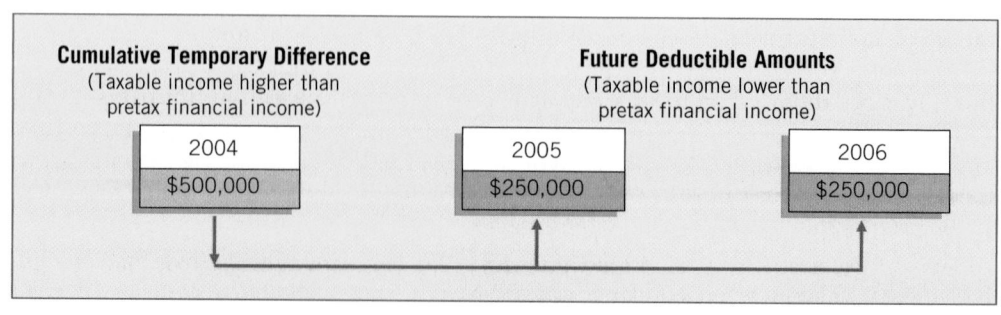

Deferred Tax Asset

A **deferred tax asset** is the deferred tax consequence attributable to deductible temporary differences. In other words, a **deferred tax asset represents the increase in taxes refundable (or saved) in future years as a result of deductible temporary differences existing at the end of the current year**.

To illustrate, assume that Hunt Co. accrues a loss and a related liability of $50,000 in 2004 for financial reporting purposes because of pending litigation. This amount is not deductible for tax purposes until the period the liability is paid, which is expected to be 2005. As a result, a deductible amount will occur in 2005 when the liability (Estimated Litigation Liability) is settled, causing taxable income to be lower than pretax financial income. The computation of the deferred tax asset at the end of 2004 (assuming a 40% tax rate) is as follows.

Book basis of litigation liability	$50,000
Tax basis of litigation liability	–0–
Cumulative temporary difference at the end of 2004	50,000
Tax rate	40%
Deferred tax asset at the end of 2004	$20,000

Illustration 14-14
Computation of Deferred Tax Asset, End of 2004

Another way to compute the deferred tax asset is to prepare a schedule that indicates the deductible amounts scheduled for the future as a result of deductible temporary differences. This schedule is shown in Illustration 14-15.

	Future Years
Future deductible amounts	$50,000
Tax rate	40%
Deferred tax asset at the end of 2004	$20,000

Illustration 14-15
Schedule of Future Deductible Amounts

Assuming that 2004 is Hunt's first year of operations, and income tax payable is $100,000, the income tax expense is computed as follows.

Deferred tax asset at end of 2004	$ 20,000
Deferred tax asset at beginning of 2004	–0–
Deferred tax expense (benefit) for 2004	(20,000)
Current tax expense for 2004 (Income tax payable)	100,000
Income tax expense (total) for 2004	$ 80,000

Illustration 14-16
Computation of Income Tax Expense, 2004

The **deferred tax benefit** results from the increase in the deferred tax asset from the beginning to the end of the accounting period. The deferred tax benefit is a negative component of income tax expense. The total income tax expense of $80,000 on the income statement for 2004 is thus comprised of two elements—current tax expense of $100,000 and deferred tax benefit of $20,000. For Hunt Co. the journal entry that is made at the end of 2004 to record income tax expense, deferred income taxes, and income tax payable is shown on the next page.

Income Tax Expense	80,000	
Deferred Tax Asset	20,000	
Income Tax Payable		100,000

At the end of 2005 (the second year), the difference between the book value and the tax basis of the litigation liability is zero. Therefore, there is no deferred tax asset at this date. Assuming that income tax payable for 2005 is $140,000, the computation of income tax expense for 2005 is as follows.

Illustration 14-17
Computation of Income Tax Expense, 2005

Deferred tax asset at the end of 2005	$ –0–
Deferred tax asset at the beginning of 2005	20,000
Deferred tax expense (benefit) for 2005	20,000
Current tax expense for 2005 (Income tax payable)	140,000
Income tax expense (total) for 2005	$160,000

The journal entry to record income taxes for 2005 is as follows.

Income Tax Expense	160,000	
Deferred Tax Asset		20,000
Income Tax Payable		140,000

The total income tax expense of $160,000 on the income statement for 2005 is thus comprised of two elements—current tax expense of $140,000 and deferred tax expense of $20,000.

The Deferred Tax Asset account would appear as follows at the end of 2005.

Illustration 14-18
Deferred Tax Asset Account after Reversals

Deferred Tax Asset

2004	20,000	2005	20,000

WHAT DO THE NUMBERS MEAN?

"REAL ASSETS"

A key issue in accounting for income taxes is whether a deferred tax asset should be recognized in the financial records. Based on the conceptual definition of an asset, a deferred tax asset meets the three main conditions for an item to be recognized as an asset:

⟨1⟩ *It results from a past transaction.* In the Hunt Co. example, the accrual of the loss contingency is the past event that gives rise to a future deductible temporary difference.

⟨2⟩ *It gives rise to a probable benefit in the future.* Taxable income is higher than pretax financial income in the current year (2004). However, in the next year the exact opposite occurs; that is, taxable income is lower than pretax financial income. Because this deductible temporary difference reduces taxes payable in the future, a probable future benefit exists at the end of the current period.

> ◈ **The entity controls access to the benefits.** Hunt Co. has the ability to obtain the benefit of existing deductible temporary differences by reducing its taxes payable in the future. Hunt Co. has the exclusive right to that benefit and can control others' access to it.
>
> Market analysts' reaction to the **write-off** of deferred tax assets also supports their treatment as assets. When Bethlehem Steel reported a $1 billion charge in 2001 to write off a deferred tax asset, analysts believed that Bethlehem was signaling that it would be unable to realize the future benefits of the tax deductions; thus, the asset should be written down like other assets.[3]

Deferred Tax Asset — Valuation Allowance

A deferred tax asset is recognized for all deductible temporary differences. However, a deferred tax asset should be reduced by a **valuation allowance** if, based on all available evidence, **it is more likely than not** that some portion or all of the deferred tax asset **will not be realized**. "More likely than not" means a level of likelihood that is at least slightly more than 50 percent.

Assume that Jensen Co. has a deductible temporary difference of $1,000,000 at the end of its first year of operations. Its tax rate is 40 percent, which means a deferred tax asset of $400,000 ($1,000,000 × 40%) is recorded. Assuming that income taxes payable are $900,000, the journal entry to record income tax expense, the deferred tax asset, and income tax payable is as follows.

> **OBJECTIVE 4**
> Explain the purpose of a deferred tax asset valuation allowance.

Income Tax Expense	500,000	
Deferred Tax Asset	400,000	
Income Tax Payable		900,000

After careful review of all available evidence, it is determined that it is more likely than not that $100,000 of this deferred tax asset will not be realized. The journal entry to record this reduction in asset value is as follows.

Income Tax Expense	100,000	
Allowance to Reduce Deferred Tax Asset		
to Expected Realizable Value		100,000

In this journal entry, income tax expense is increased in the current period because a favorable tax benefit is not expected to be realized for a portion of the deductible temporary difference. **A valuation allowance is simultaneously established to recognize the reduction in the carrying amount of the deferred tax asset.** This valuation account is a contra account and may be reported on the financial statements in the following manner.

Deferred tax asset	$400,000
Less: Allowance to reduce deferred tax	
asset to expected realizable value	100,000
Deferred tax asset (net)	$300,000

Illustration 14-19
Balance Sheet Presentation of Valuation Allowance Account

---

[3]J. Weil and S. Liesman, "Stock Gurus Disregard Most Big Write-offs But They Often Hold Vital Clues to Outlook," *Wall Street Journal, Interactive Edition* (December 31, 2001).

This allowance account is evaluated at the end of each accounting period. If, at the end of the next period, the deferred tax asset is still $400,000, but now $350,000 of this asset is expected to be realized, then the following entry is made to adjust the valuation account.

Allowance to Reduce Deferred Tax Asset to Expected Realizable Value	50,000	
Income Tax Expense		50,000

All available evidence, both positive and negative, should be carefully considered to determine whether, based on the weight of available evidence, a valuation allowance is needed. For example, if the company has been experiencing a series of loss years, a reasonable assumption is that these losses will continue and the benefit of the future deductible amounts will be lost. The use of a valuation account under other conditions will be discussed later in the chapter.

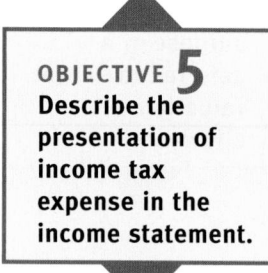

OBJECTIVE **5**
Describe the presentation of income tax expense in the income statement.

Income Statement Presentation

Whether the change in deferred income taxes should be added to or subtracted from income tax payable in computing income tax expense depends on the circumstances. For example, an increase in a deferred tax liability would be added to income tax payable. On the other hand, an increase in a deferred tax asset would be subtracted from income tax payable. The formula to compute income tax expense (benefit) is as follows.

Illustration 14-20
Formula to Compute Income Tax Expense

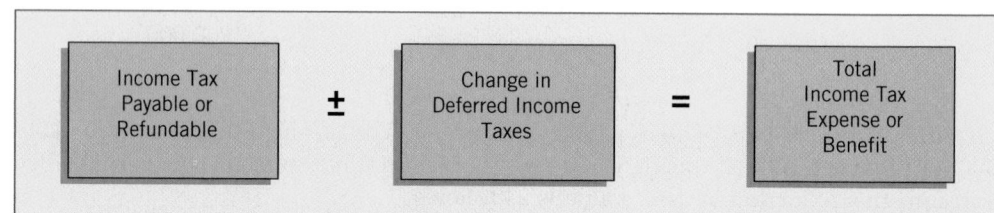

In the income statement or in the notes to the financial statements, the significant components of income tax expense attributable to continuing operations should be disclosed. Given the information related to Chelsea Inc. on page 688, Chelsea's income statement is reported as follows.

Illustration 14-21
Income Statement Presentation of Income Tax Expense

CHELSEA INC. INCOME STATEMENT FOR THE YEAR ENDING DECEMBER 31, 2004		
Revenues		$130,000
Expenses		60,000
Income before income taxes		70,000
Income tax/expense		
Current	$16,000	
Deferred	12,000	28,000
Net income		$ 42,000

As illustrated, both the current portion (amount of income tax payable for the period) and the deferred portion of income tax expense are reported. Another option is to simply report the total income tax expense on the income statement, and then in the notes to the financial statements indicate the current and deferred portions. Income tax expense is often referred to as "Provision for income taxes." Using this terminology, the current provision is $16,000, and the provision for deferred taxes is $12,000.

Specific Differences

Numerous items create differences between pretax financial income and taxable income. For purposes of accounting recognition, these differences are of two types: (1) temporary, and (2) permanent.

OBJECTIVE 6
Describe various temporary and permanent differences.

Temporary Differences

Temporary differences that will result in taxable amounts in future years when the related assets are recovered are often called **taxable temporary differences**. Temporary differences that will result in deductible amounts in future years when the related book liabilities are settled are often called **deductible temporary differences**. Taxable temporary differences give rise to recording deferred tax liabilities; deductible temporary differences give rise to recording deferred tax assets. Examples of temporary differences are provided in Illustration 14-22.[4]

Illustration 14-22
Examples of Temporary Differences

A. **Revenues or gains are taxable after they are recognized in financial income.**
   An asset (e.g., accounts receivable or investment) may be recognized for revenues or gains that will result in **taxable amounts in future years** when the asset is recovered. Examples:
   1. Sales accounted for on the accrual basis for financial reporting purposes and on the installment (cash) basis for tax purposes.
   2. Contracts accounted for under the percentage-of-completion method for financial reporting purposes and a portion of related gross profit deferred for tax purposes.
   3. Investments accounted for under the equity method for financial reporting purposes and under the cost method for tax purposes.
   4. Gain on involuntary conversion of nonmonetary asset which is recognized for financial reporting purposes but deferred for tax purposes.

B. **Expenses or losses are deductible after they are recognized in financial income.**
   A liability (or contra asset) may be recognized for expenses or losses that will result in **deductible amounts in future years** when the liability is settled. Examples:
   1. Product warranty liabilities.
   2. Estimated liabilities related to discontinued operations or restructurings.
   3. Litigation accruals.
   4. Bad debt expense recognized using the allowance method for financial reporting purposes; direct write-off method used for tax purposes.

C. **Revenues or gains are taxable before they are recognized in financial income.**
   A liability may be recognized for an advance payment for goods or services to be provided in future years. For tax purposes, the advance payment is included in taxable income upon the receipt of cash. Future sacrifices to provide goods or services (or future refunds to those who cancel their orders) that settle the liability will result in **deductible amounts in future years**. Examples:
   1. Subscriptions received in advance.
   2. Advance rental receipts.
   3. Sales and leasebacks for financial reporting purposes (income deferral) and reported as sales for tax purposes.
   4. Prepaid contracts and royalties received in advance.

D. **Expenses or losses are deductible before they are recognized in financial income.**
   The cost of an asset may have been deducted for tax purposes faster than it was expensed for financial reporting purposes. Amounts received upon future recovery of the amount of the asset for financial reporting (through use or sale) will exceed the remaining tax basis of the asset and thereby result in **taxable amounts in future years**. Examples:
   1. Depreciable property, depletable resources, and intangibles.
   2. Deductible pension funding exceeding expense.
   3. Prepaid expenses that are deducted on the tax return in the period paid.

---

[4]*SFAS No. 109* gives more examples of temporary differences. We have presented the most common types.

Determining a company's temporary differences may prove difficult. A company should prepare a balance sheet for tax purposes that can be compared with its GAAP balance sheet; many of the differences between the two balance sheets would be temporary differences.

Originating and Reversing Aspects of Temporary Differences. An **originating temporary difference** is the initial difference between the book basis and the tax basis of an asset or liability, regardless of whether the tax basis of the asset or liability exceeds or is exceeded by the book basis of the asset or liability. A **reversing difference**, on the other hand, occurs when a temporary difference that originated in prior periods is eliminated and the related tax effect is removed from the deferred tax account.

For example, assume that Sharp Co. has tax depreciation in excess of book depreciation of $2,000 in 2000, 2001, and 2002, and that it has an excess of book depreciation over tax depreciation of $3,000 in 2003 and 2004 for the same asset. Assuming a tax rate of 30 percent for all years involved, the Deferred Tax Liability account would reflect the following.

Illustration 14-23

Tax Effects of Originating and Reversing Differences

Tax Effects of Reversing Differences		**Deferred Tax Liability**		Tax Effects of Originating Differences
2003	900	2000	600	
2004	900	2001	600	
		2002	600	

The originating differences for Sharp in each of the first 3 years would be $2,000, and the related tax effect of each originating difference would be $600. The reversing differences in 2003 and 2004 would each be $3,000, and the related tax effect of each would be $900.

Permanent Differences

Some differences between taxable income and pretax financial income are permanent. **Permanent differences** are caused by items that (1) enter into pretax financial income but **never** into taxable income, or (2) enter into taxable income but **never** into pretax financial income.

Congress has enacted a variety of tax law provisions in an effort to attain certain political, economic, and social objectives. Some of these provisions exclude certain revenues from taxation, limit the deductibility of certain expenses, and permit the deduction of certain other expenses in excess of costs incurred. A corporation that has tax-free income, nondeductible expenses, or allowable deductions in excess of cost has an effective tax rate that is different from the statutory (regular) tax rate.

Since permanent differences affect only the period in which they occur, they do not give rise to future taxable or deductible amounts. As a result, **there are no deferred tax consequences to be recognized.** Examples of permanent differences are shown in Illustration 14-24 on page 697.

Temporary and Permanent Differences Illustrated

To illustrate the computations used when both temporary and permanent differences exist, assume that Bio-Tech Company reports pretax financial income of $200,000 in each of the years 2002, 2003, and 2004. The company is subject to a 30 percent tax rate, and has the following differences between pretax financial income and taxable income.

1. An installment sale of $18,000 in 2002 is reported for tax purposes over an 18-month period at a constant amount per month beginning January 1, 2003. The entire sale is recognized for book purposes in 2002.

2. Premium paid for life insurance carried by the company on key officers is $5,000 in 2003 and 2004. This is not deductible for tax purposes, but is expensed for book purposes.

Illustration 14-24
Examples of Permanent Differences

A. **Items are recognized for financial reporting purposes but not for tax purposes.**
   Examples:
   1. Interest received on state and municipal obligations.
   2. Expenses incurred in obtaining tax-exempt income.
   3. Proceeds from life insurance carried by the company on key officers or employees.
   4. Premiums paid for life insurance carried by the company on key officers or employees (company is beneficiary).
   5. Fines and expenses resulting from a violation of law.
   6. Compensation expense associated with certain employee stock options.
B. **Items are recognized for tax purposes but not for financial reporting purposes.**
   Examples:
   1. "Percentage depletion" of natural resources in excess of their cost.
   2. The deduction for dividends received from U.S. corporations, generally 70% or 80%.

The installment sale is a temporary difference, and the life insurance premium is a permanent difference. The reconciliation of Bio-Tech Company's pretax financial income to taxable income and the computation of income tax payable is shown in Illustration 14-25.

Illustration 14-25
Reconciliation and Computation of Income Taxes Payable

	2002	2003	2004
Pretax financial income	$200,000	$200,000	$200,000
Permanent difference			
Nondeductible expense		5,000	5,000
Temporary difference			
Installment sale	(18,000)	12,000	6,000
Taxable income	182,000	217,000	211,000
Tax rate	30%	30%	30%
Income tax payable	$ 54,600	$ 65,100	$ 63,300

Note that differences causing pretax financial income to exceed taxable income are **deducted** from pretax financial income when determining taxable income. Conversely, differences causing pretax financial income to be less than taxable income are **added to** pretax financial income in determining taxable income.

Both permanent and temporary differences are considered in reconciling pretax financial income to taxable income. Since the permanent difference (nondeductible expense) does not result in future taxable or deductible amounts, deferred income taxes are not recorded for this difference.

The journal entries to record income taxes for Bio-Tech for 2002, 2003, and 2004 are as follows.

December 31, 2002

Income Tax Expense ($54,600 + $5,400)	60,000	
Deferred Tax Liability ($18,000 × 30%)		5,400
Income Tax Payable ($182,000 × 30%)		54,600

December 31, 2003

Income Tax Expense ($65,100 − $3,600)	61,500	
Deferred Tax Liability ($12,000 × 30%)	3,600	
Income Tax Payable ($217,000 × 30%)		65,100

December 31, 2004

Income Tax Expense ($63,300 − $1,800)	61,500	
Deferred Tax Liability ($6,000 × 30%)	1,800	
Income Tax Payable ($211,000 × 30%)		63,300

Bio-Tech has one temporary difference, which originates in 2002 and reverses in 2003 and 2004. A deferred tax liability is recognized at the end of 2002 because the temporary difference causes future taxable amounts. As the temporary difference reverses, the deferred tax liability is reduced. There is no deferred tax amount associated with the difference caused by the nondeductible insurance expense because it is a permanent difference.

Although a statutory (enacted) tax rate of 30 percent applies for all 3 years, the effective rate is different. The **effective tax rate** is computed by dividing total income tax expense for the period by pretax financial income. The effective rate is 30 percent for 2002 ($60,000 ÷ $200,000 = 30%) and 30.75 percent for 2003 and 2004 ($61,500 ÷ $200,000 = 30.75%).

Tax Rate Considerations

In our previous illustrations, the enacted tax rate did not change from one year to the next. Thus, to compute the deferred income tax amount to be reported on the balance sheet, the cumulative temporary difference is simply multiplied by the current tax rate. Using Bio-Tech as an example, the cumulative temporary difference of $18,000 is multiplied by the enacted tax rate, 30 percent in this case, to arrive at a deferred tax liability of $5,400 ($18,000 × 30%) at the end of 2002.

Future Tax Rates

What happens if tax rates are different for future years? In this case, the **enacted tax rate** expected to apply should be used. Therefore, presently enacted changes in the tax rate that become effective for a particular future year(s) must be considered when determining the tax rate to apply to existing temporary differences. For example, assume that Warlen Co. at the end of 2001 has the following cumulative temporary difference of $300,000, computed as follows.

Illustration 14-26
Computation of Cumulative Temporary Difference

Book basis of depreciable assets	$1,000,000
Tax basis of depreciable assets	700,000
Cumulative temporary difference	$ 300,000

Furthermore, assume that the $300,000 will reverse and result in taxable amounts in the following years when the enacted tax rates are as follows.

Illustration 14-27
Deferred Tax Liability Based on Future Rates

	2002	2003	2004	2005	2006	Total
Future taxable amounts	$80,000	$70,000	$60,000	$50,000	$40,000	$300,000
Tax rate	40%	40%	35%	30%	30%	
Deferred tax liability	$32,000	$28,000	$21,000	$15,000	$12,000	$108,000

The total deferred tax liability at the end of 2001 is $108,000. Tax rates other than the current rate may be used only when the future tax rates have been enacted into law, as is apparently the case in this example. **If new rates are not yet enacted into law for future years, the current rate should be used.**

In determining the appropriate enacted tax rate for a given year, companies are required to use the **average tax rate**. The Internal Revenue Service and other taxing jurisdictions tax income on a graduated tax basis. For a U.S. corporation, the first $50,000 of taxable income is taxed at 15 percent, the next $25,000 at 25 percent, with higher incremental levels of income being taxed at rates as high as 39 percent. In computing deferred income taxes, companies for which graduated tax rates are a significant factor are therefore required to **determine the average tax rate and use that rate**.

Revision of Future Tax Rates

When a change in the tax rate is enacted into law, its effect on the existing deferred income tax accounts should be recorded immediately. **The effect is reported as an adjustment to income tax expense in the period of the change.**

Assume that on December 10, 2001, a new income tax act is signed into law that lowers the corporate tax rate from 40 percent to 35 percent, effective January 1, 2003. If Hostel Co. has one temporary difference at the beginning of 2001 related to $3 million of excess tax depreciation, then it has a Deferred Tax Liability account with a balance of $1,200,000 ($3,000,000 × 40%) at January 1, 2001. If taxable amounts related to this difference are scheduled to occur equally in 2002, 2003, and 2004, the deferred tax liability at the end of 2001 should be $1,100,000, computed as follows.

	2002	2003	2004	Total
Future taxable amounts	$1,000,000	$1,000,000	$1,000,000	$3,000,000
Tax rate	40%	35%	35%	
Deferred tax liability	$ 400,000	$ 350,000	$ 350,000	$1,100,000

Illustration 14-28
Schedule of Future Taxable Amounts and Related Tax Rates

An entry, therefore, would be made at the end of 2001 to recognize the decrease of $100,000 ($1,200,000 − $1,100,000) in the deferred tax liability as follows.

Deferred Tax Liability	100,000	
Income Tax Expense		100,000

Corporate tax rates do not change often and, therefore, the current rate will usually be employed. However, state and foreign tax rates change more frequently and they require adjustments in deferred income taxes accordingly.[5]

ACCOUNTING FOR NET OPERATING LOSSES

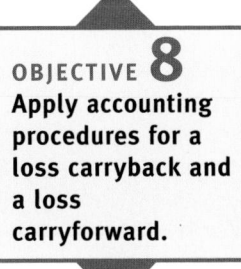

OBJECTIVE **8**
Apply accounting procedures for a loss carryback and a loss carryforward.

A **net operating loss (NOL)** occurs for tax purposes in a year when tax-deductible expenses exceed taxable revenues. An inequitable tax burden would result if companies were taxed during profitable periods without receiving any tax relief during periods of net operating losses. Under certain circumstances, therefore, the federal tax laws per-

[5]Tax rate changes nearly always will have a substantial impact on income numbers and the reporting of deferred income taxes on the balance sheet. As a result, you can expect to hear an economic consequences argument every time that Congress decides to change the tax rates. For example, when Congress raised the corporate rate from 34 percent to 35 percent in 1993, companies took an additional "hit" to earnings if they were in a deferred tax liability position.

mit taxpayers to use the losses of one year to offset the profits of other years. This income-averaging provision is accomplished through the **carryback and carryforward of net operating losses**. Under this provision, a company pays no income taxes for a year in which it incurs a net operating loss. In addition, it may select one of the two options discussed below.

Loss Carryback

Through use of a **loss carryback**, a company may carry the net operating loss back 2 years and receive refunds for income taxes paid in those years. The loss must be applied to the earlier year first and then to the second year. Any loss remaining after the 2-year carryback may be **carried forward** up to 20 years to offset future taxable income.[6] The following diagram illustrates the loss carryback procedure, assuming a loss in 2004.

Illustration 14-29
Loss Carryback Procedure

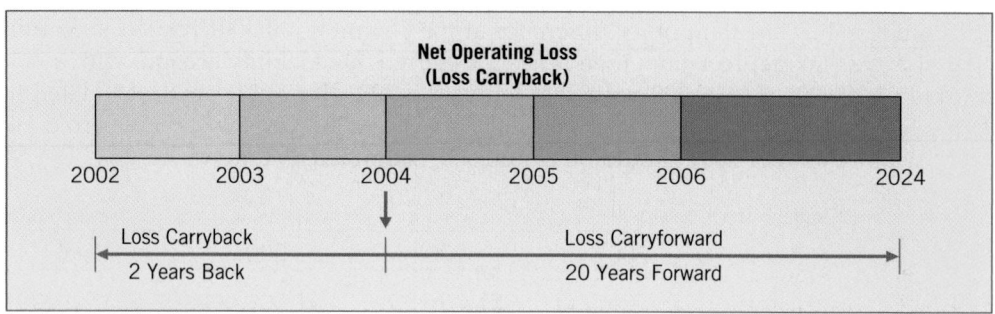

Loss Carryforward

A company may elect to forgo the loss carryback and use only the **loss carryforward** option, offsetting future taxable income for up to 20 years. Illustration 14-30 shows this approach.

Illustration 14-30
Loss Carryforward
Procedure

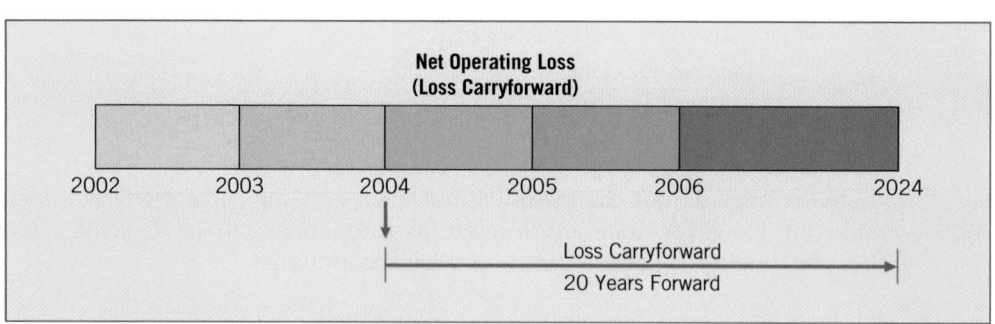

Operating losses can be substantial. **IBM Corporation**'s total losses exceeded $15 billion dollars for the years 1992 and 1993, representing billions of dollars in potential tax savings. Companies that have suffered substantial losses are often attractive merger candidates because in certain cases the acquirer may use these losses to reduce its own income taxes.

---

[6]For net operating losses arising in tax years 2001 and 2002, companies can carry back up to 5 years. This temporary change was designed to stimulate the economy in the wake of the terrorist attacks on 9/11/2001. For homework purposes, we will use a 2-year carryback period.

Loss Carryback Illustrated

To illustrate the accounting procedures for a net operating loss carryback, assume that Groh Inc. has no temporary or permanent differences. Groh experiences the following.

Year	Taxable Income or Loss	Tax Rate	Tax Paid
2000	$ 50,000	35%	$17,500
2001	100,000	30%	30,000
2002	200,000	40%	80,000
2003	(500,000)	—	–0–

In 2003, Groh Inc. incurs a net operating loss that it decides to carry back. Under the law, the carryback must be applied first to the **second year preceding the loss year**. Therefore, the loss would be carried back first to 2001. Any unused loss would then be carried back to 2002. Accordingly, Groh would file amended tax returns for 2001 and 2002, receiving refunds for the $110,000 ($30,000 + $80,000) of taxes paid in those years.

For accounting as well as tax purposes, the $110,000 represents the **tax effect (tax benefit) of the loss carryback**. This tax effect should be recognized in 2003, the loss year. Since the tax loss gives rise to a refund that is both measurable and currently realizable, the associated tax benefit should be recognized in this loss period.

The following journal entry is appropriate for 2003.

Income Tax Refund Receivable	110,000	
Benefit Due to Loss Carryback (Income Tax Expense)		110,000

The account debited, **Income Tax Refund Receivable**, is reported on the balance sheet as a current asset at December 31, 2003. The account credited is reported on the income statement for 2003 as follows.

GROH INC.	
INCOME STATEMENT (PARTIAL) FOR 2003	
Operating loss before income taxes	$(500,000)
Income tax benefit	
Benefit due to loss carryback	110,000
Net loss	$(390,000)

Illustration 14-31
Recognition of Benefit of the Loss Carryback in the Loss Year

Since the $500,000 net operating loss for 2003 exceeds the $300,000 total taxable income from the 2 preceding years, the remaining $200,000 loss is to be carried forward.

Loss Carryforward Illustrated

If a net operating loss is not fully absorbed through a carryback, or if the company decides not to carry the loss back, then it can be carried forward for up to 20 years.[7] Be-

---

[7]The length of the carryforward period has varied. It has increased from 7 years to 20 years over a period of time.

cause carryforwards are used to offset future taxable income, the **tax effect of a loss carryforward** represents **future tax savings**. Realization of the future tax benefit depends upon future earnings, the prospect of which may be highly uncertain.

The key accounting issue is whether there should be different requirements for recognition of a deferred tax asset for (a) deductible temporary differences, and (b) operating loss carryforwards. The FASB's position is that in substance these items are the same—both are amounts that are deductible on tax returns in future years. As a result, the Board concluded that there **should not be different requirements** for recognition of a deferred tax asset from deductible temporary differences and operating loss carryforwards.[8]

Carryforward without Valuation Allowance

To illustrate the accounting for an operating loss carryforward, return to the Groh Inc. example from the preceding section. In 2003 the company would record the tax effect of the $200,000 loss carryforward as a deferred tax asset of $80,000 ($200,000 × 40%) assuming that the enacted future tax rate is 40 percent. The journal entries to record the benefits of the carryback and the carryforward in 2003 would be as follows.

To recognize benefit of loss carryback

Income Tax Refund Receivable	110,000	
Benefit Due to Loss Carryback (Income Tax Expense)		110,000

To recognize benefit of loss carryforward

Deferred Tax Asset	80,000	
Benefit Due to Loss Carryforward (Income Tax Expense)		80,000

The income tax refund receivable of $110,000 will be realized immediately as a refund of taxes paid in the past. A Deferred Tax Asset is established for the benefits of future tax savings. The two accounts credited are contra income tax expense items, which would be presented on the 2003 income statement as follows.

Illustration 14-32
Recognition of the Benefit of the Loss Carryback and Carryforward in the Loss Year

GROH INC.		
INCOME STATEMENT (PARTIAL) FOR 2003		
Operating loss before income taxes		$(500,000)
Income tax benefit		
Benefit due to loss carryback	$110,000	
Benefit due to loss carryforward	80,000	190,000
Net loss		$(310,000)

The $110,000 **current tax benefit** is the income tax refundable for the year, which is determined by applying the carryback provisions of the tax law to the taxable loss for 2003. The $80,000 is the **deferred tax benefit** for the year, which results from an increase in the deferred tax asset.

For 2004, assume that Groh Inc. returns to profitable operations and has taxable income of $250,000 (prior to adjustment for the NOL carryforward) subject to a 40 per-

---

[8]This requirement is controversial because many do not believe it is appropriate to recognize deferred tax assets except when they are assured beyond a reasonable doubt. Others argue that deferred tax assets for loss carryforwards should never be recognized until income is realized in the future.

cent tax rate. Groh Inc. would then realize the benefits of the carryforward for tax purposes in 2004 which were recognized for accounting purposes in 2003. The income tax payable for 2004 is computed as follows.

Illustration 14-33
Computation of Income
Tax Payable with Realized
Loss Carryforward

Taxable income prior to loss carryforward	$ 250,000
Loss carryforward deduction	(200,000)
Taxable income for 2004	50,000
Tax rate	40%
Income tax payable for 2004	$ 20,000

The journal entry to record income taxes in 2004 would be as follows.

Income Tax Expense	100,000	
Deferred Tax Asset		80,000
Income Tax Payable		20,000

The Deferred Tax Asset account is reduced because the benefits of the NOL carryforward are realized in 2004.

The 2004 income statement that appears below would **not report** the tax effects of either the loss carryback or the loss carryforward, because both had been reported previously.

Illustration 14-34
Presentation of the Benefit of Loss Carryforward
Realized in 2004, Recognized in 2003

GROH INC.		
INCOME STATEMENT (PARTIAL) FOR 2004		
Income before income taxes		$250,000
Income tax expense		
Current	$20,000	
Deferred	80,000	100,000
Net income		$150,000

Carryforward with Valuation Allowance

Return to the Groh Inc. example. Assume that it is more likely than not that the entire NOL carryforward will not be realized in future years. In this situation, Groh Inc. records the tax benefits of $110,000 associated with the $300,000 NOL carryback, as previously described. In addition, it records a Deferred Tax Asset of $80,000 ($200,000 × 40%) for the potential benefits related to the loss carryforward, and an allowance to reduce the deferred tax asset by the same amount. The journal entries in 2003 are as follows.

To recognize benefit of loss carryback

Income Tax Refund Receivable	110,000	
Benefit Due to Loss Carryback (Income Tax Expense)		110,000

To recognize benefit of loss carryforward

Deferred Tax Asset	80,000	
Benefit Due to Loss Carryforward (Income Tax Expense)		80,000

To record allowance amount

Benefit Due to Loss Carryforward (Income Tax Expense)	80,000	
Allowance to Reduce Deferred Tax Asset		
to Expected Realizable Value		80,000

The latter entry indicates that because positive evidence of sufficient quality and quantity is not available to counteract the negative evidence, a valuation allowance is needed. The presentation in the 2003 income statement would be as follows.

Illustration 14-35
Recognition of Benefit of
Loss Carryback Only

GROH INC.	
INCOME STATEMENT (PARTIAL) FOR 2003	
Operating loss before income taxes	$(500,000)
Income tax benefit	
Benefit due to loss carryback	110,000
Net loss	$(390,000)

In 2004, assuming that the company has taxable income of $250,000 (before considering the carryforward) subject to a tax rate of 40 percent, the deferred tax asset is realized and the allowance is no longer needed. The following entries would be made.

To record current and deferred income taxes

Income Tax Expense	100,000	
Deferred Tax Asset		80,000
Income Tax Payable		20,000

To eliminate allowance and recognize loss carryforward

Allowance to Reduce Deferred Tax Asset to		
Expected Realizable Value	80,000	
Benefit Due to Loss Carryforward (Income Tax Expense)		80,000

The $80,000 Benefit Due to the Loss Carryforward is computed by multiplying the $200,000 loss carryforward by the 40 percent tax rate. This amount is reported on the 2004 income statement because it was not recognized in 2003. Assuming that the income for 2004 is derived from continuing operations, the income statement would be:

Illustration 14-36
Recognition of Benefit of
Loss Carryforward When
Realized

GROH INC.		
INCOME STATEMENT (PARTIAL) FOR 2004		
Income before income taxes		$250,000
Income tax expense		
Current	$ 20,000	
Deferred	80,000	
Benefit due to loss carryforward	(80,000)	20,000
Net income		$230,000

Another method is to report only one line for total income tax expense of $20,000 on the face of the income statement and disclose the components of income tax expense in the notes to the financial statements.

Valuation Allowance Revisited

All positive and negative information should be considered in determining whether a valuation allowance is needed. Whether a deferred tax asset will be realized depends on whether sufficient taxable income exists or will exist within the carryback or carryforward period available under tax law. The following possible sources of taxable income may be available under the tax law to realize a tax benefit for deductible temporary differences and carryforwards.

Taxable Income Sources

a. Future reversals of existing taxable temporary differences

b. Future taxable income exclusive of reversing temporary differences and carryforwards

c. Taxable income in prior carryback year(s) if carryback is permitted under the tax law

d. **Tax-planning strategies** that would, if necessary, be implemented to:
   (1) Accelerate taxable amounts to utilize expiring carryforwards
   (2) Change the character of taxable or deductible amounts from ordinary income or loss to capital gain or loss
   (3) Switch from tax-exempt to taxable investments.[9]

Illustration 14-37
Possible Sources of Taxable Income

If any one of these sources is sufficient to support a conclusion that a valuation allowance is not necessary, other sources need not be considered.

Forming a conclusion that a valuation allowance is not needed is difficult when there is negative evidence such as cumulative losses in recent years. Companies may also cite positive evidence indicating that a valuation allowance is not needed. Examples (not prerequisites) of evidence to consider when determining the need for a valuation allowance are presented in Illustration 14-38.

Negative Evidence

a. A history of operating loss or tax credit carryforwards expiring unused

b. Losses expected in early future years (by a presently profitable entity)

c. Unsettled circumstances that, if unfavorably resolved, would adversely affect future operations and profit levels on a continuing basis in future years

d. A carryback, carryforward period that is so brief that it would limit realization of tax benefits if (1) a significant deductible temporary difference is expected to reverse in a single year or (2) the enterprise operates in a traditionally cyclical business.

Positive Evidence

a. Existing contracts or firm sales backlog that will produce more than enough taxable income to realize the deferred tax asset based on existing sale prices and cost structures

b. An excess of appreciated asset value over the tax basis of the entity's net assets in an amount sufficient to realize the deferred tax asset

c. A strong earnings history exclusive of the loss that created the future deductible amount (tax loss carryforward or deductible temporary difference) coupled with evidence indicating that the loss (for example, an unusual, infrequent, or extraordinary item) is an aberration rather than a continuing condition.[10]

Illustration 14-38
Evidence to Consider in Evaluating the Need for a Valuation Account

INTERNATIONAL INSIGHT

Under international accounting standards *(IAS 12)*, a deferred tax asset may not be recognized unless realization is "probable." However, "probable" is not defined in the standard, leading to diversity in the recognition of deferred tax assets.

---

[9]"Accounting for Income Taxes," *Statement of Financial Accounting Standards No. 109* (Norwalk, Conn.: FASB, 1992). A tax-planning strategy is an action that would be implemented to realize a tax benefit for an operating loss or tax credit carryforward before it expires. Tax-planning strategies are considered when assessing the need for and amount of a valuation allowance for deferred tax assets.

[10]Ibid., par. 23 and 24.

The use of a valuation allowance provides management with an opportunity to manage its earnings. As one accounting expert notes, "The 'more likely than not' provision is perhaps the most judgmental clause in accounting." What some companies might do is set up valuation accounts and then use the valuation account to increase income as needed. Others could take the income immediately to increase capital or to offset large negative charges to income.

WHAT DO THE NUMBERS MEAN?

READ THOSE NOTES

A recent study of companies' valuation allowances indicates that the allowances are related to the factors identified as positive and negative evidence. And though there is little evidence that the valuation allowance is used to manage earnings,[11] the press sometimes understates the impact of reversing the deferred tax valuation allowance. For example, **Verity, Inc.** eliminated its entire valuation allowance of $18.9 million in 2000 but focused on a net deferred tax gain of $2.9 million in its press release. Why the difference? As revealed in Verity's financial statement notes, other deferred tax expense amounts totaled over $16 million. Thus, the one-time valuation reversal gave an $18.9 million bump to income, not the net $2.9 million reported in the press. The lesson: After you read the morning paper, read the financial statement notes.

FINANCIAL STATEMENT PRESENTATION

Balance Sheet

OBJECTIVE 9
Describe the presentation of deferred income taxes in financial statements.

Deferred tax accounts are reported on the balance sheet as assets and liabilities. They should be classified as a net current amount and a net noncurrent amount. **An individual deferred tax liability or asset is classified as current or noncurrent based on the classification of the related asset or liability for financial reporting purposes.** A deferred tax asset or liability is considered to be related to an asset or liability if reduction of the asset or liability will cause the temporary difference to reverse or turn around. A deferred tax liability or asset that is not related to an asset or liability for financial reporting, including a deferred tax asset related to a loss carryforward, should be classified according to the expected reversal date of the temporary difference.

To illustrate, assume that Morgan Inc. records bad debt expense using the allowance method for accounting purposes and the direct write-off method for tax purposes. The company currently has Accounts Receivable and Allowance for Doubtful Accounts balances of $2 million and $100,000, respectively. In addition, given a 40 percent tax rate, it has a debit balance in the Deferred Tax Asset account of $40,000 (40% × $100,000). The $40,000 debit balance in the Deferred Tax Asset account is considered to be related to the Accounts Receivable and the Allowance for Doubtful Accounts balances because collection or write-off of the receivables will cause the temporary difference to reverse. Therefore, the Deferred Tax Asset account is classified as current, the same as the Accounts Receivable and Allowance for Doubtful Accounts balances.

In practice, most companies engage in a large number of transactions that give rise to deferred taxes. The balances in the deferred tax accounts should be analyzed and classified on the balance sheet in two categories: one for the **net current amount**, and one for the **net noncurrent amount**. This procedure is summarized as follows.

[11]G. S. Miller and D. J. Skinner, "Determinants of the Valuation Allowance for Deferred Tax Assets under *SFAS No. 109*," *The Accounting Review* (April 1998).

⟨1⟩ *Classify the amounts as current or noncurrent.* If they are related to a specific asset or liability, the amounts should be classified in the same manner as the related asset or liability. If not so related, they should be classified on the basis of the expected reversal date of the temporary difference.

⟨2⟩ *Determine the net current amount* by summing the various deferred tax assets and liabilities classified as current. If the net result is an asset, report it on the balance sheet as a current asset; if a liability, report it as a current liability.

⟨3⟩ *Determine the net noncurrent amount* by summing the various deferred tax assets and liabilities classified as noncurrent. If the net result is an asset, report it on the balance sheet as a noncurrent asset; if a liability, report it as a long-term liability.

To illustrate, assume that K. Scott Company has four deferred tax items at December 31, 2004. An analysis reveals the following.

Illustration 14-39
Classification of Temporary Differences as Current or Noncurrent

Temporary Difference	Resulting Deferred Tax (Asset)	Liability	Related Balance Sheet Account	Classification
1. Rent collected in advance: recognized when earned for accounting purposes and when received for tax purposes.	$(42,000)		Unearned Rent	Current
2. Use of straight-line depreciation for accounting purposes and accelerated depreciation for tax purposes.		$214,000	Equipment	Noncurrent
3. Recognition of profits on installment sales during period of sale for accounting purposes and during period of collection for tax purposes.		45,000	Installment Accounts Receivable	Current
4. Warranty liabilities: recognized for accounting purposes at time of sale; for tax purposes at time paid.	(12,000)		Estimated Liability under Warranties	Current
Totals	$(54,000)	$259,000		

The deferred taxes to be classified as current net to a $9,000 asset ($42,000 + $12,000 − $45,000). The deferred taxes to be classified as noncurrent net to a $214,000 liability. Consequently, deferred income taxes would appear on K. Scott's December 31, 2004, balance sheet, as shown in Illustration 14-40.

Illustration 14-40
Balance Sheet Presentation of Deferred Income Taxes

Current assets	
Deferred tax asset	$ 9,000
Long-term liabilities	
Deferred tax liability	$214,000

As indicated earlier, a deferred tax asset or liability **may not be related** to an asset or liability for financial reporting purposes. One example is an operating loss carryforward. In this case, a deferred tax asset is recorded, but there is no related, identifiable asset or liability for financial reporting purposes. In these limited situations, deferred income taxes should be classified according to the **expected reversal date** of the temporary difference. That is, the tax effect of any temporary difference reversing next year should be reported as current, and the remainder should be reported as noncurrent. If a deferred tax asset is noncurrent, it should be classified in the "Other assets" section.

The total of all deferred tax liabilities, the total of all deferred tax assets, and the total valuation allowance should be disclosed. In addition, the following should be disclosed: (1) any net change during the year in the total valuation allowance, and (2) the types of temporary differences, carryforwards, or carrybacks that give rise to significant portions of deferred tax liabilities and assets.

Income tax payable is shown as a current liability on the balance sheet. Corporations are required to make estimated tax payments to the Internal Revenue Service quarterly. These estimated payments are recorded by a debit to Prepaid Income Taxes. As a result, the balance of the Income Tax Payable is offset by the balance of the Prepaid Income Taxes account when reporting income taxes on the balance sheet.

Income Statement

Expanded Discussion of Intraperiod Tax Allocation

Income tax expense (or benefit) should be allocated to continuing operations, discontinued operations, extraordinary items, the cumulative effect of accounting changes, and prior period adjustments. This approach is referred to as intraperiod tax allocation.

In addition, the significant components of income tax expense attributable to continuing operations should be disclosed:

1. Current tax expense or benefit.
2. Deferred tax expense or benefit, exclusive of other components listed below.
3. Investment tax credits.
4. Government grants (to the extent they are recognized as a reduction of income tax expense).
5. The benefits of operating loss carryforwards (resulting in a reduction of income tax expense).
6. Tax expense that results from allocating certain tax benefits either directly to paid-in capital or to reduce goodwill or other noncurrent intangible assets of an acquired entity.
7. Adjustments of a deferred tax liability or asset for enacted changes in tax laws or rates or a change in the tax status of an enterprise.
8. Adjustments of the beginning-of-the-year balance of a valuation allowance because of a change in circumstances that causes a change in judgment about the realizability of the related deferred tax asset in future years.

Additional Examples of Deferred Tax Disclosures

In the notes, companies are also required to reconcile (using percentages or dollar amounts) income tax expense attributable to continuing operations with the amount that results from applying domestic federal statutory tax rates to pretax income from continuing operations. The estimated amount and the nature of each significant reconciling item should be disclosed. An example from the 2000 Annual Report of **PepsiCo, Inc.** is presented in Illustration 14-41.

PEPSICO

Illustration 14-41
Disclosure of Income
Taxes—PepsiCo, Inc.

PEPSICO, INC.
(in millions)

Note 13: Income Taxes

U.S. and foreign income before income taxes:

	2000	1999
U.S.	$2,126	$2,771
Foreign	1,084	885
	$3,210	$3,656

Provision for income taxes:

		2000	1999
Current:	Federal	$ 771	$ 730
	Foreign	157	306
	State	36	40
		964	1,076
Deferred:	Federal	60	519
	Foreign	(10)	(12)
	State	13	23
		63	530
		$1,027	$1,606

Reconciliation of the U.S. Federal statutory tax rate to our effective tax rate:

	2000	1999
U.S. Federal statutory tax rate	35.0%	35.0%
State income tax, net of Federal tax benefit	1.0	1.1
Lower taxes on foreign results	(3.0)	(2.7)
Bottling transactions	–	10.6
Other, net	(1.0)	(0.1)
Effective tax rate	32.0%	43.9%

Deferred taxes are recorded to give recognition to temporary differences between the tax bases of assets or liabilities and their reported amounts in the financial statements. We record the tax effect of these temporary differences as deferred tax assets or deferred tax liabilities. Deferred tax assets generally represent items that can be used as a tax deduction or credit in future years. Deferred tax liabilities generally represent items that we have taken a tax deduction for, but have not yet recorded in the Consolidated Statement of income.

Deferred tax liabilities (assets):

	2000	1999
Investments in unconsolidated affiliates	$ 672	$ 667
Property, plant, and equipment	576	545
Safe harbor leases	94	101
Zero-coupon notes	73	76
Intangible assets other than nondeductible goodwill	54	47
Other	404	328
Gross deferred tax liabilities	1,873	1,764
Net operating loss carryforwards	(443)	(450)
Postretirement benefits	(187)	(179)
Various current liabilities and other	(640)	(626)
Gross deferred tax assets	(1,270)	(1,255)
Deferred tax assets valuation allowances	464	461
Deferred tax assets, net of valuation allowances	(806)	(794)
Net deferred tax liabilities	$ 1,067	$ 970
Included in:		
Prepaid expenses and other current assets	$ (294)	$ (239)
Deferred income taxes	1,361	1,209
	$ 1,067	$ 970

Net operating loss carryforwards totaling $2.9 billion at year-end 2000 are being carried forward and are available to reduce future taxable income of certain subsidiaries in a number of foreign and state jurisdictions. These net operating losses will expire as follows: $0.1 billion in 2001, $2.5 billion between 2002 and 2016, and $0.3 billion may be carried forward indefinitely.

Valuation allowances have been established primarily for deferred tax assets related to net operating losses in certain state and foreign tax jurisdictions where the amount of expected future taxable income from operations does not support the recognition of these deferred tax assets.

These income tax disclosures are required for several reasons. Three of these reasons are:

① *Assessing Quality of Earnings.* Many investors seeking to assess the quality of a company's earnings are interested in the reconciliation of pretax financial income to taxable income. Earnings that are enhanced by a favorable tax effect should be examined carefully, particularly if the tax effect is nonrecurring. For example, the tax disclosure in Illustration 14-41 indicates that **PepsiCo**'s effective tax rate declined from 43.9 percent in 1999 to 32 percent in 2000. The decline translates into a tax savings of $579 million. That savings offset the decline in income before taxes and allowed PepsiCo to report a slight increase in bottom-line income from 1999 to 2000.

② *Making Better Predictions of Future Cash Flows.* Examination of the deferred portion of income tax expense provides information as to whether taxes payable are likely to be higher or lower in the future. In **PepsiCo**'s case, significant future taxable amounts and higher tax payments are expected, due to lower depreciation in the future and realization of gains on equity investments. As a result, it may be possible to predict future reductions in deferred tax liabilities leading to a loss of liquidity because actual tax payments will be higher than the tax expense reported on the income statement.[12]

③ *Predicting Future Cash Flows from Operating Loss Carryforwards.* The amounts and expiration dates of any operating loss carryforwards for tax purposes should be disclosed. From this disclosure, the reader can determine the amount of income that may be recognized in the future on which no income tax will be paid. For example, the **PepsiCo** disclosure in Illustration 14-41 indicates that PepsiCo has $2.9 billion in net operating loss carryforwards that can be used to reduce future taxes up to the year 2016 and beyond.

Loss carryforwards can be extremely valuable to a potential acquirer. At one time, **Dalfort Company** received nearly $360 million in operating loss carryforwards and other credits as a result of its ownership of **Braniff Airlines**. Many speculate that Dalfort bought **Levitz Furniture Corp.** (a large discounter of quality furniture) so that it could offset its carryforward losses from Braniff against Levitz's earnings. Companies that have suffered substantial losses may find themselves worth more "dead" than alive because their tax losses have little value to themselves but great value to other enterprises. In short, substantial tax carryforwards can have real economic value.[13]

REVIEW OF THE ASSET-LIABILITY METHOD

OBJECTIVE **10**
Indicate the basic principles of the asset-liability method.

The FASB believes that the **asset-liability method** (sometimes referred to as the liability approach) is the most consistent method for accounting for income taxes. One objective of this approach is to recognize the amount of taxes payable or refundable for the current year. A second objective is to recognize **deferred tax liabilities and assets**

[12]An article by R. P. Weber and J. E. Wheeler, "Using Income Tax Disclosures to Explore Significant Economic Transactions," *Accounting Horizons* (September 1992), discusses how deferred tax disclosures can be used to assess the quality of earnings and to predict future cash flows.

[13]The IRS frowns on acquisitions done solely to obtain operating loss carryforwards. If the merger is determined to be solely tax motivated, then the deductions will be disallowed. But because it is very difficult to determine whether a merger is or is not tax motivated, the "purchase of operating loss carryforwards" continues.

SHELTERED

WHAT DO THE NUMBERS MEAN?

As mentioned in the opening story, companies employ various tax strategies to reduce their tax bills. The following table reports some recent high-profile cases in which profitable companies during the 1996–2000 time period paid little income tax, and in some cases got tax refunds.

Company	Pre-Tax Income ($ millions)	Federal Tax Paid (Refund) ($ millions)	Tax Rate (%)
Enron	$ 1,785	$(381)	(21.34)%
El Paso Energy	1,638	(254)	(15.51)
Goodyear	442	(23)	(5.20)
Navistar	1,368	28	2.05
General Motors	12,468	740	5.94

These companies used various tools to lower their tax bills, including off-shore tax shelters, tax deferrals, and hefty use of stock options, the cost of which reduce taxable income but do not affect pretax financial income.[14] Thus, companies can use various provisions in the tax code to reduce their effective tax rate well below the statutory rate of 35 percent.

One IRS provision designed to curb excessive tax avoidance is the **alternative minimum tax (AMT)**, in which companies compute their potential tax liability, after adjusting for various preference items that reduce their tax bills under the regular tax code. (Examples of such preference items are accelerated depreciation methods and the installment method for revenue recognition.) Companies must pay the higher of the two tax obligations computed under the AMT and the regular tax code. But, as indicated by the cases above, some profitable companies are able to avoid high tax bills, even in the presence of the AMT. Maybe we are in for some more tax reform?

for the **future tax consequences** of events that have been recognized in the financial statements or tax returns.

To implement the objectives, the following basic principles are applied in accounting for income taxes at the date of the financial statements.

Basic Principles

a. A current tax liability or asset is recognized for the estimated taxes payable or refundable on the tax return for the current year.

b. A deferred tax liability or asset is recognized for the estimated future tax effects attributable to temporary differences and carryforwards.

c. The measurement of current and deferred tax liabilities and assets is based on provisions of the enacted tax law; the effects of future changes in tax laws or rates are not anticipated.

d. The measurement of deferred tax assets is reduced, if necessary, by the amount of any tax benefits that, based on available evidence, are not expected to be realized.[15]

Illustration 14-42
Basic Principles of the Asset-Liability Method

Discussion of Conceptual Approaches to Interperiod Tax Allocation

[14]H. Gleckman, D. Foust, M. Arndt, and K. Kerwin, "Tax Dodging: Enron Isn't Alone," *Business Week* (March 4, 2002), pp. 40-41.

[15]"Accounting for Income Taxes" (1992), par. 6 and 8.

The procedures for implementing the asset-liability method are shown in Illustration 14-43.

Illustration 14-43

Procedures for Computing and Reporting Deferred Income Taxes

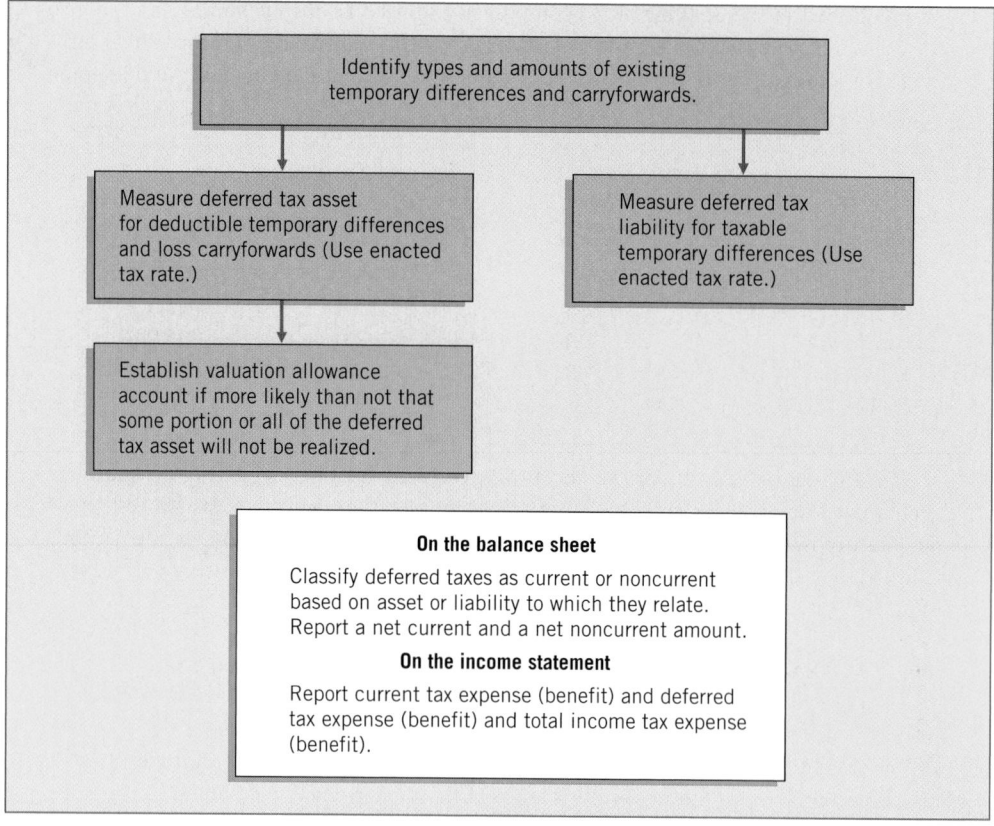

As an aid to understanding deferred income taxes, we provide the following glossary.[16]

KEY DEFERRED INCOME TAX TERMS

CARRYBACKS. Deductions or credits that cannot be utilized on the tax return during a year and that may be carried back to reduce taxable income or taxes paid in a prior year. An **operating loss carryback** is an excess of tax deductions over gross income in a year; a **tax credit carryback** is the amount by which tax credits available for utilization exceed statutory limitations.

CARRYFORWARDS. Deductions or credits that cannot be utilized on the tax return during a year and that may be carried forward to reduce taxable income or taxes payable in a future year. An **operating loss carryforward** is an excess of tax deductions over gross income in a year; a **tax credit carryforward** is the amount by which tax credits available for utilization exceed statutory limitations.

CURRENT TAX EXPENSE (BENEFIT). The amount of income taxes paid or payable (or refundable) for a year as determined by applying the provisions of the enacted tax law to the taxable income or excess of deductions over revenues for that year.

---

[16]"Accounting for Income Taxes," Appendix E.

DEDUCTIBLE TEMPORARY DIFFERENCE. Temporary differences that result in deductible amounts in future years when the related asset or liability is recovered or settled, respectively.

DEFERRED TAX ASSET. The deferred tax consequences attributable to deductible temporary differences and carryforwards.

DEFERRED TAX CONSEQUENCES. The future effects on income taxes as measured by the enacted tax rate and provisions of the enacted tax law resulting from temporary differences and carryforwards at the end of the current year.

DEFERRED TAX EXPENSE (BENEFIT). The change during the year in an enterprise's deferred tax liabilities and assets.

DEFERRED TAX LIABILITY. The deferred tax consequences attributable to taxable temporary differences.

INCOME TAXES. Domestic and foreign federal (national), state, and local (including franchise) taxes based on income.

INCOME TAXES CURRENTLY PAYABLE (REFUNDABLE). Refer to current tax expense (benefit).

INCOME TAX EXPENSE (BENEFIT). The sum of current tax expense (benefit) and deferred tax expense (benefit).

TAXABLE INCOME. The excess of taxable revenues over tax deductible expenses and exemptions for the year as defined by the governmental taxing authority.

TAXABLE TEMPORARY DIFFERENCE. Temporary differences that result in taxable amounts in future years when the related asset or liability is recovered or settled, respectively.

TAX-PLANNING STRATEGY. An action that meets certain criteria and that would be implemented to realize a tax benefit for an operating loss or tax credit carryforward before it expires. Tax-planning strategies are considered when assessing the need for and amount of a valuation allowance for deferred tax assets.

TEMPORARY DIFFERENCE. A difference between the tax basis of an asset or liability and its reported amount in the financial statements that will result in taxable or deductible amounts in future years when the reported amount of the asset or liability is recovered or settled, respectively.

VALUATION ALLOWANCE. The portion of a deferred tax asset for which it is more likely than not that a tax benefit will not be realized.

INTERNATIONAL INSIGHT

Nations that recognize deferred taxes using the liability method include, among others, Australia, Germany, the United Kingdom, and Spain. IASB standards for taxes also use the liability method. The European Directives do not specify the accounting for deferred taxes.

SUMMARY OF LEARNING OBJECTIVES

❶ Identify differences between pretax financial income and taxable income. Pretax financial income (or income for book purposes) is computed in accordance with generally accepted accounting principles. Taxable income (or income for tax purposes) is computed in accordance with prescribed tax regulations. Because tax regulations and GAAP are different in many ways, pretax financial income and taxable income frequently differ. Differences may exist, for example, in the timing of revenue recognition and the timing of expense recognition.

❷ Describe a temporary difference that results in future taxable amounts. A credit sale that is recognized as revenue for book purposes in the period it is earned but is deferred and reported as revenue for tax purposes in the period it is collected will result in future taxable amounts. The future taxable amounts will occur in the periods the

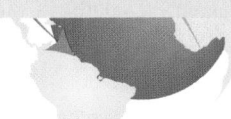

KEY TERMS

alternative minimum tax, *711*
asset-liability method, *710*
average tax rate, *699*
current tax benefit (expense), *702*
deductible amounts, *686*
deductible temporary difference, *695*
deferred tax asset, *691*

deferred tax expense
(benefit), *688, 690*

deferred tax liability, *687*

effective tax rate, *698*

enacted tax rate, *698*

Income Tax Refund
Receivable, *701*

loss carryback, *700*

loss carryforward, *700*

more likely than not, *693*

net current amount, *706*

net noncurrent amount,
706

net operating loss (NOL),
699

originating temporary
difference, *696*

permanent difference, *696*

pretax financial income, *684*

reversing difference, *696*

taxable amounts, *686*

taxable income, *684*

taxable temporary
difference, *695*

tax effect (tax benefit), *701*

temporary difference, *686*

valuation allowance, *693*

receivable is recovered and the collections are reported as revenue for tax purposes. This results in a deferred tax liability.

❸ Describe a temporary difference that results in future deductible amounts. An accrued warranty expense that is paid for and is deductible for tax purposes in a period later than the period in which it is incurred and recognized for book purposes will result in future deductible amounts. The future deductible amounts will occur in the periods during which the related liability for book purposes is settled. This results in a deferred tax asset.

❹ Explain the purpose of a deferred tax asset valuation allowance. A deferred tax asset should be reduced by a valuation allowance if, based on all available evidence, it is more likely than not (a level of likelihood that is at least slightly more than 50 percent) that some portion or all of the deferred tax asset will not be realized. All available evidence, both positive and negative, should be carefully considered to determine whether, based on the weight of available evidence, a valuation allowance is needed.

❺ Describe the presentation of income tax expense in the income statement. The significant components of income tax expense should be disclosed in the income statement or in the notes to the financial statements. The most commonly encountered components are the current expense (or benefit) and the deferred expense (or benefit).

❻ Describe various temporary and permanent differences. Examples of temporary differences are: (1) revenue or gains that are taxable after they are recognized in financial income; (2) expenses or losses that are deductible after they are recognized in financial income; (3) revenues or gains that are taxable before they are recognized in financial income; (4) expenses or losses that are deductible before they are recognized in financial income. Examples of permanent differences are: (1) items recognized for financial reporting purposes but not for tax purposes, and (2) items recognized for tax purposes but not for financial reporting purposes.

❼ Explain the effect of various tax rates and tax rate changes on deferred income taxes. Tax rates other than the current rate may be used only when the future tax rates have been enacted into law. When a change in the tax rate is enacted into law, its effect on the deferred income tax accounts should be recognized immediately. The effects are reported as an adjustment to income tax expense in the period of the change.

❽ Apply accounting procedures for a loss carryback and a loss carryforward. A company may carry a net operating loss back 2 years and receive refunds for income taxes paid in those years. The loss must be applied to the earlier year first and then to the second year. Any loss remaining after the 2-year carryback may be carried forward up to 20 years to offset future taxable income. A company may forgo the loss carryback and use the loss carryforward, offsetting future taxable income for up to 20 years.

❾ Describe the presentation of deferred income taxes in financial statements. Deferred tax accounts are reported on the balance sheet as assets and liabilities. They should be classified as a net current and a net noncurrent amount. An individual deferred tax liability or asset is classified as current or noncurrent based on the classification of the related asset or liability for financial reporting. A deferred tax liability or asset that is not related to an asset or liability for financial reporting, including a deferred tax asset related to a loss carryforward, should be classified according to the expected reversal date of the temporary difference.

❿ Indicate the basic principles of the asset-liability method. The following basic principles are applied in accounting for income taxes at the date of the financial statements: (1) A current tax liability or asset is recognized for the estimated taxes payable or refundable on the tax return for the current year. (2) A deferred tax liability or asset is recognized for the estimated future tax effects attributable to temporary differences and carryforwards using the enacted tax rate. (3) The measurement of current and deferred tax liabilities and assets is based on provisions of the enacted tax law. (4) The mea-

Comprehensive Illustration of Interperiod Tax Allocation

surement of deferred tax assets is reduced, if necessary, by the amount of any tax benefits that, based on available evidence, are not expected to be realized.

REVIEW EXERCISE

Johnny Bravo Company began operations in 2002 and has provided the following information.

1. Pretax financial income for 2002 is $100,000.

2. The tax rate enacted for 2002 and future years is 40%.

3. Differences between the 2002 income statement and tax return are listed below.
   (a) Warranty expense accrued for financial reporting purposes amounts to $5,000. Warranty deductions per the tax return amount to $2,000.
   (b) Gross profit on construction contracts using the percentage-of-completion method for books amounts to $92,000. Gross profit on construction contracts for tax purposes amounts to $62,000.
   (c) Depreciation of property, plant, and equipment for financial reporting purposes amounts to $60,000. Depreciation of these assets amounts to $80,000 for the tax return.
   (d) A $3,500 fine paid for violation of pollution laws was deducted in computing pretax financial income.
   (e) Interest revenue earned on an investment in tax-exempt municipal bonds amounts to $1,400.
   Assume (a) is short-term in nature; assume (b) and (c) are long-term in nature.

4. Taxable income is expected for the next few years.

Instructions
(a) Compute taxable income for 2002.
(b) Compute the deferred taxes at December 31, 2002, that relate to the temporary differences described above.
(c) Prepare the journal entry to record income tax expense, deferred taxes, and income taxes payable for 2002.
(d) Draft the income tax expense section of the income statement beginning with "Income before income taxes."
(e) Assume that in 2003 Johnny Bravo reported a pretax operating loss of $100,000. There were no other temporary or permanent differences in tax and book income for 2003. Prepare the journal entry to record income tax expense for 2003. Johnny Bravo expects to return to profitability in 2004.

SOLUTION TO REVIEW EXERCISE

(a)		
Pretax financial income		$100,000
Permanent differences		
Fine for pollution		3,500
Tax-exempt interest		(1,400)
Originating temporary differences		
Excess warranty expense per books		
($5,000 – $2,000)		3,000
Excess construction profits per books		
($92,000 – $62,000)		(30,000)
Excess depreciation per tax		
($80,000 – $60,000)		(20,000)
Taxable income		$ 55,100

(b)

Temporary Difference	Future Taxable (Deductible) Amounts	Tax Rate	Deferred Tax (Asset)	Liability
Warranty costs	$ (3,000)	40%	$(1,200)	
Construction contracts	30,000	40%		$12,000
Depreciation	20,000	40%		8,000
Totals	$47,000		$(1,200)	$20,000*

*Because of a flat tax rate, these totals can be reconciled: $47,000 × 40% = $(1,200) + $20,000.

(c)

```
Income Tax Expense              40,840
Deferred Tax Asset               1,200
     Deferred Tax Liability              20,000
     Income Tax Payable                  22,040
```

Taxable income for 2002 [from part (a)]	$ 55,100
Tax rate	40%
Income tax payable for 2002	$ 22,040

Deferred tax liability at the end of 2002 [from part (b)]	$ 20,000
Deferred tax liability at the beginning of 2002	–0–
Deferred tax expense for 2002	$ 20,000

Deferred tax asset at the end of 2002	$ 1,200
Deferred tax asset at the beginning of 2002	–0–
Deferred tax benefit for 2002	$ (1,200)

(d)

Income before income taxes		$100,000
Income tax expense		
Current	$22,040	
Deferred	18,800	40,840
Net income		$ 59,160

(e)

```
Income Tax Refund Receivable*        22,040
Deferred Tax Asset**                 17,960
     Benefit from Operating Loss Carryback        22,040
     Benefit from Operating Loss Carryforward     17,960
```

2003 Loss $100,000
*Carryback   (55,100) × 40% = $22,040 refund
**Carryforward $ 44,900 × 40% = $17,960 deferred tax asset

No valuation allowance is needed, since Johnny Bravo is expected to return to profitability in 2004. This is positive evidence that the deferred tax asset will be realized.

QUESTIONS

1 Explain the difference between pretax financial income and taxable income.

2 What are the two objectives of accounting for income taxes?

3 Interest on municipal bonds is referred to as a permanent difference when determining the proper amount to report for deferred taxes. Explain the meaning of permanent differences, and give two other examples.

4 Explain the meaning of a temporary difference as it relates to deferred tax computations, and give three examples.

5 Differentiate between an originating temporary difference and a reversing difference.

6 The book basis of depreciable assets for Guinan Co. is $900,000, and the tax basis is $700,000 at the end of 2004. The enacted tax rate is 34% for all periods. Determine the amount of deferred taxes to be reported on the balance sheet at the end of 2004.

7 Borg Inc. has a deferred tax liability of $68,000 at the beginning of 2004. At the end of 2004, it reports accounts receivable on the books at $80,000 and the tax basis at zero (its only temporary difference). If the enacted tax rate is 34% for all periods, and income tax payable for the period is $230,000, determine the amount of total income tax expense to report for 2004.

8 What is the difference between a future taxable amount and a future deductible amount? When is it appropriate to record a valuation account for a deferred tax asset?

9 Pretax financial income for Mott Inc. is $300,000, and its taxable income is $100,000 for 2004. Its only temporary difference at the end of the period relates to a $90,000 difference due to excess depreciation for tax purposes. If the tax rate is 40% for all periods, compute the amount of income tax expense to report in 2004. No deferred income taxes existed at the beginning of the year.

10 How are deferred tax assets and deferred tax liabilities reported on the balance sheet?

11 Describe the procedures involved in segregating various deferred tax amounts into current and noncurrent categories.

12 How is it determined whether deferred tax amounts are considered to be "related" to specific assets or liability amounts?

13 At the end of the year, North Carolina Co. has pretax financial income of $550,000. Included in the $550,000 is $70,000 interest income on municipal bonds, $30,000 fine for dumping hazardous waste, and depreciation of $60,000. Depreciation for tax purposes is $45,000. Compute income taxes payable, assuming the tax rate is 30% for all periods.

14 Raleigh Co. has one temporary difference at the beginning of 2004 of $500,000. The deferred tax liability established for this amount is $150,000, based on a tax rate of 30%. The temporary difference will provide the following taxable amounts: $100,000 in 2005; $200,000 in 2006, and $200,000 in 2007. If a new tax rate for 2007 of 25% is enacted into law at the end of 2004, what is the journal entry necessary in 2004 (if any) to adjust deferred taxes?

15 What are some of the reasons that the components of income tax expense should be disclosed and a reconciliation between the effective tax rate and the statutory tax rate be provided?

16 Differentiate between "carryback" and "carryforward." Which can be accounted for with the greater certainty when it arises? Why?

17 What are the possible treatments for tax purposes of a net operating loss? What are the circumstances that determine the option to be applied? What is the proper treatment of a net operating loss for financial reporting purposes?

18 What controversy relates to the accounting for net operating loss carryforwards?

BRIEF EXERCISES

BE14-1 In 2004, Speedy Gonzalez Corporation had pretax financial income of $168,000 and taxable income of $110,000. The difference is due to the use of different depreciation methods for tax and accounting purposes. The effective tax rate is 40%. Compute the amount to be reported as income taxes payable at December 31, 2004.

BE14-2 Murphy Corporation began operations in 2004 and reported pretax financial income of $225,000 for the year. Murphy's tax depreciation exceeded its book depreciation by $30,000. Murphy's tax rate for 2004 and years thereafter is 30%. In its December 31, 2004 balance sheet, what amount of deferred tax liability should be reported?

BE14-3 Using the information from BE14-2, assume this is the only difference between Murphy's pretax financial income and taxable income. Prepare the journal entry to record the income tax expense, deferred income taxes, and income tax payable, and show how the deferred tax liability will be classified on the December 31, 2004, balance sheet.

BE14-4 At December 31, 2003, Yserbius Corporation had a deferred tax liability of $25,000. At December 31, 2004, the deferred tax liability is $42,000. The corporation's 2004 current tax expense is $43,000. What amount should Yserbius report as total 2004 tax expense?

BE14-5 At December 31, 2004, Deep Space Nine Corporation had an estimated warranty liability of $125,000 for accounting purposes and $0 for tax purposes. (The warranty costs are not deductible until paid.) The effective tax rate is 40%. Compute the amount Deep Space Nine should report as a deferred tax asset at December 31, 2004.

BE14-6 At December 31, 2003, Next Generation Inc. had a deferred tax asset of $35,000. At December 31, 2004, the deferred tax asset is $59,000. The corporation's 2004 current tax expense is $61,000. What amount should Next Generation report as total 2004 tax expense?

BE14-7 At December 31, 2004, Stargate Corporation has a deferred tax asset of $200,000. After a careful review of all available evidence, it is determined that it is more likely than not that $80,000 of this deferred tax asset will not be realized. Prepare the necessary journal entry.

BE14-8 Steven Seagal Corporation had income before income taxes of $175,000 in 2004. Seagal's current income tax expense is $40,000, and deferred income tax expense is $30,000. Prepare Seagal's 2004 income statement, beginning with income before income taxes.

BE14-9 Tazmania Inc. had pretax financial income of $154,000 in 2004. Included in the computation of that amount is insurance expense of $4,000 which is not deductible for tax purposes. In addition, depreciation for tax purposes exceeds accounting depreciation by $14,000. Prepare Tazmania's journal entry to record 2004 taxes, assuming a tax rate of 45%.

BE14-10 Terminator Corporation has a cumulative temporary difference related to depreciation of $630,000 at December 31, 2004. This difference will reverse as follows: 2005, $42,000; 2006, $294,000; and 2007, $294,000. Enacted tax rates are 34% for 2005 and 2006, and 40% for 2007. Compute the amount Terminator should report as a deferred tax liability at December 31, 2004.

BE14-11 At December 31, 2003, Tick Corporation had a deferred tax liability of $680,000, resulting from future taxable amounts of $2,000,000 and an enacted tax rate of 34%. In May 2004, a new income tax act is signed into law that raises the tax rate to 38% for 2004 and future years. Prepare the journal entry for Tick to adjust the deferred tax liability.

BE14-12 Valis Corporation had the following tax information.

Year	Taxable Income	Tax Rate	Taxes Paid
2001	$300,000	35%	$105,000
2002	$325,000	30%	$ 97,500
2003	$400,000	30%	$120,000

In 2004 Valis suffered a net operating loss of $450,000, which it elected to carry back. The 2004 enacted tax rate is 29%. Prepare Valis's entry to record the effect of the loss carryback.

BE14-13 Zoop Inc. incurred a net operating loss of $500,000 in 2004. Combined income for 2002 and 2003 was $400,000. The tax rate for all years is 40%. Prepare the journal entries to record the benefits of the carryback and the carryforward.

BE14-14 Use the information for Zoop Inc. given in BE14-13. Assume that it is more likely than not that the entire net operating loss carryforward will not be realized in future years. Prepare all the journal entries necessary at the end of 2004.

BE14-15 Vectorman Corporation has temporary differences at December 31, 2004, that result in the following deferred taxes.

Deferred tax liability—current	$38,000
Deferred tax asset—current	$(52,000)
Deferred tax liability—noncurrent	$96,000
Deferred tax asset—noncurrent	$(27,000)

Indicate how these balances would be presented in Vectorman's December 31, 2004, balance sheet.

EXERCISES

E14-1 **(One Temporary Difference, Future Taxable Amounts, One Rate, No Beginning Deferred Taxes)** South Carolina Corporation has one temporary difference at the end of 2004 that will reverse and cause taxable amounts of $55,000 in 2005, $60,000 in 2006, and $65,000 in 2007. South Carolina's pretax financial income for 2004 is $300,000, and the tax rate is 30% for all years. There are no deferred taxes at the beginning of 2004.

Instructions
(a) Compute taxable income and income taxes payable for 2004.
(b) Prepare the journal entry to record income tax expense, deferred income taxes, and income taxes payable for 2004.
(c) Prepare the income tax expense section of the income statement for 2004, beginning with the line "Income before income taxes."

E14-2 **(Two Differences, No Beginning Deferred Taxes, Tracked through 2 Years)** The following information is available for Wenger Corporation for 2003.

1. Excess of tax depreciation over book depreciation, $40,000. This $40,000 difference will reverse equally over the years 2004–2007.
2. Deferral, for book purposes, of $20,000 of rent received in advance. The rent will be earned in 2004.
3. Pretax financial income, $300,000.
4. Tax rate for all years, 40%.

Instructions
(a) Compute taxable income for 2003.
(b) Prepare the journal entry to record income tax expense, deferred income taxes, and income taxes payable for 2003.
(c) Prepare the journal entry to record income tax expense, deferred income taxes, and income taxes payable for 2004, assuming taxable income of $325,000.

E14-3 **(One Temporary Difference, Future Taxable Amounts, One Rate, Beginning Deferred Taxes)** Bandung Corporation began 2004 with a $92,000 balance in the Deferred Tax Liability account. At the end of 2004, the related cumulative temporary difference amounts to $350,000, and it will reverse evenly over the next 2 years. Pretax accounting income for 2004 is $525,000, the tax rate for all years is 40%, and taxable income for 2004 is $405,000.

Instructions
(a) Compute income taxes payable for 2004.
(b) Prepare the journal entry to record income tax expense, deferred income taxes, and income taxes payable for 2004.
(c) Prepare the income tax expense section of the income statement for 2004 beginning with the line "Income before income taxes."

E14-4 **(Three Differences, Compute Taxable Income, Entry for Taxes)** Zurich Company reports pretax financial income of $70,000 for 2004. The following items cause taxable income to be different than pretax financial income.

1. Depreciation on the tax return is greater than depreciation on the income statement by $16,000.
2. Rent collected on the tax return is greater than rent earned on the income statement by $22,000.
3. Fines for pollution appear as an expense of $11,000 on the income statement.

Zurich's tax rate is 30% for all years, and the company expects to report taxable income in all future years. There are no deferred taxes at the beginning of 2004.

Instructions
(a) Compute taxable income and income taxes payable for 2004.
(b) Prepare the journal entry to record income tax expense, deferred income taxes, and income taxes payable for 2004.
(c) Prepare the income tax expense section of the income statement for 2004, beginning with the line "Income before income taxes."
(d) Compute the effective income tax rate for 2004.

E14-5 **(Two Temporary Differences, One Rate, Beginning Deferred Taxes)** The following facts relate to Krung Thep Corporation.

1. Deferred tax liability, January 1, 2004, $40,000.
2. Deferred tax asset, January 1, 2004, $0.
3. Taxable income for 2004, $95,000.
4. Pretax financial income for 2004, $200,000.
5. Cumulative temporary difference at December 31, 2004, giving rise to future taxable amounts, $240,000.
6. Cumulative temporary difference at December 31, 2004, giving rise to future deductible amounts, $35,000.
7. Tax rate for all years, 40%.
8. The company is expected to operate profitably in the future.

Instructions

(a) Compute income taxes payable for 2004.
(b) Prepare the journal entry to record income tax expense, deferred income taxes, and income taxes payable for 2004.
(c) Prepare the income tax expense section of the income statement for 2004, beginning with the line "Income before income taxes."

E14-6 (Identify Temporary or Permanent Differences) Listed below are items that are commonly accounted for differently for financial reporting purposes than they are for tax purposes.

Instructions

For each item below, indicate whether it involves:

(1) A temporary difference that will result in future deductible amounts and, therefore, will usually give rise to a deferred income tax asset.
(2) A temporary difference that will result in future taxable amounts and, therefore, will usually give rise to a deferred income tax liability.
(3) A permanent difference.

Use the appropriate number to indicate your answer for each.

(a) _____ An accelerated depreciation method is used for tax purposes, and the straight-line depreciation method is used for financial reporting purposes for some plant assets.
(b) _____ A landlord collects some rents in advance. Rents received are taxable in the period when they are received.
(c) _____ Expenses are incurred in obtaining tax-exempt income.
(d) _____ Costs of guarantees and warranties are estimated and accrued for financial reporting purposes.
(e) _____ Installment sales of investments are accounted for by the accrual method for financial reporting purposes and the installment method for tax purposes.
(f) _____ For some assets, straight-line depreciation is used for both financial reporting purposes and tax purposes but the assets' lives are shorter for tax purposes.
(g) _____ Interest is received on an investment in tax-exempt municipal obligations.
(h) _____ Proceeds are received from a life insurance company because of the death of a key officer. (The company carries a policy on key officers.)
(i) _____ The tax return reports a deduction for 80% of the dividends received from U.S. corporations. The cost method is used in accounting for the related investments for financial reporting purposes.
(j) _____ Estimated losses on pending lawsuits and claims are accrued for books. These losses are tax deductible in the period(s) when the related liabilities are settled.

E14-7 (Terminology, Relationships, Computations, Entries)

Instructions

Complete the following statements by filling in the blanks.

(a) In a period in which a taxable temporary difference reverses, the reversal will cause taxable income to be _____ (less than, greater than) pretax financial income.

(b) If a $76,000 balance in Deferred Tax Asset was computed by use of a 40% rate, the underlying cumulative temporary difference amounts to $_____.

(c) Deferred taxes _____ (are, are not) recorded to account for permanent differences.

(d) If a taxable temporary difference originates in 2004, it will cause taxable income of 2004 to be _____ (less than, greater than) pretax financial income for 2004.

(e) If total tax expense is $50,000 and deferred tax expense is $65,000, then the current portion of the expense computation is referred to as current tax _____ (expense, benefit) of $_____.

(f) If a corporation's tax return shows taxable income of $100,000 for Year 2 and a tax rate of 40%, how much will appear on the December 31, Year 2, balance sheet for "Income tax payable" if the company has made estimated tax payments of $36,500 for Year 2? $_____.

(g) An increase in the Deferred Tax Liability account on the balance sheet is recorded by a _____ (debit, credit) to the Income Tax Expense account.

(h) An income statement that reports current tax expense of $82,000 and deferred tax benefit of $23,000 will report total income tax expense of $_____.

(i) A valuation account is needed whenever it is judged to be _____ that a portion of a deferred tax asset _____ (will be, will not be) realized.

(j) If the tax return shows total taxes due for the period of $75,000 but the income statement shows total income tax expense of $55,000, the difference of $20,000 is referred to as deferred tax _____ (expense, benefit).

E14-8 (Two Temporary Differences, One Rate, 3 Years) Button Company has two temporary differences between its income tax expense and income taxes payable. The following information is available.

	2004	2005	2006
Pretax financial income	$840,000	$910,000	$945,000
Excess of depreciation expense on tax return	(30,000)	(40,000)	(10,000)
Excess of warranty expense on financial income	20,000	10,000	8,000
Taxable income	$830,000	$880,000	$943,000

The income tax rate for all years is 40%.

Instructions

(a) Prepare the journal entry to record income tax expense, deferred income taxes, and income tax payable for 2004, 2005, and 2006.

(b) Assuming there were no temporary differences prior to 2004, indicate how deferred taxes will be reported on the 2006 balance sheet. Button's product warranty is for 12 months.

(c) Prepare the income tax expense section of the income statement for 2006, beginning with the line "Pretax financial income."

E14-9 (Carryback and Carryforward of NOL, No Valuation Account, No Temporary Differences) The pretax financial income (or loss) figures for Jenny Spangler Company are as follows.

1999	$160,000
2000	250,000
2001	80,000
2002	(160,000)
2003	(380,000)
2004	120,000
2005	100,000

Pretax financial income (or loss) and taxable income (loss) were the same for all years involved. Assume a 45% tax rate for 1999 and 2000 and a 40% tax rate for the remaining years.

Instructions

Prepare the journal entries for the years 2001 to 2005 to record income tax expense and the effects of the net operating loss carrybacks and carryforwards assuming Jenny Spangler Company uses the carryback provision. All income and losses relate to normal operations. (In recording the benefits of a loss carryforward, assume that no valuation account is deemed necessary.)

E14-10 (2 NOLs, No Temporary Differences, No Valuation Account, Entries and Income Statement) Felicia Rashad Corporation has pretax financial income (or loss) equal to taxable income (or loss) from 1996 through 2004 as follows.

	Income (Loss)	Tax Rate
1996	$29,000	30%
1997	40,000	30%
1998	17,000	35%
1999	48,000	50%
2000	(150,000)	40%
2001	90,000	40%
2002	30,000	40%
2003	105,000	40%
2004	(60,000)	45%

Pretax financial income (loss) and taxable income (loss) were the same for all years since Rashad has been in business. Assume the carryback provision is employed for net operating losses. In recording the benefits of a loss carryforward, assume that it is more likely than not that the related benefits will be realized.

Instructions

(a) What entry(ies) for income taxes should be recorded for 2000?

(b) Indicate what the income tax expense portion of the income statement for 2000 should look like. Assume all income (loss) relates to continuing operations.

(c) What entry for income taxes should be recorded in 2001?

(d) How should the income tax expense section of the income statement for 2001 appear?

(e) What entry for income taxes should be recorded in 2004?

(f) How should the income tax expense section of the income statement for 2004 appear?

E14-11 (Three Differences, Classify Deferred Taxes) At December 31, 2003, Surya Bonilay Company had a net deferred tax liability of $375,000. An explanation of the items that compose this balance is as follows.

Temporary Differences	Resulting Balances in Deferred Taxes
1. Excess of tax depreciation over book depreciation	$200,000
2. Accrual, for book purposes, of estimated loss contingency from pending lawsuit that is expected to be settled in 2004. The loss will be deducted on the tax return when paid.	(50,000)
3. Accrual method used for book purposes and installment method used for tax purposes for an isolated installment sale of an investment.	225,000
	$375,000

In analyzing the temporary differences, you find that $30,000 of the depreciation temporary difference will reverse in 2004, and $120,000 of the temporary difference due to the installment sale will reverse in 2004. The tax rate for all years is 40%.

Instructions

Indicate the manner in which deferred taxes should be presented on Surya Bonilay Company's December 31, 2003, balance sheet.

 **E14-12 (Two Temporary Differences, One Rate, Beginning Deferred Taxes, Compute Pretax Financial Income)** The following facts relate to Sabrina Duncan Corporation.

1. Deferred tax liability, January 1, 2004, $60,000.
2. Deferred tax asset, January 1, 2004, $20,000.
3. Taxable income for 2004, $105,000.
4. Cumulative temporary difference at December 31, 2004, giving rise to future taxable amounts, $230,000.
5. Cumulative temporary difference at December 31, 2004, giving rise to future deductible amounts, $95,000.
6. Tax rate for all years, 40%. No permanent differences exist.
7. The company is expected to operate profitably in the future.

Instructions
(a) Compute the amount of pretax financial income for 2004.
(b) Prepare the journal entry to record income tax expense, deferred income taxes, and income taxes payable for 2004.
(c) Prepare the income tax expense section of the income statement for 2004, beginning with the line "Income before income taxes."
(d) Compute the effective tax rate for 2004.

E14-13 (One Difference, Multiple Rates, Effect of Beginning Balance versus No Beginning Deferred Taxes) At the end of 2003, Lucretia McEvil Company has $180,000 of cumulative temporary differences that will result in reporting future taxable amounts as follows.

2004	$ 60,000
2005	50,000
2006	40,000
2007	30,000
	$180,000

Tax rates enacted as of the beginning of 2002 are:

2002 and 2003	40%
2004 and 2005	30%
2006 and later	25%

McEvil's taxable income for 2003 is $320,000. Taxable income is expected in all future years.

Instructions
(a) Prepare the journal entry for McEvil to record income taxes payable, deferred income taxes, and income tax expense for 2003, assuming that there were no deferred taxes at the end of 2002.
(b) Prepare the journal entry for McEvil to record income taxes payable, deferred income taxes, and income tax expense for 2003, assuming that there was a balance of $22,000 in a Deferred Tax Liability account at the end of 2002.

E14-14 (Deferred Tax Asset with and without Valuation Account) Jennifer Capriati Corp. has a deferred tax asset account with a balance of $150,000 at the end of 2003 due to a single cumulative temporary difference of $375,000. At the end of 2004 this same temporary difference has increased to a cumulative amount of $450,000. Taxable income for 2004 is $820,000. The tax rate is 40% for all years. No valuation account related to the deferred tax asset is in existence at the end of 2003.

Instructions
(a) Record income tax expense, deferred income taxes, and income taxes payable for 2004, assuming that it is more likely than not that the deferred tax asset will be realized.
(b) Assuming that it is more likely than not that $30,000 of the deferred tax asset will not be realized, prepare the journal entry at the end of 2004 to record the valuation account.

E14-15 (Deferred Tax Asset with Previous Valuation Account) Assume the same information as E14-14, except that at the end of 2003, Jennifer Capriati Corp. had a valuation account related to its deferred tax asset of $45,000.

Instructions

(a) Record income tax expense, deferred income taxes, and income taxes payable for 2004, assuming that it is more likely than not that the deferred tax asset will be realized in full.

(b) Record income tax expense, deferred income taxes, and income taxes payable for 2004, assuming that it is more likely than not that none of the deferred tax asset will be realized.

E14-16 **(Deferred Tax Liability, Change in Tax Rate, Prepare Section of Income Statement)**   Jana Novotna Inc.'s only temporary difference at the beginning and end of 2003 is caused by a $3 million deferred gain for tax purposes for an installment sale of a plant asset, and the related receivable (only one-half of which is classified as a current asset) is due in equal installments in 2004 and 2005. The related deferred tax liability at the beginning of the year is $1,200,000. In the third quarter of 2003, a new tax rate of 34% is enacted into law and is scheduled to become effective for 2005. Taxable income for 2003 is $5,000,000, and taxable income is expected in all future years.

Instructions

(a) Determine the amount reported as a deferred tax liability at the end of 2003. Indicate proper classification(s).

(b) Prepare the journal entry (if any) necessary to adjust the deferred tax liability when the new tax rate is enacted into law.

(c) Draft the income tax expense portion of the income statement for 2003. Begin with the line "Income before income taxes." Assume no permanent differences exist.

E14-17 **(Two Temporary Differences, Tracked through 3 Years, Multiple Rates)**   Taxable income and pretax financial income would be identical for Anke Huber Co. except for its treatments of gross profit on installment sales and estimated costs of warranties. The following income computations have been prepared.

Taxable income	2003	2004	2005
Excess of revenues over expenses (excluding two temporary differences)	$160,000	$210,000	$90,000
Installment gross profit collected	8,000	8,000	8,000
Expenditures for warranties	(5,000)	(5,000)	
(5,000)			
Taxable income	$163,000	$213,000	$93,000

Pretax financial income	2003	2004	2005
Excess of revenues over expenses (excluding two temporary differences)	$160,000	$210,000	$90,000
Installment gross profit earned	24,000	–0–	–0–
Estimated cost of warranties	(15,000)	–0–	–0–

The tax rates in effect are: 2003, 40%; 2004 and 2005, 45%. All tax rates were enacted into law on January 1, 2003. No deferred income taxes existed at the beginning of 2003. Taxable income is expected in all future years.

Instructions

Prepare the journal entry to record income tax expense, deferred income taxes, and income tax payable for 2003, 2004, and 2005.

E14-18 **(Three Differences, Multiple Rates, Future Taxable Income)**   During 2004, Anna Nicole Smith Co.'s first year of operations, the company reports pretax financial income at $250,000. Smith's enacted tax rate is 45% for 2004 and 40% for all later years. Smith expects to have taxable income in each of the next 5 years. The effects on future tax returns of temporary differences existing at December 31, 2004, are summarized on the next page.

	Future Years					
	2005	2006	2007	2008	2009	Total
Future taxable (deductible) amounts:						
Installment sales	$32,000	$32,000	$32,000			$ 96,000
Depreciation	6,000	6,000	6,000	$6,000	$6,000	30,000
Unearned rent	(50,000)	(50,000)				(100,000)

Instructions

(a) Complete the schedule below to compute deferred taxes at December 31, 2004.

(b) Compute taxable income for 2004.

(c) Prepare the journal entry to record income tax payable, deferred taxes, and income tax expense for 2004.

	Future Taxable		December 31, 2004	
	(Deductible)	Tax	Deferred Tax	
Temporary Difference	Amounts	Rate	(Asset)	Liability
Installment sales	$ 96,000			
Depreciation	30,000			
Unearned rent	(100,000)		_____	_____
Totals	$ _____		_____	_____

E14-19 (Two Differences, One Rate, Beginning Deferred Balance, Compute Pretax Financial Income) Sharon Stone Co. establishes a $100 million liability at the end of 2004 for the estimated costs of closing two of its manufacturing facilities. All related closing costs will be paid and deducted on the tax return in 2005. Also, at the end of 2004, the company has $50 million of temporary differences due to excess depreciation for tax purposes, $7 million of which will reverse in 2005.

The enacted tax rate for all years is 40%, and the company pays taxes of $64 million on $160 million of taxable income in 2004. Stone expects to have taxable income in 2005.

Instructions

(a) Determine the deferred taxes to be reported at the end of 2004.

(b) Indicate how the deferred taxes computed in (a) are to be reported on the balance sheet.

(c) Assuming that the only deferred tax account at the beginning of 2004 was a deferred tax liability of $10,000,000, draft the income tax expense portion of the income statement for 2004, beginning with the line "Income before income taxes." (*Hint:* You must first compute (1) the amount of temporary difference underlying the beginning $10,000,000 deferred tax liability, then (2) the amount of temporary differences originating or reversing during the year, then (3) the amount of pretax financial income.)

E14-20 (Two Differences, No Beginning Deferred Taxes, Multiple Rates) Teri Hatcher Inc., in its first year of operations, has the following differences between the book basis and tax basis of its assets and liabilities at the end of 2003.

	Book Basis	Tax Basis
Equipment (net)	$400,000	$340,000
Estimated warranty liability	$200,000	$ –0–

It is estimated that the warranty liability will be settled in 2004. The difference in equipment (net) will result in taxable amounts of $20,000 in 2004, $30,000 in 2005, and $10,000 in 2006. The company has taxable income of $520,000 in 2003. As of the beginning of 2003, the enacted tax rate is 34% for 2003–2005, and 30% for 2006. Hatcher expects to report taxable income through 2006.

Instructions

(a) Prepare the journal entry to record income tax expense, deferred income taxes, and income tax payable for 2003.

(b) Indicate how deferred income taxes will be reported on the balance sheet at the end of 2003.

E14-21 (Two Temporary Differences, Multiple Rates, Future Taxable Income) Svetlana Boginskaya Inc. has two temporary differences at the end of 2003. The first difference stems from installment sales, and the second one results from the accrual of a loss contingency. Boginskaya's accounting department has developed a schedule of future taxable and deductible amounts related to these temporary differences as follows.

	2004	2005	2006	2007
Taxable amounts	$40,000	$50,000	$60,000	$80,000
Deductible amounts		(15,000)	(19,000)	
	$40,000	$35,000	$41,000	$80,000

As of the beginning of 2003, the enacted tax rate is 34% for 2003 and 2004, and 38% for 2005–2008. At the beginning of 2003, the company had no deferred income taxes on its balance sheet. Taxable income for 2003 is $500,000. Taxable income is expected in all future years.

Instructions

(a) Prepare the journal entry to record income tax expense, deferred income taxes, and income taxes payable for 2003.

(b) Indicate how deferred income taxes would be classified on the balance sheet at the end of 2003.

E14-22 (Two Differences, One Rate, First Year) The differences between the book basis and tax basis of the assets and liabilities of JoAnn Castle Corporation at the end of 2003 are presented below.

	Book Basis	Tax Basis
Accounts receivable	$50,000	$-0-
Litigation liability	30,000	-0-

It is estimated that the litigation liability will be settled in 2004. The difference in accounts receivable will result in taxable amounts of $30,000 in 2004 and $20,000 in 2005. The company has taxable income of $350,000 in 2003 and is expected to have taxable income in each of the following 2 years. Its enacted tax rate is 34% for all years. This is the company's first year of operations. The operating cycle of the business is 2 years.

Instructions

(a) Prepare the journal entry to record income tax expense, deferred income taxes, and income tax payable for 2003.

(b) Indicate how deferred income taxes will be reported on the balance sheet at the end of 2003.

E14-23 (NOL Carryback and Carryforward, Valuation Account versus No Valuation Account) Spamela Hamderson Inc. reports the following pretax income (loss) for both financial reporting purposes and tax purposes. (Assume the carryback provision is used for a net operating loss.)

Year	Pretax Income (Loss)	Tax Rate
2002	$120,000	34%
2003	90,000	34%
2004	(280,000)	38%
2005	220,000	38%

The tax rates listed were all enacted by the beginning of 2002.

Instructions

(a) Prepare the journal entries for the years 2002–2005 to record income tax expense (benefit) and income tax payable (refundable) and the tax effects of the loss carryback and carryforward, assuming that at the end of 2004 the benefits of the loss carryforward are judged more likely than not to be realized in the future.

(b) Using the assumption in (a), prepare the income tax section of the 2004 income statement beginning with the line "Operating loss before income taxes."

(c) Prepare the journal entries for 2004 and 2005, assuming that based on the weight of available evidence, it is more likely than not that one-fourth of the benefits of the carryforward will not be realized.

(d) Using the assumption in (c), prepare the income tax section of the 2004 income statement beginning with the line "Operating loss before income taxes."

E14-24   (NOL Carryback and Carryforward, Valuation Account Needed)   Denise Beilman Inc. reports the following pretax income (loss) for both book and tax purposes. (Assume the carryback provision is used where possible for a net operating loss.)

Year	Pretax Income (Loss)	Tax Rate
2002	$120,000	40%
2003	90,000	40%
2004	(280,000)	45%
2005	120,000	45%

The tax rates listed were all enacted by the beginning of 2002.

Instructions

(a) Prepare the journal entries for years 2002–2005 to record income tax expense (benefit) and income tax payable (refundable), and the tax effects of the loss carryback and carryforward, assuming that based on the weight of available evidence, it is more likely than not that one-half of the benefits of the carryforward will not be realized.

(b) Prepare the income tax section of the 2004 income statement beginning with the line "Operating loss before income taxes."

(c) Prepare the income tax section of the 2005 income statement beginning with the line "Income before income taxes."

E14-25   (NOL Carryback and Carryforward, Valuation Account Needed)   Meyer reported the following pretax financial income (loss) for the years 2002–2006.

2002	$240,000
2003	350,000
2004	120,000
2005	(570,000)
2006	180,000

Pretax financial income (loss) and taxable income (loss) were the same for all years involved. The enacted tax rate was 34% for 2002 and 2003, and 40% for 2004–2006. Assume the carryback provision is used first for net operating losses.

Instructions

(a) Prepare the journal entries for the years 2004–2006 to record income tax expense, income tax payable (refundable), and the tax effects of the loss carryback and carryforward, assuming that based on the weight of available evidence, it is more likely than not that one-fifth of the benefits of the carryforward will not be realized.

(b) Prepare the income tax section of the 2005 income statement beginning with the line "Income (loss) before income taxes."

PROBLEMS

P14-1 (Three Differences, No Beginning Deferred Taxes, Multiple Rates) The following information is available for Swanson Corporation for 2003.

1. Depreciation reported on the tax return exceeded depreciation reported on the income statement by $100,000. This difference will reverse in equal amounts of $25,000 over the years 2004–2007.
2. Interest received on municipal bonds was $10,000.
3. Rent collected in advance on January 1, 2003, totaled $60,000 for a 3-year period. Of this amount, $40,000 was reported as unearned at December 31, for book purposes.
4. The tax rates are 40% for 2003 and 35% for 2004 and subsequent years.
5. Income taxes of $360,000 are due per the tax return for 2003.
6. No deferred taxes existed at the beginning of 2003.

Instructions

(a) Compute taxable income for 2003.
(b) Compute pretax financial income for 2003.
(c) Prepare the journal entries to record income tax expense, deferred income taxes, and income taxes payable for 2003 and 2004. Assume taxable income was $980,000 in 2004.
(d) Prepare the income tax expense section of the income statement for 2003, beginning with "Income before income taxes."

P14-2 (One Temporary Difference, Tracked for 4 Years, One Permanent Difference, Change in Rate) The pretax financial income of Kristal Parker-Gregory Company differs from its taxable income throughout each of 4 years as follows.

Year	Pretax Financial Income	Taxable Income	Tax Rate
2004	$280,000	$180,000	35%
2005	320,000	225,000	40%
2006	350,000	270,000	40%
2007	420,000	580,000	40%

Pretax financial income for each year includes a nondeductible expense of $30,000 (never deductible for tax purposes). The remainder of the difference between pretax financial income and taxable income in each period is due to one depreciation temporary difference. No deferred income taxes existed at the beginning of 2004.

Instructions

(a) Prepare journal entries to record income taxes in all 4 years. Assume that the change in the tax rate to 40% was not enacted until the beginning of 2005.
(b) Draft the income tax section of the income statement for 2005.

P14-3 (Second Year of Depreciation Difference, Two Differences, Single Rate, Extraordinary Item) The following information has been obtained for the Tracy Kerdyk Corporation.

1. Prior to 2003, taxable income and pretax financial income were identical.
2. Pretax financial income is $1,700,000 in 2003 and $1,400,000 in 2004.
3. On January 1, 2003, equipment costing $1,000,000 is purchased. It is to be depreciated on a straight-line basis over 5 years for tax purposes and over 8 years for financial reporting purposes. (*Hint:* Use the half-year convention for tax purposes—see Chapter 9.)
4. Interest of $60,000 was earned on tax-exempt municipal obligations in 2004.
5. Included in 2004 pretax financial income is an extraordinary gain of $200,000, which is fully taxable.
6. The tax rate is 35% for all periods.
7. Taxable income is expected in all future years.

Instructions

(a) Compute taxable income and income tax payable for 2004.

(b) Prepare the journal entry to record 2004 income tax expense, income tax payable, and deferred taxes.

(c) Prepare the bottom portion of Kerdyk's 2004 income statement, beginning with "Income before income taxes and extraordinary item."

(d) Indicate how deferred income taxes should be presented on the December 31, 2004, balance sheet.

P14-4 (Permanent and Temporary Differences, One Rate) The accounting records of Anderson Inc. show the following data for 2004.

1. Life insurance expense on officers was $9,000.
2. Equipment was acquired in early January for $200,000. Straight-line depreciation over a 5-year life is used, with no salvage value. For tax purposes, Anderson used a 30% rate to calculate depreciation.
3. Interest revenue on State of New York bonds totaled $4,000.
4. Product warranties were estimated to be $60,000 in 2004. Actual repair and labor costs related to the warranties in 2004 was $10,000. The remainder is estimated to be incurred evenly in 2005 and 2006.
5. Sales on an accrual basis was $100,000. For tax purposes, $75,000 was recorded on the installment method.
6. Fines incurred for pollution violations were $4,200.
7. Pretax financial income was $850,000. The tax rate is 30%.

Instructions

(a) Prepare a schedule starting with pretax financial income and ending with taxable income.

(b) Prepare the journal entry for 2004 income tax payable and expense.

P14-5 (Actual NOL without Valuation Account) Mark O'Meara Inc. reported the following pretax income (loss) and related tax rates during the years 1999–2005.

	Pretax Income (loss)	Tax Rate
1999	$ 40,000	30%
2000	25,000	30%
2001	60,000	30%
2002	80,000	40%
2003	(200,000)	45%
2004	70,000	40%
2005	90,000	35%

Pretax financial income (loss) and taxable income (loss) were the same for all years since O'Meara began business. The tax rates from 2002–2005 were enacted in 2002.

Instructions

(a) Prepare the journal entries for the years 2003–2005 to record income tax payable (refundable), income tax expense (benefit), and the tax effects of the loss carryback and carryforward. Assume that O'Meara elects the carryback provision where possible and expects to realize the benefits of any loss carryforward in the year that immediately follows the loss year.

(b) Indicate the effect the 2003 entry(ies) has on the December 31, 2003, balance sheet.

(c) Indicate how the bottom portion of the income statement, starting with "Operating loss before income taxes," would be reported in 2003.

(d) Indicate how the bottom portion of the income statement, starting with "Income before income taxes," would be reported in 2004.

P14-6 (Two Differences, Two Rates, Future Income Expected) Presented below are two independent situations related to future taxable and deductible amounts resulting from temporary differences existing at December 31, 2003.

1. Pirates Co. has developed the following schedule of future taxable and deductible amounts.

	2004	2005	2006	2007	2008
Taxable amounts	$300	$300	$300	$ 300	$300
Deductible amount	—	—	—	(1,400)	—

2. Eagles Co. has the following schedule of future taxable and deductible amounts.

	2004	2005	2006	2007
Taxable amounts	$300	$300	$ 300	$300
Deductible amount	—	—	(2,000)	—

Both Pirates Co. and Eagles Co. have taxable income of $3,000 in 2003 and expect to have taxable income in all future years. The tax rates enacted as of the beginning of 2003 are 30% for 2003–2006 and 35% for years thereafter. All of the underlying temporary differences relate to noncurrent assets and liabilities.

Instructions

For each of these two situations, compute the net amount of deferred income taxes to be reported at the end of 2003, and indicate how it should be classified on the balance sheet.

P14-7 (One Temporary Difference, Tracked 3 Years, Change in Rates, Income Statement Presentation)
Gators Corp. sold an investment on an installment basis. The total gain of $60,000 was reported for financial reporting purposes in the period of sale. The company qualifies to use the installment method for tax purposes. The installment period is 3 years; one-third of the sale price is collected in the period of sale. The tax rate was 35% in 2003, and 30% in 2004 and 2005. The 30% tax rate was not enacted in law until 2004. The accounting and tax data for the 3 years is shown below.

	Financial Accounting	Tax Return
2003 (35% tax rate)		
Income before temporary difference	$ 70,000	$70,000
Temporary difference	60,000	20,000
Income	$130,000	$90,000
2004 (30% tax rate)		
Income before temporary difference	$ 70,000	$70,000
Temporary difference	–0–	20,000
Income	$ 70,000	$90,000
2005 (30% tax rate)		
Income before temporary difference	$ 70,000	$70,000
Temporary difference	–0–	20,000
Income	$ 70,000	$90,000

Instructions

(a) Prepare the journal entries to record the income tax expense, deferred income taxes, and the income tax payable at the end of each year. No deferred income taxes existed at the beginning of 2003.

(b) Explain how the deferred taxes will appear on the balance sheet at the end of each year. (Assume the Installment Accounts Receivable is classified as a current asset.)

(c) Draft the income tax expense section of the income statement for each year, beginning with "Income before income taxes."

P14-8 (Two Differences, 2 Years, Compute Taxable Income and Pretax Financial Income) The following information was disclosed during the audit of Thomas Muster Inc.

1.

Year	Amount Due per Tax Return
2003	$140,000
2004	112,000

2. On January 1, 2003, equipment costing $400,000 is purchased. For financial reporting purposes, the company uses straight-line depreciation over a 5-year life. For tax purposes, the company uses the elective straight-line method over a 5-year life. (*Hint:* For tax purposes, the half-year convention must be used—see Chapter 9.)

3. In January 2004, $225,000 is collected in advance rental of a building for a 3-year period. The entire $225,000 is reported as taxable income in 2004, but $150,000 of the $225,000 is reported as unearned revenue in 2004 for financial reporting purposes. The remaining amount of unearned revenue is to be earned equally in 2005 and 2006.

4. The tax rate is 40% in 2003 and all subsequent periods. (*Hint:* To find taxable income in 2003 and 2004, the related income tax payable amounts will have to be grossed up.)

5. No temporary differences existed at the end of 2002. Muster expects to report taxable income in each of the next 5 years.

Instructions

(a) Determine the amount to report for deferred income taxes at the end of 2003, and indicate how it should be classified on the balance sheet.

(b) Prepare the journal entry to record income taxes for 2003.

(c) Draft the income tax section of the income statement for 2003 beginning with "Income before income taxes." (*Hint:* You must compute taxable income and then combine that with changes in cumulative temporary differences to arrive at pretax financial income.)

(d) Determine the deferred income taxes at the end of 2004, and indicate how they should be classified on the balance sheet.

(e) Prepare the journal entry to record income taxes for 2004.

(f) Draft the income tax section of the income statement for 2004, beginning with "Income before income taxes."

P14-9 (Five Differences, Compute Taxable Income and Deferred Taxes, Draft Income Statement) Martha King Company began operations at the beginning of 2004. The following information pertains to this company.

1. Pretax financial income for 2004 is $100,000.

2. The tax rate enacted for 2004 and future years is 40%

3. Differences between the 2004 income statement and tax return are listed below:

    (a) Warranty expense accrued for financial reporting purposes amounts to $5,000. Warranty deductions per the tax return amount to $2,000.

    (b) Gross profit on construction contracts using the percentage-of-completion method for books amounts to $92,000. Gross profit on construction contracts for tax purposes amounts to $62,000.

    (c) Depreciation of property, plant, and equipment for financial reporting purposes amounts to $60,000. Depreciation of these assets amounts to $80,000 for the tax return.

    (d) A $3,500 fine paid for violation of pollution laws was deducted in computing pretax financial income.

    (e) Interest revenue earned on an investment in tax-exempt municipal bonds amounts to $1,400. (Assume (a) is short-term in nature; assume (b) and(c) are long-term in nature.)

4. Taxable income is expected for the next few years.

Instructions

(a) Compute taxable income for 2004.

(b) Compute the deferred taxes at December 31, 2004, that relate to the temporary differences described above. Clearly label them as deferred tax asset or liability.

(c) Prepare the journal entry to record income tax expense, deferred taxes, and income taxes payable for 2004.

(d) Draft the income tax expense section of the income statement beginning with "Income before income taxes."

CONCEPTUAL CASES

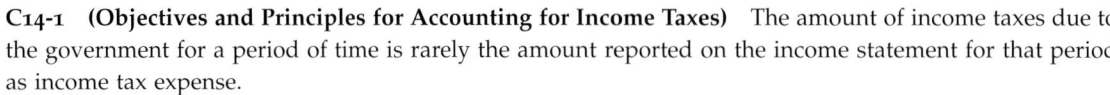 **C14-1 (Objectives and Principles for Accounting for Income Taxes)** The amount of income taxes due to the government for a period of time is rarely the amount reported on the income statement for that period as income tax expense.

Instructions

(a) Explain the objectives of accounting for income taxes in general purpose financial statements.

(b) Explain the basic principles that are applied in accounting for income taxes at the date of the financial statements to meet the objectives discussed in (a).

(c) List the steps in the annual computation of deferred tax liabilities and assets.

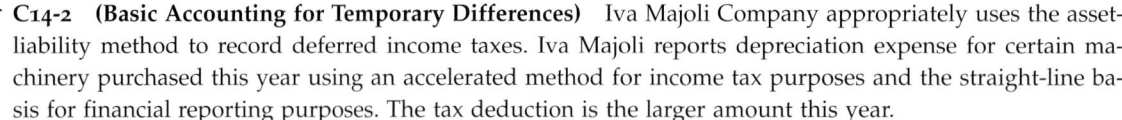 **C14-2 (Basic Accounting for Temporary Differences)** Iva Majoli Company appropriately uses the asset-liability method to record deferred income taxes. Iva Majoli reports depreciation expense for certain machinery purchased this year using an accelerated method for income tax purposes and the straight-line basis for financial reporting purposes. The tax deduction is the larger amount this year.

Iva Majoli received rent revenues in advance this year. These revenues are included in this year's taxable income. However, for financial reporting purposes, these revenues are reported as unearned revenues, a current liability.

Instructions

(a) What are the principles of the asset-liability approach?

(b) How would Majoli account for the temporary differences?

(c) How should Majoli classify the deferred tax consequences of the temporary differences on its balance sheet?

C14-3 (Identify Temporary Differences and Classification Criteria) The asset-liability approach for recording deferred income taxes is an integral part of generally accepted accounting principles.

Instructions

(a) Indicate whether each of the following independent situations should be treated as a temporary difference or as a permanent difference, and explain why.

    (1) Estimated warranty costs (covering a 3-year warranty) are expensed for financial reporting purposes at the time of sale but deducted for income tax purposes when paid.

    (2) Depreciation for book and income tax purposes differs because of different bases of carrying the related property, which was acquired in a trade-in. The different bases are a result of different rules used for book and tax purposes to compute the basis of property acquired in a trade-in.

    (3) A company properly uses the equity method to account for its 30% investment in another company. The investee pays dividends that are about 10% of its annual earnings.

    (4) A company reports a gain on an involuntary conversion of a nonmonetary asset to a monetary asset. The company elects to replace the property within the statutory period using the total proceeds so the gain is not reported on the current year's tax return.

(b) Discuss the nature of the deferred income tax accounts and possible classifications in a company's balance sheet. Indicate the manner in which these accounts are to be reported.

C14-4 (Accounting and Classification of Deferred Income Taxes)

Part A

This year Lindsay Davenport Company has each of the following items in its income statement.

1. Gross profits on installment sales.

2. Revenues on long-term construction contracts.

3. Estimated costs of product warranty contracts.
4. Premiums on officers' life insurance with Davenport as beneficiary.

Instructions

(a) Under what conditions would deferred income taxes need to be reported in the financial statements?

(b) Specify when deferred income taxes would need to be recognized for each of the items above, and indicate the rationale for such recognition.

Part B

Davenport Company's president has heard that deferred income taxes can be classified in different ways in the balance sheet.

Instructions

Identify the conditions under which deferred income taxes would be classified as a noncurrent item in the balance sheet. What justification exists for such classification?

(AICPA adapted)

C14-5 (Explain Computation of Deferred Tax Liability for Multiple Tax Rates) At December 31, 2004, Martina Hingis Corporation has one temporary difference which will reverse and cause taxable amounts in 2005. In 2004 a new tax act set taxes equal to 45% for 2004, 40% for 2005, and 34% for 2006 and years thereafter.

Instructions

Explain what circumstances would call for Martina Hingis to compute its deferred tax liability at the end of 2004 by multiplying the cumulative temporary difference by:

(a) 45%.
(b) 40%.
(c) 34%.

C14-6 (Explain Future Taxable and Deductible Amounts, How Carryback and Carryforward Affects Deferred Taxes) Mary Joe Fernandez and Meredith McGrath are discussing accounting for income taxes. They are currently studying a schedule of taxable and deductible amounts that will arise in the future as a result of existing temporary differences. The schedule is as follows.

	Current Year	Future Years			
	2004	2005	2006	2007	2008
Taxable income	$850,000				
Taxable amounts		$375,000	$375,000	$ 375,000	$375,000
Deductible amounts				(2,400,000)	
Enacted tax rate	50%	45%	40%	35%	30%

Instructions

(a) Explain the concept of future taxable amounts and future deductible amounts as illustrated in the schedule.

(b) How do the carryback and carryforward provisions affect the reporting of deferred tax assets and deferred tax liabilities?

C14-7 (Deferred Taxes, Income Effects) Henrietta Aguirre, CPA, is the newly hired director of corporate taxation for Mesa Incorporated, which is a publicly traded corporation. Ms. Aguirre's first job with Mesa was the review of the company's accounting practices on deferred income taxes. In doing her review, she noted differences between tax and book depreciation methods that permitted Mesa to realize a sizable deferred tax liability on its balance sheet. As a result, Mesa did not have to report current income tax expenses.

Aguirre also discovered that Mesa has an explicit policy of selling off fixed assets before they reversed in the deferred tax liability account. This policy, coupled with the rapid expansion of its fixed asset base, allowed Mesa to "defer" all income taxes payable for several years, even though it always has reported positive earnings and an increasing EPS. Aguirre checked with the legal department and found the policy to be legal, but she's uncomfortable with the ethics of it.

Instructions
Answer the following questions.

(a) Why would Mesa have an explicit policy of selling assets before they reversed in the deferred tax liability account?

(b) What are the ethical implications of Mesa's "deferral" of income taxes?

(c) Who could be harmed by Mesa's ability to "defer" income taxes payable for several years, despite positive earnings?

(d) In a situation such as this, what are Ms. Aguirre's professional responsibilities as a CPA?

USING YOUR JUDGMENT

FINANCIAL REPORTING PROBLEM

3M COMPANY
The financial statements of 3M Company were provided with your book or can be accessed on the Take Action! CD.

Instructions
Refer to 3M's Company financial statements and the accompanying notes to answer the following questions.

(a) What amounts relative to income taxes does 3M report in its:
  (1) 2001 income statement?
  (2) December 31, 2001, balance sheet?
  (3) 2001 statement of cash flows?

(b) 3M's provision for income taxes in 1999, 2000, and 2001 was computed at what effective tax rates? (See notes to the financial statements.)

(c) How much of 3M's 2001 total provision for income taxes was current tax expense, and how much was deferred tax expense?

(d) What did 3M report as the significant components (the details) of its December 31, 2001, deferred tax assets and liabilities?

FINANCIAL STATEMENT ANALYSIS CASE

HOMESTAKE MINING COMPANY
Homestake Mining Company is a 120-year-old international gold mining company with substantial gold mining operations and exploration in the United States, Canada, and Australia. At year-end, Homestake reported the following items related to income taxes (thousands of dollars).

Total current taxes	$ 26,349
Total deferred taxes	(39,436)
Total income and mining taxes (the provision for taxes per its income statement)	(13,087)
Deferred tax liabilities	$303,050
Deferred tax assets, net of valuation allowance of $207,175	95,275
Net deferred tax liability	$207,775

Note 6: The classification of deferred tax assets and liabilities is based on the related asset or liability creating the deferred tax. Deferred taxes not related to a specific asset or liability are classified based on the estimated period of reversal.

Tax loss carryforwards (U.S., Canada, Australia, and Chile)	$71,151
Tax credit carryforwards	$12,007

Instructions

(a) What is the significance of Homestake's disclosure of "Current taxes" of $26,349 and "Deferred taxes" of $(39,436)?

(b) Explain the concept behind Homestake's disclosure of gross deferred tax liabilities (future taxable amounts) and gross deferred tax assets (future deductible amounts).

(c) Homestake reported tax loss carryforwards of $71,151 and tax credit carryforwards of $12,007. How do the carryback and carryforward provisions affect the reporting of deferred tax assets and deferred tax liabilities?

COMPARATIVE ANALYSIS CASE

THE COCA-COLA COMPANY AND PEPSICO, INC.

Instruction

Go to the Take Action! CD and use information found there to answer the following questions related to The Coca-Cola Company and PepsiCo, Inc.

(a) What are the amounts of Coca-Cola's and PepsiCo's provision for income taxes for the year 2001? Of each company's 2001 provision for income taxes, what portion is current expense and what portion is deferred expense?

(b) What amount of cash was paid in 2001 for income taxes by Coca-Cola and by PepsiCo?

(c) What was the U.S. federal statutory tax rate in 2001? What was the effective tax rate in 2001 for Coca-Cola and PepsiCo? Why might their effective tax rates differ?

(d) For the year-end 2001, what amounts were reported by Coca-Cola and PepsiCo as (a) gross deferred tax assets and (b) gross deferred tax liabilities?

(e) Do either Coca-Cola or PepsiCo disclose any net operating loss carrybacks and/or carryforwards at year-end 2001? What are the amounts, and when do the carryforwards expire?

INTERNATIONAL REPORTING CASE

TOMKINS PLC

Tomkins PLC is a British company that operates in four business sectors: industrial and automotive engineering; construction components; food manufacturing; and professional, garden, and leisure products. Tomkins prepares its accounts in accordance with United Kingdom (U.K.) accounting standards. Like U.S. reporting, U.K. financial reporting is investor-oriented. As a result, British companies report different income amounts for tax and financial reporting purposes. British companies receive different tax treatment for such items as depreciation (capital allowances), and they receive tax credits for operating losses. Tomkins reported income of £305 million in a recent year and reported total shareholders' funds of £2,221 million at year-end. Tomkins provided disclosures related to taxes in its annual report as shown at the top of page 736.

If Tomkins had used U.S. GAAP for deferred taxes, its income would have been lower by £8.2 million in the current year. Stockholders' equity at year-end would have been £87.5 million higher if Tompkins had applied U.S. GAAP.

TOMPKINS PLC

Principal Accounting Policies — Tax

The tax charge is based on the profit for the year and takes into account tax deferred due to timing differences between the treatment of certain items for tax and accounting purposes. Deferred tax is calculated under the liability method and it is considered probable that all liabilities will crystallise. Deferred tax assets are not recognized in respect of provision for post-retirement benefits.

Note 5: Tax on Profit on Ordinary Activities

	Current Year £ million	Prior Year £ million
Corporation tax at 31%	56.6	69.6
Overseas tax	85.5	95.8
Deferred tax–UK (see note 16)	5.1	(7.1)
–Overseas (see note 16)	7.3	9.2
Associated undertakings' tax	0.7	3.0
	155.2	170.5

The tax charge on exceptional items in 1999 and 1998 is £nil.

Note 16: Provisions for Liabilities and Charges

	Current Year	Prior Year
The deferred tax provision comprises:	98.5	102.9
Excess of capital allowances over depreciation charged	40.8	25.5
Other timing differences	—	(30.3)
Advance corporation tax recoverable	139.3	98.1

Results Under U.S. Accounting Principles

The consolidated financial statements are prepared in conformity with accounting principles generally accepted in the UK (UK GAAP) which differ in certain respects from those generally accepted in the United States (US GAAP). The significant areas of difference affecting the Tomkins consolidated financial statements are described below:

Deferred Income Tax. In Tomkins consolidated financial statements, deferred tax is calculated under the liability method and it is considered probable that all liabilities will crystallise. Deferred tax assets are not recognised in respect of provision for post-retirement benefits. Under US GAAP, deferred taxes are provided for all temporary differences on a full liability basis. Deferred tax assets are also recognized to the extent that their realisation is more likely than not.

Instructions

Use the information in the Tomkins disclosure to answer the following.

(a) Prepare the journal entry that would be required to reconcile Tomkins' income to U.S. GAAP for the differences in deferred taxes under U.S. and U.K. accounting standards.

(b) Prepare the journal entry that would be required to reconcile Tomkins' shareholders' equity to U.S. GAAP for the differences in deferred taxes under U.S. and U.K. accounting standards at the end of the current year.

(c) In light of the information disclosed under "Principal Accounting Policies—Tax," explain why you think Tomkins' equity under U.S. GAAP would be higher at year-end in the current year.

(d) Tomkins indicates that "Deferred tax is calculated under the liability method and it is considered probable that all (deferred tax) liabilities will crystallise [be realized]." Does this approach cause any problems in comparing the financial statements of U.S. and U.K. companies? Explain.

*Remember to check the **Take Action! CD**
and the book's **companion Web site**
to find additional resources for this chapter.*

ACCOUNTING FOR COMPENSATION

CHAPTER

15

MORE DEPENDS ON THE MARKET

LEARNING
OBJECTIVES

After studying this chapter, you should be able to:

❶ Explain the accounting for salary and bonuses.

❷ Describe the accounting for stock compensation plans under generally accepted accounting principles.

❸ Explain the controversy surrounding stock compensation plans.

❹ Identify types of pension plans and their characteristics.

❺ Identify the components of pension expense.

❻ Utilize a work sheet for employer's pension plan entries.

❼ Explain the accounting for prior service cost and gains and losses.

❽ Describe the reporting requirements for pension plans in financial statements.

In addition to their salary, executives also may earn annual and long-term incentives if their companies perform well. But if the stock market does not perform, their stock options can wind up providing no financial payoff. As indicated in the charts below, more and more of executive pay is related to stock price.

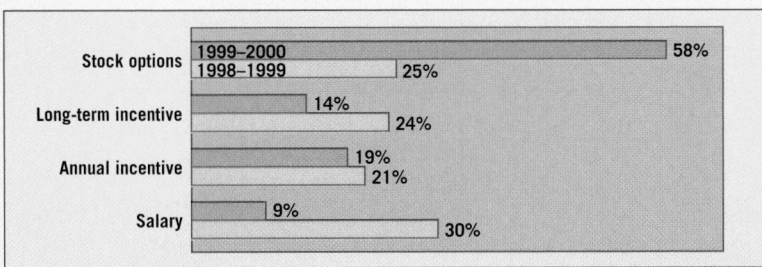

Pay elements for CEOs from the top 200 industrial and service companies ranked by revenues

For dot-com executives the percentage is much higher, as shown below.

Stock options as a portion of 1999–2000 renumeration for 100 dot-com companies' CEOs and for the top 200 companies' CEOs; figures are in millions of dollars

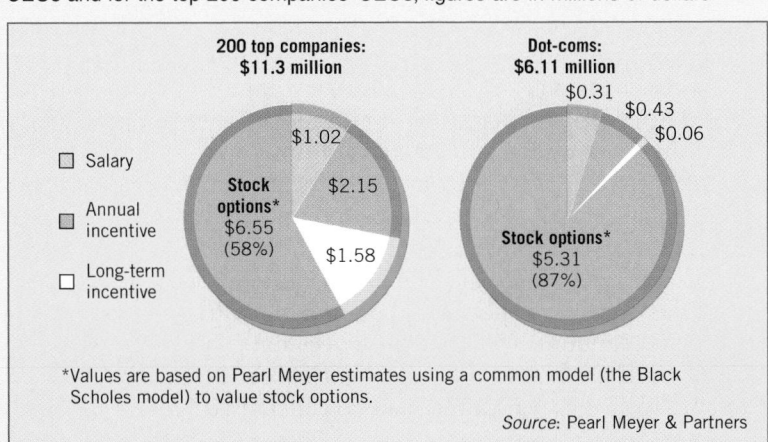

*Values are based on Pearl Meyer estimates using a common model (the Black Scholes model) to value stock options.

Source: Pearl Meyer & Partners

What these figures show is the dramatic change in the way many top executives (and for that matter, regular employees) are compensated.[1] In addition, many companies have postretirement plans that include pensions, health care benefits, and life insurance benefits. It is no wonder that compensation consultants are in high demand.

[1]Adapted from Ruth Simon and Lunthe Jeanne Dugan, "Options Overdose," *Wall Street Journal* (June 4, 2001).

As indicated in the opening story, various forms of compensation are used to compensate employees. Compensation expense can include salary, wages, bonuses, fringe benefits (such as health insurance, life insurance, pensions, and other postretirement benefits), and stock options. The purpose of the chapter is to discuss the accounting issues related to these various forms of compensation. The content and organization of the chapter are as follows.

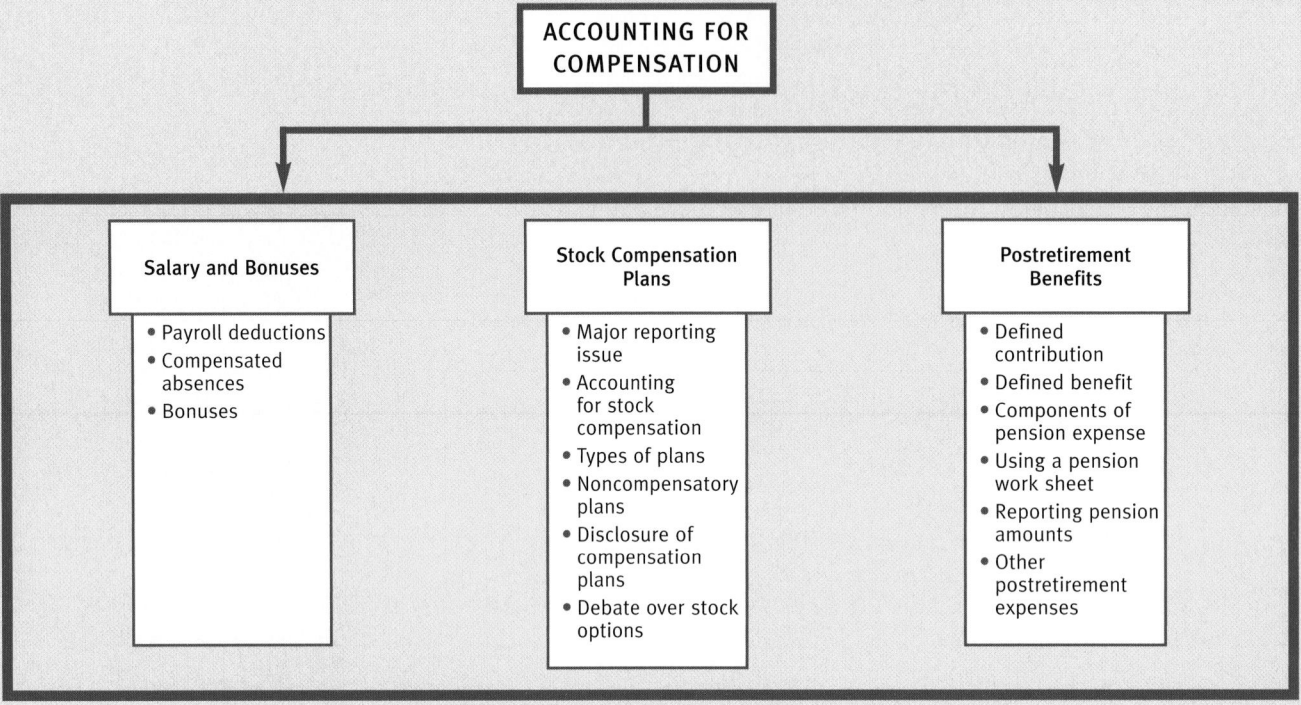

SALARY AND BONUSES

Effective compensation programs are ones that do the following: (1) motivate employees to high levels of performance, (2) help retain key employees and allow for recruitment of new talent, (3) base compensation on employee and company performance, (4) maximize the employee's after-tax benefit and minimize the employer's after-tax cost, and (5) use performance criteria over which the employer's has control. Straight cash compensation plans (salary and, perhaps, bonus) are an important part of any compensation program.

The accounting for salary (wages) is relatively straightforward. Amounts paid to employees for salaries and wages per the employment contract should be reported as compensation expense. Amounts owed to employees for salaries and wages at the end of the accounting period are reported as a current liability. In addition, the following items related to employee compensation must be considered.

- Payroll deductions
- Compensated absences
- Bonuses

Payroll Deductions

The most common types of payroll deductions are taxes, insurance premiums, employee savings, and union dues. **To the extent the amounts deducted have not been remitted to the proper authority at the end of the accounting period, they should be recognized as current liabilities.**

Social Security Taxes

Since January 1, 1937, Social Security legislation has provided federal old age, survivor, and disability insurance (O.A.S.D.I.) benefits for certain individuals and their families through taxes levied on both the employer and the employee. All employers covered are required to collect the employee's share of this tax, by deducting it from the employee's gross pay, and to remit it to the government along with the employer's share. Both the employer and the employee are taxed at the same rate, currently 6.2 percent based on the employee's gross pay up to an $84,900 annual limit.

In 1965 Congress passed the first federal health insurance program for the aged—popularly known as Medicare. It is a two-part program designed to alleviate the high cost of medical care for those over age 65. The Basic Plan, which provides hospital and other institutional services, is financed by a separate Hospital Insurance tax paid by both the employee and the employer at the rate of 1.45 percent on the employee's total compensation. The Voluntary Plan takes care of the major part of doctors' bills and other medical and health services and is financed by monthly payments from all who enroll plus matching funds from the federal government.

The combination of the O.A.S.D.I. tax, usually called Federal Insurance Contribution Act (F.I.C.A.) tax, and the federal Hospital Insurance Tax is commonly referred to as the **Social Security tax**. The combined rate for these taxes, 7.65 percent on an employee's wages to $84,900 and 1.45 percent in excess of $84,900, is changed intermittently by acts of Congress. **The amount of unremitted employee and employer Social Security tax on gross wages paid should be reported by the employer as a current liability.**

Unemployment Taxes

Another payroll tax levied by the federal government in cooperation with state governments provides a system of unemployment insurance. All employers who (1) paid wages of $1,500 or more during any calendar quarter in the year or preceding year, or (2) employed at least one individual on at least one day in each of 20 weeks during the current or preceding calendar year are subject to the Federal Unemployment Tax Act (F.U.T.A.). This tax is levied only on the employer, at a rate of 6.2 percent on the first $7,000 of compensation paid to each employee during the calendar year. The employer is allowed a tax credit not to exceed 5.4 percent for contributions paid to a state plan for unemployment compensation. Thus, if an employer is subject to a state unemployment tax of 5.4 percent or more, only 0.8 percent tax is due the federal government.

State unemployment compensation laws differ from the federal law and differ among various states. Therefore, employers must be familiar with the unemployment tax laws in each state in which they pay wages and salaries. Although the normal state tax may range from 3 percent to 7 percent or higher, all states provide for some form of merit rating, under which a reduction in the state contribution rate is allowed. Employers who display by their benefit and contribution experience that they have provided steady employment may be entitled to this reduction—if the size of the state fund is adequate to provide the reduction. In order not to penalize an employer who has earned a reduction in the state contribution rate, federal law allows a credit of 5.4 percent, even when the effective state contribution rate is less than 5.4 percent.

To illustrate, Appliance Repair Co., which has a taxable payroll of $100,000, is subject to a federal rate of 6.2 percent and a state contribution rate of 5.7 percent. But because of stable employment experience, the company's state rate has been reduced to 1 percent. The computation of the federal and state unemployment taxes for Appliance Repair Co. is:

State unemployment tax payment (1% × $100,000)	$1,000
Federal unemployment tax [(6.2% − 5.4%) × $100,000]	800
Total federal and state unemployment tax	$1,800

Illustration 15-1
Computation of Unemployment Taxes

The federal unemployment tax is paid quarterly with a tax form filed annually. State contributions generally are required to be paid quarterly. Because both the federal and the state unemployment taxes accrue on earned compensation, the amount of accrued but unpaid employer contributions **should be recorded as an operating expense and as a current liability when financial statements are prepared at year-end**.

Income Tax Withholding

Federal and some state income tax laws require employers to withhold from the pay of each employee the applicable income tax due on those wages. The amount of income tax withheld is computed by the employer according to a government-prescribed formula or withholding tax table. That amount depends on the length of the pay period and each employee's taxable wages, marital status, and claimed dependents. If the income tax withheld plus the employee and the employer Social Security taxes exceeds specified amounts per month, the employer is required to make remittances to the government during the month. Illustration 15-2 summarizes various payroll deductions and liabilities.

Illustration 15-2
Summary of Payroll Liabilities

Item	Who Pays	
Income tax withholding		
FICA taxes—employee share	Employee	
Union dues		Employer reports these amounts as liabilities until remitted.
FICA taxes—employer share		
Federal unemployment	Employer	
State unemployment		

Illustration

Assume a weekly payroll of $10,000 entirely subject to F.I.C.A. and Medicare (7.65%), federal (0.8%) and state (4%) unemployment taxes with income tax withholding of $1,320 and union dues of $88 deducted. The entry to record the wages and salaries paid and the **employee payroll deductions** would be:

Wages and Salaries Expense	10,000	
Withholding Taxes Payable		1,320
F.I.C.A. Taxes Payable		765
Union Dues Payable to Local No. 257		88
Cash		7,827

The entry to record the **employer payroll taxes** would be:

Payroll Tax Expense	1,245	
F.I.C.A. Taxes Payable		765
Federal Unemployment Tax Payable		80
State Unemployment Tax Payable		400

The employer is required to remit to the government its share of F.I.C.A. tax along with the amount of F.I.C.A. tax deducted from each employee's gross compensation.

All unremitted employer F.I.C.A. taxes should be recorded as payroll tax expense and payroll tax payable.[2]

Compensated Absences

Compensated absences are absences from employment—such as vacation, illness, and holidays—for which employees are paid anyway. A liability should be accrued for the cost of compensation for future absences if **all of the following conditions** are met.[3]

UNDERLYING CONCEPTS

When these four conditions exist, all elements in the definition of a liability exist. In addition, the matching concept requires that the period receiving the services also should report the related expense.

(a) The employer's obligation relating to employees' rights to receive compensation for future absences is attributable to employees' services **already rendered**.

(b) The obligation relates to the rights that **vest or accumulate**.

(c) Payment of the compensation is **probable**.

(d) The amount can be **reasonably estimated**.[4]

An example of an accrual for compensated absences is shown below in an excerpt from the balance sheet of **Clarcor Inc.** presented in its annual report.

CLARCOR INC.

Current liabilities	
Accounts payable	$ 6,308
Accrued salaries, wages, and commissions	2,278
Compensated absences	2,271
Accrued pension liabilities	1,023
Other accrued liabilities	4,572
	$16,452

Illustration 15-3
Balance Sheet Presentation of Accrual for Compensated Absences

If an employer meets conditions (a), (b), and (c) but does not accrue a liability because of a failure to meet condition (d), that fact should be disclosed.

Vested rights exist when an employer has an obligation to make payment to an employee even if his or her employment is terminated. Thus, vested rights are not contingent on an employee's future service. **Accumulated rights** are those that can be carried forward to future periods if not used in the period in which earned. For example, assume that you have earned four days of vacation pay as of December 31, the end of your employer's fiscal year, and that you will be paid for this vacation time even if you terminate employment. In this situation, your four days of vacation pay are considered

---

[2]In a manufacturing enterprise, all of the payroll costs (wages, payroll taxes, and fringe benefits) are allocated to appropriate cost accounts such as Direct Labor, Indirect Labor, Sales Salaries, Administrative Salaries, and the like. This abbreviated and somewhat simplified discussion of payroll costs and deductions is not indicative of the volume of records and clerical work that may be involved in maintaining a sound and accurate payroll system.

[3]"Accounting for Compensated Absences," *Statement of Financial Accounting Standards No. 43* (Stamford, Conn.: FASB, 1980), par. 6.

[4]These same four conditions are to be applied to accounting for **postemployment benefits**. **Postemployment benefits** are benefits provided by an enterprise to past or inactive employees **after employment but prior to retirement**. Examples include salary continuation, supplemental unemployment benefits, severance pay, job training, and continuation of health and life insurance coverage.

vested and must be accrued. Now assume that your vacation days are not vested, but that you can carry the four days over into later periods. Although the rights are not vested, they are accumulated rights for which the employer must provide an accrual, allowing for estimated forfeitures due to turnover.

A modification of the general rules relates to the issue of **sick pay**. If sick pay benefits vest, accrual is required. If sick pay benefits accumulate but do not vest, accrual is permitted but not required. The reason for this distinction is that compensation that is designated as sick pay may be administered in one of two ways. In some companies, employees receive sick pay only if they are absent because of illness. Accrual of a liability is permitted but not required because its payment is contingent upon future employee illness. In other companies, employees are allowed to accumulate unused sick pay and take compensated time off from work even though they are not ill. For this type of sick pay, a liability must be accrued because it will be paid whether or not employees ever become ill.

The expense and related liability for compensated absences should be recognized in the year earned by employees. For example, if new employees receive rights to two weeks' paid vacation at the beginning of their second year of employment, the vacation pay is considered to be earned during the first year of employment.

What rate should be used to accrue the compensated absence cost—the current rate or an estimated future rate? *FASB Statement No. 43* is silent on this subject. Therefore, it is likely that companies will use the current rather than future rate. The future rate is less certain and raises issues concerning the time value of money. To illustrate, assume that Amutron Inc. began operations on January 1, 2003. The company employs ten individuals who are paid $480 per week. Vacation weeks earned by all employees in 2003 were 20 weeks, but none were used during this period. In 2004, the vacation weeks were used when the current rate of pay was $540 per week for each employee. The entry at December 31, 2003 to accrue the accumulated vacation pay is as follows.

Wages Expense	9,600	
Vacation Wages Payable ($480 × 20)		9,600

At December 31, 2003 the company would report on its balance sheet a liability of $9,600. In 2004, the vacation pay related to 2003 would be recorded as follows.

Vacation Wages Payable	9,600	
Wages Expense	1,200	
Cash ($540 × 20)		10,800

In 2004 the vacation weeks were used, and so the liability is extinguished. Note that the difference between the amount of cash paid and the reduction in the liability account is recorded as an adjustment to Wages Expense in the period when paid. This difference arises because the liability account was accrued at the rates of pay in effect during the period when compensated time was earned. The cash paid, however, is based on the rates in effect during the period when compensated time is used. If the future rates of pay had been used to compute the accrual in 2003, then the cash paid in 2004 would have been equal to the liability.[5]

---

[5]Some companies have obligations for benefits paid to employees after they retire. The accounting and reporting standards for postretirement benefit payments are complex. These standards relate to two different types of **postretirement benefits**: (1) pensions, and (2) postretirement health care and life insurance benefits. These issues are discussed later in this chapter.

Bonuses

Many companies give a **bonus** to certain or all officers and employees in addition to their regular salaries or wages. Frequently the bonus amount is dependent on the company's yearly profit. For example, **Ford Motor Company** has a plan whereby employees share in the success of the company's operations on the basis of a complicated formula using net income as its primary basis for computation. From the standpoint of the enterprise, **bonus payments to employees** may be considered additional wages and should be included as a deduction in determining the net income for the year.

To illustrate the entries for an employee bonus, assume a company whose income for the year 2004 is $100,000 will pay out bonuses of $10,700 in January 2005. An adjusting entry dated December 31, 2004, is made to record the bonus as follows.

Employees' Bonus Expense	10,700	
Profit-Sharing Bonus Payable		10,700

Additional Discussion on Bonus Computations

In January 2005, when the bonus is paid, the journal entry would be:

Profit-Sharing Bonus Payable	10,700	
Cash		10,700

The expense account should appear in the income statement as an operating expense. **The liability, Profit-Sharing Bonus Payable, is usually payable within a short period of time and should be included as a current liability in the balance sheet.**

STOCK COMPENSATION PLANS

Many companies recognize that a more long-term compensation plan is often needed, in addition to a cash component. Long-term compensation plans attempt to develop in key employees a strong loyalty toward the company. An effective way to accomplish this goal is to give the employees "a piece of the action"—that is, an equity interest based on changes in long-term measures such as increases in earnings per share, revenues, stock price, or market share. These plans, generally referred to as **stock option plans**, come in many different forms. Essentially, they provide key employees with the opportunity to receive stock or cash in the future if the stock price performance of the company is satisfactory. As mentioned in the opening story, this form of compensation is being used extensively to compensate employees.

The Major Reporting Issue

Suppose that you are an employee for Hurdle Inc. and you are granted options to purchase 10,000 shares of the firm's common stock as part of your compensation. The date you receive the options is referred to as the **grant date**. The options are good for 10 years. The market price and the exercise price for the stock are both $20 at the grant date. **What is the value of the compensation you just received?**

Some believe you have not received anything: That is, the difference between the market price and the exercise price is zero, and therefore no compensation results. Others argue these options have value: If the stock price goes above $20 any time over the next 10 years and you exercise these options, substantial compensation results. For example, if at the end of the fourth year, the market price of the stock is $30 and you exercise your options, you will have earned $100,000 [10,000 options × ($30 − $20)], ignoring income taxes.

How should the granting of these options be reported by Hurdle Inc.? In the past, GAAP required that compensation cost be measured by the excess of the market price of the stock over its exercise price at the grant date. This approach is referred to as the **intrinsic value method** because the computation is not dependent on external circumstances: **it is the difference between the market price of the stock and the exercise price of the options at the grant date**. Hurdle would therefore not recognize any compensation expense related to your options because at the grant date the market price and exercise price were the same.

The FASB **encourages but does not require recognition of compensation cost for the fair value of stock-based compensation paid to employees for their services.**[6] The FASB position is that the accounting for the cost of employee services should be based on the value of compensation paid, which is presumed to be a measure of the value of the services received. Accordingly, the compensation cost arising from employee stock options should be measured based on the fair value of the stock options granted.[7] To determine this value, acceptable option pricing models are used to value options at the date of grant. This approach is referred to as the **fair value method** because the option value is estimated based on the many factors that determine its underlying value.[8]

The FASB met considerable resistance when it proposed requiring the fair value method for recognizing the costs of stock options in the financial statements. As a result, it was decided that a company **can choose** to use **either** the intrinsic value method or the fair value method when accounting for compensation cost on the income statement. However, if a company uses the intrinsic value method to recognize compensation costs for employee stock options, it must provide expanded disclosures on these costs. Specifically, companies that choose the intrinsic value method are required to disclose in a note to the financial statements pro-forma net income and earnings per share (if presented by the company), **as if it had used the fair value method**.

Accounting for Stock Compensation

OBJECTIVE 2
Describe the accounting for stock compensation plans under generally accepted accounting principles.

A company is given a choice in the recognition method for stock compensation. However, **the FASB encourages adoption of the fair value method**. Our discussion in this section illustrates both methods. Stock option plans involve two main accounting issues:

⟨**1**⟩ How should compensation expense be determined?

⟨**2**⟩ Over what periods should compensation expense be allocated?

Determining Expense
Under the fair value method, total compensation expense is computed based on the fair value of the options expected to vest on the date the options are granted to the

---

[6]"Accounting for Stock-Based Compensation," *Statement of Financial Accounting Standards No. 123* (Norwalk, Conn.: FASB, 1995).

[7]Stock options issued to non-employees in exchange for other goods or services must be recognized according to the fair value method in *SFAS 123.*

[8]These factors include the volatility of the underlying stock, the expected life of the options, the risk-free rate during the option life, and expected dividends during the option life.

employee(s) (i.e., the **grant date**).[9] Fair value for public companies is to be estimated using an option pricing model, with some adjustments for the unique factors of employee stock options. No adjustments are made after the grant date, in response to subsequent changes in the stock price—either up or down.[10]

Under the intrinsic value method, total compensation cost is computed as the excess of the market price of the stock over the option price on the date when both the number of shares to which employees are entitled and the option or purchase price for those shares are known. This date is called the **measurement date**. For many plans, this measurement date is the **grant date**. However, the measurement date may be later for plans with variable terms (either number of shares and/or option price are not known) that depend on events after the date of grant. For such variable plans, compensation expense may have to be estimated on the basis of assumptions as to the final number of shares and the option price (usually at the exercise date).

ACCOUNTS DECEIVABLE

WHAT DO THE NUMBERS MEAN?

Businesses—especially tech firms that issue lots of stock options—say they shouldn't have to account for the value of stock options when figuring earnings. So far, they've prevailed against the Financial Accounting Standards Board, which says they should. Bear Stearns analyst Pat McConnell calculated the impact of options on earnings at S&P 500 companies using FASB-recommended accounting—and it isn't a pretty picture. The following companies had the biggest changes in earnings.

Company/Business	1999 Reported EPS	Share Earnings (Loss) with Stock Options	Percent Decline
McDermott Int'l./Energy services	$0.01	$(0.06)	700%
Yahoo!/Internet search engine	0.10	(0.50)	600
Autodesk/CAD software	0.16	(0.74)	563
Conexant/Semiconductors	0.06	(0.10)	267
Broadcom/Integrated circuits	0.36	(0.53)	247

Source: "Accounts Deceivable," *Business Week* (September 2000).

Allocating Compensation Expense

In general, under both the fair and intrinsic value methods, compensation expense is recognized in the periods in which the employee performs the service—the **service period**. Unless otherwise specified, the service period is the vesting period—the time between the grant date and the vesting date. Thus, total compensation cost is determined at the grant date and allocated to the periods benefited by the employees' services.

[9]"To vest" means "to earn the rights to." An employee's award becomes vested at the date that the employee's right to receive or retain shares of stock or cash under the award is no longer contingent on remaining in the service of the employer.

[10]Nonpublic companies frequently do not have data with which to estimate the fair-value element. Therefore, nonpublic companies are permitted to use a minimum value method to estimate the value of the options. The minimum value method does not consider the volatility of the stock price when estimating option value.

Illustration

To illustrate the accounting for a stock option plan, assume that on November 1, 2002, the stockholders of Chen Company approve a plan that grants the company's five executives options to purchase 2,000 shares each of the company's $1 par value common stock. The options are granted on January 1, 2003, and may be exercised at any time within the next ten years. The option price per share is $60, and the market price of the stock at the date of grant is $70 per share. **Under the intrinsic value method**, the total compensation expense is computed below.

Market value of 10,000 shares at date of grant ($70 per share)	$700,000
Option price of 10,000 shares at date of grant ($60 per share)	600,000
Total compensation expense (intrinsic value)	$100,000

Under the fair value method, total compensation expense is computed by applying an acceptable fair value option pricing model (such as the Black-Scholes option pricing model). To keep this illustration simple, we will assume that the fair value option pricing model determines total compensation expense to be $220,000.

Basic Entries. The value of the options under either method is recognized as an expense in the periods in which the employee performs services. In the case of Chen Company, assume that the expected period of benefit is 2 years, starting with the grant date. The journal entries to record the transactions related to this option contract using both the intrinsic value and fair value method are shown below.

Illustration 15-4
Comparison of Entries for Option Contract—Intrinsic Value and Fair Value Methods

Intrinsic Value	Fair Value
At date of grant (January 1, 2003)	
No entry	No entry
To record compensation expense for 2003 (December 31, 2003)	

Compensation Expense 50,000
  Paid-in Capital—Stock Options
  ($100,000 ÷ 2) 50,000
	Compensation Expense 110,000
	  Paid-in Capital—Stock Options
	  ($220,000 ÷ 2) 110,000

To record compensation expense for 2004 (December 31, 2004)	

Compensation Expense 50,000
  Paid-in Capital—Stock Options 50,000
	Compensation Expense 110,000
	  Paid-in Capital—Stock Options 110,000

Under both methods, compensation expense is allocated evenly over the 2-year service period. The only difference between the two methods is the amount of compensation recognized.

Exercise. If 20 percent, or 2,000, of the 10,000 options were exercised on June 1, 2006 (3 years and 5 months after date of grant), the following journal entry would be recorded using the **intrinsic value method**.

June 1, 2006

Cash (2,000 × $60)	120,000	
Paid-in Capital—Stock Options (20% × $100,000)	20,000	
Common Stock (2,000 × $1.00)		2,000
Paid-in Capital in Excess of Par		138,000

Under the **fair value approach**, the entry would be:

June 1, 2006

Cash (2,000 × $60)	120,000	
Paid-in Capital—Stock Options (20% × $220,000)	44,000	
Common Stock (2,000 × $1.00)		2,000
Paid-in Capital in Excess of Par		162,000

Expiration. If the remaining stock options are not exercised before their expiration date, the balance in the Paid-in Capital—Stock Options account should be transferred to a more properly titled paid-in capital account, such as Paid-in Capital from Expired Stock Options. The entry to record this transaction at the date of expiration would be as follows.

Illustration 15-5
Comparison of Entries for Stock Option Expiration—Intrinsic Value and Fair Value Methods

Intrinsic Value		Fair Value	
January 1, 2013 (expiration date)			
Paid-in Capital—Stock Options	80,000	Paid-in Capital—Stock Options	176,000
Paid-in Capital from Expired Stock		Paid-in Capital from Expired Stock	
Options (80% × $100,000)	80,000	Options (80% × $220,000)	176,000

Adjustment. The fact that a stock option is not exercised does not nullify the propriety of recording the costs of services received from executives and attributable to the stock option plan. Under GAAP, compensation expense is, therefore, not adjusted upon expiration of the options. However, if a stock option is forfeited because **an employee fails to satisfy a service requirement** (e.g., leaves employment), the estimate of compensation expense recorded in the current period should be adjusted (as a change in estimate). This change in estimate would be recorded by debiting Paid-in Capital—Stock Options and crediting Compensation Expense, thereby decreasing compensation expense in the period of forfeiture.

Types of Plans

Many different types of plans are used to compensate key employees. In all these plans the amount of the reward depends upon future events. Consequently, continued employment is a necessary element in almost all types of plans. The popularity of a given plan usually depends on the firm's prospects in the stock market and on tax considerations. For example, if it appears that appreciation will occur in a company's stock, a plan that offers the option to purchase stock is attractive. Conversely, if it appears that price appreciation is unlikely, then compensation might be tied to some performance measure such as an increase in book value or earnings per share.

*Expanded Discussion of
Stock Compensation Plans*

Three common compensation plans that illustrate different objectives are:

1. Stock option plans (incentive or nonqualified).
2. Stock appreciation rights plans.
3. Performance-type plans.

Most plans follow the general guidelines for reporting established in the previous sections.

Noncompensatory Plans

In some companies, stock purchase plans permit all employees to purchase stock at a discounted price for a short period of time. These plans are usually classified as noncompensatory. Noncompensatory means that the primary purpose of the plan is not to compensate the employees but, rather, to enable the employer to secure equity capital or to induce widespread ownership of an enterprise's common stock among employees. Thus, compensation expense is not reported for these plans. **Noncompensatory plans** have three characteristics:

1. Substantially all full-time employees may participate on an equitable basis.
2. The discount from market price is small. That is, it does not exceed the greater of a per share discount reasonably offered to stockholders or the per share amount of costs avoided by not having to raise cash in a public offering.
3. The plan offers no substantive option feature.

For example, Masthead Company had a stock purchase plan under which employees who meet minimal employment qualifications are entitled to purchase Masthead stock at a 5 percent reduction from market price for a short period of time. The reduction from market price is not considered compensatory because the per share amount of the costs avoided by not having to raise the cash in a public offering is equal to 5 percent. **Plans that do not possess all of the above mentioned three characteristics are classified as compensatory.**

Disclosure of Compensation Plans

To comply with *SFAS No. 123*, companies offering stock-based compensation plans must determine the fair value of the options. Companies must then decide whether to use the fair value method and recognize expense in the income statement, or to use the intrinsic value approach and disclose in the notes the pro forma impact on net income and earnings per share (if presented), as if the fair value method had been used.

Regardless of whether the intrinsic value or fair value method is used, full disclosure should be made about the status of these plans at the end of the periods presented, including the number of shares under option, options exercised and forfeited, the weighted average option prices for these categories, the weighted average fair value of options granted during the year, and the average remaining contractual life of the options outstanding.[11] In addition to information about the status of the stock option plans, companies must also disclose the method and significant assumptions used to estimate the fair values of the stock options.

---

[11]These data should be reported separately for each different type of plan offered to employees.

If the intrinsic value method is used in the financial statements, companies must still disclose the pro forma net income and pro forma earnings per share (if presented), as if the fair value method had been used to account for the stock-based compensation cost. Illustration 15-6 illustrates this disclosure, as provided by **Gateway, Inc.**

	2001	2000	1999
GATEWAY, INC.			

Had compensation expense for employee and director stock options been determined based on the fair value of the options on the date of grant, net income (loss) and net income (loss) per share would have resulted in the pro forma amounts indicated below (in thousands, except per share amounts):

	2001	2000	1999
Net income (loss)—as reported	$(1,033,915)	$241,483	$427,944
Net income (loss)—pro forma	$(1,106,376)	$ (53,675)	$319,494
Net income (loss) per share—as reported			
Basic	$ (3.20)	$ 0.75	$ 1.36
Diluted	$ (3.20)	$ 0.73	$ 1.32
Net income (loss) per share—pro forma			
Basic	$ (3.42)	$ (0.17)	$ 1.02
Diluted	$ (3.42)	$ (0.17)	$ 0.98

The pro forma effect on net income (loss) for 2001, 2000, and 1999 is not fully representative of the pro forma effect on net income (loss) in future years because it does not take into consideration pro forma compensation expense related to the vesting of grants made prior to 1997.

Illustration 15-6

Disclosure of Pro-Forma Effect of Stock Option Plans

Debate over Stock Option Accounting

In general, use of the fair value approach results in greater compensation costs relative to the intrinsic value models. For example, a study of the companies in the Standard & Poor's 500 stock index documented that, on average, earnings in 1998 were overstated by 5 percent through the use of the intrinsic value method. And some companies, such as **Guidant**, **3Com**, and **Cendant**, reported earnings under the intrinsic value model that were up to three times higher than earnings using the fair value method.

It is an understatement to say that corporate America is unhappy with the fair value method to record compensation expense for these plans. Many small high-technology companies are particularly vocal in their opposition, arguing that only through offering stock options can they attract top professional management. They contend that if they are forced to recognize large amounts of compensation expense under these plans, they will be at a competitive disadvantage with larger companies that can withstand higher compensation charges. As one high-tech executive stated, "If your goal is to attack fat-cat executive compensation in multi-billion dollar firms, then please do so! But not at the expense of the people who are 'running lean and mean,' trying to build businesses and creating jobs in the process."

The stock option saga is a classic example of the difficulty the FASB faces in issuing an accounting standard. Many powerful interests aligned against the Board; even some who initially appeared to support the Board's actions later reversed themselves. The whole incident is troubling because the debate for the most part is not about the **proper accounting** but more about the **economic consequences** of the standards. If we continue to write standards so that some social, economic, or public

OBJECTIVE 3
Explain the controversy involving stock compensation plans.

UNDERLYING CONCEPTS

The stock option controversy involves economic-consequence issues. The FASB believes the neutrality concept should be followed. Others disagree, noting that factors other than accounting theory should be considered.

policy goal is achieved, it will not be too long before financial reporting will lose its credibility.

POSTRETIREMENT BENEFITS

Other long-term forms of compensation in addition to stock options are pensions and other postretirement benefits, such as health care and other social-welfare benefits. Many companies have pension plans that provide benefits (payments) to employees after they retire for services provided while they are working. Pension plans are of two general types:

1. Defined contribution plans
2. Defined benefit plans

Defined Contribution Plan

OBJECTIVE 4
Identify types of pension plans and their characteristics.

In a **defined contribution plan**, the employer agrees to contribute to a pension trust a certain sum each period, based on a formula. This formula may consider such factors as age, length of employee service, employer's profits, and compensation level. **Only the employer's contribution is defined**; no promise is made regarding the ultimate benefits paid out to the employees. A common form of this plan is a "401(k)" plan.

WHAT DO THE NUMBERS MEAN?

THE DANGERS OF NOT DIVERSIFYING

The defined contribution plan is very popular with employees. A recent report by **Fidelity Investments** noted that approximately three-quarters of eligible employees contribute to a defined contribution plan. Participants are saving an average of 7 percent of their gross income for retirement. However, most investors tend to concentrate their funds in just a few investments, as shown below.

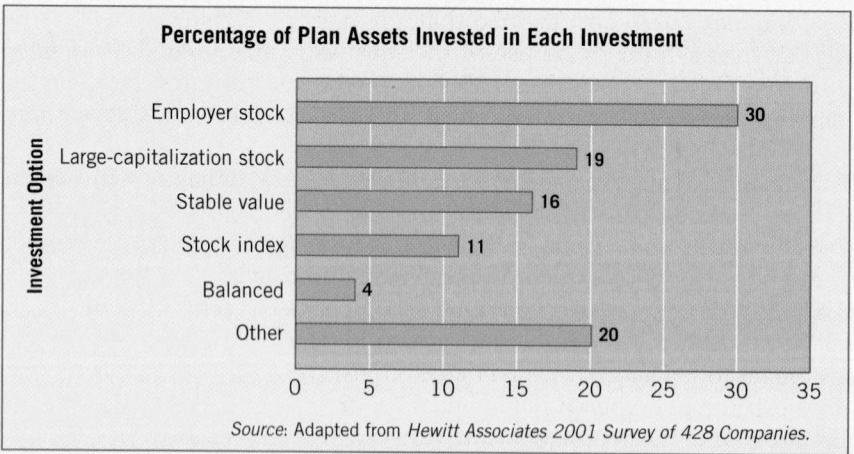

Percentage of Plan Assets Invested in Each Investment

Source: Adapted from *Hewitt Associates 2001 Survey of 428 Companies.*

As the graph shows, a significant percentage of participants invest in their company's stock. However, the dangers of having all your retirement assets in one stock are considerable. With the collapse of the tech bubble and recent failures such as **Enron** and **WorldCom** wiping out the assets of many current and retired employees, the need for diversification is apparent.

The size of the pension benefits that the employee finally collects under the plan depends on the amounts originally contributed to the pension trust, the income accumulated in the trust, and the treatment of forfeitures of funds caused by early terminations of other employees. The amounts originally contributed are usually turned over to an **independent third-party trustee** who acts on behalf of the beneficiaries—the participating employees. The trustee assumes ownership of the pension assets and is accountable for their investment and distribution. The trust is separate and distinct from the employer.

The accounting for a defined contribution plan is straightforward. The employee gets the benefit of gain or the risk of loss from the assets contributed to the pension plan. The employer's responsibility is simply to make a contribution each year based on the formula established in the plan. As a result, the employer's annual cost (pension expense) is simply the amount that it is obligated to contribute to the pension trust. A liability is reported on the employer's balance sheet only if the contribution has not been made in full, and an asset is reported only if more than the required amount has been contributed.

In addition to pension expense, the only disclosures required by the employer under a defined contribution plan are a plan description, including employee groups covered, the basis for determining contributions, and the nature and effect of significant matters affecting comparability from period to period.[12]

Disclosures for Defined Contribution Plans

Defined Benefit Plan

A **defined benefit plan** defines the benefits that the employee will receive at the time of retirement. The formula that is typically used provides for the benefits to be a function of the employee's years of service and the employee's compensation level when he or she nears retirement. It is necessary to determine what the contribution should be today to meet the pension benefit commitments that will arise at retirement (a time value of money computation). Many different contribution approaches could be used. Whatever funding method is employed, it should provide enough money at retirement to meet the benefits defined by the plan.

The employees are the beneficiaries of a defined contribution trust, but the employer is the beneficiary of a defined benefit trust. The trust's primary purpose under a defined benefit plan is to safeguard assets and to invest them so that there will be enough to pay the employer's obligation to the employees. **In form**, the trust is a separate entity. **In substance**, the trust assets and liabilities belong to the employer. That is, **as long as the plan continues, the employer is responsible for the payment of the defined benefits (without regard to what happens in the trust).** Any shortfall in the accumulated assets held by the trust must be made up by the employer. Any excess accumulated in the trust can be recaptured by the employer, either through reduced future funding or through a reversion of funds.

The accounting for a defined benefit plan is complex. Because the benefits are defined in terms of uncertain future variables, an appropriate funding pattern must be established to ensure that enough funds will be available at retirement to provide the benefits promised. This funding level depends on a number of factors such as turnover, mortality, length of employee service, compensation levels, and interest earnings.

Employers are at risk with defined benefit plans because they must be sure to make enough contributions to meet the cost of benefits that are defined in the plan. The expense recognized each period is not necessarily equal to the cash contribution. Similarly, the liability is controversial because its measurement and recognition relate to unknown future variables. Thus, the accounting issues related to this type of plan are complex. **Our discussion in the following sections primarily deals with defined benefit plans.**

INTERNATIONAL INSIGHT

Outside the U.S., private pension plans are less common because many other nations tend to rely on government-sponsored pension plans. Consequently, accounting for defined benefit pension plans is typically a less important issue elsewhere.

---

[12]"Employers' Accounting for Pension Plans," *Statement of Financial Accounting Standards No. 87* (Stamford, Conn.: FASB, 1985), pars. 63–66.

Components of Pension Expense

There is broad agreement that pension cost should be accounted for on the **accrual basis**.[13] The profession recognizes that **accounting for pension plans requires measurement of the cost and its identification with the appropriate time periods.** The determination of pension cost, however, is extremely complicated because it is a function of the following components.

① Service Cost. Service cost is the expense caused by the increase in pension benefits payable (the **projected benefit obligation**) to employees because of their services rendered during the current year. Actuaries[14] compute **service cost** as the present value of the new benefits earned by employees during the year.

② Interest on the Liability. Because a pension is a deferred compensation arrangement, there is a time value of money factor. As a result, it is recorded on a discounted basis. **Interest expense accrues each year on the projected benefit obligation just as it does on any discounted debt.** The accountant receives help from the actuary in selecting the interest rate, referred to as the **settlement rate.**

③ Actual Return on Plan Assets. The return earned by the accumulated pension fund assets in a particular year is relevant in measuring the net cost to the employer of sponsoring an employee pension plan. Therefore, **annual pension expense should be adjusted for interest and dividends that accumulate within the fund as well as increases and decreases in the market value of the fund assets.**

④ Amortization of Unrecognized Prior Service Cost. Pension plan amendments (including initiation of a pension plan) often include provisions to increase benefits (or in rare situations, to decrease benefits) for employee service provided in prior years. Because plan amendments are granted with the expectation that the employer will realize economic benefits in future periods, **the cost (prior service cost) of providing these retroactive benefits is allocated to pension expense in the future, specifically to the remaining service-years of the affected employees.**

⑤ Gain or Loss. Volatility in pension expense can be caused by sudden and large changes in the market value of plan assets and by changes in the projected benefit obligation (which changes when actuarial assumptions are modified or when actual experience differs from expected experience). Two items comprise this gain or loss: (1) the difference between the actual return and the expected return on plan assets, and (2) amortization of the unrecognized net gain or loss from previous periods. This computation is complex and will be discussed later in the chapter.

---

[13]Until the mid-1960s, with few exceptions, companies applied the **cash basis** of accounting to pension plans by recognizing the amount paid in a particular accounting period as the pension expense for the period. The problem was that the amount paid or funded in a fiscal period depended on financial management and was too often discretionary. For example, funding could be based on the availability of cash, the level of earnings, or other factors unrelated to the requirements of the plan. Application of the cash basis made it possible to manipulate the amount of pension expense appearing in the income statement simply by varying the cash paid to the pension fund.

[14]Actuaries are individuals who are trained through a long and rigorous certification program to assign probabilities to future events and their financial effects. The insurance industry employs actuaries to assess risks and to advise on the setting of premiums and other aspects of insurance policies. Employers rely heavily on actuaries for assistance in developing, implementing, and funding pension plans.

The **components of pension expense** and their effect on total pension expense (increase or decrease) are shown in Illustration 15-7.

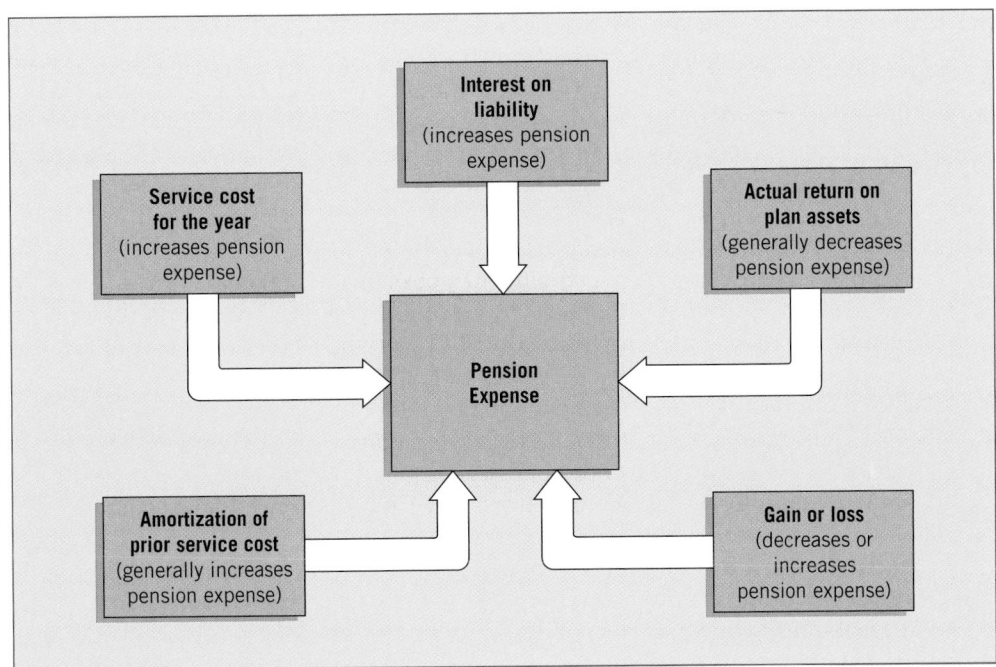

Illustration 15-7
Components of Annual
Pension Expense

Service Cost

The **service cost** component recognized in a period is **the actuarial present value of benefits attributed by the pension benefit formula to employee service during the period**. That is, the actuary predicts the additional benefits that must be paid under the plan's benefit formula as a result of the employees' current year's service and then discounts the cost of those future benefits back to their present value.

Future compensation levels are considered in measuring the present obligation and periodic pension expense if the plan benefit formula incorporates them. In other words, the present obligation resulting from a promise to pay a benefit of 1 percent of an employee's **final pay** is different from an employer's promise to pay 1 percent of **current pay**. To ignore this fact is to ignore an important aspect of pension expense. Thus, the **benefits/years-of-service actuarial method** is the approach adopted by the FASB.

Some object to this determination, arguing that a company should have more freedom to select an expense recognition pattern. Others believe that incorporating future salary increases into current pension expense is accounting for events that have not happened yet. They argue that if the plan were terminated today, only liabilities for accumulated benefits would have to be paid. **Nevertheless, the FASB indicates that the projected benefit obligation provides a more realistic measure of the employer's obligation under the plan on a going-concern basis and, therefore, should be used as the basis for determining service cost.**

Interest on the Liability

The second component of pension expense is **interest on the liability**, or **interest expense**. As indicated earlier, a pension is a deferred compensation arrangement under which this element of wages is deferred and a liability is created. Because the liability is not paid until maturity, it is recorded on a discounted basis and accrues interest over the life of the employee. **The interest component is the interest for the period on the projected benefit obligation outstanding during the period.** The FASB did not address the question of how often to compound the interest cost. To simplify our illustrations and problem materials, we use a simple interest computation, applying it to the beginning-of-the-year balance of the projected benefit liability.

How is the interest rate determined? The Board states that the assumed discount rate should **reflect the rates at which pension benefits could be effectively settled** (**settlement rates**). In determining these rates, it is appropriate to look to available information about rates implicit in current prices of annuity contracts that could be used to effect settlement of the obligation. (Under an annuity contract an insurance company unconditionally guarantees to provide specific pension benefits to specific individuals in return for a fixed consideration or premium.) Other rates of return on high-quality fixed-income investments might also be employed.

Actual Return on Plan Assets

Pension plan assets are usually investments in stocks, bonds, other securities, and real estate that are held to earn a reasonable return, generally at minimum risk. Pension plan assets are increased by employer contributions and actual returns on pension plan assets; they are decreased by benefits paid to retired employees. As indicated, the actual return earned on these assets increases the fund balance and correspondingly reduces the employer's net cost of providing employees' pension benefits. That is, the higher the actual return on the pension plan assets, the less the employer has to contribute eventually and, therefore, the less pension expense that needs to be reported.

The actual return on the plan assets is the increase in pension funds from interest, dividends, and realized and unrealized changes in the fair market value of the plan assets. If the actual return on the plan assets is positive (a gain) during the period, it is subtracted in the computation of pension expense. If the actual return is negative (a loss) during the period, it is added in the computation of pension expense.[15]

Using a Pension Work Sheet

Important to accounting for pensions is the fact that **several significant items of the pension plan are unrecognized in the accounts and in the financial statements**. Among the compromises the FASB made was the nonrecognition (noncapitalization) of the following pension items:

1. Projected benefit obligation.
2. Pension plan assets.
3. Unrecognized prior service costs.
4. Unrecognized net gain or loss.

OBJECTIVE 6
Utilize a work sheet for employer's pension plan entries.

A company is required to **disclose in notes** to the financial statements all of these four noncapitalized items, but they are not recognized in the body of the financial statements. The exact amount of these items must be known at all times because they are used in the computation of annual pension expense. **In order to track these off-balance-sheet pension items, memo entries and accounts have to be maintained outside the formal general ledger accounting system**. A work sheet unique to pension accounting is utilized to record both the formal entries and the memo entries to keep track of all the company's relevant pension plan items and components.[16]

[15]At this point, we are using the actual rate of return. As shown later, for purposes of computing pension expense, the expected rate of return is used.

[16]The use of this pension entry work sheet is recommended and illustrated by Paul B. W. Miller, "The New Pension Accounting (Part 2)," *Journal of Accountancy* (February 1987), pp. 86–94.

The format of the **pension work sheet** is shown below.

Illustration 15-8
Basic Format of Pension
Work Sheet

Pension Work Sheet

	General Journal Entries			Memo Record	
Items	Annual Pension Expense	Cash	Prepaid/ Accrued Cost	Projected Benefit Obligation	Plan Assets

The "General Journal Entries" columns of the work sheet (near the left side) record entries in the formal general ledger accounts. The "Memo Record" columns (on the right side) maintain balances on the unrecognized (noncapitalized) pension items. On the first line of the work sheet, the beginning balances (if any) are recorded. Subsequently, transactions and events related to the pension plan are recorded, using debits and credits and using both sets of records as if they were one for recording the entries. For each transaction or event, the debits must equal the credits. **The balance in the Prepaid/Accrued Cost column should equal the net balance in the memo record.**

2003 Entries and Work Sheet

To illustrate the use of a work sheet and how it helps in accounting for a pension plan, assume that on January 1, 2003, Zarle Company adopts a defined benefit pension plan. The following facts apply to the pension plan for the year 2003.

Plan assets, January 1, 2003, are $100,000.

Projected benefit obligation, January 1, 2003, is $100,000.

Annual service cost is $9,000.

Settlement rate is 10%.

Actual return on plan assets is $10,000.

Contributions are $8,000.

Benefits paid to retirees during the year are $7,000.

Using the data presented above, the work sheet in Illustration 15-9 (page 756) presents the beginning balances and all of the pension entries recorded by Zarle Company in 2003. The beginning balances for the projected benefit obligation and the pension plan assets are recorded on the first line of the work sheet in the memo record. They are not recorded in the formal general journal and, therefore, are not reported as a liability and an asset in the financial statements of Zarle Company. These two significant pension items are off-balance-sheet amounts that affect pension expense but are not recorded as assets and liabilities in the employer's books.

Entry (a) in Illustration 15-9 records the service cost component, which increases pension expense $9,000 and increases the liability (projected benefit obligation) $9,000. Entry (b) accrues the interest expense component, which increases both the liability and the pension expense by $10,000 (the beginning projected benefit obligation multiplied

Items	General Journal Entries			Memo Record	
	Annual Pension Expense	Cash	Prepaid/ Accrued Cost	Projected Benefit Obligation	Plan Assets
Balance, Jan. 1, 2003			—	100,000 Cr.	100,000 Dr.
(a) Service cost	9,000 Dr.			9,000 Cr.	
(b) Interest cost	10,000 Dr.			10,000 Cr.	
(c) Actual return	10,000 Cr.				10,000 Dr.
(d) Contributions		8,000 Cr.			8,000 Dr.
(e) Benefits				7,000 Dr.	7,000 Cr.
Journal entry for 2003	9,000 Dr.	8,000 Cr.	1,000 Cr.*		
Balance, Dec. 31, 2003			1,000 Cr.**	112,000 Cr.	111,000 Dr.

*$9,000 − $8,000 = $1,000
**$112,000 − $111,000 = $1,000

Illustration 15-9
Pension Work Sheet— 2003

by the settlement rate of 10%). Entry (c) records the actual return on the plan assets, which increases the plan assets and decreases the pension expense. Entry (d) records Zarle Company's contribution (funding) of assets to the pension fund; cash is decreased $8,000 and plan assets are increased $8,000. Entry (e) records the benefit payments made to retirees, which results in equal $7,000 decreases to the plan assets and the projected benefit obligation.

The "formal journal entry" on December 31, which is the entry made to formally record the pension expense in 2003, is as follows.

2003

Pension Expense	9,000	
Cash		8,000
Prepaid/Accrued Pension Cost		1,000

The credit to Prepaid/Accrued Pension Cost for $1,000 represents the difference between the 2003 pension expense of $9,000 and the amount funded of $8,000. Prepaid/Accrued Pension Cost (credit) is a liability because the plan is underfunded by $1,000. The Prepaid/Accrued Pension Cost account balance of $1,000 also equals the net of the balances in the memo accounts. This reconciliation of the off-balance-sheet items with the prepaid/accrued pension cost reported in the balance sheet is shown in Illustration 15-10.

Illustration 15-10
Pension Reconciliation Schedule—December 31, 2003

Projected benefit obligation (Credit)	$(112,000)
Plan assets at fair value (Debit)	111,000
Prepaid/accrued pension cost (Credit)	$ (1,000)

If the net of the memo record balances is a credit, the reconciling amount in the prepaid/accrued cost column will be a credit equal in amount. If the net of the memo record balances is a debit, the prepaid/accrued cost amount will be a debit equal in amount. The work sheet is designed to produce this reconciling feature, which will be useful later in the preparation of the required notes related to pension disclosures.

In this illustration, the debit to Pension Expense exceeds the credit to Cash, resulting in a credit to Prepaid/Accrued Pension Cost—the recognition of a liability. If the credit to Cash exceeded the debit to Pension Expense, Prepaid/Accrued Pension Cost would be debited—the recognition of an asset.

Amortization of Unrecognized Prior Service Cost (PSC)

When a defined benefit plan is either initiated (adopted) or amended, credit is often given to employees for years of service provided before the date of initiation or amendment. As a result of prior service credits, the projected benefit obligation is usually greater than it was before. In many cases, the increase in the projected benefit obligation is substantial.

One question that arises is whether an expense and related liability for these **prior service costs (PSC)** should be fully reported at the time a plan is initiated or amended. The FASB has taken the position that no expense for these costs, and in some cases no liability, should be recognized at the time of the plan's adoption or amendment. The Board's rationale is that the employer would not provide credit for past years of service unless it expected to receive benefits in the future. As a result, **the retroactive benefits should not be recognized as pension expense entirely in the year of amendment but should be recognized during the service periods of those employees who are expected to receive benefits under the plan (the remaining service life of the covered active employees).**

The cost of the retroactive benefits (including benefits that are granted to existing retirees) is the increase in the projected benefit obligation at the date of the amendment. The amount of the prior service cost is computed by an actuary. The computation of the amount to recognize each period for the amortization of the unrecognized prior service cost is generally based on the average remaining service of employees in the plan (referred to as the **years-of-service method**).

OBJECTIVE **7**
Explain the accounting for prior service cost and gains and losses.

Gain or Loss

Of great concern to companies that have pension plans are the uncontrollable and unexpected swings in pension expense that could be caused by (1) sudden and large changes in the market value of plan assets, and (2) changes in actuarial assumptions that affect the amount of the projected benefit obligation. If these gains or losses were to impact fully the financial statements in the period of realization or incurrence, substantial fluctuations in pension expense would result. Therefore, the profession decided to reduce the volatility associated with pension expense by using **smoothing techniques** that dampen and in some cases fully eliminate the fluctuations.

Smoothing Unexpected Gains and Losses on Plan Assets. One component of pension expense, actual return on plan assets, reduces pension expense (assuming the actual return is positive). A large change in the actual return can substantially affect pension expense for a year. Assume a company has a 40 percent return in the stock market for the year. Should this substantial, and perhaps one-time, event affect current pension expense?

Actuaries ignore current fluctuations when they develop a funding pattern to pay expected benefits in the future. They develop an **expected rate of return** and multiply it by an asset value weighted over a reasonable period of time to arrive at an **expected return on plan assets**. This return is then used to determine its funding pattern.

The FASB adopted the actuary's approach to dampen wide swings that might occur in the actual return. That is, the **expected return** on the plan assets is to be included as a component of pension expense, not the actual return in a given year. To achieve this goal, the expected rate of return is multiplied by the fair value of the plan assets or a market-related asset value of the plan assets. (Throughout our Zarle Company illustrations, market-related value and fair value of plan assets are assumed equal.) The

market-related asset value is a calculated value that recognizes changes in fair value in a systematic and rational manner over not more than five years.[17]

What happens to the difference between the expected return and the actual return, often referred to as the **unexpected gain or loss**—also called **asset gains and losses** by the FASB? Asset gains (occurring when actual return is greater than expected return) and asset losses (occurring when actual return is less than expected return) are recorded in an Unrecognized Net Gain or Loss account and are combined with unrecognized gains and losses accumulated in prior years.

WHAT DO THE NUMBERS MEAN?

PENSION COSTS UPS AND DOWNS

For some companies, having a pension plan had become a real profit generator in the late 1990s. The income generated in those plans was so strong that the plans not only paid for themselves but also increased earnings. This happens when the expected returns on pension assets are greater than the company's annual costs. At **Norfolk Southern**, pension income amounted to 12 percent of operating profit, and it tallied 11 percent of such profit at **Lucent Technologies, Coastal Corp**, and **Unisys Corp**. The issue is important because in these cases management is not driving the operating income — pension income is. And as a result, income can change quickly. Unfortunately, the stock market has stopped booming, and now pension expense for many companies has increased substantially. The reason: Expected return on a smaller asset base no longer is sufficient to offset pension service costs and interest on the projected benefit obligation. As a result, many companies are finding it difficult to meet their earnings targets.

Smoothing Unexpected Gains and Losses on the Pension Liability. In estimating, the projected benefit obligation (the liability), actuaries make assumptions about such items as mortality rate, retirement rate, turnover rate, disability rate, and salary amounts. Any change in these actuarial assumptions changes the amount of the projected benefit obligation. Seldom does actual experience coincide exactly with the actuarial predictions. These unexpected gains or losses from changes in the projected benefit obligation are called **liability gains and losses**.

Liability gains (resulting from unexpected decreases in the liability balance) and liability losses (resulting from unexpected increases) are deferred (unrecognized). The liability gains and losses are combined in the same Unrecognized Net Gain or Loss account used for asset gains and losses. They are accumulated from year to year, off-balance-sheet, in a memo account. The amortization of the net gain or loss that results from either or both asset and liability gains and losses is a complex calculation beyond the scope of this text.

2004 Entries and Work Sheet

Continuing the Zarle Company illustration into 2004, we note that a January 1, 2004, amendment to the pension plan grants to employees prior service benefits. The following facts apply to the pension plan for the year 2004.

On January 1, 2004, Zarle Company grants prior service benefits having a present value of $80,000.

Annual service cost is $9,500.

[17]Different ways of calculating market-related value may be used for different classes of assets. For example, an employer might use fair value for bonds and a five-year-moving-average for equities. But the manner of determining market-related value should be applied consistently from year to year for each asset class.

Settlement rate is 10%, and expected rate of return on pension assets is 9%.

Actual return on plan assets is $11,100.

Annual funding contributions are $20,000.

Benefits paid to retirees during the year are $8,000.

Amortization of prior service cost (PSC) using the years-of-service method is $27,200.

The following work sheet presents all of the pension entries and information recorded by Zarle Company in 2004.

Illustration 15-11

Pension Work Sheet—2004

	General Journal Entries			Memo Record			
Items	Annual Pension Expense	Cash	Prepaid/ Accrued Cost	Projected Benefit Obligation	Plan Assets	Unrecog- nized Prior Service Cost	Unrecog- nized Net Gain or Loss
Balance, Dec. 31, 2003			1,000 Cr.	112,000 Cr.	111,000 Dr.		
(f) Prior service cost				80,000 Cr.		80,000 Dr.	
Balance, Jan. 1, 2004			1,000 Cr.	192,000 Cr.	111,000 Dr.	80,000 Dr.	
(g) Service cost	9,500 Dr.			9,500 Cr.			
(h) Interest cost	19,200 Dr.ª			19,200 Cr.			
(i) Actual return	11,100 Cr.				11,100 Dr.		
(j) Unexpected gain	1,110 Dr.						1,110 Cr.
(k) Amortization of PSC	27,200 Dr.					27,200 Cr.	
(l) Contributions		20,000 Cr.			20,000 Dr.		
(m) Benefits				8,000 Dr.	8,000 Cr.		
Journal entry for 2004	45,910 Dr.	20,000 Cr.	25,910 Cr.				
Balance, Dec. 31, 2004			26,910 Cr.	212,700 Cr.	134,100 Dr.	52,800 Dr.	1,110 Cr.

ª$19,200 = $192,000 × 10%.

The first line of the work sheet shows the beginning balances of the Prepaid/Accrued Pension Cost account and the memo accounts. Entry (f) records Zarle Company's granting of prior service cost by adding $80,000 to the projected benefit obligation and to the unrecognized (noncapitalized) prior service cost. Entries (g) and (h) are similar to the corresponding entries in 2003.

Entries (i) and (j) are related: Recording the actual return in entry (i) has been illustrated in 2003; it is recorded similarly in 2004. In 2003 it was assumed that the actual return on plan assets was equal to the expected return on plan assets. In 2004, the actual return was different from the expected return. The actual return was $11,100 and the expected return was $9,990 (9% × $111,000). Therefore an Unexpected Gain of $1,110 ($11,100 − $9,990) occurred and is recorded in an Unrecognized Gain or Loss account.[18] As a result of this adjustment, the expected return on the plan assets is the amount actually used to compute pension expense. This unexpected gain increases pension expense.

[18]What happens to the unrecognized gain or loss over time? Because the asset gains and losses and the liability gain and losses can be offsetting, the accumulated total unrecognized net gain or loss may not grow very large. But, it is possible that no offsetting will occur and that the balance in the Net Gain or Loss account will continue to grow. To limit its growth, the FASB has developed approaches to amortize the Unrecognized Gain or Loss if it gets too large. These approaches are complex and beyond the scope of this text.

Entry (k) records the 2004 amortization of unrecognized prior service cost by debiting Pension Expense by $27,200 and crediting the new Unrecognized Prior Service Cost account by the same amount. Entries (l) and (m) are similar to the corresponding entries in 2003.

The journal entry on December 31 to formally record the pension expense—the sum of the annual pension expense column—for 2004 is as follows.

2004

Pension Expense	45,910	
Cash		20,000
Prepaid/Accrued Pension Cost		25,910

Because the expense exceeds the funding, the Prepaid/Accrued Pension Cost account is credited for the $25,910 difference and is a liability. In 2004, as in 2003, the balance of the Prepaid/Accrued Pension Cost account ($26,910) is equal to the net of the balances in the memo accounts, as shown in Illustration 15-12.

Illustration 15-12

Pension Reconciliation Schedule—December 31, 2004

Projected benefit obligation (Credit)	$(212,700)
Plan assets at fair value (Debit)	134,100
Funded status	(78,600)
Unrecognized prior service cost (Debit)	52,800
Unrecognized net gain (Credit)	(1,110)
Prepaid/accrued pension cost (Credit)	$ (26,910)

The reconciliation is the formula that makes the work sheet work. It relates the components of pension accounting, recorded and unrecorded, to one another.

Reporting Pension Amounts

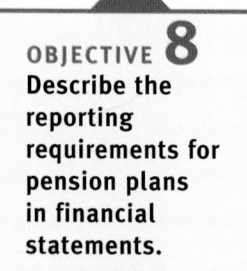

OBJECTIVE **8**
Describe the reporting requirements for pension plans in financial statements.

One might suspect that a phenomenon as significant and complex as pensions would involve extensive reporting and disclosure requirements. We will cover these requirements in two categories: (1) those within the financial statements, and (2) those within the notes to the financial statements.

Within the Financial Statements

If the amount funded (credit to Cash) by the employer to the pension trust is **less than the annual expense** (debit to Pension Expense), a credit balance accrual of the difference arises in the long-term liability section. It might be described as Accrued Pension Cost, Liability for Pension Expense Not Funded, or Pension Liability. A liability is classified as current when it requires the disbursement of cash within the next year.

If the amount funded to the pension trust during the period is **greater than the amount charged to expense**, an asset equal to the difference arises. This asset is reported as Prepaid Pension Cost or Prepaid Pension Expense in the current assets section if it is current in nature. If it is long-term in nature, it is reported in the other assets section.

Within the Notes to the Financial Statements

Pension plans are frequently important to an understanding of financial position, results of operations, and cash flows of a company. Therefore, the following information, if not disclosed in the body of the financial statements, should be disclosed in the notes.[19]

1 A schedule showing all the major components of pension expense should be reported.
Rationale: Information provided about the components of pension expense helps users better understand how pension expense is determined and is useful in forecasting a company's net income.

2 A **reconciliation** showing how the projected benefit obligation and the fair value of the plan assets changed from the beginning to the end of the period is required.
Rationale: Disclosing the projected benefit obligation, the fair value of the plan assets, and changes in them should help users understand the economics underlying the obligations and resources of these plans. The Board believes that explaining the changes in the projected benefit obligation and fair value of plan assets in the form of a reconciliation provides a more complete disclosure and makes the financial statements more understandable.

3 The **funded status** of the plan (difference between the projected benefit obligation and fair value of the plan assets) and the amounts recognized and not recognized in the financial statements must be disclosed.
Rationale: Providing a reconciliation of the plan's funded status to the amount reported in the balance sheet highlights the difference between the funded status and the balance sheet presentation.

4 A disclosure of the rates used in measuring the benefit amounts (discount rate, expected return on plan assets, rate of compensation) should be disclosed.
Rationale: Disclosure of these rates permits the reader to determine the reasonableness of the assumptions applied in measuring the pension liability and pension expense.

In summary, the disclosure requirements are extensive, and purposely so. One factor that has been a challenge for useful pension reporting in the past has been the lack of consistency in terminology. Furthermore, a substantial amount of offsetting is inherent in the measurement of pension expense and the pension liability. These disclosures are designed to address these concerns and take some of the mystery out of pension reporting.

Illustration of Pension Note Disclosure
In the following sections we provide illustrations and explain the key pension disclosure elements.

Components of Pension Expense. The Board requires disclosure of the individual pension expense components: (1) service cost, (2) interest cost, (3) expected return on assets, (4) other deferrals and amortization. The purpose of such disclosure is to make clear to more sophisticated readers how pension expense is determined. Providing information on the components should also be useful in predicting future pension expense.

An example of this part of the disclosure in presented in Illustration 15-13. It uses the information from the Zarle Company illustration, specifically the expense component information from the work sheets in Illustration 15-9 and Illustration 15-11.

---

[19]"Employers' Disclosure about Pensions and Other Postretirement Benefits," *Statement of Financial Accounting Standards No. 132* (Stamford, Conn.: FASB, 1998). This statement modifies the disclosure requirements of *SFAS No. 87*. In our view, these new disclosure requirements are easier to understand and more streamlined than the disclosure requirements mandated prior to *SFAS No. 132*.

Illustration 15-13
Summary of Expense
Components—2003, 2004

ZARLE COMPANY		
Components of Net Periodic Pension Expense	2003	2004
Service cost	$ 9,000	$ 9,500
Interest cost	10,000	19,200
Expected return on plan assets	(10,000)	(9,990)*
Amortization of prior service cost	–0–	27,200
Net periodic pension expense	$ 9,000	$45,910

*Note that the expected return must be disclosed, not the actual. In 2004, the expected return is $9,990, which is the actual gain of $11,100 adjusted by the unrecognized gain of $1,110.

✦ **UNDERLYING CONCEPTS**

This represents another compromise between relevance and reliability. The disclosure of the unrecognized items attempts to balance these objectives.

Reconciliation and Funded Status of Plan. Having a reconciliation of the changes in the assets and liabilities from the beginning of the year to the end of the year, statement readers can better understand the underlying economics of the plan. In essence, this disclosure (reconciliation) contains the information in the pension work sheet for the projected benefit obligation and plan asset columns.

In addition, the FASB also requires a disclosure of the funded status of the plan. That is, the off-balance-sheet assets, liabilities, and unrecognized gains and losses must be reconciled with the on-balance-sheet liability or asset. Many believe this is the key to understanding the accounting for pensions. Why is such a disclosure important? The delayed recognition of some pension elements may exclude the most current and the most relevant information about the pension plan from the financial statements. This important information, however, is provided within this disclosure.

Using the information for Zarle Company, the following schedule provides an example of the reconciliation.

Illustration 15-14
Pension Disclosure for
Zarle Company—2003
and 2004

ZARLE COMPANY PENSION DISCLOSURE		
	2003	2004
Change in benefit obligation		
Benefit obligation at beginning of year	$100,000	$112,000
Service cost	9,000	9,500
Interest cost	10,000	19,200
Amendments (Prior service cost)	–0–	80,000
Benefits paid	(7,000)	(8,000)
Benefit obligation at end of year	112,000	212,700
Change in plan assets		
Fair value of plan assets at beginning of year	100,000	111,000
Actual return on plan assets	10,000	11,100
Contributions	8,000	20,000
Benefits paid	(7,000)	(8,000)
Fair value of plan assets at end of year	111,000	134,100
Funded status	(1,000)	(78,600)
Unrecognized net gain	–0–	(1,110)
Unrecognized prior service cost	–0–	52,800
Prepaid (accrued) benefit cost	$ (1,000)	$ (26,910)

The 2003 column reveals that the projected benefit obligation is underfunded by $1,000. The 2004 column reveals that the underfunded liability of $78,600 is reported in the balance sheet at $26,910, due to unrecognized net gain of $1,110 and the unrecognized prior service cost of $52,800.

Other Postretirement Expenses

In addition to pensions, companies often provide other types of postretirement benefits as well. These other benefits include life insurance offered outside a pension plan, dental, eye, and medical care, legal and tax services, tuition assistance, day care, and housing assistance. The costs related to these benefits can be substantial.

Why didn't the FASB cover these other types of postretirement benefits in the earlier pension accounting statement? Because the apparent similarities between the two benefits mask some significant differences. These differences are shown in Illustration 15-15.

UNDERLYING CONCEPTS

Does it make a difference to users of financial statements whether pension information is recognized in the financial statements or disclosed only in the notes? The FASB was not sure, so in accord with the full disclosure principle, it decided to provide extensive pension plan disclosures.

Illustration 15-15
Differences between Pensions and Postretirement Health Care Benefits

Item	Pensions	Health Care Benefits
Funding	Generally funded.	Generally NOT funded.
Benefit	Well-defined and level dollar amount.	Generally uncapped and great variability.
Beneficiary	Retiree (maybe some benefit to surviving spouse).	Retiree, spouse, and other dependents.
Benefit payable	Monthly.	As needed and used.
Predictability	Variables are reasonably predictable.	Utilization difficult to predict. Level of cost varies geographically and fluctuates over time.

Expanded Discussion of Other Postretirement Benefits

Two of the differences presented in Illustration 15-15 highlight why measuring the future payments for health care benefit plans is so much more difficult than for pension plans.

1. Many postretirement plans do not set a limit on health care benefits. No matter how serious the illness or how long it lasts, the benefits continue to flow. (Even if the employer uses an insurance company plan, the premiums will escalate according to the increased benefits provided.)

2. The level of health care benefit utilization and health care costs is difficult to predict. The increased longevity and unexpected illnesses (e.g., AIDS) along with new medical technologies (e.g., MRI scans) and cures (e.g., radiation) cause changes in health care utilization.

Additionally, although health care benefits are generally covered by the fiduciary and reporting standards for employee benefit funds under government regulations, the stringent minimum vesting, participation, and funding standards that apply to pensions do not apply to health care benefits. Nevertheless, many of the basic concepts and much of the accounting terminology and measurement methodology applicable to pensions are also applicable to other postretirement benefits. As a result, the accounting entries and work sheet treatment are essentially the same as for pensions, and therefore a worksheet for other postretirement benefits, is not illustrated here.

The disclosures required for other postretirement benefit plans are also similar to, and just as detailed and extensive as, those required for pensions. By recognizing these

Examples of Pension and Other Postretirement Benefit Disclosures

similarities, under the provisions of *FASB Statement No. 132* pension and other postretirement benefit disclosures can be combined. The following disclosures are required.

① Postretirement expense for the period, separately identifying all components of that cost.

② A schedule showing changes in postretirement benefit obligations and plan assets during the year.

③ A schedule reconciling the funded status of the plan with amounts reported in the employer's balance sheet, separately identifying the reconciling items.

④ The assumptions and rates used in computing the future benefit amounts, including the following: assumed health care cost trend rates; assumed discount rates; and the effect of a one-percentage-point increase in the assumed health care cost trend rate on the measurement of the accumulated benefit obligation, the service cost, and the interest cost.

CONCLUDING REMARKS

Accounting for compensation at one time was relatively straightforward. However, employment agreements have become more complex, making it more difficult to determine the proper expense and related liability. Today, compensation is often in the form of bonuses, stock options, and other non-cash forms. These compensation arrangements make it more difficult to determine in what period compensation should be reported. In addition, the measurement of the related liability becomes more complex. As a result, it is not surprising that much effort is being expended to determine the proper accounting and reporting for these various compensation arrangements.

SUMMARY OF LEARNING OBJECTIVES

❶ **Explain the accounting for salary and bonuses.** Amounts paid to employees for salaries and wages should be reported as compensation expense. The most common types of payroll deductions are taxes and miscellaneous items such as insurance premiums, employee savings, and union dues. Any amounts deducted from payroll but not yet remitted to the proper authority at the end of the accounting period should be recognized as current liabilities.

❷ **Describe the accounting for stock compensation plans under GAAP.** Companies are given a choice in the recognition approach to stock compensation; the FASB encourages adoption of the fair value method. Using the fair value approach, total compensation expense is computed based on the fair value of the options that are expected to vest on the grant date. Under the intrinsic value approach, total compensation cost is computed as the excess of the market price of the stock over the option price on the date when both the number of shares to which employees are entitled and the option or purchase price for those shares are known. Under both the fair and intrinsic value methods, compensation expense is recognized in the periods in which the employee performs the services.

❸ **Explain the controversy surrounding stock compensation plans.** When first proposed, there was considerable opposition to the recognition provisions contained in the fair value approach, because that approach could result in substantial compensation expense that was not previously recognized. Corporate America, particularly the high-technology sector, was quite vocal in its opposition to the proposed standard. They believed that they would be placed at a competitive disadvantage with larger companies that can withstand higher compensation charges. In response to this opposition, which was based primarily on economic-consequences arguments, the FASB decided to en-

KEY TERMS

Accumulated rights, *741*

Actual return on the plan assets, *754*

Actuarial present value, *753*

Asset gains and losses, *758*

Bonus, *743*

Compensated absences, *741*

Components of pension expense, *753*

Defined benefit plan, *751*

Defined contribution plan, *750*

Expected rate of return, *757*

Expected return on plan assets, *757*

Fair value method, *744*

Funded status, *761*

Grant date, *743*

Interest on the liability/ Interest expense, *753*

Intrinsic value method, *744*

Liability gains and losses, *758*

Measurement date, *745*

Noncompensatory plans, *748*

Pension work sheet, *755*

Prior service costs (PSC), *757*

Projected benefit obligation, *752*

Reconciliation, *761*

Retroactive benefits, *757*

Service cost, *753*

Service period, *745*

Settlement rates, *754*

Social Security tax, *739*

Stock option plans, *743*

courage, rather than require, recognition of compensation cost based on the fair value method and to require expanded disclosures.

Unexpected gain or loss, *758*
Vested rights, *741*
Years-of-service method, *757*

④ Identity types of pension plans and their characteristics. The two most common types of pension arrangements are defined contribution plans and defined benefit plans. In *defined contribution plans,* the employer agrees to contribute to a pension trust a certain sum each period, based on a formula. This formula may consider such factors as age, length of employee service, employer's profits, and compensation level. Only the employer's contribution is defined; no promise is made regarding the ultimate benefits paid out to the employees. *Defined benefit plans* specify the benefits that the employee will receive at the time of retirement. The formula typically used provides for the benefits to be a function of the employee's years of service and the employer's compensation level when he or she nears retirement.

⑤ Identify the components of pension expense. Pension expense is a function of the following components: (1) service cost, (2) interest on the liability, (3) return on plan assets, (4) amortization of unrecognized prior service cost, and (5) gain or loss.

⑥ Utilize a work sheet for pension plan entries. A work sheet unique to pension accounting may be utilized to record both the formal entries and the memo entries to keep track of all the employer's relevant pension plan items and components.

⑦ Explain the accounting for prior service cost and gains and losses. The amount of prior service cost is computed by an actuary. Amortization of the unrecognized prior service cost is an accounting function performed with the assistance of an actuary.

The difference between the expected return and the actual return is called asset gains and losses. This component defers the difference between the actual return and expected return on plan assets in computing current-year pension expense.

In estimating the projected benefit obligation (the liability), actuaries make assumptions about such items as mortality rate, retirement rate, turnover rate, disability rate, and salary amounts. Any change in these actuarial assumptions changes the amount of the projected benefit obligation. These unexpected gains or losses from changes in the projected benefit obligation are liability gains and losses. Liability gains (resulting from unexpected decreases in the liability balance) and liability losses (resulting from unexpected increases) are deferred (unrecognized). The liability gains and losses are combined in the same Unrecognized Net Gain or Loss account used for asset gains and losses and are accumulated from year to year, off-balance-sheet, in a memo record account.

⑧ Describe the reporting requirements for pension plans in financial statements. The current financial statement disclosure requirements for pension plans are as follows: (1) The components of net periodic pension expense for the period. (2) A schedule showing changes in the benefit obligation and plan assets during the year. (3) A schedule reconciling the funded status of the plan with amounts reported in the employer's statement of financial position. (4) The weighted-average assumed discount rate, the rate of compensation increase used to measure the projected benefit obligation, and the weighted-average expected long-term rate of return on plan assets.

REVIEW EXERCISE

Morgan Company provides you with the following information related to its compensation program for its employees.

1. Total payroll for 2004 was $5,000,000, of which $1,400,000 is exempt from Social Security tax because it represent amounts paid in excess of $84,900 to certain employees. The amount paid to employees who earn in excess of $7,000 was $4,200,000. The state unemployment tax is 3.5%, but Morgan Company is allowed a credit of 2.3% by the state for its low unemployment record. Assume the current F.I.C.A. tax is 7.65% on wages to $84,900 and 1.45% in excess of $84,900. The federal unemployment tax rate is 0.8% after the state credit.

2. On January 2, 2003, Morgan granted options to key executives to purchase 40,000 shares of the company's $1 par value common stock. The option price was set at $40, and the fair value option-pricing model determined total compensation to be $450,000. The market price of the stock at the date of grant was $40. The service period for the award is 2 years. The market price at December 31, 2004, was $62.

3. For the year 2004, Morgan was provided the following pension plan information from its actuary.

Service cost	$ 70,000
Prior service cost amortization	12,000
Contribution to the plan	65,000
Benefits paid	50,000
Projected benefit obligation, January 1, 2004	900,000
Plan assets at January 1, 2004	1,000,000
Actual and expected return on plan assets	90,000
Interest (settlement) rate	8%

Instructions

(a) Compute:
  (1) The amount of Social Security taxes that Morgan will report as an expense in 2004.
  (2) The amount of federal and state unemployment taxes that Morgan will report as expense in 2004.

(b) Compute the amount, if any, of compensation expense to be reported for the stock option plan for key executives in 2004. The company uses the intrinsic value method for determining compensation expense. Also determine the amount of compensation expense to be reported in 2004 assuming the company uses the fair value method.

(c) Compute the amount of pension expense to be reported by Morgan for the year 2004.

SOLUTION TO REVIEW EXERCISE

(a) (1)
Total payroll	$5,000,000
Exempt payroll	1,400,000
	3,600,000
FICA tax rate	7.65%
FICA taxes	$ 275,400
Exempt payroll subject to additional tax	$1,400,000
Hospital insurance tax rate	1.45%
Hospital insurance taxes (HIT)	$ 20,300
FICA taxes	$275,400
HIT	20,300
Social Security taxes	$295,700

(2)
Total payroll	$5,000,000
Exempt payroll	4,200,000
	800,000
Federal employment tax rate	0.8%
Federal employment taxes	$ 6,400
Payroll subject to unemployment taxes	$800,000
State unemployment tax rate (3.5% − 2.3%)	1.2%
State unemployment taxes	$ 9,600

(b) Under the intrinsic value method, there is zero (no) computation because the market price of Morgan's stock and the exercise price of the options granted are the same.

Under the fair value method, compensation expense is $225,000 ($450,000 ÷ 2).

(c)		
Service cost		$70,000
Interest on the liability ($900,000 × 8%)		72,000
Expected return on plan assets		(90,000)
Prior service cost amortization		12,000
Pension expense		$64,000

QUESTIONS

1 What are compensated absences?

2 Under what conditions must an employer accrue a liability for the cost of compensated absences?

3 Under what conditions is an employer required to accrue a liability for sick pay? Under what conditions is an employer permitted but not required to accrue a liability for sick pay?

4 Caitlin Carter operates a health food store, and she has been the only employee. Her business is growing, and she is considering hiring some additional staff to help her in the store. Explain to her the various payroll deductions that she will have to account for, including their potential impact on her financial statements, if she hires additional staff.

5 Briefly explain the accounting requirements for stock compensation plans under *Statement of Financial Accounting Standards No. 123.*

6 Weiland Corporation has an employee stock purchase plan which permits all full-time employees to purchase 10 shares of common stock on the third anniversary of their employment and an additional 15 shares on each subsequent anniversary date. The purchase price is set at the market price on the date purchased and no commission is charged. Discuss whether this plan would be considered compensatory.

7 What date or event does the profession believe should be used in determining the value of a stock option? What arguments support this position?

8 Over what period of time should compensation cost of stock options be allocated?

9 How is the compensation expense of stock options computed using the fair value approach?

10 Differentiate between a defined contribution pension plan and a defined benefit pension plan. Explain how the employer's obligation differs between the two types of plans.

11 What factors must be considered by the actuary in measuring the amount of pension benefits under a defined benefit plan?

12 Explain how cash basis accounting for pension plans differs from accrual basis accounting for pension plans. Why is cash basis accounting generally considered unacceptable for pension plan accounting?

13 Identify the five components that comprise pension expense. Briefly explain the nature of each component.

14 What is service cost and what is the basis of its measurement?

15 In computing the interest component of pension expense, what interest rates may be used?

16 Explain the difference between service cost and prior service cost.

17 What is meant by "prior service cost"? When is prior service cost recognized as pension expense?

18 If pension expense recognized in a period exceeds the current amount funded by the employer, what kind of account arises? How should that account be reported in the financial statements? If the reverse occurs—that is, current funding by the employer exceeds the amount recognized as pension expense—what kind of account arises, and how should it be reported?

19 How does an "asset gain or loss" develop in pension accounting? How does a "liability gain or loss" develop in pension accounting?

20 Of what value to the financial statement reader is the schedule reconciling the funded status of the plan with amounts reported in the employer's balance sheet?

21 What are postretirement benefits other than pensions?

22 What are the major differences between postretirement health care benefits and pension benefits?

BRIEF EXERCISES

BE15-1 Future Zone Corporation's weekly payroll of $23,000 included FICA taxes withheld of $1,426, federal taxes withheld of $2,990, state taxes withheld of $920, and insurance premiums withheld of $250. Prepare the journal entry to record Future Zone's payroll.

BE15-2 Tale Spin Inc. provides paid vacations to its employees. At December 31, 2004, 30 employees have each earned 2 weeks of vacation time. The employees' average salary is $600 per week. Prepare Tale Spin's December 31, 2004, adjusting entry.

BE15-3 Gargoyle Corporation provides its officers with bonuses based on income. For 2004, the bonuses total $450,000 and are paid on February 15, 2005. Prepare Gargoyle's December 31, 2004, adjusting entry and the February 15, 2005, entry.

BE15-4 On January 1, 2004, Johnson Corporation granted 5,000 options to executives. Each option entitles the holder to purchase one share of Johnson's $5 par value common stock at $50 per share at any time during the next 5 years. The market price of the stock is $65 per share on the date of grant. The period of benefit is 2 years. Prepare Johnson's journal entries for January 1, 2004, and December 31, 2004 and 2005, using the intrinsic value method.

BE15-5 Use the information given for Johnson Corporation in BE15-4. Assume the fair value option pricing model determines that total compensation expense is $140,000. Prepare Johnson's journal entries for January 1, 2004, and December 31, 2004, and 2005, using the fair value method.

BE15-6 The following information is available for Jack Borke Corporation for 2004.

Service cost	$29,000
Interest on projected benefit obligation	22,000
Return on plan assets	20,000
Amortization of unrecognized prior service cost	15,200
Amortization of unrecognized net loss	500

Compute Borke's 2004 pension expense.

BE15-7 At January 1, 2004, Uddin Company had plan assets of $250,000 and a projected benefit obligation of the same amount. During 2004, service cost was $27,500, the settlement rate was 10%, actual and expected return on plan assets were $25,000, contributions were $20,000, and benefits paid were $17,500. Prepare a pension work sheet for Uddin Company for 2004.

BE15-8 For 2004, Potts Company had pension expense of $32,000 and contributed $25,000 to the pension fund. Prepare Potts Company's journal entry to record pension expense and funding.

BE15-9 At December 31, 2004, Conway Corporation had a projected benefit obligation of $510,000, plan assets of $322,000, unrecognized prior service cost of $127,000, and accrued pension cost of $61,000. Prepare a pension reconciliation schedule for Conway.

BE15-10 Caleb Corporation has the following information available concerning its postretirement benefit plan for 2003.

Service cost	$40,000
Interest cost	52,400
Return on plan assets	26,900

Compute Caleb's 2003 postretirement expense.

EXERCISES

E15-1 **(Compensated Absences)** Zero Mostel Company began operations on January 2, 2003. It employs 9 individuals who work 8-hour days and are paid hourly. Each employee earns 10 paid vacation days and 6 paid sick days annually. Vacation days may be taken after January 15 of the year following the year in which they are earned. Sick days may be taken as soon as they are earned; unused sick days accumulate. Additional information is as follows.

	Actual Hourly Wage Rate		Vacation Days Used by Each Employee		Sick Days Used by Each Employee	
	2003	2004	2003	2004	2003	2004
	$10	$11	0	9	4	5

Zero Mostel Company has chosen to accrue the cost of compensated absences at rates of pay in effect during the period when earned and to accrue sick pay when earned.

Instructions

(a) Prepare journal entries to record transactions related to compensated absences during 2003 and 2004.

(b) Compute the amounts of any liability for compensated absences that should be reported on the balance sheet at December 31, 2003 and 2004.

E15-2 (Compensated Absences) Assume the facts in the preceding exercise, except that Zero Mostel Company has chosen not to accrue paid sick leave until used, and has chosen to accrue vacation time at expected future rates of pay without discounting. The company used the following projected rates to accrue vacation time.

Year in Which Vacation Time Was Earned	Projected Future Pay Rates Used to Accrue Vacation Pay
2003	$10.75
2004	11.60

Instructions

(a) Prepare journal entries to record transactions related to compensated absences during 2003 and 2004.

(b) Compute the amounts of any liability for compensated absences that should be reported on the balance sheet at December 31, 2003, and 2004.

E15-3 (Payroll Tax Entries) The total payroll of Rene Auber Company for September 2003 was $480,000, of which $110,000 is exempt from F.I.C.A. tax because it represented amounts paid in excess of $84,900 to certain employees. The amount paid to employees in excess of $7,000 was $400,000. Income taxes in the amount of $90,000 were withheld, as well as $9,000 in union dues. The state unemployment tax is 3.5%, but Auber Company is allowed a credit of 2.3% by the state for its unemployment experience. Also, assume that the current F.I.C.A. tax is 7.65% on an employee's wages to $84,900 and 1.45% in excess of $84,900. No employee for Auber makes more than $125,000. The federal unemployment tax rate is 0.8% after state credit.

Instructions

Prepare the necessary journal entries if the wages and salaries paid and the employer payroll taxes are recorded separately.

E15-4 (Payroll Tax Entries) Green Day Hardware Company's payroll for November 2004 is summarized below.

			Amount Subject to Payroll Taxes	
			Unemployment Tax	
Payroll	Wages Due	F.I.C.A.	Federal	State
Factory	$120,000	$120,000	$40,000	$40,000
Sales	44,000	32,000	4,000	4,000
Administrative	36,000	36,000	—	—
Total	$200,000	$188,000	$44,000	$44,000

At this point in the year some employees have already received wages in excess of those to which payroll taxes apply. Assume that the state unemployment tax is 2.5%. The F.I.C.A. rate is 7.65% on an employee's wages to $84,900 and 1.45% in excess of $84,900. Of the $188,000 wages subject to F.I.C.A. tax, $20,000 is in excess of $84,900 related to the sales wages. Federal unemployment tax rate is 0.8% after credits. Income tax withheld amounts to $16,000 for factory, $7,000 for sales, and $6,000 for administrative.

Instructions

(a) Prepare a schedule showing the employer's total cost of wages for November by function. (Round all computations to nearest dollar.)

(b) Prepare the journal entries to record the factory, sales, and administrative payrolls including the employer's payroll taxes.

E15-5 (Issuance and Exercise of Stock Options) On November 1, 2003, Columbo Company adopted a stock option plan that granted options to key executives to purchase 30,000 shares of the company's $10 par value common stock. The options were granted on January 2, 2004, and were exercisable 2 years after the date of grant if the grantee was still an employee of the company; the options expired 6 years from date of grant. The option price was set at $40, and the fair value option pricing model determines the total compensation expense to be $450,000.

All of the options were exercised during the year 2006: 20,000 on January 3 when the market price was $67, and 10,000 on May 1 when the market price was $77 a share.

Instructions

Prepare journal entries relating to the stock option plan for the years 2004, 2005, and 2006 under the fair value method. Assume that the employee performs services equally in 2004 and 2005.

E15-6 (Issuance, Exercise, and Termination of Stock Options) On January 1, 2004, Titania Inc. granted stock options to officers and key employees for the purchase of 20,000 shares of the company's $10 par common stock at $25 per share. The options were exercisable within a 5-year period beginning January 1, 2006, by grantees still in the employ of the company, and expiring December 31, 2010. The service period for this award is 2 years. Assume that the fair value option pricing model determines total compensation expense to be $350,000.

On April 1, 2005, 2,000 option shares were terminated when the employees resigned from the company. The market value of the common stock was $35 per share on this date.

On March 31, 2006, 12,000 option shares were exercised when the market value of the common stock was $40 per share.

Instructions

Prepare journal entries using the fair value method to record issuance of the stock options, termination of the stock options, exercise of the stock options, and charges to compensation expense, for the years ended December 31, 2004, 2005, and 2006.

E15-7 (Issuance, Exercise, and Termination of Stock Options) On January 1, 2002, Nichols Corporation granted 10,000 options to key executives. Each option allows the executive to purchase one share of Nichols' $5 par value common stock at a price of $20 per share. The options were exercisable within a 2-year period beginning January 1, 2004, if the grantee is still employed by the company at the time of the exercise. On the grant date, Nichols' stock was trading at $25 per share, and a fair value option-pricing model determines total compensation to be $400,000.

On May 1, 2004, 8,000 options were exercised when the market price of Nichols' stock was $30 per share. The remaining options lapsed in 2006 because executives decided not to exercise their options.

Instructions

Prepare the necessary journal entries related to the stock option plan for the years 2002 through 2006. Nichols uses the fair value approach to account for stock options.

E15-8 (Pension Expense, Journal Entries) The following information is available for the pension plan of Kiley Company for the year 2003.

Actual and expected return on plan assets	$ 12,000
Benefits paid to retirees	40,000
Contributions (funding)	95,000
Interest/discount rate	10%
Prior service cost amortization	8,000
Projected benefit obligation, January 1, 2003	500,000
Service cost	60,000

Instructions

(a) Compute pension expense for the year 2003.

(b) Prepare the journal entry to record pension expense and the employer's contribution to the pension plan in 2003.

E15-9 (Computation of Pension Expense) Rebekah Company provides the following information about its defined benefit pension plan for the year 2004.

Service cost	$ 90,000
Contribution to the plan	105,000
Prior service cost amortization	10,000
Actual and expected return on plan assets	64,000
Benefits paid	40,000
Accrued pension cost liability at January 1, 2004	10,000
Plan assets at January 1, 2004	640,000
Projected benefit obligation at January 1, 2004	800,000
Unrecognized prior service cost balance at January 1, 2004	150,000
Interest/discount (settlement) rate	10%

Instructions

Compute the pension expense for the year 2004.

E15-10 (Preparation of Pension Work Sheet with Reconciliation) Using the information in E15-9, prepare a pension work sheet inserting January 1, 2004, balances, showing December 31, 2004, balances and the journal entry recording pension expense.

E15-11 (Basic Pension Work Sheet) The following facts apply to the pension plan of Trudy Borke Inc. for the year 2004.

Plan assets, January 1, 2004	$490,000
Projected benefit obligation, January 1, 2004	490,000
Settlement rate	8.5%
Annual pension service cost	40,000
Contributions (funding)	30,000
Actual return on plan assets	49,700
Benefits paid to retirees	33,400

Instructions

Using the preceding data, compute pension expense for the year 2004. As part of your solution, prepare a pension work sheet that shows the journal entry for pension expense for 2004 and the year-end balances in the related pension accounts.

E15-12 (Basic Pension Work Sheet) The following defined benefit pension data of Doreen Corp. apply to the year 2004.

Projected benefit obligation, January 1, 2004 (before amendment)	$560,000
Plan assets, January 1, 2004	546,200
Prepaid/accrued pension cost (credit)	13,800
On January 1, 2004, Doreen Corp., through plan amendment, grants prior service benefits having a present value of	100,000
Settlement rate	9%
Annual pension service cost	58,000
Contributions (funding)	55,000
Actual return on plan assets	52,280
Benefits paid to retirees	40,000
Prior service cost amortization for 2004	17,000

Instructions

For 2004, prepare a pension work sheet for Doreen Corp. that shows the journal entry for pension expense and the year-end balances in the related pension accounts.

E15-13 **(Disclosures: Pension Expense and Reconciliation Schedule)** Mildred Enterprises provides the following information relative to its defined benefit pension plan.

Balances or Values at December 31, 2004

Projected benefit obligation	$2,737,000
Fair value of plan assets	2,278,329
Unrecognized prior service cost	205,000
Unrecognized net loss (January 1, 2004, balance, –0–)	45,680
Accrued pension cost liability	207,991
Other pension plan data:	
Service cost for 2004	$ 94,000
Unrecognized prior service cost amortization for 2004	45,000
Actual return on plan assets in 2004	130,000
Expected return on plan assets in 2004	175,680
Interest on January 1, 2004, projected benefit obligation	253,000
Contributions to plan in 2004	92,329
Benefits paid	140,000

Instructions
(a) Prepare the note disclosing the components of pension expense for the year 2004.
(b) Reconcile the funded status of the plan with the amount reported in the December 31, 2004, balance sheet.

PROBLEMS

P15-1 **(Payroll Tax Entries)** Star Wars Company pays its office employee payroll weekly. Below is a partial list of employees and their payroll data for August. Because August is their vacation period, vacation pay is also listed.

Employee	Earnings to July 31	Weekly Pay	Vacation Pay to Be Received in August
Mark Hamill	$4,200	$180	—
Carrie Fisher	3,500	150	$300
Harrison Ford	2,700	110	220
Alec Guinness	7,400	250	—
Peter Cushing	8,000	290	580

Assume that the federal income tax withheld is 10% of wages. Union dues withheld are 2% of wages. Vacations are taken the second and third weeks of August by Fisher, Ford, and Cushing. The state unemployment tax rate is 2.5% and the federal is 0.8%, both on a $7,000 maximum. The F.I.C.A. rate is 7.65% on employee and employer on a maximum of $84,900 per employee. In addition, a 1.45% rate is charged both employer and employee for an employee's wage in excess of $84,900.

Instructions
Make the journal entries necessary for each of the four August payrolls. The entries for the payroll and for the company's liability are made separately. Also make the entry to record the monthly payment of accrued payroll liabilities.

P15-2 **(Payroll Tax Entries)** Below is a payroll sheet for Empire Import Company for the month of September 2004. The company is allowed a 1% unemployment compensation rate by the state; the federal unemployment tax rate is 0.8% and the maximum for both is $7,000. Assume a 10% federal income tax rate for all employees and a 7.65% F.I.C.A. tax on employee and employer on a maximum of $84,900. In addition, 1.45% is charged both employer and employee for an employee's wage in excess of $84,900 per employee.

Name	Earnings to Aug. 31	September Earnings	Income Tax Withholding	F.I.C.A.	State U.C.	Federal U.C.
B.D. Williams	$ 6,800	$ 800				
D. Prowse	6,300	700				
K. Baker	7,600	1,100				
F. Oz	13,600	1,900				
A. Daniels	105,000	15,000				
P. Mayhew	112,000	16,000				

Instructions

(a) Complete the payroll sheet and make the necessary entry to record the payment of the payroll.

(b) Make the entry to record the payroll tax expenses of Empire Import Company.

(c) Make the entry to record the payment of the payroll liabilities created. Assume that the company pays all payroll liabilities at the end of each month.

P15-3 (Stock Option Plan) ISU Company adopted a stock option plan on November 30, 2001, that provided that 70,000 shares of $5 par value stock be designated as available for the granting of options to officers of the corporation at a price of $8 a share. The market value was $12 a share on November 30, 2001.

On January 2, 2002, options to purchase 28,000 shares were granted to president Don Pedro—15,000 for services to be rendered in 2002 and 13,000 for services to be rendered in 2003. Also on that date, options to purchase 14,000 shares were granted to vice president Beatrice Leonato—7,000 for services to be rendered in 2002 and 7,000 for services to be rendered in 2003. The market value of the stock was $14 a share on January 2, 2002. The options were exercisable for a period of one year following the year in which the services were rendered.

In 2003 neither the president nor the vice president exercised their options because the market price of the stock was below the exercise price. The market value of the stock was $7 a share on December 31, 2003, when the options for 2002 services lapsed.

On December 31, 2004, both president Pedro and vice president Leonato exercised their options for 13,000 and 7,000 shares, respectively, when the market price was $16 a share.

Instructions

Prepare the necessary journal entries in 2001 when the stock option plan was adopted, in 2002 when options were granted, in 2003 when options lapsed, and in 2004 when options were exercised. The company elects to use the intrinsic value method.

P15-4 (Two-Year Work Sheet and Reconciliation Schedule) On January 1, 2004, Diana Peter Company has the following defined benefit pension plan balances.

Projected benefit obligation	$4,200,000
Fair value of plan assets	4,200,000

The interest (settlement) rate applicable to the plan is 10%. On January 1, 2005, the company amends its pension agreement so that prior service costs of $500,000 are created. Other data related to the pension plan are as follows.

	2004	2005
Service costs	$150,000	$180,000
Unrecognized prior service costs amortization	–0–	90,000
Contributions (funding) to the plan	140,000	185,000
Benefits paid	200,000	280,000
Actual return on plan assets	252,000	260,000
Expected rate of return on assets	6%	8%

Instructions

(a) Prepare a pension work sheet for the pension plan for 2004 and 2005.

(b) As of December 31, 2005, prepare a schedule reconciling the funded status with the reported liability (accrued pension cost).

P15-5 (Pension Expense, Journal Entries) Mantle Company sponsors a defined benefit pension plan. The following information related to the pension plan is available for 2003.

	2003
Plan assets (fair value), January 1	$380,000
Projected benefit obligation, January 1	600,000
Prepaid/(accrued) pension cost balance, January 1	(40,000)
Unrecognized prior service cost, January 1	180,000
Service cost	60,000
Actual and expected return on plan assets	24,000
Amortization of prior service cost	10,000
Contributions (funding)	110,000
Interest/settlement rate	9%

Instructions

(a) Compute pension expense for 2003.

(b) Prepare the journal entries to record the pension expense and the company's funding of the pension plan for 2003.

P15-6 (Comprehensive 2-Year Work Sheet) Ingrid Mount Co. has the following defined benefit pension plan balances on January 1, 2002.

Projected benefit obligation	$4,500,000
Fair value of plan assets	4,500,000

The interest (settlement) rate applicable to the plan is 10%. On January 1, 2003, the company amends its pension agreement so that prior service costs of $600,000 are created. Other data related to the pension plan are as follows.

	2002	2003
Service costs	$150,000	$170,000
Unrecognized prior service costs amortization	–0–	90,000
Contributions (funding) to the plan	150,000	184,658
Benefits paid	220,000	280,000
Actual return on plan assets	252,000	250,000
Expected rate of return on assets	6%	8%

Instructions

(a) Prepare a pension work sheet for the pension plan in 2002.

(b) Prepare any journal entries related to the pension plan that would be needed at December 31, 2002.

(c) Prepare a pension work sheet for 2003 and any journal entries related to the pension plan as of December 31, 2003.

(d) As of December 31, 2003, prepare a schedule reconciling the funded status with the reported liability (accrued pension cost).

CONCEPTUAL CASES

C15-1 **(Stock Compensation Plans)** Presented below is an excerpt from a speech given by SEC Commissioner J. Carter Beese, Jr.

> . . . I believe investors will be far better off if the value of stock options is reported in a footnote rather than on the face of the income statement. By allowing footnote disclosures, we will protect shareholders' current and future investments by not raising the cost of capital for the innovative, growth companies that depend on stock options to attract and retain key employees. I've said it before and I'll say it again: the stock option accounting debate essentially boils down to one thing—the cost of capital. And as long as we can adequately protect investors without raising the cost of capital to such a vital segment of our economy, why would we want to do it any other way?
>
> The FASB has made the assertion that when it comes to public policy, they lack the competence to weigh various national goals. I also agree with the sentiment that, as a general matter, Congress should not be in the business of writing accounting standards.
>
> But the SEC has the experience and the capability to determine exactly where to draw the regulatory lines to best serve investors and our capital markets. That is our mandate, and that is what we do, day in and day out.
>
> But we may have to act sooner rather than later. As we speak, the FASB's proposals are raising the cost of venture capital. That's because venture capitalists are pricing deals based on their exit strategies, which usually include cashing out in public offerings. The FASB's proposals, however, provide incentives for companies to stay private longer—they are able to use options more freely to attract and retain key employees, and they avoid the earnings hit that going public would entail. Even worse, as venture capital deals become less profitable because of the FASB's proposed actions, venture capitalists are starting to look overseas for alternative investment opportunities that lack the investment drag now associated with certain American ventures.
>
> I acknowledge that the FASB deserves some degree of freedom to determine what they believe is the best accounting approach. At the same time, however, I cannot stand by idly for long and watch venture capital increase in price or even flee this country because of a myopic search for an accounting holy grail. At some point, I believe that the SEC must inject itself into this debate, and help the FASB determine what accounting approach is ultimately in the best interests of investors as a whole.
>
> We owe it to shareholders, issuers and all market participants, and indeed our country, to make the best decision in accordance with the public good, not just technical accounting theory.

Instructions
(a) What are the major recommendations of *SFAS No. 123* on "Accounting for Stock-Based Compensation Plans"?
(b) Write a response to Commissioner Beese, defending the use of the concept of neutrality in financial accounting and reporting.

C15-2 **(Pension Termination)** Cardinal Technology recently merged with College Electronix, a computer graphics manufacturing firm. In performing a comprehensive audit of CE's accounting system, Richard Nye, internal audit manager for Cardinal Technology, discovered that the new subsidiary did not capitalize pension assets and liabilities, subject to the requirements of *FASB Statement No. 87*.

The net present value of CE's pension assets was $15.5 million, the vested benefit obligation was $12.9 million, and the projected benefit obligation was $17.4 million. Nye reported this audit finding to Renée Selma, the newly appointed controller of CE. A few days later Selma called Nye for his advice on what to do. Selma started her conversation by asking, "Can't we eliminate the negative income effect of our pension dilemma simply by terminating the employment of nonvested employees before the end of our fiscal year?"

Instructions
How should Nye respond to Selma's remark about firing nonvested employees?

C15-3 **(Postretirement Health Care Benefits)** Philip Regan, Chief Executive Officer of Relief Dynamics Inc., a large defense contracting firm, is considering ways to improve the company's financial position after several years of sharply declining profitability. One way to do this is to reduce or completely eliminate Relief's commitment to present and future retirees who have full medical and dental benefits coverage. Despite financial problems, Relief still is committed to providing excellent pension benefits.

Instructions

Answer the following questions.

(a) What factors should Regan consider before making his decision to cut postretirement health benefits?

(b) Does your answer to the above question change if Relief Dynamics was paying Phil Regan, CEO, a salary of $30 million per year?

(c) In your opinion, how did FASB's *Statement No. 106* influence the commitment of many organizations to its employees?

USING YOUR JUDGMENT

FINANCIAL REPORTING PROBLEM

3M COMPANY

The financial statements of **3M** were provided with your book or can be accessed on the Take Action! CD.

Instructions

Refer to 3M's financial statements and the accompanying notes to answer the following questions.

(a) What kind of pension plan does 3M provide its employees in the United States?

(b) What was 3M's pension expense for 2001, 2000, and 1999 for the U.S.?

(c) What is the impact of 3M's pension plans for 2001 on its financial statements?

COMPARATIVE ANALYSIS CASE

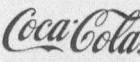

THE COCA-COLA COMPANY AND PEPSICO, INC.

Instructions

Go to the Take Action! CD and use information found there to answer the following questions related to **The Coca-Cola Company** and **PepsiCo, Inc.**

(a) What kind of pension plans do Coca-Cola and PepsiCo provide their employees?

(b) What net periodic pension expense (cost) did Coca-Cola and PepsiCo report in 2001?

(c) What relevant rates were used by Coca-Cola and PepsiCo in computing their pension amounts?

(d) What are (1) pro forma income and (2) pro forma income per share related to *FAS 123* for Coca-Cola and PepsiCo in 2001?

INTERNATIONAL REPORTING CASE

VOLVO

Volvo, a Swedish company that operates in the automotive and transport equipment industry, prepares its financial statements in accordance with Swedish accounting standards. In 1998, Volvo had income of 8,638 million SEK (Swedish Kronor) with assets of 204,426 million SEK at December 31, 1998. Volvo sponsors a pension plan for its employees in Sweden and the U.S. and provided the following disclosure related to its pension provisions in the notes to its financial statements.

VOLVO

Note 22: Provisions for postemployment benefits

	1996	1997	1998
Provisions for pensions	1,937	1,905	1,451
Provisions for other postemployment benefits	1,213	1,391	1,485
Total	3,150	3,296	2,936

The amounts shown for Provisions for postemployment benefits correspond to the actuarially calculated value of obligations not insured with a third party or secured through transfers of funds to pension foundations. The amount of pensions falling due within one year is included. The Swedish Group companies have insured their pension obligations with third parties. Group pension costs in 1998 amounted to 3,567. The greater part of pension costs consist of continuing payments to independent organizations that administer pension plans. Assets in pension foundations at market value exceeded the corresponding pension obligations by 425.

Volvo's shares trade on the NASDAQ in the United States (and on several European stock exchanges as well). As a consequence of listing its shares in the U.S., Volvo provides additional disclosure in its notes on the differences in accounting for its pension plans under U.S. and Swedish accounting standards. If Volvo had applied U.S. GAAP to its pensions, income would have been 313 million SEK higher in 1998, and stockholders' equity would have been 1,548 higher at December 31, 1998. The following excerpt about pension accounting differences between the U.S. and Sweden was taken from Volvo's notes.

Significant differences between Swedish and U.S. accounting principles

Note J: *Provision for pensions and other postemployment benefits.* The greater part of the Volvo Group's pension commitments are defined contribution plans; that is, they are met through regular payments to independent authorities or organs that administer pension plans. There is no difference between U.S. and Swedish accounting principles in accounting for these pension plans.

Other pension commitments are defined benefit plans; that is, the employee is entitled to receive a certain level of pension, usually related to the employee's final salary. In these cases the annual pension cost is calculated based on the current value of future pension payments. In Volvo's consolidated accounts, provisions for pensions and pension costs for the year in the individual companies are calculated based on local rules and directives. In accordance with U.S. GAAP provisions for pensions and pension costs for the year should always be calculated as specified in SFAS 87, "Employers Accounting for Pensions". The difference lies primarily in the choice of discount rates and the circumstance that U.S. calculations of capital-valuation, in contrast to the Swedish, are based on salaries calculated at time of retirement.

Instructions

Use the information on Volvo to answer the following questions.

(a) What are the key differences in accounting for pensions under U.S. and Swedish standards?

(b) Briefly explain how differences in U.S. and Swedish standards for pensions would affect the amounts reported in the financial statements.

(c) In light of the differences identified above, what are the likely reason(s) that Volvo's income and equity would be higher under U.S. GAAP than under Swedish accounting standards?

*Remember to check the **Take Action! CD**
and the book's **companion Web site**
to find additional resources for this chapter.*

ACCOUNTING FOR LEASES

MORE COMPANIES ASK, "WHY BUY?"

LEARNING OBJECTIVES

After studying this chapter, you should be able to:

1. Explain the advantages of lease transactions.
2. Describe the accounting criteria and procedures for capitalizing leases by the lessee.
3. Contrast the operating and capitalization methods of recording leases.
4. Identify the classifications of leases for the lessor.
5. Describe the lessor's accounting for direct financing leases.
6. Describe the lessor's accounting for sales-type leases.
7. Describe the disclosure requirements for leases.

Leasing has grown tremendously in popularity and today is the fastest growing form of capital investment. Instead of borrowing money to buy an airplane, a computer, a nuclear core, or a satellite, a company makes periodic payments to lease it. Even gambling casinos lease their slot machines. Airlines and railroads lease huge amounts of equipment; many hotel and motel chains lease their facilities; and most retail chains lease the bulk of their retail premises and warehouses. The popularity of leasing is evidenced in the fact that 558 of 600 companies surveyed by the AICPA in 2001 disclosed lease data.[1]

A classic example is the airline industry. Many travelers on airlines such as United, Delta, and Southwest believe the planes they are flying are owned by these airlines. But in many cases nothing could be further from the truth. Here are the lease percentages for the major U.S. airlines.

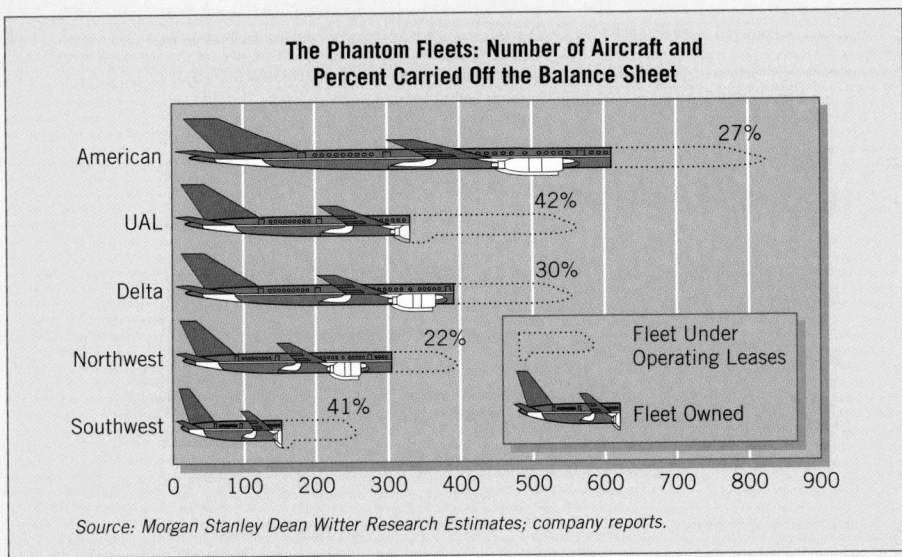

The Phantom Fleets: Number of Aircraft and Percent Carried Off the Balance Sheet

Source: Morgan Stanley Dean Witter Research Estimates; company reports.

Why do airline companies lease many of their airplanes? One reason is the favorable accounting treatment that airlines receive if they lease rather than purchase. By not reporting the airplane and related borrowing on their balance sheets, companies lower their debt to equity ratios. In addition, companies that lease often report higher net income in the earlier years of the life of the airplane.

---

[1]AICPA, *Accounting Trends and Techniques—2001.*

Because of the increased significance and prevalence of lease arrangements indicated in the opening story, the need for uniform accounting and complete informative reporting of these transactions has intensified. In this chapter, we will look at the accounting issues related to leasing. The content and organization of this chapter are as follows.

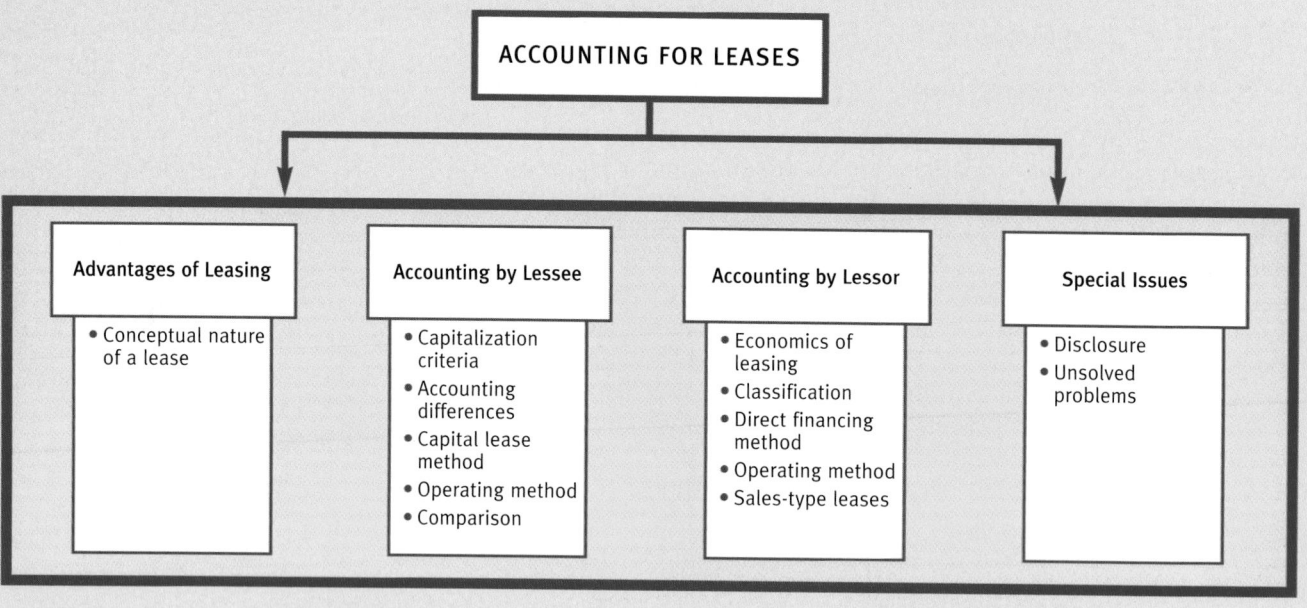

ADVANTAGES OF LEASING

OBJECTIVE 1
Explain the advantages of lease transactions.

A **lease** is a contractual agreement between a **lessor** and a **lessee** that gives the lessee the right to use specific property, owned by the lessor, for a specified period of time, in return for stipulated, and generally periodic, cash payments (rents). An essential element of the lease agreement is that the lessor conveys less than the total interest in the property.

The growth in leasing indicates that it often has a genuine advantage over owning property. Some of the advantages to the lessee of leasing are:

1. *100% Financing at Fixed Rates.* Leases are often signed without requiring any money down from the lessee, which helps the lessee conserve scarce cash—an especially desirable feature for new and developing companies. In addition, lease payments often remain fixed, which protects the lessee against inflation and increases in the cost of money.

2. *Protection against Obsolescence.* Leasing equipment reduces risk of obsolescence to the lessee, and in many cases passes the risk of residual value to the lessor. For example, **Merck** (a pharmaceutical maker) leases computers. Merck is permitted under the lease agreement to turn in an old computer for a new model at any time, canceling the old lease and writing a new one. The cost of the new lease is added to the balance due on the old lease, less the old computer's trade-in value.

3. *Flexibility.* Lease agreements may contain less restrictive provisions than other debt agreements. Innovative lessors can tailor a lease agreement to the lessee's special needs. For instance, rental payments can be structured to meet the timing of cash revenues generated by the equipment so that payments are made when the equipment is productive.

④ *Less Costly Financing.* Some companies find leasing cheaper than other forms of financing. For example, start-up companies in depressed industries or companies in low tax brackets may lease as a way of claiming tax benefits that might otherwise be lost. Depreciation deductions offer no benefit to companies that have little if any taxable income. Through leasing, these tax benefits are used by the leasing companies or financial institutions, which can pass some of these tax benefits back to the user of the asset in the form of lower rental payments.

⑤ *Off-Balance-Sheet Financing.* Certain leases do not add debt on a balance sheet or affect financial ratios, and they may add to borrowing capacity. Such **off-balance-sheet financing** is critical to some companies. As demonstrated later in this chapter, certain types of lease arrangements are not capitalized on the balance sheet. The liability section is thereby relieved of large future lease commitments that, if recorded, would adversely affect the debt-to-equity ratio.

⑥ *Tax Advantages.* In some cases, companies can "have their cake and eat it too." That is, companies do not report an asset or a liability for the lease arrangement for financial reporting purposes. However, for tax purposes, the asset is capitalized and depreciated. As a result, the company takes deductions earlier rather than later and also saves on its taxes. A common vehicle for this type transaction is a "synthetic lease" arrangement. An expanded discussion of a synthetic lease used by **Krispy Kreme** is on page 793.

INTERNATIONAL INSIGHT

Some companies "double dip" on the international level too. The leasing rules of the lessor's and lessee's countries may be different, permitting both parties to be an owner of the asset. Thus, both lessor and lessee receive the tax benefits related to depreciation.

OFF-BALANCE-SHEET FINANCING

As shown in our opening story, the airlines use lease arrangements extensively, which results in a great deal of off-balance-sheet financing. The following chart indicates that debt levels are understated by a substantial amount for many airlines that lease aircraft.

WHAT DO THE NUMBERS MEAN?

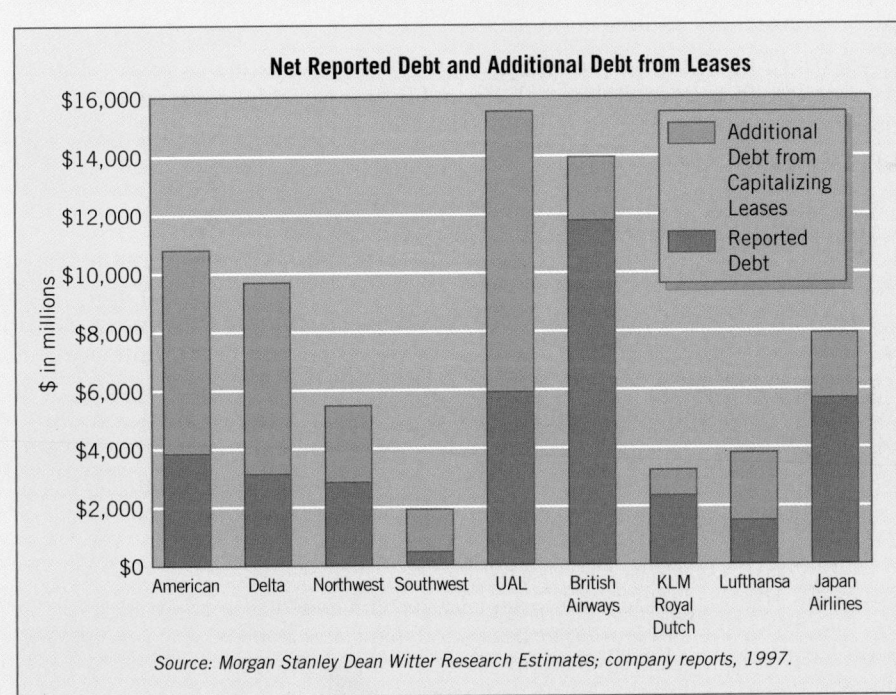

Source: Morgan Stanley Dean Witter Research Estimates; company reports, 1997.

Thus, analysts must adjust reported debt levels for the effects of non-capitalized leases. A methodology for making this adjustment is discussed in Eugene A. Imhoff, Jr., Robert C. Lipe, and David W. Wright, "Operating Leases: Impact of Constructive Capitalization," *Accounting Horizons* (March 1991).

Conceptual Nature of a Lease

If United Airlines borrows $47 million on a 10-year note from National City Bank to purchase a Boeing 757 jet plane, it is clear that an asset and related liability should be reported on United's balance sheet at that amount. If United purchases the 757 for $47,000,000 directly from Boeing through an installment purchase over 10 years, it is equally clear that an asset and related liability should be reported (i.e., the installment transaction should be "capitalized"). However, if United **leases** the Boeing 757 for 10 years through a noncancelable lease transaction with payments of the same amount as the installment purchase transaction, differences of opinion start to develop over how this transaction should be reported. The various views on **capitalization of leases** are as follows.

① *Do Not Capitalize Any Leased Assets.* In this view, because the lessee does not have ownership of the property, capitalization is considered inappropriate. Furthermore, a lease is an **"executory" contract** requiring continuing performance by both parties. Because other executory contracts (such as purchase commitments and employment contracts) are not capitalized at present, leases should not be capitalized, either.

② *Capitalize Leases That Are Similar to Installment Purchases.* In this view, transactions should be reported in accordance with their economic substance. Therefore, if installment purchases are capitalized, so also should leases that have similar characteristics. For example, United Airlines is committed to the same payments over a 10-year period for either a lease or an installment purchase; lessees make rental payments, whereas owners make mortgage payments. Why shouldn't the financial statements report these transactions in the same manner?

③ *Capitalize All Long-Term Leases.* Under this approach, the only requirement for capitalization is the long-term right to use the property. This property-rights approach capitalizes all long-term leases.[2]

④ *Capitalize Firm Leases Where the Penalty for Nonperformance Is Substantial.* A final approach is to capitalize only "firm" (noncancelable) contractual rights and obligations. "Firm" means that it is unlikely that performance under the lease can be avoided without a severe penalty.[3]

UNDERLYING CONCEPTS

The issue of how to report leases is the classic case of substance versus form. Although legal title does not technically pass in lease transactions, the benefits from the use of the property do transfer.

In short, the various viewpoints range from no capitalization to capitalization of all leases. The FASB apparently agrees with the capitalization approach when the lease is similar to an installment purchase, noting that **a lease that transfers substantially all of the benefits and risks of property ownership should be capitalized**. Transfer of ownership can be assumed only if there is a high degree of performance to the transfer, that is, the lease is noncancelable. **Noncancelable** means that the lease contract is cancelable only upon the outcome of some remote contingency, or that the cancellation provisions and penalties of the contract are so costly to the lessee that cancellation probably will not occur. Only noncancelable leases may be capitalized.

---

[2]The property rights approach was originally recommended in a research study by the AICPA: John H. Myers, "Reporting of Leases in Financial Statements," *Accounting Research Study No. 4* (New York: AICPA, 1964), pp. 10–11. Recently, this view has received additional support. See Peter H. Knutson, "Financial Reporting in the 1990s and Beyond," Position Paper (Charlottesville, Va.: AIMR, 1993), and Warren McGregor, "Accounting for Leases: A New Approach," Special Report (Norwalk, Conn.: FASB, 1996).

[3]Yuji Ijiri, *Recognition of Contractual Rights and Obligations,* Research Report (Stamford, Conn.: FASB, 1980).

This viewpoint leads to three basic conclusions: (1) The characteristics that indicate that substantially all of the benefits and risks of ownership have been transferred must be identified. (2) The same characteristics should apply consistently to the lessee and the lessor. (3) Those leases that do **not** transfer substantially all the benefits and risks of ownership are operating leases. They should not be capitalized but rather accounted for as rental payments and receipts.

ACCOUNTING BY LESSEE

If a lessee **capitalizes** a lease, the **lessee** records an asset and a liability generally equal to the present value of the rental payments. The **lessor**, having transferred substantially all the benefits and risks of ownership, recognizes a sale by removing the asset from the balance sheet and replacing it with a receivable. The typical journal entries for the lessee and the lessor, assuming equipment is leased and is capitalized, appear as follows.

Lessee			Lessor		
Leased Equipment	XXX		Lease Receivable	XXX	
Lease Liability		XXX	Equipment		XXX

OBJECTIVE 2
Describe the accounting criteria and procedures for capitalizing leases by the lessee.

Illustration 16-1
Journal Entries for Capitalized Lease

Having capitalized the asset, the lessee records the depreciation. The lessor and lessee treat the lease rental payments as consisting of interest and principal.

If the lease is not capitalized, no asset is recorded by the lessee and no asset is removed from the lessor's books. When a lease payment is made, the lessee records rental expense and the lessor recognizes rental revenue.

For a lease to be recorded as a **capital lease**, the lease must be noncancelable, and it must meet one or more of the following four criteria.

Capitalization Criteria (Lessee)

- The lease transfers ownership of the property to the lessee.
- The lease contains a bargain purchase option.[4]
- The lease term is equal to 75 percent or more of the estimated economic life of the leased property.
- The present value of the minimum lease payments (excluding executory costs) equals or exceeds 90 percent of the fair value of the leased property.[5]

Illustration 16-2
Capitalization Criteria for Lessee

Leases that **do not meet any of the four criteria** are classified and accounted for by the lessee as **operating leases**. Illustration 16-3 (page 784) shows that a lease meeting any one of the four criteria results in the lessee having a capital lease.

[4]A bargain purchase option is defined in the next section.

[5]"Accounting for Leases," *FASB Statement No. 13* as amended and interpreted through May 1980 (Stamford, Conn.: FASB, 1980), par. 7.

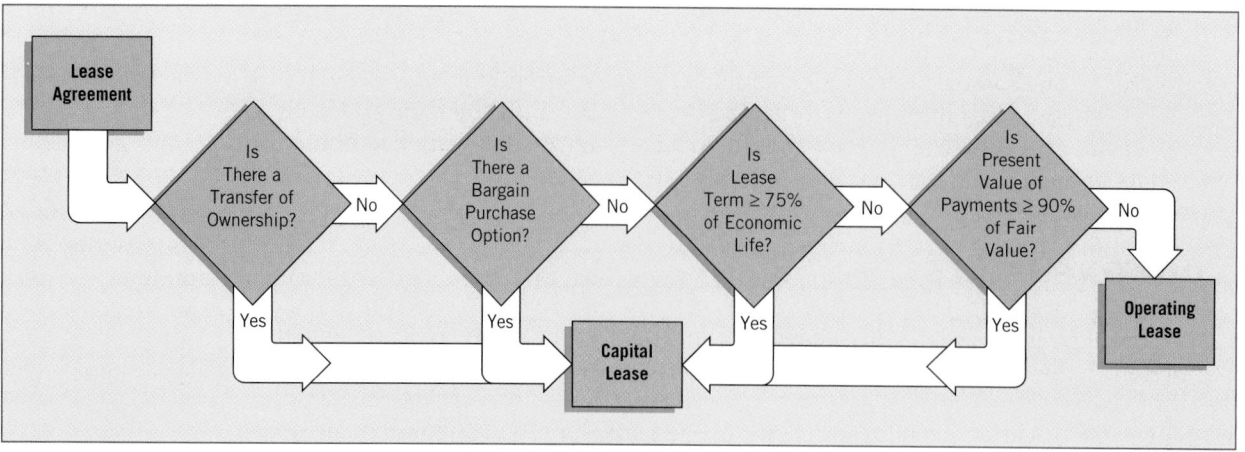

Illustration 16-3
Diagram of Lessee's
Criteria for Lease
Classification

In keeping with the FASB's reasoning that a significant portion of the value of the asset is consumed in the first 75 percent of its life, neither the third nor the fourth criterion is to be applied when the inception of the lease occurs during the last 25 percent of the life of the asset.

Capitalization Criteria

The four **capitalization criteria** that apply to lessees are controversial and can be difficult to apply in practice. They are discussed in detail in the following pages.

Transfer of Ownership Test

If the lease transfers ownership of the asset to the lessee, it is a capital lease. This criterion is not controversial and is easily implemented in practice.

Bargain Purchase Option Test

UNDERLYING CONCEPTS

Capitalization of leases illustrates the necessity for good definitions. The lease fits the definition of an asset, as it gives the lessee the economic benefits that flow from the possession or the use of the asset.

A **bargain purchase option** is a provision allowing the lessee to purchase the leased property for a price that is **significantly lower** than the property's expected fair value at the date the option becomes exercisable. At the inception of the lease, the difference between the option price and the expected fair market value must be large enough to make exercise of the option reasonably assured.

Economic Life Test (75% Test)

If the lease period equals or exceeds 75 percent of the asset's economic life, most of the risks and rewards of ownership are transferred to the lessee, and capitalization is therefore appropriate. However, determining the lease term and the economic life of the asset can be troublesome.

The **lease term** is generally considered to be the fixed, noncancelable term of the lease. However, this period can be extended if a bargain renewal option is provided in the lease agreement. A **bargain renewal option** is a provision allowing the lessee to renew the lease for a rental that is lower than the expected fair rental at the date the option becomes exercisable. At the inception of the lease, the difference between the renewal rental and the expected fair rental must be great enough to make exercise of the option to renew reasonably assured.

Determining estimated economic life can also pose problems, especially if the leased item is a specialized item or has been used for a significant period of time. For example, determining the economic life of a nuclear core is extremely difficult because it is subject to much more than normal "wear and tear." The FASB takes the position that if the lease starts during the last 25 percent of the life of the asset, the economic life test cannot be used as a basis to classify a lease as a capital lease.

Recovery of Investment Test (90% Test)

If the present value of the minimum lease payments equals or exceeds 90 percent of the fair market value of the asset, then the leased asset should be capitalized. The rationale for this test is that if the present value of the minimum lease payments is reasonably close to the market price of the asset, the asset is effectively being purchased.

In determining the present value of the minimum lease payments, three important concepts are involved: (1) minimum lease payments, (2) executory costs, and (3) discount rate.

Minimum Lease Payments. **Minimum lease payments** are payments the lessee is obligated to make or can be expected to make in connection with the leased property. They include the following.

1. *Minimum Rental Payments*—Minimum payments the lessee is obligated to make to the lessor under the lease agreement. In some cases, the minimum rental payments may be equal to the minimum lease payments. However, the minimum lease payments also may include a guaranteed residual value (if any), penalty for failure to renew, or a bargain purchase option (if any), as noted below.

2. *Guaranteed Residual Value*—The residual value is the estimated fair (market) value of the leased property at the end of the lease term. The lessor often transfers the risk of loss to the lessee or to a third party through a guarantee of the estimated residual value. The **guaranteed residual value** is (1) the certain or determinable amount at which the lessor has the right to require the lessee to purchase the asset, or (2) the amount the lessee or the third-party guarantor guarantees the lessor will realize. If it is not guaranteed in full, the **unguaranteed residual value** is the estimated residual value exclusive of any portion guaranteed.

3. *Penalty for Failure to Renew or Extend the Lease*—The amount payable that is required of the lessee if the agreement specifies that the lease must be extended or renewed and the lessee fails to do so.

4. *Bargain Purchase Option*—As indicated earlier (in item 1), an option given to the lessee to purchase the equipment at the end of the lease term at a price that is fixed sufficiently below the expected fair value, so that, at the inception of the lease, purchase appears to be reasonably assured.

Executory costs (defined below) are not included in the lessee's computation of the present value of the minimum lease payments.

Executory Costs. Like most assets, leased tangible assets require the incurrence of insurance, maintenance, and tax expenses—called **executory costs**—during their economic life. If the lessor retains responsibility for the payment of these "ownership-type costs," a portion of each lease payment that represents executory costs **should be excluded** in computing the present value of the minimum lease payments because it does not represent payment on or reduction of the obligation. If the portion of the minimum lease payments that represents executory costs is not determinable from the provisions of the lease, an estimate of such amount must be made. Many lease agreements, however, specify that executory costs be paid to the appropriate third parties directly by the lessee. In these cases, the rental payment can be used **without adjustment** in the present value computation.

Discount Rate. The lessee computes the present value of the minimum lease payments using the **lessee's incremental borrowing rate**, which is defined as: "The rate that, at the inception of the lease, the lessee would have incurred to borrow the funds necessary to buy the leased asset on a secured loan with repayment terms similar to the payment schedule called for in the lease."[6] Assume, for example, that Mortenson Inc. decides to lease computer equipment for a 5-year period at a cost of $10,000 a year. To determine whether the present value of these payments is less than 90 percent of the fair market value of the property, the lessee discounts the payments using its incremental borrowing rate. Determining that rate will often require judgment because it is based on a hypothetical purchase of the property.

However, there is one exception to this rule: If (1) the lessee knows the **implicit interest rate computed by the lessor** and (2) it is less than the lessee's incremental borrowing rate, then the **lessee must use the lessor's implicit rate**. The **interest rate implicit in the lease** is the discount rate that, when applied to the minimum lease payments and any unguaranteed residual value accruing to the lessor, causes the aggregate present value to be equal to the fair value of the leased property to the lessor.[7]

The purpose of this exception is twofold: First, **the implicit rate of the lessor is generally a more realistic rate** to use in determining the amount (if any) to report as the asset and related liability for the lessee. Second, the guideline is provided to ensure that the lessee **does not use an artificially high incremental borrowing rate** that would cause the present value of the minimum lease payments to be less than 90 percent of the fair market value of the property. Use of such a rate would thus make it possible to avoid capitalization of the asset and related liability. The lessee may argue that it cannot determine the implicit rate of the lessor and therefore the higher rate should be used. However, in many cases, the implicit rate used by the lessor can be approximated. The determination of whether or not a reasonable estimate could be made will require judgment, particularly where the result from using the incremental borrowing rate comes close to meeting the 90 percent test. Because **the lessee may not capitalize the leased property at more than its fair value** (as discussed later), the lessee is prevented from using an excessively low discount rate.

The elements that comprise the present value of minimum lease payments are summarized in Illustration 16-4.

Illustration 16-4

Computation of Present Value of Minimum Lease Payments

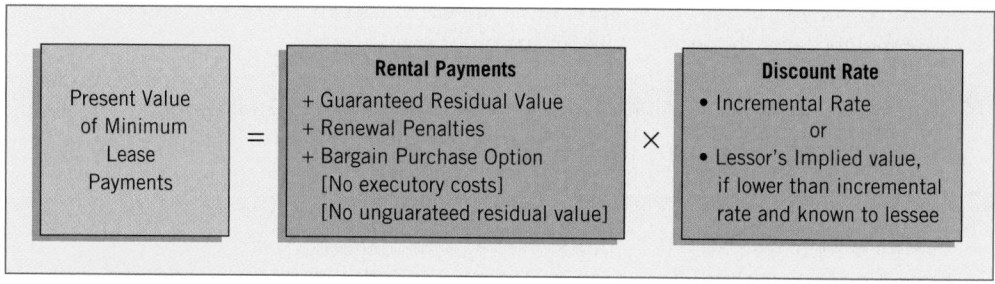

Asset and Liability Accounted for Differently

In a capital lease transaction, the lessee is using the lease as a source of financing. The lessor finances the transaction (provides the investment capital) through the leased asset, and the lessee makes rent payments, which actually are installment payments. Therefore, over the life of the property rented, **the rental payments to the lessor constitute a payment of principal plus interest**.

Asset and Liability Recorded

Under the capital lease method, the lessee treats the lease transaction as if an asset were being purchased in a financing transaction in which an asset is acquired and an obligation created. Therefore, the lessee records a capital lease as an asset and a liability at the lower of (1) the present value of the minimum lease payments (excluding execu-

---

[6]*FASB Statement No. 13*, op. cit., par. 5 (l).

[7]Ibid., par. 5 (k).

tory costs) or (2) the fair market value of the leased asset at the inception of the lease. The rationale for this approach is that the leased asset should not be recorded for more than its fair market value.

Depreciation Period

One troublesome aspect of accounting for the depreciation of the capitalized leased asset relates to the period of depreciation. If the lease agreement transfers ownership of the asset to the lessee (criterion 1) or contains a bargain purchase option (criterion 2), the leased asset is depreciated in a manner consistent with the lessee's normal depreciation policy for owned assets, **using the economic life of the asset**. On the other hand, if the lease does not transfer ownership or does not contain a bargain purchase option, then it is depreciated over the **term of the lease**. In this case, the leased asset reverts to the lessor after a certain period of time.

Effective Interest Method

Throughout the term of the lease, the **effective interest method** is used to allocate each lease payment between principal and interest. This method produces a periodic interest expense equal to a constant percentage of the carrying value of the lease obligation.

The discount rate used by the lessee to determine the present value of the minimum lease payments must be used by the lessee when applying the effective interest method to capital leases.

Depreciation Concept

Although the amounts initially capitalized as an asset and recorded as an obligation are computed at the same present value, the **depreciation of the asset and the discharge of the obligation are independent accounting processes** during the term of the lease. The lessee should depreciate the leased asset by applying conventional depreciation methods: straight-line, sum-of-the-years'-digits, declining-balance, units of production, etc.

The FASB uses the term "amortization" more frequently than "depreciation" to recognize intangible leased property rights. The authors prefer "depreciation" to describe the write-off of a tangible asset's expired services.

Capital Lease Method (Lessee)

Lessor Company and Lessee Company sign a lease agreement dated January 1, 2004, that calls for Lessor Company to lease equipment to Lessee Company beginning January 1, 2004. The terms and provisions of the lease agreement and other pertinent data are as follows.

1. The term of the lease is 5 years, and the lease agreement is noncancelable, requiring equal rental payments of $25,981.62 at the beginning of each year (annuity due basis).
2. The equipment has a fair value at the inception of the lease of $100,000, an estimated economic life of 5 years, and no residual value.
3. Lessee Company pays all of the executory costs directly to third parties except for the property taxes of $2,000 per year, which are included in the annual payments to the lessor.
4. The lease contains no renewal options, and the equipment reverts to Lessor Company at the termination of the lease.
5. Lessee Company's incremental borrowing rate is 11 percent per year.
6. Lessee Company depreciates on a straight-line basis similar equipment that it owns.

⑦ Lessor Company set the annual rental to earn a rate of return on its investment of 10 percent per year. This fact is known to Lessee Company.[8]

The lease meets the criteria for classification as a capital lease for the following reasons: (1) The lease term of 5 years, being equal to the equipment's estimated economic life of 5 years, satisfies the 75 percent test. (2) The present value of the minimum lease payments ($100,000 as computed below) exceeds 90 percent of the fair value of the property ($100,000).

The minimum lease payments are $119,908.10 ($23,981.62 × 5). The amount capitalized as leased assets is computed as the present value of the minimum lease payments (excluding executory costs—property taxes of $2,000) as follows.

Illustration 16-5
Computation of
Capitalized Lease
Payments

Capitalized amount = ($25,981.62 − $2,000) × Present value of an annuity due of 1 for
5 periods at 10% (Appendix A, Table 5)

= $23,981.62 × 4.16986
= $100,000

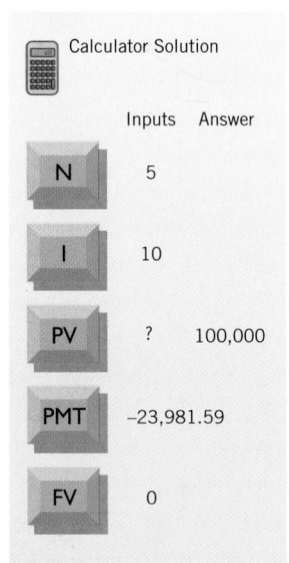

Calculator Solution

	Inputs	Answer
N	5	
I	10	
PV	?	100,000
PMT	−23,981.59	
FV	0	

The lessor's implicit interest rate of 10 percent is used instead of the lessee's incremental borrowing rate of 11 percent because (1) it is lower and (2) the lessee has knowledge of it.

The entry to record the capital lease on Lessee Company's books on January 1, 2004, is:

Leased Equipment under Capital Leases	100,000	
Lease Liability		100,000

Note that the preceding entry records the obligation at the net amount of $100,000 (the present value of the future rental payments) rather than at the gross amount of $119,908.10 ($23,981.62 × 5).

The journal entry to record the **first lease payment on January 1, 2004,** is:

Property Tax Expense	2,000.00	
Lease Liability	23,981.62	
Cash		25,981.62

Each lease payment of $25,981.62 consists of three elements: (1) a reduction in the lease liability, (2) a financing cost (interest expense), and (3) executory costs (property taxes). The total financing cost (interest expense) over the term of the lease is $19,908.10, the difference between the present value of the lease payments ($100,000) and the actual cash disbursed, net of executory costs ($119,908.10). Therefore, the annual interest

[8]If Lessee Company had an incremental borrowing rate of, say, 9 percent (lower than the 10 percent rate used by Lessor Company) and it did not know the rate used by Lessor Company, the present value computation would have yielded a capitalized amount of $101,675.35 ($23,981.62 × 4.23972). And, because this amount exceeds the $100,000 fair value of the equipment, Lessee Company would have had to capitalize the $100,000 and use 10 percent as its effective rate for amortization of the lease obligation.

expense, applying the effective interest method, is a function of the outstanding obligation, as shown in Illustration 16-6.

Illustration 16-6
Lease Amortization
Schedule for Lessee—
Annuity Due Basis

	LESSEE COMPANY				
	LEASE AMORTIZATION SCHEDULE				
	(ANNUITY DUE BASIS)				
Date	Annual Lease Payment	Executory Costs	Interest (10%) on Unpaid Obligation	Reduction of Lease Liability	Lease Liability
	(a)	(b)	(c)	(d)	(e)
1/1/04					$100,000.00
1/1/04	$ 25,981.62	$ 2,000	$ –0–	$ 23,981.62	76,018.38
1/1/05	25,981.62	2,000	7,601.84	16,379.78	59,638.60
1/1/06	25,981.62	2,000	5,963.86	18,017.76	41,620.84
1/1/07	25,981.62	2,000	4,162.08	19,819.54	21,801.30
1/1/08	25,981.62	2,000	2,180.32*	21,801.30	–0–
	$129,908.10	$10,000	$19,908.10	$100,000.00	

(a) Lease payment as required by lease.
(b) Executory costs included in rental payment.
(c) Ten percent of the preceding balance of (e) except for 1/1/04; since this is an annuity due, no time has elapsed at the date of the first payment and no interest has accrued.
(d) (a) minus (b) and (c).
(e) Preceding balance minus (d).
*Rounded by 19 cents.

At the end of Lessee Company's fiscal year, December 31, 2004, **accrued interest** is recorded as follows.

Interest Expense	7,601.84	
Interest Payable		7,601.84

Depreciation of the leased equipment over its lease term of 5 years, applying Lessee Company's normal depreciation policy (straight-line method), results in the following entry on December 31, 2004.[9]

Depreciation Expense—Capital Leases	20,000	
Accumulated Depreciation—Capital Leases		20,000
($100,000 ÷ 5 years)		

At December 31, 2004, the assets recorded under capital leases are separately identified on the lessee's balance sheet. Similarly, the related obligations are separately

---

[9]If Lessee Company guarantees a residual value, the guaranteed residual value is subtracted from the cost of the leased asset for depreciation purposes. For example, if Lessee Company in illustration 16-5 guarantees a residual value of $10,000, depreciation expense would be $18,000 [($100,000 − $10,000) ÷ 5] per year. Conversely an unguaranteed residual value is not subtracted from the cost of the leased asset for depreciation purposes. In this case, the lessee does not have to make a payment at the end of the lease term, and therefore the total cost of the asset should be depreciated.

identified. The portion due within one year or the operating cycle, whichever is longer, is classified with current liabilities and the rest with noncurrent liabilities. For example, the current portion of the December 31, 2004, total obligation of $76,018.38 in the lessee's amortization schedule is the amount of the reduction in the obligation in 2005, or $16,379.78. The liabilities section as it relates to lease transactions at December 31, 2004, is shown in Illustration 16-7.

Illustration 16-7

Reporting Current and
Noncurrent Lease
Liabilities

Current liabilities	
Interest payable	$ 7,601.84
Lease liability	16,379.78
Noncurrent liabilities	
Lease liability	$59,638.60

The journal entry to record the lease payment of January 1, 2005, is as follows.

Property Tax Expense	2,000.00	
Interest Expense (or Interest Payable)	7,601.84	
Lease Liability	16,379.78	
Cash		25,981.62

Entries through 2008 would follow the pattern above. Other executory costs (insurance and maintenance) assumed by Lessee Company would be recorded in a manner similar to that used to record any other operating costs incurred on assets owned by Lessee Company.

Upon expiration of the lease, the amount capitalized as leased equipment is fully amortized, and the lease obligation is fully discharged. If not purchased, the equipment would be returned to the lessor, and the leased equipment and related accumulated depreciation accounts would be removed from the books.

If the equipment is purchased at termination of the lease at a price of $5,000 and the estimated life of the equipment is changed from 5 to 7 years, the following entry might be made.

Equipment ($100,000 + $5,000)	105,000	
Accumulated Depreciation—Capital Leases	100,000	
Leased Equipment under Capital Leases		100,000
Accumulated Depreciation—Equipment		100,000
Cash		5,000

If the lessee guarantees the residual value, the present value of this residual value should be reported as part of the lease liability. For example, assume that Hogan Co. enters into a 3-year lease of machinery on January 1, 2004. The lease requires three annual payments of $20,000, beginning January 1, 2004. In addition, Hogan Co. guarantees the lessor a residual value of $10,000 at the end of the lease. The interest rate used to discount the lease payments is 9 percent. In this case, the present value of the minimum lease payments would be computed as shown in Illustration 16-8.

If a **bargain purchase option** exists instead of a guaranteed residual value, the lessee should increase the present value of the minimum lease payments by the present value of the option price. In both the guaranteed residual value and the bargain purchase option cases, the lessee is committed to making these payments, and therefore the payments should be reported as an increase to the lease liability and related asset.

Rental payment	$ 20,000	
Present value of annuity due for 3 years at 9%	× 2.75911	
Present value of rental payments	$55,182.20	
Present value of guaranteed residual value is $7,721.80 [$10,000 × .77218 (PVF$_{3,9\%}$)]		
Present value of rental payments	$55,182.20	
Present value of guaranteed residual value	7,721.80	
Total present value of minimum lease payments	$62,904.00	

Illustration 16-8
Computation of Present
Value of Minimum Lease
Payments

Operating Method (Lessee)

Under the **operating method**, rent expense (and the associated liability) accrues day by day to the lessee as the property is used. **The lessee assigns rent to the periods benefiting from the use of the asset and ignores, in the accounting, any commitments to make future payments.** Appropriate accruals or deferrals are made if the accounting period ends between cash payment dates.

For example, assume that the capital lease illustrated in Illustration 16-6 did not qualify as a capital lease and was therefore to be accounted for as an operating lease. The first-year charge to operations would have been $25,981.62, the amount of the rental payment. The journal entry to record this payment on January 1, 2004, would be as follows.

Rent Expense	25,981.62	
Cash		25,981.62

The rented asset, as well as any long-term liability for future rental payments, is not reported on the balance sheet. Rent expense would be reported on the income statement. In addition, **note disclosure is required for all operating leases that have non-cancelable lease terms in excess of one year**. An illustration of the type of note disclosure required for an operating lease (as well as other types of leases) is provided in Illustrations 16-17 to 16-19 later in this chapter.

Comparison of Capital Lease with Operating Lease

As indicated, if the lease had been accounted for as an operating lease, the first-year charge to operations would have been $25,981.62, the amount of the rental payment. Treating the transaction as a capital lease, however, resulted in a first-year charge of $29,601.84: depreciation of $20,000 (assuming straight-line), interest expense of $7,601.84 (per Illustration 16-9), and executory costs of $2,000. Illustration 16-9 shows that **while the total charges to operations are the same over the lease term whether the lease is accounted for as a capital lease or as an operating lease, under the capital lease treatment the charges are higher in the earlier years and lower in the later years.**[10]

OBJECTIVE 3
Contrast the operating and capitalization methods of recording leases.

[10]The higher charges in the early years is one reason lessees are reluctant to adopt the capital lease accounting method. Lessees (especially those of real estate) claim that it is really no more costly to operate the leased asset in the early years than in the later years. Thus, they advocate an even charge similar to that provided by the operating method.

Illustration 16-9

Comparison of Charges to Operations—Capital vs. Operating Leases

	Capital Lease				Operating	
Year	Depreciation	Executory Costs	Interest	Total Charge	Lease Charge	Difference
2004	$ 20,000	$ 2,000	$ 7,601.84	$ 29,601.84	$ 25,981.62	$ 3,620.22
2005	20,000	2,000	5,963.86	27,963.86	25,981.62	1,982.24
2006	20,000	2,000	4,162.08	26,162.08	25,981.62	180.46
2007	20,000	2,000	2,180.32	24,180.32	25,981.62	(1,801.30)
2008	20,000	2,000	—	22,000.00	25,981.62	(3,981.62)
	$100,000	$10,000	$19,908.10	$129,908.10	$129,908.10	$ –0–

LESSEE COMPANY
SCHEDULE OF CHARGES TO OPERATIONS
CAPITAL LEASE VERSUS OPERATING LEASE

If an accelerated method of depreciation is used, the differences between the amounts charged to operations under the two methods would be even larger in the earlier and later years.

In addition, using the capital lease approach would have resulted in an asset and related liability of $100,000 initially reported on the balance sheet. No such asset or liability would be reported under the operating method. Therefore, the following differences occur if a capital lease instead of an operating lease is employed:

1. an increase in the amount of reported debt (both short-term and long-term),
2. an increase in the amount of total assets (specifically long-lived assets), and
3. a lower income early in the life of the lease and, therefore, lower retained earnings.

Thus, many companies believe that capital leases have a detrimental impact on their financial position: Their debt to total equity ratio increases, and their rate of return on total assets decreases. As a result, the business community resists capitalizing leases.

Whether this resistance is well founded is a matter of debate. From a cash flow point of view, the company is in the same position whether the lease is accounted for as an operating or a capital lease. The reason why managers often argue against capitalization is that it can more easily lead to **violation of loan covenants**; it can affect the **amount of compensation received by owners** (for example, a stock compensation plan tied to earnings); and finally, it can **lower rates of return** and **increase debt to equity relationships**, thus making the company less attractive to present and potential investors.[11]

---

[11]One study indicates that management's behavior did change as a result of *FASB No. 13*. For example, many companies restructure their leases to avoid capitalization; others increase their purchases of assets instead of leasing; and others, faced with capitalization, postpone their debt offerings or issue stock instead. However, it is interesting to note that the study found no significant effect on stock or bond prices as a result of capitalization of leases. A. Rashad Abdel-khalik, "The Economic Effects on Lessees of *FASB Statement No. 13*, Accounting for Leases," Research Report (Stamford, Conn.: FASB, 1981).

WHAT DO THE NUMBERS MEAN?

Krispy Kreme, a chain of 217 donut shops, has caught the attention—some good, some bad—of Wall Street. On the good side, investors are impressed by the company's ability to grow rapidly on a relatively small bit of capital. For the first 9 months of fiscal 2002, the company's capital expenditures fell to $38 million, from $59 million the year before. Yet Krispy Kreme expanded along with its customers' waistlines during the same period: Its earnings rose 73 percent, to $18 million, on sales that were up 27 percent to $277 million.

That's an impressive feat if you care about return on capital. But there's a hole in this donut. Amid much hoopla, the company announced in 2001 that it would spend $30 million on a new 187,000 square foot mixing plant and warehouse in Effingham, Illinois. Yet the investments and obligations associated with that $30 million are not apparent in the financial statements.

By financing through a synthetic lease, Krispy Kreme can keep the investment and obligation off the books. In a synthetic lease, a financial institution like **Bank of America** sets up a *special purpose entity* (SPE) that borrows money to build the plant and then leases it to Krispy Kreme. For accounting purposes, Krispy Kreme reports an operating lease, but for tax purposes the company is considered the owner of the asset and gets depreciation tax deductions.

In response to negative publicity about the use of SPEs to get favorable financial reporting and tax benefits, Krispy Kreme announced it was going to change its method of financing construction of its dough-making plant.

Source: Adapted from Seth Lubore and Elizabeth MacDonald, "Debt? Who, Me?" *Forbes* (February 18, 2002), p. 56.

ACCOUNTING BY LESSOR

Earlier in this chapter we discussed leasing's advantages to the lessee. Three important benefits are available to the lessor:

1. *Interest Revenue.* Leasing is a form of financing; therefore, financial institutions and leasing companies find leasing attractive because it provides competitive interest margins.

2. *Tax Incentives.* In many cases, companies that lease cannot use the tax benefit, but leasing provides them with an opportunity to transfer such tax benefits to another party (the lessor) in return for a lower rental rate on the leased asset. To illustrate, **Boeing Aircraft** at one time sold one of its 767 jet planes to a wealthy investor who didn't need the plane but could use the tax benefit. The investor then leased the plane to a foreign airline, for whom the tax benefit was of no use. Everyone gained. Boeing was able to sell its 767, the investor received the tax benefit, and the foreign airline found a cheaper way to acquire a 767.[12]

3. *Residual Value Profits.* Another advantage to the lessor is the return of the property at the end of the lease term. Residual values can produce very large profits. **Citigroup** at one time assumed that the commercial aircraft it was leasing to the airline industry would have a residual value of 5 percent of their purchase price. It turned out that they were worth 150 percent of their cost—a handsome profit.

---

[12]Some would argue that there is a loser—the U.S. government. The tax benefits enable the profitable investor to reduce or eliminate taxable income.

However, 3 years later these same planes slumped to 80 percent of their cost, but still far more than 5 percent.

Economics of Leasing

The lessor determines the amount of the rental, basing it on the rate of return—the implicit rate—needed to justify leasing the asset. The key factors considered in establishing the rate of return are the credit standing of the lessee, the length of the lease, and the status of the residual value (guaranteed versus unguaranteed). In the Lessor Company/Lessee Company example on pages 787–790, the implicit rate of the lessor was 10 percent, the cost of the equipment to the lessor was $100,000 (also fair market value), and the estimated residual value was zero. Lessor Company determined the amount of the lease payment in the following manner.

Illustration 16-10
Computation of
Lease Payments

Fair market value of leased equipment	$100,000.00
Less: Present value of the residual value	–0–
Amount to be recovered by lessor through lease payments	$100,000.00
Five beginning-of-the-year lease payments to yield a 10% return ($100,000 ÷ 4.16986ᵃ)	$ 23,981.62

ᵃPV of an annuity due of 1 for 5 years at 10% (Appendix A, Table 5)

If a residual value were involved (whether guaranteed or not), the lessor would not have to recover as much from the lease payments. Therefore, the lease payments would be less.

Classification of Leases by the Lessor

OBJECTIVE 4
Identify the classifications of leases for the lessor.

From the standpoint of the **lessor**, all leases may be classified for accounting purposes as one of the following:

① Operating leases.
② Direct financing leases.
③ Sales-type leases.

Referring to Illustration 16-11, if at the date of the lease agreement (inception) the lessor is party to a lease that meets **one or more** of the Group I criteria (1, 2, 3, and 4) and **both** of the Group II criteria (1 and 2), the lessor shall classify and account for the arrangement as a direct financing lease or as a sales-type lease.[13] (Note that the Group I criteria are identical to the criteria that must be met in order for a lease to be classified as a capital lease by a lessee, as shown in Illustration 16-2.)

Why the Group II requirements? The answer is that the profession wants to make sure that the lessor has really transferred the risks and benefits of ownership. If collectibility of payments is not predictable or if performance by the lessor is incomplete, then the criteria for revenue recognition have not been met, and it should be accounted for as an operating lease.

For example, computer leasing companies at one time used to buy **IBM** equipment, lease it, and remove the leased assets from their balance sheets. In leasing the asset, the computer lessors stated that they would be willing to substitute new IBM

---

[13]*FASB Statement No. 13*, op. cit., pars. 6, 7, and 8.

Illustration 16-11
Capitalization Criteria
for Lessor

Capitalization Criteria (Lessor)

Group I

- The lease transfers ownership of the property to the lessee.
- The lease contains a bargain purchase option.
- The lease term is equal to 75 percent or more of the estimated economic life of the leased property.
- The present value of the minimum lease payments (excluding executory costs) equals or exceeds 90 percent of the fair value of the leased property.

Group II

- Collectibility of the payments required from the lessee is reasonably predictable.
- No important uncertainties surround the amount of unreimbursable costs yet to be incurred by the lessor under the lease (lessor's performance is substantially complete or future costs are reasonably predictable).

equipment if obsolescence occurred. However, when IBM introduced a new computer line, IBM refused to sell it to the computer leasing companies. As a result, a number of the lessors could not meet their contracts with their customers and were forced to take back the old equipment. What the computer leasing companies had taken off the books now had to be reinstated. Such a case demonstrates one reason for the Group II requirements.

The distinction for the lessor between a direct financing lease and a sales-type lease is the presence or absence of a manufacturer's or dealer's profit (or loss): A sales-type lease involves a manufacturer's or dealer's profit, and a direct financing lease does not. The profit (or loss) to the lessor is evidenced by the difference between the fair value of the leased property at the inception of the lease and the lessor's cost or carrying amount (book value). Normally, sales-type leases arise when manufacturers or dealers use leasing as a means of marketing their products. For example, a computer manufacturer will lease its computer equipment to businesses and institutions. Direct financing leases generally result from arrangements with lessors that are primarily engaged in financing operations, such as lease-finance companies, banks, insurance companies, and pension trusts. However, a lessor need not be a manufacturer or dealer to recognize a profit (or loss) at the inception of a lease that requires application of sales-type lease accounting.

All leases that do not qualify as direct financing or sales-type leases are classified and accounted for by the lessors as operating leases. Illustration 16-12 shows the circumstances under which a lease is classified as operating, direct financing, or sales-type for the lessor.

Illustration 16-12
Diagram of Lessor's
Criteria for Lease
Classification

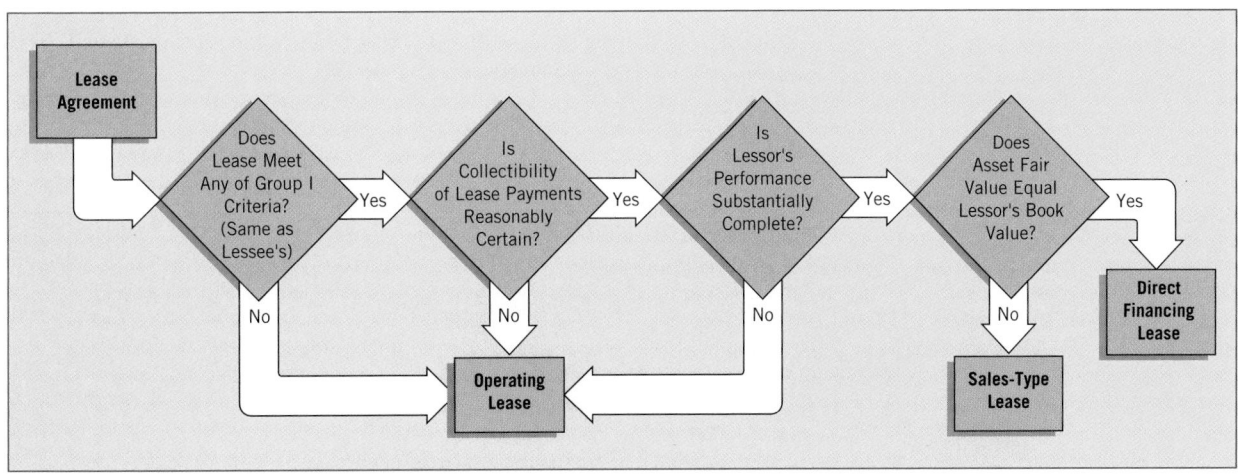

As a consequence of the additional Group II criteria for lessors, it is possible that a lessor having not met both criteria will classify a lease as an **operating** lease but the lessee will classify the same lease as a **capital** lease. In such an event, both the lessor and lessee will carry the asset on their books, and both will depreciate the capitalized asset.

Direct Financing Method (Lessor)

<table>
<tr><td>OBJECTIVE **5**
Describe the lessor's accounting for direct financing leases.</td></tr>
</table>

Leases that are in substance the financing of an asset purchase by the lessee are called **direct financing leases**. In this type of lease, the 1 lessor records a **lease receivable** instead of a leased asset.

The lease receivable is the present value of the minimum lease payments. Remember that "minimum lease payments" includes:

1. Rental payments (excluding executory costs).
2. Bargain purchase option (if any).
3. Guaranteed residual value (if any).
4. Penalty for failure to renew (if any).

Recall that if the lessor pays any executory costs, then the rental payment should be reduced by that amount for purposes of computing minimum lease payments.

The following presentation, utilizing the data from the preceding Lessor Company/Lessee Company illustration on pages 787–790, illustrates the accounting treatment accorded a direct financing lease. The information relevant to Lessor Company in accounting for this lease transaction is repeated as follows.

1. The term of the lease is 5 years beginning January 1, 2004, noncancelable, and requires equal rental payments of $25,981.62 at the beginning of each year. Payments include $2,000 of executory costs (property taxes).
2. The equipment has a cost of $100,000 to Lessor Company, a fair value at the inception of the lease of $100,000, an estimated economic life of 5 years, and no residual value.
3. No initial direct costs were incurred in negotiating and closing the lease transaction.
4. The lease contains no renewable options and the equipment reverts to Lessor Company at the termination of the lease.
5. Collectibility is reasonably assured, and no additional costs (with the exception of the property taxes being collected from the lessee) are to be incurred by Lessor Company.
6. Lessor Company set the annual lease payments to ensure a rate of return of 10 percent (implicit rate) on its investment as follows.

Illustration 16-13
Computation of Lease Payments

Fair market value of leased equipment	$100,000.00
Less: Present value of residual value	–0–
Amount to be recovered by lessor through lease payments	$100,000.00
Five beginning-of-the-year lease payments to yield a 10% return ($100,000 ÷ 4.16986ᵃ)	$ 23,981.62

ᵃPV of an annuity due of 1 for 5 years at 10% (Appendix A, Table 5).

The lease meets the criteria for classification as a direct financing lease because (1) the lease term exceeds 75 percent of the equipment's estimated economic life, (2) the present value of the minimum lease payments exceeds 90 percent of the equipment's fair value, (3) collectibility of the payments is reasonably assured, and (4) there are no further costs to be incurred by Lessor Company. It is not a sales-type lease because there is no difference between the fair value ($100,000) of the equipment and the lessor's cost ($100,000).

The Lease Receivable is the present value of the minimum lease payments (excluding executory costs minus property taxes of $2,000) and is computed as follows.

Illustration 16-14
Computation of Lease Receivable

Lease receivable = ($25,981.62 − $2,000) × Present value of an annuity due of 1 for 5 periods at 10% (Appendix A, Table 5)
= $23,981.62 × 4.16986
= $100,000

The lease of the asset and the resulting receivable are recorded January 1, 2004 (the inception of the lease), as follows.

Lease Receivable	100,000	
Equipment		100,000

The lease receivable is often **reported** in the balance sheet as "Net investment in capital leases." It is classified either as current or noncurrent, depending upon when the net investment is to be recovered.

The leased equipment with a cost of $100,000, which represents Lessor Company's investment, is replaced with a lease receivable. In a manner similar to the lessee's treatment of interest, Lessor Company applies the effective interest method and recognizes interest revenue as a function of the lease receivable balance, as shown in Illustration 16-15.

Illustration 16-15
Lease Amortization Schedule for Lessor— Annuity Due Basis

			LESSOR COMPANY		
			LEASE AMORTIZATION SCHEDULE		
			(ANNUITY DUE BASIS)		
Date	Annual Lease Payment	Executory Costs	Interest (10%) on Lease Receivable	Lease Receivable Recovery	Lease Receivable
	(a)	(b)	(c)	(d)	(e)
1/1/04					$100,000.00
1/1/04	$ 25,981.62	$ 2,000.00	$ –0–	$ 23,981.62	76,018.38
1/1/05	25,981.62	2,000.00	7,601.84	16,379.78	59,638.60
1/1/06	25,981.62	2,000.00	5,963.86	18,017.76	41,620.84
1/1/07	25,981.62	2,000.00	4,162.08	19,819.54	21,801.30
1/1/08	25,981.62	2,000.00	2,180.32*	21,801.30	–0–
	$129,908.10	$10,000.00	$19,908.10	$100,000.00	

(a) Annual rental that provides a 10% return on net investment.
(b) Executory costs included in rental payment.
(c) Ten percent of the preceding balance of (e) except for 1/1/04.
(d) (a) minus (b) and (c).
(e) Preceding balance minus (d).
*Rounded by 19 cents.

On January 1, 2004, the journal entry to record receipt of the first year's lease payment is as follows.

Cash	25,981.62	
Lease Receivable		23,981.62
Property Tax Expense/Property Taxes Payable		2,000.00

On December 31, 2004, the interest revenue earned during the first year is recognized through the following entry.

Interest Receivable	7,601.84	
Interest Revenue—Leases		7,601.84

At December 31, 2004, the lease receivable is reported in the lessor's balance sheet among current assets or noncurrent assets, or both. The portion due within one year or the operating cycle, whichever is longer, is classified as a current asset, and the rest with noncurrent assets.

The assets section as it relates to lease transactions at December 31, 2004, would appear as follows.

Illustration 16-16
Reporting Lease
Transactions by Lessor

Current assets	
Interest receivable	$ 7,601.84
Lease receivable	16,379.78
Noncurrent assets (investments)	
Lease receivable	$59,638.60

The following entries record receipt of the second year's lease payment and recognition of the interest earned.

January 1, 2005

Cash	25,981.62	
Lease Receivable		16,379.78
Interest Receivable		7,601.84
Property Tax Expense/Property Taxes Payable		2,000.00

December 31, 2005

Interest Receivable	5,963.86	
Interest Revenue—Leases		5,963.86

Journal entries through 2008 would follow the same pattern except that no entry would be recorded in 2008 (the last year) for earned interest. Because the receivable is fully collected by January 1, 2008, no balance (investment) is outstanding during 2008 to which Lessor Company could attribute any interest. **Lessor Company recorded no depreciation**. If the equipment is sold to Lessee Company for $5,000 upon expiration of the lease, Lessor Company would recognize disposition of the equipment as follows.

Cash	5,000	
Gain on Sale of Leased Equipment		5,000

Operating Method (Lessor)

Under the **operating method**, each rental receipt by the lessor is recorded as rental revenue. The **leased asset is depreciated in the normal manner**, with the depreciation expense of the period matched against the rental revenue. The amount of revenue recognized in each accounting period is a level amount (straight-line basis) regardless of the lease provisions, unless another systematic and rational basis is more representative of the time pattern in which the benefit is derived from the leased asset. In addition to the depreciation charge, maintenance costs and the cost of any other services rendered under the provisions of the lease that pertain to the current accounting period are charged to expense. Costs paid to independent third parties, such as appraisal fees, finder's fees, and costs of credit checks, **are amortized over the life of the lease,** usually on a straight-line basis.

To illustrate the operating method, assume that the direct financing lease illustrated in the previous section did not qualify as a capital lease and was therefore to be accounted for as an operating lease. The entry to record the cash rental receipt, assuming the $2,000 was for property tax expense, would be as follows.

Cash	25,981.62	
Rental Revenue		25,981.62

Depreciation is recorded by the lessor as follows (assuming a straight-line method, a cost basis of $100,000, and a 5-year life).

Depreciation Expense—Leased Equipment	20,000	
Accumulated Depreciation—Leased Equipment		20,000

If property taxes, insurance, maintenance, and other operating costs during the year are the obligation of the lessor, they are recorded as expenses chargeable against the gross rental revenues.

If the lessor owned plant assets that it used in addition to those leased to others, **the leased equipment and accompanying accumulated depreciation would be separately classified** as Equipment Leased to Others or Investment in Leased Property. If significant in amount or in terms of activity, the rental revenues and accompanying expenses are separated in the income statement from sales revenue and cost of goods sold.

Sales-Type Leases (Lessor)

A **sales-type lease** recognizes interest revenue like a direct financing lease. However it also recognizes a manufacturer's or dealer's profit. In a sales-type lease, the lessor records the sale price of the asset, the cost of goods sold and related inventory reduction, and the lease receivable.

To illustrate, assume that Hartland Co. manufacturers tractors. On January 1, 2004, it leased to Potts Company a tractor that cost $100,000 to manufacture and has a fair value of $140,000. The lease agreement covers the 10-year useful life of the tractor and requires 10 equal payments at the end of each year of $22,784 ($140,000 ÷ PVF–

OBJECTIVE 6
Describe the lessor's accounting for sales-type leases.

$OA_{10,10\%}$). An interest rate of 10 percent is implicit in the lease agreement. Collectibility of rentals is reasonably assured, and there are no important uncertainties concerning future lessor costs. Given that the conditions for a capital lease are met, the journal entry on the books of the lessor is as follows.

Cost of Goods Sold	100,000	
Lease Receivable	140,000	
Sales Revenue		140,000
Inventory		100,000

The lessor in this case recognizes a gross profit of $40,000 ($140,000 − $100,000) on January 1, 2004. At the end of the year it would also report interest revenue of $14,000 (10% × $140,000).

Many manufactures or dealers of equipment use the sales-type lease because in essence they have sold the product and then finance the sale. Companies that use sales-type leases therefore recognize income earlier than if a direct financing or operating lease is used.

WHAT DO THE NUMBERS MEAN?

XEROX TAKES ON THE SEC

Much of **Xerox**'s income is derived from leasing equipment. Reporting such leases as sales leases, Xerox records a lease contract as a sale, with income therefore being recognized immediately. One problem is that each lease receipt is comprised of payments for various items such as supplies, services, financing, and equipment.

The SEC *accused* Xerox of inappropriately allocating lease receipts, which affects the timing of income that is reported. If SEC guidelines were applied, income would be reported in different time periods. Xerox contended that its methods were correct and also noted that when the lease term is up, the bottom line is the same using either the SEC's recommended allocation method or the method used by Xerox.

Although Xerox can refuse to change its method, the SEC has the right to prevent a company from selling stock or bonds to the public if filings of the company have been rejected by the agency.

Apparently, being able to access public markets is very valuable to Xerox. The company agreed to change its accounting according to SEC wishes, and paid a fine of $10 million due to its past accounting practices.

Source: Adapted from "Xerox Takes on the SEC," *Accounting Web* (January 9, 2002) (www.accountingweb.com).

SPECIAL ISSUES

Disclosing Lease Data

OBJECTIVE 7
Describe the disclosure requirements for leases.

Disclosures Required of the Lessee
The FASB requires that the following information with respect to leases be disclosed in the **lessee's** financial statements or in the notes.[14]

---

[14]"Accounting for Leases," *FASB Statement No. 13,* as amended and interpreted through May 1980 (Stamford, Conn.: FASB, 1980), par. 16.

Illustration 16-17
Lessee's Disclosures

(a) For capital leases:
   i. The gross amount of assets at each balance sheet date categorized by nature or function. This information may be combined with comparable information for owned assets.
   ii. Future *minimum lease payments* as of the latest balance sheet date, in the aggregate and for each of five succeeding fiscal years. Separate deductions for *executory costs* included in the *minimum lease payments* and for the amount of imputed interest necessary to reduce net *minimum lease payments* to present value.
   iii. Total noncancelable minimum sublease rentals to be received in the future, as of the latest balance sheet date.
   iv. Total *contingent rentals*.
   v. Assets recorded under capital leases and the accumulated amortization thereon shall be separately identified in the lessee's balance sheet or notes. Likewise, related obligations shall be separately identified as obligations under capital leases. Depreciation on capitalized leased assets should be separately disclosed.

(b) For operating leases having initial or remaining noncancelable *lease terms* in excess of one year:
   i. Future minimum rental payments required as of the latest balance sheet date, in the aggregate and for each of the five succeeding fiscal years.
   ii. Total minimum rentals to be received in the future under noncancelable subleases as of the latest balance sheet date.

(c) For all operating leases, rental expense for each period with separate amounts for minimum rentals, *contingent rentals*, and sublease rentals. Rental payments under leases with *terms* of a month or less that were not renewed need not be included.

(d) A general description of the lessee's arrangements including, but not limited to:
   i. The basis on which *contingent rental* payments are determined.
   ii. The existence and terms of renewal or purchase options and escalation clauses.
   iii. Restrictions imposed by lease agreements, such as those concerning dividends, additional debt, and further leasing.

Disclosures Required of the Lessor

The FASB requires that **lessors** disclose in the financial statements or in the notes the following information when leasing "is a significant part of the lessor's business activities in terms of revenue, net income, or assets."[15]

Illustration 16-18
Lessor's Disclosures

(a) For sales-type and direct financing leases:
   i. The components of the net investment in sales-type and direct financing leases as of each balance sheet date:
      a. Future *minimum lease payments* to be received, with separate deductions for (i) *executory costs* and (ii) the accumulated allowance for uncollectible *minimum lease payments* receivable.
      b. The *unguaranteed residual values* accruing to the lessor.
      c. Unearned revenue.
   ii. Future *minimum lease payments* to be received for each of the five succeeding fiscal years.
   iii. The amount of unearned revenue included in income to offset *initial direct costs* charged against income for each period for which an

income statement is presented. (For direct financing leases only.)
   iv. Total *contingent rentals* included in income for each period for which an income statement is presented.

(b) For operating leases:
   i. The cost and carrying amount, if different, of leased property according to nature or function, and total amount of accumulated depreciation.
   ii. Minimum future rentals on noncancelable leases as of the latest balance sheet date, in aggregate and for each of five succeeding fiscal years.
   iii. Total *contingent rentals* included in income for each period for which an income statement is presented.

(c) A general description of the lessor's leasing arrangements.

Disclosures Illustrated

The financial statement excerpts from the 2001 Annual Report of **The Penn Traffic Company** in Illustration 16-19 (page 802) present the statement and note disclosures typical of a **lessee** having both capital leases and operating leases.

[15]Ibid., par. 23.

PENN TRAFFIC COMPANY
(Dollar amounts in thousands)

Capital Leases (Note 12)	2001	2000
Capital leases	$60,405	$66,119
Less: Accumulated amortization	(9,593)	(5,052)
	50,812	61,067
Current Liabilities		
Current portion of obligations under capital leases (Note 12)	$ 7,878	$ 9,667
Noncurrent Liabilities		
Obligations under capital leases (Note 12)	73,396	82,537

Note 12: Leases (in part)

The Company principally operates in leased store facilities with terms of up to 20 years with renewable options for additional periods. The Company follows the provisions of Statement of Financial Accounting Standards No. 13, "Accounting for Leases" ("SFAS 13"), in determining the criteria for capital leases. Leases that do not meet such criteria are classified as operating leases and related rentals are charged to expense in the year incurred. In addition to minimum rentals, substantially all store leases provide for the Company to pay real estate taxes and other expenses. The majority of store leases also provide for the Company to pay contingent rentals based on a percentage of the store's sales in excess of stipulated amounts.

For 2001, 2000, and 1999, capital lease amortization expense was $7.6 million, $9.0 million, and $11.8 million, respectively.

The following is a summary by year of future minimum rental payments for capitalized leases and for operating leases that have initial or remaining noncancelable terms in excess of one year as of February 3, 2001:

Fiscal Years Ending	Total	Operating	Capital
	(in thousands of dollars)		
2002	$ 50,392	$ 33,460	$ 16,932
2003	47,866	32,092	15,774
2004	42,818	29,279	13,539
2005	40,443	27,237	13,206
2006	38,381	25,509	12,872
Later years	243,463	179,614	63,849
Total minimum lease payments	$463,363	$327,191	136,172
Less: Estimated amount representing interest			(54,898)
Present value of net minimum capital lease payments			81,274
Less: Current portion			(7,878)
Long-term obligations under capital leases at February 3, 2001			$ 73,396

Minimum rental payments for operating leases, including contingent rentals and net of sublease payments in 2001, 2000, and 1999 were $30,604, $30,036, and $35,832, respectively.

The following note from the 2001 Annual Report of Dana Corporation illustrates the disclosures of a **lessor**.

Illustration 16-20
Disclosure of Leases
by Lessor

DANA CORPORATION
Notes to Financial Statements
(in millions)

Note 1 (In Part): Summary of Significant Accounting Policies
Lease Financing

Lease financing consists of direct financing leases, leveraged leases and equipment on operating leases. Income on direct financing leases is recognized by a method which produces a constant periodic rate of return on the outstanding investment in the lease. Income on leveraged leases is recognized by a method which produces a constant rate of return on the outstanding net investment in the lease, net of the related deferred tax liability, in the years in which the net investment is positive. Initial direct costs are deferred and amortized using the interest method over the lease period. Equipment under operating leases is recorded at cost, net of accumulated depreciation. Income from operating leases is recognized ratably over the term of the leases.

The components of the net investment in direct financing leases are as follows:

	December 31	
	2000	2001
Total minimum lease payments	$154	$125
Residual values	42	38
Deferred initial direct costs	2	2
	198	165
Less: Unearned income	57	47
	$141	$118

The following is a schedule, by year, of total minimum lease payments receivable on direct financing and operating leases as of December 31, 2001:

Year Ending December 31:	Direct Financing	Operating
2002	$ 23	$20
2003	21	16
2004	18	12
2005	16	10
2006	12	8
Later years	35	15
Total minimum lease payments receivable	$125	$81

Unsolved Problems

As indicated at the beginning of this chapter, lease accounting is a much abused area in which strenuous efforts are being made to circumvent *Statement No. 13*. In practice, the accounting rules for capitalizing leases have been rendered partially ineffective by the strong desires of lessees to resist capitalization. Leasing generally involves large dollar amounts that when capitalized materially increase reported liabilities and adversely affect the debt-to-equity ratio. Lease capitalization is also resisted because charges to expense made in the early years of the lease term are higher under the capital lease method than under the operating method, frequently without tax benefit. As a consequence, "let's beat *Statement No. 13*" is one of the most popular games in town.

To avoid leased asset capitalization, lease agreements are designed, written, and interpreted so that none of the four capitalized lease criteria are satisfied from the lessee's viewpoint. Devising lease agreements in such a way has not been too difficult when the following specifications have been met.

1 Make certain that the lease does not specify the transfer of title of the property to the lessee.

2 Do not write in a bargain purchase option.

3 Set the lease term at something less than 75 percent of the estimated economic life of the leased property.

4 Arrange for the present value of the minimum lease payments to be less than 90 percent of the fair value of the leased property.

The real challenge lies in disqualifying the lease as a capital lease to the lessee while having the same lease qualify as a capital (sales or financing) lease to the lessor. Unlike lessees, lessors try to avoid having lease arrangements classified as operating leases.[16]

Avoiding the first three criteria is relatively simple, but it takes a little ingenuity to avoid the "90 percent recovery test" for the lessee while satisfying it for the lessor. Two of the factors involved in this effort are: (1) the use of the incremental borrowing rate by the lessee when it is higher than the implicit interest rate of the lessor, by making information about the implicit rate unavailable to the lessee; and (2) residual value guarantees.

The lessee's use of the higher interest rate is probably the more popular subterfuge. While lessees are knowledgeable about the fair value of the leased property and, of course, the rental payments, they generally are not aware of the estimated residual value used by the lessor. Therefore the lessee who does not know exactly the lessor's implicit interest rate might use a different incremental borrowing rate.

The residual value guarantee is the other unique, yet popular, device used by lessees and lessors. In fact, a whole new industry has emerged to circumvent symmetry between the lessee and the lessor in accounting for leases. The residual value guarantee has spawned numerous companies whose principal, or even sole, function is to guarantee the residual value of leased assets. These **third-party guarantors** (insurers), for a fee, assume the risk of deficiencies in leased asset residual value.

Because the guaranteed residual value is included in the minimum lease payments for the lessor, the 90 percent recovery of fair market value test is satisfied. The lease is a nonoperating lease to the lessor. **But because the residual value is guaranteed by a third party, the minimum lease payments of the lessee do not include the guarantee.** Thus, by merely transferring some of the risk to a third party, lessees can alter substantially the accounting treatment by converting what would otherwise be capital leases to operating leases.[17]

[16]The reason is that most lessors are financial institutions and do not want these types of assets on their balance sheets. In fact, banks and savings and loans are not permitted to report these assets on their balance sheets except for relatively short periods of time. Furthermore, the capital lease transaction from the lessor's standpoint provides higher income flows in the earlier periods of the lease.

[17]As an aside, third-party guarantors have experienced some difficulty. **Lloyd's of London**, at one time, insured the fast-growing U.S. computer-leasing industry in the amount of $2 billion against revenue losses and losses in residual value if leases were canceled. Because of "overnight" technological improvements and the successive introductions of more efficient and less expensive computers by computer manufacturers, lessees in abundance canceled their leases. As the market for second-hand computers became flooded and residual values plummeted, third-party guarantor Lloyd's of London projected a loss of $400 million. Much of the third-party guarantee business was stimulated by the lessees' and lessors' desire to circumvent *FASB Statement No. 13.*

Much of this circumvention is encouraged by the nature of the criteria, which stem from weaknesses in the basic objective of *Statement No. 13.* Accounting standards-setting bodies continue to have poor experience with arbitrary break points or other size and percentage criteria—that is, rules like "90 percent of," "75 percent of," etc. Some believe that a more workable solution would be to require capitalization of all leases that extend for some defined period (such as one year) on the basis that the lessee has acquired an asset (a property right) and a corresponding liability, rather than on the basis that the lease transfers substantially all the risks and rewards of ownership.

Three years after it issued *Statement No. 13,* a majority of the FASB expressed "the tentative view that, if *Statement 13* were to be reconsidered, they would support a property right approach in which all leases are included as 'rights to use property' and as 'lease obligations' in the lessee's balance sheet." Recently, the FASB and other international standard setters have issued a report on lease accounting that proposes the capitalization of more leases.[18]

SUMMARY OF LEARNING OBJECTIVES

① Explain the advantages of lease transactions. A lease is a contractual agreement between a lessor and a lessee that conveys to the lessee the right to use specific property (real or personal), owned by the lessor, for a specified period of time. In return for this right, the lessee agrees to make periodic cash payments (rents) to the lessor. The advantages of lease transactions are: (1) 100 percent financing; (2) protection against obsolescence, (3) flexibility, (4) less costly financing, (5) off-balance-sheet financing, and (6) possible tax advantages.

② Describe the accounting criteria and procedures for capitalizing leases by the lessee. A lease is a capital lease if one or more of the following criteria are met: (1) The lease transfers ownership of the property to the lessee. (2) The lease contains a bargain purchase option. (3) The lease term is equal to 75 percent or more of the estimated economic life of the leased property. (4) The present value of the minimum lease payments (excluding executory costs) equals or exceeds 90 percent of the fair value of the leased property. For a capital lease, the lessee records an asset and a liability at the lower of (1) the present value of the minimum lease payments, or (2) the fair market value of the leased asset at the inception of the lease.

③ Contrast the operating and capitalization methods of recording leases. The total charges to operations are the same over the lease term whether the lease is accounted for as a capital lease or as an operating lease. Under the capital lease treatment, the charges are higher in the earlier years and lower in the later years. If an accelerated method of depreciation is used, the differences between the amounts charged to operations under the two methods would be even larger in the earlier and later years. The following occurs if a capital lease instead of an operating lease is employed: (1) an increase in the amount of reported debt (both short-term and long-term), (2) an increase in the amount of total assets (specifically long-lived assets), and (3) a lower income early in the life of the lease and, therefore, lower retained earnings.

④ Identify the classifications of leases for the lessor. From the standpoint of the lessor, all leases may be classified for accounting purpose as follows: (1) operating leases, (2) direct financing leases, (3) sales-type leases. The lessor should classify and account for an arrangement as a direct financing lease or a sales-type lease if, at the date of the lease agreement, one or more of the Group I criteria (as shown in learning objective 2 for lessees) are met and both of the following Group II criteria are met. *Group II:* (1) Collectibility of the payments required from the lessee is reasonably predictable; and (2) no important uncertainties surround the amount of unreimbursable costs yet to be

[18]H. Nailor and A. Lennard, "Capital Leases: Implementation of a New Approach," *Financial Accounting Series No. 206A* (Norwalk, Conn.: FASB, 2000).

KEY TERMS

bargain purchase option, *784*
bargain renewal option, *784*
capital lease, *783*
capitalization criteria, *784*
capitalization of leases, *782*
direct financing lease, *796*
effective interest method, *787*
executory costs, *785*
guaranteed residual value, *785*
implicit interest rate, *786*
incremental borrowing rate, *785*
lease, *780*
lease term, *784*
lessee, *780*
lessor, *780*
manufacturer's or dealer's profit, *795*
minimum lease payments, *785*
noncancelable, *782*
off-balance-sheet financing, *781*
operating lease, *783*
sales-type lease, *799*
third-party guarantors, *804*

incurred by the lessor under the lease. All leases that fail to meet the criteria are classified and accounted for by the lessor as operating leases.

5 Describe the lessor's accounting for direct financing leases. Leases that are in substance the financing of an asset purchase by a lessee require the lessor to substitute a "lease receivable" for the leased asset. Payments received from lessees reduce the Lease Receivable. Interest revenue is accrued by applying the effective interest rate to the Lease Receivable balance.

6 Describe the lessor's accounting for sales-type leases. A sales-type lease recognizes interest revenue like a direct financing lease. It also recognizes a manufacturer's or dealer's profit. In a sales-type lease, the lessor records at the inception of the lease the sales price of the asset, the cost of goods sold and related inventory reduction, and the lease receivable.

7 Describe the disclosure requirements for leases. The disclosure requirements for the **lessee** are classified as follows: (1) capital leases; (2) operating leases having initial or remaining noncancelable lease terms in excess of one year; (3) all operating leases; and (4) a general description of the lessee's arrangements. The disclosure requirements for the **lessor** are classified as follows: (1) sales-type and direct financing leases; (2) operating leases; and (3) a general description of the lessor's leasing arrangements.

Expanded Discussion of Real Estate Leases and Leveraged Leases

REVIEW EXERCISE

Assume that Morgan Bakeries is involved in two different lease situations. Each of these leases is noncancelable, and in no case does Morgan receive title to the properties leased during or at the end of the lease term. All leases start on January 1, 2004, with the first rental due at the beginning of the year. The additional information is shown below.

	Harmon, Inc.	Mendota Truck Co.
Type of property	Cabinets	Truck
Yearly rental	$6,000	$5,582.62
Lease term	20 years	3 years
Estimated economic life	30 years	7 years
Purchase option	None	None
Fair market value at inception of lease	$60,000	$20,000
Cost of asset to lessor	$60,000	$15,000
Residual value		
Guaranteed	– 0 –	$7,000
Unguaranteed	$5,000	– 0 –
Incremental borrowing rate of lessee	12%	12%
Executory costs paid by	*Lessee*	*Lessee*
	$300 per year	$500 per year
Present value of minimum lease payments		
Using incremental borrowing rate of lessee	$50,194.68	$20,000
Using implicit rate of lessor	Not known	Not known
Estimated fair market value at end of lease	$5,000	Not available

Instructions

(a) (1) Determine for Morgan Bakeries and Harman Co. whether the lease is a capital or operating lease, and (2) record the journal entries for both the lessee and the lessor on January 1, 2004.

(b) (1) Determine for Morgan Bakeries and Mendota Truck Co. whether the lease is a capital or operating lease, and (2) record the journal entries for both the lessee and the lessor on January 1, 2004.

SOLUTION TO REVIEW EXERCISE

(a) (1) The following is an analysis of the Harmon, Inc. lease.

1. **Transfer of title?** No.

2. **Bargain purchase option?** No.

3. **Economic life test (75% test).** The lease term is 20 years and the estimated economic life is 30 years. Thus it does **not** meet the 75 percent test.

4. **Recovery of investment test (90% test):**

Fair market value	$60,000	Rental payments	$ 6,000
Rate	90%	PV of annuity due for	
90% of fair market value	$54,000	20 years at 12%	× 8.36578
		PV of rental payments	$50,194.68

Because the present value of the minimum lease payments is less than 90 percent of the fair market value, the 90 percent test is not met. Both Morgan and Harmon should account for this lease as an operating lease.

(2) The journal entries to record the lease transaction on January 1, 2004, are as follows.

Morgan Bakeries (Lessee)			Harmon, Inc. (Lessor)		
Rent Expense	6,000		Cash	6,000	
Cash		6,000	Rental Revenue		6,000

(b) (1) The following is an analysis of the Mendota Truck Co. lease.

1. **Transfer of title?** No.

2. **Bargain purchase option?** No.

3. **Economic life test (75% test):** The lease term is three years and the estimated economic life is seven years. Thus it does **not** meet the 75 percent test.

4. **Recovery of investment test (90% test):**

Fair market value	$20,000	Rental payments	$ 5,582.62
Rate	90%	PV of annuity due for	
90% of fair market value	$18,000	3 years at 12%	× 2.69005
		PV of rental payments	$15,017.54

(Note: adjusted for $.01 due to rounding)

PV of guaranteed residual value: = $7,000(PVF$_{3,12\%}$) = $7,000(.71178) = $4,982.46

PV of rental payments	$15,017.54
PV of guaranteed residual value	4,982.46
PV of minimum lease payments	$20,000.00

The present value of the minimum lease payments is greater than 90 percent of the fair market value. Therefore, the 90 percent test is met. Morgan accounts for the lease as a capital lease, and Mendota has a sales-type lease.

(2) Assuming that Mendota's implicit rate is the same as Morgan's incremental borrowing rate, the following entries are made on January 1, 2004.

Morgan Bakeries (Lessee)				Mendota Truck Co. (Lessor)		
Leased Asset — Truck	20,000			Lease Receivable	20,000	
Lease Liability		20,000		Cost of Goods Sold	15,000	
				Inventory — Truck		15,000
				Sales		20,000

QUESTIONS

1 Jackie Remmers Co. is expanding its operations and is in the process of selecting the method of financing this program. After some investigation, the company determines that it may (1) issue bonds and with the proceeds purchase the needed assets, or (2) lease the assets on a long-term basis. Without knowing the comparative costs involved, answer the following questions.

(a) What might be the advantages of leasing the assets instead of owning them?

(b) What might be the disadvantages of leasing the assets instead of owning them?

(c) In what way will the balance sheet be differently affected by leasing the assets as opposed to issuing bonds and purchasing the assets?

2 Mildred Natalie Corp. is considering leasing a significant amount of assets. The president, Joan Elaine Robinson, is attending an informal meeting in the afternoon with a potential lessor. Because her legal advisor cannot be reached, she has called on you, the controller, to brief her on the general provisions of lease agreements to which she should give consideration in such preliminary discussions with a possible lessor. Identify the general provisions of the lease agreement that the president should be told to include in her discussion with the potential lessor.

3 Identify the two recognized lease accounting methods for lessees, and distinguish between them.

4 Wayne Higley Company rents a warehouse on a month-to-month basis for the storage of its excess inventory. The company periodically must rent space whenever its production greatly exceeds actual sales. For several years the company officials have discussed building their own storage facility, but this enthusiasm wavers when sales increase sufficiently to absorb the excess inventory. What is the nature of this type of lease arrangement, and what accounting treatment should be accorded it?

5 Distinguish between minimum rental payments and minimum lease payments, and indicate what is included in minimum lease payments.

6 Explain the distinction between a direct financing lease and a sales-type lease for a lessor.

7 Outline the accounting procedures involved in applying the operating method by a lessee.

8 Outline the accounting procedures involved in applying the capital lease method by a lessee.

9 Identify the lease classifications for lessors and the criteria that must be met for each classification.

10 Outline the accounting procedures involved in applying the direct financing method.

11 Outline the accounting procedures involved in applying the operating method by a lessor.

12 Joan Elbert Company is a manufacturer and lessor of computer equipment. What should be the nature of its lease arrangements with lessees if the company wishes to account for its lease transactions as sales-type leases?

13 Gordon Graham Corporation's lease arrangements qualify as sales-type leases at the time of entering into the transactions. How should the corporation recognize revenues and costs in these situations?

14 Joann Skabo, M.D. (lessee) has a noncancelable 20-year lease with Cheryl Countryman Realty, Inc. (lessor) for the use of a medical building. Taxes, insurance, and maintenance are paid by the lessee in addition to the fixed annual payments, of which the present value is equal to the fair market value of the leased property. At the end of the lease period, title becomes the lessee's at a nominal price. Considering the terms of the lease described above, comment on the nature of the lease transaction and the accounting treatment that should be accorded it by the lessee.

15 Describe the effect of a "bargain purchase option" on accounting for a capital lease transaction by a lessee.

16 What disclosures should be made by a lessee if the leased assets and the related obligation are not capitalized?

BRIEF EXERCISES

BE16-1 WarpSpeed Corporation leased equipment from Photon Company. The lease term is 5 years and requires equal rental payments of $30,000 at the beginning of each year. The equipment has a fair value at the inception of the lease of $138,000, an estimated useful life of 8 years, and no residual value. WarpSpeed pays all executory costs directly to third parties. Photon set the annual rental to earn a rate of return of 10%, and this fact is known to WarpSpeed. The lease does not transfer title or contain a bargain purchase option. How should WarpSpeed classify this lease?

BE16-2 Waterworld Company leased equipment from Costner Company. The lease term is 4 years and requires equal rental payments of $37,283 at the beginning of each year. The equipment has a fair value at the inception of the lease of $130,000, an estimated useful life of 4 years, and no salvage value. Waterworld pays all executory costs directly to third parties. The appropriate interest rate is 10%. Prepare Waterworld's January 1, 2004, journal entries at the inception of the lease.

BE16-3 Rick Kleckner Corporation recorded a capital lease at $200,000 on January 1, 2004. The interest rate is 12%. Kleckner Corporation made the first lease payment of $35,947 on January 1, 2004. The lease requires eight annual payments. The equipment has a useful life of 8 years with no salvage value. Prepare Kleckner Corporation's December 31, 2004, adjusting entries.

BE16-4 Use the information for Rick Kleckner Corporation from BE16-3. Assume that at December 31, 2004, Kleckner made an adjusting entry to accrue interest expense of $19,686 on the lease. Prepare Kleckner's January 1, 2005, journal entry to record the second lease payment of $35,947.

BE16-5 Jana Kingston Corporation enters into a lease on January 1, 2004, that does not transfer ownership or contain a bargain purchase option. It covers 3 years of the equipment's 8-year useful life, and the present value of the minimum lease payments is less than 90% of the fair market value of the asset leased. Prepare Jana Kingston's journal entry to record its January 1, 2004, annual lease payment of $37,500.

BE16-6 Karen A. Henkel Corporation leased equipment that was carried at a cost of $150,000 to Sharon Swander Company. The term of the lease is 6 years beginning January 1, 2004, with equal rental payments of $30,677 at the beginning of each year. All executory costs are paid by Swander directly to third parties. The fair value of the equipment at the inception of the lease is $150,000. The equipment has a useful life of 6 years with no salvage value. The lease has an implicit interest rate of 9%, no bargain purchase option, and no transfer of title. Collectibility is reasonably assured with no additional cost to be incurred by Henkel. Prepare Karen A. Henkel Corporation's January 1, 2004, journal entries at the inception of the lease.

BE16-7 Use the information for Karen A. Henkel Corporation from BE16-6. Assume the direct financing lease was recorded at a present value of $150,000. Prepare Karen A. Henkel's December 31, 2004, entry to record interest.

BE16-8 Jennifer Brent Corporation owns equipment that cost $72,000 and has a useful life of 8 years with no salvage value. On January 1, 2004, Jennifer Brent leases the equipment to Donna Havaci Inc. for one year with one rental payment of $15,000 on January 1. Prepare Jennifer Brent Corporation's 2004 journal entries.

BE16-9 Indiana Jones Corporation enters into a 6-year lease of machinery on January 1, 2004, which requires 6 annual payments of $30,000 each, beginning January 1, 2004. In addition, Indiana Jones guarantees the lessor a residual value of $20,000 at lease-end. The machinery has a useful life of 6 years. Prepare Indiana Jones' January 1, 2004, journal entries assuming an interest rate of 10%.

BE16-10 Starfleet Corporation manufactures replicators. On January 1, 2004, it leased to Ferengi Company a replicator that had cost $110,000 to manufacture. The lease agreement covers the 5-year useful life of the replicator and requires 5 equal annual rentals of $45,400 each. An interest rate of 12% is implicit in the lease agreement. Collectibility of the rentals is reasonably assured, and there are no important uncertainties concerning costs. Prepare Starfleet's January 1, 2004, journal entries.

EXERCISES

E16-1 **(Lessee Entries; Capital Lease)** On January 1, 2003, Burke Corporation signed a 5-year noncancelable lease for a machine. The terms of the lease called for Burke to make annual payments of $8,668 at the beginning of each year, starting January 1, 2003. The machine has an estimated useful life of 6 years. The machine reverts back to the lessor at the end of the lease term. Burke uses the straight-line method of depreciation for all of its plant assets. Burke's incremental borrowing rate is 10%, and the Lessor's implicit rate is unknown.

Instructions

(a) What type of lease is this? Explain.

(b) Compute the present value of the minimum lease payments.

(c) Prepare all necessary journal entries for Burke for this lease through January 1, 2004.

E16-2 (Lessee Computations and Entries; Capital Lease with Guaranteed Residual Value) Pat Delaney Company leases an automobile with a fair value of $8,725 from John Simon Motors, Inc., on the following terms.

1. Noncancelable term of 50 months.
2. Rental of $200 per month (at end of each month; present value at 1% per month is $7,840).
3. Estimated residual value after 50 months is $1,180. (The present value at 1% per month is $715.) Delaney Company guarantees the residual value of $1,180.
4. Estimated economic life of the automobile is 60 months.
5. Delaney Company's incremental borrowing rate is 12% a year (1% a month). Simon's implicit rate is unknown.

Instructions

(a) What is the nature of this lease to Delaney Company?

(b) What is the present value of the minimum lease payments?

(c) Record the lease on Delaney Company's books at the date of inception.

(d) Record the first month's depreciation on Delaney Company's books. (Assume straight-line.)

(e) Record the first month's lease payment.

E16-3 (Lessee Entries; Capital Lease with Executory Costs) On January 1, 2004, Lahey Paper Co. signs a 10-year noncancelable lease agreement to lease a storage building from Sheffield Storage Company. The following information pertains to this lease agreement.

1. The agreement requires equal rental payments of $72,000 beginning on January 1, 2004.
2. The fair value of the building on January 1, 2004 is $440,000.
3. The building has an estimated economic life of 12 years, with an unguaranteed residual value of $10,000. Lahey Paper Co. depreciates similar buildings on the straight-line method.
4. The lease is nonrenewable. At the termination of the lease, the building reverts to the lessor.
5. Lahey Paper's incremental borrowing rate is 12% per year. The lessor's implicit rate is not known by Lahey Paper Co.
6. The yearly rental payment includes $2,470.51 of executory costs related to taxes on the property.

Instructions

Prepare the journal entries on the lessee's books to reflect the signing of the lease agreement and to record the payments and expenses related to this lease for the years 2004 and 2005. Lahey Paper's corporate year end is December 31.

E16-4 (Type of Lease; Amortization Schedule) Mike Maroscia Leasing Company leases a new machine that has a cost and fair value of $95,000 to Maggie Sharrer Corporation on a 3-year noncancelable contract. Maggie Sharrer Corporation agrees to assume all risks of normal ownership including such costs as insurance, taxes, and maintenance. The machine has a 3-year useful life and no residual value. The lease was signed on January 1, 2004. Mike Maroscia Leasing Company expects to earn a 9% return on its investment. The annual rentals are payable on each December 31.

Instructions

(a) Discuss the nature of the lease arrangement and the accounting method that each party to the lease should apply.

(b) Prepare an amortization schedule that would be suitable for both the lessor and the lessee and that covers all the years involved.

E16-5 (Lessor Entries; Sales-Type Lease) Crosley Company, a machinery dealer, leased a machine to Dexter Corporation on January 1, 2003. The lease is for an 8-year period and requires equal annual payments of

$35,013 at the beginning of each year. The first payment is received on January 1, 2003. Crosley had purchased the machine during 2002 for $160,000. Collectibility of lease payments is reasonably predictable, and no important uncertainties surround the amount of costs yet to be incurred by Crosley. Crosley set the annual rental to ensure an 11% rate of return. The machine has an economic life of 10 years with no residual value and reverts to Crosley at the termination of the lease.

Instructions

Prepare all necessary journal entries for Crosley for 2003.

E16-6 (Lessee-Lessor Entries; Sales-Type Lease) On January 1, 2003, Bensen Company leased equipment to Flynn Corporation. The following information pertains to this lease.

1. The term of the noncancelable lease is 6 years, with no renewal option. The equipment reverts to the lessor at the termination of the lease.
2. Equal rental payments are due on January 1 of each year, beginning in 2003.
3. The fair value of the equipment on January 1, 2003, is $150,000, and its cost is $120,000.
4. The equipment has an economic life of 8 years. Flynn depreciates all of its equipment on a straight-line basis.
5. Bensen set the annual rental to ensure an 11% rate of return. Flynn's incremental borrowing rate is 12%, and the implicit rate of the lessor is unknown.
6. Collectibility of lease payments is reasonably predictable, and no important uncertainties surround the amount of costs yet to be incurred by the lessor.

Instructions

(a) Discuss the nature of this lease to Bensen and Flynn.
(b) Calculate the amount of the annual rental payment.
(c) Prepare all the necessary journal entries for Flynn for 2003.
(d) Prepare all the necessary journal entries for Bensen for 2003.

4.79079 = 245,000

E16-7 (Computation of Rental; Journal Entries for Lessor) Morgan Marie Leasing Company signs an agreement on January 1, 2003, to lease equipment to Cole William Company. The following information relates to this agreement.

1. The term of the noncancelable lease is 6 years with no renewal option. The equipment has an estimated economic life of 6 years.
2. The cost of the asset to the lessor is $245,000. The fair value of the asset at January 1, 2003, is $245,000.
3. The asset will revert to the lessor at the end of the lease term at which time the asset is expected to have a residual value of $43,622, none of which is guaranteed.
4. Cole William Company assumes direct responsibility for all executory costs.
5. The agreement requires equal annual rental payments, beginning on January 1, 2003.
6. Collectibility of the lease payments is reasonably predictable. There are no important uncertainties surrounding the amount of costs yet to be incurred by the lessor.

Instructions

(a) Assuming the lessor desires a 10% rate of return on its investment, calculate the amount of the annual rental payment required. (*Hint:* Be sure to deduct the present value of the residual value to determine the amount to recover in the lease payments.) Round to the nearest dollar.
(b) Prepare an amortization schedule that would be suitable for the lessor for the lease term.
(c) Prepare all of the journal entries for the lessor for 2003 and 2004 to record the lease agreement, the receipt of lease payments, and the recognition of income. Assume the lessor's annual accounting period ends on December 31.

E16-8 (Amortization Schedule and Journal Entries for Lessee) Laura Potts Leasing Company signs an agreement on January 1, 2003, to lease equipment to Janet Plote Company. The following information relates to this agreement.

1. The term of the noncancelable lease is 5 years with no renewal option. The equipment has an estimated economic life of 5 years.

2. The fair value of the asset at January 1, 2003, is $80,000.
3. The asset will revert to the lessor at the end of the lease term, at which time the asset is expected to have a residual value of $7,000, none of which is guaranteed.
4. Plote Company assumes direct responsibility for all executory costs, which include the following annual amounts: (1) $900 to Rocky Mountain Insurance Company for insurance, and (2) $1,600 to Laclede County for property taxes.
5. The agreement requires equal annual rental payments of $18,142.95 to the lessor, beginning on January 1, 2003.
6. The lessee's incremental borrowing rate is 12%. The lessor's implicit rate is 10% and is known to the lessee.
7. Plote Company uses the straight-line depreciation method for all equipment.
8. Plote uses reversing entries when appropriate.

Instructions

(Round all numbers to the nearest cent.)

(a) Prepare an amortization schedule that would be suitable for the lessee for the lease term.
(b) Prepare all of the journal entries for the lessee for 2003 and 2004 to record the lease agreement, the lease payments, and all expenses related to this lease. Assume the lessee's annual accounting period ends on December 31.

E16-9 (Accounting for an Operating Lease) On January 1, 2003, Doug Nelson Co. leased a building to Patrick Wise Inc. The relevant information related to the lease is as follows.

1. The lease arrangement is for 10 years.
2. The leased building cost $4,500,000 and was purchased for cash on January 1, 2003.
3. The building is depreciated on a straight-line basis. Its estimated economic life is 50 years.
4. Lease payments are $275,000 per year and are made at the end of the year.
5. Property tax expense of $85,000 and insurance expense of $10,000 on the building were incurred by Nelson in the first year. Payment on these two items was made at the end of the year.
6. Both the lessor and the lessee are on a calendar-year basis.

Instructions

(a) Prepare the journal entries that Nelson Co. should make in 2003.
(b) Prepare the journal entries that Wise Inc. should make in 2003.
(c) If Nelson paid $30,000 to a real estate broker on January 1, 2003, as a fee for finding the lessee, how much should be reported as an expense for this item in 2003 by Nelson Co.?

E16-10 (Accounting for an Operating Lease) On January 1, 2004, a machine was purchased for $900,000 by Tom Young Co. The machine is expected to have an 8-year life with no salvage value. It is to be depreciated on a straight-line basis. The machine was leased to St. Leger Inc. on January 1, 2004, at an annual rental of $210,000. Other relevant information is as follows.

1. The lease term is for 3 years.
2. Tom Young Co. incurred maintenance and other executory costs of $25,000 in 2004 related to this lease.
3. The machine could have been sold by Tom Young Co. for $940,000 instead of leasing it.
4. St. Leger is required to pay a rent security deposit of $35,000 and to prepay the last month's rent of $17,500.

Instructions

(a) How much should Tom Young Co. report as income before income tax on this lease for 2004?
(b) What amount should St. Leger Inc. report for rent expense for 2004 on this lease?

E16-11 (Operating Lease for Lessee and Lessor) On February 20, 2003, Barbara Brent Inc., purchased a machine for $1,500,000 for the purpose of leasing it. The machine is expected to have a 10-year life, no residual value, and will be depreciated on the straight-line basis. The machine was leased to Chuck Rudy Company on March 1, 2003, for a 4-year period at a monthly rental of $19,500. There is no provision for the renewal of the lease or purchase of the machine by the lessee at the expiration of the lease term. Brent paid $30,000 of commissions associated with negotiating the lease in February 2003.

Instructions

(a) What expense should Chuck Rudy Company record as a result of the facts above for the year ended December 31, 2003? Show supporting computations in good form.

(b) What income or loss before income taxes should Brent record as a result of the facts above for the year ended December 31, 2003? (*Hint:* Amortize commissions over the life of the lease.)

PROBLEMS

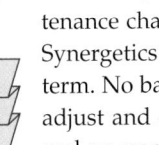

P16-1 **(Lessee-Lessor Entries; Operating Lease)** Synergetics Inc. leased a new crane to M. K. Gumowski Construction under a 5-year noncancelable contract starting January 1, 2004. Terms of the lease require payments of $22,000 each January 1, starting January 1, 2004. Synergetics will pay insurance, taxes, and maintenance charges on the crane, which has an estimated life of 12 years, a fair value of $160,000, and a cost to Synergetics of $160,000. The estimated fair value of the crane is expected to be $45,000 at the end of the lease term. No bargain purchase or renewal options are included in the contract. Both Synergetics and Gumowski adjust and close books annually at December 31. Collectibility of the lease payments is reasonably certain, and no uncertainties exist relative to unreimbursable lessor costs. Gumowski's incremental borrowing rate is 10%, and Synergetics' implicit interest rate of 9% is known to Gumowski.

Instructions

(a) Identify the type of lease involved and give reasons for your classification. Discuss the accounting treatment that should be applied by both the lessee and the lessor.

(b) Prepare all the entries related to the lease contract and leased asset for the year 2004 for the lessee and lessor, assuming:

  (1) Insurance, $500.

  (2) Taxes, $2,000.

  (3) Maintenance, $650.

  (4) Straight-line depreciation and salvage value, $10,000.

(c) Discuss what should be presented in the balance sheet and income statement and related notes of both the lessee and the lessor at December 31, 2004.

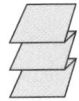

P16-2 **(Lessee-Lessor Entries, Balance Sheet Presentation; Sales-Type Lease)** Cascade Industries and Barbara Hardy Inc. enter into an agreement that requires Barbara Hardy Inc. to build three diesel-electric engines to Cascade's specifications. Upon completion of the engines, Cascade has agreed to lease them for a period of 10 years and to assume all costs and risks of ownership. The lease is noncancelable, becomes effective on January 1, 2004, and requires annual rental payments of $620,956 each January 1, starting January 1, 2004.

Cascade's incremental borrowing rate is 10%, and the implicit interest rate used by Barbara Hardy Inc. and known to Cascade is 8%. The total cost of building the three engines is $3,900,000. The economic life of the engines is estimated to be 10 years with residual value set at zero. Cascade depreciates similar equipment on a straight-line basis. At the end of the lease, Cascade assumes title to the engines. Collectibility of the lease payments is reasonably certain and no uncertainties exist relative to unreimbursable lessor costs.

Instructions

(Round all numbers to the nearest dollar.)

(a) Discuss the nature of this lease transaction from the viewpoints of both lessee and lessor.

(b) Prepare the journal entry or entries to record the transaction on January 1, 2004, on the books of Cascade Industries.

(c) Prepare the journal entry or entries to record the transaction on January 1, 2004, on the books of Barbara Hardy Inc.

(d) Prepare the journal entries for both the lessee and lessor to record the first rental payment on January 1, 2004.

(e) Prepare the journal entries for both the lessee and lessor to record interest expense (revenue) at December 31, 2004. (Prepare a lease amortization schedule for 2 years.)

(f) Show the items and amounts that would be reported on the balance sheet (not notes) at December 31, 2004, for both the lessee and the lessor.

P16-3 **(Balance Sheet and Income Statement Disclosure—Lessee)** The following facts pertain to a non-cancelable lease agreement between Ben Alschuler Leasing Company and John McKee Electronics, a lessee, for a computer system.

Inception date:	October 1, 2003
Lease term	6 years
Economic life of leased equipment	6 years
Fair value of asset at October 1, 2003	$200,255
Residual value at end of lease term	–0–
Lessor's implicit rate	10%
Lessee's incremental borrowing rate	10%
Annual lease payment due at the beginning of each year, beginning with October 1, 2003	$41,800

The collectibility of the lease payments is reasonably predictable, and there are no important uncertainties surrounding the costs yet to be incurred by the lessor. The lessee assumes responsibility for all executory costs, which amount to $5,500 per year and are to be paid each October 1, beginning October 1, 2003. (This $5,500 is not included in the rental payment of $41,800.) The asset will revert to the lessor at the end of the lease term. The straight-line depreciation method is used for all equipment.

The following amortization schedule has been prepared correctly for use by both the lessor and the lessee in accounting for this lease. The lease is to be accounted for properly as a capital lease by the lessee and as a direct financing lease by the lessor.

Date	Annual Lease Payment/ Receipt	Interest (10%) on Unpaid Liability/ Receivable	Reduction of Lease Liability/ Receivable	Balance of Lease Liability/ Receivable
10/01/03				$200,255
10/01/03	$ 41,800		$ 41,800	158,455
10/01/04	41,800	$15,846	25,954	132,501
10/01/05	41,800	13,250	28,550	103,951
10/01/06	41,800	10,395	31,405	72,546
10/01/07	41,800	7,255	34,545	38,001
10/01/08	41,800	3,799*	38,001	–0–
	$250,800	$50,545	$200,255	

*Rounding error is $1.

Instructions

(Round all numbers to the nearest cent.)

(a) Assuming the lessee's accounting period ends on September 30, answer the following questions with respect to this lease agreement.
   (1) What items and amounts will appear on the lessee's income statement for the year ending September 30, 2004?
   (2) What items and amounts will appear on the lessee's balance sheet at September 30, 2004?
   (3) What items and amounts will appear on the lessee's income statement for the year ending September 30, 2005?
   (4) What items and amounts will appear on the lessee's balance sheet at September 30, 2005?
(b) Assuming the lessee's accounting period ends on December 31, answer the following questions with respect to this lease agreement.
   (1) What items and amounts will appear on the lessee's income statement for the year ending December 31, 2003?
   (2) What items and amounts will appear on the lessee's balance sheet at December 31, 2003?

(3) What items and amounts will appear on the lessee's income statement for the year ending December 31, 2004?

(4) What items and amounts will appear on the lessee's balance sheet at December 31, 2004?

P16-4 (Balance Sheet and Income Statement Disclosure—Lessor) Assume the same information as in P16-3.

Instructions

(Round all numbers to the nearest cent.)

(a) Assuming the lessor's accounting period ends on September 30, answer the following questions with respect to this lease agreement.

(1) What items and amounts will appear on the lessor's income statement for the year ending September 30, 2004?

(2) What items and amounts will appear on the lessor's balance sheet at September 30, 2004?

(3) What items and amounts will appear on the lessor's income statement for the year ending September 30, 2005?

(4) What items and amounts will appear on the lessor's balance sheet at September 30, 2005?

(b) Assuming the lessor's accounting period ends on December 31, answer the following questions with respect to this lease agreement.

(1) What items and amounts will appear on the lessor's income statement for the year ending December 31, 2003?

(2) What items and amounts will appear on the lessor's balance sheet at December 31, 2003?

(3) What items and amounts will appear on the lessor's income statement for the year ending December 31, 2004?

(4) What items and amounts will appear on the lessor's balance sheet at December 31, 2004?

P16-5 (Lessee Entries and Balance Sheet Presentation; Capital Lease) Hilary Brennan Steel Company as lessee signed a lease agreement for equipment for 5 years, beginning December 31, 2003. Annual rental payments of $32,000 are to be made at the beginning of each lease year (December 31). The taxes, insurance, and the maintenance costs are the obligation of the lessee. The interest rate used by the lessor in setting the payment schedule is 10%; Brennan's incremental borrowing rate is 12%. Brennan is unaware of the rate being used by the lessor. At the end of the lease, Brennan has the option to buy the equipment for $1, considerably below its estimated fair value at that time. The equipment has an estimated useful life of 7 years, and no salvage value has been added. Brennan uses the straight-line method of depreciation on similar owned equipment.

Instructions

(Round all numbers to the nearest dollar.)

(a) Prepare the journal entry or entries, with explanations, that should be recorded on December 31, 2003, by Brennan. (Assume no residual value.)

(b) Prepare the journal entry or entries, with explanations, that should be recorded on December 31, 2004, by Brennan. (Prepare the lease amortization schedule for all five payments.)

(c) Prepare the journal entry or entries, with explanations, that should be recorded on December 31, 2005, by Brennan.

(d) What amounts would appear on Brennan's December 31, 2005, balance sheet relative to the lease arrangement?

P16-6 (Lessee Entries and Balance Sheet Presentation; Capital Lease) On January 1, 2004, Charlie Doss Company contracts to lease equipment for 5 years, agreeing to make a payment of $94,732 (including the executory costs of $6,000) at the beginning of each year, starting January 1, 2004. The taxes, the insurance, and the maintenance, estimated at $6,000 a year, are the obligations of the lessee. The leased equipment is to be capitalized at $370,000. The asset is to be amortized on a double-declining-balance basis, and the obligation is to be reduced on an effective-interest basis. Doss's incremental borrowing rate is 12%, and the implicit rate in the lease is 10%, which is known by Doss. Title to the equipment transfers to Doss when the lease expires. The asset has an estimated useful life of 5 years and no residual value.

Instructions

(Round all numbers to the nearest dollar.)

(a) Explain the probable relationship of the $370,000 amount to the lease arrangement.

(b) Prepare the journal entry or entries that should be recorded on January 1, 2004, by Charlie Doss Company.

(c) Prepare the journal entry to record depreciation of the leased asset for the year 2004.

(d) Prepare the journal entry to record the interest expense for the year 2004.

(e) Prepare the journal entry to record the lease payment of January 1, 2005, assuming reversing entries are not made.

(f) What amounts will appear on the lessee's December 31, 2004, balance sheet relative to the lease contract?

P16-7 **(Lessee Entries, Capital Lease with Monthly Payments)** John Roesch Inc. was incorporated in 2002 to operate as a computer software service firm with an accounting fiscal year ending August 31. Roesch's primary product is a sophisticated on-line inventory-control system; its customers pay a fixed fee plus a usage charge for using the system.

Roesch has leased a large, Alpha-3 computer system from the manufacturer. The lease calls for a monthly rental of $50,000 for the 144 months (12 years) of the lease term. The estimated useful life of the computer is 15 years.

Each scheduled monthly rental payment includes $4,000 for full-service maintenance on the computer to be performed by the manufacturer. All rentals are payable on the first day of the month beginning with August 1, 2003, the date the computer was installed and the lease agreement was signed.

The lease is noncancelable for its 12-year term, and it is secured only by the manufacturer's chattel lien on the Alpha-3 system. Roesch can purchase the Alpha-3 system from the manufacturer at the end of the 12-year lease term for 75% of the computer's fair value at that time.

This lease is to be accounted for as a capital lease by Roesch, and it will be depreciated by the straight-line method with no expected salvage value. Borrowed funds for this type of transaction would cost Roesch 12% per year (1% per month). Following is a schedule of the present value of $1 for selected periods discounted at 1% per period when payments are made at the beginning of each period.

Periods (months)	Present Value of $1 per Period Discounted at 1% per Period
1	1.000
2	1.990
3	2.970
143	76.658
144	76.899

Instructions

Prepare, in general journal form, all entries Roesch should have made in its accounting records during August 2003 relating to this lease. Give full explanations and show supporting computations for each entry. Remember, August 31, 2003, is the end of Roesch's fiscal accounting period and it will be preparing financial statements on that date. Do not prepare closing entries.

(AICPA adapted)

P16-8 **(Basic Lessee Accounting with Difficult PV Calculation)** In 2001 Judy Yin Trucking Company negotiated and closed a long-term lease contract for newly constructed truck terminals and freight storage facilities. The buildings were erected to the company's specifications on land owned by the company. On January 1, 2002, Judy Yin Trucking Company took possession of the lease properties. On January 1, 2002 and 2003, the company made cash payments of $1,048,000 that were recorded as rental expenses.

Although the terminals have a composite useful life of 40 years, the noncancelable lease runs for 20 years from January 1, 2002, with a bargain purchase option available upon expiration of the lease.

The 20-year lease is effective for the period January 1, 2002, through December 31, 2021. Advance rental payments of $900,000 are payable to the lessor on January 1 of each of the first 10 years of the lease term. Advance rental payments of $320,000 are due on January 1 for each of the last 10 years of the lease. The company has an option to purchase all of these leased facilities for $1 on December 31, 2021. It also must make annual payments to the lessor of $125,000 for property taxes and $23,000 for insurance. The lease was negotiated to assure the lessor a 6% rate of return.

Instructions

(Round all numbers to the nearest dollar.)

(a) Prepare a schedule to compute for Judy Yin Trucking Company the discounted present value of the terminal facilities and related obligation at January 1, 2002.

(b) Assuming that the discounted present value of terminal facilities and related obligation at January 1, 2002, was $8,400,000, prepare journal entries for Judy Yin Trucking Company to record the following.

(1) Cash payment to the lessor on January 1, 2004.

(2) Amortization of the cost of the leased properties for 2004, using the straight-line method and assuming a zero salvage value.

(3) Accrual of interest expense at December 31, 2004.

Selected present value factors are as follows:

Periods	For an Ordinary Annuity of $1 at 6%	For $1 at 6%
1	.943396	.943396
2	1.833393	.889996
8	6.209794	.627412
9	6.801692	.591898
10	7.360087	.558395
19	11.158117	.330513
20	11.469921	.311805

(AICPA adapted)

P16-9 (Operating Lease vs. Capital Lease) You are auditing the December 31, 2002, financial statements of Sarah Shamess, Inc., manufacturer of novelties and party favors. During your inspection of the company garage, you discovered that a 2001 Shirk automobile not listed in the equipment subsidiary ledger is parked in the company garage. You ask Sally Straub, plant manager, about the vehicle, and she tells you that the company did not list the automobile because the company was only leasing it. The lease agreement was entered into on January 1, 2002, with Jack Hayes New and Used Cars.

You decide to review the lease agreement to ensure that the lease should be afforded operating lease treatment, and you discover the following lease terms.

1. Noncancelable term of 50 months.
2. Rental of $180 per month (at the end of each month; present value at 1% per month is $7,055.)
3. Estimated residual value after 50 months is $1,100. (The present value at 1% per month is $699.) Shamess guarantees the residual value of $1,100.
4. Estimated economic life of the automobile is 60 months.
5. Shamess's incremental borrowing rate is 12% per year (1% per month).

Instructions

You are a senior auditor writing a memo to your supervisor, the audit partner in charge of this audit, to discuss the above situation. Be sure to include (a) why you inspected the lease agreement, (b) what you determined about the lease, and (c) how you advised your client to account for this lease. Explain every journal entry that you believe is necessary to record this lease properly on the client's books. (It is also necessary to include the fact that you communicated this information to your client.)

CONCEPTUAL CASES

C16-1 (Lessee Accounting and Reporting) On January 1, 2004, Sandy Hayes Company entered into a noncancelable lease for a machine to be used in its manufacturing operations. The lease transfers ownership of the machine to Yen Quach by the end of the lease term. The term of the lease is 8 years. The minimum lease payment made by Yen Quach on January 1, 2004, was one of eight equal annual payments. At the inception of the lease, the criteria established for classification as a capital lease by the lessee were met.

Instructions

(a) What is the theoretical basis for the accounting standard that requires certain long-term leases to be capitalized by the lessee? Do not discuss the specific criteria for classifying a specific lease as a capital lease.

(b) How should Hayes account for this lease at its inception and determine the amount to be recorded?

(c) What expenses related to this lease will Hayes incur during the first year of the lease, and how will they be determined?

(d) How should Hayes report the lease transaction on its December 31, 2004, balance sheet?

C16-2 (Lessor and Lessee Accounting and Disclosure) Laurie Gocker Inc. entered into a lease arrangement with Nathan Morgan Leasing Corporation for a certain machine. Morgan's primary business is leasing, and it is not a manufacturer or dealer. Gocker will lease the machine for a period of 3 years, which is 50% of the machine's economic life. Morgan will take possession of the machine at the end of the initial 3-year lease and lease it to another, smaller company that does not need the most current version of the machine. Gocker does not guarantee any residual value for the machine and will not purchase the machine at the end of the lease term.

Gocker's incremental borrowing rate is 15%, and the implicit rate in the lease is 14%. Gocker has no way of knowing the implicit rate used by Morgan. Using either rate, the present value of the minimum lease payments is between 90% and 100% of the fair value of the machine at the date of the lease agreement.

Gocker has agreed to pay all executory costs directly and no allowance for these costs is included in the lease payments.

Morgan is reasonably certain that Gocker will pay all lease payments, and because Gocker has agreed to pay all executory costs, there are no important uncertainties regarding costs to be incurred by Morgan. Assume that no indirect costs are involved.

Instructions

(a) With respect to Gocker (the lessee), answer the following.
   (1) What type of lease has been entered into? Explain the reason for your answer.
   (2) How should Gocker compute the appropriate amount to be recorded for the lease or asset acquired?
   (3) What accounts will be created or affected by this transaction and how will the lease or asset and other costs related to the transaction be matched with earnings?
   (4) What disclosures must Gocker make regarding this leased asset?
(b) With respect to Morgan (the lessor), answer the following.
   (1) What type of leasing arrangement has been entered into? Explain the reason for your answer.
   (2) How should this lease be recorded by Morgan, and how are the appropriate amounts determined?
   (3) How should Morgan determine the appropriate amount of earnings to be recognized from each lease payment?
   (4) What disclosures must Morgan make regarding this lease?

(AICPA adapted)

C16-3 (Lessee Capitalization Criteria) On January 1, Melanie Shinault Company, a lessee, entered into three noncancelable leases for brand-new equipment, Lease L, Lease M, and Lease N. None of the three leases transfers ownership of the equipment to Melanie Shinault at the end of the lease term. For each of the three leases, the present value at the beginning of the lease term of the minimum lease payments, excluding that portion of the payments representing executory costs such as insurance, maintenance, and taxes to be paid by the lessor, is 75% of the fair value of the equipment.

The following information is peculiar to each lease.

1. Lease L does not contain a bargain purchase option. The lease term is equal to 80% of the estimated economic life of the equipment.

2. Lease M contains a bargain purchase option. The lease term is equal to 50% of the estimated economic life of the equipment.

3. Lease N does not contain a bargain purchase option. The lease term is equal to 50% of the estimated economic life of the equipment.

Instructions

(a) How should Melanie Shinault Company classify each of the three leases above, and why? Discuss the rationale for your answer.

(b) What amount, if any, should Melanie Shinault record as a liability at the inception of the lease for each of the three leases above?

(c) Assuming that the minimum lease payments are made on a straight-line basis, how should Melanie Shinault record each minimum lease payment for each of the three leases above?

(AICPA adapted)

C16-4 (Comparison of Different Types of Accounting by Lessee and Lessor)

Part 1

Capital leases and operating leases are the two classifications of leases described in FASB pronouncements from the standpoint of the **lessee**.

Instructions

(a) Describe how a capital lease would be accounted for by the lessee both at the inception of the lease and during the first year of the lease, assuming the lease transfers ownership of the property to the lessee by the end of the lease.

(b) Describe how an operating lease would be accounted for by the lessee both at the inception of the lease and during the first year of the lease, assuming equal monthly payments are made by the lessee at the beginning of each month of the lease. Describe the change in accounting, if any, when rental payments are not made on a straight-line basis.

Do **not** discuss the criteria for distinguishing between capital leases and operating leases.

Part 2

Sales-type leases and direct financing leases are two of the classifications of leases described in FASB pronouncements from the standpoint of the **lessor**.

Instructions

Compare and contrast a sales-type lease with a direct financing lease as follows.

(a) Lease receivable.

(b) Interest revenue.

(c) Manufacturer's or dealer's profit.

Do **not** discuss the criteria for distinguishing between the leases described above and operating leases.

(AICPA adapted)

C16-5 (Lease Capitalization and Bargain Purchase Option) Brad Hayes Corporation is a diversified company with nationwide interests in commercial real estate developments, banking, copper mining, and metal fabrication. The company has offices and operating locations in major cities throughout the United States. Corporate headquarters for Brad Hayes Corporation is located in a metropolitan area of a mid-western state, and executives connected with various phases of company operations travel extensively. Corporate management is currently evaluating the feasibility of acquiring a business aircraft that can be used by company executives to expedite business travel to areas not adequately served by commercial airlines. Proposals for either leasing or purchasing a suitable aircraft have been analyzed, and the leasing proposal was considered to be more desirable.

The proposed lease agreement involves a twin-engine turboprop Viking that has a fair market value of $1,000,000. This plane would be leased for a period of 10 years beginning January 1, 2004. The lease agreement is cancelable only upon accidental destruction of the plane. An annual lease payment of $141,780 is due on January 1 of each year; the first payment is to be made on January 1, 2004. Maintenance operations are strictly scheduled by the lessor, and Brad Hayes Corporation will pay for these services as they are performed. Estimated annual maintenance costs are $6,900. The lessor will pay all insurance premiums and local property taxes, which amount to a combined total of $4,000 annually and are included in the annual lease payment of $141,780. Upon expiration of the 10-year lease, Brad Hayes Corporation can purchase the Viking for $44,440. The estimated useful life of the plane is 15 years, and its salvage value in the used plane market is estimated to be $100,000 after 10 years. The salvage value probably will never be less than $75,000 if the engines are overhauled and maintained as prescribed by the manufacturer. If the purchase option is not exercised, possession of the plane will revert to the lessor, and there is no provision for renewing the lease agreement beyond its termination on December 31, 2013.

Brad Hayes Corporation can borrow $1,000,000 under a 10-year term loan agreement at an annual interest rate of 12%. The lessor's implicit interest rate is not expressly stated in the lease agreement, but this rate appears to be approximately 8% based on ten net rental payments of $137,780 per year and the initial market value of $1,000,000 for the plane. On January 1, 2004, the present value of all net rental payments and the purchase option of $44,440 is $888,890 using the 12% interest rate. The present value of all net rental payments and the $44,440 purchase option on January 1, 2004, is $1,022,226 using the 8% interest rate implicit in the lease agreement. The financial vice-president of Brad Hayes Corporation has established that this lease agreement is a capital lease as defined in *Statement of Financial Accounting Standards No. 13, "Accounting for Leases."*

Instructions

(a) What is the appropriate amount that Brad Hayes Corporation should recognize for the leased aircraft on its balance sheet after the lease is signed?

(b) Without prejudice to your answer in part (a), assume that the annual lease payment is $141,780 as stated in the question, that the appropriate capitalized amount for the leased aircraft is $1,000,000 on January 1, 2004, and that the interest rate is 9%. How will the lease be reported in the December 31, 2004, balance sheet and related income statement? (Ignore any income tax implications.)

(CMA adapted)

C16-6 (Lease Capitalization, Bargain Purchase Option) Cuby Corporation entered into a lease agreement for 10 photocopy machines for its corporate headquarters. The lease agreement qualifies as an operating lease in all terms except there is a bargain purchase option. After the 5-year lease term, the corporation can purchase each copier for $1,000, when the anticipated market value is $2,500.

Glenn Beckert, the financial vice president, thinks the financial statements must recognize the lease agreement as a capital lease because of the bargain purchase agreement. The controller, Donna Kessinger, disagrees: "Although I don't know much about the copiers themselves, there is a way to avoid recording the lease liability." She argues that the corporation might claim that copier technology advances rapidly and that by the end of the lease term the machines will most likely not be worth the $1,000 bargain price.

Instructions

Answer the following questions.

(a) What ethical issue is at stake?

(b) Should the controller's argument be accepted if she does not really know much about copier technology? Would it make a difference if the controller were knowledgeable about the pace of change in copier technology?

(c) What should Beckert do?

USING YOUR JUDGMENT

FINANCIAL REPORTING PROBLEM

3M COMPANY

The financial statements of 3M were provided with your book or can be accessed on the Take Action! CD

Instructions

Refer to 3M's financial statements and the accompanying notes to answer the following questions.

(a) What types of leases are used by 3M?

(b) What amount of rental expense (net of minor sublease income) was reported by 3M in 1999, 2000, and 2001?

(c) What minimum annual rental commitments under all noncancelable leases at December 31, 2001, did 3M disclose?

FINANCIAL STATEMENT ANALYSIS CASE

PENN TRAFFIC COMPANY

Presented in Illustration 16-19 are the financial statement disclosures from the 2001 Annual Report of **The Penn Traffic Company.**

Instructions
Answer the following questions related to these disclosures.

(a) What is the total obligation under capital leases at February 3, 2001, for Penn Traffic?
(b) What is the book value of the assets under capital lease at February 3, 2001, for Penn Traffic? Explain why there is a difference between the amounts reported for assets and liabilities under capital leases.
(c) What is the total rental expense reported for leasing activity for the year-ended February 3, 2001, for Penn Traffic?
(d) Estimate the off-balance-sheet liability due to Penn Traffic's operating leases at fiscal year-end 2001.

COMPARATIVE ANALYSIS CASE

UAL, INC. AND SOUTHWEST AIRLINES

Instructions

Go to the Take Action! CD and use information found there to answer the following questions related to **UAL, Inc.** and **Southwest Airlines.**

(a) What types of leases are used by Southwest and on what assets are these leases primarily used?
(b) How long-term are some of Southwest's leases? What are some of the characteristics or provisions of Southwest's (as lessee) leases?
(c) What did Southwest report in 2001 as its future minimum annual rental commitments under non-cancelable leases?
(d) At year-end 2001, what was the present value of the minimum rental payments under Southwest's capital leases? How much imputed interest was deducted from the future minimum annual rental commitments to arrive at the present value?
(e) What were the amounts and details reported by Southwest for rental expense in 2001, 2000, and 1999?
(f) How does UAL's use of leases compare with Southwest's?

INTERNATIONAL REPORTING CASE

As discussed in the chapter, U.S. GAAP accounting for leases allows companies to use off-balance-sheet financing for the purchase of operating assets. International accounting standards are similar to U.S. GAAP in that under these rules, companies can keep leased assets and obligations off their balance sheets. However, under *International Accounting Standard No. 17 (IAS 17)*, leases are capitalized based on the subjective evaluation of whether the risks and rewards of ownership are transferred in the lease. In Japan, virtually all leases are treated as operating leases. Furthermore, unlike U.S. and IAS standards, the Japanese rules do not require disclosure of future minimum lease payments.

Presented below are recent financial data for three major airlines that lease some part of their aircraft fleet. **American Airlines** prepares its financial statements under U.S. GAAP and leases approximately 27% of its fleet. **KLM Royal Dutch Airlines** and **Japan Airlines (JAL)** present their statements in accordance with their home country GAAP (Netherlands and Japan respectively). KLM leases about 22% of its aircraft, and JAL leases approximately 50% of its fleet.

Financial Statement Data	American Airlines (millions of dollars)	KLM Royal Dutch Airlines (millions of guilders)	Japan Airlines (millions of yen)
As-reported			
Assets	20,915	19,205	2,042,761
Liabilities	14,699	13,837	1,857,800
Income	985	606	4,619
Estimated impact of capitalizing operating leases on:[1]			
Assets	5,897	1,812	244,063
Liabilities	6,886	1,776	265,103
Income	(143)	24	(9,598)

[1]Based on *Apples to Apples: Global Airlines: Flight to Quality* (New York: N.Y.: Morgan Stanley Dean Witter, October 1998).

Instructions

(a) Using the as-reported data for each of the airlines, compute the rate of return on assets and the debt to assets ratio. Compare these companies on the basis of this analysis.

(b) Adjust the as-reported numbers of the three companies for the effects of non-capitalization of leases, and then redo the analysis in part (a).

(c) The following statement was overheard in the library: "Non-capitalization of operating leases is not that big a deal for profitability analysis based on rate of return on assets, since the operating lease payments (under operating lease accounting) are about the same as the sum of the interest and depreciation expense under capital lease treatment." Do you agree? Explain.

(d) Since the accounting for leases worldwide is similar, does your analysis above suggest there is a need for an improved accounting standard for leases? (*Hint:* Reflect on comparability of information about these companies' leasing activities, when leasing is more prevalent in one country than in others.)

*Remember to check the **Take Action! CD*** *and the book's **companion Web site*** *to find additional resources for this chapter.*

WHEN DO I GET MY MONEY BACK?

Recently investors have lost money when companies report restatements. Restatements arise when companies discover errors or irregularities in their prior years' accounting reports. For example, in 2000 **Microstrategy** restated previously reported revenue amounts such that profits for 1998 and 1999 turned into losses. And in 2001 **Enron** restated its results for the gains on the sale of assets to one of its subsidiaries, which were improperly recorded. In both cases, the company's stock price took a beating when the market discovered that the prior periods' numbers were in error. Microstrategy's stock dropped from $227 to $87; Enron's shares dropped from over $80 to under $1 per share and the firm declared bankruptcy shortly after.

What are investors to do if a company misleads them by misstating its financial results? Join other investors in a class action suit against the company and in some cases, the auditor. In the Microstrategy case, investors laid claim to a $155 million settlement. Class action activity has picked up in recent years, with 307 class action suits in 2000, up from 196 in 1996.

Though the settlements can be large (a total of over $4.3 billion in 2000), only about half of investors who are eligible join a class action suit. To find out about class actions, investors can go online to see if they are eligible to join any class actions. Below are some recent examples.

Company	Settlement Amount	Contact for Claim
Econnect	$ 400,000	www.dberdon.com
Olston	24,100,000	www.dberdon.com
Quaker Oats	10,400,000	www.gilardi.com
Smart Choice Automotive	2,500,000	www.gilardi.com
Sunbeam	110,000,000	www.gilardi.com

The amounts reported are before attorney's fees, which can range from 15 to 30 percent of the total. And there can be taxes owed if the settlement results in a capital gain on the investment. Thus, investors can get back some of the money they lost due to restatements, but they should be prepared to pay an attorney and the tax man first.[1]

After studying this chapter, you should be able to:

1. Describe various accounting changes.
2. Understand how to account for cumulative-effect accounting changes.
3. Understand how to account for retroactive accounting changes.
4. Describe the accounting for changes of estimates.
5. Describe the accounting for correction of errors.
6. Compute earnings per share in a simple capital structure.
7. Compute earnings per share in a complex capital structure.

---

[1] Adapted from C. Coolidge, "Lost and Found," *Forbes* (October 1, 2001), pp. 124–125.

PREVIEW OF CHAPTER 17

As the opening story indicates, investors can be affected adversely by misstatements of financial information. When misstatements occur, companies must follow specific accounting and reporting requirements. In addition, to ensure comparability among companies, the reporting of accounting changes, accounting estimates, and earnings per share information has been standardized to help investors better understand a company's financial condition. The content and organization of the chapter are as follows.

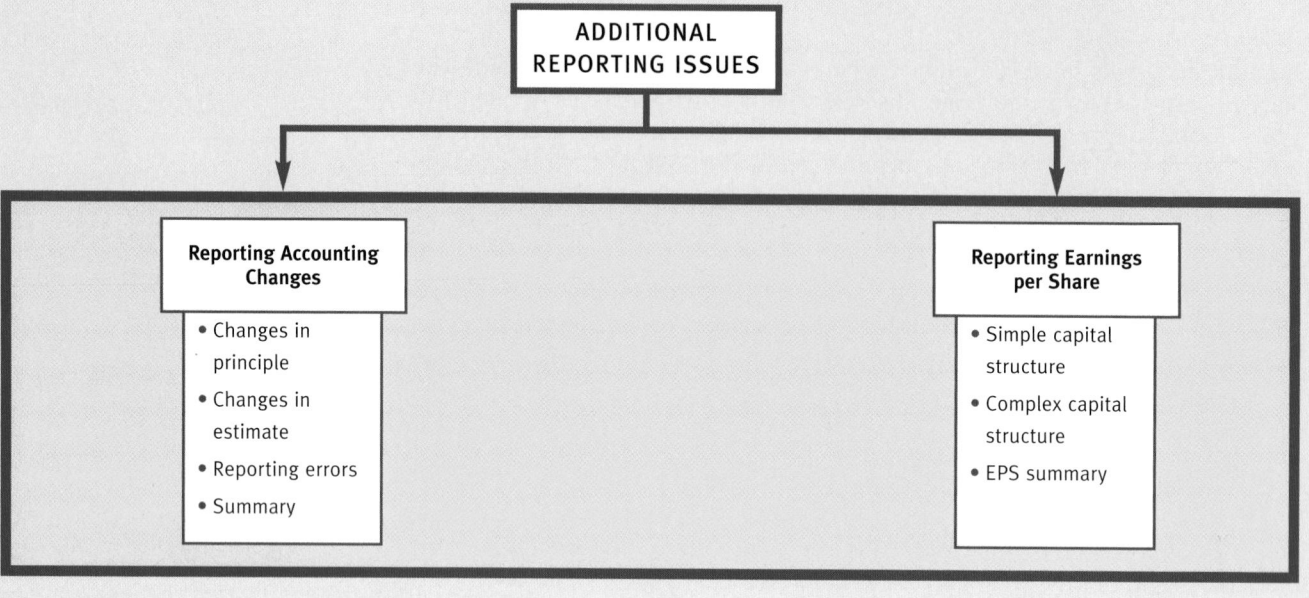

REPORTING ACCOUNTING CHANGES

OBJECTIVE 1
Describe various accounting changes.

As indicated above, when changes in accounting occur, the comparability of financial information between periods and between companies is diminished and useful historical trend data are obscured. The two major types of accounting change[2] are:

① *Change in Accounting Principle.* A change from one generally accepted accounting principle to another generally accepted accounting principle. Example: A change in the method of depreciation from double-declining to straight-line depreciation of plant assets.

② *Change in Accounting Estimate.* A change that occurs as the result of new information or as additional experience is acquired. Example: A change in the estimate of the useful lives of depreciable assets.[3]

[2]"Accounting Changes," *Opinions of the Accounting Principles Board No. 20* (New York: AICPA, 1971).

[3]In its survey of 600 annual reports *Accounting Trends and Techniques—2001* identified the following specific types of accounting changes reported:

Revenue recognition 92	Reporting entity 8
Software development costs 13	Derivatives and hedging 6
Start-up costs 9	Depreciable lives 3
Inventories 9	Other 42

Another situation that necessitates changes in the accounting, though it is not classified as an accounting change are **accounting errors**. **Errors in financial statements** occur as a result of mathematical mistakes, mistakes in the application of accounting principles, or oversight or misuse of facts that existed at the time financial statements were prepared. Example: The incorrect application of the revenue recognition principle in determining revenue.

Each of these items is discussed separately to investigate its unusual characteristics and to determine how each item should be reported in the accounts and how the information should be disclosed in comparative statements.

Changes in Accounting Principle

A change in accounting principle involves a change from one generally accepted accounting principle to another. For example, a company might change the basis of inventory pricing from average cost to LIFO. Or it might change the method of depreciation on plant assets from accelerated to straight-line, or vice versa. Yet another change might be from the completed-contract to percentage-of-completion method of accounting for construction contracts.

Cumulative-Effect Type Accounting Change

The **current, or "catch-up," method is generally used to account for changes in accounting principle**. The general requirements of this approach are:

① The **cumulative effect** of the change in accounting principle should be reported in the income statement between the captions "Extraordinary items" and "Net income."

② Financial statements for prior periods included for comparative purposes should not be restated.

③ Income before extraordinary items and net income, computed on a **pro-forma (as-if)** basis should be shown on the face of the income statement for all periods. They are presented **as if the newly adopted principle had been applied during all periods affected**. Related earnings per share data should also be reported. The reader, then, has some understanding of how restated financial statements appear.[4]

Illustration   Assume that Lang Inc. decided at the beginning of 2004 to change from the sum-of-the-years'-digits method of depreciation to the straight-line method for financial reporting for its buildings. For tax purposes, the company has employed the straight-line method and will continue to do so. The assets originally cost $120,000 in 2002 and have an estimated useful life of 15 years. The data assumed for this illustration are as follows.

Year	Sum-of-the-Years'-Digits Depreciation	Straight-Line Depreciation	Difference	Tax Effect 40%	Effect on Income (net of tax)
2002	$15,000[a]	$ 8,000[b]	$ 7,000	$2,800	$4,200
2003	14,000	8,000	6,000	2,400	3,600
	$29,000	$16,000	$13,000	$5,200	$7,800

[a]$120,000 × $\frac{15}{120}$ = $15,000   [b]$120,000 ÷ 15 = $8,000

[4]Ibid., par. 21.

UNDERLYING CONCEPTS

While the qualitative characteristic of *usefulness* may be enhanced by changes in accounting, the characteristics of *comparability* and *consistency* may be adversely affected.

INTERNATIONAL INSIGHT

In Canada, Hong Kong, and the United Kingdom, changes in accounting principle are accounted for retroactively. That is, the changes are accounted for as prior year adjustments.

OBJECTIVE **2**
Understand how to account for cumulative-effect accounting changes.

Illustration 17-1
Data for Change in Depreciation Method

Lang Inc. has income before extraordinary items and cumulative effect of changes in accounting principle of $130,000 in 2004 and $111,000 in 2003. Also, Lang Inc. has an extraordinary loss (net of tax) of $30,000 in 2004 and an extraordinary gain (net of tax) of $10,000 in 2003.

Journal Entry Although the journal entry can be made any time during the year, it is effective **as of the beginning of the year**. The entry made to record this change to straight-line depreciation in 2004 should be:

Accumulated Depreciation	13,000	
Deferred Tax Asset		5,200
Cumulative Effect of Change in Accounting		
Principle—Depreciation		7,800

The debit of $13,000 to Accumulated Depreciation is the excess of the sum-of-the-years'-digits depreciation over the straight-line depreciation. The credit to the Deferred Tax Asset of $5,200 is recorded to eliminate this account from the financial statements. Prior to the change in accounting principle, sum-of-the-years'-digits was used for book but not tax purposes, which gave rise to a debit balance in the Deferred Tax Asset account of $5,200. The cumulative effect on income resulting from the difference between sum-of-the-years'-digits depreciation and straight-line depreciation is reduced by the tax effect on that difference. Now that the company intends to use the straight-line method for both tax and book purposes, no deferred income taxes related to depreciation should exist, and the Deferred Tax Asset account should be eliminated.

Income Statement Presentation The cumulative effect of the change in accounting principle should be reported on the income statement between the captions "Extraordinary items" and "Net income." The cumulative effect is not an extraordinary item, but it is reported on a net-of-tax basis similar to that used for extraordinary items. This information is shown in Illustration 17-2.

Illustration 17-2
Income Statement without Pro-Forma Amounts

	2004	2003
Income before extraordinary item and cumulative effect of a change in accounting principles	$130,000	$111,000
Extraordinary item, net of tax	(30,000)	10,000
Cumulative effect on prior years of retroactive application of new depreciation method, net of tax	7,800	
Net income	$107,800	$121,000
Per share amounts		
Earnings per share (10,000 shares)		
Income before extraordinary item and cumulative effect of a change in accounting principle	$13.00	$11.10
Extraordinary item	(3.00)	1.00
Cumulative effect on prior years of retroactive application of new depreciation method	0.78	
Net income	$10.78	$12.10

UNDERLYING CONCEPTS

The pro-forma treatment attempts to restore the comparability of the income statements.

Note that depreciation expense for 2004 is computed on the straight-line basis.

Pro-Forma Amounts Pro-forma amounts permit financial statement users to determine the net income that would have been shown if the newly adopted principle had been in effect in earlier periods. In other words, how would Lang Inc.'s income be reported if the straight-line method had been used in 2003? To determine this amount, the prior year (2003) is restated, assuming that the straight-line method is used. The computation is as follows.

Income before extraordinary item (2003) not restated	$111,000
Excess of sum-of-the-years-digits over straight-line depreciation, net of tax	3,600
Pro-forma income before extraordinary item (2003)	$114,600

Illustration 17-3
Computation of Pro-Forma Income, 2003

This and other information is shown on the face of the income statement as follows.

Illustration 17-4
Income Statement with Pro-Forma Amounts

Pro-forma (as-if) amounts, assuming retroactive application of new depreciation method:

	2004	2003
Income before extraordinary item	$130,000	$114,600
Earnings per common share	$13.00	$11.46
Net income	$100,000[a]	$124,600[b]
Earnings per common share	$10.00	$12.46

[a]($130,000 − $30,000 = $100,000)
[b]($114,600 + $10,000 = $124,600)

The $130,000 of 2004 income before extraordinary item needs no restatement like the 2003 income because the new straight-line method of depreciation is used in 2004.

Pro-forma information is useful to individuals interested in assessing the trend of earnings over a period of time. Pro-forma information, which is shown only as supplementary information, may be reported in the income statement, in a separate schedule, or in the notes to the financial statements.

The pro-forma amounts should include both (1) the direct effects of a change, and (2) nondiscretionary adjustments in items based on income before taxes or net income (such as profit-sharing expense and certain royalties) that would have been recognized if the newly adopted principle had been followed in prior periods. Related income tax effects should be recognized for both (1) and (2). If an income statement is presented for the current period only, the actual and pro-forma amounts (including earnings per share) for the immediately preceding period should be disclosed.

Summary Illustration Illustration 17-5 indicates how this information is presented on the income statement.[5] The appropriate note disclosure is also provided.

Retroactive-Effect Type Accounting Change

In certain circumstances, a change in accounting principle may be handled retroactively. Under the **retroactive treatment** the cumulative effect of the new method on the financial statements at the beginning of the period is computed. A retroactive adjustment of the financial statements presented is made by **recasting the statements of prior years on a basis consistent with the newly adopted principle. Any part of the**

OBJECTIVE **3**
Understand how to account for retroactive accounting changes.

[5]In practice, three-year comparative income statements are prepared. For reasons of simplicity, we have presented two-year comparative statements.

Illustration 17-5
Cumulative-Effect Type
Accounting Change

CUMULATIVE-EFFECT TYPE ACCOUNTING CHANGE REPORTING THE CHANGE IN TWO-YEAR COMPARATIVE STATEMENTS		
	2004	2003
Income before extraordinary item and cumulative effect of a change in accounting principles	$130,000	$111,000
Extraordinary item, net of tax	(30,000)	10,000
Cumulative effect on prior years of retroactive application of new depreciation method, net of tax (Note A)	7,800	
Net income	$107,800	$121,000
Per share amounts		
Earnings per share (10,000 shares)		
Income before extraordinary item and cumulative effect of a change in accounting principle	$13.00	$11.10
Extraordinary item	(3.00)	1.00
Cumulative effect on prior years of rectroactive application of new depreciation method	0.78	
Net income	$10.78	$12.10

Pro-forma (as-if) amounts, assuming retroactive application of new depreciation method:

	2004	2003
Income before extraordinary item	$130,000	$114,600
Earnings per common share	$13.00	$11.46
Net income	$100,000	$124,600
Earnings per common share	$10.00	$12.46

Note A: Change in Depreciation Method for Plant Assets. In 2004 depreciation of plant assets is computed by use of the straight-line method. In prior years, beginning in 2002, depreciation of buildings was computed by the sum-of-the-years'-digits method. The new method of depreciation was adopted in recognition of . . . (state justification for the change of depreciation method) . . . and has been applied retroactively to building acquisitions of prior years to determine the cumulative effect. The effect of the change in 2004 was to increase income before extraordinary item by approximately $3,000 (or 30 cents per share). The adjustment necessary for retroactive application of the new method, amounting to $7,800, is included in income of 2004. The pro-forma amounts shown on the income statement have been adjusted for the effect of retroactive application on depreciation, and the pro-forma effect for related income taxes.

cumulative effect attributable to years prior to those presented is treated as an adjustment of beginning retained earnings of the earliest year presented. In such situations, the nature of and justification for the change and the effect on net income and related per share amounts should be disclosed for each period presented. The five situations that require the restatement of all prior period financial statements are:

① A change from the LIFO inventory valuation method to another method.

② A change in the method of accounting for long-term construction-type contracts.

③ A change to or from the "full-cost" method of accounting in the extractive industries.

④ Issuance of financial statements by a company for the first time to obtain additional equity capital, to effect a business combination, or to register securities. (This procedure may be used only by closely held companies and then only once.)

⑤ A professional pronouncement recommends that a change in accounting principle be treated retroactively. For example, *FASB No. 11* requires that retroactive treatment be given for changes in "Accounting for Contingencies."

Why did the profession provide for these exceptions? Though the reasons are varied, the major one is that reporting the cumulative adjustment in the period of the change might have such a large effect on net income that the income figure would be misleading. A perfect illustration is the experience of **Chrysler Corporation** (now **DaimlerChrysler**) when it changed its inventory accounting from LIFO to FIFO. If the change had been handled as a cumulative effect, Chrysler would have had to report a $53,500,000 adjustment to net income, which would have resulted in net income of $45,900,000 instead of a net loss of $7,600,000. Such situations lend support to restatement so that comparability is not seriously affected.

Illustration To illustrate the retroactive method, assume that Denson Construction Co. has accounted for its income from long-term construction contracts using the completed-contract method. In 2004, the company changed to the percentage-of-completion method because management believes that this approach provides a more appropriate measure of the income earned. For tax purposes (assume a 40 percent enacted tax rate), the company has employed the completed-contract method and plans to continue using this method in the future. Illustration 17-6 provides the information for analysis.

INTERNATIONAL INSIGHT

IAS 8 generally requires restatement of prior years for accounting changes. However, IAS 8 permits the cumulative effect method or prospective method if the amounts to restate prior periods are not reasonably determinable.

Year	Pretax Income from Percentage-of-Completion	Pretax Income from Completed-Contract	Difference	Tax Effect 40%	Income Effect (net of tax)
Prior to 2003	$600,000	$400,000	$200,000	$80,000	$120,000
In 2003	180,000	160,000	20,000	8,000	12,000
Total at beginning of 2004	$780,000	$560,000	$220,000	$88,000	$132,000
Total in 2004	$200,000	$190,000	$ 10,000	$ 4,000	$ 6,000

Illustration 17-6
Data for Change in Accounting for Long-Term Construction Contracts

The entry to record the change in 2004 would be:

Construction in Process	220,000	
Deferred Tax Liability		88,000
Retained Earnings		132,000

The Construction in Process account is increased by $220,000, representing the adjustment in prior years' income of $132,000 and the adjustment in prior years' tax expense of $88,000. The Deferred Tax Liability account is used to recognize a tax liability for future taxable amounts. That is, in future periods taxable income will be higher than book income as a result of current temporary differences, and, therefore, a deferred tax liability must be reported in the current year.

Income Statement Presentation The bottom portion of the income statement for Denson Construction Co. **before giving effect to the retroactive change in accounting principle** would be as follows.

Illustration 17-7
Income Statement before
Retroactive Change

Income Statement	2004	2003
Net income	$114,000ª	$96,000ª
Per Share Amounts		
Earnings per share (100,000 shares)	$1.14	$.96

ªThe net income for the two periods is computed as follows.
2004 $190,000 − .40($190,000) = $114,000
2003 $160,000 − .40($160,000) = $96,000

The bottom portion of the income statement for Denson Construction Co. **after giving effect to the retroactive change in accounting principle** would be as follows.

Illustration 17-8
Income Statement after
Retroactive Change

Income Statement	2004	2003
Net income	$120,000ª	$108,000ª
Per Share Amounts		
Earnings per share (100,000 shares)	$1.20	$1.08

ªThe net income for the two periods is computed as follows.
2004 $200,000 − .40($200,000) = $120,000
2003 $180,000 − .40($180,000) = $108,000

Note that the two-year comparative income statement (Illustration 17-8) has a major difference from the earlier two-year comparative income statement (Illustration 17-5). No pro-forma information is necessary when changes in accounting principles are handled retroactively, because the income numbers for previous periods are restated.

Retained Earnings Statement Assuming a retained earnings balance of $1,600,000 at the beginning of 2003, the retained earnings statement **before giving effect to the retroactive change in accounting principle** would appear as follows.

Illustration 17-9
Retained Earnings
Statement before
Retroactive Change

RETAINED EARNINGS STATEMENT		
	2004	2003
Balance at beginning of year	$1,696,000	$1,600,000
Net income	114,000	96,000
Balance at end of year	$1,810,000	$1,696,000

A comparative retained earnings statement **after giving effect to the retroactive change in accounting principle** is shown in Illustration 17-10.

An expanded retained earnings statement is included in this two-year comparative presentation to indicate the type of adjustment that is needed to restate the beginning balance of retained earnings. In 2003, the beginning balance was adjusted for the excess of the percentage-of-completion income over the completed-contract income prior to 2003 ($120,000). In 2004, the beginning balance was adjusted for the $120,000 cumulative difference plus the additional $12,000 for 2003.

No such adjustments are necessary when the current or catch-up method is employed. The reason is that the cumulative effect of the change on net income is reported

RETAINED EARNINGS STATEMENT		
	2004	2003
Balance at beginning of year, as previously reported	$1,696,000	$1,600,000
Add: Adjustment for the cumulative effect on prior years of applying retroactively the new method of accounting for long-term contracts (Note A)	132,000	120,000
Balance at beginning of year, as adjusted	1,828,000	1,720,000
Net income	120,000	108,000
Balance at end of year	$1,948,000	$1,828,000

Note A: Change in Method of Accounting for Long-Term Contracts. The company has accounted for revenue and costs for long-term construction contracts by the percentage-of-completion method in 2004, whereas in all prior years revenue and costs were determined by the completed-contract method. The new method of accounting for long-term contracts was adopted to recognize . . . (state justification for change in accounting principle) . . . and financial statements of prior years have been restated to apply the new method retroactively. For income tax purposes, the completed-contract method has been continued. The effect of the accounting change on income of 2004 was an increase of $6,000 net of related taxes and on income of 2003 as previously reported was an increase of $12,000 net of related taxes. The balances of retained earnings for 2003 and 2004 have been adjusted for the effect of applying retroactively the new method of accounting.

Illustration 17-10
Retained Earnings Statement after Retroactive Change

in the income statement of the current year and no prior period reports are restated. It is ordinarily appropriate to prepare a retained earnings or stockholders' equity statement when presenting comparative statements, regardless of what type of accounting change is involved. An illustration was provided for the retroactive method only to explain the additional computations required.

Change to LIFO Method

As indicated, the cumulative effect of any accounting change should be shown in the income statement between "Extraordinary items" and "Net income," except for the conditions mentioned in the preceding section. In addition, this rule does not apply when a company changes to the LIFO method of inventory valuation. In such a situation, **the base-year inventory for all subsequent LIFO calculations is the opening inventory in the year the method is adopted. There is no restatement of prior years' income because it is impractical to do so.** A restatement to LIFO would be subject to assumptions as to the different years that the layers were established, and these assumptions would ordinarily result in the computation of a number of different earnings figures. The only adjustment necessary may be to restate the beginning inventory to a cost basis from a lower of cost or market approach.

Disclosure, then, is limited to showing the effect of the change on the results of operations in the period of change. Also the reasons for omitting the computations of the cumulative effect and the pro-forma amounts for prior years should be explained.

Additional Observations

A careful examination must be made in each circumstance to ensure that a change in principle has actually occurred. **A change in accounting principle is not considered to result from the adoption of a new principle in recognition of events that have occurred for the first time or that were previously immaterial.** For example, when a depreciation method that is adopted for **newly** acquired plant assets is different from the method or methods used for **previously recorded** assets of a similar class, a change in accounting principle **has not occurred.** Certain marketing expenditures that were previously immaterial and expensed in the period incurred may become

INTERNATIONAL INSIGHT

In some countries, changes in accounting principles are made by adjusting current period income and disclosing the effects on current and/or prior period income.

material and acceptably deferred and amortized without a change in accounting principle occurring.

Finally, **if the accounting principle previously followed was not acceptable**, or if **the principle was applied incorrectly, a change to a generally accepted accounting principle is considered a correction of an error**. A switch from the cash or income tax basis of accounting to the accrual basis is considered a correction of an error. If the company deducted salvage value when computing double-declining depreciation on plant assets and later recomputed depreciation without deduction of estimated salvage value, an error is corrected.

Changes in accounting principle are considered appropriate only when the enterprise demonstrates that the alternative generally accepted accounting principle that is adopted is **preferable** to the existing one. In applying the profession's guidelines, preferability among accounting principles should be determined on the basis of whether the new principle constitutes an **improvement in financial reporting**, not on the basis of the income tax effect alone. But it is not always easy to determine what is an improvement in financial reporting.

Even though the criterion of preferability is difficult to apply, the general guidelines established have acted as a deterrent to capricious changes in accounting principles.[6] **If an FASB standard creates a new principle or expresses preference for or rejects a specific accounting principle, a change is considered clearly acceptable.**

Changes in Accounting Estimate

OBJECTIVE **4**
Describe the accounting for changes in estimates.

The preparation of financial statements requires estimating the effects of future conditions and events. The following are examples of items that require estimates.

1. Uncollectible receivables.
2. Inventory obsolescence.
3. Useful lives and salvage values of assets.
4. Liabilities for warranty costs and income taxes.

INTERNATIONAL INSIGHT

In most nations changes in accounting estimates are treated prospectively. International differences occur in the degree of disclosure required.

Future conditions and events and their effects cannot be perceived with certainty. Therefore, estimating requires the exercise of judgment. Accounting estimates will change as new events occur, as more experience is acquired, or as additional information is obtained.

Changes in estimates must be handled prospectively. That is, no changes should be made in previously reported results. Opening balances are not adjusted, and no attempt is made to "catch-up" for prior periods. Financial statements of prior periods are not restated, and pro-forma amounts for prior periods are not reported. Instead, the effects of all changes in estimate are accounted for in (1) the period of change if the change affects that period only, or (2) the period of change and future periods if the change affects both. As a result, changes in estimates are viewed as **normal recurring corrections and adjustments**, the natural result of the accounting process, and retroactive treatment is prohibited.

The circumstances related to a change in estimate are different from those surrounding a change in accounting principle. If changes in estimates were handled on a retroactive basis, or on a cumulative-effect basis, continual adjustments of prior years' income would occur. It seems proper to accept the view that because new conditions

---

[6]If management has not provided reasonable justification for the change in accounting principle, the auditor should express a qualified opinion, or if the effect of the change is sufficiently material, the auditor should express an adverse opinion on the financial statements. "Reports on Audited Financial Statements," *Statement on Auditing Standards No. 58* (New York: AICPA, 1988).

or circumstances exist, the revision fits the new situation and should be handled in the current and future periods.

To illustrate, Underwriters Labs Inc. purchased for $300,000 a building that was originally estimated to have a useful life of 15 years and no salvage value. Depreciation has been recorded for 5 years on a straight-line basis. On January 1, 2004, the estimate of the useful life is revised so that the asset is considered to have a total life of 25 years. Assume that the useful life for financial reporting and tax purposes is the same. The accounts at the beginning of the sixth year are as follows.

Building	$300,000
Less: Accumulated depreciation—building (5 × $20,000)	100,000
Book value of building	$200,000

Illustration 17-11
Book Value after 5 Years' Depreciation

The entry to record depreciation for the year 2004 is:

Depreciation Expense	10,000	
Accumulated Depreciation—Building		10,000

The $10,000 depreciation charge is computed as follows.

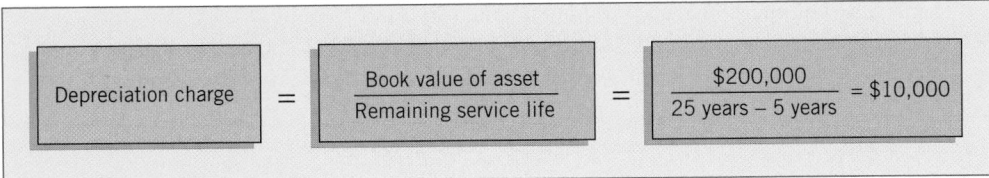

$$\text{Depreciation charge} = \frac{\text{Book value of asset}}{\text{Remaining service life}} = \frac{\$200,000}{25 \text{ years} - 5 \text{ years}} = \$10,000$$

Illustration 17-12
Depreciation after Change in Estimate

The disclosure of a change in estimated useful lives appeared in the Annual Report of **Ampco–Pittsburgh Corporation.**

Ampco–Pittsburgh Corporation

Note 11: Change in Accounting Estimate. The Corporation revised its estimate of the useful lives of certain machinery and equipment. Previously, all machinery and equipment, whether new when placed in use or not, were in one class and depreciated over 15 years. The change principally applies to assets purchased new when placed in use. Those lives are now extended to 20 years. These changes were made to better reflect the estimated periods during which such assets will remain in service. The change had the effect of reducing depreciation expense and increasing net income by approximately $991,000 ($.10 per share).

Illustration 17-13
Disclosure of Change in Estimated Useful Lives

Differentiating between a change in an estimate and a change in an accounting principle is sometimes difficult. Is it a change in principle or a change in estimate when a company changes from deferring and amortizing certain marketing costs to recording them as an expense as incurred because future benefits of these costs have become doubtful? In such a case, **whenever it is impossible to determine whether a change in principle or a change in estimate has occurred, the change should be considered a change in estimate.**

A similar problem occurs in differentiating between a change in estimate and a correction of an error, although the answer is more clear cut. How do we determine whether the information was overlooked in earlier periods (an error), or whether the information is now available for the first time (change in estimate)? Proper classification is important because corrections of errors have a different accounting treatment from that given changes in estimates. The general rule is that **careful estimates that later prove to be incorrect should be considered changes in estimate**. Only when the estimate was obviously computed incorrectly because of lack of expertise or in bad faith should the adjustment be considered an error. There is no clear demarcation line here, and good judgment must be used in light of all the circumstances.[7]

WHAT DO THE NUMBERS MEAN?

WHY CHANGE?

Why do companies change accounting methods or estimates? Many changes are implemented because the FASB or SEC mandates them in a new rule. For example, in 2000, many companies adopted new revenue recognition rules as required by the SEC and so recorded cumulative effect adjustments that reduced earnings. **Alcoa Co.**, **Mead Corporation**, and **Murphy Oil**, for example, reported earnings decreases of up to 3 percent in adopting these new rules.

Other accounting changes are voluntary. **Goodyear Tire and Rubber** changed from LIFO to FIFO and reported a $44.4 million increase in income in 2000. Conceptually, such voluntary changes have merit if the revised methods result in more representative reporting of financial results. However, observing negative earnings effects for mandatory changes but positive earnings effects from voluntary changes raises concerns that managers' voluntary changes are implemented in order to present their financial performance in the most favorable light. Such reporting could help managers achieve compensation targets or relax debt restrictions, which are based on reported earnings.

Reporting a Correction of an Error

OBJECTIVE 5
Describe the accounting for correction of errors.

No business, large or small, is immune from errors. The risk of material errors, however, may be reduced through the installation of good internal control and the application of sound accounting procedures. Authoritative guidance for how **correction of an error** should be handled is addressed in *FASB Statement No. 16*.[8]

The following are examples of accounting errors.

1. A change from an accounting principle that is **not** generally accepted to an accounting principle that is acceptable. The rationale adopted is that the prior periods were incorrectly presented because of the application of an improper accounting principle. Example: A change from the cash or income tax basis of accounting to the accrual basis.

---

[7]In evaluating reasonableness, the auditor should use one or a combination of the following approaches.

(a) Review and test the process used by management to develop the estimate.
(b) Develop an independent expectation of the estimate to corroborate the reasonableness of management's estimate.
(c) Review subsequent events or transactions occurring prior to completion of fieldwork.

"Auditing Accounting Estimates," *Statement on Auditing Standards No. 57* (New York: AICPA, 1988).

[8]"Prior Period Adjustments," *Statement of Financial Accounting Standards No. 16* (Stamford, Conn.: FASB, 1977), p. 5.

② Mathematical mistakes that result from adding, subtracting, and so on. Example: The totaling of the inventory count sheets incorrectly in computing the inventory value.

③ Changes in estimate that occur because the estimates are not prepared in good faith. Example: The adoption of a clearly unrealistic depreciation rate.

④ An oversight, such as the failure to accrue or defer certain expenses and revenues at the end of the period.

⑤ A misuse of facts, such as the failure to use salvage value in computing the depreciation base for the straight-line approach.

⑥ The incorrect classification of a cost as an expense instead of an asset, and vice versa.

As soon as they are discovered, errors must be corrected by proper entries in the accounts and reported in the financial statements. **The profession requires that corrections of errors be treated as prior period adjustments**, be recorded in the year in which the error was discovered, and be reported in the financial statements as an adjustment to the beginning balance of retained earnings. If comparative statements are presented, the prior statements affected should be restated to correct for the error. The disclosures need not be repeated in the financial statements of subsequent periods.

Illustration To illustrate, in 2004 the bookkeeper for Selectric Company discovered that in 2003 the company failed to record in the accounts $20,000 of depreciation expense on a newly constructed building. The depreciation is correctly included in the tax return. Because of numerous temporary differences, reported net income for 2003 was $150,000 and taxable income was $110,000. The following entry was made for income taxes. (Assume a 40 percent effective tax rate in 2003.)

Income Tax Expense	60,000	
Income Tax Payable		44,000
Deferred Tax Liability		16,000

As a result of the $20,000 omission error in 2003.

Depreciation expense (2003) **was** understated	$20,000
Accumulated depreciation **is** understated	20,000
Income tax expense (2003) **was** overstated ($20,000 × 40%)	8,000
Net income (2003) **was** overstated	12,000
Deferred tax liability **is** overstated ($20,000 × 40%)	8,000

The entry made in 2004 to correct the omission of $20,000 of depreciation in 2003 would be:

2004 Correcting Entry

Retained Earnings	12,000	
Deferred Tax Liability	8,000	
Accumulated Depreciation—Buildings		20,000

The journal entry to record the correction of the error is the same whether single-period or comparative financial statements are prepared, but presentation on the financial statements will differ. If single-period (noncomparative) statements are presented, the error should be reported as an adjustment to the opening balance of retained earnings of the period in which the error is discovered, as shown below.

Illustration 17-14
Reporting an Error—
Single-Period Financial
Statement

Retained earnings, January 1, 2004		
As previously reported		$350,000
Correction of an error (depreciation)	$20,000	
Less: Applicable income tax reduction	8,000	(12,000)
Adjusted balance of retained earnings, January 1, 2004		338,000
Add: Net income 2004		400,000
Retained earnings, December 31, 2004		$738,000

Comparative Statements   If comparative financial statements are prepared, adjustments should be made to correct the amounts for all affected accounts reported in the statements for all periods reported. The data for each year being presented should be restated to the correct basis, and any **catch-up adjustment should be shown as a prior period adjustment to retained earnings for the earliest period being reported.** For example, in the case of Selectric Company, the error of omitting the depreciation of $20,000 in 2003, which was discovered in 2004, results in the restatement of the 2003 financial statements when presented in comparison with those of 2004. The following accounts in the 2003 financial statements (presented in comparison with those of 2004) would have been restated.

Illustration 17-15
Reporting an Error—
Comparative Financial
Statements

In the Balance Sheet:

Accumulated depreciation—buildings	$20,000 increase
Deferred tax liability	$ 8,000 decrease
Retained earnings, ending balance	$12,000 decrease

In the Income Statement:

Depreciation expense—buildings	$20,000 increase
Tax expense	$ 8,000 decrease
Net income	$12,000 decrease

In the Retained Earnings Statement:

Retained earnings, ending balance (due to lower net income for the period)	$12,000 decrease

The 2004 financial statements in comparative form with those of 2003 are prepared as if the error had not occurred. At a minimum, such comparative statements in 2004 would include a note in the financial statements. This note would call attention to restatement of the 2003 statements and disclose the effect of the correction on income before extraordinary items, net income, and the related per share amounts.

Summary of Accounting Changes and Corrections of Errors

The development of guidelines in reporting accounting changes and corrections has helped resolve several significant and long-standing accounting problems. Yet, because of diversity in situations and characteristics of the items encountered in practice, the application of professional judgment is of paramount importance. In applying these guidelines, the primary objective is to serve the user of the financial statements. Achieving such service requires accuracy, full disclosure, and an absence of misleading inferences. The principal distinctions and treatments presented in the earlier discussion are summarized in Illustration 17-16.

Illustration 17-16

Summary of Guidelines
for Accounting Changes
and Errors

- **Changes in Accounting Principle**

  General rule:

  Employ the current or catch-up approach by:
  a. Reporting current results on the new basis.
  b. Reporting the cumulative effect of the adjustment in the current income statement between the captions "Extraordinary items" and "Net income."
  c. Presenting prior period financial statements as previously reported.
  d. Presenting pro-forma data on income and earnings per share for all prior periods presented.

  Exceptions:

  Employ the retroactive approach by:
  a. Restating the financial statements of all prior periods presented.
  b. Disclosing in the year of the change the effect on net income and earnings per share for all prior periods presented.
  c. Reporting an adjustment to the beginning retained earnings balance in the statement of retained earnings.
  Employ the change to LIFO approach by:
  a. Not restating prior years' income.
  b. Using opening inventory in the year the method is adopted as the base-year inventory for all subsequent LIFO computations.
  c. Disclosing the effect of the change on the current year, and the reasons for omitting the computation of the cumulative effect and pro-forma amounts for prior years.

- **Changes in Accounting Estimate**

  Employ the current and prospective approach by:
  a. Reporting current and future financial statements on the new basis.
  b. Presenting prior period financial statements as previously reported.
  c. Making no adjustments to current period opening balances for purposes of catch-up, and making no pro-forma presentations.

- **Changes Due to Error**

  Employ the retroactive approach by:
  a. Correcting all prior period statements presented.
  b. Restating the beginning balance of retained earnings for the first period presented when the error effects occur in a period prior to that one.

REPORTING EARNINGS PER SHARE

As indicated in this chapter, per share amounts are commonly reported for the effects of accounting changes. Earnings per share data also are frequently reported in the financial press and are widely used by stockholders and potential investors in evaluating the profitability of a company. **Earnings per share** indicates the income earned by each share of common stock. Thus, **earnings per share is reported only for common stock**. For example, if Oscar Co. has net income of $300,000 and a weighted average of 100,000 shares of common stock outstanding for the year, earnings per share is $3 ($300,000 ÷ 100,000).

Because of the importance of earnings per share information, most companies are required to report this information on the face of the income statement.[9] The exception is nonpublic companies. Because of cost-benefit considerations they do not have to re-

---

[9]"Earnings per Share," *Statement of Financial Accounting Standards No. 128* (Norwalk, Conn.: FASB, 1997).

port this information.[10] Generally, earnings per share information is reported below net income in the income statement. For Oscar Co. the presentation would be as follows.

Illustration 17-17
Income Statement
Presentation of EPS

Net income	$300,000
Earnings per share	$3.00

When the income statement contains intermediate components of income, earnings per share should be disclosed for each component. The following is representative.

Illustration 17-18
Income Statement Presentation of EPS Components

Earnings per share:	
Income from continuing operations	$4.00
Loss from discontinued operations, net of tax	0.60
Income before extraordinary item and	
cumulative effect of change in accounting principle	3.40
Extraordinary gain, net of tax	1.00
Cumulative effect of change in accounting principle, net of tax	0.50
Net income	$4.90

These disclosures enable the user of the financial statements to recognize the effects on EPS of income from continuing operations, as distinguished from income or loss from irregular items.[11]

Earnings Per Share — Simple Capital Structure

OBJECTIVE 6
Compute earnings per share in a simple capital structure.

A corporation's capital structure is **simple** if it consists only of common stock or includes no **potential common stock** that upon conversion or exercise could dilute earnings per common share. A capital structure is **complex** if it includes securities that could have a dilutive effect on earnings per common share.

The computation of earnings per share for a simple capital structure involves two items (other than net income)—preferred stock dividends and weighted average number of shares outstanding.

Preferred Stock Dividends

As indicated earlier, earnings per share relates to earnings per common share. When a company has both common and preferred stock outstanding, **the current year preferred stock dividend is subtracted from net income to arrive at** income available to common stockholders. The formula for computing earnings per share is then as follows.

[10]A nonpublic enterprise is an enterprise other than (1) whose debt or equity securities are traded in a public market on a foreign or domestic stock exchange or in the over-the-counter market (including securities quoted locally or regionally), or (2) that is required to file financial statements with the SEC. An enterprise is no longer considered a nonpublic enterprise when its financial statements are issued in preparation for the sale of any class of securities in a public market.

[11]Per share amounts for discontinued operations, an extraordinary item, or the cumulative effect of an accounting change in a period should be presented either on the face of the income statement or in the notes to the financial statements.

Earnings Per Share	=	Net Income – Preferred Dividends
		Weighted Average Number of Shares Outstanding

Illustration 17-19
Formula for Computing Earnings per Share

In reporting earnings per share information, dividends on preferred stock should be subtracted from each of the intermediate components of income (income from continuing operations and income before extraordinary items) and finally from net income to arrive at income available to common stockholders. If dividends on preferred stock are declared and a net loss occurs, **the preferred dividend is added to the loss** for purposes of computing the loss per share. If the preferred stock is cumulative and the dividend is not declared in the current year, **an amount equal to the dividend that should have been declared for the current year only** should be subtracted from net income or added to the net loss. Dividends in arrears for previous years should have been included in the previous years' computations.

Weighted Average Number of Shares Outstanding

In all computations of earnings per share, the **weighted average number of shares outstanding** during the period constitutes the basis for the per share amounts reported. Shares issued or purchased during the period affect the amount outstanding and must be **weighted by the fraction of the period they are outstanding**. The rationale for this approach is to find the equivalent number of whole shares outstanding for the year.

To illustrate, assume that Stallone Inc. has the following changes in its common stock shares outstanding for the period.

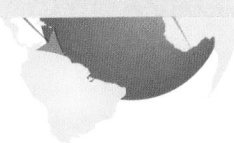

Date	Share Changes	Shares Outstanding
January 1	Beginning balance	90,000
April 1	Issued 30,000 shares for cash	30,000
		120,000
July 1	Purchased 39,000 shares	39,000
		81,000
November 1	Issued 60,000 shares for cash	60,000
December 31	Ending balance	141,000

Illustration 17-20
Shares Outstanding, Ending Balance—Stallone Inc.

To compute the weighted average number of shares outstanding, the following computation is made.

Dates Outstanding	(A) Shares Outstanding	(B) Fraction of Year	(C) Weighted Shares (A × B)
Jan. 1—Apr. 1	90,000	3/12	22,500
Apr. 1—July 1	120,000	3/12	30,000
July 1—Nov. 1	81,000	4/12	27,000
Nov. 1—Dec. 31	141,000	2/12	23,500
Weighted average number of shares outstanding			103,000

Illustration 17-21
Weighted Average Number of Shares Outstanding

As illustrated, 90,000 shares were outstanding for three months, which translates to 22,500 whole shares for the entire year. Because additional shares were issued on April 1, the shares outstanding change and these shares must be weighted for the time outstanding. When 39,000 shares were purchased on July 1, the shares outstanding were reduced, and again a new computation must be made to determine the proper weighted shares outstanding.

Stock Dividends and Stock Splits When **stock dividends** or **stock splits** occur, computation of the weighted average number of shares requires restatement of the shares outstanding before the stock dividend or split. For example, assume that a corporation had 100,000 shares outstanding on January 1 and issued a 25 percent stock dividend on June 30. For purposes of computing a weighted average for the current year, the additional 25,000 shares outstanding as a result of the stock dividend are assumed to have been **outstanding since the beginning of the year**. Thus the weighted average for the year would be 125,000 shares.

The issuance of a stock dividend or stock split is restated, but the issuance or repurchase of stock for cash is not. Why? The reason is that stock splits and stock dividends do not increase or decrease the net assets of the enterprise; only additional shares of stock are issued and, therefore, the weighted average shares must be restated. By restating, valid comparisons of earnings per share can be made between periods before and after the stock split or stock dividend. Conversely, the issuance or purchase of stock for cash changes the amount of net assets. As a result, the company either earns more or less in the future as a result of this change in net assets. Stated another way, **a stock dividend or split does not change the shareholders' total investment**—it only increases (unless it is a reverse stock split) the number of common shares representing this investment.

To illustrate how a stock dividend affects the computation of the weighted average number of shares outstanding, assume that Rambo Company has the following changes in its common stock shares during the year.

Illustration 17-22
Shares Outstanding,
Ending Balance—Rambo
Company

Date	Share Changes	Shares Outstanding
January 1	Beginning balance	100,000
March 1	Issued 20,000 shares for cash	20,000
		120,000
June 1	60,000 additional shares (50% stock dividend)	60,000
		180,000
November 1	Issued 30,000 shares for cash	30,000
December 31	Ending balance	210,000

The computation of the weighted average number of shares outstanding would be as follows.

Illustration 17-23
Weighted Average
Number of Shares
Outstanding—Stock Issue
and Stock Dividend

Dates Outstanding	(A) Shares Outstanding	(B) Restatement	(C) Fraction of Year	(D) Weighted Shares (A × B × C)
Jan. 1—Mar. 1	100,000	1.50	2/12	25,000
Mar. 1—June 1	120,000	1.50	3/12	45,000
June 1—Nov. 1	180,000		5/12	75,000
Nov. 1—Dec. 31	210,000		2/12	35,000
Weighted average number of shares outstanding				180,000

The shares outstanding prior to the stock dividend must be restated. The shares outstanding from January 1 to June 1 are adjusted for the stock dividend, so that these shares are stated on the same basis as shares issued subsequent to the stock dividend. Shares issued after the stock dividend do not have to be restated because they are on the new basis. The stock dividend simply restates existing shares. **The same type of treatment applies to a stock split.**

If a stock dividend or stock split occurs after the end of the year, but before the financial statements are issued, the weighted average number of shares outstanding for the year (and any other years presented in comparative form) must be restated. For example, assume that Hendricks Company computes its weighted average number of shares to be 100,000 for the year ended December 31, 2003. On January 15, 2004, before the financial statements are issued, the company splits its stock 3 for 1. In this case, the weighted average number of shares used in computing earnings per share for 2003 would be 300,000 shares. If earnings per share information for 2002 is provided as comparative information, it also must be adjusted for the stock split.

Comprehensive Illustration

Let's study a comprehensive illustration. Sylvester Corporation has income before extraordinary item of $580,000 and an extraordinary gain, net of tax of $240,000. In addition, it has declared preferred dividends of $1 per share on 100,000 shares of preferred stock outstanding. Sylvester Corporation also has the following changes in its common stock shares outstanding during 2003.

Dates	Share Changes	Shares Outstanding
January 1	Beginning balance	180,000
May 1	Purchased 30,000 treasury shares	30,000
		150,000
July 1	300,000 additional shares (3 for 1 stock split)	300,000
		450,000
December 31	Issued 50,000 shares for cash	50,000
December 31	Ending balance	500,000

Illustration 17-24
Shares Outstanding, Ending Balance— Sylvester Corp.

To compute the earnings per share information, the weighted average number of shares outstanding is determined as follows.

Dates Outstanding	(A) Shares Outstanding	(B) Restatement	(C) Fraction of Year	(D) Weighted Shares (A × B × C)
Jan. 1—May 1	180,000	3	4/12	180,000
May 1—Dec. 31	150,000	3	8/12	300,000
Weighted average number of shares outstanding				480,000

Illustration 17-25
Weighted Average Number of Shares Outstanding

In computing the weighted average number of shares, the shares sold on December 31, 2003, are ignored because they have not been outstanding during the year. The weighted average number of shares is then divided into income before extraordinary item and net income to determine earnings per share. Sylvester Corporation's preferred dividends of $100,000 are subtracted from income before extraordinary item ($580,000) to arrive at income before extraordinary item available to common stockholders of $480,000 ($580,000 − $100,000).

Deducting the preferred dividends from the income before extraordinary item has the effect of also reducing net income without affecting the amount of the extraordinary item. The final amount is referred to as **income available to common stockholders**.

Illustration 17-26
Computation of Income Available to Common Stockholders

	(a) Income Information	(b) Weighted Shares	(c) Earnings per Share (A ÷ B)
Income before extraordinary item available to common stockholders	$480,000*	480,000	$1.00
Extraordinary gain (net of tax)	240,000	480,000	.50
Income available to common stockholders	$720,000	480,000	$1.50

*$580,000 − $100,000

Disclosure of the per share amount for the extraordinary item (net of tax) must be reported either on the face of the income statement or in the notes to the financial statements. Income and per share information reported on the face of Sylvester Corporation's income statement would be as follows.

Illustration 17-27
Earnings per Share, with Extraordinary Item

Income before extraordinary item	$580,000
Extraordinary gain, net of tax	240,000
Net income	$820,000
Earnings per share:	
Income before extraordinary item	$1.00
Extraordinary item, net of tax	0.50
Net income	$1.50

Earnings Per Share — Complex Capital Structure

OBJECTIVE 7
Compute earnings per share in a complex capital structure.

One problem with a **basic EPS** computation is that it fails to recognize the potentially dilutive impact on outstanding stock when a corporation has dilutive securities in its capital structure. **Dilutive securities** are securities that can be converted to common stock and that upon conversion or exercise reduce (dilute) earnings per share. Dilutive securities present a serious problem because of their adverse effect on earnings per share. This adverse effect can be significant and, more important, unexpected unless financial statements call attention to the potential dilutive effect in some manner.

A complex capital structure exists when a corporation has convertible securities, options, warrants or other rights that upon conversion or exercise could dilute earnings per share. Therefore when a company has a complex capital structure, both a basic and diluted earnings per share are generally reported.

The computation of **diluted EPS** is similar to the computation of basic EPS. The difference is that diluted EPS includes the effect of all dilutive potential common shares that were outstanding during the period. The formula in Illustration 17-28 shows the relationship between basic EPS and diluted EPS.

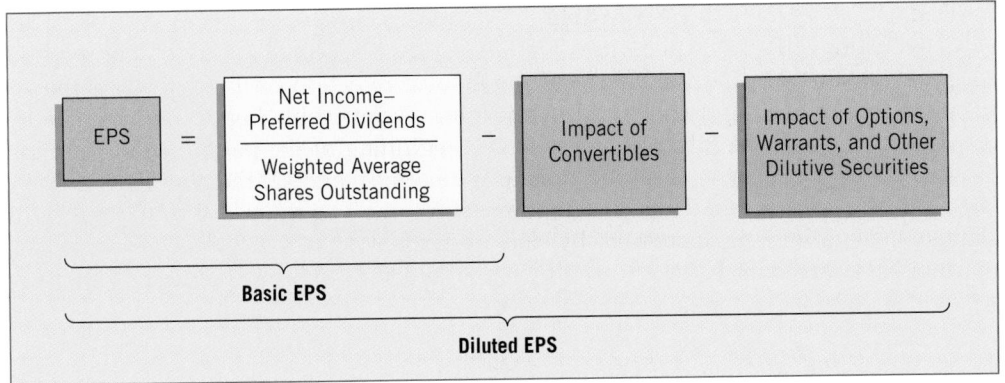

Illustration 17-28
Relation between Basic and Diluted EPS

INTERNATIONAL INSIGHT

The provisions in U.S. GAAP are substantially the same as those in International Accounting Standard No. 33, *Earnings per Share*, recently issued by the IASC. The FASB and IASC worked together on this standard to achieve international comparability related to EPS presentations.

Note that companies with complex capital structures will not report diluted EPS if the securities in their capital structure are antidilutive. **Antidilutive securities** are securities which upon conversion or exercise increase earnings per share (or reduce the loss per share). The purpose of the dual presentation is to inform financial statement users of situations that will likely occur and to provide "worst case" dilutive situations. If the securities are antidilutive, the likelihood of conversion or exercise is considered remote. Thus, companies that have only antidilutive securities are not permitted to increase earnings per share and are required to report only the basic EPS number.

The computation of basic EPS was illustrated in the prior section. The discussion in the following sections addresses the effects of convertible and other dilutive securities on EPS calculations.

THE SOURCE OF MY DILUTION

WHAT DO THE NUMBERS MEAN?

What is the source of dilutive securities, which give rise to complex capital structures? Merger activity is a major source.

Typical mergers in the 1990s were combinations of information, entertainment, or financial (banking) companies. For example, **Bell Atlantic Corp.** and **Nynex Corp.** combined in a $22.7 billion deal, **Time** acquired **Warner Communications** for $10.1 billion, and **Walt Disney Co.** purchased **Capital Cities/ABC, Inc.** Even larger were the mergers of **Nations Bank** and **BankAmerica** ($62 billion), and **Bell Atlantic** and **GTE** ($71 billion) in 1998.

One consequence of heavy merger activity is an increase in the use of securities such as convertible bonds, convertible preferred stocks, stock warrants, and contingent shares to structure these deals. Although not common stock in form, these securities enable their holders to obtain common stock upon exercise or conversion.

During the 1960s, corporate officers recognized that the issuance of dilutive securities in a merger did not have the same immediate adverse effect on earnings per share as the issuance of common stock. In addition, many companies found that issuance of convertible securities did not seem to upset common stockholders, even though the common stockholders' interests were substantially diluted when these securities were later converted or exercised.

As a consequence of the massive mergers in the 1990s, the presence of dilutive securities on corporate balance sheets is now very prevalent. As discussed in Chapter 15, the use of stock option plans, which also are dilutive in nature, is increasing. These option plans are used mainly to attract and retain executive talent and to provide tax relief for executives in high tax brackets.

Source: Farrell Kramer, "Mergers Have Been in Fashion in 1996, With Seven Big Ones," *St. Louis Post-Dispatch* (December 16, 1996), p. A7; and Geoffrey Colvin, "The Year of the Mega Merger," *Fortune* (January 11, 1999), p. 62.

Diluted EPS—Convertible Securities

At conversion, convertible securities are exchanged for common stock. The method used to measure the dilutive effects of potential conversion on EPS is called the **if-converted method**. The if-converted method for a convertible bond assumes: (1) the conversion of the convertible securities at the beginning of the period (or at the time of issuance of the security, if issued during the period), and (2) the elimination of related interest, net of tax. Thus the **denominator**—the weighted average number of shares outstanding—is increased by the additional shares assumed issued. The **numerator**—net income—is increased by the amount of interest expense, net of tax associated with those potential common shares.

Comprehensive Illustration—If-Converted Method As an example, Marshy Field Corporation has net income of $210,000 for the year and a weighted average number of common shares outstanding during the period of 100,000 shares. The basic earnings per share is, therefore, $2.10 ($210,000 ÷ 100,000). The company has two convertible debenture bond issues outstanding. One is a 6 percent issue sold at 100 (total $1,000,000) in a prior year and convertible into 20,000 common shares. The other is a 10 percent issue sold at 100 (total $1,000,000) on April 1 of the current year and convertible into 32,000 common shares. The tax rate is 40 percent.

As shown in Illustration 17-29, to determine the numerator, we add back the interest on the if-converted securities, less the related tax effect. Because the if-converted method assumes conversion as of the beginning of the year, no interest on the convertibles is assumed to be paid during the year. The interest on the 6 percent convertibles is $60,000 for the year ($1,000,000 × 6%). The increased tax expense is $24,000 ($60,000 × 0.40), and the interest added back net of taxes is $36,000 [$60,000 − $24,000, or simply $60,000 × (1 − 0.40)].

Because 10 percent convertibles are issued subsequent to the beginning of the year, the shares assumed to have been issued on that date (April 1) are weighted as outstanding from April 1 to the end of the year. In addition, the interest adjustment to the numerator for these bonds would only reflect the interest for nine months. Thus the interest added back on the 10 percent convertible would be $45,000 [$1,000,000 × 10% × 9/12 year × (1 − 0.4)]. The computation of earnings (the numerator) for diluted earnings per share is shown in Illustration 17-29.

Illustration 17-29
Computation of Adjusted Net Income

Net income for the year	$210,000
Add: Adjustment for interest (net of tax)	
6% debentures ($60,000 × [1 − 0.40])	36,000
10% debentures ($100,000 × 9/12 × [1 − 0.40])	45,000
Adjusted net income	$291,000

The computation for shares adjusted for dilutive securities (the denominator) for diluted earnings per share is shown in Illustration 17-30.

Illustration 17-30
Computation of Weighted Average Number of Shares

Weighted average number of shares outstanding	100,000
Add: Shares assumed to be issued:	
6% debentures (as of beginning of year)	20,000
10% debentures (as of date of issue, April 1; 9/12 × 32,000)	24,000
Weighted average number of shares adjusted for dilutive securities	144,000

Marshy Field would then report earnings per share based on a dual presentation on the face of the income statement; basic and diluted earnings per share are reported.[12] The presentation is shown in Illustration 17-31.

Net Income for the year	$210,000
Earnings per Share (Note X)	
Basic earnings per share ($210,000 ÷ 100,000)	$2.10
Diluted earnings per share ($291,000 ÷ 144,000)	$2.02

Illustration 17-31
Earnings per Share
Disclosure

Other Factors The example above assumed that Marshy Field's bonds were sold at the face amount. If the bonds are sold at a premium or discount, interest expense must be adjusted each period to account for this occurrence. Therefore, the amount of interest expense added back, net of tax, to net income is the interest expense reported on the income statement, not the interest paid in cash during the period.

In addition, the conversion rate on a dilutive security may change over the period during which the dilutive security is outstanding. In this situation, for the diluted EPS computation, the **most advantageous conversion rate available to the holder is used**. For example, assume that a convertible bond was issued January 1, 2002, with a conversion rate of 10 common shares for each bond starting January 1, 2004; beginning January 1, 2007, the conversion rate is 12 common shares for each bond; and beginning January 1, 2011, it is 15 common shares for each bond. In computing diluted EPS in 2002, the conversion rate of 15 shares to one bond is used.

Finally, if the 6 percent convertible debentures were instead 6 percent convertible preferred stock, the convertible preferred would be considered potential common shares and included in shares outstanding in diluted EPS calculations. Preferred dividends are not subtracted from net income in computing the numerator. Why not? Because it is assumed that the convertible preferreds are converted and are outstanding as common stock for purposes of computing EPS. Net income is used as the numerator—**no tax effect** is computed because preferred dividends generally are not deductible for tax purposes.

Diluted EPS—Options and Warrants

Stock options and warrants outstanding (whether or not presently exercisable) are included in diluted earnings per share unless they are antidilutive. Options and warrants and their equivalents are included in earnings per share computations through the **treasury stock method**.

The treasury stock method assumes that the options or warrants are exercised at the beginning of the year (or date of issue if later) and that the proceeds from the exercise of options and warrants are used to purchase common stock for the treasury. If the exercise price is lower than the market price of the stock, then the proceeds from exercise are not sufficient to buy back all the shares. The incremental shares remaining are added to the weighted average number of shares outstanding for purposes of computing diluted earnings per share.

For example, if the exercise price of a warrant is $5 and the fair market value of the stock is $15, the treasury stock method would increase the shares outstanding. Exercise of the warrant would result in one additional share outstanding, but the $5 received for the one share issued is not sufficient to purchase one share in the market at $15. Three warrants would have to be exercised (and three additional shares issued) to produce enough money ($15) to acquire one share in the market. Thus, a net increase of two shares outstanding would result.

[12]Conversion of bonds is dilutive because EPS with conversion ($2.02) is less than basic EPS ($2.10).

Thus, if the exercise price of the option or warrant is **lower** than the market price of the stock, dilution occurs. If the exercise price of the option or warrant is **higher** than the market price of the stock, common shares are reduced. In this case, the options or warrants are **antidilutive** because their assumed exercise leads to an increase in earnings per share.

For both options and warrants, exercise is not assumed unless the average market price of the stock is above the exercise price during the period being reported.[13] As a practical matter, a simple average of the weekly or monthly prices is adequate, so long as the prices do not fluctuate significantly.

Comprehensive Illustration — Treasury Stock Method To illustrate application of the treasury stock method, assume that Kubitz Industries, Inc. has net income for the period of $220,000. The average number of shares outstanding for the period was 100,000 shares. Hence, basic EPS—ignoring all dilutive securities—is $2.20. The average number of shares under outstanding options (although not exercisable at this time), at an option price of $20 per share, is 5,000 shares. The average market price of the common stock during the year was $28. The computation is shown below.

Illustration 17-32

Computation of Earnings per Share—Treasury Stock Method

	Basic Earnings per Share	Diluted Earnings per Share
Average number of shares under option outstanding:		5000
Option price per share		× $20
Proceeds upon exercise of options		$100,000
Average market price of common stock		$28
Treasury shares that could be repurchased with proceeds ($100,000 ÷ $28)		3,571
Excess of shares under option over the treasury shares that could be repurchased (5,000 − 3,571)— Potential common incremental shares		1,429
Average number of common shares outstanding	100,000	100,000
Total average number of common shares outstanding and potential common shares	100,000 (A)	101,429 (C)
Net income for the year	$220,000 (B)	$220,000 (D)
Earnings per share	$2.20 (B ÷ A)	$2.17 (D ÷ C)

Antidilution Revisited

In computing diluted EPS, the aggregate of all dilutive securities must be considered. But first we must determine which potentially dilutive securities are in fact individually dilutive and which are antidilutive. **Any security that is antidilutive should be excluded** and cannot be used to offset dilutive securities.

Recall that antidilutive securities are securities whose inclusion in earnings per share computations would increase earnings per share (or reduce net loss per share). Convertible debt is antidilutive if the addition to income of the interest (net of tax) causes a greater percentage increase in income (numerator) than conversion of the bonds causes a percentage increase in common and potentially dilutive shares (denominator). In other words, convertible debt is antidilutive if conversion of the security causes common stock earnings to increase by a greater amount per additional common share than earnings per share was before the conversion.

[13]It might be noted that options and warrants have essentially the same assumptions and computational problems, although the warrants may allow or require the tendering of some other security, such as debt, in lieu of cash upon exercise. In such situations, the accounting becomes quite complex. *FASB No. 128* explains the proper disposition in this situation.

To illustrate, assume that Kohl Corporation has a 6 percent, $1,000,000 debt issue that is convertible into 10,000 common shares. Net income for the year is $210,000, the weighted average number of common shares outstanding is 100,000 shares, and the tax rate is 40 percent. In this case assumed conversion of the debt into common stock at the beginning of the year requires the following adjustments of net income and the weighted average number of shares outstanding.

Net income for the year	$210,000	Average number of shares outstanding	100,000
Add: Adjustment for interest (net of tax) on 6% debentures		Add: Shares issued upon assumed conversion of debt	10,000
$60,000 × (1 − .40)	36,000	Average number of common and potential common shares	110,000
Adjusted net income	$246,000		

Basic EPS = $210,000 ÷ 100,000 = $2.10
Diluted EPS = $246,000 ÷ 110,000 = $2.24 = **Antidilutive**

Illustration 17-33
Test for Antidilution

As a shortcut, the convertible debt also can be identified as antidilutive by comparing the EPS resulting from conversion, $3.60 ($36,000 additional earnings ÷ 10,000 additional shares), with EPS before inclusion of the convertible debt, $2.10.

With options or warrants, whenever the exercise price is higher than the market price, the security is antidilutive. **Antidilutive securities should be ignored in all calculations and should not be considered in computing diluted earnings per share.** This approach is reasonable because the profession's intent was to inform the investor of the **possible dilution** that might occur in reported earnings per share and not to be concerned with securities that, if converted or exercised, would result in an increase in earnings per share.

Example of Antidilution with Multiple Securities

EPS Presentation and Disclosure

If a corporation's capital structure is complex, the earnings per share presentation would be as follows.

Earnings per common share	
Basic earnings per share	$3.30
Diluted earnings per share	$2.70

Illustration 17-34
EPS Presentation—
Complex Capital Structure

When the earnings of a period include irregular items, per share amounts (where applicable) should be shown for income from continuing operations, income before extraordinary items, or income before accounting change, and net income. Companies that report a discontinued operation, an extraordinary item, or the cumulative effect of an accounting change should present per share amounts for those line items either on the face of the income statement or in the notes to the financial statements. A presentation reporting extraordinary items only is presented in Illustration 17-35.

Earnings per share amounts must be shown for all periods presented. Also, all prior period earnings per share amounts presented should be restated for stock dividends and stock splits. If diluted EPS data are reported for at least one period, such data should be reported for all periods presented, even if it is the same as basic EPS. When results of operations of a prior period have been restated as a result of a prior period adjustment, the earnings per share data shown for the prior periods should also be restated. The effect of the restatement should be disclosed in the year of the restatement.

Illustration 17-35
EPS Presentation, with
Extraordinary Item

Basic earnings per share	
Income before extraordinary item	$3.80
Extraordinary item	0.80
Net income	$3.00
Diluted earnings per share	
Income before extraordinary item	$3.35
Extraordinary item	0.65
Net income	$2.70

Complex capital structures and dual presentation of earnings per share require the following additional disclosures in note form.

1. Description of pertinent rights and privileges of the various securities outstanding.
2. A reconciliation of the numerators and denominators of the basic and diluted per share computations, including individual income and share amount effects of all securities that affect EPS.
3. The effect given preferred dividends in determining income available to common stockholders in computing basic EPS.
4. Securities that could potentially dilute basic EPS in the future that were not included in the computation because they would be antidilutive.
5. Effect of conversions subsequent to year-end, but before statements have been issued.

Illustration 17-36 presents the reconciliation and the related disclosure that is needed to meet disclosure requirements of this standard.

Illustration 17-36
Reconciliation for Basic
and Diluted EPS

	For the Year Ended 2004		
	Income (Numerator)	Shares (Denominator)	Per-Share Amount
Income before extraordinary item and accounting change	$7,500,000		
Less: Preferred stock dividends	(45,000)		
Basic EPS			
Income available to common stockholders	7,455,000	3,991,666	$1.87
Warrants		30,768	
Convertible preferred stock	45,000	308,333	
4% convertible bonds (net of tax)	60,000	50,000	
Diluted EPS			
Income available to common stockholders— assumed conversions	$7,560,000	4,380,767	$1.73

Stock options to purchase 1,000,000 shares of common stock at $85 per share were outstanding during the second half of 2004 but were not included in the computation of diluted EPS because the options' exercise price was greater than the average market price of the common shares. The options were still outstanding at the end of year 2004 and expire on June 30, 2014.[14]

[14]Note that *Statement No. 123* has specific disclosure requirements as well regarding stock option plans and earnings per share disclosures.

Summary of EPS Computation

As you can see, computation of earnings per share is a complex issue. It is a controversial area because many securities, although technically not common stock, have many of its basic characteristics. Some companies have issued these types of securities rather than common stock in order to avoid an adverse dilutive effect on earnings per share.

Illustration 17-37 displays graphically the elementary points of calculating earnings per share in a simple capital structure.

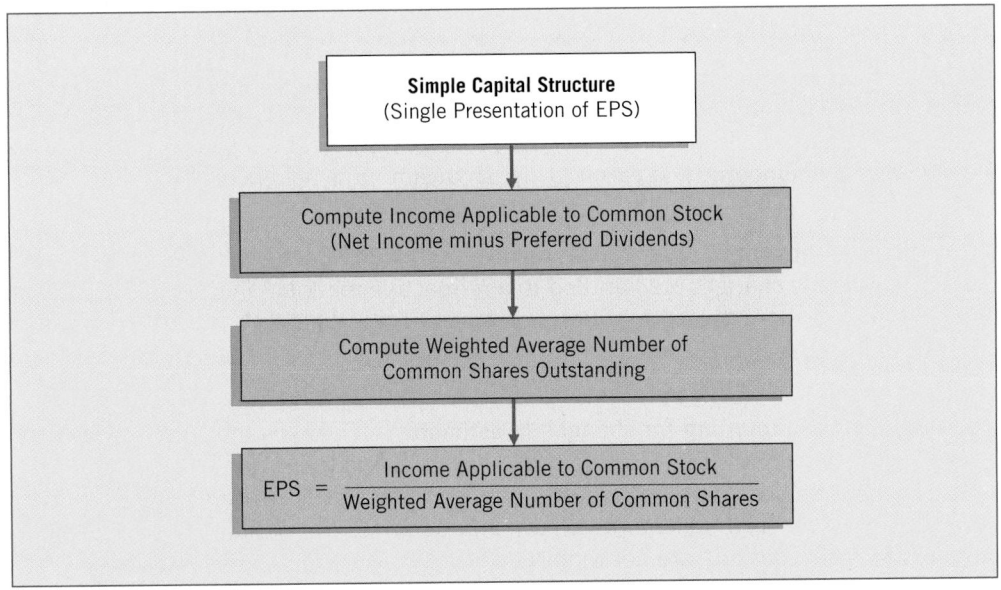

Illustration 17-37
Calculating EPS, Simple Capital Structure

Illustration 17-38 shows the calculation of earnings per share for a complex capital structure.

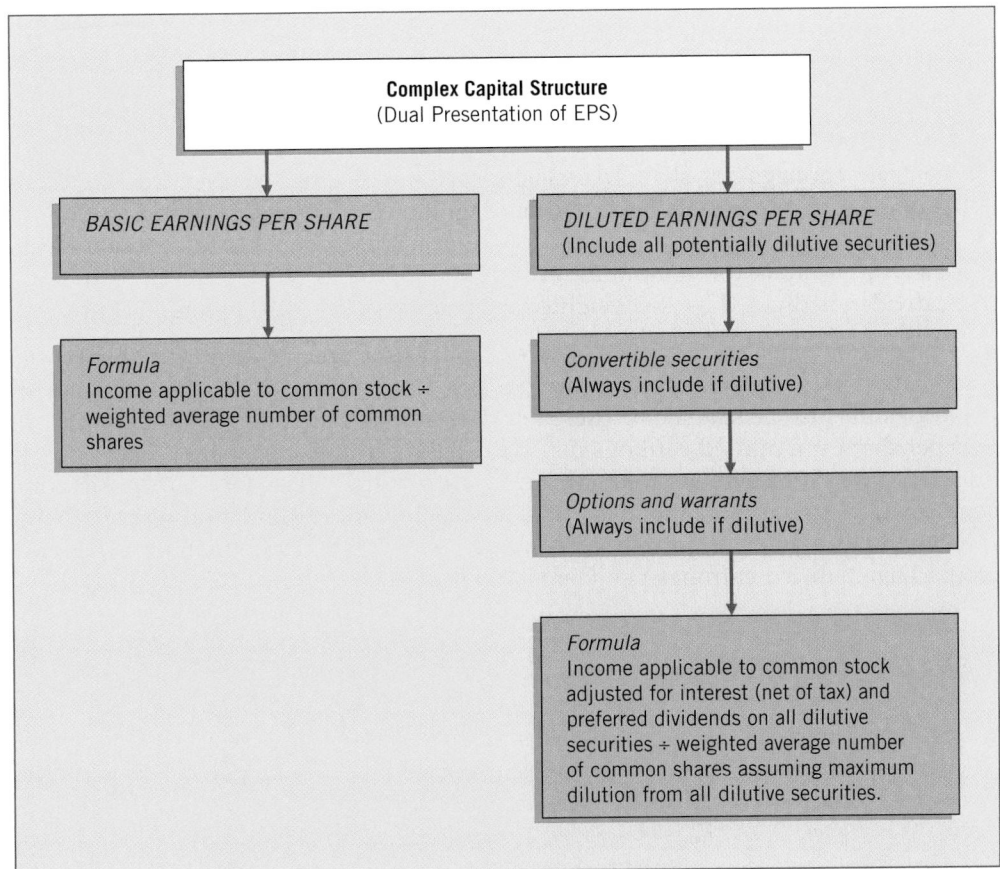

Illustration 17-38
Calculating EPS, Complex Capital Structure

KEY TERMS

antidilutive securities, *843*

basic EPS, *842*

change in accounting
  estimate, *824*

change in accounting
  principle, *824*

complex capital structure,
  838

correction of an error, *834*

cumulative effect, *825*

diluted EPS, *842*

dilutive securities, *842*

earnings per share, *837*

errors in financial statements, *825*

if-converted method, *844*

income available to common
  stockholders, *838*

pro-forma, *825*

prospective changes, *832*

retroactive changes, *827*

simple capital structure,
  838

treasury stock method, *845*

weighted average number of
  shares outstanding, *839*

SUMMARY OF LEARNING OBJECTIVES

❶ Describe various accounting changes.   A change in accounting principle involves a change from one generally accepted accounting principle to another. A change in accounting principle is not considered to result from the adoption of a new principle in recognition of events that have occurred for the first time or that were previously immaterial. If the accounting principle previously followed was not acceptable, or if the principle was applied incorrectly, a change to a generally accepted accounting principle is considered a correction of an error.

❷ Understand how to account for cumulative-effect accounting changes.   The general requirement for changes in accounting principle is that the cumulative effect of the change (net of tax) be shown at the bottom of the current year's income statement and that pro-forma net income and earnings per share amounts be reported for all prior periods presented.

❸ Understand how to account for retroactive accounting changes.   A number of accounting principle changes are handled in a retroactive manner. That is, prior years' financial statements are recast on a basis consistent with the newly adopted principle, and any part of the effect attributable to years prior to those presented is treated as an adjustment of the earliest retained earnings presented.

❹ Describe the accounting for changes in estimates.   Changes in estimates must be handled prospectively. That is, no changes should be made in previously reported results. Opening balances are not adjusted, and no attempt is made to "catch up" for prior periods. Financial statements of prior periods are not restated, and pro-forma amounts for prior periods are not reported.

❺ Describe the accounting for correction of errors.   As soon as they are discovered, errors must be corrected by proper entries in the accounts and reported in the financial statements. The profession requires that corrections of errors be treated as prior period adjustments, be recorded in the year in which the error was discovered, and be reported in the financial statements as an adjustment to the beginning balance of retained earnings. If comparative statements are presented, the prior statements affected should be restated to correct for the error. The disclosures need not be repeated in the financial statements of subsequent periods.

❻ Compute earnings per share in a simple capital structure.   When a company has both common and preferred stock outstanding, the current-year preferred stock dividend is subtracted from net income to arrive at income available to common stockholders. The formula for computing earnings per share is net income less preferred stock dividends divided by the weighted average of shares outstanding.

❼ Compute earnings per share in a complex capital structure.   A complex capital structure requires a dual presentation of earnings per share, each with equal prominence on the face of the income statement. These two presentations are referred to as basic earnings per share and diluted earnings per share. Basic earnings per share is based on the number of weighted average common shares outstanding (i.e., equivalent to EPS for a simple capital structure). Diluted earnings per share indicates the dilution of earnings per share that would have occurred if all potential issuances of common stock that would have reduced earnings per share had taken place.

REVIEW EXERCISE

Garner Company began operations on January 1, 2002, and uses the average cost method of pricing inventory. Management is contemplating a change in inventory methods for 2005. The following information is available for the years 2002–2005.

	Net Income Computed Using		
	Average Cost Method	FIFO Method	LIFO Method
2002	$15,000	$20,000	$12,000
2003	18,000	24,000	14,000
2004	20,000	27,000	17,000

On January 1, 2004, Garner issued 10-year, $200,000 face value, 6% bonds, at par. Each $1,000 bond is convertible into 30 shares of Garner common stock. The company has had 10,000 common shares outstanding throughout its life. None of the bonds have been exercised as of the end of 2005. (Ignore tax effects.)

Instructions

(a) Prepare the journal entry necessary to record a change from the average cost method to the FIFO method in 2005.

(b) Assume Garner Company used the LIFO method instead of the average cost method during the years 2002–2004. In 2005, Garner changed to the FIFO method. Prepare the journal entry necessary to record the change in accounting principle.

(c) Assuming Garner had the accounting change described in (b), Garner's income in 2005 was $30,000. Compute basic and diluted earnings per share for Garner Company for 2005. Show how income and EPS will be reported for 2005 and 2004.

SOLUTION TO REVIEW EXERCISE

(a)

Inventory	18,000*	
Cumulative Effect of Change in		
Accounting Principle—Inventory		18,000

*($20,000 + $24,000 + $27,000) − ($15,000 + $18,000 + $20,000)

(b)

Inventory	28,000*	
Retained Earnings		28,000

*($20,000 + $24,000 + $27,000) − ($12,000 + $14,000 + $17,000)

(c) Basic EPS = $30,000 ÷ 10,000 = <u>$3.00</u>

Diluted EPS

Net income	$30,000
Add: Interest savings ($200,000 × 6%)	12,000
Adjusted net income	$42,000

$200,000 ÷ $1,000 = 200 bonds
× 30
6,000 shares

Diluted EPS: $42,000 ÷ (10,000 + 6,000) = <u>$2.63</u>

	2005	2004
Net income	$30,000	$27,000
Basic EPS	$ 3.00	$ 2.70*
Diluted EPS	$ 2.63	$ 2.44*

*2004 Income $27,000
Add: Interest   12,000
$39,000 ÷ 16,000 shares = $2.44

REPORTING CASH FLOWS

In Chapter 6 we learned that the primary purpose of the **statement of cash flows** is to provide information about an entity's cash receipts and cash payments during a period. A secondary objective is to provide information on a cash basis about its operating, investing, and financing activities. **The statement of cash flows therefore reports cash receipts, cash payments, and net change in cash resulting from operating, investing, and financing activities of an enterprise during a period, in a format that reconciles the beginning and ending cash balances.**

In this appendix we review the structure of the statement of cash flows and examine some complexities in its preparation.

CLASSIFICATION OF CASH FLOWS

OBJECTIVE 8

After studying Appendix 17A, you should be able to: Identify the major classifications of cash flows.

The statement of cash flows classifies cash receipts and cash payments by operating, investing, and financing activities.[1] Transactions and other events characteristic of each kind of activity are as follows.

(1) **Operating activities** involve the cash effects of transactions that enter into the determination of net income, such as cash receipts from sales of goods and services and cash payments to suppliers and employees for acquisitions of inventory and expenses.

(2) **Investing activities** generally involve long-term assets and include (a) making and collecting loans, and (b) acquiring and disposing of investments and productive long-lived assets.

(3) **Financing activities** involve liability and stockholders' equity items and include (a) obtaining cash from creditors and repaying the amounts borrowed, and (b) obtaining capital from owners and providing them with a return on, and a return of, their investment.

Illustration 17A-1 classifies the typical cash receipts and payments of a business enterprise that are classified according to operating, investing, and financing activities.

Some cash flows relating to investing or financing activities are classified as operating activities.[2] For example, receipts of investment income (interest and dividends)

[1]The basis recommended by the FASB for the statement of cash flows is actually "cash and cash equivalents." **Cash equivalents** are short-term, highly liquid investments that are both: (a) readily convertible to known amounts of cash, and (b) so near their maturity that they present insignificant risk of changes in interest rates. Generally, only investments with original maturities of three months or less qualify under this definition. Examples of cash equivalents are Treasury bills, commercial paper, and money market funds purchased with cash that is in excess of immediate needs.

Although we use the term "cash" throughout our discussion and illustrations in this appendix, we mean cash and cash equivalents when reporting the cash flows and the net increase or decrease in cash.

[2]For exceptions to the treatment of purchases and sales of loans and securities by banks and brokers, see *Statement of Financial Accounting Standards No. 102* (February 1989). Banks and brokers are required to classify cash flows from purchases and sales of loans and securities specifically for resale and carried at market value **as operating activities.** This requirement recognizes that for these firms these assets are similar to inventory in other businesses.

Operating

Cash inflows
    From sales of goods or services.
    From returns on loans (interest) and on equity
       securities (dividends).
Cash outflows
    To suppliers for inventory.
    To employees for services.
    To government for taxes.
    To lenders for interest.
    To others for expenses.

Income Statement Items

Investing

Cash inflows
    From sale of property, plant, and equipment.
    From sale of debt or equity securities of other entities.
    From collection of principal on loans to other entities.
Cash outflows
    To purchase property, plant, and equipment.
    To purchase debt or equity securities of other entities.
    To make loans to other entities.

Generally Long-Term Asset Items

Financing

Cash inflows
    From sale of equity securities.
    From issuance of debt (bonds and notes).
Cash outflows
    To stockholders as dividends.
    To redeem long-term debt or reacquire capital stock.

Generally Long-Term Liability and Equity Items

Illustration 17A-1
Classification of Typical Cash Inflows and Outflows

INTERNATIONAL INSIGHT

According to International Accounting Standards, "cash and cash equivalents" can be defined as "net monetary assets," that is, "cash and demand deposits and highly liquid investments less short-term borrowings."

and payments of interest to lenders are classified as operating activities. Conversely, some cash flows relating to operating activities are classified as investing or financing activities. For example, the cash received from the sale of property, plant, and equipment at a gain, although reported in the income statement, is classified as an investing activity, and the effects of the related gain would not be included in net cash flow from operating activities. Likewise, a gain or loss on the payment (extinguishment) of debt would generally be part of the cash outflow related to the repayment of the amount borrowed and therefore is a financing activity.

FORMAT OF THE STATEMENT OF CASH FLOWS

The three activities discussed in the preceding paragraphs constitute the general format of the statement of cash flows. The cash flows from operating activities section always appears first, followed by the investing and financing activities sections. The individual inflows and outflows from investing and financing activities are reported separately. That is, they are reported gross, not netted against one another. Thus, cash outflow from the purchase of property is reported separately from the cash inflow from the sale of property. Similarly, the cash inflow from the issuance of debt is reported separately from the cash outflow from its retirement. The net increase or decrease in cash reported during the period should reconcile the beginning and ending cash balances as reported in the comparative balance sheets.

The skeleton format of the statement of cash flows is as follows.

COMPANY NAME		
STATEMENT OF CASH FLOWS		
PERIOD COVERED		
Cash flows from operating activities		
Net income		XXX
Adjustments to reconcile net income to net		
cash provided by operating activities:		
(List of individual items)	XX	XX
Net cash flow from operating activities		XXX
Cash flows from investing activities		
(List of individual inflows and outflows)	XX	
Net cash provided (used) by investing activities		XXX
Cash flows from financing activities		
(List of individual inflows and outflows)	XX	
Net cash provided (used) by financing activities		XXX
Net increase (decrease) in cash		XXX
Cash at beginning of period		XXX
Cash at end of period		XXX

STEPS IN PREPARATION

Unlike the other major financial statements, the statement of cash flows is not prepared from the adjusted trial balance. The information to prepare this statement usually comes from three sources:

1. **Comparative balance sheets** provide the amount of the changes in assets, liabilities, and equities from the beginning to the end of the period.

2. **Current income statement** data help the reader determine the amount of cash provided by or used by operations during the period.

3. **Selected transaction data** from the general ledger provide additional detailed information needed to determine how cash was provided or used during the period.

Preparing the statement of cash flows from the data sources above involves three major steps:

Step 1. Determine the change in cash. This procedure is straightforward because the difference between the beginning and the ending cash balance can be easily computed from an examination of the comparative balance sheets.

Step 2. Determine the net cash flow from operating activities. This procedure is complex. It involves analyzing not only the current year's income statement but also comparative balance sheets as well as selected transaction data.

Step 3. Determine net cash flows from investing and financing activities. All other changes in the balance sheet accounts must be analyzed to determine their effects on cash.

On the following pages we work through these three steps in the process of preparing the statement of cash flows for a company.

Illustration

To illustrate a statement of cash flows, we will use the **first year of operations** for Tax Consultants Inc. The company started on January 1, 2002, when it issued 60,000 shares of $1 par value common stock for $60,000 cash. The company rented its office space and furniture and equipment and performed tax consulting services throughout the first year. The comparative balance sheets at the beginning and end of the year 2002 appear as follows.

<table>
<tr><td colspan="4" align="center">**TAX CONSULTANTS INC.**
COMPARATIVE BALANCE SHEET</td></tr>
<tr><td>**Assets**</td><td>Dec. 31, 2002</td><td>Jan. 1, 2002</td><td>Change
Increase/Decrease</td></tr>
<tr><td>Cash</td><td>$49,000</td><td>$-0-</td><td>$49,000 Increase</td></tr>
<tr><td>Accounts receivable</td><td>36,000</td><td>-0-</td><td>36,000 Increase</td></tr>
<tr><td>Total</td><td>$85,000</td><td>$-0-</td><td></td></tr>
<tr><td>**Liabilities and Stockholders' Equity**</td><td></td><td></td><td></td></tr>
<tr><td>Accounts payable</td><td>$ 5,000</td><td>$-0-</td><td>5,000 Increase</td></tr>
<tr><td>Common stock ($1 par)</td><td>60,000</td><td>-0-</td><td>60,000 Increase</td></tr>
<tr><td>Retained earnings</td><td>20,000</td><td>-0-</td><td>20,000 Increase</td></tr>
<tr><td>Total</td><td>$85,000</td><td>$-0-</td><td></td></tr>
</table>

Illustration 17A-3
Comparative Balance Sheet, Tax Consultants Inc., 2002

The income statement and additional information for Tax Consultants Inc. are as follows.

<table>
<tr><td colspan="2" align="center">**TAX CONSULTANTS INC.**
INCOME STATEMENT
FOR THE YEAR ENDED DECEMBER 31, 2002</td></tr>
<tr><td>Revenues</td><td>$125,000</td></tr>
<tr><td>Operating expenses</td><td>85,000</td></tr>
<tr><td>Income before income taxes</td><td>40,000</td></tr>
<tr><td>Income tax expense</td><td>6,000</td></tr>
<tr><td>Net income</td><td>$ 34,000</td></tr>
</table>

Additional Information
Examination of selected data indicates that a dividend of $14,000 was paid during the year.

Illustration 17A-4
Income Statement, Tax Consultants Inc., 2002

Step 1: Determine the Change in Cash

To prepare a statement of cash flows, the first step is to **determine the change in cash**. This is a simple computation. Tax Consultants Inc. had no cash on hand at the beginning of the year 2002, but $49,000 was on hand at the end of 2002. Thus, the change in cash for 2002 was an increase of $49,000.

The other two steps are more complex and involve additional analysis.

OBJECTIVE **9**
Differentiate between net income and net cash flows from operating activities.

Step 2: Determine Net Cash Flow from Operating Activities

A useful starting point in **determining net cash flow from operating activities**[3] is to understand why net income must be converted. Under generally accepted accounting principles, most companies must use the accrual basis of accounting, which requires that revenue be recorded when earned and that expenses be recorded when incurred. Net income may include credit sales that have not been collected in cash and expenses incurred that may not have been paid in cash. Thus, under the accrual basis of accounting, net income will not indicate the net cash flow from operating activities.

To arrive at net cash flow from operating activities, it is necessary to report revenues and expenses on a **cash basis. This is done by eliminating the effects of income statement transactions that did not result in a corresponding increase or decrease in cash.** The relationship between net income and net cash flow from operating activities is graphically depicted as follows.

Illustration 17A-5

Net Income versus Net Cash Flow from Operating Activities

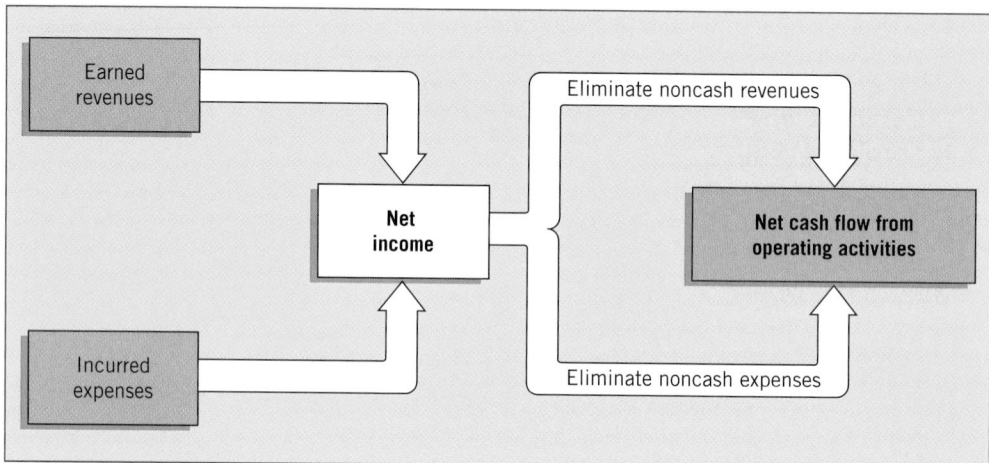

In this appendix, we use the term net income to refer to accrual-based net income. The conversion of net income to net cash flow from operating activities may be done through either a direct method or an indirect method as explained in the following discussion.

OBJECTIVE **10**
Contrast the direct and indirect methods of calculating net cash flow from operating activities.

Direct Method The **direct method** (also called the income statement method) reports cash receipts and cash disbursements from operating activities. The difference between these two amounts is the net cash flow from operating activities. In other words, the direct method deducts from operating cash receipts the operating cash disbursements. The direct method results in the presentation of a condensed cash receipts and cash disbursements statement.

As indicated from the accrual-based income statement, Tax Consultants Inc. reported revenues of $125,000. However, because the company's accounts receivable increased during 2002 by $36,000, only $89,000 ($125,000 − $36,000) in cash was collected on these revenues. Similarly, Tax Consultants Inc. reported operating expenses of $85,000, but accounts payable increased during the period of $5,000. Assuming that these payables related to operating expenses, cash operating expenses were $80,000 ($85,000 − $5,000). Because no taxes payable exist at the end of the year, the $6,000 income tax expense for 2002 must have been paid in cash during the year. Then the computation of net cash flow from operating activities is as follows.

---

[3]"Net cash flow from operating activities" is a generic phrase, which is replaced in the statement of cash flows with either "Net cash **provided by** operating activities" if operations increase cash, or "Net cash **used by** operating activities" if operations decrease cash.

Cash collected from revenues	$89,000	
Cash payments for expenses	80,000	
Income before income taxes	9,000	
Cash payments for income taxes	6,000	
Net cash provided by operating activities	$ 3,000	

Illustration 17A-6
Computation of Net Cash
Flow from Operating
Activities, 2002—Direct
Method

"Net cash provided by operating activities" is the equivalent of cash basis net income. ("Net cash used by operating activities" would be equivalent to cash basis net loss.)

Indirect Method   The **indirect method** (or reconciliation method) starts with net income and converts it to net cash flow from operating activities. In other words, **the indirect method adjusts net income for items that affected reported net income but did not affect cash**. To compute net cash flow from operating activities, noncash charges in the income statement are added back to net income and noncash credits are deducted. Explanations for the two adjustments to net income in this example, namely, the increases in accounts receivable and accounts payable, are as follows.

Increase in Accounts Receivable—Indirect Method.   When accounts receivable increase during the year, revenues on an accrual basis are higher than revenues on a cash basis because goods sold on account are reported as revenues. In other words, operations of the period led to increased revenues, but not all of these revenues resulted in an increase in cash. Some of the increase in revenues resulted in an increase in accounts receivable. To convert net income to net cash flow from operating activities, the increase of $36,000 in accounts receivable must be deducted from net income.

Increase in Accounts Payable—Indirect Method.   When accounts payable increase during the year, expenses on an accrual basis are higher than they are on a cash basis because expenses are incurred for which payment has not taken place. To convert net income to net cash flow from operating activities, the increase of $5,000 in accounts payable must be added to net income.

As a result of the accounts receivable and accounts payable adjustments, net cash provided by operating activities is determined to be $3,000 for the year 2002. This computation is shown as follows.

Net income		$34,000
Adjustments to reconcile net income to net cash provided by operating activities:		
Increase in accounts receivable	$(36,000)	
Increase in accounts payable	5,000	(31,000)
Net cash provided by operating activities		$ 3,000

Illustration 17A-7
Computation of Net Cash
Flow from Operating
Activities, 2002—
Indirect Method

Note that net cash provided by operating activities is the same whether the direct or the indirect method is used. Because just about all companies use the indirect method in computing cash flow from operations, it is used in the subsequent more complex illustration.[4]

More Complex Illustration

A more complex illustration is based on the 2002 operations of Account Services Inc. Similar to Tax Consultants, Account Services also provides accounting and bookkeeping services. In addition, Account Services sells computer software used for vari-

OBJECTIVE 11
**Prepare a
statement of cash
flows.**

[4]*Accounting Trends and Techniques—2001* (AICPA, 2001) reports that 593 out of 600 surveyed companies use the indirect method.

ous accounting and tax processes. Account Services Inc. experienced operating success in 2002. Thus, inventories is one of the assets appearing in Account Services' December 31, 2002, balance sheet. The comparative balance sheets, income statements, and selected data for 2002 are shown in Illustrations 17A-8 and 17A-9.

Illustration 17A-8

Comparative Balance Sheet, Account Services Inc., 2002

ACCOUNT SERVICES INC. COMPARATIVE BALANCE SHEET DECEMBER 31			
Assets	2002	2001	Change Increase/Decrease
Cash	$ 54,000	$ 37,000	$ 17,000 Increase
Accounts receivable	68,000	26,000	42,000 Increase
Inventories	54,000	–0–	54,000 Increase
Prepaid expenses	4,000	6,000	2,000 Decrease
Land	45,000	70,000	25,000 Decrease
Buildings	200,000	200,000	–0–
Accumulated depreciation—buildings	(21,000)	(11,000)	10,000 Increase
Equipment	193,000	68,000	125,000 Increase
Accumulated depreciation—equipment	(28,000)	(10,000)	18,000 Increase
Totals	$569,000	$386,000	
Liabilities and Stockholders' Equity			
Accounts payable	$ 33,000	$ 40,000	7,000 Decrease
Bonds payable	110,000	150,000	40,000 Decrease
Common stock ($1 par)	220,000	60,000	160,000 Increase
Retained earnings	206,000	136,000	70,000 Increase
Totals	$569,000	$386,000	

Illustration 17A-9

Income Statement, Account Services Inc., 2002

ACCOUNT SERVICES INC. INCOME STATEMENT FOR THE YEAR ENDED DECEMBER 31, 2002		
Revenues		$890,000
Cost of goods sold	$465,000	
Operating expenses	221,000	
Interest expense	12,000	
Loss on sale of equipment	2,000	700,000
Income from operations		190,000
Income tax expense		65,000
Net income		$125,000

Additional Information

(a) Operating expenses include depreciation expense of $33,000 and amortization of prepaid expenses of $2,000.
(b) Land was sold at its book value for cash.
(c) Cash dividends of $55,000 were paid in 2002.
(d) Interest expense of $12,000 was paid in cash.
(e) Equipment with a cost of $166,000 was purchased for cash. Equipment with a cost of $41,000 and a book value of $36,000 was sold for $34,000 cash.
(f) Bonds were redeemed at their book value for cash.
(g) Common stock ($1 par) was issued for cash.

Step 1: Determine the Change in Cash
The first step in the preparation of the statement of cash flows is to determine the change in cash. As is shown in the comparative balance sheet, cash increased $17,000 in 2002.

The second and third steps are discussed below and on the following pages.

Step 2: Determine Net Cash Flow from Operating Activities
Explanations of the adjustments to net income of $125,000 are as follows.

Increase in Accounts Receivable The increase in accounts receivable of $42,000 represents recorded accrual basis revenues in excess of cash collections in 2002. The increase is deducted from net income to convert from the accrual basis to the cash basis.

Increase in Inventories The increase in inventories of $54,000 represents an operating use of cash for which an expense was not incurred. This amount is therefore deducted from net income to arrive at cash flow from operations. In other words, when inventory purchased exceeds inventory sold during a period, cost of goods sold on an accrual basis is lower than on a cash basis.

Decrease in Prepaid Expenses The decrease in prepaid expenses of $2,000 represents a charge to the income statement for which there was no cash outflow in the current period. The decrease is added back to net income to arrive at net cash flow from operating activities.

Decrease in Accounts Payable When accounts payable decrease during the year, cost of goods sold and expenses on a cash basis are higher than they are on an accrual basis, because on a cash basis the goods and expenses are recorded as expense when paid. To convert net income to net cash flow from operating activities, the decrease of $7,000 in accounts payable must be deducted from net income.

Depreciation Expense (Increase in Accumulated Depreciation) Accumulated Depreciation—Buildings increased $10,000 ($21,000 − $11,000). The Buildings account did not change during the period, which means that $10,000 of depreciation was recorded in 2002.

Accumulated Depreciation—Equipment increased by $18,000 ($28,000 − $10,000) during the year. But Accumulated Depreciation—Equipment was decreased by $5,000 as a result of the sale during the year. Thus, depreciation for the year was $23,000. The reconciliation of Accumulated Depreciation—Equipment is as follows.

Beginning balance	$10,000
Add: Depreciation for 2002	23,000
	33,000
Deduct: Sale of equipment	5,000
Ending balance	$28,000

The total depreciation of $33,000 ($10,000 + $23,000) charged to the income statement must be added back to net income to determine net cash flow from operating activities.

Loss on Sale of Equipment Equipment having a cost of $41,000 and a book value of $36,000 was sold for $34,000. As a result, the company reported a loss of $2,000 on its sale. To arrive at net cash flow from operating activities, it is necessary to add back to net income the loss on the sale of the equipment. The reason is that the loss is a noncash charge to the income statement. It did not reduce cash, but it did reduce net income.

From the foregoing items, the operating activities section of the statement of cash flows is prepared as shown in Illustration 17A-10.

Illustration 17A-10

Operating Activities
Section of Cash Flows
Statement for Account
Services Inc., 2002

Cash flows from operating activities		
Net income		$125,000
Adjustments to reconcile net income to		
net cash provided by operating activities:		
Depreciation expense	$33,000	
Increase in accounts receivable	(42,000)	
Increase in inventories	(54,000)	
Decrease in prepaid expenses	2,000	
Decrease in accounts payable	(7,000)	
Loss on sale of equipment	2,000	(66,000)
Net cash provided by operating activities		59,000

Step 3: Determine Net Cash Flows from Investing and Financing Activities

By analyzing the remaining changes in the balance sheet accounts, we can identify cash flows from investing and financing activities.

Land   Land decreased $25,000 during the period. As indicated from the information presented, land was sold for cash at its book value. This transaction is an investing activity reported as a $25,000 source of cash.

Equipment   An analysis of the equipment account indicates the following.

Beginning balance	$ 68,000
Purchase of equipment	166,000
	234,000
Sale of equipment	41,000
Ending balance	$193,000

Equipment with a fair value of $166,000 was purchased for cash—an investing transaction reported as a cash outflow. The sale of the equipment for $34,000 is also an investing activity, but one that generates a cash inflow.

Bonds Payable   Bonds payable decreased $40,000 during the year. As indicated from the additional information, bonds were redeemed at their book value. This financing transaction used cash of $40,000.

Common Stock   The common stock account increased $160,000 during the year. As indicated from the additional information, common stock of $160,000 was issued at par. This is a financing transaction that provided cash of $160,000.

Retained Earnings   Retained earnings changed $70,000 ($206,000 − $136,000) during the year. The $70,000 change in retained earnings is the result of net income of $125,000 from operations and the financing activity of paying cash dividends of $55,000.

Statement of Cash Flows

The statement of cash flows as shown in Illustration 17A-11 is prepared by combining the foregoing items.

Illustration 17A-11
Statement of Cash Flows,
Account Services Inc.,
2002

ACCOUNT SERVICES INC. STATEMENT OF CASH FLOWS FOR THE YEAR ENDED DECEMBER 31, 2002 INCREASE (DECREASE) IN CASH		
Cash flows from operating activities		
Net income		$125,000
Adjustments to reconcile net income to net cash provided by operating activities:		
Depreciation expense	$ 33,000	
Increase in accounts receivable	(42,000)	
Increase in inventories	(54,000)	
Decrease in prepaid expenses	2,000	
Decrease in accounts payable	(7,000)	
Loss on sale of equipment	2,000	(66,000)
Net cash provided by operating activities		59,000
Cash flows from investing activities		
Sale of land	25,000	
Sale of equipment	34,000	
Purchase of equipment	(166,000)	
Net cash used by investing activities		(107,000)
Cash flows from financing activities		
Redemption of bonds	(40,000)	
Sale of common stock	160,000	
Payment of dividends	(55,000)	
Net cash provided by financing activities		65,000
Net increase in cash		17,000
Cash, January 1, 2002		37,000
Cash, December 31, 2002		$ 54,000

SPECIAL PROBLEMS IN STATEMENT PREPARATION

Some of the special problems related to preparing the statement of cash flows were discussed in connection with the preceding illustrations. Other problems that arise with some frequency in the preparation of this statement may be categorized as follows.

OBJECTIVE 12
Identify special problems in preparing a statement of cash flows.

1. Adjustments similar to depreciation.
2. Accounts receivable (net).
3. Other working capital changes.
4. Net losses.
5. Gains.
6. Significant noncash transactions.

Adjustments Similar to Depreciation

Depreciation expense is the most common adjustment to net income that is made to arrive at net cash flow from operating activities. But there are numerous other noncash expense or revenue items. Examples of expense items that must be added back to net income are the **amortization of intangible assets** such as patents, and the **amortization of deferred costs** such as bond issue costs. These charges to expense involve expenditures made in prior periods that are being amortized currently and reduce net income without affecting cash in the current period.

Also, **amortization of bond discount or premium** on long-term bonds payable affects the amount of interest expense, but neither changes cash. As a result, amortization of these items should be added back to (discount) or subtracted from (premium) net income to arrive at net cash flow from operating activities. In a similar manner, **changes in deferred income taxes** affect net income but have no effect on cash. For example, Kroger Co. at one time experienced an increase in its liability for deferred taxes of approximately $42 million. Tax expense was increased and net income was decreased by this amount, but cash was not affected. Therefore, $42 million would be added back to net income on Kroger's statement of cash flows.

Another common adjustment to net income is **a change related to an investment in common stock** when income or loss is accrued under the equity method. Recall that under the equity method, the investor (1) debits the investment account and credits revenue for its share of the investee's net income, and (2) credits dividends received to the investment account. Therefore, the net increase in the investment account does not affect cash flow and must be deducted from net income in arriving at net cash flow from operating activities. To illustrate, assume that Victor Co. owns 40 percent of Milo Inc., and during the year Milo Inc. reports net income of $100,000 and pays a cash dividend of $30,000. This information is reported in Victor Co.'s statement of cash flows as a deduction from net income in the following manner—Equity in earnings of Milo Co., net of dividends, $28,000.

If the fair value method is used, income of the investee is not recognized, and any cash dividend received is recorded as revenue. In this case, no adjustment to net income in the statement of cash flows is necessary for any cash dividend received.

Accounts Receivable (Net)

Up to this point, we have assumed that no allowance for doubtful accounts—a contra account—was needed to offset accounts receivable. However, if an allowance for doubtful accounts is needed, how does it affect the determination of net cash flow from operating activities? For example, assume that Redmark Co. reports net income of $40,000 and has the following balances related to accounts receivable.

Illustration 17A-12
Accounts Receivable
Balances, Redmark Co.

	2004	2003	Change Increase/Decrease
Accounts receivable	$105,000	$90,000	$15,000 Increase
Allowance for doubtful accounts	10,000	4,000	6,000 Increase
Accounts receivable (net)	$ 95,000	$86,000	9,000 Increase

Because an increase in the Allowance for Doubtful Accounts is caused by a charge to bad debts expense, an increase in the Allowance for Doubtful Accounts should be added back to net income to arrive at net cash flow from operating activities. One method for presenting this information in a statement of cash flows is shown in Illustration 17A-13.

As indicated, the increase in the Allowance for Doubtful Accounts balance is caused by a charge to bad debt expense for the year. Because bad debt expense is a noncash charge, it must be added back to net income in arriving at net cash flow from operating activities.

REDMARK CO.
STATEMENT OF CASH FLOWS (PARTIAL)
FOR THE YEAR 2004

Cash flows from operating activities		
Net income		$40,000
Adjustments to reconcile net income to net cash provided by operating activities:		
Increase in accounts receivable	$(15,000)	
Increase in allowance for doubtful accounts	6,000	(9,000)
		$31,000

Instead of separately analyzing the allowance account, a short-cut approach is to net the allowance balance against the receivable balance and compare the change in accounts receivable on a net basis. This presentation would be as follows.

REDMARK CO.
STATEMENT OF CASH FLOWS (PARTIAL)
FOR THE YEAR 2004

Cash flows from operating activities	
Net income	$40,000
Adjustments to reconcile net income to net cash provided by operating activities:	
Increase in accounts receivable (net)	(9,000)
	$31,000

This short-cut procedure works also if the change in the allowance account was caused by a writeoff of accounts receivable. In this case, both the Accounts Receivable and the Allowance for Doubtful Accounts are reduced, and no effect on cash flows occurs. Because of its simplicity, **you should use the net approach on your homework assignments**.

Other Working Capital Changes

Up to this point, all of the changes in working capital items (current asset and current liability items) have been handled as adjustments to net income in determining net cash flow from operating activities. You must be careful, however, because **some changes in working capital, although they affect cash, do not affect net income**. Generally, these are investing or financing activities of a current nature.

One example would be the purchase of **short-term available-for-sale securities**. For example, the purchase of short-term available-for-sale securities for $50,000 cash has no effect on net income but it does cause a $50,000 decrease in cash.[5] This transaction is reported as a cash flow from investing activities and reported gross as follows.[6]

Cash flows from investing activities	
Purchase of short-term available-for-sale securities	$(50,000)

[5]If the basis of the statement of cash flows is cash **and cash equivalents** and the short-term investment is considered a cash equivalent, then nothing would be reported in the statement because the balance of cash and cash equivalents does not change as a result of this transaction.

[6]"Accounting for Certain Investments in Debt and Equity Securities," *Statement of Financial Accounting Standards No. 115* (Norwalk, CT: 1993), par. 118.

Another example is the issuance of a **short-term nontrade note payable** for cash. This change in a working capital item has no effect on income from operations but it increases cash by the amount of the note payable. For example, the issuance of a $10,000 short-term note payable for cash is reported in the statement of cash flows as follows.

Cash flows from financing activities
Issuance of short-term note $10,000

Another change in a working capital item that has no effect on income from operations or on cash is a **cash dividend payable**. Although the cash dividends when paid will be reported as a financing activity, the declared but unpaid dividend is not reported on the statement of cash flows.

Because **trading securities** are bought and held principally for the purpose of selling them in the near term, the cash flows from purchases and sales of trading securities should be classified as cash flows from **operating activities**.[7]

Net Losses

If an enterprise reports a net loss instead of a net income, the net loss must be adjusted for those items that do not result in a cash inflow or outflow. The net loss after adjusting for the charges or credits not affecting cash may result in a negative or a positive cash flow from operating activities.

For example, if the net loss was $50,000 and the total amount of charges to be added back was $60,000, then net cash provided by operating activities is $10,000, as shown in this computation.

Illustration 17A-15
Computation of Net Cash Flow from Operating Activities—Cash Inflow

Net loss		$(50,000)
Adjustments to reconcile net income to net cash provided by operating activities:		
Depreciation of plant assets	$55,000	
Amortization of patents	5,000	60,000
Net cash provided by operating activities		$ 10,000

If the company experiences a net loss of $80,000 and the total amount of the charges to be added back is $25,000, the presentation appears as follows.

Illustration 17A-16
Computation of Net Cash Flow from Operating Activities—Cash Outflow

Net loss	$(80,000)
Adjustments to reconcile net income to net cash used by operating activities:	
Depreciation of plant assets	25,000
Net cash used by operating activities	$(55,000)

Although it is not illustrated in this appendix, a negative cash flow may result even if the company reports a net income.

Gains

In the illustration for Account Services Inc., the company experienced a loss of $2,000 from the sale of equipment. This loss was added to net income to compute net cash

[7]Ibid., par. 118.

flow from operating activities because **the loss is a noncash charge in the income state-ment.** If a **gain** from a sale of equipment is experienced, it too requires that net income be adjusted. Because the gain is reported in the statement of cash flows as part of the cash proceeds from the sale of equipment under investing activities, **the gain is de-ducted from net income to avoid double counting**—once as part of net income, and again as part of the cash proceeds from the sale.

Significant Noncash Transactions

Because the statement of cash flows reports only the effects of operating, investing, and financing activities in terms of cash flows, some **significant noncash transactions** and other events that are investing or financing activities are omitted from the body of the statement. Among the more common of these noncash transactions that should be re-ported or disclosed in some manner are the following.

Examples of Cash Flow Statements, Including Disclosure of Significant Noncash Transactions

1. Acquisition of assets by assuming liabilities (including capital lease obligations) or by issuing equity securities.
2. Exchanges of nonmonetary assets.
3. Refinancing of long-term debt.
4. Conversion of debt or preferred stock to common stock.
5. Issuance of equity securities to retire debt.

   These noncash items are not to be incorporated in the statement of cash flows. If material in amount, these disclosures may be either narrative or summarized in a separate schedule at the bottom of the statement, or they may appear in a separate note or supplementary schedule to the financial statements. The presentation of these sig-nificant noncash transactions or other events in a separate schedule at the bottom of the statement of cash flows is shown as follows.

Net increase in cash	$3,717,000
Cash at beginning of year	5,208,000
Cash at end of year	$8,925,000
Noncash investing and financing activities	
Purchase of land and building through issuance of 250,000 shares	
of common stock	$1,750,000
Exchange of Steadfast, NY, land for Bedford, PA, land	$2,000,000
Conversion of 12% bonds to 50,000 shares of common stock	$ 500,000

Illustration 17A-17
Schedule Presentation of Noncash Investing and Financing Activities

   Alternatively, these noncash transactions might be presented in a separate note, as follows.

Note G: Significant noncash transactions. During the year the company engaged in the following significant noncash investing and financing transactions:	
Issued 250,000 shares of common stock to purchase land and building	$1,750,000
Exchanged land in Steadfast, NY, for land in Bedford, PA	$2,000,000
Converted 12% bonds due 2004 to 50,000 shares of common stock	$ 500,000

Illustration 17A-18
Note Presentation of Noncash Investing and Financing Activities

Certain other significant noncash transactions or other events are generally not reported in conjunction with the statement of cash flows. Examples of these types of transactions are **stock dividends**, **stock splits**, **and restrictions on retained earnings**. These items, neither financing nor investing activities, are generally reported in conjunction with the statement of stockholders' equity or schedules and notes pertaining to changes in capital accounts.

<table>
<tr><td>

KEY TERMS

cash equivalents, *852(n)*
direct method, *856*
financing activities, *852*
indirect method, *857*
investing activities, *852*
operating activities, *852*
significant noncash transactions, *865*
statement of cash flows, *852*

</td></tr>
</table>

SUMMARY OF LEARNING OBJECTIVES

⑧ Identify the major classifications of cash flows. The cash flows are classified as: (1) *Operating activities*—transactions that result in the revenues, expenses, gains, and losses that determine net income. (2) *Investing activities*—lending money and collecting on those loans, and acquiring and disposing of investments, plant assets, and intangible assets. (3) *Financing activities*—obtaining cash from creditors and repaying loans, issuing and reacquiring capital stock, and paying cash dividends.

⑨ Differentiate between net income and net cash flows from operating activities. Net income on an accrual basis must be adjusted to determine net cash flow from operating activities because some expenses and losses do not cause cash outflows and some revenues and gains do not provide cash inflows.

⑩ Contrast the direct and indirect methods of calculating net cash flow from operating activities. Under the direct approach, major classes of operating cash receipts and cash disbursements are calculated. The computations are summarized in a schedule of changes from the accrual to the cash basis income statement. The indirect method adds back to net income the noncash expenses and losses and subtracts the noncash revenues and gains.

⑪ Prepare a statement of cash flows. Preparing the statement involves three major steps: (1) Determine the change in cash. This is the difference between the beginning and the ending cash balance shown on the comparative balance sheets. (2) Determine the net cash flow from operating activities. This procedure is complex; it involves analyzing not only the current year's income statement but also the comparative balance sheets and the selected transaction data. (3) Determine cash flows from investing and financing activities. All other changes in the balance sheet accounts must be analyzed to determine the effects on cash.

⑫ Identify special problems in preparing a statement of cash flows. These special problems are: (1) adjustments similar to depreciation; (2) accounts receivable (net); (3) other working capital changes; (4) net losses; (5) gains; and (6) significant noncash transactions.

Note: All **asterisked** Brief Exercises, Exercises, and Problems relate to material contained in the appendix to the chapter.

QUESTIONS

1 In recent years, the *Wall Street Journal* has indicated that many companies have changed their accounting principles. What are the major reasons why companies change accounting methods?

2 State how each of the following items is reflected in the financial statements.

(a) Change from straight-line method of depreciation to sum-of-the-years'-digits.

(b) Change from FIFO to LIFO method for inventory valuation purposes.

(c) Charge for failure to record depreciation in a previous period.

(d) Litigation won in current year, related to prior period.

(e) Change in the realizability of certain receivables.

(f) Writeoff of receivables.

(g) Change from the percentage-of-completion to the completed-contract method for reporting net income.

3 What are the advantages of employing the current or catch-up method for handling changes in accounting principle?

4 Explain when pro-forma amounts are reported, and why these amounts are useful to financial statement readers.

5 Define a change in estimate and provide an illustration. When is a change in accounting estimate affected by a change in accounting principle?

6 Indicate how the following items are recorded in the accounting records in the current year of Tami Agler Co.

(a) Large writeoff of goodwill.

(b) A change in depreciating plant assets from accelerated depreciation to the straight-line method.

(c) Large writeoff of inventories because of obsolescence.

(d) Change from the cash basis to accrual basis of accounting.

(e) Change from LIFO to FIFO method for inventory valuation purposes.

(f) Change in the estimate of service lives for plant assets.

7 E. A. Basler Inc. wishes to change from the sum-of-the-years'-digits to the straight-line depreciation method for financial reporting purposes. The auditor indicates that a change would be permitted only if it is to a preferable method. What difficulties develop in assessing preferability?

8 Discuss how a change to the LIFO method of inventory valuation is handled.

9 Clara Beverage Co., a closely held corporation, is in the process of preparing financial statements to accompany an offering of its common stock. The company at this time has decided to switch from the accelerated depreciation method to the straight-line method of depreciation to better present its financial operations. How should this change in accounting principle be reported in the financial statements?

10 Discuss and illustrate how a correction of an error in previously issued financial statements should be handled.

11 Lou Brady Corp. failed to record accrued salaries for 2001, $2,000; 2002, $2,100; and 2003, $3,900. What is the amount of the overstatement or understatement of Retained Earnings at December 31, 2004?

12 At December 31, 2003, Amad Company had 600,000 shares of common stock issued and outstanding, 400,000 of which had been issued and outstanding throughout the year, and 200,000 of which were issued on October 1, 2003. Net income for 2003 was $3,000,000, and dividends declared on preferred stock were $400,000. Compute Amad's earnings per common share (round to the nearest penny).

13 What effect do stock dividends or stock splits have on the computation of the weighted average number of shares outstanding?

14 Define the following terms.

(a) Basic earnings per share.

(b) Potentially dilutive security.

(c) Diluted earnings per share.

(d) Complex capital structure.

(e) Potential common stock.

15 What are the computational guidelines for determining whether a convertible security is to be reported as part of diluted earnings per share?

16 Discuss why options and warrants may be considered potentially dilutive common shares for the computation of diluted earnings per share.

17 Explain how convertible securities are determined to be potentially dilutive common shares and how those convertible senior securities that are not considered to be potentially dilutive common shares enter into the determination of earnings per share data.

18 Explain the treasury stock method as it applies to options and warrants in computing dilutive earnings per share data.

19 What is meant by the term antidilution? Give an example.

20 What type of earnings per share presentation is required in a complex capital structure?

★21 Differentiate between investing activities, financing activities, and operating activities.

★22 What are the major sources of cash (inflows) in a statement of cash flows? What are the major uses (outflows) of cash?

★23 Identify and explain the major steps involved in preparing the statement of cash flows.

★24 Unlike the other major financial statements, the statement of cash flows is not prepared from the adjusted trial balance. From what sources does the information to prepare this statement come and what information does each source provide?

★25 Differentiate between the direct method and the indirect method by discussing each method.

BRIEF EXERCISES

BE17-1 Larry Beaty Corporation decided at the beginning of 2004 to change from double-declining balance depreciation to straight-line depreciation for financial reporting. The company will continue to use an accelerated method for tax purposes. For years prior to 2004, depreciation expense under the two methods was as follows: double-declining balance $128,000, and straight-line $80,000. The tax rate is 35%. Prepare Beaty's 2004 journal entry to record the change in accounting principle.

BE17-2 Robert Boey, Inc. changed from the LIFO cost flow assumption to the FIFO cost flow assumption in 2004. The increase in the prior year's income before taxes is $1,000,000. The tax rate is 40%. Prepare Boey's 2004 journal entry to record the change in accounting principle.

BE17-3 Nancy Castle Company purchased a computer system for $60,000 on January 1, 2002. It was depreciated based on a 7-year life and an $18,000 salvage value. On January 1, 2004; Castle revised these estimates to a total useful life of 4 years and a salvage value of $10,000. Prepare Castle's entry to record 2004 depreciation expense.

BE17-4 In 2004, John Hiatt Corporation discovered that equipment purchased on January 1, 2002, for $75,000 was expensed at that time. The equipment should have been depreciated over 5 years, with no salvage value. The effective tax rate is 30%. Prepare Hiatt's 2004 journal entry to correct the error.

BE17-5 Haley Corporation had 2004 net income of $1,200,000. During 2004, Haley paid a dividend of $2 per share on 100,000 shares of preferred stock. During 2004, Haley had outstanding 250,000 shares of common stock. Compute Haley's 2004 earnings per share.

BE17-6 Barkley Corporation had 120,000 shares of stock outstanding on January 1, 2004. On May 1, 2004, Barkley issued 45,000 shares. On July 1, Barkley purchased 10,000 treasury shares, which were reissued on October 1. Compute Barkley's weighted average number of shares outstanding for 2004.

BE17-7 Green Corporation had 200,000 shares of common stock outstanding on January 1, 2004. On May 1, Green issued 30,000 shares. **(a)** Compute the weighted average number of shares outstanding if the 30,000 shares were issued for cash. **(b)** Compute the weighted average number of shares outstanding if the 30,000 shares were issued in a stock dividend.

BE17-8 Strickland Corporation earned net income of $300,000 in 2004 and had 100,000 shares of common stock outstanding throughout the year. Also outstanding all year was $400,000 of 10% bonds, which are convertible into 16,000 shares of common. Strickland's tax rate is 40%. Compute Strickland's 2004 diluted earnings per share.

BE17-9 Sabonis Corporation reported net income of $400,000 in 2004 and had 50,000 shares of common stock outstanding throughout the year. Also outstanding all year were 5,000 shares of cumulative preferred stock, each convertible into 2 shares of common. The preferred stock pays an annual dividend of $5 per share. Sabonis' tax rate is 40%. Compute Sabonis' 2004 diluted earnings per share.

BE17-10 Sarunas Corporation reported net income of $300,000 in 2004 and had 200,000 shares of common stock outstanding throughout the year. Also outstanding all year were 30,000 options to purchase common stock at $10 per share. The average market price of the stock during the year was $15. Compute diluted earnings per share.

*BE17-11 Red October Corporation reported net income of $50,000 in 2004. Depreciation expense was $17,000. The following working capital accounts changed:

Accounts receivable	$11,000 increase
Available-for-sale securities	16,000 increase
Inventory	7,400 increase
Nontrade note payable	15,000 decrease
Accounts payable	9,300 increase

Compute net cash provided by operating activities.

*BE17-12 American Gladhanders Corporation had the following activities in 2004.

Sale of land	$130,000
Purchase of inventory	$845,000
Purchase of treasury stock	$ 72,000
Purchase of equipment	$415,000
Issuance of common stock	$320,000
Purchase of available-for-sale securities	$ 59,000

Compute the amount American Gladhanders should report as net cash provided (used) by investing activities in its statement of cash flows.

*BE17-13   Chrono Trigger Corporation had the following activities in 2004.

Payment of accounts payable,	$770,000
Issuance of common stock,	$250,000
Payment of dividends,	$300,000
Collection of note receivable,	$100,000
Issuance of bonds payable,	$510,000
Purchase of treasury stock,	$ 46,000

Compute the amount Chrono Trigger should report as net cash provided (used) by financing activities in its 2004 statement of cash flows.

EXERCISES

E17-1   (Error and Change in Principle—Depreciation)   Joy Cunningham Co. purchased a machine on January 1, 2001, for $550,000. At that time it was estimated that the machine would have a 10-year life and no salvage value. On December 31, 2004, the firm's accountant found that the entry for depreciation expense had been omitted in 2002. In addition, management has informed the accountant that they plan to switch to straight-line depreciation, starting with the year 2004. At present, the company uses the sum-of-the-years'-digits method for depreciating equipment.

Instructions
Prepare the general journal entries the accountant should make at December 31, 2004. (Ignore tax effects.)

E17-2   (Change in Principle and Change in Estimate—Depreciation)   Kathleen Cole Inc. acquired the following assets in January of 2001.

Equipment, estimated service life, 5 years; salvage value, $15,000	$525,000
Building, estimated service life, 30 years; no salvage value	$693,000

The equipment has been depreciated using the sum-of-the-years'-digits method for the first 3 years for financial reporting purposes. In 2004, the company decided to change the method of computing depreciation to the straight-line method for the equipment, but no change was made in the estimated service life or salvage value. It was also decided to change the total estimated service life of the building from 30 years to 40 years, with no change in the estimated salvage value. The building is depreciated on the straight-line method.

The company has 100,000 shares of capital stock outstanding. Results of operations for 2004 and 2003 are shown below.

	2004	2003
Income before cumulative effect of change in computing depreciation for 2004: depreciation for 2004 has been computed on the straight-line basis for both the equipment and building[a]	$385,000	$380,000
Income per share before cumulative effect of change in computing depreciation for 2004	$3.85	$3.80

[a]The computation for depreciation expense for 2004 and 2003 for the building was based on the original estimate of service life for 30 years.

Instructions
(a)   Compute the cumulative effect of the change in accounting principle to be reported in the income statement for 2004, and prepare the journal entry to record the change. (Ignore tax effects.)

(b)   Present comparative data for the years 2003 and 2004, starting with income before cumulative effect of accounting change. Prepare pro-forma data. Do not prepare the footnote. (Ignore tax effects.)

E17-3 (Change in Estimate—Depreciation) Peter M. Dell Co. purchased equipment for $510,000 which was estimated to have a useful life of 10 years with a salvage value of $10,000 at the end of that time. Depreciation has been entered for 7 years on a straight-line basis. In 2004, it is determined that the total estimated life should be 15 years with a salvage value of $5,000 at the end of that time.

Instructions

(a) Prepare the entry (if any) to correct the prior years' depreciation.

(b) Prepare the entry to record depreciation for 2004.

E17-4 (Change in Principle—Depreciation) Gerald Englehart Industries changed from the double-declining balance to the straight-line method in 2004 on all its plant assets. For tax purposes, assume that the amount of tax depreciation is higher than the double-declining balance depreciation for each of the 3 years. The appropriate information related to this change is as follows.

Year	Double-Declining Balance Depreciation	Straight-Line Depreciation	Difference
2002	$250,000	$125,000	$125,000
2003	225,000	125,000	100,000
2004	202,500	125,000	77,500

Net income for 2003 was reported at $270,000; net income for 2004 was reported at $300,000, excluding any adjustment for the cumulative effect of a change in depreciation methods. The straight-line method of depreciation was employed in computing net income for 2004.

Instructions

(a) Assuming a tax rate of 34%, what is the amount of the cumulative effect adjustment in 2004?

(b) Prepare the journal entry(ies) to record the cumulative effect adjustment in the accounting records.

(c) Starting with income before cumulative effect of change in accounting principle, prepare the remaining portion of the income statement for 2003 and 2004. Indicate the pro-forma net income that should be reported. Ignore per share computations and note disclosures.

E17-5 (Change in Principle—Long-term Contracts) Pam Erickson Construction Company changed from the completed-contract to the percentage-of-completion method of accounting for long-term construction contracts during 2004. For tax purposes, the company employs the completed-contract method and will continue this approach in the future. (*Hint:* Adjust all tax consequences through the Deferred Tax Liability account.) The appropriate information related to this change is as follows.

	Pretax Income from:		
	Percentage-of-Completion	Completed-Contract	Difference
2003	$780,000	$590,000	$190,000
2004	700,000	480,000	220,000

Instructions

(a) Assuming that the tax rate is 35%, what is the amount of net income that would be reported in 2004?

(b) What entry(ies) are necessary to adjust the accounting records for the change in accounting principle?

E17-6 (Various Changes in Principle—Inventory Methods) Below is the net income of Anita Ferreri Instrument Co., a private corporation, computed under the three inventory methods using a periodic system.

	FIFO	Average Cost	LIFO
2001	$26,000	$24,000	$20,000
2002	30,000	25,000	21,000
2003	28,000	27,000	24,000
2004	34,000	30,000	26,000

Instructions (Ignore tax considerations.)

(a) Assume that in 2004 Ferreri decided to change from the FIFO method to the average cost method of pricing inventories. Prepare the journal entry necessary for the change that took place during 2004, and show all the appropriate information needed for reporting on a comparative basis.

(b) Assume that in 2004 Ferreri, which had been using the LIFO method since incorporation in 2001, changed to the FIFO method of pricing inventories. Prepare the journal entry necessary for the change, and show all the appropriate information needed for reporting on a comparative basis.

E17-7 (Change in Principle and Error; Financial Statements) Presented below are the comparative statements for Denise Habbe Inc.

	2004	2003
Sales	$340,000	$270,000
Cost of sales	200,000	142,000
Gross profit	140,000	128,000
Expenses	88,000	50,000
Net income	$ 52,000	$ 78,000
Retained earnings (Jan. 1)	$125,000	$ 72,000
Net income	52,000	78,000
Dividends	(30,000)	(25,000)
Retained earnings (Dec. 31)	$147,000	$125,000

The following additional information is provided.

1. In 2004, Denise Habbe Inc. decided to switch its depreciation method from sum-of-the-years'-digits to the straight-line method. The differences in the two depreciation methods for the assets involved are:

	2004	2003
Sum-of-the-years'-digits	$30,000ª	$40,000
Straight-line	25,000	25,000

ªThe 2004 income statement contains depreciation expense of $30,000.

2. In 2004, the company discovered that the ending inventory for 2003 was overstated by $24,000; ending inventory for 2004 is correctly stated.

Instructions

(a) Prepare the revised income and retained earnings statement for 2003 and 2004, assuming comparative statements (Ignore income tax effects.) Do not prepare footnotes or pro-forma amounts.

(b) Prepare the revised income and retained earnings statement for 2004, assuming a noncomparative presentation. (Ignore income tax effects.) Do not prepare footnotes or pro-forma amounts.

E17-8 (Weighted Average Number of Shares) Newton Inc. uses a calendar year for financial reporting. The company is authorized to issue 9,000,000 shares of $10 par common stock. At no time has Newton issued any potentially dilutive securities. Listed below is a summary of Newton's common stock activities.

1. Number of common shares issued and outstanding at December 31, 2001	2,000,000
2. Shares issued as a result of a 10% stock dividend on September 30, 2002	200,000
3. Shares issued for cash on March 31, 2003	2,000,000
Number of common shares issued and outstanding at December 31, 2003	4,200,000

4. A 2-for-1 stock split of Newton's common stock took place on March 31, 2004.

Instructions

(a) Compute the weighted average number of common shares used in computing earnings per common share for 2002 on the 2003 comparative income statement.

(b) Compute the weighted average number of common shares used in computing earnings per common share for 2003 on the 2003 comparative income statement.

(c) Compute the weighted average number of common shares to be used in computing earnings per common share for 2003 on the 2004 comparative income statement.

(d) Compute the weighted average number of common shares to be used in computing earnings per common share for 2004 on the 2004 comparative income statement.

(CMA adapted)

E17-9 (EPS: Simple Capital Structure) On January 1, 2004, Wilke Corp. had 480,000 shares of common stock outstanding. During 2004, it had the following transactions that affected the common stock account.

February 1	Issued 120,000 shares
March 1	Issued a 10% stock dividend
May 1	Acquired 100,000 shares of treasury stock
June 1	Issued a 3-for-1 stock split
October 1	Reissued 60,000 shares of treasury stock

Instructions

(a) Determine the weighted average number of shares outstanding as of December 31, 2004.

(b) Assume that Wilke Corp. earned net income of $3,456,000 during 2004. In addition, it had 100,000 shares of 9%, $100 par nonconvertible, noncumulative preferred stock outstanding for the entire year. Because of liquidity considerations, however, the company did not declare and pay a preferred dividend in 2004. Compute earnings per share for 2004, using the weighted average number of shares determined in part (a).

(c) Assume the same facts as in part (b), except that the preferred stock was cumulative. Compute earnings per share for 2004.

(d) Assume the same facts as in part (b), except that net income included an extraordinary gain of $864,000 and a loss from discontinued operations of $432,000. Both items are net of applicable income taxes. Compute earnings per share for 2004.

E17-10 (EPS: Simple Capital Structure) Ace Company had 200,000 shares of common stock outstanding on December 31, 2004. During the year 2005 the company issued 8,000 shares on May 1 and retired 14,000 shares on October 31. For the year 2005 Ace Company reported net income of $249,690 after a casualty loss of $40,600 (net of tax).

Instructions

What earnings per share data should be reported at the bottom of its income statement, assuming that the casualty loss is extraordinary?

E17-11 (EPS: Simple Capital Structure) Flagstad Inc. presented the following data.

Net income	$2,500,000
Preferred stock: 50,000 shares outstanding,	
$100 par, 8% cumulative, not convertible	5,000,000
Common stock: Shares outstanding 1/1	750,000
Issued for cash, 5/1	300,000
Acquired treasury stock for cash, 8/1	150,000
2-for-1 stock split, 10/1	

Instructions

Compute earnings per share.

E17-12 (EPS with Convertible Bonds, Various Situations) In 2003 Bonaparte Enterprises issued, at par, 60 $1,000, 8% bonds, each convertible into 100 shares of common stock. Bonaparte had revenues of $17,500 and expenses other than interest and taxes of $8,400 for 2004. (Assume that the tax rate is 40%.) Throughout 2004, 2,000 shares of common stock were outstanding; none of the bonds was converted or redeemed.

Instructions

(a) Compute diluted earnings per share for 2004.

(b) Assume the same facts as those assumed for part (a), except that the 60 bonds were issued on September 1, 2004 (rather than in 2003), and none have been converted or redeemed.

(c) Assume the same facts as assumed for part (a), except that 20 of the 60 bonds were actually converted on July 1, 2003.

E17-13 (EPS with Convertible Bonds and Preferred Stock) Simon Corporation issued 10-year, $5,000,000 par, 7% callable convertible subordinated debentures on January 2, 2003. The bonds have a par value of $1,000, with interest payable annually. The current conversion ratio is 14:1, and in 2 years it will increase to 18:1. At the date of issue, the bonds were sold at 98. Bond discount is amortized on a straight-line basis. Simon's effective tax was 35%. Net income in 2003 was $9,500,000, and the company had 2,000,000 shares outstanding during the entire year.

Instructions
(a) Prepare a schedule to compute both basic and diluted earnings per share.
(b) Discuss how the schedule would differ if the security was 7% cumulative convertible preferred stock.

E17-14 (EPS with Convertible Bonds and Preferred Stock) On January 1, 2003, Crocker Company issued 10-year, $2,000,000 face value, 6% cumulative bonds, at par. Each $1,000 bond is convertible into 15 shares of Crocker common stock. Crocker's net income in 2003 was $300,000, and its tax rate was 40%. The company had 100,000 common stock outstanding throughout 2003. None of the bonds were exercised in 2003.

Instructions
(a) Compute diluted earnings per share for 2003.
(b) Compute diluted earnings per share for 2003, assuming the same facts as above, except that $1,000,000 of 6% cumulative convertible preferred stock was issued instead of the bonds. Each $100 preferred share is convertible into 5 shares of Crocker common stock.

E17-15 (EPS with Options, Various Situations) Venzuela Company's net income for 2003 is $50,000. The only potentially dilutive securities outstanding were 1,000 options issued during 2002, each exercisable for one share at $6. None has been exercised, and 10,000 shares of common were outstanding during 2003. The average market price of Venzuela's stock during 2003 was $20.

Instructions
(a) Compute diluted earnings per share. (Round to nearest cent.)
(b) Assume the same facts as those assumed for part (a), except that the 1,000 options were issued on October 1, 2003 (rather than in 2002). The average market price during the last 3 months of 2003 was $20.

E17-16 (EPS with Warrants) Howat Corporation earned $360,000 during a period when it had an average of 100,000 shares of common stock outstanding. The common stock sold at an average market price of $15 per share during the period. Also outstanding were 15,000 warrants that could be exercised to purchase one share of common stock for $10 for each warrant exercised.

Instructions
(a) Are the warrants dilutive?
(b) Compute basic earnings per share.
(c) Compute diluted earnings per share.

*E17-17 (Statement Presentation of Transactions—Indirect Method) Each of the following items must be considered in preparing a statement of cash flows (indirect method) for Turbulent Indigo Inc. for the year ended December 31, 2003.

(a) Plant assets that had cost $20,000 6 years before and were being depreciated on a straight-line basis over 10 years with no estimated scrap value were sold for $5,300.
(b) During the year, 10,000 shares of common stock with a stated value of $10 a share were issued for $43 a share.
(c) Uncollectible accounts receivable in the amount of $27,000 were written off against the Allowance for Doubtful Accounts.
(d) The company sustained a net loss for the year of $50,000. Depreciation amounted to $22,000, and a gain of $9,000 was realized on the sale of land for $39,000 cash.
(e) A 3-month U.S. Treasury bill was purchased for $100,000. The company uses a cash and cash equivalents basis for its cash flow statement.

(f) Patent amortization for the year was $20,000.

(g) The company exchanged common stock for a 70% interest in Tabasco Co. for $900,000.

(h) During the year, treasury stock costing $47,000 was purchased.

Instructions

State where each item is to be shown in the statement of cash flows, if at all.

*E17-18 (SCF—Indirect Method) Condensed financial data of Pat Metheny Company for 2004 and 2003 are presented below.

PAT METHENY COMPANY
COMPARATIVE BALANCE SHEET
AS OF DECEMBER 31, 2004 AND 2003

	2004	2003
Cash	$ 1,800	$ 1,150
Receivables	1,750	1,300
Inventory	1,600	1,900
Plant assets	1,900	1,700
Accumulated depreciation	(1,200)	(1,170)
Long-term investments (Held-to-maturity)	1,300	1,420
	$ 7,150	$ 6,300
Accounts payable	$ 1,200	$ 900
Accrued liabilities	200	250
Bonds payable	1,400	1,550
Capital stock	1,900	1,700
Retained earnings	2,450	1,900
	$ 7,150	$ 6,300

PAT METHENY COMPANY
INCOME STATEMENT
FOR THE YEAR ENDED DECEMBER 31, 2004

Sales	$6,900
Cost of goods sold	4,700
Gross margin	2,200
Selling and administrative expense	930
Income from operations	1,270
Other revenues and gains	
Gain on sale of investments	80
Income before tax	1,350
Income tax expense	540
Net income	810
Cash dividends	260
Income retained in business	$ 550

Additional information:

During the year, $70 of common stock was issued in exchange for plant assets. No plant assets were sold in 2004.

Instructions

Prepare a statement of cash flows using the indirect method.

*E17-19 **(SCF—Indirect Method)** Presented below are data taken from the records of Antonio Brasileiro Company.

	December 31, 2004	December 31, 2003
Cash	$ 15,000	$ 8,000
Current assets other than cash	85,000	60,000
Long-term investments	10,000	53,000
Plant assets	335,000	215,000
	$445,000	$336,000
Accumulated depreciation	$ 20,000	$ 40,000
Current liabilities	40,000	22,000
Bonds payable	75,000	–0–
Capital stock	254,000	254,000
Retained earnings	56,000	20,000
	$445,000	$336,000

Additional information:

1. Held-to-maturity securities carried at a cost of $43,000 on December 31, 2003, were sold in 2004 for $34,000. The loss (not extraordinary) was incorrectly charged directly to Retained Earnings.
2. Plant assets that cost $50,000 and were 80% depreciated were sold during 2004 for $8,000. The loss (not extraordinary) was incorrectly charged directly to Retained Earnings.
3. Net income as reported on the income statement for the year was $57,000.
4. Dividends paid amounted to $10,000.
5. Depreciation charged for the year was $20,000.

Instructions
Prepare a statement of cash flows for the year 2004 using the indirect method.

PROBLEMS

P17-1 **(Change in Estimate, Principle, and Error Correction)** Roland Company is in the process of having its financial statements audited for the first time as of December 31, 2003. The auditor has found the following items that occurred in previous years.

1. Roland purchased equipment on January 2, 2000, for $65,000. At that time, the equipment had an estimated useful life of 10 years with a $5,000 salvage value. The equipment is depreciated on a straight-line basis. On January 2, 2003, as a result of additional information, the company determined that the equipment had a total estimated useful life of 7 years with a $3,000 salvage value.
2. During 2003 Roland changed from the double-declining balance method for its building to the straight-line method. The auditor provided the following computations which present depreciation on both bases.

	2003	2002	2001
Straight-line	$27,000	$27,000	$27,000
Declining-balance	48,600	54,000	60,000

3. Roland purchased a machine on July 1, 2000, at a cost of $80,000. The machine has a salvage value of $8,000 and a useful life of 8 years. Roland's bookkeeper recorded straight-line depreciation during each year but failed to consider the salvage value.

Instructions
(a) Prepare the necessary journal entries to record each of the preceding changes or errors. Depreciation expense for 2003 has not been recorded.
(b) Compute the 2003 depreciation expense on the equipment.
(c) Show the comparative statements for 2002 and 2003, starting with income before the cumulative effect of change in accounting principle. Income before depreciation expense was $300,000 in 2003, and net income was $210,000 in 2002.

P17-2 (Comprehensive Accounting Change and Error Analysis Problem)   On December 31, 2004, before the books were closed, the management and accountants of Eloise Keltner Inc. made the following determinations about three depreciable assets.

1. Depreciable asset A was purchased January 2, 2001. It originally cost $495,000 and, for depreciation purposes, the straight-line method was originally chosen. The asset was originally expected to be useful for 10 years and to have a zero salvage value. In 2004, the decision was made to change the depreciation method from straight-line to sum-of-the-years'-digits, and the estimates relating to useful life and salvage value remained unchanged.
2. Depreciable asset B was purchased January 3, 2000. It originally cost $120,000 and, for depreciation purposes, the straight-line method was chosen. The asset was originally expected to be useful for 15 years and have a zero salvage value. In 2004, the decision was made to shorten the total life of this asset to 9 years and to estimate the salvage value at $3,000.
3. Depreciable asset C was purchased January 5, 2000. The asset's original cost was $140,000, and this amount was entirely expensed in 2000. This particular asset has a 10-year useful life and no salvage value. The straight-line method was chosen for depreciation purposes.

Additional data:

1. Income in 2004 before depreciation expense amount to $400,000.
2. Depreciation expense on assets other than A, B, and C totaled $55,000 in 2004.
3. Income in 2003 was reported at $370,000.
4. Ignore all income tax effects.
5. 100,000 shares of common stock were outstanding in 2003 and 2004.

Instructions
(a) Prepare all necessary entries in 2004 to record these determinations.
(b) Prepare comparative income statements for Eloise Keltner Inc. for 2003 and 2004, starting with income before the cumulative effects of any change in accounting principle.
(c) Prepare comparative retained earnings statements for Eloise Keltner Inc. for 2003 and 2004. The company had retained earnings of $200,000 at December 31, 2002.

P17-3 (Change in Principle)   Plato Corporation performs year-end planning in November of each year before its calendar year ends in December. The preliminary estimated net income is $3 million. The CFO, Mary Sheets, meets with the company president, S. A. Plato, to review the projected numbers. She presents the following projected information.

PLATO CORPORATION		
PROJECTED INCOME STATEMENT		
FOR THE YEAR ENDED DECEMBER 31, 2003		
Sales		$29,000,000
Cost of goods sold	$14,000,000	
Depreciation	2,600,000	
Operating expenses	6,400,000	23,000,000
Income before income taxes		$ 6,000,000
Provision for income taxes		3,000,000
Net income		$ 3,000,000

PLATO CORPORATION	
SELECTED BALANCE SHEET INFORMATION	
AT DECEMBER 31, 2003	
Estimated cash balance	$ 5,000,000
Available-for-sale securities (at cost)	10,000,000
Security fair value adjustment account (1/1/03)	200,000

Estimated market value at December 31, 2003:

Security	Cost	Estimated Market
A	$ 2,000,000	$ 2,200,000
B	4,000,000	3,900,000
C	3,000,000	3,000,000
D	1,000,000	2,800,000
Total	$10,000,000	$11,900,000

Equipment	$3,000,000
Accumulated depreciation (5-year SL)	1,200,000
New robotic equipment (purchased 1/1/03)	5,000,000
Accumulated depreciation (5-year DDB)	2,000,000

The corporation has never before used robotic equipment, and Sheets assumed an accelerated depreciation method because of the rapidly changing technology in robotic equipment. The company normally uses straight-line depreciation for production equipment.

Plato explains to Sheets that it is important for the corporation to show an $8,000,000 net income before taxes because Plato receives a $1,000,000 bonus if the income before taxes and bonus reaches $8,000,000. He also cautions that he will not pay more than $3,000,000 in income taxes to the government.

Instructions

(a) What can Sheets do within GAAP to accommodate the president's wishes to achieve $8,000,000 income before taxes and bonus? Present the revised income statement based on your decision.

(b) Are the actions ethical? Who are the stakeholders in this decision, and what effect do Sheets' actions have on their interests?

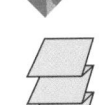

P17-4 (EPS with Complex Capital Structure) Diane Leto, controller at Dewey Yaeger Pharmaceutical Industries, a public company, is currently preparing the calculation for basic and diluted earnings per share and the related disclosure for Yaeger's external financial statements. Below is selected financial information for the fiscal year ended June 30, 2004.

DEWEY YAEGER PHARMACEUTICAL INDUSTRIES	
SELECTED STATEMENT OF	
FINANCIAL POSITION INFORMATION	
JUNE 30, 2004	
Long-term debt	
Notes payable, 10%	$ 1,000,000
7% convertible bonds payable	5,000,000
10% bonds payable	6,000,000
Total long-term debt	$12,000,000
Shareholders' equity	
Preferred stock, 8.5% cumulative, $50 par value, 100,000 authorized, 25,000 shares issued and outstanding	$ 1,250,000
Common stock, $1 par, 10,000,000 shares authorized, 1,000,000 shares issued and outstanding	1,000,000
Additional paid-in capital	4,000,000
Retained earnings	6,000,000
Total shareholders' equity	$12,250,000

The following transactions have also occurred at Yaeger.

1. Options were granted in 2002 to purchase 100,000 shares at $15 per share. Although no options were exercised during 2004, the average price per common share during fiscal year 2004 was $20 per share.

2. Each bond was issued at face value. The 7% convertible debenture will convert into common stock at 50 shares per $1,000 bond. It is exercisable after 5 years and was issued in 2003.
3. The 8.5% preferred stock was issued in 2002.
4. There are no preferred dividends in arrears; however, preferred dividends were not declared in fiscal year 2004.
5. The 1,000,000 shares of common stock were outstanding for the entire 2004 fiscal year.
6. Net income for fiscal year 2004 was $1,500,000, and the average income tax rate is 40%.

Instructions

For the fiscal year ended June 30, 2004, calculate the following for Dewey Yaeger Pharmaceutical Industries.

(a) Basic earnings per share.
(b) Diluted earnings per share.

P17-5 (Simple EPS and EPS with Stock Options) As auditor for Banquo & Associates, you have been assigned to check Duncan Corporation's computation of earnings per share for the current year. The controller, Mac Beth, has supplied you with the following computations.

Net income	$3,374,960
Common shares issued and outstanding:	
Beginning of year	1,285,000
End of year	1,200,000
Average	1,242,500

Earnings per share:

$$\frac{\$3,374,960}{1,242,500} = \$2.72 \text{ per share}$$

You have developed the following additional information.

1. There are no other equity securities in addition to the common shares.
2. There are no options or warrants outstanding to purchase common shares.
3. There are no convertible debt securities.
4. Activity in common shares during the year was as follows.

Outstanding, Jan. 1	1,285,000
Treasury shares acquired, Oct. 1	(250,000)
	1,035,000
Shares reissued, Dec. 1	165,000
Outstanding, Dec. 31	1,200,000

Instructions

(a) On the basis of the information above, do you agree with the controller's computation of earnings per share for the year? If you disagree, prepare a revised computation of earnings per share.
(b) Assume the same facts as those in (a), except that options had been issued to purchase 140,000 shares of common stock at $10 per share. These options were outstanding at the beginning of the year and none had been exercised or canceled during the year. The average market price of the common shares during the year was $25, and the ending market price was $35. Prepare a computation of earnings per share.

P17-6 (EPS Computation of Basic and Diluted EPS) Edmund Halvor of the controller's office of East Aurora Corporation was given the assignment of determining the basic and diluted earnings per share values for the year ending December 31, 2003. Halvor has compiled the information listed below.

1. The company is authorized to issue 8,000,000 shares of $10 par value common stock. As of December 31, 2002, 3,000,000 shares had been issued and were outstanding.
2. The per share market prices of the common stock on selected dates were as follows.

	Price per Share
July 1, 2002	$20.00
January 1, 2003	21.00
April 1, 2003	25.00
July 1, 2003	11.00
August 1, 2003	10.50
November 1, 2003	9.00
December 31, 2003	10.00

3. A total of 700,000 shares of an authorized 1,200,000 shares of convertible preferred stock had been issued on July 1, 2002. The stock was issued at its par value of $25, and it has a cumulative dividend of $3 per share. The stock is convertible into common stock at the rate of one share of convertible preferred for one share of common. The rate of conversion is to be automatically adjusted for stock splits and stock dividends. Dividends are paid quarterly on September 30, December 31, March 31, and June 30.

4. East Aurora Corporation is subject to a 40% income tax rate.

5. The after-tax net income for the year ended December 31, 2003, was $13,550,000.

The following specific activities took place during 2003.

1. January 1: A 5% common stock dividend was issued. The dividend had been declared on December 1, 2002, to all stockholders of record on December 29, 2002.

2. April 1: A total of 200,000 shares of the $3 convertible preferred stock was converted into common stock. The company issued new common stock and retired the preferred stock. This was the only conversion of the preferred stock during 2003.

3. July 1: A 2-for-1 split of the common stock became effective on this date. The board of directors had authorized the split on June 1.

4. August 1: A total of 300,000 shares of common stock were issued to acquire a factory building.

5. November 1: A total of 24,000 shares of common stock were purchased on the open market at $9 per share. These shares were to be held as treasury stock and were still in the treasury as of December 31, 2003.

6. Common stock cash dividends: Cash dividends to common stockholders were declared and paid as follows.
   April 15: $0.30 per share
   October 15: $0.20 per share

7. Preferred stock cash dividends: Cash dividends to preferred stockholders were declared and paid as scheduled.

Instructions

(a) Determine the number of shares used to compute basic earnings per share for the year ended December 31, 2003.

(b) Determine the number of shares used to compute diluted earnings per share for the year ended December 31, 2003.

(c) Compute the adjusted net income to be used as the numerator in the basic earnings per share calculation for the year ended December 31, 2003.

P17-7 **(Computation of Basic and Diluted EPS)** The following information pertains to Prancer Company for 2003.

Net income for the year	$1,200,000
8% convertible bonds issued at par ($1,000 per bond). Each bond is convertible into 40 shares of common stock.	2,000,000
6% convertible, cumulative preferred stock, $100 par value. Each share is convertible into 3 shares of common stock.	3,000,000
Common stock, $10 par value	6,000,000
Common stock options (granted in a prior year) to purchase 50,000 shares of common stock at $20 per share	500,000
Tax rate for 2003	40%
Average market price of common stock	$25 per share

There were no changes during 2003 in the number of common shares, preferred shares, or convertible bonds outstanding. There is no treasury stock.

Instructions

(a) Compute basic earnings per share for 2003.
(b) Compute diluted earnings per share for 2003.

*P17-8 **(SCF)** The following is Method Man Corp.'s comparative balance sheet accounts worksheet at December 31, 2004 and 2003, with a column showing the increase (decrease) from 2003 to 2004.

COMPARATIVE BALANCE SHEET			
	2004	2003	Increase (Decrease)
Cash	$ 807,500	$ 700,000	$ 107,500
Accounts receivable	1,128,000	1,168,000	(40,000)
Inventories	1,850,000	1,715,000	135,000
Property, plant and equipment	3,307,000	2,967,000	340,000
Accumulated depreciation	(1,165,000)	(1,040,000)	(125,000)
Investment in Blige Co.	305,000	275,000	30,000
Loan receivable	262,500	—	262,500
Total assets	$ 6,495,000	$ 5,785,000	$ 710,000
Accounts payable	$ 1,015,000	$ 955,000	$ 60,000
Income taxes payable	30,000	50,000	(20,000)
Dividends payable	80,000	100,000	(20,000)
Capital lease obligation	400,000	—	400,000
Capital stock, common, $1 par	500,000	500,000	—
Additional paid-in capital	1,500,000	1,500,000	—
Retained earnings	2,970,000	2,680,000	290,000
Total liabilities and stockholders' equity	$ 6,495,000	$ 5,785,000	$ 710,000

Additional information:

1. On December 31, 2003, Method Man acquired 25% of Blige Co.'s common stock for $275,000. On that date, the carrying value of Blige's assets and liabilities, which approximated their fair values, was $1,100,000. Blige reported income of $120,000 for the year ended December 31, 2004. No dividend was paid on Blige's common stock during the year.
2. During 2004, Method Man loaned $300,000 to TLC Co., an unrelated company. TLC made the first semi-annual principal repayment of $37,500, plus interest at 10%, on December 31, 2004.
3. On January 2, 2004, Method Man sold equipment costing $60,000, with a carrying amount of $35,000, for $40,000 cash.
4. On December 31, 2004, Method Man entered into a capital lease for an office building. The present value of the annual rental payments is $400,000, which equals the fair value of the building. Method Man made the first rental payment of $60,000 when due on January 2, 2005.
5. Net income for 2004 was $370,000.
6. Method Man declared and paid cash dividends for 2004 and 2003 as follows.

	2004	2003
Declared	December 15, 2004	December 15, 2003
Paid	February 28, 2005	February 28, 2004
Amount	$80,000	$100,000

Instructions

Prepare a statement of cash flows for Method Man Corp. for the year ended December 31, 2004, using the indirect method.

(AICPA adapted)

CONCEPTUAL CASES

C17-1 **(Analysis of Three Accounting Changes and Errors)** Listed below are three independent, unrelated sets of facts relating to accounting changes.

Situation 1 Penelope Millhouse Company is in the process of having its first audit. The company's policy with regard to recognition of revenue is to use the installment method. However, *APB No. 10* states that the installment method of revenue recognition is not a generally accepted accounting principle except in certain circumstances, which are not present here. Millhouse president, A. G. Shumway, is willing to change to an acceptable method.

Situation 2 Cheri Nestor Co. decides in January 2004 to adopt the straight-line method of depreciation for plant equipment. The straight-line method will be used for new acquisitions as well as for previously acquired plant equipment for which depreciation had been provided on an accelerated basis.

Situation 3 Laura Osmund Co. determined that the depreciable lives of its fixed assets are too long at present to fairly match the cost of the fixed assets with the revenue produced. The company decided at the beginning of the current year to reduce the depreciable lives of all of its existing fixed assets by 5 years.

Instructions

For each of the situations described, provide the information indicated below.

(a) Type of accounting change.
(b) Manner of reporting the change under current generally accepted accounting principles including a discussion, where applicable, of how amounts are computed.
(c) Effect of the change on the balance sheet and income statement.

C17-2 **(Analysis of Various Accounting Changes and Errors)** Mischelle Reiners, controller of Lisa Terry Corp., is aware that an opinion on accounting changes has been issued. After reading the opinion, she is confused about what action should be taken on the following items related to Terry Corp. for the year 2003.

1. In 2003, Terry decided to change its policy on accounting for certain marketing costs. Previously, the company had chosen to defer and amortize all marketing costs over at least 5 years because Terry believed that a return on these expenditures did not occur immediately. Recently, however, the time differential has considerably shortened, and Terry is now expensing the marketing costs as incurred.
2. In 2003, the company examined its entire policy relating to the depreciation of plant equipment. Plant equipment had normally been depreciated over a 15-year period, but recent experience has indicated that the company was incorrect in its estimates and that the assets should be depreciated over a 20-year period.
3. One division of Terry Corp., Ralph Rosentiel Co., has consistently shown an increasing net income from period to period. On closer examination of its operating statement, it is noted that bad debt expense and inventory obsolescence charges are much lower than in other divisions. In discussing this with the controller of this division, it has been learned that the controller has increased his net income each period by knowingly making low estimates related to the writeoff of receivables and inventory.
4. In 2003, the company purchased new machinery that should increase production dramatically. The company has decided to depreciate this machinery on an accelerated basis, even though other machinery is depreciated on a straight-line basis.
5. All equipment sold by Terry is subject to a 3-year warranty. It has been estimated that the expense ultimately to be incurred on these machines is 1% of sales. In 2003, because of a production breakthrough, it is now estimated that $\frac{1}{2}$ of 1% of sales is sufficient. In 2001 and 2002, warranty expense was computed as $64,000 and $70,000, respectively. The company now believes that these warranty costs should be reduced by 50%.
6. In 2003, the company decided to change its method of inventory pricing from average cost to the FIFO method. The effect of this change on prior years is to increase 2001 income by $65,000 and increase 2002 income by $20,000.

Instructions

Mischelle Reiners has come to you, as her CPA, for advice about the situations above. Prepare a memorandum to Reiners, indicating the appropriate accounting treatment that should be given each of these situations.

C17-3 (Comprehensive Accounting Changes and Error Analysis) Charlene Rydell Manufacturing Co. is preparing its year-end financial statements. The controller, Kimbria Shumway, is confronted with several decisions about statement presentation with regard to the following items.

1. The vice president of sales had indicated that one product line has lost its customer appeal and will be phased out over the next 3 years. Therefore, a decision has been made to lower the estimated lives on related production equipment from the remaining 5 years to 3 years.

2. Estimating the lives of new products in the Leisure Products Division has become very difficult because of the highly competitive conditions in this market. Therefore, the practice of deferring and amortizing preproduction costs has been abandoned in favor of expensing such costs as they are incurred.

3. The Hightone Building was converted from a sales office to offices for the Accounting Department at the beginning of this year. Therefore, the expense related to this building will now appear as an administrative expense rather than a selling expense on the current year's income statement.

4. When the year-end physical inventory adjustment was made for the current year, the controller discovered that the prior year's physical inventory sheets for an entire warehouse were mislaid and excluded from last year's count.

5. The method of accounting used for financial reporting purposes for certain receivables has been approved for tax purposes during the current tax year by the Internal Revenue Service. This change for tax purposes will cause both deferred and current taxes payable to change substantially.

6. Management has decided to switch from the FIFO inventory valuation method to the LIFO inventory valuation method for all inventories.

7. Rydell's Custom Division manufactures large-scale, custom-designed machinery on a contract basis. Management decided to switch from the completed-contract method to the percentage-of-completion method of accounting for long-term contracts.

Instructions

(a) *APB Opinion No. 20*, "Accounting Changes," identifies the following types of accounting changes—changes in accounting principle, changes in estimates, and changes due to error. For each of these types of accounting changes, do the following.
   (1) Define the type of change.
   (2) Explain the general accounting treatment required according to *APB Opinion No. 20* with respect to the current year and prior years' financial statements.
(b) For each of the seven changes Rydell Manufacturing Co. has made in the current year, identify and explain whether the change is a change in accounting principle, in estimate, or due to error. If any of the changes is not one of these types, explain why.

(CMA adapted)

C17-4 (EPS: Preferred Dividends, Options, and Convertible Debt) Earnings per share (EPS) is the most featured single financial statistic about modern corporations. Daily published quotations of stock prices have recently been expanded to include for many securities a "times earnings" figure that is based on EPS. Stock analysts often focus their discussions on the EPS of the corporations they study.

Instructions

(a) Explain how dividends or dividend requirements on any class of preferred stock that may be outstanding affect the computation of EPS.
(b) One of the technical procedures applicable in EPS computations is the treasury stock method. Briefly describe the circumstances under which it might be appropriate to apply the treasury stock method.
(c) Convertible debentures are considered potentially dilutive common shares. Explain how convertible debentures are handled for purposes of EPS computations.

(AICPA adapted)

C17-5 (EPS Concepts and Effect of Transactions on EPS) Fernandez Corporation, a new audit client of yours, has not reported earnings per share data in its annual reports to stockholders in the past. The treasurer, Angelo Balthazar, requested that you furnish information about the reporting of earnings per share data in the current year's annual report in accordance with generally accepted accounting principles.

Instructions

(a) Define the term earnings per share as it applies to a corporation with a capitalization structure composed of only one class of common stock, and explain how earnings per share should be computed and how the information should be disclosed in the corporation's financial statements.

(b) Discuss the treatment, if any, that should be given to each of the following items in computing earnings per share of common stock for financial statement reporting.

    (1) Outstanding preferred stock issued at a premium with a par value liquidation right.

    (2) The exercise at a price below market value but above book value of a common stock option issued during the current fiscal year to officers of the corporation.

    (3) The replacement of a machine immediately prior to the close of the current fiscal year at a cost 20% above the original cost of the replaced machine. The new machine will perform the same function as the old machine that was sold for its book value.

    (4) The declaration of current dividends on cumulative preferred stock.

    (5) The acquisition of some of the corporation's outstanding common stock during the current fiscal year. The stock was classified as treasury stock.

    (6) A 2-for-1 stock split of common stock during the current fiscal year.

*C17-6 **(SCF Theory and Analysis of Improper SCF)** Gloria Estefan and Flaco Jimenez are examining the following statement of cash flows for Tropical Clothing Store's first year of operations.

TROPICAL CLOTHING STORE	
STATEMENT OF CASH FLOWS	
FOR THE YEAR ENDED JANUARY 31, 2004	
Sources of cash	
From sales of merchandise	$ 362,000
From sale of capital stock	400,000
From sale of investment	120,000
From depreciation	80,000
From issuance of note for truck	30,000
From interest on investments	8,000
Total sources of cash	1,000,000
Uses of cash	
For purchase of fixtures and equipment	340,000
For merchandise purchased for resale	253,000
For operating expenses (including depreciation)	170,000
For purchase of investment	85,000
For purchase of truck by issuance of note	30,000
For purchase of treasury stock	10,000
For interest on note	3,000
Total uses of cash	891,000
Net increase in cash	$ 109,000

Gloria claims that Tropical's statement of cash flows is an excellent portrayal of a superb first year with cash increasing $109,000. Flaco replies that it was not a superb first year, that the year was an operating failure, that the statement was incorrectly presented, and that $109,000 is not the actual increase in cash.

Instructions

(a) With whom do you agree, Gloria or Flaco? Explain your position.

(b) Using the data provided, prepare a statement of cash flows in proper indirect method form. The only noncash items in income are depreciation and the gain from the sale of the investment (purchase and sale are related).

USING YOUR JUDGMENT

FINANCIAL REPORTING PROBLEM

3M COMPANY

The financial statements of 3M were provided with your book or can be accessed on the Take Action! CD.

Instructions

Refer to 3M's financial statements and the accompanying notes to answer the following questions.

(a) Were there changes in accounting principles reported by 3M during the three years covered by its income statements (1999–2001)? If so, describe the nature of the change and the year of change.
(b) For each change in accounting principle, identify, if possible, the effect of each change on prior years, and the effect on operating results in the year of change.
(c) Were any changes in estimates made by 3M in 2001?
(d) What were the basic and diluted earnings per share for 3M in 2001? Briefly discuss the securities that give rise to 3M's complex capital structure.

FINANCIAL STATEMENT ANALYSIS CASE

TRI INC.

Twin Ricky Inc. (TRI) manufactures a variety of consumer products. The company's founders have run the company for 30 years and are now interested in retiring. Consequently, they are seeking a purchaser who will continue its operations, and a group of investors, Donna Inc., is looking into the acquisition of TRI.

To evaluate its financial stability and operating efficiency, TRI was requested to provide the latest financial statements and selected financial ratios. Summary information provided by TRI is presented below.

Additional Financial Statement Analysis Problems

TRI STATEMENT OF INCOME FOR THE YEAR ENDED NOVEMBER 30, 2003 (IN THOUSANDS)	
Sales (net)	$30,500
Interest income	500
Total revenue	31,000
Costs and expenses	
Cost of goods sold	17,600
Selling and administrative expense	3,550
Depreciation and amortization expense	1,890
Interest expense	900
Total costs and expenses	23,940
Income before taxes	7,060
Income taxes	2,900
Net income	$ 4,160

TRI
STATEMENT OF FINANCIAL POSITION
AS OF NOVEMBER 30
(IN THOUSANDS)

	2003	2002
Cash	$ 400	$ 500
Marketable securities (at cost)	500	200
Accounts receivable (net)	3,200	2,900
Inventory	5,800	5,400
Total current assets	9,900	9,000
Property, plant, & equipment (net)	7,100	7,000
Total assets	$17,000	$16,000
Accounts payable	$ 3,700	$ 3,400
Income taxes payable	900	800
Accrued expenses	1,700	1,400
Total current liabilities	6,300	5,600
Long-term debt	2,000	1,800
Total liabilities	8,300	7,400
Common stock ($1 par value)	2,700	2,700
Paid-in capital in excess of par	1,000	1,000
Retained earnings	5,000	4,900
Total shareholders' equity	8,700	8,600
Total liabilities and shareholders' equity	$17,000	$16,000

SELECTED FINANCIAL RATIOS

	TRI		Current Industry Average
	2001	2002	
Current ratio	1.62	1.61	1.63
Acid-test ratio	.63	.64	.68
Times interest earned	8.50	8.55	8.45
Net profit margin	12.1%	13.2%	13.0%
Total debt to net worth	1.02	.86	1.03
Total asset turnover	1.83	1.84	1.84
Inventory turnover	3.21	3.17	3.18

Instructions
(a) Calculate a new set of ratios for the fiscal year 2003 for TRI based on the financial statements presented.
(b) Explain the analytical use of each of the seven rations presented, describing what the investors can learn about TRI's financial stability and operating efficiency.
(c) Identify two limitations of ratio analysis.

(CMA adapted)

COMPARATIVE ANALYSIS CASE

 **THE COCA-COLA COMPANY AND PEPSICO, INC.**

Instructions
Go to the Take Action! CD and use information found there to answer the following questions related to
The Coca-Cola Company and PepsiCo, Inc.

(a) Identify the changes in accounting principles reported by Coca-Cola during the three years covered by its income statements (1999–2001). Describe the nature of the change and the year of change.

(b) Identify the changes in accounting principles reported by PepsiCo during the three years covered by its income statements (1999–2001). Describe the nature of the change and the year of change.

(c) For each change in accounting principle by Coca-Cola and PepsiCo, identify, if possible, the cumulative effect, the pro-forma effect of each change on prior years, and the effect on operating results in the year of change.

(d) What are the weighted average number of shares used by Coca-Cola and PepsiCo in 2001, 2000, and 1999 to compute diluted earnings per share?

(e) What was the diluted net income per share for Coca-Cola and PepsiCo for 2001, 2000, and 1999?

*Remember to check the **Take Action! CD**
and the book's **companion Web site**
to find additional resources for this chapter.*

In accounting (and finance), the term **time value of money** is used to indicate a relationship between time and money—that a dollar received today is worth more than a dollar promised at some time in the future. Why? Because of the opportunity to invest today's dollar and receive interest on the investment. Yet, when you have to decide among various investment or borrowing alternatives, it is essential to be able to compare today's dollar and tomorrow's dollar on the same footing—to "compare apples to apples." We do that by using the concept of **present value**, which has many applications in accounting.

APPLICATIONS OF TIME VALUE CONCEPTS

Financial reporting uses different measurements in different situations. Present value is one of these measurements, and its usage has been increasing.[1] Some of the applications of present value-based measurements to accounting topics are listed below, several of which are discussed in this textbook.

PRESENT VALUE-BASED ACCOUNTING MEASUREMENTS

1. *Notes.* Valuing noncurrent receivables and payables that carry no stated interest rate or a lower than market interest rate.

2. *Leases.* Valuing assets and obligations to be capitalized under long-term leases and measuring the amount of the lease payments and annual leasehold amortization.

3. *Pensions and Other Postretirement Benefits.* Measuring service cost components of employers' postretirement benefits expense and postretirement benefits obligation.

4. *Long-Term Assets.* Evaluating alternative long-term investments by discounting future cash flows. Determining the value of assets acquired under deferred payment contracts. Measuring impairments of assets.

5. *Sinking Funds.* Determining the contributions necessary to accumulate a fund for debt retirements.

6. *Business Combinations.* Determining the value of receivables, payables, liabilities, accruals, and commitments acquired or assumed in a "purchase."

7. *Disclosures.* Measuring the value of future cash flows from oil and gas reserves for disclosure in supplementary information.

8. *Installment Contracts.* Measuring periodic payments on long-term purchase contracts.

OBJECTIVE 1
Identify accounting topics where the time value of money is relevant.

[1]Many of the recent standards, such as FASB Statements No. 106, 107, 109, 113, 114, 116, 141, 142, and 144, have addressed the issue of present value somewhere in the pronouncement or related basis for conclusions.

In addition to accounting and business applications, compound interest, annuity, and present value concepts apply to personal finance and investment decisions. In purchasing a home or car, planning for retirement, and evaluating alternative investments, you will need to understand time value of money concepts.

THE NATURE OF INTEREST

Interest is payment for the use of money. It is the excess cash received or repaid over and above the amount lent or borrowed (**principal**). For example, if the Corner Bank lends you $1,000 with the understanding that you will repay $1,150, then the excess over $1,000, or $150, represents interest expense. Or if you lend your roommate $100 and then collect $110 in full payment, the $10 excess represents interest revenue.

The amount of interest to be paid is generally stated as a rate over a specific period of time. For example, if you used $1,000 for one year before repaying $1,150, the rate of interest is 15% per year ($150 ÷ $1,000). The custom of expressing interest as a percentage rate is an established business practice.[2] In fact, business managers make investing and borrowing decisions on the basis of the rate of interest involved rather than on the actual dollar amount of interest to be received or paid.

How is the interest rate determined? One of the most important factors is the level of credit risk (risk of nonpayment) involved. Other factors being equal, the higher the credit risk, the higher the interest rate. Low-risk borrowers like **Microsoft** or **Intel** can probably obtain a loan at or slightly below the going market rate of interest. You or the neighborhood delicatessen, on the other hand, would probably be charged several percentage points above the market rate, if you can get a loan at all!

The amount of interest involved in any financing transaction is a function of three variables:

VARIABLES IN INTEREST COMPUTATION

① *Principal.* The amount borrowed or invested.

② *Interest Rate.* A percentage of the outstanding principal.

③ *Time.* The number of years or fractional portion of a year that the principal is outstanding.

The larger the principal amount, or the higher the interest rate, or the longer the time period, the larger the dollar amount of interest.

SIMPLE INTEREST

OBJECTIVE 2
Distinguish between simple and compound interest.

Simple interest is computed on the amount of the principal only. It is the return on (or growth of) the principal for one time period. Simple interest is commonly expressed as follows.[3]

$$\text{Interest} = p \times i \times n$$

[2]Federal law requires the disclosure of interest rates on an **annual basis** in all contracts. That is, instead of stating the rate as "1% per month," it must be stated as "12% per year" if it is simple interest or "12.68% per year" if it is compounded monthly.

[3]Simple interest is traditionally expressed in textbooks in business mathematics or business finance as: $I(\text{interest}) = P(\text{principal}) \times R(\text{rate}) \times T(\text{time})$.

where

p = principal

i = rate of interest for a single period

n = number of periods

To illustrate, if you borrow $1,000 for 3 years with a simple interest rate of 15% per year, the total interest you will pay is $450, computed as follows.

$$\text{Interest} = p \times i \times n$$

$$= \$1,000 \times .15 \times 3$$

$$= \$450$$

If you borrow $1,000 for 3 months at 15%, the interest is $37.50, computed as follows.

$$\text{Interest} = \$1,000 \times .15 \times .25$$

$$= \$37.50$$

COMPOUND INTEREST

John Maynard Keynes, the legendary English economist, supposedly called it magic. Mayer Rothschild, the founder of the famous European banking firm, is said to have proclaimed it the eighth wonder of the world. Today people continue to extol its wonder and its power. The object of their affection is compound interest.

Compound interest is computed on principal **and** on any interest earned that has not been paid or withdrawn. It is the return on (or growth of) the principal for two or more time periods. Compounding computes interest not only on the principal but also on the interest earned to date on that principal, assuming the interest is left on deposit.[4]

To illustrate the difference between simple and compound interest, assume that you deposit $1,000 in the Last National Bank, where it will earn simple interest of 9% per year, and you deposit another $1,000 in the First State Bank, where it will earn compound interest of 9% per year compounded annually. Also assume that in both cases you will not withdraw any interest until 3 years from the date of deposit. The computation of interest to be received and the accumulated year-end balance are indicated in Illustration A-1.

Illustration A-1

Simple vs. Compound Interest

Last National Bank				First State Bank		
Simple Interest Calculation	Simple Interest	Accumulated Year-end Balance		Compound Interest Calculation	Compound Interest	Accumulated Year-end Balance
Year 1 $1,000.00 × 9%	$ 90.00	$1,090.00		Year 1 $1,000.00 × 9%	$ 90.00	$1,090.00
Year 2 $1,000.00 × 9%	90.00	$1,180.00		Year 2 $1,090.00 × 9%	98.10	$1,188.10
Year 3 $1,000.00 × 9%	90.00	$1,270.00		Year 3 $1,188.10 × 9%	106.93	$1,295.03
	$270.00		→ $25.03 ←		$295.03	
			Difference			

[4]Here is an illustration of the power of *time* and *compounding* interest on money. In 1626, Peter Minuit bought Manhattan Island from the Manhattoe Indians for $24 worth of trinkets and beads. If the Indians had taken a boat to Holland, invested the $24 in Dutch securities returning just 6% per year, and kept the money and interest invested at 6%, by 1971 they would have had $13 billion, enough to buy back Manhattan and still have a couple of billion dollars left for doodads (*Forbes,* June 1, 1971). By 2002, 376 years after the trade, the $24 would have grown to approximately $79 billion.

Note in the illustration above that simple interest uses the initial principal of $1,000 to compute the interest in all 3 years. **Compound interest uses the accumulated balance (principal plus interest to date) at each year-end to compute interest in the succeeding year**—which explains why your compound interest account is larger.

Obviously if you had a choice between investing your money at simple interest or at compound interest, you would choose compound interest, all other things—especially risk—being equal. In the example, compounding provides $25.03 of additional interest revenue. For practical purposes compounding assumes that unpaid interest earned becomes a part of the principal, and the accumulated balance at the end of each year becomes the new principal sum on which interest is earned during the next year.

Compound interest is the typical interest computation applied in business situations, particularly in our economy where large amounts of long-lived assets are used productively and financed over long periods of time. Financial managers view and evaluate their investment opportunities in terms of a series of periodic returns, each of which can be reinvested to yield additional returns. Simple interest is usually applicable only to short-term investments and debts that involve a time span of one year or less.

Compound Interest Tables (see pages A40–A49)

OBJECTIVE 3
Learn how to use appropriate compound interest tables.

Five different types of compound interest tables are presented at the end of this appendix. These tables should help you study this appendix as well as solve other problems involving interest. The titles of these five tables and their contents are:

INTEREST TABLES AND CONTENTS

1. *Future Value of 1* table. Contains the amounts to which 1 will accumulate if deposited now at a specified rate and left for a specified number of periods. (Table 1)
2. *Present Value of 1* table. Contains the amounts that must be deposited now at a specified rate of interest to equal 1 at the end of a specified number of periods. (Table 2)
3. *Future Value of an Ordinary Annuity of 1* table. Contains the amounts to which periodic rents of 1 will accumulate if the payments (rents) are invested at the **end** of each period at a specified rate of interest for a specified number of periods. (Table 3)
4. *Present Value of an Ordinary Annuity of 1* table. Contains the amounts that must be deposited now at a specified rate of interest to permit withdrawals of 1 at the **end** of regular periodic intervals for the specified number of periods. (Table 4)
5. *Present Value of an Annuity Due of 1* table. Contains the amounts that must be deposited now at a specified rate of interest to permit withdrawals of 1 at the **beginning** of regular periodic intervals for the specified number of periods. (Table 5)

Illustration A-2 indicates the general format and content of these tables. It shows how much principal plus interest a dollar accumulates to at the end of each of five periods at three different rates of compound interest.

FUTURE VALUE OF 1 AT COMPOUND INTEREST			
(EXCERPT FROM TABLE 1, PAGE A41)			
Period	9%	10%	11%
1	1.09000	1.10000	1.11000
2	1.18810	1.21000	1.23210
3	1.29503	1.33100	1.36763
4	1.41158	1.46410	1.51807
5	1.53862	1.61051	1.68506

Illustration A-2
Excerpt from Table 1

The compound tables are computed using basic formulas. For example, the formula to determine the future value factor (*FVF*) for 1 is:

$$FVF_{n,i} = (1 + i)^n$$

where

$FVF_{n,i}$ = future value factor for n periods at i interest

n = number of periods

i = rate of interest for a single period

The $FVF_{n,i}$ and other time value of money formulas are programmed into financial calculators. The use of these tools to solve time value of money problems is illustrated in Appendix B.

To illustrate the use of interest tables to calculate compound amounts, assuming an interest rate of 9%, the future value to which 1 accumulates (the future value factor) is shown below.

Period	Beginning-of-Period Amount	×	Multiplier $(1 + i)$	=	End-of-Period Amount*	Formula $(1 + i)^n$
1	1.00000		1.09		1.09000	$(1.09)^1$
2	1.09000		1.09		1.18810	$(1.09)^2$
3	1.18810		1.09		1.29503	$(1.09)^3$

*Note that these amounts appear in Table 1 in the 9% column.

Illustration A-3
Accumulation of
Compound Amounts

Throughout the discussion of compound interest tables the use of the term **periods** instead of **years** is intentional. Interest is generally expressed in terms of an annual rate, but in many business circumstances the compounding period is less than one year. In such circumstances the annual interest rate must be converted to correspond to the length of the period. The process is to convert the "annual interest rate" into the "compounding period interest rate" by **dividing the annual rate by the number of compounding periods per year**.

In addition, the number of periods is determined by **multiplying the number of years involved by the number of compounding periods per year**. To illustrate, assume that $1.00 is invested for 6 years at 8% annual interest compounded **quarterly**. Using Table 1, page A40, we can determine the amount to which this $1.00 will accumulate: Read the factor that appears in the 2% column on the 24th row—6 years × 4 compounding periods per year, namely 1.60844, or approximately $1.61. Thus, the term **periods**, not **years**, is used in all compound interest tables to express the quantity of n.

Illustration A-4 shows how to determine (1) the interest rate per compounding period and (2) the number of compounding periods in four situations of differing compounding frequency.[5]

Illustration A-4

Frequency of
Compounding

12% Annual Interest Rate over 5 Years Compounded	Interest Rate per Compounding Period	Number of Compounding Periods
Annually (1)	.12 ÷ 1 = .12	5 years × 1 compounding per year = 5 periods
Semiannually (2)	.12 ÷ 2 = .06	5 years × 2 compoundings per year = 10 periods
Quarterly (4)	.12 ÷ 4 = .03	5 years × 4 compoundings per year = 20 periods
Monthly (12)	.12 ÷ 12 = .01	5 years × 12 compoundings per year = 60 periods

How often interest is compounded can make a substantial difference in the rate of return. For example, a 9% annual interest compounded **daily** provides a 9.42% yield, or a difference of .42%. The 9.42% is referred to as the **effective yield**.[6] The annual interest rate (9%) is called the **stated, nominal,** or **face rate.** When the compounding frequency is greater than once a year, the effective interest rate will always be greater than the stated rate.

Illustration A-5 shows how compounding for five different time periods affects the effective yield and the amount earned by an investment of $10,000 for one year.

Illustration A-5

Comparison of Different
Compounding Periods

Interest Rate	Compounding Periods				
	Annually	**Semiannually**	**Quarterly**	**Monthly**	**Daily**
8%	8.00% $800	8.16% $816	8.24% $824	8.30% $830	8.33% $833
9%	9.00% $900	9.20% $920	9.31% $931	9.38% $938	9.42% $942
10%	10.00% $1,000	10.25% $1,025	10.38% $1,038	10.47% $1,047	10.52% $1,052

[5]Because interest is theoretically earned (accruing) every second of every day, it is possible to calculate interest that is **compounded continuously.** Computations involving continuous compounding are facilitated through the use of the natural, or Napierian, system of logarithms. As a practical matter, however, most business transactions assume interest to be compounded no more frequently than daily.

[6]The formula for calculating the **effective rate** in situations where the compounding frequency (n) is greater than once a year is as follows.

$$\text{Effective rate} = (1 + i)^n - 1$$

To illustrate, if the stated annual rate is 8% compounded quarterly (or 2% per quarter), the effective annual rate is:

$$\text{Effective rate} = (1 + .02)^4 - 1$$
$$= (1.02)^4 - 1$$
$$= 1.0824 - 1$$
$$= .0824$$
$$= 8.24\%$$

FUNDAMENTAL VARIABLES

The following four variables are fundamental to all compound interest problems.

FUNDAMENTAL VARIABLES

① *Rate of Interest.* This rate, unless otherwise stated, is an annual rate that must be adjusted to reflect the length of the compounding period if less than a year.

② *Number of Time Periods.* This is the number of compounding periods. (A period may be equal to or less than a year.)

③ *Future Value.* The value at a future date of a given sum or sums invested assuming compound interest.

④ *Present Value.* The value now (present time) of a future sum or sums discounted assuming compound interest.

The relationship of these four fundamental variables is depicted in the following **time diagram**.

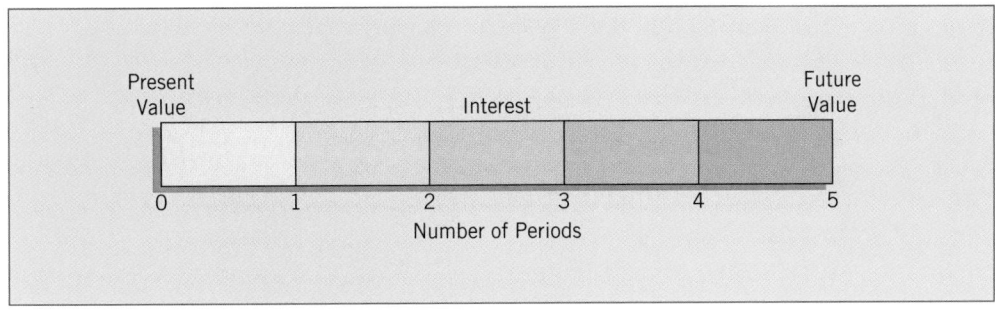

Illustration A-6
Basic Time Diagram

In some cases all four of these variables are known, but in many business situations at least one variable is unknown. As an aid to better understanding the problems and to finding solutions, we encourage you to sketch compound interest problems in the form of the preceding time diagram.

SINGLE-SUM PROBLEMS

Many business and investment decisions involve a single amount of money that either exists now or will in the future. Single-sum problems can generally be classified into one of the following two categories.

① Computing the **unknown future value** of a known single sum of money that is invested now for a certain number of periods at a certain interest rate.

② Computing the **unknown present value** of a known single sum of money in the future that is discounted for a certain number of periods at a certain interest rate.

When analyzing the information provided, you determine first whether it is a future value problem or a present value problem. **If you are solving for a future value**, all cash flows must be *accumulated* to a future point. In this instance, the effect of interest is to increase the amounts or values over time so that the future value is greater than the present value. However, **if you are solving for a present value**, all cash flows must be *discounted* from the future to the present. In this case, the **discounting** reduces the amounts or values so that the present value is less than the future amount.

Preparation of time diagrams aids in identifying the unknown as an item in the future or the present. Sometimes it is neither a future value nor a present value that is to be determined but, rather, the interest or discount rate or the number of compounding or discounting periods.

Future Value of a Single Sum

To determine the **future value** of a single sum, multiply the future value factor by its present value (principal), as follows.

$$FV = PV \ (FVF_{n,i})$$

where

$$FV = \text{future value}$$

$$PV = \text{present value (principal or single sum)}$$

$$FVF_{n,i} = \text{future value factor for } n \text{ periods at } i \text{ interest}$$

To illustrate, Bruegger Co. wants to determine the future value of $50,000 invested for 5 years compounded annually at an interest rate of 11%. In time-diagram form, this investment situation would appear as follows.

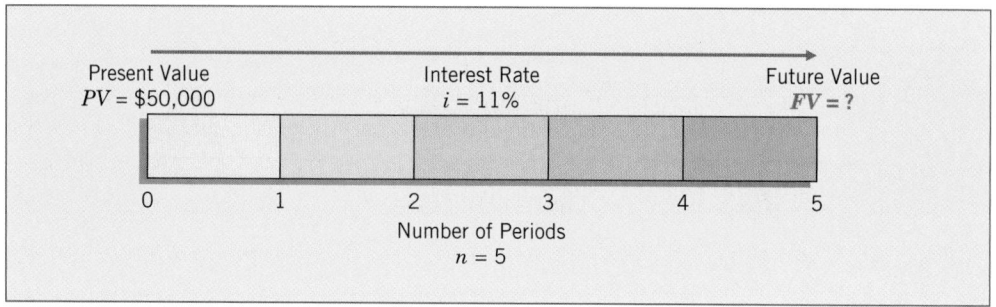

Using the formula, this investment problem is solved as follows.

$$\text{Future value} = PV \ (FVF_{n,i})$$

$$= \$50,000 \ (FVF_{5,11\%})$$

$$= \$50,000 \ (1 + .11)^5$$

$$= \$50,000 \ (1.68506)$$

$$= \$84,253$$

To determine the future value factor of 1.68506 in the formula above, use a financial calculator or read the appropriate table, in this case Table 1 (11% column and the 5-period row).

This time diagram and formula approach can be applied to a routine business situation. To illustrate, **Commonwealth Edison Company** deposited $250 million in an escrow account with the **Northern Trust Company** at the beginning of 2002 as a commitment toward a power plant to be completed December 31, 2005. How much will be on deposit at the end of 4 years if interest is 10%, compounded semiannually?

With a known present value of $250 million, a total of 8 compounding periods (4 × 2), and an interest rate of 5% per compounding period (.10 ÷ 2), this problem can be time diagrammed and the future value determined as follows.

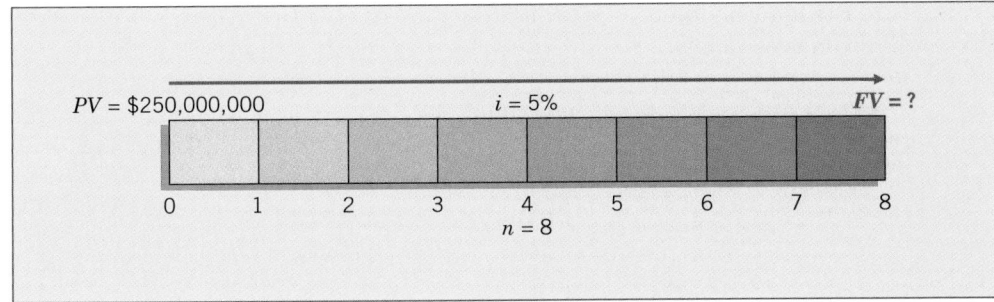

Future value = $250,000,000 $(FVF_{8,5\%})$

$$= \$250,000,000 \ (1 + .05)^8$$

$$= \$250,000,000 \ (1.47746)$$

$$= \$369,365,000$$

Using a future value factor found in Table 1 (5% column, 8-period row), we find that the deposit of $250 million will accumulate to $369,365,000 by December 31, 2005.

Present Value of a Single Sum

The Bruegger Co. example on page A8 showed that $50,000 invested at an annually compounded interest rate of 11% will be worth $84,253 at the end of 5 years. It follows, then, that $84,253, 5 years in the future is worth $50,000 now. That is, $50,000 is the present value of $84,253. The **present value** is the amount that must be invested now to produce the known future value. **The present value is always a smaller amount than the known future value because interest will be earned and accumulated on the present value to the future date.** In determining the future value, we move forward in time using a process of **accumulation**. In determining present value, we move backward in time using a process of **discounting**.

As indicated earlier, a "present value of 1 table" appears at the end of this appendix as Table 2. Illustration A-7 demonstrates the nature of such a table. It shows the present value of 1 for five different periods at three different rates of interest.

PRESENT VALUE OF 1 AT COMPOUND INTEREST (EXCERPT FROM TABLE 2, PAGE A41)			
Period	9%	10%	11%
1	0.91743	0.90909	0.90090
2	0.84168	0.82645	0.81162
3	0.77218	0.75132	0.73119
4	0.70843	0.68301	0.65873
5	0.64993	0.62092	0.59345

Illustration A-7
Excerpt from Table 2

The present value of 1 (present value factor) may be expressed as a formula:

$$PVF_{n,i} = \frac{1}{(1 + i)^n}$$

where

$PVF_{n,i}$ = present value factor for n periods at i interest

To illustrate, assuming an interest rate of 9%, the present value of 1 discounted for three different periods is as follows.

Illustration A-8
Present Value of $1
Discounted at 9% for
Three Periods

Discount Periods	1	÷ $(1 + i)^n$	=	Present Value*	Formula $1/(1 + i)^n$
1	1.00000	1.09		.91743	$1/(1.09)^1$
2	1.00000	$(1.09)^2$		.84168	$1/(1.09)^2$
3	1.00000	$(1.09)^3$		.77218	$1/(1.09)^3$

*Note that these amounts appear in Table 2 in the 9% column.

The present value of any single sum (future value), then, is as follows.

$$PV = FV\ (PVF_{n,i})$$

where

$$PV = \text{present value}$$
$$FV = \text{future value}$$
$$PVF_{n,i} = \text{present value factor for } n \text{ periods at } i \text{ interest}$$

To illustrate, what is the present value of $84,253 to be received or paid in 5 years discounted at 11% compounded annually? In time-diagram form, this problem is drawn as follows.

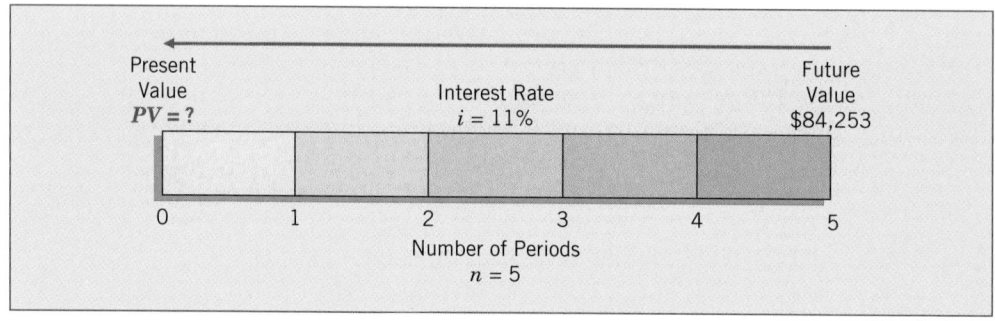

Using the formula, this problem is solved as follows.

$$\text{Present value} = FV\ (PVF_{n,i})$$
$$= \$84{,}253\ (PVF_{5,11\%})$$
$$= \$84{,}253\left(\frac{1}{(1 + .11)^5}\right)$$
$$= \$84{,}253\ (.59345)$$
$$= \$50{,}000$$

To determine the present value factor of .59345, use a financial calculator or read the present value of a single sum in Table 2 (11% column, 5-period row).

The time diagram and formula approach can be applied in a variety of situations. For example, assume that your rich uncle proposes to give you $2,000 for a trip to Europe when you graduate from college 3 years from now. He proposes to finance the trip by investing a sum of money now at 8% compound interest that will provide you with $2,000 upon your graduation. The only conditions are that you graduate and that you tell him how much to invest now.

To impress your uncle, you might set up the following time diagram and solve this problem as follows.

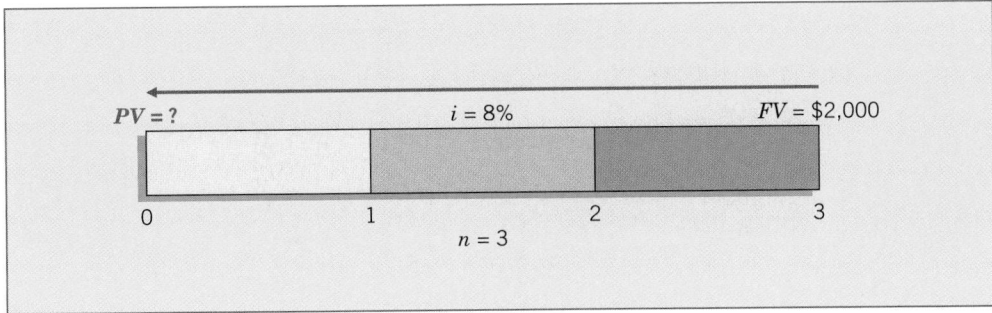

$$\text{Present value} = \$2{,}000 \ (PVF_{3,8\%})$$

$$= \$2{,}000 \left(\frac{1}{(1 + .08)^3} \right)$$

$$= \$2{,}000 \ (.79383)$$

$$= \$1{,}587.66$$

Advise your uncle to invest $1,587.66 now to provide you with $2,000 upon graduation. To satisfy your uncle's other condition, you must pass this course, and many more.

Solving for Other Unknowns in Single-Sum Problems

In computing either the future value or the present value in the previous single-sum illustrations, both the number of periods and the interest rate were known. In many business situations, both the future value and the present value are known, but the number of periods or the interest rate is unknown. The following two illustrations are single-sum problems (future value and present value) with either an unknown number of periods (n) or an unknown interest rate (i). These illustrations and the accompanying solutions demonstrate that if any three of the four values (future value, FV; present value, PV; number of periods, n; interest rate, i) are known, the remaining unknown variable can be derived.

Illustration—Computation of the Number of Periods

The Village of Somonauk wants to accumulate $70,000 for the construction of a veterans monument in the town square. If at the beginning of the current year the Village deposited $47,811 in a memorial fund that earns 10% interest compounded annually, how many years will it take to accumulate $70,000 in the memorial fund?

In this illustration, both the present value ($47,811) and the future value ($70,000) are known along with the interest rate of 10%. A time diagram of this investment problem is as follows.

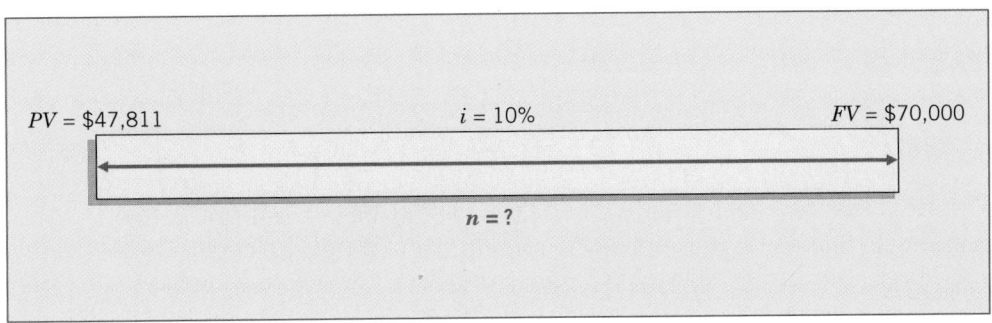

Because both the present value and the future value are known, we can solve for the unknown number of periods using either the future value or the present value formulas as shown below.

Illustration A-9
Solving for Unknown
Number of Periods

Future Value Approach	Present Value Approach
$FV = PV \, (FVF_{n,10\%})$	$PV = FV \, (PVF_{n,10\%})$
$\$70,000 = \$47,811 \, (FVF_{n,\,10\%})$	$\$47,811 = \$70,000 \, (PVF_{n,10\%})$
$FVF_{n,10\%} = \dfrac{\$70,000}{\$47,811} = 1.46410$	$PVF_{n,10\%} = \dfrac{\$47,811}{\$70,000} = .68301$

Using the future value factor of 1.46410, refer to Table 1 and read down the 10% column to find that factor in the 4-period row. Thus, it will take 4 years for the $47,811 to accumulate to $70,000 if invested at 10% interest compounded annually. Using the present value factor of .68301, refer to Table 2 and read down the 10% column to find that factor in the 4-period row.

Illustration—Computation of the Interest Rate

Advanced Design, Inc. wishes to have $1,409,870 for basic research 5 years from now. The firm currently has $800,000 to invest for that purpose. At what rate of interest must the $800,000 be invested to fund basic research projects of $1,409,870, 5 years from now?

A time diagram of this investment situation is as follows.

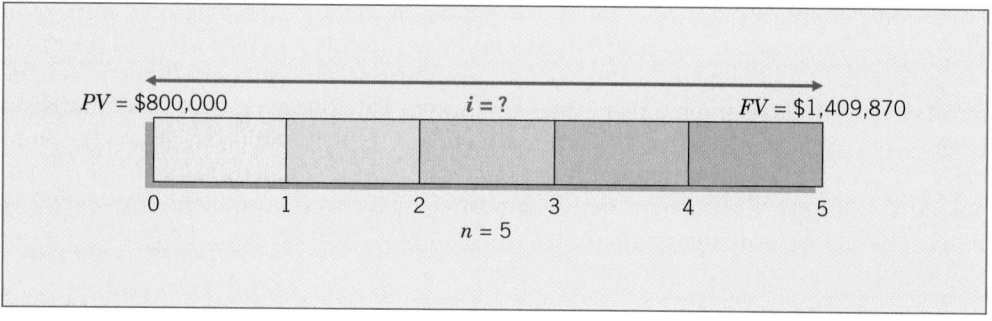

The unknown interest rate may be determined from either the future value approach or the present value approach as shown in Illustration A-10.

Illustration A-10
Solving for Unknown
Interest Rate

Future Value Approach	Present Value Approach
$FV = PV \, (FVF_{5,i})$	$PV = FV \, (PVF_{5,i})$
$\$1,409,870 = \$800,000 \, (FVF_{5,i})$	$\$800,000 = \$1,409,870 \, (PVF_{5,i})$
$FVF_{5,i} = \dfrac{\$1,409,870}{\$800,000} = 1.76234$	$PVF_{5,i} = \dfrac{\$800,000}{\$1,409,870} = .56743$

Using the future value factor of 1.76234, refer to Table 1 and read across the 5-period row to find that factor in the 12% column. Thus, the $800,000 must be invested at 12% to accumulate to $1,409,870 in 5 years. And, using the present value factor of .56743 and Table 2, again find that factor at the juncture of the 5-period row and the 12% column.

ANNUITIES

The preceding discussion involved only the accumulation or discounting of a single principal sum. Individuals frequently encounter situations in which a series of dollar amounts are to be paid or received periodically, such as loans or sales to be repaid in installments, invested funds that will be partially recovered at regular intervals, or cost savings that are realized repeatedly. A life insurance contract is probably the most common and most familiar type of transaction involving a series of equal payments made at equal intervals of time. Such a process of periodic saving represents the accumulation of a sum of money through an annuity. An **annuity**, by definition, requires that (1) the periodic payments or receipts (called **rents**) always be the same amount, (2) the **interval** between such rents always be the same, and (3) the **interest be compounded** once each interval. The **future value of an annuity** is the sum of all the rents plus the accumulated compound interest on them.

It should be noted that the rents may occur at either the beginning or the end of the periods. To distinguish annuities under these two alternatives, an annuity is classified as an **ordinary annuity** if the rents occur at the end of each period, and as an **annuity due** if the rents occur at the beginning of each period.

Future Value of an Ordinary Annuity

One approach to the problem of determining the future value to which an annuity will accumulate is to compute the value to which **each** of the rents in the series will accumulate and then total their individual future values. For example, assume that $1 is deposited at the **end** of each of 5 years (an ordinary annuity) and earns 12% interest compounded annually. The future value can be computed as follows using the "future value of 1" table (Table 1) for each of the five $1 rents.

END OF PERIOD IN WHICH $1.00 IS TO BE INVESTED						Value at End of Year 5
Present	1	2	3	4	5	
--------------$1.00———————————→						$1.57352
----------------------------$1.00————————→						1.40493
--------------------------------------$1.00———————→						1.25440
--$1.00———→						1.12000
--$1.00						1.00000
Total (future value of an ordinary annuity of $1.00 for 5 periods at 12%)						$6.35285

Illustration A-11

Solving for the Future Value of an Ordinary Annuity

Because the rents that compose an ordinary annuity are deposited at the end of the period, they can earn no interest during the period in which they are originally deposited. For example, the third rent earns interest for only two periods (periods four and five). Obviously the third rent earns no interest for the first two periods since it is not deposited until the third period. Furthermore, it can earn no interest for the third period since it is not deposited until the end of the third period. Any time the future value of an ordinary annuity is computed, the number of compounding periods will always be **one less than the number of rents**.

Although the foregoing procedure for computing the future value of an ordinary annuity will always produce the correct answer, it can become cumbersome if the number of rents is large. A more efficient way of expressing the future value of an ordinary annuity of 1 is in a formula that is a summation of the individual rents plus the compound interest:

$$FVF\text{-}OA_{n,i} = \frac{(1+i)^n - 1}{i}$$

where

$$FVF\text{-}OA_{n,i} = \text{future value factor of an ordinary annuity}$$

$$i = \text{rate of interest per period}$$

$$n = \text{number of compounding periods}$$

For example, $FVF\text{-}OA_{5,12\%}$ refers to the value to which an ordinary annuity of 1 will accumulate in 5 periods at 12% interest.

Using the formula above, tables have been developed similar to those used for the "future value of 1" and the "present value of 1" for both an ordinary annuity and an annuity due. The table in Illustration A-12 is an excerpt from the "future value of an ordinary annuity of 1" table.

Illustration A-12

Excerpt from Table 3

	FUTURE VALUE OF AN ORDINARY ANNUITY OF 1 (EXCERPT FROM TABLE 3, PAGE A45)		
Period	10%	11%	12%
1	1.00000	1.00000	1.00000
2	2.10000	2.11000	2.12000
3	3.31000	3.34210	3.37440
4	4.64100	4.70973	4.77933
5	6.10510	6.22780	6.35285*

*Note that this annuity table factor is the same as the sum of the future values of 1 factors shown in Illustration A-11.

Interpreting the table, if $1.00 is invested at the end of each year for 4 years at 11% interest compounded annually, the value of the annuity at the end of the fourth year will be $4.71 (4.70973 × $1.00). Multiply the factor from the appropriate line and column of the table by the dollar amount of **one rent** involved in an ordinary annuity. The result: the accumulated sum of the rents and the compound interest to the date of the last rent.

The future value of an ordinary annuity is computed as follows.

$$\text{Future value of an ordinary annuity} = R \ (FVF\text{-}OA_{n,i})$$

where

$$R = \text{periodic rent}$$

$$FVF\text{-}OA_{n,i} = \text{future value of an ordinary annuity factor}$$
$$\text{for } n \text{ periods at } i \text{ interest}$$

To illustrate, what is the future value of five $5,000 deposits made at the end of each of the next 5 years, earning interest of 12%? In time-diagram form, this problem is drawn as follows.

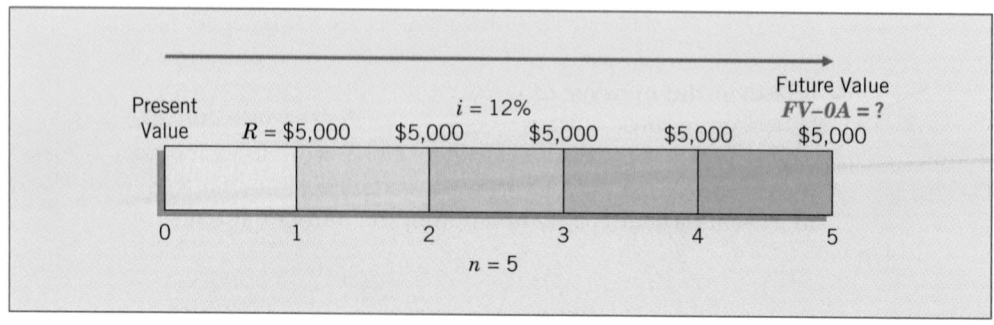

Using the formula, this investment problem is solved as follows.

$$\text{Future value of an ordinary annuity} = R\ (FVF\text{-}OA_{n,i})$$

$$= \$5{,}000\ (FVF\text{-}OA_{5,12\%})$$

$$= \$5{,}000 \left(\frac{(1 + .12)^5 - 1}{.12} \right)$$

$$= \$5{,}000\ (6.35285)$$

$$= \$31{,}764.25$$

We can determine the future value of an ordinary annuity factor of 6.35285 in the formula above using a financial calculator or by reading the appropriate table, in this case Table 3 (12% column and the 5-period row).

To illustrate these computations in a business situation, assume that Hightown Electronics decides to deposit $75,000 at the end of each 6-month period for the next 3 years for the purpose of accumulating enough money to meet debts that mature in 3 years. What is the future value that will be on deposit at the end of 3 years if the annual interest rate is 10%?

The time diagram and formula solution are as follows.

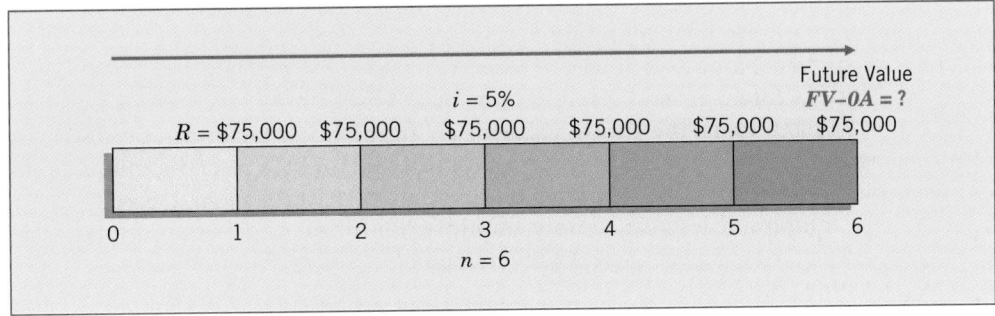

$$\text{Future value of an ordinary annuity} = R\ (FVF\text{-}OA_{n,i})$$

$$= \$75{,}000\ (FVF\text{-}OA_{6,5\%})$$

$$= \$75{,}000 \left(\frac{(1 + .05)^6 - 1}{.05} \right)$$

$$= \$75{,}000\ (6.80191)$$

$$= \$510{,}143.25$$

Thus, six 6-month deposits of $75,000 earning 5% per period will grow to $510,143.25.

Future Value of an Annuity Due

The preceding analysis of an ordinary annuity was based on the assumption that the periodic rents occur at the **end** of each period. An **annuity due** assumes periodic rents occur at the **beginning** of each period. This means an annuity due will accumulate interest during the first period, whereas an ordinary annuity rent will earn no interest during the first period because the rent is not received or paid until the end of the period. In other words, the significant difference between the two types of annuities is in the number of interest accumulation periods involved.

If rents occur at the end of a period (ordinary annuity), in determining the **future value of an annuity** there will be one less interest period than if the rents occur at the beginning of the period (annuity due). The distinction is shown in Illustration A-13.

Illustration A-13

Comparison of the Future Value of an Ordinary Annuity with an Annuity Due

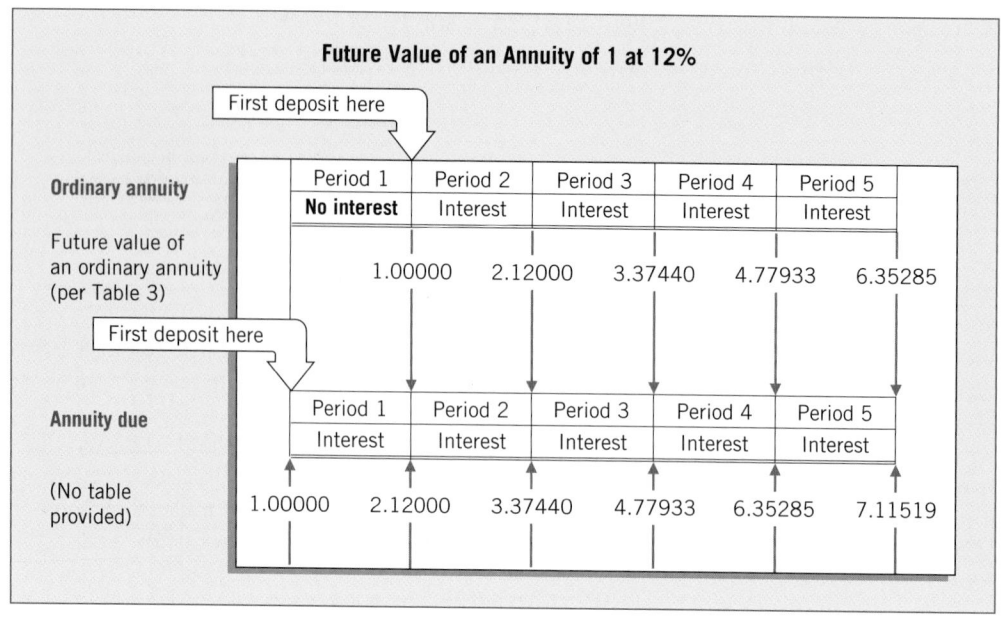

In this example, because the cash flows from the annuity due come exactly one period earlier than for an ordinary annuity, the future value of the annuity due factor is exactly 12% higher than the ordinary annuity factor. For example, the value of an ordinary annuity factor at the end of period one at 12% is 1.00000, whereas for an annuity due it is 1.12000. **Thus, the future value of an annuity due factor can be found by multiplying the future value of an ordinary annuity factor by 1 plus the interest rate.** For example, to determine the future value of an annuity due interest factor for 5 periods at 12% compound interest, simply multiply the future value of an ordinary annuity interest factor for 5 periods (6.35285) by one plus the interest rate $(1 + .12)$, to arrive at 7.11519 (6.35285×1.12).

To illustrate the use of the ordinary annuity tables in converting to an annuity due, assume that Sue Lotadough plans to deposit $800 a year on each birthday of her son Howard, starting today, his tenth birthday, at 12% interest compounded annually. Sue wants to know the amount she will have accumulated for college expenses by her son's eighteenth birthday. If the first deposit is made on Howard's tenth birthday, Sue will make a total of 8 deposits over the life of the annuity (assume no deposit on the eighteenth birthday). Because all the deposits will be made at the beginning of the periods, they represent an annuity due.

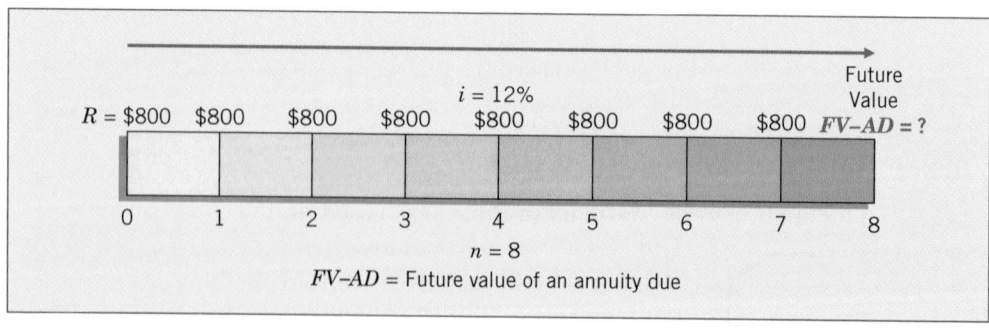

Referring to the "future value of an ordinary annuity of 1" table for 8 periods at 12%, we find a factor of 12.29969. This factor is then multiplied by $(1 + .12)$ to arrive at the future value of an annuity due factor. As a result, the accumulated value on Howard's eighteenth birthday is $11,020.52, as shown in Illustration A-14.

1. Future value of an ordinary annuity of 1 for 8 periods at 12% (Table 3)	12.29969
2. Factor $(1 + .12)$	$\times$ 1.12
3. Future value of an annuity due of 1 for 8 periods at 12%	13.77565
4. Periodic deposit (rent)	$\times$ \$800
5. Accumulated value on son's eighteenth birthday	\$11,020.52

Depending on the college he chooses, Howard may have only enough to finance his first year of school.

Illustrations of Future Value of Annuity Problems

In the foregoing annuity examples three values were known—amount of each rent, interest rate, and number of periods. They were used to determine the fourth value, future value, which was unknown. The first two future value problems presented illustrate the computations of (1) the amount of the rents and (2) the number of rents. The third problem illustrates the computation of the future value of an annuity due.

Computation of Rent

Assume that you wish to accumulate \$14,000 for a down payment on a condominium apartment 5 years from now; for the next 5 years you can earn an annual return of 8% compounded semiannually. How much should you deposit at the end of each 6-month period?

The \$14,000 is the future value of 10 (5 $\times$ 2) semiannual end-of-period payments of an unknown amount, at an interest rate of 4% (8% $\div$ 2). This problem appears in the form of a time diagram as follows.

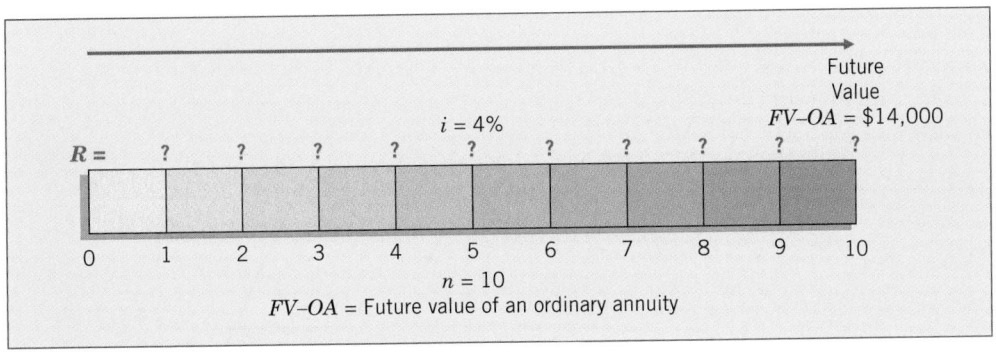

Using the formula for the future value of an ordinary annuity, the amount of each rent is determined as follows.

$$\text{Future value of an ordinary annuity} = R \; (FVF\text{-}OA_{n,i})$$

$$\$14,000 = R \; (FVF\text{-}OA_{10,4\%})$$

$$\$14,000 = R(12.00611)$$

$$\frac{\$14,000}{12.00611} = R$$

$$R = \$1,166.07$$

Thus, you must make 10 semiannual deposits of \$1,166.07 each in order to accumulate \$14,000 for your down payment.

Computation of the Number of Periodic Rents

Suppose that your company wishes to accumulate $117,332 by making periodic deposits of $20,000 at the end of each year that will earn 8% compounded annually while accumulating. How many deposits must be made?

The $117,332 represents the future value of $n(?)$ $20,000 deposits, at an 8% annual rate of interest. This problem appears in the form of a time diagram as follows.

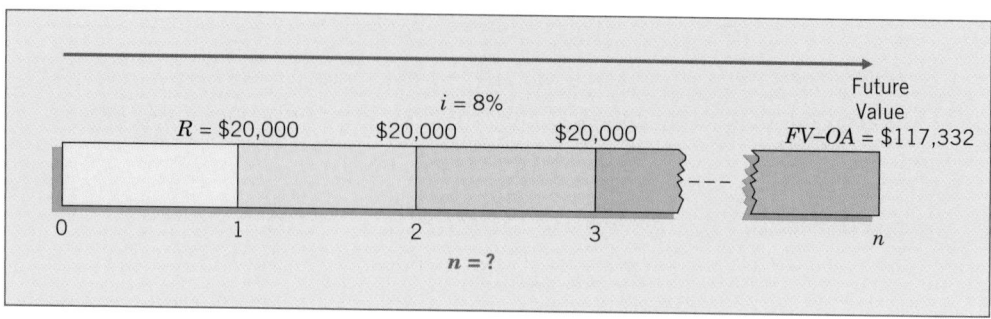

Using the future value of an ordinary annuity formula, we obtain the following factor.

$$\text{Future value of an ordinary annuity} = R \, (FVF\text{-}OA_{n,i})$$

$$\$117,332 = \$20,000 \, (FVF\text{-}OA_{n,8\%})$$

$$FVF\text{-}OA_{n,8\%} = \frac{\$117,332}{\$20,000} = 5.86660$$

Using Table 3 and reading down the 8% column, we find 5.86660 in the 5-period row. Thus, five deposits of $20,000 each must be made.

Computation of the Future Value

Walter Goodwrench, a mechanic, has taken on weekend work in the hope of creating his own retirement fund. Mr. Goodwrench deposits $2,500 today in a savings account that earns 9% interest. He plans to deposit $2,500 every year for a total of 30 years. How much cash will have accumulated in Mr. Goodwrench's retirement savings account when he retires in 30 years? This problem appears in the form of a time diagram as follows.

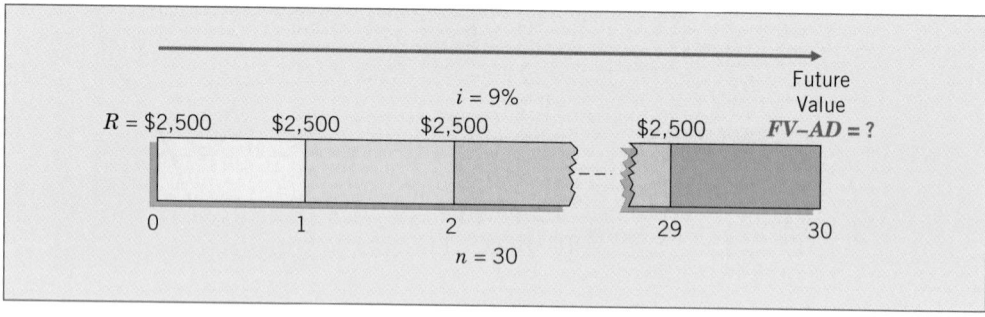

Using the "future value of an ordinary annuity of 1" table, the solution is computed as follows.

Illustration A-15

Computation of Accumulated Value of an Annuity Due

1. Future value of an ordinary annuity of 1 for 30 periods at 9%	136.30754
2. Factor (1 + .09)	× 1.09
3. Future value of an annuity due of 1 for 30 periods at 9%	148.57522
4. Periodic rent	× $2,500
5. Accumulated value at end of 30 years	$371,438

Present Value of an Ordinary Annuity

The present value of an annuity is **the single sum** that, if invested at compound interest now, would provide for an annuity (a series of withdrawals) for a certain number of future periods. In other words, the present value of an ordinary annuity is the present value of a series of equal rents to be withdrawn at equal intervals.

One approach to finding the present value of an annuity is to determine the present value of each of the rents in the series and then total their individual present values. For example, an annuity of $1.00 to be received at the **end** of each of 5 periods may be viewed as separate amounts; the present value of each is computed from the table of present values (see pages A42–A43), assuming an interest rate of 12%.

OBJECTIVE **7**
Solve present value of ordinary and annuity due problems.

END OF PERIOD IN WHICH $1.00 IS TO BE RECEIVED

Present Value at Beg. of Year 1	1	2	3	4	5
$0.89286 ← $1.00					
.79719 ← $1.00					
.71178 ← $1.00					
.63552 ← $1.00					
.56743 ← $1.00					
$3.60478 Total (present value of an ordinary annuity of $1.00 for five periods at 12%)					

Illustration A-16
Solving for the Present Value of an Ordinary Annuity

This computation tells us that if we invest the single sum of $3.60 today at 12% interest for 5 periods, we will be able to withdraw $1.00 at the end of each period for 5 periods. This cumbersome procedure can be summarized by:

$$PVF\text{-}OA_{n,i} = \frac{1 - \dfrac{1}{(1+i)^n}}{i}$$

The expression $PVF\text{-}OA_{n,i}$ refers to the present value of an ordinary annuity of 1 factor for n periods at i interest. Using this formula, present value of ordinary annuity tables are prepared. An excerpt from such a table is shown below.

Illustration A-17
Excerpt from Table 4

PRESENT VALUE OF AN ORDINARY ANNUITY OF 1 (EXCERPT FROM TABLE 4, PAGE A47)			
Period	10%	11%	12%
1	0.90909	0.90090	0.89286
2	1.73554	1.71252	1.69005
3	2.48685	2.44371	2.40183
4	3.16986	3.10245	3.03735
5	3.79079	3.69590	3.60478*

*Note that this annuity table factor is equal to the sum of the present value of 1 factors shown in Illustration A-16.

The general formula for the present value of any ordinary annuity is as follows.

Present value of an ordinary annuity = $R \, (PVF\text{-}OA_{n,i})$

where

$$R = \text{periodic rent (ordinary annuity)}$$

$$PVF\text{-}OA_{n,i} = \text{present value of an ordinary annuity of 1}$$
$$\text{for } n \text{ periods at } i \text{ interest}$$

To illustrate, what is the present value of rental receipts of $6,000 each to be received at the end of each of the next 5 years when discounted at 12%? This problem may be time-diagrammed and solved as follows.

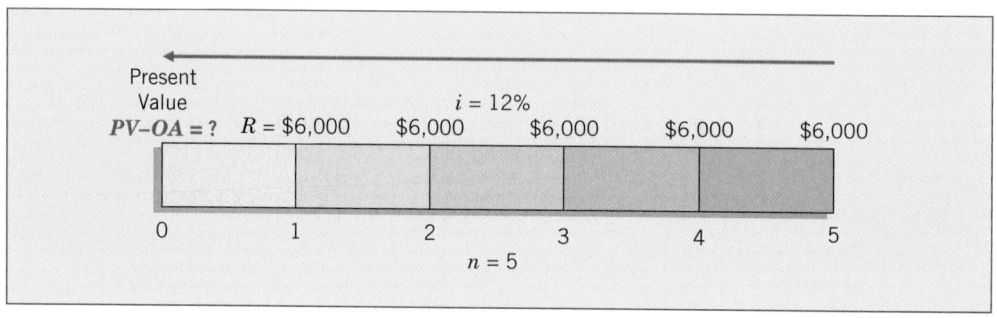

$$\text{Present value of an ordinary annuity} = R \ (PVF\text{-}OA_{n,i})$$

$$= \$6,000 \ (PVF\text{-}OA_{5,12\%})$$

$$= \$6,000 \ (3.60478)$$

$$= \$21,628.68$$

The present value of the 5 ordinary annuity rental receipts of $6,000 each is $21,628.68. Determining the present value of the ordinary annuity factor 3.60478 can be accomplished using a financial calculator or by reading the appropriate table, in this case Table 4 (12% column and 5-period row).

Present Value of an Annuity Due

In the discussion of the present value of an ordinary annuity, the final rent was discounted back the same number of periods that there were rents. In determining the present value of an annuity due, there is always one fewer discount period. This distinction is shown graphically in Illustration A-18.

Because each cash flow comes exactly one period sooner in the present value of the annuity due, the present value of the cash flows is exactly 12% higher than the present value of an ordinary annuity. Thus, **the present value of an annuity due factor can be found by multiplying the present value of an ordinary annuity factor by 1 plus the interest rate**.

To determine the present value of an annuity due interest factor for 5 periods at 12% interest, take the present value of an ordinary annuity for 5 periods at 12% interest (3.60478) and multiply it by 1.12 to arrive at the present value of an annuity due, 4.03735 (3.60478 × 1.12). Because the payment and receipt of rentals at the beginning of periods (such as leases, insurance, and subscriptions) are as common as those at the end of the periods (referred to as "in arrears"), we have provided present value annuity due factors in the form of Table 5.

Space Odyssey, Inc., rents a communications satellite for 4 years with annual rental payments of $4.8 million to be made at the beginning of each year. If the relevant annual interest rate is 11%, what is the present value of the rental obligations?

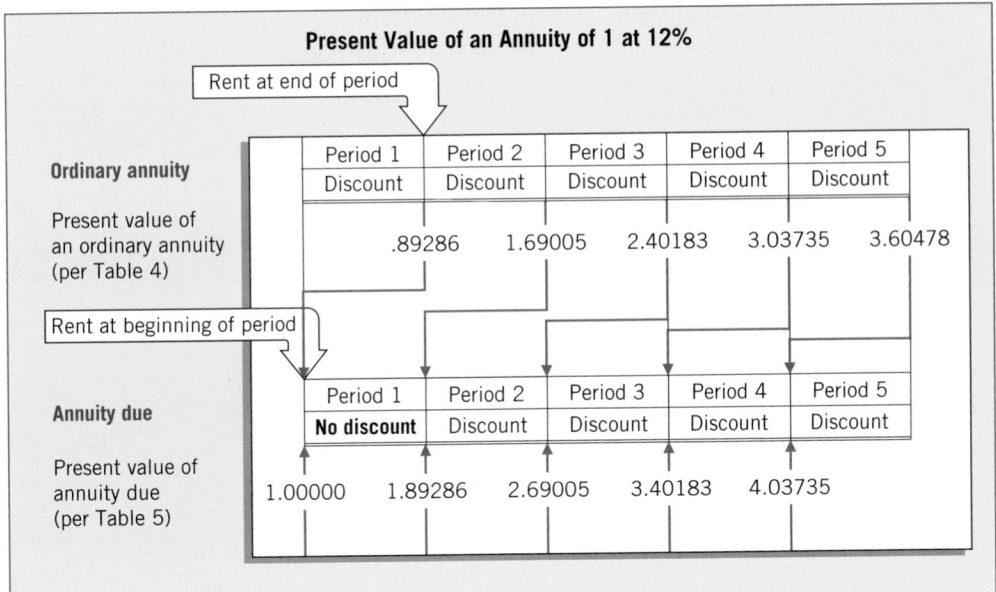

Illustration A-18
Comparison of Present Value of an Ordinary Annuity with an Annuity Due

This problem is time-diagrammed as follows.

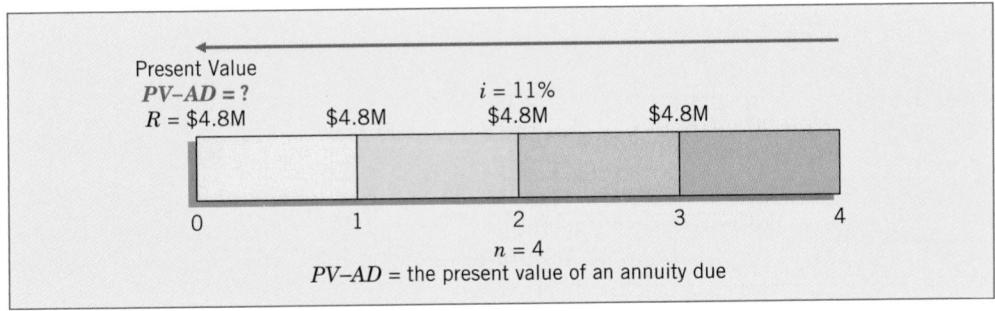

This problem is solved in the following manner.

1. Present value of an ordinary annuity of 1 for 4 periods at 11% (Table 4)	3.10245
2. Factor $(1 + .11)$	× 1.11
3. Present value of an annuity due of 1 for 4 periods at 11%	3.44372
4. Periodic deposit (rent)	× $4,800,000
5. Present value of payments	$16,529,856

Illustration A-19
Computation of Present Value of an Annuity Due

Since we have Table 5 for present value of an annuity due problems, we can also locate the desired factor 3.44372 and compute the present value of the lease payments to be $16,529,856.

Illustrations of Present Value of Annuity Problems

The following three illustrations demonstrate the computation of (1) the present value, (2) the interest rate, and (3) the amount of each rent.

Computation of the Present Value of an Ordinary Annuity

You have just won a lottery totaling $4,000,000 and learned that you will be paid the money by receiving a check in the amount of $200,000 at the end of each of the next 20 years. What amount have you really won? That is, what is the present value of the $200,000 checks you will receive over the next 20 years? A time diagram of this enviable situation is as follows (assuming an appropriate interest rate of 10%).

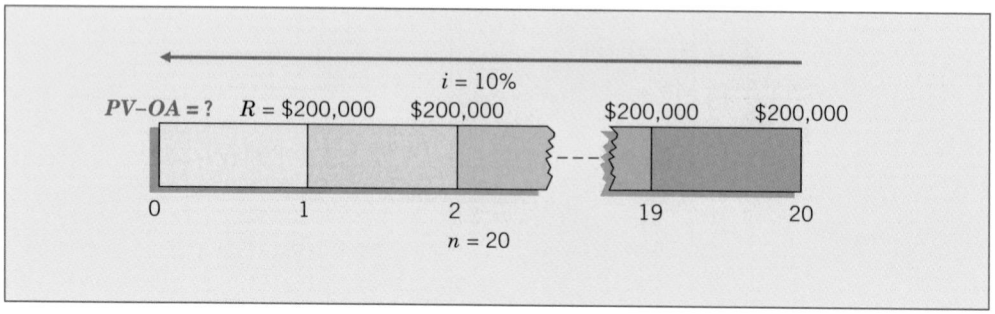

The present value is determined as follows:

$$\text{Present value of an ordinary annuity} = R\ (PVF\text{-}OA_{n,i})$$

$$= \$200,\!000\ (PVF\text{-}OA_{20,10\%})$$

$$= \$200,\!000\ (8.51356)$$

$$= \$1,\!702,\!712$$

As a result, if the state deposits $1,702,712 now and earns 10% interest, it can withdraw $200,000 a year for 20 years to pay you the $4,000,000.

Computation of the Interest Rate

Many shoppers make purchases by using a credit card. When you receive the invoice for payment you may pay the total amount due or you may pay the balance in a certain number of payments. For example, if you receive an invoice from VISA with a balance due of $528.77 and you are invited to pay it off in 12 equal monthly payments of $50 each, with the first payment due one month from now, what rate of interest would you be paying?

The $528.77 represents the present value of the 12 payments of $50 each at an unknown rate of interest. This situation in the form of a time diagram appears as follows.

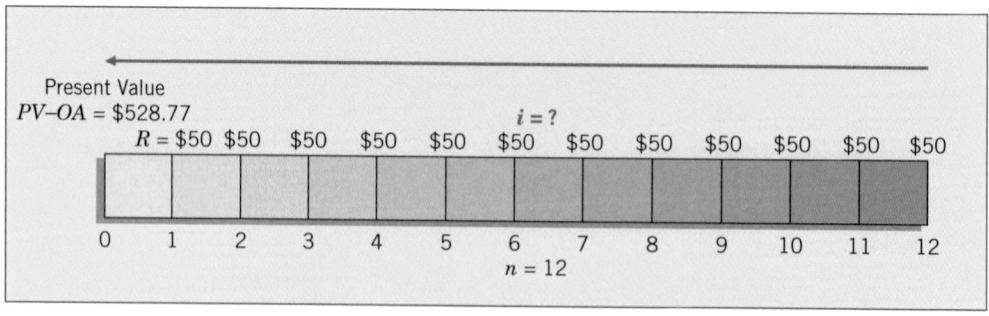

The rate is determined as follows.

$$\text{Present value of an ordinary annuity} = R\ (PVF\text{-}OA_{n,i})$$

$$\$528.77 = \$50\ (PVF\text{-}OA_{12,i})$$

$$(PVF\text{-}OA_{12,i}) = \frac{\$528.77}{\$50} = 10.57540$$

Referring to Table 4 and reading across the 12-period row, we find 10.57534 in the 2% column. Since 2% is a monthly rate, the nominal annual rate of interest is 24% (12 × 2%), and the effective annual rate is 26.82413% $[(1 + .02)^{12} - 1]$. Obviously, you're better off paying the entire bill now if you possibly can.

Computation of a Periodic Rent

Norm and Jackie Remmers have saved $18,000 to finance their daughter Dawna's college education. The money has been deposited in the Bloomington Savings and Loan Association and is earning 10% interest compounded semiannually. What equal amounts can their daughter withdraw at the end of every 6 months during the next 4 years while she attends college, without exhausting the fund? This situation is time-diagrammed as follows.

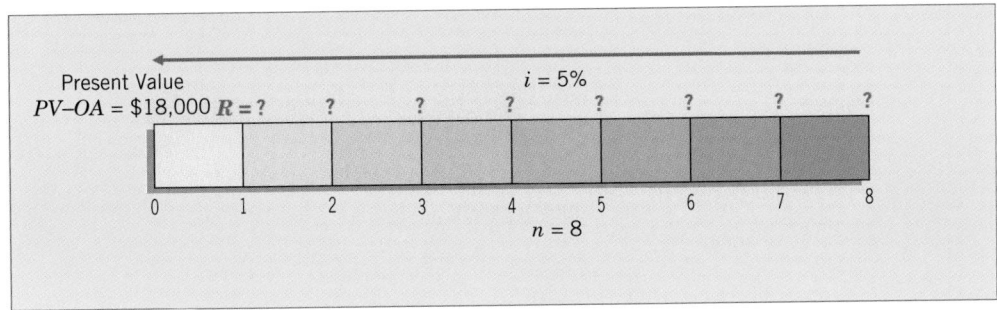

The answer is not determined simply by dividing $18,000 by 8 withdrawals because that would ignore the interest earned on the money remaining on deposit. Taking into consideration that interest is compounded semiannually at 5% (10% ÷ 2) for 8 periods (4 years × 2), and using the same present value of an ordinary annuity formula, we determine the amount of each withdrawal that she can make as follows.

$$\text{Present value of an ordinary annuity} = R\ (PVF\text{-}OA_{n,i})$$

$$\$18,000 = R\ (PVF\text{-}OA_{8,5\%})$$

$$\$18,000 = R\ (6.46321)$$

$$R = \$2,784.99$$

MORE COMPLEX SITUATIONS

Often it is necessary to use more than one table to solve time value problems. The business problem encountered may require that computations of both present value of a single sum and present value of an annuity be made. Two common situations are:

1. Deferred annuities.
2. Bond problems.

OBJECTIVE **8**
Solve present value problems related to deferred annuities and bonds.

Deferred Annuities

A **deferred annuity** is an annuity in which the rents begin after a specified number of periods. A deferred annuity does not begin to produce rents until 2 or more periods have expired. For example, "an **ordinary annuity** of six annual rents deferred 4 years" means that no rents will occur during the first 4 years, and that the first of the six rents will occur at the end of the fifth year. "An **annuity due** of six annual rents deferred 4 years" means that no rents will occur during the first 4 years, and that the first of six rents will occur at the beginning of the fifth year.

Future Value of a Deferred Annuity

In the case of the future value of a deferred annuity the computations are relatively straightforward. Because there is no accumulation or investment on which interest may accrue, the future value of a deferred annuity is the same as the future value of an annuity not deferred. That is, the deferral period is ignored in computing the future value.

To illustrate, assume that Sutton Corporation plans to purchase a land site in 6 years for the construction of its new corporate headquarters. Because of cash flow problems, Sutton is able to budget deposits of $80,000 that are expected to earn 12% annually only at the end of the fourth, fifth, and sixth periods. What future value will Sutton have accumulated at the end of the sixth year?

A time diagram of this situation is as follows.

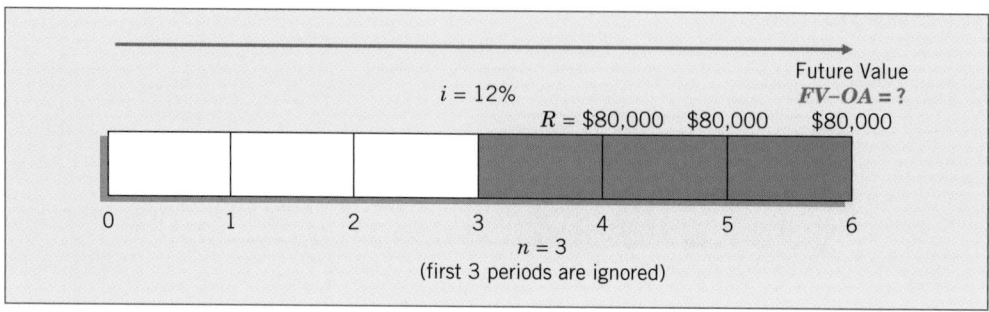

The value accumulated is determined by using the standard formula for the future value of an ordinary annuity:

$$\text{Future value of an ordinary annuity} = R\ (FVF\text{-}OA_{n,i})$$

$$= \$80,000\ (FVF\text{-}OA_{3,12\%})$$

$$= \$80,000\ (3.37440)$$

$$= \$269,952$$

Present Value of a Deferred Annuity

In computing the present value of a deferred annuity, the interest that accrues on the original investment during the deferral period must be recognized.

To compute the present value of a deferred annuity, we compute the present value of an ordinary annuity of 1 as if the rents had occurred for the entire period, and then subtract the present value of rents which were not received during the deferral period. We are left with the present value of the rents actually received subsequent to the deferral period.

To illustrate, Tom Bytehead has developed and copyrighted a software computer program that is a tutorial for students in advanced accounting. He agrees to sell the copyright to Campus Micro Systems for six annual payments of $5,000 each. The payments are to begin 5 years from today. Given an annual interest rate of 8%, what is the present value of the six payments?

This situation is an ordinary annuity of 6 payments deferred 4 periods. The following time diagram helps to visualize this sales agreement.

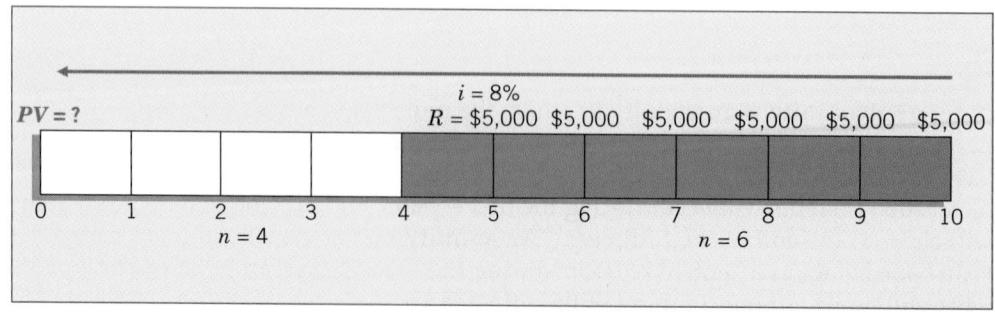

Two options are available to solve this problem. The first is to use only Table 4 as follows.

Illustration A-20
Computation of the
Present Value of a
Deferred Annuity

1. Each periodic rent		$5,000
2. Present value of an ordinary annuity of 1 for total periods (10) [number of rents (6) plus number of deferred periods (4)] at 8%	6.71008	
3. Less: Present value of an ordinary annuity of 1 for the number of deferred periods (4) at 8%	−3.31213	
4. Difference		× 3.39795
5. Present value of six rents of $5,000 deferred 4 periods		$16,989.75

The subtraction of the present value of an annuity of 1 for the deferred periods eliminates the nonexistent rents during the deferral period and converts the present value of an ordinary annuity of $1.00 for 10 periods to the present value of 6 rents of $1.00, deferred 4 periods.

Alternatively, the present value of the 6 rents could be computed using both Table 2 and Table 4. One can first discount the annuity 6 periods, but because the annuity is deferred 4 periods, the present value of the annuity must then be treated as a future amount to be discounted another 4 periods. A time diagram illustrates this two-step process as follows.

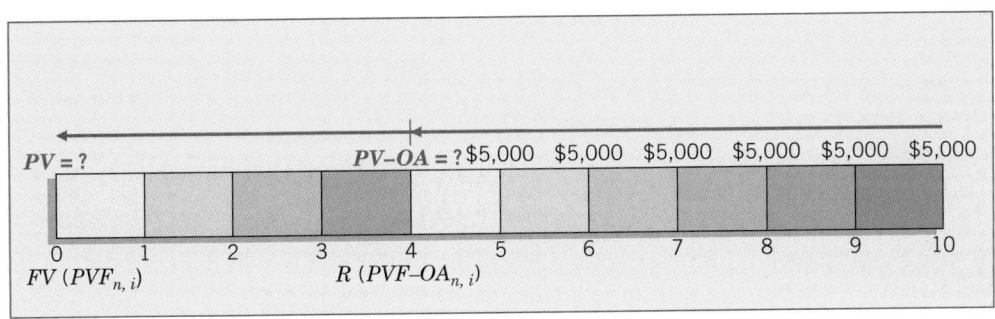

Step 1: Present value of
an ordinary annuity

$= R \ (PVF\text{-}OA_{n,i})$

$= \$5,000 \ (PVF\text{-}OA_{6,8\%})$

$= \$5,000 \ (4.62288)$
(Table 4, Present value of an ordinary annuity)

$= \$23,114.40$

Step 2: Present value

$= FV \ (PVF_{n,i})$

$= \$23,114.40 \ (PVF_{4,8\%})$

$= \$23,114.40 \ (.73503)$
(Table 4, Present value of a single sum)

$= \$16,989.78$

The present value of $16,989.78 computed above is the same result although computed differently from the first illustration.

Valuation of Long-Term Bonds

A long-term bond produces two cash flows: (1) periodic interest payments during the life of the bond, and (2) the principal (face value) paid at maturity. At the date of issue, bond buyers determine the present value of these two cash flows using the market rate of interest.

The periodic interest payments represent an annuity, and the principal represents a single-sum problem. The current market value of the bonds is the combined present values of the interest annuity and the principal amount.

To illustrate, Alltech Corporation on January 1, 2003, issues $100,000 of 9% bonds due in 5 years with interest payable annually at year-end. The current market rate of interest for bonds of similar risk is 11%. What will the buyers pay for this bond issue.

The time diagram depicting both cash flows is shown below.

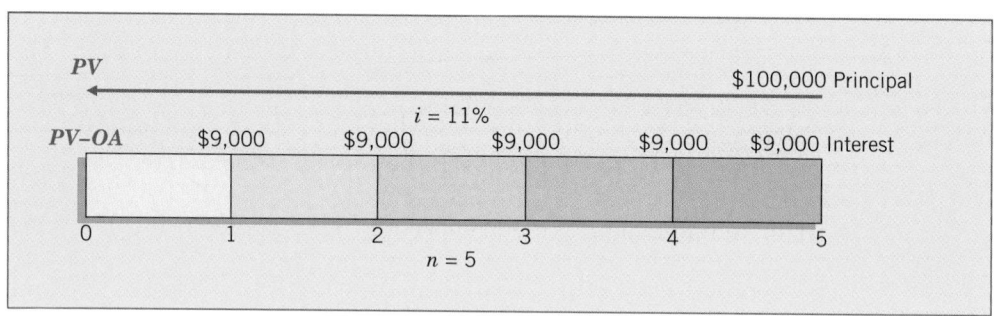

The present value of the two cash flows is computed by discounting at 11% as follows.

Illustration A-21
Computation of the Present Value of an Interest-Bearing Bond

1. Present value of the principal: FV $(PVF_{5,11\%}) = \$100,000$ (.59345) $59,345.00
2. Present value of the interest payments: R $(PVF\text{-}OA_{5,11\%}) = \$9,000$ (3.69590)   33,263.10
3. Combined present value (market price) — carrying value of bonds $92,608.10

By paying $92,608.10 at date of issue, the buyers of the bonds will realize an effective yield of 11% over the 5-year term of the bonds. This is true because the cash flows were discounted at 11%.

PRESENT VALUE MEASUREMENT

OBJECTIVE 9
Apply expected cash flows to present value measurement.

In the past, most accounting calculations of present value were based on the most likely cash flow amount. *Concepts Statement No. 7*[7] introduces an **expected cash flow approach** that uses a range of cash flows and incorporates the probabilities of those cash flows to provide a more relevant measurement of present value.

To illustrate the expected cash flow model, assume that there is a 30% probability that future cash flows will be $100, a 50% probability that they will be $200, and a 20% probability that they will be $300. In this case, the expected cash flow would be $190 [($100 × 0.3) + ($200 × 0.5) + ($300 × 0.2)]. Under traditional present value approaches, the most likely estimate ($200) would be used, but that estimate does not consider the different probabilities of the possible cash flows.

---

[7]"Using Cash Flow Information and Present Value in Accounting Measurements," *Statement of Financial Accounting Concepts No. 7* (Norwalk, Conn.: FASB, 2000).

After determining expected cash flows, the proper interest rate must then be used to discount the cash flows. The interest rate used for this purpose has three components:

THREE COMPONENTS OF INTEREST

① *Pure Rate of Interest (2%–4%).* This would be the amount a lender would charge if there were no possibilities of default and no expectation of inflation.

② *Expected Inflation Rate of Interest (0%–?).* Lenders recognize that in an inflationary economy, they are being paid back with less valuable dollars. As a result, they increase their interest rate to compensate for this loss in purchasing power. When inflationary expectations are high, interest rates are high.

③ *Credit Risk Rate of Interest (0%–5%).* The government has little or no credit risk (i.e., risk of nonpayment) when it issues bonds. A business enterprise, however, depending upon its financial stability, profitability, etc., can have a low or a high credit risk.

The FASB takes the position that after the expected cash flows are computed, they should be discounted by the **risk-free rate of return**, which is defined as **the pure rate of return plus the expected inflation rate**. The Board notes that the expected cash flow framework adjusts for credit risk because it incorporates the probability of receipt or payment into the computation of expected cash flows. Therefore the rate used to discount the expected cash flows should consider only the pure rate of interest and the inflation rate.

Expected Cash Flow Illustration

To illustrate application of these concepts, assume that Al's Appliance Outlet offers a 2-year warranty on all products sold. In 2003, Al sold $250,000 of a particular type of clothes dryer. Al's Appliance has entered into an agreement with Ralph's Repair to provide all warranty service on the dryers sold in 2003. Al's Appliance wishes to measure the fair value of the agreement to determine the warranty expense to record in 2003 and the amount of warranty liability to record on the December 31, 2003, balance sheet. Since there is not a ready market for these warranty contracts, Al's Appliance uses expected cash flow techniques to value the warranty obligation.

Based on prior warranty experience, Al's Appliance estimates the following expected cash outflows associated with the dryers sold in 2003.

Year	Cash Flow Estimate	×	Probability Assessment	=	Expected Cash Flow
2004	$3,800		20%		$ 760
	6,300		50%		3,150
	7,500		30%		2,250
			Total		$6,160
2005	$5,400		30%		$1,620
	7,200		50%		3,600
	8,400		20%		1,680
			Total		$6,900

Illustration A-22
Expected Cash Outflows–
Warranties

Applying expected cash flow concepts to these data, Al's Appliance estimates warranty cash outflows of $6,160 in 2004 and $6,900 in 2005.

The present value of these cash flows, assuming a risk-free rate of 5 percent and cash flows occurring at the end of the year, is shown in the following schedule.

Illustration A-23
Present Value of
Cash Flows

Year	Expected Cash Flow	×	PV Factor, $i = 5\%$	=	Present Value
2004	$6,160		0.95238		$ 5,870
2005	6,900		0.90703		6,260
				Total	$12,130

KEY TERMS

annuity, A13

annuity due, A13

compound interest, A3

deferred annuity, A23

discounting, A8

effective yield, A6

expected cash flow
    approach, A26

face rate, A6

future value, A8

interest, A2

nominal rate, A6

ordinary annuity, A13

present value, A9

principal, A2

risk-free rate of return, A27

simple interest, A2

stated rate, A6

time value of money, A1

SUMMARY OF LEARNING OBJECTIVES

❶ Identify accounting topics where the time value of money is relevant. Some of the applications of present value–based measurements to accounting topics are: (1) notes, (2) leases, (3) pensions and other postretirement benefits, (4) long-term assets, (5) sinking funds, (6) business combinations, (7) disclosures, and (8) installment contracts.

❷ Distinguish between simple and compound interest. See Fundamental Concepts following this Summary.

❸ Learn how to use appropriate compound interest tables. In order to identify the appropriate compound interest table to use, of the five given, you must identify whether you are solving for (1) the future value of a single sum, (2) the present value of a single sum, (3) the future value of a series of sums (an annuity), or (4) the present value of a series of sums (an annuity). In addition, when a series of sums (an annuity) is involved, you must identify whether these sums are received or paid (1) at the beginning of each period (annuity due) or (2) at the end of each period (ordinary annuity).

❹ Identify variables fundamental to solving interest problems. The following four variables are fundamental to all compound interest problems: (1) *Rate of interest:* unless otherwise stated, an annual rate that must be adjusted to reflect the length of the compounding period if less than a year. (2) *Number of time periods:* the number of compounding periods (a period may be equal to or less than a year). (3) *Future value:* the value at a future date of a given sum or sums invested assuming compound interest. (4) *Present value:* the value now (present time) of a future sum or sums discounted assuming compound interest.

❺ Solve future and present value of 1 problems. See Fundamental Concepts following this Summary, items 5(a) and 6(a).

❻ Solve future value of ordinary and annuity due problems. See Fundamental Concepts following this Summary, item 5(b).

❼ Solve present value of ordinary and annuity due problems. See Fundamental Concepts following this Summary, item 6(b).

❽ Solve present value problems related to deferred annuities and bonds. Deferred annuities are annuities in which rents begin after a specified number of periods. The future value of a deferred annuity is computed the same as the future value of an annuity not deferred. The present value of a deferred annuity is found by computing the present value of an ordinary annuity of 1 as if the rents had occurred for the entire period, and then subtracting the present value of rents not received during the deferral period. The current market value of bonds is the combined present values of the interest annuity and the principal amount.

◆ **Apply expected cash flows to present value measurement.** The expected cash flow approach uses a range of cash flows and the probabilities of those cash flows to provide the most likely estimate of expected cash flows. The proper interest rate used to discount the cash flows is the risk-free rate of return.

FUNDAMENTAL CONCEPTS

1. *Simple Interest.* Interest on principal only, regardless of interest that may have accrued in the past.

2. *Compound Interest.* Interest accrues on the unpaid interest of past periods as well as on the principal.

3. *Rate of Interest.* Interest is usually expressed as an annual rate, but when the compounding period is shorter than one year, the interest rate for the shorter period must be determined.

4. *Annuity.* A series of payments or receipts (called rents) that occur at equal intervals of time. Types of annuities:

   (a) *Ordinary Annuity.* Each rent is payable (receivable) at the end of the period.

   (b) *Annuity Due.* Each rent is payable (receivable) at the beginning of the period.

5. *Future Value.* Value at a later date of a single sum that is invested at compound interest.

   (a) *Future Value of 1* (or value of a single sum). The future value of $1.00 (or a single given sum), FV, at the end of n periods at i compound interest rate (Table 1).

   (b) *Future Value of an Annuity.* The future value of a series of rents invested at compound interest. In other words, the accumulated total that results from a series of equal deposits at regular intervals invested at compound interest. Both deposits and interest increase the accumulation.

      (1) *Future Value of an Ordinary Annuity.* The future value on the date of the last rent.

      (2) *Future Value of an Annuity Due.* The future value one period after the date of the last rent. When an annuity due table is not available, use Table 3 with the following formula.

$$\text{Value of annuity due of 1 for } n \text{ rents} = \text{(Value of ordinary annuity for } n \text{ rents)} \times (1 + \text{interest rate})$$

6. *Present Value.* The value at an earlier date (usually now) of a given future sum discounted at compound interest.

   (a) *Present Value of 1* (or present value of a single sum). The present value (worth) of $1.00 (or a given sum), due n periods hence, discounted at i compound interest (Table 2).

   (b) *Present Value of an Annuity.* The present value (worth) of a series of rents discounted at compound interest; in other words, it is the sum when invested at compound interest that will permit a series of equal withdrawals at regular intervals.

(1) *Present Value of an Ordinary Annuity.* The value now of $1.00 to be received or paid at the end of each period (rents) for *n* periods, discounted at *i* compound interest (Table 4).

(2) *Present Value of an Annuity Due.* The value now of $1.00 to be received or paid at the beginning of each period (rents) for *n* periods, discounted at *i* compound interest (Table 5). To use Table 4 for an annuity due, apply this formula.

Present value of annuity due of 1 for *n* rents = (Present value of an ordinary annuity of *n* rents) × (1 + interest rate)

EXERCISES

(Interest rates are per annum unless otherwise indicated.)

EA-1 **(Using Interest Tables)** For each of the following cases, indicate **(a)** to what rate columns, and **(b)** to what number of periods you would refer in looking up the interest factor.

1. In a future value of 1 table

Annual Rate	Number of Years Invested	Compounded
a. 9%	9	Annually
b. 12%	5	Quarterly
c. 10%	15	Semiannually

2. In a present value of an annuity of 1 table

Annual Rate	Number of Years Involved	Number of Rents Involved	Frequency of Rents
a. 9%	25	25	Annually
b. 10%	15	30	Semiannually
c. 12%	7	28	Quarterly

EA-2 **(Expected Cash Flows)** For each of the following, determine the expected cash flows.

	Cash Flow Estimate	Probability Assessment
(a)	$ 3,800	20%
	6,300	50%
	7,500	30%
(b)	$ 5,400	30%
	7,200	50%
	8,400	20%
(c)	$(1,000)	10%
	2,000	80%
	5,000	10%

EA-3 **(Expected Cash Flows and Present Value)** Andrew Kelly is trying to determine the amount to set aside so that he will have enough money on hand in 2 years to overhaul the engine on his vintage used car.

While there is some uncertainty about the cost of engine overhauls in 2 years, by conducting some research online, Andrew has developed the following estimates.

Engine Overhaul Estimated Cash Outflow	Probability Assessment
$200	10%
450	30%
550	50%
750	10%

Instructions

How much should Andrew Kelly deposit today in an account earning 6%, compounded annually, so that he will have enough money on hand in 2 years to pay for the overhaul?

EA-4 (Simple and Compound Interest Computations) Alan Jackson invests $20,000 at 8% annual interest, leaving the money invested without withdrawing any of the interest for 8 years. At the end of the 8 years, Alan withdrew the accumulated amount of money.

Instructions

(a) Compute the amount Alan would withdraw assuming the investment earns simple interest.
(b) Compute the amount Alan would withdraw assuming the investment earns interest compounded annually.
(c) Compute the amount Alan would withdraw assuming the investment earns interest compounded semi-annually.

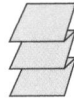

EA-5 (Computation of Future Values and Present Values) Using the appropriate interest table, answer each of the following questions. (Each case is independent of the others.)

(a) What is the future value of $7,000 at the end of 5 periods at 8% compounded interest?
(b) What is the present value of $7,000 due 8 periods hence, discounted at 11%?
(c) What is the future value of 15 periodic payments of $7,000 each made at the end of each period and compounded at 10%?
(d) What is the present value of $7,000 to be received at the end of each of 20 periods, discounted at 5% compound interest?

EA-6 (Computation of Future Values and Present Values) Using the appropriate interest table, answer the following questions. (Each case is independent of the others.)

(a) What is the future value of 20 periodic payments of $4,000 each made at the beginning of each period and compounded at 8%?
(b) What is the present value of $2,500 to be received at the beginning of each of 30 periods, discounted at 10% compound interest?
(c) What is the future value of 15 deposits of $2,000 each made at the beginning of each period and compounded at 10%? (Future value as of the end of the fifteenth period.)
(d) What is the present value of 6 receipts of $1,000 each received at the beginning of each period, discounted at 9% compounded interest?

EA-7 (Computation of Present Value) Using the appropriate interest table, compute the present values of the following periodic amounts due at the end of the designated periods.

(a) $30,000 receivable at the end of each period for 8 periods compounded at 12%.
(b) $30,000 payments to be made at the end of each period for 16 periods at 9%.
(c) $30,000 payable at the end of the seventh, eighth, ninth, and tenth periods at 12%.

EA-8 (Future Value and Present Value Problems) Presented below are three unrelated situations.

(a) Horace Grant Company recently signed a lease for a new office building, for a lease period of 10 years. Under the lease agreement, a security deposit of $12,000 is made, with the deposit to be returned at the expiration of the lease, with interest compounded at 10% per year. What amount will the company receive at the time the lease expires?

(b) Sharone Wright Corporation, having recently issued a $20 million, 15-year bond issue, is committed to make annual sinking fund deposits of $600,000. The deposits are made on the last day of each year, and yield a return of 10%. Will the fund at the end of 15 years be sufficient to retire the bonds? If not, what will the deficiency be?

(c) Under the terms of his salary agreement, president Rex Walters has an option of receiving either an immediate bonus of $40,000, or a deferred bonus of $70,000, payable in 10 years. Ignoring tax considerations, and assuming a relevant interest rate of 8%, which form of settlement should Walters accept?

EA-9 (Computation of Bond Prices) What would you pay for a $50,000 debenture bond that matures in 15 years and pays $5,000 a year in interest if you wanted to earn a yield of:

(a) 8%?   **(b)** 10%?   **(c)** 12%?

EA-10 (Computations for a Retirement Fund) Clarence Weatherspoon, a super salesman contemplating retirement on his fifty-fifth birthday, decides to create a fund on an 8% basis that will enable him to withdraw $20,000 per year on June 30, beginning in 2008, and continuing through 2011. To develop this fund, Clarence intends to make equal contributions on June 30 of each of the years 2004–2007.

Instructions

(a) How much must the balance of the fund equal on June 30, 2007, in order for Clarence Weatherspoon to satisfy his objective?
(b) What are each of Clarence's contributions to the fund?

 EA-11 (Unknown Rate) LEW Company purchased a machine at a price of $100,000 by signing a note payable, which requires a single payment of $123,210 in 2 years. Assuming annual compounding of interest, what rate of interest is being paid on the loan?

EA-12 (Unknown Periods and Unknown Interest Rate) Consider the following independent situations.

(a) Jerry Stackhouse wishes to become a millionaire. His money market fund has a balance of $92,296 and has a guaranteed interest rate of 10%. How many years must Jerry leave that balance in the fund in order to get his desired $1,000,000?
(b) Assume that Russell Maryland desires to accumulate $1 million in 15 years using his money market fund balance of $182,696. At what interest rate must Russell's investment compound annually?

EA-13 (Evaluation of Purchase Options) Sosa Excavating Inc. is purchasing a bulldozer. The equipment has a price of $100,000. The manufacturer has offered a payment plan that would allow Sosa to make 10 equal annual payments of $16,274.53, with the first payment due one year after the purchase.

Instructions

(a) How much total interest will Sosa pay on this payment plan?
(b) Sosa could borrow $100,000 from its bank to finance the purchase at an annual rate of 9%. Should Sosa borrow from the bank or use the manufacturer's payment plan to pay for the equipment?

EA-14 (Analysis of Alternatives) The Black Knights Inc., a manufacturer of high-sugar, low-sodium, low-cholesterol TV dinners, would like to increase its market share in the Sunbelt. In order to do so, Black Knights has decided to locate a new factory in the Panama City area. Black Knights will either buy or lease a site depending upon which is more advantageous. The site location committee has narrowed down the available sites to the following three buildings.

Building A: Purchase for a cash price of $600,000, useful life 25 years.

Building B: Lease for 25 years with annual lease payments of $69,000 being made at the beginning of the year.

Building C: Purchase for $650,000 cash. This building is larger than needed; however, the excess space can be sublet for 25 years at a net annual rental of $7,000. Rental payments will be received at the end of each year. The Black Knights Inc. has no aversion to being a landlord.

Instructions
In which building would you recommend that The Black Knights Inc. locate, assuming a 12% cost of funds?

EA-15 (Computation of Bond Liability) Katarina Witt Inc. manufactures skating equipment. Recently the vice president of operations of the company has requested construction of a new plant to meet the increasing demand for the company's skates. After a careful evaluation of the request, the board of directors has decided to raise funds for the new plant by issuing $2,000,000 of 11% term corporate bonds on March 1, 2003, due on March 1, 2018, with interest payable each March 1 and September 1. At the time of issuance, the market interest rate for similar financial instruments is 10%.

Instructions
As the controller of the company, determine the selling price of the bonds.

EA-16 (Computation of Pension Liability) Nerwin, Inc. is a furniture manufacturing company with 50 employees. Recently, after a long negotiation with the local labor union, the company decided to initiate a pension plan as a part of its compensation plan. The plan will start on January 1, 2003. Each employee covered by the plan is entitled to a pension payment each year after retirement. As required by accounting standards, the controller of the company needs to report the pension obligation (liability). On the basis of a discussion with the supervisor of the Personnel Department and an actuary from an insurance company, the controller develops the following information related to the pension plan.

Average length of time to retirement	15 years
Expected life duration after retirement	10 years
Total pension payment expected each year after retirement for all employees. Payment made at the end of the year.	$700,000 per year

The interest rate to be used is 8%.

Instructions
On the basis of the information above, determine the present value of the pension obligation (liability).

EA-17 (Investment Decision) Scottie Pippen just received a signing bonus of $1,000,000. His plan is to invest this payment in a fund that will earn 8%, compounded annually.

Instructions
(a) If Pippen plans to establish the Scottie Pippen Foundation once the fund grows to $1,999,000, how many years until he can establish the foundation?
(b) Instead of investing the entire $1,000,000, Pippen invests $300,000 today and plans to make 9 equal annual investments into the fund beginning one year from today. What amount should the payments be if Pippen plans to establish the $1,999,000 foundation at the end of 9 years?

EA-18 (Retirement of Debt) Jesper Parnevik borrowed $70,000 on March 1, 2002. This amount plus accrued interest at 12% compounded semiannually is to be repaid March 1, 2012. To retire this debt, Jesper plans to contribute to a debt retirement fund five equal amounts starting on March 1, 2007, and for the next 4 years. The fund is expected to earn 10% per annum.

Instructions
How much must be contributed each year by Jesper Parnevik to provide a fund sufficient to retire the debt on March 1, 2012?

EA-19 (Computation of Amount of Rentals) Your client, Vince Gill Leasing Company, is preparing a contract to lease a machine to Souvenirs Corporation for a period of 25 years. Gill has an investment cost of $365,755 in the machine, which has a useful life of 25 years and no salvage value at the end of that time. Your client is interested in earning an 11% return on its investment and has agreed to accept 25 equal rental payments at the end of each of the next 25 years.

Instructions
You are requested to provide Gill with the amount of each of the 25 rental payments that will yield an 11% return on investment.

EA-20 (Least Costly Payoff) Sonic Hedgehog Corporation has outstanding a contractual debt. The corporation has available two means of settlement: It can either make immediate payment of $2,600,000, or it can make annual payments of $300,000 for 15 years, each payment due on the last day of the year.

Instructions
Which method of payment do you recommend, assuming an expected effective interest rate of 8% during the future period?

EA-21 (Least Costly Payoff) Assuming the same facts as those in EA-20 except that the payments must begin now and be made on the first day of each of the 15 years, what payment method would you recommend?

PROBLEMS

(Interest rates are per annum unless otherwise indicated.)

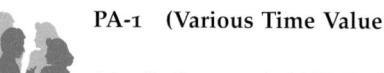

PA-1 (Various Time Value Situations) Answer each of these unrelated questions.

(a) On January 1, 2003, Rather Corporation sold a building that cost $250,000 and that had accumulated depreciation of $100,000 on the date of sale. Rather received as consideration a $275,000 non-interest-bearing note due on January 1, 2006. There was no established exchange price for the building, and the note had no ready market. The prevailing rate of interest for a note of this type on January 1, 2003, was 9%. At what amount should the gain from the sale of the building be reported?

(b) On January 1, 2003, Rather Corporation purchased 200 of the $1,000 face value, 9%, 10-year bonds of Walters Inc. The bonds mature on January 1, 2013, and pay interest annually beginning January 1, 2004. Rather Corporation purchased the bonds to yield 11%. How much did Rather pay for the bonds?

(c) Rather Corporation bought a new machine and agreed to pay for it in equal annual installments of $4,000 at the end of each of the next 10 years. Assuming that a prevailing interest rate of 8% applies to this contract, how much should Rather record as the cost of the machine?

(d) Rather Corporation purchased a special tractor on December 31, 2003. The purchase agreement stipulated that Rather should pay $20,000 at the time of purchase and $5,000 at the end of each of the next 8 years. The tractor should be recorded on December 31, 2003, at what amount, assuming an appropriate interest rate of 12%?

(e) Rather Corporation wants to withdraw $100,000 (including principal) from an investment fund at the end of each year for 9 years. What should be the required initial investment at the beginning of the first year if the fund earns 11%?

PA-2 (Various Time Value Situations) Using the appropriate interest table, provide the solution to each of the following four questions by computing the unknowns.

(a) What is the amount of the payments that Tom Brokaw must make at the end of each of 8 years to accumulate a fund of $70,000 by the end of the eighth year, if the fund earns 8% interest, compounded annually?

(b) Peter Jennings is 40 years old today and he wishes to accumulate $500,000 by his sixty-fifth birthday so he can retire to his summer place on Lake Hopatcong. He wishes to accumulate this amount by making equal deposits on his fortieth through his sixty-fourth birthdays. What annual deposit must Peter make if the fund will earn 12% interest compounded annually?

(c) Jane Pauley has $20,000 to invest today at 9% to pay a debt of $56,253. How many years will it take her to accumulate enough to liquidate the debt?

(d) Maria Shriver has a $27,600 debt that she wishes to repay 4 years from today; she has $18,181 that she intends to invest for the 4 years. What rate of interest will she need to earn annually in order to accumulate enough to pay the debt?

PA-3 (Analysis of Alternatives) Derrick Coleman Inc. has decided to surface and maintain for 10 years a vacant lot next to one of its discount-retail outlets to serve as a parking lot for customers. Management is considering the following bids involving two different qualities of surfacing for a parking area of 12,000 square yards.

Bid A: A surface that costs $5.25 per square yard to install. This surface will have to be replaced at the end of 5 years. The annual maintenance cost on this surface is estimated at 20 cents per square yard for each year except the last year of its service. The replacement surface will be similar to the initial surface.

Bid B: A surface that costs $9.50 per square yard to install. This surface has a probable useful life of 10 years and will require annual maintenance in each year except the last year, at an estimated cost of 9 cents per square yard.

Instructions

Prepare computations showing which bid should be accepted by Derrick Coleman Inc. You may assume that the cost of capital is 9%, that the annual maintenance expenditures are incurred at the end of each year, and that prices are not expected to change during the next 10 years.

PA-4 (Evaluating Payment Alternatives) Terry O'Malley has just learned he has won a $900,000 prize in the lottery. The lottery has given him two options for receiving the payments: (1) If Terry takes all the money today, the state and federal governments will deduct taxes at a rate of 46% immediately. (2) Alternatively, the lottery offers Terry a payout of 20 equal payments of $62,000 with the first payment occurring when Terry turns in the winning ticket. Terry will be taxed on each of these payments at a rate of 25%.

Instructions

Assuming Terry can earn an 8% rate of return (compounded annually) on any money invested during this period, which pay-out option should he choose?

PA-5 (Analysis of Alternatives) Sally Brown died, leaving to her husband Linus an insurance policy contract that provides that the beneficiary (Linus) can choose any one of the following four options.

(a) $55,000 immediate cash.
(b) $3,700 every 3 months payable at the end of each quarter for 5 years.
(c) $18,000 immediate cash and $1,600 every 3 months for 10 years, payable at the beginning of each 3-month period.
(d) $4,000 every 3 months for 3 years and $1,200 each quarter for the following 25 quarters, all payments payable at the end of each quarter.

Instructions

If money is worth 2½% per quarter, compounded quarterly, which option would you recommend that Linus exercise?

PA-6 (Expected Cash Flows and Present Value) Larry's Lawn Equipment sells high-quality lawn mowers and offers a 3-year warranty on all new lawn mowers sold. In 2003, Larry sold $300,000 of new specialty mowers for golf greens for which Larry's service department does not have the equipment to do the service. Larry has entered into an agreement with Mower Mavens to provide all warranty service on the special mowers sold in 2003. Larry wishes to measure the fair value of the agreement to determine the warranty liability for sales made in 2003. The controller for Larry's Lawn Equipment estimates the following expected warranty cash outflows associated with the mowers sold in 2003.

Year	Cash Flow Estimate	Probability Assessment
2004	$2,000	20%
	4,000	60%
	5,000	20%
2005	$2,500	30%
	5,000	50%
	6,000	20%
2006	$3,000	30%
	6,000	40%
	7,000	30%

Instructions

Using expected cash flow and present value techniques, determine the value of the warranty liability for the 2003 sales. Use an annual discount rate of 5%. Assume all cash flows occur at the end of the year.

PA-7 (Expected Cash Flows and Present Value) At the end of 2003, Richards Company is conducting an impairment test and needs to develop a fair value estimate for machinery used in its manufacturing operations. Given the nature of Richard's production process, the equipment is for special use. (No second-hand market values are available.) The equipment will be obsolete in 2 years, and Richard's accountants have developed the following cash flow information for the equipment.

Year	Cash Flow Estimate	Probability Assessment
2004	$6,000	40%
	8,000	60%
2005	$ (500)	20%
	2,000	60%
	3,000	20%
	Scrap Value	
2005	$ 500	50%
	700	50%

Instructions

Using expected cash flow and present value techniques, determine the fair value of the machinery at the end of 2003. Use a 6% discount rate, and assume all cash flows occur at the end of the year.

PA-8 (Purchase Price of a Business) During the past year, Nicole Bobek planted a new vineyard on 150 acres of land that she leases for $27,000 a year. She has asked you as her accountant to assist her in determining the value of her vineyard operation.

The vineyard will bear no grapes for the first 5 years (1–5). In the next 5 years (6–10), Nicole estimates that the vines will bear grapes that can be sold for $60,000 each year. For the next 20 years (11–30) she expects the harvest will provide annual revenues of $100,000. But during the last 10 years (31–40) of the vineyard's life she estimates that revenues will decline to $80,000 per year.

During the first 5 years the annual cost of pruning, fertilizing, and caring for the vineyard is estimated at $9,000; during the years of production, 6–40, these costs will rise to $10,000 per year. The relevant market rate of interest for the entire period is 12%. Assume that all receipts and payments are made at the end of each year.

Instructions

Dick Button has offered to buy Nicole's vineyard business by assuming the 40-year lease. On the basis of the current value of the business, what is the minimum price Nicole should accept?

PA-9 (Time Value Concepts Applied to Solve Business Problems) Answer the following questions related to Mark Grace Inc.

(a) Mark Grace Inc. has $572,000 to invest. The company is trying to decide between two alternative uses of the funds. One alternative provides $80,000 at the end of each year for 12 years, and the other is to receive a single lump sum payment of $1,900,000 at the end of the 12 years. Which alternative should Grace select? Assume the interest rate is constant over the entire investment.

(b) Mark Grace Inc. has completed the purchase of new IBM computers. The fair market value of the equipment is $824,150. The purchase agreement specifies an immediate down payment of $200,000 and semi-annual payments of $76,952 beginning at the end of 6 months for 5 years. What is the interest rate, to the nearest percent, used in discounting this purchase transaction?

(c) Mark Grace Inc. loans money to John Kruk Corporation in the amount of $600,000. Grace accepts an 8% note due in 7 years with interest payable semiannually. After 2 years (and receipt of interest for 2 years), Grace needs money and therefore sells the note to Chicago National Bank, which demands interest on the note of 10% compounded semiannually. What is the amount Grace will receive on the sale of the note?

(d) Mark Grace Inc. wishes to accumulate $1,300,000 by December 31, 2013, to retire bonds outstanding. The company deposits $300,000 on December 31, 2003, which will earn interest at 10% compounded quarterly, to help in the retirement of this debt. In addition, the company wants to know how much should be deposited at the end of each quarter for 10 years to ensure that $1,300,000 is available at the end of 2013. (The quarterly deposits will also earn at a rate of 10%, compounded quarterly.) Round to even dollars.

PA-10 (Analysis of Alternatives) Homer Simpson Inc., a manufacturer of steel school lockers, plans to purchase a new punch press for use in its manufacturing process. After contacting the appropriate vendors, the purchasing department received differing terms and options from each vendor. The Engineering Department has determined that each vendor's punch press is substantially identical and each has a useful life of 20 years. In addition, Engineering has estimated that required year-end maintenance costs will be $1,000 per year for the first 5 years, $2,000 per year for the next 10 years, and $3,000 per year for the last 5 years. Following is each vendor's sale package.

Vendor A: $45,000 cash at time of delivery and 10 year-end payments of $15,000 each. Vendor A offers all its customers the right to purchase at the time of sale a separate 20-year maintenance service contract, under which Vendor A will perform all year-end maintenance at a one-time initial cost of $10,000.

Vendor B: Forty seminannual payments of $8,000 each, with the first installment due upon delivery. Vendor B will perform all year-end maintenance for the next 20 years at no extra charge.

Vendor C: Full cash price of $125,000 will be due upon delivery.

Instructions
Assuming that both Vendor A and B will be able to perform the required year-end maintenance, that Simpson's cost of funds is 10%, and the machine will be purchased on January 1, from which vendor should the press be purchased?

PA-11 (Analysis of Business Problems) Jean-Luc is a financial executive with Starship Enterprises. Although Jean-Luc has not had any formal training in finance or accounting, he has a "good sense" for numbers and has helped the company grow from a very small company ($500,000 sales) to a large operation ($45 million in sales). With the business growing steadily, however, the company needs to make a number of difficult financial decisions in which Jean-Luc feels a little "over his head." He therefore has decided to hire a new employee with "numbers" expertise to help him. As a basis for determining whom to employ, he has decided to ask each prospective employee to prepare answers to questions relating to the following situations he has encountered recently. Here are the questions.

(a) In 2001, Starship Enterprises negotiated and closed a long-term lease contract for newly constructed truck terminals and freight storage facilities. The buildings were constructed on land owned by the company. On January 1, 2002, Starship took possession of the leased property. The 20-year lease is effective for the period January 1, 2002, through December 31, 2021. Advance rental payments of $800,000 are payable to the lessor (owner of facilities) on January 1 of each of the first 10 years of the lease term. Advance payments of $300,000 are due on January 1 for each of the last 10 years of the lease term. Starship has an option to purchase all the leased facilities for $1.00 on December 31, 2021. At the time the lease was negotiated, the fair market value of the truck terminals and freight storage facilities was approximately $7,200,000. If the company had borrowed the money to purchase the facilities, it would have had to pay 10% interest. Should the company have purchased rather than leased the facilities?

(b) Last year the company exchanged a piece of land for a noninterest-bearing note. The note is to be paid at the rate of $12,000 per year for 9 years, beginning one year from the date of disposal of the land. An appropriate rate of interest for the note was 11%. At the time the land was originally purchased, it cost $90,000. What is the fair value of the note?

(c) The company has always followed the policy to take any cash discounts on goods purchased. Recently the company purchased a large amount of raw materials at a price of $800,000 with terms 2/10, n/30 on which it took the discount. Starship has recently estimated its cost of funds at 10%. Should Starship continue this policy of always taking the cash discount?

PA-12 (Analysis of Lease vs. Purchase) Jose Rijo Inc. owns and operates a number of hardware stores in the New England region. Recently the company has decided to locate another store in a rapidly growing area of Maryland. The company is trying to decide whether to purchase or lease the building and related facilities.

Purchase: The company can purchase the site, construct the building, and purchase all store fixtures. The cost would be $1,650,000. An immediate down payment of $400,000 is required, and the remaining $1,250,000 would be paid off over 5 years at $300,000 per year (including interest). The property is expected to have a useful life of 12 years, and then it will be sold for $500,000. As the owner of the property, the company will have the following out-of-pocket expenses each period.

Property taxes (to be paid at the end of each year)	$40,000
Insurance (to be paid at the beginning of each year)	27,000
Other (primarily maintenance which occurs at the end of each year)	16,000
	$83,000

Lease: First National Bank has agreed to purchase the site, construct the building, and install the appropriate fixtures for Rijo Inc. if Rijo will lease the completed facility for 12 years. The annual costs for the lease would be $240,000. Rijo would have no responsibility related to the facility over the 12 years. The terms of the lease are that Rijo would be required to make 12 annual payments (the first payment to be made at the time the store opens and then each following year). In addition, a deposit of $100,000 is required when the store is opened. This deposit will be returned at the end of the twelfth year, assuming no unusual damage to the building structure or fixtures.

Currently the cost of funds for Rijo Inc. is 10%.

Instructions
Which of the two approaches should Rijo Inc. follow?

PA-13 (Pension Funding) You have been hired as a benefit consultant by Maugarite Alomar, the owner of Attic Angels. She wants to establish a retirement plan for herself and her three employees. Maugarite has provided the following information: The retirement plan is to be based upon annual salary for the last year before retirement and is to provide 50% of Maugarite's last-year annual salary and 40% of the last-year annual salary for each employee. The plan will make annual payments at the beginning of each year for 20 years from the date of retirement. Maugarite wishes to fund the plan by making 15 annual deposits beginning January 1, 2003. Invested funds will earn 12% compounded annually. Information about plan participants as of January 1, 2003, is as follows.

Maugarite Alomar, owner: Current annual salary of $40,000; estimated retirement date January 1, 2028.
Kenny Rogers, flower arranger: Current annual salary of $30,000; estimated retirement date January 1, 2033.
Anita Baker, sales clerk: Current annual salary of $15,000; estimated retirement date January 1, 2023.
Willie Nelson, part-time bookkeeper: Current annual salary of $15,000; estimated retirement date January 1, 2018.

In the past, Maugarite has given herself and each employee a year-end salary increase of 4%. Maugarite plans to continue this policy in the future.

Instructions
(a) Based upon the above information, what will be the annual retirement benefit for each plan participant? (Round to the nearest dollar.) (*Hint:* Maugarite will receive raises for 24 years.)
(b) What amount must be on deposit at the end of 15 years to ensure that all benefits will be paid? (Round to the nearest dollar.)
(c) What is the amount of each annual deposit Maugarite must make to the retirement plan?

TABLE 1   FUTURE VALUE OF 1 (FUTURE VALUE OF A SINGLE SUM)

$$FVF_{n,i} = (1 + i)^n$$

(n) Periods	2%	2½%	3%	4%	5%	6%
1	1.02000	1.02500	1.03000	1.04000	1.05000	1.06000
2	1.04040	1.05063	1.06090	1.08160	1.10250	1.12360
3	1.06121	1.07689	1.09273	1.12486	1.15763	1.19102
4	1.08243	1.10381	1.12551	1.16986	1.21551	1.26248
5	1.10408	1.13141	1.15927	1.21665	1.27628	1.33823
6	1.12616	1.15969	1.19405	1.26532	1.34010	1.41852
7	1.14869	1.18869	1.22987	1.31593	1.40710	1.50363
8	1.17166	1.21840	1.26677	1.36857	1.47746	1.59385
9	1.19509	1.24886	1.30477	1.42331	1.55133	1.68948
10	1.21899	1.28008	1.34392	1.48024	1.62889	1.79085
11	1.24337	1.31209	1.38423	1.53945	1.71034	1.89830
12	1.26824	1.34489	1.42576	1.60103	1.79586	2.01220
13	1.29361	1.37851	1.46853	1.66507	1.88565	2.13293
14	1.31948	1.41297	1.51259	1.73168	1.97993	2.26090
15	1.34587	1.44830	1.55797	1.80094	2.07893	2.39656
16	1.37279	1.48451	1.60471	1.87298	2.18287	2.54035
17	1.40024	1.52162	1.65285	1.94790	2.29202	2.69277
18	1.42825	1.55966	1.70243	2.02582	2.40662	2.85434
19	1.45681	1.59865	1.75351	2.10685	2.52695	3.02560
20	1.48595	1.63862	1.80611	2.19112	2.65330	3.20714
21	1.51567	1.67958	1.86029	2.27877	2.78596	3.39956
22	1.54598	1.72157	1.91610	2.36992	2.92526	3.60354
23	1.57690	1.76461	1.97359	2.46472	3.07152	3.81975
24	1.60844	1.80873	2.03279	2.56330	3.22510	4.04893
25	1.64061	1.85394	2.09378	2.66584	3.38635	4.29187
26	1.67342	1.90029	2.15659	2.77247	3.55567	4.54938
27	1.70689	1.94780	2.22129	2.88337	3.73346	4.82235
28	1.74102	1.99650	2.28793	2.99870	3.92013	5.11169
29	1.77584	2.04641	2.35657	3.11865	4.11614	5.41839
30	1.81136	2.09757	2.42726	3.24340	4.32194	5.74349
31	1.84759	2.15001	2.50008	3.37313	4.53804	6.08810
32	1.88454	2.20376	2.57508	3.50806	4.76494	6.45339
33	1.92223	2.25885	2.65234	3.64838	5.00319	6.84059
34	1.96068	2.31532	2.73191	3.79432	5.25335	7.25103
35	1.99989	2.37321	2.81386	3.94609	5.51602	7.68609
36	2.03989	2.43254	2.89828	4.10393	5.79182	8.14725
37	2.08069	2.49335	2.98523	4.26809	6.08141	8.63609
38	2.12230	2.55568	3.07478	4.43881	6.38548	9.15425
39	2.16474	2.61957	3.16703	4.61637	6.70475	9.70351
40	2.20804	2.68506	3.26204	4.80102	7.03999	10.28572

TABLE 1   FUTURE VALUE OF 1

8%	9%	10%	11%	12%	15%	(n) Periods
1.08000	1.09000	1.10000	1.11000	1.12000	1.15000	1
1.16640	1.18810	1.21000	1.23210	1.25440	1.32250	2
1.25971	1.29503	1.33100	1.36763	1.40493	1.52088	3
1.36049	1.41158	1.46410	1.51807	1.57352	1.74901	4
1.46933	1.53862	1.61051	1.68506	1.76234	2.01136	5
1.58687	1.67710	1.77156	1.87041	1.97382	2.31306	6
1.71382	1.82804	1.94872	2.07616	2.21068	2.66002	7
1.85093	1.99256	2.14359	2.30454	2.47596	3.05902	8
1.99900	2.17189	2.35795	2.55803	2.77308	3.51788	9
2.15892	2.36736	2.59374	2.83942	3.10585	4.04556	10
2.33164	2.58043	2.85312	3.15176	3.47855	4.65239	11
2.51817	2.81267	3.13843	3.49845	3.89598	5.35025	12
2.71962	3.06581	3.45227	3.88328	4.36349	6.15279	13
2.93719	3.34173	3.79750	4.31044	4.88711	7.07571	14
3.17217	3.64248	4.17725	4.78459	5.47357	8.13706	15
3.42594	3.97031	4.59497	5.31089	6.13039	9.35762	16
3.70002	4.32763	5.05447	5.89509	6.86604	10.76126	17
3.99602	4.71712	5.55992	6.54355	7.68997	12.37545	18
4.31570	5.14166	6.11591	7.26334	8.61276	14.23177	19
4.66096	5.60441	6.72750	8.06231	9.64629	16.36654	20
5.03383	6.10881	7.40025	8.94917	10.80385	18.82152	21
5.43654	6.65860	8.14028	9.93357	12.10031	21.64475	22
5.87146	7.25787	8.95430	11.02627	13.55235	24.89146	23
6.34118	7.91108	9.84973	12.23916	15.17863	28.62518	24
6.84847	8.62308	10.83471	13.58546	17.00000	32.91895	25
7.39635	9.39916	11.91818	15.07986	19.04007	37.85680	26
7.98806	10.24508	13.10999	16.73865	21.32488	43.53532	27
8.62711	11.16714	14.42099	18.57990	23.88387	50.06561	28
9.31727	12.17218	15.86309	20.62369	26.74993	57.57545	29
10.06266	13.26768	17.44940	22.89230	29.95992	66.21177	30
10.86767	14.46177	19.19434	25.41045	33.55511	76.14354	31
11.73708	15.76333	21.11378	28.20560	37.58173	87.56507	32
12.67605	17.18203	23.22515	31.30821	42.09153	100.69983	33
13.69013	18.72841	25.54767	34.75212	47.14252	115.80480	34
14.78534	20.41397	28.10244	38.57485	52.79962	133.17552	35
15.96817	22.25123	30.91268	42.81808	59.13557	153.15185	36
17.24563	24.25384	34.00395	47.52807	66.23184	176.12463	37
18.62528	26.43668	37.40434	52.75616	74.17966	202.54332	38
20.11530	28.81598	41.14479	58.55934	83.08122	232.92482	39
21.72452	31.40942	45.25926	65.00087	93.05097	267.86355	40

TABLE 2   PRESENT VALUE OF 1 (PRESENT VALUE OF A SINGLE SUM)

$$PVF_{n,i} = \frac{1}{(1 + i)^n} = (1 + i)^{-n}$$

(n) Periods	2%	2½%	3%	4%	5%	6%
1	.98039	.97561	.97087	.96154	.95238	.94340
2	.96117	.95181	.94260	.92456	.90703	.89000
3	.94232	.92860	.91514	.88900	.86384	.83962
4	.92385	.90595	.88849	.85480	.82270	.79209
5	.90573	.88385	.86261	.82193	.78353	.74726
6	.88797	.86230	.83748	.79031	.74622	.70496
7	.87056	.84127	.81309	.75992	.71068	.66506
8	.85349	.82075	.78941	.73069	.67684	.62741
9	.83676	.80073	.76642	.70259	.64461	.59190
10	.82035	.78120	.74409	.67556	.61391	.55839
11	.80426	.76214	.72242	.64958	.58468	.52679
12	.78849	.74356	.70138	.62460	.55684	.49697
13	.77303	.72542	.68095	.60057	.53032	.46884
14	.75788	.70773	.66112	.57748	.50507	.44230
15	.74301	.69047	.64186	.55526	.48102	.41727
16	.72845	.67362	.62317	.53391	.45811	.39365
17	.71416	.65720	.60502	.51337	.43630	.37136
18	.70016	.64117	.58739	.49363	.41552	.35034
19	.68643	.62553	.57029	.47464	.39573	.33051
20	.67297	.61027	.55368	.45639	.37689	.31180
21	.65978	.59539	.53755	.43883	.35894	.29416
22	.64684	.58086	.52189	.42196	.34185	.22751
23	.63416	.56670	.50669	.40573	.32557	.26180
24	.62172	.55288	.49193	.39012	.31007	.24698
25	.60953	.53939	.47761	.37512	.29530	.23300
26	.59758	.52623	.46369	.36069	.28124	.21981
27	.58586	.51340	.45019	.34682	.26785	.20737
28	.57437	.50088	.43708	.33348	.25509	.19563
29	.56311	.48866	.42435	.32065	.24295	.18456
30	.55207	.47674	.41199	.30832	.23138	.17411
31	.54125	.46511	.39999	.29646	.22036	.16425
32	.53063	.45377	.38834	.28506	.20987	.15496
33	.52023	.44270	.37703	.27409	.19987	.14619
34	.51003	.43191	.36604	.26355	.19035	.13791
35	.50003	.42137	.35538	.25342	.18129	.13011
36	.49022	.41109	.34503	.24367	.17266	.12274
37	.48061	.40107	.33498	.23430	.16444	.11579
38	.47119	.39128	.32523	.22529	.15661	.10924
39	.46195	.38174	.31575	.21662	.14915	.10306
40	.45289	.37243	.30656	.20829	.14205	.09722

TABLE 2   PRESENT VALUE OF 1

8%	9%	10%	11%	12%	15%	(n) Periods
.92593	.91743	.90909	.90090	.89286	.86957	1
.85734	.84168	.82645	.81162	.79719	.75614	2
.79383	.77218	.75132	.73119	.71178	.65752	3
.73503	.70843	.68301	.65873	.63552	.57175	4
.68058	.64993	.62092	.59345	.56743	.49718	5
.63017	.59627	.56447	.53464	.50663	.43233	6
.58349	.54703	.51316	.48166	.45235	.37594	7
.54027	.50187	.46651	.43393	.40388	.32690	8
.50025	.46043	.42410	.39092	.36061	.28426	9
.46319	.42241	.38554	.35218	.32197	.24719	10
.42888	.38753	.35049	.31728	.28748	.21494	11
.39711	.35554	.31863	.28584	.25668	.18691	12
.36770	.32618	.28966	.25751	.22917	.16253	13
.34046	.29925	.26333	.23199	.20462	.14133	14
.31524	.27454	.23939	.20900	.18270	.12289	15
.29189	.25187	.21763	.18829	.16312	.10687	16
.27027	.23107	.19785	.16963	.14564	.09293	17
.25025	.21199	.17986	.15282	.13004	.08081	18
.23171	.19449	.16351	.13768	.11611	.07027	19
.21455	.17843	.14864	.12403	.10367	.06110	20
.19866	.16370	.13513	.11174	.09256	.05313	21
.18394	.15018	.12285	.10067	.08264	.04620	22
.17032	.13778	.11168	.09069	.07379	.04017	23
.15770	.12641	.10153	.08170	.06588	.03493	24
.14602	.11597	.09230	.07361	.05882	.03038	25
.13520	.10639	.08391	.06631	.05252	.02642	26
.12519	.09761	.07628	.05974	.04689	.02297	27
.11591	.08955	.06934	.05382	.04187	.01997	28
.10733	.08216	.06304	.04849	.03738	.01737	29
.09938	.07537	.05731	.04368	.03338	.01510	30
.09202	.06915	.05210	.03935	.02980	.01313	31
.08520	.06344	.04736	.03545	.02661	.01142	32
.07889	.05820	.04306	.03194	.02376	.00993	33
.07305	.05340	.03914	.02878	.02121	.00864	34
.06763	.04899	.03558	.02592	.01894	.00751	35
.06262	.04494	.03235	.02335	.01691	.00653	36
.05799	.04123	.02941	.02104	.01510	.00568	37
.05369	.03783	.02674	.01896	.01348	.00494	38
.04971	.03470	.02430	.01708	.01204	.00429	39
.04603	.03184	.02210	.01538	.01075	.00373	40

TABLE 3 FUTURE VALUE OF AN ORDINARY ANNUITY OF 1

$$\text{FVF-OA}_{n,i} = \frac{(1 + i)^n - 1}{i}$$

(n) Periods	2%	2½%	3%	4%	5%	6%
1	1.00000	1.00000	1.00000	1.00000	1.00000	1.00000
2	2.02000	2.02500	2.03000	2.04000	2.05000	2.06000
3	3.06040	3.07563	3.09090	3.12160	3.15250	3.18360
4	4.12161	4.15252	4.18363	4.24646	4.31013	4.37462
5	5.20404	5.25633	5.30914	5.41632	5.52563	5.63709
6	6.30812	6.38774	6.46841	6.63298	6.80191	6.97532
7	7.43428	7.54743	7.66246	7.89829	8.14201	8.39384
8	8.58297	8.73612	8.89234	9.21423	9.54911	9.89747
9	9.75463	9.95452	10.15911	10.58280	11.02656	11.49132
10	10.94972	11.20338	11.46338	12.00611	12.57789	13.18079
11	12.16872	12.48347	12.80780	13.48635	14.20679	14.97164
12	13.41209	13.79555	14.19203	15.02581	15.91713	16.86994
13	14.68033	15.14044	15.61779	16.62684	17.71298	18.88214
14	15.97394	16.51895	17.08632	18.29191	19.59863	21.01507
15	17.29342	17.93193	18.59891	20.02359	21.57856	23.27597
16	18.63929	19.38022	20.15688	21.82453	23.65749	25.67253
17	20.01207	20.86473	21.76159	23.69751	25.84037	28.21288
18	21.41231	22.38635	23.41444	25.64541	28.13238	30.90565
19	22.84056	23.94601	25.11687	27.67123	30.53900	33.75999
20	24.29737	25.54466	26.87037	29.77808	33.06595	36.78559
21	25.78332	27.18327	28.67649	31.96920	35.71925	39.99273
22	27.29898	28.86286	30.53678	34.24797	38.50521	43.39229
23	28.84496	30.58443	32.45288	36.61789	41.43048	46.99583
24	30.42186	32.34904	34.42647	39.08260	44.50200	50.81558
25	32.03030	34.15776	36.45926	41.64591	47.72710	54.86451
26	33.67091	36.01171	38.55304	44.31174	51.11345	59.15638
27	35.34432	37.91200	40.70963	47.08421	54.66913	63.70577
28	37.05121	39.85980	42.93092	49.96758	58.40258	68.52811
29	38.79223	41.85630	45.21885	52.96629	62.32271	73.63980
30	40.56808	43.90270	47.57542	56.08494	66.43885	79.05819
31	42.37944	46.00027	50.00268	59.32834	70.76079	84.80168
32	44.22703	48.15028	52.50276	62.70147	75.29883	90.88978
33	46.11157	50.35403	55.07784	66.20953	80.06377	97.34316
34	48.03380	52.61289	57.73018	69.85791	85.06696	104.18376
35	49.99448	54.92821	60.46208	73.65222	90.32031	111.43478
36	51.99437	57.30141	63.27594	77.59831	95.83632	119.12087
37	54.03425	59.73395	66.17422	81.70225	101.62814	127.26812
38	56.11494	62.22730	69.15945	85.97034	107.70955	135.90421
39	58.23724	64.78298	72.23423	90.40915	114.09502	145.05846
40	60.40198	67.40255	75.40126	95.02552	120.79977	154.76197

TABLE 3   FUTURE VALUE OF AN ORDINARY ANNUITY OF 1

8%	9%	10%	11%	12%	15%	(n) Periods
1.00000	1.00000	1.00000	1.00000	1.00000	1.00000	1
2.08000	2.09000	2.10000	2.11000	2.12000	2.15000	2
3.24640	3.27810	3.31000	3.34210	3.37440	3.47250	3
4.50611	4.57313	4.64100	4.70973	4.77933	4.99338	4
5.86660	5.98471	6.10510	6.22780	6.35285	6.74238	5
7.33592	7.52334	7.71561	7.91286	8.11519	8.75374	6
8.92280	9.20044	9.48717	9.78327	10.08901	11.06680	7
10.63663	11.02847	11.43589	11.85943	12.29969	13.72682	8
12.48756	13.02104	13.57948	14.16397	14.77566	16.78584	9
14.48656	15.19293	15.93743	16.72201	17.54874	20.30372	10
16.64549	17.56029	18.53117	19.56143	20.65458	24.34928	11
18.97713	20.14072	21.38428	22.71319	24.13313	29.00167	12
21.49530	22.95339	24.52271	26.21164	28.02911	34.35192	13
24.21492	26.01919	27.97498	30.09492	32.39260	40.50471	14
27.15211	29.36092	31.77248	34.40536	37.27972	47.58041	15
30.32428	33.00340	35.94973	39.18995	42.75328	55.71747	16
33.75023	36.97371	40.54470	44.50084	48.88367	65.07509	17
37.45024	41.30134	45.59917	50.39593	55.74972	75.83636	18
41.44626	46.01846	51.15909	56.93949	63.43968	88.21181	19
45.76196	51.16012	57.27500	64.20283	72.05244	102.44358	20
50.42292	56.76453	64.00250	72.26514	81.69874	118.81012	21
55.45676	62.87334	71.40275	81.21431	92.50258	137.63164	22
60.89330	69.53194	79.54302	91.14788	104.60289	159.27638	23
66.76476	76.78981	88.49733	102.17415	118.15524	184.16784	24
73.10594	84.70090	98.34706	114.41331	133.33387	212.79302	25
79.95442	93.32398	109.18177	127.99877	150.33393	245.71197	26
87.35077	102.72314	121.09994	143.07864	169.37401	283.56877	27
95.33883	112.96822	134.20994	159.81729	190.69889	327.10408	28
103.96594	124.13536	148.63093	178.39719	214.58275	377.16969	29
113.28321	136.30754	164.49402	199.02088	241.33268	434.74515	30
123.34587	149.57522	181.94343	221.91317	271.29261	500.95692	31
134.21354	164.03699	201.13777	247.32362	304.84772	577.10046	32
145.95062	179.80032	222.25154	275.52922	342.42945	644.66553	33
158.62667	196.98234	245.47670	306.83744	384.52098	765.36535	34
172.31680	215.71076	271.02437	341.58955	431.66350	881.17016	35
187.10215	236.12472	299.12681	380.16441	484.46312	1014.34568	36
203.07032	258.37595	330.03949	422.98249	543.59869	1167.49753	37
220.31595	282.62978	364.04343	470.51056	609.83053	1343.62216	38
238.94122	309.06646	401.44778	523.26673	684.01020	1546.16549	39
259.05652	337.88245	442.59256	581.82607	767.09142	1779.09031	40

TABLE 4 PRESENT VALUE OF AN ORDINARY ANNUITY OF 1

$$PVF\text{-}OA_{n,i} = \frac{1 - \dfrac{1}{(1 + i)^n}}{i}$$

(n) Periods	2%	2½%	3%	4%	5%	6%
1	.98039	.97561	.97087	.96154	.95238	.94340
2	1.94156	1.92742	1.91347	1.88609	1.85941	1.83339
3	2.88388	2.85602	2.82861	2.77509	2.72325	2.67301
4	3.80773	3.76197	3.71710	3.62990	3.54595	3.46511
5	4.71346	4.64583	4.57971	4.45182	4.32948	4.21236
6	5.60143	5.50813	5.41719	5.24214	5.07569	4.91732
7	6.47199	6.34939	6.23028	6.00205	5.78637	5.58238
8	7.32548	7.17014	7.01969	6.73274	6.46321	6.20979
9	8.16224	7.97087	7.78611	7.43533	7.10782	6.80169
10	8.98259	8.75206	8.53020	8.11090	7.72173	7.36009
11	9.78685	9.51421	9.25262	8.76048	8.30641	7.88687
12	10.57534	10.25776	9.95400	9.38507	8.86325	8.38384
13	11.34837	10.98319	10.63496	9.98565	9.39357	8.85268
14	12.10625	11.69091	11.29607	10.56312	9.89864	9.29498
15	12.84926	12.38138	11.93794	11.11839	10.37966	9.71225
16	13.57771	13.05500	12.56110	11.65230	10.83777	10.10590
17	14.29187	13.71220	13.16612	12.16567	11.27407	10.47726
18	14.99203	14.35336	13.75351	12.65930	11.68959	10.82760
19	15.67846	14.97889	14.32380	13.13394	12.08532	11.15812
20	16.35143	15.58916	14.87747	13.59033	12.46221	11.46992
21	17.01121	16.18455	15.41502	14.02916	12.82115	11.76408
22	17.65805	16.76541	15.93692	14.45112	13.16300	12.04158
23	18.29220	17.33211	16.44361	14.85684	13.48857	12.30338
24	18.91393	17.88499	16.93554	15.24696	13.79864	12.55036
25	19.52346	18.42438	17.41315	15.62208	14.09394	12.78336
26	20.12104	18.95061	17.87684	15.98277	14.37519	13.00317
27	20.70690	19.46401	18.32703	16.32959	14.64303	13.21053
28	21.28127	19.96489	18.76411	16.66306	14.89813	13.40616
29	21.84438	20.45355	19.18845	16.98371	15.14107	13.59072
30	22.39646	20.93029	19.60044	17.29203	15.37245	13.76483
31	22.93770	21.39541	20.00043	17.58849	15.59281	13.92909
32	23.46833	21.84918	20.38877	17.87355	15.80268	14.08404
33	23.98856	22.29188	20.76579	18.14765	16.00255	14.23023
34	24.49859	22.72379	21.13184	18.41120	16.19290	14.36814
35	24.99862	23.14516	21.48722	18.66461	16.37419	14.49825
36	25.48884	23.55625	21.83225	18.90828	16.54685	14.62099
37	25.96945	23.95732	22.16724	19.14258	16.71129	14.73678
38	26.44064	24.34860	22.49246	19.36786	16.86789	14.84602
39	26.90259	24.73034	22.80822	19.58448	17.01704	14.94907
40	27.35548	25.10278	23.11477	19.79277	17.15909	15.04630

TABLE 4 PRESENT VALUE OF AN ORDINARY ANNUITY OF 1

8%	9%	10%	11%	12%	15%	(n) Periods
.92593	.91743	.90909	.90090	.89286	.86957	1
1.78326	1.75911	1.73554	1.71252	1.69005	1.62571	2
2.57710	2.53130	2.48685	2.44371	2.40183	2.28323	3
3.31213	3.23972	3.16986	3.10245	3.03735	2.85498	4
3.99271	3.88965	3.79079	3.69590	3.60478	3.35216	5
4.62288	4.48592	4.35526	4.23054	4.11141	3.78448	6
5.20637	5.03295	4.86842	4.71220	4.56376	4.16042	7
5.74664	5.53482	5.33493	5.14612	4.96764	4.48732	8
6.24689	5.99525	5.75902	5.53705	5.32825	4.77158	9
6.71008	6.41766	6.14457	5.88923	5.65022	5.01877	10
7.13896	6.80519	6.49506	6.20652	5.93770	5.23371	11
7.53608	7.16073	6.81369	6.49236	6.19437	5.42062	12
7.90378	7.48690	7.10336	6.74987	6.42355	5.58315	13
8.24424	7.78615	7.36669	6.98187	6.62817	5.72448	14
8.55948	8.06069	7.60608	7.19087	6.81086	5.84737	15
8.85137	8.31256	7.82371	7.37916	6.97399	5.95424	16
9.12164	8.54363	8.02155	7.54879	7.11963	6.04716	17
9.37189	8.75563	8.20141	7.70162	7.24967	6.12797	18
9.60360	8.95012	8.36492	7.83929	7.36578	6.19823	19
9.81815	9.12855	8.51356	7.96333	7.46944	6.25933	20
10.01680	9.29224	8.64869	8.07507	7.56200	6.31246	21
10.20074	9.44243	8.77154	8.17574	7.64465	6.35866	22
10.37106	9.58021	8.88322	8.26643	7.71843	6.39884	23
10.52876	9.70661	8.98474	8.34814	7.78432	6.43377	24
10.67478	9.82258	9.07704	8.42174	7.84314	6.46415	25
10.80998	9.92897	9.16095	8.48806	7.89566	6.49056	26
10.93516	10.02658	9.23722	8.54780	7.94255	6.51353	27
11.05108	10.11613	9.30657	8.60162	7.98442	6.53351	28
11.15841	10.19828	9.36961	8.65011	8.02181	6.55088	29
11.25778	10.27365	9.42691	8.69379	8.05518	6.56598	30
11.34980	10.34280	9.47901	8.73315	8.08499	6.57911	31
11.43500	10.40624	9.52638	8.76860	8.11159	6.59053	32
11.51389	10.46444	9.56943	8.80054	8.13535	6.60046	33
11.58693	10.51784	9.60858	8.82932	8.15656	6.60910	34
11.65457	10.56682	9.64416	8.85524	8.17550	6.61661	35
11.71719	10.61176	9.67651	8.87859	8.19241	6.62314	36
11.77518	10.65299	9.70592	8.89963	8.20751	6.62882	37
11.82887	10.69082	9.73265	8.91859	8.22099	6.63375	38
11.87858	10.72552	9.75697	8.93567	8.23303	6.63805	39
11.92461	10.75736	9.77905	8.95105	8.24378	6.64178	40

TABLE 5 PRESENT VALUE OF AN ANNUITY DUE OF 1

$$\text{PVF-AD}_{n,i} = 1 + \frac{1 - \dfrac{1}{(1+i)^{n-1}}}{i}$$

(n) Periods	2%	2½%	3%	4%	5%	6%
1	1.00000	1.00000	1.00000	1.00000	1.00000	1.00000
2	1.98039	1.97561	1.97087	1.96154	1.95238	1.94340
3	2.94156	2.92742	2.91347	2.88609	2.85941	2.83339
4	3.88388	3.85602	3.82861	3.77509	3.72325	3.67301
5	4.80773	4.76197	4.71710	4.62990	4.54595	4.46511
6	5.71346	5.64583	5.57971	5.45182	5.32948	5.21236
7	6.60143	6.50813	6.41719	6.24214	6.07569	5.91732
8	7.47199	7.34939	7.23028	7.00205	6.78637	6.58238
9	8.32548	8.17014	8.01969	7.73274	7.46321	7.20979
10	9.16224	8.97087	8.78611	8.43533	8.10782	7.80169
11	9.98259	9.75206	9.53020	9.11090	8.72173	8.36009
12	10.78685	10.51421	10.25262	9.76048	9.30641	8.88687
13	11.57534	11.25776	10.95400	10.38507	9.86325	9.38384
14	12.34837	11.98319	11.63496	10.98565	10.39357	9.85268
15	13.10625	12.69091	12.29607	11.56312	10.89864	10.29498
16	13.84926	13.38138	12.93794	12.11839	11.37966	10.71225
17	14.57771	14.05500	13.56110	12.65230	11.83777	11.10590
18	15.29187	14.71220	14.16612	13.16567	12.27407	11.47726
19	15.99203	15.35336	14.75351	13.65930	12.68959	11.82760
20	16.67846	15.97889	15.32380	14.13394	13.08532	12.15812
21	17.35143	16.58916	15.87747	14.59033	13.46221	12.46992
22	18.01121	17.18455	16.41502	15.02916	13.82115	12.76408
23	18.65805	17.76541	16.93692	15.45112	14.16300	13.04158
24	19.29220	18.33211	17.44361	15.85684	14.48857	13.30338
25	19.91393	18.88499	17.93554	16.24696	14.79864	13.55036
26	20.52346	19.42438	18.41315	16.62208	15.09394	13.78336
27	21.12104	19.95061	18.87684	16.98277	15.37519	14.00317
28	21.70690	20.46401	19.32703	17.32959	15.64303	14.21053
29	22.28127	20.96489	19.76411	17.66306	15.89813	14.40616
30	22.84438	21.45355	20.18845	17.98371	16.14107	14.59072
31	23.39646	21.93029	20.60044	18.29203	16.37245	14.76483
32	23.93770	22.39541	21.00043	18.58849	16.59281	14.92909
33	24.46833	22.84918	21.38877	18.87355	16.80268	15.08404
34	24.98856	23.29188	21.76579	19.14765	17.00255	15.23023
35	25.49859	23.72379	22.13184	19.41120	17.19290	15.36814
36	25.99862	24.14516	22.48722	19.66461	17.37419	15.49825
37	26.48884	24.55625	22.83225	19.90828	17.54685	15.62099
38	26.96945	24.95732	23.16724	20.14258	17.71129	15.73678
39	27.44064	25.34860	23.49246	20.36786	17.86789	15.84602
40	27.90259	25.73034	23.80822	20.58448	18.01704	15.94907

TABLE 5   PRESENT VALUE OF AN ANNUITY DUE OF 1

8%	9%	10%	11%	12%	15%	(n) Periods
1.00000	1.00000	1.00000	1.00000	1.00000	1.00000	1
1.92593	1.91743	1.90909	1.90090	1.89286	1.86957	2
2.78326	2.75911	2.73554	2.71252	2.69005	2.62571	3
3.57710	3.53130	3.48685	3.44371	3.40183	3.28323	4
4.31213	4.23972	4.16986	4.10245	4.03735	3.85498	5
4.99271	4.88965	4.79079	4.69590	4.60478	4.35216	6
5.62288	5.48592	5.35526	5.23054	5.11141	4.78448	7
6.20637	6.03295	5.86842	5.71220	5.56376	5.16042	8
6.74664	6.53482	6.33493	6.14612	5.96764	5.48732	9
7.24689	6.99525	6.75902	6.53705	6.32825	5.77158	10
7.71008	7.41766	7.14457	6.88923	6.65022	6.01877	11
8.13896	7.80519	7.49506	7.20652	6.93770	6.23371	12
8.53608	8.16073	7.81369	7.49236	7.19437	6.42062	13
8.90378	8.48690	8.10336	7.74987	7.42355	6.58315	14
9.24424	8.78615	8.36669	7.98187	7.62817	6.72448	15
9.55948	9.06069	8.60608	8.19087	7.81086	6.84737	16
9.85137	9.31256	8.82371	8.37916	7.97399	6.95424	17
10.12164	9.54363	9.02155	8.54879	8.11963	7.04716	18
10.37189	9.75563	9.20141	8.70162	8.24967	7.12797	19
10.60360	9.95012	9.36492	8.83929	8.36578	7.19823	20
10.81815	10.12855	9.51356	8.96333	8.46944	7.25933	21
11.01680	10.29224	9.64869	9.07507	8.56200	7.31246	22
11.20074	10.44243	9.77154	9.17574	8.64465	7.35866	23
11.37106	10.58021	9.88322	9.26643	8.71843	7.39884	24
11.52876	10.70661	9.98474	9.34814	8.78432	7.43377	25
11.67478	10.82258	10.07704	9.42174	8.84314	7.46415	26
11.80998	10.92897	10.16095	9.48806	8.89566	7.49056	27
11.93518	11.02658	10.23722	9.54780	8.94255	7.51353	28
12.05108	11.11613	10.30657	9.60162	8.98442	7.53351	29
12.15841	11.19828	10.36961	9.65011	9.02181	7.55088	30
12.25778	11.27365	10.42691	9.69379	9.05518	7.56598	31
12.34980	11.34280	10.47901	9.73315	9.08499	7.57911	32
12.43500	11.40624	10.52638	9.76860	9.11159	7.59053	33
12.51389	11.46444	10.56943	9.80054	9.13535	7.60046	34
12.58693	11.51784	10.60858	9.82932	9.15656	7.60910	35
12.65457	11.56682	10.64416	9.85524	9.17550	7.61661	36
12.71719	11.61176	10.67651	9.87859	9.19241	7.62314	37
12.77518	11.65299	10.70592	9.89963	9.20751	7.62882	38
12.82887	11.69082	10.73265	9.91859	9.22099	7.63375	39
12.87858	11.72552	10.75697	9.93567	9.23303	7.63805	40

USING FINANCIAL CALCULATORS

LEARNING OBJECTIVE

After studying this appendix, you should be able to:

 Use a financial calculator to solve time value of money problems.

Business professionals, once they have mastered the underlying concepts in Appendix A, will often use a financial (business) calculator to solve time value of money problems. In many cases, calculators must be used if interest rates or time periods do not correspond with the information provided in the compound interest tables.

Financial calculators allow you to solve present and future value problems by entering the time value of money variables into the calculator. The five most common keys used to solve time value of money problems are pictured below:[1]

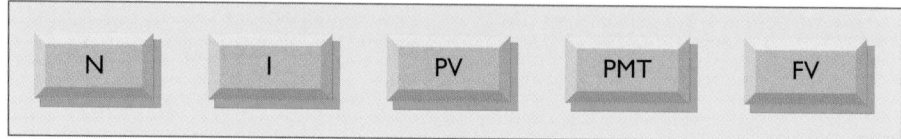

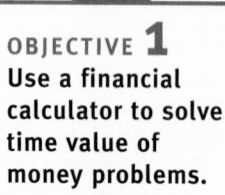

OBJECTIVE 1
Use a financial calculator to solve time value of money problems.

where

N = number of periods

I = interest rate per period (some calculators use I/YR or i)

PV = present value (occurs at the beginning of the first period)

PMT = payment (all payments are equal, and none are skipped)

FV = future value (occurs at the end of the last period)

In solving time value of money problems in this appendix, you will generally be given three of four variables and will have to solve for the remaining variable. The fifth key (the key not used) is given a value of zero to ensure that this variable is not used in the computation.

FUTURE VALUE OF A SINGLE SUM

To illustrate the use of a financial calculator, let's assume that you want to know the future value of $50,000 invested to earn 11%, compounded annually for 5 years.

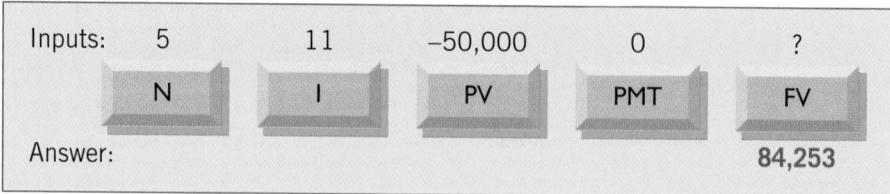

The diagram shows you the information (inputs) to enter into the calculator: N = 5, I = 11, PV = −50,000, and PMT = 0. FV is then pressed to yield the answer: $84,253. This is the same answer as shown on page A8, when compound interest tables were used to compute the future value of a single sum. As in-

---

[1]On many calculators, these keys are actual buttons on the face of the calculator; on others, they are shown on the display after accessing a present value menu.

dicated, the PMT key was given a value of zero because a series of payments did not occur in this problem.

Plus and Minus

The use of plus and minus signs in time value of money problems using a financial calculator can be confusing. Most financial calculators are programmed so that the positive and negative cash flows in any problem offset each other. In the future value problem above, we identified the 50,000 initial investment as a negative (outflow); the answer 84,253 was shown as a positive, reflecting a cash inflow. If the 50,000 were entered as a positive, then the final answer would have been reported as a negative (−84,253). Hopefully, the sign convention will not cause confusion. If you understand what is required in a problem, you should be able to interpret a positive or negative amount in determining the solution to a problem.

Compounding Periods

In the problem above, we assumed that compounding occurs once a year. Some financial calculators have a default setting, which assumes that compounding occurs 12 times a year. You must determine what default period has been programmed into your calculator and change it as necessary to arrive at the proper compounding period.

Rounding

Most financial calculators store and calculate using 12 decimal places. As a result, because compound interest tables generally have factors only up to 5 decimal places, a slight difference in the final answer can result. In most time value of money problems, the final answer will not include more than two decimal points.

PRESENT VALUE OF A SINGLE SUM

To illustrate how a present value problem is solved using a financial calculator, assume that you want to know the present value of $84,253 to be received in 5 years, discounted at 11% compounded annually.

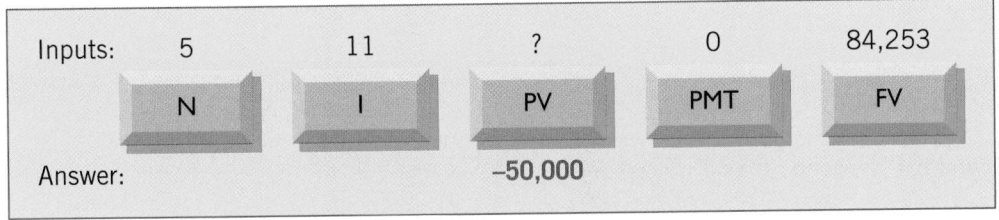

In this case, you enter N = 5, I = 11, PMT = 0, FV = 84,253, and then press the PV key to find the present value of $50,000.

FUTURE VALUE OF AN ORDINARY ANNUITY

To illustrate the future value of an ordinary annuity, assume that you are asked to determine the future value of five $5,000 deposits made at the end of each of the next 5 years, each of which earns interest at 12%, compounded annually.

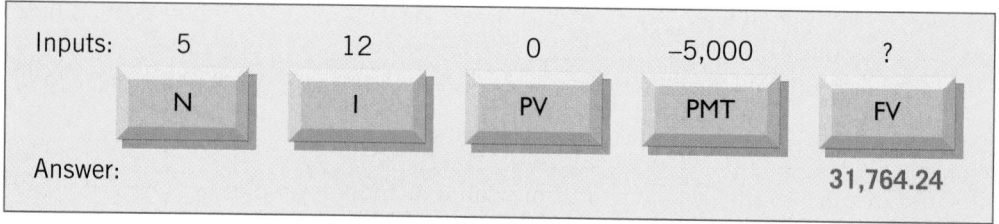

In this case, you enter N = 5, I = 12, PV = 0, PMT = −5,000, and then press FV to arrive at the answer of $31,764.24.[2] The $5,000 payments are shown as negatives because the deposits represent cash outflows that will accumulate with interest to the amount to be received (cash inflow) at the end of 5 years.

FUTURE VALUE OF AN ANNUITY DUE

Recall from the discussion in Appendix A that in any annuity problem you must determine whether the periodic payments occur at the beginning or the end of the period. If the first payment occurs at the beginning of the period, most financial calculators have a key marked "Begin" (or "Due") that you press to switch from the end-of-period payment mode (for an ordinary annuity) to beginning-of-period payment mode (for an annuity due). For most calculators, the word BEGIN is displayed to indicate that the calculator is set for an annuity due problem. (Some calculators use DUE.)

To illustrate a future value of an annuity due problem, let's revisit a problem from Appendix A: Sue Lotadough plans to deposit $800 per year in a fund on each of her son's birthdays, starting today (his tenth birthday). All amounts on deposit in the fund will earn 12% compounded annually. Sue wants to know the amount she will have accumulated for college expenses on her son's eighteenth birthday. She will make 8 deposits into the fund. (Assume no deposit will be made on the eighteenth birthday.)

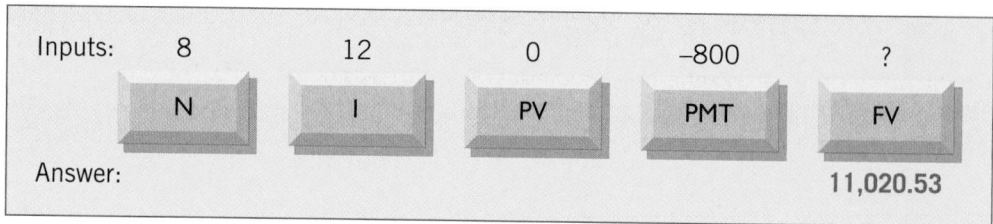

In this case, you enter N = 8, I = 12, PV = 0, PMT = −800, and then press FV to arrive at the answer of $11,020.53. You must be in the BEGIN or DUE mode to solve this problem correctly. Before starting to solve any annuity problem, make sure that your calculator is switched to the proper mode.

PRESENT VALUE OF AN ORDINARY ANNUITY

To illustrate how to solve a present value of an ordinary annuity problem using a financial calculator, assume that you are asked to determine the present value of rental receipts of $6,000 each to be received at the end of each of the next 5 years, when discounted at 12%.

---

[2]Note on page A15 that the answer using the compound interest tables is $31,764.25—a difference of 1 cent due to rounding.

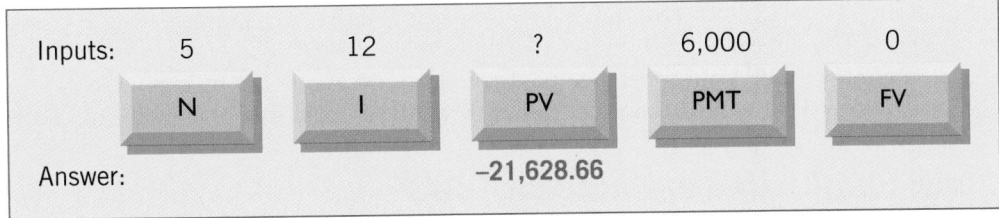

In this case, you enter N = 5, I = 12, PMT = 6,000, FV = 0, and then press PV to arrive at the answer of $21,628.66.[3]

USEFUL FEATURES OF THE FINANCIAL CALCULATOR

With a financial calculator you can solve for any interest rate or for any number of periods in a time value of money problem. Here are some illustrations of these features.

Auto Loan

Assume you are financing a new car with a 3-year loan. The loan has a 9.5% nominal annual interest rate, compounded monthly. The price of the car is $6,000, and you want to determine the monthly payments, assuming that the payments start one month after the purchase.

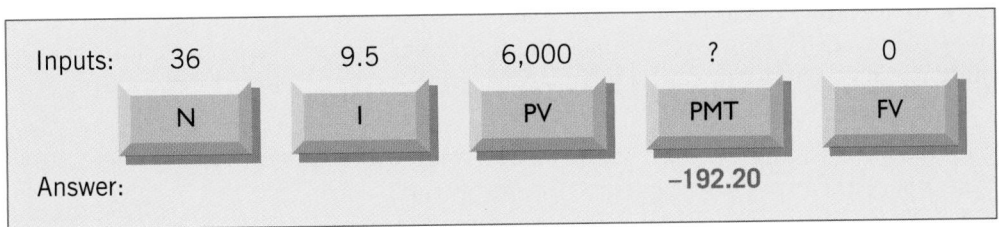

Thus, by entering N = 36 (12 × 3), I = 9.5, PV = 6,000, FV = 0, and then pressing PMT, you can determine that the monthly payments will be $192.20. Note that the payment key is usually programmed for 12 payments per year. Thus, you must change the default (compounding period) if the payments are different than monthly.

Mortgage Loan Amount

Let's say you are evaluating financing options for a loan on your house. You decide that the maximum mortgage payment you can afford is $700 per month. The annual interest rate is 8.4%. If you get a mortgage that requires you to make monthly payments over a 15-year period, what is the maximum purchase price you can afford?

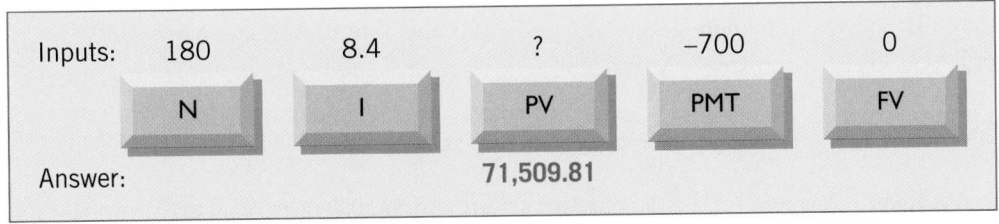

[3]If the rental payments were received at the beginning of the year, then it would be necessary to switch to the BEGIN or DUE mode. In this case, the present value of the payments would be $24,224.10.

Entering N = 180 (12 × 15 years), I = 8.4, PMT = −700, FV = 0, and pressing PV, you find a present value of $71,509.81—the maximum house price you can afford, given that you want to keep your mortgage payments at $700. Note that by changing any of the variables, you can quickly conduct "what-if" analyses for different factual situations.

Individual Retirement Account (IRA)

Assume you opened an IRA on April 15, 1992, with a deposit of $2,000. Since then you have deposited $100 in the account every 2 weeks (26 deposits per year, with the first $100 deposit made on April 29, 1992). The account pays 7.6% annual interest compounded semi-monthly (with each deposit). How much will be in the account on April 15, 2002?

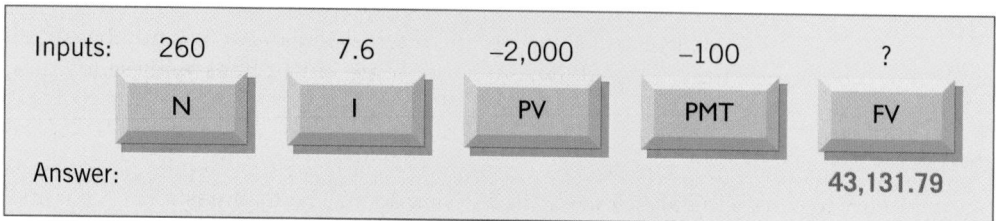

By entering N = 260 (26 × 10 years), I = 7.6, PV = −2,000, PMT = −100, and pressing FV, you determine the future value of $43,131.79. This is the amount that the IRA will grow to over the 10-year period. Note that in this problem we use four of the keys and solve for the fifth. Thus, we combine the future value of a single sum and of an annuity.

SUMMARY OF LEARNING OBJECTIVE

❶ Use a financial calculator to solve time value of money problems. A financial calculator can be used to solve time value of money problems. By entering into the calculator amounts for all but one of the unknown elements (periods, interest rate, payments, future or present value), a financial calculator can be used to solve the same and additional problems as those solved with the time value of money tables. Particularly useful situations involve interest rates and compounding periods not presented in the tables.

EXERCISES

EB-1 (Determine Interest Rate)   Reba McEntire wishes to invest $19,000 on July 1, 2003, and have it accumulate to $49,000 by July 1, 2013.

Instructions
Use a financial calculator to determine at what exact annual rate of interest Reba must invest the $19,000.

EB-2 (Determine Interest Rate)   On July 17, 2002, Tim McGraw borrowed $42,000 from his grandfather to open a clothing store. Starting July 17, 2003, Tim has to make ten equal annual payments of $6,500 each to repay the loan.

Instructions
Use a financial calculator to determine what interest rate Tim is paying.

EB-3 (Determine Interest Rate) As the purchaser of a new house, Patty Loveless has signed a mortgage note to pay the Memphis National Bank and Trust Co. $14,000 every 6 months for 20 years, at the end of which time she will own the house. At the date the mortgage is signed the purchase price was $198,000, and a down payment of $20,000 was made. The first payment will be made 6 months after the date the mortgage is signed.

Instructions
Using a financial calculator, compute the exact rate of interest earned on the mortgage by the bank.

PROBLEMS

PB-1 (Various Time Value of Money Situations) Using a financial calculator, provide a solution to each of the following questions.

(a) What is the amount of the payments that Karla Zehms must make at the end of each of 8 years to accumulate a fund of $70,000 by the end of the eighth year, if the fund earns 7.25% interest, compounded annually?

(b) Bill Yawn is 40 years old today, and he wishes to accumulate $500,000 by his sixty-fifth birthday so he can retire to his summer place on Lake Winnebago. He wishes to accumulate this amount by making equal deposits on his fortieth through sixty-fourth birthdays. What annual deposit must Bill make if the fund will earn 9.65% interest compounded annually?

(c) Jane Mayer has a $26,000 debt that she wishes to repay 4 years from today; she has $17,000 that she intends to invest for the 4 years. What rate of interest will she need to earn annually in order to accumulate enough to pay the debt?

PB-2 (Various Time Value of Money Situations) Using a financial calculator, solve for the unknowns in each of the following situations.

(a) Wayne Eski wishes to invest $150,000 today to ensure payments of $20,000 to his son at the end of each year for the next 15 years. At what interest rate must the $150,000 be invested? (Round the answer to two decimal points.)

(b) On June 1, 2003, Shelley Long purchases lakefront property from her neighbor, Joey Brenner, and agrees to pay the purchase price in seven payments of $16,000 each, the first payment to be payable June 1, 2004. (Assume that interest compounded at an annual rate of 7.35% is implicit in the payments.) What is the purchase price of the property?

(c) On January 1, 2003, Cooke Corporation purchased 200 of the $1,000 face value, 8% coupon, 10-year bonds of Howe Inc. The bonds mature on January 1, 2013, and pay interest annually beginning January 1, 2004. Cooke purchased the bonds to yield 10.65%. How much did Cooke pay for the bonds?

PB-3 (Various Time Value of Money Situations) Using a financial calculator, provide a solution to each of the following situations.

(a) On March 12, 2004, William Scott invests in a $180,000 insurance policy that earns 5.25% compounded annually. The annuity policy allows William to receive annual payments, the first of which is payable to William on March 12, 2005. What will be the amount of each of the 20 equal annual receipts?

(b) Bill Schroeder owes a debt of $35,000 from the purchase of his new sport utility vehicle. The debt bears annual interest of 9.1% compounded monthly. Bill wishes to pay the debt and interest in equal monthly payments over 8 years, beginning one month hence. What equal monthly payments will pay off the debt and interest?

(c) On January 1, 2004, Sammy Sosa offers to buy Mark Grace's used snowmobile for $8,000, payable in five equal installments, which are to include 8.25% interest on the unpaid balance and a portion of the principal. If the first payment is to be made on January 1, 2004, how much will each payment be?

(d) Repeat the requirements in part (c), assuming Sosa makes the first payment on December 31, 2004.

As introduced in Chapter 2, financial reporting and accounting within general purpose financial statements are guided by a conceptual framework. The peculiar nature of some industries and business concerns sometimes requires departure from general concepts or use of special accounting measurement techniques. For example, in the software industry, there are contexts in which certain research and development costs are capitalized. And in the retail industry, estimation methods are used to provide timely and reliable information about inventories. These departures from basic theory have been developed to provide useful accounting information in these special industry contexts.

The purpose of the following four appendixes is to discuss the reporting practices characteristic of various industries. Topics addressed are the retail inventory method, accounting for natural resources, accounting for software development costs, and accounting for troubled debt. The content and organization of these appendixes are as follows.

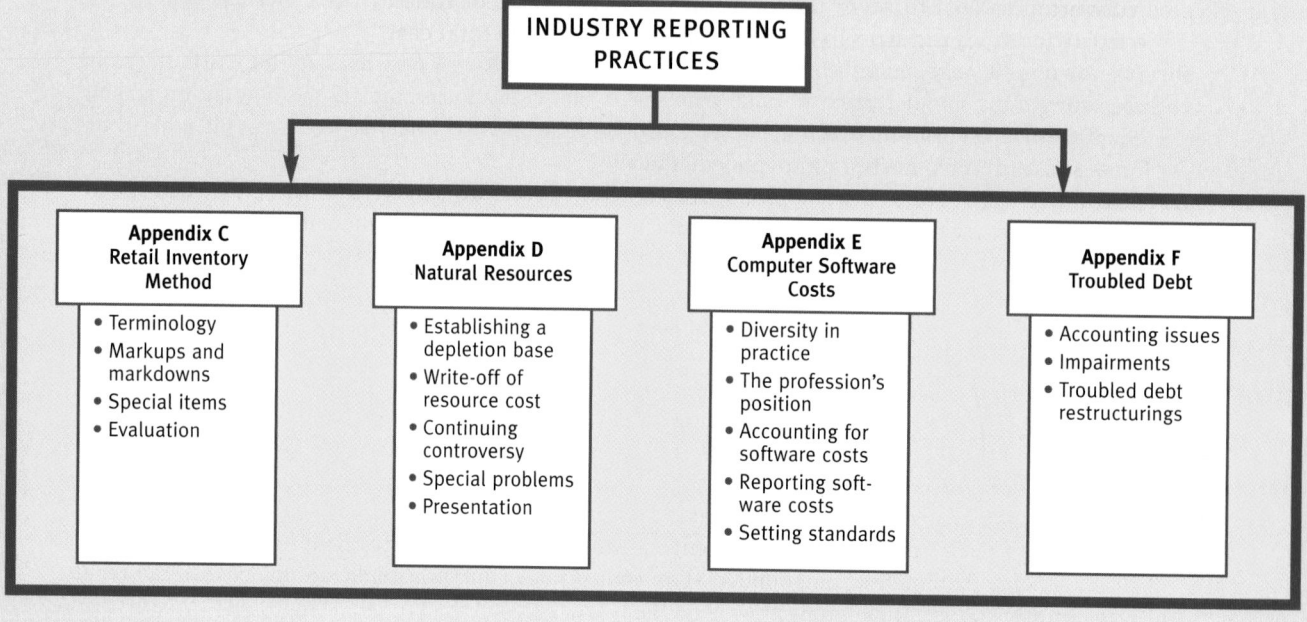

INDUSTRY REPORTING PRACTICES

Appendix C
Retail Inventory Method

- Terminology
- Markups and markdowns
- Special items
- Evaluation

Appendix D
Natural Resources

- Establishing a depletion base
- Write-off of resource cost
- Continuing controversy
- Special problems
- Presentation

Appendix E
Computer Software Costs

- Diversity in practice
- The profession's position
- Accounting for software costs
- Reporting software costs
- Setting standards

Appendix F
Troubled Debt

- Accounting issues
- Impairments
- Troubled debt restructurings

LEARNING
OBJECTIVE

After studying this appendix, you should be able to:

1 Determine ending inventory by applying the retail inventory method.

Accounting for inventory in a retail operation presents several challenges. Retailers with certain types of inventory may use the specific identification method to value their inventories. Such an approach makes sense when individual inventory units are significant, such as automobiles, pianos, or fur coats. However, imagine attempting to use such an approach at **Wal-Mart, True-Value Hardware, Sears,** or **Bloomingdale's**—high-volume retailers that have many different types of merchandise. It would be extremely difficult to determine the cost of each sale, to enter cost codes on the tickets, to change the codes to reflect declines in value of the merchandise, to allocate costs such as transportation, and so on.

An alternative is to compile the inventories at retail prices. In most retail concerns, an observable pattern between cost and price exists. Retail prices can therefore be converted to cost through use of a formula. This method, called the **retail inventory method, requires that a record be kept of (1) the total cost and retail value of goods purchased, (2) the total cost and retail value of the goods available for sale, and (3) the sales for the period**.

Here is how it works: The sales for the period are deducted from the retail value of the goods available for sale, to produce an estimated inventory (goods on hand) at retail. The ratio of cost to retail for all goods passing through a department or firm is then determined by dividing the total goods available for sale at cost by the total goods available at retail. The inventory valued at retail is converted to ending inventory at cost by applying the cost-to-retail ratio. Use of the retail inventory method is very common. For example, **Safeway** supermarkets uses the retail inventory method as do the department stores of **Target Corp.** The retail inventory method is illustrated below for Jordan-Guess Inc.

OBJECTIVE **1**
Determine ending inventory by applying the retail inventory method.

JORDAN-GUESS INC. (current period)	Cost	Retail
Beginning inventory	$14,000	$ 20,000
Purchases	63,000	90,000
Goods available for sale	$77,000	110,000
Deduct: Sales		85,000
Ending inventory, at retail		$ 25,000
Ratio of cost to retail ($77,000 ÷ $110,000)		70%
Ending inventory at cost (70% of $25,000)		$ 17,500

Illustration C-1
Retail Inventory Method

To avoid a potential overstatement of the inventory, periodic inventory counts are made, especially in retail operations where loss due to shoplifting and breakage is common.

There are different versions of the retail inventory method—the conventional (lower of average cost or market) method, the cost method, the LIFO retail method, and the dollar-value LIFO retail method. Regardless of which version is used, the retail inventory method is sanctioned by the IRS, various retail associations, and the accounting profession. One of its advantages is that the inventory balance **can be approximated without a physical count**.

The retail inventory method is particularly useful for any type of interim report, because a fairly quick and reliable measure of the inventory value is usually needed. Insurance adjusters often use this approach to estimate losses from fire, flood, or other type of casualty. This method also acts as a **control device** because any deviations from a physical count at the end of the year have to be explained. In addition, the retail method **expedites the physical inventory count** at the end of the year. The crew taking the physical inventory need record only the retail price of each item; there is no need to look up each item's invoice cost, thereby saving time and expense.

RETAIL METHOD TERMINOLOGY

The amounts shown in the Retail column of Illustration C-1 represent the original retail prices, assuming no price changes. Sales prices are frequently marked up or down. For retailers, the term **markup** means an additional markup of the original retail price. (In another context, such as the gross profit discussion in Chapter 8, we often think of markup on the basis of cost.) **Markup cancellations** are decreases in prices of merchandise that had been marked up above the original retail price.

Markdowns below the original sales prices may be necessary because of a decrease in the general level of prices, special sales, soiled or damaged goods, overstocking, and competition. Markdowns are common in retailing these days. **Markdown cancellations** occur when the markdowns are later offset by increases in the prices of goods that had been marked down—such as after a one-day sale, for example. Neither a markup cancellation nor a markdown cancellation can exceed the original markup or markdown.

To illustrate these different concepts, assume that Designer Clothing Store recently purchased 100 dress shirts from Marroway, Inc. The cost for these shirts was $1,500, or $15 a shirt. Designer Clothing established the selling price on these shirts at $30 a shirt. The manager noted that the shirts were selling quickly, so he added a markup of $5 per shirt. This markup made the price too high for customers, and sales lagged. The manager then reduced the price to $32. At this point we would say that Designer Clothing has had a markup of $5 and a markup cancellation of $3. As soon as the major marketing season passed, the manager marked the remaining shirts down to a sales price of $23. At this point, an additional markup cancellation of $2 has taken place, and a $7 markdown has occurred. If the shirts are later written up to $24, a markdown cancellation of $1 would occur.

RETAIL INVENTORY METHOD WITH MARKUPS AND MARKDOWNS—CONVENTIONAL METHOD

Retailers use markup and markdown concepts in developing the proper inventory valuation at the end of the accounting period. To obtain the appropriate inventory figures, proper treatment must be given to markups, markup cancellations, markdowns, and markdown cancellations.

To illustrate the different possibilities, consider the data for In-Fashion Stores Inc., shown in Illustration C-2. In-Fashion's ending inventory at cost can be calculated under two assumptions, A and B. (The reasons for the two will be explained later.)

Assumption A: Computes a cost ratio after markups (and markup cancellations) but before markdowns.

Assumption B: Computes a cost ratio after both markups and markdowns (and cancellations).

	Cost	Retail
Beginning inventory	$ 500	$ 1,000
Purchases (net)	20,000	35,000
Markups		3,000
Markup cancellations		1,000
Markdowns		2,500
Markdown cancellations		2,000
Sales (net)		25,000

IN-FASHION STORES INC.

	Cost		Retail	
Beginning inventory	$ 500		$ 1,000	
Purchases (net)	20,000		35,000	
Merchandise available for sale	20,500		36,000	
Add:				
Markups		$ 3,000		
Less: Markup cancellations		(1,000)		
Net markups			2,000	
	20,500		38,000	

Cost-to-retail ratio $\dfrac{\$20,500}{\$38,000} = 53.9\%$ .... **(A)**

	Cost		Retail	
Deduct:				
Markdowns		2,500		
Less: Markdown cancellations		(2,000)		
Net markdowns			500	
	$20,500		37,500	

Cost-to-retail ratio $\dfrac{\$20,500}{\$37,500} = 54.7\%$ .... **(B)**

			Retail	
Deduct: Sales (net)			25,000	
Ending inventory at retail			$12,500	

Illustration C-2
Retail Inventory Method with Markups and Markdowns

The computations for In-Fashion Stores are:

Ending inventory at retail	×	Cost ratio	=	Value of ending inventory
Assumption A: $12,500	×	53.9%	=	$6,737.50
Assumption B: $12,500	×	54.7%	=	$6,837.50

Illustration C-3
Value of Ending Inventory Computation

The question becomes: Which assumption and which percentage should be employed to compute the ending inventory valuation?

The answer depends on the retail inventory method chosen. **The conventional retail inventory method uses assumption A only. It is designed to approximate the lower of average cost or market.** We will refer to this approach as the **lower of cost or market approach** or the **conventional retail inventory method**. To understand why the markups but not the markdowns are considered in the cost percentage, we must understand how a retail outlet operates. Markup normally indicates that the market value of the item has increased. On the other hand, a markdown means that a decline in the utility of that item has occurred. Therefore, if we attempt to approximate the lower of cost or market, markdowns are considered a current loss and are not involved in the calculation of the cost-to-retail ratio. Thus, the cost-to-retail ratio is lower, which leads to an approximate lower of cost or market.

An example will make this clear. Two items were purchased for $5 apiece, and the original sales price was established at $10 each. One item was subsequently written down to $2. Assuming no sales for the period, **if markdowns are considered** in the cost-to-retail ratio (assumption B, above), we compute the ending inventory in the following manner.

Illustration C-4
Retail Inventory Method
Including Markdowns—
Cost Method

MARKDOWNS INCLUDED IN COST-TO-RETAIL RATIO		
	Cost	Retail
Purchases	$10.00	$20.00
Deduct: Markdowns		8.00
Ending inventory, at retail		$12.00

Cost-to-retail ratio $\dfrac{\$10.00}{\$12.00} = 83.3\%$

Ending inventory at cost ($12.00 × .833) = $10.00

This approach is the **cost method**. It reflects an average cost of the two items of the commodity without considering the loss on the one item.

If markdowns are not considered, the result is the lower of cost or market method (assumption A). The calculation is made as shown below.

Illustration C-5
Retail Inventory Method
Excluding Markdowns—
Conventional Method
(LCM)

MARKDOWNS NOT INCLUDED IN COST-TO-RETAIL RATIO		
	Cost	Retail
Purchases	$10.00	$20.00

Cost-to-retail ratio $\dfrac{\$10.00}{\$20.00} = 50\%$

Deduct: Markdowns		8.00
Ending inventory, at retail		$12.00

Ending inventory, at cost ($12 × .50) = $6.00

Under the conventional retail inventory method (when markdowns are **not** considered in computing the cost-to-retail ratio), the ratio would be 50% ($10/$20), and ending inventory would be $6 ($12 × 0.50).

The inventory valuation of $6 reflects two inventory items, one inventoried at $5, the other at $1. Basically, the sales price was reduced from $10 to $2, and the cost was reduced from $5 to $1.[1] To approximate the lower of cost or market, therefore, the

---

[1]This figure is really not market (replacement cost), but is net realizable value less the normal margin that is allowed. In other words, the sale price of the goods written down is $2, but subtracting a normal margin of 50% ($5 cost, $10 price), the figure becomes $1.

cost-to-retail ratio must be established by dividing the cost of goods available by the sum of the original retail price of these goods plus the net markups; the markdowns and markdown cancellations are excluded. The basic format for the retail inventory method using the lower of cost or market approach is shown in Illustration C-6 using the In-Fashion Stores information.

IN-FASHION STORES INC.		
	Cost	Retail
Beginning inventory	$ 500.00	$ 1,000.00
Purchases (net)	20,000.00	35,000.00
Totals	20,500.00	36,000.00
Add: Net markups		
Markups	$3,000.00	
Markup cancellations	1,000.00	2,000.00
Totals	$20,500.00	38,000.00
Deduct: Net markdowns		
Markdowns	2,500.00	
Markdown cancellations	2,000.00	500.00
Sales price of goods available		37,500.00
Deduct: Sales (net)		25,000.00
Ending inventory, at retail		$12,500.00

$$\text{Cost-to-retail ratio} = \frac{\text{Cost of goods available}}{\text{Original retail price of goods available, plus net markups}}$$

$$= \frac{\$20,500}{\$38,000} = 53.9\%$$

Ending inventory at lower of cost or market (53.9% × $12,500.00) $ 6,737.50

Illustration C-6
Comprehensive Conventional Retail Inventory Method Format

Because an averaging effect occurs, an exact lower of cost or market inventory valuation is ordinarily not obtained, but an adequate approximation can be achieved. In contrast, adding net markups **and** deducting net markdowns yields **approximate cost**.

SPECIAL ITEMS RELATING TO RETAIL METHOD

The retail inventory method becomes more complicated when such items as freight-in, purchase returns and allowances, and purchase discounts are involved. **Freight costs** are treated as a part of the purchase cost. **Purchase returns** are ordinarily considered as a reduction of the price at both cost and retail. And **purchase discounts and allowances** usually are considered as a reduction of the cost of purchases. When the purchase allowance is not reflected by a reduction in the selling price, no adjustment is made to the retail column. In short, the treatment for the items affecting the cost column of the retail inventory approach follows the computation for cost of goods available for sale.

Note also that **sales returns and allowances** are considered as proper adjustments to gross sales; **sales discounts**, however, are not recognized when sales are recorded gross. To adjust for the sales discount account in such a situation would provide an ending inventory figure at retail that would be overvalued.

In addition, a number of special items require careful analysis. **Transfers-in** from another department, for example, should be reported in the same way as purchases from an outside enterprise. **Normal shortages** (breakage, damage, theft, shrinkage) should reduce the retail column because these goods are no longer available for sale. Such costs are reflected in the selling price because a certain amount of shortage is considered normal in a retail enterprise. As a result, this amount is not considered in computing the cost to retail percentage. Rather, it is shown as a deduction similar to sales to arrive at ending inventory at retail. **Abnormal shortages** should be deducted from both the cost and retail columns and reported as a special inventory amount or as a loss. To do otherwise distorts the cost-to-retail ratio and overstates ending inventory. Finally, companies often provide their employees with special discounts to encourage loyalty, better performance, and so on. **Employee discounts** should be deducted from the retail column in the same way as sales. These discounts should not be considered in the cost-to-retail percentage because they do not reflect an overall change in the selling price.

Illustration C-7 shows some of these concepts. The company, Feminine Executive Apparel, determines its inventory using the conventional retail inventory method.

Illustration C-7

Conventional Retail Inventory Method—Special Items Included

Tutorial on LIFO Retail Method

FEMININE EXECUTIVE APPAREL		
	Cost	Retail
Beginning inventory	$ 1,000	$ 1,800
Purchases	30,000	60,000
Freight-in	600	—
Purchase returns	(1,500)	(3,000)
Totals	30,100	58,800
Net markups		9,000
Abnormal shortage	(1,200)	(2,000)
Totals	$28,900 ⟶	65,800
Deduct:		
Net markdowns		1,400
Sales	$36,000	
Sales returns	(900)	35,100
Employee discounts		800
Normal shortage		1,300
		$27,200

$$\text{Cost-to-retail ratio} = \frac{\$28,900}{\$65,800} = 43.9\%$$

Ending inventory at lower of cost or market (43.9% × $27,200) = $11,940.80

EVALUATION OF RETAIL INVENTORY METHOD

The retail inventory method of computing inventory is used widely (1) to permit the computation of net income without a physical count of inventory, (2) as a control measure in determining inventory shortages, (3) in regulating quantities of merchandise on hand, and (4) for insurance information.

One characteristic of the retail inventory method is that it **has an averaging effect on varying rates of gross profit**. When applied to an entire business where rates of gross profit vary among departments, no allowance is made for possible distortion of results because of such differences. Some companies refine the retail method under such conditions by computing inventory separately by departments or by classes of merchandise with similar gross profits. In addition, the reliability of this method assumes that the distribution of items in inventory is similar to the "mix" in the total goods available for sale.

SUMMARY OF LEARNING OBJECTIVE

1 **Determine ending inventory by applying the retail inventory method.** The steps to determine ending inventory by applying the conventional retail method are: (1) The sales for the period are deducted from the retail value of the goods available for sale to produce an estimated inventory at retail. (2) The ratio of cost to retail for all goods passing through a department or firm is then determined by dividing the total goods available for sale at cost by the total goods available at retail. (3) The inventory valued at retail is converted to approximate cost by applying the cost-to-retail ratio.

EXERCISES

EC-1 **(Retail Inventory Method)** Presented below is information related to Bobby Engram Company.

	Cost	Retail
Beginning inventory	$ 58,000	$100,000
Purchases (net)	122,000	200,000
Net markups		10,345
Net markdowns		26,135
Sales		186,000

Instructions
(a) Compute the ending inventory at retail.
(b) Compute a cost-to-retail percentage for the following cases. (Round to two decimals.)
   (1) Excluding both markups and markdowns.
   (2) Excluding markups but including markdowns.
   (3) Excluding markdowns but including markups.
   (4) Including both markdowns and markups.
(c) Which of the methods in (b) above (1, 2, 3, or 4):
   (1) Provides the most conservative estimate of ending inventory?
   (2) Provides an approximation of lower of cost or market?
   (3) Is used in the conventional retail method?
(d) Compute ending inventory at lower of cost or market. (Round to nearest dollar.)
(e) Compute cost of goods sold based on (d).
(f) Compute gross margin based on (d).

EC-2 **(Retail Inventory Method)** Presented below is information related to Ricky Henderson Company.

	Cost	Retail
Beginning inventory	$ 200,000	$ 280,000
Purchases	1,375,000	2,140,000
Markups		95,000
Markup cancellations		15,000
Markdowns		35,000
Markdown cancellations		5,000
Sales		2,200,000

Instructions
Compute the inventory by the conventional retail inventory method.

EC-3 **(Retail Inventory Method)** The records of Ellen's Boutique report the following data for the month of April.

Sales	$99,000	Purchases (at cost)	$48,000
Sales returns	2,000	Purchases (at sales price)	88,000
Additional markups	10,000	Purchase returns (at cost)	2,000
Markup cancellations	1,500	Purchase returns (at sales price)	3,000
Markdowns	9,300	Beginning inventory (at cost)	30,000
Markdown cancellations	2,800	Beginning inventory (at sales price)	46,500
Freight on purchases	2,400		

Instructions

Compute the ending inventory by the conventional retail inventory method.

PROBLEMS

PC-1 (Retail Inventory Method) The records for the Clothing Department of Magdalena Aguilar's Discount Store are summarized below for the month of January.

Inventory; January 1: at retail $25,000; at cost $17,000
Purchases in January: at retail $137,000; at cost $86,500
Freight-in: $7,000
Purchase returns: at retail $3,000; at cost $2,300
Purchase allowances: $2,200
Transfers in from suburb branch: at retail $13,000; at cost $9,200
Net markups: $8,000
Net markdowns: $4,000
Inventory losses due to normal breakage, etc.: at retail $400
Sales at retail: $85,000
Sales returns: $2,400

Instructions

Compute the inventory for this department as of January 31, at **(a)** retail and **(b)** lower of average cost or market.

PC-2 (Retail Inventory Method) Presented below is information related to Edward Braddock Inc.

	Cost	Retail
Inventory, 12/31/03	$250,000	$ 390,000
Purchases	914,500	1,460,000
Purchase returns	60,000	80,000
Purchase discounts	18,000	—
Gross sales (after employee discounts)	—	1,460,000
Sales returns	—	97,500
Markups	—	120,000
Markup cancellations	—	40,000
Markdowns	—	45,000
Markdown cancellations	—	20,000
Freight-in	79,000	—
Employee discounts granted	—	8,000
Loss from breakage (normal)	—	2,500

Instructions

Assuming that Edward Braddock Inc. uses the conventional retail inventory method, compute the cost of its ending inventory at December 31, 2004.

PC-3 (Retail Inventory Method) Jared Jones Inc. uses the retail inventory method to estimate ending inventory for its monthly financial statements. The following data pertain to a single department for the month of October 2004.

Inventory, October 1, 2004	
At cost	$ 52,000
At retail	78,000
Purchases (exclusive of freight and returns)	
At cost	262,000
At retail	423,000
Freight-in	16,600
Purchase returns	
At cost	5,600
At retail	8,000
Additional markups	9,000
Markup cancellations	2,000
Markdowns (net)	3,600
Normal spoilage and breakage	10,000
Sales	380,000

Instructions

(a) Using the conventional retail method, prepare a schedule computing estimated lower of cost or market inventory for October 31, 2004.

(b) A department store using the conventional retail inventory method estimates the cost of its ending inventory as $60,000. An accurate physical count reveals only $47,000 of inventory at lower of cost or market. List the factors that may have caused the difference between the computed inventory and the physical count.

LEARNING
OBJECTIVE

*After studying this appendix,
you should be able to:*

 Explain the accounting for
natural resources.

OBJECTIVE **1**
**Explain the
accounting for
natural resources.**

Natural resources, often called wasting assets, include petroleum, minerals, and timber. They are characterized by two main features: (1) the complete removal of the asset, and (2) replacement of the asset only by an act of nature. Unlike plant and equipment, natural resources are consumed physically over the period of use and do not maintain their physical characteristics. Still, the accounting problems associated with natural resources are similar to those encountered with fixed assets. The questions to be answered are:

1. How is the cost basis for write-off of natural resources (**depletion**) established?

2. What pattern of allocation should be employed?

ESTABLISHING A DEPLETION BASE

How do we determine the depletion base for natural resources? Sizable expenditures are needed to find these natural resources, and for every successful discovery there are many "failures." Furthermore, long delays are encountered between the time the costs are incurred and the benefits are obtained from the extracted resources. As a result, a conservative policy frequently is adopted in accounting for the expenditures incurred in finding and extracting natural resources. The computation of the depletion base involves four factors: (1) acquisition cost of the deposit, (2) exploration costs, (3) development costs, and (4) restoration costs.

Acquisition Costs

Acquisition cost is the price paid to obtain the property right to search and find an undiscovered natural resource or the price paid for an already discovered resource. In some cases, property is leased and special royalty payments paid to the owner if a productive natural resource is found and is commercially profitable. Generally, the acquisition cost is placed in an account titled Undeveloped Property and assigned to the natural resource if exploration efforts are successful. If they are unsuccessful, the cost is written off as a loss.

Exploration Costs

As soon as a company has the right to use the property, **exploration costs** are often needed to find the resource. In most cases, these costs are expensed as incurred. When these costs are substantial and the risks of finding the resource uncertain (such as in the oil and gas industry), capitalization may occur. The unique issues related to the oil and gas industry are examined on pages D3–D4.

Development Costs

Development costs are divided into: (1) tangible equipment and (2) intangible development costs. Tangible equipment includes all of the transportation and other heavy equipment necessary to extract the resource and get it ready for production or shipment. Because the asset can be moved from one drilling or mining site to another, **tangible equipment costs are normally not considered in the depletion base**. Instead, separate depreciation charges are employed. Tangible assets that cannot be moved should be depreciated over their useful life or the life of the resource, whichever is shorter. **Intangible development costs, on the other hand, are considered part of the depletion base**. These costs are for such items as the drilling costs, tunnels, shafts, and wells, which have no tangible characteristics but are needed for the production of the natural resource.

Restoration Costs

Companies sometimes incur substantial costs to restore property to its natural state after extraction has occurred. These **restoration costs** should be added to the depletion base for purposes of computing the depletion cost per unit. It follows that any salvage value received on the property should be deducted from the depletion base.

WRITE-OFF OF RESOURCE COST

As soon as the depletion base is established, the next problem is to determine how the cost of the natural resource should be allocated to accounting periods. Normally, depletion is computed on the **units of production method** (activity approach), which means that depletion is a function of the number of units withdrawn during the period. In adopting this approach, the total cost of the natural resource less salvage value is divided by the number of units estimated to be in the resource deposit, to obtain a cost per unit of product. This cost per unit is multiplied by the number of units extracted to compute depletion.

For example, MaClede Co. has acquired the right to use 1,000 acres of land in Alaska to mine for gold. The lease cost is $50,000; the related exploration costs on the property are $100,000; and intangible development costs incurred in opening the mine are $850,000. Total costs related to the mine before the first ounce of gold is extracted are, therefore, $1,000,000. MaClede estimates that the mine will provide approximately 100,000 ounces of gold. The depletion rate established is computed in the following manner.

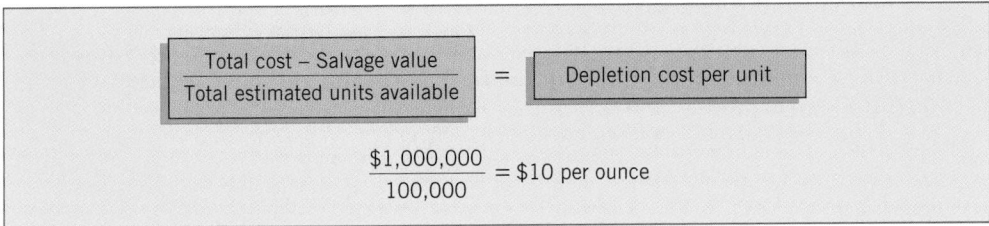

$$\frac{\text{Total cost} - \text{Salvage value}}{\text{Total estimated units available}} = \boxed{\text{Depletion cost per unit}}$$

$$\frac{\$1,000,000}{100,000} = \$10 \text{ per ounce}$$

Illustration D-1
Computation of Depletion Rate

If 25,000 ounces are extracted in the first year, then the depletion for the year is $250,000 (25,000 ounces at $10). The entry to record the depletion is:

Inventory	250,000	
Accumulated Depletion		250,000

Inventory is first debited for the total depletion for the year, and then is credited for the cost of materials sold during the year. The amount not sold remains in inventory and is reported in the current assets section.

In some instances an Accumulated Depletion account is not used, and the credit goes directly to the natural resources asset account. The balance sheet presents the cost of the property and the amount of accumulated depletion entered to date as follows.

Gold mine (at cost)	$1,000,000	
Less: Accumulated depletion	250,000	$750,000

Illustration D-2
Balance Sheet Presentation of Natural Resource

In the income statement, the depletion cost is part of the cost of goods sold.

The tangible equipment used in extracting the gold may also be depreciated on a units of production basis, especially if the estimated lives of the equipment can be directly assigned to one given resource deposit. If the equipment is used on more than one job, other cost allocation methods such as straight-line or accelerated depreciation methods would be more appropriate.

CONTINUING CONTROVERSY

A major controversy relates to the accounting for exploration costs in the oil and gas industry. Conceptually, the question is whether unsuccessful exploration costs are a cost of those that are successful. Some believe that unsuccessful ventures are a cost of those that are successful. This is called the **full cost concept.** Its rationale is that the cost of drilling a dry hole is a cost that is needed to find the commercially profitable wells. Others believe that only the costs of successful projects should be capitalized. This is the **successful efforts concept.** Its rationale is that an unsuccessful company will end up capitalizing many costs that will make it, over a short period of time, show no less income than does one that is successful.[1] In addition, in the view of successful efforts proponents, the only relevant measure for a single property unit is the cost directly related to that unit. The remainder of the costs should be reported as period charges.

The FASB has attempted to narrow the available alternatives but has met with little success. Here is a brief history of the debate.

<1> **1977—The FASB issued *Statement No. 19,* which required oil and gas companies to follow successful efforts accounting.** However, after small oil and gas producers, voicing strong opposition, lobbied extensively in Congress, governmental agencies assessed the implications of this standard from a public interest perspective and reacted contrary to the FASB's position.[2]

<2> **1978–1979—In response to criticisms of the FASB's actions, the SEC reexamined the issue and found both successful efforts and full cost accounting inadequate because neither reflects the economic substance of oil and gas exploration.** As a substitute, the SEC argued in favor of a yet-to-be developed method, **reserve recognition accounting (RRA),** which it believed would provide more useful information. Under RRA, as soon as a company discovers oil, it reports the value of the oil on the balance sheet and in the income statement. Thus, RRA is a **current value** approach as opposed to full costing and successful efforts, which are **historical cost** approaches.[3]

---

[1] Large international oil companies such as **Exxon Mobil** use the successful efforts approach. Full-cost accounting is used by most of the smaller, exploration-oriented companies. The differences in net income figures under the two methods can be staggering. It was estimated that **ChevronTexaco**'s full-cost accounting increased its reported profits by $500 million over a 10-year period.

[2] The Department of Energy indicated that companies using the full-cost method at that time would reduce their exploration activities because of the unfavorable earnings impact associated with successful efforts accounting. The Justice Department asked the SEC to postpone adoption of one uniform method of accounting in the oil and gas industry until the SEC could determine whether the information reported to investors would be enhanced and competition constrained by adoption of the successful efforts method.

[3] The use of RRA would make a substantial difference in the balance sheets and income statements of oil companies. For example, **Atlantic Richfield Co.** at one time reported net producing property of $2.6 billion. If RRA were adopted, the same properties would be valued at $11.8 billion. Similarly, **Standard Oil of Ohio,** which reported net producing properties of $1.7 billion, would have reported approximately $10.7 billion under RRA.

As a result of the SEC's actions, the FASB had no choice but to issue another standard that suspended the requirement that companies follow successful efforts accounting (FASB *Statement No. 25*, "Suspension of Certain Accounting Requirements for Oil and Gas Producing Companies"). Therefore, full costing again became permissible.

3 **1982**—The SEC encountered practical problems in attempting to implement RRA, because estimates are needed for **(1) the amount of the reserves, (2) the future production costs, (3) the periods of expected disposal, (4) the discount rate, and (5) the selling price.** Due to the subjectivity inherent in these estimates, the SEC indicated that RRA does not currently possess the required degree of reliability for use as a primary method of financial reporting. However, the SEC continued to stress that some form of value-based disclosure was needed for oil and gas reserves. As a result, the FASB issued *Statement No. 69*, "Disclosure about Oil and Gas Producing Activities," which requires current value disclosures.[4]

Either the full-cost approach or the successful efforts approach is currently acceptable. It does seem ironic that Congress directed the FASB to develop one method of accounting for the oil and gas industry, and when the FASB did so, the government chose not to accept it. Subsequently, the government (SEC) attempted to develop a new approach, failed, and then urged the FASB to develop the disclosure requirements in this area. After all these changes, alternatives still exist in the oil and gas industry.

This controversy in the oil and gas industry provides a number of lessons to the student in accounting. First, it demonstrates the strong influence that the federal government has in financial reporting matters. Second, the concern for economic consequences places considerable pressure on the FASB to weigh the economic effects of any required standard. Third, the experience with RRA highlights the problems that are encountered when a change from an historical cost to a current value approach is proposed. Fourth, this controversy illustrates the difficulty of establishing standards when affected groups have differing viewpoints. And finally, it reinforces the need for a conceptual framework with carefully developed guidelines for recognition, measurement, and reporting, so that issues of this nature hopefully may be more easily resolved in the future.

UNDERLYING CONCEPTS

Failure to consider the economic consequences of accounting principles is a frequent criticism of the profession. However, the neutrality concept requires that the statements be free from bias. Freedom from bias requires that the statements reflect economic reality, even if undesirable effects occur.

SPECIAL PROBLEMS IN DEPLETION ACCOUNTING

Accounting for natural resources has some interesting problems that are uncommon to most other types of assets. These problems are divided into four categories.

1 Difficulty of estimating recoverable reserves.

2 Problems of discovery value.

3 Tax aspects of natural resources.

4 Accounting for liquidating dividends.

---

[4]**Under full-cost accounting, costs can be capitalized only up to a ceiling, the height of which is determined by the present value of company reserves.** Capitalized costs above that ceiling have to be expensed. In 1986 the price of oil plummeted, and as a result a number of companies faced massive write-offs of their reserves because capitalized costs exceeded the present value of the companies' reserves. For example, **Mesa Limited Partnerships'** $31 million profit was restated to a $169 million loss, and **Pacific Lighting's** $44.5 million profit was changed to a $70.5 million loss.

Estimating Recoverable Reserves

Not infrequently the estimate of recoverable reserves has to be changed either because new information has become available or because production processes have become more sophisticated. Natural resources such as oil and gas deposits and some rare metals have recently provided the greatest challenges. Estimates of these reserves are in large measure "knowledgeable guesses."

This problem is the **same as accounting for changes in estimates for the useful lives of plant and equipment**. The procedure is to revise the depletion rate on a prospective basis by dividing the remaining cost by the estimate of the new recoverable reserves. This approach has much merit because the required estimates are so tenuous.

Discovery Value

Discovery value accounting and reserve recognition accounting are similar. RRA is specifically related to the oil and gas industry, whereas **discovery value** is a broader term associated with the whole natural resources area. As indicated earlier, accountants do not recognize discovery values. However, if discovery value were to be recorded, an asset account would be debited and an Unrealized Appreciation account would be credited. Unrealized Appreciation is part of stockholders' equity. Unrealized Appreciation would then be transferred to revenue as the natural resources are sold.

A similar issue arises with resources such as growing timber, aging liquor, and maturing livestock that increase in value over time. One method is to record the increase in value as the accretion occurs: Debit the asset account and credit revenue or an unrealized revenue account. These increases can be substantial. **Boise Cascade**'s timber resources were at one time valued at $1.7 billion, whereas its book value was approximately $289 million. Accountants have been hesitant to record these increases because of the uncertainty regarding the final sales price and the problem of estimating the costs involved in getting the resources ready for sale.

Tax Aspects of Natural Resources

The tax aspects of accounting for most natural resources have comprised some of the most controversial provisions of the Internal Revenue Code. The tax law has long provided a deduction for the greater of **cost** or **percentage depletion** against revenue from oil, gas, and most minerals. The percentage or statutory depletion allows a write-off ranging from 5 percent to 22 percent (depending on the natural resource) of gross revenue received. As a result, the amount of depletion may exceed the cost assigned to a given natural resource. An asset's carrying amount may be zero, but a depletion deduction may still be taken if the enterprise has gross revenue. The significance of the percentage depletion allowance is now greatly reduced because it has been repealed for most oil and gas companies and is of only limited use in most other situations.

Liquidating Dividends

A company often owns as its only major asset a certain property from which it intends to extract natural resources. If the company does not expect to purchase additional properties, it may distribute gradually to stockholders their capital investments by paying dividends greater than the amount of accumulated net income. The major accounting problem is to distinguish between dividends that are a return of capital and those that are not. The company issuing a **liquidating dividend** should debit Paid-in Capital in Excess of Par for that portion related to the original investment instead of Retained Earnings, because the dividend is a return of part of the investor's original contribution.

To illustrate, at year-end, Callahan Mining had a retained earnings balance of $1,650,000, accumulated depletion on mineral properties of $2,100,000, and paid-in capital in excess of par of $5,435,493. Callahan's board declared a dividend of $3 a share on the 1,000,000 shares outstanding. The entry to record the $3,000,000 cash dividend is as follows.

Retained Earnings	1,650,000	
Paid-in Capital in Excess of Par	1,350,000	
Cash		3,000,000

Stockholders must be informed that $1.35 of each $3 dividend ($1,350,000 ÷ 1,000,000 shares) represents a liquidating dividend.

PRESENTATION OF NATURAL RESOURCES

Special disclosure requirements relate to the oil and gas industry. Companies engaged in these activities must disclose the following in their financial statements: (1) the basic method of accounting for those costs incurred in oil and gas producing activities (e.g., full cost versus successful efforts), and (2) the manner of disposing of costs relating to oil and gas producing activities (e.g., expensing immediately versus depreciation and depletion). Public companies, in addition to these two required disclosures, must include as supplementary information numerous schedules reporting reserve quantities; capitalized costs; acquisition, exploration, and development activities; and a standardized measure of discounted future net cash flows related to proved oil and gas reserve quantities.[5]

SUMMARY OF LEARNING OBJECTIVE

❶ Explain the accounting for natural resources. The accounting procedures for depletion of natural resources are (1) establishment of depletion base, and (2) write-off of resource cost. Four factors are involved in establishing the depletion base: (a) *acquisition costs*, (b) *exploration costs*, (c) *development costs*, and (d) *restoration costs*. To write off resource cost, depletion is normally computed on the units of production method, which means that depletion is a function of the number of units withdrawn during the period. In adopting this approach, the total cost of the natural resource less salvage value is divided by the number of units estimated to be in the resource deposit, to obtain a cost per unit of product. This cost per unit is multiplied by the number of units withdrawn to compute depletion.

> **KEY TERMS**
>
> acquisition cost, *D1*
> depletion, *D1*
> development costs, *D1*
> discovery value, *D5*
> exploration costs, *D1*
> full cost concept, *D3*
> liquidating dividend, *D5*
> natural resources, *D1*
> percentage depletion, *D5*
> reserve recognition
>   accounting (RRA), *D3*
> restorations costs, *D2*
> successful efforts concept,
>   *D3*

EXERCISES

ED-1 (Depletion Computations—Timber) Stanislaw Timber Company owns 9,000 acres of timberland purchased in 1992 at a cost of $1,400 per acre. At the time of purchase the land without the timber was valued at $400 per acre. In 1993, Stanislaw built fire lanes and roads, with a life of 30 years, at a cost of $84,000. Every year Stanislaw sprays to prevent disease at a cost of $3,000 per year and spends $7,000 to maintain the fire lanes and roads. During 1994, Stanislaw selectively logged and sold 700,000 board feet of timber, of the estimated 3,500,000 board feet. In 1995, Stanislaw planted new seedlings to replace the trees cut at a cost of $100,000.

---

[5]"Disclosures about Oil and Gas Producing Activities," *Statement of Financial Accounting Standards Board No. 69* (Stamford, Conn.: FASB, 1982).

Instructions

(a) Determine the depreciation expense and the cost of timber sold related to depletion for 1994.

(b) Stanislaw has not logged since 1994. If Stanislaw logged and sold 900,000 board feet of timber in 2005, when the timber cruise (appraiser) estimated 5,000,000 board feet, determine the cost of timber sold related to depletion for 2005.

ED-2 **(Depletion Computations—Oil)** Diderot Drilling Company has leased property on which oil has been discovered. Wells on this property produced 18,000 barrels of oil during the past year that sold at an average sales price of $15 per barrel. Total oil resources of this property are estimated to be 250,000 barrels.

The lease provided for an outright payment of $500,000 to the lessor before drilling could be commenced and an annual rental of $31,500. A premium of 5% of the sales price of every barrel of oil removed is to be paid annually to the lessor. In addition, the lessee is to clean up all the waste and debris from drilling and to bear the costs of reconditioning the land for farming when the wells are abandoned. It is estimated that this clean-up and reconditioning will cost $30,000.

Instructions

From the provisions of the lease agreement, you are to compute the cost per barrel for the past year, exclusive of operating costs, to Diderot Drilling Company.

ED-3 **(Depletion Computations—Timber)** Forda Lumber Company owns a 7,000-acre tract of timber purchased in 1997 at a cost of $1,300 per acre. At the time of purchase the land was estimated to have a value of $300 per acre without the timber. Forda Lumber Company has not logged this tract since it was purchased. In 2004, Forda had the timber cruised. The cruise (appraiser) estimated that each acre contained 8,000 board feet of timber. In 2004, Forda built 10 miles of roads at a cost of $7,840 per mile. After the roads were completed, Forda logged and sold 3,500 trees containing 850,000 board feet.

Instructions

(a) Determine the cost of timber sold related to depletion for 2004.

(b) If Forda depreciates the logging roads on the basis of timber cut, determine the depreciation expense for 2004.

(c) If Forda plants five seedlings at a cost of $4 per seedling for each tree cut, how should Forda treat the reforestation?

ED-4 **(Depletion Computations—Minerals)** At the beginning of 2003, Aristotle Company acquired a mine for $970,000. Of this amount, $100,000 was ascribed to the land value and the remaining portion to the minerals in the mine. Surveys conducted by geologists have indicated that approximately 12,000,000 units of the ore appear to be in the mine. Aristotle incurred $170,000 of development costs associated with this mine prior to any extraction of minerals. It estimates that it will require $40,000 to prepare the land for an alternative use when all of the mineral has been removed. During 2003, 2,500,000 units of ore were extracted, and 2,100,000 of these units were sold.

Instructions

Compute (a) the total amount of depletion for 2003, and (b) the amount that is charged as an expense for 2003 for the cost of the minerals sold during 2003.

PROBLEMS

PD-1 **(Depletion and Depreciation—Mining)** Richard Wright Mining Company has purchased a tract of mineral land for $600,000. It is estimated that this tract will yield 120,000 tons of ore with sufficient mineral content to make mining and processing profitable. It is further estimated that 6,000 tons of ore will be mined the first and last year, and 12,000 tons every year in between. The land will have a residual value of $30,000.

The company builds necessary structures and sheds on the site at a cost of $36,000. It is estimated that these structures can serve 15 years, but because they must be dismantled if they are to be moved, they have no scrap value. The company does not intend to use the buildings elsewhere. Mining machinery installed at the mine was purchased second-hand at a cost of $48,000. This machinery cost the former owner $100,000 and was 50% depreciated when purchased. Richard Wright Mining estimates that about half of this machinery will still be useful when the present mineral resources have been exhausted, but that dismantling and removal costs will just about offset its value at that time. The company does not intend to use the machinery elsewhere. The remaining machinery will last until about one-half the present estimated mineral ore has been removed and will then be worthless. Cost is to be allocated equally between these two classes of machinery.

Instructions

(a) As chief accountant for the company, you are to prepare a schedule showing estimated depletion and depreciation costs for each year of the expected life of the mine.

(b) Also compute the depreciation and depletion for the first year, assuming actual production of 7,000 tons. Nothing occurred during the year to cause the company engineers to change their estimates of either the mineral resources or the life of the structures and equipment.

PD-2 (Depletion, Timber, and Extraordinary Loss) Ted Koppel Logging and Lumber Company owns 3,000 acres of timberland on the north side of Mount St. Helens, which was purchased in 1968 at a cost of $550 per acre. In 1980, Kopple began selectively logging this timber tract. In May 1980, Mount St. Helens erupted, burying the timberland of Koppel under a foot of ash. All of the timber on the Koppel tract was downed. In addition, the logging roads, built at a cost of $150,000, were destroyed, as well as the logging equipment with a net book value of $300,000.

At the time of the eruption, Koppel had logged 20% of the estimated 500,000 board feet of timber. Prior to the eruption, Koppel estimated the land to have a value of $200 per acre after the timber was harvested. Koppel includes the logging roads in the depletion base.

Koppel estimates it will take 3 years to salvage the downed timber at a cost of $700,000. The timber can be sold for pulp wood at an estimated price of $3 per board foot. The value of the land is unknown, but must be considered nominal due to future uncertainties.

Instructions

(a) Determine the depletion cost per board foot for the timber harvested prior to the eruption of Mount St. Helens.

(b) Prepare the journal entry to record the depletion prior to the eruption.

(c) If this tract represents approximately half of the timber holdings of Koppel, determine the amount of the estimated loss, and show how the losses of roads, machinery, and timber and the salvage of the timber should be reported in the financial statements of Koppel for the year ended December 31, 1980.

PD-3 (Natural Resources—Timber) Western Paper Products purchased 10,000 acres of forested timberland in March 2004. The company paid $1,700 per acre for this land, which was above the $800 per acre most farmers were paying for cleared land. During April, May, June, and July 2004, Western cut enough timber to build roads using moveable equipment purchased on April 1, 2004. The cost of the roads was $195,000, and the cost of the equipment was $189,000. This equipment was expected to have a $9,000 salvage value and would be used for the next 15 years. Western selected the straight-line method of depreciation for the moveable equipment. Western began actively harvesting timber in August, and by December had harvested and sold 472,500 board feet of timber of the estimated 6,750,000 board feet available for cutting.

In March 2005, Western planted new seedlings in the area harvested during the winter. Cost of planting these seedlings was $120,000. In addition, Western spent $8,000 in road maintenance and $6,000 for pest spraying during calendar-year 2005. The road maintenance and spraying are annual costs. During 2005 Western harvested and sold 774,000 board feet of timber of the estimated 6,450,000 board feet available for cutting.

In March 2006, Western again planted new seedlings at a cost of $150,000, and also spent $15,000 on road maintenance and pest spraying. During 2006, the company harvested and sold 650,000 board feet of timber of the estimated 6,500,000 board feet available for cutting.

Instructions

Compute the amount of depreciation and depletion expense for each of the 3 years. Assume that the roads are usable only for logging and therefore are included in the depletion base.

The development of computer software products takes on increasing importance as our economy continues to change from a manufacturing process orientation (tangible outputs) to an information flow society (intangible outputs).[1] This appendix discusses the basic issues involved in accounting for computer software.

DIVERSITY IN PRACTICE

Computer software may be either **purchased** or **created** by a company. It may be purchased or created for **external use** (such as spreadsheet applications like Excel or Lotus 1-2-3) or for **internal use** (e.g., to establish a better internal accounting system). Should costs incurred in developing the software be expensed immediately or capitalized and amortized in the future? Prior to 1985, some companies expensed all software costs, and others capitalized such costs. Still others differentiated such costs on the basis of whether the software was purchased or created, or whether it was used for external or internal purposes.

THE PROFESSION'S POSITION

OBJECTIVE **1**
Identify the accounting treatment for computer software costs.

A major question is whether the costs involved in developing software are research and development costs. If they are actually R & D, then the profession requires that they be expensed as incurred. If they are not research and development costs, then a strong case can be made for capitalization. As one financial executive of a software company, who argues for capitalization, noted, "The key distinction between our spending and R & D is recoverability. We know we are developing something we can sell."

In an attempt to resolve this issue (at least for companies that sell computer software), the FASB issued *Statement of Financial Accounting Standards No. 86,* "Accounting for the Costs of Computer Software to Be Sold, Leased, or Otherwise Marketed."[2] The major recommendations of this pronouncement are:

① Costs incurred in creating a computer software product should be charged to research and development expense when incurred until **technological feasibility** has been established for the product.

② Technological feasibility is established upon completion of a detailed program design or working model.

In short, the FASB has taken a conservative position in regard to computer software costs. All costs must be expensed until the company has completed planning, designing, coding, and testing activities necessary to establish that

---

[1]A major contributing factor was **IBM**'s decision in 1969 to "unbundle" its hardware and software, that is, to state the cost of the hardware and software separately. Prior to the unbundling, most applications software was provided free with the hardware. This unbundling led to the creation of a whole new industry, the software industry, whose members began selling software to hardware users.

[2]"Accounting for the Cost of Computer Software to Be Sold, Leased, or Otherwise Marketed," *Statement of Financial Accounting Standards No. 86* (Stamford, Conn.: FASB, 1985). Also see, Robert W. McGee, *Accounting for Software* (Homewood, Ill.: Dow Jones-Irwin, 1985).

the product can be produced to meet its design specifications. Subsequent costs incurred should be capitalized and amortized to current and future periods.

Two additional points should be emphasized. First, **if the software is purchased and it has alternative future uses, then it may be capitalized.** Second, **this standard applies only to the development of software that is to be sold, leased, or otherwise marketed to third parties** (i.e., for external use).

The profession has also indicated how to account for computer software to be used internally. Activities performed during the preliminary project stage of development (conceptual formulation and evaluation of alternatives, for example) are similar to R & D costs and should be expensed immediately. However, once the software is at the application development stage (at the coding or installation into hardware stages, for example), its future economic benefits become probable and so capitalization of costs is required. Costs subsequent to the application development stage related to training and application maintenance should be expensed as incurred.[3]

ACCOUNTING FOR CAPITALIZED SOFTWARE COSTS

If software costs are capitalized, then a proper amortization pattern for these costs must be established. **Companies are required to use the greater of (1) the ratio of current revenues to current and anticipated revenues (percent of revenue approach) or (2) the straight-line method over the remaining useful life of the asset (straight-line approach) as a basis for amortization.** These rules can result in the use of the ratio method one year and the straight-line method in another.

To illustrate, assume that **AT&T** has capitalized software costs of $10 million, and its current (first-year) revenues from sales of this product are $4 million. AT&T anticipates earning $16 million in additional future revenues from this product, which is estimated to have an economic life of 4 years. Using the percent of revenue approach, the current (first) year's amortization would be $2 million ($10,000,000 × $4,000,000/ $20,000,000). Using the straight-line approach, the amortization would be $2.5 million ($10,000,000/4 years). Thus the straight-line approach would be employed because it results in the greater amortization charge.

REPORTING SOFTWARE COSTS

Because much concern exists about the reliability of an asset such as software, the FASB indicated that capitalized software costs should be valued at the **lower of unamortized cost or net realizable value.** If net realizable value is lower, then the capitalized software costs should be written down to this value. Once written down, **it may not be written back up.** In addition to the regular disclosures for R & D costs, the following should be reported in the financial statements.

1. Unamortized software costs.
2. The total amount charged to expense and amounts, if any, written down to net realizable value.

Once again these accounting and reporting requirements apply only to software **developed for external purposes.**

[3]"Accounting for the Costs of Computer Software Developed or Obtained for Internal Use," *Statement of Position 98-1* (New York: AICPA, 1998).

An example of software development cost disclosure, taken from the annual report of **Micrografx Inc.**, is shown below.

MICROGRAFX INC.

Capitalized software development costs and acquired product rights consist of the following (in thousands).

	June 30,	
	1998	1997
Capitalized software development costs	$ 9,077	$ 5,270
Less: Accumulated amortization	(5,886)	(1,986)
Capitalized software development costs, net	$ 3,191	$3,284
Acquired product rights	$6,477	$5,940
Less: Accumulated amortization	(3,784)	(2,359)
Acquired product rights, net	$2,693	$3,581

Significant Accounting Policies:

In accordance with Statement of Financial Accounting Standards ("SFAS") No. 86, "Accounting for the Costs of Computer Software to be Sold, Leased, or Otherwise Marketed," the Company capitalizes certain software development costs incurred after technological feasibility is achieved and also capitalizes costs of acquiring certain product rights in connection with the development of its computer software products. Capitalized costs are reported at the lower of unamortized cost or net realizable value. Capitalized software development costs and acquired product rights are amortized straight-line over the estimated economic life of the products, generally 12 to 18 months, which approximates amortization based on the ratio of current net sales over future estimated net sales. The Company begins amortization when the products are available for general release to customers. All other research and development expenditures are charged to research and development expense in the period incurred.

SETTING STANDARDS FOR SOFTWARE ACCOUNTING

"It's unreasonable to expense all software costs, and it's unreasonable to capitalize all software costs," said **IBM**'s director of financial reporting. "If you subscribe to those two statements, then it follows that there is somewhere in between where development ends and capitalization begins. Now you have to define that point."[4] The FASB defined that point as "technological feasibility," which is established upon completion of a detailed program design or working model.

The difficulty of applying this criterion to software is that "there is no such thing as a real, specific, baseline design. But you could make it look like you have one as early or as late as you like," says Osman Erlop of **Hambrecht & Quist**.[5] That is, if you wish to capitalize, draw up a detailed program design quickly. If you want to expense lots of development costs, simply hold off writing a detailed program design. And, once capitalized, the costs are amortized over the useful life specified by the developer,

[4]"When Does Life Begin?" *Forbes* (June 16, 1986), pp. 72–74.
[5]Ibid.

which because of either constant redesign or supersession is generally quite short (2 to 4 years).

As another example, some companies "manage by the numbers." That is, they are very careful to identify projects that are worthwhile and capitalize the computer software costs associated with them. They believe that good projects must be capitalized and amortized in the future; otherwise, the concept of properly matching expense and revenues is abused.

Other companies choose not to manage by the numbers and simply expense all these costs. Companies that expense all these costs have no use for a standard that requires capitalization. In their view, it would mean only that a more complex, more expensive cost accounting system would be required, one that would provide little if any benefit.

Financial analysts have reacted almost uniformly against any capitalization. They believe software costs should be expensed because of the rapid obsolescence of software and the potential for abuse that may result from capitalizing costs inappropriately. As Donald Kirk, a former chairman of the FASB, stated, "The Board is now faced with the problem of balancing what it thought was good theory with the costs for some companies of implementing a new accounting system with the concerns of users about the potential for abuse of the standard."[6]

Resolving the software accounting problem again demonstrates the difficulty of establishing reporting standards.

SUMMARY OF LEARNING OBJECTIVE

1 **Identify the accounting treatment for computer software costs.** Costs incurred in creating a software product should be charged to R & D expense when incurred until technological feasibility has been established for the product. Subsequent costs should be capitalized and amortized to current and future periods. Software that is purchased for sale or lease to third parties and has alternative future uses may be capitalized and amortized using the greater of the percent of revenue approach or the straight-line approach.

EXERCISES

EE-1 (Accounting for Computer Software Costs) New Jersey Inc. has capitalized computer software costs of $3,600,000 on its new Trenton software package. Revenues from 2003 (first-year) sales are $2,000,000. Additional future revenues from "Trenton" for the remainder of its economic life, through 2007, are estimated to be $10,000,000.

Instructions
(a) What method or methods of amortization are to be applied in the write-off of capitalized computer software costs?
(b) Compute the amount of amortization for 2003 for "Trenton."

EE-2 (Accounting for Computer Software Costs) During 2003, Delaware Enterprises spent $5,000,000 developing its new Dover software package. Of this amount, $2,200,000 was spent before technological feasibility was established for the product, which is to be marketed to third parties. The package was completed at December 31, 2003. Delaware expects a useful life of 8 years for this product with total revenues of $16,000,000. During the first year (2004), Delaware realizes revenues of $3,200,000.

[6]Donald J. Kirk, "Growing Temptation & Rising Expectation = Accelerating Regulation," *FASB Viewpoints* (June 12, 1985), p. 7.

Instructions

(a) Prepare journal entries required in 2003 for the foregoing facts.

(b) Prepare the entry to record amortization at December 31, 2004.

(c) At what amount should the computer software costs be reported in the December 31, 2004, balance sheet? Could the net realizable value of this asset affect your answer?

(d) What disclosures are required in the December 31, 2004, financial statements for the computer software costs?

(e) How would your answers for (a), (b), and (c) be different if the computer software was developed for internal use?

During periods of depressed economic conditions or other financial hardship, some debtors have difficulty meeting their financial obligations. For example, owing to rising interest rates and corporate mismanagement, the savings and loan industry experienced a decade of financial crises. The banking industry also faced credit concerns: During the late 1980s bad energy loans and the rescheduling of loans between "less developed countries," such as Argentina, Brazil, and Mexico, and major U.S. banks created considerable uncertainty about the soundness of our banking system. Electric utilities with large nuclear plant construction programs suffered from the financial strains of illiquidity. More recently, companies such as **Xerox**, **Kmart**, and **Polaroid** had to restructure their debts or in some other way be bailed out of negative cash flow situations when the economy, technology, competition, or a combination thereof, turned against them.

LEARNING OBJECTIVE

After studying this appendix, you should be able to:

 Distinguish among and account for: (1) a loss on loan impairment, (2) a troubled debt restructuring that results in the settlement of a debt, and (3) a troubled debt restructuring that results in a continuation of debt with modification of terms.

ACCOUNTING ISSUES

The major accounting issues related to troubled debt situations involve recognition and measurement. In other words, when should a loss be recognized and at what amount?

To illustrate the major issue related to recognition, assume that Metro Bank has a $10,000,000, 5-year, 10% loan to Brazil, with interest receivable annually. At the end of the third year, Metro Bank has determined that it probably will be able to collect only $7,000,000 of this loan at maturity. Should it wait until the loan becomes uncollectible, or should it record a loss immediately? The general recognition principle is this: **Losses should be recorded immediately if it is probable that the loss will occur**.

Assuming that Metro Bank decides to record a loss, at what amount should the loss be recorded? Three alternatives are:

1. *Aggregate Cash Flows.* Some argue that a loss should not be recorded unless the aggregate cash flows from the loan are less than its carrying amount. In the Metro Bank example, the aggregate cash flows expected are $7,000,000 of principal and $2,000,000 of interest ($10,000,000 × 10% × 2), for a total of $9,000,000. Thus, a loss of only $1,000,000 ($10,000,000 − $9,000,000) would be reported.

   Advocates of this position argue that Metro Bank will recover $9,000,000 of the $10,000,000 and, therefore, its loss is only $1,000,000. Others disagree, noting that this approach ignores present values. That is, the present value of the future cash flows is much less than $9,000,000, and therefore the loss is much greater than $1,000,000.

2. *Present Value—Historical Effective Rate.* Those who argue for the use of present value, however, disagree about the interest rate to use to discount the expected future cash flows. The two rates discussed are the **historical (original) effective rate** and the **market rate** at the time the loan is recognized as troubled.

   Those who favor the historical effective rate believe that losses should reflect only a deterioration in credit quality. When the historical effective loan rate is used, the value of the investment will change only if some of the legally contracted cash flows are reduced. A loss in this case is recognized because the expected future cash flows have changed. Interest rate changes caused by current economic events that affect the fair value of the loan are ignored.

OBJECTIVE **1**
Distinguish among and account for: (1) a loss on loan impairment, (2) a troubled debt restructuring that results in the settlement of a debt, and (3) a troubled debt restructuring that results in a continuation of debt with modification of terms.

③ *Present Value—Market Rate.* Others believe that expected future cash flows of a troubled loan should be discounted at market interest rates, which reflect current economic events and conditions that are commensurate with the risks involved. The historical effective interest rate reflects the risk characteristics of the loan at the time it was originated or acquired, but not at the time it is troubled. In short, proponents of the market rate believe that a fair value measure should be used.

This appendix addresses issues concerning the accounting by debtors and creditors for troubled debt. Two different types of situations result with troubled debt:

① Impairments.
② Restructurings:

    a. Settlements.
    b. Modification of terms.

In a troubled debt situation, the creditor usually first recognizes a loss on impairment. Subsequently either the terms of the loan are modified or the loan is settled on terms unfavorable to the creditor. In unusual cases, the creditor forces the debtor into bankruptcy in order to ensure the highest possible collection on the loan. Illustration F-1 shows this continuum.

Illustration F-1
Usual Progression in Troubled Debt Situations

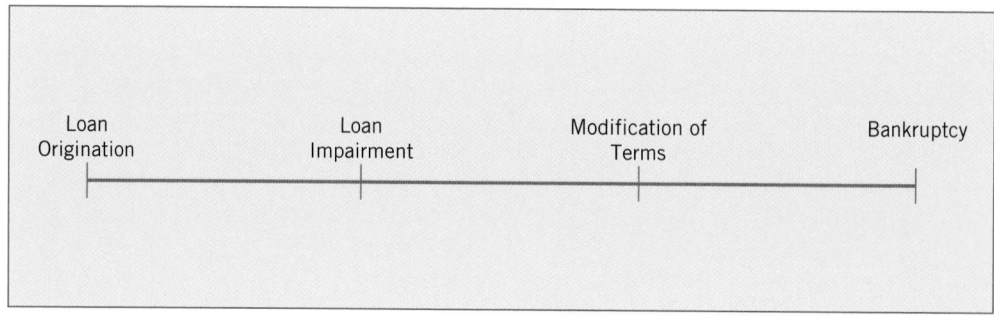

IMPAIRMENTS
| Loan Origination | Loan Impairment | Modification of Terms | Bankruptcy |

IMPAIRMENTS

A loan[1] is considered **impaired** when it is **probable**,[2] based on current information and events, that the creditor will be unable to collect all amounts due (both principal and interest) according to the contractual terms of the loan. Creditors should apply their normal review procedures in making the judgment as to the probability of collection.[3] If a loan is considered impaired, the loss due to the **impairment** should be measured as the difference between the investment in the loan (generally the principal plus ac-

---

[1]*FASB Statement No. 114,* "Accounting by Creditors for Impairment of a Loan," (Norwalk, Conn.: FASB, May 1993), defines a loan as "a contractual right to receive money on demand or on fixed and determinable dates that is recognized as an asset in the creditor's statement of financial position." For example, accounts receivable with terms exceeding one year are considered loans.

[2]Recall the definitions of probable, reasonably possible, and remote with respect to contingencies, as defined in *FASB Statement No. 5.*

[3]Normal review procedures include examination of "watch lists," review of regulatory reports of examination, and examination of management reports of total loan amounts by borrower.

crued interest) and the expected future cash flows discounted at the loan's historical effective interest rate.[4] In estimating future cash flows the creditor should employ all reasonable and supportable assumptions and projections.[5]

Illustration of Loss on Impairment

On December 31, 2003, Prospect Inc. issued a $500,000, 5-year, zero-interest-bearing note to Community Bank. The note was issued to yield 10% annual interest. As a result, Prospect received and Community Bank paid $310,460 ($500,000 × .62092) on December 31, 2003.[6] A time diagram illustrates the factors involved:

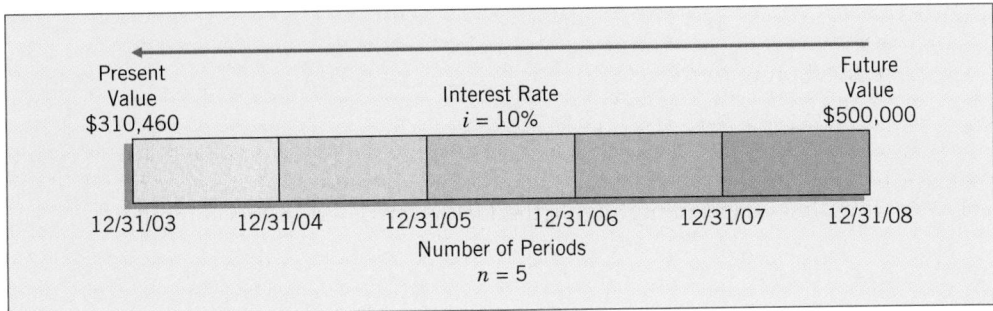

The entries to record this transaction on the books of Community Bank (creditor) and Prospect Inc. (debtor) are as follows.

December 31, 2003			
Community Bank (Creditor)		**Prospect Inc. (Debtor)**	
Notes Receivable	500,000	Cash	310,460
Discount on Notes		Discount on Notes	
Receivable	189,540	Payable	189,540
Cash	310,460	Notes Payable	500,000

Illustration F-2
Creditor and Debtor Entries to Record Note

Assuming that Community Bank and Prospect Inc. use the effective interest method to amortize discounts, Illustration F-3 (on page F4) shows the amortization of the discount and the increase in the carrying amount of the note over the life of the note.

Unfortunately, during 2005 Prospect's business deteriorated due to increased competition and a faltering regional economy. After reviewing all available evidence at December 31, 2005, Community Bank determined that it was probable that Prospect would pay back only $300,000 of the principal at maturity. As a result, Community Bank decided that the loan was impaired, and that a loss should be recorded immediately.

---

[4]The creditor may also, for the sake of expediency, use the market price of the loan (if such a price is available) or the fair value of collateral if it is a collateralized loan. *FASB Statement No. 114,* par. 13.

[5]*FASB Statement No. 114,* par. 15.

[6]Present value of $500,000 due in 5 years at 10%, annual compounding (Appendix A, Table 2) equals $500,000 × .62092.

Illustration F-3
Schedule of Interest and
Discount Amortization
(Before Impairment)

	COMMUNITY BANK			
Date	Cash Received (0%)	Interest Revenue (10%)	Discount Amortized	Carrying Amount of Note
12/31/03				$310,460
12/31/04	$0	$ 31,046[a]	$ 31,046	341,506[b]
12/31/05	0	34,151	34,151	375,657
12/31/06	0	37,566	37,566	413,223
12/31/07	0	41,322	41,322	454,545
12/31/08	0	45,455	45,455	500,000
Total	$0	$189,540	$189,540	

[a]$31,046 = \$310,460 \times .10$
[b]$341,506 = \$310,460 + \$31,046$

To determine the loss, the first step is to compute the present value of the expected cash flows discounted at the historical effective rate of interest. This amount is $225,396. The following time diagram highlights the factors involved in this computation.

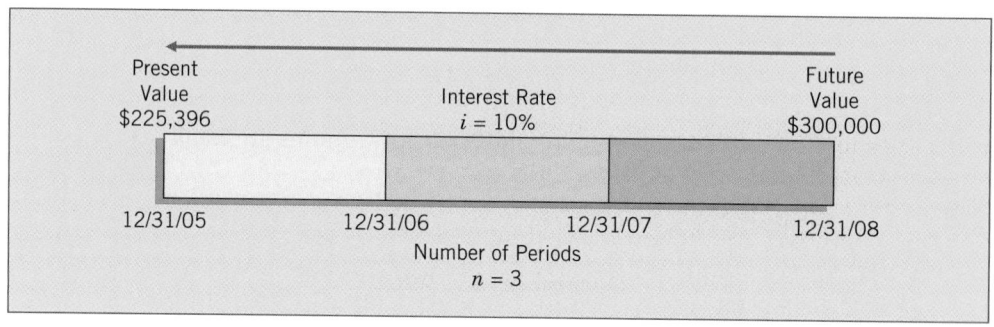

The loss due to impairment is equal to the difference between the present value of the expected future cash flows and the recorded carrying amount of the investment in the loan. The calculation of the loss is shown in Illustration F-4.

Illustration F-4
Computation of Loss Due
to Impairment

Carrying amount of investment (12/31/05)—Illustration F-3	$375,657
Less: Present value of $300,000 due in 3 years at 10% interest compounded annually (Appendix A, Table 2); $FV(PVF_{3,10\%})$; ($300,000 \times .75132$)	225,396
Loss due to impairment	$150,261

The loss due to the impairment is $150,261, not $200,000 ($500,000 − $300,000). The reason is that the loss is measured at a present value amount, not an undiscounted amount, at the time the loss is recorded.

The entry to record the loss is as follows.

Illustration F-5
Creditor and Debtor
Entries to Record Loss
on Note

December 31, 2005		
Community Bank (Creditor)		**Prospect Inc. (Debtor)**
Bad Debt Expense	150,261	No entry
Allowance for Doubtful Accounts	150,261	

Community Bank (creditor) debits Bad Debt Expense for the expected loss. At the same time, it reduces the overall value of its loan receivable by crediting Allowance for Doubtful Accounts.[7] On the other hand, Prospect Inc. (debtor) makes no entry because it still legally owes $500,000.[8]

TROUBLED DEBT RESTRUCTURINGS

A **troubled debt restructuring** occurs when a creditor "for economic or legal reasons related to the debtor's financial difficulties grants a concession to the debtor that it would not otherwise consider."[9] Thus a **troubled debt restructuring** does not apply to modifications of a debt obligation that reflect general economic conditions that dictate a reduction in interest rates. Nor does it apply to the refunding of an old debt with new debt having an effective interest rate approximately equal to that of similar debt issued by nontroubled debtors.

A troubled debt restructuring involves one of two basic types of transactions:

◇**1** Settlement of debt at less than its carrying amount.

◇**2** Continuation of debt with a modification of terms.

Settlement of Debt

A transfer of noncash assets (real estate, receivables, or other assets) or the issuance of the debtor's stock can be used to settle a debt obligation in a troubled debt restructuring. In these situations, **the noncash assets or equity interest given should be accounted for at their fair market value**. The debtor is required to determine the excess of the carrying amount of the payable over the fair value of the assets or equity transferred (gain). Likewise, the creditor is required to determine the excess of the receivable over the fair value of those same assets or equity interests transferred (loss). The debtor recognizes a gain equal to the amount of the excess, and the creditor normally would charge the excess (loss) against Allowance for Doubtful Accounts. In addition, the debtor recognizes a gain or loss on disposition of assets to the extent that the fair value of those assets differs from their carrying amount (book value).

Transfer of Assets

Assume that American City Bank has loaned $20,000,000 to Union Mortgage Company. Union Mortgage in turn has invested these monies in residential apartment buildings, but because of low occupancy rates it cannot meet its loan obligations. American City Bank agrees to accept from Union Mortgage real estate with a fair market value of $16,000,000 in full settlement of the $20,000,000 loan obligation. The real estate has a recorded value of $21,000,000 on the books of Union Mortgage Company.

---

[7]In the event that the loan is written off, the loss is charged against the allowance. In subsequent periods, if the estimated expected cash flows are revised based on new information, the allowance account and bad debt account are adjusted (either increased or decreased depending whether conditions improved or worsened) in the same fashion as the original impairment. The terms "loss" and "bad debt expense" are used interchangeably throughout this discussion. Losses related to receivables transactions should be charged to Bad Debt Expense or the related Allowance for Doubtful Accounts because these are the accounts used to recognize changes in values affecting receivables.

[8]Many alternatives are permitted to recognize income in subsequent periods. See *FASB Statement No. 118*, "Accounting by Creditors for Impairment of a Loan—Income Recognition and Disclosures" (Norwalk, Conn.: FASB, October 1994) for appropriate methods.

[9]"Accounting by Debtors and Creditors for Troubled Debt Restructurings," *FASB Statement No. 15* (Norwalk, Conn.: FASB, June, 1977), par. 1.

The entry to record this transaction on the books of American City Bank (creditor) is as follows.

Real Estate	16,000,000	
Allowance for Doubtful Accounts	4,000,000	
Note Receivable from Union Mortgage Company		20,000,000

The real estate is recorded at fair market value, and a charge is made to the Allowance for Doubtful Accounts to reflect the bad debt write-off.

The entry to record this transaction on the books of Union Mortgage Company (debtor) is as follows.

Note Payable to American City Bank	20,000,000	
Loss on Disposition of Real Estate	5,000,000	
Real Estate		21,000,000
Gain on Restructuring of Debt		4,000,000

Union Mortgage Company has a loss on the disposition of real estate in the amount of $5,000,000 (the difference between the $21,000,000 book value and the $16,000,000 fair market value), which should be shown as an ordinary loss on the income statement. In addition, it has a gain on restructuring of debt of $4,000,000 (the difference between the $20,000,000 carrying amount of the note payable and the $16,000,000 fair market value of the real estate).

Granting of Equity Interest

Assume that American City Bank had agreed to accept from Union Mortgage Company 320,000 shares of Union's common stock ($10 par) that has a fair market value of $16,000,000 in full settlement of the $20,000,000 loan obligation. The entry to record this transaction on the books of American City Bank (creditor) is as follows.

Investment	16,000,000	
Allowance for Doubtful Accounts	4,000,000	
Note Receivable from Union Mortgage Company		20,000,000

The stock received by American City Bank is recorded as an investment at the fair market value at the date of restructure.

The entry to record this transaction on the books of Union Mortgage Company (debtor) is as follows.

Note Payable to American City Bank	20,000,000	
Common Stock		3,200,000
Additional Paid-in Capital		12,800,000
Gain on Restructuring of Debt		4,000,000

The stock issued by Union Mortgage Company is recorded in the normal manner with the difference between the par value and the fair value of the stock recorded as additional paid-in capital.

Modification of Terms

In some cases, a debtor will have serious short-run cash flow problems that lead it to request one or a combination of the following modifications:

① Reduction of the stated interest rate.

② Extension of the maturity date of the face amount of the debt.

③ Reduction of the face amount of the debt.

④ Reduction or deferral of any accrued interest.

Under *FASB Statement No. 114*, the creditor's loss is based upon cash flows discounted at the historical effective rate of the loan. The FASB concluded that, "because loans are recorded originally at discounted amounts, the ongoing assessment for impairment should be made in a similar manner."[10] The debtor's gain is calculated based upon **undiscounted amounts**, as required by the previous standard. As a consequence, **the gain recorded by the debtor will not equal the loss recorded by the creditor under many circumstances.**[11]

Two illustrations demonstrate the accounting for a troubled debt restructuring by debtors and creditors:

① The debtor does not record a gain.

② The debtor does record a gain.

In both instances the creditor has a loss.

Illustration 1 — No Gain for Debtor

This illustration demonstrates a restructuring in which no gain is recorded by the debtor.[12] On December 31, 2003, Morgan National Bank enters into a debt restructuring agreement with Resorts Development Company, which is experiencing financial difficulties. The bank restructures a $10,500,000 loan receivable issued at par (interest paid to date) by:

① Reducing the principal obligation from $10,500,000 to $9,000,000;

② Extending the maturity date from December 31, 2003, to December 31, 2007; and

③ Reducing the interest rate from 12% to 8%.

---

[10]*FASB Statement No. 114*, par. 42.

[11]In response to concerns expressed about this nonsymmetric treatment, the FASB stated that *Statement No. 114* does not address debtor accounting because the FASB was concerned that expansion of the scope of the statement would delay its issuance.

[12]Note that the examples given for restructuring assume no previous entries were made by the creditor for impairment. In actuality it is likely that, in accordance with *Statement No. 114*, the creditor would have already made an entry when the loan initially became impaired, and restructuring would simply require an adjustment of the initial estimated bad debt by the creditor. Recall, however, that the debtor makes no entry upon impairment.

Debtor Calculations. The total future cash flow after restructuring of $11,880,000 ($9,000,000 of principal plus $2,880,000 of interest payments[13]) exceeds the total pre-restructuring carrying amount of the debt of $10,500,000. Consequently, **no gain is recorded, and no adjustment is made by the debtor** to the carrying amount of the payable. As a result, no entry is made by Resorts Development Co. (debtor) at the date of restructuring.

A new effective interest rate must be computed by the debtor in order to record interest expense in future periods. The new effective interest rate equates the present value of the future cash flows specified by the new terms with the pre-restructuring carrying amount of the debt. In this case, the new rate is computed by relating the pre-restructure carrying amount ($10,500,000) to the total future cash flow ($11,880,000). The rate necessary to discount the total future cash flow ($11,880,000) to a present value equal to the remaining balance ($10,500,000) is 3.46613%.[14]

On the basis of the effective rate of 3.46613%, the schedule shown in Illustration F-6 is prepared.

Illustration F-6

Schedule Showing Reduction of Carrying Amount of Note

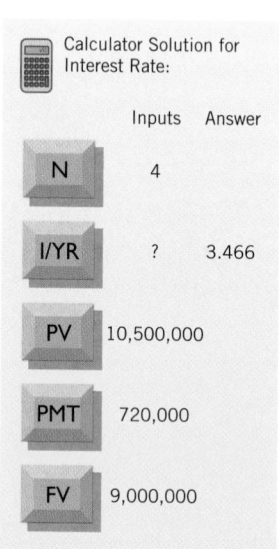

Calculator Solution for Interest Rate:

	Inputs	Answer
N	4	
I/YR	?	3.466
PV	10,500,000	
PMT	720,000	
FV	9,000,000	

RESORTS DEVELOPMENT CO. (DEBTOR)

Date	Interest Paid (8%)	Interest Expense (3.46613%)	Reduction of Carrying Amount	Carrying Amount of Note
12/31/03				$10,500,000
12/31/04	$ 720,000[a]	$ 363,944[b]	$ 356,056[c]	10,143,944
12/31/05	720,000	351,602	368,398	9,775,546
12/31/06	720,000	338,833	381,167	9,394,379
12/31/07	720,000	325,621	394,379	9,000,000
	$2,880,000	$1,380,000	$1,500,000	

[a]$720,000 = $9,000,000 × .08
[b]$363,944 = $10,500,000 × 3.46613%
[c]$356,056 = $720,000 − $363,944

Thus, on December 31, 2004 (date of first interest payment after restructure), the debtor makes the following entry.

December 31, 2004

Notes Payable	356,056	
Interest Expense	363,944	
Cash		720,000

[13]Total interest payments are: $9,000,000 × .08 × 4 years = $2,880,000.

[14]An accurate interest rate *i* can be found by using the formulas given at the tops of Tables 2 and 4 in Appendix A to set up the following equation.

$$\$10,500,000 = \frac{1}{(1 + i)^4} \times \$9,000,000 + \frac{1 - \dfrac{1}{(1 + i)^4}}{i} \times \$720,000$$

(from Table 2, Appendix A)   (from Table 4, Appendix A)

Solving algebraically for *i*, we find that *i* = 3.46613%.

A similar entry (except for different amounts for debits to Notes Payable and Interest Expense) is made each year until maturity. At maturity, the following entry is made.

December 31, 2007

Notes Payable	9,000,000	
Cash		9,000,000

Creditor Calculations.   Morgan National Bank (creditor) is required to calculate its loss based upon the expected future cash flows discounted at the historical effective rate of the loan. This loss is calculated as follows.

Pre-restructure carrying amount		$10,500,000
Present value of restructured cash flows:		
Present value of $9,000,000 due in 4 years		
at 12%, interest payable annually (Appendix A, Table 2);		
$FV(PVF_{4,12\%})$; ($9,000,000 × .63552)	$5,719,680	
Present value of $720,000 interest payable annually for 4		
years at 12% (Appendix A, Table 4); $R(PVF\text{-}OA_{4,12\%})$;		
($720,000 × 3.03735)	2,186,892	
Present value of restructured cash flows		7,906,572
Loss on restructuring		$ 2,593,428

Illustration F-7
Computation of Loss to
Creditor on Restructuring

As a result, Morgan National Bank records a bad debt expense account as follows (assuming no allowance balance has been established from recognition of an impairment).

Bad Debt Expense	2,593,428	
Allowance for Doubtful Accounts		2,593,428

In subsequent periods, interest revenue is reported based on the historical effective rate. Illustration F-8 provides the following interest and amortization information.

Illustration F-8
Schedule of Interest and
Amortization after Debt
Restructuring

MORGAN NATIONAL BANK (CREDITOR)				
Date	Interest Received (8%)	Interest Revenue (12%)	Increase of Carrying Amount	Carrying Amount of Note
12/31/03				$7,906,572
12/31/04	$ 720,000[a]	$ 948,789[b]	$ 228,789[c]	8,135,361
12/31/05	720,000	976,243	256,243	8,391,604
12/31/06	720,000	1,006,992	286,992	8,678,596
12/31/07	720,000	1,041,404[d]	321,404[d]	9,000,000
Total	$2,880,000	$3,973,428	$1,093,428	

[a]$720,000 = $9,000,000 × .08
[b]$948,789 = $7,906,572 × .12
[c]$228,789 = $948,789 − $720,000
[d]$28 adjustment to compensate for rounding.

On December 31, 2004, Morgan National Bank would make the following entry.

December 31, 2004

Cash	720,000	
Allowance for Doubtful Accounts	228,789	
Interest Revenue		948,789

A similar entry (except for different amounts debited to Allowance for Doubtful Accounts and credited to Interest Revenue) is made each year until maturity. At maturity, the following entry is made.

December 31, 2007

Cash	9,000,000	
Allowance for Doubtful Accounts	1,500,000	
Notes Receivable		10,500,000

Illustration 2—Gain for Debtor

If the pre-restructure carrying amount exceeds the total future cash flows as a result of a modification of the terms, the debtor records a gain. To illustrate, assume the facts in the previous example except that Morgan National Bank reduced the principal to $7,000,000 (and extended the maturity date to December 31, 2007, and reduced the interest from 12% to 8%). The total future cash flow is now $9,240,000 ($7,000,000 of principal plus $2,240,000 of interest[15]), which is $1,260,000 less than the pre-restructure carrying amount of $10,500,000. Under these circumstances, Resorts Development Company (debtor) would reduce the carrying amount of its payable $1,260,000 and record a gain of $1,260,000. On the other hand, Morgan National Bank (creditor) would debit its Bad Debt Expense for $4,350,444. This computation is shown in Illustration F-9.

Illustration F-9
Computation of Loss to
Creditor on Restructuring

Pre-restructure carrying amount		$10,500,000
Present value of restructured cash flows:		
Present value of $7,000,000 due in 4 years at 12%, interest payable annually (Appendix A, Table 2); $FV(PVF_{4,12\%})$; ($7,000,000 × .63552)	$4,448,640	
Present value of $560,000 interest payable annually for 4 years at 12% (Appendix A, Table 4); $R(PVF\text{-}OA_{4,12\%})$; ($560,000 × 3.03735)	1,700,916	6,149,556
Creditor's loss on restructuring		$ 4,350,444

Entries to record the gain and loss on the debtor's and creditor's books at the date of restructure, December 31, 2003, are shown in Illustration F-10.

For Resorts Development (debtor), because the new carrying value of the note ($10,500,000 − $1,260,000 = $9,240,000) equals the sum of the undiscounted cash flows ($9,240,000), the imputed interest rate is 0 percent. Consequently, all of the future cash flows reduce the principal balance, and no interest expense is recognized. For Morgan

[15]Total interest payments are: $7,000,000 × .08 × 4 years = $2,240,000.

December 31, 2003 (date of restructure)		
Resorts Development Co. (Debtor)		**Morgan National Bank (Creditor)**
Notes Payable 1,260,000		Bad Debt Expense 4,350,444
Gain on Restructuring of		Allowance for Doubtful Accounts 4,350,444
Debt	1,260,000	

Illustration F-10
Debtor and Creditor
Entries to Record Gain
and Loss on Note

National the interest revenue would be reported in the same fashion as the previous example, that is, using the historical effective interest rate applied toward the newly discounted value of the note. Interest computations are shown in Illustration F-11.

Illustration F-11
Schedule of Interest and
Amortization after Debt
Restructuring

		MORGAN NATIONAL BANK (CREDITOR)			
Date	Interest Received (8%)	Interest Revenue (12%)	Increase in Carrying Amount	Carrying Amount of Note
12/31/03				$6,149,556
12/31/04	$ 560,000ª	$ 737,947ᵇ	$177,947ᶜ	6,327,503
12/31/05	560,000	759,300	199,300	6,526,803
12/31/06	560,000	783,216	223,216	6,750,019
12/31/07	560,000	809,981ᵈ	249,981ᵈ	7,000,000
Total	$2,240,000	$3,090,444	$850,444	

ª$560,000 = $7,000,000 × .08
ᵇ$737,947 = $6,149,556 × .12
ᶜ$177,947 = $737,947 − $560,000
ᵈ$21 adjustment to compensate for rounding.

Illustration F-12
Debtor and Creditor
Entries to Record Periodic
Interest and Final
Principal Payments

The following journal entries illustrate the accounting by debtor and creditor for periodic interest payments and final principal payment.

Resorts Development Co. (Debtor)		**Morgan National Bank (Creditor)**	
December 31, 2004 (date of first interest payment following restructure)			
Notes Payable 560,000		Cash	560,000
Cash	560,000	Allowance for Doubtful Accounts	177,947
		Interest Revenue	737,947
December 31, 2005, 2006, and 2007 (dates of 2nd, 3rd, and last interest payments)			
(Debit and credit same accounts as 12/31/04			
using applicable amounts from appropriate amortization schedules.)			
December 31, 2007 (date of principal payment)			
Notes Payable 7,000,000		Cash	7,000,000
Cash	7,000,000	Allowance for Doubtful Accounts	3,500,000
		Notes Receivable	10,500,000

SUMMARY OF LEARNING OBJECTIVE

❶ Distinguish among and account for: (1) a loss on loan impairment, (2) a troubled debt restructuring that results in the settlement of a debt, and (3) a troubled debt restructuring that results in a continuation of debt with modification of terms. An impairment loan loss is based on the difference between the present value of the future cash flows and the carrying amount of the note. There are two types of settlement of debt restructurings: (1) transfer of noncash assets, and (2) granting of equity interest. For accounting purposes there are also two types of restructurings with continuation of debt with modified terms: (1) the carrying amount of debt is less than the future cash flows, and (2) the carrying amount of debt is greater than the total future cash flows.

EXERCISES

EF-1 (Settlement of Debt) Larisa Nieland Company owes $200,000 plus $18,000 of accrued interest to First State Bank. The debt is a 10-year, 10% note. During 2003, Larisa Nieland's business deteriorated due to a faltering regional economy. On December 31, 2003, First State Bank agrees to accept an old machine and cancel the entire debt. The machine has a cost of $390,000, accumulated depreciation of $221,000, and a fair market value of $190,000.

Instructions

(a) Prepare journal entries for Larisa Nieland Company and First State Bank to record this debt settlement.

(b) How should Larisa Nieland report the gain or loss on the disposition of machine and on restructuring of debt in its 2003 income statement?

(c) Assume that, instead of transferring the machine, Larisa Nieland decides to grant 15,000 shares of its common stock ($10 par) which has a fair market value of $190,000 in full settlement of the loan obligation. If First State Bank treats Larisa Nieland's stock as a trading investment, prepare the entries to record the transaction for both parties.

EF-2 (Term Modification without Gain—Debtor's Entries) On December 31, 2003, Firstar Bank enters into a debt restructuring agreement with Nicole Bradtke Company, which is now experiencing financial trouble. The bank agrees to restructure a 12%, issued at par, $2,000,000 note receivable by the following modifications.

1. Reducing the principal obligation from $2,000,000 to $1,600,000.
2. Extending the maturity date from December 31, 2003, to December 31, 2006.
3. Reducing the interest rate from 12% to 10%.

Bradtke pays interest at the end of each year. On January 1, 2007, Bradtke Company pays $1,600,000 in cash to Firstar Bank.

Instructions

(a) Based on *FASB Statement No. 114*, will the gain recorded by Bradtke be equal to the loss recorded by Firstar Bank under the debt restructuring?

(b) Can Bradtke Company record a gain under the term modification mentioned above? Explain.

(c) Assuming that the interest rate Bradtke should use to compute interest expense in future periods is 1.4276%, prepare the interest payment schedule of the note for Bradtke Company after the debt restructuring.

(d) Prepare the interest payment entry for Bradtke Company on December 31, 2005.

(e) What entry should Bradtke make on January 1, 2007?

EF-3 (Term Modification without Gain—Creditor's Entries) Using the same information as in EF-2 above, answer the following questions related to Firstar Bank (creditor).

Instructions

(a) What interest rate should Firstar Bank use to calculate the loss on the debt restructuring?

(b) Compute the loss that Firstar Bank will suffer from the debt restructuring. Prepare the journal entry to record the loss.

(c) Prepare the interest receipt schedule for Firstar Bank after the debt restructuring.

(d) Prepare the interest receipt entry for Firstar Bank on December 31, 2005.

(e) What entry should Firstar Bank make on January 1, 2007?

EF-4 **(Debtor/Creditor Entries for Settlement of Troubled Debt)** Petra Langrova Co. owes $199,800 to Mary Joe Fernandez Inc. The debt is a 10-year, 11% note. Because Petra Langrova Co. is in financial trouble, Mary Joe Fernandez Inc. agrees to accept some property and cancel the entire debt. The property has a book value of $80,000 and a fair market value of $120,000.

Instructions

(a) Prepare the journal entry on Langrova's books for debt restructure.

(b) Prepare the journal entry on Fernandez's books for debt restructure.

EF-5 **(Debtor/Creditor Entries for Modification of Troubled Debt)** Steffi Graf Corp. owes $225,000 to First Trust. The debt is a 10-year, 12% note due December 31, 2003. Because Graf Corp. is in financial trouble, First Trust agrees to extend the maturity date to December 31, 2005, reduce the principal to $200,000, and reduce the interest rate to 5%, payable annually on December 31.

Instructions

(a) Prepare the journal entries on Graf's books on December 31, 2003, 2004, and 2005.

(b) Prepare the journal entries on First Trust's books on December 31, 2003, 2004, and 2005.

EF-6 **(Impairments)** On December 31, 2002, Iva Majoli Company borrowed $62,092 from Paris Bank, signing a 5-year, $100,000 non-interest-bearing note. The note was issued to yield 10% interest. Unfortunately, during 2004, Majoli began to experience financial difficulty. As a result, at December 31, 2004, Paris Bank determined that it was probable that it would receive back only $75,000 at maturity. The market rate of interest on loans of this nature is now 11%.

Instructions

(a) Prepare the entry to record the issuance of the loan by Paris Bank on December 31, 2002.

(b) Prepare the entry (if any) to record the impairment of the loan on December 31, 2004, by Paris Bank.

(c) Prepare the entry (if any) to record the impairment of the loan on December 31, 2004, by Majoli Company.

EF-7 **(Impairments)** On December 31, 2001, Conchita Martinez Company signed a $1,000,000 note to Sauk City Bank. The market interest rate at that time was 12%. The stated interest rate on the note was 10%, payable annually. The note matures in 5 years. Unfortunately, because of lower sales, Conchita Martinez's financial situation worsened. On December 31, 2003, Sauk City Bank determined that it was probable that the company would pay back only $600,000 of the principal at maturity. However, it was considered likely that interest would continue to be paid, based on the $1,000,000 loan.

Instructions

(a) Determine the amount of cash Conchita Martinez received from the loan on December 31, 2001.

(b) Prepare a note amortization schedule for Sauk City Bank up to December 31, 2003.

(c) Determine the loss on impairment that Sauk City Bank should recognize on December 31, 2003.

PROBLEMS

PF-1 **(Loan Impairment Entries)** On January 1, 2003, Bostan Company issued a $1,200,000, 5-year, zero-interest-bearing note to National Organization Bank. The note was issued to yield 8% annual interest. Unfortunately, during 2004, Bostan fell into financial trouble due to increased competition. After reviewing all available evidence on December 31, 2004, National Organization Bank decided that the loan was impaired. Bostan will probably pay back only $800,000 of the principal at maturity.

Instructions

(a) Prepare journal entries for both Bostan Company and National Organization Bank to record the issuance of the note on January 1, 2003. (Round to the nearest $10.)

(b) Assuming that both Bostan Company and National Organization Bank use the effective interest method to amortize the discount, prepare the amortization schedule for the note.

(c) Under what circumstances can National Organization Bank consider Bostan's note to be "impaired"?

(d) Compute the loss National Organization Bank will suffer from Bostan's financial distress on December 31, 2004. What journal entries should be made to record this loss?

 **PF-2** **(Debtor/Creditor Entries for Continuation of Troubled Debt)** Jeremy Hillary is the sole shareholder of Hillary Inc., which is currently under protection of the U.S. bankruptcy court. As a "debtor in possession," he has negotiated the following revised loan agreement with Valley Bank. Hillary Inc.'s $400,000, 12%, 10-year note was refinanced with a $400,000, 5%, 10-year note.

Instructions

(a) What is the accounting nature of this transaction?

(b) Prepare the journal entry to record this refinancing:

    (1) On the books of Hillary Inc.

    (2) On the books of Valley Bank.

(c) Discuss whether generally accepted accounting principles provide the proper information useful to managers and investors in this situation.

It has been said that until the early 1970s most financial managers worked in a cozy, if unthrilling world. Since then, however, constant change caused by volatile markets, new technology, and deregulation has increased the risks to businesses. The response from the financial community was to develop products to manage the risks due to changes in market prices.

These products—called **derivatives**—are useful for risk management because the fair values or cash flows of these instruments can be used to offset the changes in fair values or cash flows of the assets that are at risk. The growth in use of derivatives has been aided by the development of powerful computing and communication technology, which provides new ways to analyze information about markets as well as the power to process high volumes of payments.

LEARNING
OBJECTIVES

After studying this appendix, you should be able to:

1. Explain who uses derivatives and why.
2. Understand the basic guidelines for accounting for derivatives.
3. Describe the accounting for derivative financial instruments.
4. Explain how to account for a fair value hedge.
5. Explain how to account for a cash flow hedge.
6. Identify special reporting issues related to derivative financial instruments that cause unique accounting problems.
7. Describe the disclosure requirements for traditional and derivative financial instruments.

UNDERSTANDING DERIVATIVES

In order to understand derivatives, consider the following examples.

Illustration 1—Forward Contract. Let's assume that you believe that the price of **Microsoft**'s stock will increase substantially in the next 3 months. Unfortunately, you do not have the cash resources to purchase the stock today. You therefore enter into a contract with your broker for delivery of 100 shares of Microsoft stock in 3 months at the price of $110 per share. As a result of the contract, you **have received the right** to receive 100 shares of Microsoft stock in 3 months and you **have an obligation** to pay $110 per share at that time. You have entered into a **forward contract**, a type of derivative. The benefit of this derivative contract to you is that you are able to buy Microsoft stock today and take delivery in 3 months. If the price goes up, as you expect, you win. If the price goes down, you lose.

Illustration 2—Option Contract. Let's suppose that instead of entering into the forward contract for delivery of the stock in 3 months, you tell your broker that you are undecided about whether to purchase Microsoft stock and need 2 weeks to decide. You enter into a different type of contract with your broker, one that gives you the right to purchase Microsoft stock at its current price any time within the next 2 weeks. As part of the contract, the broker charges you $300 for holding the contract open for 2 weeks at a set price. You have entered into an **option contract**, another type of derivative. As a result of this contract, **you have received the right**, **but not the obligation** to purchase this stock. If the price of the Microsoft stock increases in the next 2 weeks, you exercise your option. In this case, the cost of the stock to you is the price of the stock stated in the contract plus the cost of the option contract. If the price does not increase, you do not exercise the contract, but you incur a cost for the option.

For both the forward contract and the option contract, the delivery of the stock was for a future date, and the value of the contract was based on the underlying asset—the Microsoft stock. These financial instruments are referred to as **derivatives** because their value **is derived from** values of other assets (for example, stocks, bonds, or commodities) or is related to a market-determined indicator (for example, interest rates or the Standard and Poor's 500 stock composite index).

In this appendix, we will discuss the accounting for three different types of derivatives:

① Financial forwards or financial futures.
② Options.
③ Swaps.

Who Uses Derivatives, and Why?

OBJECTIVE **1**
Explain who uses derivatives and why.

Whether it is protection for changes in interest rates, the weather, stock prices, oil prices, or foreign currencies, derivative contracts can be used to smooth the fluctuations caused by various types of risks. Any individual or company that wants to ensure against certain types of business risks often can use derivative contracts to achieve this objective.

Producers and Consumers

To illustrate who might use derivatives, assume that Heartland Ag is a large producer of potatoes for the consumer market. The present price for potatoes is excellent, but unfortunately it will take Heartland 2 months to harvest its potatoes and deliver them to the market. Because Heartland is concerned that the price of potatoes will drop, it signs a contract agreeing to sell its potatoes today at the current market price for delivery in 2 months.

Who would buy this contract? Suppose on the other side of the contract is **McDonald's Corporation** who wants to have potatoes (for French fries) in 2 months and is worried that prices will increase. McDonald's is therefore agreeable to delivery in 2 months at current prices. McDonald's knows that it will need potatoes in 2 months and that it can make an acceptable profit at this price level.

In this situation, if the price of potatoes increases before delivery, you might conclude that Heartland loses and McDonald's wins. Conversely, if prices decrease, Heartland wins and McDonald's loses. However the objective is not to gamble on the outcome. Regardless of which way the price moves, both Heartland and McDonald's should be pleased because both have received a price at which an acceptable profit is obtained. In this case, Heartland is a **producer** and McDonald's is a **consumer**. Both companies are referred to as **hedgers** because they are hedging their positions to ensure an acceptable financial result.

Commodity prices are volatile and depend on weather, crop disasters, and general economic conditions. For the producer and the consumer to plan effectively, it makes good sense to lock in specific future revenues or costs in order to run their businesses successfully.

Speculators and Arbitrageurs

In some cases, instead of McDonald's taking a position in the forward contract, a speculator may purchase the contract from Heartland. The **speculator** is betting that the price of potatoes will increase and therefore the value of the forward contract will increase. The speculator, who may be in the market for only a few hours, will then sell the forward contract to another speculator or to a company like McDonald's.

Another user of derivatives is **arbitrageurs**. These market players attempt to exploit inefficiencies in various derivative markets. They seek to lock in profits by simultaneously entering into transactions in two or more markets. For example, an arbitrageur might trade in a futures contract and at the same time in the commodity underlying the futures contract, hoping to achieve small price gains on the difference between the two. Speculators and arbitrageurs are very important to markets because they keep the market liquid on a daily basis.

In these illustrations, we explained why Heartland Ag (the producer) and McDonald's (the consumer) would become involved in a derivative contract. Consider other types of situations that companies face.

1. Airlines, like **Delta**, **Southwest**, and **United**, are affected by changes in the price of jet fuel.
2. Financial institutions, such as **Citigroup**, **Bankers Trust**, and **M&I Bank**, are involved in borrowing and lending funds which are affected by changes in interest rates.
3. Multinational corporations, like **Cisco Systems**, **Coca-Cola**, and **General Electric**, are subject to changes in foreign exchange rates.

It is not surprising that you find most corporations involved in some form of derivatives transactions. Here are some reasons given by companies in their annual reports as to why they use derivatives.

1. **Exxon Mobil** uses derivative instruments primarily to hedge its exposure to fluctuations in interest rates, foreign currency exchange rates, and hydrocarbon prices.
2. **Caterpillar** uses derivative financial instruments to manage foreign currency exchange rates, interest rates, and commodity price exposure.
3. **Johnson & Johnson** uses derivative financial instruments to manage the impact of interest rate and foreign exchange rate changes on earnings and cash flows.

Many corporations use derivatives extensively and successfully. However, derivatives can be dangerous, and it is critical that all parties involved understand the risks and rewards associated with these contracts.[1]

BASIC PRINCIPLES IN ACCOUNTING FOR DERIVATIVES

In *SFAS No. 133,* the FASB concluded that derivatives such as forwards and options are assets and liabilities and should be reported in the balance sheet at **fair value**.[2] The Board believes that fair value will provide statement users the best information about derivative financial instruments.[3] Relying on some other basis of valuation for derivatives, such as historical cost, does not make sense because many derivatives have a historical cost of zero. Furthermore, given the well-developed markets for derivatives and

OBJECTIVE 2
Understand the basic guidelines for accounting for derivatives.

[1]There are some well-publicized examples of companies that have suffered considerable losses using derivatives. For example, companies such as **Enron** (U.S.), **Showa Shell Sekiyu** (Japan), **Metallgesellschaft** (Germany), **Procter & Gamble** (U.S.), and **Air Products & Chemicals** (U.S.) have incurred significant losses from investments in derivative instruments.

[2]Accounting for Derivative Instruments and Hedging Activities," *Statement of Financial Accounting Standards No. 133* (Stamford, Conn.: FASB, 1998). All derivative instruments, whether financial or not, are covered under this standard. Our discussion in this chapter focuses on derivative financial instruments because of their widespread use in practice.

[3]*Fair value* is defined as the amount at which an asset (or liability) could be bought (incurred) or sold (settled) between two willing parties (i.e., not forced or in liquidation). Quoted market prices in active markets are the best evidence of fair value and should be used if available. In the absence of market prices, the prices of similar assets or liabilities or accepted present value techniques can be used. "Disclosures About Fair Value of Financial Instruments," *Statement of Financial Accounting Standards No. 107* (Stamford, Conn.: FASB, 1991) paras. 5–6, 11. The Board's long-term objective is to require fair value measurement and recognition for all financial instruments (*SFAS No. 133,* para. 216).

for the assets upon which derivatives' values are based, the Board believed that reliable fair value amounts could be determined for derivative instruments.

On the income statement, any unrealized gain or loss should be recognized in income if the derivative is used for speculation purposes. If the derivative is used for hedging purposes, the accounting for any gain or loss depends on the type of hedge used. The accounting for hedged transactions is discussed later in the appendix.

In summary, the following guidelines are used in accounting for derivatives.

① Derivatives should be recognized in the financial statements as assets and liabilities.

② Derivatives should be reported at fair value.

③ Gains and losses resulting from speculation in derivatives should be recognized immediately in income.

④ Gains and losses resulting from hedge transactions are reported in different ways, depending upon the type of hedge.

Illustration of Derivative Financial Instrument — Speculation

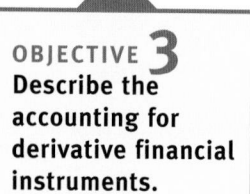

OBJECTIVE 3
Describe the accounting for derivative financial instruments.

To illustrate the measurement and reporting of a derivative financial instrument for speculative purposes, we examine a derivative whose value is related to the market price of Laredo Inc. common stock. As in the previous Microsoft example, you could realize a gain from the increase in the value of the Laredo shares with the use of a derivative financial instrument, such as a call option.[4] A **call option** gives the holder the right, but not the obligation, to buy shares at a preset price (often referred to as the **strike price** or the **exercise price**).

For example, assume you enter into a call option contract with Baird Investment Co., which gives you the option to purchase Laredo stock at $100 per share.[5] If the price of Laredo stock increases above $100, you can exercise this option and purchase the shares for $100 per share. If Laredo's stock never increases above $100 per share, the call option is worthless and you recognize a loss.

Accounting Entries

To illustrate the accounting for a call option, assume that you purchased a call option contract on January 2, 2003, when Laredo shares are trading at $100 per share. The terms of the contract give you the option to purchase 1,000 shares (referred to as the **notional amount**) of Laredo stock at an option price of $100 per share. The option expires on April 30, 2003. You purchase the call option for $400 and make the following entry.

January 2, 2003

Call Option	400	
Cash		400

This payment, referred to as the **option premium**, is generally much less than the cost of purchasing the shares directly. The option premium is comprised of two amounts: (1) intrinsic value and (2) time value. The formula to compute the option premium is shown in Illustration G-1.

---

[4]You could use a different type of option contract—a **put option**—to realize a gain if you speculate that the Laredo stock will decline in value. A put option gives the holder the option to sell shares at a preset price. Thus, a put option **increases** in value when the underlying asset **decreases** in value.

[5]Baird Investment Company is referred to as the **counterparty**. Counterparties frequently are investment bankers or other entities that hold inventories of financial instruments.

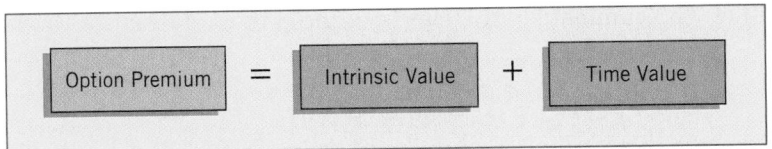

Intrinsic value is the difference between the market price and the preset strike price at any point in time. It represents the amount realized by the option holder if the option were exercised immediately. On January 2, 2003, the intrinsic value is zero because the market price is equal to the preset strike price.

Time value refers to the option's value over and above its intrinsic value. Time value reflects the possibility that the option has a fair value greater than zero because there is some expectation that the price of Laredo shares will increase above the strike price during the option term. As indicated, the time value for the option is $400.[6]

On March 31, 2003, the price of Laredo shares has increased to $120 per share. The intrinsic value of the call option contract is now $20,000. That is, you could exercise the call option and purchase 1,000 shares from Baird Co. for $100 per share and then sell the shares in the market for $120 per share. This gives you a gain of $20,000 ($120,000 − $100,000) on the option contract.[7] The entry to record the increase in the intrinsic value of the option is as follows.

March 31, 2003

Call Option	20,000	
Unrealized Holding Gain or Loss—Income		20,000

A market appraisal indicates that the time value of the option at March 31, 2003, is $100.[8] The entry to record this change in value of the option is as follows.

March 31, 2003

Unrealized Holding Gain or Loss—Income	300	
Call Option ($400 − $100)		300

At March 31, 2003, the call option is reported in your balance sheet at fair value of $20,100.[9] The unrealized holding gain increases net income for the period, and the loss on the time value of the option decreases net income.

On April 1, 2003, the entry to record the settlement of the call option contract with Baird Investment Co. is as follows.

April 1, 2003

Cash	20,000	
Loss on Settlement of Call Option	100	
Call Option		20,100

[6]This cost is estimated using option-pricing models, such as the Black-Scholes model. The fair value estimate is affected by the volatility of the underlying stock, the expected life of the option, the risk-free rate of interest, and expected dividends on the underlying stock during the option term.

[7]In practice, you generally do not have to actually buy and sell the Laredo shares to settle the option and realize the gain. This is referred to as the **net settlement** feature of option contracts.

[8]The decline in value reflects both the decreased likelihood that the Laredo shares will continue to increase in value over the option period and the shorter time to maturity of the option contract.

[9]As indicated earlier, the total value of the option at any point in time is equal to the intrinsic value plus the time value.

Illustration G-2 summarizes the effects of the call option contract on net income.

Illustration G-2

Effect on Income—
Derivative Financial
Instrument

Date	Transaction	Income (Loss) Effect
March 31, 2003	Net increase in value of call option ($20,000 − $300)	$19,700
April 1, 2003	Settle call option	(100)
	Total net income	$19,600

The accounting summarized in Illustration G-2 is in accord with *SFAS No. 133*. That is, because the call option meets the definition of an asset, it is recorded in the balance sheet on March 31, 2003. Furthermore, the call option is reported at fair value, with any gains or losses reported in income.

Differences between Traditional and Derivative Financial Instruments

What is the difference between a traditional and derivative financial instrument? A derivative financial instrument has three basic characteristics.[10]

1. **The instrument has (1) one or more underlyings and (2) an identified payment provision.** An **underlying** is a specified interest rate, security price, commodity price, index of prices or rates, or other market-related variable. Payment is determined by the interaction of the underlying with the face amount or the number of units specified in the derivative contract (the notional amounts). For example, the value of the call option increased in value when the value of the Laredo stock increased. In this case, the underlying was the stock price. The change in the stock price is multiplied by the number of shares (notional amount) to arrive at the payment provision.

2. **The instrument requires little or no investment at the inception of the contract.** To illustrate, you paid a small premium to purchase the call option—an amount much less than if the Laredo shares were purchased as a direct investment.

3. **The instrument requires or permits net settlement.** As indicated in the call option example, you could realize a profit on the call option without taking possession of the shares. This **net settlement** feature serves to reduce the transaction costs associated with derivatives.

Illustration G-3 on the next page summarizes the differences between traditional and derivative financial instruments. We use a trading security for the traditional financial instrument and a call option as an example of a derivative financial instrument.

These distinctions between traditional and derivative financial instruments explain in part the popularity of derivatives but also suggest that the accounting might be different.

[10]In *SFAS No. 133*, the FASB identifies these same features as the key characteristics of derivatives. The FASB used these broad characteristics so that the definitions and hence the standard could be applied to yet-to-be-developed derivatives (para 249).

Illustration G-3
Features of Traditional and Derivative Financial Instruments

Feature	Traditional Financial Instrument (Trading Security)	Derivative Financial Instrument (Call Option)
Payment provision	Stock price times the number of shares.	Change in stock price (underlying) times number of shares (notional amount).
Initial investment	Investor pays full cost.	Initial investment is much less than full cost.
Settlement	Deliver stock to receive cash.	Receive cash equivalent, based on changes in stock price times the number of shares.

DERIVATIVES USED FOR HEDGING

Flexibility in use and the low-cost features of derivatives relative to traditional financial instruments explain why derivatives have become so popular in recent years. An additional use for derivatives is in risk management. For example, companies such as **Coca-Cola**, **Exxon Mobil**, and **General Electric**, which borrow and lend substantial amounts in credit markets are exposed to significant **interest rate risk**. That is, they face substantial risk that the fair values or cash flows of interest-sensitive assets or liabilities will change if interest rates increase or decrease. These same companies also have significant international operations and so are exposed to **exchange rate risk**—the risk that changes in foreign currency exchange rates will negatively impact the profitability of their international businesses.

Derivatives can be used to offset the risks that a firm's fair values or cash flows will be negatively impacted by changes in interest rates or foreign currency exchange rates. This use of derivatives is referred to as **hedging**.

SFAS No. 133 established accounting and reporting standards for derivative financial instruments used in hedging activities.[11] Special accounting is allowed for two types of hedges—fair value and cash flow hedges.[12]

Fair Value Hedge

In a **fair value hedge**, a derivative is used to hedge (offset) the exposure to changes in the fair value of a recognized asset or liability or of an unrecognized commitment. In a perfectly hedged position, the gain or loss on the fair value of the derivative and that of the hedged asset or liability should be equal and offsetting. A common type of fair value hedge is the use of interest rate swaps to hedge the risk that changes in interest rates will impact the fair value of debt obligations. Another typical fair value hedge is the use of put options to hedge the risk that an equity investment will decline in value.

OBJECTIVE 4
Explain how to account for a fair value hedge.

[11]The hedge accounting provisions of *SFAS No. 133* are the major new elements in the standard and contain some of the more difficult accounting issues. The provisions were needed because of growth in the quantity and variety of derivative financial instruments used for hedging and due to the lack of, and inconsistency in, existing accounting standards for derivatives used in hedging transactions.

[12]*SFAS No. 133* also addresses the accounting for certain foreign currency hedging transactions. In general, these transactions are special cases of the two hedges discussed here. Understanding of foreign currency hedging transactions requires knowledge of consolidation of multinational entities, which is beyond the scope of this textbook.

Interest Rate Swap—A Fair Value Hedge

Options and futures have certain disadvantages. First, because they are traded on organized securities exchanges, options and futures have standardized terms and lack the flexibility needed to tailor contracts to specific circumstances. In addition, most types of derivatives have relatively short time horizons and therefore cannot be used to reduce any type of long-term risk exposure.

As a result, a very popular type of derivative used by many corporations is a swap. A **swap** is a transaction between two parties in which the first party promises to make a payment to the second party. Similarly, the second party promises to make a simultaneous payment to the first party. The most common type of swap is the **interest rate swap**: one party makes payments based on a fixed or floating rate, and the second party does just the opposite. In most cases, large money-center banks find the two parties and handle the flow of payments between the two parties, as shown below.

Illustration G-4

Swap Transaction

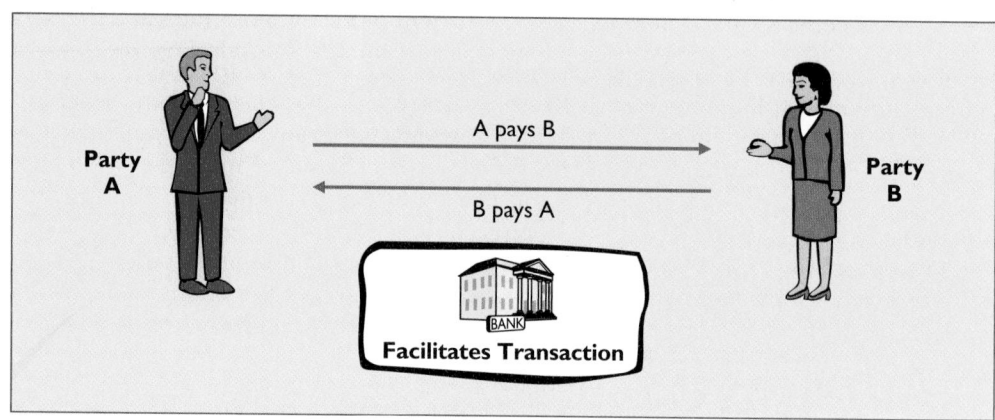

Accounting Entries

To illustrate the accounting for a fair value hedge, assume that Jones Company issues $1,000,000 of 5-year, 8% fixed-rate bonds on January 2, 2003. The entry to record this transaction is as follows.

January 2, 2003

Cash	1,000,000	
Bonds Payable		1,000,000

A fixed interest rate was offered to appeal to investors. But Jones is concerned that if market interest rates decline, the fair value of the liability will increase and the company will suffer an economic loss.[13] To protect against the risk of loss, Jones decides to hedge the risk of a decline in interest rates by entering into a 5-year **interest rate swap** contract. The terms of the swap contract to Jones are:

1. Jones will receive fixed payments at 8% (based on the $1,000,000 amount).
2. Jones will pay variable rates, based on the market rate in effect for the life of the swap contract. The variable rate at the inception of the contract is 6.8%.

As depicted in Illustration G-5, by using this swap Jones can change the interest on the bonds payable from a fixed rate to a variable rate.

---

[13]This economic loss arises because Jones is locked into the 8% interest payments even if rates decline.

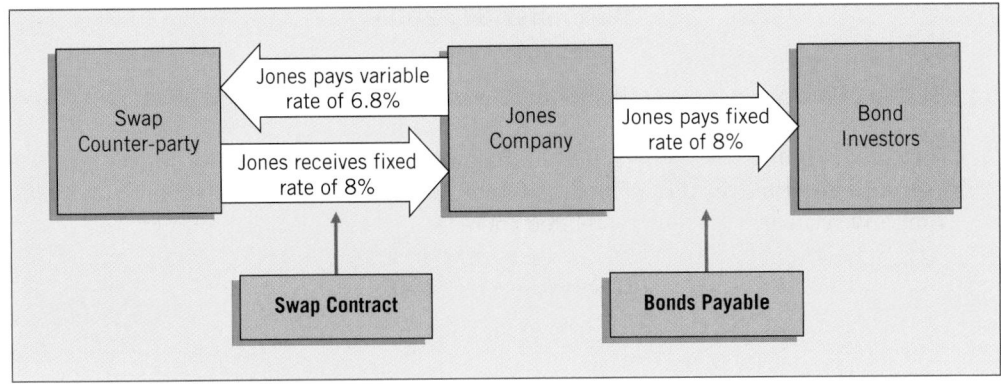

Illustration G-5
Interest Rate Swap

The settlement dates for the swap correspond to the interest payment dates on the debt (December 31). On each interest payment (settlement) date, Jones and the counterparty will compute the difference between current market interest rates and the fixed rate of 8% and determine the value of the swap.[14] If interest rates decline, the value of the swap contract to Jones increases (Jones has a gain), while at the same time Jones's fixed-rate debt obligation increases (Jones has an economic loss). The swap is an effective risk-management tool in this setting. Its value is related to the same underlying (interest rates) that will affect the value of the fixed-rate bond payable. Thus, if the value of the swap goes up, it offsets the loss related to the debt obligation.

Assuming that the swap was entered into on January 2, 2003 (the same date as the issuance of the debt), the swap at this time has no value. Therefore no entry is necessary.

January 2, 2003

No entry required. Memorandum to indicate that the swap contract is signed.

At the end of 2003, the interest payment on the bonds is made. The journal entry to record this transaction is as follows.

December 31, 2003

Interest Expense	80,000	
Cash (8% × $1,000,000)		80,000

At the end of 2003, market interest rates have declined substantially. Therefore the value of the swap contract has increased. Recall (see Illustration G-5) that in the swap, Jones is to receive a fixed rate of 8%, or $80,000 ($1,000,000 × 8%), and pay a variable rate (which in this case is 6.8%), or $68,000. Jones therefore receives $12,000 ($80,000 − $68,000) as a settlement payment on the swap contract on the first interest payment date. The entry to record this transaction is as follows.

December 31, 2003

Cash	12,000	
Interest Expense		12,000

In addition, a market appraisal indicates that the value of the interest rate swap has increased $40,000. This increase in value is recorded as follows.[15]

---

[14]The underlying for an interest rate swap is some index of market interest rates. The most commonly used index is the London Interbank Offer Rate, or LIBOR. In this example, we assumed the LIBOR is 6.8%.

[15]Theoretically, this fair value change reflects the present value of expected future differences in variable and fixed interest rates.

December 31, 2003

Swap Contract	40,000	
Unrealized Holding Gain or Loss—Income		40,000

This swap contract is reported in the balance sheet, and the gain on the hedging transaction is reported in the income statement. Because interest rates have declined, the company records a loss and a related increase in its liability as follows.

December 31, 2003

Unrealized Holding Gain or Loss—Income	40,000	
Bonds Payable		40,000

The loss on the hedging activity is reported in net income, and bonds payable in the balance sheet is adjusted to fair value.

Financial Statement Presentation

Illustration G-6 indicates how the asset and liability related to this hedging transaction are reported on the balance sheet.

Illustration G-6
Balance Sheet
Presentation of
Fair Value Hedge

JONES COMPANY BALANCE SHEET (PARTIAL) DECEMBER 31, 2003	
Current assets	
Swap contract	$40,000
Long-term liabilities	
Bonds payable	$1,040,000

The effect on the Jones Company balance sheet is the addition of the swap asset and an increase in the carrying value of the bonds payable. Illustration G-7 indicates how the effects of this swap transaction are reported in the income statement.

Illustration G-7
Income Statement Presentation of Fair Value Hedge

JONES COMPANY INCOME STATEMENT (PARTIAL) FOR THE YEAR ENDED DECEMBER 31, 2003		
Interest expense ($80,000 − $12,000)		$68,000
Other income		
Unrealized holding gain—swap contract	$40,000	
Unrealized holding loss—bonds payable	(40,000)	
Net gain (loss)		$0

On the income statement, interest expense of $68,000 is reported. Jones has effectively changed the debt's interest rate from fixed to variable. That is, by receiving a fixed rate and paying a variable rate on the swap, the fixed rate on the bond payable is converted to variable, which results in an effective interest rate of 6.8% in 2003.[16]

[16]Similar accounting and measurement will be applied at future interest payment dates. Thus, if interest rates increase, Jones will continue to receive 8% on the swap (records a loss) but will also be locked into the fixed payments to the bondholders at an 8% rate (records a gain).

Also, the gain on the swap offsets the loss related to the debt obligation. Therefore the net gain or loss on the hedging activity is zero.

The overall impact of the swap transaction on the financial statements is shown in Illustration G-8.

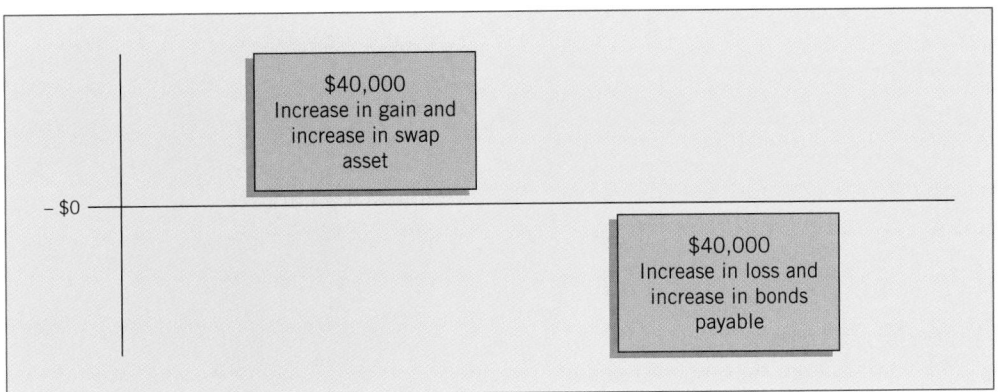

Illustration G-8
Impact on Financial Statements of Fair Value Hedge

In summary, the accounting for fair value hedges (as illustrated in the Jones example) **records the derivative at its fair value in the balance sheet with any gains and losses recorded in income**. Thus, the gain on the swap offsets or hedges the loss on the bond payable, due to the decline in interest rates. By adjusting the hedged item (the bond payable in the Jones case) to fair value, with the gain or loss recorded in earnings, the accounting for the Jones bond payable deviates from amortized cost. This special accounting is justified in order to report accurately the nature of the hedging relationship between the swap and the bond payable in the balance sheet (both the swap and the debt obligation are recorded at fair value) and in the income statement (offsetting gains and losses are reported in the same period).

Cash Flow Hedge

OBJECTIVE **5**
Explain how to account for a cash flow hedge.

Cash flow hedges are used to hedge exposures to **cash flow risk**, which is exposure to the variability in cash flows. Special accounting is allowed for cash flow hedges. Generally, derivatives are measured and reported at fair value on the balance sheet, and gains and losses are reported directly in net income. However, derivatives used in cash flow hedges are accounted for at fair value on the balance sheet, but **gains or losses are recorded in equity, as part of other comprehensive income**.

To illustrate the accounting for cash flow hedges, assume that in September 2002 Allied Can Co. anticipates purchasing 1,000 metric tons of aluminum in January 2003. Allied is concerned that prices for aluminum will increase in the next few months, and it wants to protect against possible price increases for aluminum inventory. To hedge the risk that it might have to pay higher prices for inventory in January 2003, Allied enters into an aluminum futures contract.

A **futures contract** gives the holder the right and the obligation to purchase an asset at a preset price for a specified period of time.[17] In this case, the aluminum futures contract gives Allied the right and the obligation to purchase 1,000 metric tons of aluminum for $1,550 per ton. This contract price is good until the contract expires in January 2003. The underlying for this derivative is the price of aluminum. If the price of aluminum rises above $1,550, the value of the futures contract to Allied increases,

INTERNATIONAL INSIGHT

Under IAS, unrealized holding gains or losses on cash flow hedges are recorded as adjustments to the value of the hedged item, not in other comprehensive income.

[17]A **futures contract** is a firm contractual agreement between a buyer and seller for a specified asset on a fixed date in the future. The contract also has a standard specification so both parties know exactly what is being traded. A **forward** is similar but is not traded on an exchange and does not have standardized conditions.

because Allied will be able to purchase the aluminum at the lower price of $1,550 per ton.[18]

Assuming that the futures contract was entered into on September 1, 2002, and that the price to be paid today for inventory to be delivered in January—the **spot price**—was equal to the contract price, the futures contract has no value. Therefore no entry is necessary.

September 2002

No entry required. Memorandum to indicate that the futures contract is signed.

At December 31, 2002, the price for January delivery of aluminum has increased to $1,575 per metric ton. Allied would make the following entry to record the increase in the value of the futures contract.

December 31, 2002

Futures Contract	25,000	
Unrealized Holding Gain or Loss—Equity		25,000
([$1,575 − $1,550] × 1,000 tons)		

The futures contract is reported in the balance sheet as a current asset. The gain on the futures contract is reported as part of other comprehensive income. Since Allied has not yet purchased and sold the inventory, this is an **anticipated transaction**. In this type of transaction, gains or losses on the futures contract are accumulated in equity as part of other comprehensive income until the period in which the inventory is sold and earnings is affected.

In January 2003, Allied purchases 1,000 metric tons of aluminum for $1,575 and makes the following entry.[19]

January 2003

Aluminum Inventory	1,575,000	
Cash ($1,575 × 1,000 tons)		1,575,000

At the same time, Allied makes final settlement on the futures contract and makes the following entry.

January 2003

Cash	25,000	
Futures Contract ($1,575,000 − $1,550,000)		25,000

Through use of the futures contract derivative, Allied has been able to fix the cost of its inventory. The $25,000 futures contract settlement offsets the amount paid to purchase the inventory at the prevailing market price of $1,575,000. The result is that the net cash outflow is at $1,550 per metric ton, as desired. In this way, Allied has hedged the cash flow for the purchase of inventory, as depicted in Illustration G-9 on the next page.

There are no income effects at this point. The gain on the futures contract is accumulated in equity as part of other comprehensive income until the period when the inventory is sold and earnings is affected through cost of goods sold.

For example, assume that the aluminum is processed into finished goods (cans). The total cost of the cans (including the aluminum purchases in January 2003) is

[18]As with the earlier call option example, the actual aluminum does not have to be exchanged. Rather, the parties to the futures contract settle by paying the cash difference between the futures price and the price of aluminum on each settlement date.

[19]In practice, futures contracts are settled on a daily basis; for our purposes we show only one settlement for the entire amount.

Anticipated Cash Flows		Actual Cash Flows	
Wish to fix cash paid for inventory at $1,550,000	=	Actual cash paid	$1,575,000
		Less: Cash received on futures contract	(25,000)
		Final cash paid	$1,550,000

$1,700,000. Allied sells the cans in July 2003 for $2,000,000. The entry to record this sale is as follows.

July 2003

Cash	2,000,000	
Sales Revenue		2,000,000
Cost of Goods Sold	1,700,000	
Inventory (Cans)		1,700,000

Since the effect of the anticipated transaction has now affected earnings, Allied makes the following entry related to the hedging transaction.

July 2003

Unrealized Holding Gain or Loss—Equity	25,000	
Cost of Goods Sold		25,000

The gain on the futures contract, which was reported as part of other comprehensive income, now reduces cost of goods sold. As a result, the cost of aluminum included in the overall cost of goods sold is $1,550,000. The futures contract has worked as planned to manage the cash paid for aluminum inventory and the amount of cost of goods sold.

OTHER REPORTING ISSUES

The preceding examples illustrate the basic reporting issues related to the accounting for derivatives. Additional issues of importance are as follows.

1. The accounting for embedded derivatives.
2. Qualifying hedge criteria.
3. Disclosures about financial instruments and derivatives.

OBJECTIVE 6
Identify special reporting issues related to derivative financial instruments that cause unique accounting problems.

Embedded Derivatives

As indicated at the beginning of this appendix, a major impetus for unifying and improving the accounting standards for derivatives was the rapid innovation in the development of complex financial instruments. In recent years, this innovation has led to the development of **hybrid securities**. These securities have characteristics of both debt and equity, and they often are a combination of traditional and derivative financial instruments. For example, a convertible bond (as discussed in Chapter 11) is a hybrid instrument because it is comprised of a debt security, referred to as the **host security**, combined with an option to convert the bond to shares of common stock, the **embedded derivative**.

To provide consistency in accounting for similar derivative instruments, embedded derivatives are required to be accounted for similarly to other derivative instruments. Therefore, a derivative that is embedded in a hybrid security should be **separated from the host security** and accounted for using the accounting for derivatives. This separation process is referred to as **bifurcation**.[20] Thus, an investor in a convertible bond is required to separate the stock option component of the instrument. He or she then accounts for the derivative (the stock option) at fair value and the host instrument (the debt) according to GAAP, as if there were no embedded derivative.[21]

Qualifying Hedge Criteria

The FASB identified certain criteria that hedging transactions must meet before the special accounting for hedges is required. These criteria are designed to ensure that hedge accounting is used in a consistent manner across different hedge transactions. The general criteria relate to the following areas.

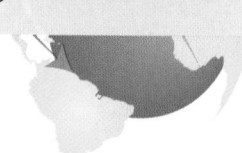 **Designation, documentation, and risk management.** At inception of the hedge, there must be formal **documentation** of the hedging relationship, the entity's **risk management** objective, and the strategy for undertaking the hedge. **Designation** refers to identifying the hedging instrument, the hedged item or transaction, the nature of the risk being hedged, and how the hedging instrument will offset changes in the fair value or cash flows attributable to the hedged risk.

The FASB decided that designation and documentation are critical to the implementation of the special hedge accounting model. Without these requirements, there was concern that companies would try to apply the hedge accounting provisions retroactively only in response to negative changes in market conditions, in order to offset the negative impact of a transaction on the financial statements. Allowing special hedge accounting in such a setting could mask the speculative nature of the original transaction.

Effectiveness of the hedging relationship. At inception and on an ongoing basis, the hedging relationship is expected to be **highly effective** in achieving offsetting changes in fair value or cash flows. Assessment of effectiveness is required whenever financial statements are prepared. The general guideline for effectiveness is that the fair values or cash flows of the hedging instrument (the derivative) and the hedged item exhibit a high degree of correlation. In practice, high effectiveness is assumed when the correlation is close to one (for example, within plus or minus .10). In our earlier hedging examples (interest rate swap and the futures contract on aluminum inventory), the fair values and cash flows were exactly correlated. That is, when the cash payment for the inventory purchase increased, it was offset dollar for dollar by the cash received on the futures contract.

If the effectiveness criterion is not met, either at inception or because of changes following inception of the hedging relationship, special hedge accounting is no longer allowed, and the derivative should be accounted for as a free-standing derivative.[22]

Effect on reported earnings of changes in fair values or cash flows. A change in the fair value of a hedged item or variation in the cash flow of a hedged fore-

[20]Such a derivative can also be designated as a hedging instrument, and the hedge accounting provisions outlined earlier in the chapter would be applied.

[21]The **issuer** of the convertible bonds would not bifurcate the option component of the convertible bonds payable. *SFAS No. 133* explicitly precludes embedded derivative accounting for an embedded derivative that is indexed to an entity's own common stock. If the conversion feature was tied to **another company's** stock, this derivative would be bifurcated.

[22]The accounting for the part of a derivative that is not effective in a hedge is at fair value with gains and losses recorded in income.

casted transaction must have the potential to change the amount recognized in reported earnings. There is no need for special hedge accounting if both the hedging instrument and the hedged item are accounted for at fair value under existing GAAP. In this case, the offsetting gains and losses will be properly reflected in earnings. For example, special accounting is not needed for a fair value hedge of a trading security, because both the investment and the derivative are accounted for at fair value on the balance sheet with gains or losses reported in earnings. Thus, "special" hedge accounting is necessary only when there is a mismatch of the accounting effects for the hedging instrument and the hedged item under GAAP.[23]

Disclosure Provisions

Because *SFAS No. 133* provides comprehensive accounting guidance for derivatives, this standard replaces the disclosure provisions in *SFAS No. 105* and *SFAS No. 119* and amends the disclosure rules in *SFAS No. 107*.[24] Thus, *SFAS No. 107* provides general guidance for traditional financial instrument disclosures, and *SFAS No. 133* addresses the disclosures for derivative financial instruments.

> **OBJECTIVE 7**
> Describe the disclosure requirements for traditional and derivative financial instruments.

As a consequence of these two pronouncements, the primary requirements for disclosures related to financial instruments are as follows.

1. A company should disclose the fair value and related carrying value of its financial instruments in the body of the financial statements, in a note, or in a summary table form that makes it clear whether the amounts represent assets or liabilities.

2. The fair value disclosures should distinguish between financial instruments held or issued for purposes other than trading. For derivative financial instruments, the firm should disclose its objectives for holding or issuing those instruments (speculation or hedging), the hedging context (fair value or cash flow), and its strategies for achieving risk management objectives.

3. In disclosing fair values of financial instruments, a company should not combine, aggregate, or net the fair value of separate financial instruments, even if those instruments are considered to be related.

4. A company should display as a separate classification of other comprehensive income the net gain or loss on derivative instruments designated in cash flow hedges.

5. Companies are encouraged, but not required, to provide quantitative information about market risks of derivative financial instruments, and also of its other assets and liabilities. Such information should be consistent with the way the company manages and adjusts risks, and it should be useful for comparing the results of its use of derivative financial instruments.

While these additional disclosures of fair value provide useful information to financial statement users, they are generally provided as supplemental information only.

---

[23]An important criterion specific to cash flow hedges is that the forecasted transaction in a cash flow hedge "is likely to occur." This probability (defined as significantly greater than the term "more likely than not") should be supported by observable facts such as frequency of similar past transactions and the firm's financial and operational ability to carry out the transaction.

[24]*SFAS No. 105* refers to "Disclosure of Information about Financial Instruments with Off-Balance Sheet Risk and Financial Instruments with Concentrations of Credit Risk," *Statement of Financial Accounting Standards No. 105* (Stamford, Conn.: FASB, 1990). *SFAS No. 119* refers to "Disclosure about Derivative Financial Instruments and Fair Value of Financial Instruments," *Statement of Financial Accounting Standards No. 119* (Stamford, Conn.: FASB, 1994).

The balance sheet continues to rely primarily on historical cost. Exceptions to this general rule are the fair value requirements for certain investment securities and derivative financial instruments, as illustrated earlier. Illustration G-10 provides a fair value disclosure for **The Gillette Company**.

Illustration G-10
The Gillette Company
Fair Value Disclosure

THE GILLETTE COMPANY
Financial Instruments

The estimated fair values of the Company's financial instruments are summarized below.

(in millions)	December 31, 2000 Carrying Amount	December 31, 2000 Fair Value	December 31, 1999 Carrying Amount	December 31, 1999 Fair Value
Long-term investments	$ 186	$ 187	$ 188	$ 188
Long-term debt	(2,281)	(2,308)	(3,289)	(3,186)
Derivative instruments				
Debt-related contracts	(28)	(19)	140	93
Other currency forwards				
Purchase contracts	23	27	—	—
Sell contracts	(1)	(5)	—	—
Currency options	—	—	1	1
Equity contracts	7	7	1	1
Commodity contracts	—	(2)	—	5

UNDERLYING CONCEPTS

Providing supplemental information on the fair values of financial instruments illustrates application of the full disclosure principle.

The fair values of cash and cash equivalents, short-term investments, and short-term debt approximate cost because of the immediate and short-term maturities of these financial instruments. The fair value of long-term investments (and some derivatives) is based on quoted market prices at the reporting date. The fair value of long-term debt and some derivatives is based on market prices for similar instruments or by discounting expected cash flows at rates currently available to the company for instruments with similar risks and maturities.

If a company is unable to arrive at an estimate of fair value, it must disclose information relevant to the estimate of fair value (such as the terms of the instrument) and the reason why it is unable to arrive at an estimate of fair value.[25]

Summary of *SFAS No. 133*

Illustration G-11 on the next page provides a summary of the accounting provisions for derivatives and hedging transactions.

As indicated, the general accounting for derivatives is based on fair values. *SFAS No. 133* also establishes **special accounting guidance** when derivatives are used **for hedging purposes**. For example, when an interest rate swap was used to hedge the bonds payable in a fair value hedge (see Jones Co. earlier), unrealized losses on the bonds payable were recorded in earnings, which is not GAAP for bonds issued without such a hedge. This special accounting is justified in order to accurately report the nature of the hedging relationship in the balance sheet (both the swap and the liability are recorded at fair value) and in the income statement (offsetting gains and losses are reported in the same period).

---

[25]*SFAS No. 107* lists a number of exceptions to this requirement; most of these exceptions are covered in other standards. The exception list includes such items as: pension and post-retirement benefits; employee stock options; insurance contracts; lease contracts; warranties, rights, and obligations; purchase obligations; equity method investments; minority interests; and instruments classified as stockholders' equity in the entity's balance sheet.

Illustration G-11
Summary of Derivative
Accounting Under *SFAS*
133

Derivative Use	Accounting for Derivative	Accounting for Hedged Item	Common Example
Speculation	At fair value with unrealized holding gains and losses recorded in income.	Not applicable	Call or put option on an equity security.
Hedging			
Fair value	At fair value with holding gains and losses recorded in income.	At fair value with gains and losses recorded in income.	Interest rate swap hedge of a fixed-rate debt obligation.
Cash flow	At fair value with unrealized holding gains and losses from the hedge recorded in other comprehensive income, and reclassified in income when the hedged transaction's cash flows affect earnings.	Use other generally accepted accounting principles for the hedged item.	Use of a futures contract to hedge a forecasted purchase of inventory.

Special accounting also is used for cash flow hedges. Derivatives used in qualifying cash flow hedges are accounted for at fair value on the balance sheet, but unrealized holding gains or losses are recorded in other comprehensive income until the hedged item is sold or settled. In a cash flow hedge, the hedged item continues to be recorded at its historical cost.

COMPREHENSIVE HEDGE ACCOUNTING EXAMPLE

To demonstrate a comprehensive example of the hedge accounting provisions, using a fair value hedge, let's assume that on April 1, 2002, Hayward Co. purchased 100 shares of Sonoma stock at a market price of $100 per share. Hayward does not intend to actively trade this investment and consequently classifies the Sonoma investment as available-for-sale. Hayward makes the following entry to record this available-for-sale investment.

April 1, 2002

Available-for-Sale Securities	10,000	
Cash		10,000

Available-for-sale securities are recorded at fair value on the balance sheet, and unrealized gains and losses are reported in equity as part of other comprehensive income.[26] Fortunately for Hayward, the value of the Sonoma shares increases to $125 per share during 2002. Hayward makes the following entry to record the gain on this investment.

December 31, 2002

Security Fair Value Adjustment (Available-for-Sale)	2,500	
Unrealized Holding Gain or Loss—Equity		2,500

[26]The distinction between trading and available-for-sale investments is discussed in Chapter 13.

Illustration G-12 indicates how the Sonoma investment is reported in Hayward's balance sheet.

Illustration G-12

Balance Sheet
Presentation of
Available-for-Sale
Securities

HAYWARD CO. BALANCE SHEET (PARTIAL) DECEMBER 31, 2002	
Assets	
Available-for-sale securities (at fair value)	$12,500
Stockholders' Equity	
Accumulated other comprehensive income Unrealized holding gain	$2,500

While Hayward has benefited from an increase in the price of Sonoma shares, it is exposed to the risk that the price of the Sonoma stock will decline. To hedge this risk, Hayward locks in its gain on the Sonoma investment by purchasing a put option on 100 shares of Sonoma stock.

Hayward enters into the put option contract on January 2, 2003, and designates the option as a fair value hedge of the Sonoma investment. This put option (which expires in 2 years) gives Hayward the option to sell Sonoma shares at a price of $125. Since the exercise price is equal to the current market price, no entry is necessary at inception of the put option.[27]

January 2, 2003

No entry required. Memorandum to indicate that put option contract is signed and is designated as a fair value hedge for the Sonoma investment.

At December 31, 2003, the price of the Sonoma shares has declined to $120 per share. Hayward records the following entry for the Sonoma investment.

December 31, 2003

Unrealized Holding Gain or Loss—Income	500	
Security Fair Value Adjustment (Available-for-Sale)		500

Note that upon designation of the hedge, the accounting for the available-for-sale security changes from regular GAAP in that the unrealized holding loss is recorded in income, not in equity. If Hayward had not followed this accounting, a mismatch of gains and losses in the income statement would result. Thus, special accounting for the hedge item (in this case, an available-for-sale security) is necessary in a fair value hedge.

The following journal entry records the increase in value of the put option on Sonoma shares.

December 31, 2003

Put Option	500	
Unrealized Holding Gain or Loss—Income		500

The decline in the price of Sonoma shares results in an increase in the fair value of the put option. That is, Hayward could realize a gain on the put option by purchasing

---

[27]To simplify the example, we assume no premium is paid for the option.

100 shares in the open market for $120 and then exercise the put option, selling the shares for $125. This results in a gain to Hayward of $500 (100 shares × [$125 − $120]).[28]

Illustration G-13 indicates how the amounts related to the Sonoma investment and the put option are reported.

HAYWARD CO. BALANCE SHEET (PARTIAL) DECEMBER 31, 2003	
Assets	
Available-for-sale securities (at fair value)	$12,000
Put option	$500

ILLUSTRATION G-13
Balance Sheet Presentation of Fair Value Hedge

The increase in fair value on the option offsets or hedges the decline in value on Hayward's available-for-sale security. By using fair value accounting for both financial instruments, the financial statements reflect the underlying substance of Hayward's net exposure to the risks of holding Sonoma stock. By using fair value accounting for both these financial instruments, the balance sheet reports the amount that Hayward would receive on the investment and the put option contract if they were sold and settled respectively.

Illustration G-14 illustrates the reporting of the effects of the hedging transaction on income for the year ended December 31, 2003.

HAYWARD CO. INCOME STATEMENT (PARTIAL) FOR THE YEAR ENDED DECEMBER 31, 2003	
Other Income	
Unrealized holding gain—put option	$500
Unrealized holding loss—available-for-sale securities	(500)

Illustration G-14
Income Statement Presentation of Fair Value Hedge

The income statement indicates that the gain on the put option offsets the loss on the available-for-sale securities.[29] The reporting for these financial instruments, even when they reflect a hedging relationship, illustrates why the FASB argued that fair value accounting provides the most relevant information about financial instruments, including derivatives.

CONTROVERSY AND CONCLUDING REMARKS

SFAS No. 133 represents the FASB's effort to develop accounting guidance for derivatives. Many believe that these new rules are needed to properly measure and report derivatives in financial statements. Others argue that reporting derivatives at fair value

---

[28]In practice, Hayward generally does not have to actually buy and sell the Sonoma shares to realize this gain. Rather, unless the counterparty wants to hold Hayward shares, the contract can be "closed out" by having the counterparty pay Hayward $500 in cash. This is an example of the net settlement feature of derivatives.

[29]Note that the fair value changes in the option contract will not offset **increases** in the value of the Hayward investment. Should the price of Sonoma stock increase above $125 per share, Hayward would have no incentive to exercise the put option.

results in unrealized gains and losses that are difficult to interpret. Concerns also were raised about the complexity and cost of implementing the standard, since prior to *SFAS No. 133*, many derivatives were not recognized in financial statements.

The FASB, as part of its due process, worked to respond to these concerns. From the beginning of the project in 1992, the FASB held over 100 meetings and received comments from over 400 constitutents or constituent groups. In response to these comments, the FASB revised the original proposal to make the provisions easier to apply. The FASB also delayed the effective date for *SFAS No. 133*, to give preparers more time to understand the standard and to develop the information systems necessary to implement the standard. More than 120 companies requested the delay, arguing that the rule could complicate companies' efforts to deal with the year 2000 (Y2K) problem.[30]

The authors believe that the long-term benefits of this standard will far outweigh any short-term implementation costs. As the volume and complexity of derivatives and hedging transactions continue to grow, the risk that investors and creditors will be exposed to unexpected losses arising from derivative transactions also increases. Without this standard, statement readers do not have comprehensive information in financial statements concerning many derivative financial instruments and the effects of hedging transactions using derivatives.

KEY TERMS

anticipated transaction, *G12*
bifurcation, *G14*
call option, *G4*
cash flow hedge, *G11*
counterparty, *G4(n)*
derivative financial instrument, derivative, *G1*
designation, *G14*
documentation, *G14*
embedded derivative, *G13*
fair value, *G3*
fair value hedge, *G7*
futures contract, *G11*
hedging, *G7*
highly effective, *G14*
host security, *G13*
hybrid security, *G13*
interest rate swap, *G8*
intrinsic value, *G5*
net settlement, *G5(n)*
notional amount, *G4*
option premium, *G4*
put option, *G4(n)*
risk management, *G14*
spot price, *G12*
strike (exercise) price, *G4*
swap, *G8*
time value, *G5*
underlying, *G6*

SUMMARY OF LEARNING OBJECTIVES FOR APPENDIX G

1 Explain who uses derivatives and why. Any company or individual that wants to ensure against different types of business risks may use derivative contracts to achieve this objective. In general, these transactions involve some type of hedge. Speculators also use derivatives, attempting to find an enhanced return. Speculators are very important to the derivatives market because they keep it liquid on a daily basis. Arbitrageurs attempt to exploit inefficiencies in various derivative contracts. Derivatives are used primarily for purposes of hedging a company's exposure to fluctuations in interest rates, foreign currency exchange rates, and commodity prices.

2 Understand the basic guidelines for accounting for derivatives. Derivatives should be recognized in the financial statements as assets and liabilities and reported at fair value. Gains and losses resulting from speculation should be recognized immediately in income. Gains and losses resulting from hedge transactions are reported in different ways, depending upon the type of hedge.

3 Describe the accounting for derivative financial instruments. Derivative financial instruments are reported in the balance sheet and recorded at fair value. Except for derivatives used in hedging, realized and unrealized gains and losses on derivative financial instruments are recorded in income.

4 Explain how to account for a fair value hedge. The derivative used in a qualifying fair value hedge is recorded at its fair value in the balance sheet, with any gains and losses recorded in income. In addition, the item being hedged with the derivative is also accounted for at fair value. By adjusting the hedged item to fair value, with the gain or loss recorded in earnings, the accounting for the hedged item may deviate from GAAP in the absence of a hedge relationship. This special accounting is justified in order to report accurately the nature of the hedging relationship between the derivative hedging instruments and the hedged item. Both are reported in the balance sheet, with offsetting gains and losses reported in income in the same period.

[30]Interestingly, some companies adopted the standard early because the rules provide better accounting for some derivatives relative to the rules in place before *SFAS No. 133*. Paula Froelich, "U.S. Companies Find New Accounting Rule Costly, Inefficient," Dow Jones News Service (March 2, 1999). In June 2000, the FASB issued guidance to ease implementation of the provisions of *SFAS No. 133*: "Accounting for Certain Derivative Hedging Instruments and Certain Hedging Activities—An Amendment to FASB Statement No. 133," *Statement of Financial Accounting Standards No. 138* (Stamford, Conn.: FASB, 2000).

⑤ Explain how to account for a cash flow hedge. Derivatives used in qualifying cash flow hedges are accounted for at fair value on the balance sheet, but gains or losses are recorded in equity as part of other comprehensive income. These gains or losses are accumulated and reclassified in income when the hedged transaction's cash flows affect earnings. Accounting is according to GAAP for the hedged item.

⑥ Identify special reporting issues related to derivative financial instruments that cause unique accounting problems. A derivative that is embedded in a hybrid security should be separated from the host security and accounted for using the accounting for derivatives. This separation process is referred to as bifurcation. Special hedge accounting is allowed only for hedging relationships that meet certain criteria. The main criteria are: (1) There is formal documentation of the hedging relationship, the entity's risk management objective, and the strategy for undertaking the hedge, and the derivative is designated as either a cash flow or fair value hedge. (2) The hedging relationship is expected to be highly effective in achieving offsetting changes in fair value or cash flows. (3) "Special" hedge accounting is necessary only when there is a mismatch of the accounting effects for the hedging instrument and the hedged item under GAAP.

⑦ Describe the disclosure requirements for traditional and derivative financial instruments. Companies must disclose the fair value and related carrying value of its financial instruments, and these disclosures should distinguish between amounts that represent assets or liabilities. The disclosures should distinguish between financial instruments held or issued for purposes other than trading. For derivative financial instruments, the firm should disclose whether the instruments are used for speculation or hedging. In disclosing fair values of financial instruments, a company should not combine, aggregate, or net the fair value of separate financial instruments, even if those instruments are considered to be related. A company should display as a separate classification of other comprehensive income the net gain or loss on derivative instruments designated in cash flow hedges. Companies are encouraged, but not required, to provide quantitative information about market risks of derivative financial instruments.

QUESTIONS

1 What is meant by the term underlying as it relates to derivative financial instruments?

2 What are the main distinctions between a traditional financial instrument and a derivative financial instrument?

3 What is the purpose of a fair value hedge?

4 In what situation will bonds payable carrying amounts not be reported at cost or amortized cost?

5 Why might a company become involved in an interest rate swap contract to receive fixed interest payments and pay variable?

6 What is the purpose of a cash flow hedge?

7 Where are gains and losses related to cash flow hedges involving anticipated transactions reported?

8 What are hybrid securities? Give an example of a hybrid security.

EXERCISES

EG-1 (Derivative Transaction) On January 2, 2002, Jones Company purchases a call option for $300 on Merchant common stock. The call option gives Jones the option to buy 1,000 shares of Merchant at a strike price of $50 per share. The market price of a Merchant share is $50 on January 2, 2002 (the intrinsic value is therefore $0). On March 31, 2002, the market price for Merchant stock is $53 per share, and the time value of the option is $200.

Instructions

(a) Prepare the journal entry to record the purchase of the call option on January 2, 2002.

(b) Prepare the journal entry(ies) to recognize the change in the fair value of the call option as of March 31, 2002.

(c) What was the effect on net income of entering into the derivative transaction for the period January 2 to March 31, 2002?

EG-2 (Fair Value Hedge) On January 2, 2003, MacCloud Co. issued a 4-year, $100,000 note at 6% fixed interest, interest payable semiannually. MacCloud now wants to change the note to a variable-rate note.

As a result, on January 2, 2003, MacCloud Co. enters into an interest rate swap where it agrees to receive 6% fixed and pay LIBOR of 5.7% for the first 6 months on $100,000. At each 6-month period, the variable rate will be reset. The variable rate is reset to 6.7% on June 30, 2003.

Instructions

(a) Compute the net interest expense to be reported for this note and related swap transaction as of June 30, 2003.

(b) Compute the net interest expense to be reported for this note and related swap transaction as of December 31, 2003.

EG-3 (Cash Flow Hedge) On January 2, 2002, Parton Company issues a 5-year, $10,000,000 note at LIBOR, with interest paid annually. The variable rate is reset at the end of each year. The LIBOR rate for the first year is 5.8%.

Parton Company decides it prefers fixed-rate financing and wants to lock in a rate of 6%. As a result, Parton enters into an interest rate swap to pay 6% fixed and receive LIBOR based on $10 million. The variable rate is reset to 6.6% on January 2, 2003.

Instructions

(a) Compute the net interest expense to be reported for this note and related swap transactions as of December 31, 2002.

(b) Compute the net interest expense to be reported for this note and related swap transactions as of December 31, 2003.

EG-4 (Fair Value Hedge) Sarazan Company issues a 4-year, 7.5% fixed-rate interest only, nonprepayable $1,000,000 note payable on December 31, 2002. It decides to change the interest rate from a fixed rate to variable rate and enters into a swap agreement with M&S Corp. The swap agreement specifies that Sarazan will receive a fixed rate at 7.5% and pay variable with settlement dates that match the interest payments on the debt. Assume that interest rates have declined during 2003 and that Sarazan received $13,000 as an adjustment to interest expense for the settlement at December 31, 2003. The loss related to the debt (due to interest rate changes) was $48,000. The value of the swap contract increased $48,000.

Instructions

(a) Prepare the journal entry to record the payment of interest expense on December 31, 2003.

(b) Prepare the journal entry to record the receipt of the swap settlement on December 31, 2003.

(c) Prepare the journal entry to record the change in the fair value of the swap contract on December 31, 2003.

(d) Prepare the journal entry to record the change in the fair value of the debt on December 31, 2003.

EG-5 (Fair Value Hedge) Using the same information from EG-4, consider the effects of the swap on M&S Corp. The $1,000,000 nonprepayable note is classified as an available-for-sale security by M&S Corp.

Instructions

(a) Prepare the journal entry to record the receipt of interest revenue on December 31, 2003.

(b) Prepare the journal entry to record the payment of the swap settlement on December 31, 2003.

(c) Prepare the journal entry to record the change in the fair value of the swap contract on December 31, 2003.

(d) Prepare the journal entry to record the change in the fair value of the available-for-sale debt security on December 31, 2003.

PROBLEMS

PG-1 (Derivative Financial Instrument) The treasurer of Miller Co. has read on the Internet that the stock price of Ewing Inc. is about to take off. In order to profit from this potential development, Miller Co. purchased a call option on Ewing common shares on July 7, 2002, for $240. The call option is for 200 shares (notional value), and the strike price is $70. The option expires on January 31, 2003. The following data are available with respect to the call option.

Date	Market Price of Ewing Shares	Time Value of Call Option
September 30, 2002	$77 per share	$180
December 31, 2002	75 per share	65
January 4, 2003	76 per share	30

Instructions

Prepare the journal entries for Miller Co. for the following dates.

(a) July 7, 2002—Investment in call option on Ewing shares.
(b) September 30, 2002—Miller prepares financial statements.
(c) December 31, 2002—Miller prepares financial statements.
(d) January 4, 2003—Miller settles the call option on the Ewing shares.

PG-2 (Derivative Financial Instrument) Johnstone Co. purchased a put option on Ewing common shares on July 7, 2002, for $240. The put option is for 200 shares, and the strike price is $70. The option expires on January 31, 2003. The following data are available with respect to the put option.

Date	Market Price of Ewing Shares	Time Value of Put Option
September 30, 2002	$77 per share	$125
December 31, 2002	75 per share	50
January 31, 2003	78 per share	0

Instructions

Prepare the journal entries for Johnstone Co. for the following dates.

(a) January 7, 2002—Investment in put option on Ewing shares.
(b) September 30, 2002—Johnstone prepares financial statements.
(c) December 31, 2002—Johnstone prepares financial statements.
(d) January 31, 2003—Put option expires.

PG-3 (Free-standing Derivative) Warren Co. purchased a put option on Echo common shares on January 7, 2003, for $360. The put option is for 400 shares, and the strike price is $85. The option expires on July 31, 2003. The following data are available with respect to the put option.

Date	Market Price of Echo Shares	Time Value of Put Option
March 31, 2003	$80 per share	$200
June 30, 2003	82 per share	90
July 6, 2003	77 per share	25

Instructions

Prepare the journal entries for Warren Co. for the following dates.

(a) January 7, 2003—Investment in put option on Echo shares.
(b) March 31, 2003—Warren prepares financial statements.
(c) June 30, 2003—Warren prepares financial statements.
(d) July 6, 2003—Warren settles the call option on the Echo shares.

PG-4 (Fair Value Hedge Interest Rate Swap) On December 31, 2002, Mercantile Corp. had a $10,000,000, 8% fixed-rate note outstanding, payable in 2 years. It decides to enter into a 2-year swap with Chicago First Bank to convert the fixed-rate debt to variable-rate debt. The terms of the swap indicate that Mercantile will receive interest at a fixed rate of 8.0% and will pay a variable rate equal to the 6-month LIBOR rate, based on the $10,000,000 amount. The LIBOR rate on December 31, 2002, is 7%. The LIBOR rate will be reset every 6 months and will be used to determine the variable rate to be paid for the following 6-month period.

Mercantile Corp. designates the swap as a fair value hedge. Assume that the hedging relationship meets all the conditions necessary for hedge accounting. The 6-month LIBOR rate and the swap and debt fair values are as follows.

Date	6-Month LIBOR Rate	Swap Fair Value	Debt Fair Value
December 31, 2002	7.0%	—	$10,000,000
June 30, 2003	7.5%	(200,000)	9,800,000
December 31, 2003	6.0%	60,000	10,060,000

Instructions

(a) Present the journal entries to record the following transactions.
   (1) The entry, if any, to record the swap on December 31, 2002.
   (2) The entry to record the semiannual debt interest payment on June 30, 2003.
   (3) The entry to record the settlement of the semiannual swap amount receivables at 8%, less amount payable at LIBOR, 7%.
   (4) The entry to record the change in the fair value of the debt on June 30, 2003.
   (5) The entry to record the change in the fair value of the swap at June 30, 2003.
(b) Indicate the amount(s) reported on the balance sheet and income statement related to the debt and swap on December 31, 2002.
(c) Indicate the amount(s) reported on the balance sheet and income statement related to the debt and swap on June 30, 2003.
(d) Indicate the amount(s) reported on the balance sheet and income statement related to the debt and swap on December 31, 2003.

PG-5 (Cash Flow Hedge) LEW Jewelry Co. uses gold in the manufacture of its products. LEW anticipates that it will need to purchase 500 ounces of gold in October 2002, for jewelry that will be shipped for the holiday shopping season. However, if the price of gold increases, LEW's cost to produce its jewelry will increase, which would reduce its profit margins.

To hedge the risk of increased gold prices, on April 1, 2002, LEW enters into a gold futures contract and designates this futures contract as a cash flow hedge of the anticipated gold purchase. The notional amount of the contract is 500 ounces, and the terms of the contract give LEW the option to purchase gold at a price of $300 per ounce. The price will be good until the contract expires on October 31, 2002.

Assume the following data with respect to the price of the call options and the gold inventory purchase.

Date	Spot Price for October Delivery
April 1, 2002	$300 per ounce
June 30, 2002	310 per ounce
September 30, 2002	315 per ounce

Instructions

Prepare the journal entries for the following transactions.

(a) April 1, 2002—Inception of the futures contract, no premium paid.
(b) June 30, 2002—LEW Co. prepares financial statements.
(c) September 30, 2002—LEW Co. prepares financial statements.
(d) October 10, 2002—LEW Co. purchases 500 ounces of gold at $315 per ounce and settles the futures contract.
(e) December 20, 2002—LEW sells jewelry containing gold purchased in October 2002 for $350,000. The cost of the finished goods inventory is $200,000.
(f) Indicate the amount(s) reported on the balance sheet and income statement related to the futures contract on June 30, 2002.
(g) Indicate the amount(s) reported in the income statement related to the futures contract and the inventory transactions on December 31, 2002.

PG-6 (Fair Value Hedge) On November 3, 2003, Sprinkle Co. invested $200,000 in 4,000 shares of the common stock of Johnstone Co. Sprinkle classified this investment as available-for-sale. Sprinkle Co. is considering making a more significant investment in Johnstone Co. at some point in the future but has decided to wait and see how the stock does over the next several quarters.

To hedge against potential declines in the value of Johnstone stock during this period, Sprinkle also purchased a put option on the Johnstone stock. Sprinkle paid an option premium of $600 for the put option, which gives Sprinkle the option to sell 4,000 Johnstone shares at a strike price of $50 per share. The option expires on July 31, 2004. The following data are available with respect to the values of the Johnstone stock and the put option.

Date	Market Price of Johnstone Shares	Time Value of Put Option
December 31, 2003	$50 per share	$375
March 31, 2004	45 per share	175
June 30, 2004	43 per share	40

Instructions

(a) Prepare the journal entries for Sprinkle Co. for the following dates.

(1) November 3, 2003—Investment in Johnstone stock and the put option on Johnstone shares.
(2) December 31, 2003—Sprinkle Co. prepares financial statements.
(3) March 31, 2004—Sprinkle prepares financial statements.
(4) June 30, 2004—Sprinkle prepares financial statements.
(5) July 1, 2004—Sprinkle settles the put option and sells the Johnstone shares for $43 per share.

(b) Indicate the amount(s) reported on the balance sheet and income statement related to the Johnstone investment and the put option on December 31, 2003.
(c) Indicate the amount(s) reported on the balance sheet and income statement related to the Johnstone investment and the put option on June 30, 2004.

Logo Credits

The following companies have granted permission for their logos to be included in this text.

3M
Alterra Healthcare Corporation
Anchor BanCorp Wisconsin Inc.
Avon Rubber p.l.c. The Avon logo is a registered trademark supplied by kind permission of Avon Rubber p.l.c.
Bayer US
Brown Shoe Company, Inc.
The Coca-Cola Company
The Walt Disney Company
Gateway, Inc.
The Gillette Company

Johnson & Johnson
Kellogg Company, KELLOGG'S™ is a trademark of Kellogg Company. All rights reserved. Used with permission.
Mack Trucks, Inc.
Mattel, Inc. Mattel logo courtesy of Mattel, Inc.
Merck & Co. Inc.
Occidental Petroleum Corporation
PepsiCo, Inc. © 2002 PepsiCo, Inc. All rights reserved. Used with permission.

Quaker Oats Company. The Quaker name and Quaker Oats logo are registered trademarks of the Quaker Oats Company.
Southwest Airlines
Tompkins PLC
Tootsie Roll Industries, Inc.
Union Planters Corporation
Uniroyal Technology Corporation
Westinghouse Electric Corporation

COMPANY INDEX

Abbott Laboratories, 130
Aldephia Communications, 539
Adolph Coors Company, 291, 347, 539
AES Corporation, 185, 515
Air Products & Chemicals, G3n.1
Alberto-Culver Company, 144, 600
Alcatel, 123
Alcoa Co., 834
Allied Products Corporation, 589
Altera International, 649
Alterra Healthcare Corporation, 128
Amazon.com, 134, 171, 352, 478, 649
American Airlines, 77, 125, 779, 821–822
American Express, 304, 575
America Online, 472
America West, 125
Ameritrade, 598
Ampco—Pittsburgh Corporation, 833
Anadarko Petroleum Corporation, 412
Anchor BanCorp Wisconsin Inc., 129
AOL Time Warner, Inc., 483
A&P. *See* The Great Atlantic & Pacific Tea Company
Apple Computer, Inc., 380, 533
April-Marcus, Inc., 350
Atlantic Richfield Co., D3n.3
AT&T, 68, 575, 610, E2
Autodesk, 745
Avon Rubber PLC, 219–220

Bank America, 843
Bankers Trust, G3
Bank of America, 61, 793
BankOne Corporation, 4, 298
Barnesandnoble.com, 478
Barrick Gold Corporation, 405
Basis Technology, 649
Baskin-Robbins, 477
Bayer, 513–514
Bear Stearns, 745
Bell Atlantic Corporation, 843
Best Buy Co., 541–544
Bethlehem Steel, 693
Bloomingdales, C2
BMC Industries, Inc., 530
Boeing Aircraft, 142, 221, 346, 594, 793
Boise Cascade, D5
Braniff Airlines, 125, 710, F1
Broadcom, 745
Brown Group, Inc., 599
Brown Shoe, Inc., 358, 365
Buybackletter.com, 585

Calpine, 515
Capital Cities/ABC, Inc., 843
Casio, 367
Caterpillar, G3
CBS, 594
Cendant, 14, 749
Century 21, 477
Chesapeake Corporation, 139
Chrysler Corporation, 829. *See also* DaimlerChrysler
Circuit City, 543

Cisco Systems, 32, 123, 173, 407, 539, G3
Citicorp (Citigroup), 187n.21, 793–794, G3
Coastal Corporation, 758
Coca-Cola Amatil, 633
The Coca-Cola Company, 59, 121, 168, 218–219, 282, 342, 372, 405–406, 468, 472, 477, 479, 513, 571–572, 575, 630–631, 633, 634, 646, 681, 735, 776, 885–886, G3, G7
Coca-Cola Enterprises, 633
Columbia Tri-Star, 39
Commonwealth Edison Company, 570–571, A8
Conexant, 745
Consolidated Papers, Inc., 144
ContiFinancial, 285
Continental Airlines, 125
Continental Illinois Bank, F1
CPC International, 297

DaimlerChrylser, 425n.14, 647
Dalfort Company, 710
Dana Corporation, 803
Datapoint Corp, 231
DebtforSale.com, 298
Delta Airlines, 77, 779, G3
Diners Club, 304
Discover, 304
Dresser Industries, 218
Drugs.com, 475
Drugstore.com, 352, 649
DuPont, 426, 594
Dynergy, 641

Eagle Clothes, Inc., 350
Earthweb, 236
Eastern Airlines, 125
Eastman Kodak Corporation, 58, 120, 167, 187n.21, 217, 281, 297, 342, 403, 468, 512, 570, 629–630, 680, 734, 776, 820–821
Econnect, 823
E.F. Hutton, 289n.4
El Paso Energy, 711
Embraer, 282–283
Enron, 14, 126, 515, 539, 641, 650, 711, 823, G3n.1
eToys.com, 352
Exxon Mobil, 68, 346, 575, D3n.1, G3, G7
Eziba.com, 649

Federal Express Corporation, 593–594
Fidelity Investments, 750
Fifth Third Bancorp, 4
First Chicago, 304
Footstar, 185
Ford Motor Company, 346, 425n. 14, 743
Fortune Brands, Inc., 373
Fuqua Industries, 364

Gap Inc., 472
Gateway, 310–311
Gateway 2000, 123, 125–126

General Dynamics, 43
General Electric, 173, 186, 297, 522, 575, G3, G7
General Electric Capital Corporation, 522
General Mills, 407
General Motors Acceptance Corporation (GMAC), 304
General Motors (GM), 304, 425n.14, 576–577, 594, 711
General Tire and Rubber, 366n.21
Georgia Pacific, 125
The Gillette Company, G16
GM. *See* General Motors
GMAC. *See* General Motors Acceptance Corporation
Goodyear Tire and Rubber, 602, 603, 711, 834
Gould Inc., 61
The Great Atlantic & Pacific Tea Company (A&P), 135, 434
GTE, 843
Guidant, 749
Gulf Oil, 577

Halliburton Company, 134
Hambrecht & Quist, E3
Hoechst A.G., 572–573
Holiday Inn, 477
Home Depot, 409
Homestake Mining Company, 734–735
Honeywell, Inc., 584

IBM Corporation, 29, 173, 247, 346, 700, 794, 795, E1n.1, E3
Intel Corporation, 126, 142, 143
International Paper, 14, 482
International Thoroughbred Breeders, 288
Ivillage, 236

Japan Airlines (JAL), 821–822
J.C. Penney, 367, 524
JDS-Uniphase, 171
Jim Walter's Corporation, 412
Johnson Controls, 14, 482
Johnson & Johnson, 512–513, G3
J.P. Morgan, 304

Kellogg Corporation, 120–121, 374, 630
Keystone Consolidated industries, Inc., 185, 186
Kimco Realty, 424
KLM Royal Dutch Airlines, 821–822
Knight Ridder, Inc., 131
Krispy Kreme, 539, 793
Kroger Co., 862

Level 8 Systems, 32
Levitz Furniture Corporation, 710
Lions Capital, F1
LIRR (Long Island Railroad), 61
Lloyd's of London, 804n.17
Loans.com, 475
Long Island Railroad (LIRR), 61
LTV Corporation, 589

Lucent Technologies, 38, 225, 407, 598, 758

Mack Trucks, Inc., 130
Manufacturers Hanover Trust Co., 287
MasterCard, 304, 306n.20
Mattell, Inc., 132
Maxwell House, 292
McDermott Int'l., 745
McDonald's, 176, 468–469, 477, 575, G2
Mead Corporation, 834
Merck & Co., Inc., 478, 492, 494, 512–514, 575, 780
Merrill Lynch & Co., 594
Mesa Limited Partnerships, D4n.4
Metallgesellschaft, G3n.1
M&I Bank, G3
Micrografx Inc., E3
Microsoft, 173, 478, 595
MicroStrategy, 174, 823
Midway Airlines, 125
Minnesota Mining and Manufacturing Company (3M), 884
Minute-Maid, 372
Mitsubishi Motors, 647
Molex, 587
Monsanto, 297
Moody's Investors Service, 525
Motorola, Inc., 132, 346
Multex.com, 182
Mumford of Wyoming, 372–373
Murphy Oil, 834

Nations Bank, 843
Navistar, 475, 711
Nestlé SA, 469–470
Nissan, 475
Norfolk Southern, 758
Nortel, 407
Northern Trust Company, A8
Northland Cranberries, 372, 570–571
Northwest Airlines, 779
NRG Energy, 515
Nynex Corporation, 843

Occidental Petroleum Corporation, 342–343
Ocean Spray, 372
Olston, 823
Owens Corning, Inc., 128–129

Pacific Lighting, D4n.4
Paramount, 39
Penn Traffic Company, 801–802, 821
Pepsi Bottling Group, 14, 482
PepsiCo, Inc., 29, 59, 121, 133, 168, 186, 218–219, 282, 342, 372, 405–406, 468,

513, 571–572, 630–631, 681, 708–710, 735, 776, 885–886
PMC-Sierra, 171
Polaroid, 478
Priceline.com, 25, 236, 478
Prime Motor Inn, 242
Primerica, 475
Procter & Gamble, 346, G3n.1

The Quaker Oats Company, 143–144, 823
Qualcomm Inc., 598
Quanex Corporation, 136
Quest Medical, Inc., 593–594

Ranchers Exploration and Development Corporation, 594
Really Useful Group, 477
Rent-Way, Inc., 174
Rex Stores, 594
R.G. Barry & Co., 68
Rite Aid, 14
R.J. Reynolds, 31
RJR Nabisco, 523n.9

Safeway, C2
Salon.com, 236
Santa Fe Southern Pacific, 594
S.C. Johnson, 182
Seaboard Corporation, 291
Sears, 294, 304, C2
Sears Roebuck Acceptance Corporation (SRAC), 304
ServiceMaster, 526
Sherwin-Williams Company, 167–168
Showa Shell Sekiyu, G3n.1
Smart Choice Automotive, 823
Smithkline Beecham, 513–514
Sonic, Inc., 404–405
Southern California Edison, 589
Southwest Airlines, 407, 779, 821, G3
SRAC (Sears Roebuck Acceptance Corporation), 304
Standard Oil of Ohio, D3n.3
Standard & Poor's Corporation, 525
Staples, 368
Stauffer Chemical Company, 363
Sunbeam, 14, 225, 823
Sunshine Mining, 26–27, 524
Suntrust Banks, 4, 297–298
Superior Bank FSB, 285

Target Corporation, C2
Tenneco, Inc., 609
Texaco, 297, 477, D3n.1

3Com, 749
3M. See Minnesota Mining and Manufacturing Company
Tomkins PLC, 168–169, 735–736
Tootsie Roll Industries, 433, 470
Toyota, 477
Tropicana, 372
True-Value Hardware, C2
TWA, 125
20th Century Fox, 39
Tyco International, 515

UAL. See United Air Lines
Ugly Duckling Corporation, 285
Underwriters Labs Inc., 833
Union Electric Company (Ameren UE), 434
Union Planters, 680–681
Uniroyal Technology Corporation (UTC), 167
Unisys Corporation, 758
United Air Lines (UAL), 77, 125, 521, 779, 782, 821, G3
United Parcel Service (UPS), 30
USX Corporation, 297, 475, 577
UTC. See Uniroyal Technology Corporation

Verity, Inc., 706
VISA, 304, 306n.20
Volvo, 776–778

Wal-Mart, 346–348, 407, 409, C2
Walt Disney Company, 477, 843
Warner Communications, 843
Webvan, 598
Westinghouse Electric Corporation, 281–282
Weyerhaeuser Company, 58–59, 130, 184
Wherehouse Entertainment Inc, 608n.1
Wiebold, Incorporated, 630
Willamette Industries, Inc., 145, 426–427
Williams Companies, 641
Woolworth Corporation, 380
WorldCom, 525
W.R. Grace, 174
W.T. Grant, 237, 242

Xerox Inc., 14, 304, 478, 800

Yahoo!, 32, 171, 745

Subject Index

Abnormal shortages, C7
Absences, compensated, *see* Compensated absences
Accelerated depreciation method, 422
Account(s), 69. *See also specific headings*: adjunct, 145, 527; classification of, 126–138; and balance sheet format, 135–138; current assets, 127–131; liabilities, 133–135; non-current assets, 131–133; stockholders' equity, 135; contra, 145, 527, 693; definition of, 63; numbering systems for, 70–71; real, 63; stockholders' equity, 64; T-accounts, 69, 71
Accounting: basic equation in, 64–66; financial, *see* Financial accounting; goals/purposes of, 27, 311; income numbers and method of, 173; managerial, 2
Accounting cycle, 68–86: adjusted trial balance, 82; adjusting entries, 72–82; closing process, 83–85; identifying/recording transactions and events, 68–69; journalizing, 69–70; post-closing trial balance, 85; posting, 70–71; reversing entries, 85, 96–98; steps in, 68; trial balance, 71–72
Accounting information systems, 6–93. *See also* Accounting cycle: basic equation in, 64–66; debits and credits in, 64; definition of, 62; reversing entries, 96–98; for accruals, 96–97; for prepayments, 97–98; and stockholders' equity relationships, 66–67; terminology related to, 63; work sheet used in, 86–93; adjusting entries on, 86–88; closing process on, 92; columns on, 88–89; financial statements, preparing, 89–92; interim financial statements, preparing, 92–93
Accounting policies, 138, 139
Accounting principles, 6n.5, 35–41. *See also* Accounting standards changes in, *see* Changes in accounting principles: for derivatives, G3–G4; exercises related to, 51–52, 53–54; full disclosure principle, 40–41; historical cost principle, 35–36; matching principle, 38–39; revenue recognition principle, 36–38
Accounting Principles Board (APB), 8–10, 11. *See also* APB *Opinions*
Accounting Research Bulletins, 7–8: and GAAP, 12; "Long-Term Construction-Type Contracts" (No. 45), 227n.10; "Restatement and Revision of Accounting Research Bulletins" (No. 43), 353n.7, 368n.24
Accounting standards. *See also* FASB *Statements of Financial Accounting Standards*: for computer software costs, E3–E4; conceptual case exercises related to, 18–23; conceptual framework for, 26; enforcement of, 7; and expectations gap, 14–15; global, 15; international, 15; need for, 5–6; neutrality in, 31; organizations involved with, 6–11;

political influences on, 13–14; for reporting of pro forma numbers, 171
Accounting Standards Executive Committee (AcSEC), 11
Accounting systems. *See also* Accounting information systems: accrual basis, 5; double-entry, 64; for inventories, 347–349
Accounts payable: as current liabilities, 133, 518; exercises related to, 555; increase in (indirect method), 857
Accounts receivable, 290–291: and cash discounts (sales discounts), 292–293; collection of written-off accounts, 298; as current asset, 128; disposition of, 304–309; exercises/problems related to, 323, 332, 333, 338–339; indirect method for increases in, 857; nonrecognition of interest on, 293; recognition of, 292–293; on statement of cash flows, 862–863; and trade discounts, 292; uncollectible, 294–298; valuation of, 128, 294–298
Accruals: adjusting entries for, 78–82; reversing entries for, 96–97
Accrual basis accounting: information based on, 5; objective of, 5; for pension costs, 752; problems related to, 563; warranty costs under, 534
Accrued expenses: adjusting entries for, 79–82; bad debts, 81–82; interest, 79–80; salaries, 80–81; definition of, 79; reversing entries for, 96–97
Accrued interest: adjusting entries for, 79–80; with capital leases, 789
Accrued revenues: adjusting entries for, 78–79; definition of, 78
Accumulated balance, A4
Accumulated other comprehensive income, 196
Accumulated rights, 743–744
Acid-test (quick) ratio, 543
Acquisition(s): and historical cost principle, 35–36; and obtaining loss carryforwards, 710n.13; of property, plant, and equipment, 408–425; buildings, 409–410; cash discounts, 412–413; contributions, 414–415; costs subsequent to, 415–418; equipment, 410; interest costs during construction, 410–412; land, 409; lump sum purchase, 413; self-constructed assets, 410; stock issuance, 413–414
Acquisition cost, D1
AcSEC, *see* Accounting Standards Executive Committee
Activity depreciation method, 421
Activity ratios, 247, 248
Actual rate of return, 752, 754
Actuarial present value (of pension benefits), 753
Actuaries, 752n.14
Additional paid-in capital (stockholders' equity), 136
Additions (PP&E), 416
Adjunct accounts, 145, 527
Adjusted trial balance, 82, 88

Adjusting entries (adjustments), 72–82: for accruals, 78–82; expenses, 79–82; revenues, 78–79; definition of, 63; and depreciation, 861–862; errors, correction of, 835; estimates, changes in, 832; exercises/problems related to, 103–106, 110–119, 328–329, 335–336; for prepayments; expenses, 73–77; revenues, 77–78; for retroactive-effect accounting changes, 828; on work sheets, 86–88
Advances (to subsidiaries), 133
Advertising supplies, 74–75, 131
Affiliated companies, investments in, 131
After costs, 533
Aging of accounts, 296, 297n.12
Agricultural crops, 43
AICPA, *see* American Institute of Certified Public Accountants
AICPA *Statements of Position (SOPs)*, 11, 12: "Accounting for Certain Costs and Activities Related to Property, Plant, and Equipment" (proposed), 418n.7; "Accounting for Performance of Construction-Type and Certain Production-Type Contracts" *(81-1)*, 226n.9; "Accounting for the Costs of Computer Software Developed or Obtained for Internal Use" *(98-1)*, E2n.3; "Disclosure of Certain Significant Risks and Uncertainties" *(94-6)*, 139n.14; "Reporting on the Costs of Startup Activities" *(98-5)*, 491n.18
AICPA *Statements on Auditing Standards (SASs)*: "Auditing Accounting Estimates" (No. 57), 834n.7; "Audit Risk and Materiality in Conducting an Audit" (No. 47), 42n.16; "The Meaning of 'Present Fairly in Conformity With Generally Accepted Accounting Principles' in the Independent Auditor's Report" (No. 69), 12; "Reports on Audited Financial Statements" (No. 58), 31n.9, 832n.6; "Subsequent Events" (No. 1), 141n.16
Airline industry, 418n.7, 420n.9, 779, 821–822
All-inclusive approach (income measurement), 181, 212–213
Allowance for doubtful accounts, 862–863
Allowance method, 294, 295
Alternative minimum tax (AMT), 711
Altman, E. I., 138
American Bar Association, 577
American Institute of Certified Public Accountants (AICPA), 6–8, 11, 19, E2n.3. *See also* AICPA: *Statements of Position (SOPs)*; AICPA *Statements on Auditing Standards (SASs)*
Amortization: on bond investments, 662–665; at bond reacquisition, 528; of discount related to debt securities, 656n.14; effective interest (present value) method, 549–553; exercises/problems related to, 501–502, 561,

565–566; of franchise costs, 477; and going concern assumption, 34; of goodwill, 482; of intangible assets, 473–474; of patent costs, 478; of premiums and discounts, A1

Amortized cost: of debt securities, 636; of held-to-maturity securities, 636

AMT (alternative minimum tax), 711

Annual entries, 252

Annual interest rate, A6

Annuities, A13–A25: deferred, A23–A25; future value of, A24; present value of, A24–A25; due, annuities; future value of, A15–A17; present value of, A20–A21; future value of, A13–A18; annuities due, A15–A17; deferred, A24; ordinary annuities, A13–A15; ordinary; future value of, A13–A15; present value of, A19–A20; present value of, A19–A23; annuities due, A20–A21; deferred, A24–A25; ordinary annuities, A19–A20

Antidilutive securities, 843, 846–847

APB, see Accounting Principles Board

APB *Opinions*, 8, 10, 12: "Accounting Changes" (No. 20), 187n.22, 824n.2; "Accounting for Nonmonetary Transactions" (No. 29), 428n.16; "Disclosure of Accounting Policies" (No. 22), 139; "Interest on Receivables and Payables" (No. 21), 293n.8, 302n.16, 518n.6, 527, 552n.3; "Omnibus Opinion—1966" (No. 10), 233, 234n.13; "Omnibus Opinion—1967" (No. 12), 433n.20; "Reporting the Results of Operations" (No. 30), 183n.16, 184n.17; "The Equity Method of Accounting for Investments in Common Stock" (No. 18), 64, 646n.10, 647, 649n.12

Appropriated Retained Earnings, 194

Approximate cost, C6

Approximation of inventories, 378–381

Arbitrageurs, G2

AROs, see Asset retirement obligations

Articles of incorporation, 576

Articulation, 33

Artistic-related intangible assets, 476–477

Asian financial crisis, 1

Assessment(s), 532–533: of cash flows, 4, 5; unasserted, 533

Assets. *See also specific headings*: on balance sheet; current, 127–131; intangible, 132–133; non-current, 131–133; "other assets," 133; book value of, 76–77; classification of, 126–127; current, see Current assets; deferred tax assets, 686, 690–694; definition of, 32, 68, 127; fixed, 146, 408. See also Property, plant, and equipment; gains/losses, asset, 758; intangible, see Intangible assets; under lease agreements, 786–787; long-term, A1; non-current, see Non-current assets; self-constructed, 410; soft, 4; useful life of, 75

Asset accounts: adjusting entries on, 73, 78–79; debiting and crediting, 64

Asset-liability method, 710–712

Asset-linked bonds, 524

Asset retirement obligations (AROs), 536–538, 558

Asset turnover ratio, 433, 434

Assumptions (in financial accounting), 34–35, 51–52

Audit and Accounting Guidelines (AICPA), 11, 12

Auditing Standards Board (AICPA), 11

Australia, 712, 839

Auto loan feature (financial calculators), B4

Available-for-sale securities, 129: debt, 637–641; definition of, 635; equity, 644–646; exercises/problems related to, 668, 671–677; portfolio of securities, 638–639; presentation of, 640–641; recording of, 644; sale of, 639–640; short-term; single security, 637–638; unrealized gains/losses on, 194; valuation of, 644–646

Average cost method: for equity securities, 643n.8; for inventory valuation, 354–355

Average days to sell inventory ratio, 374

Average tax rate, 699

Avoidable interest, 440

Bad debts, see Uncollectible accounts

Badwill, 483

Balance(s): compensating, 289; credit, 64; debit, 64

Balance sheet, 123–147: accounting policies explained on, 139; accumulated other comprehensive income on, 196; adjunct accounts on, 145; adjusting entries for accruals on, 78; cash on, 128–129; classification of accounts on, 126–138; and balance sheet format, 135–138; current assets, 127–131; liabilities, 133–135; non-current assets, 131–133; stockholders' equity, 135; contingencies explained on, 139; contra accounts on, 145; contractual situations explained on, 140; cross references on, 145; current assets on, 127–131; cash, 128–129; inventories, 130; prepaid expenses, 130; receivables, 130; short-term investments, 129; current liabilities on, 133–134; definition of, 63; disclosure techniques for, 143–146; adjunct accounts, 145; contra accounts, 145; cross references, 145; notes, 143–145; parenthetical explanations, 143; supporting schedules, 145–146; terminology, 146; exercises/problems related to, 108–109, 113, 151–166; fair values explained on, 143; format of, 135–138; income taxes on, 706–708; intangible assets on, 132–133; inventories on, 130; lease presentation on, 813–815; liabilities on, 133–135; current, 133–134; current liabilities, 133–134; long-term, 135; long-term liabilities, 135; limitations of, 125–126; long-term investments on, 131–132; long-term liabilities on, 135; non-current assets on, 131–133; intangible assets, 132–133; long-term investments, 131–132; "other assets" section, 133; property, plant, and equipment, 132; notes to, 143–145; "other assets" section of, 133; parenthetical explanations on, 143; post-balance-sheet events on, 140–142; prepaid expenses on, 130; property, plant, and equipment on, 132; receivables on, 130; short-term investments on, 129; stockholders' equity on, 135, 600–601; supplemental information on, 138–143; accounting policies, 139; contingencies, 139; contractual situations, 140; fair values, 143; post-balance-sheet events, 140–142; supporting schedules for, 145–146; terminology explained on, 146; usefulness of, 124–125; and work sheets, 88–92

Balance sheet approach, *see* Percentage-of-receivables valuation approach

Bank accounts, 314: charges, 317; credits, 317; drafts, 286; errors, 317; overdrafts, 289, 290; reconciliation of balances, 316–319, 328–329, 335–337; statements, 316

Bargain purchase, 483, 819–820

Bargain purchase option, 784, 790

Bargain renewal option, 784

Base, depreciation, 419

Basic EPS, 842

Basic equation, 64–66

Bearer (coupon) bonds, 524

Belgium, 527

Benefits/years-of-service actuarial method, 753

Betterments, 416. *See also* Improvements

Bias, freedom from, D4

Billings account, 251–252

"Blue-chip" stocks, 575

Bonds, 131, 523–529: conversion of, 845n.12; convertible, 524, 608–609, 611, 872–873; with detachable warrants, 620; exercises/problems related to, 556, 557, 561–562, 565, 567, 620–621, 627, A32, A33; investments in, 662–665; discount amortization on, 662–664; premium amortization on, 664–665; issued at discount or premium on interest date, 527; issued at par on interest date, 526–527; issuing, 523; long-term, valuation of, A26; as long-term liabilities, 135; ratings of, 525; types of, 523–524; valuation of bonds payable, 524–529

Bond discount, 525, 862

Bond indenture, 523

Bond premium, 525, 862

Bond warrants, 611

Bonuses, 743

Book of original entry, *see* Journals

Book value, 76–77, 549n.1, 604. *See also* Carrying value

Book value method, 590

Borrowing: incremental borrowing rate, 785; and restricted cash, 289; secured, 305, 308–309

Brazil, 415

Buildings, cost of, 409–410. *See also* Property, plant, and equipment

Burden, 410

Burton, John C., 7n.6

Business combinations, present value-based measurements for, A1

Business organization, forms of, 576

Calculators, *see* Financial calculators
Callable bonds, 524, 528n.11
Callable preferred stock, 589
Canada, 4, 7, 825
CAP, *see* Committee on Accounting Procedure
Capital, working, 134
Capital allocation, 3
Capital expenditures, 416
Capitalization: of computer software costs, E2; of costs under full-cost accounting, D4n.4; of development expenditures, 489; of goodwill, 480; of interest costs, *see* Interest capitalization; of leases, 782–786, 795, 803–804, 818–820; of R & D costs, 491–492
Capitalization period, 439
Capital leases, 796: example of, 786–791; exercises/problems related to, 809–810, 817; lease presentation on, 815–816; operating leases vs., 791–793; as source of financing, 786
Capital maintenance approach, 175n.5
Capital stock, 136, 577–578, 579
Carrybacks, 700, 701, 712
Carryforwards, 700–706, 710, 712
Carrying value, 549
Cash, 286–290: on balance sheet, 128–129; bank overdrafts, 289; and cash equivalents, 289; control of, 314–319; with bank accounts, 314; with imprest petty cash system, 314–316; by physical protection, 316; and reconciliation of bank balances, 316–319; as current asset, 128; determining change in, 855; management/control of, 287–288; reporting of, 288–289; restricted, 288–289
Cash balance, exercises/problems related to, 322, 329
Cash basis accounting: for pension costs, 752n.13; problems related to, 563; warranty costs under, 534
Cash debt coverage ratio, 243
Cash discounts (sales discounts), 292–293, 412–413
Cash dividends, 593–594, 624–626, 629
Cash dividends payable, 520, 864
Cash equivalents, 237n.17, 289, 290, 852n.1
Cash flows, 236–244, 852–866: accounting method and assessment of, 5; classification of, 852–853; conceptual case exercises related to, 280–281; expected, A26–A28, A30–A31, A34–A35; information for assessment of, 4, 5; SFAC No. 7 on, 27, 36; statement of, *see* Statement of cash flows; use of term, 5n.3
Cash flow hedge, G11–G13
Cash flow risk, G11
Cashier's checks, 286
Catch-up method (accounting changes), 825, 830, 831
CDs (certificates of deposit), 287
Ceiling limits, 368–369
Certified checks, 286
Certified Public Accountants (CPAs), 7, 11
Change funds, 287, 290
Changes in accounting estimates, 832–834: correction of errors vs., 834;

criteria for, 833–834; cumulative catch-up accounting for, 229; exercises/problems related to, 869–870, 875; income statement information on, 188; reporting issues with, 832–834
Changes in accounting principles, 825–832: cumulative-effect, 825–827, 838n.11; exercises/problems related to, 206, 869–871, 875–877, 881–882; income statement information on, 187–188; justification for, 187; to LIFO method, 831; retroactive-effect type, 827–831
Channel stuffing, 225
Checks, 286, 316n.1, 317
Claims, 532–533
Class action suits, 823
Closing entries: definition of, 63; exercises/problems related to, 106, 107, 110, 112–115, 118–119; preparation of, 83; on work sheets, 92
Closing process, 83–85, 92
"Cockroach theory," 182
Code of Professional Conduct (AICPA), 12
Codified law, 8
Cohen, Abby Joseph, 1, 483
Coin, 286
Collateral, receivables pledged as, 130
Collateral trust bonds, 523
Collection, debt, 298
Collection float, 314
Columnar format (statement of stockholders' equity), 602
Columns, work sheet, 88–89
Combined income statement, 194, 195
Commercial paper, 287n.1, 289
Committee on Accounting Procedure (CAP), 7–8
Committee on Accounting Procedure (CAP) (AICPA), 20, 595
Commodity-backed bonds, 524
Common law, 8
Common stock, 131, 578: classes of, 587; exercises related to, 614–615; reporting of, 66, 67
Company names, 475
Comparability, 31: and changes in accounting, 825; and pro-forma treatment, 826; and R & D cost expensing, 491
Comparative statements, adjustments to, 836
Compensated absences, 741–742, 768–769
Compensating balances, 289, 290
Compensation, 737–765: bonuses, 743; with capital vs. operating leases, 792; salary, *see* Salary(-ies); stock compensation plans, *see* Stock compensation plans
Completed-contract revenue recognition, 235: long-term contracts, 226–227, 229, 230, 252–253; problems related to, 273
Completion-of-production revenue recognition, 230, 235
Complex capital structure, 842–848: antidilution, 846–847; diluted EPS, 844–846; EPS presentation and disclosure, 847–848
Components, discontinued operations as, 182
Composite rate, 296

Compound interest, A3–A12: continuous compounding, A6n.5; exercises related to, A31; fundamental variables with, A7; future value of single sum, A8–A9; interest rate, computation of, A12; interest tables for, A4–A6; number of periods, computation of, A11–A12; and present value of single sum, A9–A11; single-sum problems, A7–A12; tables for, A40–A49
Comprehensive income: definition of, 33; exercises/problems related to, 206, 217, 669, 674–675; on income statements, 194–196; and unrealized gains/losses, 637
Computer software costs, E1–E4: capitalization of, E2; standards for, E3–E4
Concepts, FASB, see FASB Statements of Financial Accounting Concepts
Conceptual framework, 25–45: basic assumptions in, 34–35; basic principles of accounting in, 35–41; full disclosure principle, 40–41; historical cost principle, 35–36; matching principle, 38–39; revenue recognition principle, 36–38; case exercises related to, 54–55; conservatism constraint in, 43; constraints in, 41–43; cost-benefit relationship in, 41–42; definition of, 26; economic entity assumption in, 34; FASB development of, 27–28; fundamental concepts (level 2) of, 29–33; basic elements of financial statements, 32–33; qualitative characteristics of information, 29–32; going concern assumption in, 34–35; and industry practices, 43; materiality constraint in, 42–43; monetary unit assumption in, 35; need for, 26–27; objectives (level 1) of, 28–29; periodicity assumption in, 35; qualitative characteristics of information in, 29–32; comparability, 31; consistency, 31; relevance, 29–30; reliability, 29–31; understandability, 29; recognition and measurement concepts (level 3) of, 33–43; assumptions in, 34–35; constraints in, 41–43; principles of accounting in, 35–41
Condensed income statements, 178, 180, 205
Conditional promises (pledges), 415
Conservatism, 43, 130, 367, 491
Consigned goods, 350–351
Consistency: and changes in accounting, 825; of information, 31; and R & D cost expensing, 491
Consolidated financial statements, 649–650
"Constant currency" financial reports, 35
Constraint(s), 41–43: conservatism as, 43; cost-benefit relationship as, 41–42; and costs of reporting, 41–42; exercises related to, 51–52; industry practices as, 43; materiality as, 42–43
Construction: contracts, construction, 226, 249–253; interest costs during, 410–412, 463–464
Contingencies, 530–539: definition of, 138; exercises related to, 557; explanations

of, on balance sheet, 139; gain, 530; loss, 531–539; presentation of, 541, 543

Contingent liabilities, 531, 580

Contra accounts, 145, 527, 693

Contracts, long-term, see Long-term contracts

Contract-related intangible assets, 477

Contract services, R & D activities accounting for, 489

Contractual situations, 138, 140

Contributed (paid-in) capital, 579

Contributions (for property, plant, and equipment), 414–415

Controlling interest, 649

Conventional retail inventory method, C4

Convertible bonds, 524, 608–609, 611, 872–873

Convertible debt, 608–609, 611, 882

Convertible preferred stock, 589

Convertible securities, reporting issues related to, 844–845

"Cookie jar" reserves, 174

Copyrights, 132, 476–477

Corporations, 67, 576–578: capital stock (share system) of, 577–578; ownership interests in, 578; and state law, 576–577

Cost(s): of buildings, 409–410; of equipment, 410; of equity securities, 642, 643; of guarantees/warranties, 533–536; historical cost principle, 35–36; of intangible assets, 473; interest, see Interest costs; and inventory valuation, 351–352; of issuing stock, 583–584; and matching principle, 38–39; of natural resources, D5; period, 39, 351; product, 39, 351; subsequent to acquisition of PP&E, 415–418

Cost-benefit relationship, 41–42, 611

Cost flow assumptions: average cost method, 354–355; FIFO method, 355–356; for inventory valuation, 353–357; LIFO method, 356–367; specific identification methods, 353–354

Cost method, C4: for investment valuation, 644n.9; with treasury stock, 585–587

Cost-recovery accounting method, 233–234, 235, 265

Cost-to-cost basis (contract completion), 227–229

Counterparty, G4n.5

Coupon bonds, 524

Coupon rate, 299n.14, 524

Covenants, 522, 523n.9

Coverage ratios, 247, 248

CPAs, see Certified Public Accountants

Credits, 64

Credit balance, 64

Credit card companies, 304

Crediting, 64

Credit quality, evaluation of, 522

Credit risk: concentrations of, 309n.23; interest rate and level of, A2

Credit risk rate of interest, A27

"Credit squeeze," 304

Cross references (on balance sheet), 145

Cumulative catch-up, 229

Cumulative-effect changes in accounting principle, 177, 825–827

Cumulative preferred stock, 589

Currency, 286

Current assets: on balance sheet, 127–131; cash, 128–129; exercises related to, 154–155; inventories, 130; prepaid expenses, 130; receivables, 130; short-term investments, 129; classification of, 162–163; deferred tax assets as, 706; definition of, 127–128; exercises related to, 155; inventories as, 128

Current cash debt coverage ratio, 242–243

Current liabilities, 516–522: accounts payable, 518; analysis of, 543–544; on balance sheet, 133–134, 154–155; classification of, 162–163; current maturity of long-term debt, 520; deferred tax liabilities as, 706; definition of, 517; dividends payable, 520–521; exercises/problems related to, 155–156, 562, 565, 567; notes payable, 518–520; payroll deductions as, 738; presentation of, 541; unearned revenues, 521–522

Current maturities of long-term debt, 520

Current method (accounting changes), 825, 830, 831

Current operating performance approach (income reporting), 181–182, 212–213

Current ratio, 365, 543

Current receivables, 290

Current tax expense (benefit), 702, 712

Customer-related intangible assets, 476

Date of declaration, 593

Date of payment, 593

Date of record, 593

Day care (as postretirement expense), 763

Days outstanding, 311n.24

Days to collect accounts receivable, 311n.24

Dealer's profit (or loss), 795

Debenture bonds, 523

Debits, 64

Debit balance, 64

Debiting, 64

Debt(s). See also Liabilities: bad, see Uncollectible accounts; conceptual case exercises related to, 569–570; convertible, 608–609, 611, 882; extinguishment of, 528–529; growth rates for corporate/consumer, 529; long-term; analysis of, 544–545; current maturity of, 520; exercises related to, 559; presentation of, 541, 542; policies for managing, 522; preferred stock and, 516; troubled, F1–F11; accounting issues, F1–F2; impairments, F2–F5; restructurings of, F5–F11

Debt securities: amortization of discount related to, 656n.14; fair value controversy related to, 657–658; impairment test for, 656; investments in, 129, 635–642; available-for-sale securities, 637–641; held-to-maturity securities, 636–637; trading securities, 641–642; problems related to, 672, 676–677

Debt to total assets ratio, 544

Decision usefulness, 28–29, 29

Declared cash dividends, 593

Declining-balance depreciation method, 422–423

Decreasing-charge depreciation method, 422–423

Deductible amounts (income taxes), 686, 690–694

Deductible temporary differences, 695, 713

Deep discount bonds, 524

Defaults, revenue recognition with, 258–259

Deferred annuities, value of, A23–A25

Deferred charges, 133

Deferred charge account, 527

Deferred costs, amortization of, 862

Deferred income taxes, 133: on balance sheet, 706–708; changes in, 862; exercises/problems related to, 718–720, 722–723, 725–726, 731–733; and future deductible amounts, 690–694; and future taxable amounts, 686–690; as long-term liabilities, 135; terms related to, 712–713

Deferred payment, 458–459

Deferred tax amount, 686

Deferred tax asset, 686, 690–694, 713, 723–724

Deferred tax consequences, 713

Deferred tax expense (benefit), 688, 691, 702, 713

Deferred tax liability, 686–689, 713, 724, 733–734

Deficiency letters, 7

Defined benefit plans, 751–754

Defined contribution plans, 750–751

Deflation, monetary unit assumption and, 35

Delaware (as state of incorporation), 577

Delivery: revenue recognition after, 230–235; revenue recognition before, 226–230

Demolition costs, 409–410

Depletion base (natural resources), D1–D2

Deposits: legally restricted, 289; restricted, 289; in transit, 317

Deposit accounting method, 234, 235

Depositor errors, 317

Depreciation: adjusting entries for, 75–76; adjustments similar to, on statement of cash flows, 861–862; after change in estimate, 833; capital leases, 787, 789; as cost allocation vs. valuation, 427; definition of, 75; direct financing leases, 797, 798; exercises/problems related to, 451–454, 459–461, 465–466, 869–870; and going concern assumption, 34; operating leases, 799; of property, plant, and equipment, 418–427; activity method for, 421; base for, 419; declining-balance method for, 422–423; decreasing-charge methods for, 422–423; estimation of service lives, 419–420; methods of, 420–424; and partial periods, 424–425; and revision of depreciation rates, 425–426; straight-line method for, 421–422; sum-of-the-years'-digits method for, 422, 423

Depreciation base, 419

Derivatives, G1–G21: accounting principles for, G3–G4; disclosure provisions for, G15–G17; embedded, G13–G14; for hedging, G7–G15; cash flow hedge, G11–G13; comprehensive example of, G17–G19; fair value hedge, G7–G11; interest rate swap, G8–G11; qualifying hedge criteria, G14–G15; for speculation, G4–G6; traditional financial instruments vs., G6–G7; uses of, G2–G3
Designated market value, 369–370
Designation (hedging), G14
Detachable warrants: bonds, 611; stock, 609–610
Development activities, 489
Development costs, D1–D2
Diluted EPS, 842, 844–846
Dilution of ownership, 577, 627–628
Dilutive securities, 842, 843
Direct financing leases, 794–799
Direct write-off method, 294, 295
Disclosure, 1. See also Notes; Supplementary information: on balance sheet, 143–146; for derivatives, G15–G17; and full disclosure principle, 40–41; of interest rates on annual basis, A2n.2; present value-based measurements for, A1
Discontinued operations, 182–183: definition of, 182; income statement information on, 182–183; on income statements, 177; as irregular items, 181; per share amounts for, 838n.11
Discount(s): bonds issued at, 527, 549–551; bonds sold at, 525; cash, for plant assets, 412–413; classification of, 527; on leases, 785–786; on long-term liabilities, 135; on notes, 300–302; present value-based measurements for, A1; on trading securities, 641
Discount amortization, 662–664
Discounting, A9
Discovery value (natural resources), D5
Disposal, impairment of assets held for, 488
Disposition(s): of accounts receivable, 304–309; sales of receivables, 306–309; secured borrowing, 305, 308–309; exercises/problems related to, 454–455, 462; of notes receivable, 304–309; of property, plant, and equipment, 427–432; by exchanges, 428–432; by involuntary conversion, 428; by sale of assets, 427–428
Dissimilar nonmonetary assets, exchange of, 429–430
Distributions to owners, 33
Dividend(s), 590–600: in arrears, 589; cash, 593–594; exercises related to, 616, 618–620, 624–626, 628–629; financial condition and distributions of, 591–592; in kind, 594. See also Property dividends; liquidating, 594–595; payable, dividends, 520–521; preferred stock, reporting of, 838–839; property, 594; reporting of, 66, 67; share buybacks vs., 594; stock, 595–597; stock dividends vs., 599; types of, 592–597; yield, dividend, 604n.25
DJIA (Dow Jones Industrial Average), 575

Dollar-value LIFO, 360–362, 390–391, 395–397, 401–402
Double-declining-balance depreciation method, 423
Double-entry accounting system, 64–66
Dow Jones Industrial Average (DJIA), 575
Due on demand, 520
Due process system (FASB), 9

Earned capital, 579
Earned revenues, 36, 37, 222
Earnings, quality of, 173–175
Earnings management, 174, 213–215
Earnings per share (EPS), 837–849: complex capital structure, 842–848; antidilution, 846–847; diluted EPS (convertible securities), 844–845; diluted EPS (options and warrants), 845–846; presentation and disclosure, EPS, 847–848; computation of, 191; exercises/problems related to, 204–206, 872–873, 877–880, 882–883; on income statements, 177, 191–193, 204; simple capital structure, 838–842; preferred stock dividends, 838–839; weighted average number of shares outstanding, 839–841
Economic consequences (of accounting standards), 14, 22–23
Economic entity assumption, 34, 652
Economic factors (in retiring assets), 419–420
Economic life test (75% test), 784
Effective interest amortization, 549–553: accruing interest, 552; bonds issued at discount, 549–551; bonds issued at premium, 551–552; exercises related to, 671–672; lease payments, 787; premium or discount, amortization of, 662
Effective interest rate, 299–301, A6n.6
Effective tax rate, 698
Effective yield, 525, A6
EITF, see Emerging Issues Task Force Statements
Electric utilities, F1
Elements (of financial statements), 27, 28, 32–33, 51
Embedded derivatives, G13–G14
Emerging Issues Task Force Statements (EITF), 10–11, 185
Employee discounts, C7
Enacted tax rate, 698
Energy companies, 641
Entries: adjusting, 63, 72–82; closing, 63, 83; to general journal, 70; reversing, 85, 96–98
Environment, operating, 184
Environmental liabilities, 536–538
Environmental Protection Agency (EPA), 536
EPS, see Earnings per share
Equipment. See also Property, plant, and equipment: acquisition of, 449; cost of, 410; for R&D activities, 489
Equipment costs, D1
Equity, 127. See also Stockholders' (owners') equity
Equity interest, granting of, F6

Equity method: disclosures under, 651; exercises related to, 669–671, 679; for investment accounting, 647–649
Equity method accounting, 633
Equity securities, 129: available-for-sale, 644–646; exercises/problems related to, 669–670, 672, 678–679; impairment test for, 656; investments in, 642–650; between 20% and 50%, holdings of, 646–649; less than 20%, holdings of, 643–646; more than 50%, holdings of, 649–650; trading, 646
Equity value per share (stock), 604
Erlop, Osman, E3
Errors: in bank balances, 317; correction of, in financial statements; for changes in accounting principles, 832; changes of estimates vs., 834; on comparative statements, 836; exercises/problems related to, 869, 871, 875–876, 881–882; as prior period adjustments, 835; in prior income measurement, 181; reporting correction of, 834–836; in trial balances, 71–72
Estimate(s): of asset service lives, 419–420; of balance sheet items, 125–126; changes in, see Changes in accounting estimates; depreciation as, 76; of recoverable reserves, D5
Estimated tax payments, 708
Ethics, 11, 15–16
Europe: copyrights in, 477; lack of financial disclosure in, 1; non-check payments in, 287n.1; primary accounting objective in, 4
Events: definition of, 63; external, 69; as extraordinary items, 183, 184; identifying/recording, 68–69; internal, 69; post-balance-sheet, 140–142; subsequent, 140–142
Excess of fair value over cost acquired, 483
Exchange: dispositions of nonmonetary assets by, 428–432; for noncash consideration, 643
Exchange price, 292
Exchange rate risk, 310, G7
Executive pay, stock price and, 737
Executory contracts, 782
Executory costs (leases), 785, 810
Exercise price, G4
Expectations gap, 14–15
Expected cash flows, A26–A28, A30–A31, A34–A35
Expected inflation rate of interest, A27
Expected rate of return, 757
Expenditures, major types of, 416
Expenses: adjusting entries for; accrued, 79–82; prepaid, 73–77; classification of, 177, 178; deferred tax expense, 688; definition of, 33, 175; forms of, 175; general and administrative, 351; losses vs., 176; matching principle and recognition of, 38–39; prepaid, on balance sheet, 130; reporting of, 66, 67; reversing entries for; accrued, 96–97; prepaid, 97–98; selling, 351
Expense accounts: adjusting entries on; for accrued expenses, 79–81; for prepaid expenses, 73; closing entries on, 83–84; debiting and crediting, 64
Expense warranty approach, 534

Exploration costs, D1
Extended warranties, 535–536
External events, 69
Extinguishment of debt, 528–529
Extraordinary items, 183–186: definition of, 183; exceptions to, 184–185; exercises/problems related to, 203, 213; gains/losses not included in, 184; on income statements, 177; involuntary conversions as, 428; as irregular items, 181; net of tax, 190–191

Face rate, 299n.14, A6
Face value: of bonds, 524–525; notes issued at, 299–300
Facilities, 489. *See also* Property, plant, and equipment
Factors, 306
Factoring receivables, 306
FAF (Financial Accounting Foundation), 8
Fair market value, 596
Fair value(s). *See also specific topics, e.g.:* Goodwill: controversy over, 657–658; of debt securities, 636; definition of, 138; exercises/problems related to, 670–671, 679–680; explanations of, on balance sheet, 143; and gains trading, 658; of investment securities vs. liabilities, 658; par value as basis for, 580; readily determinable, 636n.3; reporting of changes in, 637; of stock, 595; and subjective classifications of securities, 657–658; subjectivity of, 658; unresolved controversies over, 657–658
Fair value hedge, G7–G11
Fair value information: and historical cost principle, 36; requirements for, 4; SFAC No. 7 on, 36
Fair value method: exercises/problems related to, 669, 673–674; for investment valuation, 644; for stock compensation plans, 744–747; for transfers between investment categories, 656–657
Fair value test, 486
FASAC, *see* Financial Accounting Standards Advisory Council
FASB, *see* Financial Accounting Standards Board
FASB *Concepts (SFACs), see* FASB *Statements of Financial Accounting Concepts*
FASB *Discussion Memorandum,* 26n.2
FASB *Interpretations,* 10, 12: "Criteria for Applying the Equity Method of Accounting for Investments in Common Stock" (No. 35), 647; "Reasonable Estimation of the Amount of Loss" (No. 14), 538, F2n.2
FASB *Standards, see* FASB *Statements of Financial Accounting Standards*
FASB *Statements of Financial Accounting Concepts (SFACs),* D3, 10, 12, 21–22, 829, A1n.1: "Accounting by Creditors for Impairment of a Loan" (No. 114), F2n.1, F3nn.4–5, F7; "Accounting by Debtors and Creditors for Troubled Debt Restructurings" (No. 15), F5n.9, F7; "Elements of Financial

Statements" (No. 6), 27, 32, 32n.10, 69n.1, 127n.8, 175n.7, 517n.4, 579n.2, 689; "Elements of Financial Statements of Business Enterprises" (No. 3), 27, 527–528; "Objectives of Financial Reporting by Business Enterprises" (No. 1), 5nn.2–3, 27; "Objectives of Financial Reporting by Nonbusiness Organizations" (No. 4), 27n.3; "Qualitative Characteristics of Accounting Information" (No. 2), 27, 29–30, 42n.16; "Recognition and Measurement in Financial Statements of Business Enterprises" (No. 5), 27, 33–35, 37n.13, 40n.14, 181n.10, 224n.3, 226n.7, 230n.11; "Reporting Income, Cash Flows, and Financial Position of Business Enterprises" (proposed), 124n.4, 125n.5, 126n.7; "Suspension of Certain Accounting Requirements for Oil and Gas Producing Companies" (No. 25), D4; "Using Cash Flow Information and Present Value in Accounting Measurements" (No. 7), 27, 36, A26
FASB *Statements of Financial Accounting Standards (SFASs),* 10, 852n.2: "Accounting by Creditors for Impairment of a Loan—Income Recognition and Disclosures" (No. 118), F5n.8; "Accounting for Asset Retirement Obligations" (No. 143), 537n.19; "Accounting for Certain Derivative Hedging Instruments and Certain Hedging Activities" (No. 138), G20n.30; "Accounting for Certain Investments in Debt and Equity Securities" (No 115), 129n.9, 634n.2, 657, 863n.6, 864n.7; "Accounting for Compensated Absences" (No. 43), 741n.3, 742; "Accounting for Contingencies" (No. 5), 530n.12, 538, 538n.20, 539n.21, F2n.2; "Accounting for Contributions Received and Made" (No. 116), 414nn.4–5; "Accounting for Derivative Instruments and Hedging Activities" (No. 133), G3, G6, G7, G14n.21, G15, G16, G19–G20; "Accounting for Franchise Fee Revenue" (No. 45), 234; "Accounting for Income Taxes" (No. 109), 689n.2, 695n.4, 705n.9, 705nn.9–10, 711n.15, 712n.16; "Accounting for Leases" (No. 13), 783, 786nn.6–7, 792n.11, 794n.13, 800n.14, 801n.15, 803, 804n.17, 805; "Accounting for Research and Development Costs" (No. 2), 489nn.15–16, 490nn.17; "Accounting for Sales of Real Estate" (No. 66), 231n.12, 234; "Accounting for Stock-Based Compensation" (No. 123), 744nn.6–7, 748, 848n.14; "Accounting for the Costs of Computer Software to Be Sold, Leased, or Otherwise Marketed" (No. 86), E1, E3; "Accounting for the Impairment or Disposal of Long-Lived Assets" (No. 144), 183n.15, 184n.17, 484n.12; "Accounting for Transfers and Servicing of Financial Assets and Extinguishments of Liabilities" (No. 140), 306n.21;

"Business Combinations" (No. 141), 475n.6, 481n.11; "Capitalization of Interest Cost" (No. 34), 351n.6, 411n.2, 441n.2; and changes in accounting principle, 832; "Classification of Obligations That Are Callable by the Creditor" (No. 78), 520n.8; "Classification of Short-term Obligations Expected to Be Refinanced" (No. 6), 133n.11; "Disclosure about Derivative Financial Instruments and Fair Value of Financial Instruments" (No. 119), G15; "Disclosure about Oil and Gas Producing Activities" (No. 69), D4, D6n.5; "Disclosure of Information about Capital Structure" (No. 129), 135n.12, 590n.11, 601n.22; "Disclosure of Information about Financial Instruments with Off-Balance Sheet Risk and Financial Instruments with Concentrations of Credit Risk" (No. 105), G15; "Disclosures About Fair Value of Financial Instruments" (No. 107), 309n.23, G3n.3, G15, G16n.25; "Earnings Per Share" (No. 128), 193n.25, 837n.9; "Employers' Accounting for Pension Plans" (No. 87), 751n.12, 761n.19; "Employers' Disclosure about Pensions and Other Postretirement Benefits" (No. 132), 761n.19, 764; "Exposure Draft: Accounting for Financial Instruments with Characteristics of Liabilities, Equity, or Both" (proposed), 516n.3, 590n.10, 608n.1; "Goodwill and Other Intangible Assets" (No. 142), 472n.4, 474n.5, 476n.8; "Prior Period Adjustments" (No. 16), 834; "Recission of FASB Statements No. 4, 44, and 64 and Technical Corrections" (No. 145), 184n.19; "Reporting Comprehensive Income" (No. 130), 194n.28, 602n.23, 640n.6; "Revenue Recognition When Right of Return Exists" (No. 48), 224n.4; "Statement of Cash Flows" (No. 95), 237n.16
FASB *Technical Bulletins,* 10, 12: "Accounting for Separately Extended Warranty and Product Maintenance Contracts" *(90-91),* 535n.17, 536n.18; "Purpose and Scope of FASB Technical Bulletins and Procedures for Issuance" *(79-1),* 10
Federal Insurance Contribution Act (F.I.C.A.), 739–741
Federal Reserve, 288
Federal Unemployment Tax Act (F.U.T.A.), 739
Feedback value (of information), 30
FFO (funds from operations), 424n.13
F.I.C.A., *see* Federal Insurance Contribution Act
Fiduciary responsibility, 5n.4
FIFO, *see* First-in, first-out method
Final pay, 753
Financial accounting: basic assumptions in, 34–35; challenges facing, 3–4; conceptual case exercises related to, 18; definition of, 2; ethics in, 15–16
Financial Accounting Foundation (FAF), 8

Financial Accounting Standards Advisory Council (FASAC), 8, 9

Financial Accounting Standards Board (FASB), 6–11: conceptual case exercises related to, 19; conceptual framework developed by, 26–28; and IASC Standard No. 33, 843; interest costs ruling by, 351; and off-balance-sheet financing, 430; SPE guidelines from, 650; *Statements of, see* FASB *Statements of Financial Accounting Concepts (SFACs)*; FASB *Statements of Financial Accounting Standards (SFASs)*; user group pressure on, 13–14

Financial calculators, B1–B5: auto loan feature of, B4; future values, calculation of; annuity due, B3; ordinary annuity, B2–B3; single sum, B1–B2; individual retirement account feature of, B5; mortgage loan amount feature of, B4–B5; present values, calculation of; ordinary annuity, B3–B4; single sum, B2

Financial components approach, 307

Financial flexibility, 125: and cash debt coverage ratio, 243; statement of cash flows and evaluation of, 239

Financial instruments: with both debt and equity characteristics, 608–612; conceptual questions related to, 611; convertible debt, 608–609; stock warrants issued with other securities, 609–611; classification of, 517; convertible debt, 608–609; derivatives vs. traditional, G6–G7; stock warrants issued with other securities, 609–611

Financial reporting, 1, 823–866: of accounting changes, 824–837; in accounting estimates, 832–834; changes in accounting principle, 825–832; reporting correction of errors, 834–836; and capital allocation, 3; of cash flows, 852–866; classification of, 852–853; statement of cash flows, 853–866; challenges facing, 3–4; of changes in accounting estimates, 832–834; of changes in accounting principle, 825–832; cumulative-effect type, 825–827; to LIFO method, 831; retroactive-effect type, 827–831; of computer software costs, E1–E4; capitalization of costs, E2; standards for, E3–E4; constraints on, 41–42; on correction of errors, 834–836; of earnings per share, 837–849; complex capital structure, 842–848; simple capital structure, 838–842; ethics involved in, 15–16; and expectations gap, 14–15; financial statements vs., 2; international, 1, 15; of natural resources, D1–D6; discovery value, D5; establishing depletion base, D1–D2; estimation of recoverable reserves, D5; liquidating dividends, D5–D6; major controversy in, D3–D4; presentation, D5–D6; tax aspects of, D5; write-off of resource cost, D2–D3; need for standards in, 5–6; objectives of, 4–5, 18, 27–29, 55; and politics of standard-setting process, 13–14; retail inventory method of, C1–C8; evaluation of, C7; with markups and markdowns, C3–C6; special items relating to, C6–C7;

terminology related to, C3; *SFAC No. 1* on, 27; *SFAC No. 4* on, 27n.3; and statement of cash flows, 236; tax reporting vs., 684–686; of troubled debt, F1–F13; accounting issues, F1–F2; impairments, F2–F5, F12–F13; restructurings, troubled debt, F5–F13

Financial statements, 2: basic elements of, 32–33; comparative, adjustments to, 836; correction of errors on, *see* Errors; definition of, 63; depreciation presentation on, 76–77; disclosure in, 40; financial reporting vs., 2; general-purpose, 5, 28–29; interim, work sheets for, 92–93; notes to, 40; presentation of information on, *see specific topics*; problems related to, 110–111, 112–113, 114–117; reporting pension amounts within, 760; *SFACs* on, 27, 32; timeliness of, 4; work sheet information for, 89–92

Financing: leasing as form of, 780, 781, 786, 793; off-balance-sheet, 539–543

Financing activities: determining net cash flow from, 860–862; on statement of cash flows, 239, 240

Finished goods inventory, 346

First-in, first-out (FIFO) method: exercises/problems related to, 386–389, 393–395, 401, 402; for inventory valuation, 355–356; for investments, 643n.8

Fixed assets, 146, 408. *See also* Property, plant, and equipment

Fleming, Sir Alexander, 478

Flexibility, financial, *see* Financial flexibility

Floor limits, 368–369

F.o.b. destination, 350

F.o.b. shipping point, 350

Foreign Corrupt Practices Act, 61

Forgery, 287n.1, 316n.1

"Fortune 500" companies, 576

Forward contracts, G1, G11n.17

Forward-looking information, 3

401(k) plans, 750

Fractional-year depreciation policies, 424–425

Framework, *see* Conceptual framework

France, EPS disclosure in, 839

Franchises, 132: as contract-related intangible assets, 477; exercises/problems related to, 503–504, 508; installment-sales accounting method for, 231

Fraud, 14–15, 316n.1

Free cash flow, 243

Freights costs, C6

Full cost concept, D3–D4

Full disclosure principle, 40–41, 138: exercises related to, 52–53; for pension plans, 763

Functional expense classification, 178

Funds from operations (FFO), 424n.13

Funds on deposit, 286

Funded status (of pension plan), 761

F.U.T.A. (Federal Unemployment Tax Act), 739

Futures contracts, G11–G13

Future cash flows: predicting, from loss carryforwards, 710; risk or uncertainty of, 173; *SFAC No. 7* on, 27

Future deductible amounts (deferred income taxes), 690–694

Future income tax rates, 698–699

Future taxable amounts, 686–690, 718–719, 724–726, 729–730

Future value: of annuities, A13–A18; annuities due, A15–A17, B3; deferred annuities, A24; ordinary annuities, A13–A15; exercises related to, A31–A32, B2–B3; of single sum, A8–A9, B1–B2; tables for calculating, A40–A41, A44–A45; using financial calculators for; annuities due, B3; ordinary annuities, B2–B3; single sum, B1–B2

GAAP, *see* Generally accepted accounting principles

Gains: definition of, 33, 175; extraordinary, 190; forms of, 175; holding, 641; not included in extraordinary items, 184; revenues vs., 176; on statement of cash flows, 864–865; unexpected, 757–760; unrealized, 173; unusual, 185–187

Gain contingencies, 139, 530

Gain from extinguishment, 528

Gains trading, 640–641, 658

Gas companies, D3–D4

General and administrative expenses, 351

General checking accounts, 314

General journal, 69–70

General ledger, 69, 70

Generally accepted accounting principles (GAAP), 5–6, 12–13: conceptual case exercises related to, 19; definition of, 12; goodwill under, 14; and *Opinion No. 21*, 527; organizations involved with, 6–11; American Institute of Certified Public Accountants, 6–8, 11; Financial Accounting Standards Board, 6–11; Securities and Exchange Commission, 6–7; and *SAS No. 69*, 12; and *SFAC No. 3*, 528; tax reporting vs. reporting under, 684–686

General-purpose financial statements, 5, 28–29

Germany: corporate governance and finance in, 578; credit information in, 29; deferred tax recognition in, 712; depreciation of fixed assets in, 422; revaluations of fixed assets in, 415

Going concern assumption, 34–35

Goods: notes received for, 302–303; in transit, 350

Goodwill, 132, 479–483: economic consequences of, 14; exercises/problems related to, 504–505, 509–510; impairment rule for, 486–487; negative, 483; recording, 480–482; write-off of, 482–483

Grant date, 743–745

Great Britain, *see* United Kingdom

Greenspan, Alan, 1, 288

Gross margin method, *see* Gross profit method

Gross margin percentage, 379n.3

Gross profit: deferred, 254, 260; exercises related to, 263–264, 269–270; on income statement, 178; percentage, gross profit, 379; on selling price, 379, 380; varying rates of, C7

Gross profit method (inventory approximation), 378–381: and computation of gross profit percentage, 379–380; evaluation of, 381; exercises related to, 392, 403

"Growth" companies, 593

Guarantees, 533–536: accrual basis, 534–535; cash basis, 534; sales warranty approach, 535–536

Guaranteed residual value, 785, 804, 810

Health care benefits: conceptual case exercises related to, 775–776; as postretirement expense, 763

Hedgers, G2

Hedging, G7–G15: cash flow hedge, G11–G13; comprehensive example of, G17–G19; fair value hedge, G7–G11; interest rate swap, G8–G11; qualifying hedge criteria, G14–G15

Held-to-maturity securities, 129: definition of, 635; exercises/problems related to, 667–668, 671–673; investments in, 636–637

High rate of returns, 224

Historical cost, 35–36, D3: on balance sheets, 125; under international accounting standards, 410; and lower of cost of market rule, 367; for property, plant, and equipment valuation, 408–409

Historical effective rate, F1

Holding gain or loss, 641

Holidays, paid, see Compensated absences

Hollywood studios, accounting by, 39

Hong Kong, 7, 825

Hopkins, Deborah, 221

Hospital Insurance Tax, 739

Host securities, G13

Household net worth, stock as percentage of, 575

Housing assistance, postretirement, 763

Human resource accounting, 68–69

Hybrid securities, G13

IASB, see International Accounting Standards Board

IASC, see International Accounting Standards Committee

IAS (International Accounting Standards), 15

Identifying transactions and events, 68–69

If-converted method, 844–845

IGBE (International Gold Bullion Exchange), 61

Impaired notes receivable, 303–304

Impairment(s), 483–488: of assets to be disposed of, 488; exercises/problems related to, 505–506, 509–510; of goodwill, 486–487; of indefinite-life intangibles, 486; of investment value, 655–656; of limited-life intangibles, 485–486; of property, plant, and equipment, 484–485; restoration of, 487–488; troubled debt, F2–F5, F12–F13

Impairment loss, 484, 485

Implicit interest rate, 300, 786

Imprest bank accounts, 314

Imprest petty cash system, 314–316

Improvements: conceptual case exercises related to, 464–465; with limited lives, 409; to property, plant, and equipment, 416–417; special assessments for, 409

Imputation, 303

Imputed interest rates, 303

Income: common stockholders, income available to, 842; comprehensive, see Comprehensive income; items included in, 180–181; net, see Net income; from operations, 178, 182; pretax, 684; recognition of, from investments, 648–649; taxable, 684; work sheet columns for, 89

Income bonds, 524

"Income from continuing operations," 183

Income statement(s), 171–197: adjusting entries for accruals on, 78; changes in accounting principle on, 187–188; changes in estimates on, 188; comprehensive income on, 194–196; condensed, 178, 180; cumulative-effect accounting changes on, 826; definition of, 63; discontinued operations on, 182–183; earnings per share on, 191–193; elements of, 175–176; extraordinary items on, 183–186; format of, 175–180: condensed, 178, 180; and elements of statement, 175–176; multiple-step, 177–179; single-step, 176; income taxes on, 694–695, 708–710; intraperiod tax allocation on, 190–191; and items included in income, 180–181; lease presentation on, 814–815; limitations of, 173; multiple-step format for, 177–179; and quality of earnings, 173–175; reporting of irregular items in, 180–189; changes in accounting principle, 187–188; changes in estimates, 188; discontinued operations, 182–183; extraordinary items, 183–186; summary of, 188–189; unusual gains/losses, 185–187; retained earnings statement on, 193–194; retroactive-effect accounting changes on, 829–830; second, 194, 195; single-step for, 176; special reporting issues with, 190–196; comprehensive income, 194–196; earnings per share, 191–193; intraperiod tax allocation, 190–191; retained earnings statement, 193–194; unusual gains/losses on, 185–187; usefulness of, 172–173; work sheet columns for, 88–89; work sheet information for, 89, 90

Income taxes, 683–715: asset-liability accounting method for, 710–712; currently payable (refundable), 713; deferred, 133; and future deductible amounts, 690–694; and future taxable amounts, 686–690; as long-term liabilities, 135; terms related to, 712–713; estimated payments of, 708; future deductible amounts, 690–694; future taxable amounts, 686–690;

intraperiod tax allocation, 190–191; and net operating losses, 699–706; loss carryback, 700, 701; loss carryforward, 700–706; payroll deductions for, 740; permanent differences, 696–698; presentation of, 706–710; balance sheet, 706–708; income statement, 694–695, 708–710; specific differences in, 695–698; tax rate considerations in, 698–699; temporary differences, 695–698; work sheet columns for, 89

Income taxes currently payable (refundable), 713

Income tax expense (benefit), 713

Income tax section (income statements), 177

Increasing-charge method (depreciation), 424

Incremental borrowing rate, 785

Incremental method: lump-sum sales, 582; stock warrants issued with other securities, 610–611

Indefinite-life intangible assets, 132: accounting treatment for, 474; impairment of, 486

Independent third-party trustee, 751

Indirect costs, R & D activities accounting for, 490

Indirect method (reconciliation method), 857

Individual retirement account feature (financial calculators), B5

Industry practices, 43

Inflation: and "constant currency" financial reports, 35; and monetary unit assumption, 35

"Inflation accounting," 35

Inflation rate of interest, expected, A27

Installment contracts, present value-based measurements for, A1

Installment-sales accounting, 230–233, 235: defaults and repossessions, 258–259; exercises/problems related to, 265, 270, 272–273, 276; interest on installment contracts, 257; presentation of transactions, 259–260; revenue recognition with, 253–260; defaults and repossessions, 258–259; interest on installment contracts, 257; presentation of transactions, 259–260; uncollectible accounts, 257

Insurance: adjusting entries for, 75; life, 131, 763; prepayment of, 131; self-insurance, 538–539

Intangible assets, 471–496: amortization of, 473–474, 862; artistic-related, 476–477; on balance sheet, 132–133; categories of, 475; characteristics of, 472–473; contract-related, 477; customer-related, 476; goodwill, see Goodwill; impairments, 483–488; of assets to be disposed of, 488; of goodwill, 486–487; of indefinite-life intangibles, 486; of limited-life intangibles, 485–486; of property, plant, and equipment, 484–485; restoration of, 487–488; marketing-related, 475; presentation of related items and, 492–494; research and development costs of,

488–492; technology-related, 478–479; valuation of, 473

Interest. *See also specific headings*: on accounts receivable, 293; adjusting entries for, 79–80; avoidable, 440; compound, *see* Compound interest; definition of, A2; effective interest amortization, *see* Effective interest amortization; exercises/problems related to, 561, 565–566; on installment contracts, 257; on pension fund liabilities, 752; simple, A2–A3, A31; tables, interest, A4–A6, A30, A40–A49

Interest-bearing notes, 298, 301–302, 518–519

Interest capitalization, 351, 439–443: amount for, 440–441; assets qualifying for, 439; capitalization period for, 439; during construction, 410–412; exercises/problems related to, 455–456, 464; illustration of, 441–443; for property, plant, and equipment, 410–412

Interest costs, 351: capitalization of, 439–443; during construction, 410–412; pensions, 753–754

Interest rates, 299n.14: annual basis disclosure of, A2n.2; on bonds, 524–526; compounding of, A12; definition of, A2; effective, 299–301, A6n.6; exercises related to, A32; implicit, 300, 786; imputed, 303; for notes receivable, 303; principles for selecting, 440–441; pure rate of interest, A27; stated, 299n.14

Interest rate risk, G7

Interest rate swap, G8–G11

Interest revenue, 412

Interim financial statements, 92–93

Internal control (cash), 287

Internal events, 69

Internally-created intangibles, 473, 480

Internal Revenue Code, 684

Internal Revenue Service (IRS), 61, 683–686

International accounting: accounting changes, 829; accounting estimates, changes in, 832; accounting principles, changes in, 825, 831; accounting standards and practices, 7; cash and cash equivalents, 853; cash flow hedges, G11; cash flow statements, 240; consolidated and parent company financial statements, 649; "constant currency" financial reports, 35; contingencies, disclosures about, 541; convertible debt, recording of, 611; copyrights, 477; corporate governance and finance, 578; currencies used by multinational corporations, 314; deferred tax asset recognition, 705; deferred tax recognition, 712; development expenditures, capitalization of, 489; earnings per share, presentation/disclosure of, 839, 843; equity reduction and dividend amounts, 593; exchange rate risks, 310; extraordinary items, classification of, 184; financial assets, classification of, 642; financial reporting, objectives of, 4; fixed assets, 415, 422; general contingencies, 538; hedge criteria,

qualifying, G14; historical cost, 410; and IASC conceptual framework, 27; income, reported, 176; income reserves, 600; information, stockholder access to, 577; interest, capitalization of, 412, 439; leasing, 781, 795; LIFO method, 356, 366; long-term debt, valuation of, 527; "modified all-inclusive" income statements, 181; pension plans, 751; receivables, sale of, 308; recoveries of impairments, write-ups for, 488; reserves, excessive, 297; restricted cash, 289; significant-influence investments, 648

International Accounting Standards Board (IASB), 15, 59–60

International Accounting Standards Committee (IASC), 15, 843

International Accounting Standards (IAS), 15

International financial reporting, 1

International Gold Bullion Exchange (IGBE), 61

International Organization of Securities Commissions (IOSCO), 6

Internet companies, 134

Internet domain names, 475

Interpretations, FASB, *see* FASB *Interpretations*

Intraperiod tax allocation, 190–191, 708

Intrinsic value method, 744–746

Intrinsic value (of option), G5

Inventories, 345–375: accounting systems for, 347–349; periodic system, 348–349; perpetual system, 347–348; analysis of, 373–374; on balance sheet, 130; classification of, 346–347; Commerce Department reports on, 345; as current asset, 128; definition of, 346; gross profit method approximation of, 378–381; computation of gross profit percentage, 379–380; evaluation of, 381; last-in, first-out method for, 356–367; advantages of, 363–364; comparison of approaches to, 362–363; disadvantages of, 364–367; dollar-value LIFO, 360–362; LIFO liquidation, 358–360; LIFO reserve, 357–358; lower of cost or market rule for; application methods, 370–371; ceiling and floor, 368–369; evaluation of, 371–372; illustration of, 369–370; modified perpetual system for, 348n.4; periodic system, 348–349; perpetual system, 347–348; presentation of, 372–373; valuation of, 128, 350–372; average cost method for, 354–355; cost flow assumptions for, 353–357; costs included in, 351–352; first-in, first-out method for, 355–356; last-in, first-out method for, 356–367; lower of cost or market rule for, 367–372; physical goods, 350–351; specific identification method for, 353–354

Inventory accounts, closing process for, 84–85

Inventory methods, 870–871

Inventory profits, 364

Inventory systems, closing process for, 83–85

Inventory turnover ratio, 374

Investee, 642

Investing activities: determining net cash flow from, 860–862; on statement of cash flows, 239

Investments, 633–660: on balance sheet; long-term, 131–132; short-term, 129; in bonds, 662–665; discount amortization on, 662–664; premium amortization on, 664–665; in debt securities, 129, 635–642; available-for-sale securities, 637–641; held-to-maturity securities, 636–637; trading securities, 641–642; in equity securities, 642–650; between 20% and 50%, holdings, 646–649; less than 20%, holdings of, 643–646; more than 50%, holdings of, 649–650; fair value controversy over, 657–658; impairment of value of, 655–656; land as, 409; by owners, 33; presentation of, 650–655; transfers between categories of, 656–657

Investor, 642

Involuntary conversions, 428

IOSCO (International Organization of Securities Commissions), 6

I.O.U.s, 287, 290

Irregular items: all-inclusive approach to, 181; current operating performance approach to, 181–182; definition of, 175n.6; discontinued operations as, 182–183; extraordinary items as, 183–186; on income statements, 180–189; changes in accounting principle, 187–188; changes in estimates, 188; discontinued operations, 182–183; extraordinary items, 183–186; summary of, 188–189; unusual gains/losses, 185–187; modified all-inclusive approach to, 182; problems related to, 208, 209, 210–211; restructuring charges as, 181; summary of, 188–189

IRS, *see* Internal Revenue Service

Japan: corporate governance and finance in, 578; EPS disclosure in, 839; leases in, 821; non-check payments in, 287n.1; revaluations of fixed assets in, 415; valuation of assets/liabilities in, 43; valuation of long-term debt in, 527

Jenkins, Edmund, 171, 471

Journals, 69: cumulative-effect accounting changes, entries for, 826; definition of, 63; general, 69–70; special, 70; trial balance and errors in, 71, 72

Journalizing, 69–70

Judgments (of balance sheet items), 125–126

Junk bonds, 523

Keynes, John Maynard, A3

Kiechel, Walter, 471

Kirk, Donald, 471, E4

Korea, 7, 29

Land. *See also* Property, plant, and equipment: cost of, 409; demolition of old buildings on, 409–410; installment-sales accounting method for development of, 231; interest capitalization and expenditures for,

411–412; reductions in price of, 409; stock issued for (exercise), 615

Large stock dividends, 599

Last-in, first-out (LIFO) method: advantages of, 363–364; comparison of approaches to, 362–363; disadvantages of, 364–367; dollar-value LIFO, 360–362; exercises/problems related to, 386–390, 393–397, 401–403; for inventory valuation, 356–367; liquidation, LIFO, 358–360; reporting change to, 831; reserve, LIFO, 357–358

LBOs (leveraged buyouts), 584

LCM rule, see Lower of cost or market rule

Lease(s)/leasing, 779–806: accounting problems related to, 803–805, A37–A38; advantages of, 780–781; capital vs. operating, 783; classification, 794–796; conceptual nature of, 782–783; definition of, 780; disclosure of lease data, 800–803; lessee, accounting by, see Lessees; lessor, accounting by, see Lessors; as long-term liabilities, 135; present value-based measurements for, A1; synthetic, 793

Lease receivable, 796, 797

Lease term, 784

Ledger (term), 63

Legal fees, 478

Legally restricted deposits, 289

Legal services (as postretirement expense), 763

Legal systems, 8

Lessees, 783–793: assets vs. liabilities, accounting for, 786–787; capitalization criteria, 784–786; capital lease method, 787–793; operating method, 791–793

Lessors, 793–800: classification of leases, 794–796; direct financing method, 796–799; economics of leasing, 794; operating method, 799; sales-type leases, 799–800

Leverage, 40

Leveraged buyouts (LBOs), 584

Liabilities, 515–553: analysis of, 543–545; on balance sheet, 133–135; current, 133–134; current liabilities, 133–134; long-term, 135; long-term liabilities, 135; bonds, 523–529; issuing, 523; types of, 523–524; valuation of bonds payable, 524–529; classification of, 126–127, 555, 556; compensated absences as, 741; contingencies, 530–539; gain contingencies, 530; loss contingencies, 531–539; and contingencies, 530–539; current, 516–522; accounts payable, 518; current maturity of long-term debt, 520; dividends payable, 520–521; notes payable, 518–520; unearned revenues, 521–522; deferred tax liability, 686–689; definition of, 32, 127, 516–517; and historical cost principle, 36; under lease agreements, 786–787; long-term, 522–529; and off-balance-sheet financing, 539–543; presentation of, 541–543

Liability accounts: adjusting entries on, 77–81; debiting and crediting, 64

Liability gains and losses, 758

LIBOR (London Interbank Offer Rate), G9n.14

Licenses (permits), 477

License operations, installment-sales accounting method for, 231

Liens, disclosure of, 132

Life insurance, 131, 763

LIFO, see Last-in, first-out method

LIFO effect, 357

LIFO liquidation, 358–360

LIFO reserve, 357–358, 365

Limitations (on balance sheet), 125–126

Limited-life intangible assets, 132: amortization of, 473–474; impairment of, 485–486

Lines of credit, 304

Liquidating dividends, 592, 594–595, D5–D6

Liquidity, 124–125: current assets presented in order of, 128; current cash debt coverage ratio, 242–243; statement of cash flows and evaluation of, 239; and working capital, 134

Liquidity ratios, 247, 248

Litigation, 139, 532–533

Loan covenants, violation of, 792

Lockbox accounts, 314

London Interbank Offer Rate (LIBOR), G9n.14

Long-term assets, present value-based measurements for, A1

Long-term borrowing, 289

Long-term contracts: exercises/problems related to, 263–265, 271–274, 279, 870; presentation by percentage of completion, 251–252; revenue recognition with, 249–253

Long-term debt: analysis of, 544–545; current maturity of, 520; exercises related to, 559; presentation of, 541, 542

Long-term investments: on balance sheet, 131–132; problems related to, 677

Long-term liabilities, 522–529: on balance sheet, 135, 154–155; bonds, 523–529; conceptual case exercises related to, 568; deferred income taxes as, 135

Long-term notes, 131, 299

Loss(es). See also Net operating loss: definition of, 33, 175; due to impairments, F2–F5; expenses vs., 176; from extinguishment, 528; extraordinary, 190; forms of, 175; holding, 641; from investments, 649; with long-term contracts, 229–230; manufacturer's/dealer's, 795; not included in extraordinary items, 184; unexpected, 757–760; unrealized, 173; unusual, 185–187

Loss carryback, 700, 701, 712, 721–722, 726–727

Loss carryforward, 700–706, 710, 712, 721–722, 726–727

Loss contingencies, 139, 531–539: environmental liabilities, 536–538; exercises/problems related to, 563–564, 568–569; guarantee and warranty costs, 533–536; accrual basis, 534–535; cash basis, 534; sales warranty approach, 535–536;

litigation, claims, and assessments, 532–533; self-insurance, 538–539

Lower (floor) limits, 368–369

Lower of cost or market (LCM) rule, C4: application methods, 370–371; ceiling and floor, 368–369; evaluation of, 371–372; exercises/problems related to, 391–392, 397–399, 402; illustration of, 369–370; for inventory valuation, 367–372

Lump sum price, 413, 458–459

Lump-sum sales (stock), 581–582, 615, 623

McConnell, Pat, 745

Major repairs, 417

Maker, 298

Managerial accounting, 2

Manhattan Island, purchase of, A3n.4

Manufacturer's profit (or loss), 795

Manufacturing concerns, 346

Markdown cancellations, C3

Markdowns, C3

Market (for LCM), 367

Marketing-related intangible assets, 475

Market rate, 525, F2

Market-related value, 758n.17

Market value, 77: of property, plant, and equipment, 409; of stock issued for property acquisition, 413

Mark-to-market accounting, 641

Markups, 379, C3

MasterNet, 61

Master valuation account, 480

Master valuation approach, 481–482

Matching principle, 38–39: and adjusting entries, 72; for compensated absences, 741; completed-contract method vs., 229; conceptual case exercises related to, 55–58; and depreciation, 422; and pension costs, 752; and percentage-of-sales valuation approach, 295; and revenue recognition, 38–39; with warranties, 535

Material items, nonrecurring, 183

Materiality, 42–43, 293: expensing ash trays/waste baskets, 416; and methods used, 636; SFAC No. 2 on, 42n.16

Materials, R & D activities accounting for, 489

Maturity value of bonds, 524. See also Face value

Measurement, 27, 28: of asset retirement obligations, 537; of income, 173, 175, 181–182; SFAC No. 5 on, 27, 33–35; SFAC No. 7 on, 27

Measurement date, 745

Merchandise inventory, 346

Mergers, dilutive securities and, 843

Mexico, 577, 839

Mezzanine, 590n.10

Minimum lease payments, 785, 796, 804

Minimum value method (for stock option value), 745n.10

Model Business Corporate Act, 577

Modified all-inclusive income statements, 181, 182

Modified perpetual inventory system, 348n.4

Monetary exchanges, nonmonetary vs., 429n.17
Monetary unit assumption, 35
Money market funds, 287, 289
Money market savings certificates, 287
Money orders, 286
Monthly financial statements, work sheets for, 92–93
More likely than not, 693
Mortgage bonds, 523
Mortgage loan amount feature (financial calculators), B4–B5
Moving-average method (for inventory valuation), 355
Mulally, Alan, 221
Multiple-step income statements, 177–179: exercises/problems related to, 202–204, 207–209; sections of, 177

Natural expense classification, 178
Natural resources, D1–D6: depletion base for, D1–D2; discovery value of, D5; and estimation of recoverable reserves, D5; liquidating dividends, D5–D6; presentation of, D6; tax aspects of, D5; write-off of, D2–D3
Negative goodwill (badwill), 483
Negotiable instruments, 286
Net approach (cash flows), 862–863
Net carrying amount, 528
Net current amount (deferred taxes), 706–707
Netherlands, 4, 7
Net income: adjustments to, 861–862; for available-for-sale securities, 644–645; debt securities as part of, 637, 640, 641; effect of change of accounting principles on, 187; for evaluation of company, 182; exercises related to, 202; items included in, 181; for trading securities, 646; work sheet columns for, 89
Net income per share, see Earnings per share
Net losses, 864
Net noncurrent amount (deferred taxes), 706–707
Net of tax, 187, 190
Net operating loss (NOL), 699–706: loss carryback, 700, 701; loss carryforward, 700–706; problems related to, 729
Net proceeds, 308
Net realizable value (NRV), 294, 368
Net sales revenue, 178
Net settlement (options), G5n.7, G6
Net working capital, 134
Net worth (household), stock as percentage of, 575
Neutrality: and fair value requirements, 595; and freedom from bias, D4; of information, 31; and stock option controversy, 749
New York Stock Exchange, 595, 598
90% test (recovery of investment test), 785, 804
NOL, see Net operating loss
Nominal accounts, 63
Nominal rate, 524, A6
Noncancelable leases, 782
Noncash transactions, 865–866

Noncompensatory stock option plans, 748
Nonconsolidated subsidiaries, 131, 539–540
Non-current assets, 131–133: intangible assets, 132–133; long-term investments, 131–132; "other assets," 133; property, plant, and equipment, 132
Noncurrent liabilities, 567
Noncurrent receivables, 133, 290
Nondetachable warrants, 609n.5, 611
Nonfinancial measurements, 3, 25
Noninterest-bearing notes, 298, 341
Nonmonetary assets, exchanges of, 428–432, 454, 458–459, 461–462, 466
Nonoperating section (income statements), 177
Nonpublic enterprises, 838n.10
Nonreciprocal transfers, 414
Nonrecognition of interest, 293
Nonrecurring material items, 0
Nontrade receivables, 130, 290, 291
No-par stock, 580–581
Normal shortages, C6–C7
"No take-back" rule, 225
Notes (fiscal). See also Notes payable; Notes receivable: as current liabilities, 133, 134; interest-bearing, 298; issuance of, at face value, 299–300; issuance of, at other than face value, 300–303; long-term, 131, 135; present value-based measurements for, A1; promissory, 298; for property, goods, or services, 302–303; zero-interest-bearing, 298
Notes (informational): on balance sheet, 143–145; for changes in estimates, 833; for disclosure of pension items, 754; and full disclosure principle, 40; with leases, 800–803; reporting pension amounts in, 760–763; for restrictions on retained earnings, 600; on securities outstanding, 135n.12
Notes payable: as current liabilities, 518–520; exercises related to, 555; short-term nontrade, 864
Notes receivable: choice of interest rate for, 303; disposition of, 304–309; exercises/problems related to, 326–327, 332–333, 338–341; interest-bearing notes, 301–302; issuance of, at face value, 299–300; issuance of, at other than face value, 300–303; notes for property, goods, or services, 302–303; recognition of, 298–303; valuation of, 303–304; zero-interest-bearing notes, 300–301
Notional amount, G4
Not-sufficient-funds (NSF) checks, 317
NRV, see Net realizable value
NSF (not-sufficient-funds) checks, 317

O.A.S.D.I. (old age, survivor, and disability insurance) benefits, 739
Off-balance-sheet financing, 539–543, 781
Office supplies, 74, 131
Oil companies, D3–D4
Old age, survivor, and disability insurance (O.A.S.D.I.) benefits, 739
"One-time items," 187n.21
Operating activities, 852n.2: determining

net cash flow from, 856–860; on statement of cash flows, 239, 240; trading securities as, 864
Operating cycles, 127
Operating leases, 540, 783, 795–796: capital leases vs., 791–793; exercises/problems related to, 812–813, 817; lessee's accounting under, 791; lessor's accounting under, 799
Operating loss carryback, 712
Operating loss carryforward, 712
Operating section (income statements), 177, 178
Operating supplies, 131
Operations, income from, 178, 182
Opinions, APB, see APB Opinions
Options, 845–846, G1, G4–G5
Ordinary repairs, 417
Ordinary stock dividends, 596
Originating temporary differences, 696
"Other assets" (on balance sheet), 133
Other comprehensive income, 194
Outstanding checks, 317
Outstanding stock, 587
Over (cash), 315
Overhead, 410
Owners, 33
Owners' equity, see Stockholders' equity
Ownership (ownership interests): in corporations, 578; dilution of, 577, 627–628; under leases, 782–784; as residual interest, 579; structure, 67

PAB (public accountability board), 14
Pacioli, Luca, 471
Paid-in (contributed) capital, 579
"Paper" profits, 364
Parent company, 649
Parenthetical explanations (on balance sheet), 143
Par method (treasury stock), 585
Partial periods, depreciation and, 424–425
Participating preferred stock, 589
Partnerships, 67
Par value: of bonds, 524. See also Face value; of stock, 579–580
Patents, 132, 478, 503, 507–508, 511–512
Payee, 298
Payout ratio, 604
Payroll deductions, 738–741: exercises/problems related to, 769–770, 772–773; income tax withholding, 740; Social Security, 739; unemployment taxes, 739–740
Pending litigation, 532
Pension plans: components of pension expense, 752–754; exercises/problems related to, 770–771, 774, 775, A33, A38; as long-term liabilities, 135; present value-based measurements for, A1; reporting amounts for, 760–763
Pension work sheets, 754–760, 771, 773–774
Percentage depletion, D5
Percentage markup, 379n.3
Percentage-of-completion revenue recognition, 235: exercises/problems related to, 271–272, 279; long-term contracts, 226–230, 251–252
Percentage-of-receivables valuation approach, 296–298

Percentage-of-sales valuation approach, 295–296

Periods (compound interest computations), A5, A11–A12

Period costs, 39, 351–352

Periodic inventory system, 348–349: balance sheet preparation with, 157–158; closing process for, 85; exercises/problems related to, 107, 157–158, 207–208, 385–386

Periodicity assumption, 35, 141

Permanent differences (income taxes), 696, 720, 729

Permits, 477

Perpetual inventory system, 347–348: closing process for, 83–85; exercises related to, 385, 386

Personal checks, 286

Personnel, R & D activities accounting for, 489

Petty cash, 287, 290, 314–316, 327–328, 335

Pharmaceutical industry, 478

Physical factors (in retiring assets), 419–420

Physical goods (in inventory valuation), 350–351

Physical protection (of cash), 316

Plant assets, 408. See also Property, plant, and equipment

Pledge, 305n.18

Point of sale, revenue recognition at, 223–225

Politics, standard setting and, 13–14, 19–20

Pollution expenditure (case exercise), 510–511

Postage stamps on hand, 287, 290

Post-balance-sheet events: on balance sheet, 140–142; conceptual case exercises related to, 166; definition of, 138

Post-closing trial balance, 85

Postdated checks, 287, 290

Postemployment benefits, 741n.4

Posting, 70–71: definition of, 63; trial balance and errors in, 72, 7171

Post-sale costs, 533

PP&E, see Property, plant, and equipment

Practice Bulletins (AICPA), 11

Predictive value (of information), 30

Preemptive right, 577, 627–628

Preferred dividends: in arrears, 520; conceptual case exercise related to, 882; reporting issues with, 838–839

Preferred stock, 578, 588–590: accounting for, 590; convertible, 589; elements of debt with, 516; exercises related to, 614–616, 873; features of, 589–590; reporting of, 590

Premium(s): bonds issued at, 527, 551–552; bonds sold at, 525; classification of, 527; on long-term liabilities, 135; present value-based measurements for, A1; on trading securities, 641

Premium amortization (bond), 664–665

Pre-opening costs (case exercise), 511

Prepayments: adjusting entries for, 73–78; expenses, 73–77; revenues,

77–78; as current asset, 128; expenses, prepaid; adjusting entries for, 73–77; on balance sheet, 130; depreciation, 75–76; insurance, 75; reversing entries for, 97–98; supplies, 74–75; revenues, prepaid, 77–78; reversing entries for, 97–98; valuation of, 128

Present value factor of a single sum (PVF), 299n.15

Present value of an ordinary annuity (PV-OA), 299n.15

Present value (PV), A1: accounting measurements based on, A1–A2; of annuities, A19–A23; annuities due, A20–A21; deferred annuities, A24–A25; ordinary annuities, A19–A20; of bond issues, 526; of bonds, 524–525; exercises/problems related to, A30–A32, A34–A35; of expected future net cash flows, 484; with leasing, 816–817; SFAC No. 7 on, 27, 36; for short-term notes, 293; of single sum; with compound interest, A9–A11; using financial calculator for, B2

Pretax financial income, 684, 722–723, 725, 731

Pricing, disclosure of method for, 130

Principal: of bonds, 524. See also Face value; definition of, A2

Principles of accounting, see Accounting principles

Prior period adjustments, 181n.11: definition of, 193; problems related to, 210

Prior service costs (PSC), 752, 757

Probable contingencies, 532

Probable violations, 520

Process patents, 478

Product costs, 39, 351

Product guarantee, 533. See also Warranties

Production, and revenue recognition, 37

Product maintenance contracts, 535n.16

Product patents, 478

Profit. See also Gross profit: manufacturer's/dealer's, 795; transitory, 364

Profitability ratios, 247, 248

Profit margin on sales ratio, 434

Pro-forma information, 826–827

Pro-forma measures, comparison of, 32

Pro-forma reporting practices, 171

Projected benefit obligation, 752

Promissory notes, 298

Property: notes received for, 302–303; shares of stock issued for, 582–593

Property, plant, and equipment (PP&E), 407–437: acquisition and valuation of, 408–425; buildings, cost of, 409–410; cash discounts, 412–413; contributions, 414–415; equipment, cost of, 410; interest costs during construction, 410–412; land, cost of, 409; lump sum purchase, 413; self-constructed assets, 410; stock issuance, 413–414; additions to, 416; analysis of, 433–435; on balance sheet, 132, 165–166; costs subsequent to acquisition, 415–418; additions, 416; improvements, 416–417;

rearrangement and reinstallation, 417; repairs, 417–418; replacements, 416–417; depreciation of, 418–427; activity method for, 421; base for, 419; declining-balance method for, 422–423; decreasing-charge methods for, 422–423; estimation of service lives, 419–420; methods of, 420–424; and partial periods, 424–425; and revision of depreciation rates, 425–426; straight-line method for, 421–422; sum-of-the-years'-digits method for, 422, 423; dispositions of, 427–432; by exchanges, 428–432; by involuntary conversion, 428; by sale of assets, 427–428; impairments of, 484–485; improvements to, 416–417; presentation of, 432–433; rearrangement and reinstallation of, 417; repairs to, 417–418; replacement of, 416–417

Property dividends, 594

Property held for sale, 133

Property-rights approach (leasing), 782

Proportional method: lump-sum sales, 581–582; stock warrants issued with other securities, 610–611

Proprietorships, 67

Prospective changes, 832

PSC, see Prior service costs

Public accountability board (PAB), 14

Purchased intangibles, 473: goodwill, 480–482; R & D activities accounting for, 489

Purchase discounts and allowances, C6

Purchase returns, C6

Pure rate of interest, A27

Put options, G4n.4

PV, see Present value

PVF (present value factor of a single sum), 299n.15

PV-OA (present value of an ordinary annuity), 299n.15

Qualitative characteristics (of accounting information), 27–32: comparability, 31; consistency, 31; exercises related to, 50–51, 55–57; relevance, 29–30; reliability, 29–31; SFAC No. 2 on, 29–30; understandability, 29

Quality of earnings, 173–174

Quarterly financial statements, work sheets for, 92–93

Quick ratio, 543

Quinn, James, 471

Rate of gross profit, 379n.3

Rate of return: with capital vs. operating leases, 792; on common stock equity, 602; risk-free, A27; on total assets, 434–435

Rate of return on assets (ROA), 435

Ratios, 247

Ratio analysis, 247–248. See also specific ratios

Raw materials inventory, 346

R & D costs, see Research and development costs

Reacquisition of shares, 584–588: purchase of treasury stock, 585–587; retiring treasury stock, 588; sale of treasury stock, 587–588

Reacquisition price, 528
Readily determinable fair value, 636n.3
Real accounts (term), 63
Real estate: acquisition costs of, 447; depreciation choices for, 424
Real estate investment trusts (REITs), 424n.13
Realizable revenues, 36–37, 222
Realized revenues, 36, 222
Rearrangement costs, 417
Reasonableness (accounting changes), 834n.7
Reasonably possible contingencies, 532
Receipt of cash, revenue recognition upon, 37–38
Receivables, 290–311: accounts receivable, see Accounts receivable; analysis of, 310–311; on balance sheet, 130; and cash discounts (sales discounts), 292–293; current, 290; disposition of, 304–309; sales of receivables, 306–309; secured borrowing, 305, 308–309; noncurrent, 290; nonrecognition of interest on, 293; nontrade, 290; notes receivable, see Notes receivable; presentation of, 309–310, 322–323; trade, 290; and trade discounts, 292; transfer of, 304; types of, 290–291
Receivables turnover ratio, 310
Reclassification adjustments, 651–653
Recognition, 27, 28, 33–34, 68
Reconciliation: of bank accounts, 316–319, 328–329, 335–337; exercises/problems related to, 328–329, 335–337, 771, 773–774; in pension plan reporting, 761–763
Reconciliation method (indirect method), 857
Recording transactions and events, 68–69
Recourse, 306–308
Recoverability test, 484
Recoverable reserves, estimation of (natural resources), D5
Recovery of investment test (90% test), 785, 804
Redeemable preferred stock, 590n.10
Reductions in price of land, 409
Refunding, 529
Registered bonds, 524
Registrars, 578
Reinstallation costs, 417
REITs (real estate investment trusts), 424n.13
Relative size (of items), 42–43
Relevance, 29–30: and disclosure of pension plan items, 762; of fair value of debt securities, 636; and lower of cost or market, 371; and R & D cost expensing, 491
Reliability, 29–31: and disclosure of pension plan items, 762; of fair value of debt securities, 636; and lower of cost or market, 371; and R & D cost expensing, 491
Remote contingencies, 532
Rent, prepaid, 131
Renting, see Lease(s)/leasing
Rents (annuities), A13
Repairs, 417–418
Replacements (PP&E), 416–417
Replacement cost, 368–369

Report form (balance sheet), 136–137
Reporting, see Financial reporting
Repossessions: exercises related to, 269–270; revenue recognition with, 258–259
Representational faithfulness, 30, 31
Research and development (R & D) costs: accounting for, 489–490; activities included in, 489; exercises/problems related to, 503, 506–507, 509, 512; for intangible assets, 488–492; for patentable products/processes, 478; presentation of, 492, 494; start-up costs, 491
Reserves, "cookie jar," 174
Reserve recognition accounting (RRA), D3–D4
Reserve (term), 146
Residual interest, 579
Residual value, guaranteed, 785, 804
Residual value profits (leasing), 793–794
Restoration costs, D2
Restoration of impairments, 487–488
Restricted cash and cash flows, 288–289
Restricted deposits, 289
Restrictions on long-term debt, 522
Restructuring: charges for, 181, 186; of troubled debt, F5–F11
Retail inventory method, C1–C8: evaluation of, C7; with markups and markdowns, C3–C6; special items relating to, C6–C7; terminology related to, C3
Retained earnings, 579: and dividend amounts, 591; exercises/problems related to, 204, 207–209, 619; reporting of, 66, 67; restrictions on, 193–194; in stockholders' equity section, 136
Retained earnings statements: exercises/problems related to, 205, 210; on income statements, 193–194; retroactive-effect accounting changes on, 830–831
Retirement of debt, A33
Retroactive benefits, 757
Retroactive-effect changes in accounting principle, 827–831
Returns, high rate of, 224
Revenues. See also Revenue recognition: adjusting entries for, 77–79; definition of, 33, 175; earned, 36, 37, 222; forms of, 175; gains vs., 176; net sales, 178; realizable, 222; reporting of, 66, 67; unearned, 77
Revenue accounts: adjusting entries on, 77–79; closing entries for, 83; debiting and crediting, 64
Revenue bonds, 524
Revenue expenditures, 416
Revenue recognition, 222–236: after delivery, 230–235; cost-recovery accounting method, 233–234; deposit accounting method, 234; installment-sales accounting method, 230–233; bases or methods for, 235–236; conceptual case exercises related to, 55–56; before delivery, 226–230; at end of production, 37; with installment sales, 253–260; defaults and repossessions, 258–259; interest on installment contracts, 257; presentation of transactions, 259–260;

uncollectible accounts, 257; and level of ownership, 649; with long-term contracts, 249–253; and matching principle, 38–39; at point of sale (delivery), 223–225; during production, 37; upon receipt of cash, 37–38
Revenue recognition principle, 36–38, 72, 222
Reversing differences, 696
Reversing entries, 85, 96–98: for accruals, 96–97; exercises related to, 110; for prepayments, 97–98
Risks: balance sheet disclosure of, 139; cash flow, G11; exchange rate, G7; interest rate, G7
Risk-free rate of return, A27
ROA (rate of return on assets), 435
Rothschild, Mayer, A3
RRA, see Reserve recognition accounting

Sack, Robert, 15
Salary(-ies), 738–743: adjusting entries for, 80–81; and bonuses, 743; compensated absences, 741–742; payroll deductions, 738–741; income tax withholding, 740; Social Security taxes, 739; unemployment taxes, 739–740
Sales: of assets, 427–428; channel stuffing, 225; Commerce Department reports on, 345; cost-recovery accounting method for, 233–234; deposit accounting method for, 234; installment, see Installment-sales accounting; of property, plant, and equipment, 427–428; of receivables, 306–309; with recourse, 306–308; without recourse, 306–307; revenue recognition for, 222–235; after delivery, 230–235; before delivery, 226–230; at point of sale, 223–225; secured borrowing vs., 308–309; trade loading, 224–225; when right of return exists, 224
Sales discounts, 292–293, C6
Sales returns and allowances, C6
Sales-type leases, 794, 795, 799–800, 810–811, 813–814
Sales warranty approach, 535
Salvage value, 419
SASs, see AICPA Statements on Auditing Standards
Savings accounts, 286
SEC, see Securities and Exchange Commission
Second income statements, 194, 195
Secret processes, 132
Secret reserves, 583
Secured bonds, 523
Secured borrowing, 305, 308–309
Security(-ies). See also specific headings: antidilutive, 843, 846–847; available-for-sale, 129, 637–641; debt, 635–642; definition of, 634n.2; diluted, 842; equity, 129; between 20% and 50%, holdings, 646–649; investments in, 642–650; less than 20%, holdings of, 643–646; more than 50%, holdings of, 649–650; held-to-maturity, 129, 636–637; host, G13; hybrid, G13;

as long-term investments, 131–132; trading, 129, 641–642

Securities and Exchange Commission (SEC), 6–7: and abuses of financial reporting process, 236; and accounting scandals, 14; conceptual case exercises related to, 21; creation of, 21; and disclosure of dividend policy, 592; and EITF statements, 10; and environmental liabilities, 538; on manipulation of earnings reports, 174; and public accountability board, 14; realized/realizable and earned revenue criteria, 223n.2; and reserve recognition accounting, D3–D4; and 20–25 percent rule, 599n.18

Securities Fair Value Adjustment (Available-for-Sale) account, 638

Securitization, 285, 306

Self-constructed assets, 410, 449–450, 457–458, 465

Self-insurance, 538–539

Selling expenses, 351

Serial bonds, 524

Services: notes received for, 302–303; shares of stock issued for, 582–593

Service cost, 752, 753

Service lives, estimation of, 419–420

Service period, 745

Settlement rates, 752, 754

75% test (economic life test), 784

SFACs, see FASB Statements of Financial Accounting Concepts

SFASs, see FASB Statements of Financial Accounting Standards

Share buybacks, 594, 595

Sharpe, Michael, 24

Short (cash), 315

Short-term borrowing, 289

Short-term investments: on balance sheet, 129; as current asset, 128; valuation of, 128

Short-term notes, 293, 298–299

Short-term paper, 287, 290

Short-term receivables, 294

Sick pay, 742. *See also* Compensated absences

Significant influence, 646–647

Significant noncash transactions, 865

Similar nonmonetary assets, exchange of, 429–432

Simple capital structure, 838–842: preferred stock dividends, 838–839; weighted average number of shares outstanding, 839–841

Simple interest, A2–A3, A31

Singapore, 7

Single-step income statements, 176, 202–203, 207–209

Single sums, compound interest for, A7–A12

Sinking funds, present value-based measurements for, A1

Small (ordinary) stock dividends, 596

Smoothing techniques, 757–758

Social Security taxes, 739

Soft assets, 4

Software costs, *see* Computer software costs

Solvency, 125, 239

SOPs, see AICPA Statements of Position

Spain, 712

Special assessments, 409

Special Committee on Financial Reporting (AICPA), 41–42, 188

Special funds, 131, 133

Special journals, 70

Special purpose entities (SPEs), 540, 650, 793

Specific goods approach (LIFO valuation), 358

Specific goods pooled LIFO approach, 359–360

Specific identification method (for inventory valuation), 353–354

Speculation, derivatives for, G4–G6

Speculators, G2

SPEs, *see* Special purpose entities

Standards, FASB, *see* FASB *Statements of Financial Accounting Standards (SFASs)*

Standard & Poors' 500 index, 182

Standards, *see* Accounting standards

Start-up costs, 491

State corporate laws, 576–577

Stated rate, 299n.14, 524, A6

Stated value, 581

Stated value method (treasury stock), 585

Statements: AICPA, *see* AICPA *Statements of Position*; AICPA, *see* AICPA *Statements on Auditing Standards*; FASB, *see* FASB *Statements of Financial Accounting Concepts*; FASB *Statements of Financial Accounting Standards*

Statement of cash flows, 852–866: accounts receivable (net) on, 862–863; adjustments similar to depreciation on, 861–862; change in cash, determination of, 855; and classification of cash flows, 852–853; content of, 238; definition of, 63; exercises/problems related to, 266–269, 274–275, 873–875, 880, 883; and financial reporting, 236; format of, 238–239, 853–854; gains on, 864–865; net cash flow from investing and financing activities, determination of, 860–862; net cash flow from operating activities, determination of, 856–860; net losses on, 864; preparation of, 239–241; purpose of, 237; significant noncash transactions on, 865–866; steps in preparation of, 854–861; usefulness of, 241–244; working capital changes on, 863–864

Statement of earnings, *see* Income statement(s)

Statement of financial position, *see* Balance sheet

Statement of income, *see* Income statement(s)

Statement of retained earnings, 63, 89, 90

Statement of stockholders' equity, 194–196, 602, 603

Stock(s). *See also* Earnings per share; Stockholders' equity: capital, 136; common, *see* Common stock; costs of issuing, 583–584; earnings per share reporting for, 837; issuance of, 579–584; costs of, 583–584; exercises related to, 614–615; in noncash transactions, 582–583; no-par stock, 580–581; with other securities (lump-sum sales), 581–582; par value stock, 579–580; no-par, 580–581; outstanding, 587; par value of, 579–580; PP&E acquired by issuance of, 413–414, 467; preferred, *see* Preferred stock; reacquisition of shares, 584–588; purchase of Treasury Stock, 585–587; retirement of Treasury Stock, 588; sale of Treasury Stock, 587–588; stated value of, 581; Treasury stock, *see* Treasury stock; U.S. vs. British use of term, 146; watered, 583

Stock buybacks, 594, 595

Stock compensation plans, 743–750: accounting for, 744–747; allocating compensation expense, 745; conceptual case exercises related to, 775; determining expense, 744–745; disclosure of, 748–749; and noncompensatory plans, 748; recognition of value with, 743–744; and stock option accounting, 749–750; types of, 747–750

Stock dividends, 520–521, 595–599: and computation of weighted average number of shares, 840–841; preferred stock, 838–839

Stockholders' (owners') equity, 66–67, 575–606: analysis of, 602, 604; on balance sheet, 135; classification of, 127; corporate capital, 579–588; issuance of stock, 579–584; reacquisition of shares, 584–588; and corporate form of organization, 576–578; debiting and crediting accounts for, 64; dividend policy, 590–600; disclosure of restrictions on retained earnings, 600; financial condition and dividend distributions, 591–592; stock split, 597–600; types of dividends, 592–597; preferred stock, 588–590; presentation of, 600–603; statement of, 194–196

Stock market indexes, 575

Stock options: exercises/problems related to, 770, 878, 882; non-employees, issuance to, 744n.7

Stock option plans, 743, 773. *See also* Stock compensation plans

Stock right, 577n.1

Stock splits, 597–600: and computation of weighted average number of shares, 840–841; exercises related to, 618, 624–626, 628

Stock warrants, 577n.1: detachable, 609–610; issuance of, with other securities, 609–611; nondetachable, 609n.5

Straight-line method: depreciation, 421–422; interest amortization, 552

Strike price, G4

Sub-prime lending, 285

Subsequent costs/expenditures, 415–418, 450–451

Subsequent events, 140–142, 161–162

Subsidiary(-ies): advances to, 133; definition of, 649; transfer of accounts/notes receivable to, 304

Substitution approach (PP&E), 416–417

Successful efforts approach, D3–D4

Summa de Arithmetica, Geometrica (Luca Pacioli), 471

Summary of Significant Accounting Policies, 139

Summers, Lawrence, 1, 15

Sum-of-the-years'-digits method (depreciation), 422, 423

Supplementary information. *See also* Notes; Supporting schedules: on balance sheet, 138–143; and full disclosure principle, 40–41; on long-term liabilities, 135

Supplies, adjusting entries for, 74–75

Supporting schedules: for balance sheet, 145–146; for income statements, 178.180

Surplus (term), 146

Swaps, G8

Sweden, 527

Switzerland, 29, 538, 600

Synthetic leases, 793

T-accounts, 69, 71

Take-or-pay contracts, 540

Tangible fixed assets, investments in, 131

Taxes: and advantages of leasing, 781; avoidance of, 683; contingencies related to, 139; as current liability, 133; exercises/problems related to, 718–726, 728–730; income, *see* Income taxes; intraperiod tax allocation, 190–191; and natural resources accounting, D5; payroll deductions for, 738–741; planning strategy for, 705n.9, 713; prepayment of, 131; reporting for, 684–686; Social Security, 739; unemployment, 739–740

Taxable income, 684, 686–687, 713, 731–732

Taxable temporary differences, 695, 713

Tax credit carryback, 712

Tax credit carryforward, 712

Tax effect (tax benefit), 701

Tax incentives (leases), 793

Tax services (as postretirement expense), 763

Technical Bulletins, FASB, *see* FASB *Technical Bulletins*

Technological feasibility, E1, E3

Technology-related intangible assets, 478–479

Temporary difference (income tax), 686–687, 695–696, 713: deductible, 713; exercises/problems related to, 718–726; expected reversal date of, 708; taxable, 713

Term bonds, 524

Term of lease, 787

Third-party guarantors, 804

Threatened litigation, 532

Time, 843

Times interest earned ratio, 544

Timeliness, 4, 30

Time period assumption, 141

Time value of money, A1–A30: annuities, A13–A25; deferred, A23–A25; future value of, A13–A18; present value of, A19–A23; applications of concepts, A1–A2; and expected cash flows, A27–A28; future value, *see* Future value; interest,

A2–A12; components of, A27; compound, A3–A12; exercises related to, A30; nature of, A2; simple, A2–A3; variables in computation of, A2; long-term bonds valuation, A26; and plus/minus signs with calculator, B2; present value, *see* Present value; problems related to, A34, A36–A37

Time value (of option), G5

Trade accounts payable, 517, 518. *See also* Accounts payable

Trade discounts, 292

Trade loading, 224–225

Trademarks, 132, 475

Trade names, 132, 475, 502–503, 508

Trade notes payable, 518. *See also* Notes payable

Trade receivables, 290

Trading on the equity, 604, 620

Trading securities, 129: debt, 641–642; definition of, 635; equity, 646; problems related to, 672–673; recording of, 646; on statement of cash flows, 864

Traditional LIFO, 358

Transactions: balance sheet reporting of, 162; definition of, 63; exercises/problems related to, 101, 109–111; as extraordinary items, 183, 184; identifying/recording, 68–69; in installment sales, presentation of, 259–260; types of, 69

Transaction approach (income measurement), 175

Transfer agents, 578

Transfers-in, C6

Transitory profits, 364

Travel advances, 287, 290

Treasury bills, 287n.1, 289

Treasury shares, 585

Treasury stock, 585: exercises related to, 616, 622–624, 629; purchase of, 585–587; retiring, 588; sale of, 587–588

Treasury stock method, 845–846

Trial balance, 71–72: adjusted, 82; definition of, 63; exercises related to, 101–103; post-closing, 85; work sheet columns for, 88

Troubled debt, F1–F11: accounting issues, F1–F2; impairments, F2–F5; restructurings of, F5–F11

Trucks, acquisition costs of, 447–448

Tuition assistance (as postretirement expense), 763

Turner, Lynn, 32, 236

20–25 percent rule, 599

Unasserted claims and assessments, 533

Uncertainties, balance sheet disclosure of, 139

Uncollectible accounts (bad debts), 130: adjusting entries for, 81–82; and age of accounts, 297n.12; exercises/problems related to, 323–325, 329–332, 337–339, 341–342; methods for recording, 294–295; revenue recognition with, 257

Uncollectible accounts receivable, 294–298

Unconditional promises (pledges), 414–415

Underlyings, G6

Understandability, 29, 40, 143

Unearned revenues: adjusting entries for, 77–78; as current liabilities, 133, 521–522

Unemployment taxes, 739–740

Unexpected gain or loss, 757–760

Unfiled suits, 533

Uniform Commercial Code, 578

Uniform Stock Transfer Act, 578

United Kingdom, 415, 578: changes in accounting principle, 825; deferred tax recognition, 712; primary accounting objective in, 4; professional accounting bodies in, 7

U.S. Commerce Department, 345

U.S. Department of Energy, D3n.2

U.S. Federal Reserve, 288

Unit LIFO, 358

Units of production method (activity approach), D2

Unsecured bonds, 523

Upper (ceiling) limits, 368–369

Useful life (of assets), 75

Usefulness, changes in accounting and, 825

User groups, standards and, 13

Vacation time, *see* Compensated absences

Valuation: of accounts receivable, 294–298; of bonds payable, 524–529; disclosure of basis for, 130; fair market value of stock for, 414n.3; fair values, 143; and historical cost principle, 35–36; of intangible assets, 133, 473; of inventories, 128, 350–372; average cost method for, 354–355; cost flow assumptions for, 353–357; costs included in, 351–352; first-in, first-out method for, 355–356; last-in, first-out method for, 356–367; lower of cost or market rule for, 367–372; physical goods, 350–351; specific identification method for, 353–354; of long-term bonds, A26; of notes receivable, 303–304; percentage-of-receivables valuation approach, 296–298; percentage-of-sales approach to, 295–296; of property, plant, and equipment, 408–425; buildings, cost of, 409–410; cash discounts, 412–413; contributions, 414–415; costs subsequent to, 415–418; equipment, cost of, 410; interest costs during construction, 410–412; land, cost of, 409; lump sum purchase, 413; self-constructed assets, 410; stock issuance, 413–414; of short-term receivables, 294; of stock issued in noncash transactions, 582–583; of stock issued with other securities, 581–582

Valuation allowance, 693–694: carryforward with, 702–704; carryforward without, 702–703; definition of, 713; exercises related to, 723–724, 726–727; need for, 705–706

Value: future, *see* Future value; market-related, 758n.17; present, *see* Present value

Verifiability, 30–31
Vested rights, 743–745
Violation of loan covenants, 792
Virtual companies, 34n.11

Wages, *see* Salary(-ies)
Wages payable (as current liability), 133
Wall Street Journal, 182, 287
Warrants: detachable; bond, 611; exercises related to, 620; stock, 609–610; exercises related to, 873; issuance of, with other securities, 609–611; nondetachable; bond, 611; stock, 609n.5; reporting issues with, 845–846; stock, 577n.1, 609–611
Warranties, 533–536: exercises/problems related to, 556–557, 563; tax deductions for, 690

Wasting assets, D1. *See also* Natural resources
Watch lists, F2n.3
Watered stock, 583
Webber, Andrew Lloyd, 477
Weighted-average accumulated expenditures, 440
Weighted-average method, 354
Weighted average number of shares outstanding, 839–841, 871–872
Wheat, Francis, 8
Wheat Committee, 8
Without recourse, 306–307, 326
With recourse, 306–308, 326
Working capital, 134, 863–864
Working capital ratio, 543
Work in process inventory, 346
Work sheets, 86–93: adjusting entries on, 86–88; closing process on, 92; columns on, 88–89; exercises/problems related to, 106–109, 113; financial statement preparation from, 89–92; for income statements, 88–90; for interim financial statements, 92–93
World Trade Center bombing, 185
World Wide Web, financial reports on, 4
Write-off(s), 182, 294, 295: of goodwill, 482–483; of natural resource cost, D2–D3

Years-of-service method, 757

Zero-interest-bearing notes, 298, 300–301, 519–520
Zero-interest debenture bonds, 524